For Reference

Not to be taken from this room

THE CONCISE ENCYCLOPEDIA
OF WORLD WAR II

THE CONCISE ENCYCLOPEDIA OF WORLD WAR II

Two Volumes

Cathal J. Nolan

AN IMPRINT OF ABC-CLIO, LLC
Santa Barbara, California • Denver, Colorado • Oxford, England

Library of Congress Cataloging-in-Publication Data

Nolan, Cathal J.
    The Concise Encyclopedia of World War II / Cathal J. Nolan.
        p. cm.
    Includes bibliographical references and index.
    ISBN 978-0-313-33050-6 (set : alk. paper) — ISBN 978-0-313-36527-0
(set : ebook)
1. World War, 1939–1945—Encyclopedias.   I. Title.   II. Title: Encyclopedia of World War Two,
1937–1945.   III. Title: Encyclopedia of World War 2, 1937–1945.
    D740.N65   2010
    940.5303—dc22   2009036965

14   13   12   11   10   1   2   3   4   5

This book is also available on the World Wide Web as an eBook.
Visit www.abc-clio.com for details.

ABC-CLIO, LLC
130 Cremona Drive, P.O. Box 1911
Santa Barbara, California 93116-1911

This book is printed on acid-free pap∞
Manufactured in the United States of America

But what I want is annihilation!

> *—Adolf Hitler in 1944, upon learning that the V-2 rocket*
> *would not be as destructive as he hoped.*

Victors are not judged.

> *—One of the favorite sayings of Joseph Stalin, repeated in his*
> *major postwar speech commemorating the "Great Fatherland War," 1945.*

If you are cursed with any imagination at all, you have at least one horrid glimpse of a child in bed with a ton of masonry tumbling down on top of him, or a three-year-old girl crying *"Mutter, Mutter,"* because she has been burned. You have to turn away from that picture if you intend to retain your sanity and do the work your nation expects of you.

—General Curtis LeMay, USAAF, writing in 1965 on the bombing of Germany.

CONTENTS

LIST OF ENTRIES

PREFACE

The main challenge in writing this encyclopedia was to compress the vast scope and complexity of World War II into a relatively short work, without substituting a mere rendition of facts for deeper understanding of the war. While focusing principally on military aspects of the war, as opposed to life on the various home fronts or the minutiae of cabinet diplomacy, I have endeavored to present the war in larger terms than battle or operational history. Interpretive issues dealt with include the evolution of total war strategic doctrines in the mid-20th century, as well as the profoundly difficult questions of the determinants of victory and defeat that attend the writing of all good military history: economic and political goals pursued and whether these matched the military means and logistical reach available; institutional and national cultures and military traditions; command personalities, training, doctrine, and weapons.

Other questions that inform the text include the following: Why did the Allies win the war and the Axis states lose? How were victory and defeat defined by participants? What role was played by factors of production, moral commitment, planned or unplanned attrition, as well as by the personalities of democratic leaders and dictators alike and specific policies leaders followed or abjured? What did the major powers hope to gain from pursuing certain military and political strategies and not others? Were their choices wise and prudent, or reckless and self-destructive, or inescapable, given contemporary knowledge and options as well as known outcomes? What effects did the war have on minor participants, neutral states, and ordinary people whose lives it pounded and uprooted or utterly destroyed? To the degree possible in a general work such as this, I tried to weave in a sense of the extreme clash of will and force that characterizes all war, of the blood and smashed bone and suffering that always attends real war as waged by real people.

In a deep sense, World War II was a resumption of mass violence after "an armistice of twenty years," as Maréchal Ferdinand Foch accurately predicted in 1919 would be the fate of the Treaty of Versailles with Germany. The greatest war the world has ever known, or fears to know, was closely linked to that other stupendous clash of nations, of will and arms, economies and technology, of mass emotion and mass armies, called the "Great War" by the generation that fought it. Not least of these connections was a sense of horror and exhaustion among those who waged the first world war of the 20th century. Too often forgotten, however, are accompanying feelings of triumph and vindication among those who won the war. Instead, near-caricature images portray World War I as an utterly futile conflict on all sides, a dreary slog of mud-splattered lambs led to their slaughter by abysmally inept and dull-witted generals. Better known is that dread of more war and satisfaction with the peace on the winning side was opposed by a deep desire for revenge and a revolutionary overthrow of the Great War's outcome by many of those in the losing camp. Dissatisfaction in support of violence was even felt by populations in some countries, most notably Italy and Japan, which numbered among the victors of 1918.

Historians point to many other connections between the world wars: German and other national dissatisfaction with the Versailles system and international order; competitive, militant nationalisms among a host of injured or newly minted countries that nursed real and imagined grievances across several generations; conflicting imperial ideologies and interests; unresolved territorial issues; the growing capacity for total mobilization of whole societies and economies for industrialized war; emergence of new military technologies accompanied by aggressive, offensive fighting doctrines; and ever more clearly as time recedes, the path to genocide that is traceable from the Ottoman slaughter of Armenians in 1915 to the Shoah, the mass murder of European Jews, and to multiple other ethnic holocausts and horrors of the early 1940s.

The persistent conflicts of the first half of the 20th century encouraged erection of "war states" by several Great Powers, both in response to World War I and in preparation for what became World War II. Germany and the Soviet Union, and in some measure Japan, mobilized tens of millions to war and reorganized their economies and societies in readiness to fight with radical drive to impose their political and ideological will on enemies. Latterly, and to a degree neither they nor their opponents foresaw, after first disarming voluntarily to levels that matched the forced disarmament of Germany, Britain and the United States proved even more capable of organizing their peoples and market economies for war. Under pressures of making total war, many countries underwent root social and governmental reorganization deemed necessary by elites to harness national or imperial economic capabilities. Multiple societies witnessed new commitments in the scale and depth of public loyalty and sacrifice demanded from citizens, a call to arms and workplace, to supreme effort for the nation, reinforced by intense propaganda that aimed to inculcate ideological motivation and emotional commitment among mass populations. There was also a great deal of raw coercion.

There were some continuities, but more important discontinuities, in military lessons drawn from World War I about operational as against merely tactical mobility. New offensive doctrines were introduced by all sides that strove to overcome profound defensive advantages and quicken the pace of battle. Not all were successful, as realities of industrial attrition meant that by 1945 the killing rate in battle exceeded that of the Great War. At the same time, old ideas about sea power and armies on the move had to be adjusted to incorporate new ideas and realities of air power. Everywhere, there was newfound devotion of government and science to weapons development. That process meant the means of destruction available were vastly greater by 1945 than when the war began, more than a single technological generation ahead of what planners anticipated just a few years before it started. Armies and navies were subjected to protracted attritional combat for which few had planned and none were really prepared, even as military leaders searched for alternate strategies that might provide a quicker route to "decisive victory." Everyone learned better utilization of combined arms and radio-linked command and control systems so that more powerful killing machines became more efficient as well as more numerous in late-war battles. Accompanying rising military capabilities was a deterioration in moral and operational restraint, until World War II became a true total war.

World War II was more truly global in its causes and theaters of extraordinary violence, and perhaps in lasting demographic and geopolitical consequences, than the preceding world war. It had a pronounced and ultimate character as a war not just among opposing national militaries, but as a "race" war: a conflict so deep in the ambition of hatred that some parties sought not just permanent political and economic domination, but biological extermination of their enemies. Perhaps the most important difference between the world wars was that World War II was fought not mainly to adjust national borders or gain imperial provinces or colonies. Right from the start, it was waged by Nazi Germany as a *Vernichtungskrieg* ("war of annihilation"), a war of "race and blood" beyond the normal clash of nations, wherein whole peoples and civilizations were marked off to disappear from the face of the Earth. Some very nearly did.

On the German side, World War II was a total war in ends sought from the first day to the last. Dedication to total victory by any means did not mark, at least at first, the goals pursued or methods employed by most other participants. Neither the French nor British began the fight dedicated to total destruction of the German enemy. Far from it; the RAF spent much of the first winter of the war dropping leaflets instead of bombs on the Ruhr. That changed starting in mid-1940, as progressive decisions were made to smash Germany's war production from the air, then to destroy its cities and morale by targeting its people for bombing. Despite the horrors of Shanghai and Nanjing, the Japanese war of aggression underway in China was essentially a traditional war of conquest of territory and for regional geopolitical and economic dominance. Once fighting in Asia and the Pacific merged with war in Europe from the end of 1941, however, those theaters also took on the general character and methods of total war. Ultimately, the main Axis partners accelerated into climactic cults of dominance and death, while the major Allied powers turned away from pity to deliberate targeting of civilians for vengeance sake or to carpet a quicker path to victory.

Cathal J. Nolan
International History Institute
Boston University
May 25, 2009

ACKNOWLEDGMENTS

I have concentrated in this encyclopedia on the military, diplomatic, and political history of World War II. This is a work mostly about fighting the war and the people who organized, directed, or waged it. The home front is discussed, especially for occupied countries and major belligerents. However, I have not attempted to recount or comment on the many and wide domestic issues that draw many social and cultural historians to the events of 1937–1945. I strove to provide even-handed coverage, not to serve any ideological or nationalist agendas. I may only hope that I have been properly morally aware of the significance of such extraordinary times and their unprecedented horrors. That said, humility of conclusion about the meaning of events is the proper role for any historian writing about so complex and devastating a conflict. This is, after all, an encyclopedia: a compact summary of many topics and facts. The deepest meanings of the war, of Nazism, Soviet partisan resistance, of the Shoah, must be sought in full-length works by scholars who devote lifetimes to their study and in eyewitness accounts that provide a direct human connection that no historian can replicate. I have done the best that I can to present the most reliable knowledge and honest summary conclusions of those scholars, insofar as I have understood them.

I owe an overwhelming intellectual debt to hundreds of scholars from whose close studies of specific issues and events of the war I greatly benefited while researching and writing this *Encyclopedia of World War II*. I am additionally grateful to students in my senior and graduate seminar on "World War II: Causes, Course, Consequences," which I teach at Boston University. I want to give special thanks to students who took that course between 2006 and 2009. Their questions and challenges sharpened my thinking and helped me correct errors as I worked simultaneously to answer their queries and compose this encyclopedia. In particular, I wish to express my gratitude to Jessica Talarico for her research assistance on the darkest of topics: the Shoah, testimony and events detailed at the International Military Tribunals, and war crimes issues more generally. I am confident that Jessica is about to embark on a stellar career in military history and museum studies. Also helpful was Dr. Carl Hodge of the University of British Columbia. His counsel on certain German sources and issues of language is much appreciated. Lieutenant Colonel Erik Rundquist, a National Defense Fellow at Boston University in 2008–2009, was especially helpful concerning entries dealing with airborne warfare. I am grateful also to my friend and colleague William Keylor. As his students know, he is the deepest of all fonts of knowledge on the international history of the 20th century. Any mistakes that survived consultation of sources and colleagues to find their way into this very large text are mine alone.

AUTHOR'S NOTE

I have taken care to make the *Encyclopedia of World War II* especially useful to readers by providing cross-references from multiple directions. For instance, where I provide a main entry under the Soviet operational name for a battle or campaign, I also include a cross-reference from the German term and vice versa. Similarly, where I use a conventional military history reference such as *Ardennes campaign,* I add cross-references to the nearly exclusively American term, *Battle of the Bulge,* and the German code name *Wacht Am Rhein.* To avoid cluttering the text unduly with cross-references, I do not italicize ordinary terms such as "artillery," "battleship," or "infantry" in all cases. Where such common terms are italicized it means the cross-reference has especially pertinent information to the main entry concerned. To additionally ease visual clutter, I do not place names of major statesmen in italics; Adolf Hitler, Benito Mussolini, Franklin D. Roosevelt, Winston Churchill, and Joseph Stalin are therefore never italicized unless there is a special reason for doing so in a particular main entry. Similarly, I do not italicize major militaries such as British Army, Red Army, Wehrmacht, Royal Navy, or Kriegsmarine, again with limited special exceptions. Foreign language words are italicized only in the main entry headers to avoid sending readers on a mistaken search for a cross-reference that does not exist.

I do not use noble titles or reference subsequent knighthoods or peerages, in preference for use of contemporary military or civilian government titles. Hence, Lord Louis Mountbatten, or 1st Earl Mountbatten of Burma, is rendered simply as Louis Mountbatten, preceded by the appropriate naval rank he held at the time of the reference. Similarly, Field Marshal 1st Earl Alexander of Tunis is rendered simply as General or Field Marshal Harold Alexander, according to his rank at the time. Comparable treatment is given to German officers with noble titles, such as

Wilhelm Ritter von Leeb, who is entered simply as Wilhelm von Leeb, with his appropriate military rank. Exceptions are made in the case of major royalty such as Emperor *Haile Selassie* and the Shōwa Emperor, *Hirohito,* and when noble title was the primary form of international address used at the time, as with Count *Galeazzo Ciano.* Certain Japanese princes and barons were most notable for their connection to the Royal Family and the political implications this had. Their titles are usually provided for that reason. In most cases, Japanese noble titles did not clash with or unduly clutter contemporary military titles, so they actually help to better identify the individual concerned.

Military titles in general entries or secondary references are provided as they were on the date in question. In biographical entries, they are given initially at the highest level achieved in a career, though without pointing out finer distinctions between gradations of major ranks even if these existed in fact. Thus, a German general officer of whatever gradation ("Colonel General," or "of the Cavalry," "of the Army," or "der Panzergruppen") is just a general or field marshal for main entry identification. Normally, ranks are given in English-language equivalents. I use some common acronyms in the text, such as USN, or SS, or ETO, but I provide main entries and cross-references to all such usages in the entry headers. Use of Arabic or Roman numerals in military unit designations varied across armies as well as within them. For instance, the Wehrmacht used Arabic numerals for divisions and corps but Roman numerals for armies and army groups. Some German units mixed Arabic and Roman numerals for their district and unit numbers on flags, or for battalions and regiments, respectively. For the sake of clarity and consistency, I use Arabic numerals for all unit designations at all levels for all armed forces, including U.S. Army and British and Commonwealth military enumeration. Thus, "U.S. Third Army" is rendered as "U.S. 3rd Army," while the Wehrmacht designation "IV Panzerarmee" is given as "4th Panzer Army." "German 6th Army" is used when "Soviet 6th Army" was also engaged in the campaign, or comparable potential confusion exists.

I follow contemporary practice of regional specialists in using the pinyin system for romanizing Chinese personal and place names. Names long familiar to older readers in their Wade-Giles form are cross-referenced. Wade-Giles forms were commonly used during the war and among historians for several decades after it. Contemporary maps, memoirs, official histories, and other historical accounts also employed the older transliterations. In this Encyclopedia, the wartime usage "Chiang Kai-shek" is given in pinyin modern form as *Jiang Jieshi,* with a cross-reference to and from *Chiang Kai-shek,* just as "Nanking" is rendered "Nanjing." Names of certain European cities that vary, as in Polish or German, or German and Russian, are usually given consistently in one form, with the other in parentheses where there may be confusion. Even the two great democratic militaries of the war were often divided by a common language, with British and Commonwealth troops using one term and Americans using another for the same thing; for instance, "passage of lines" and "leapfrogging," or "combat zone" and "forward area." I cross-reference these and other terms. I also provide a limited sampling of contemporary military slang.

German operational code names are sometimes used for main entry heads, but cross-referenced to an English-language term so that readers will have no difficulty finding the entry. Campaign terminology in Soviet and Russian histories is often lengthy and awkward in English translation, as in *Rzhev-Viazma strategic operation*. Nevertheless, it is used in this encyclopedia as delineating an important historiographical tradition. I am fully aware that, on occasion, that tradition was deliberately misleading to serve postwar Stalinist interests. I compensate for that problem in descriptive and analytical text. Where appropriate, English-language cross-references are provided for preferred Soviet or German terminology, such as *Battle of Moscow* to lead readers to the main entry *Moscow offensive operation (December 5, 1941–January 7, 1942)* and *Battle of France* to guide readers to the main entry *FALL GELB*. Casualty figures are hugely problematic for many battles and campaigns. Wherever possible, I provide them from official sources. Where opposing official sources clash or are suspect for other reasons, I supply current consensus figures from specialist historians.

MAPS

Poland and Eastern Europe, 1939–1940. (United States at War Database)

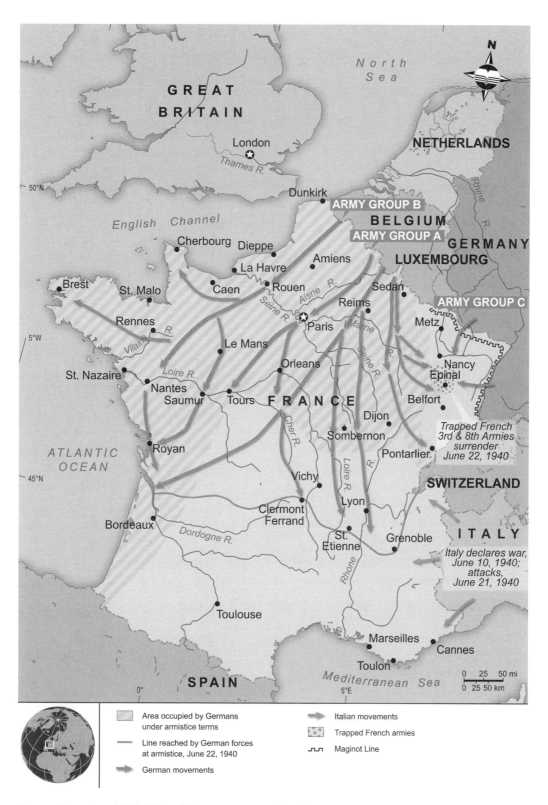

France Campaign, 1940. (United States at War Database)

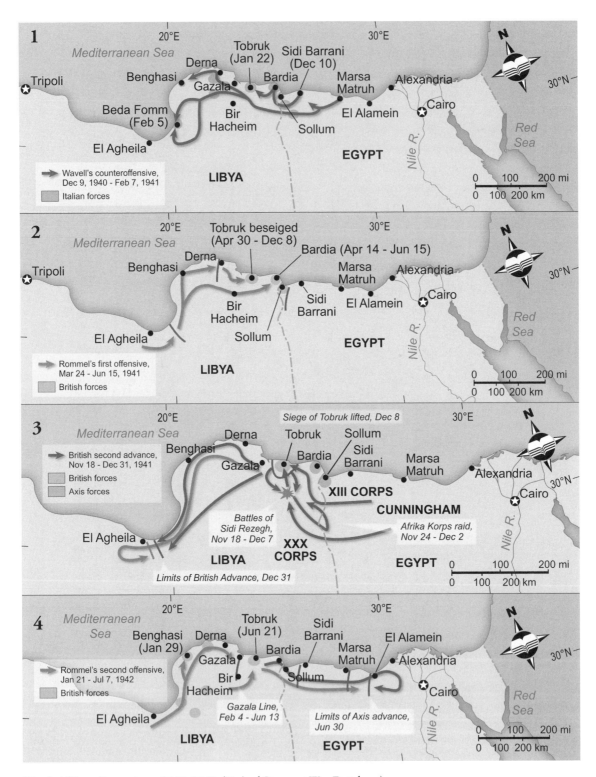

North African Operations, 1940–1942. (United States at War Database)

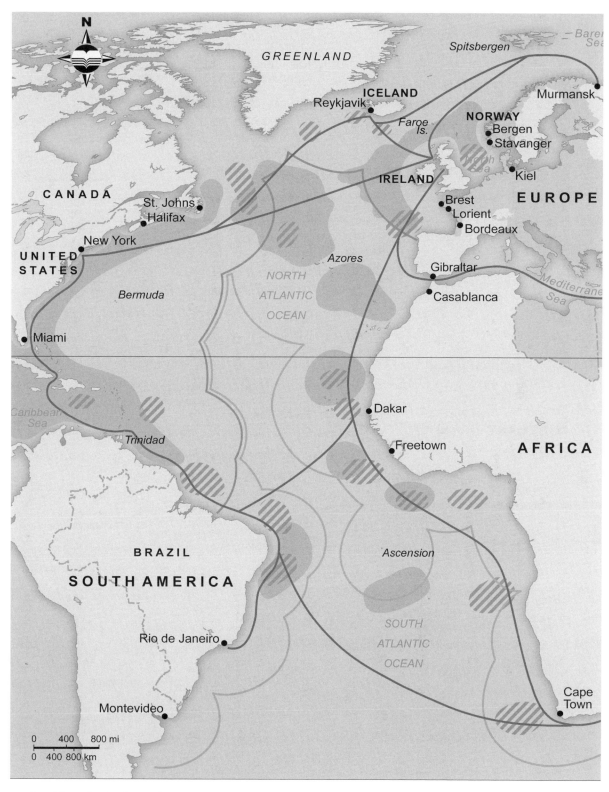

Battle of the Atlantic. (United States at War Database)

Operation BARBAROSSA, the German Plan, 1941. (United States at War Database)

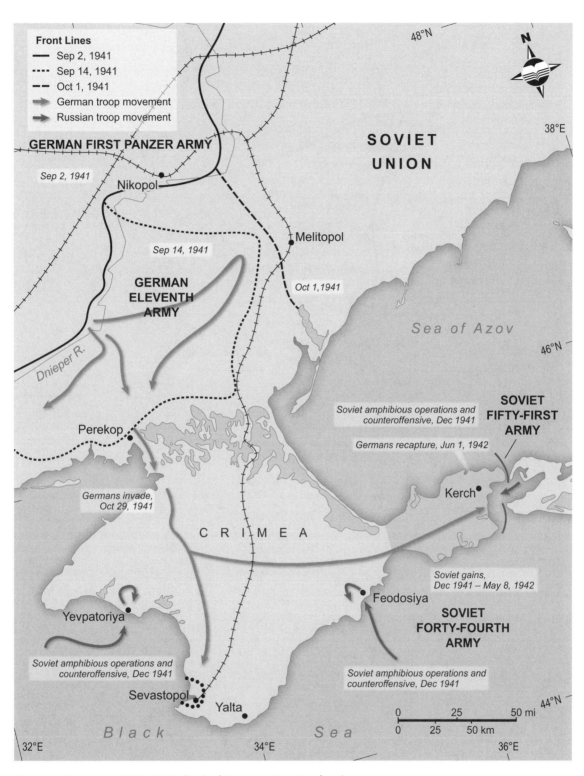

Crimean Campaign, 1941–1942. (United States at War Database)

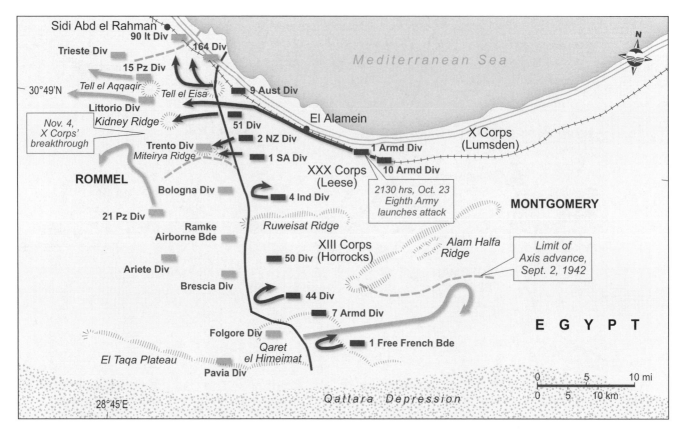

Battle of El Alamein, 1942. (United States at War Database)

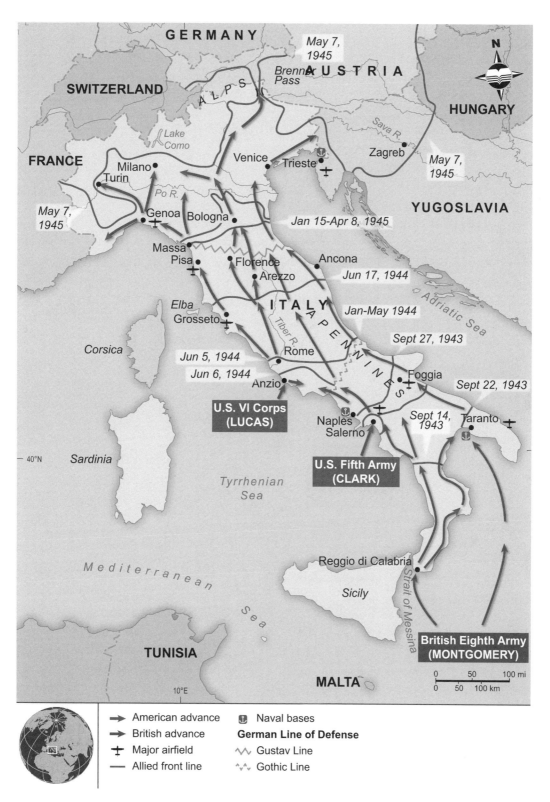

Italy, 1943–1945. (United States at War Database)

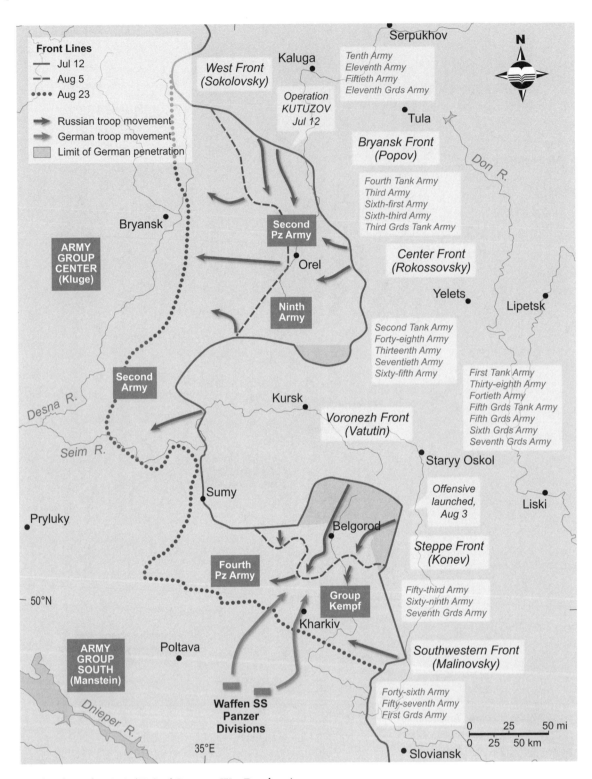

Battle of Kursk, 1943. (United States at War Database)

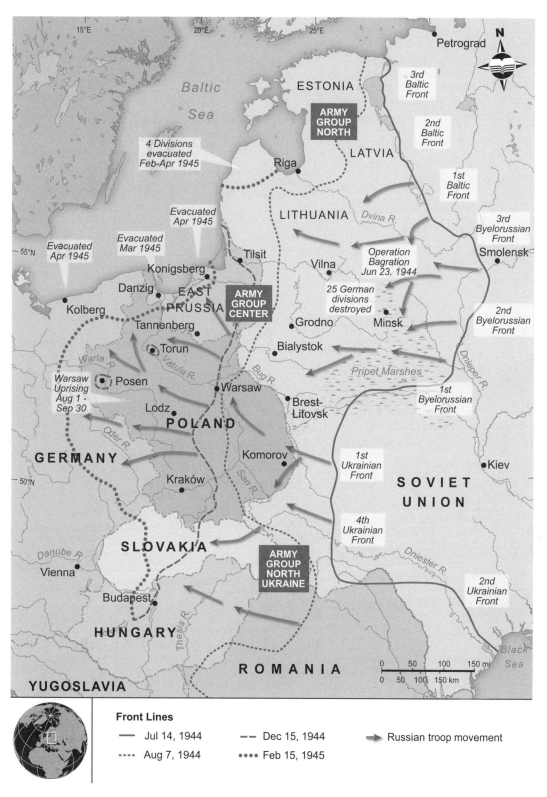

Petrograd

15°E   20°E   25°E

Baltic Sea

ESTONIA

3rd Baltic Front

ARMY GROUP NORTH

2nd Baltic Front

4 Divisions evacuated Feb-Apr 1945

Riga

LATVIA

1st Baltic Front

Evacuated Apr 1945

LITHUANIA

Dvina R.

3rd Byelorussian Front

Evacuated Apr 1945

Evacuated Mar 1945

—55°N

Tilsit

Vilna

Operation Bagration Jun 23, 1944

Smolensk

Konigsberg

Danzig

EAST PRUSSIA

ARMY GROUP CENTER

25 German divisions destroyed

Grodno

Minsk

2nd Byelorussian Front

Kolberg

Tannenberg

Torun

Warta

Vistula R.

Bialystok

Pripet Marshes

Dnieper R.

Warsaw Uprising Aug 1 - Sep 30

Posen

Warsaw

Bug R.

1st Byelorussian Front

Lodz

POLAND

Brest-Litovsk

GERMANY

Oder R.

Kraków

Komorov

San R.

1st Ukrainian Front

Kiev

—50°N

S O V I E T

U N I O N

4th Ukrainian Front

SLOVAKIA

ARMY GROUP NORTH UKRAINE

Danube R.

Vienna

Budapest

Dniester R.

Tisza R.

2nd Ukrainian Front

HUNGARY

Black Sea

YUGOSLAVIA

R O M A N I A

0   50   100   150 mi

0   50 100 150 km

Front Lines

—— Jul 14, 1944   - - - Dec 15, 1944   ➡ Russian troop movement

···· Aug 7, 1944   •••• Feb 15, 1945

Eastern Front, 1944. (United States at War Database)

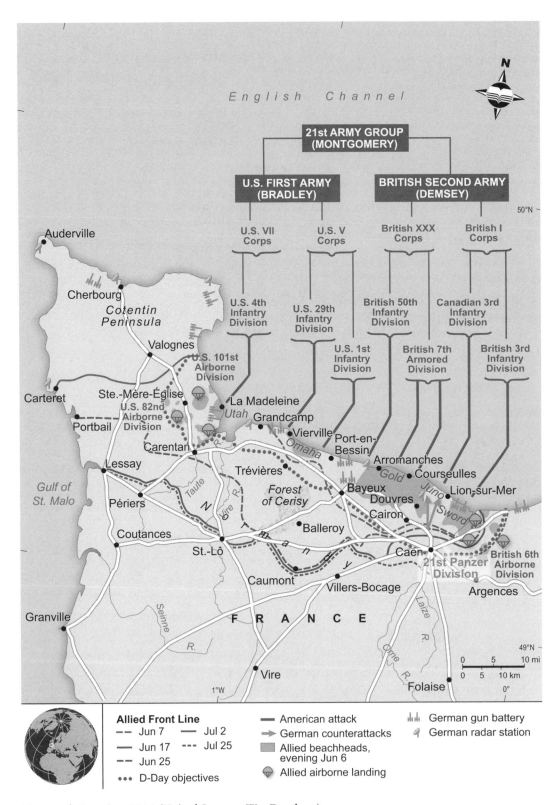

Normandy Invasion, 1944. (United States at War Database)

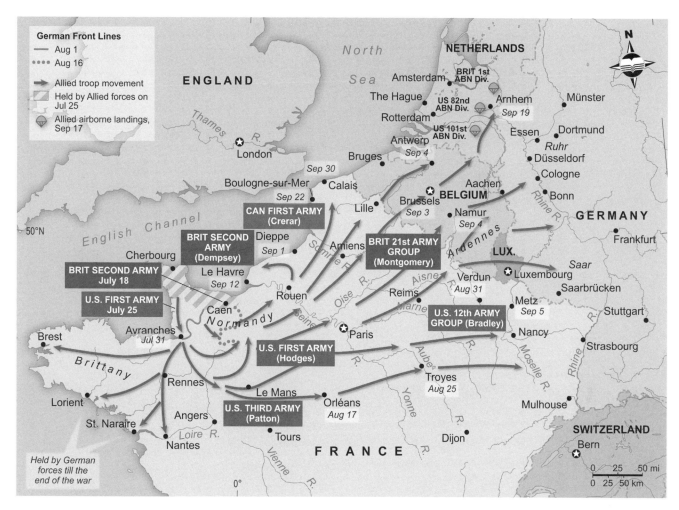

German Front Lines
— Aug 1
···· Aug 16

→ Allied troop movement
Held by Allied forces on Jul 25
Allied airborne landings, Sep 17

North Sea

NETHERLANDS

ENGLAND

Amsterdam

BRIT 1st ABN Div.

The Hague

US 82nd ABN Div.

Arnhem
Sep 19

Münster

Rotterdam

Essen

Dortmund

Antwerp
Sep 4

US 101st ABN Div.

Ruhr

Düsseldorf

Bruges

Cologne

Thames R.

London

Aachen

Bonn

GERMANY

Boulogne-sur-Mer
Sep 22

Sep 30

Calais

Brussels
Sep 3

BELGIUM

Namur
Sep 4

Rhine R.

Lille

CAN FIRST ARMY (Crerar)

English Channel

Dieppe
Sep 1

BRIT SECOND ARMY (Dempsey)

Amiens

BRIT 21st ARMY GROUP (Montgomery)

Ardennes

LUX.

Frankfurt

50°N

Somme R.

Luxembourg

Cherbourg

BRIT SECOND ARMY July 18

Le Havre
Sep 12

Rouen

Oise R.

Reims

Aisne R.

Verdun
Aug 31

Saar

Saarbrücken

U.S. FIRST ARMY July 25

Caen

Normandy

Seine R.

Marne R.

Metz
Sep 5

Stuttgart

Avranches
Jul 31

Paris

U.S. 12th ARMY GROUP (Bradley)

Nancy

Rhine

Brest

U.S. FIRST ARMY (Hodges)

Moselle R.

Strasbourg

Brittany

Rennes

Le Mans

Troyes
Aug 25

Aube R.

Lorient

Angers

U.S. THIRD ARMY (Patton)

Orléans
Aug 17

R.

Mulhouse

St. Naraire

Loire R.

Tours

Yonne R.

Dijon

SWITZERLAND

Bern

Nantes

FRANCE

R.

Vienne R.

Held by German forces till the end of the war

0°

0   25   50 mi
0 25 50 km

Caen to the Rhine, 1944. (United States at War Database)

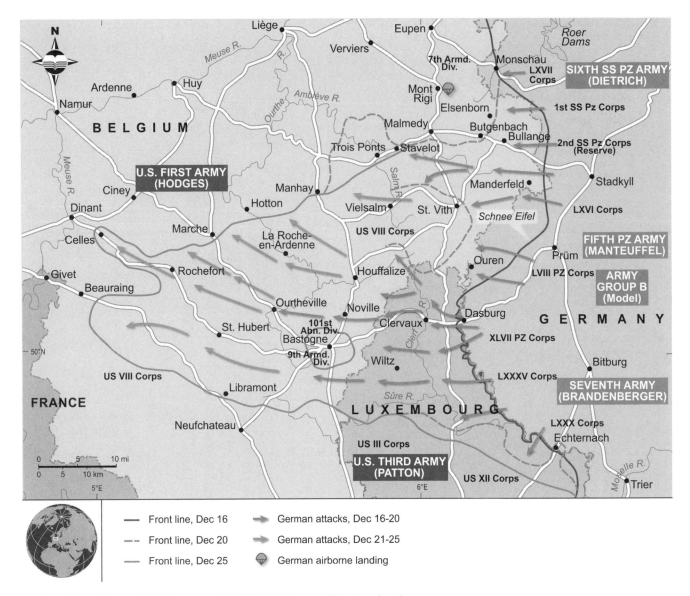

Battle of the Ardennes (Bulge), 1944–1945. (United States at War Database)

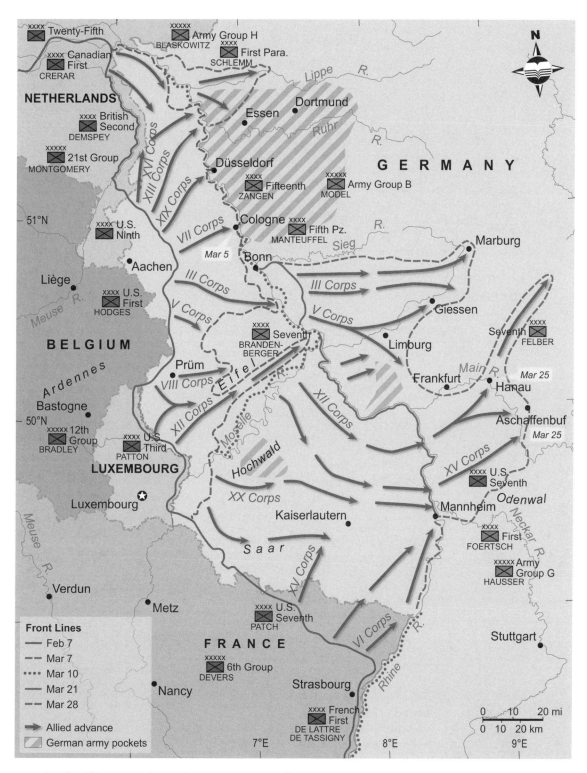

Crossing the Rhine, 1945. (United States at War Database)

Collapse of Germany, April–May 1945. (United States at War Database)

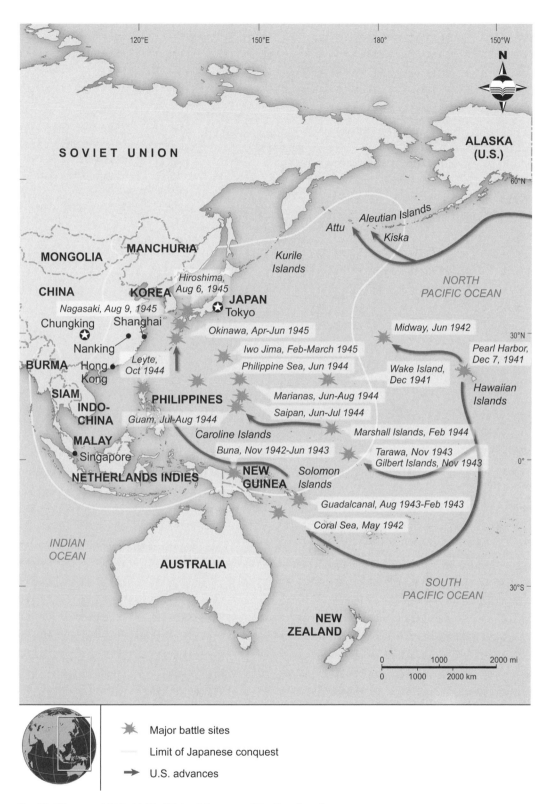

Pacific Theater, 1941–1945. (United States at War Database)

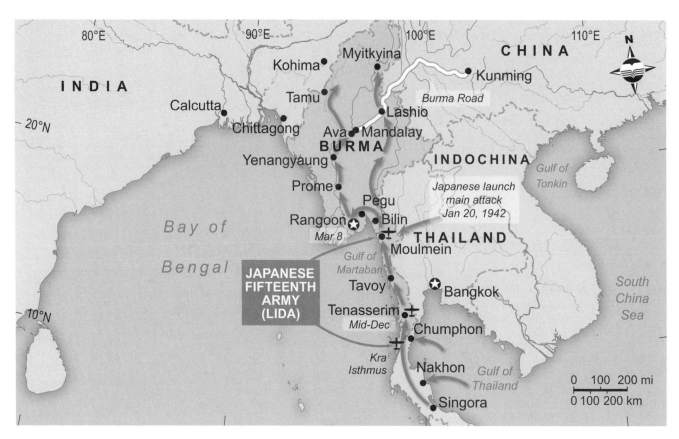

Japanese Invasion of Burma, 1941–1942. (United States at War Database)

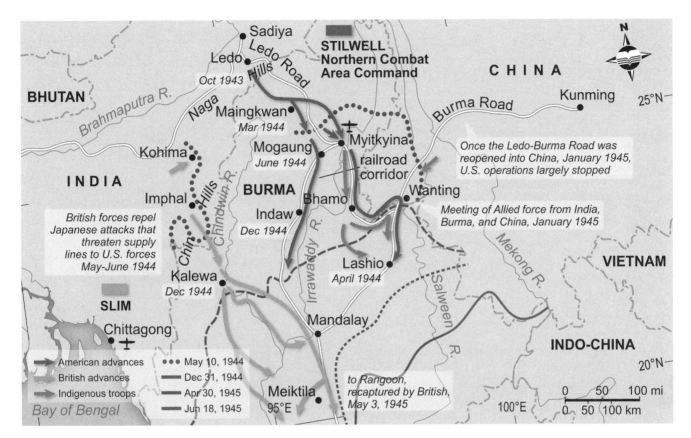

Burman-China Theater, 1943–1945. (United States at War Database)

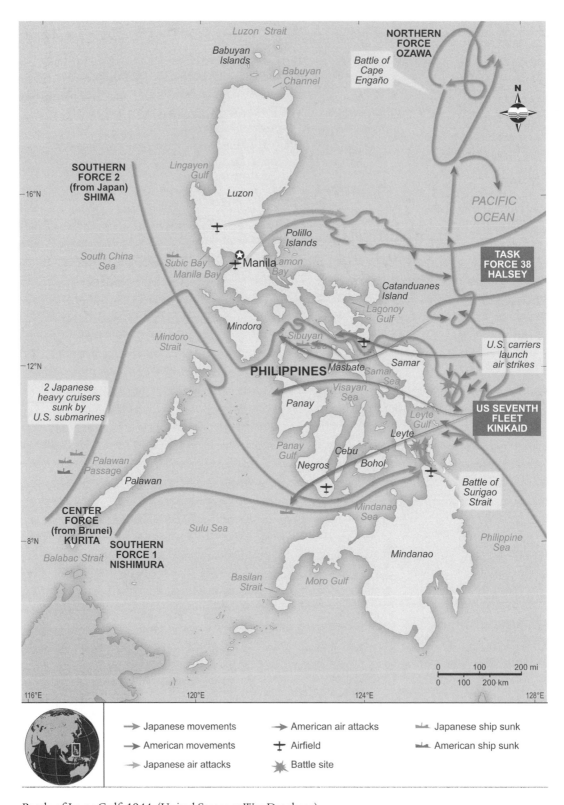

Battle of Leyte Gulf, 1944. (United States at War Database)

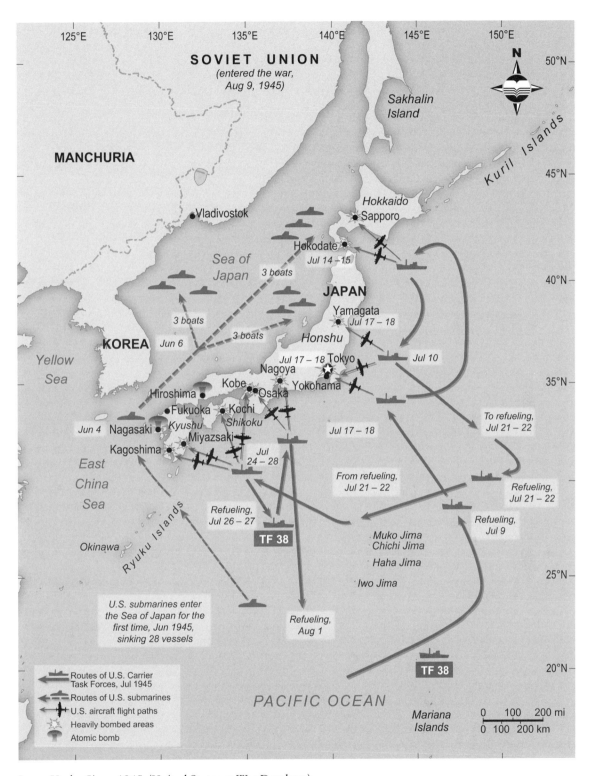

Japan Under Siege, 1945. (United States at War Database)

A-2   Allied air intelligence. Alternately, a specific air intelligence officer assigned to an air group.

A-10   German experimental intercontinental ballistic missile (ICBM).
See V-weapons program.

AA   Anti-aircraft artillery.
See anti-aircraft guns; Flak.

AACHEN   French: Aix-la-Chapelle. This former capital of Charlemagne was surrounded by U.S. forces on October 16, 1944. Hard resistance delayed the American advance for five weeks. American troops were also withdrawn from the sector to deal with the *Ardennes offensive.*

AAF   Army Air Forces.
See United States Army Air Forces.

ABC-1 PLAN   A joint American, British, and Canadian war plan framed in March 1941. The still neutral United States agreed that it would coordinate strategic planning with the other Western democracies upon entering the war. Early coordination actually preceded that event. Also agreed was a *Germany first strategy* should war ensue with all major Axis powers. That left sending aid to the *Guomindang* in China a distant priority. The strategic outlines of the ABC-1 Plan survived well into the war, leading to a strategy of early containment of Germany while peripheral attacks were made on the outlying Axis powers and colonies. The main early actions aimed at Germany were blockade by sea and pounding from the air, while the Western Allies strove to win the vital *Battle of the Atlantic (1939–1945)*. Meanwhile, Western Allied strength was gathered preparatory to a massive invasion of Western Europe, while such aid as could be spared and delivered was sent to the Soviet Union through *Lend-Lease* and *Mutual Aid*.

See also *Arcadia Conference; Rainbow Plans*.

ABDA COMMAND American-British-Dutch-Australian Command. The first Western Allied joint command of the Pacific War. At the *Arcadia Conference* in December 1941, the Western Allies agreed to establish an ABDA headquarters under General *Archibald Wavell*. The Command commenced operations on January 15, 1942. Its area of responsibility was all Dutch and British colonies in the southwest Pacific, Thailand, Burma, and the northern coast of Australia. Its subordinate naval command was called ABDAFLOAT. The Command marshaled pitifully few land, naval, or air resources against a confusion of bold Japanese strokes and stunning and rapid advances. Given command confusion and professional jealousies, ABDA proved unable to organize effective resistance. It survived only until the Japanese drove the HQ from Java on February 25, 1942. Thereafter, the United States took effective charge in the Pacific, the British commanded Allied efforts from Burma to Suez, while *Jiang Jieshi* was in nominal command in China.

See also *Burma; Java Sea (1942); South East Asia Command (SEAC)*.

ABSOLUTE NATIONAL DEFENSE SPHERE An inner strategic zone proclaiming total defense of an "inner" security perimeter for Japan, comprising Burma, Malaya, western New Guinea, the Dutch East Indies, Carolines, Marianas, and Kuriles. Territory held by Japanese forces outside the sphere was considered strategically expendable, useful only to delay the enemy's advance to the vital core of Japan's empire.

ABTEILUNG(EN) "Department(s)." A standard unit of the *Wehrmacht* with a paper strength of about a battalion. The term was also used to denote a specific military unit or detachment.

See also *Abwehr*.

ABWEHR "Amt Ausland Abwehr." German military intelligence. It was formed in the shadow of defeat in World War I, in violation of terms of the *Treaty of Versailles*. The Abwehr was headed during most of World War II by Admiral *Wilhelm Canaris,* who took command in 1935. Like most other prewar intelligence agencies, the Abwehr had limited espionage capabilities and few established foreign networks when war broke out in 1939. Internally, it was organized into an "Amtsgruppe Ausland" that gathered diplomatic intelligence and four "Abteilungen," or Departments I, II, III, and Z. Respectively, they conducted agent-based espionage, sabotage and subversion operations, counterespionage, and central administration. The Abwehr left most signals, electronic, and other technical intelligence to the Wehrmacht. The Abwehr sought to maintain an apolitical military professionalism, though that should not be misread as suggesting that it was out of sympathy with the aggressive nationalism of the regime and Wehrmacht. Still, its aloofness from overt Nazism brought its leadership under deep suspicion by the *Gestapo* and *SD* (*Sicherheitsdienst*), bitter rivals of the Abwehr within the *Schutzstaffel (SS)*. In 1942 a modus operandi was worked out that permitted the SD to conduct counterintelligence operations. That freed the Abwehr from having to conduct Party political espionage on the German population.

Abwehr human intelligence (HUMINT) networks had a toehold in France, but were rolled up quickly once war broke out in September 1939. Abteilung I never succeeded in penetrating Great Britain, the United States, or the Soviet Union. Its most successful wartime foreign operations were based in Spain, where it concentrated on monitoring ship movements past the Strait of Gibraltar and on liaison with foreign intelligence agencies—Spain was a major base for agents from all sides. Abteilung I had lesser successes in the Balkans. Its greatest wartime failure was in Britain, where every Abwehr agent was intercepted and either executed or turned by the *XX Committee's* "double-cross system." Abteilung II had a better record. It helped subvert Czechoslovakia by stirring Sudeten Germans in the run-up to the *Munich Conference* in 1938. However, one of its field units invaded Poland by itself after failing to receive Adolf Hitler's recall order for *FALL WEISS* in late August 1939. It crossed the border and occupied a designated target inside Poland, then hurriedly pulled out. It returned with the real invasion a few days later. From mid-1941 special units of Abteilung II *Brandenburgers* operated behind Soviet lines as expert saboteurs. Others shepherded into combat non-German units recruited from amongst desperate Soviet prisoners of war. Partly duplicating the success of the XX Committee, Abteilung III was able to turn a number of captured British agents and run radio disinformation (*Funkspeil*) through them back to Britain. A notable counterintelligence success was breaking up the *Rote Kapelle* espionage ring. Abteilung III tried to make contact with the IRA to foment subversion against the British in Ulster. It sent agents into the *Irish Free State*, but little came of that initiative. The Abwehr in general, and Abteilung III in particular, cooperated extensively with the Gestapo in ferreting out enemy agents, and with the SD in brutal preemption and repression of *resistance* movements inside German-occupied Europe.

As the war turned against Germany in 1942–1943, political loyalty increasingly trumped military professionalism as Nazi Party agencies looked to purge and control all organs of the state. Abwehr cooperation with the Gestapo and SD thus broke down. Canaris even used the Abwehr to protect anti-Nazi resisters in the intelligence and officer corps, notably the so-called *Schwarze Kapelle*, which was actively engaged in plotting to assassinate Hitler as early as 1938. Abwehr officers were involved in several wartime assassination and coup plots against Hitler. In late 1942 suspicion of the Abwehr led to arrests and torture of a number of its officers, seriously weakening the anti-Nazi movement within it. Failed operations in Spain led to further discrediting. On February 12, 1944, the Abwehr was dissolved by Hitler. *Heinrich Himmler,* head of the SS and an insatiable empire-builder, then absorbed Abwehr functions and some politically vetted officers into the SD. After the *July Plot* to kill Hitler failed later in the year, Canaris was arrested, tortured, and tried for treason. In April 1945 he was hanged by his Gestapo and SD jailors and enemies to prevent his liberation by U.S. forces.

See also BARCLAY; BLAU; COCKADE; FORTITUDE; FUSAG; *Indian Legion;* LUCY; *maskirovka;* MINCEMEAT.

ABYSSINIA   Also known as Ethiopia, prior to World War II the ancient kingdom and empire of Abyssinia was the only African nation besides Liberia that remained independent of European imperial conquest. At the end of the 19th century, Italy annexed neighboring Eritrea, which imperialists in Abyssinians also coveted. Along with a misread treaty and ongoing border dispute, that act led to war. The Abyssinians decisively defeated the Italians at Adowa in 1896, a humiliation of the Regio Esercito that Italian nationalists and imperialists could not forget or forgive. Border skirmishes with Italian forces from Eritrea or Italian Somaliland occurred into the 1930s. This long-running dispute with Italy was then referred to the *League of Nations.* Benito Mussolini did not wait upon a legal ruling. Instead, he ordered an invasion of Abyssinia in 1935, which began the *Abyssinian War (1935–1936).* Some Regio Esercito commanders and troops behaved with sadistic and racist cruelty during the war, using *poison gas* against retreating Abyssinian columns and callously murdering prisoners of war. Emperor *Haile Selassie* was forced into exile. The League denounced the aggression but imposed only weak sanctions on Italy, notably excluding oil, principally because the Western Allies were concerned that strict sanctions would push Mussolini and Italy closer to Adolf Hitler and Nazi Germany. That concern was dissolved into the larger European war when Italy declared war on Great Britain and France in June 1940. Abyssinia was the first Axis-occupied country to be liberated, as a result of the *East African campaign (1940–1941).* The fighting pitted a superior raw number of Italians against a combined force of British, African colonial, and Indian Army troops. The British and Commonwealth coalition forces were supported by Abyssinians fighting as guerillas (*Patriots*) inside the country, with others accompanying and fighting with the British columns in repeated routs of the Italians. Emperor Haile Selassie was restored to his throne in Addis Ababa on May 5, 1941.

See also Badoglio, Pietro; Gideon Force; Stresa Front.

ABYSSINIAN WAR (1935–1936)   During the early 1930s Italy progressively encroached on Abyssinian territory from colonial bases in Eritrea and Italian Somaliland. The ostensible casus belli under which Italy invaded in 1935 was a disputed border in the Ogaden peninsula. The real cause was Benito Mussolini's desire to extend Italy's empire in East Africa, along with nationalist pursuit of blood revenge for humiliation inflicted by the Abyssinians on an Italian army at Adowa in 1896. A border skirmish between Abyssinian and Italian troops occurred at Wal Wal on December 5, 1934. For 10 months tensions built in the region and internationally. London tried to appease Rome by offering a strip of Abyssinian land to Italy, but Mussolini personally wanted war to "erase the shame" of the defeat at Adowa and to celebrate the cult of violence and of "action" that underlay his *fascist* movement. Italian armed forces therefore invaded Abyssinia in October 1935. Until that point, Britain and France had sought to accommodate Italy's imperial ambitions in Africa to avoid pushing Mussolini closer to Adolf Hitler and Nazi Germany in Europe. Some in London and Paris still thought it might be possible to bring Italy back into the old anti-German alliance, the Triple Entente that fought the Great War in the west from 1915 to 1918, or at least the *Stresa Front* formed in April 1935 to oppose Hitler's rearmament of Germany. But given Mussolini's sharp and relentless aggression, the Stresa Front soon lay in ruin. The *Hoare-Laval Pact (1935)* was hastily negotiated as a last-ditch diplomatic effort to again appease Italy at Abyssinia's direct expense. But it also failed.

Mussolini sent a huge force of 400,000 troops, 100,000 supporting civilians, and 500 combat aircraft crashing into Abyssinia starting on October 3, 1935. That military commitment was extraordinary for a colonial war, constituting the largest invasion in the history of European colonialism. Against such numbers the Abyssinians stood little chance. Italian technological superiority in aircraft and armor, as well as ruthless use of illicit blister gas, quickly bested more lightly armed Abyssinian troops. Along with tons of bombs, blister agents killed thousands out of 20,000 Abyssinian soldiers retreating in long columns. Biological agents were also approved for use by Mussolini, in a measure of his ruthlessness and nature as a war criminal. The Abyssinians had no anti-aircraft guns to repel low-flying crop dusters of the Regia Aeronautica spraying poison, or biplane bombers and fighters that attacked and strafed panicking columns. Addis Ababa fell on May 5, 1936, to an Italian army led by Field Marshal *Pietro Badoglio*. Italy now possessed the enlarged East African empire it had coveted since the 19th century. Four days later, Mussolini proclaimed from a balcony in Rome: "Italy finally has its empire . . . It is a Fascist empire, an empire of peace, an empire of civilization and humanity."

Mussolini had initial trouble gaining recognition of his new conquest, which remained incomplete in any case. The League of Nations denounced Italy as an aggressor state on October 11, 1935, but it authorized only limited sanctions that specifically excluded oil and steel. Many in high policy circles in London and Paris thought that an accommodation with Mussolini was still possible. Indeed, some would believe that also about Hitler into January 1939. The weak Western response deeply discredited an already tottering League and gutted any meaning of its proposed service as an instrument of *collective security*. As one result, Hitler concluded that the Western powers were feeble, speeded his rearmament program, and moved more quickly to overturn the international order established by the *Treaty of Versailles*. Mussolini sidled ever closer to Hitler, despite continuing Anglo-French efforts at *appeasement*, and whipped up nationalist sentiment against the League and against London. In wake of the weak response to his aggression, Mussolini concluded that the Western Allies were morally "decadent" and in terminal geopolitical decline, while the fascist states were supposedly "virile" and ascendant powers. It was stuff and nonsense, but played well enough to the *blackshirt* faithful.

Field Marshal *Rodolfo Graziani* was appointed Italy's viceroy in Abyssinia. His occupation policy was overtly racist, harsh, and highly punitive as resistance continued in the two-thirds of Abyssinia that remained uncontrolled by the Italian occupiers. In July 1936, Mussolini ordered "a systematic policy of terror and extermination against rebels and any population who favors them." Prisoners were used for live target practice, more poison gas was sprayed on villages, and thousands more Abyssinian civilians died in Italian *concentration camps*. A failed assassination attempt against Graziani in 1937 led to a rampaging massacre of several thousand Abyssinian civilians by Italian troops. Such brutal mistreatment only encouraged the Abyssinians to continue to resist. As a result of the efforts of ex-Abyssinian Army troops and other guerillas, who became known as *Patriots,* the Italians never effectively controlled the country outside its main cities, and even those were linked by heavily guarded railway lines constantly subject to Patriot sabotage and other attacks. The protracted fighting and heavy garrison needs that resulted added an enormous strain to Italy's already very weak economic and fiscal circumstances. Sanctions further cut into Italian foreign markets around the world. More money had to be spent on shipping and armaments as troops were kept in the field in Abyssinia whom the government desperately wanted to demobilize and stop paying.

Italian troops based in Abyssinia tried to advance into Kenya, Sudan, and British Somaliland in 1940, all neighboring British colonies or protectorates. That was another failed attempt to expand Italy's East Africa empire into vulnerable Western colonies, this time at a moment of aching British military and political weakness in Europe. But the British Empire proved far more resilient than Mussolini or Hitler calculated. The Italian declaration of war against Britain and attempt to pick off vulnerable East African colonies posed a strategic threat to the Suez Canal. In British eyes, it thereby converted the war in East Africa into an important theater of the larger war of imperial self-defense against Germany. In the end, Italy could not hold onto any of its fresh East African gains or even its older colonies. Abyssinia seethed with rebellion against Italian occupation, and the countryside became dangerous for Italian patrols. Patriots flocked to fight alongside the British and set up guerilla operations in Italian rear areas. The country was liberated by invading British, Indian Army, and Abyssinian troops in May 1941, a major achievement of the *East African campaign* fought from 1940 to 1941. Emperor *Haile Selassie* was restored to the throne. The rest of the Italian colonial empire in East Africa quickly fell to British and Commonwealth armies operating from forward bases in Abyssinia. None of those colonies were returned to Italy after the war, although Eritrea was designated a United Nations Trust Territory under Italian supervision.

Note: The usual dating of this war, used in this entry for reasons of familiarity, reflects Italian propaganda as well as international recognition of Rome's claim to the "conquest" of Abyssinia. In fact, the fighting that began in late 1935 did not end in most of rural Abyssinia until the Italians were defeated and expelled from the country in mid-1941.

See also Gideon Force.

Suggested Reading: G. Baer, *Test Case* (1976); F. Hardie, *The Abyssinian Crisis* (1974).

ACE   Any fighter pilot with at least five confirmed "kills." The Luftwaffe had the highest number of aces of the war, with claims by 3,000 Luftwaffe flyers to the status of "experten." Nine German flyers were recognized as each making over 200 "Abschüsse" (shootdowns). Erich Hartmann and Gerhard Barkhorn were the top aces of any air force, with official credit for 352 and 301 victories, respectively. Hartmann's last shootdown was over Brno in Czechoslovakia on May 8, 1945, the last day of the war. He was taken prisoner the next day and spent 10 years in Soviet labor camps. Although the Japanese discouraged individual kill counts in favor of collective credit, records of shootdowns were kept by pilots and fighter squadrons nonetheless. Most were recorded as painted cherry blossoms on the sides of fighters. The leading Japanese Army ace was Hiroyoshi Nishizawa, credited with 102 kills. He was shot down while seated as a passenger on a transport aircraft. Next in line were fighter pilots with 87 and 80 victories. Japanese naval aces included Saburo Saki with 60 kills. He was severely wounded over Guadalcanal, but returned to air combat in 1944. The lesser Axis air forces also produced aces. The top Finnish ace had 94 kills, while the top fighter pilot in Italy's *Regia Aeronautica* was credited with 26 shootdowns. Croatia produced an unusual number of aces proportionate to its small population.

The greatest Allied ace of the war was Red Army Air Force (VVS) pilot Ivan Kozhedub, who had 62 confirmed kills as the top "asy" of the VVS. Among British and Commonwealth air forces the top ace was a New Zealander, Marmaduke Pattle. He was credited with destroying 51 enemy aircraft. The top American ace was Richard Bong, who was accorded 40 corroborated kills. The leading Frenchman was Marcel Albert, who had 33 recorded victories. Some of his shootdowns were scored over France in 1940. More came later in the war when he flew Yak-3 fighters over the *Eastern Front,* alongside other *Free French* pilots who flew for the VVS with the *Normandie-Niemen* squadron. Many other Allied nations also had fighter aces. The RCAF had over 150, while the air forces of Australia and New Zealand each produced dozens of air aces or had pilots declared aces while flying with the RAF.

U-boat captains of the Kriegsmarine were celebrated as "sea aces." They were elevated in Nazi propaganda as feted national heroes. The most famous were Günther Prien, Joachim Schepke, Otto Schuhart, and Herbert Schultze, among others. U-boat aces were in fact disproportionately responsible for sinking Allied ships, with just 20 U-boat captains accounting for 23 percent of tonnage sunk by all U-boats: tonnage as well as raw numbers of ships, was the measurement by which one became a submarine ace. Few U-boat aces survived the war, however, as the arm had the highest casualty rate of any in the Wehrmacht. The Royal Navy, Dutch Navy, and other navies produced submarine aces as well. Confirmed sinkings by U.S. Navy submarine captains were reappraised after the war and in many cases lowered, fairly or not.

ACHSE "AXIS" Code name for the 1943 German operation to disarm all Italian armed forces and take control of alpine France and those parts of the Balkans under Italian administration. It was slated to be implemented in the event Italy surrendered separately. It was originally code named "ALARICH." In modified form, ACHSE was put into effect during the muddled and muffed Italian surrender to the Western Allies in early September 1943. Hundreds of thousands of Italians were disarmed and shipped off to labor camps in the Reich. But in parts of the Balkans some Italian divisions resisted the Germans. Wehrmacht and *Waffen-SS* reprisals were severe: in just one instance, 5,000 Italian prisoners were shot.

ACK-ACK Onomatopoeic British term for anti-aircraft fire, derived from signals code for anti-aircraft guns. It does not appear to have been a play on the term for the superb German 88 mm anti-aircraft gun, or acht-acht (8-8), but it may have been.

See also Flak.

ACTION FRANÇAISES French anti-Semitic organization. It was founded in 1899 by Charles Maurras (1868–1952) during the protracted "Dreyfus Affair" that tore apart the French Army. Action Françaises helped undermine French national morale before World War II, as it also did prior to the Great War. Members were mainstays of the fascist wing of the Vichy regime, helping prepare for murderous collaboration with Nazi and Vichy race laws that led to deportation and murder of many thousands of French and foreign Jews.

See also fascism; France.

ADEN A key British naval base on the Arabian peninsula, protecting the *"All Red" route* from India to the Suez Canal. It was the main base from which Indian Army troops retook British Somaliland from the Italians in March 1941, while other British and Commonwealth armies penetrated Abyssinia (Ethiopia).

ADIGE LINE A German defensive line built across northern Italy along the Adige River. It was a World War I–style system of interlocking trenches and pillboxes, usually 1,000 to 5,000 meters in depth. It was intended to cover the Wehrmacht's withdrawal into the last corner of northeast Italy, thence into Austria. It was breached before it could be fully manned, overrun by the rapid advance of U.S. 5th Army during the campaign for the *Argenta Gap* in April 1945.

ADLERANGRIFF Code name for a two-week long Luftwaffe assault on RAF airbases that initiated the *Battle of Britain* on August 13, 1940, which the Germans called "Adlertag" or "Eagle Day."

ADLERHORST

See Hitler's headquarters.

ADLERTAG **(AUGUST 13, 1940)**   "Eagle Day."
   See ADLERANGRIFF; Britain, Battle of.

ADMIN BOX, BATTLE OF (FEBRUARY 5–23, 1944)   Also known as the "Battle of Ngayedauk" or "Battle of Sinzweya." It took place during the British campaign to expel the Japanese from Burma. British 14th Army was actually heavily manned by *Indian Army* troops. Their fight began with a Japanese spoiling attack on advance units of British 15th Corps. The Japanese code named that operational maneuver "Ha-Gō." It was intended to distract from the main action of the *Imphal offensive,* which in fact crashed into a simultaneous Western Allied offensive in Burma. Japanese commanders hoped to pin down British and Indian Army forces that might otherwise be shifted against the drive to Imphal, which was slated to open in March. The fighting developed around a compact British administrative HQ and supply base that formed a 1,100 square meter "Box" near Sinzweya. Japanese 55th Division, an all-infantry force without tank or heavy artillery support, struck with total surprise against defending 7th Indian Division. The Indians were quickly surrounded, but contrary to prior Japanese experience with British and Indian Army troops in Burma, refused to surrender or run. Instead, they stood and fought back hard. Nor were they overwhelmed by the firepower deficient Japanese infantry, who had been unable to haul heavy weapons over dense jungle trails to Sinzweya.

British airlifts and highly accurate tactical bombing added strength to several tanks used in a defensive role by determined Indian troops within the Box. The Japanese did not expect the Indians or other British troops to fight as hard or as well as they did, based on prior experience. But the resistance proved that British and Indian Army forces had learned much. Japanese 55th Division's supply situation also became critical when it failed to take the well-stocked base at the outset, as had been foolhardily planned by HQ planners. Other Indian Army divisions fought into Sinzweya to relieve the siege. Then they enveloped and utterly destroyed Japanese 55th Division. Allied casualties totaled just over 3,500 killed, wounded, or missing. Japanese official casualties exceeded 5,300, including 3,106 dead. About 400 Japanese survivors got away from the carnage only by withdrawing against orders on February 24. And that was a sure sign of fatal decline in Japanese morale in the Burma theater. The fight was viewed as a significant defeat by *Imperial General Headquarters* in Tokyo. In fact, it was only the opening act in a far greater disaster for the Japanese soon to play out at Imphal: victory at Sinzweya enabled British and Indian Army reinforcements to be sent to Imphal, where defeat unhinged the Japanese offensive and started a cascading catastrophe for all Japanese forces in-country. On the Western Allied side, the February battle showed how far Indian Army troops had advanced in training, combat skill, discipline, motivation, and equipment from the calamitous defeats of 1942.

ADMIRALTY
   See Royal Navy (RN).

ADMIRALTY ISLANDS A South Pacific island group 200 miles northeast of New Guinea, forming part of the larger *Bismarck Archipelago*. The Japanese occupied the Admiralties in April 1942. Some islands were retaken by Western Allied forces in 1944; others were bypassed in the *island-hopping* campaign. Los Negros was secretly scouted on February 27, 1944. Poor Japanese dispositions enabled American troops to get ashore on the far side of that island two days later, with General *Douglas MacArthur* on hand to watch the preliminary bombardment. The attackers quickly established a perimeter around a captured air strip. The Japanese struck back with small infiltration attacks that night, but were repulsed. On March 3 the Japanese commander realized the mistake of his initial dispositions and launched a main attack on the now firm American perimeter. The attackers came under close naval gunfire, but persisted. Parts of the perimeter were overrun in hand-to-hand fighting that lasted through the night, killing 61 Americans but some 750 Japanese. Not one Japanese soldier surrendered: all wounded or able-bodied survivors killed themselves. A number of small garrisons on other Admiralty islets were quickly overcome by Western Allied air, naval, and ground forces. The most significant fight took place on Manus Island starting on March 15. Australian and American aircraft and ground forces attacked and overran the Japanese airfield on Manus on the 16th, but fighting continued against Japanese bitterenders until March 25. U.S. forces took two more islets in the chain on April 1, reaching them in stealthy native canoes. By the time all fighting ended in the Admiralties the invaders suffered 330 dead and nearly 1,200 wounded. Japanese dead numbered 3,300. Just 75 Japanese allowed themselves to be taken prisoner, and most of them were too badly wounded to prevent capture.

See also Alamo Force; Bismarck Sea, Battle of the; Rabaul.

ADSEC Advance Section, Communications Zone. The logistics section directly supporting U.S. troops during the cross-Channel invasion of France in 1944.

AEAF Allied Expeditionary Air Force. The senior air command of the Western Allies, under *SHAEF.*

AEF Allied Expeditionary Force. The formal nomenclature for all Western Allied armies involved in the 1944–1945 campaign in northwestern Europe under the unitary command of General *Dwight Eisenhower.*

See also SHAEF.

AEGEAN ISLANDS

See Crete; Dodecanese campaign.

AFGHANISTAN This isolated and mountainous Muslim land was occupied by the British out of India from 1857, but it was never fully "pacified." Afghans achieved unruly independence after a bloody rebellion in the 1920s. Feudal emirs and provincial warlords thereafter ruled in uneasy coexistence under a loose and weak central king. Afghanistan joined the *League of Nations* in 1935. It subsequently signed nonaggression pacts with its more powerful neighbors: the Soviet Union, Turkey, and Iran. Nazi Germany achieved some influence with anti-British Afghan emirs, although Afghanistan remained formally neutral from 1939 to 1941. Thereafter, Soviet and British victories over Germany and intense Anglo-Soviet pressure compelled Afghans to sever all ties with the Axis states.

See also New Order.

AFHQ

See Allied Forces Headquarters (AFHQ).

AFRICAN AMERICANS   Discrimination against prewar enlistment of African Americans meant that just 5,000 black enlisted men and a handful of black officers served in the U.S. Army when the war began. Even with the onset of a world war, Army leaders ensured that blacks were far less likely to be recruited than whites. The Army was forced to admit many more blacks from December 1942, however, when President Franklin Roosevelt issued executive order #9279, forcing all branches of the military to end racially-based restrictions. But not even a direct order from the commander in chief ended in-service discrimination. The Army responded by segregating most black enlistees into the Quartermaster and Engineering Corps, where they were employed as drivers, road builders, and ammunition depot workers. Even when trained for combat and deployed in forward combat zones, black units were often reassigned to noncombat support duties. Active discrimination by white soldiers against their black countrymen in overseas bases sometimes led to violent individual confrontations and even a few riots. There were additional race riots on bases and nearby towns in the United States. Over 700,000 black soldiers served in the U.S. Army by the end of the war, of whom nearly 400,000 deployed overseas. The first black unit to enter combat was the 25th Regiment, which fought on *Bougainville* in March 1944. Among larger combat units, the 92nd and 93rd Infantry Divisions and the 2nd Cavalry had the largest number of African American troops.

The USAAF strongly resisted admitting black pilots until forced to do so by presidential order. Then it trained blacks at segregated facilities, most notably airfields at Tuskegee, Alabama. The first all-black fighter squadron to be deployed overseas saw action in the Mediterranean starting in April 1943. It was followed by just three more black squadrons before the war ended—fewer than would have been available had there not been such prejudicial resistance to giving blacks officer commissions. The U.S. Navy also restricted African American recruitment. It traditionally employed black sailors in menial noncombat positions aboard ships and in navy yards, including working as loaders of ammunition on supply ships. That pattern continued for most black sailors during the war, by the end of which about 165,000 African Americans had served in the Navy. Another

17,000 joined the U.S. Marine Corps, while several thousand served in the Coast Guard. Black ammunition workers were drawn into heavy combat on *Iwo Jima* and several other Pacific islands, while black sailors saw combat on numerous ships that came under Japanese or German attack or which hunted enemy shipping or submarines.

Despite the many and enormous obstacles presented to African American recruitment, training, and deployment, once in combat all-black units generally fought at least as well as most all-white units. Some fought with true distinction. Individual African American soldiers, sailors, and pilots fought so well they received the highest awards for valor. That was true despite deep institutional and social prejudice against acknowledging the superior combat performance of individual blacks: some had to wait decades to receive much belated awards, up to and including the Medal of Honor. Discrimination extended to auxiliary women's formations. The WAVES refused to accept black women for most of the war. The first African American women were admitted only in July 1945, too late to see any overseas service. The National Maritime Union, the American *merchant marine* personnel service, had no color barrier. It therefore saw large enlistments of black crewmen. More generally, African Americans migrated outside the South in large numbers during World War II, mostly to find work in booming factories and ports in the North and West, and on the coasts. The return of black servicemen to segregated facilities and social life in the United States following their participation in liberation of foreign lands from racist regimes proved hard and left much justified bitterness. Return home was on occasion attended by murderous violence against black veterans by some of the people they had fought to defend. The U.S. military stayed racially segregated until President Harry Truman ended the practice in 1948.

See also Forrestal, James; medals; Patton, George; rape; Red Ball Express; Stimson, Henry.

Suggested Reading: Bryan Booker, *African-Americans in the U.S. Army in World War II* (2008).

AFRICAN TROOPS

See Abyssinian War (1935–1936); Allies; Armée d'Afrique; Argenta Gap; Chindits; desert campaign (1940–1943); East African campaign (1940–1941); Fezzan campaign (1941–1943); DRAGOON; Elba; FALL GELB; Free French; French Expeditionary Corps; French Somaliland; French West Africa; Gabon; Gold Coast; Goumiers; Monte Casino; Nigeria; Patriots; Sierra Leone; South Africa; Tirailleurs; Tirailleurs Senegalese; West African Military Labor Corps; Western Desert Air Force; Zouaves.

AFRIKA KORPS "Deutsches Afrika Korps (DAK)." A *Sperrverband* originally comprising one German light infantry division and a single Panzer division. It was formed on Adolf Hitler's order in February 1941 and deployed in haste to Tripoli starting in March. Hitler never regarded the Mediterranean as a primary theater of operations for the Wehrmacht. The DAK was assembled from scratch and rushed into combat to assist the beleaguered Italians in North Africa, who were on the verge of catastrophic defeat by British and Commonwealth forces. Hitler could not allow that collapse on the eve of launching Operation *BARBAROSSA* against the Soviet Union. Other German air and ground units followed as the *desert campaign (1940–1943)* developed a logic of its own. Some Regio Esercito units were attached to Afrika Korps command, although nominally the DAK was under overall Italian authority. In practice, German troops responded exclusively to German officers.

The original Afrika Korps commander was Major General *Erwin Rommel*. He genuinely inspired the men of the DAK to exceptional battlefield acts and made tactical innovations in armored warfare and anti-tank fighting that won legendary status on either side of the lines. In fact, an inflated reputation of the Afrika Korps among British and Commonwealth troops was a real problem. It had to be overcome with training, but also with hard won victories, before British 8th Army was able to regain the initiative in North Africa and drive the Germans and Italians back into Tunisia. As the scale of fighting expanded in the western desert in 1942, the Afrika Korps was given progressively larger paper formation titles, though it was only marginally larger than the original DAK in fact. It was finally absorbed into Italian 1st Army in early 1943. Throughout the DAK's time in Africa it suffered from severe shortages of tanks, aircraft, and fuel and ammunition. It increasingly faced much superior Western Allied logistics and larger forces, along with sea and air blockade of its own supplies conducted by the Royal Navy in the Mediterranean and RAF interdiction along extended desert roads. It fared poorly in terms of resupply and reinforcement because Hitler's attention was always primarily on the *Eastern Front*, which bled vast numbers of Wehrmacht men and vehicles during 1941 and 1942.

See also BATTLEAXE; Kasserine Pass; El Alamein; Montgomery; TORCH; Tunisia.

AFV Armored Fighting Vehicle. Western Allied designation for all types of armored vehicles, from tanks and tank destroyers to self-propelled guns and half-tracks.

AGENCY AFRICA A French–Polish joint intelligence operation set up by Major Rygor Slowikowski after he escaped to France upon the defeat of Poland in Operation *FALL WEISS* (1939). Slowikowski worked for the French until the armistice of June 22, 1940. He then set up a spy network in North Africa in mid-1941, believing that he was acting on orders from the Polish government-in-exile. But the London Poles were themselves acting at the behest of *MI6*. Later, the *Office of Strategic Services (OSS)* became involved. Slowikowski was remarkably effective running a network of local French agents across North Africa and parts of West Africa, under control of Polish intelligence officers who had joined him in exile. His network provided valuable information about Vichy defenses to the Western Allies prior to the *TORCH* landings in November 1942. However, the effect of that information should not be exaggerated: TORCH depended little on intelligence gleaned from within the region; its planning was determined by strategic, operational, and large-scale geopolitical considerations. After the Western Allied invasion and liberation of North Africa, Slowikowski's agents worked mainly in counterintelligence and on interrogations of Axis prisoners.

See also amphibious operations.

A-Gō *Imperial Japanese Navy (IJN)* code name for its late-war strategy of seeking to deny control of the Marianas Islands to U.S. forces. From May 1944, the IJN planned and hoped for a "decisive battle" with the U.S. Navy somewhere between the Philippines and Marianas Islands. The central concept of the Japanese operational plan was to use gravely weakened naval aviation, including land-based aircraft, to distract the U.S. fleet carriers long enough for IJN fast battleships and cruisers to close and hammer the enemy landing force with naval shellfire. The plan added preference for night action, with the surface ships supported by most of Japan's remaining attack submarines. That concept led to massing of IJN assets and wild destruction and disaster at the *Battle of the Philippine Sea*.

AIF (SECOND)   Australian Imperial Forces.
See Australian Army.

AIR ARMY   "vozdushnaia armiia." The largest Soviet air formation, roughly comparable to a Luftwaffe *Fliegerkorps*. They were not constituted until May 1942. Once formed, they helped counteract the early Luftwaffe advantage in large-scale air formations. However, unlike more flexibly deployed Fliegerkorps, Soviet air armies were attached to individual Fronts and under the control of ground force commanders.
See also Red Army Air Force (VVS).

AIRBORNE   Infantry and weapons delivered to a battlefield by parachute and glider. The Soviet Union was a pioneer in airborne warfare, experimenting as early as 1922 with both parachutists and gliders. It trained so many youths in sports jump and glider clubs of the *Komsomol* and *Osoaviakhim* that by 1940 over one million citizens had received some airborne training. The Red Army Air Force (VVS) also made advances in development of advance gliders and other specialized aircraft. This lead in airborne tactics and resources was squandered during the late 1930s purge of VVS top commands. An effort was made to reorganize in the late spring of 1941, but it came too late to affect the outcome of the opening battles of the German invasion of the Soviet Union in mid-1941. Preoccupied with defending against deep German penetrations during *BARBAROSSA*, the Red Army did not attempt strategic airborne operations. The Red Army and VVS had experimented with prototype flying tanks that were intended to accompany infantry into *deep battle* operations. That experiment stopped in early 1942 as more basic combat demands took priority in planning, production, and battlefield execution. Facing catastrophic manpower losses, the Red Army abandoned its prewar plans to form airborne tank, artillery, and infantry corps. Instead, it reorganized all airborne forces on a brigade-level. The Stavka thereafter mostly used airborne troops as light or regular infantry in desperate ground fighting, with only small drops conducted near Kiev and Odessa. Surviving gliders were used to resupply pockets of regulars trapped behind German lines. In that respect, the German and Soviet airborne experience was similar.

A Soviet corps-level airborne operation was assayed during a Red Army counter-offensive at Viazma in February–March, 1942. It formed part of the *Rzhev-Viazma strategic operation* (January 8–April 20, 1942). In the *Demiansk offensive operation* that spring, over 7,000 Soviet paratroopers died. They landed well enough behind German lines, but were overpowered when left without sufficient follow-on support. From 1942 the VVS employed its glider fleet mainly to resupply *partisans* in German rear areas and to fly in demolition specialists and explosives to assist partisans carrying out sabotage missions. *NKVD* men were also parachuted or glided behind German lines with instructions to establish tight central control over the partisans. Some Red Army airborne were employed in local attacks in the Crimea in 1943, during advances that retook part of the peninsula and surrounding Black Sea region. But most airborne were converted into *rifle divisions* and thrown into hard fighting as regular infantry. Another large Soviet airborne operation was tried at Kanev on September 24, 1943. Having broken up the prewar airborne divisions, the Stavka deployed a scratch corps of ill-trained or even untrained recruits. Some were making their first jump of any kind right into combat, over the Dnieper River at night. They were simply ordered into transport aircraft and told to jump. The operation failed with extremely heavy losses. The fiasco contributed directly to Soviet failure in the larger *Battle of the Dnieper (1943),* and Stalin forbade future night jumps. The most successful Soviet airborne assaults of the war came at its end, against the Japanese during the *Manchurian offensive operation* of August 1945. In that operation all three Red Army Fronts engaged against the Japanese employed airborne troops in, by then, well-practiced deep insertions.

German military observers in the Soviet Union in the 1920s were intrigued by Soviet airborne experiments, although senior officers in the Reichswehr were not. Germany built some secret airborne capability in the 1920s and speeded the program in the early 1930s. The Luftwaffe worked openly on an airborne capability from 1938, once Adolf Hitler backed the project. A full airborne corps was thus in place before the war, led by Luftwaffe General *Kurt Student*. Limited airborne operations were planned for the occupation of Czechoslovakia in 1938 and again for the invasion of Poland in 1939. Neither plan was carried out due to settlement of the Czech crisis at the *Munich Conference* in September 1938 and the short duration of the *FALL WEISS* campaign in Poland. The corps eventually comprised one Luftwaffe division and a Heer division, seconded to the Luftwaffe. That was an unusual arrangement. In most militaries, airborne units were placed under army rather than air force control. The main aircraft employed in Luftwaffe airborne operations was the three-engine Ju-52. It could deliver *Fallschirmjäger* (paratroopers) directly or tow them in a small specialty glider. The DFS-230 "attack glider" carried 10 Fallschirmjäger or a 2,500 lb. payload of equipment. The Luftwaffe later built the huge Me-323 Gigant ("Giant"), which could carry 200 men. Typically in late-war German weapons design, that super-glider was beyond Luftwaffe logistical and transport capabilities as it needed three other planes to tow it, and the German aircraft industry had by then gone over to nearly exclusive fighters production. The Me-323 thus made an equivalent contribution to the German war effort as did Howard Hughes' infamous, giant "Spruce Goose" HK-1 *flying boat* to Western Allied operations; that is, none whatever.

The first ever use of airborne assault troops in combat took place in Denmark on April 9, 1940, when Student's men seized key airports by surprise. Within hours Fallschirmjäger also landed across Norway. At *Dombås* near Trondheim, they were defeated by the Norwegian Army after five days of fighting. At Narvik advance Fallschirmjäger engaged in extensive fighting with British forces that had landed amphibiously. At the outset of *FALL GELB* on May 10, 1940, Fallschirmjäger parachutist and glider-borne assaults achieved notable success in Belgium, where they landed near or atop several key forts. Their most spectacular success came with capture of the key fortress at *Eban Emael*. In France, Fallschirmjäger took key bridges over the Meuse and other forward sites on the first day, then awaited arrival of the Panzers. The most important element of their attacks was to mislead Western Allied commanders into believing the main weight of effort (*Schwerpunkt*) of the German offensive was in the north, when it actually came later through the Ardennes. Two more sets of landings were conducted on the first day of the campaign in the Netherlands. One was carried out near The Hague, with the intention of seizing the airport to permit *airlanding* forces to fly in. It met sharp resistance from the Dutch Army and saw huge losses of Ju-52 transports. A more successful operation led to seizure of key bridges over the Maas and several canals, allowing 9th Panzer to move quickly across country.

Fallschirmjäger carried out glider attacks in Greece during the *Balkan campaign* (1940–1941). There followed the largest German airborne action of the war: a large-scale attack against British and Commonwealth forces on *Crete* (Operation MERKUR). Parachute and glider-borne assaults quickly took the main airport, but Student's exposed and lightly armed Fallschirmjäger took 25 percent casualties and had to be heavily reinforced before the island was secured from stunned and poorly deployed, but determined, British and Greek defenders. The casualty rate among Fallschirmjäger on Crete convinced Hitler to forbid further large airborne operations. Germany only used Fallschirmjäger and glider troops afterwards for special missions such as the rescue of Mussolini (September 12, 1943). It also used gliders in very small reinforcement or espionage insertions and to deliver supplies to isolated troops on the Eastern Front. Otherwise, the Fallschirmjäger of "3rd Parachute Army" were used after Crete exclusively as light infantry in support of regular ground forces. They fought on the ground in Italy in 1943; on the Eastern Front from November 1943 to May 1944; and in Normandy, Brittany, and across the Netherlands during the second half of 1944. On several occasions, such as in Normandy and the Netherlands, Fallschirmjäger faced equally elite Western Allied paratroopers who dropped on top of them and who were also trained to fight as light infantry. The Germans made a successful surprise airborne assault on *Tito*'s headquarters in western Bosnia in May 1944. The last significant German use of glider troops was to land on the *Vercors* in southern France in an anti-*Résistance* operation in mid-1944. No other Axis military in Europe used gliders.

Axis commanders also used the elite Italian airborne Folgore ("Lightning") Division mainly on the ground. It suffered massive casualties at *El Alamein* in 1942. The San Marco Marines of the Regia Marina also had a parachute unit, the Battaglione Nuotatori. Only the Japanese developed airborne capabilities among other Axis forces. These saw limited action from mid-1942 due to low numbers and because Japan quickly went over to a strict defensive posture around its Pacific perimeter. Before that, the Imperial Japanese Army drew upon German experience and advisers to train a limited number of men in parachute attack. Its "Raiding Group" (teishin dan) comprised 2 parachute regiments of 600 men each. They had organic transport and were complemented by an attached glider regiment. The Imperial Japanese Navy separately trained two battalions of *Rikusentai* from the Yokosuka base. These airborne marines were deployed on Celebes and Sumatra during the invasion of the Dutch East Indies in early 1942, and later on Timor. As Japan moved into a wholly defensive posture in 1943, the Yokosuka regiments were employed as airborne troops only in local raids and other small-scale special operations. They were largely wiped out fighting as regular light infantry in defense of *Saipan* in 1944.

The British responded to early German success by rapidly organizing their own airborne and airlanding units. The most basic early problem Britain faced was limited strategic options. From June 1940, Britain was especially strained—to the defensive limit, but not beyond—by Italy's entry into the war and the consequent opening of new East African and Mediterranean fronts. Proposals to develop an offensive airborne capability initially met determined institutional opposition from RAF Bomber Command and from the British Army, which protested against releasing scarce aircraft and elite recruits to airborne training units. However, airborne operations fit well the *Chiefs of Staff* strategy and the prime minister's strong preference for peripheral assaults around the edges of the Nazi empire. Rather than division-scale drops in support of conventional ground forces, which were no longer engaged on the continent in any case, the first British airborne operations were conceived as commando-style raids. The first raid dropped British paratroopers into Italy in February 1941. Other small-scale raids saw drops into France, but the British also took a very different lesson from defending against the Fallschirmjäger assault on Crete than did the Germans after carrying out that operation. Where Hitler was most and adversely impressed by high Fallschirmjäger casualties, the British viewed Crete as a successful airborne assault that took an important military objective. From late 1941, therefore, British airborne capability preparation was elevated to division-level, and planning resumed for future large-scale operations.

Starting from scratch, the RAF and British Army had to design and produce specialist aircraft for airborne operations. The British did not have resources to spare at first. Hence, they initially relied on an inadequate aircraft adaptation: drop holes were simply cut in the floor of two-engine Whitley medium bombers, then of two-engine Albemarle medium bombers. Once heavy bombers became available in large numbers, the British switched to four-engine Stirling and Halifax aircraft for their airborne deliveries. When American C-47 Dakotas became available through *Lend-Lease*, the British switched to that highly capable and purpose-built airborne delivery aircraft. The C-47 was slow and unarmored, but it was a highly reliable transport for airborne troops heading to drops zones. And it allowed men to jump from a side door designed to accommodate fast drops with bulky equipment. British wooden glider types also evolved until, in combination, the Hotspur, Horsa, and Hamilcar far exceeded the lift capabilities of the small German DFS-230. Where the early Hotspur carried just 8 men, the Horsa carried 32. The still larger Hamilcar achieved a carrying capacity of 40 parachutists or seven tons of equipment, jeeps, or even a light tank. Over 4,000 of the two larger glider types were built. A powered version of the 40-seat Hamilcar was designed for the Pacific War but never went into action.

The first effort to carry out a large-scale airborne assault out came with Operation *TORCH,* the Western Allied landings in North Africa in November 1942. British 1st Airborne Division next jumped into Sicily in 1943 during Operation *HUSKY,* flying from North African bases. British 1st Airborne was joined in the order of battle by 6th Airborne and dropped into hard fighting in Normandy at the outset of *OVERLORD* late on June 5, 1944, and into *D-Day (June 6, 1944)*. British airborne jumped into total disaster around Arnhem during *MARKET GARDEN* that September. The experience shattered an entire airborne division and badly shook command confidence in the practice of exposing paratroopers and lightly armed glider troops deep behind enemy lines. It should be noted that British airborne divisions were multinational. Dropping or airlanding alongside British troops in Normandy and again in the Netherlands were paratroopers of several nationalities, including a Polish Parachute Brigade and a battalion of Canadians with the *Red Devils* of 6th Airborne. Free French also served. The British also recruited a brigade of paratroopers from the *Indian Army* and another of *Gurkhas* from Nepal. *Chindit* glider airlandings were carried out in Burma with the aid of the U.S. Army Air Force in March 1944. The 50th Indian Parachute Brigade was used on the ground as light infantry, not as airborne, during the *Imphal campaign*. The Gurkha airborne brigade dropped near Rangoon in May 1945.

The United States began development of a large-scale airborne capability in 1941. Until then its only operational airborne unit was the 501st Parachute Battalion. By the end of 1944 the U.S. Army trained and fielded five full airborne divisions. Each had an authorized complement of 8,505 men, comprising a parachute regiment and two glider regiments. U.S. airborne troops dropped in front of the first assault waves that carried out HUSKY, the invasion of Sicily. They were heavily engaged in perimeter defense against German and Italian counterattacks. General *George S. Patton* then called upon 2,000 more to jump as critical reinforcements behind the American invasion beach. A terrible friendly fire incident led USN and U.S. Army anti-aircraft gunners to shoot down 10 percent of the reinforcements, with significant loss of both aircraft and lives. But the airborne troops who landed were crucial to holding off a German armored counterattack that pressed hard against the narrow beachhead. Two U.S. airborne divisions jumped or glided into the Côtentin peninsula in Normandy on D-Day: the 82nd "All American" and 101st "Screaming Eagles" landed behind UTAH and OMAHA beaches. They were nearly all badly scattered and dispersed and took high casualties as they engaged in hard fighting over the first week of the *Normandy campaign*, including against veteran Fallschirmjäger deployed as light infantry in the Côtentin peninsula hedgerow country (bocage). The same American divisions made a second combat jump into the Netherlands during MARKET GARDEN. They were deployed on the ground as emergency, veteran infantry during the opening confusion of the Wehrmacht's *Ardennes offensive* in December 1944. They were critical in disrupting the German drive toward Antwerp, with the 101st notably holding out at Bastogne after becoming completely surrounded.

None of the five U.S. airborne divisions fielded during the war had organic air transport. They were delivered to their drop zones by USAAF C-47 Dakotas or in towed-gliders, notably the Waco CG-4A. U.S. 13th and 17th Divisions completed training stateside and were deployed to the ETO before the end of 1944. The 11th Division was sent to the Pacific, where it carried out several combat drops on Luzon in late 1944. The four American airborne divisions in the ETO were expanded to an official complement of 12,979 men each in December 1944. That was only a paper reform that had little or no impact on airborne operations. The last Western airborne operation of the European war was a joint combat jump made by British 6th Division and American 17th Division across the Rhine on March 23, 1945, in Operation VARSITY. Despite the fact that other American ground forces and elements of French 1st Army were already over the Rhine farther south, VARSITY was carried off as planned. Regardless of exhaustive advance preparation by Field Marshal *Bernard Law Montgomery*, the jumps incurred heavy casualties among the airborne component.

See also Air Commando; recoilless guns; Otto Skorzeny; Slovak Uprising; WESERÜBUNG.

AIR COMMANDO   A small U.S. Army Air Force command in Burma and India. It operated in support of British and Commonwealth forces fighting the Japanese. Its gliders carried *Chindit* fighters into action behind Japanese lines, while its small complement of fighters and bombers interdicted Japanese air and ground formations. It subsequently flew supplies to the *Guomindang* in southern China.

AIR CORPS   "aviatsionnaia korpus." A large Soviet air formation.
See Fliegerkorps; Red Army Air Force (VVS).

AIR CORPS FERRYING SERVICE
See Air Transport Command.

AIRCRAFT
See selected land and sea battles and: *aircraft carriers; airborne; airlanding; air power; anti-aircraft weapons; anti-submarine warfare; balloons; blimps; bombers; bombing; fighters; float planes; French Air Force; helicopters; Italian Air Force; Jabo-rei; Jabo; Jagd-bomber; Japanese Army Air Force; Japanese Naval Air Force; jets; kamikaze; Kondor; Luft-waffe; radio; Royal Air Force (RAF); Royal Australian Air Force (RAAF); Royal Canadian*

Air Force (RAF); recoilless guns; Red Army Air Force (VVS); Swordfish; United States Army Air Forces; VLR (Very Long Range) aircraft; Zerstoerer.

AIRCRAFT CARRIERS   In 1914 the Royal Navy conducted the first ever aircraft carrier-launched air attack. *Escort carriers* were also used to guard shipping routes during World War I. At the *Washington Naval Conference* in 1922, the strategic importance of carriers was misunderstood by many involved. Construction was limited in the final treaties mainly because it was feared that some navy might seek to convert such large-hulled ships into battleships, still thought to be the most powerful and decisive naval weapons platforms. In fact, the United States and Japan later converted old *battleships* and *battlecruisers* —which also were limited by treaty in 1922—into carriers. Germany and Italy remained solely reliant on battleships, battlecruisers, and heavy cruisers, and these were mainly confined to port during the war for fear of loss. All major navies continued to overestimate the utility of battleships and to build more of them before and during the war. Only the three largest navies—the American, British, and Japanese—came to see a vital future role for carriers during the interwar period, in long-distance reconnaissance and then as a strike weapon of great power. The Royal Navy deployed the largest carrier fleet in Europe in 1939, but it had too few trained crew and no offensive carrier doctrine. Its naval aircraft were also of poor relative quality. As the true importance of aircraft carriers emerged through 1940, the British were compelled to convert cruisers, liners, and even a few large merchantmen into ersatz carriers. These were used in convoy escort duty on an emergency basis in 1939–1940. These inadequate ships were later replaced by true escort carriers.

The Regia Marina, French Navy, and Kriegsmarine did not complete their carrier programs before the war. They all laid the greatest shipbuilding emphasis on other types of capital warships. The shared inclination away from deploying carriers in the Mediterranean arose partly from "gun club" conservatism, but more from a strategic judgment that in Europe's confined spaces land-based bombers could be expected to operate at will. That compared to ocean-spanning needs and outlooks of the USN and IJN, and to a lesser extent of the globe-spanning Royal Navy. For instance, the Italians entirely relied on land-based torpedo and dive bombers. They spent all naval appropriations on battleships and heavy cruisers and on smaller escort warships or attack craft. They built no carriers, despite aspirations to dominate the Mediterranean. The French enlisted just one converted carrier by 1939, with only one new fleet carrier under construction. Interservice rivalry limited cooperation that might have led to France developing more sound naval aviation, but so did a primary consciousness that France was a land power and that it faced the gravest threat on the ground along the Rhine. The Royal Navy therefore began the war with a substantial lead in naval aviation in Europe: it had seven carriers. These were initially used—some historians say misused—in close *anti-submarine warfare.* As a result, HMS Courageous was sunk by a U-boat on September 17, 1939, just two weeks into the critical *Battle of the Atlantic (1939–1945).* The RN deployed its carriers to deter or block a potential German invasion of Britain after June 1940. When that danger passed, some were employed to soundly defeat the Regia Marina's battleships in the Mediterranean. They also served to convoy fighters to Malta and the Middle East to establish theater air superiority. The ascendance of carriers over old-fashioned battleships was conclusively demonstrated by the British when carrier biplanes sank or damaged several Regia Marina battleships at anchor at *Taranto* in 1940.

Adolf Hitler's *Z-Plan* called for a carrier fleet capable of sustaining 12 squadrons of naval aircraft. Germany started construction of the first of two proposed fleet carriers, or "Flugzeugträger," before the war. But the idea of German carriers was sabotaged from the start by Luftwaffe insistence that it could destroy enemy ships at sea using land-based aircraft and by *Hermann Göring*'s refusal of even basic cooperation with any effort to develop a Kriegsmarine air arm. Work on the Flugzeugträger B was abandoned in late 1940. Desultory work on its sister ship, DKM Graf Zeppelin, continued into January 1943. Then it, too, was discontinued upon Admiral *Karl Dönitz* taking over from Admiral *Erich Raeder*. Dönitz shifted all carrier and other large surface ship construction and crews to U-boats. In addition to material and labor shortages, a major reason for not launching a carrier fleet was Hitler's utter lack of understanding of sea power, in general, and of naval air power, in particular. Just as important, Hermann Göring and his coterie of young but untalented aides petulantly but profoundly frustrated the Kriegsmarine's carrier ambitions at every turn. The only reason for doing so was that Göring feared creation of what might become a rival air force to his Luftwaffe.

Japan used a loophole—the absence of limits on warships under 10,000 tons—in the *Washington Naval Treaty* of 1922 to build small aircraft carriers whose combat punch more than compensated for size. The IJN initially planned to use its carriers for reconnaissance, to protect their battlefleets, and to scout and hunt down enemy warships. It also held an alluring promise for the IJN of closing the "battleship gap" between it and larger Western navies, especially the U.S. Navy. The Japanese also suffered from a cult of the offensive more generally. Therefore, the IJN concentrated on development of naval attack aircraft—dive bombers and torpedo bombers—during the 1930s. It built a great carrier fleet, which it first used in an opening sequence of highly successful assaults along the coast of China at the start of the *Sino-Japanese War (1937–1945)*. In 1936 the IJN formally adopted a combat doctrine of a mass carrier strike force. Under this theory carriers were to be concentrated for assault rather than dispersed as fleet protectors. That was a pioneering new doctrine. It would be imitated by other navies, including the rival U.S. Navy. The Japanese proved its worth in the opening battles of the Pacific War. The IJN deployed the world's largest carrier force by November 1941: six older fleet carriers and four larger and newer fleet carriers, with a total complement and reserve of 1,400 planes and 2,500 pilots. These carriers and the new Japanese battle doctrine enjoyed huge success in the opening raid on *Pearl Harbor* and even more in rapid expansion across Southeast Asia during the "Hundred Days" of December 1941–March 1942.

However, the IJN lost four fleet carriers and many of its best pilots and naval bomber crews at *Midway* in June 1942. It never recovered from that blow because the IJN had not calculated or prepared for a protracted war of attrition at sea. Japan's economy was also insufficiently developed to keep pace with the astonishing productive capacity of the United States. The IJN built 14 carriers during the war (all types), including conversion of a super battleship hull into the massive IJN Shinano. The IJN also turned to smaller seaplane carriers, using these not as a strike force but to ferry aircraft into increasingly isolated Pacific outposts. The IJN could no longer stock its fleet carriers with naval aircraft by early 1944, while pilot quality and general morale had also badly deteriorated. The Japanese were reduced to using their last fleet carriers as planeless lures at *Leyte Gulf*. By the end of the war the Japanese lost all their carriers to enemy action, either sunk or so heavily damaged they were put out of action. In contrast, the United States started the war in 1941 with seven fleet carriers. Before the fighting ended in August 1945, the U.S. Navy commissioned an astonishing 104 carriers (all types). It thereby claimed a naval air power preponderance it has yet to surrender.

U.S. carrier types included prewar fleet and experimental carriers, escort carriers, and three other main classes: Independence-class light carriers, Saipan-class light carriers, and Midway-class fleet carriers. U.S. and Japanese carriers began the war with wooden flight decks, but both navies moved to armored flight decks as their earlier designs proved vulnerable to dive bombers. Like the IJN and U.S. Navy, the Royal Navy experimented with carrier design during the interwar period. Most British carriers had armored decks from the start of the war because the British anticipated operating within range of land-based aircraft while intending to use their carriers for a primary reconnaissance role for surface battle groups. A key feature of USN fleet carriers was their ability to embark more aircraft than either Japanese or British carriers. American carriers also could launch and recover planes more quickly than the Japanese, a trait that provided an important advantage in the great carrier battles of 1942.

See various naval battles and operations. *See also Catapult Aircraft Merchant (CAM); Doolittle raid; Habakkuk; Merchant Aircraft Carrier (MAC); Okinawa.*

AIR DEFENCE OF GREAT BRITAIN (ADGB)   The original and unified RAF command in charge of home defense from 1925 to 1936. It was replaced by separate RAF commands from 1936 to 1943: Fighter Command (active air defense) and Bomber Command (deterrence and retaliation). The ADGB was revived and reshaped in 1943. The principal reasons for doing so were the changed nature of the air war with Germany and to accommodate Western Allied fighter and anti-aircraft defenses needed to protect invasion airfields, marshalling areas, embarkation points, and shipping before and during *OVERLORD*. ADGB thereafter carried out anti-submarine recce and patrols and provided air cover over the landing beaches and lodgement areas at the start of the invasion. To those ends, the ADGB was subsumed under the *Allied Expeditionary Air Force (AEAF)*. The ADGB deployed 45 squadrons hosting over 800 aircraft on June 5, 1944. Another 12 squadrons were attached from the 2nd Tactical Air Force (TAF), which was also part of the AEAF. The 2nd TAF assumed forward operations once the beachhead was secure and inland airstrips became available, except over the Côtentin Peninsula. ADGB anti-aircraft guns were active and effective in shooting down V-1 rockets fired against Britain in late 1944.

AIR DEFENSE

See Air Defense Force (PVO); Air Defence of Great Britain (ADGB); Anderson shelters; anti-aircraft guns; Berlin bomber offensive; Blitz; Chain Home radar; Combined Bomber Offensive; fighters; Flak; Flakhelfer; Flak towers; Freya; intruders; Kammhuber Line; Lichtenstein-Gerät; Luftschutz; Malta; Nachtjagd; Ploesti; proximity fuze; radar; radio; Reichsluftschutzbund; Reichsverteidigung; Ruhr; Raumnachtjadg; strategic bombing; Wilde Sau; Würzburg; Zahme Sau.

AIR DEFENSE FORCE (PVO) The fighter-interceptor forces of the Soviet Union. In June 1941 the PVO numbered 183,000 personnel.

See Red Army Air Force (VVS).

AIR DIVISION A Soviet air formation equivalent to a *Fliegerdivision*. The USAAF also used this term later in the war for its large bomber formations, previously called "bombardment groups," then "combat wings."

See also Red Army Air Force (VVS); United States Army Air Forces (USAAF).

AIRDROP Dropping military or humanitarian relief supplies by parachute.

See airborne.

AIR FLEET

See Luftflotte.

AIR GAPS Several large areas of ocean could not be reached by Western Allied aircraft during the *Battle of the Atlantic (1939–1945)*. The most important was a large area in the mid-Atlantic south of Iceland alternately known as the mid-Atlantic Gap or Greenland Gap. Air gaps were prime killing grounds for U-boats. British and Canadian troops set up air bases on Iceland and in the Faeroe Islands to partly close the gap, but it was not until 1941 that Britain operated full-scale reconnaissance and hunting from these northern bases. The delay was mainly caused by a shortage of aircraft and by improper types. Over time, longer-range aircraft further shrank the mid-Atlantic gap, though it was a struggle to prise these loose from the RAF. "The Gap" in the Atlantic was not completely closed until 1943, when British and American bases were established on the *Azores* after enormous pressure was brought to bear on the Portuguese government, and Lisbon felt more secure from Axis bombing retaliation from Italy. *VLR (Very Long Range) aircraft* were deployed from the Azores. VLR patrols and the appearance of more and better *escort carriers* provided continuous air cover to convoys.

See also Black Pit; Habakkuk.

AIRLANDING Western Allied term for airborne troops, weapons, and equipment inserted onto a battlefield by glider.

See airborne.

AIRMINDEDNESS   A general interwar trend in both popular imagination and among leadership in most countries, holding that *air power* would emerge as a unique war-winning weapon and that aircraft had changed the entire relationship between civil populations and war-fighting. It imbued air forces with a common mystique and populations with both admiration and fear of aircraft and air men. It deeply affected planning by the Western Allies, surrounding air force doctrine with the aura of a promised "knock-out blow" that would vitiate the need for calamitous battles on land or water.

See also total war.

AIR OFFENSIVE   A Red Army Air Force (VVS) doctrine that developed after the catastrophic losses of *BARBAROSSA* in 1941. It matched well with reviving VVS strength, as new aircraft models came into large-scale production from 1942. It proposed massive preparatory tactical bombing ahead of Red Army ground offensives, including pounding more distant Luftwaffe airfields and supply depots. A second stage called for the VVS to provide close support to advancing ground forces. Insofar as long-range bombers were employed at all, their role was interdiction of enemy troop or armor concentrations.

AIR POWER   Balloons proved to be effective artillery observation platforms during World War I. Germany also developed Zeppelins as mobile bombing platforms, using rigid airships to bomb London in 1915. Zeppelins and other dirigibles were used most extensively at sea. Dirigibles proved to be a design dead end as a bomber because of their inability to fly in bad weather and high vulnerability to hostile ground fire and fighter interception. The first use of fixed-wing aircraft as observer platforms in preference to fixed balloons was by the Italians in 1911, during their campaign to conquer Tripoli. From the start of the Great War rigid aircraft were employed to supplement balloons in unarmed spotting for artillery, or in reconnaissance of enemy ground forces. They were used at sea to scout for enemy ships. By 1915 some fixed-wing bombers saw action, but engine power and payload remained core restrictions just over a decade after the first powered flight. Still, rigid bombers provoked deployment of purpose-built, rigid fighter interceptors. The threat to valuable spotter balloons and unarmed scout planes in turn required deployment of fighters to serve as protectors and escorts. Over 200,000 military aircraft of all types, on all sides, were produced by 1918, and 40,000 air crew died, but most elements of military aviation were well on the way to full-fledged lethality. One area that stayed underdeveloped in World War I, but saw dramatic expansion in World War II, was transport by air of military supply and *airborne* troops.

Those who sought to curtail general military spending in several countries in the 1920s touted air power as a cheap alternative defense to large ground forces. That contrasted with theories of the Italian air power writer Giulio Douhet, who published his influential *Command of the Air* in 1921. Douhet argued that in the next Great Power war aircraft would be the most powerful offensive weapon system. Indeed, air power would be strategically decisive. Like H. G. Wells before the Great War, Douhet foresaw vast fleets of bombers overflying enemy armies to attack war industries, factories, and cities in strategic rear areas. The idea of *strategic bombing* grew from this and other kernels, but mainly as a cheap deterrent to war rather than as an offensive doctrine. Rudimentary efforts at strategic bombing had been tried by Germany and Great Britain in 1917–1918, and by the early 1930s, several powers deployed fleets of bombers they hoped would provide a deterrent to keep the peace. But few as yet considered the bomber as a potentially and massively destructive offensive force. On the other hand, theories about *morale bombing*, or terror bombing, were already taking shape. Adolf Hitler only ever thought of bombing as a terror weapon. He did not understand that the RAF had come to see the strategic bomber as a potential decisive weapon of economic blockade and destruction, with terror or morale effects as incidental to a primary economic purpose. The bomber as a terror weapon was unveiled to an already frightened world at *Guernica* on April 26, 1937. Bombing of that undefended Basque town by aircraft of the *Kondor Legion* dramatically increased fear among all civilian populations, while encouraging airmen on all sides who thought that they could win the next war on their own by bombing. As air war historian Richard Overy succinctly put it: "It was . . . movement of ships and men and the occupying of land that won the day [in World War II]. Air power had a complementary rather than an autonomous role to play." That said, the contribution of air power to the defeat of the Axis states was substantial.

The Red Army Air Force (VVS) had over 14,000 aircraft in 1939, making it the largest air fleet in the world by a factor of four or five. Most VVS planes were obsolete types: nearly all its 20,000 aircraft in 1941 would be destroyed by the end of the first six months of the German–Soviet war. However, the sheer scale of the Soviet aircraft industry permitted rapid recovery in 1942, then production of vast quantities of new models. Germany's *Luftwaffe* ranked second to the VVS in 1939 with over 3,600 front-line military aircraft. But the lead was somewhat illusory, as production of its newer models was already behind that of the aircraft production of the Western Allies. The RAF and Armée de l'Air had 1,900 and 1,700 first-line planes, respectively, in 1939. But Britain and France were both accelerating production of all types of military aircraft. The RAF concentrated on building fighters because it had overestimated the size of the Luftwaffe and exaggerated projections of future German production. As a result of the error, British fighter production soon surpassed Germany's. The Luftwaffe would not ramp up its own production until two years into the war. That meant German production continued at a slightly higher than prewar rate even while producing outmoded dive bomber and medium bombers, while the RAF was developing and deploying new four-engine heavy bombers and more advanced fighters. The aircraft industry of the other Axis states was in even worse shape. The *Regia Aeronautica* had almost as many operational aircraft as either Great Britain or France, but most Italian models were woefully inadequate and hardly counted as frontline planes. In the entire war, the Italian aircraft industry produced just over 7,000 new planes.

The Japanese Army Air Force (JAAF) and Japanese Navy Air Force (JNAF) had a combined frontline strength of 3,000 aircraft when Japan attacked China in 1937. China could put just 700 obsolete warplanes into the air in its defense. Japan's aircraft industry produced fewer than 1,500 planes in 1937 and did not ramp up sufficiently after that. As a result, the IJN still had only 3,089 combat aircraft, along with another 370 trainers, when it attacked *Pearl Harbor* and other Western targets in Southeast Asia and the Pacific in December 1941. Production reached 4,768 aircraft by 1940 but was divided between the intensely rival and uncooperative JAAF and JNAF. Only 5,088 military aircraft of all types left Japanese assembly lines in 1941. Production rose during 1943–1944 but was confined mainly to light fighters and obsolete and highly vulnerable medium bombers. Japan also uniquely failed to expand its pilot training schools, so pilot skills deteriorated dramatically from 1943. In contrast, the United States Army Air Forces (USAAF) expanded over 120-fold within just 18 months. A projected total USAAF strength of 62,000 aircraft, of all types, was agreed in Air War Plans Division-1 (AWPD-1). That became the basis for U.S. air strategy in December 1941, until superceded in August 1942, by AWPD-2. The revised plan called for a frontline force of 19,250 aircraft and a total force of 146,000 aircraft by 1943, including trainers and a large reserve. That figure was later reduced to a constant of 127,000 operational aircraft by 1943. In August 1945, when the war ended, the USAAF was the most potent and far-reaching air force in the world with 80,000 operational aircraft and nearly 2.4 million men. Its increasingly confident pilots and crews had started behind some enemy air forces, but in the end flew excellent aircraft in final conditions of air supremacy over both Germany and Japan.

Japan, Great Britain, and the United States had a significant portion of their aircraft dedicated to naval aviation in 1939. The Japanese were the most tactically advanced air power among all major combatants at the start of the war, with pilots and bombardiers having accrued many combat hours in the opening years of the *Sino-Japanese War (1937–1945)*. Advanced Japanese aerial skills showed clearly in the remarkable daring and professionalism with which they carried out the extraordinary naval air strike against Pearl Harbor, and in early airborne and bombing operations across the Pacific in the first three months of 1942. Yet, they quickly as well as progressively fell behind the Americans and British in aircraft production, air power capabilities, and pilot skills as the war continued in Burma and the South Pacific. German airmen were next in skill and experience in 1939, dating to the activities of the *Kondor Legion* during the *Spanish Civil War (1936–1939)*. Soviet and Italian pilots, too, learned from experience in that war but were handicapped by inadequate aircraft. The VVS additionally suffered from savaging by prewar purges that notably targeted its Spanish Civil War veterans. Pilots and air crews of all other Western air forces were combat virgins in 1939; and in the case of most American pilots, until late 1941.

All major air powers were dedicated to tactical rather than strategic air operations in 1939, to bombing, strafing, and providing fighter cover in direct support of ground forces. The Luftwaffe was ruthlessly effective at these techniques during *FALL WEISS* in Poland in 1939, where the small Polish Air Force was outclassed and outnumbered five to one in modern combat aircraft. The Germans employed airborne troops and airlift capacity to great effect in Denmark and Norway during *WESERÜBUNG* in early April 1940. The Luftwaffe enjoyed airborne surprise and real tactical success during the *FALL GELB* invasions of the Low Countries and France a month later. The Luftwaffe was more evenly matched numerically by Western Allied air forces in that campaign than is sometimes realized or reported, but it displayed superior pilot and ground control skills. French and British fighter and bomber squadrons were deeply attrited until the RAF held back fighter reinforcements after it became clear the ground campaign was lost. The RAF made a final defensive stand over *Dunkirk,* then withdrew to home airfields. From there the RAF continued a protracted fight for air supremacy over the Channel, leading into the *Battle of Britain* later that summer and fall. The RAF built up fighter and anti-aircraft defenses from November 1940 to June 1941, while pouring new resources into Bomber Command and testing new bombers and navigation aids in small-scale raids over occupied France, the Low Countries, and against the Ruhr. All that was preparatory to launching strategic bombing over the rest of Germany. The RAF continued in a tactical role against Italian ground and air forces in East and North Africa and lent fresh support to Royal Navy convoy protection and *anti-submarine warfare* in the burgeoning *Battle of the Atlantic.* Most air combat and bombing in and around the Mediterranean in 1942–1943 revolved around ground or convoy operations, with the RAF and USAAF on one side and the Luftwaffe and Regia Aeronautica lined up on the other. Captured African and Italian air bases were used by Western Allied bombers flying strategic missions into southern Germany and over the Balkans after that.

Not everyone learned the lessons of air power well or in time. Many in the Royal Navy were blithely convinced that capital warships had nothing to fear from air attack. It focused mainly on other navies, fixing primarily on the threat from the German and Italian surface navies and to a lesser degree on submarine threats. Such faith in surface defense was shaken in the waters off *Crete* starting on May 20, 1941. The Royal Navy suffered heavy ship losses in brave efforts first to reinforce, then to evacuate, the defeated garrison. Its ships were sunk or damaged mainly by German land-based aircraft, as the island fell to assault by German *Fallschirmjäger* and *air landing* troops. Any lingering illusion of naval immunity to land-based aircraft was finally shattered for the British on December 10, 1941, when the Royal Navy battleships HMS Prince of Wales and HMS Repulse were sunk off Malaya by Japanese land-based torpedo and dive bombers. Naval myopia was all the more remarkable given the intense fear in Britain before the war that "the bomber will always get through." That conviction led to procurement of an effective land-based fighter force as well as a rudimentary strategic bomber fleet. But there was another factor at work in Britain and the United States from mid-1940, after the British were pushed off the continent three times by the Wehrmacht. Development of a strategic bomber force looked to be the only strategic option left open to the British, as well as the quickest way for the Americans to strike hard at Germany. That Western Allied calculus was only advanced by Hitler's invasion of the Soviet Union, which committed so great a share of Germany's resources to land combat that it could not afford to divert resources to the Luftwaffe, whose potential strategic bombing role Hitler never really understood. That left the Luftwaffe playing a distant second fiddle to the Heer, where the Western powers committed to the air war as a central part of their strategy for ultimate victory.

A mutual bias toward a tactical role for air power continued throughout four years of fighting on the Eastern Front, from June 1941 to May 1945. Although the Germans and Soviets devoted some resources to developing heavy and long-range bombers, most aircraft and crews were chewed up in ground support roles during vast offensives and counteroffensives. The Luftwaffe began the fight in the east even more spectacularly than the Heer during *BARBAROSSA,* destroying thousands of Soviet aircraft on the ground in the first days and weeks while shooting down thousands more overmatched enemy planes in aerial dogfights. Cocky with success, within a year the Luftwaffe found itself with too few planes and far too many missions to be flown against an enemy air force that had recovered and improved, even as it suffered astounding losses of men, matériel, and aircraft. Initial German technological advantages did not last: British and American fighters supplied through *Lend-Lease* helped close the air gap that yawned wide with opening VVS losses. Then Soviet aircraft production ramped up, and highly talented aircraft designers brought out a series of superb new fighters and fighter-bombers. By 1943 VVS pilots were already flying aircraft superior to anything but the pitifully few late-war jets that came out of German factories, and in numbers that were literally and fatally unimagined by Hitler or Göring. The limits of German air power became clear also in the failure of Luftwaffe transports to supply German 6th Army at *Stalingrad* in December 1942–January 1943. The fighting edge of German air power was then blunted in huge air battles over enormous ground fights at *Kursk* in mid-1943 and all along the Eastern Front in 1944. From mid-1943 the Luftwaffe was nearly exclusively on defense in the east, just like the Heer and *Waffen-SS* ground formations it once protected in deep offensive operations. Having permanently lost the air initiative to the VVS, the Luftwaffe only undertook occasional tactical counteroffensives that grew evermore feeble into 1945. Meanwhile, Soviet efforts and capabilities increased until air superiority, and then air supremacy, was achieved over every battlefield.

That VVS accomplishment was greatly aided by the Western Allies' bombing campaign over Germany, which absorbed the lion's share of new fighters coming off German production lines and of new pilots from Luftwaffe training schools. As importantly, bombing Germany also soaked up most production of the magnificent and deadly 88 mm *anti-aircraft gun,* easily the best anti-aircraft gun produced by any military during the war. Had more '88s been freed for use in the east, they certainly would have destroyed many more thousands of Red Army tanks while acting in a comparably deadly role as anti-tank guns. That additional defensive firepower might have bogged down or at least slowed several Soviet counteroffensives. In the great campaigns fought by the Wehrmacht against the Western Allies in 1943–1944 in North Africa, Italy, France, and the Low Countries, the Luftwaffe played an ever-diminishing tactical role. Ultimately, German ground forces could only safely move at night. Only in German skies did the Luftwaffe maintain an effective presence as a defensive force into early 1945, until it also nearly disappeared during the last two months of the air war. Other than handfuls of desperate sorties by technologically immature jets made as the regime expired, the Luftwaffe mainly left the skies over Germany to vast fleets of Western Allied bombers and fighters in March–April, 1945.

Neither before nor during World War II did any Axis air force develop an effective strategic bomber force or doctrine. The Luftwaffe, Regia Aeronautica, and Japanese Army Air Force all employed their bomber strength tactically rather than strategically, in support of ground attacks or against enemy naval forces and shipping. Germany developed the first ballistic missile in the form of the V-2 rocket late in the war, but that weapon was—as the name suggested and Hitler conceived of it—a vengeance weapon rather than a strategic or war-winning weapon. The Japanese experimented with incendiary bombing and dissemination of germ weapons by high-altitude balloons (*Fugos*), but these had such limited success they were a nonfactor in the air war. While theorists in all air forces considered the role of bombing in psychological warfare, until mid-1940 no air force engaged in terror bombing against enemies capable of retaliation in kind: the Luftwaffe brutally bombed Warsaw and Rotterdam but not Paris or London, while the French and British failed to carry out their prewar threats to massively bomb the Ruhr and other parts of Germany within reach of their planes. The Battle of Britain changed that equation, but only slowly. Hitler concluded that economic bombing was ineffective. In any case, the Wehrmacht needed the Luftwaffe to continue its primary tactical role supporting ground forces on the Eastern Front and lacked the proper aircraft to conduct a campaign of strategic bombing.

It was thus the RAF that crept toward deliberate targeting of civilians, both as a primary form of economic warfare and as a means of trying to crumble German morale. The real difference from the Luftflotte was that the British poured more of their resources into bomber production to match their growing and grim dedication to a hard doctrine of *area bombing*. Once the means became available in the form of new four-engine heavy bombers, the British used these to strike at the German economy. RAF Bomber Command reached deep into the enemy heartland in an effort to destroy war production. But once it was discovered that *precision bombing* was ineffective, RAF Bomber Command accepted as a corollary of area bombing that it must kill German workers and level their homes; "dehouse" them, was the way Winston Churchill put it. RAF doctrine thus evolved from attempting precise targeting of military and economic targets into an effort to foment a popular uprising against the Nazis. It was hoped and argued by air power advocates that Britain might thereby avoid the necessity of invading the continent, where it must surely face another series of great land battles comparable to the Somme, Ypres, and Mons. It was the British followed by the Americans who most employed terror bombing, or "morale bombing." That was because the Western Allies developed the physical means to conduct a strategic campaign on a scale that seemed able to fulfill the war-winning promise made by radical adherents of the doctrine, which during the war turned into a dogma for the Allied bomber chiefs.

It is generally agreed that strategic bombing as promoted by air power radicals failed. Bombing Germany proved less than effective on several levels. A secret 1941 study reported to Churchill and the combined chiefs of staff that 30 percent of

British bombers dropped their loads within five miles of the designated target, a number that fell to just 10 percent over the critical, heavily defended region of the Ruhr Valley. As one historian bluntly and brutally put it: "Bomber Command's crews . . . were dying largely to crater the German countryside." With new navigation aids and improved bombs, accuracy improved in 1943 and again from late 1944. With later improvements in bombsights and targeting, and upon deployment of long-distance fighter escorts, the Western Allies achieved air superiority over most of Western Europe in 1944, and air supremacy over Germany itself in 1945. They took advantage to conduct *thousand bomber raids* and *carpet bomb* German cities. Western Allied heavy bombers were highly effective in damaging the German war economy during the last year of the war. Bombing had by then already forced dispersal of much vital German production to caves and forests, or driven it underground. By *Albert Speer's* calculation, bombing occupied 1.5–2.0 million German workers just to repair bomb damage. The air war also tied down at least 1.5 million German troops and channeled a large share of gun production into 88 mm anti-aircraft tubes. It also diverted much of Germany's military effort into servicing anti-aircraft guns with heavy ammunition: 50,000 anti-aircraft guns were deployed inside Germany by 1944. German defenders also replied with still the first experimental jet fighters, but these proved too crude and few in number to make a decisive impact.

The Western Allies lost 22,000 bombers and 110,000 air crew in Europe and Asia combined. As lessons were learned, air power proved tactically decisive over land and at sea in Europe. While air power contributed importantly to the strategic victory over the Axis in Europe, it was not the main cause or instrument of that victory: it took physical defeat and occupation of Nazi Germany by vast land armies to win the war. When used to destroy Axis armies or attack or protect warships and convoys, air power was hugely successful. It helped bring about victory only when backed by the threat or reality of ground invasion. Only in the case of Japan might a good argument be made that air power—principally long-range area bombing that culminated in delivery of two atomic bombs— was strategically decisive. Even then, in the Pacific, Southeast Asia, and China, it also took much hard fighting on land and water to bring the decision air weapon within range so that it could be brought to bear on the war production, morale, and will to resist of the Japanese people and military.

See also individual naval battles, and *Blitzkrieg; Dresden; Combined Bomber Offensive; electronic warfare; grand strategy; The Hump; kamikaze; Malta; Normandy campaign; Okinawa; oil; radar.*

Suggested Reading: Richard Overy, *The Air War, 1939–1945* (1980).

AIR RAID   Any attack on ground targets by aircraft, but especially if conducted by bombers against an urban target.

AIR REGIMENT   "aviatsionnyi polk." A core *Red Army Air Force (VVS)* unit comprising fighters or bombers, but not usually both. It was roughly equivalent to a *Gruppe* in the Luftwaffe, or about 30 aircraft.

AIR–SEA RESCUE Rescuing downed air crew from open water was highly risky and required specialized boats and training. Initially, both sides in Europe recognized and respected rescue operations conducted under the *Red Cross* emblem. German and British air–sea rescue missions involving clearly marked *float planes* and small rescue ships were usually unmolested as they recovered pilots and crew from the North Sea, at least during 1939. Even as the situation deteriorated for the Western Allies during *FALL GELB* in May–June, 1940, and throughout the *Battle of Britain* that summer, this mutual courtesy of war extended to the Channel. But not always: British fighters shot down several clearly marked German rescue aircraft looking for downed Luftwaffe pilots in the Channel, while German gunboats shot up well-marked British rescue boats. German air–sea rescue was initially more successful than its British counterpart, largely because the Germans pioneered a portable rescue transmitter. After the British captured one they closely copied it to produce the *"Gibson Girl,"* which helped save thousands of ditched aircrew over the duration of the war. RAF and Coastal Command greatly expanded air–sea rescue programs in tandem with the maturing *strategic bombing* of Germany. That included mounting deep rescue operations searching for ditched bomber crews in much more distant waters than the Channel.

By 1942 British rescue technique was significantly enhanced by providing bomber crews with dinghies, marker dies to enhance spotting, and Gibson Girl transmitters. Addition to air survival kits of a crystal oscillator in 1943 permitted precise radar tracking of downed crews. If they bailed out of the aircraft with the oscillator intact they were far more likely to be picked up by rescue ships vectored to their position. The Royal Canadian Navy also carried out extensive rescue efforts off North America early in the *Battle of the Atlantic*. The British and Canadians were later joined in the North Sea, Atlantic, and Mediterranean by a parallel American air–sea rescue operation that ultimately achieved a remarkable success rate. USAAF and U.S. Navy rescue efforts in the Pacific faced huge difficulties of long-distance operations over vast stretches of open water. Yet, rescues were successful in many instances. Initially, rescues were carried out ad hoc by diverting regular patrol squadrons to suspected bail-out or crash sites. Air–Sea Rescue Squadrons were formed in the U.S. Pacific Fleet as of April 1944, as U.S. naval assets reached a level of abundance the Japanese could not imagine. Some rescues were made from one side of a coral reef with Japanese infantry shooting at the downed crew and rescue team from a nearby island. The Royal Australian Navy pioneered flotillas of small rescue craft in the Arafura Sea, Timor Sea, around New Guinea, and off the Dutch East Indies. Japanese air–sea rescue was increasingly hampered from the end of 1942, as were virtually all Japanese military operations in the Pacific, as Japan's naval forces were heavily attrited and its so-called defense perimeter was tightly compressed.

See also carrier pigeons; Convoy Rescue Ships; helicopters; Laconia Order.

AIR TRANSPORT AUXILIARY (ATA) A British volunteer aviation unit comprised mainly of civilian pilots. For reasons of age, gender, or health—there were several one-armed or one-eyed ATA pilots—these pilots were not draftable into active duty with the RAF. Although the ATA was administered and clerked by British Airways civilians, it was nonetheless put under command of the RAF, and its pilots were issued an RAF-style uniform. As military pilots were pulled from RAF ferry duties into combat, the ATA took up the load of flying urgent supplies within Britain, then the still more urgent business of ferrying aircraft from factories and storage facilities to forward air bases. ATA tasks included long-haul ferries of *Lend-Lease* aircraft manufactured in the United States and flown to the southern UK via Newfoundland, Iceland, and Scotland. Despite early RAF resistance to allowing women pilots into the ATA, a group of eight women began ferrying single-engine Tiger Moth trainers as early as November 1939—wartime necessity proved a partial gender equalizer. By the end of the war, 166 women pilots served in the ATA. They ferried all types of RAF aircraft during the war, including several Meteor jets. Twelve women qualified to fly four-engine heavy bombers, while 82 were certified on various medium bombers. Other women served as ATA grounds crew or mechanics. ATA male pilots ferried combat aircraft directly to bases in France from mid-1944. They were joined in that duty by female pilots from September. Civilian pilots of the ATA—representing 30 Allied nationalities—ferried 300,000 military aircraft by the end of the war.

See also logistics; Women's Airforce Service Pilots.

AIR TRANSPORT COMMAND (ATC)   The USAAF air transport system. It was established as the "Air Corps Ferrying Service" in May 1941, principally to ferry *Lend-Lease* military supplies and aircraft to Britain. It was recommissioned as the Air Transport Command in July 1942 and made responsible for rushing critical aircraft, supplies, and personnel to the Pacific theater of operations. It cooperated fairly effectively with the U.S. Navy once the usual interservice arguments were resolved. The ATC ferried Lend-Lease planes and supplies to the Soviet Union across the Atlantic through Iran and via the Alaska–Aleutian route to Siberia. It flew a smaller operation over the *Hump* to supply the *Guomindang* in southern China. ATC transport planes were used to ferry troops and supplies deep into combat zones during combat emergencies. The ATC operated numerous overseas forward bases in all major theaters of war, carrying in supplies and reinforcements and ferrying out the most seriously wounded men. Its 200,000 personnel ultimately operated a constant fleet of over 3,500 aircraft, in addition to ferrying 250,000 military aircraft to various theaters of operations.

See logistics.

AIX-LA-CHAPELLE
See Aachen.

AKTION REINHARD   A *Schutzstaffel* (SS) "honorific" given to an extermination program carried out in new *death camps* designed and built under the authority of *Reinhard Heydrich*. The program conducted mass killings of Jews following

Heydrich's assassination in Prague, though it was planned long in advance of that event.

See also Belzec; Lublin-Majdanek; Sobibor; Treblinka; Wannsee conference.

ALAMEIN, BATTLE OF
See El Alamein, Second Battle of.

ALAM EL-HALFA, BATTLE OF (AUGUST 30–SEPTEMBER 7, 1942)   Also known as "Second Alamein." This fight was Field Marshal *Erwin Rommel's* last opportunity to win in the desert and to break through to Egypt and the Suez Canal. In a well-conceived battle plan, General *Bernard Law Montgomery* ordered British 8th Army to conduct a fighting withdrawal intended to draw Rommel upon fixed guns and waiting armor along the Alam el-Halfa Ridge. Rommel took the bait, sending two Panzer divisions to attack. These were slowed by mines and a lightly armored screening force. The Panzers therefore fell hours behind the attack schedule. They also ran so low on fuel that Rommel diverted them north after taking barely a third of the planned-for ground. That brought the Panzers precisely against the main strength of waiting British artillery and armor. The Germans were savaged, and Rommel was forced to recall his tanks. Yet again, Montgomery showed his mastery of a set-piece battle. Not for the last time, he also failed to properly or promptly pursue. On September 4th, he belatedly sent an infantry division, which lacked the needed speed, to cut off Rommel's retreating tanks. Some fighting continued for another three days before the Germans finally pulled away. After Alam el-Halfa the British went over to permanent offensive in North Africa, beginning with the critical victory at the *Second Battle of El Alamein* in October. It was later revealed that actionable *ULTRA* intelligence played a key role in Montgomery's plans. The battle also represented a breakthrough for restored British morale and for new skill in air–land coordination.

ALAMO FORCE   Initially called "New Britain Force," this Western Allied task force was set up in early 1942 by General *Douglas MacArthur* and served directly under his GHQ. In clear radio transmissions it was called "Alamo Force," but in secret communications it was encoded as "Escalator Force." It was charged with isolating and reducing *Rabaul,* but never got that chance after the assault proposed in *CARTWHEEL* was canceled and the Western Allies instead leap-frogged over Rabaul. Alamo Force was largely American in composition—U.S. 6th Army formed its core—but it incorporated Australian air, land, and sea units as well. In 1943 the Australians were reorganized into *New Guinea Force.* Alamo Force thereafter was an all-American command except for its logistical support, which was provided by U.S. and Australian services. It fought in the campaigns to retake Dutch New Guinea, New Britain, the Admiralty Islands, and the Philippines.

ALASKA   Alaska was the American territory most targeted for enemy military action in World War II. The Japanese shelled Dutch Harbor and invaded and occupied the *Aleutian Islands* of Attu and Kiska. Alaska was also hit toward the end of the war by *Fugos*. The Aleutians were liberated by a U.S. Navy task force after hard fighting. Otherwise, Alaska was defended by the "Tundra Army," or Alaska Territorial Guard, a force of some 2,700 local whites and Inuit formed in 1941. Alaska's main role in the war was as a supply base for various Pacific campaigns and a stopover for *Lend-Lease* aircraft flying on to Siberia. The Japanese threat to Alaska encouraged postwar public acceptance of Alaskan statehood by the lower 48 states, just as the *Pearl Harbor* attack contributed to statehood for Hawaii.

See also war aims: Japan.

ALASKAN HIGHWAY
See Alcan Military Highway.

ALBANIA Mountainous Albania has most often been part of other people's empires: the ancient Greeks, Romans, and Byzantines all held some or all of Albania under their sway, as did the Ottoman Empire from the 15th century until 1913. Many Albanians converted to Islam as they adjusted to life as an Ottoman province. Albania became an independent principality in 1913 as a result of the First and Second Balkan Wars. It sank into anarchy during World War I, but its precarious sovereignty was widely recognized after the war and confirmed in 1921 by agreement among Italy, Greece, and Yugoslavia. All those states coveted some Albanian territory, but they could not agree on how to partition the country. Albania was proclaimed a republic in 1925, but then turned back to monarchy under King *Zog I*. It was invaded by Italy on April 7, 1939, in a long-contemplated but still impulsive act of aggression ordered by Benito Mussolini. Minor resistance delayed even the poorly prepared Italians only long enough for the royal family to flee into exile. Ethnic Albanian resistance began in neighboring Kosovo. Matériel aid was provided by the British *Special Operations Executive (SOE)*, but nationalist resistance flagged with German occupation of Kosovo and much of Yugoslavia from April 1941.

Albanian Communists launched a small-scale guerrilla campaign in the mountains following the German invasion of the Soviet Union in June 1941. Led by *Enver Hoxha*, they were also assisted by *Tito's* Communist partisan movement operating in Yugoslavia. A few nationalists and other non-Communists, mainly organized around family and clan associations, began a separate resistance in the south of Albania. Tribal-based resistance was organized in the center of the country. British agents coordinated only minimal supplies to the Albanian resistance and so exercised little real influence. Instead, ancient internal rivalries and a fast-moving military situation drove events in 1943–1944. The overthrow of Mussolini and looming surrender of Italy was critical, provoking uprisings across Albania. Two Italian divisions surrendered to Albanian partisans and were disarmed. Others simply fled. Some Italian Communists and antifascists joined the Albanian partisans. Other Italian troops continued to fight alongside German units, which poured into Albania in September to secure the country for the Axis and keep open supply and communications routes to German forces in Greece. Typical Nazi techniques of mass reprisal for the smallest act of resistance soon cowed most of the population. A Nazi-puppet regime was set up in Tirana. It had a presence in a few other towns, but most of the countryside remained no-go territory for Axis troops. The resistance split and a multisided civil war ensued when Hoxha and the Communists turned against all other Albanian resisters as German defeat approached outside the country. This confused situation allowed German forces retreating from Greece to pass through Albania with minimal interference during September 1944. Hoxha's partisans took control of Albania, with Yugoslav support, as the Germans departed. A quixotic Stalinist regime was established in which Hoxha ruled as absolute dictator until his death in 1985.

See also Victor Emmanuel.

ALCAN MILITARY HIGHWAY   An American–Canadian joint project that cut a mountain road over 1,500 miles long to Alaska, linking supply bases in the United States and Canada. It was opened to military traffic on October 29, 1942, but not completed until 1943. It was made possible because the mutual threat from Japan, along with logistics pressures of making *Lend-Lease* deliveries to Siberia, finally overcame traditional Canadian objection to a highway connecting Alaska to the lower 48 U.S. states.

ALCOHOL
   See battle stress; Churchill, Winston; extraordinary events; Göring, Hermann; Hitler, Adolf; Imperial Japanese Army; Nanjing, Rape of; politruk; Rabe, John; rations; Red Army; Smith, Holland; Stalin, Joseph; Timoshenko, Semyon.

ALEUTIAN ISLANDS   An Alaskan archipelago extending toward eastern Siberia. Dutch Harbor was shelled by the Japanese. Attu and Kiska, two islands in the far western Aleutians, were invaded at the beginning of June 1942. The attack was part of a diversion intended to draw U.S. Navy forces away from the fight at *Midway* (June 4–5, 1942). Admiral *Chester Nimitz* did not take the bait because he knew from *ULTRA* intercepts that the main blow would fall on Midway Island. Nimitz ordered TF8 under Rear Admiral Robert Theobald to the Aleutians to intercept the Japanese invasion, while he retained all his carriers at Midway. Theobald had 5 cruisers, 14 destroyers, a complement of submarines and supply ships, and air support from land-based bombers. Already in the Aleutians was Japanese 5th Fleet, commanded by Vice Admiral Hosagaya Boshiro. He had divided his attack force into four groups: a mobile force with two light carriers and a seaplane carrier at its core, along with support ships; two strike forces, one each for Attu and Kiska; and his flagship group, comprising a heavy cruiser and two destroyers, protecting supply ships. A separate and more distant Aleutian Screening Force was hurriedly pulled back to Midway, too late to save Admiral *Isoroku Yamamoto's* four fleet carriers once the battle turned against Japan. After Midway, the U.S. Navy was free to send additional assets to the Aleutians, including a battleship and an escort carrier. Despite the devastating loss of four fleet carriers at Midway, the Japanese ill-advisedly proceeded to occupy isolated Aleutian outposts.

With TF8 wrongly positioned by Theobald, the Japanese landed unopposed on Attu on June 5 and on Kiska on June 7. They were not discovered until June 10. Air raids were mounted by long-range bombers against the Japanese on Kiska. Theobald also conducted a naval bombardment, but to little effect. The Japanese garrison on Attu was temporarily transferred to Kiska in late August, then 2,700 men were reinserted on Attu. In awful weather conditions for both sides, the standoff in the Aleutians continued through the winter months. American engineers built 5,000-foot airstrips on Adak and Amchitka starting at the end of August. These fields permitted short-range bombing of Kiska while bringing Attu within range of U.S. land-based bombers for the first time. However, heavy seas and winter storms limited air and sea operations until March 1943. A naval engagement was then fought at the *Komandorski Islands* (March 26, 1943). On May 11, 11,000 men of the U.S. 7th Infantry Division landed on Attu. Fighting was bitter and often hand-to-hand. Surviving Japanese launched a *banzai* charge that partly overran American lines on May 29. There followed sustained fighting all through the night and into the following morning. Just 28 enlisted Japanese were taken prisoner when it was over: No officer surrendered. Americans counted another 2,351 Japanese corpses, all killed in the fighting or choosing suicide over surrender. Hundreds more Japanese were assumed killed and buried by bombs on other parts of the island, or were thought to have been buried earlier by their countrymen. U.S. casualties were 600 dead and 1,200 wounded.

A worse fight was anticipated on Kiska, where twice as many Japanese troops were dug in. However, the Japanese Navy secretly evacuated Kiska on July 28–29. The departing ships slipped past the American destroyer picket line in the dark and fog. Unaware that the enemy was gone, U.S. 7th Division landed on Kiska in assault deployment. It formed the core of a force of 34,000 men who landed on August 15, with 5,300 in a brigade from Canadian 6th Division as well as the Canadian contingent of the 1st Special Service Force (SSF) (later dubbed the *Devil's Brigade*). Nearly sixty soldiers were killed or injured by friendly fire. The main cause was fog and taut confusion during a landing in which severe opposition was expected, but none materialized. Over 200 more troops were wounded by Japanese booby traps or suffered severe frostbite. Plans to use the Aleutians as a base for the invasion of Japan were soon shelved, though bombing missions were eventually flown against targets in the Kuriles. The main Aleutian islands were garrisoned for the remainder of the war. Otherwise the chain returned to historical obscurity.

See also Pips, Battle of.

Suggested Reading: Brian Garfield, *The Thousand-Mile War* (1969).

ALEXANDER, HAROLD (1891–1961)   British field marshal. Alexander had extensive combat experience during World War I and was a rising star within the

British Army during the 1930s. He commanded a division during *FALL GELB* (1940) from May to June, then oversaw the general evacuation of Western Allied troops from *Dunkirk*. He went to Burma in March 1942 to shore up British and Commonwealth forces then retreating pell-mell into India under heavy assault. He was sent to North Africa to command British 1st Army against the Regio Esercito and *Afrika Korps*. He was appointed to overall command in the Middle East in August 1942. Alexander was excellent when it came to marshaling resources. He was superb in smoothing over inter-Allied disputes and handling difficult subordinates, especially General *Bernard Law Montgomery*. Alexander impressed many at the *Casablanca Conference*. His obvious political skills led to high appointment on February 20, 1943, as ground forces commander of all Western Allied armies in the Mediterranean theater and as deputy to General *Dwight Eisenhower*. Alexander pushed home the attack that began badly in Tunisia in November 1942, until all Axis forces in North Africa were defeated and surrendered by early May 1943. Elevated to command 15th Army Group, Alexander oversaw the invasion of Sicily in Operation *HUSKY,* with General Montgomery and General *George Patton* serving as his main subcommanders. Some of Alexander's decisions in Sicily were criticized for supposed favoritism of the more cautious approach taken by Montgomery. The dispute over how to proceed contributed to the growing strain that marked operations in the Mediterranean and Anglo-American relations more generally. Alexander was next given command of all Allied forces in Italy. He conducted the difficult and controversial *Italian campaign (1943–1945),* which kept him out of the *Normandy campaign* in 1944. He rose to commander in chief for the entire Mediterranean in November 1944 and was promoted to field marshal. He fought in Italy to the end of the war, formally accepting the German military surrender there on April 29, 1945.

ALGERIA   Algeria occupied a special place in the history of the French Empire. During the 19th century it was a kind of French Siberia, full of political exiles. It was also a preferred locale of settlement by colons, or ethnic French migrants to Africa. In the century before 1940 one million poor French and other colons migrated to Algerian lands that were forcibly cleared of local Arab and Berber populations by the French Army. General *Maxime Weygand* was sent to Algeria as the Vichy governor after the fall of France in June 1940. He and other Vichy officials enforced severe anti-Semitic laws that were alien to Algeria's long religious tradition of relative tolerance, but which found a welcome home among colons and fascist-minded Vichyites. The Western Allies pushed aside Vichy officials once they secured the country in early 1943, following the *TORCH* landings and heavy fighting against German forces from November 1942. The Germans were then attacked in Tunisia from secure bases in Algeria. The *Free French* slowly took political control over Algeria in the wake of the Axis defeat. French rule was fully restored in 1945, but only after violent repression of local Arab nationalism. Anticolonial grievances and French political and military weakness in the aftermath of defeat in World War II led to the bitter and bloody Algerian War of Independence from 1954 to 1962.

ALIAKMON LINE   A Greek defensive line running from the River Aliakmon to the Yugoslav frontier. It was outflanked by the Axis invasion of Greece in April 1940.

ALLGEMEINE SS
See Schutzstaffel (SS); Totenkopfverbände; Waffen-SS.

ALLIED CONTROL COMMISSIONS   Command structures (Kommandatura) were set up by the main Allied powers in Germany and Austria immediately after the war. They operated under the auspices of formal Allied Control Commissions. These military governments initially comprised representatives from Great Britain, the Soviet Union, and the United States. French representatives were added once a small French occupation zone was carved out of previously agreed British and American zones. Berlin and Vienna were also subdivided into four discrete occupation zones. Vienna was reunited once the Allies withdrew from Austria in 1955. Berlin remained divided until 1989, physically as well as politically by the Berlin Wall from 1961. Allied troops remained in Berlin until September 8, 1994. The United States held exclusive authority in Japan, though it permitted observers from other Allied states. Lesser territories had more limited commissions: the British and Americans jointly oversaw occupation policy in Italy; the Soviets were prime authorities in Finland, though Western Allied observers were allowed. In Rumania, the Allied Control Commission was used by Moscow to impose a Communist regime on Bucharest in March 1945.
See also Allied Military Government of Occupied Territories (AMGOT); war crimes trials.

ALLIED EXPEDITIONARY AIR FORCE (AEAF)   A limited-duration air command created upon the insistence of General *Dwight Eisenhower* that he have tactical control over all available air power during *OVERLORD*, especially the heavy bomber forces of the RAF and USAAF. The air chiefs had remained obdurate in insistence on continuing *strategic bombing* of German cities even in the build-up to the invasion. A new air command was therefore needed to compel the bomber chiefs to direct the heavies to tactically bomb transportation and communications targets in Normandy and the Pas de Calais, the latter as a ruse and to delay transfer of German 15th Army to Normandy. The AEAF had operational control over RAF 2nd Tactical Air Force and U.S. 9th Air Force, along with the resources of the *Air Defence of Great Britain (ADGB)*.

ALLIED FORCES HEADQUARTERS (AFHQ)   The first Western Allied HQ formed on a basis of equality between Great Britain and the United States. It was General *Dwight Eisenhower's* HQ during the *TORCH* landings and follow-on fighting in Algeria and Tunisia. It was located in Algiers until July 1944, when it moved to Italy in tandem with the slow advance of Western Allied armies up that peninsula during the *Italian campaign (1943–1945)*. It thereafter served as Field Marshal *Harold Alexander's* HQ for the entire Mediterranean theater of operations.

ALLIED INTELLIGENCE BUREAU (AIB)   The main clearing house for Western Allied intelligence gathering and field operations in the Southwest Pacific theater of operations. Its HQ was in Brisbane. It was a joint effort of Australia, Great Britain, and the United States, with surviving officers and assets of Dutch intelligence also taking part.

See also coast watchers.

ALLIED MILITARY GOVERNMENT OF OCCUPIED TERRITORIES (AMGOT)   An occupation government set up to deal with liberated enemy territory in Europe, starting with Sicily in 1943. Although AMGOT remained under military command, the main administrative work was done by civilians who moved in after active military operations ceased. AMGOT was progressively extended to the rest of Italy over the course of the *Italian campaign (1943–1945),* but the AMGOT experience was not a happy one, and the model was not applied to other liberated territory.

See also Allied Control Commissions.

ALLIES   Common term for the members of the wartime coalition formally called the *United Nations alliance* from January 1, 1942. The principal Allies were the United States, the Soviet Union, and Great Britain. China was a nominal fourth major ally, but it was divided on the ground between *Guomindang* and *Chinese Communists* and in any case exercised little to no influence over Allied councils. It is commonplace to use "Allies" in a more confined sense, comprising only the major Western democracies and smaller attached powers but excluding the Soviet Union. References to the Western powers alone in this work are instead rendered as "Western Allies." That more restrictive term meant primarily Britain and France and their satellites and minor allies to June 1940; Britain, its Commonwealth, and several governments-in-exile from June 1940 to December 1941; and Britain, the United States, and all other smaller Western powers (including the *Free French*) from December 1941 to the end of the war. The most notable minor Western Allies were Australia in the Pacific and Canada in the Battle of the Atlantic and in Western Europe. Others of varying note were Brazil, the Netherlands, Norway, Poland, South Africa, and in a distant sense only, Greece and Yugoslavia. Belgium was knocked out of the war very quickly in May 1940, as was the Netherlands. They along with Greece and several other European countries established governments-in-exile and kept some forces in the field with British aid.

Lesser allies in the early period included the Free French and Abyssinia, with "Fighting France" contributing substantially more militarily from 1943 to 1945. In Asia, Burma and the Philippines also had governments-in-exile claiming to be their rightful representatives and recognized as such in Western Allied capitals. By the end of the war 40 smaller nations and territories joined the United Nations alliance. Many contributed nothing to the war effort beyond signatures to varied proclamations. Most of these nonactive "belligerents" were in Latin America. Two million troops of the *Indian Army* fought for the British cause. It is possible that without them Britain might have lost control of the Middle East. Other than Abyssinians and white South Africans, most Africans who fought for the Allies did so within various colonial forces such as the *Armée d'Afrique* or *Tirailleurs Senagalese* or in colonial units of the British Army. British West Indies colonies contributed men in varying degree. Burmese, Tonkinese, Filipinos, and other Asian peoples were associated by connection to larger imperial powers. Some fought as *resistance* fighters against the Japanese, receiving Allied matériel aid and advisers. In Burma, Malaya, and elsewhere in Southeast Asia others chose to fight against the former colonial power alongside the Japanese. The formal name of the Allied wartime alliance was transferred to the postwar security organization founded in 1945 by the major victor nations.

See also Axis alliance; Big Four; Big Three.

ALL RED ROUTE   The sea and air route from India to the Suez Canal. It was called "All Red" because of the predominance of British imperial territory in the region, marked in red on every schoolchild's map.

ALPENFESTUNG   "Mountain Redoubt." The Western Allies feared that "bitterenders" and other fanatics of the Hitlerite regime would hole up for a last stand in the Alps. General *Dwight Eisenhower* feared that development and moved significant numbers of Western Allies troops into southern Germany to meet it. The threat proved a chimera, however, partly because Adolf Hitler chose to remain to the end in the Führerbunker in surrounded Berlin.

See also National Redoubts; werewolf guerillas.

ALSACE-LORRAINE   France lost these two border provinces to Germany in 1871, following crushing defeat in the Franco–Prussian War (1870–1871). Recovery of the "lost provinces" was the central aim of all French war plans before World War I, a known fact that greatly influenced Otto von Bismarck's balance of power diplomacy and underlay operational assumptions of the Reichswehr's "Schlieffen Plan" in 1914. Reunification was achieved by France in the *Treaty of Versailles* in 1919. Reclamation of the territories to Germany thereafter became a core demand of the Nazis and other extreme German nationalists. Alsace and Lorraine were declared re-annexed by Germany immediately upon the fall of France in late June 1940. Many ethnic French residents were expelled, while ethnic Germans were declared German citizens and young males were conscripted into the Wehrmacht. The provinces were liberated and returned to France in 1944. Their continuing French status was assured by the military and political outcome of World War II.

See also malgré-nous; Oradour-sur-Glane.

ALSIB   Code name of the *Lend-Lease* supply route via Alaska to Siberia. *See Alcan Military Highway.*

ALSOS MISSIONS
See nuclear weapons programs.

AMAU DOCTRINE (1934)   A prewar Japanese declaration that warned other powers not to aid China's economic reconstruction or otherwise interfere in Japan's proclaimed "special interest" in China and Manchuria. It was a fundamental challenge to the "Open Door" policy of the United States and an indirect challenge to the *Washington Treaty* system.
See also Greater East Asian Co-Prosperity Sphere.

AMBROSIO, VITTORIO (1879–1958)   Italian general. He was experienced in war, having fought in the Italo-Ottoman (Tripolitanian) War in 1911 and as a divisional staff officer during World War I. He led the Italian occupation army that accompanied the German invasion of Yugoslavia in 1941. He next served in the *Comando Supremo,* rising to chief of staff in February 1943. He failed to persuade Benito Mussolini to bring home Italian divisions from the *Eastern Front* and to exit the war with the Soviet Union. Upon the Western Allied invasion of Sicily in mid-1943, Ambrosio again failed to persuade Mussolini to pull out of the Axis and negotiate a separate exit from the war. Ambrosio was intimately involved in the plot that deposed Mussolini. He was also closely involved in secret negotiations to permit the Western Allies to enter Rome peacefully, but did not complete the talks in time to prevent massive German intervention. He escaped from Rome just before the Germans arrived. He served briefly as minister for war in Marshal *Pietro Badoglio's* pro-Allied government. Untrusted by the Western Allies or Badoglio, Ambrosio was reduced to a quiet supervisory command at the end of 1943.

AMERICA FIRST COMMITTEE (AFC)   The major American isolationist organization. It began as a campus movement during the 1940 presidential campaign. It quickly grew into a national organization with over 800,000 members. It attracted leading businessman, anti–New Deal politicians, celebrities, German and Irish American Anglophobes, and some liberal peace activists. Speaking with such disparate voices, members of the AFC opposed *Lend-Lease* to Britain and the Soviet Union, but they agreed with national defense preparedness measures as long as these did not involve overseas deployments or commitments. Charles Lindbergh emerged as principal spokesman for the AFC, lacing isolationism with his personal xenophobia and *anti-Semitism*. The AFC presented real opposition to several key preparedness measures during 1941, but it did not stop them. It quietly disbanded after *Pearl Harbor*.
See also Committee to Defend America by Aiding the Allies.

AMERICAL DIVISION   One of just two named divisions of the U.S. Army during World War II. The other was the Philippine Division. It was an American division first activated in New Caledonia in May 1942, from scratch units rushed there in haste at the start of the war in the midst of Japanese successes across the southwest Pacific. The division fought on *Guadalcanal, Bougainville,* and in the Philippines.

AMERICANISTAS   Anti-Japanese guerillas in the Philippines. Nationalists who accepted American military aid and were officered by Filipinos with experience in the prewar army, they numbered about 30,000 in 1943. They frequently fought Communist *Huks* as well as the Japanese on Luzon.

AMERICAN MILITARY MISSION TO CHINA
See China-Burma-India Theater (CBI); Joseph Stilwell.

AMERICAN VOLUNTEER GROUP (AVG)   Also known as the "Flying Tigers" or "Fei Hu." One hundred American fighter pilots joined the Chinese Air Force from September 1941, prior to formal U.S. entry into the war against Japan. They were discharged from U.S. service with permission—indeed, active connivance—by the USAAF and U.S. Navy, with behind-the-scenes approval by President Franklin Roosevelt. Another 200 grounds crew joined up to service three volunteer fighter squadrons. The AVG was commanded by General *Claire Chennault,* who proposed the scheme. It flew 100 P-40 fighters provided by the United States to the *Guomindang* forces in southern China. Britain provided an air base in Burma to facilitate training and supply. The noses of the fighters were painted to look like shark or tiger jaws, hence the popular name of the unit. The AVG provided *Jiang Jieshi* with air cover his forces otherwise lacked. Plans for additional fighter squadrons and a bomber group were preempted by the Japanese attack on *Pearl Harbor (December 7, 1941).* In the first desperate weeks of the new war with Japan the AVG split. One squadron fought in Burmese skies above British ground forces, while the rest of the AVG remained in China protecting the terminus of the *Burma Road.* It was assisted in that role by a small number of RAF fighters. The AVG squadron in Burma saw heavy action over Rangoon in early 1942. The two squadrons still based in China were in near-continuous combat with Japanese fighters and bombers through February 1942, and intermittently thereafter. The majority of pilots left the AVG to rejoin U.S. forces upon expiration of their one-year contracts in July 1942. All told, AVG fighters accounted for nearly 300 Japanese warplanes in exchange for 50 of their own, and the lives of 14 pilots. Their colorful imagery was retained by Chennault for his successor unit within U.S. 14th Air Force.

AMERIKA BOMBER
See bombers; strategic bombing.

AMIENS RAID
See Résistance (French).

AMIS German slang for Americans, comparable to "*Tommies*" for the British and "*Ivans*" for Russians.

AMMUNITION

See air power; anti-aircraft weapons; anti-tank weapons; armor; artillery; B.A.R.; BAR-BAROSSA (1941); Bari raid (1943); bombs; elephants; Flak; Germany, conquest of; Gross-transportraum; horses; Imperial Japanese Army; Leningrad, siege of; Luftwaffe; machine guns; marching fire; mules; Panzerfaust; Panzerschreck; Quartermaster Corps; rockets; shrapnel; Singapore; Sino-Japanese War (1937–1945); Stalingrad, Battle of; strategic bombing; white phosphorus.

AMPHIBIOUS OPERATIONS   The British term was "combined operations." Amphibious operations are generally agreed to be the most difficult to carry out of any military endeavor. Amphibious assaults engaged all the military capabilities of an attacker: intelligence, logistics, and air, land, and sea power. The Japanese Army trained two divisions in amphibious assault, the 5th and 11th. They pioneered modern amphibious assault at the outset of the *Sino-Japanese War (1937–1945)*, when they landed troops along parts of the coast of northern China. An especially ambitious set of landings were made during the major campaign around Shanghai, where the Japanese first used their top secret *Military Landing Craft Carrier*. Japanese Army engineers also invented the bow-ramp *landing craft* later copied by the Western Allies. Interservice rivalry between the Japanese Army and the Imperial Japanese Navy over allocation of troops and shipping in amphibious operations was intense. The Army generally brooked no Navy interference once its troops were ashore. As was generally true of Japanese naval tactics, amphibious landings at night were preferred because they took advantage of extensive nighttime training by the IJN.

From 1937 to 1942 the Japanese carried out an unbroken succession of successful amphibious assaults. Usually meeting utterly surprised defenders, they landed from southern China to the Dutch East Indies, across the southern Pacific, and on Guam and Wake Islands. That string of victories was broken in May 1942, when the Japanese were forced to cancel an assault on Port Moresby because of a close-run naval battle in the *Coral Sea*. A planned amphibious operation against Midway Island in the first week of June was called off as the great carrier battle of *Midway* unfolded. Although originally intended only as a diversion from the attack on Midway, Japanese troops landed unopposed on Attu and Kiska in the *Aleutian Islands*. Amphibious operations were also carried out to reinforce the large Japanese garrison on *Guadalcanal*, but ultimately failed to keep pace with enemy reinforcements. On numerous South and Central Pacific islands Japanese proved highly adept at defending against amphibious operations, or at the least inflicting heavy casualties on their enemies. They initially tried to meet and stop enemy landings on the beaches, through concentrated firepower and aggressive counterattacks against ill-formed enemy perimeters. The Japanese specialized in night attacks. This manner of defense proved highly costly in lives and quickly eroded garrison strength. The Japanese adapted new defensive doctrine in response to massive Western Allied preliminary bombardments of beach defenses. Japanese commanders moved progressively toward static inland defense from dug-in or underground positions. That approach marked major fights for control of *Iwo Jima* and *Okinawa,* among other Pacific locales.

Other than Japan at the outset of the China War and the beginning of the Pacific War, the Axis states were seldom faced with having to conduct seaborne operations. It was their fate to defend against them instead. Still, some Axis amphibious operations were carried out. The Germans conducted a combined amphibious and airborne assault on Norway in April 1940, with mixed success on both scores. The Heer and Kriegsmarine reluctantly prepared to assault Britain across the Channel that September, until the proposed invasion, Operation *SEELÖWE,* was canceled by Adolf Hitler. Planning revealed that the Germans were utterly unprepared to carry out such a major landing. They lacked any purpose-built landing craft and therefore proposed to cross men and supplies on converted river barges. That meant also attempting to move tens of thousands of draught horses across the Channel by methods not much advanced from those of William the Conqueror in 1066, or Philip II's plan in 1588. Smaller German amphibious assaults were carried out against Soviet defenses at various places in the Baltic. At the start of the German–Soviet war in 1941 and again at its close in 1945, the Germans moved men and supplies and launched amphibious attacks against various Baltic islands and along the mainland Baltic coast. More extensive German operations took place in the Black Sea, notably on the Crimean peninsula and against its opposing western and Caucasus shores. Even more significant amphibious withdrawals were carried out in those areas and in the Baltic later in the war. A remarkable amphibious withdrawal by the Wehrmacht was also conducted from Sicily to the toe of the boot of Italy in 1943. Smaller withdrawals were carried out by garrisons from the eastern Mediterranean and the Baltic in 1944. Spectacular marine evacuations of troops and civilians from East Prussia were conducted with just weeks remaining in the war, accompanied by several of history's greatest maritime calamities.

Several sea evacuations were conducted by the Red Army in the first year of the German–Soviet war. Disaster attended hasty evacuation of troops from the Baltic coast in the last week of June 1941. Colossal losses accompanied a massive evacuation across the Kerch Straits in May 1942. The Soviet Navy made the first offensive amphibious landing by any Allied power in December 1941: it carried out two large-scale landings at *Kerch-Feodosiia,* small ports on the Kerch peninsula in the eastern Crimea. Otherwise, the Red Army did not usually have to cross large bodies of water to engage the enemy. Other than two more Black Sea assaults and several small attacks later in the war in the Baltic, the Red Army did not concentrate on preparation for amphibious operations. Instead, it improvised whenever required. Soviet sea assaults during 1941–1942 were thus ad hoc relief or counterattack missions conducted around the Black Sea. They were not primarily defensive in character; they were instead a premature application of prewar Soviet offensive doctrine forced on the Red Army by the goading and orders of Joseph Stalin. They were implemented with minimal planning and without specialized boats or vehicles. Two more amphibious operations were assayed as the Red Army went over to permanent offense. Overall, a lack of purpose-built landing craft hampered Soviet operations, which put a premium on improvisation by local commanders and combat engineers. Excluded from this abbreviated list are remarkable logistical and reinforcement operations conducted across the open water of Lake Ladoga during successive summers of the *siege of Leningrad*. The Red Army recorded all major river crossings as amphibious operations. Soviet historians therefore count several crossings of the Danube in 1944–1945 as amphibious operations. Amphibious operations were much better planned and conducted as Red Army strength grew in all arenas later in the war. The Soviet Navy also trained several hundred thousand marines by 1945, although the principal focus of the Baltic Fleet remained interdiction of shipping. By the end of the war the Soviets had a significant amphibious capability, including specialized landing craft imported via *Lend-Lease*.

Once the British were expelled from France in June 1940, the Western Allies were forced to develop amphibious capabilities to cross several oceans and then the Channel to get at their Axis enemies with ground forces. The British had a long tradition of fighting over water, but even they had to start essentially from scratch. After the fall of France and British expulsion from Greece, there was no friendly port on the Continent. To fight the Heer or Regio Esercito the British Army had to fight its way ashore first. It is a testament to long-range planning, and to British fortitude, that thinking about amphibious vehicle and ship design to enable a return to the Continent began just a month after the disaster of *FALL GELB (1940)*. Even as the *Battle of Britain* was underway and preparations for defense against invasion were undertaken, planners also worked on offensive amphibious projects. Starting with *commando* raids and a landing on Madagascar in May 1942, British and Commonwealth forces built up a "combined operations" capability through hard experience. The worst but most valuable lessons came with a large-scale Anglo-Canadian commando assault at *Dieppe* on August 19, 1942. That ended in total disaster for the attackers, but two central lessons were drawn from the failure: any landing needed to achieve surprise to be successful, and landings must be preceded by intense bombing and naval bombardment. Smaller lessons called for prior close scouting of the gradient and weight-bearing load of the sand of a given landing beach; continuous close support fire from off-shore craft in the initial phase of the landing; quick clearance of beach obstacles and mines; and improved shore-to-ship communications. The British did better in subsequent landings in North Africa. They did very well in Italy in September 1943, where they began to perfect use of innovative *Combined Operations Pilotage Parties*. British and Canadian troops applied the lessons of Dieppe and landings in Africa and Italy with real success on three of the five *D-Day* beaches on June 6, 1944.

The Americans learned bloody lessons about how not to carry out amphibious operations during the *TORCH* landings in North Africa on November 8, 1942. Despite access to reports from the *Agency Africa* network, inadequate intelligence led to near disaster along the beaches and needless losses in the harbors of Algiers and Casablanca. Inadequate training of too many units rushed into combat, some without proper weapons training, meant that more GIs died than was necessary, while precious landing craft and ships were lost. Beach management was also chaotic and unloading of heavy equipment too slow and poorly conceived. The next American amphibious operation in the ETO went more smoothly, at Sicily in *HUSKY*. Problems returned for the Americans at *Anzio* due to a failure to expand the lodgement with sufficient speed to prevent the Germans bringing artillery to range against overcrowded beaches. On the other side of these assaults, even improvised Vichy French opposition to the TORCH landings had caused great difficulty, while more effective Axis opposition in Sicily and again at Anzio taught hard lessons about how to fight one's way ashore as well as how to defend a perimeter. Both sides brought lessons from prior landings to France in June 1944. Field Marshal *Erwin Rommel* clung to an older view about how to meet seaborne invaders: directly on the beaches, before the enemy gained a lodgement. Others disagreed, rejecting Rommel's view in preference for the argument that the best time and place to stop an amphibious invasion was with an armored counterattack once the enemy was onshore. Combined with a failure of strategic intelligence and planning, Hitler and the Wehrmacht allowed the Western Allies to come ashore in Normandy against relatively light opposition and to secure a defensible lodgement. Instead of launching a concentrated counterattack with mobile forces, they succumbed to enemy *deception operations,* then fed arriving divisions piecemeal into the fight.

U.S. Marines and the U.S. Army and Navy learned especially difficult lessons about the nature of amphibious assault half a world away against tenacious Japanese defenders in the Pacific. There was protracted fighting on *Guadalcanal* that tested naval resupply by both sides and briefer but intense violence and carnage on *Tarawa*. Those battles taught the Japanese new lessons about how to defend, moving them back from the beaches into fortified dugouts and caves. U.S. marines developed improved amphibious doctrine and taught it to the U.S. Army, which also learned directly by fighting alongside marines across the Pacific. The revised assault doctrine reduced reliance on operational surprise in favor of heavier advance bombing and bombardment; careful mapping by frogmen or mini-submarines of coral reefs, precise water depths, and tides; underwater demolition of offshore reef obstacles and advance beach clearance; continuous bombardment with prepositioned artillery, if possible from nearby islets or by close-in naval bombardment just before the assault; much closer deployment of LSTs so that a shorter run-in to the beach was made by the smallest and most vulnerable landing craft; use of armored and well-armed *amphibious vehicles* such as amphtracs to provide close-in protection and suppressing fire during the assault; a heavy first assault wave; rapid exploitation of captured air strips to permit land-based fighter cover and tactical bombing; a specialized HQ ship to oversee the operation; and dedicated supply and protective perimeter fleets that remained on station until the target island was declared secure, especially including naval air cover.

In addition to direct beach assaults into the teeth of dug-in Japanese defenders, U.S. commanders in the Pacific learned to use amphibious landings to bypass enemy strongpoints. On New Guinea and elsewhere they cut off and isolated whole Japanese garrisons that lacked coastal transport in areas were roads were also nonexistent. U.S. and Australian forces thereby leaped down lengths of coastline, instead of fighting overland through jungle, over mountains, and past pestilential coastal swamps. This technique was advanced during campaigns conducted by General *Douglas MacArthur* in New Guinea, but found its greatest application in the Central Pacific. Not all Pacific lessons were applicable in the radically different conditions of the ETO, or against a different enemy than the Japanese. But many more lessons were transferable than were actually learned by resistant planners in the ETO. Learning on smaller islands should have helped a great deal when it came to carrying out the largest amphibious operations in the history of armed conflict: the Western Allied invasion of Europe. But Marine advisers sent to Europe encountered smug condescension instead.

See discrete island chains and campaigns. *See also Balikpapan; combat loaded; Guam; H-Hour; Okinawa; Peleliu; Saipan; SEALION; second front; Soviet Navy; storm boats; storm landings; Tinian; Wake.*

AMPHIBIOUS VEHICLES A series of specialized assault vehicles and aircraft produced mainly by the Western Allies to enable beach landings along the European coastline and across the Pacific theater of operations. They were also used in *recce* missions. The British Terrapin MkI was an amphibious truck that saw limited action in Italy and France. A superior and ubiquitous amphibian was the *DUKW* boat-truck. The principal amphibious vehicle for the U.S. Army, it quickly displaced the Terrapin for British and Commonwealth forces once it became available in greater numbers. The U.S. developed an armored amphibious tractor called amphtrac (AmTrac) or LVT (Land Vehicle Tracked). The LVT was designed for use in the Pacific war. British and Commonwealth forces called the LVT a "Buffalo." The Wehrmacht had two amphibious vehicles used mainly in river crossings: the Type 166 Schwimmwagen, which was a light amphibious boat-like car equipped with side paddles, and a larger Trippel SG6 Amphibian. The Japanese developed six amphibious light tank types and a semiamphibious truck for transporting supplies in coastal areas marked by swamps. The Red Army developed a number of light amphibious tanks before the war, including the T-38 scout tank, which was transportable by air. The T-38 proved incapable of standing up to German tanks in 1941. Its lack of any radio also made it a poor scout vehicle. At the end of 1941 most surviving T-38s were withdrawn to rear areas for use as military tractors. The Soviets planned the T-39 and T-40 as successors, but few were built. Amphibious aircraft employed by all major armies included *float planes* and *flying boats*. The Japanese built small seaplane carriers and seaplane bases to support amphibious operations and defend landings.

See also DD tanks.

AMPHTRAC "amphibious tractor."
See amphibious vehicles.

AMTRAC "amphibious tractor."
See amphibious vehicles.

ANAMI KORCHIKA (1887–1945)   Japanese general. He was instrumental in framing the policy of military aggression pursued by Japan against China, and a forceful advocate of war with the Western powers. He backed General *Hideki Tōjō* in the final decision to attack the United States and Great Britain. Korchika held active commands in China and Manchuria. He took charge of all Japanese forces in New Guinea in November 1943. He returned to Japan to take charge of the *Japanese Army Air Force*. He was minister of war from April 1945. He was intimately involved in high level debate over whether Japan should seek terms, arguing for "honor before surrender." After failure of an attempted coup by junior officers intent on preventing surrender even after the twin atomic bombings, and after public announcement of the emperor's call for submission was made, Anami committed ritual suicide (seppuku).

ANDAMAN AND NICOBAR ISLANDS   British forces withdrew from this Indian Ocean chain once the loss of Burma made them vulnerable. Japan occupied the islands in March 1942. Nominal control of the chain was granted to *Subhas Chandra Bose* in late 1943, though the islands remained under Japanese control rather than that of the *Indian National Army*. Once the Japanese outer defense perimeter was breached and the IJN shredded, the garrison scattered across this chain was totally isolated. The Western Allies decided to bomb intermittently but did not invade. The Japanese garrison surrendered along with all other Japanese forces in August–September, 1945.

ANDERS, WLADYSLAW (1892–1970)   Polish general. A cavalry officer by training, he was wounded during the Soviet invasion of Poland in September 1939. He was imprisoned in Moscow, but escaped the fate of many thousands of other Polish officers who were murdered by the *NKVD* in the *Katyn Forest*. Released in 1941 upon the German invasion of the Soviet Union, Anders was appointed to command *Polish Army* units reconstituted from prisoners released by the Soviets. His divisions departed Russia for Iraq and Egypt within a year to join the British in hard fighting in Italy from 1944 to the end of the war. "Anders' Army" saw bitter fighting at *Monte Cassino,* along the *Gothic Line,* and at the *Argenta Gap*. Like most of his men, Anders was bitterly opposed to the Soviet-backed government set up under the *Lublin Poles*. Stripped of his citizenship, he spent the rest of his life in exile from the country he served so well.

ANDERSON SHELTERS   Primitive, corrugated-steel, garden air-raid shelters for civilians in Great Britain. Kits were issued and construction recommended by Civil Defence authorities. The shelters provided more psychological comfort than physical protection.

ANGAU
See New Guinea, Dutch.

ANGLO-GERMAN NAVAL AGREEMENT (JUNE 18, 1935) Britain agreed to German naval rearmament up to 35 percent of Royal Navy tonnage in capital warships, in direct violation of the disarmament clauses of the *Treaty of Versailles* (1919) and of the *Locarno Treaties*. The main German interest had been to engage Britain in rejection of Versailles and the international security system it supported. Adolf Hitler succeeded completely in that purpose. The principal British interest was political *appeasement,* at that stage more from sincere belief or hope that war could be avoided through concessions to Germany than from motivation to buy time for rearmament, a motive that later emerged in British policy circles once Hitler's true aggressive intentions became undeniably clear. The Naval Agreement weakened the *Stresa Front* before it had a chance to show any deterrent value. It reverberated in world capitals because the British failed to consult their French allies, or the Italians, Americans, or Soviets, before kicking out of place one of the main supporting pillars of the post-1918 international order of which Britain was a principal architect. With truly remarkable lack of strategic foresight, London agreed to 45 percent equivalent tonnage in submarines and even to *U-boat* parity "should Germany deem it necessary." This credulous agreement permitted the Kriegsmarine to lay hulls for more destroyers (64), cruisers (21), battleships (5), and *pocket battleships* (3) than its shipyards could complete and brought its secret U-boat program into the open. Three weeks after the signing ceremony, Hitler announced a naval building program of two capital ships and 28 U-boats. Secret planning continued on a battleship and aircraft carrier fleet. The submarine agreement ultimately proved the great disaster. Submarines quickly emerged as the crucial weapon against Western Allied surface ships and convoys once hostilities began. Germany renounced the Naval Agreement in April 1939 and began to build as many warships as its shipyards could turn out.

See also Canaris, Wilhelm; Dönitz, Karl; Z-plan.

ANGLO-SOVIET TREATY (MAY 26, 1942) Signed in London by *Vyacheslav Molotov* in behalf of the Soviet Union and *Anthony Eden* for Great Britain, its essential point of agreement was stipulation that neither side would seek a separate peace with Germany. The treaty was really more a declaration than a binding legal agreement among sovereign nations. It was also notable for what it did not say: Britain refused to recognize Moscow's annexations of eastern Poland and the Baltic States that stemmed from the *Nazi–Soviet Pact* of August 1939.

ANIMALS All armies relied heavily on animal power and services in certain theaters of operation. They relied even more heavily on animals for supplies of meat, either on the hoof or in tinned form. In North Africa the principal beasts of burden were camels and *mules*. In India, Burma, and across Southeast Asia water buffalo, bullocks, and *elephants* were widely used as pack animals and on road, railway, and airfield construction details. The Wehrmacht and Red Army were each highly dependent on *horses* for transportation and logistics. *Carrier pigeons* remained in wide use, despite the advance of radio and field telephones. The Japanese relied heavily on pigeons in the Pacific.

See also anti-tank guns; dogs; falcons; logistics.

ANNEXATIONS

See Abyssinia; Albania; Alsace-Lorraine; Anglo-Soviet Treaty; Anschluss; Austria; BARBAROSSA; Beck, Ludwig; Belgium; Belorussia; Bessarabia; Bosnia; Brest-Litovsk; Bukovina; Bulgaria; China; Ciano, Galeazzo; concentration camps; Courland; Curzon Line; Czechoslovakia; desertion; Estonia; ethnic cleansing; Eupen and Malmedy; Finland; Finnish–Soviet War (1939–1940); French Indochina; Germanics; Germany; Gestapo; Hitler, Adolf; Holocaust; Hungary; Junkers; Korea; Kuriles; Latvia; Lebensraum; Lithuania; Luxembourg; Malaya; Malgré-nous; Manchuria; Memel; mines; Molotov Line; Munich Conference; Nazi–Soviet Pact; NKVD; Norway; Oder–Neisse line; Poland; Red Army; Reichskommissariat Ostland; Rhineland; Rumania; Ryukyus; Sakhalin Island; Schleswig-Holstein; Silesia; Soviet Union; Stalin Line; St. Germain, Treaty of; Sudetenland; Tehran Conference; Teschen; Thailand; Treaties of Paris; Tripartite Pact; Ukraine; Ukrainian Insurgent Army (UPA); Voivodina; Wehrmacht; Western Belorussia; Yalta Conference; Yugoslavia; Zog I.

ANSCHLUSS The forced union of Austria and Germany effected on March 11–13, 1938. Union was forbidden by the terms of the *Treaties of Versailles* and *St. Germain.* An attempt to establish a simple customs union (Zollverein) was therefore blocked by France in 1931. Austrian Nazis mounted an abortive coup d'etat in July 1934, murdering Chancellor *Englebert Dollfuss* during the attempt. The Putsch was halted by Austrian police and army units led by *Kurt von Schuschnigg* and by promises of Italian military support for Austria's independence: Benito Mussolini deployed several divisions to the *Brenner Pass* and threatened direct intervention, the only foreign leader to do so. Strategic collaboration between Italy and Germany after 1936 left Austria isolated. France was internally weakened by the heated ideological conflicts of the Third Republic, while Britain turned to a policy of *appeasement.* Schuschnigg, now Chancellor of Austria, was curtly summoned to meet Hitler in early 1938 and was browbeaten into accepting several Nazi ministers in his government. When Nazi *fifth columnists* sparked anti-Jewish pogroms and political riots in favor of Anschluss, the newly appointed Nazi minister in charge of Austrian police, Seyss-Inquart (1892–1946), did nothing to stop the agitation. Seeking to preempt the drive to Anschluss, Schuschnigg called for a plebiscite on union with Germany on just three days notice, but he lost his nerve in the face of stepped-up German intimidation and canceled the vote.

With Austria facing imminent German military intervention, Seyss-Inquart implemented Hitler's demand that Austria "invite" the Wehrmacht across the border on March 11, 1938. Anschluss was proclaimed two days later. Britain, France, and Italy did nothing. Schuschnigg and thousands of other Austrians were sent to *concentration camps.* Over two dozen senior officers were sent to *Dachau,* and some senior officers were murdered. Worst of all, Austria's Jews fell into Nazi hands.

Hitler cynically held a plebiscite on April 10. His toadies and propaganda machine reported the vote as 99 percent in favor of Anschluss, and his personal rule as Führer of a nation that was thereupon reduced to a province of the Greater German Reich. This easy success greatly enhanced Hitler's reputation with the Wehrmacht and German diplomatic corps, even as it deepened his already profound contempt for the West and inflated his pathological sense of personal destiny. Anschluss briefly relieved Germany's foreign currency shortage, expanded the Wehrmacht long term, threateningly positioned German forces around Czechoslovakia, and gave Germany new borders with Hungary, Italy, and Yugoslavia. Anschluss was not reversed—Austria was not reestablished as state separate from Germany—until the total defeat of Nazi Germany in 1945. Four-power Allied occupation of Austria followed from 1945 to 1955, when Austria was governed by an *Allied Control Commission*.

ANT FREIGHT

See Tokyo Express.

ANTI-AIRCRAFT ARTILLERY/GUNS

All major combatants produced a wide variety of increasingly effective and longer-range anti-aircraft guns as the war deepened. Fixed anti-aircraft artillery was deployed in defense of cities, though some German guns in the Ruhr Valley were mounted on trains to enable them to follow the bomber stream for many miles. More anti-aircraft guns were deployed on warships and merchantmen as the air threat to shipping was better understood. U.S. Navy warships sported many dozens of anti-aircraft guns each by the end of the war, of greatly varying caliber and range for distant or close-in air defense. These proved highly effective against *kamikaze* and other late-war, poorly trained Japanese pilots. All major power armies were protected in the field by vehicle-mounted anti-aircraft guns, with airfields and base areas also deploying larger fixed guns. Most anti-aircraft guns were derivatives of normal artillery tubes but employed different forms of ammunition than standard field artillery, anti-tank guns, or big naval guns. Smaller caliber (20 mm–40 mm), rapid-firing cannons were usually mounted on trucks or half-tracks or on obsolete tank chassis. They functioned best in defense of infantry or armor against low-flying enemy aircraft making strafing or bomb runs. Comparable naval calibers (popularly called "pom-poms" by Western Allied crew) provided close-in defense of ships. Larger calibers of up to 120 mm employed explosive heavy ordnance that sought out high altitude *heavy bombers*. From 1943 they were usually fitted out with firing *radars* and worked together with radar-guided searchlights.

See also aircraft carriers; air power; anti-tank weapons; Flak; Flak Towers; proximity fuze.

ANTI-COMINTERN PACT (NOVEMBER 25, 1936)

A joint declaration by Nazi Germany and Imperial Japan that affirmed opposition to the *Comintern*. Secret codicils pledged economic and diplomatic, but not military, assistance should either state go to war with the Soviet Union. *Joachim von Ribbentrop* inspired Adolf Hitler to pursue alliances with Italy and Japan that aimed at Great Britain. Ribbentrop regarded the Anti-Comintern Pact as a triumph worthy of German recognition of the Japanese puppet state of "Manchukuo" (*Manchuria*). Italy adhered to the Pact on November 6, 1937. It also recognized Manchukuo but did not agree to the secret protocol. Benito Mussolini's interest was driven by Italy's deteriorating relations with Great Britain and an old personal claim to anti-Communist fame. A right-wing regime in Hungary signed in 1939, paying obeisance to Germany. Deeply anti-Communist Poland refused to join. Spain signed in secret in 1939, out of deep-seated anti-Communism on the part of the *Francisco Franco* regime and partly to more closely support Hitler. Germany's smaller puppets and minor allies adhered to the Pact in 1941: Croatia, Finland, Slovakia, Rumania, and Bulgaria signed, as did the collaborationist governments of Denmark and Japan's client regimes in Nanjing, Inner Mongolia, and Manchuria. The Pact was renewed for five years on November 25, 1941. That did nothing strategically for Germany or Japan. Instead, the Pact enhanced Western concerns about Axis military cooperation while fusing perception about the kindred nature of the regimes in Berlin, Tokyo, and Rome. That perception was not accurate about Italy, and perhaps not about Japan. Yet, the perception in Washington in general and by President Franklin Roosevelt personally, that both regimes were akin to the Nazis, importantly colored views and hardened U.S. policies from 1940.

See also Axis alliance.

ANTI-SEMITISM   In the late 19th century, religious hatred of Jews in Europe was supplemented with racial motivations, as theories of *Aryan* superiority and social-Darwinism took root. In the first half of the 20th century, anti-Semitism took a new ultra-nationalist form of hostility to communities of Jews as "alien" elements living within homogenous national societies. That view took root even where Jews had coexisted more or less peacefully for several centuries as quiet or moderately autonomous minorities. This type of hatred of Jews was most pronounced in ethnically German and Slavic regions of eastern and central Europe, but also found numerous adherents in France, Belgium, Italy, and Spain. Anti-Semitism was not just an important component of the twisted psychological make-up of Adolf Hitler and his admirers in the *Nazi Party*. Populist mythologizing of "the Jew" as a figure of abstract, conspiratorial and antinationalist evil was widespread in Christian-rightist and nationalist politics across Europe during the 1920s and 1930s, as well as within the United States and Canada. It was a profound prejudice shared by figures as ideologically distant as Joseph Stalin and Benito Mussolini, among many other tyrants. In a more traditional and milder form, anti-Semitism was shared by more than a few democratic leaders. *Édouard Daladier* indulged it in France. Such sentiments also found adherents among segments of the general population of many countries. French pacifists turned to anti-Semitism from 1937 to 1939, expressing fear that Jews and Communists were pulling France into a new war with Germany.

A radical and newly racialized anti-Semitism gained adherents in Germany and parts of central Europe in the 1920s. The view of "the Jew" as not just religiously and socially different, but as racially distinct from and inferior to the "Volk," fed directly into the rise and popular appeal of *Nazism*. Race hatred conduced to an ultimately exterminationist ideology that in a more distant sense underlay the origins and conduct of World War II in Europe and led directly to the *Holocaust.* Important arguments persist among historians about the essential connections between anti-Semitism and the extermination programs of the Nazis and others, such as the *Ustaše*. In 1996 sociologist Daniel Goldhagen used the term "eliminationist" to characterize what he saw as the historical logic of German anti-Semitism, which supposedly led inexorably into genocidal conclusions along a clear *Sonderweg*. Other scholars strongly disagreed that the German variant was peculiarly or even especially eliminationist before Hitler and the Nazis turned it in that direction.

On specific forms, expressions, and instances of anti-Semitism *see also Action Françaises; Algeria; America First Committee; Anschluss; Antonescu, Ion; Auschwitz; British Union of Fascists; Bulgaria; Einsatzgruppen; Einstein, Albert; fascism; genocide; ghettos; Iron Guard; Italian Army; Joyce, William; Nuremberg Laws; Palestine; Pius XI; Pius XII; Poland; Protocols of the Elders of Zion; Rumania; Schutzstaffel (SS); Sonderweg; Sovinformburo; Vatican; Wannsee conference; Warsaw Ghetto.*

ANTI-SUBMARINE WARFARE (ASW) All passive or active measures taken to defend against submarines. The ASW doctrine of the main Western Allied navies was well-advanced by the end of World War I, but lapsed badly during the interwar years. Instead of building large flotillas of smaller escort ships, the Royal Navy reverted to construction of capital warships such as battleships and cruisers, and discredited and failed to practice often or well necessary anti-submarine escort drills. The Admiralty also failed to prevent successive peacetime governments from adopting and following a highly damaging "Ten Year Rule" in annual budgets: the assumption that Britain would not engage in a naval war in the next 10 years, rolled over year after year. Cuts led to elimination of the Anti-Submarine and Trade (convoy support) Divisions and sharp curtailment of scientific research. Fortunately, some research continued on underwater detection systems. It culminated in a technological breakthrough that led to *ASDIC,* which proved critical to ultimate Royal Navy success in the war against the U-boats. For all those reasons, the main ASW technique employed by British and Commonwealth navies at the outset of the war was passive: to steam vulnerable cargo, tanker, and troopships in *convoy,* though even that tactic was opposed by some important naval officers. For a number of months the Admiralty quite wishfully thought that fast single ships ("independents") could avoid U-boats by running blacked-out and with zigzag navigation. So-called fast merchantmen were therefore not forced into "slow convoys" early in the *Battle of the Atlantic.*

Another passive technique was routing convoys around known U-boat positions and picket lines, a measure greatly aided by *ULTRA* reading of Kriegsmarine signals intercepts. It became clear that passive tactics would not suffice as sinkings rose to crisis levels in 1940–1941. A hasty expedient while awaiting arrival from shipyards of new and better escorts was to arm as many merchantmen as the scarce supply of weapons allowed, and far beyond what prewar rules of *cruiser warfare* ostensibly permitted. That decision reflected a general breakdown of the laws of war at sea, dating at least to the Kriegsmarine announcement before the war that the German navy would regard even legal armament of any merchant as constituting its conversion into an auxiliary warship, hence making it a legitimate target for "sink on sight" rules of engagement. Early merchant defenses were primitive and ineffective. An armed merchant might mount no more than a single small or medium-caliber deck gun, alongside a few rockets and parachute mines for illuminating and frightening surfaced U-boats at night. As long as British and Commonwealth navies lacked sufficient small warships to serve as convoy escorts and were also unable to provide continuous air cover through the mid-Atlantic *air gaps,* ASW tactics also were limited. Rather than seeking to kill U-boats, convoy escorts in the early period more often spread *depth charge* patterns in an effort to force the enemy to submerge and thereby lose contact with the convoy, which sped away as best it could.

Killing U-Boats in preference to merely suppressing them required refinements in detection technology and improved ASW weapons that just were not available in the first year of the war at sea. That was true even though prewar advances in underwater detection technology meant that from the outset all Royal Navy destroyers were fitted with ASDIC. Depth charge delivery systems compounded limitations of the ASDIC sound detection system so that contact with a U-boat was lost by the attacking escort just before the moment of attack. *Depth charges* were only deliverable from the stern so that loss of contact from forward-pinging ASDIC meant that a charging destroyer could only lay a spread across the last known position of the U-boat. Because depth charges took time to sink before detonating, many U-boats were detected by ASDIC-equipped escorts but escaped destruction by turning hard or diving deep, even as the escort closed at high speed to depth charge an area or depth from which the U-boats had since departed. These limitations of depth detection and sink speed were not overcome until 1943, and even then the stern-only deployment of depth charges limited their usefulness when combined with short-range technical limitations of ASDIC. Long neglected and urgent work on a forward-throwing ASW bomb was recommended just before the war began. The solution took longer to achieve. The problem was not solved until a variety of forward-throwing charges were deployed, notably the *Hedgehog* and its *Squid* and *Mousetrap* cousins. However, even after new ASW weapons were made available, some escort ship captains evidenced a preference for ramming U-boats they had forced to the surface. This was much discouraged: even when successful, ramming almost always damaged the attacking surface ship as well, taking a badly needed escort out of service to undergo lengthy repairs that occupied over-tasked shipyards already straining to meet construction schedules. The most effective measures to force a U-Boat to submerge, and to concuss it or otherwise damage or sink it, proved to be surveillance and hunter aircraft working alone from land bases or from *escort carriers* that were part of hunter-killer task forces. Aircraft-mounted

ASW weapons were as badly neglected by the Royal Navy as shipborne weapons. RAF Coastal Command started the war with inadequate aircraft and only a few small, ineffective specialized anti-submarine bombs. But already, the great arms race at sea was on.

Admiral *Karl Dönitz,* head of the Kriegsmarine U-boat arm to January 1943 and the full Kriegsmarine after that, easily countered the threat from ASDIC by ordering U-boat captains to attack only on the surface at night. That gave U-boats a speed advantage over slower merchants while reducing their silhouette so that they became nearly undetectable by escorts. Surface night attacks led to a long run of early U-boat successes. The tactic was ultimately countered by new Allied surface *radars* and limited by the developing sophistication of the convoy system. Dönitz then countered the convoys and met growing numbers of escorts with new tactics of group attack, commonly known as the *"wolf pack."* The new method overwhelmed escorts by vectoring in more U-boats from a long picket line than they could defend simultaneously, so that some boats were in position to attack while scarce escorts were chasing away others. The Allies took progressively more effective countermeasures against wolf packs by deploying quickly produced *corvettes* and *destroyer escorts.* To free ocean-capable escort warships for Atlantic duty, U.S. shipyards built several hundred small warships in two controversial classes of coastal boats called *"sub-chasers."* These proved a waste of resources and trained seamen: they were credited with just one U-boat sinking in the Atlantic. The weight of Allied production told against the U-boats over time. Technical advances that increased the lethality of Allied aircraft included short-wave and more portable *Huff-Duff* detection devices and the *Leigh Light* mounted on long-range bombers. More and longer-range aircraft fitted with powerful search radars hunted along known picket lines. *VLR (Very Long-Range)* bombers and new bases closed the air gaps. Ersatz *escort carriers* were deployed, then replaced by the real thing. Other important technical breakthroughs were new *Direction-Finding (D/F)* equipment, critically important 10-centimetric radar, shipborne Huff-Duff provided to escorts from July 1941, and much greater numbers of escort ships of all types from 1942. Additional anti-submarine devices included air-deployed sonobuoys, acoustic homing torpedoes, and *Magnetic Anomaly Detectors* (MAD). Aerial-deployed homing torpedoes were another technological leap forward that led to many U-boat kills.

Reinforcing technical advances, and ultimately more important than any of them, was new tactical doctrine that insisted that reconnaissance aircraft and VLR bombers work in concert with surface escorts. This was not as obvious then as it seems in retrospect. It was also delayed by serious interservice rivalry. Thus, the USAAF initially repeated some of the original errors of RAF Bomber Command in refusing to release heavy bombers for anti-submarine warfare, then made a new mistake all its own: for the first eight months of 1942, most U.S. aircraft in the Atlantic were deployed in ineffective and premature hunter groups instead of convoy protection. Once a convergence was achieved of escorts and aircraft, better D/F equipment, and new radars and shipborne Huff-Duff, the Allied navies went over to permanent offense against the U-boats. The culmination of offensive thinking was the concept of the "Support Group," an independent task force of hunter-killer warships and aircraft operating outside the convoy system. The first Support Group was formed by the British in September 1942. The *TORCH* landings delayed full implementation of the program by drawing off escorts to protect the troop convoys to North Africa. But as more and better escorts became available, new sea tactics were perfected with the singular contribution of RN Captain *John Walker,* commander of Second Support Group. For the rest of the war U-boats were more hunted than hunters.

See also *cork patrols; Foxer; frigates; LORAN; mines; Pillenwerfer; Swordfish; torpedoes.*

ANTI-TANK WEAPONS Specialized weapons to penetrate tank armor were developed in tandem with the arrival of tanks on the battlefield during World War I. The first effective anti-tank weapon was the *mine.* Anti-tank mines remained a staple of defense by all armies against enemy armor throughout World War II. The Red Army developed anti-tank doctrine that employed heavy mines laid in dense and deep fields to delay or channel attacking *Panzers* or fix them under the fire of waiting Soviet armor and anti-tank infantry and artillery positions. British 8th Army employed comparable tactics against Panzers in the *desert campaign,* notably at *Second El Alamein* in 1942. Tanks used in a deep defensive role could be dug-in or deployed as mobile counterattack forces. In either deployment, tanks proved the single most effective anti-tank weapons system on all sides for most of the war until the Allies established air supremacy on all fronts. Rocket-armed *tank-buster* aircraft were deployed in *cab ranks* to be called down to target individual enemy tanks. The effectiveness of tanks vs. tanks was greatly enhanced by infantry and artillery support and progressive development of additional fixed, mobile, infantry, and specialized aircraft-mounted anti-tank weapons.

A major difference in tank defense between World War I and World War II was development of large-caliber, high-velocity anti-tank guns by most major armies. That led to a gun-vs.-armor race that began before World War II and continued for decades after it. By the start of the war in Europe armor had leaped ahead of most prewar anti-tank guns, which proved too small in caliber and ineffective in early battles in Poland and France. Useful anti-tank guns awaited larger calibers introduced as a result of combat experience. For instance, the Wehrmacht entered the war with various models of anti-tank guns designated as PAK ("Panzerabwehr-kanone"). Most were towed weapons, small enough to be hauled behind one or two horses; some were towable by two or three men. As with comparable anti-tank guns of the Polish Army and Red Army, PAK calibers under 50 mm proved incapable of harming the heavier armor plate deployed on most tanks at anything beyond point-blank range. The Germans therefore built 50 mm and 75 mm anti-tank guns by 1942–1943, and a 76 mm gun after that. But they also turned the superb 88 mm anti-aircraft gun to a level trajectory and supplied crews with armor-piercing ammunition. The German '88 became the most effective anti-tank gun of the war on any side. It was even mounted as the main gun in Tiger (Mark VI) heavy tanks, primarily to contend with late-model Soviet heavy tanks. However, demands for homeland *air defense* kept the bulk of production of '88 mm tubes in an anti-aircraft artillery role and hence far from ground combat on the frontlines.

Allied armies eventually caught up to the Germans in the race to build large-caliber anti-tank guns. The British Army deployed 6-pounders, 12-pounders, and eventually 17-pounders in an anti-tank role. The latter was an equivalent bore to a 77 mm gun, but it fired a very high-velocity, armor-piercing round. The most popular U.S. anti-tank gun was a towed 3-inch tube. The Red Army continued to use outmoded small-caliber anti-tank weapons as late as the fall of 1942, mainly out of desperation while awaiting new tubes to arrive with *Lend-Lease* or from relocated Soviet factories. The Red Army achieved superior firepower that was used to blunt the last German strategic offensives in the east in 1943, once tube production ramped up. By the end of the war the Soviet Union fielded many tens of thousands and several types of big anti-tank guns, including two of the three largest guns of the war at 100 mm and 122 mm, respectively. The Germans countered by building a few massive 128 mm guns that threw a 28 kg shell to an effective range of 4,000 meters. Such size and weight extremes made the largest anti-tank guns effectively immobile, which vitiated their battlefield purpose. At the other end of the production scale, reflecting the early departure of Italy from the war and the paucity of Italian industrial capacity, the Italian Army never built or deployed anti-tank guns larger than 47 mm. That left Italian troops badly exposed to assaults by Western Allied medium tanks and Soviet medium and heavy tanks.

The Japanese did not face more than a handful of medium tanks in China before 1942, and no heavies. Japan thus built anti-tank guns only in calibers of 37 mm and 57 mm, which were sufficient to deal with the prewar French, British, and Soviet light tanks available to the *Guomindang*. At the start of the *Sino-Japanese War (1937–1945)* the Chinese fielded a few dozen Renault FT-17s (Model 1918), Carden Lloyd Mk VI patrol tanks, Vickers 6-ton light tanks, Vickers medium tanks, and Italian L.3/35 tankettes and German Pz-1As. In 1938 the Guomindang acquired Soviet T-26s, BA-10s, and BA-20s. It was not until the Japanese faced much heavier American Shermans in the Pacific and Lend-Lease Grants and Shermans in southern China that the need for larger caliber anti-tank guns became apparent. Isolated Japanese garrisons already in the South Pacific improvised almost pathetic defenses against enemy tanks. For instance, it was common to hurl bags of mud or lime at vision slits in hopes of blinding tank drivers, or throw homemade coconut or glass bombs. Japanese suicide troops hurled themselves against the sides or rear of enemy tanks, exploding satchel-charges attached to their bodies. Large tank traps modeled on tiger pits were dug in roadways, only with mines rather than stakes at the bottom. Smaller holes were dug across open fields. Inside each hole a Japanese soldier waited with a 250-pound bomb, which he hoped to detonate should a Sherman pass overhead. Opposing troops learned to crawl up to these holes and shoot or grenade the man-mine inside. Heavy preset mines and artillery were the only effective Japanese anti-tank weapons. The other expedient was to retreat into a cave or tunnel system to avoid facing tanks directly.

As anti-tank guns grew in caliber they greatly increased in weight. Smaller, animal-towed guns mostly disappeared, replaced by larger tubes mounted on the chaises of outmoded tanks. Heavy guns were also mounted on purpose-built chaises as older models proved too small. The Germans produced several hybrid anti-tank guns starting with the *Panzerjäger* ("tank hunter") and *Jagdpanzer* ("hunting tank"), moving to the more dubious because lumbering *Elefant* (or Ferdinand). The Wehrmacht named other heavy anti-tank or *self-propelled guns* after animals, including the Jagdpanther ("hunting panther") and Nashorn ("Rhinoceros"). Mobile anti-tank guns were much more lightly armored than the heavy tanks they faced. Most were fixed: lacking any turret, the weapon was aimed only by moving the vehicle so that it had to face an enemy tank to fire upon it. That meant anti-tank guns were best fought by crews who took up preset, static defensive positions. Self-propelled or anti-tank guns accordingly carried most armor at the front, making them more susceptible to flank fire or close infantry assault than comparable medium tanks. So why build them? Germany built mobile anti-tank guns because they were a quick and cheap alternative to tanks: they required less complex engineering, less assembly line time, and took much less weight of steel to complete. The latter consideration was especially important to German production from 1943, despite the oddity of Germany producing super-heavies like the Elefant and wasting vast amounts of steel on a late-war *U-boat* construction program that hardly led to action at sea.

The logic was quite different in the U.S. Army, which called mobile anti-tank guns "tank destroyers." The United States produced and deployed massed tank destroyers as a prewar doctrinal response to *Blitzkrieg*. The idea was to counter German armor with fast, massed, high velocity anti-tank guns that would "seek, strike, and destroy" Panzers. The Army was ordered by General *George C. Marshall* to organize a Tank Destroyer Force in November 1941. Units were equipped with towed anti-tank guns as well as self-propelled M-1, M-3, M-5, or M-10 Wolverine tank destroyers. The latter had a main weapon with a 3-inch bore, the standard U.S. tank destroyer gun from 1943. The British refitted Lend-Lease M10s with their superb 17-pounder gun. They called this hybrid "Achilles," an unfortunate and unintended—but perhaps not inaccurate—acknowledgment of thin-armor vulnerability to German tanks and anti-tank guns that these vehicles faced in battle. The later M18 Hellcat mounted a 76 mm gun, while the M36 had a powerful 90 mm tube. All U.S. tank destroyers carried a .50 caliber machine gun for defense against infantry. By the end of the war, U.S. tank destroyer battalions proved to be much less effective in stopping German tanks than simply using Shermans in a defensive role.

Anti-tank ammunition evolved with changes in the thickness and sloped design of opposing armor. Armor-Piercing (AP) solid shot worked by kinetic energy. The Germans improved this by ballistic shaping of the round, then by adding a soft nose cap that prevented a shell from shattering on impact. These Armor-Piercing, Capped (APC) shells were further improved by adding a second hollow ballistic cap (APCBC). Another German anti-tank round was the "Hartkernmunition," or what the British called an Armor-Piercing Composite Rigid (APCR) round. This had a hard tungsten core but a narrow diameter, making it somewhat arrow-like in flight. Some shells thus required fins to stabilize them in flight to the target. Other armies followed the German lead, until every one deployed Armor-Piercing High Explosive (APHE) shells for large caliber guns. Prior to the war the French Army developed the Armor-Piercing Discarding Sabot (APDS). This employed reduced tungsten-alloy shot—tungsten does not shatter as easily as steel, yet is more dense and heavy—surrounded by a discardable casing or "sabot." French shell designers retreated to Great Britain with the defeat of France in *FALL GELB* in 1940. They assisted the British Army in producing APDS shells for 17-pounder tubes. The new shell was first used on the battlefield in 1944. The Wehrmacht was forced to abandon APDS anti-tank shot late in the war due to a severe shortage of tungsten caused by Western Allied preemptive buying then blockade of Germany's Iberian suppliers. The Germans retained the sabot principle for anti-aircraft guns whose lighter shells attained a higher muzzle-velocity. High Explosive Anti-Tank (HEAT) rockets were fired from towed guns such as the R-Werfer 43, which was used extensively by the Wehrmacht in North Africa and Italy. Hollow-charge shells were also developed. These did not try to penetrate armor with kinetic impact. Instead, they injected a stream of liquid metal and gas at extreme high pressures that cut through armor into the vitals of an enemy tank at preset ranges and terminal velocities up to 85 meters per second.

New types of warhead led to a small anti-tank weapons innovation focused on delivery by infantry. Prewar and early war anti-tank rifles quickly disappeared from all armies once they proved incapable of penetrating heavier armor. All major combatants instead developed high-explosive anti-tank warheads, including hollow-charge and rocket weapons. Several types of hollow-charge or smooth-bore infantry weapons quickly found their way into battle, among them the British *PIAT,* American *bazooka,* and German *Panzerfaust* and *Panzerschreck*. These new weapons displaced earlier HEAT rocket weapons such as the R-Werfer 43. Few of the latter were seen in Normandy beyond deployment in fixed defenses, whereas numerous Panzerfäuste and Panzerschrecke were encountered to the end of the war. The Germans gathered their anti-tank infantry into specialized companies called *Panzerzerstörer*. When times grew even more desperate as Soviet and Western Allied tank superiority climbed, German anti-tank defenses were organized into misnamed *Panzerjägdgruppe*. As the Red Army and Western Allied armies commenced the *conquest of Germany* in 1945, they ran into still more ill-organized units of boys and old men of the *Volkssturm,* armed mainly with Panzerfäuste.

See also assault guns; Belgian Gate; dogs; recoilless guns.

Suggested Reading: Wolfgang Fleischer, *German Motorized Artillery and Panzer Artillery in World War II* (2004); Ian Hogg, *Allied Guns of World War II* (1998).

ANTONESCU, ION (1882–1946) Rumanian field marshal; minister of war, 1932–1944; dictator, 1940–1944. Antonescu established a dictatorship in September 1940, closely modeled on that of Benito Mussolini in Italy. He was initially supported by the radical *Iron Guard* but broke with the Guardists after they failed in a coup attempt in January 1941. Antonescu made a strong impression on Adolf Hitler when they met and was similarly impressed with the German Führer. Antonescu was informed of German plans for *BARBAROSSA* 10 days before that massive assault on the Soviet Union commenced. He immediately promised Hitler, "I'll be there from the start! When it's a question of action against the Slavs, you can always count on Rumania." True to his intemperate declamation, two Rumanian armies flanked German Army Group South in the invasion of Ukraine and the Crimea. Rumanian support for the war against the Soviet Union was bolstered by anger over the earlier annexation of Bessarabia and Bukovina, territorial fops thrown back to Antonescu by Hitler to win Rumania support for the reckless war in the east. However, Rumanian opinion turned hard against the war with rising casualties. It collapsed upon utter destruction of two Rumanian armies at *Stalingrad* over the winter of 1942–1943. During his four-year dictatorship Antonescu oversaw a discrete Rumanian holocaust carried out against Jews and Roma that extinguished over 300,000 lives. He failed to take advantage of Soviet operational interests to secure a more generous armistice in early 1944. Instead, the Red Army crossed the Dniester from Ukraine into Rumania on August 23, 1944. A panicking King Michael dismissed Antonescu and tried to negotiate a separate exit from the war. The result was a total Rumania military collapse. Antonescu was tried and shot in 1946.

ANTONOV, ALEXEI A. (1895–1962) Soviet general. Antonov served in the Tsarist Army in World War I before joining the Red Army in 1919 to fight for the Bolsheviks in the Russian Civil War (1918–1921). He survived the terrible purges of the 1930s, rising to serve on the General Staff. He spent most of 1941–1942 fighting in the Caucasus. He was reassigned to the Operations Directorate of the General Staff in late 1942 and appointed to the Stavka during the great fight around *Stalingrad*. He rose to chief of the General Staff following reassignment to a Front command of *Alexander M. Vasilevsky* in February 1945. Marshal *Georgi Zhukov* thought highly of Antonov. He continued to serve in high positions with the Red Army after the war, rising high within the command structure of the Warsaw Pact.

ANTWERP
   See Ardennes offensive; Belgium; G-4; MARKET GARDEN; Scheldt Estuary campaign.

ANVIL Original code name for the Western Allied invasion of the Mediterranean coast of France, staged from Italy. It was changed to *DRAGOON* prior to the actual landing on August 15, 1944.

ANZAC AREA A short-lived command of Australian, New Zealand, and American ships and other assets organized as "Anzac Force." It was set up in haste in January 1942 at the start of the war against Japan in the South Pacific. It was disbanded four months later as the strategic situation changed and more permanent command structures were developed.

ANZACS Popular term for soldiers from Australia and New Zealand, derived from their common service in a single corps—the Australia and New Zealand Army

Corps, or ANZAC—from 1914 to mid-1918. The nomenclature was changed even before the end of World War I, but survived unofficially as a common daily reference to Australian and New Zealander soldiers, sailors, and airmen.

ANZIO (JANUARY 22–MAY 24, 1944) Following the Western Allied landing at Salerno (September 9, 1943), commanders set out an ambitious plan to leapfrog far up the Italian coast and liberate Rome via *amphibious operation.* Competitive demands for *landing craft* in other theaters, as well as preparations for the invasion of France in mid-1944, led to a reduced force going ashore at Anzio. The landings took place on January 22, 1944. They were well-covered by air and sea power and unopposed other than by a few Luftwaffe straffings and hasty *E-boat* attacks. Rather than taking advantage of the tactical surprise that was achieved, Major General John Lucas dug in along a shallow perimeter. He then advanced beyond the beachhead perimeter at a markedly slow pace. This supremely frustrated Winston Churchill, who was the principal enthusiast for the Anzio plan. Lucas thus denied the Western Allies the chance to seize Rome quickly and easily. Lucas displayed a pronounced command tardiness, a tendency Americans were deeply critical of when they perceived it in Field Marshal *Bernard Law Montgomery.* The delay at Anzio prevented defense-in-depth of the lodgement and created a massive backup of reinforcements and supplies on the beaches, which were then exposed to German bombing and artillery that was brought within range and began heavy shelling.

Lucas' failure to advance quickly out of the landing zone presented Field Marshal *Albert Kesselring* with time to recover and counterattack. Kesselring quickly gathered together a force equivalent to six German divisions, scratching units together from across Italy. He then mounted a highly effective counterattack on the lodgement at Anzio. German infantry surrounded the beachhead perimeter, while heavy artillery brought fire crashing down on overcrowded beaches and rear areas, causing extremely heavy casualties. The Anzio operation thus bore a striking resemblance to German defense of the Kerch Peninsula in the Crimea in November 1943. As the fight continued German casualties also mounted. Allied air power and precise operational intelligence, gathered through air recce as well as from *ULTRA* intercepts, enabled the defenders to blunt a major counteroffensive launched by Kesselring on February 16. Over 5,000 German casualties were inflicted and suffered over the next four days. Hard fighting continued along a bloody, slowly expanding perimeter. Meanwhile, other Allied thrusts to the south met determined resistance and prevented the Americans from forming a single front across Italy. Perimeter fighting continued into early May. Although there were no large engagements over the period following the third battle of *Monte Cassino,* fighting was still intense as terrain and toughness on either side reminded men of World War I: fighting surged back and forth over the same entrenchments and strongpoints, while men under near-constant bombardment lived troglodyte lives in bunkers, cellars, and trenches. The breakout came with the launch of Operation DIADEM on May 11. Anzio forces thereafter linked with 2nd Corps of General *Mark Clark's*

U.S. 5th Army. A broad advance followed, attended by much controversy then and since over the manner and timing of Clark's liberation of Rome on June 4, 1944, for Clark allowed much of German 10th Army to escape to the north. That was a beaten force that should have been trapped and annihilated. It lived to fight and kill more Allied troops over the remaining 11 months of the *Italian campaign (1943–1945)* because Clark's vanity pulled him toward Rome instead of into the rear of the retreating 10th Army.

See also Kleinkampfverbände.

Suggested Reading: Carlo d'Este, *Fatal Decision: Anzio and the Battle for Rome* (1991); David Eisenhower, *They Fought at Anzio* (2007).

APPEARANCE
See East African campaign (1940–1941).

APPEASEMENT   Pacifying an aggressor with local or nonvital concessions, often territorial in nature. The policy pursued by the Western Allies toward Italy and Germany in the second half of the 1930s morally presumed that a duty to resist aggression was trumped by a higher duty to seek peace. That view rested on practices of a post–World War I international society founded not on Wilsonian conceptions of rights—sovereign, national, or minority—but on traditional instruments of constant readjustment to threats and to the naked exercise of power. Practically, appeasement was a limited political tactic within the balance of power system, an interim measure employed by British and French leaders to gain time to work out a general settlement with Germany and, later, for rearmament and deterrent alliance building. It amounted to seeking sequential local solutions that avoided a general war. It arose from a certainty among Britain's leaders that their global empire must be drawn into any general war, whatever its origin in some distant local quarrel. The British approach to the Axis was also part of a grand, accepted, well-understood, and frequently successful tradition of British diplomacy dating to Lord Palmerston, if not earlier. It was pursued by successive British and French governments toward Fascist Italy and Nazi Germany during the 1930s, with broad elite and wide public approval. Appeasement of the Axis states also had strong support from Britain's Commonwealth allies and most *neutral states*.

The first test of the policy when applied to Nazi Germany came in 1935, when Britain helped undermine the international order it helped create at the Paris Peace Conference in 1919 by agreeing to the *Anglo-German Naval Agreement*. That decision was taken without consultation with Britain's major allies, for whom it also eviscerated the *Treaty of Versailles (1919)*. In a traditional Great Power answer to a territorial challenge to the balance of power, Britain tried to avert the *Abyssinian War (1935–1936)* by offering Italy a piece of that small country's territory. However, the Abyssinians refused to surrender any of their sovereign territory. Modified appeasement was still practiced toward Italy following its aggression against Abyssinia, and again regarding Italian assistance to *Francisco Franco* in the *Spanish Civil War (1936–1939)*. A more important test occurred when Adolf Hitler remilitarized the *Rhineland* in 1936. The Western democracies did nothing: appeasement was habitual by then, and there was no public appetite for armed confrontation of the dictators. Appeasement was becoming the only alternative to a general European war, which the Western Allies did not want and for which they were not ready economically, politically, or militarily. The policy of seeking local settlements with Hitler at the expense of smaller powers culminated in surrender of the *Sudetenland* to Germany at the *Munich Conference* in September 1938. Hitler expected more opposition from the Western democracies than he encountered. The British initially viewed the settlement as a great diplomatic success that averted a European war. Prime Minister *Neville Chamberlain* regarded it as a personal and political triumph. In fact, Hitler was always unappeasable. He wanted war and was taken aback and disgusted by the Munich settlement. Munich also discouraged Joseph Stalin from seeking a deal with the West for the Soviet Union to deter Germany and Japan. The great dictator of the east instead sought a separate peace with Hitler, while opposing Japan with demonstrations of Red Army strength in 1938 and again at *Nomonhan* in 1939. The shift in the East Asia Squadron led to the *Nazi–Soviet Pact (August 23, 1939)*, which divided eastern and central Europe between the Nazi and Soviet empires and cleared the way for a joint invasion of Poland in September.

Appeasement of Italy by the western powers predated and outlasted appeasement of Germany. The French view was somewhat different than the British. The French concurred in early British appeasement of Italy in response to Benito Mussolini's bullying campaign leading into the invasion of Abyssinia, but Paris was not always subservient to London when it came to Mediterranean policy. Admiral *Jean Louis Darlan,* among others, pressed for a much stronger response to Italian aggression and ambition for empire. Other French leaders cleaved to Chamberlain's side of the argument, fearing to lose the only major ally France had left. That ensured continued division and debate inside the French government through the Munich crisis and throughout the nine months of the *Phoney War*. Disputes within the Western Allied camp were shrewdly aggravated by Mussolini. Chamberlain was convinced until May 1940 that appeasement of Mussolini was both necessary and possible. His policy was demonstrated to be a total failure when Italy attacked France on June 10, 1940, with the German *FALL GELB* campaign already effectively decided. Chamberlain even then personally thought that Italy might be lured out of alliance with Germany. That extraordinary view was based on overestimation of Italy's real military power and potential by British analysts, and on utter misreading by British diplomats of Mussolini's true intentions and worldview. The worst misunderstandings were communicated to London by the British ambassador in Rome, Sir Percy Loraine.

Policy toward Italy was also shaped by wishful thinking born of a rising sense of strategic desperation during the late 1930s: the Western Allies feared to face Italy and Germany in war at the same time. Upon the defeat of France and withdrawal of the French Navy from the Allied order of battle, the Royal Navy was indeed stretched thin against the Kriegsmarine in the North Sea and North

Atlantic. Nevertheless, the British took on and defeated the Regia Marina in the Mediterranean in fairly short order. British naval and army planners were also deeply worried about a possible third front opening against Japanese forces in the Far East, a region they had stripped of real defenses to call home the legions to defend the British homeland. Britain therefore also tried appeasement when facing Japanese threats, such as demands to close the *Burma road* to British supplies heading to the *Guomindang* in southern China. It was American policy toward Japan that progressively hardened over the course of 1940–1941, as confrontation and threats of economic sanctions by Washington displaced conciliation and any thought of appeasement. The result of abandoning appeasement of Japan was, in fact, war in the Far East even as the Western Allies agreed that the real threat was Nazi Germany. The capitulation of moral principle and real strategic advantage that flowed from appeasement until Munich gave the old diplomatic tactic such a bad name that whenever it was practiced by statesmen after World War II they have always called it something else.

Suggested Reading: Robert Caputi, *Neville Chamberlain and Appeasement* (2000); Reynolds Salerno, *Vital Crossroads: Mediterranean Origins of the Second World War* (2002).

ARAB LEGION The Trans-Jordanian Army. It was commanded by a British officer, John B. Glubb, from 1921 to 1956.

ARAKAN CAMPAIGN (FEBRUARY 1944) A diversionary attack made by the Japanese in February 1944 intended to draw British forces away from the main target of their *Imphal offensive*: Kohima. The Japanese called the action "Ha-Gō." The British termed it *Battle of the Admin Box.* The attack failed badly from poor Japanese preparation and tough resistance by *Indian Army* troops so that reinforcements were able to reach Kohima in time.

ARAKI, SADAO Japanese general.
See Kodo-ha.

ARAWE PENINSULA
See New Britain; Rabaul.

ARBEITSLAGER "labor camp."
See concentration camps; Holocaust; Ostarbeiter.

ARCADIA CONFERENCE (DECEMBER 22, 1941–JANUARY 14, 1942) The first Western Allied conference held after U.S. entry into the war. Top British and American political and military authorities met to set short-range and medium-term strategic goals. They discussed immediate force dispositions, production requirements, and personnel for specific joint commands. They discussed *Lend-Lease* aid and national production quotas and approved the *United Nations Declaration*. Winston Churchill and Franklin Roosevelt dominated proceedings, of course, but both were closely guided by respective military chiefs. Decisions reached included a *Germany first strategy*, proposed landings in North Africa, pooling of raw material and shipping resources, and establishment of the *Combined Chiefs of Staff* committee.

See also *ABC-1 plan; ABDA Command.*

ARCTIC CONVOYS

See *convoys.*

ARCTIC WARFARE

See *convoys; Finland; Greenland; LACHSFANG; Norway.*

ARDEATINE CAVE MASSACRE (MARCH 24, 1944)

Also known as the "Fosse Ardeatine" massacre. A massacre of 335 hostages, prisoners, Jews, and several casual passersby rounded up for revenge killing. It was carried out by German troops in retaliation for an Italian partisan attack the day before, in which 33 men of a *Schutzstaffel (SS)* police battalion were killed. The victims were marched into the Ardeatine Cave outside Rome in groups of five and shot. Corpses were stacked against the cave walls. The scene of the massacre was concealed for a year by German military engineers who blew up the entrance to the cave. In 1947 a British military court convicted Field Marshal *Albert Kesselring* of ordering the shootings.

ARDENNES

A heavily wooded area straddling northern France and southern Belgium and incorporating much of Luxembourg. It is often written that the Ardennes was thought by French interwar strategists to be impenetrable by armor. French intelligence actually did foresee a threat of penetration, but did not think the Germans could make it through as quickly as they did in May 1940. The French did not believe that Panzers could cross the Meuse without strong infantry support and certainly not before the 10th day of any campaign. The Ardennes was therefore not fortified and only lightly defended by weak French infantry divisions at the start of *FALL GELB,* during which the goal of penetration of the Ardennes by German armor was actually the *Schwerpunkt* of the assault. The Wehrmacht turned the flank of the *Maginot Line* by descending onto the plains of northern France out of the Ardennes hills much faster than the French High Command anticipated. More critically, the Panzers then swiftly crossed the Meuse without waiting for leg infantry to catch up. Then they raced to the coast in the face of orders to stop issued by the OKH and even by Adolf Hitler. The thrust was only weakly counterattacked. It therefore cut off French, British, and Belgian armies on its northern flank, forced a panicked Allied retreat out of Belgium, and compelled evacuation from *Dunkirk.*

ARDENNES OFFENSIVE (DECEMBER 16, 1944–JANUARY 25, 1945)
Known by Americans as the "Battle of the Bulge." The last German offensive in the west in World War II was launched by armor massed in the *Ardennes* in an attempt to repeat the German success of May 1940. The Germans concentrated their weight of effort at a weak point in the American lines identified as the *Schwerpunkt* of the Western Front in late 1944. Only five weak American rifle divisions guarded the Ardennes because the Western Allies were most concerned with their own offensive operations on the north and south flanks of the Ardennes. Although *ULTRA* intercepts showed that the Germans were massing armor and infantry in northern Germany, they did not reveal to analysts the final destination of those formations. Nor did General *Dwight Eisenhower* or his subordinates or civilian leaders believe that Germany was even capable of launching a major winter offensive. Hitler threw all remaining strategic reserves into an offensive he personally codenamed "Wacht Am Rhein" ("Watch on the Rhine"). Over 1,000 carefully hoarded fighters were assigned to preemptively attack enemy airfields, though the Luftwaffe could not hope to recover air parity let alone achieve air superiority. Thirty ground divisions, including most of Germany's remaining Panzer and mechanized divisions, many of which had been transferred from the Eastern Front, moved off the line on December 16, 1944.

The strategic conceit was recapture of the port of Antwerp, thereby again cutting Western Allied armies in two. The specific goal was to divide British and Canadian armies to the north from American armies farther south, while also capturing vast stocks of war matériel and closing Antwerp as a supply conduit. German operational plans counted on achieving total surprise, sustained bad weather to limit enemy air power, and most recklessly of all, capturing fuel depots along the route as an essential condition of Panzers finishing their advance to Antwerp. Hitler ordered an attack by Army Group B to make the main penetration. He assembled two concentrations of his dwindling Panzers. SS-6th Panzerarmee was assigned to SS-General *Sepp Dietrich*. He was to lead the main attack in the north while 5th Panzer Army under Field Marshal *Hasso von Manteuffel* supported in the center. Protecting the southern flank of the overall advance was German 7th Army under Lieutenant General Erich Brandenberger. Field Marshal *Gerd von Rundstedt* was in nominal command of Army Group B, but Field Marshal *Walter Model* was given the real operational authority. The final plan as implemented bore no resemblance to Rundstedt's original "Plan Martin." Neither commander believed that the offensive could achieve its stated goal of reaching the Atlantic and splitting the Western Allied armies. Nor did their paper order of battle comport with actual divisions on the ground. Worst of all, Hitler's plan required bad weather to keep enemy air forces from destroying the Panzer columns.

Special operations and airborne troops deployed in advance of the main assault were led by another of Hitler's favorite soldiers, *Otto Skorzeny*. Some were English speakers dressed in American uniforms, driving captured U.S. jeeps. They sowed some confusion in immediate rear areas that delayed and misdirected initial U.S. reinforcements. But most of the German agents were discovered and killed in skirmishes, while 16 were summarily executed after capture and in accordance with the normal rules of war that forbade combat concealment in the enemy's uniform. Special operations that sought to capture key bridges across the Meuse also failed. The main attack was partly illuminated by searchlights reflecting off low clouds to provide light to the assault troops. It took the Americans by complete surprise. Two U.S. rifle divisions were shattered as the Panzers achieved a breakthrough and raced toward the key towns of Bastogne and St. Vith. No Western Allied commander had foreseen the attack. Critical intelligence on the German build-up had been ignored or explained away, while a widespread belief within *SHAEF* that the Wehrmacht was a spent force delayed effective response during the first hours. American mobility then proved decisive: armor and infantry were rushed to the front to firm the "shoulders" of the defense so that the force of Manteuffel's main attack produced a "bulge" in the center of the American line that reached 60 miles in depth. Large numbers of stunned, green American riflemen had surrendered. But the veteran 101st Airborne was rushed into Bastogne to hold that key crossroads town. After a three-day delay caused by confusion over the scale of the German assault, Eisenhower ordered all offensive operations in other regions of the front to halt. General *George Patton* was ordered to disengage part of 3rd Army in the south and swing north to attack into the southern flank of the German bulge. He did so with remarkable speed and verve. Field Marshal *Bernard Law Montgomery* also attacked with British 30th Corps into the northern German flank. "Monty" was given command of two American armies from General *Omar Bradley's* 12th Army Group. The transfer was made over Bradley's vehement objection and produced lasting bitterness on Bradley's part that proved deeply harmful to the Western Allied war effort before the end of the war.

Having left armies unprepared to meet a full German offensive, Eisenhower was finally making the right calls: to stand at Bastogne, send 3rd Army north, and release to Montgomery American ground forces on the northern flank. General *Courtney Hodges* pivoted 7th Corps to concentrate and carry out a counterattack, but he also bled divisions into hard fighting to hold the Germans from reaching the Meuse. The many flaws in the German plan now came into play, especially the requirement to capture fuel dumps: Rundstedt's Panzers started out with just one-quarter of the minimum fuel supply necessary to reach their final objectives. As the central thrust by Manteuffel failed and surrounded American troops in Bastogne held out against heavy odds, Hitler thinned the shoulders of the advance to reinforce the center. Winter skies cleared on December 22. That allowed thousands of bombers and fighters to waste exposed Panzer columns and break up and burn vital follow-on supplies. Ground resistance also toughened, then held against the wilting German tanks and infantry. Bastogne was relieved on December 26. The last major Luftwaffe attack in the West was made on January 1, 1945, as nearly 160 enemy aircraft were caught by surprise at various air fields and destroyed on the ground. However, over 300 German planes were lost. The Western Allies could easily replace their lost aircraft; the Luftwaffe could not. By the end of the battle nearly all 1,000 aircraft committed by Hitler were destroyed.

The American counterattack began on January 3. Eisenhower's decision to attack the center as well as all around the perimeter of the German bulge, rather than concentrate for a deep pincer maneuver into the exposed flanks as Patton and Montgomery wanted, may have delayed the end of the battle and led to higher casualties than necessary. It also permitted many Germans to escape, albeit without their heavy weapons or fighting morale intact. Even given that failure to pinch off and destroy most German units inside the bulge, the Wehrmacht's losses were severe: 100,000 men, 800 tanks, and 1,000 combat aircraft. It thus proved impossible to hold the Western Allies along the Rhine or keep the Soviets from the Carpathians or the east bank of the Vistula: the Red Army launched the *Vistula-Oder operation* on the other side of Germany on January 12. The Ardennes offensive was among Hitler's last great blunders of the war, one of the few in which he was principally responsible for operational failure because he acted against clear advice from his generals. The offensive spent Germany's final military reserves. More importantly, it broke the will of most ordinary *Landser* to continue to resist in the West. It thereby hastened the collapse of resistance once the Western powers crossed the Rhine. It probably quickened the end of Hitler's regime, and hastened his death, by several months. One unforeseen consequence was that the attack in the Ardennes thereby spared Germany attack with atomic bombs, which only became operational two months after the Nazi surrender in May.

See also V-weapons program.

Suggested Reading: Hugh Cole, *The Ardennes: Battle of the Bulge* (1993); John S. Eisenhower, *The Bitter Woods* (1969); C. Macdonald, *Battle of the Bulge* (1984).

ARDITI Italian elite assault troops during World War I. Many arditi veterans were members of the original *fascist* gangs of thugs, or "squadristi," which plagued Italy in the immediate aftermath of the Great War.

AREA BOMBING British term for mass bombing of enemy cities and urban populations. Americans called the same practice "carpet bombing." The first area or city attacks were carried out by the Luftwaffe against Warsaw, Rotterdam, and London. In Richard Overy's words, the practice was adopted by RAF Bomber Command "by a process of elimination." It was not accepted until after British airmen tried *precision bombing,* then slowly came to accept that they could not hit specific targets at which they aimed gravity bombs. The key moment for the RAF came in 1941 when a secret bombing study proved the inefficacy of RAF efforts and methods. The study was ordered by Winston Churchill's scientific adviser, Frederick Lindeman, and carried out by D. M. Butt. The "Butt Report" assessed accuracy based on hundreds of aerial reconnaissance photos: more were available because bomber cameras were more widely used from 1941. Butt concluded that one-third of RAF bombers never reached or bombed their targets. He noted that just 30 percent even dropped their bomb loads within five miles of a designated target, a number that plunged to just 10 percent over the critical and heavily defended region of the Ruhr Valley. That conclusion had the paradoxical effect of becoming instrumental in Bomber Command adopting a strategy of area bombing, while also seeking to improve accuracy in the long term. An additional inducement to area bombing was bad weather. Winter cloud cover made it impossible for aircraft at high altitudes to see ground targets, even those the size of a city.

Area bombing also had roots in prewar doctrines about bombing to suppress the morale of an enemy's civilian population, a practice known as *morale bombing*. Fleets of British bombers dropped high explosive and incendiary ordnance in destructive patterns over wide areas, rather than continuing to aim at specific targets such as aircraft plants or refineries. The British developed doctrine to support area bombing as the practice itself unfolded. But once committed, Bomber Command carried out area bombing of German cities with a vigor that amounted in some cases to fanaticism. Area bombing of vital workers in French towns along the coast of the Bay of Biscay was also assayed once it became clear that targeting U-boat pens even with blockbuster bombs was totally ineffective. The USAAF initially resisted area bombing by night in Europe, in favor of repeated attempts at daylight precision bombing of high priority economic and military targets. That created a pattern wherein the USAAF sought to achieve air supremacy over Germany by targeting its aircraft and other vital industries by day, while Bomber Command pursued city bombing as a strategy of generalized economic disruption and suppression of morale, hoping that bombing alone could be a war-winning weapon.

As American crew casualties reached unsustainable levels and the morally numbing effects of protracted war eroded early objections, the USAAF accepted in practice to area bomb Germany from late 1944. Several missions flown by the USAAF were so inaccurate that they actually hit the wrong country: three blacked-out towns in Switzerland were hit by loads of bombs in April 1944 or later, errors for which the United States paid compensation in 1949. When the USAAF was able to bring *strategic bombing* to Japan, its air campaign became progressively more indiscriminate and ruthless. Once the policy and practice of area bombing was accepted, RAF and USAAF leaders alike found it difficult to disengage—even when precision technology improved and more accurate bombing became genuinely possible late in the air war. Under rising domestic criticism and with the war nearly won, the RAF halted area bombing of German cities on April 1, 1945, though *Arthur Harris* insisted the decision remain secret. Western bombers had by then killed over 600,000 civilians in Germany, including women, children, and other noncombatants. Some died by the direct effects of explosions, others were crushed under fallen rubble. Many were burned alive. The RAF alone dropped over one million tons of ordnance on 131 German cities. The USAAF area bombed Japan's cities from January 1945, ceasing only when atomic bombs were used to try to bring the war to a swifter end.

See also air power; Bomber Command; Hiroshima; leaflet bombing; Nagasaki; Royal Air Force (RAF); thousand bomber raids; total war.

ARGENTA GAP, BATTLE OF (APRIL 9–19, 1945)   The final Western Allied offensive of the *Italian campaign (1943–1945)* was conducted down the Po Valley by 15th Army Group, led by Field Marshal *Harold Alexander*. British 8th Army was led by Lieutenant General *Oliver Leese*. He faced wholly immobile but veteran units in German Army Group C, under command of General Heinrich von Vietinghoff.

The Germans had no air cover but were still given a "stand and fight" *Haltebefehl order* by Adolf Hitler. The British began with a daring *commando* assault. They forced a path around Lake Comacchio from April 9, thence through the Argenta Gap toward Ferrara. British 8th Army was supported from April 15 by a second powerful attack made by U.S. 5th Army under Lieutenant General *Lucian Truscott*. The main British and American advances were supported by Brazilian and South African troops, among others. U.S. forces included a unit of Japanese Americans from the 442d Regimental Combat Team. All Western Allied troops enjoyed over-whelming artillery and air superiority. Truscott shifted the axis of advance to take advantage of collapsing German positions, even "bouncing" the Po with an improvised fleet of small boats and river ferries. He broke through the *Adige Line* before the bewildered Germans could properly man it. It took just over a week for the Western Allied armies to link and encircle what was left of Army Group C. In rapid succession, Bologna, Ferrara, Genoa, Milan, and Venice were liberated. All German forces in Italy surrendered on April 29, effective at 12:00 hours on May 2.

ARGENTINA   Buenos Aires was home to many *Axis* agents and sympathizers. Argentina maintained formal neutrality until just weeks before the end of the war. That pleased its many citizens of Italian and German descent while still permit-ting export of large amounts of beef to Britain. Argentina fended off strong efforts by Washington to force it to enter into hemispheric defense arrangements. While profiting from trade with the Western Allies, Argentina hosted extensive Axis spy networks. Part of the governing elite reconsidered neutrality as the tide of war turned against the Axis. The shift away from the Axis became easier once Italy signed an armistice, then formally switched sides in September 1943. Argentina severed relations with Germany and Japan on January 26, 1944. That provoked a palace coup by General Juan Perón, who was decidedly pro-Axis and also a quasi-fascist in the mold of Benito Mussolini. The United States, Britain, and other Allied states recalled their ambassadors and brought great economic pressure against the junta. Even Perón was finally forced to bend to economic threats and the looming defeat of the main Axis powers: Argentina declared war on Germany and Japan on March 27, 1945. The declaration was meaningless and treated as such by all parties. The United States and Britain recognized the Perón regime on April 7, but the pro-Axis leanings of the junta led to a rebuff to Argentine hopes to seat a delegation at the *San Francisco conference*. Postwar Argentina was a safe haven for *Schutzstaffel (SS)* officers, collaborators, and a number of war criminals (including Josef Mengele). Many escaped justice to enjoy protected exile in Argentina, with aid from the Vatican or other *ratlines*.

ARGONAUT   Allied code name for the *Yalta conference*.

ARGUMENT   Code name for the "Big Week" bombing of Germany during the *Combined Bomber Offensive*.

ARMED MERCHANT CRUISER (AMC)   The designation of several dozen British passenger liners hastily converted for *convoy* escort duties during the early stages of the *Battle of the Atlantic (1939–1945)*. This repeated an exercise by the Royal Navy during World War I. AMCs were hybrids of inferior speed, armament, and firepower, with overlarge crews and high maintenance costs. Some naval officers thought they were barely better than no escorts at all. Worse, conversions removed these large ships from more effective duty as troop transports. That said, they filled a desperate need for escorts during the most dangerous period of *U-boat* threat to British shipping. They presented a small threat to surface attack, helped hunt German resupply ships, and enforced the difficult northern blockade. Over 50 were placed in service, including some in the Royal Australian Navy and others with Canadian or other non-British crews. Fifteen were sunk; several fell victim to powerful German surface raiders; the rest were torpedoed by U-boats. The low military value of AMCs conduced to reconversion as the escort ship crisis passed. The last AMCs were decommissioned or converted to troop ships by the end of 1943. Surplus crew were diverted to *escort carriers* by then coming into service in greater numbers.

See also Athenia, sinking of.

ARMEEABTEILUNG   "Army detachment." An improvised Wehrmacht formation larger on paper than a corps, but smaller than an army. They were usually named for their commander of the moment, as in "Armeeabteilung Kempf." Late in the war, Adolf Hitler and the OKH increasingly resorted to this type of formation. The rough Red Army equivalent was an "operational group."

ARMÉE D'AFRIQUE   The large French colonial army based in Algeria. Before the war it policed the French Empire in Africa. It included units of Turcos, or Algerian infantry; *Zouaves,* or European "colons" in all-white units who dressed Berber-style in brightly colored uniforms; Spahis, or Arab-style light cavalry; and polyglot soldiers of the *Foreign Legion*. The Armée d'Afrique formed 12 divisions in the French order of battle in 1939. By June 1940, 80,000 of its troops were deployed in metropolitan France. The rest guarded overseas colonies. Most of the latter remained loyal to *Vichy,* spurning the *Free French* and the Western Allies alike. As the French Army was confined to just 100,000 men inside France by the armistice imposed by Germany, Vichy authorized an expansion of overseas garrisons to 225,000. Most were deployed to fight the *Free French* and oppose Western Allied landings in outposts of colonial empire, not to take on the German conqueror and occupier of the home country. Some troops shifted to support for General *Charles de Gaulle* as the tide turned in the Mediterranean from the end of 1942. They were merged with Free French forces to fight on the southern flank in the Tunisian campaign. Some fought in the *Italian campaign (1943–1945),* made the *DRAGOON* landings in France on August 15, 1944, and fought into Germany in 1945.

See also Tirailleurs Senegalese.

ARMÉE DE L'AIR
See French Air Force.

ARMÉE DE L'AIR DE VICHY
See French Air Force.

ARMÉE DE L'ARMISTICE
See armistice; French Army.

ARMIA KRAJOWA   "Home Army."
See Polish Army.

ARMISTICES   An armistice is an agreement on cessation of hostilities in the expectation that a full peace settlement will follow, but does not in itself constitute the product of final negotiations, though it may lay out basic terms. The Finns and Soviets agreed to an armistice to end the *Finnish–Soviet War (1939–1940),* effective on March 13, 1940. That war resumed when Finland joined the attack on the Soviet Union in 1941, launching what the Finns call the "Continuation War." France agreed to an armistice with Germany on June 22, 1940, that left French prisoners of war in Germany until the "end of the war." It split France into occupied and unoccupied zones, disarmed it to a level of 100,000 men, docked the French Navy, and forced France to pay for the cost of German occupation troops. France and Italy agreed to an armistice on June 24, ending a two-week war begun by Benito Mussolini to muscle in on French defeat at German hands. No formal peace followed between France and either Axis power. The rump state of Vichy was instead occupied by the Germans in the wake of the *TORCH* landings by Western Allied forces in Algiers in November 1942. Vichy forces agreed to a local armistice with the British in Lebanon on July 14, 1941. Simple ceasefires rather than armistices with local Vichy officials were arranged across North Africa, as overseas Vichy laid down its arms after initially resisting the landings in Algiers. Joseph Stalin wanted an armistice to stop the German onslaught during the opening weeks of *BARBAROSSA,* preliminary to surrender of large swaths of Soviet territory to Germany, but Adolf Hitler was interested only in total victory and a war of racial annihilation in the east, a position that converted Stalin to a policy of all-out resistance.

A secret armistice was arranged by the Western Allies with the new Italian government of Marshal *Pietro Badoglio* in the summer of 1943. A more detailed armistice was agreed in talks held on Malta, but the occupation was then badly botched, permitting German troops to occupy all of north and central Italy. Rumania signed an armistice with representatives of the three major Allied powers in Moscow on September 12, 1944. The Finns signed an armistice on September 19 that required them to attack German forces still on their territory. Bulgaria signed an armistice with the Soviet Union and the Western Allies on October 28. A Hungarian–Soviet armistice was agreed in mid-October but aborted by German military intervention. A second armistice was signed by Hungary on January 20, 1945. Germany was not permitted to sign an armistice, although several top Nazi officials offered various formulas to the Western Allies without Hitler's knowledge. All such offers were emphatically rejected, as the United Nations Alliance enforced *unconditional surrender* by Germany. The Japanese government agreed to a preliminary armistice with the Allies on August 15, 1945, though that did not stop the Red Army from carrying through with the *Manchurian offensive operation (August 1945)*. Japan's representatives signed a formal "Instrument of Surrender" on September 2. Although a proviso was agreed whereby Japan retained its emperor system (*kokutai*) in name, the surrender was essentially unconditional and complete. It included American occupation and lesser Western Allied administration of the home islands, and subsequent imposition of a fundamentally reformed constitutional system.

See also FALL GELB; FALL WEISS.

ARMOR During World War II the tank came into its own as an offensive weapon. This was made clear with the stunning German *Blitzkrieg* into Poland in *FALL WEISS* (1939), then again in France and the Low Countries in *FALL GELB* in 1940, and on a vast scale in the opening months of *BARBAROSSA* in the Soviet Union in 1941. Tanks also became the major defensive system against enemy tanks, a trend that led to the largest armored battle ever fought at *Kursk* in 1943, where 12 Panzer divisions met massed Soviet armor and thousands of anti-tank guns. The second largest armor fight of the war took place at *Falaise* in 1944. Topographical features limited use of tanks in mountainous areas such as the Caucasus and Balkans. They were also less used in fighting in Asia before 1945 than in North Africa, Europe, or the western Soviet Union. Otherwise, tanks were a signature weapon of World War II. They came in multiple varieties, from prewar tankettes that proved worse than useless even during the *Spanish Civil War (1936–1939),* to fast light versions and solid medium models, to late war heavy and super heavy types that crushed roads and broke stone bridges as they passed. Uniquely, the Wehrmacht fielded a small artillery observer tank ("Beobachtungswagen").

The Regio Esercito had the worst tanks in Europe. Italian tankettes were fine for crushing unarmed and unarmored Abyssinians in 1936, but they proved woefully inadequate when facing British armor in 1940–1941. They were merely death traps for their own crews when deployed on the Eastern Front in 1942. The L3/35 weighed 7.5 tons, had a two-man crew, and mounted a 20 mm main gun incapable of piercing opposing armor. Among lesser Axis armies, Hungarian tanks were only slightly better than Italian tankettes. The Toldi III three-man light tank weighed 10.3 tons and mounted a 40 mm gun. The Turan II was a 20-ton tank with a five-man crew that carried a 75 mm gun. The Axis states also used captured Czech Skoda Type-36 and -38 light tanks on the Eastern Front. The Type-38 was produced for several years after the extinction of Czechoslovakia, while some were still used in battle as late as 1945. Germany's armor spanned a wide range of capabilities and designs. Panzer I and II prewar models were used in Spain and in small numbers by China, but were obsolete by 1939. Panzer divisions attacking into Poland were mostly equipped with the 25-ton medium Panzer III. Still effective in France and the Low Countries in 1940, Panzer III armor proved inadequate and its 50 mm main gun useless against anything but enemy light tanks by the time of the BARBAROSSA campaign a year later. About 5,500 Panzer IIIs were built. The Panzer IV was about the same weight as the Panzer III but had heavier protective armor, a 75 mm main gun, and reached battle speed of 25 mph. The Panzer V, or "Panther," was a 50-ton tank that originally mounted a 75 mm gun. While it was an effective heavy tank, only 5,976 were built. The Panzer VI/E, or "Tiger I," was a monster at 63 tons. Its five-man crew operated a deadly and very long-range 88 mm main gun, but Tigers only had a top speed of 23 mph. The Panzer VI/II, or "King Tiger" or "Tiger II," was even heavier at 77 tons and actually three mph faster than the Panzer VI/E Tiger. It also mounted an 88 mm main gun in a Henschel turret. Its front armor was nearly impenetrable. However, the Tiger II was mechanically unreliable, proved difficult to maneuver in urban fighting, and was much too heavy for many older bridges. Most importantly, it took far too much skilled labor and steel and was therefore not produced in decisive numbers: only 1,354 Tiger Is were built and another 500 Tiger IIs, and not all of those found a way into battle.

Some Chinese warlords and the *Guomindang* had a hodgepodge of tanks imported during the 1920s, notably several dozen Renault FT-17s (Model 1918). During the early 1930s, China acquired Carden Lloyd Mk VI patrol tanks, about 20 Vickers 6-ton light tanks, and several dozen Vickers medium tanks, as well as Italian L.3/35 tankettes and German Pz-1As. The Guomindang acquired Soviet tanks and armored cars in 1938, mainly T-26s, BA-10s, and BA-20s. The United States provided some *Lend-Lease* Shermans to China from 1944 to 1945. The Japanese were only marginally better off than the Chinese in terms of tank design, but they had many more tanks. Most were light or tankette types, copies of early French Renaults or British Vickers models. The standard Japanese tank from 1932 was the 10-ton Mitsubishi Type-89 Chi-Ro medium, which was basically an infantry assault vehicle mounting a small 57 mm gun. It was produced until 1942. A few Type-95 "heavy" tanks were built. The first Mitsubishi Type-97 Chi-Ha medium tank rolled off the assembly line in 1937. It weighed under 16 tons and mounted a small 57 mm gun. It became the standard Japanese model of the war. The Japanese Army also used its tanks differently. It deployed armor in "tank groups" (sensha dan) of three or more regiments of 80 tanks each. Japanese doctrine dictated that all armor act in an infantry support role, until the Japanese experienced what massed Red Army tank divisions could do at *Nomonhan* in 1939. It still took Japan until 1943 to deploy its first true armored division, which was sent to Manchuria and saw little to no action. Shortages of all critical materials meant that Japan only produced five light tanks in 1945. Despite improvements to Japanese tanks and doctrine, Soviet armor again rolled over the Japanese during the *Manchurian offensive operation (August 1945)*. The major Western Allied nations fighting in Asia used the same models built in abundance to fight Italy and Germany in Africa and Europe. The topography of Southeast Asia and the South Pacific was not generally conducive to armored warfare. The central plains of *Okinawa* saw more tanks used by both sides than in any other battle outside China.

U.S. Army doctrine favored lighter tanks both before and throughout the war. That was partly a result of fighting doctrine that favored mobility and deep maneuver over raw firepower. But it also arose from the extraordinary logistical difficulty of transporting every American tank across an ocean before it could fight in Asia, Africa, or Europe. U.S. forces began the war with several light tank types, all named for Civil War generals. The M3 Stuart was a 4-man tank weighing 12 tons and mounting an inadequate 37 mm main gun. The M5 Stuart was a 15-ton light tank also armed with a 37 mm cannon. The M3 Lee (the designation when issued to U.S. forces) and Grant (British and Commonwealth forces) were mediums, weighing 27 tons. They had a 75 mm main gun plus an anti-aircraft machine gun. The last U.S. light tank built was the M24 Chaffee, which had a 76 mm gun. The M4 Sherman was the main U.S. battle tank. Over 50,000 were built. It was provided in quantity to British and Commonwealth forces and in smaller numbers to the Red Army. Depending on mark, it weighed 29–32 tons and mounted a 75 mm or 76 mm main gun, along with two .30 caliber anti-infantry machine guns and an anti-aircraft machine gun. U.S. tanks were usually overmatched on the battlefield during the second half of the war by better-armored and bigger-gun German models. Still, the medium-over-heavy tank preference of U.S. forces proved mostly sound. Unlike late-war German or Japanese tanks, American tanks were on perpetual offense after landing on some distant beach in Europe or Asia. That meant the U.S. Army needed medium tanks that could cross canals and rivers on hastily built pontoon bridges, because the enemy nearly always blew available permanent structures. Wehrmacht tankers discovered in 1944–1945 that while oversize heavies were far more powerful than a Sherman, they were less effective in urban settings and too heavy for most French, Belgian, or Dutch bridges. And there were always more Shermans on the horizon. Western Allied forces also developed armored tactics in which speed and greater numbers of smaller and less powerful tanks outflanked and overwhelmed Tiger Is and IIs. The U.S. finally fielded a limited number of its own heavy tanks late in the war. Although the M26 Pershing mounted a 90 mm gun plus the usual complement of machine guns, it only weighed 41 tons.

In addition to domestic tanks such as the inadequate Mk III "Valentine" infantry tank, the British Army received thousands of U.S.-built tanks via Lend-Lease. Among the first received was the M3A1 supplied in mid-1942 by a diverted emergency convoy. It was used extensively in the *desert campaign* beginning with the two battles of *El Alamein*. It was known to Tommies as the "Honey." British and Canadian armored divisions were also consigned M3 Grants. The British were not always content to use undergunned American tanks. They re-equipped Shermans with more powerful 17-pounder tubes to create an upgunned British version in 1944: the "Firefly." Royal Engineers also developed a series of highly specialized tanks for the *OVERLORD* invasion of France. The most famous were formally known as "Armored Vehicles, Royal Engineers"(AVRE). These were amphibious assault tank adaptations inspired by Major General Percy Hobart, and thus most commonly referred to as "Hobart's Funnies". The "Funnies" were usually modified British "Churchills." They included "swimming" tanks fitted with rubber floats and canvas screens; "crab" tanks, equipped with thrashers and flails for clearing mines; "bobbin" tanks that rolled out mesh as a temporary road over sand and clay; bulldozer tanks; "Crocodile" flame-throwing tanks; Armored Ramp Carriers; and other tanks fitted with specialty tools such as demolition frames or fascine layers. One AVRE was fitted with a petard spigot mortar that fired a 40 lb bomb—called "flying dustbins" by British troops—for demolishing pillboxes. All these fine adaptations helped British and Canadian troops get onto their beaches in Normandy on *D-Day (June 6, 1944)*, then get off them and move inland.

Soviet armor was plentiful before the German invasion on June 22, 1941, but varied greatly in quality. The 11-ton T-26 was the most numerous Soviet tank when the war broke out. T-60s weighed 6.4 tons, had a crew of two, and mounted a 20 mm gun. They were the Red Army scout tank equivalent of the Italian L3/35 tankette. The 10-ton T-70 was still rolling off the line in 1942. It was a death trap for its two-man crew when facing Panzers or anti-tank guns. Yet, with the main medium and heavy tank factories lost at Kharkov and surrounded at Leningrad, a critical decision was made to concentrate on producing T-60s in automobile plants while fevered completion of new tank factories was underway, notably at Chelyabinsk ("Tankograd"). Chelyabinsk became the main manufacturing center of the superb T-34 medium battle tank, the mainstay of Soviet tank armies by mid-1942. The 1940 model weighed 28.5 tons while mounting a powerful 76 mm gun. Its four-man crew could attain a battle speed of 34 mph, faster than any Panzer. The 1943 model was nearly six tons heavier; the extra weight came from additional armor. The 1943 T-34 was turned out at the extraordinary rate of 1,200 per month. The T-34-85 did not add much weight. Its great advance over earlier models was its 85 mm high velocity gun, which could smash the heaviest Panzers. Its turret was also enlarged and modified, providing better sighting and gun handling. Even with the extra weight it still attained a top speed of 34 mph. About 11,000 were built in 1944 and 18,500 in 1945. The T-44 was comparable to the T-34, but with thicker armor (3.5 inches frontal).

Alongside T-26s, T-60s, and the first T-34s, the Red Army deployed the KV-1 in 1941. Named for *Kliment Voroshilov*, it weighed 53 tons. It outmatched the armored protection and weight of shell of German Panzer IIIs and IVs, could withstand multiple hits, and mounted a powerful 76 mm gun of its own. Protection and firepower made up for a slow, 22 mph top speed. The KV-1 so impressed the Wehrmacht that German tank designers modeled the Panther and Tiger types on it. The Soviets introduced a new series of heavy tanks late in the war. The KV-2 weighed 57 tons and mounted a 152 mm howitzer. Capable of just 16 mph and with insufficient frontal armor, it proved highly vulnerable. The 1943 KV-5 was a 50-ton tank with an 85 mm gun. The "Joseph Stalin," or JS II, was a variation of the KV line under a new name. It weighed over 50 tons and had a top speed of 23 mph. It mounted a 122 mm gun and had 3.5–4.7-inch frontal armor, along with a remarkable 3.5-inch side armor. The JS III weighed an additional 1.5 tons but was two mph faster. It had an exceptional 4.7–6.0 inches of frontal armor. Some 2,300 "Stalin" tanks were built in 1944, and 1,500 in 1945.

See also anti-tank weapons; armored infantry; bazooka pants; combat cars; half-track; Panzerjägdgruppe; tank buster; tank panic; Wunderwaffen.

Suggested Reading: K. Macksey, *Tank vs. Tank* (1991).

ARMORED DIVISION
See United States Army.

ARMORED INFANTRY American mechanized infantry incorporated into armored divisions. In weapons they varied little from regular *rifle divisions*. The key difference was that they kept up with tanks by riding in half-tracks or other mechanized vehicles that formed part of their division's organic transport. The Wehrmacht term for comparable troops was *Panzergrenadiers*.

ARMY In most militaries, a large ground combat formation comprising a single HQ that controlled two or more *corps*, dedicated artillery, plus attached nondivisional combat and support troops. Soviet armies replaced the corps echelon for the first two years of the war on the Eastern Front. They were thus smaller and far more numerous than Wehrmacht armies. German armies shrank in actual size and combat power due to protracted attrition, but the Wehrmacht did not expand beyond 16 Army HQs designated in the east, including 4 Panzerarmee HQs. Japanese armies comprised two or more reinforced divisions and thus were corps-sized in the wartime parlance of the Western Allies.

ARMY AIR FORCES (AAF)
See United States Army Air Forces (USAAF).

ARMY DETACHMENT
See Armeeabteilung; operational group.

ARMY GROUND FORCES (AGF)
See United States Army.

ARMY GROUP A massive command comprising several subordinate armies and anywhere from 500,000 to 1.5 million men. An army group was the largest formation of ground forces under one commander used by any military in the war, or indeed in the history of war. The Red Army used *Direction* to designate army groups from 1941 to 1942, but thereafter shifted nomenclature to *Front*. During the last campaign of the war, the *Manchurian offensive operation* against Japan in August 1945, the Red Army reverted to use of "Direction." There were 11 Wehrmacht army groups, or *Heeresgruppen,* by 1944, commanding 26 armies: 18 of infantry, 6 so-called Panzerarmee, 1 airborne army, and 1 mountain army. After three years of fighting on the Eastern Front, every Heeresgruppe and German army was but a shadow of its former size and combat power by 1944. Meanwhile, opposing Soviet Fronts and whole groups of Fronts were larger and vastly more powerful than in 1941. The Western Allies also deployed some of the most powerful army groups seen in the history of war from 1944 to 1945. The

British formed 21st Army Group under Field Marshal *Bernard Law Montgomery*. It included American, Polish, and *Free French* divisions fighting alongside British divisions, as well as Canadian 1st Army. The U.S. Army formed three army groups in 1944: the 12th under General *Omar Bradley* fighting in northern France and central Germany; the 15th under General *Mark Clark* in Italy; and the 6th under General *Jacob Devers,* which landed in southern France in August 1944 and fought to the lower Rhine. U.S. 6th Army Group included French 1st Army.

ARMY SERVICE FORCES (ASF)
See United States Army.

ARNHEM
See MARKET GARDEN.

ARNIM, HANS-JÜRGEN VON (1889–1962) German colonel general.
See Kasserine Pass; TORCH.

ARNOLD, HENRY (1886–1950) "Hap" or "Happy." American general. Taught
to fly by Orville Wright in 1911, Arnold rose to head the U.S. Army Air Corps during the interwar years. He then served as deputy to General *George C. Marshall*. Arnold subsequently served as one of the *Joint Chiefs of Staff*. During the war he oversaw a remarkable expansion of the *United States Army Air Forces (USAAF),* from modest prewar beginnings until it became by far the largest air force in the war, flying missions across several continents and operating an enormous global logistical system. Arnold's greatest contributions were his organizational vision for the USAAF, emphasis on high levels of training, and keen awareness of the importance of logistics to efficient operation of so large and complex an enterprise. He had an extraordinary personal work ethic, which took a real toll on his health. He was universally liked.

ARNOLD SCHEME
See British Commonwealth Air Training Scheme; Royal Air Force (RAF).

ARROW CROSS A Hungarian *fascist* movement that took power in Budapest in
a coup on October 15, 1944, with considerable German help. The coup meant that no separate peace was agreed with Moscow and the Western Allies and ensured that the campaign to murder Hungary's Jews continued.

ARSENAL OF DEMOCRACY
See Lend-Lease; Roosevelt, Franklin D.

ARTILLERY A revolution in artillery occurred in 1870s as French designers perfected breech-loaders to vastly increase rates of fire. New recoilless gun carriages, in which the carriage held place while the tube returned to firing position, made it unnecessary to resight guns after every firing. Artillery was the dominant battlefield weapon by World War I, delivering explosive ordnance as well as poison gas shells. Ranges of a few giant guns exceeded 70 kilometers, though the effective range of sustained barrages was 5,000–6,000 meters by 1918. Large numbers of artillery pieces on either side of the lines provided a powerful defensive ability to break up mass attacks. Artillery was thus the major factor leading to and then sustaining the operational stalemate of trench warfare. Artillery so dominated the battlefield it became the principal producer of casualties in the Great War, even as it drove millions of men deep underground and into complex trench systems in an effort to avoid its steel rain. Aerial reconnaissance and early mathematically projected firing techniques made artillery the overwhelming weapon in the final Allied offensive in 1918, as firepower finally displaced flesh as the major instrument of victory in industrial warfare. Technological development continued after the war so that by the start of World War II artillery was even more accurate, rapid-fire, and plentiful. Once again it would prove the main killer of men, causing over half the total combat casualties of the second great war of the 20th century.

Except for small, all-mechanized units of the professional core of the *British Expeditionary Force*, in 1939 most artillery was still hauled into battle the same way Karl XII, Friedrich II, and Napoleon hauled big guns to war: behind *horses*. Horse-towed artillery was ubiquitous in the 1939 *FALL WEISS* campaign in Poland, and again in the *FALL GELB* fight in the west in 1940. A few gargantuan pieces were mounted on iron horses as *railway guns*. Horse-towed field artillery remained important throughout the war in the Wehrmacht, Japanese Army, and Red Army, supplemented by motorized guns or tubes towed by truck. All major armies also developed tracked or *self-propelled guns*, while the Wehrmacht and Red Army developed closely related *assault guns* and attendant doctrine. British and American armies used self-propelled guns in a similar manner, essentially as more highly mobile field artillery that advanced before concentrating in batteries to provide *indirect fire* support. This differed from German and Soviet practice, wherein self-propelled or assault guns provided close *direct fire* to support assaulting infantry. The exceptional industrial capacity of the United States permitted the U.S. Army, and most other Western Allied armies, to move toward fully motorized and mechanized artillery. The U.S. Army thus soon caught up in mobility to the British Army, and then surpassed it in terms of overall mobility. The main change in artillery in World War II was this fresh mobility. In addition, better fire control techniques were made possible by integration of *radio* and preset *fire plans*, as well as "Fire Direction Centers" and spotter planes. Also increasing as the war continued was the size and effective range—up to 12,000 meters or more—of the largest calibers, as all armies advanced beyond the small calibers with which they began the fight.

Italy had the least developed artillery among the Axis states entering the war. Most Italian tubes were model types from the mid-to-late 1930s, useful against underarmed Abyssinians and Spanish leftists but not capable of stopping British,

Soviet, or American armor. The Japanese built several high-velocity guns and still more *howitzer* models, but none in sufficient numbers to meet the firepower demands of their hard-pressed garrisons and field armies. That partly reflected a bias in Japanese military culture against defense by firepower, in preference for frequent infantry counterattacks using artillery in a direct support role. As a result, even those guns available were often underused in limited preliminary bombardments, and even then only in daylight. Counterbattery fire was also discouraged, in part due to ammunition shortages as Japan's war economy and *merchant marine* entered permanent crisis. German artillery was the most varied of any combatant nation, as measured by types of guns produced. Wehrmacht doctrine stressed directed fire against enemy batteries, anti-tank guns, and armor, then a shift to interdiction and counterbattery roles. Forward observers (FOs) trailed a phone line that usually led back to a concealed battery. The Wehrmacht alone fielded a small artillery observer tank, or "Beobachtungswagen." That was partly because German units lacked full radio communications between FOs and batteries, which reduced the timeliness and effectiveness of fire support. The Germans did not use a grid system for fire control. Instead, the FO worked out estimates of range and angle to target. That required him to have advanced skills in mathematics needed to read printed logarithm tables and work out firing solutions on mechanical calculators. All that took time, usually more than 10 minutes. But it ensured unusually accurate shelling once coordinates were communicated to the guns.

The British Army deployed 6-pounders, 12-pounders, 17-pounders, and 25-pounders as *field guns*. Using armor-piercing ammunition, these calibers also served as anti-tank guns. The 25-pounder emerged as the mainstay British field gun. British and Commonwealth forces also used a variety of howitzers and heavy *mortars*. After catastrophic defeat in *FALL GELB* in 1940, the British Army changed its fire-control practices as fire by grid coordinates was introduced. British divisional artillery was also equipped with radio trucks, needed to cart heavy electric batteries that powered long-distance field radios. A single FO could control concentrated fire from several batteries via radio. This system was adopted by all Commonwealth armies and, in a modified form, by the U.S. Army. U.S. light field guns included a 75 mm pack howitzer mounted on an M8 rubber-tired carriage. The main U.S. field gun was the 105 mm M2A1 howitzer, of which 8,500 were made. Another 4,000 155 mm heavy M1s and M1A1s were shipped out. By the end of the war the U.S. Army deployed 111 battalions of heavy artillery, alongside more than 100 battalions equipped with medium guns. All field batteries with guns heavier than 155 mm were pooled at the corps or army level, where commanders also controlled a reserve of light and medium tubes. American units had more radios than the British. Therefore, instead of a single FO directing all divisional batteries, smaller combat units might call in direct fire coordinates from forward positions. All that radio chatter necessitated a Fire Control Center at the nearest HQ, which set fire priorities and directed guns onto selected priority targets. Under either system and depending on the skill of a given unit, from the time a FO called in target grid numbers to the time batteries fired might be as little as two minutes. By 1945, Western Allied fire control was so precise that up to 200 guns could put shells on the same target at nearly the same moment.

Artillery used a form of sound ranging that dated to World War I on more static fronts, with buried microphones recording time of flight of shells to determine range. Western Allied commanders used heavy artillery for suppressing fire in offensive operations, *creeping barrages* ahead of the infantry in a style learned and practiced on the western front later in World War I. In the east, poor quality of Soviet fire control, maps, radio communications, and forward observers led to an important difference in artillery doctrine and usage from Western armies. The Red Army used *rolling barrages* instead. Overall, the Soviets tended to concentrate on artillery's active destructive effects in saturation bombardment and to rely on sheer volume of a bombardment in a manner more reminiscent of early battles of the Great War. For that reason, and because the Soviets lacked sophisticated fire control systems and training, the Red Army organized artillery into corps and armies separate from its *rifle divisions* or *tank armies*. No combatant's artillery underwent more quantitative increase during the war than did the Red Army, or with fewer changes to production models. That was because the Soviets suffered such huge losses of artillery tubes over the first six months of fighting that emergency quotas of gun and ammunition production concentrated on delivering large volumes of existing and simplified gun models, rather than experimenting with new calibers or designs. Once factories forced to relocate to the Urals were up and running again by mid-1942, continuing heavy attrition on the Eastern Front kept up demand for existing tube calibers and models. That said, by 1943 Soviet quantitative advantage in artillery had a qualitative effect in protracted battles with the Wehrmacht.

As the tides of combat and war production alike turned, the Soviets built new carriages and chaises types that allowed the Red Army to alter deployment and use of existing guns. Most tubes were retained as conventional artillery, but some were converted into mobile anti-tank guns, while others became *assault guns*. The new, tracked anti-tank guns were first used to effect in continuous offensives that cleared Army Group South from Ukraine over the winter of 1943–1944. The Soviet Union was producing an extraordinary volume of artillery tubes by 1945, along with tracked and towed carriages to give its artillery more mobility. In combat, Soviet artillery concentrations per footage of frontline, and Soviet preliminary barrages, were easily the densest and heaviest of the war. The Red Army achieved over 400 guns per mile of front on several occasions, not including masses of *Katyusha* rocket artillery capable of blanketing whole areas of the enemy's rear with terrifying saturation attacks in just minutes. The Germans were so impressed by Soviet rocket artillery they developed a counter in the form of heavier versions of their own *Nebelwerfer* rocket launcher. They also learned to use these weapons in assault and anti-tank roles in the later battles of the war in the East.

See also anti-aircraft guns; anti-tank weapons; concentration of fire; counterbattery fire; division; electronic warfare; elephants; fire for effect; flash spotting; horses; mules; murder; prearranged fire; recoilless guns; reconnaissance by fire; rockets; serenade; standing barrage; stonk; superimposed fire; time on target.

Suggested Reading: I. V. Hogg, *Germany Artillery of World War II* (1975); I. V. Hogg, *British and American Artillery of World War II* (1978); John Norris, *Artillery: A History* (2000).

ARYAN In Nazi race theory and ideology: a non-Jewish, north European Caucasian; the "superior race" supposedly responsible for creating all higher civilization, including lost Atlantis. Adolf Hitler believed that the Dutch, English, French, Norwegians, Swedes, and other Nordic peoples, along with some Italians, were of "Aryan stock." The utter speciousness of this racialist claim, even for Nazis, was demonstrated late in World War II when the *Schutzstaffel (SS)*—desperate for new *Waffen-SS* recruits—fortuitously "discovered" that many Croatians in the *Ustaše* shared an Aryan bloodline. Benito Mussolini issued a specious "Manifesto of Racial Scientists" in 1938, without goading from the Nazis, proclaiming that Italians were also of Aryan descent and that "Jews do not belong to the higher Italian race."

See also anti-Semitism; Chamberlain, Houston Stewart; fascism; Germanics; Herrenvolk; National Socialism; Untermenschen.

ASCENSION ISLAND Located in the South Atlantic midway between Africa and South America, from mid-1942 it hosted a U.S. airbase. Western Allied aircraft flew from Ascension to participate in convoy protection and *anti-submarine warfare*. It was also a stopover for aircraft being ferried to Africa, and thence to Sicily and Italy or on to the Soviet Union.

See also Takoradi air route.

ASDIC From "Anti-Submarine Detection Investigation Committee," dating to British, French, and American *anti-submarine warfare* research during World War I. All Royal Navy destroyers were fitted with ASDIC during the early 1930s. This underwater detection device to locate *U-boats* using sound echoes was refined before and during World War II by British and other anti-Nazi scientists. Improved hydrophones had long been able to detect a U-boat's bearing. When grouped to receive echoes of sound pulses, they also determined range. ASDIC worked by sending out acoustical pulses that echoed off hulls of U-boats, but also sometimes off the sides of whales or schools of fish. The echoes were heard by grouped hydrophones on the sending ship, so that an ASDIC screen and operator provided the escort's captain with estimated range and position of the enemy submarine. It was limited by the sounds of other ships' screws, rough seas, and onboard machinery of its host ship. Such interference enabled U-boats to hide from escorts inside the "noise barrier" created by a *convoy*. More importantly, even in optimum conditions early ASDIC could not determine a U-boat's depth.

British and Commonwealth ASDIC operators could locate U-boats to a distance of 2,000 meters by 1940. However, from 200 meters range to source, pulse and echo merged. That meant U-boats were lost to detection before the moment of attack, just as a destroyer closed on its position. Because forward-throwing technology for *depth charges* had not been developed, the explosives were dropped astern of the charging destroyer across the last known position of the U-boat. Loss of contact, stern attack, and the time it took charges to sink to explosive depth combined to permit many U-boats to escape destruction simply by turning hard away from the closing destroyer or corvette. Admiral *Karl Dönitz*, head of the Kriegsmarine U-boat arm, countered the threat from ASDIC by instructing U-boat captains to attack only on the surface and at night. That countermeasure was lost to U-boats once the Western Allies deployed aircraft equipped with *Leigh Lights*. Dönitz next ordered research into absorbent coating and rubber hull paints to reduce the ASDIC signature of his U-boats, but with little success. Similarly, release of a *Pillenwerfer* noise-maker only tricked inexperienced ASDIC operators. An advanced Type 147 ASDIC set was developed later in the war that tracked U-boats in three dimensions, giving readouts of bearing as well as range and depth. Note: All Western Allied navies adopted the U.S. Navy term for ASDIC in 1943: *sonar*.

ASIA FIRST STRATEGY A U.S. media and political faction, with some military supporters, wanted the Pacific theater of operations to receive priority over any African and European operations against Germany. They tended to rally around anything proposed by General *Douglas MacArthur*, notably his proposals to lead the main offensive against Japan. In a narrower sense, Admiral *Ernest King* shared an "Asia first" perspective. President Franklin D. Roosevelt showed solid leadership in instead sticking to the "*Germany first strategy*" and commitment made to Winston Churchill even before U.S. entry into the war.

See also Three Demands.

ASIA FOR ASIANS Propaganda slogan under which Japan pursued hegemony in East Asia before the war. It touched a responsive cord in a region dominated by white foreigners and colonial regimes. Even after Japanese conquests and brutal occupations it was not always obvious to all local leaders and populations that the slogan in fact disguised a policy of "Asia for the Japanese."

See also Greater East Asian Co-Prosperity Sphere; resistance.

ASSAULT GUNS A subclassification of artillery referring to *howitzers* or other *field guns* mounted on tracked carriages, usually of surplus or outmoded tanks. They moved and fired in close support of attacking infantry. Although sharing the outer appearance of tanks they usually lacked turrets and sacrificed armor for speed and weight of gun. The main German assault gun was the Stug III (Sturmgeschütz III). It was equipped with a low-velocity 75 mm howitzer. From 1942 that gun was replaced by a high-velocity tube as Stugs took on Soviet or Western Allied tanks more often than they supported German infantry assaults. The Wehrmacht deployed increasing numbers of assault guns ("Sturmartillerie") as the war continued, often in place of Panzers, which took far more steel, labor, and funds to build. Over time, production considerations meant that units supposed to be equipped with Panzers were instead given assault guns. These served primarily in an anti-tank role as the

Wehrmacht moved to permanent defense in 1944–1945. The Stug III was built in large numbers as Panzer Mk III chaises were released with battlefield obsolescence of that model tank. The Stug IV was an upgunned, turretless, wider-tracked vehicle than the Stug III. Very late war German assault guns included squat urban fighting vehicles such as the Brummbär ("Grizzly") and Sturmtiger ("Storm Tiger"). Their appearance was part of a general trend in design toward gigantism that ill-served actual combat needs, but it also reflected recognition that fighting in the east had shifted into big cities, away from the "happy days" of broken-field running by the fast Panzers of 1941–1943. Not many of the new urban warfare–type assault guns left German factories, fewer than 300 Brummbär and just a few dozen Sturmtiger.

Early model Soviet assault guns such as the KV-2, which mounted a howitzer on a KV-1 heavy tank chassis, were easily knocked out during *BARBAROSSA* in 1941 and again in 1942. By the end of the war, however, the Red Army adapted and deployed a range of powerful and effective assault guns that served in a "tank destroyer" role; that is, as anti-tank guns. The Soviets mass produced the SU-class assault gun calibers of 76 mm and 122 mm and deployed huge SU-152 mm and ISU-152 mm guns. The SU-152 was called "zverboi" ("beast-killer") by Red Army *krasnoarmeets* because of its success in destroying Tigers, Panthers, Elephants, and other German fighting vehicles with feral or animal names. British, Commonwealth, and U.S. armies did not deploy assault guns as such, relying instead on *heavy artillery, air power,* and an abundance of tanks. The Western Allies modified some battle tank chaises—including the Sherman, Centaur, and Churchill—in the direction of what the Wehrmacht and Red Army called assault guns, replacing the main high-velocity gun with a howitzer. But Western armies used these primarily in an anti-tank role rather than for close infantry support. Americans termed such armored vehicles "tank destroyers," not assault guns. On the whole, they did not perform as well as hoped by designers or in early U.S. Army doctrine.

See also self-propelled guns.

AT "Anti-Tank."
See anti-tank weapons; assault guns.

ATHENIA, SINKING OF (SEPTEMBER 3, 1939) On the first day of the naval war between Great Britain and Germany U-30 sank the 13,600-ton British passenger liner "Athenia." U-30's captain believed the Athenia was an *Armed Merchant Cruiser.* Among more than 1,100 passengers onboard, about 300 were American citizens. The ship settled slowly, permitting rescue of all but those killed by the initial explosions: 118 souls, among them 28 Americans, died. Concerned lest a *U-boat* campaign again provoke the United States to hostility as it had in 1917, Adolf Hitler ordered that no more liners were to be targeted even if they were traveling in *convoy.* U-30's logs were also falsified. In 1941 the captain who sank Athenia was killed when his U-110 was surfaced and machine gunned. U-110's *Enigma* machine was captured.

See also Atlantic, Battle of; unrestricted submarine warfare.

ATLANTIC, BATTLE OF THE (1939–1945) The greatest naval contest in history, lasting for all but two days of World War II, counting from the start of Operation *FALL WEISS*: September 3, 1939–May 8, 1945. This greatest of all naval contests for control of the major sea lanes was termed the "Battle of the Atlantic" by Winston Churchill in 1940, when Allied fortunes at sea were at their bleakest. It was not a battle in the traditional sense of a single encounter at sea by battle fleets, or even a series of sea fights. It was instead a full-scale naval war, a guerre de course of surface raiders and *wolf packs* against *convoy* escorts and hunter-killer groups. It lasted nearly six years, drawing in ships, squadrons, and whole fleets from four major navies and several minor ones, along with supporting air units, intelligence operations, and much of the *merchant marine* of the Atlantic world. It coursed over the deepest regions of the North Atlantic and South Atlantic Oceans, seared shipping in the Caribbean, Baltic, and Barents seas, spilled into the Indian Ocean, and illuminated with fire and death the coastlines of five continents. It drew in the major surface and *U-boat* assets of the Kriegsmarine and Royal Navy (RN), led to a remarkable expansion of the Royal Canadian Navy (RCN), then pulled in a major share of the assets of the United States Navy (USN). Also engaged were ships and crews of several small European and South American navies and elements of the Italian Navy and French Navy. The Battle of the Atlantic was waged for control of great sea lanes from the Americas to Africa and Western Europe that were critical to providing essential war matériel to Britain, and later, also to the Soviet Union via sea to the Indian Ocean and thence overland across Iran. Looming over the naval battle was the promise of convoying millions of troops from North America to participate in the several Western Allied invasions of Africa and Europe.

The Battle of the Atlantic was mostly about attrition and logistics, but also about deeper contests in shipbuilding, crew training, and technological innovation. The fighting men of all sides showed moral and physical courage and remarkable endurance. Forgotten lessons from World War I were learned again by Axis and Allied navies over its grey course, at great cost in ships, men, blood, and national treasure. As remarkable as it seems in retrospect, the first and most important of these forgotten lessons was the sheer efficacy of U-boats as commerce raiders. German U-boats sank over 11 million gross tons of shipping worldwide from 1914 to 1918. During World War II they would sink nearly 15 million gross tons, most of it British and much of it in cold North Atlantic waters. Yet, Allied navies were again ill-prepared to defend their vital shipping against the U-boat threat in 1939, and hardly armed or prepared at all to fight back. Fortunately, the Axis navies were similarly unready to wage all-out submarine warfare. Before the Kriegsmarine might deploy a potentially decisive fleet of U-boats into the North Atlantic, bitterly divisive intraservice arguments among senior officers had to be resolved. Top admirals competed to persuade Adolf Hitler to complete, or to completely discontinue, his *Z-Plan*. That prewar commitment to a 10-year naval construction program called for German yards to build a battlefleet of powerful surface ships capable of challenging the Royal Navy, and then the U.S. Navy, for supremacy at sea. Interservice quarrels between the Kriegsmarine and Luftwaffe over who would control naval aviation, and about shared research into specialized anti-ship weapons, hampered interdiction of Allied shipping by air, while limiting arial scouting for prey in aid of U-boat operations. The always difficult *Hermann Göring* played a pernicious and obstructionist role, resisting all efforts to commission an adequate naval air arm that might compete with his Luftwaffe. Allied navies had finally proven the value of convoys during World War I only after bitter and deeply costly argument. They built many more and smaller escorts in lieu of capital warships by 1918. They additionally and conclusively demonstrated the utility and necessity of seaborne and land-based aircraft in the conduct of *anti-submarine warfare (ASW)*. Yet, all Allied navies as well as the neutral U.S. Navy began the war grossly deficient in numbers of small escorts, did not train properly in convoy escort duty, and did not evidence either the will or confidence needed to defeat the U-boat threat. They rushed to construct new escorts but wrongly equipped, wrongly assigned, or wrongly designed some; they still relied on inappropriate and too short-range aircraft; and they followed mediocre-to-primitive ASW doctrine and had inadequate ASW weapons.

The prelude to the fight came on August 19, 1939, during the building Polish crisis. Admiral *Karl Dönitz,* head of the Kriegsmarine U-boat arm, ordered 36 operational U-boats to battle stations. They moved stealthily into positions around the approaches to the British Isles and in the English Channel and Gibraltar Strait. The Royal Navy was also on alert during the weeks of diplomatic crisis leading to war. However, British attention and naval planning was focused on escorting the British Expeditionary Force (BEF) across the Channel, or on blocking egress from the Baltic Sea by major German surface ships seeking to engage as commerce raiders. Dönitz's U-boats therefore had the upper hand. For many officers on either side from the generation that experienced the naval war of 1914–1918, strong memories were aroused by news that followed expiration of the British ultimatum to Germany at noon on September 3, 1939. Across Germany, Britain, and in the neutral United States, memory of the "Lusitania" sinking was stirred by news that the first ship sunk in the new naval war was a passenger liner, the "*Athenia.*" Allied and American citizens on an unarmed passenger ship had again died in the Atlantic at the hands of a German U-boat, whose captain had fired without warning then left, without offering help to survivors. As happened in 1915 and again in 1917, deep controversy erupted over application of the rules of *cruiser warfare.* The Germans argued from the start for a right of submarines to follow *shoot on sight* practices and wage *unrestricted submarine warfare,* at least within formally declared *War Zones.* Yet, Hitler initially reacted to adverse world opinion by banning U-boats from sinking any more liners. He reversed that decision on September 23, allowing small passenger liners to be attacked by U-boats operating under formal cruiser rules. Loud objection by many neutral governments soon caused him to reimpose the ban. Hitler initially refused to permit attacks against French shipping for similar pragmatic and reinforcing diplomatic reasons. Despite these restrictions, U-boat captains spoke of their first "happy time" in the Atlantic, during which there was good hunting for "grey wolves" unhurried and unharried in pursuing their lethal work. For many months the Kriegsmarine set the terms of engagement by sending out surface raiders and waves of U-boats at times and to hunting areas of its choosing. Allied navies reacted with varying degrees of initial but ineffective dash, then with more sober courage through mid-1940. After that came increasing desperation and near despair in the second half of 1940 and all of 1941.

Battle against German surface raiders was intermittent, but dramatic, and lasted several years. The *pocket battleships* DKM Graf Spee and DKM Deutschland sailed before September 1, 1939. "Graf Spee" sank nine merchants before it was forced to fight a British hunter group off the River Plate on December 13. Damaged and outgunned, it retreated into neutral Montevideo harbor. There it faced a 72-hour internment deadline from the government of Uruguay, while more British warships took up station outside the harbor. Hitler issued fateful orders to "Graf Spee" to avoid internment or capture. On December 17, the still-wounded ship moved out of the harbor toward the British picket line. Before it could be engaged it was scuttled by Captain Langsdorff, who later committed suicide on shore. The scuttling was captured by the News Reels and shown around the world. Sinking a dangerous opponent such as "Graf Spee" in exchange for the loss of just nine merchantmen was seen as a victory by the Royal Navy, as well as proving a passing distraction for a world public growing bored by the "*Phoney War.*" Just as dangerous to Allied shipping as the "Graf Spee" was the German *auxiliary cruiser* ("Handelsstörkreuzer" or "commerce disruption cruiser"). Nine steamed out of Baltic or French ports between 1939 and 1942. They raided from the Atlantic and Antarctic, into the South Pacific and Indian Ocean. Their presence in a given sea compelled widespread dispersal of scarce Allied warships, pulling escorts from the convoys and the main fight against the U-boats in the North Atlantic. Sent out in two waves of six and then three ships, Admiral *Erich Raeder's* auxiliary cruisers sank over three-quarters of a million tons of Allied shipping. By the end of 1942 seven were sunk, one was destroyed when it caught fire, and one was cannibalized. A 10th raider set out in February 1943, but was quickly bombed back into port. An 11th was wrecked by bombs while residing in its shipyard.

Two sister ships classed as *battlecruisers*, DKM Scharnhorst and DKM Gneisenau, made a sweep off Iceland in November 1939, where they sank a British *Armed Merchant Cruiser* and deeply frightened the Royal Navy. They set out again in early 1940, causing consternation in London when they sank the Royal Navy carrier HMS Glorious and two destroyers from her screen. A third battlecruiser raid was assayed from January to March 1941. The two "Scharnhorsts," as these ships were jointly known, savaged a convoy before running to lay up in Brest. On Hitler's personal order, they made the *Channel Dash* back north in February 1942, embarrassing the Royal Navy but also taking themselves out of the fight against Atlantic commerce while freeing British warships that had been committed to blockading the "Scharnhorsts" in port. The order revealed that Hitler never understood the concept of a "fleet in being," while also grossly overvaluing Norway strategically and seeking to defend it with his major surface ships and too many U-boats. DKM Scharnhorst was sunk in December 1943. DKM Gneisenau was stripped of weapons by Dönitz. Its guns were redeployed in Norwegian coastal forts and its hulk used as a blockship off Poland in March 1945, a most inglorious end for such an important warship.

Still more dangerous German battleships steamed out to fight on rare occasions. Hitler restricted their cruises because he feared to risk such prestigious warships in battle. The most dramatic episode occurred when DKM Bismarck accompanied by the heavy cruiser DKM Prince Eugen made a dramatic run from Norway around Iceland and back toward the coast of France from May 21–26, 1941. Salvoes from Bismarck found and battered HMS Prince of Wales and blew up HMS Hood, leaving just three men alive in the water from a complement of 1,419. Tracked, missed, then found again by Royal Navy hunting groups, the "Bismarck" was torpedoed by *Swordfish* biplanes from the carrier HMS Ark Royal. Two hits below-the-waterline destroyed Bismarck's rudder and left her steering in circles, dangerous and wounded but incapable of fleeing her pursuers. Contact was lost for a time, until DKM Bismarck's enforced circling brought her back onto British radar screens some 400 miles out of Brest. The German battleship was finished off the next day, after fighting it out with several British battleships and cruisers. Over 2,000 German sailors perished, some by fire, others abandoned in the water when a false U-boat sighting compelled the British to stop rescuing survivors. DKM Prince Eugen survived the war. It was then blasted into slag by atomic fire in a U.S. nuclear test in the South Pacific in 1946. DKM Tirpitz was the biggest and most powerful battleship ever built for a European navy. It was commissioned late, in February 1941, but its mere existence served to create a "fleet in being" effect, forcing the Royal Navy to maintain a powerful battlefleet at Scapa Flow even though "Tirpitz" never fired a shot in battle with the enemy. Its sole war cruise led to bombardment of the coast and coal mines of the *Spitzbergen Islands* in September 1943. The shelling started a coal fire that burned for 14 years. After the Spitzbergen raid, "Tirpitz" sought safety deep inside a Norwegian fiord. She was found and damaged by British *midget submarines*. Thereafter, she was repeatedly bombed by the RAF. "Tirpitz" was moved to Tromsö where she was battered into a hulk during late 1943. She finally sank on November 12, 1944, upon being hit by huge "Tallboy" bombs dropped by the RAF. She took more than 1,200 men down with her.

German U-boats accompanied Kriegsmarine destroyers into misadventure in Norway in 1940, during Operation *WESERÜBUNG*. Too many remained in Norwegian waters throughout the war, deployed there upon Hitler's personal insistence and in support of one of his odder flank commitments. The major, and far grimmer, German naval effort in the Atlantic was made by U-boats against convoys. The Western Allies initially responded to the threat with a combination of passive measures such as laying dense fields of sea mines. That constricted U-boat routes in the North Sea and other key areas where minefields were laid , including the Dover Strait. Several U-boats were lost to British mines. In more open water, individual ships and then whole convoys steamed zigzag courses while running blacked out at night. Most merchantmen remained unarmed for many months. The fastest, those capable of 15 knots, and the slowest, those running under 9 knots, sailed as "independents" rather than in convoy, until it was demonstrated by high loss rates that convoys were a superior defense to speed. Above all, it was progressive adoption of a convoy system that proved the most effective passive defense. The Germans gained a huge advantage when Dönitz moved the U-boat fleet to Atlantic bases in July 1940, after the conquest of France and the Low Countries. U-boats operated from pens built by the *Todt organization* in Bordeaux, Brest, la Pallice, Lorient, and St. Nazaire until mid-1944 and the start of the *Normandy campaign*. The pens proved impenetrable by bombs, despite many heavy raids. They still stand today.

The Germans initially stationed weather trawlers deep in the Atlantic. After they were sunk or chased away, Dönitz ordered weather stations set up on land in the Canadian Arctic and Greenland. Most of these were undiscovered by the Allies and provided critical information supporting Dönitz's direction of U-boat operations. Western Allied air bases were established on Iceland and in the Faeroes, but not in the Portuguese-controlled Azores until 1943 and never in southern Ireland (Eire). *VLR (Very Long-Range)* aircraft finally closed the *air gap* in the mid-Atlantic once they began to operate from the Azores, Iceland, and southern England. U-boats moved on the surface until then without fear of Allied aircraft, to kill many hundreds of ships in the target-rich air gap. Each side employed *float planes* in the Battle of the Atlantic. The RAF's "Sunderland" could reach Iceland and the Bay of Biscay from U.K. bases. It was countered by a Luftwaffe fleet of reconnaissance squadrons equipped with Bv138s and Bv222s, Do-18s, and He-115s. These spotted for an original force of 18 squadrons of He-111 medium bombers, trained before the war to bomb ships and lay mines. Longer-range German aircraft came on stream as the battle developed, notably the Fw200 or *Kondor*. Continuing interservice arguments between the Kriegsmarine and Luftwaffe, which Hitler characteristically declined to resolve, were especially marked by petulant obstruction of cooperation by Göring. That permitted the Kriegsmarine too few of the right planes to properly scout for the U-boat fleet. Other interservice arguments concerned whether to develop an aircraft-delivered torpedo or specialized antiship bomb. The Luftwaffe ignored all Kriegsmarine design advice on the way to developing an ineffective ship bomb on its own. In the meantime, improving air cover and fighter interception of Kondors by fighters launched from *escort carriers* pushed back the German air threat to Allied shipping.

The Royal Navy was stretched thin in the Arctic, Atlantic, and Mediterranean to the end of 1941, despite a remarkable expansion of the corvette and destroyer fleet of the RCN. Canadians escorted almost half of all Atlantic convoys by that point, and there was growing assistance from the formally neutral U.S. Navy. Still, during 1941 the loss rate reached 300,000 GRT (Gross Register Tonnage) per month, while ships totaling nearly two million more GRT were receiving maintenance or under repair. U.S. *shipyards* began turning out the first *Liberty Ships* in September 1941. Smaller U.S. and Canadian yards also produced new types of fast, purpose-built escorts, in ever larger numbers. Much of the USN destroyer fleet entered the fight even before the United States entered the war, while 50 older destroyers were granted to Britain in the *destroyers-for-bases* deal. Although officially a nonbelligerent navy, the USN was already escorting convoys deep into the North Atlantic, greatly relieving the burden on the RCN and RN. President Franklin D. Roosevelt ordered U.S. escorts into the War Zone under cover of enforcing a discrete hemispheric security zone he unilaterally declared, specifically to exclude U-boats. Roosevelt then extended the exclusion zone to include Iceland. The USN thus took over escort duties from the "Western Ocean Meeting Point" (WOMP) off Newfoundland to a more easterly "Mid-Ocean Meeting Point" (MOMP), where convoys were handed off to RN protection for the final leg through the *Western Approaches* to Great Britain. U.S. destroyers attacked U-boats on several occasions before formal hostilities commenced. Two U.S. warships, USS Kearney and USS Reuben James, were engaged in turn by U-boats. The "Kearney" was badly damaged and the "Reuben James" was sunk with the loss of 115 American lives. Upon Germany's declaration of war against the United States on December 11, 1941, the USN made an all-out commitment to the battle, even as it struggled with internal and political pressures to look first to the naval war in the Pacific.

The USN entered the fight without enough escorts to protect the enormous cargo traffic along the eastern seaboard of the United States and within the Caribbean. Oil tankers from the Gulf of Mexico were especially vulnerable to U-boat attacks until convoys could be organized or new inland pipelines completed. Admiral *Ernest King* shucked off British advice and immediately ordered unprotected ships to steam as independents and told unescorted convoys to proceed at high speed without taking basic evasive action. The USN had to learn the hard way, as the RN learned before it, that speed alone was no defense against a skilled U-boat captain. Fortunately for his new American enemy, Hitler intervened in U-boat operations to insist on widely dispersing too many boats to Norwegian waters and to the Mediterranean. German submarine cruising ranges were also still limited, curtailing cruising times in American or Caribbean waters. The U.S. merchant marine and much shipping heading north out of the Caribbean or neutral ports in South America was nonetheless ravaged by U-boats prowling U.S. coastal waters. Dönitz's captains spoke of a second "happy time," as Operation PAUKENSCHLAG (Drumroll), the assault on American shipping, began on January 13, 1942. By the time that campaign ended seven months later, U-boats sank three million GRT, or 15 percent of all Allied losses in the entire war. Just 22 U-boats were lost in exchange. Why were losses so great? Largely because Admiral King accepted the argument for convoys in principle but resisted unescorted or weakly escorted convoys in practice. He thought such groupings of unarmed and unprotected ships only invited attack. Like others in the Royal Navy before him, King preferred to see the fastest ships sail as independents. It was an argument two wars and several hard sea campaigns old when the Americans revisited it. As always, only deadly shipping loss statistics eroded the anticonvoy position over time.

It was only blood and terror and loss of ships and men in plain view that taught Americans to blackout all ships and coastal cities, plot evasive courses, and establish effective coastal air and sea patrols. Some RN and RCN escorts moved south to support USN efforts in American coastal waters, escorting ships to the main convoy routes from Canada until new transatlantic routes could be established from various American ports. Germany complicated matters by adding a fourth rotor to its naval *Enigma machines,* reducing Allied ability to locate wolf packs and divert convoys around them by reading Dönitz's signals intelligence. The Germans also broke the Allied escort code, Naval Code #3. That gave the U-boats an advantage that lasted until new codes were introduced in May 1943. But it was principally lack of coastal convoys and sufficient escorts to form them that permitted the extraordinary slaughter: 65 out of 71 ships sunk in February had steamed as independents. The USN formed coastal *Bucket Brigades* in April as an interim measure that proved partially successful. Dönitz therefore shifted many of his U-boats from Florida into the Caribbean, where Gulf Coast oil tankers abounded and many still sailed unescorted. The main North Atlantic convoys were less molested during this period, as most U-boats were happily sinking ships farther south. The situation improved over the second half of 1942. The RN, RCN, and USN coordinated and systematized convoy planning, added more escort ships, deployed the first true escort carriers, and stretched land-based air cover from every available base using new and longer-range aircraft. Older twin-engine bombers were handed over to Coastal Command and the USN, as four-engine heavy bomber types replaced them in the air war over Germany. A few four-engine aircraft were provided, and more fighters were redeployed from southern England to intercept Kondors and other German aircraft operating out of the Bay of Biscay. Not all went smoothly, and the naval war remained in doubt to those fighting it. After ONS154 lost 14 of its 46 ships in December 1942, the Royal Navy sharply rebuked the responsible RCN escort group and temporarily withdrew all Canadian escort groups from the battle, ordering crews to undergo intensive ASW retraining. They were replaced by RN groups returning from North Africa after escorting troop and supply ships of the *TORCH* landings. It was a real humiliation for the Canadians, but mostly reflected the fact that too many RCN crews were necessarily rushed into escort duty only half-trained during the dark days when even a poorly trained crew was desperately needed. Once retrained and back in battle the same RCN crews and their successors achieved an admirable record.

The Germans were having troubles of their own. If measured by *BdU's* key metric of tonnage sunk per U-boat per day ("Tonnagekrieg"), the tide of war in the Atlantic appears to have turned by the end of 1941. That was even before full commitment by the USN to the fight. Some historians have even argued that the battle at sea against the U-boats was already won by that date and that only secret British calculation to frighten and manipulate the Americans into committing major naval forces to the Atlantic explains the nearly universal wartime view that the fight was far from over at the start of 1942. Statistics are tricky things, but they support marking a much later date as the point the fortunes of battle actually turned in the Atlantic. U-boats sank nearly 1,300 ships in 1941, and another 1,662 during 1942. That meant the Allies lost 8 million GRT in 1942 alone, a figure greatly increased by losses of unescorted independents in American seas in the first half of the year. Even though Allied shipyards were producing more ships at faster rates, and escorts and aircraft were sinking more U-boats, German production of U-boats meant more attack craft were also available to Dönitz. In German and British propaganda, public perception at the time, and in secret intelligence appraisals, the final shift of fortunes in the Atlantic did not truly favor the Allies until mid-1943. U.S. shipyards were by then building far more Liberty

Ships than even an expanded U-boat fleet could sink, with construction averaging three months per ship and 1,500 ships per year at its peak. U.S. shipyards alone were also turning out 200 escorts per year, which subsequently sank more U-boats than Germany could build or crew. But not all that was clear to either side until mid-1943.

A new Western Approaches commander, Admiral Max Horton, organized hunter-killer groups of ASW aircraft, escort carriers, and fast escorts as greater supplies of each weapons system became available. More U-boats failed to return to home ports as a result. Also notable were pioneering ASW tactics developed by Royal Navy Captain *John Walker,* first in his role in convoy escort duty then as commander of Second Support Group. This new offensive-mindedness was approved by Allied leaders at the *Casablanca Conference (January 14–24, 1943).* Five full Support Groups, each with at least one escort carrier, were now formed to take the fight in the Atlantic to the U-boats. Where escorts previously sought to suppress U-boats while their convoy steamed away, Support Groups instead steamed at flank speed toward any convoy that reported U-boat action. They then remained in the area to hunt down and kill the enemy, long enough that he could no longer stay submerged or actively driving him to the surface or sending him to the bottom. An Atlantic Convoy Conference, held in Washington in March 1943, redistributed area responsibility among the three major navies. The RCN assumed control of convoys north of New York and west of 47° longitude, the USN henceforth made its major effort farther south, while the RN controlled the Western Approaches and home waters. German production meant that Dönitz just then achieved his "decisive" 400 U-boat fleet. The protracted, climactic phase of the Battle of the Atlantic thus took place from January to July, 1943. A record 170 U-boats were actively deployed in March, attacking 11 convoys and sinking numerous merchantmen. But most convoys got through to Britain unsighted by any German, while improved ASW tactics took a count of 15 U-boats. Such attrition of experienced crews and skippers could not be borne for long by the Kriegsmarine. More U-boats went down in April, while 40 boats were lost to Dönitz in May. In return, just six convoyed merchantmen were sunk.

The losses included Dönitz's younger son. He would lose his eldest son in the silent service later in the war. Otherwise, he seemed unconcerned with crew losses in anything but operational terms, and they had become unsustainable. Dönitz ordered an end to attacks on northern convoys in the late spring of 1943, shifting most boats to concentrate on less well-defended routes. He admitted at least temporary defeat and recalled all U-boats from deep Atlantic operations on May 23. The Battle of the Atlantic had been won by the Allied navies and sailors of the merchant marine, even though it was far from over, which is essentially what Winston Churchill told the House of Commons on September 21. In a climactic four month period from April to July, 1943, 109 U-boats had been sunk. Many succumbed to aircraft patrolling the Bay of Biscay; others fell to powerful surface Support Groups and increasingly confident and numerous Escort Groups. U-boats sank just two ships in the North Atlantic in August, even as Allied warship strength markedly increased. By mid-1943 the USN alone operated four Support Groups in the Atlantic, while most Escort Groups were also strong enough to detach some ships to stay to hunt any U-boat that dared attack a passing convoy. Allied warship numbers and capabilities were so overwhelming by early 1944 that a single U-boat might find several Support Groups bearing down on it, which meant little chance of survival. Intelligence advances and coups, better air and surface radars, true VLR aircraft patrols, new mid-ocean island air bases in the Azores, more escort carriers with portable air power, and an established and reliable convoy system were the critical components of Allied victory.

Dönitz's fleet was reduced to hugging the coasts of Europe or huddling inside concrete pens, more hunted than hunters: The U-boats were finished as a strategic threat. They would return to the Atlantic in September 1944, equipped with *Schnorchel* gear. A new Type XXI Elektroboote was entering production, and Dönitz had big plans for resumption of the U-boat war. Before he could do so, millions of North American troops crossed the Atlantic to join British, Polish, Free French, and other Allied soldiers in breaching the crust of Hitler's so-called *Festung Europa*. Not even the Elektroboote and excellent new German homing *torpedoes* permitted U-boats to renew the assault on convoys without high risk of their own destruction. Dönitz recognized that reality and sent 13 precious boats to plant mines instead. Five were lost, while the mine fields did little damage to enemy shipping. Ten more U-boats were sent out in a wolf pack to test the hunting in the Caribbean. Seven were lost in exchange for just 16,000 GRT of shipping. Wolf pack tactics, too, were abandoned in preference for more stealthy and solitary killing. However, sending a lone U-boat against a well-defended convoy was a virtual suicide mission by late 1943, and few independents of any value were found anymore. Dönitz therefore sent some boats to looked for targets in still more distant waters: the Indian Ocean and South Pacific. While those boats were far away and most others were hidden from air attack in concrete pens, great convoys plied back and forth untouched atop the Atlantic, delivering more men and vast quantities of food and war matériel to finish the liberation of Western Europe. Even Dönitz finally realized that his U-boats could only hope to harass or contain enemy traffic, not stop it. Not even he believed any longer in massed wolf pack attacks or a final victory at sea, although he claimed that he did in boastful conversations with his Führer well into 1945. What he offered instead was what all top Nazis were reduced to by that point in the war: a means to extend it, to stave off defeat and cling to power a while longer, before the Götterdämmerung.

The U-boats made a contribution to the German war effort until mid-1943. They significantly slowed supplies of war matériel to Britain and the Soviet Union and delayed the Anglo-American build-up needed to launch a second front. They helped prolong the war, with all its agony. Yet, they failed to prevent vital supply of Britain or transport of the men and machines who carried out invasions of North Africa (1942), Sicily and Italy (1943), and France (June and again in August, 1944). The U-boats were driven from French ports after mid-1944, to die in the Mediterranean or scurry back to relative safety but strategic uselessness in the cold waters of the Baltic. Individual boats sallied to the end of the war. The U-boat captains and crews were brave men, however repugnant the cause for which they fought.

But enemy superiority in ASW warships, aircraft, and technology was so great that most U-boat crew never saw their home port or families again. There were still more than 400 boats in the German fleet in October 1944, most in Baltic ports with more in Norway and a handful scattered across several oceans. Limits imposed by fuel shortages and lack of trained crew, along with superior enemy escort strength, weapons, and tactics, meant that fewer than 40 U-boats went to sea at the same time, and those to little purpose: Dönitz's vaunted hunters made not one kill that month. By the end of the year, 20 percent of operational U-boats were lost each month, nearly all with their full crews. U-boat operations staff were forced from their HQ by the advancing Red Army in January 1945. Bombing shut down most yards along the Baltic coast the next month. There was a final massacre of U-boats off Norway in April, including seven of the new Type XXIs.

On May 4, 1945, Dönitz—then Führer of the "Third Reich" in succession to the suicide of Adolf Hitler—recalled all U-boats and sent out a final order. In a display of vulgar despair disguised as military grace, he instructed the entire fleet to scuttle for "honor's sake." Operation REGENBOGEN sent 218 U-boats to the bottom at the hands of their own skippers and crews. Just 43 surviving U-boats surrendered or were overrun and captured while in pens and shipyards. Over the chill course of the bloody battle in the Atlantic, 1,170 German submarines were commissioned, achieving a peak force of 460 boats. The Kriegsmarine lost 739 U-boats sent to do harm or into harm's way. The casualty rate for crews was 63 percent dead and 12 percent captured, out of more than 40,000 submariners sent on war patrols. That was the highest death rate of any arm of any service of any country in the war. The Western Allies also suffered grievous losses in the Atlantic: 2,452 merchant ships and 175 warships were sunk by submarine attack, with more ships lost to enemy aircraft. Nearly 13 million GRT of merchant shipping was bottomed by 1945, lost along with many tens of thousands of seamen, servicemen, and merchantmen crews.

See also Azores; B-Dienst; Black Pit; Direction-Finding (D/F); Huff-Duff; Italian Navy; Q-ships; radio; Spain; troop ships.

Suggested Reading: Bernard Ireland, *Battle of the Atlantic* (2003); Marc Milner, *Battle of the Atlantic* (2003).

ATLANTIC CHARTER (AUGUST 14, 1941) A statement of principles drafted by Franklin Roosevelt and Winston Churchill at the end of two days of meetings aboard the American heavy cruiser USS Augusta and British battlecruiser HMS Prince of Wales in Placentia Bay, Newfoundland. It was a remarkably aggressive declaration of what amounted to anti-German *war aims,* considering that the United States was officially neutral. It was viewed by Churchill as another step by Roosevelt along the path to war with Germany and the other *Axis* states. Its terms were liberal, although many nations signing later were not. That realism cloaked in democratic idealism spoke to hard lessons of prewar diplomacy, to Depression-era economic realities, Axis aggression, Roosevelt's domestic political needs, and long-term Anglo-American aspirations for world governance. The terms of the Charter were: (1) no territorial aggrandizement to follow victory; (2) postwar border changes permitted only with popular consent; (3) reaffirmation of self-determination and self-government as core international principles; (4) free trade to replace beggar-thy-neighbor protectionist policies practiced by all in the 1930s, including Great Britain and the United States; (5) international economic cooperation, including on traditional domestic issues such as labor, poverty, and social security (in FDR's eyes, a "New Deal" for the world); (6) global freedom from want (poverty) and fear (of aggression), phrasing drawing upon FDR's *Four Freedoms*; (7) freedom of the seas, the most longstanding and deeply shared Anglo-American policy; and (8) defeat and disarmament of the Axis states. The Atlantic Charter was subsequently endorsed as a statement of official war aims by the *United Nations alliance*. Like Woodrow Wilson's "Fourteen Points" address in 1917, the rhetoric of the Atlantic Charter stirred worldwide enthusiasm and fed illusions that the peace to follow would be permanent and liberal. Indian nationalists' hopes were dashed sooner than most, as Churchill clarified that the Charter did not apply to India, Burma, or other parts of the British Empire. Nor did later adherence by Joseph Stalin and the Soviet Union advance any liberal-internationalist goal. Nevertheless, principles enunciated in the Charter found some postwar resonance in the founding conferences and language of the United Nations Organization and in the Bretton Woods trading system and institutions.

See also *Declaration on Liberated Europe*.

ATLANTIC FERRY ORGANIZATION (AFTERO) An air ferry delivering military aircraft to Great Britain. The first planes were fabricated in the United States and secretly shipped to the Canadian border to avoid the *Neutrality Acts*, dragged across and flown across the Atlantic via Newfoundland and Iceland to Scotland. AFTERO subsequently openly delivered early *Lend-Lease* aircraft. It operated only from November 1940 to August 1941, when it was absorbed into *RAF Ferry Command*.

See also *Air Transport Auxiliary (ATA); Air Transport Command (ATC); Neutrality Acts*.

ATLANTIC WALL "Atlantik wal." Adolf Hitler designated German fortifications and related defenses along the Atlantic perimeter of his European empire "der Atlantik Wal." It incorporated all coastal fortification from the French border with Spain through Belgium, the Netherlands, and Denmark—over 3,000 miles of coastline. Nearly 500,000 workers and slave laborers built the Atlantic Wall from 1941 to 1944, mainly under control of the *Todt Organization*. Dense minefields and 15,000 discrete structures—bunkers, pillboxes, machine gun and observation posts—were supposed to be built. Many were, but not all: the fortification system along the Atlantic coast was never contiguous or completed. Field Marshal *Gerd von Rundstedt* did not believe in defending against invasion by meeting the enemy on the beaches. Work was desultory at best on his watch, from 1941 to 1943. Rundstedt later described the Atlantic Wall as "sheer humbug" that would not hold the enemy back more than 24 hours. Most work was done in late 1943 and early 1944, under direction of Field Marshal

Erwin Rommel. When the invasion came on June 6, 1944, Western troops breached the Atlantic Wall in multiple places in Normandy in under 24 hours.

See also *Dieppe; Festung Europa*.

Suggested Reading: Allan Wilt, *The Atlantic Wall* (1975).

ATOMIC BOMBS

See *Hiroshima; Japan; Nagasaki; nuclear weapons programs; Peenemünde*.

ATROCITIES

World War II was an armed conflict without parallel in history for the sophisticated savagery and raw hatred with which it was waged. Cruel, murderous acts committed against defenseless civilians or *prisoners of war* by opposing military forces were commonplace. Individuals, families, and clutches of neighbors or strangers were subject as always in war to spontaneous brutality by rogue soldiers. During World War II the normal horrors of war broke all precedents: hostages were butchered, torture was widespread, armies ran amok in the ruins of great cities, whole populations were callously and brutally uprooted and deported, and systematic slaughter of unarmed peoples became deliberate policy of the most powerful states in the world. So many real atrocities on the grandest of scales marked World War II that it is hard to remember that the war also saw many false "atrocity stories." Lurid tales about enemy cruelty abound in all wars form an integral part of the *propaganda* of belligerents. Fake atrocities were used by propaganda services throughout World War II to stir domestic and international support and bring approbation down upon enemies, or to distract from an atrocity performed by one's own side and subsequently discovered by some third party. The truth about most real atrocities waited liberation from the occupying power, and in many cases took years and even decades to be fully uncovered.

For specific incidents, sustained policies, and controversies concerning atrocities see *Antonescu, Ion; Ardeatine Cave massacre; Auschwitz; Babi Yar; Bataan death march; biological warfare; Biscari massacres; commando order; Commissar order; concentration camps; Coventry; death camps; desertion; Einsatzgruppen; Eisenbahntruppen; ethnic cleansing; genocide; Gestapo; Goldap operation; Guernica; GULAG; Hiroshima; Hitler, Adolf; Holocaust; Homma, Masaharu; Hong Kong; hostages; Ianfu; Katyn massacre; Laconia order; Malmédy massacre; Manila; Moscow Conference; Nagasaki; Nanjing, Rape of; NKVD; Oradour-sur-Glane; partisans; Poland; Pripet Marshes; Rassenkampf; Red Army; Reichenau order; Singapore; Sino-Japanese War (1937–1945); Slovak Uprising; Smersh; Sonderkommando; special action; special orders; Stalin, Joseph; strategic bombing; Ukraine; Unit 731; unrestricted submarine warfare; Vernichtungskrieg; V-weapons program; Warsaw Ghetto; Warsaw Uprising; war treason*.

ATTACK AIRCRAFT

See *bombers*.

ATTACK CARGO SHIP (AKA)

See *landing ships*.

ATTENTISME "wait and see." The most common attitude of the French, as well as other peoples in German-occupied Europe, toward the see-saw military contest between the *Axis* and *Allies*. A wide range of complex attitudes is subsumed under the term, ranging from fear of the *Résistance* as most likely to provoke Germans into making reprisals against French prisoners in Germany or within France, to broad, if rather passive, support for the Vichy regime as a guarantor of some semblance of peace and even independence. The attitude eroded in favor of the Allies throughout the occupation, accelerating from November 1942, when the Germans occupied the *zone libre* in response to the *TORCH landings* in North Africa on November 8, 1942. After a brief revival of feeling for Marshal *Philippe Pétain* in the bombing run-up to the *OVERLORD* invasion of France in early 1944, waiting dissolved for a significant minority of French into active resistance against German military and political authorities, or assistance to arriving Western armies.

See also collaboration; resistance.

ATTLEE, CLEMENT (1883–1967) British prime minister, 1945. Attlee fought at Gallipoli in 1915, suffering a grievous wound. In the interwar period he rose to leadership of the Labour Party. He forced *Neville Chamberlain's* resignation as prime minister at the outset of *FALL GELB* in 1940, by withdrawing confidence over the handling of the expedition to Norway. He served in Winston Churchill's wartime cabinet, hugely assisting the cause of national unity in prosecution of the war. Attlee was elevated to deputy prime minister in 1942. In 1945 he served on the British delegation at the *San Francisco conference,* returning home in July to lead the Labour Party to a solid victory in the general election. He replaced Churchill as prime minister and as head of the British delegation to the *Potsdam Conference.*

ATTU

See Aleutian Islands.

AUCHINLECK, CLAUDE (1884–1981) British general. His early career was spent almost entirely with the Indian Army. His first active command came during the ill-fated Western Allied expedition to Norway in 1940. He then commanded British and Commonwealth forces in the *desert campaigns (1940–1943)* when a dissatisfied Winston Churchill sacked General *Archibald Wavell* and appointed "Auk." Churchill subsequently sacked Auchinleck as commander in chief Middle East, replacing him with General *Harold Alexander,* while General *Bernard Law Montgomery* took charge of 8th Army. Auchinleck was appointed commander in chief of the Indian Army in 1943, after a year without an active command. He played an important but rear area role in support of the second *Burma campaign (1943–1945).*

AUFBAU OST

See BARBAROSSA.

AUGUST STORM (1945)
See Manchurian offensive operation.

AUNG SAN (1914?–1947)   Burmese nationalist. In 1941 he was part of a group called "The Thirty," which studied guerrilla tactics in Japan. He then fought alongside the Japanese as a major general of the *Burma National Army,* under the political authority of *Ba Maw.* As it became clear that Japan would lose the war, Aung San secretly organized an anti-Japanese political and military movement. In March 1945, he led a revolt against Japanese occupation forces. His military experience propelled him to the political forefront as the war ended. He briefly claimed the premiership of Burma during the struggle for power attendant on British withdrawal after the war. Aung San would have been independent Burma's first prime minister, but he was assassinated six months before formal independence.

AUSCHWITZ   Polish: "Oswiecim." The largest and most notorious of all *death camps* set up by the Nazis, it was located near a small Polish town from which it took its name. A small workers' camp was built at Auschwitz in 1916 by the Austro-Hungarian Empire. After World War I it was used by Polish horse artillery. Upon the conquest of Poland, Auschwitz I was converted in 1940 into a jail for Polish officers and political prisoners. SS Reichsführer *Heinrich Himmler* then expanded it for use by the *Schutzstaffel (SS)* as a slave labor camp, with workers servicing an IG Farben factory turning out synthetic rubber and fuel for the leading firm in the German petrochemical industry. Auschwitz II was a second and larger camp built at nearby Auschwitz-Birkenau in late 1941. It was initially used as a holding pen for slave laborers employed in a network of 36 satellite work camps run at a profit by the SS for contracted industries. It subsequently became part of the killing arena. Blueprints for turning Auschwitz into a true *death camp* were first sketched by a Polish draftsman prisoner in November 1941. By that date the first prisoners had been gassed in killing experiments using *Zyklon B.* The *Wannsee conference* followed in January 1942, overseen by *Adolf Eichmann* and *Reinhardt Heydrich.* Himmler also took a direct interest in construction of the proposed death camp. Plans for converting Auschwitz and other SS labor and concentration camps into death camps were laid out to top men of the rest of the German military and Nazi government at Wannsee. That set in motion the full and "final solution to the Jewish problem."

The SS conversion at Auschwitz started with turning a small farmhouse into a makeshift gas chamber, in which mass killings began on March 26, 1942. A second building was added in July as more trainloads of Jews arrived for "extermination." Thereafter, Jews were systematically gassed in the camp and their remains disposed of in industrial crematoria. Four crematoria and additional gas chambers were erected from March to June, 1943. They raised the camp's ability to slaughter people to an industrial scale, employing methods of modern industry to murder as many as 6,000 per day, with disposal of mountains of remains in the crematoria. Auschwitz III became the main killing camp, conducting systematic genocide of Jews and others arriving by train from March 1943. Auschwitz was also the site of the worst forms of sadism and obscene medical experimentation by Josef Mengele, as well as occasional saintly self-sacrifice by prisoners. The existence of gas chambers and crematoria at Auschwitz was subsequently denied by neo-Nazis, cranks, and others immune by reason of ideology or stupidity to historical facts and evidence. If any additional proof of the existence of gas chambers and crematoria at Auschwitz was ever needed beyond eyewitness testimony of prisoners and SS captured after the war, it was clearly provided in 2008 when late-1941 blueprints for the killing camp were discovered in Berlin.

A complex of satellite service and slave labor camps sprang up around Auschwitz. Some held Russian POWs. Others were slave labor centers rented out to German industry by the SS. Just before Auschwitz's surviving inmates were to be liberated by the Red Army, overseers of the complex were killing Jews and smaller numbers of Roma, Poles, and Russians at a rate of thousands per day. The primary method—in addition to shootings, hangings, and beatings—was mass poisoning in huge gas chambers employing Zyclon B gas pellets manufactured by I. G. Farben. That was too many dead for even the huge crematoria to handle, so bodies were also burned in immense pyres. In October 1944, an insurrection by inmates destroyed part of the death machinery, but the revolt was swiftly and utterly savagely repressed by guards. As the Red Army approached the camp complex in November 1944, the SS blew up the crematoria. In January 1945, most surviving inmates were force-marched westward. The SS tried to destroy the rest of the camp and all evidence of their crimes. When the complex was liberated by the Soviets on January 27, 1945, only a few thousand inmates were left inside, most too weak to walk. Some died soon after.

Nearly 1.5 million people are thought to have died in this one death camp complex—that toll is partly a consensus estimate by historians, but mainly it is based upon the insanely evil but highly meticulous record-keeping habits of the SS and other mass murderers, who recorded their deeds in a "Totenbuch" ("deathbook"). About 800,000 victims were Jews, including over 200,000 Hungarian Jews shipped to Auschwitz in 1944. The rest were non-Jewish Poles, Russians, Roma, and other "enemies of the Reich." The best consensus estimates are that 1,050,000 Jews were killed in Auschwitz, along with 74,000 non-Jewish Poles, 25,000 Roma, 15,000 Red Army prisoners, and perhaps another 15,000 inmates incarcerated for various reasons of the SS or Nazi state. Soviet discovery and liberation of Auschwitz was not reported to the world public until May 7, 1945. The delay was partly caused by wider issues and events involved in the *conquest of Germany* and establishment of Allied rule over all Europe during the first half of 1945. But it also resulted from moral confusion about where to rank the special suffering of Jews in a war in which Soviet propaganda had portrayed Russians as uniquely harmed by Nazi rule.

See also anti-Semitism; biological warfare; Holocaust; Speer, Albert; Warsaw Ghetto.

AUSLAND ORGANISATIONEN (AO) Foreign-based organizations of the *Nazi Party*. They were mainly concerned with propaganda, but also conducted minor espionage.

AUSSENLAGER   Satellite work camps clustered around various *concentration camps*.

AUSTRALIA   Like other Dominions of the British Empire, Australia found itself at war with the Central Powers in 1914 without any prior consultation. The doleful experience of distant battle against enemies of which Australians knew little, most notably at Gallipoli in 1915, provoked a movement to secure more foreign policy independence. The *Statute of Westminster* provided that from 1931. In Imperial consultations during the late 1930s, Australia and other Dominions strongly supported a policy of *appeasement* of the Axis states. Without real enthusiasm, Australia still joined the mother country upon the outbreak of war: Prime Minister Robert Menzies announced Australia's declaration of war against Germany on September 3, 1939, after New Zealand had already declared. Exigencies of Australia's strategic geography, along with lingering cultural and emotional ties to the Empire, led the country back into war. Yet, during the first two years there was widespread and deep-seated suspicion among the public about the wisdom of the Imperial tie and worry over the oddity of Australian boys again fighting and dying in faraway Africa and Europe for causes as yet little understood. Australia was also wholly unprepared economically for the hard and protracted war in which it found itself from 1940, as Britain's allies in Europe were overwhelmed by the Wehrmacht and London turned to the red parts of the world map for substantial and direct military assistance.

Australia rallied to train and ship out a growing *Australian Army,* which fought hard alongside the British in the disastrous *Balkan campaign* of 1940–1941, then made a significant contribution to defense of North Africa against Italian and German troops from 1941 to 1943. It did so despite rising doubts in British military leadership. It was only after a direct threat to Australia's own security arose from the initial successes of Imperial Japan in 1941–1942 that domestic opinion firmed in support of the war. Australia came under direct attack for the first time in its modern history when Japanese carrier-based and land-based bombers struck a handful of towns in the northwest. Over 200 were killed at Darwin on February 19, 1942; Japanese midget submarines also attacked shipping in Sydney harbor. There were intermittent air raids on Darwin after that, but the town was soon well-defended by *Royal Australian Air Force (RAAF)* and USAAF fighters. Those events conduced to several real invasion scares. Australia therefore redirected its effort into the Pacific theater from 1942 to 1945. It joined the *United Nations alliance* upon its formation on the first day of 1942: most Australians realized immediately that it must be the United States rather than Great Britain that henceforth provided military security to Australia in the Pacific. Australian ground, naval, and air forces were immediately drawn into heavy fighting and suffered significant losses in Malaya and on New Guinea. They saw more losses on Bougainville and Borneo, in Burma, and on several South Pacific islands.

The public's fear of invasion subsided as the Japanese were pushed back from forward air bases in the Solomons during 1942–1943. Yet, Australians continued to make an exceptional military effort for a thinly populated country. Isolated and underpopulated at just 7 million people in 1939, Australia lacked a tradition of military independence and command. At the start of the war the three chiefs of Australia's armed services were all seconded British officers, while other British officers served at various levels in command of Australian soldiers and sailors. It was accepted that newly forming Australian divisions should serve as they always had in prior wars, under their own divisional officers but integrated at higher levels into larger British and Imperial theater commands. This practice continued after American entry into the war: Australian land and air forces in the South Pacific theater served under overall command of General *Douglas MacArthur*, while *Royal Australian Navy* (RAN) ships served under *Chester Nimitz* and other U.S. admirals. The RAN had already seen action alongside the Royal Navy in operations against Italy in June 1940, but like the Army, the RAN mostly redeployed to the Pacific after Japan entered the war. Some Australian pilots of the RAAF had flown for the Royal Air Force during the *Battle of Britain* in 1940. Many remained in the RAF for the duration, breaking with the flow of Army and Navy assets to the Pacific. They were later joined by more pilots and crew, as the RAAF expanded manifold and sent fighter and bomber squadrons to all major theaters of war.

John Curtin (1885–1945) replaced Robert Menzies as wartime prime minister even as Australia turned to face Japan in the Pacific. He served from 1941 to 1945. Curtin worked well with the Americans, from whom he requested and received new security guarantees in the wake of *Pearl Harbor* and the Japanese move into the Solomons. In return, Australia became a major support base for intelligence, naval, and air operations against Japanese forces in the South Pacific from February 1942. More than a million non-Australian soldiers, marines, and sailors were operating out of Australia or supported in distant battles from its ports and airfields within a year. Not all went smoothly in Australian–American relations. Social and sexual tensions and arguments between American troops and the local population were not uncommon, and sometimes led to violence. But the overall experience was positive for both sides, and lucrative for Australians. At the government-to-government level, Menzies protested supply priorities in the "holding war" in the Pacific on April 18, 1943, stating that Australia was near the limits of its logistical and manpower capabilities. The main campaign had already moved to the central Pacific by then, leaving Australians to fight vicious but today largely forgotten battles against isolated Japanese garrisons in the South Pacific.

Larger events in North Africa, Sicily, Italy, and the bombing campaign over Germany meant that the dice of grand strategy were cast in distant Allied capitals, not Canberra. That was true even though the outcome of major gambles taken in London and Washington directly affected the lives of millions of Australians. Australian soldiers, sailors, and marines continued to slog away, largely and also unfairly unheralded then and since, alongside British and U.S. forces in New Guinea, Burma, the Bismarck Archipelago, and the Dutch East Indies. Australian troops carried out the last large amphibious landing of the war at *Balikpapan* in

July 1945. Nearly one million Australians had served in the armed forces by then, and 39,000 were dead.

See also ABDA Command; Allied Intelligence Bureau (AIB); ANZAC area; Anzacs; British Empire Air Training Scheme.

Suggested Reading: J. Robertson, *1939–1945: Australia Goes to War* (1984).

AUSTRALIAN ARMY   The Australian Army was wholly unready for war in 1939. It was predominantly a part-time force further limited by the Defence Act to serve only in Australian territory. Just 2,800 of its 82,800 men were fully trained professionals. The rest were essentially militia. Weapons and equipment stocks were at comparably low levels. Nevertheless, within two weeks Prime Minister Arthur Menzies promised to send a division to fight in Europe. That began the raising of a discrete Second Australian Imperial Force (AIF) that answered directly to the cabinet rather than the peacetime and territorial structure of the Military Boards. The term built upon the tradition of the "First AIF," which served in World War I. Part of the first Australian division to serve abroad arrived in France in time to participate in the disaster of *FALL GELB*. The AIF underwent rapid expansion from a small base and did not take part in combat again until 1941, when Australians saw action in North Africa and around the eastern Mediterranean. During the war five AIF divisions were raised: the 6th, 7th, 8th, and 9th Infantry, and the 1st Armoured Division. To enable more men to serve abroad, Australian women were enlisted in the various uniformed services starting in 1941. The Women's Auxiliary Air Force (WAAF), Women's Royal Australian Naval Service (WRANS), and the Australian Women's Army Service (AWAS) performed important services at home and often outside the country as well. Thousands of Australian women served abroad in combat zones in various capacities. Many more moved into industrial and farm jobs vacated by men who had been called to arms. Over 400,000 men and women of the RAA served outside Australia by 1945.

Joining the British in the fight against Italian forces in East and North Africa, three green divisions sailed from Australia's shores to form the 1st Australian Corps. Some Australians fought in failed British campaigns against the Germans in Greece and on Crete, and in the small but successful campaign in Syria against troops loyal to Vichy. The majority fought in North Africa. 1st Corps helped garrison Palestine but also fought in defense of Egypt and later attacked into Tripoli. From April to August 1941, 14,000 Australians made a heroic stand against encircling *Afrika Korps* forces at *Tobruk*. Then came the shock of the opening wave of unbroken Japanese advances across the South Pacific at the end of 1941 and first three months of 1942, the so-called "Hundred Days campaign." A public clamor arose to recall all Australian divisions from North Africa for critical homeland defense against what seemed a very real threat of Japanese invasion. At the urgent request of the British a single AIF division was left in North Africa through 1942. Canberra agreed to leave troops in that distant theater upon receiving a promise that an American division would be sent to defend Australia. The Australian 9th Division stayed in Egypt, where it fought alongside the famed "Desert Rats" (British 7th Armoured) in the *Western Desert Force* and later, as part of British 8th Army. It took part in the fight at *Second El Alamein* before being recalled to the Pacific.

But it was against the Japanese that Australians saw the hardest and dirtiest fighting, lasting to the very last days of the war and even a little beyond. Australian 6th and 7th divisions were pulled back from North Africa to defend Australia. On the way home some troops were diverted into a hasty defense of Java, only to be overrun and taken prisoner when that island and the rest of the Dutch East Indies fell to the Japanese in March 1942. The 8th Division was lost in fighting in Malaya when it joined the general British surrender in *Singapore*. Thousands more Australians were captured on Rabaul, or on divers South Pacific island outposts. Two-thirds of the 28,756 Australians officially taken prisoner during the war were lost in these early battles in the Pacific. More than 8,000 POWs did not survive to see liberation in August–September, 1945. Many succumbed to tropical disease and malign neglect by their Japanese guards, others fell to openly brutal and consistently harsh treatment or murder. The rest of the AIF fought under General *Douglas MacArthur* within the *South West Pacific Area* command, although Australians were initially led by their own ground forces commander, General *Thomas Blamey*. Australia deployed nearly 500,000 ground troops in the Pacific theater by August 1943, compared to just 200,000 American troops. Australians replaced Americans in ongoing and bloody, though no longer strategically significant, campaigns in New Guinea and the Solomons from October 1944. Notable Australian campaigns were conducted on *Bougainville* and *New Britain*. That commitment freed U.S. divisions to invade the Philippines and to move through the Central Pacific toward Japan itself.

See also Alamo Force; Anzac area; Anzacs; Balikpapan; Bardia; Beda Fomm; coast watchers; Digger; Guadalcanal; New Guinea campaign (1942–1945); New Guinea Force.

Suggested Reading: Horner, D. M. *Crisis of Command: Australian Generalship and the Japanese Threat, 1941–1943* (1978); Gavin Long, *The Six Years War: Australia in the 1939–1945 War* (1973).

AUSTRALIAN CORPS
See ANZAC; Australian Army.

AUSTRALIAN NAVY
See Royal Australian Navy.

AUSTRIA The "First Republic" was proclaimed in Vienna following Austria-Hungary's catastrophic defeat in 1918. The rump Austrian state that emerged from the detritus of empire was sanctioned and proscribed by the *Treaty of St. Germain (1919)*. Austria was so politically unstable it endured a brief civil war between Social Democrats and Nazis in 1934, after the latter murdered Chancellor *Englebert Dollfuss* in a failed coup attempt. The Nazis then worked from within a weakened government, and on the streets, to facilitate Adolf Hitler's and Germany's takeover of Austria. The denouement finally came when German troops marched into Austria unopposed—and cheered by some—on March 13, 1938. The *Anschluss* incorporated Austria as a province ("Ostmark") of the German Reich, a fact well-received by a majority of Austrians at the time. Late in the war, but especially after it, Austrians would claim to number among Hitler's "first victims." The Allied powers helped foment that semirevisionist claim by formally declaring Austrian victimhood in a declaration issued in Moscow in November 1943, as part of a wartime effort to encourage internal resistance in German rear areas.

Austrian resistance never materialized: while a few brave Austrians resisted the Nazis from the start, most did not. As the full range of Nazi law and policy was applied many tens of thousands of the country's approximately 200,000 Jews were forced to emigrate. They departed utterly destitute before the war began. Those left behind were confined to *concentration camps*. Nearly all were later killed as the full agenda of the *Holocaust* unfolded. Austria's small army and air force were quickly absorbed into the Wehrmacht in 1938, not as whole units but with Austrian troops scattered among more trusted German units. As the war progressed, hundreds of Austrian officers rose to high levels of command in the Wehrmacht and *Waffen-SS*. Other Austrians served at all levels in the *Nazi Party,* the *Gestapo, Schutzstaffel (SS),* and in the Nazi civil service or regular police. Although Austria was not as heavily bombed as was Germany proper, it suffered over 100,000 civilian casualties during the war. Another 250,000 Austrian soldiers or airmen were killed. Austria was invaded and occupied by the Soviets and Americans in 1945. There was much controversy in Allied circles over how to deal with Austria. There was universal agreement to undo the Anschluss and to impose four-power occupation of the country, an operation and administration carried out separately from the occupation of Germany. A number of Austrians were also tried by the *Nuremberg Tribunal* and in national trials. *Seyss-Inquart* was convicted and hanged. Austria regained full independence when Allied occupation ended in 1955.

See also prisoners of war; Schuschnigg, Kurt; Vienna offensive operation.

Suggested Reading: Evan Bukey, *Hitler's Austria, 1938–1945* (2000); R. H. Keyserlingk, *Austria in World War II* (1989).

AUTARKY Economic self-sufficiency based on highly protectionist, state overseen but often privately owned, import substitution projects and industries. In a drive for absolute "Autarkie," or total economic self-sufficiency for Germany, Adolf Hitler sought to expand extant German economic dominance of weak eastern and central European states, and to bring other countries such as Spain into Germany's dominant economic orbit in a neocolonial relationship. He decreed that it was essential that Germans secure long-term access to raw materials and agricultural lands in the east through aggressive war. The strategic aim of his drive for *Lebensraum,* or "living space," was to sustain an expanding population of German colonists and am enlarged homeland without any dependence whatsoever on foreign trade or external sources of strategic materials. Such economic independence would give Nazi Germany a large-scale economy ("Grossraumswirtschaft") that could compete in economic and military terms with the great sea empire of Britain, and with the land empires of the United States and Soviet Union. The Soviet empire and most of its peoples were slated to disappear under savage German occupation, in which war would serve merely as cover for a vast genocide. A supporting purpose of conquest was to acquire food and mineral resources needed to support a war economy capable of sustaining a protracted air, sea, and land fight with Great Britain, while preparing for an expected climactic global war with the United States in the more distant future. Hitler's economic policy toward minor Axis states and occupied territories insisted on barter agreements, which exploited and tied east and central European economies to the German war economy. Rather than increasing Germany's independence, the serial wars begun by Hitler in 1939 in fact cut off Germany's economy from vital foreign supplies. That forced Germans to turn to synthetic and ersatz substitution for many vital products, especially oil. Hitler was far from alone in pursuing the ambition of total self-reliance for Germany. It was a key part of the strategic vision of his top military advisers as well, including General *Franz Halder* and others on the General Staff and OKW. Indeed, the notion of eastward expansion to acquire food and land reserves was ensconced on the nationalist right in Germany well before 1914, let alone 1939.

Japan also pursued autarky as a primary foreign policy and war aim, within a concept of *total war* that looked to a "northern advance" (*hokushin*) to harness the raw resources of Manchuria and northern China in a single economic unit with Japan. That ambition underlay the *Sino-Japanese War (1937–1945)*, settlement policy in Manchuria, and the harsh extractive character of Japanese occupation policies and economic practices. The Japanese initially settled on a proposal roughly modeled on the British Empire: the *Greater East Asia Co-Prosperity Sphere*. But during the 1930s that concept evolved into a more German version of autarky, in which alien territory containing raw materials and space for Japanese colonization was to be directly conquered and occupied. Of course, this was portrayed—even among Japanese planners—as a defensive strategy forced upon Japan by the wiles and depredations of its enemies. After the *Nomonhan* clash with the Red Army in the summer of 1939, and with the fall of France in June 1940, Imperial General Headquarters sought a way out of the cul de sac of the China War. Military leaders thought they found it in a new "southern advance" (*nanshin*), which promised to deliver vast resources and economic independence that would permit Japan to keep its hold on China and defend against future threats from the American and Soviet empires. It could not have been more gravely wrong.

See also Great Depression; Spain; Stalin, Joseph.

AUTOBAHN   The pan-German system of four-lane highways started in 1932, but completed by the Nazi regime. Ostensibly a public works project undertaken in response to high unemployment, for Adolf Hitler the Autobahns formed a military transport system for rapid movement of troops across Germany, comparable to the railway system built in the 19th century by Otto von Bismarck. The system did serve military purposes, but not just for the Germans: U.S. 7th and 3rd Armies made use of Autobahns near Frankfurt to complete encirclement of the Ruhr in 1945.

See also New Order; Norway.

AUTOMEDON, CAPTURE OF
See nanshin.

AUXILIARY CARRIERS
See Catapult Aircraft Merchant; escort carriers; Merchant Aircraft Carrier.

AUXILIARY CRUISERS   Small to mid-sized German warships disguised as neutral or Western Allied merchantmen, and in one case as a British *Armed Merchant Cruiser*. They were intended for independent commerce raiding. The Kriegsmarine built or converted 11, all under 10,000 tons displacement. The Italian Navy built three while the Japanese commissioned two. One German auxiliary cruiser ("Handelsstörkreuzer" or "commerce disruption cruiser") had a catapult float plane to scout for prey, racks of torpedoes, and 6-inch ship's guns. Its presence in a given area, or even just rumors of its presence, forced commitments of British and Commonwealth warships that could be ill-afforded in the first years of the war at sea. One German auxiliary cruiser received assistance in the Pacific from the Soviet Union and aid and resupply from the Japanese. It sank 64,000 tons of Allied shipping. The fleet was sent out in two waves of six ships, followed by three more. They sought prey in the Antarctic, Atlantic, Indian, and Pacific Oceans. Nine Handelsstörkreuzer sank 3/4 of a million tons of shipping from 1939 to 1942, mainly merchants and whalers but also some warships, including the RAN Sydney. Of nine more Handelsstörkreuzer sent out by the end of 1942, seven were sunk, one was destroyed when it caught fire, and one was cannibalized after its cruise. A 10th raider was sent to sea alone in February 1943, but was quickly bombed back into port by the RAF. An 11th ship was undergoing conversion when it was bombed in drydock.
See also cruiser warfare.

AUXILIARY FIRE SERVICE (AFS)
See National Fire Service.

AUXILIARY PERSONNEL ATTACK SHIP (APA)
See landing ships.

AUXILIARY WARSHIPS
See Armed Merchant Cruiser; auxiliary cruisers; Catapult Aircraft Merchant; escort carriers; landing ships; Merchant Aircraft Carrier; merchant marine.

AVALANCHE   Western Allied code name for the landings at Salerno (September 9, 1943).
See Italian campaign (1943–1945).

AVG
See American Volunteer Group.

AWARDS (FOR VALOR)
See medals.

AWL "Absent Without Leave." A British and Commonwealth term for a soldier or sailor absent from official duties without permission. The U.S. equivalent was "Absent Without Official Leave (AWOL)."

AWOL
See AWL.

AXIS ALLIANCE The coalition of states centered on Nazi Germany that lost the war to the *United Nations alliance* or *Allies*. The alliance originated in a German–Italian treaty signed in secret on October 25, 1936. The term "Axis" gained currency later, from a typically bombastic rhetorical flourish by Benito Mussolini in Milan in November 1938. He used "axis" as a metaphor to describe how European and world events would revolve around the new Rome–Berlin alignment. Formal alliance came later in the *Pact of Steel* signed in May 1939. Adolf Hitler expanded the term to include Japan, seeing such an "axis" alliance as a global counterweight to the empires of Britain and France. Although Japan signed the *Anti-Comintern Pact* in 1936, Tokyo did not sign a formal alliance with Rome or Berlin until it agreed to the *Tripartite Pact* in September 1940. Minor states that joined the Axis were: Hungary (November 20, 1940), Rumania (November 23, 1940), Bulgaria (March 1, 1941), and the still smaller Nazi puppet states of Slovakia (November 23, 1940) and Croatia (June 15, 1941). Spain did not join, though many of those around *Francisco Franco* sympathized with the fascist cause. The term "Axis" is not normally applied to the alliance status of Finland, though perhaps it should be. For reasons mainly pertaining to the *Finnish–Soviet War (1939–1940)*, Finland fought as a partner of Nazi Germany from June 1941 to September 1944, the period Finns call the "Continuation War." The Finnish Army was the one minor force allied to Germany that was of high military quality. All other minor Axis states—and to a high degree, Italy as well—were weak politically and militarily and had archaic or even premodern economies that contributed little beyond natural resources to the German war effort.

The Axis alliance was divided over racial ideology, with significant tensions between Germany and its European partners arising over the question of mass murder of Jews. The great majority of Italians rejected Nazi-style anti-Semitic laws passed by Mussolini, and many hid and protected Jews. Even the Italian Army protected Jews in its administrative zone in alpine France and in Italian zones in the Balkans, until it was disarmed in September 1943 by the German operation *ACHSE*. The Rumanian government cooperated in genocide, but Bulgarian and Hungarian governments refused to do so. Bulgarian policy changed when the regime in Sophia was toppled and replaced by a Nazi-puppet and fascist regime. It changed in Hungary when that state was invaded by Germany in 1944. Race did not enter into Nazi or Japanese thinking on the question of alliance because any quack racial concerns were resolved by the Nazis declaring the Japanese to be "honorary Aryans." In addition, Hitler genuinely admired the martial spirit and warrior ethos of Japanese militarists. Racist ideology was ultimately trumped by geopolitical considerations: Japan and Germany drew close because they had shared enemies in the Soviet Union and Great Britain, to a lesser extent also in France and the Netherlands, and more distantly in the United States. Japan's territorial and imperial ambitions also complemented rather than clashed with Berlin's or Rome's. It is also clear that the Japanese had no understanding of the centrality of racism to the Nazi *Weltanschauung* and, therefore, never really understood Hitler's policies. They also failed to appreciate his all-or-nothing belief in German victory or defeat. That is the main explanation for why they persisted with advice that he make peace with the Soviet Union to concentrate against the Western Allies.

It is unknown how these misapprehensions might have played out had the Axis alliance won the war. It is likely, however, that greatly expanded and regionally dominant German and Japanese empires would have grated against one another along a newly common boundary, possibly over control of India or where to divide a prostrate and defunct Soviet Union: at the Urals or along the Volga? All winning coalitions have broken apart upon defeat of their common enemies. It is reasonable to believe that the Axis would have flown apart in much greater violence than normal among winning alliances, given what is known about the character of its members. As matters actually turned out, the long-term strength of the Axis bond was never tested by victory. Instead, it was undone by catastrophic and separate defeats in detail of all its members on all fronts. Little cooperation between the major Axis states took place. Declarations of war were not communicated in advance by Italy to Germany before its invasions of Albania in 1939 or Greece in 1940; by Germany to Japan when it attacked Poland in 1939 and the Soviet Union in June 1941; or by Japan to its European partners when it attacked the United States, Great Britain, and the Netherlands in December 1941. Hitler had concluded the *Nazi–Soviet Pact* in August 1939 without informing the Japanese of this extraordinary diplomatic revolution, even as the Japanese Army and Red Army were engaged in hostilities at *Nomonhan*. Production quotas, force deployments, and campaign planning were never coordinated over the course of the war. Fighting in what the Western Allies regarded as European and Pacific theaters of operations in a unified world war was carried out by the Axis powers as wholly discrete European and Asian wars. There was some intelligence sharing within the Axis, notably by the Italians and Japanese, but far less intelligence was shared than among the Allies, even given profound mutual suspicions of the Western powers and Soviet Union.

Economic cooperation was limited from the start by the mutually exclusive dedication of Germany and Japan to *autarky*. Very limited trade in strategic minerals was exchanged before the trade routes were closed by one Allied power or another. Some uranium shipments were made to Japan by Germany, and there was late war transfer of jet and submarine technology as well. There was some Axis cooperation on weapons research, but nothing on a scale to compare to what occurred among the Allies, again even including technology transfers to the Soviet Union. Germany sent technical information and some trade goods to Japan in exchange for raw materials critical to the German war effort. Exchanges were made by *blockade runners* and *U-boats*. Beyond support for German *auxiliary cruisers* in the Pacific and a few U-boats based in Malaya later in the war, naval cooperation between Germany and Japan was almost nonexistent. Adding injury to indifference, to the end of the war in Europe the IJN did not attempt to interfere with massive American *Lend-Lease* supplies to the Soviet Union shipped by convoys heading into Vladivostok and other Soviet ports in the Pacific. And of course, there was no equivalent of Lend-Lease among the Axis nations at all, nor any means to deliver substantial matériel aid had the will or other capacity to do so ever existed.

The Italian Navy sent several submarines into the Atlantic to intercept enemy convoys, but the Kriegsmarine treated these more as an annoyance than a contribution to the naval war. Where land and air forces of the Axis states did fight alongside one another—in Africa, the Mediterranean, Western Europe, and the Soviet Union—relations among senior officers were often marked by intense distrust and even personal contempt. Wehrmacht and *Waffen-SS* men had little general regard for their Italian counterparts. They sometimes simply ignored Italian superior officers, as General *Erwin Rommel* did throughout the *desert campaign*. To their lasting credit, many Italians in turn refused to cooperate with Nazi race laws and extermination programs, although some did. Germans held Rumanians in even more open contempt, leaving Rumanian Army divisions underequipped, without tanks or anti-tank guns or proper resupply. No wonder Rumania armies quickly collapsed on either side of *Stalingrad,* leaving German 6th Army trapped inside a grand Red Army envelopment carried out by better armed and highly motivated Red Army formations. Germans had more respect for Hungarians, with whom they were allied during World War I. But Hungarian and Rumanian armies had to be kept widely separated, or they would fight each other instead of the enemy. That was one reason why the German flanks were so weak and easily broken at Stalingrad. Hitler had turned to the minor Axis states in the spring of 1942 to make up raw numbers and smashed Wehrmacht divisions Germany had lost in the *BARBAROSSA* campaign in 1941. But the other Axis states were unable to supply either the numbers or quality of divisions equal to those in the Wehrmacht, which by 1943 was itself beginning to scrape the bottom of the replacement barrel and to skimp on basic training. With terrible losses suffered by the Italian, Hungarian, and Rumanian Armies on the Eastern Front by March 1943, the minor Axis states ceased to have frontline significance to the outcome of the war. When Italy switched sides in September 1943, German officers and Nazi authorities displayed a venomous disregard for Italian soldiers: 600,000 erstwhile allies of Germany were packed into cattle trains and sent to Austria and Germany to work as forced laborers. Many tens of thousands died under harsh conditions and from brutal treatment at the hands of their overseers. In the last months of the war, Hungarians, Rumanians, and Bulgarians suffered much the same fate.

See also Burma; Manchuria.

AXIS SALLY The sobriquet given by U.S. soldiers and sailors to an American Nazi, Mildred Gillars (1900–1988), who made wartime radio broadcasts to Western

Allied troops and populations. Her propaganda scripts were liberally sprinkled with dire warnings of impending destruction in battle and the real names of captured soldiers. Gillars was convicted of treason in 1949 and sentenced to 30 years imprisonment. She was paroled in 1961 after having declined to apply when she first became eligible for parole in 1959.

See also Joyce, William; Tokyo Rose.

AZORES A cluster of nine small islands strategically located in the Atlantic, 500 miles west of Portugal. The neutral Portuguese were cognizant of a threat from both sides during the *Battle of the Atlantic (1939–1945)* and sent a small expeditionary force to the islands to uphold their formal neutrality. The Azores were important enough that Franklin Roosevelt planned to preemptively occupy the chain in the event of a German invasion of Portugal. Winston Churchill also proposed to use force to seize the Azores, but his War Cabinet refused permission. The crucial lack of Western Allied air cover over the *Black Pit* in the mid-Atlantic was finally addressed by agreement with Portugal on October 12, 1943, permitting construction of two air bases on Terceira. One was British and the other American, though both were at first under a unified British command. A second U.S. base was built on Santa Maria in 1944. In return for this concession the Western Allies promised Lisbon they would liberate the Pacific colony of East Timor from the Japanese.

AZOV, BATTLE OF THE SEA OF (1941) German nomenclature for that part of the southern Ukrainian and Crimean campaign Russian historians call the *Donbass-Rostov Operation*.

B

B-17 "Flying Fortress."
See bombers; bombs; Combined Bomber Offensive.

B-24 "Liberator."
See bombers; Combined Bomber Offensive.

B-25 "Mitchell."
See bombers; Combined Bomber Offensive

B-26 "Marauder."
See bombers.

B-29 "Superfortress."
See blockade; bombers; Japan; United States Army Air Forces.

BABI YAR (SEPTEMBER 29–30, 1941) An *Einsatzgruppe* of the *Schutzstaffel (SS)* murdered 33,771 people over two days and nights at Babi Yar ravine outside Kiev, September 29–30, 1941. Victims were ordered to strip, climb down into anti-tank ditches, and lie atop the bodies of those already dead or dying. Then they, too, were shot. Most of the victims were Jews from Kiev, but some were Red Army *prisoners of war*. It was not just the SS who carried out the massacre Wehrmacht troops assisted in the round-up of Kiev's Jews and helped transport them to the ravine.
See also Holocaust; Rassenkampf.

BADOGLIO, PIETRO (1871–1956)   Italian marshal. Governor of Libya, 1929–1933. Badoglio first saw action on the Austrian front in World War I. During the 1930s he was chief of the General Staff ("Comando Supremo"). He commanded Italian forces in the *Abyssinian War (1935–1936)*. Even though he initially opposed the war, during it he used blister gas against the retreating Abyssinian Army. A military realist about Italy's lack of preparedness, he opposed Benito Mussolini's order for an attack on France on June 19, 1940, when the French were already effectively beaten by the Wehrmacht. Yet, Badoglio remained loyal to the Mussolini regime and carried out the command. He opposed Mussolini again over the Italian invasion of Greece in October 1940. Once again he acquiesced and personally led the assault, which went very badly. Badoglio resigned in December 1940, for squalid reasons cloaked as "personal honor" rather than any moral objection to serial aggression. He was out of power until asked by the king to form a government upon the overthrow of Mussolini in 1943. Badoglio negotiated directly with the Western Allies to take Italy out of the Axis alliance, but the armistice he arranged was bungled and led instead to German occupation of most of Italy, including Rome. Badoglio's leadership was rejected by the Italian resistance in 1944, and he retired for good. As inept as his service to the Western Allies was, it likely saved him from hanging for earlier *war crimes*.

BAEDEKER RAIDS (APRIL–JUNE, 1942)   Luftwaffe retaliatory bombings of several small British cities. They were ostensibly carried out in accordance with tourist ratings listed in a famed German guide published by Baedeker. By the standards of World War II they were minor in physical damage caused and minuscule in strategic effect. Their main role was to serve German domestic propaganda and to please Adolf Hitler's desire to retaliate for British raids on Lübeck and Rostock.

BAGRAMIAN, IVAN K. (1897–1982)   Marshal of the Soviet Union. An Armenian by birth, he joined the Red Army during the Russian Civil War (1918–1921), helping to suppress national republics in Armenia and Georgia. He survived the great purges of the 1930s. In 1941 he was a staff officer with Southwestern Front. He was commander of 16th Army during 1942–1943, which later became 11th Guards Army. He spent 1944–1945 fighting in the north in command of various Fronts. He saw action at *Kursk*, across Belorussia, and later at Riga, Memel, and in East Prussia. He was promoted to Marshal of the Soviet Union in 1955. He remained with the Red Army until retirement in 1968.

BAGRATION (JUNE 22–AUGUST 19, 1944)   Code name for the main Red Army offensive of 1944, launched against Army Group Center. It is formally known by Russian historians as the "Belorussian offensive operation," which they further subdivide into a series of individual battles. In this work, the overall operation is covered in this main entry and related cross-references.

By mid-1944 the Wehrmacht and Red Army had battered each other for two years along a more or less stalemated frontline in Belorussia. The Soviets assayed multiple but ineffective assaults over the winter of 1943–1944, before pausing for the spring *rasputitsa*. The Germans dug in and fortified, making a virtue of their diminished capacity for mobile warfare: what Adolf Hitler once called the "elegant operations" of 1939–1942 were over. However, along both flanks of the central position on the Eastern Front in Belorussia the Red Army made major gains. It pushed the Germans back 150 miles from the suburbs of Leningrad during the first quarter of 1944. More importantly, it expelled the Wehrmacht from Ukraine along the southern strategic flank. That left a deep and wide Ukrainian *"balcony,"* as the Wehrmacht called exposed flank and operational jump-off positions, overhanging Army Group Center in Belorussia. The Stavka planned to launch a sweeping deep operation to destroy Army Group Center from the Ukraine balcony. It was largely successful in carrying out that ambition by mid-August 1944, thereby creating a cascading crisis for the Wehrmacht along the entire Eastern Front.

Field Marshal Ernst Busch's Army Group Center looked strong in June 1944: it had nearly 800,000 men dug-in behind well-defined positions in highly defensible terrain marked off by woods, hills, and rivers that should have permitted an effective defense-in-depth. However, German strength was illusory. A sizeable proportion of Army Group Center was composed of *Luftwaffe field divisions* and four comparably poorly trained and ill-equipped Hungarian divisions. The crust of the Axis defense was therefore far more brittle than the OKH realized. Busch also lacked real mobile reserves—he had just three mobile infantry divisions available, and limited fuel to move even those. Worse, he did not have the command spine to demand more armor, mobile guns, and fuel from Adolf Hitler. And as was usual on the Eastern Front, German military intelligence failed to provide Busch or his army and divisional commanders in the field, or give to OKH and Hitler, advance or accurate assessments of Soviet strength, concentrations, or operational goals. An extraordinary build-up of Red Army combat power was concealed from the Germans—the *Abwehr* had been disbanded in February, but the *Schutzstaffel (SS)* proved no more competent at assembling battlefield information. The main credit for this deception must go to a remarkable *maskirovka* operation by the Soviets.

Meanwhile, Soviet commanders had advance knowledge of German dispositions in detail: precise information was gleaned in good measure from active *partisan* bands and local peasants who once despised the Soviet Union but had learned to hate their German occupiers even more. Ordinary *Landser* occupying static frontlines had no inkling of the vast Red storm that was coming to overwhelm their positions and lives as the Stavka in Moscow sent four huge Fronts into the fight in Belorussia. They were led by the most proven Soviet commanders, including General *Konstantin Rokossovsky* and Marshal *Alexander M. Vasilevsky*. In overall command was Marshal *Georgi Zhukov*, with Stalin and the rest of the Stavka hovering close over his operational maps. The Red Army began the BAGRATION offensive with a 5:1 superiority in tanks and aircraft. A vast force of 2.4 million *krasnoarmeets* was formed into 12 tank and mechanized corps and 166 rifle divisions. They were supported by similarly massive artillery formations, including tracked *assault guns* and over 5,200 new tanks. Some 5,300 combat aircraft prepared to fly cover over the ground forces, carry out interdiction raids, and strike directly at German rear positions and reinforcement columns.

Initially scheduled to start on June 19, BAGRATION was postponed for three days for technical reasons. It therefore began merely coincidentally on the third anniversary of Operation *BARBAROSSA,* not symbolically as some have suggested. Lead-off units made careful, probing assaults into the German line on June 22. The main attack commenced the next day. Stavka planners aimed to concentrate and overwhelm four key strongpoints that Hitler had declared *feste Plätze,* or fortified places: Borbruisk, Mogilev, Orsha, and Vitebsk. All four sites were quickly threatened as the Soviets unexpectedly broke through the first German line in multiple places, encircling the strongpoints. The Germans lacked sufficient mobile forces to respond, making the "feste Plätze" more traps than strongpoints. Against advice, Hitler stuck to a *Haltebefehl* strategy and an absurd order that the "feste Plätze" should actually permit themselves to be surrounded so that they could later attack into the enemy rear. The "defense line" that connected the four strongpoints in Hitler's imagination was in fact smashed within the first week, with all four fortified places succumbing. Nor did Busch perform well in Army Group command. Hitler was for once probably right to do as he did: relieve a field marshal in the middle of a great battle. Busch was replaced at the end of June by Hitler's "fireman," the devoted Nazi Field Marshal *Walter Model.* Great strategic fires were burning all around German-occupied Europe by that time, as the Western Allies established a firm lodgement in Normandy while other Western armies pressed toward Rome. Model would be flown to Normandy in August to deal with the *COBRA* breakout into the plains of France by Western armies, as Hitler desperately juggled too few men and loyal commanders on too many major fronts.

Once through Busch's and Hitler's static defense lines, Soviet tank armies galloped toward the Berezina River unopposed by sufficient Panzers or Jagdbomber. German 4th Army was encircled and trapped east of Minsk by inner pincers. Deeper Red Army pincer arms reached farther westward around that ruined city, which was liberated by the Soviets on July 3. Other armies of shattered Army Group Center were also smashed, and their remnants turned and ran. Lacking transport, armor, or any real air cover, broken German formations were pursued by swift columns of T-34-76s and T-34-85s, pounded by massed Soviet self-propelled and assault guns, and strafed and bombed by Il-2 "Shturmoviks." Hundreds of thousands of Red Army men rode atop the tanks and assault guns, or ran alongside or among them. Soviet logistics were also far superior to German supplies, efficiently brought forward in *Lend-Lease* heavy trucks, guided by peasants and partisans eager to see the Germans driven away or killed. It was the worst defeat in the history of German arms: Army Group Center lost hundreds of thousands of men, including whole divisions and armies of disconsolate prisoners. Tens of thousands were paraded through Moscow on July 17, on their way to a decade in forced labor camps before they could return to homes in Germany, or to suffer death in the snows of Siberia. Soviet losses were less heavy than in other campaigns, but still reached 125,000 killed, wounded, and missing.

Many military historians regard the pursuit phase of BAGRATION as the culmination of Red Army *deep battle* doctrine. But it also represented a marriage of doctrine with the right weapons and commanders and was carried out by soldiers steeled by good training and hard combat. Whole armies and then Fronts leaped ahead. When they were done they had moved the frontline 300 miles westward and destroyed Army Group Center beyond hope of recovery. BAGRATION also fatally weakened renamed "Army Group South Ukraine" in Rumania and Army Group North, already in retreat through the Baltic States. It thereby primed the entire Eastern Front for spectacular defeats of German forces in early 1945, by forcing Hitler and the OKH to bleed divisions from the north and south flanks to fill the huge and yawning gap in the line left by decimation of Army Group Center. Hitler characteristically blamed the failure to hold in Belorussia on everyone but himself: he sacked OKH chief of staff General *Kurt Zeitzler*. In the wake of the *July Plot,* which nearly killed Hitler while exposing a conspiracy by both retired and active duty generals, he turned over more field commands to men of "will" as against those of known military skill but suspect loyalty. A different controversy lingers over postwar Soviet propaganda contention that BAGRATION made the success of *OVERLORD* possible. There is no strong evidence to suggest that it did. In fact, it is more likely that forcing the Germans to prepare to defend the *Westwall* and breaching *Festung Europa* on the coast of France, while also conducting the *Combined Bomber Offensive,* drew critical Panzer reserves west and Luftwaffe fighters and anti-aircraft artillery back into Germany that otherwise might have slowed or perhaps even stopped BAGRATION.

Suggested Reading: Walter Dunn, *Soviet Blitzkrieg: The Battle for White Russia, 1944* (2000).

BAILEY BRIDGE   A prefabricated British Army bridge capable of spanning up to 200 feet of river, named for its inventor. Its genius lay in advancing from one side of the river via pontoons that supported sectioned construction. It proved enormously important in crossing the waterlogged Netherlands and other riverine areas such as Italy, or in crossing any river where retreating Axis forces blew the bridges. Bailey bridges entered British service in December 1941. U.S. and other Western Allied forces also used Bailey bridges. Several thousand were built during the war, totaling 200 miles of fixed bridging and 40 miles of pontoon bridge. Field Marshal *Bernard Law Montgomery* wrote and spoke in emphatic terms of their contribution to victory. He was one of many commanders who highly prized Bailey bridges.

BAKA
   See *okka.*

BALATON DEFENSIVE OPERATION (MARCH 6–15, 1945)
   See *FRÜHLINGSERWACHEN; Hungary.*

BALCONY   "Balcon." Wehrmacht term for a large, shelf-like position along an extended frontline. The Red Army called any comparable position a "step." For example, East Prussia hung like a balcony over prewar Poland, while the Baltic coast served as a German balcony threatening the Soviet advance on Berlin during the *conquest of Germany* in 1945.

See also BAGRATION; BARBAROSSA; *Pripet Marshes.*

BALDWIN, STANLEY (1867–1947)   British statesman. Conservative prime minister 1923, 1924–1929, 1936–1937. In the 1920s he faced economic dislocations stemming from World War I, including issues of war debts and *reparations*. He was mostly passive during the 1930s, clinging to the *League of Nations* well beyond that failed organization's past due date. Early tracings of full-bore *appeasement* are detectable in Baldwin's diplomacy as his government responded without vigor to several key crises: the *Abyssinian War,* during which he approved the shameful *Hoare-Laval Pact;* the *Rhineland* crisis; and the start of the *Spanish Civil War* in 1936. On the other hand, Baldwin speeded British rearmament and increased fighter production—under public pressure from Winston Churchill. He agreed to the India Act of 1935, promising eventual Home Rule. He was badly distracted from the real issues of the day by a constitutional and abdication crisis provoked by the pending marriage of King Edward VIII to an American divorcee, Wallis Simpson.

BALIKPAPAN (JULY 1–AUGUST 15, 1945)   The Australian 7th Division landed on this bit of Borneo in the Dutch East Indies in the last major *amphibious operation* of the war. Unheralded and off the front pages other than in Australia, the 7th Division retook the main oil and air facilities of Indonesia within nine days, at a cost of 863 casualties. Most of the Japanese garrison was wiped out, fighting to the last with the war nearly done. Desultory mopping up of jungle hold-outs continued to the end of the war.

BALKAN AIR FORCE (BAF)   A Western Allied joint command established in mid-1944 to coordinate operations over the Adriatic and lower Balkans. Its main responsibility was air supply of Yugoslav and Italian *partisans.* It also bombed in support of local Allied land and sea forces. It was effective in harassing German island garrisons and during German withdrawals from Greece and Yugoslavia in 1945.

See also *Dalmatian Islands.*

BALKAN CAMPAIGN (1940–1941)   Benito Mussolini committed Italy to an invasion of Albania in April 1939. That opened the door to Western power guarantees to Greece and Rumania but also led to the *Pact of Steel* signed by Germany and Italy. That posed a strategic threat to containment of the Axis powers even before Adolf Hitler's invasion of Poland on September 1. The Balkans were quiescent into mid-1940, as Adolf Hitler and the OKH concentrated on *FALL GELB*, the invasion of France and the Low Countries. But Mussolini was determined on waging a "parallel war" ("guerra parallela") in the Balkans and across the Mediterranean to keep up with German gains farther north. He ordered an invasion of Greece by the Regio Esercito on October 28, 1940. Britain was by then fighting without allies beyond the Commonwealth nations. Yet, London responded with immediate aid to Athens, principally in the form of naval and air assets but also some ground forces. RAF bombers hit Italian ports and the Royal Navy devastated the Regia Marina's Mediterranean Fleet at *Taranto* in a raid on November 11–12, 1940. Meanwhile, the Greek Army did very well against the Italians. The Greeks fielded 18 divisions in 1940. While their Army was not motorized and had little armor, it knew how to fight in its own mountains. Greek troops also had much higher morale than the invading Italians, as well as superior artillery. The ill-planned, undermanned, and poorly officered Italian offensive was thus blunted by the Greeks. The Italians had no port to unload or supply their advance and bogged down in the mountain passes in the midst of late fall rains. The Italians lacked transport to move in the high terrain, or even proper medical support for their suffering troops. Four heavy Greek infantry divisions easily held against six smaller Italian *binary divisions* along the Albanian frontier. The rest of the Greek Army manned the *Metaxas Line* around Salonika. Others held the Italians off along the *Aliakmon Line,* aided by a small number of British and Commonwealth troops. The Greeks counterattacked the Italians on November 14, driving the enemy back 30 miles into Albania in December.

However, the first Luftwaffe units now appeared in the Balkans in support of Italy: 10th *Fliegerkorps* was dispatched south from Norway. The Germans bombed Malta and British shipping in the central Mediterranean, flying from bases in Sicily. Greek and British commanders quarreled badly over disposition of forces. Still, they managed to blunt a second Italian offensive that began on March 9, 1941. German ground force intervention followed in April. Hitler was preparing to invade the Soviet Union and simply could not allow an Italian defeat in Greece and Albania to open a real Balkan front supported by the British on what was about to become his southern strategic flank. Fast-moving events in Yugoslavia moved Hitler to military intervention there and in Greece, after a pro-Axis regime in Belgrade was overthrown by a British-sponsored coup. German, Italian, and Hungarian armies invaded Yugoslavia on April 6. German 40th Panzer Corps struck toward Skopje in the south, while 1st Panzer Group launched toward Belgrade two days later. The Luftwaffe hit Belgrade with a massive terror raid on the first day, demoralizing the Yugoslavs. The British rushed three ANZAC divisions to Greece from North Africa, but the rapid collapse of the 1.2 million man Royal Yugoslav Army and quick advance of 40th Panzer Corps threatened to allow Axis troops to outflank and cut off Greek and Commonwealth forces. German 41st Panzer Corps was unleashed in the east on April 11. Belgrade fell to the Panzers the next day. The Yugoslav Army began to crumble, not just in front of the Germans but into its component ethnic parts, some of which began to fight each other. Zagreb and Sarajevo fell in short order, and the shell of the Yugoslav government capitulated on April 17th. The country was overrun in just 11 days.

The Germans broke through the Metaxas Line to take Salonika in just three days. That forced the British to fall back to Thermopylae: Winston Churchill's ill-advised Balkan gamble looked ready to devolve into another Norwegian disaster, but on a much larger scale. German intervention in Yugoslavia now broke into the Greek rear, forcing the Greeks to halt their assault on Italian positions and try to fall back out of Albania as well. However, hesitation to withdraw allowed the Germans to cut off an entire Greek Army, dividing it from British and Commonwealth forces. The British decided to evacuate from beaches at Thermopylae and Athens on April 21. The cut-off Greek army mutinied and surrendered to the Germans later that day. The British evacuation began on April 24, with heavy fighting continuing along a contracted perimeter. Although most Western Allied troops got out of Greece, the evacuation was no second *Dunkirk*: it was another bitter and serious British defeat. It was also the third time in just over a year that the British Army was thrown off the continent by the Wehrmacht. With minimal RAF air cover in the area, the Luftwaffe sank several troopships carrying evacuees to Crete or Egypt. A German airborne operation then cut off some troops at Corinth, so that a second evacuation had to be undertaken under heavy shelling and Luftwaffe attack. The total removed from Greece by April 30 was nearly 51,000. About 7,000 British troops were left ashore and forced to surrender. Others took to the mountains individually or in small groups. Some were later killed or captured, but a few eventually made it back to their units with the help of Greek *partisans*. The Greeks lost nearly 13,500 killed in the Balkan campaign and over 42,000 wounded. Just under 10,000 Greek soldiers left with the British for Crete, where they fought the Germans again before evacuating from that island to Egypt.

BALKAN PACT (1933)   In 1933 King Alexander of Yugoslavia tried to arrange an accommodation with Bulgaria, Greece, Rumania, and Turkey. Bulgaria coveted too much of Macedonia to agree, but the other Balkan states formed an entente that lasted until October 1940, when it was broken by the Italian invasion of Greece. Whatever remained of the initiative was destroyed by Adolf Hitler's aggressive Balkan diplomacy and invasion of Greece and Yugoslavia in April 1941.

BALLOONS   All types of balloons were used in World War II: blimps, barrage balloons, and Japanese high altitude *Fugos*. Barrage balloons were the most common. These large, unmanned, low-floating gas bags were tethered to steel cables tied to ships or pegged near potential ground targets. Their function was passive defense: to deter and defend from low-flying bombing or strafing runs by threatening collision with heavy cables. British barrage balloons were the most numerous. They killed a handful of German aircraft that attacked through them, only to have wings sheered off. They also knocked out a fair number of V-1 rockets. The Germans used barrage balloons extensively. All parties in Europe increasingly employed young women in balloon crews as they felt shortages of men taken into the armed forces. The U.S. Navy used barrage balloons in the Pacific from late 1943, but abandoned them when it concluded that balloons improved target spotting by the radar-poor Japanese and hence drew the enemy toward the target rather than protecting it. The Western Allies flew hundreds of barrage balloons over the invasion fleet and then the beaches at Normandy on and after *D-Day (June 6, 1944)*. Lighter-than-air rigid airships were extensively used by all European powers during World War I, when Germany sent Zeppelins across the Channel to bomb London. The U.S. Navy was the main employer of blimps in World War II. They were used as cheap patrol craft off the U.S. coastline, looking for lurking *U-boats*. Some blimps were similarly deployed as scouting platforms above *convoys*. USN blimps had onboard radar, and some carried a few *depth charges*. On a much smaller scale, a balloon radar decoy was used by U-boats. "Aphrodite" was fixed to a float or small raft and released to hover just above the waves. Trailing aluminum foil strips, the Aphrodite balloon presented a radar signature similar to a U-boat on enemy screens. However, it proved of limited effectiveness because the raft to which it was connected merely drifted rather than traveling at U-boats speeds. Nor could it mimic movement by a surfaced U-boat, all facts soon noticed by Allied radar operators.

See also air power; biological warfare.

BALTIC OFFENSIVE OPERATION (SEPTEMBER 14–NOVEMBER 24, 1944)

The Red Army offensive that overran Estonia, Latvia, and western Lithuania during the autumn of 1944. It was conducted by General *Ivan Bagramian's* 1st Baltic Front, General *Andrei Yeremenko's* 2nd Baltic Front, part of Marshal *Leonid A. Govorov's* Leningrad Front, and sundry other units. The overarching commander as well as Stavka representative was Marshal *Alexander M. Vasilevsky*. Opposing this powerful array was Army Group North, comprising German 16th and 18th Armies and various *Waffen-SS* units. Some units of Balts and 3rd Panzer Army in Lithuania fought on the German side. A Finnish–Soviet ceasefire was agreed on September 5, and Leningrad Front struck into Estonia nine days later. Tallinn was abandoned by panicked Germans and fell to the Soviets on September 23. Offshore island garrisons and several Kriegsmarine capital warships bombarded the Soviet columns, but they gave up the fight in late November. Latvia and western Lithuania were overrun by cascading assaults from three Red Army Fronts. The initial attack focused on overwhelming German defenses at Riga. Stalin and the Stavka decided to bypass Riga to cut-off Army Group North by taking Memel. The assault began on October 5. It quickly isolated the port, although the garrison in Memel held out until January 1945. A swollen refugee population and thousands of wounded *Landser* had to be evacuated by sea. Riga was also isolated as relentless pressure drove Army Group North into a shrinking pocket on the Courland peninsula. Ferocious infantry and tank battles led to heavy losses on both sides. The remnants of 33 badly attrited Wehrmacht divisions were crowded into the *Courland pocket* by October. They remained trapped there, under Soviet bombardment and threat of assault, until the last days of the war.

BALTIC SEA

On air and naval operations in the Baltic *see Baltic offensive operation; FALL WEISS; Finnish–Soviet War (1939–1940); Kriegsmarine; Soviet Navy.*

BALTIC STATES
See Baltic offensive operation; BARBAROSSA; Estonia; Holocaust; Latvia, Lithuania; Nazi–Soviet Pact; Reichskommissariat Ostland.

BA MAW (1893–1977)   Burmese nationalist leader. Prime minister under the British from 1937 to 1939, he was imprisoned from 1940 to 1942. He was released by Japanese occupation forces and anointed to lead a collaborationist government. Burmese nationalists later claimed he mitigated the worst excesses of Japanese occupation. To the extent that is true, the price paid was his authoritarian personal rule. He fled to Japan when the British regained control of Burma in 1945. After a short period in a British jail, after being arrested in Japan, Ba Maw returned to Burma in 1946.
See also Aung San; Burma National Army.

BANDA SPECIAL ATTACK CORPS
See Japanese Army Air Forces; kamikaze.

BANDENBEKÄMPFUNG   "anti-bandit warfare."
See partisans.

BANDIT   "Bandit" was a Western Allied air crew or radio signal for an identified enemy aircraft, especially a fighter. The Luftwaffe equivalent was "Indianer!" ("Indians!"), an odd signal possibly arising from prewar popularity in Germany of American western novels and films. When a German fighter pilot scored a kill it was common to cry out "Horrido!" in memory of St. Horridus, patron saint of hunters. Late in the war that cry was heard far less often, as Western Allied and Soviet pilots downed thousands of barely trained Luftwaffe recruits flying outdated aircraft. Such easy German marks were wistfully known to Luftwaffe veterans as "Nachwuchs" ("new growth"). The few missions flown by the Luftwaffe against the bomber streams during the last months of the war were cynically described by veterans as "Himmelfahrtskommando" ("missions to heaven").
See also bogey.

BANDITS   A classification of *resistance* fighters used in German antipartisan warfare. It stripped those so designated of any legal rights and exposed them to summary execution, as well as surrounding populations to hostage-taking and extreme reprisals. It was very often a euphemism for "Jew" and, as such, was employed as a semantic cover for genocide by *Einsatzgruppen*.
See also partisans.

BANGALORE TORPEDO   A simple explosive device (M1A1 Bangalore) first developed in India in 1912. It comprised 5-foot lengths of 38 mm steel tubing with threaded ends. Each section was packed with nine pounds of high explosive.

A bangalore was advanced through wire or a minefield by threading new sections to the nearest end. When detonated, it cleared a path though mines or barbed wire wide enough for infantry to pass in single-file column. Multiple bangalores could clear a path through mines for tanks or mechanized vehicles. The weapon was widely used by Western armies.

***BANZAI* CHARGES**   "Tenno heika banzai!" ("Long Live the Emperor!"). An all-in Japanese infantry attack, usually made as a desperate last-ditch measure or in a death frenzy, with little expectation of victory and none of survival. A number of banzai charges were made in the Pacific by poorly armed Japanese, some carrying only sharpened bamboo sticks. The sheer emotion and violence of a banzai charge carried the enemy's first line on occasion, but more often led to overwhelming slaughter of near-suicidal attackers. Even then, many wounded Japanese preferred to kill themselves rather than accept medical treatment or captivity. A handful gave up and survived. Western Allied soldiers found the banzai spirit frightening but also contemptible. U.S. Army researchers did little better, attributing banzai tactics to "mutual exhortation" and "mob hysteria." Yet, they correctly noted that a banzai charge developed spontaneously among ordinary Japanese soldiers as often as it did from instigation by fanatic officers.

For examples *see Aleutian Islands; Guam; Saipan; Tinian.*

B.A.R.   Browning Automatic Rifle (M1918). A .30 caliber, gas-operated, two-man American automatic rifle. It could be fired from the hip, shoulder, or from a bipod. Its heavy ammunition case was usually carried by a second man.

***BARBAROSSA* (JUNE 22–DECEMBER 5, 1941)**   The code name for the German invasion of the Soviet Union was originally "Unternehmen OTTO," or "Operation OTTO." That was changed by Adolf Hitler to "Unternehmen BARBAROSSA" in Führer Directive No. 21 on December 18, 1940. The new code invoked folk memories of Holy Roman Emperor Frederick I (1123–1190 C.E.), called "Barbarossa" or "Red Beard." As Hitler looked east as a means of bringing Britain to terms in the west by eliminating its last potential continental ally, he set the original target date for OTTO for November 1940. Also pulling Hitler east was an old dream of conquest of a continental empire that would permit the Reich to compete on a global scale with Britain and America. November passed without any invasion, and the launch date was moved to May 15, 1941, with detailed operational orders under preparation by January 1941. Hitler and his generals were properly confident in the quality and combat effectiveness of the Wehrmacht. The other two essential elements of initial German success would be secret concentration of massive assault forces and operational surprise. On the other hand, the Germans badly misread the true strength of the enemy: the *Abwehr* failed to pinpoint the location of entire Soviet armies and Fronts beyond the immediate frontier zone in the western Soviet Union; nor had military intelligence correctly estimated the depth of resources and modern industrial capacity of the Soviet command economy.

BARBAROSSA was delayed another five weeks by a combination of factors: Hitler's commitment of troops to the Balkans to rescue a failing Italian effort, and to counter a shift in regime in Yugoslavia that threatened to open a new front to the south; difficulty securing motor transport for the attack formations; the need to build forward airfields for the Luftwaffe; and unusually heavy rains of the spring *rasputitsa,* which forced the Germans to wait for roads in the invasion area to dry out. Once these difficulties were overcome, BARBAROSSA proposed to hurl four million German and other Axis soldiers against the Red Army, which was then in the midst of a fundamental reorganization of its doctrine and dispositions. Hitler told rapt Wehrmacht commanders that the greatest and most ruthless invasion in history would reach for objectives both geostrategic and racial: "to establish a defense line against Asiatic Russia from . . . the Volga River to Archangel." In fact, the true final objective was to seize *oil,* ore, and mineral reserves of a vast land sufficient to fuel the next and greater of his planned serial wars. Hitler's culminating world war would come against the power he identified in the 1920s as the ultimate enemy of German ambition: the United States. Hitler revealed in his *Second Book,* which remained unpublished during his life because it revealed too much of his strategic thinking, that America was the ultimate enemy. But war across the Atlantic was only a distant dream in 1941, an ambition for which Hitler did not have the means. More openly, immediately, and concretely, he planned to conquer the great Slav lands to fulfill the project for racial *Lebensraum* outlined in his autobiographical diatribe *Mein Kampf* (1924). He thus ordered active operational planning while the Luftwaffe was still fighting the *Battle of Britain* in mid-1940. After all, Hitler thought he had already won the hardest of all his planned wars: his invasion of France and the Low Countries succeeded beyond even his expectations, wrecking the French Army and driving the British Army from the continent in just seven weeks. Hitler expected the coming war against the Red Army to be easier still and to end almost as quickly as the battle for France. He crowed about the coming "war of annihilation" in the east. At the height of his power, he exclaimed on the eve of the invasion: "The world will hold its breath!"

Planning and Intelligence

Hitler exercised an unusual degree of control over the timing, operational conduct, and overall planning of the invasion. A few of his generals were appalled that the Wehrmacht was poised to invade a nation that had defied earlier armies, chewed them to bits, then counterinvaded its tormentors. But most were just as enthusiastic as Hitler and eagerly helped plan a war of ruthless aggression. Some were spurred by shared race hate, others by older ideologies and nationalism. Nearly all had delusions about the nature and fighting power of the enemy and themselves. Some conceits about the Soviet Union were understandable, as they arose from observable diplomatic and military blunders made by Joseph Stalin. The Soviet dictator had helped Germany destroy Poland during *FALL WEISS* in 1939. The OKW next watched a poor Red Army effort in the *Finnish–Soviet War (1939–1940).* Stalin lent critical aid to the Kriegsmarine in the conquest of Norway in April 1940 (*WESERÜBUNG*). Most importantly, the Red Army stood aside while the Wehrmacht destroyed the main armies of the Western Allies in *FALL GELB* in May–June 1940. Stalin had taken advantage of the German attack in the West to shift the Soviet frontier some 200 miles westward into the annexed Baltic States, while also stripping two provinces from Rumania. However, rather than increase German operational difficulties, that shift moved the Red Army to an ill-prepared frontier much closer to Germany, exposed it to attack in poorly prepared defense zones, and gutted the *Stalin Line* of men and guns. Most of the new Soviet positions were still unfortified or poorly entrenched in June 1941, and all were entirely surrounded by fiercely anti-Soviet populations. Finally, Stalin actually forbade the Red Army to fortify or patrol the new frontier, which now abutted directly on German-controlled territory or that of Berlin's minor allies. Stalin was unchallenged master of the Kremlin and had been for over 15 years: he was singularly responsible for the Soviet Union's lack of preparedness for the German attack. Many would later die to keep secret their knowledge of Stalin's prewar incompetence and errors of judgment, which so profoundly worsened national defenses: those purged and murdered by the *NKVD* to seal their lips numbered in the thousands.

While Stalin blundered, Hitler ordered "Aufbau Ost" ("Build-up East"), the transfer of German armies from the Western Front, which began when 18th Army moved east in July 1940. He briefed 250 Wehrmacht generals on March 30, 1941, lecturing them on the war of extermination he demanded they carry out. They sat in silent agreement as Hitler told them of plans for mass starvation of millions of civilians and Red Army conscripts, and of planned mass murder of Jews. Nor did the generals object when Hitler told them to murder all captured Communists. Some would later reissue the order with eager endorsement. Few field marshals or generals had even private qualms about openly illegal orders. It is important to appreciate that fact to understand that barbarism was built into the Wehrmacht from the planning stage of BARBAROSSA, and not just into *Einsatzgruppen* or the *Waffen-SS*. Why? Because some German and Austrian historians argued in a bitter "*Historikerstreit*" in the 1980s that Hitler's invasion was justified as a "preemptive strike," made necessary because Stalin was planning to attack Germany. Other historians demonstrated conclusively the falsity of that argument. In truth, Stalin was almost willfully blind to the German threat until the last days and hours. There is no evidence that he was planning an offensive war. Instead, he dismissed multiple warnings that Hitler was planning to attack, including from Winston Churchill and Franklin Roosevelt. *Vladimir Dekanozov*, Soviet ambassador in Berlin, reinforced a determination not to fall victim to foreign intelligence reports, which Stalin angrily dismissed as a "British provocation" ("Angliyskaya provokatisya"). As to Soviet warnings, these might be the product of counterrevolution in the ranks of the Red Army. Red Army planners were thinking about a potential preemptive strike some day, but the contingency plans they drew up as late as May 1941 were meant to deal with the mounting evidence of an impending German assault. The Red Army did not have offensive operational plans ready. It was instead untangling new dispositions and newly formed divisions, and busy mobilizing and equipping partly or even wholly untrained conscripts. It thus lacked any capability to carry out the *deep battle* strike into Germany, which revisionists accused it of planning. Moreover, Stalin was still pursuing a policy of strategic *appeasement* of Hitler until just hours before the German attack.

It is likely that Stalin seriously overestimated the real combat strength of the Red Army. What is known is that he refused to permit a full but hidden mobilization as some top generals requested. He even ordered deliberately weak defensive positioning of border troops and denied requests to intercept Luftwaffe reconnaissance flights to avoid "provoking" Hitler. Explicit orders to the Red Army to stay out of border defense zones was a problem compounded by Soviet doctrine, which was essentially offensive in an effort to fight any war outside Soviet national territory. That led to bunching of too many armies and Fronts too close to the border, rather than deployment in a defense-in-depth. In the first hours and days of battle, Soviet offensive prejudice fatally exposed millions of troops to planned Wehrmacht envelopments and forced others into premature counteroffensives that led to mass slaughter and surrender. Detailed cautions about forward Wehrmacht deployment that arrived from Soviet intelligence and border troops were ignored or angrily denied: over 80 distinct warnings about enemy preparations and intentions were sent to Stalin in the eight months before the attack. The dictator's top military advisers, Marshals *Georgi Zhukov* and *Semyon Timoshenko,* wanted full mobilization. Stalin delayed and demurred, still relying on his bad prior judgment as encoded in the *Nazi–Soviet Pact (August 23, 1939).* His tsar-like view of Russia's geopolitical situation and crude Marxist ideology convinced him that, unaided by other Western and capitalist powers, Germany would never attack. Hence, he refused to allow even basic preparedness as too provocative. Only in the failing light of June 21, the literal eve of the invasion and with *Brandenburger* infiltrators and other saboteurs already across the Soviet border, did the full meaning of accumulated warnings crash down upon him. Stalin at last accepted the compilation of intelligence arriving from Allied leaders, Soviet agents in Germany and Switzerland, and Red Army commanders on the frontier: Hitler was going to attack within the next few hours.

The operational plan for BARBAROSSA was first drafted in 1940 by the OKW. The final version assumed that the Wehrmacht would win decisive battles of encirclement that would quickly win the war in the east. The immediate aim of BARBAROSSA was total destruction of all Soviet armies bunched along the frontier. Führer Directive No. 21 proclaimed as the final operational goal: "to crush Soviet Russia in a rapid campaign." The plan called for a broad-front attack along three axes of advance. German planners thought the assault would fail if the main Soviet armies were not quickly trapped and annihilated on the western side of the Dvina and Dnieper rivers. They proposed multiple envelopments in a vast *Blitzkrieg,* utilizing massed artillery and Panzer and motorized spearheads with close air support under conditions of total political and strategic surprise. The idea of a *Vernichtungsschlacht* ("battle of annihilation") was rooted in a long tradition of strategic thinking by the General Staff. Hitler's generals stretched the idea, as had the Kaiser's men in 1914, into belief in a string of decisive battles, a campaign or *Vernichtungskrieg* ("war of annihilation") to drive in the Soviet flanks and penetrate deep into rear areas, wiping out the main force of the Red Army. What they did not know was that even if they accomplished all that in the frontier zones, massive reserves existed farther east. Hitler and his generals were so confident of quick victory they made little provision for delay and none at all for the possibility of defeat. So deep was Nazi race contempt and Wehrmacht professional hubris that all warnings were ignored that came from the OKH top logistics officer, General Eduard Wagner. He dutifully reported that the supply system could only support a maximum penetration of 500 km, and even then logistical pauses would be required.

Hitler and the OKW disregarded Wagner's warning: their invasion plan called for an initial penetration of at least 800 km. Never again would Hitler command such a concentrated force: 3,050,000 highly confident German troops massed along the border, waiting jump-off orders. They comprised 121 Wehrmacht divisions, supported by a handful of Waffen-SS divisions. But this invasion force was supported by a small reserve of just 14 Heer divisions, along with several hundred thousand Luftwaffe and Kriegsmarine personnel not yet trained or ready for ground action. Alongside the three million Germans were smaller armies from Rumania poised to retake *Bukovina* and *Bessarabia,* and some Italian and Slovakian units. Hungarians would join the assault after a few days: the delay was strictly operational, not political. The *Blue Division* from Spain and minor contingents from Axis puppet states across German-occupied Europe were not present at the launch of the invasion, but joined the campaign later. The best of the minor Axis forces was a superb 16 division Finnish Army determined to retake Karelia in what Finns would call the "Continuation War." Otherwise, Helsinki did not share Berlin's ambition to reach Moscow and Leningrad. The total invading force numbered over four million men. At least, those are the German figures. Soviet sources and historians assert that the Red Army faced a total of five million Axis troops. In either case, a mighty force was poised along a jump-off line stretching from northern Finland to the Black Sea. A northern advance would head through the Baltic states toward Leningrad. The heaviest attack was set to slice through Belorussia along the traditional invasion route through Smolensk to Moscow, while a third Axis army group battered into Ukraine toward Kiev. The bulk of the Red Army was positioned in Ukraine in accordance with Soviet doctrine, which proposed to immediately counterattack in the south at the outset of any war, while holding defensively in the denser terrain and more heavily fortified northern regions.

The German attack began at dawn on the summer solstice, Sunday, June 22, 1941, truly the "longest day" of the war. The Red Army was caught wholly unprepared, materially and psychologically. It was only during the evening of June 21, 1941—when German preparations and offensive intentions could no longer be concealed even from the willfully blind—that Stalin agreed to send a dispatch to frontline Red Army units warning of an impending attack. Even then, the thrust of his warning was not to "provoke" the Germans. Soviet communications were so poor that most frontline headquarters never received the cable, or they received it while being physically overrun. A Soviet train loaded with bulk raw material rolled across the frontier into German hands during the short night, just before an all-out attack began. Soviet mobilization, training, reorganization, planning, and deployments were all incomplete. Nearly 50 percent of Soviet troops were raw recruits called up only in April or May. They had not completed basic training and were mainly engaged as raw labor preparing weak fixed defenses along the expanded frontier of 1940. Hardly any were prepared for the stunning war of movement that was about to overwhelm them, what German doctrine called *Bewegungskrieg* and Westerners called *Blitzkrieg*. Worse, the Red Army was not positioned either to defend or preempt. That left its forward units strategically confused and destined to be overwhelmed by the attack. Here and there individual frontier commanders risked their lives by ignoring Stalin's orders not to mobilize for defense. Other factors swept aside their preparations, too, as the Axis horde moved. Paralysis afflicted the top command in Moscow during the first hours.

There was also a great flaw in Hitler's plans: the invader did not enjoy a militarily traditional or confident numerical advantage over the Red Army. In the frontier Military Districts the Soviets had 36 tank divisions, 18 motorized divisions, and 95 rifle divisions. That was a formidable force, even though Stalin refused permission to properly man forward security zones and set the *NKVD* to enforce that order. Including the defensive depth of second echelon troops, the Red Army had 186 divisions in the western regions, not the 147 divisions the Abwehr estimated. The attacking Wehrmacht and its Axis partners therefore had only slightly more troops to commit to operations in the western Soviet Union than did the enemy. Moreover, the Abwehr grossly underestimated the total Soviet order of battle: it had no idea about the existence or location of entire Fronts. Abwehr and OKW estimates of total enemy strength was placed at 222 divisions, plus 50 independent brigades. That missed 81 divisions already on the Red Army order of battle, albeit with some filled by raw recruits who were still being armed and trained; and it did not count Soviet ability to form still more *rifle divisions* and tank brigades during the campaign. As BARBAROSSA unfolded, Hitler and his generals believed they faced a force one-third less in size than the armies that actually opposed them. They would be repeatedly astonished at Soviet ability to hurl still more men and tanks into combat, long past the point German planners thought Soviet reserves were exhausted and the war should be already won.

The main German infantry weapons were tripod-mounted machine guns ("Maschinengewehr"), notably the MG-34 and MG-42. Most German infantry carried "Gewehrs" (rifles) or "Karainers" (carbines), many of World War I vintage. Most were not yet armed with the automatic weapons and powerful anti-tank infantry weapons that would dominate the last years of killing in this war. Nor did invading Axis armies enjoy a qualitative superiority in big guns or armor. German tanks were lightly gunned and underarmored compared to the Soviet T-34, let alone the heavy KV-1, both types unknown to the Abwehr before they were encountered in battle. Most German tanks were PzKpfw Mark IIs and IIIs, along with comparable prewar Czech types. Mark II Panzers were just nine tons, or barely one-third the battle weight of the revolutionary sloped-armor Soviet T-34. They had a much smaller main gun and light armor, and inferior and thinner flat armor. They were a match for the plentiful Soviet T-26 light tank, but could not stand against the new mediums and heavies. Even the more recent model Mark III Panzer gave up nine tons to an opposing T-34. It weighed less than half the armored mass of a KV-1. The latter's appearance on the battlefield shocked German troops, who were ill-armed to defend against it and psychologically unprepared to face so powerful a steel behemoth. They would have been still more shocked had they known that instead of the 10,000 tanks OKW staff planners suspected were available to the Red Army, over 23,000 tanks were in fact deployed at the front or in reserve tank parks across the Soviet Union. Only Mark IV Panzers were a direct match for the best Red Army tanks, and even they were outgunned and armored by the KV-1. The one area of real German advantage was above the planned ground assault, where the *Luftwaffe* could put into the air about 2,000 frontline combat aircraft. The *Red Army Air Force (VVS)* was many times larger than that numerically, but its aircraft were a design-generation older and slower. VVS aircraft were thus highly vulnerable. Most Soviet pilots had no combat experience in mid-1941, while many German pilots had flown numerous combat missions in several different theaters of war. Each air force was badly organized and poorly managed, but the Luftwaffe benefited from its initial technical advantages as well as complete operational surprise.

The Wehrmacht was organized into seven armies for the invasion: four *Panzergruppen* and three *Luftflotten*. Heer ground forces were supported by 600,000 motorized vehicles of all types, including 7,200 mostly towed artillery and anti-tank tubes, 3,350 Panzers of all types, and several hundred *self-propelled guns.* Transport of lead infantry units, or *Panzergrenadiers,* comprised thousands of trucks and half-tracks. Many of the trucks were commandeered from the extinct Polish and Czech Armies, or from the reduced French Army, but some were abandoned British vehicles from *Dunkirk,* while others were commercial rather than military in design and strength. Even with so many vehicles, the "Ostheer" ("eastern army") was far from a motorized force, let alone a mechanized one. Two years into the war the Wehrmacht had not yet tasted defeat or mass destruction of its men and equipment. It was at the height of its wartime strength and moral and military arrogance. Yet, the Ostheer that moved into the western Soviet Union was essentially dependent on draft animals for the overwhelming majority of its logistical supply. To the rear of the Panzers fully 90 percent of German military transport was horse-drawn. All infantry and most artillery was reliant on 750,000 draft horses to haul guns, field kitchens, ammunition, and supply wagons and to cart back the wounded in horse-pulled field ambulances. Other than the elite motorized and mechanized Panzergrenadier regiments that traveled ahead with the Panzers, all German infantry who set out to reach Kiev, Smolensk, Minsk, Leningrad, or Moscow walked the entire way. Behind the armored spearheads the main Ostheer formations moved into northern, western, and southern Russia at the same walking pace as French soldiers of Napoleon's "Grand Armée" heading for Borodino in 1812, or forlorn Swedish troops led to disaster at Poltava in Ukraine by Charles XII a hundred years earlier. Most Germans and other Axis troops entering Russia in 1941 never saw their homes again, like French and Swedish troops before them. But that is the view from 1945. The facts of German offensive imbalance in 1941 make it even more operationally remarkable that during the first three months of the campaign the Wehrmacht severely mauled and very nearly mortally wounded the Red Army, which was a superior armed force by nearly all measures except actual combat effectiveness.

The Assault

The Wehrmacht began its invasion build-up in mid-February 1941. Three massive assault waves were in place in concealed forward bases by the middle of May. The main spearhead troops, comprising 12 Panzer divisions and 12 divisions of motorized or mechanized Panzergrenadiers, moved into attack positions starting on June 3. Ethnic Ukrainians and anti-Soviet Russian exiles working with the Germans infiltrated some border areas as much as several weeks prior to the assault, reporting by radio Red Army troop movements and the locations of airfields, tank parks, and ammunition dumps. Short-range Luftwaffe attack planes moved to concealed forward airfields on June 21. German commandos went into action in Soviet rear areas during the night of June 21–22, cutting telegraph and telephone lines. Axis artillerymen moved to their guns, which had been forward deployed and camouflaged well prior to last-minute transport of their crews. A few conscripted Communists loyal to the Soviet cause rather than to Nazi Germany deserted to Red Army lines to deliver fresh warnings of impending attack, but these were all ignored. At 3:15 A.M. local time, Soviet bridge guards at Koden on the Bug River were the first to fall. The massive main assault began with heavy opening bombardments at the three selected *Schwerpunkt* starting at 3:30 A.M., with more diversionary barrages all along the frontier. First word of the attack arrived in Moscow in the form of a desperate signal from the commander of the Black Sea Fleet, who reported a devastating Luftwaffe raid was taking place against the naval base at Sevastopol. The report was disbelieved by Stalin until confirmed by direct telephone contact between Sevastopol and the Kremlin. Two hours later Ambassador *Count von der Schulenburg* delivered Germany's declaration of war to Soviet Foreign Minister *Vyacheslav Molotov*.

Luftwaffe bombers located the Black Sea Fleet at anchor in Sevastopol by the oscillating light of the city's powerful harbor lighthouse. Neither the harbor nor the city were blacked-out. Attack aircraft from other *Fliegerkorps* bombed Bialystok, Brest-Litovsk, Grodno, Kiev, Kovno, Rovno, Riga, and Tallinn without meeting any effective air or ground defense response. Two thousand outmoded VVS aircraft were destroyed in the first three days of battle, hundreds while parked in neat rows or great circles during the opening hours of the fight after dawn on June 22. Thousands more aircraft were shot from the sky by better trained and more experienced Luftwaffe pilots flying more modern planes. Some Soviet pilots crashed their slow and ill-armed monoplanes into faster and more powerful enemy aircraft, using suicide tactics to make up for the inadequacy of their planes. Such acts were not ordered, but on the first day they set a tone for the savagery to come in the east, for *total war* waged without pity on the ground or in the air, in the villages and countryside, and within hundreds of towns and cities. Thousands more VVS aircraft were abandoned on overrun airfields in ground panic over the first weeks.

The most reliable calculations place the number of lost VVS planes at just under 4,000 within the first 15 days, compared to Luftwaffe losses of 550 aircraft. Initial Luftwaffe success was unparalleled in the history of air operations. It gave German pilots total domination above the battlefield for the first six months of the war. Air supremacy in turn permitted Luftwaffe commanders to switch to critical ground support and interdiction roles, ripping apart exposed Soviet columns, strafing and bombing pockets of surrounded Soviet divisions and whole armies. For most of the rest of the BARBAROSSA campaign the Luftwaffe thus concentrated on attacking tactical targets ahead of advancing ground forces of the Ostheer, and on interdicting Red Army fuel and ammunition supplies, troop trains, and columns on the march.

The Wehrmacht attacked with three massive army groups along three main axes of advance. Army Group North (Heeresgruppe Nord) was commanded by Field Marshal *Wilhelm von Leeb*. Field Marshal *Fedor von Bock* commanded Army Group Center (Heeresgruppe Mitte). Bock would fall ill during the Soviet counteroffensive in December and be replaced on the 19th of that month by *Günther von Kluge*. Field Marshal *Gerd von Rundstedt* headed Army Group South (Heeresgruppe Süd). Army Group North thrust rapidly into the Baltic States with 26 divisions, including 3 Panzer and 3 motorized infantry divisions. Opposing the Germans in the north were 25 Red Army divisions of the Baltic Military District, including 4 tank divisions and 2 motorized divisions. Army Group North's trajectory was toward Leningrad, which Hitler intended to flatten and erase from historical memory. But capture of the city was not the main purpose of the operation. All three Army Groups were instructed to encircle and destroy the Red Army in vast *Kesselschlacht* ("cauldron battles"), after achieving multiple envelopments and double envelopments along the frontier. The champing Generalfeldmarschälle were under strict orders not to compete to take the great cities of western Russia. Yet, the golden spires of Kiev, Moscow, and Leningrad called out from history, beckoning vainglorious commanders to vie for their capture. Hitler and the OKW would also succumb to the temptation over time.

Army Group Center was the largest German formation at 50 divisions. It also had the heaviest concentration of armor: 9 Panzer divisions and 3 more of Panzergrenadiers. It was opposed by the Western Military District's 44 divisions, including 12 tank or motorized divisions. Army Group Center's distant destination was Moscow, which Hitler also slated for ultimate destruction. But once again, the primary operational goal was first to destroy all Soviet armies in the western part of the country. Army Group South attacked into Ukraine with 41 divisions, including 5 Panzer and 3 Panzergrenadier divisions. It faced the heaviest Red Army opposition because Stalin incorrectly judged that Hitler would attack with his main force into Ukraine and thus concentrated the bulk of Soviet strength there. The attack in the south was two-pronged, as dictated by the shape of the frontier and terrain factors. The greater part of Army Group South started out from southern Poland, advancing against 60 divisions of Kiev Military District, which included 16 tank and 8 motorized infantry divisions. Odessa Military District opposed the second thrust by the smaller portion of Army Group South. It launched from eastern

Rumania. Soviet forces defending Odessa comprised 22 divisions, but they were deployed close up against the frontier. The forward deployment included 4 Soviet tank divisions and 2 motorized infantry divisions that would have served far better if retained as a mobile reserve.

Following a week of unrelentingly horrendous news and left naked and exposed by his prewar misreading of Hitler's intentions, Stalin suffered some kind of collapse on June 29. As he retreated into despair and fearful seclusion at his dacha outside Moscow, he veered between panicky contemplation of surrender of the western Soviet Union and ferocious determination and defiance. He finally decided on the latter: for even as the Red Army fell back, broken and stunned, some units bloodied the Panzer spearheads and follow-on troops. Signaling the shift at the top, Stalin set up the *GKO* to help him conduct the war. He took personal command as head of the *Stavka* on July 10. What happened? As the initial shock of the onslaught passed, some Red Army men ("*krasnoarmeets*") rallied and fought hard even when hopelessly surrounded, and while legions of comrades surrendered. Fighters were ruthlessly slaughtered by the Germans, but their sacrifice entangled and bled the Cerberus of the Wehrmacht as its three grey heads snarled and bit into the vitals of the Soviet Union. That is one reason why Stalin swung to defiance even while broken remnants of his armies were in shattered retreat across hundreds of miles of territory. His top military advisers also recovered nerve in part because lower-level officers and ordinary krasnoarmeets clawed at, wounded, and slowed the advance of the mighty Ostheer as it passed over and through their positions. The other was realization that no territorial settlement in the image of the Treaty of Brest-Litovsk, which saved the Bolsheviks in power in 1918, was possible in 1941: Hitler would not be satisfied by anything short of total victory. Against that threat, there could only be a total war defense.

Army Group North launched directly out of East Prussia into the once and future Baltic states. Most troops of the defending Baltic Military District, commanded by General Fedor Kuznetov, were positioned right against the Prussian border. Support lines and echelons lay farther back of the frontier crust, garrisoned on populations deeply hostile to the recent Soviet annexation and ruthless work of the NKVD carried out over the preceding year. More honorary than real, the overall Soviet commander was Stalin's *Konarmiia* crony Marshal *Kliment Voroshilov*. He also had nominal responsibility for Northern Front. That formation was positioned to defend Leningrad, but its defense zone stretched as far north as Murmansk. It faced Germans in the Arctic, but a restless and determined Finnish Army in Karelia. Leeb sent his Panzers and motorized infantry speeding ahead in a sharp single thrust. Ably led by General *Erich von Manstein*, the Panzers seized a bridgehead over the Dvina River on June 26. A large Soviet tank force saw a flank opportunity and counterattacked, but without sufficient speed to stop Manstein breeching a second fixed defensive line. Suddenly exposed Soviet tank columns were chewed by the Luftwaffe and pounded by Leeb's artillery. Operating on a narrow front in dense terrain, Army Group North was unable to encircle and destroy all Soviet frontier forces. However, Leeb's single thrust was so powerful it broke through a third fixed Red Army line along the Velikaia River, crossing in force on July 9. Soviet forces in the Baltic, now renamed Northwestern Front, were split in two by the crossing. Each half fell back pell-mell along Leeb's expanding flanks. Kuznetov was sacked on July 4, after just two weeks of fighting. Stalin and the Stavka sent General *Nikolai Vatutin* to oversee the failing defense, to little avail. Soviet forces in the northwest quickly lost a total of 75,000 men, 4,000 guns, 2,500 tanks, and over 1,000 aircraft. Army Group North would destroy still more Soviet armies before being halted before Leningrad in November.

Army Group Center conducted a spectacular double encirclement of Western Military District forces. They caught the first contingent inside an exposed salient at Bialystok (Belostok), and the rest around Minsk. Punching through the frontier crustal defense in two places, Grodno and Brest, Bock's Panzers raced ahead 200 miles to close a steel circle behind Minsk. German leg infantry closed the inner circle around three Soviet armies at Bialystok. These operations together trapped more than 30 Soviet divisions in a deep pocket, or "Kessel" ("cauldron") as the Germans called it. Army Group Center proceeded to cook hundreds of thousands of Russians inside the Kessel with massed air and artillery pounding and steady infantry and armored compression of the perimeter. The 22 Soviet rifle divisions trapped at Minsk were crushed, and the survivors surrendered. Two huge sections of the Soviet frontier gaped open by July 8, with most of the men, tanks, and guns prepositioned there destroyed or captured. Red Army losses on the central front included nearly 5,000 tanks, 9,500 guns, and at least 340,000 men. The great majority of casualties were prisoners of war. Nearly all would be malignantly neglected to death by the Wehrmacht in the months that followed. Nor was it safe for those who refused to surrender. General Dimitri G. Pavlov and most of the senior staff of the Western Military District were arrested and executed by the NKVD. The real culprit of the great collapse in the center was Stalin.

Not everything went the way of the Wehrmacht in the weeks that followed. The hard crust of frontier static defenses was broken in the north and center, but Army Group South ran into the largest number of defenders and had a harder time against tough resistance in Ukraine. Soviet frontier forces fought back into August before succumbing. Overall, the Panzers raced across the southern steppe and the lightly forested belts of central Russia. They moved more slowly but still steadily into the deeply forested and swampy regions of the northwest. Millions of infantry and support troops followed their tracks, fanning out to burn and kill. Massive tank battles were fought in which hundreds of Mark II, III, and IV Panzers fought thousands of T-26s, supplemented by hundreds of T-34s and KV-1s. Savage, swirling armored fights chewed up hundreds of square miles of hot and dusty steppe. Others took place in open spaces between great swatches of burning forest. In a four-day tank fight near Lepel' from July 6–9, the Soviets lost over 800 armored vehicles, mostly to air and armor attacks. Hundreds of bombers and fighters clashed overhead or dived to strafe and bomb long columns of panicking Soviet conscripts, some abandoned by officers who fled in stolen divisional vehicles. Local counterattacks were mounted but were beaten back by weight of German metal: by massed artillery and nearly unopposed air power. However, whereas Polish and French armies ceased fighting when casualties became pointless in face of deep penetrations by the Panzers, some Red Army divisions and armies fought far past hope, to the death.

Army Group Center reached the "Smolensk Gate" in mid-July, entering the great land gap between bends of the Dvina and Dniepr rivers. More war without pity took place from July 10, in another huge Kesselschlacht best remembered as the *Battle of Smolensk*. Dispute continues among historians as to whether that protracted fight was a turning point leading to the ultimate failure of BARBAROSSA. Several Soviet commanders later argued that German victory after two months of heavy fighting at Smolensk was pyrrhic, that the fight so badly attrited the Panzer spearheads and eroded Wehrmacht combat power that the enemy were unable to conduct further deep encirclement operations. Several German generals later contended that the key moment in the campaign, and even in the entire war, was Hitler's decision to weaken Army Group Center by shifting the weight of Panzer forces south into Ukraine, with some Panzers also sent to reinforce Army Group North. Although that thesis found support among some military historians, it is not universally accepted. After the fall of Smolensk, but with the larger battle on the central front still underway around that smoking city, Hitler did indeed reinforce the flanks of the invasion. He was intent on crushing what he thought were the last standing Soviet armies to the north and south, but he could only do that by drawing from the center. It was at that point that the paucity of German operational and strategic reserves became manifest, along with the critical importance of hidden Soviet strength. Self-exculpating memoirs by German generals argued after the war that Hitler so weakened the offensive power of Army Group Center that he doomed the whole BARBAROSSA invasion to failure. That point is moot. Indisputable is that he left a largely infantry force much reduced in striking power to slog more slowly toward Moscow, which the Wehrmacht never reached. A more fundamental explanation of the German failure lies in fatal logistical, reserve, and other operational flaws contained in the original OKW plan and the conceit of any quick conquest of Russia.

In two "Führer orders" issued on July 19 and 23, the Panzer shift was ordered. Hitler diverted General *Hermann Hoth's* Panzergruppe northward to press home the flagging attack around Leningrad, and sent General *Heinz Guderian's* Panzergruppe southward to reinforce Rundstedt's encirclement of Kiev. On July 30, over the nearly unanimous objection of his senior generals, Hitler ordered Bock to assume a defensive posture with Army Group Center while offensive operations were underway in Ukraine. Persuaded of his own strategic vision and genius, Hitler aimed primarily at capture of food and other resources in Ukraine and beyond. He now saw these as more vital than defeat of the main forces of the Red Army, an accomplishment he and many generals assumed was already well in hand in any case. Hitler was thus lured deep into the *First Battle of Ukraine (June–September, 1941)* by opportunities for Panzer maneuvers on the steppe, and hence for more dramatic and slashing attacks than were possible in the thick forest and lake country in front of Moscow. As for reinforcing the Leningrad assault, Hitler thought that city was within Leeb's easy reach. He wanted to destroy it as a manufacturing center of tanks and other vital Soviet war matériel and end its service as a Baltic naval base for the Soviet Navy. The attack in the north flagged and failed despite reinforcement, descending into a three-year siege. But in the south Hitler seemed vindicated: Army Group South launched a fresh assault from the Belorussian *balcony* overhanging Ukraine, capturing 665,000 prisoners in two great encirclement fights at Uman and Kiev. That was the largest German success, and the worst Soviet disaster, of the entire war. That unparalleled operational achievement convinced Hitler that his vision and military talents were far superior to even his best generals. However, his critics were not wholly wrong: diversions of Panzer strength from Army Group Center greatly undermined the central thrust toward Moscow, which was not only the political capital of the Soviet Union but also a major communications hub and center of a key mining, industrial, and war-manufactures region. Whether taking Moscow would have won the war for Hitler any more than it did for Napoleon is a different question: as the Germans approached, the Soviets were already preparing a deeper defensive line along the Volga.

The speed of slashing Wehrmacht advances exacerbated deep systemic failures in Red Army communications, command, and control. The initial assault had been overwhelming and devastating. German armor punched through the brittle crust of the Military Districts in their too forward positions, then plunged deep into western Russia at speeds the Stavka never contemplated, let alone prepared to defend. The ragged holes gaped open on the Soviet frontier. The rest of the initial defense line crumbled as German flanks rapidly expanded and frontier envelopments were completed. Wehrmacht army groups destroyed entire Soviet armies and Fronts during the deep penetration phase that followed, capturing hundreds of thousands of pathetic and bewildered prisoners. The onslaught and damage was breathtaking: the Red Army lost six tanks to every Panzer it knocked out of action, with over half of Soviet losses arising from mechanical breakdown or abandonment during retreats rather than enemy action. German tank recovery and repair was superior: German advances carried positions where crews were earlier forced to abandon damaged tanks. With air cover nearly gone, Soviet artillery proved highly vulnerable. It also repeatedly failed to support exposed infantry facing German armored assaults. And that led to tank panic ("tankoboiazn") among hordes of green conscripts who lacked weapons or training to face or stop Panzers. Matters were not helped by failure of Soviet field communications as telephone and telegraph wires were cut. That exposed a systemic failure to acquire radios, a deficiency that would not be met until the first *Lend-Lease* shipments of field radios arrived from the United States in late 1942. Commanders were forced to rely on land lines, reflecting prewar expectation that the Red Army would not have to fight on Soviet soil and that existing lines would never be overrun or disrupted. The German field intelligence intercepted many panicky, poorly coded, or even uncoded Soviet signals.

For all the spectacular battlefield successes won by German arms that summer, the Red Army was not destroyed, although nearly all Soviet forces prepositioned along the frontier were. That fact vitiated the essential premise, and exposed the grave central fallacy, of BARBAROSSA. The Red Army survived and denied victory to the Wehrmacht by conducting a fighting retreat on the northern and southern flanks following collapse of the center of the front in mid-July. Much reduced and badly chastened, its men and its leaders built new defensive lines much deeper inside Russia: at Smolensk, then in front of Leningrad and Moscow, and finally along the great river barriers of the south and even along the Volga. The fight would go on. Reserves unknown to the Germans poured out of the eastern and central Soviet Union to meet the tiring Wehrmacht in the west. Nor was the Red Army always driven backwards even during the catastrophic phase of BAR-BAROSSA. It launched repeated counterattacks. Less advisedly, it assayed premature counteroffensives on Stalin's urging and orders. A major effort was assayed along the Dnieper in July, another around smoldering Smolensk in July–August, and a third by Briansk Front over the first two weeks of September. These first counterattacks were beaten off by the Wehrmacht and did most damage to freshly arriving Soviet armies thrown piecemeal and recklessly into ongoing fights. All those operations were likely undertaken from a lingering prewar offensive-mindedness on the part of the Stavka, but mainly because Stalin pushed hard for them. They proved to be beyond the Red Army's flagging abilities, as the top men of the Stavka soon realized but Stalin still did not. By late summer and the early fall, however, ordinary Russians and the Stavka were learning how to fight back against the German Blitzkrieg, already stretched beyond the end of its logistical tether. Counterblows wore down German soldiers and equipment, attrited supplies, and eroded combat power. The real question is not whether such brutal summer fights attrited German forces, because they certainly did. It is whether attrition of the Red Army, which they also caused, was so great that premature offensives opened fresh opportunities for leaping advances by the Wehrmacht in September and October.

Resistance Stiffens

The Panzers advanced again in a second wave in late summer. Germans called this the "smooth period" of the invasion, as Panzers and Panzergrenadiers rolled unopposed for hundreds of miles over the southern steppe, though less swiftly or far in northern forest and lake regions. The Germans burned thousands of villages and hundreds of towns; the Soviets burned the rest. SS death squads fanned out in the expanding Wehrmacht wake: mass murderers in *Einsatzgruppen* who systematically killed Jews, *politruks,* and *commissars.* But there were not enough Panzers and too few mechanized or motorized infantry in the spearheads to seal off all exits in western Russia's vast spaces. Some Red Army units escaped the cauldrons, even as hundreds of thousands were cooked alive inside them. Resistance forced the Panzers to halt, surround, and pound into oblivion large pockets of trapped enemy who resisted more toughly each passing day. Huge numbers of krasnoarmeets were slaughtered. Yet, Germans also died in these merciless fights. Besides, the new pockets were porous, so that the great Kessel leaked Russians. They also moved, flowing amoeba-like over the steppe as desperate men pushed against a perimeter here, then over there. T-34s smashed through German infantry at night, steel treads crushing men and horses as the tanks blew a narrow path out of some Kessel and sped away across the plain, living to fight one more day or week. Pockets of cutoff Soviet units survived all the way back to the border, at least for awhile. Those isolated pockets also had to be squeezed into surrender or annihilated, to secure the Ostheer's rear area. That hard process pulled more men and guns back from the cutting edge of the armored spearheads. And still in front of the Germans was an entire second echelon of Red Army troops, the same reserve divisions, armies, and Fronts whose existence the Abwehr entirely missed during the planning stage. Most of the Soviet frontier divisions were gone, but new armies were already forming for the defense of central Russia. The Wehrmacht swept into Kiev over the southern steppe and even entered the Crimea, but it bogged down farther north as German forces thinned while Soviet defenses thickened in front of Leningrad and Moscow.

Everywhere in front of the Panzers resistance became more stubborn and effective as the Stavka adapted and reserves were called up. Late in the Wehrmacht's "August pause," the Red Army conducted its first successful counterattack when Zhukov beat back a thrust by Guderian's Panzers in the sharply contested *Yelnia operation*. German tanks were wearing out tracks, running beyond fuel and ammunition supplies, and losing offensive momentum. Daily casualty rates among the infantry reached murder levels equal to the worst battles for the German Army in World War I: attrition was still attrition, whether it took place in a trench, atop the steppe, or inside a burning forest. As the campaign stretched into late summer it was clear that the farther the Wehrmacht penetrated the more its initial operational surprise and tactical superiority were exhausted, while the Red Army was learning how to fight by fighting. And not even the Germans could overcome the great tyrant of logistics. Russia was not Poland or France, after all. Panzers needed to halt for refitting; truck and half-track engines broke down; tank treads and tires wore out, as did gun tubes from too much firing; fuel and ammunition had to be hauled by horse power over a few bad roads that cut through western Russia. Why not use captured Soviet railways? As the Germans advanced they had to rebuild all Russian railways, even stretches captured intact that had not succumbed to Soviet scorched earth destruction: Soviet broad-gauge track would not accept German narrow-gauge rolling stock, and most Soviet rolling stock was burned or evacuated eastward before the Germans could seize it. Meanwhile, access to undamaged railways farther east gave the Red Army a significant logistics advantage. Lacking a *strategic bombing* force or doctrine, the Luftwaffe failed to destroy those railways deep behind the frontlines that ferried more and more Soviet troops to the frontlines from the far off Caucasus, Central Asia, or Siberia. To the average *Landser*, there always seemed to be more enemy soldiers arriving over the endless Russian horizon, always another river to cross, another town to assault, a new city or forest or deadly fight looming into sight.

"Friction," the inevitably of human frailty and error in action, was slowing the German advance. That should not have come as a surprise to a General Staff deeply schooled in the philosophy of war and professing to a man to admire the great Prussian military theorist Karl von Clausewitz. He had long ago identified "friction" ("Friktion") as the progressive accumulation of small difficulties and unforeseen circumstances that derange the best laid military plans, to confound the will of commanders in the conduct of battle. That hard Clausewitzian lesson was now taught to the Wehrmacht: the farther its lead Panzers penetrated the slower they moved as men and machines wore out. Panzergrenadiers converted to ordinary leg infantry as trucks and half-tracks broke down, forcing the tanks to wait for foot soldiers to catch up. Aircraft engines also wore out, or Luftwaffe pilots did from the stress of aerial combat. Forward airfields had to be built from scratch, including hangers, mechanic huts, and perimeter defenses; then they were moved again as aircraft cover ranges were exceeded. All basic supplies of food, fuel, and ammunition for the Ostheer and Luftwaffe ran low, limiting battle options and forcing men to forage locally. Exhausted troops at the end of hundreds of miles of marching and fighting resisted urging by officers and headquarters for fresh initiative, further advances. Too many old comrades were no longer sitting around the nightly campfire; too much death had been seen and killing done; home and family were too far away. Why are we here? The Wehrmacht was still winning almost all the local fights, but its general advance was slow and any movement was achieved at enormous cost. Already by July 21, after just one month of fighting, many lead Panzer divisions were down to 40 percent of paper strength. And the other side? Despite the greatest defeats and mass surrenders to that point in military history, despite one million Soviet dead and three million more lost to German captivity that summer, the Red Army fought on. The war had already moved beyond the leadership or state ideology of either side. It was a fight to the death between the Soviet and German peoples. It was mortal combat: a true, total war.

It was therefore a war without mercy in which civilians just got in the way. From the first hour of the assault the ferocity of fighting and scale and frequency of atrocity—by both sides, but especially by the Germans—set a brutal tone that would last throughout four years of Soviet–German war. When the Germans left Minsk barely 20 percent of its buildings stood, and just 40,000 souls remained from a prewar population of 250,000. Minsk's Jews were herded into ghettos, later to be transported to one or other of the new *death camps*. SS Einsatzgruppen went on "Jew hunts" in the countryside, looking for runaways and shooting any and all *partisans* or commissars they captured, or peasants or nonresisting Jews whom they accused of being *bandits solely* to justify shooting them. It is essential to understand that, before the first shot was fired, the German war plan anticipated mass starvation and millions of deaths among civilians. The partial solution to the OKW's logistics problem was to order four million troops to live off the land, whatever that did to the host population. Swarming over the countryside like so many locusts, Axis soldiers consumed all that they overran. Their explicit orders envisioned leaving almost no food or shelter for peasants, *prisoners of war,* or the poor souls confined to the *concentration camps* that sprouted like poisonous mushrooms over the ruin and rot the Wehrmacht left behind. More mass death was expected to follow in the new German race empire: extermination of most of the Slavic population by starvation was eagerly anticipated by Nazi ideologues and viewed with broad indifference by OKW planners and many Wehrmacht officers. Some 8 to 10 million tons of grain and other foodstuffs per year were ordered expropriated from the east and shipped back to the Reich. That rate of food rape was never actually achieved because too much German-occupied land was scorched, wasted, or saw production plummet as policies of unadulterated expropriation stripped peasants of any incentive to plant or harvest. What food was available would be mostly consumed by Axis armies of occupation during 1942 and after. The effects of the shortfall on local populations would be correspondingly catastrophic.

It was in the underlying murderous spirit of BARBAROSSA that Hitler's close toady on the OKW, General *Fritz Halder,* sent this cable to all German commanders on July 8, 1941: "It is Führer's firm decision to level Moscow and Leningrad and make them uninhabitable, so as to relieve us of the necessity of having to feed the populations through the winter. The cities will be razed by the Luftwaffe. Panzers must not be used for the purpose." Russia most certainly was not France: barbarization of Germany's war in the east, extermination to accompany conquest, was built-in from the outset. Out of four million Soviet soldiers taken captive in the first months of the war, 3.5 million were deliberately starved or allowed to freeze to death over the winter of 1941–1942. Five million Soviet POWs ultimately died of malice and neglect in German camps, victims not of the SS but of the Wehrmacht. As with policies of food expropriation, far fewer Russians surrendered once it was understood that captivity meant mistreatment and death. That further stiffened resistance to the invasion as ordinary men and women fought to the death, often in extraordinary circumstances. Retreating Soviet soldiers salted buildings—especially any potential HQ—with booby traps and time-delayed mines. Partisan bands formed to kill German shirkers and stragglers in the most savage ways, just as their forebears once killed freezing Frenchmen. German retaliation was swift and brutal: 100 hostages were shot for every German killed by partisans, the semiofficial rate used across Nazi-occupied Europe. Many more than that were killed in Belorussia and Ukraine. But if villagers failed to kill Germans—whom many peasants initially regarded as liberators from the hated collective farms and other policies of the city-based Bolsheviks—the NKVD found out later and shot them as accused fascists or collaborators, or just "pour encourager l'autres." The partisan war was waged without quarter from the start. Wehrmacht and SS sweeps into forests and swamps killed everyone they found, while partisans tortured and mutilated German boys, often stuffing cut-off genitals in the mouths of the dead or dying. From the start of BARBAROSSA then, tens of millions of ordinary people were trapped like barley between the great millstones of the most ruthless tyrannies known to history: National Socialism and Soviet Communism, the Wehrmacht and Red Army, the SS and NKVD, Hitler and Stalin.

Underlying German disregard for the long-term political and military effects of brutality on the local population was, to paraphrase Talleyrand, worse than a crime: it was a mistake. It led the Germans to miss a main chance to persuade non-Russian and anti-Soviet peoples into greater *collaboration*. The error arose ineluctably from the nature of the Nazi regime and from a core falsehood and assumption flowing from the idea of "Vernichtungskrieg," that the Germans did not need to tap local nationalism to help them win a big war against the Soviet Union. That was a fundamental miscalculation: it was always wishful thinking that any German war in the east would be quick and decisive, a "war of annihilation" in both

Wehrmacht operational and Nazi racial senses of that idea. The strategic plan pursued by Hitler and the OKW was fundamentally flawed at its core precisely because it was premised on quick victory over an enemy whose real military strength was a third again that determined by the Abwehr, and whose economic and reserve strengths were greater still. Moreover, no provision was made by Hitler or the Wehrmacht for protracted war should the anticipated Soviet military, political, and social collapse not take place as expected. The grand strategic strength that kept the Soviet Union fighting was temporarily disguised by spectacular German operational victories and mass Soviet surrenders in the summer and fall of 1941. Yet, ultimately insurmountable problems were already emerging for the Wehrmacht: strategic overextension, failures of logistics, and inexorable wearing logic of an industrial war of attrition against a more numerous yet equally determined foe, soon to be supported by other powerful Allies in the West.

The Long Road to Moscow

Army Group North neared Leningrad in September, approaching the city on three sides. Leeb was reinforced on his right flank by Hoth's Panzergruppe, stripped from Army Group Center by Hitler along with 400 attack aircraft sent north from 8th Fliegerkorps. Leeb's leading Panzers broke though a fourth Soviet defensive line along the Luga River in the middle of August. Leningrad's *opolchentsy* ("People's Militia") divisions were desperately thrown into the breech, without any real training and with few weapons. The tough veterans of the Wehrmacht slaughtered them; four full divisions of opolchentsy were wiped out for almost no gain after causing the enemy but little delay. Huge pine forests around the city were torched by defenders, creating fires so intense that for several days they blocked the German ground advance. As smoke rose high and thick the Luftwaffe could not fly, bomb, or strafe. The main rail line leading into Leningrad was cut on August 20 and the last rail link overrun 11 days later. The city came under direct German artillery fire on September 4. Four days after that Leeb's men cut the last land link. All that was left to supply a city engorged with refugees was a barge route across Lake Ladoga: the long nightmare of the *siege of Leningrad* had begun. The Stavka reorganized broken armies and rushed reserves to the area under two new commands: Leningrad Front and Karelian Front. Zhukov was hurried north to personally shore the defenses. It was probably more important that Hitler now shifted Panzer and Luftwaffe assets back to a resumed drive on Moscow. Disaster for the Red Army was again averted by the hubris, operational impulsiveness, and fickle error of the German Führer. Minor advances were made toward Leningrad so that the last rail link to Lake Ladoga was cut on November 8. That vital line was reopened by a Soviet counterattack on December 9, and Army Group North pushed back to Volkhov River by the end of the year. Each side dug in for a sustained winter trench battle. No one knew that Army Group North had gone as far toward the city as it would ever go. The next time the frontline around Leningrad saw real movement was January 1944. And then it would be the Red Army that advanced and the Germans who beat a panicky retreat.

The *Sumi-Kharkov operation* and *Donbass-Rostov operation* during October and November saw Army Group South advance through eastern Ukraine, then into the Crimea and the lower Don region. More Soviet divisions were destroyed or surrendered en masse; *Sebastopol* was pounded and besieged; Rostov fell to an advanced division of the Waffen-SS. But Rostov was too far forward to hold: the first real curb on German victory came when Rostov was retaken by Southern Front. Fighting in the south was then slowed by the fall rasputitsa and a developing, massive fight in front of Moscow that drew off reserves from either side. Hitler agreed in early September to return Guderian's and Hoth's Panzers to Army Group Center for a fresh drive toward the Soviet capital. Most attention and resources on both sides focused there once Operation *TAIFUN* was launched by Army Group Center on September 30. That brutal, attritional campaign did not run its course until Army Group Center froze to a halt in the snows of late November, the spires of Moscow's churches visible on the horizon to its lead units. The critical fight was a great battle along the *Ostashkov-Pochep Line,* which paralleled a north–south railway from the small but vital junction town of Viazma to Briansk, thence to Rzhev. The result of that fight was yet another German double-envelopment that destroyed the greater part of three Fronts, the single greatest catastrophe of the war for the Red Army. As many as one million Soviet troops and officers were lost to death, wounds, or captivity, along with thousands of tanks and guns and masses of war matériel. Worse, the western approaches to Moscow were ripped completely open, protected only by scratch forces and raw opolchentsy units manning the hastily constructed *Mozhaisk Line*. As the twin catastrophe at Viazma-Briansk was unfolding orders went out from the Stavka to speed work on another, deeper set of defensive positions far to the east: the *Volga Line*. The position of the next anticipated line of defense implicitly contemplated the loss of Moscow and most of European Russia.

The Wehrmacht had made its supreme effort of the war and won its greatest victory, principally by concentration of combat power but also because of deft generalship that compensated for numerical parity that should have advantaged the defense. Smashing of multiple Soviet Fronts at Viazma-Briansk was a model of combined arms control of air, armor, and infantry fighting power and a testament to the tactical skills of mid-ranking and junior officers and ordinary Landser. The Germans also won against a confused opponent suffering low morale and fighting under a badly divided command. The defeat was so sharp and complete that panic gripped Moscow, from the streets to the highest levels of the regime. The NKVD was given even more extraordinary powers than normal from October 11, and used them with exceptional brutality against panicking citizens and stragglers. Most of the government was moved 650 miles east from October 15. The General Staff left the city, as did the foreign diplomatic corps. Over 1,000 sites, many of enormous historical and cultural importance, were readied for demolition. Before Moscow fell it would be subjected to a scorched earth defense, just as it was in 1812. Panic deepened as the weak defenders of the Mozhaisk Line gave way three days later. Yet, Stalin remained in the Kremlin as the Soviet system strained to birth, mobilize, and equip new armies from its vast industrial womb. Zhukov was urgently recalled from Leningrad to take charge of the defense of Moscow. Stalin agreed on October 19 to Zhukov's insistent advice to pull back to a new defense line just 40 miles west of the Kremlin. Hasty anti-tank ditches were dug by the citizens of Moscow even as that emergency withdrawal took place. More important in slowing Army Group Center were heavy rains of the fall rasputitsa and the sea of glutinous mud they washed beneath the treads, hooves, and boots of the enemy. German military intelligence failed yet again: Hitler and the OKW were unaware that so few defenders lay between Bock and Moscow, and commanders were unhurried about finishing a campaign they believed already won.

The first hard freeze was felt in early November, making mud roads passable again. Army Group Center made its last lunge toward Moscow along a 200-mile-wide front starting on November 15. Deep penetrations were achieved by Bock's Panzers racing ahead on either flank, ever in search of a decisive victory. The bulk of the leg infantry moved directly toward the city, plodding ahead in the center. Soviet spoiling attacks were premature and feeble. But the Red Army had learned how to retreat, so that Bock failed to encircle the last straggling forces he thought he faced in front of Moscow. Bock was opposed by scratch armies thrown into Moscow's semiprepared defenses during October, and less happily, by more divisions of raw and militarily useless opolchentsy. Bock's extended delay in resuming the advance allowed freshly arriving Soviet divisions to fill in the line by late November. Additional Soviet armies assembled farther back, beyond German awareness, where they readied to make a major counterattack when the moment ripened. Withholding these formations as the Germans advanced on Moscow took supreme operational courage on the part of the Stavka, and even Stalin must receive some credit. Bock's momentum began to slow as German reserves dwindled. Wehrmacht combat units were overstretched to cover a frontline that stretched from the Baltic to the Crimea, and there had never been enough troops in strategic reserve. German supply lines and communications neared or passed snapping point; forward Luftwaffe airfields were rudimentary and few in number; every German combat arm was short on fuel and ammunition; tank and truck parts were scarce and repair facilities remote; and most Landser were bone weary from five months of marching, combat, and rising fear. Germans were no longer fighting close to home in areas hostile to the Soviet regime such as western Ukraine, Belorussia, and the Baltic States. They were deep inside territory populated by hostile, ethnic Russians: in German rear areas, broken and overrun Red Army units joined partisans to attack truck convoys, kill stragglers, and scorch everything of value.

The onset of a hard winter only confirmed that the Wehrmacht was always ill-prepared for a long campaign. As temperatures fell to -35°C Panzers stopped, literally frozen in their tracks. Oil in engines congealed; turrets froze immovably in place. "Stukas" and fighters could not fly, while bombs were set off by compression from severe cold. Shells no longer fit breaches of self-propelled guns. Men thought only about staying warm. Most German troops were still in summer-issue uniforms. They wore hodgepodge outfits stolen from local civilians kicked out of their peasant shacks or houses and left to die from exposure. By early December frostbite cases in the Ostheer approached 25 percent of its effective strength. Taking Minsk, encirclements at Uman and Kiev, warm waters off the Crimea, all were distant memories of a happier time. However, the effect of winter must not be exaggerated: the onset of bitter cold was not the main cause of the Wehrmacht's military failure, as was later argued by German generals and other apologists. Problems ran far deeper. This was revealed in relative aircraft losses: the VVS lost over 5,000 fighters and 5,200 bombers to enemy action by early December. It lost another 10,900 aircraft to accidents, scorched earth demolition, or outright abandonment in panicky retreats. Luftwaffe losses over the same period totaled 2,200 aircraft, or just 10 percent of VVS losses. Yet, aircraft losses by the Luftwaffe were less sustainable: the Germans had only 500 serviceable planes left on the entire Eastern Front by December, whereas the VVS still had 1,000 on the Moscow front alone. Matters would only worsen after that. The German aircraft industry was still running at little more than peacetime production levels into late 1941 and, thus, was far less able to replace lost planes than was the huge and highly advanced Soviet aircraft industry. The VVS was more capable of recovery, despite extraordinary losses and disruptions caused by forced relocation of its manufacturing plants during 1941. Soviet aircraft industry would start to turn out large numbers of improved aircraft types in 1942, while the Luftwaffe would struggle for the rest of the war just to replace ongoing attritional losses with ramped-up production of existing or slightly upgraded models. Despite such clear warning signs of an inability to compete in a protracted industrial war, solace was taken by Hitler and the OKW from a spectacularly erroneous Abwehr report of December 4, 1941, asserting that Red Army reserves were totally exhausted and therefore that the Soviets were incapable of launching any significant military operation.

The first blow of an exquisitely timed Soviet counteroffensive that ended the BARBAROSSA campaign fell northwest of Moscow the very next day, with a thunderclap of shock on the German side. General *Ivan S. Konev* struck hard into Army Group Center with Kalinin Front. On the 6th, Zhukov attacked with the main Soviet body, Western Front, striking deep into raw, frozen, exposed German positions. The "Battle of Moscow" entered a whole new phase of desperate German military crisis that lasted through January 1942, as the Red Army launched its first successful counteroffensive of the war. Russian historians call the turnaround the *Moscow offensive operation (December 5, 1941–January 7, 1942)*. It was immediately followed by the less successful *Rzhev-Viazma strategic operation (January 8–April 20, 1942)*. New divisions had appeared in the Soviet order of battle in front of Moscow, supplied along an intact railway system in the deep interior. VVS aircraft operated from tarmaced rather than the ersatz airfields used by the Luftwaffe, as the Soviet Union revealed reserves of strength the Wehrmacht could not hope to match. Five fresh and elite divisions even arrived by rail from distant Siberia, after Stalin finally accepted sound intelligence from his master spy in Tokyo. *Richard Sorge* had earlier reported that the Japanese military had decided to follow the *nanshin* or "southern advance" and attack Britain and the United States, rather than take the *hokushin* road of a "northern advance" into Siberia. Without warning the Western powers about the multiple blows set for delivery by Japan, the Stavka unleashed the

Siberians along with eight newly formed armies raised in haste from across what remained of European Russia. Until November, those troops had worked feverishly on the Volga Line. Now, they crashed into utterly surprised, frozen, exhausted German divisions. The Wehrmacht had been nearly victoried to death even before the Red Army threw it back from the suburbs of Moscow. Hitler responded by dealing the Ostheer additional blows: he dismissed some of its finest field generals, including Brauchitsch, Rundstedt, Guderian, Hoepner, and Leeb, and downgraded the role of the OKW in favor of the OKH on the Eastern Front. He also took direct operational command from December 1941, completing the inexorable logic of the *Führerprinzip*.

The Red Army had suffered catastrophic losses: 20,000 tanks, 41,000 guns, 22,000 aircraft, and 5 million men, including military dead numbering a staggering 1.5 million men. To that toll of combat deaths must be added 3.5 million Soviet prisoners of war, almost all of whom died in German captivity within a year or less. Among millions of Red Army personnel missing, dead, or wounded were tens of thousands of officers. Another year of bitter defensive operations and defeats lay ahead before the Red Army gained the strategic initiative and began to claw back and liberate lost Soviet territory, but it had survived BARBAROSSA. German casualties were far lower but were still great. Experienced officers were killed at a rate of 500 per week: by December 4, the Wehrmacht had lost enough combat officers to stock 40 divisions. Some 800,000 Germans, or 50 full-strength division equivalents, were casualties, including 302,000 dead. The rest were wounded, missing, or otherwise hors de combat. Unknown millions of Soviet civilians did not survive the first six months of the German–Soviet war. Many saw their villages and towns burned by their own side, torched by grim NKVD men or leveled by Red Army artillery and attack aircraft in fulfillment of the total scorched earth policy Stalin insisted upon in all areas lost to the Germans. Millions fled east with the Red Army. The order from the top was to evacuate civilians as the Red Army retreated, forcibly if necessary. That was a Russian tradition of sorts: Peter the Great did it in 1708 when Karl XII of Sweden arrived uninvited in western Russia; Alexander I did it in front of Napoleon and the Grand Armée in 1812. More Soviet civilians suffered and died under German occupation. Men were shot; women were raped, then shot. Children, too, were killed without pity. Hundreds of thousands were left to freeze or starve to death by young Landser inured to mercy by their own suffering, and by boyhoods spent under Nazi indoctrination. Ordinary Germans stole food, shelter, and winter clothing from desperately pleading women and children, people in any case marked for death by the brutal tyrant in Berlin. And for tens of millions of Soviet citizens left under German occupation at the close of BARBAROSSA, the full horrors of Nazi race war and genocide were only beginning.

See also Kerch defensive operation; panfilovtsy; Pripet Marshes; Rassenkampf; second front; special orders; Tripartite Pact; Yezhovshchina.

Suggested Reading: Gabriel Gorodetsky, *Grand Delusion: Stalin and the German Invasion of Russia* (1999); Robert Kershaw, *War Without Garlands: Operation Barbarossa, 1941–42* (2000); Evan Mawdsley, *Thunder in the East* (2005).

BARBIE, KLAUS (1913–1991) "Butcher of Lyon." *Gestapo* chief in Lyon from November 1942 to August 1944. He was infamous for sadistic pleasure taken from torture and murder of prisoners—Jews and hostages and French *Résistance* fighters, most notably *Jean Moulin*. Barbie was responsible for killing over 4,000 French Jews, including children. He deported another 7,500 to the *death camps*. In 1951 he escaped to Bolivia via a *ratline*. He was twice condemned to death in absentia by French national courts. He was identified in 1971 but not extradited to France until 1983. A deep suspicion lingered that many powerful people in Lyon did not want to see their wartime secrets come out at his trial. Nevertheless, he was tried and convicted in 1987. Barbie was defiant and unrepentant throughout the trial. Because the death penalty had been abolished in France in 1981, he was not executed. He died in prison in 1991.

BARCLAY A Western Allied *deception operation*. It was designed to conceal the *HUSKY* landings in Sicily by persuading the Comando Supremo and OKW that the landings would instead come in the Balkans. A major goal was to keep the Italian Navy concentrated near Greece. The means was creation of a sham "12th Army" comprised of 12 nonexistent divisions. The deceit was further conveyed by double agents, fake wireless traffic, obvious recruitment of Greek interpreters, and deliberately indiscreet collection of Balkan maps and money. In conjunction with the success of *MINCEMEAT,* the BARCLAY deception provided total operational surprise to the Sicily landings. The operation succeeded in good measure because it played directly on Adolf Hitler's understanding of Winston Churchill's predilection for Balkan operations and because of consistent *Abwehr* overestimation of the number of divisions in the Western Allied order of battle: to the end of the war, the Abwehr overestimated enemy strength in the Mediterranean by more than 100 percent. That persistent error aided subsequent deception operations related to *OVERLORD*.

BARDIA, BATTLE OF (JANUARY 3–4, 1941) Fought during the Western *desert campaign* of 1940–1941, in an extension of the early success of *COMPASS* at *Sidi Barrani*. British 13th Corps of the *Western Desert Force* was led by Major General Richard O'Connor in assaulting Italian 23rd Corps. The Italians were dug in around the fortified town of Bardia. This was the first fight in North Africa for the *Australian Army*. A company of *Free French* also fought at Bardia. After bombardment of the town by Royal Navy warships, the Australians overran stiff Italian resistance in a well-executed combined arms attack. Many thousands of Italians surrendered. The Western Desert Force pressed on to *Tobruk*.

BARI RAID (DECEMBER 2, 1943) A Luftwaffe raid on the British supply port of Bari on the Adriatic coast of Italy on December 2, 1943. It achieved complete surprise and did much damage. There were over 1,000 military casualties and perhaps as many civilian dead. Most were killed following sinking of two ammunition transports, one of which was carrying a secret load of mustard gas that was released by German bombs. The gas had been brought to Italy to be used in retaliation should Germans use gas weapons first. In addition to killing sailors and townsfolk, many rescuers were affected who rushed into the area unaware that they were dealing with lethal chemicals. Others died in hospital from the wrong treatment, again because the presence of mustard gas in Bari was a close secret. In 1988 the British government admitted the presence of poison gas at Bari and paid compensation to survivors.

See also chemical weapons.

BARRAGE

See artillery; balloons; creeping barrage; fire plan; murder; rolling barrage; serenade; standing barrage; stonk; time on target.

BARRAGE BALLOONS

See balloons.

BARVENKOVO SALIENT

Soviet term for what was known to Germans as the "Izium pocket." This was a 60-mile-wide Red Army bulge into the German lines some 80 miles below Kharkov, near the Donets River. Along with the *Toropets step,* it was formed during an otherwise failed set of winter offensives overseen by Marshal *Semyon Timoshenko* in January–April 1942.

See also FRIDERICUS; Izium-Barvenkovo operation; Kharkov.

BASTOGNE

See Ardennes offensive.

BATAAN DEATH MARCH (APRIL 1942)

The last significant, organized Filipino and U.S. forces resisting the Japanese in the first *Philippines campaign (1941–1942)* were hemmed into the Bataan peninsula and the island fortress of *Corregidor.* The "battling bastards of Bataan, no mama, no papa, no Uncle Sam," were indeed bereft of hope of reinforcement and ran out of food, medicine, and ammunition. They surrendered to the Japanese on April 9. The better-supplied fortress of Corregidor held out until May 6, and only fell upon being stormed. Some 78,000 captives from Bataan were marched 65 miles up the peninsula over a 12-day period, to improvised *prisoner of war* camps. Nearly 10,650 died of wounds, illness, or were murdered along the way by Japanese guards. Most victims were Filipinos, but over 1,000 Americans also died. Wounded and sick stragglers were shot, bayoneted, or beheaded by callous victors who despised any enemy who chose surrender. Others died from heat, dehydration, dysentery, or some untreated tropical disease. Another 17,600 prisoners died within a few weeks of arrival in the dreadful camps, most from maltreatment and malign neglect that aggravated their poor physical condition after months of starvation-level subsistence on Bataan. Others were simply murdered. All were routinely beaten. This cruel tale was widely disseminated in

Western countries over the following months and years. The story of the "Bataan death march" greatly hardened anti-Japanese sentiment in the United States, especially. General *Masaharu Homma* was tried after the war by a U.S. military commission in the Philippines. Convicted of ordering and condoning the atrocity despite evidence that he was not directly responsible, he was executed by firing squad.

BATTALION   In most World War II armies a battalion was the primary tactical unit below *division*. However, battalions varied significantly in paper strength and in weapons from army to army. Combat strength was also dictated by recent attrition or reinforcement. U.S. Army battalions were usually larger than French, British, or Commonwealth counterparts. Soviet, German, and Japanese battalions were all smaller. Generic battalion paper numbers were 650–1,100 men organized into 4–6 *companies*. The Italian Army and Japanese Army restricted organization to basic infantry battalions, but several major armies fielded armored reconnaissance battalions under varying designations. A U.S. Army battalion comprised three normal companies of riflemen and their standard weapons, along with a heavy weapons company that fielded eight light machine guns, three heavy machine guns, and six 81 mm mortars. Some American battalions were highly specialized. For instance, the U.S. Army fielded numerous Tank and Tank Destroyer battalions along with battalions of special forces such as Rangers. Those units existed outside the normal Army divisional structure. The British Army also had specialized Army Commando, Infantry, Motor, Parachute, and Air Landing battalions. The Red Army added Ski and Motor battalions when needed to its ordinary order of battle comprising Rifle, Cavalry, and Tank battalions. The Wehrmacht fielded Panzergrenadier and Volksgrenadier battalions at different times in the war, filling out either end of a scale from exceptional military professionalism and combat competence to desperation.

BATTLEAXE (JUNE 1941)   A British armored offensive during the *desert campaign* that began on June 15, 1941. It failed because General *Erwin Rommel* set a tank trap in the *Halfaya Pass* south of Bardia, site of an earlier fight between the Australians and Italians. Novel tank tactics by the *Afrika Korps* blunted a British armored assault by drawing the latter's tanks onto a firing line of '88 mm anti-tank guns. As British armor was severely mauled (91 tanks were lost to just 12 Panzers), German armor was freed to counterattack British and Commonwealth infantry. The stinging defeat led Winston Churchill, who had pressed hard for aggressive action in the desert, to sack General *Archibald Wavell*. He was replaced as commander in chief Middle East by General *Claude Auchinleck*.

BATTLECRUISER   A capital warship that possessed nearly the firepower of a battleship, with multiple batteries totaling eight or more 12-inch guns. However, it had much lighter deck armor, closer to that of a *cruiser*. The idea was that less weight would permit battlecruisers to make greater speed than heavier-plated battleship cousins. Battlecruisers were the brain-child of Royal Navy Admiral John Fisher, who commissioned a handful prior to World War I. The Royal Navy had

10 battlecruisers to Germany's 5 at the time of the Battle of Jutland in 1916. They proved unable to replace cruisers and singularly unable to withstand plunging fire from German battleships. At the start of the next naval war in 1939, British battlecruisers were set to fight German *pocket battleships*. They had little luck in finding the enemy. Then HMS Hood demonstrated once more that the battlecruiser was a failed concept: she exploded with the loss of all but three crewmen upon being hit by a single shell from DKM Bismarck. The Kriegsmarine also failed to learn the lessons of the Great War: it floated the powerful, expensive, sister battlecruisers DKM Scharnhorst and DKM Gneisenau in World War II, neither of which were effective as commerce raiders.

BATTLE EXHAUSTION   *See battle stress.*

BATTLE FATIGUE   *See battle stress.*

BATTLESHIP   A capital warship designed to bring to bear maximum firepower from 14″, 15″, or 16″ guns, Only the Imperial Japanese Navy built battleships with bigger guns: the 18″ gun bearing IJN Yamato and IJN Musashi. Battleships were protected by heavy armor plating on decks and the hull. Speed was thus sacrificed to firepower and armor in these massive, seaborne artillery platforms. Battleships of the World War I period were the largest and most complex weapons systems then devised. They were intended to project power to the four corners of the earth and to fight enemy battleships. By World War II they were already obsolete weapons platforms in most naval battles, where *aircraft carriers* protected by fast *cruisers* displaced them. They still saw action, notably newer "fast battleships" purpose built to keep up with fast fleet carriers. They also performed in coastal bombardments.

See various battles and naval campaigns. *See also battlecruisers; Five Power Naval Treaty; Imperial Japanese Navy; Italian Navy; Kriegsmarine; Pearl Harbor; pocket battleship; Royal Navy; Soviet Navy; U.S. Navy; Washington Naval Conference.*

BATTLE STRESS   British Army term for what U.S. forces called "battle fatigue." Known as "soldier's heart" in the American Civil War era, it was called "shell shock" by the British during World War I. After World War II it was identified as the medical condition "post traumatic stress disorder." Battle stress manifested many symptoms, including mental and moral debilitation, inaction, and psychological paralysis (convulsions, mutism, fugue states). It was brought on by exposure to the sights, noise, fear, and other stresses and horrors of prolonged combat. Western Allied armies generally recognized and treated it as a medical condition during World War II. One in four U.S. casualties was psychological, wherein mental condition was deemed sufficiently serious to terminate combat fitness. Other armies did not take so kind-hearted a view of what traditionalists regarded as hysteria or deemed cowardice. Japanese officers did not admit to the effects of battle stress on themselves or their men. Nor did most Wehrmacht or *Waffen-SS* officers. Psychiatry was deeply distrusted in the Red Army and in the Soviet Union more generally: the treatment an average *frontovik* could expect for any truly severe battle stress was relief by firing squad. It is hard to know how many Soviet deaths recorded as suicides resulted from untreated battle stress or what percentage of "accidental" injuries in the ranks were actually self-inflicted wounds. Given the huge numbers of men conscripted and the appalling conditions of the *Eastern Front,* it must have been a very great number. Red Army units did not have psychiatric medical staff below the level of Front. Later in the war, soldiers who exhibited debilitating battle stress were still kept near the front lines, but might be treated with extra rest and perhaps sedatives. Even so, only mental infirmity clearly resulting from physical trauma such as a head wound or from obvious prerecruitment mental illness was recognized as legitimate by the Red Army. In all other cases, men suffered in silence, self-medicated with alcohol, or broke under the strain and were shot or assigned to *penal battalions.*

BAYONETS

See banzai charge; Bataan death march; Imperial Japanese Army; prisoners of war; Red Army.

BAZOOKA

American, shoulder-launched, rocket warhead anti-tank weapon. First used in the ETO in Tunisia (M1A1 model), it made a real impression on German observers despite the fact that the first U.S. Army divisions to use them had been deployed so fast they had no training on the weapon. It took just weeks for German weapons designers to create a more powerful mimic, which later evolved into the *Panzerschreck.* In turn, that led the Americans to develop a larger bazooka that fired a 3.5-inch rocket warhead. Each U.S. infantry division was allotted 557 bazookas starting in 1943.

See also PIAT.

BAZOOKA PANTS

American slang for armored skirts hanging below the main armor of a tank, emplaced to deflect enemy rockets such as those fired from a *bazooka* or a *Panzerschreck.*

BBC

British Broadcasting Corporation. The critical radio instrument for maintaining civilian morale in Britain after the fall of France in 1940. It was also vital in maintaining communications with *resistance* movements inside German-occupied Europe. Later in the war, it helped undermine German morale through effective targeted propaganda. BBC reporters sent riveting though highly censored dispatches to the home front from frontlines in Africa, Europe, and the Pacific. Soldiers in the field listened more to BBC music and entertainment broadcasts and to comparable broadcasts by the enemy. BBC French-language broadcasts into occupied France were critical to building political support for General *Charles de Gaulle,* who was little known to the French public before that.

See also Force Française de l'Intérieur (FFI); Political Warfare Executive; radio.

BBR "Burn Before Reading." Humorous British shorthand for signals and SIGINT security rules.

B-DIENST "Beobachtungs-Dienst." The Kriegsmarine "Observation Service." In 1940, it partially broke the top secret Navy Cypher used by the Royal Navy, as well as the less sophisticated but still vitally important Merchant Navy Code. The first advantaged the Kriegsmarine during the campaign in Norway in 1940, though the Germans still suffered grievous surface ship losses. B-Dienst also cracked the escort code (Naval Cypher No. 3) during the *Battle of the Atlantic* in 1942, allowing the Germans to read up to 80 percent of intercepted messages. That gave U-boat command (*BdU*) the ability to predict the next waypoint for a given convoy to a high level of accuracy. Admiral *Karl Dönitz* thus vectored wolf packs onto a number of convoys during 1942–1943. Upon discovering the security breach, Western Allied navies countered with a new code (Naval Cypher No. 5) in June 1943. The Western Allies later introduced a more advanced code and transmission system called *Typex*.

BDU "Befehlshaber der Unterseeboote," or "Commanding Officer, U-boats." The position occupied by Admiral *Karl Dönitz* at the start of the war and still closely overseen by him after he became head of the Kriegsmarine in January 1943. BdU became shorthand for all references to Dönitz personally, as well as to overall and central HQ for U-boat operations. A fatal flaw in BdU was its use of high-frequency radio bursts to connect Dönitz with all supply and hunter boats in the North and South Atlantic, Baltic Sea, Caribbean, Mediterranean, and North Sea. That centralization of communications helped the Western Allies decipher U-boat codes—as many as 2,500 signals left U-boat headquarters each day—and to sink many boats.

See also B-Dienst; Enigma machines; Huff-Duff.

BEACHMASTER The naval officer in charge of disembarkment of men and equipment during an amphibious assault.

BEAMS, WAR OF THE

See Direction Finding (DF); Gee; Knickebein; LORAN; Lorenz; Oboe; Pathfinders; Würzburg; X-Gerät; Y-Gerät.

BEAVERBROOK, LORD (1879–1964) Anglo-Canadian newspaper baron. He was a key member of Prime Minister Winston Churchill's war cabinet from 1940 to 1942. He had the main responsibility for aircraft production. Beaverbrook consistently opposed *strategic bombing* on grounds that it was ineffective and that RAF heavy bombers would be better used in a tactical role supporting ground forces in the Middle East or Southeast Asia. After falling ill and leaving the cabinet he served as an important behind-the-scenes adviser to Churchill.

BECK, JÓSEF (1894–1944)   Polish foreign minister, 1932–1939. His rigidly anti-Soviet policy helped block all attempts to form an anti-German alliance in the east before *FALL WEISS*, the invasion of Poland in 1939. He was closely engaged in talks concerning the status of *Danzig* and the *Polish Corridor* and Poland's belated alliance with Britain and France in 1939.

BECK, LUDWIG (1880–1944)   German general. A staff officer during World War I, Beck rose to become chief of staff to the *OKH* in 1935. He was opposed to Adolf Hitler's aggressive plans for war and fearful that war with the Western Allies would break out over annexation of the *Sudetenland*. As a result, Beck was among the top three Wehrmacht leaders to be purged in 1938. He was replaced by *Franz Halder*. In 1943 Beck was involved in two failed plots to kill Hitler. He was the main figurehead of the *Schwarze Kapelle* and deeply involved in the *July Plot* (1944). When that coup failed he tried to kill himself, but only managed to inflict painful wounds. He was fortunate to be dragged outside and shot immediately by a tough sergeant, as other July plotters were later sadistically and slowly tortured to death or hanged.

BEDA FOMM, BATTLE OF (FEBRUARY 5–7, 1941)   British 13th Corp of the *Western Desert Force* cut off the remnants of Italian 10th Army at Beda Fomm during Operation *COMPASS*. The Italians were retreating to Tripoli following defeats at *Sidi Barrani, Bardia,* and *Tobruk*. British, Indian, and Australian troops made a surprise move through the open desert to cut the coastal road, along which the Italian column was moving. In a sharp two-day fight from February 5–7, 1941, the British took 25,000 Italian prisoners and captured 100 tanks, 216 artillery pieces, and 1,500 other vehicles.

BEDELL SMITH (1895–1961)   "Beetle." U.S. lieutenant general. He served in France as an infantry officer during World War I. He was brought to Washington as a staff officer by General *George C. Marshall,* rising to secretary of the General Staff in September 1941. Five months later he was appointed secretary of the *Combined Chiefs of Staff*. He was named General *Dwight Eisenhower*'s chief of staff in late 1942. He was a central figure in all Western Allied operations in the ETO from 1942 to 1945.

BEER HALL *PUTSCH* (NOVEMBER 9–10, 1923)   A premature attempt at a Nazi military coup in Bavaria.
    See Germany; Göring, Hermann; Hess, Rudolf; Hitler, Adolf; Kapp Putsch; Ludendorff, Erich von; Nazi Party; Ruhr.

BEF
    See British Expeditionary Force.

BELGIAN CONGO   Once Belgium was defeated in May 1940, its government-in-exile agreed to exploit the Belgian Congo in the Western Allied cause. That meant huge supplies of copper were shipped to Britain for war production, along with cobalt and radium for British atomic bomb research. Some 40,000 Congolese troops fought for the Allies against Italians in the *East African campaign (1940–1941),* then against various Axis forces across the greater Middle East.

BELGIAN GATE   "C-Element" or "Element-C" or "Cointet gate." A steel, gate-like anti-tank obstacle invented by M. Cointet. The Belgian Army deployed tens of thousands as a barrier to German Panzers along the *Dyle Line* in 1939–1940, linking them with welds and chains. Although the Wehrmacht got around Belgian Gates fairly handily in May 1940, German engineers adapted the structures in their own defenses across Europe, most notably as beach obstacles in the *Atlantic Wall*.

BELGIUM   Belgium was neutral in 1914 when it was invaded by Germany. The small Belgian Army fought bravely and well to the end of the war, although it was hemmed into a small corner of the country left unoccupied by the Germans. After a spate of postwar alliance-building with its Great War allies, Brussels retreated into renewed neutrality in the mid-to-late 1930s. That disinclined the French to extend the *Maginot Line* and reduced even General Staff cooperation until secret talks resumed in 1939. Belgium mobilized on August 25, 1939, as it became clear Germany would attack Poland and war would result with the Western Allies. Belgians then hunkered down upon the outbreak of war in the west on September 3, 1939. Brussels called up reserves, strengthened frontier defenses, and speeded secret General Staff coordination with the British and French staffs. But Belgium did not allow prepositioning of Allied forces on its soil. It only agreed to open its western border to the Allies upon an actual German attack. Belgium was invaded by Germany on May 10, 1940. Along with invasion of the Netherlands, that was the opening act of the *FALL GELB* invasion of France.

The Belgian Army comprised a not inconsiderable force of 600,000 men deployed in 18 divisions. But it was armed and organized for static defense, while the Wehrmacht planned and carried out a war of brisk movement and shocking violence, or *Blitzkrieg*. Belgian troops lacked mechanized transport and only four divisions were even partly motorized. In the entire country there were fewer than a dozen tanks. The Belgian Air Force had about 50 modern planes, and nearly half its total force of 250 aircraft was dedicated to reconnaissance. This was not a force prepared to face Panzers. If German tanks and mobile infantry could break through the hard crust of Belgian fixed fortifications , which is what happened almost immediately, it would be a short war. Brussels surrendered on May 28, after 18 days of hard fighting and enforced retreat. That cut off Anglo-French armies, which had advanced into Belgium heading for the *Dyle Line,* and forced a mass evacuation from *Dunkirk*. Over the course of the battle the Belgians lost just over 6,000 dead and many more thousands wounded. Tens of thousands of Belgians were taken to Germany as *prisoners of war,* where 2,000 subsequently died. Over 70,000 non-Flemish soldiers were deliberately separated from Flemish prisoners and kept in German camps until 1945.

Adolf Hitler annexed Eupen and Malmédy, and St. Vith, to Germany on May 18, thereby recovering all frontier areas lost to Belgium under the *Treaty of Versailles* (1919). Believing the war lost and over, King Léopold refused to lead a Belgian government-in-exile. Instead, he stayed in-country while the Belgian government was trapped in Vichy. A rival government-in-exile formed in London in July that sharply criticized the king and continued to fight the German occupation with whatever personnel escaped and military resources were provided by the Western Allies. Over the next four years the London government drew upon the distant asset of the natural resources and native troops of the *Belgian Congo*. In the meantime, Léopold met with Adolf Hitler on November 19. The King sought assurances of a moderate occupation that were neither forthcoming nor in the Führer's nature. Bitterly disappointed and increasingly out of touch following his meeting with Hitler, Léopold brooded inside his palace during four years of German occupation, until most Belgians ceased to support him. They turned instead to the government-in-exile in London.

Belgium and northern France were jointly governed by a Wehrmacht military administration under General Alexander von Falkenhausen, the least oppressive of any German governor in Western Europe. Even so, Belgians suffered the usual travails of German occupation: deportation of Jews to the *death camps* and of other citizens to Germany as forced laborers; exploitation of the national economy to German ends at the expense of Belgian consumption; *Gestapo* terror; and bombing of transportation and industrial targets. Although Belgium suffered less than most countries under Nazi occupation, the German presence exacerbated the already deep ethnic division between Flemings and Walloons. A small group of Flemish nationalists led by Staf de Clerq and the Vlaamsch Nationaal Verbond (Flemish National Union) were close collaborators not merely with the military administration, but also with Nazi social and racial policies. But they were few in number. An influential fascist movement among French-speaking Walloons was led by *Léon Degrelle*. Léopold was forcibly deported to Germany by the Nazis in June 1944, as Allied forces landed in France. Upon liberation and return of the rightful government from London in the late summer of 1944, Belgium reformed its Army until it fielded 75,000 men. They joined Allied commands in the *conquest of Germany* in 1945. Still enmeshed in bitter controversy after the war, Léopold abdicated in 1951.

See also resistance; Waffen-SS.

BELGOROD-KHARKOV OPERATION

See Kursk; RUMIANTSEV.

BELGRADE OFFENSIVE OPERATION (SEPTEMBER 28–OCTOBER 20, 1944)

See Red Army; Yugoslavia.

BELORUSSIA Eastern Belorussia suffered greatly in the 1930s from Joseph Stalin's purges and forced collectivization of peasant agriculture. Upon Poland's partition between Berlin and Moscow under terms of the *Nazi–Soviet Pact (August 23, 1939), Western Belorussia* was annexed to the Soviet Union in September 1939. Its ethnically mixed population was immediately subjected to terrors of the *NKVD* and, thereafter, to conscription into the Red Army. All Belorussia was overrun during the course of *BARBAROSSA* (June–December, 1941). It was occupied until July 1944, as part of the Nazi administrative region known as the *Reichskommissariat Ostland.* Belorussia was liberated after heavy and massively destructive fighting, but not until after failure of the *Belorussian offensive operation (November 1943–February 1944).* The NKVD returned in the wake of the Red Army, bringing renewed misery to a benighted land already denuded of Jews by the Germans and about to see its ethnic Polish population expelled westward by Stalin. Belorussian casualties are not precisely known, but probably reached two million out of a prewar population of eight million.

See also BAGRATION; *concentration camps; Holocaust; Katyn massacre; partisans; Red Army.*

BELORUSSIAN OFFENSIVE OPERATION (JUNE 22–AUGUST 19, 1944)

See BAGRATION.

BELORUSSIAN OFFENSIVE OPERATION (NOVEMBER 1943–FEBRUARY 1944)

Several Soviet efforts to retake Belorussia failed in late 1943 and early 1944, despite engaging several large Fronts on the Soviet side. Not much is known in general literature beyond the fact that fighting was hard and sustained and that the offensives failed. A planned airborne component was canceled due to bad weather, while poor winter conditions also hampered Red Army operations. By all accounts, German resistance was fierce, skillful, and successful. The Germans defended against a series of linked but poorly implemented attacks by the 1st Baltic, Western, and Belorussian Fronts. Operations by Western Front fared especially badly. The liberation of Belorussia was thus postponed until July 1944. In the meantime, German killing of Jews and *partisans* continued behind the lines. Soviet killing of accused collaborators and internal purges and deportations of local nationalists resumed wherever the Red Army advanced, until Moscow reclaimed all lands up to the expanded frontier agreed in the *Nazi–Soviet Pact* of August 23, 1939.

BELSEN

See Bergen-Belsen.

BELZEC A *concentration camp* in Poland sited to take advantage of transportation provided by the Lublin-Lvov railway. Opened as a labor camp in 1940, mass killings began in Belzec on March 17, 1942. Redesigned as a full *death camp,* it remained disguised as a slave labor camp. The murderers of Belzec originally used three wooden gas chambers employing a gas produced by petroleum products rather than *Zyclon-B.* The early wooden gas chambers were later replaced by six concrete gas chambers, to speed the pace of the killing. Belzec served as a model for two larger death camps that formed part of the *Aktion Reinhard* mass murder program. As Belzec lacked crematoria for disposing of victims' remains, and because it had already eliminated all Jews in the surrounding region, it stopped murder operations at the end of 1942. Over 600,000 had been killed at Belzec by that time, of whom at least 435,000 were Jews. The other victims were mainly Roma, Poles, and Russians.

BENEŠ, EDUARD (1884–1948)   Czech statesman. He spent World War I as a refugee in Paris, where he worked closely with *Tomáš Masaryk*. He attended the Paris Peace Conference in 1919, where he supported formation of the *League of Nations*. From 1918 to 1935 he served as foreign minister. He was also premier from 1921 to 1922. Beneš was instrumental in coordinating Czechoslovak foreign policy within the failed *Little Entente*. From 1935 to 1938 he was president of the Republic. He resigned in disgust and bitter disappointment over the *Munich Conference*, where the Western Allies surrendered the *Sudetenland* to Adolf Hitler. Beneš headed the Czechoslovak government-in-exile in Paris, which moved to London when Paris fell in 1940. His government helped organize Czech resistance, including assassination of *Reinhard Heydrich*. Beneš returned to Prague on May 16, 1945. He served as president from 1946 but resigned in June 1948, in face of a Communist coup sponsored by Moscow.

BENGAL   Bengal was the main base of political support for the Indian nationalist *Subhas Chandra Bose* before 1939. In 1943 Bengal experienced a terrible famine which took three million lives. The causes were loss of food supply from Japanese-occupied Burma, stockpiling food for military use, and a disastrous rise in rice prices as rumors of shortages led to private hoarding. Local officials reacted badly, until the British Army brought in emergency relief supplies that broke the famine. Recent research suggests that high prices rather than lack of supply was the underlying cause.

BERCHTESGADEN   A Bavarian resort town used as a retreat and southern headquarters by Adolf Hitler. Sited 6,000 feet above the town was the "Eagle's nest," a fantastical complex of bunkers and villas built and manned by the *Schutzstaffel (SS)*. Hitler entertained foreign leaders at the Berghof before the war, including *Count Ciano, Neville Chamberlain,* and former British Prime Minister David Lloyd George. However, Hitler rarely visited during the war. General *Dwight Eisenhower* feared Berchtesgaden would be used for a last-ditch, suicidal defense by Hitler, the SS, and other Nazi fanatics. It was not.

　　See also Alpenfestung.

BERGEN-BELSEN   A *concentration camp* in northwest Germany, near Hanover. It began as a holding camp for political prisoners. Many tens of thousands were killed there by sadistic guards and the commandant, though it was not a *death camp*

153

per se. Swept by typhus epidemics in 1944 and 1945, tens of thousands more died, including the Dutch girl Anne Frank. It was liberated by the British Army in April 1945. About 28,000 of the more than 38,500 inmates who were liberated were too weak or ill to survive long.

BERGHOF

See Berchtesgaden.

BERIA, LAVRENTI PAVLOVICH (1899–1953)   Soviet secret policeman. A longtime member of the terroristic CHEKA and OGPU forerunners of the *NKVD*, Beria served his fellow Georgian Joseph Stalin by heading the NKVD from 1938. He even occupied a seat on the *GKO* from 1941 to 1945. With sadistic relish, Beria oversaw the NKVD's vast archipelago of forced labor camps and orchestrated its show trials and executions, albeit murdering at a somewhat reduced rate than his predecessor during the *Yezhovshchina*. Beria was intimately involved in purges of Red Army commanders, sometimes personally beating and torturing prisoners to satisfy sadistic lust. Beria was not an ideological killer: had he been born in Germany, he surely would have just as happily served as a killer for the *Gestapo*. He was also notorious for using absolute police powers to satisfy gross sexual perversions, including kidnap and rape of children. He was hugely feared by all Soviet leaders except Stalin.

Beria's NKVD brought terror to all territories annexed to the Soviet Union under terms of the *Nazi–Soviet Pact (August 23, 1939)* and additional provinces annexed by Stalin in 1940. Punitive actions Beria carried out for Stalin included the NKVD massacre of Polish Army officers at *Katyn* and other sites, and tens of thousands more killings of "enemies of the state" that are far less famous or well documented. The *BARBAROSSA* invasion of the Soviet Union dramatically increased Beria's power, as the NKVD was used to enforce ferocious discipline at the front and in the major cities. Additional powers were granted to Beria during the military crisis before Moscow during the Wehrmacht's *TAIFUN* offensive in October–November, 1941. After the worst NKVD excesses were curbed in 1942, Beria remained in charge of political troops policing military rear areas and carrying out Stalin's mass internal deportations of suspect ethnic groups. As the Red Army assumed the strategic offensive in the second half of 1943, Beria and the NKVD followed close on its heels to ensure that liberation meant brutal reimposition of Stalinist terror and control to the expanded frontier agreed with the Nazis in 1939. Once Beria and the NKVD moved outside the borders of the Soviet Union in late 1944, they arrested and murdered potential nationalist or anti-Communist resisters and opposition leaders and seeded liberated territories with pro-Soviet Communist operatives and regimes. Beria was briefly part of a governing troika after Stalin died in March 1953. He was soon arrested and tried on show charges of treason so absurd and clearly trumped-up—that he was a British agent, among other things—that Beria might have been proud to author them. He was not executed in the name of justice, but to deny him the succession to Stalin and to remove the pall of fear he projected over even the most powerful of the Soviet nomenklatura.

See also BLAU.

BERLIN   Capital of Adolf Hitler's "Third Reich." Hitler planned to rebuild Berlin as a vulgar imperial capital to govern and intimidate the huge empire he intended to carve out of Europe and western Russia. The totally rebuilt city was to be called "Germania." It was designed by his personal architect, *Albert Speer*. Hitler tinkered with scale model plans for Germania to his final days, even as he led Berliners into moral and physical devastation. Berlin was occupied by four Allied armies from 1945. West Berlin was later formed from the British, French, and American occupation zones, while the old Soviet zone became East Berlin, capital of the German Democratic Republic (DDR). The Western Allied military presence was more voluntary than an occupation from 1949 to 1994. The Soviet occupation was rougher. The first rudimentary structures of the Berlin Wall were erected on August 13, 1961. Its cynical builders called it the "anti-fascist defense barrier." The Berlin Wall remained in place until November 9, 1989, when it was torn down and the city reunited. Allied occupation forces officially departed Berlin on September 8, 1994.

See also Berlin bomber offensive; Germany, conquest of.

BERLIN, BATTLE OF (1945)

See Germany, conquest of.

BERLIN BOMBER OFFENSIVE (1943–1944)

The last great effort of *Arthur Harris* and RAF Bomber Command to win the war by *morale bombing*. It was undertaken in the face of wider Western Allied agreement to shift to targeted bombing, and later to tactical support bombing for the invasion forces. During August and September, 1943, three giant raids cost Bomber Command nearly 8 percent of planes and crews. The decision was therefore made to bomb Berlin only on moonless winter nights, locating the city with new electronic aids at last entering service. The RAF launched the first of four November raids on the 18th, each with over 400 heavy bombers. Large-scale diversionary raids were made on other cities to draw off night-fighters. The Berlin campaign also saw introduction of *Serrate*-equipped "Mosquito" night-fighter escorts of the bomber stream. Heavy winter weather and cloud cover reduced accuracy and effectiveness of the bombing, as did the vast sprawl of Berlin: the suburbs absorbed many tons of bombs as *creep back* afflicted British bomber accuracy. Another four raids were made in December, to comparable poor strategic effect but with rising bomber losses as the Luftwaffe concentrated over 400 night-fighters and employed new *Zahme Sau* tactics. Five more massive RAF attacks were assayed in January, but only one more by mid-February. By then, the USAAF had also made several daylight raids on Berlin. Even this combined offensive failed to have the desired effect on morale or war production, which was widely dispersed and largely carried out underground. Civilian casualties were 14,000–15,000 killed and wounded, and over 450,000 made homeless. Bomber Command lost nearly 500 heavy bombers during the offensive, an attrition rate it could not sustain. The RAF is therefore widely judged to have lost the battle. Berlin was not a major target again until 1945.

Suggested Reading: M. Middlebrook, *The Berlin Raids* (1988).

BERLING'S ARMY
See Polish Army.

BERMUDA
See British West Indies.

BERNADOTTE, COUNT FOLKE (1895–1948) Swedish statesman. He tried to mediate peace during World War I, and again during World War II. He met *Heinrich Himmler* in Berlin in early April 1945 for surrender talks kept secret from Adolf Hitler. Bernadotte was seeking agreement on possible transfer of prisoners in *concentration camps* to Red Cross authority. In a second meeting held as Berlin burned under Red Army artillery, Bernadotte affirmed to Himmler that the Western Allies would accept nothing less than *unconditional surrender*. Hitler was enraged when he heard of the meetings and ordered Himmler arrested and shot for treason. Bernadotte was appointed United Nations mediator of the partition of Palestine after the war. He was assassinated by Jewish zealots (the Stern Gang) in September 1948, while arranging a ceasefire during the First Arab–Israeli War.

BERNHARD, PRINCE (1911–2004)
See Netherlands.

BERNHARDT LINE Also called the "Reinhard Line." A set of light German defensive works north of Naples. It was sited along the Garigliano River, ran across the spine of Italy, and thence to Fossacesia on the Adriatic coast. In October 1943, Adolf Hitler ordered Field Marshal *Albert Kesselring* to hold in Italy. Kesselring stopped the Western Allies along the Bernhardt Line until December, then fell back to reposition along the stronger works of the *Gustav Line*.
See also Hitler Line; Winter Line.

BESSARABIA A long-disputed region sandwiched between the Dnieper and Prut rivers, traditionally tied to Rumanian Moldavia. It was ripped away from Tsarist Russia in 1917, a change in the border never recognized in Moscow. Bessarabia and *Bukovina* were annexed by the Soviet Union in June 1940, after Joseph Stalin issued an ultimatum to Bucharest that took advantage of Adolf Hitler's preoccupation with *FALL GELB* in the west. Germany agreed to the Soviet move in secret, as the two Great Powers of the east cooperated to crush all small states between them. Most of the population of Bessarabia was non-Russian, which suggests that Stalin's main interest in annexation was strategic: to advance the Red Army to the Danube and closer to Bulgaria, which he thereafter pressured unsuccessfully for a "mutual assistance pact." Bessarabia was quickly sovietized by the *NKVD*. Ethnic Rumanians were drafted into forced labor battalions, and many were relocated deep inside the Soviet Union; others were conscripted into the Red Army. Rumania briefly recovered Bessarabia by participating in *BARBAROSSA*. From July 1941 until the Red Army returned in 1944, Bessarabia was under Rumanian control. During that time Bucharest cooperated fully with Nazi policy, including deporting Bessarabian Jews and Roma to the *death camps*. The province was joined to Soviet Moldavia in 1945, with some parts added to Ukraine.

BETIO ISLAND
See Tarawa.

BETTY BOMBER   Type-1 G4M Japanese bomber.
See bombers.

BEVIN, ERNEST (1881–1951)   British foreign secretary, 1945–1951. A trade unionist by background and from instinct, Bevin served in Winston Churchill's wartime cabinet from May 1940. He organized civilian labor during the war, his Labor roots making some measures more palatable to the working class. Bevin became foreign secretary in the postwar Labour government and oversaw peace treaties signed with the minor members of the Axis coalition: Bulgaria, Hungary, Rumania, and Italy. He coordinated closely with U.S. authorities about occupation policy in Germany. He was a key player in rebuilding and rearming West Germany and forming NATO.

BEWEGUNGSKRIEG   "war of movement." German term for the type of highly mobile operations that the Wehrmacht inherited from Prussian military tradition and the lessons of World War I. It sought to avoid positional battles of attrition, or *Stellungskrieg*, by taking advantage of the design, doctrine, and mobile capabilities of German forces. It went beyond rapid tactical movement to incorporate large-scale maneuvering of whole armies and army groups. Its minimal intention was to flank an opponent. The optimal intention was full envelopment or double envelopment of the enemy's main force, leading to a decisive victory, or *Vernichtungsschlacht*.

BIAK   This 35-mile long island off the northwest coast of New Guinea was occupied by the Japanese in early 1942. A major Japanese air facility was built there. Biak was invaded by elements of the Hurricane Task Force on May 27, 1944. Biak was well and fiercely defended by 12,600 Japanese. U.S. forces made such slow progress that the initial commander was dismissed. A pocket of desperate Japanese at

Ibdi held out to the end of July. Other Japanese hung on elsewhere. On August 17, a battalion landed at Wardo Bay, swamping the last Japanese defenders, who had gathered there to prepare a general counterattack. That broke the spirit of the defenders and scattered them into small foraging parties and stragglers. Most Japanese died before Biak was fully secured. So did 400 Americans. Another 2,000 U.S. troops suffered battle wounds, while 7,000 were incapacitated by various tropical diseases. U.S. aircraft thereafter used captured airfields on Biak to support operations on New Guinea.

Suggested Reading: Robert Smith, *The Approach to the Philippines* (1953).

BIDAULT, GEORGES (1899–1975) French *Résistance* leader. Arrested by the Germans in 1940, but freed in 1941, Bidault took over leadership of the National Council of the French *Résistance* after the arrest and murder of *Jean Moulin* in June 1943. In 1944 he became foreign minister in the *Free French* government of *Charles de Gaulle*.

BIG FOUR Wartime shorthand for China, Britain, the Soviet Union, and the United States. Alternately, it meant the leaders of those countries: Jiang Jieshi, Winston Churchill, Joseph Stalin, and Franklin Roosevelt. Churchill thought the inclusion of China, and Roosevelt's habitual, casual, and overeasy rhetoric about China being a Great Power, was "an absolute farce."

BIGOTED Description of those select few who knew the secret of the actual landing sites (codeword "Bigot") for the *OVERLORD* invasion of France.

BIG RED ONE Nickname of the U.S. Army 1st Division, taken from its red shoulder flash.

BIG THREE The United States, the Soviet Union, and Great Britain. Alternately, the leaders of those countries: Franklin Roosevelt, Joseph Stalin, and Winston Churchill.

BIG WEEK (1944)
See Combined Bomber Offensive.

BIG WING DEBATE
See Britain, Battle of; Dowding, Hugh; Leigh-Mallory, Trafford; Park, Keith; radio.

BINARY DIVISION A failed Italian experiment in which Italian Army divisions were reduced to just two *battalions* from the standard three, to increase the number of paper divisions and from a faulty theory that "binary divisions" would be faster, more mobile, and more lethal. Instead, they proved to be underarmed and understrength during the *Balkan campaign (1940–1941)* and again during the *desert campaigns (1940–1943)*.

BIOLOGICAL WARFARE Japan used biological weapons against civilian and military concentrations throughout its occupied territories, especially China, starting in the 1930s. The Japanese worked outward from facilities in Manchuria run by the ultranationalist surgeon and sadist, Shirō Ishii, who performed biological experiments on *prisoners of war* and civilians at his infamous *Unit 731*. Documentation of these horrors is only partial: the United States captured Ishii's papers at the end of the war, but they were returned to Japan in 1958. Japanese authorities have since repressed the files. However, partial file records were microfilmed before their return to Japan, the Chinese made several reports, and Western Allied interrogators also gleaned information from prisoner interrogations. What is known from these sources is that delivery of Japanese biological weapons was simple: rats with plague-infected fleas were inserted or dropped on targets, or infected grain, animals, or people were sent into target areas. At Unit 731 work was also done on more sophisticated weapons. These included the "Ha bomb" for delivery of tetanus and anthrax on the battlefield via infected shrapnel, and the "Uji bomb" to spread cholera, bubonic plague, and other plagues among civilians and hoof-and-mouth and anthrax to farm animal populations. Work was done on a variety of delivery systems to distribute animal, plant, and human diseases, including attaching infected matter to high altitude balloon bombs, or *Fugo,* to attack North America. Several thousand experimental incendiary Fugo were launched. It was hoped that later balloon barrages would carry disease across the Pacific, but Japan lost the war before this could be tried.

Japan conducted limited but widespread biological warfare throughout China and possibly also parts of Southeast Asia, from the Dutch East Indies to Burma and Malaya. There may have been targeting of some jungle tribes and hill people for complete extermination, but the majority of casualties were Chinese. Attacks were made with "germ bombs" containing anthrax, typhoid, and various other pathogens. First use likely was by local Japanese Army commanders in 1938. There is some evidence to suggest that the Japanese also used biological weapons against Russian and Mongolian troops at *Nomonhan* in 1939, delivered into the water supply by suicide troops. Biological weapons were certainly used at Ningbo in 1940, at Ch'ang-te in 1941, and on a massive scale against *Guomindang* troops in southern China in 1942. Food supplies were deliberately contaminated, though the widely believed story of infected chocolate delivered to children is based on suspect records and unreliable testimony from a postwar Soviet show trial of accused Japanese war criminals held at Khabarovsk in 1949. Plague rats and their attendant fleas were on the way for use against U.S. forces on *Saipan,* but the transport carrying them was sunk en route. The Japanese hoped to use biological weapons to attack the United States itself from a distance, utilizing Fugo. An epidemic of plague carried by lab rats released by Unit 731 at the end of the war is estimated to have taken 30,000 lives around Harbin in 1947, after a two-year incubation and migration period.

The only other known use of biological warfare occurred in 1943 in Poland, where the "Armia Krajowa" or Polish Home Army infected German soldiers and some Gestapo agents with typhoid, killing several hundred. Otherwise, only the Japanese used biological weapons during the war, although by the end of the war six other countries were conducting research: Britain, Canada, France, Germany, the Soviet Union, and the United States. Little is known about the Soviet program. The British conducted war work on botulism and anthrax from the 1930s. Tests were carried out against sheep and cattle on desolate Gruinard Island, off the coast of Scotland. The U.S. program began in 1942. It was headquartered at Fort Detrick, Maryland. Americans benefited from sharing information with the British from 1941. By 1944 the Western Allies had an anthrax bomb ready for large-scale production and were making progress on other diseases. German research was more limited than Western Allied intelligence supposed. The Germans had tried to infect North American herds with anthrax during World War I, but most of what is known to intelligence agencies about that project and interwar biological work remains classified. It is known that the Wehrmacht did not have offensive biological weapons, but instead concentrated on bio-defense. Unaware of this, the Western Allies feared that the V-1 might deliver biological infection and discussed dropping anthrax bombs on Germany. They also fed disinformation about their own capabilities into Germany as a means of bio-deterrence of Hitler and the Luftwaffe.

See also Abyssinian War (1935–1936); nerve agents.

BIR HAKEIM, BATTLE OF (MAY 26–JUNE 11, 1942)   This desert fortress at the extreme left of the British *Gazala Line* was held by the *Free French* 1st Brigade while British 8th Army withdrew to what became the *El Alamein* position. General *Erwin Rommel* attacked in force on May 26, sending the elite Italian Ariete armoured division to lead the assault. Italian tanks broke into the stronghold, but were repulsed with heavy losses. Axis forces then surrounded Bir Hakeim from June 1–10, but its Free French defenders refused to quit. With crucial support from the RAF, the French held out until ordered to withdraw under cover of night on June 10–11, having reached the end of their water and ammunition. Of 3,600 men in the garrison, 900 killed and wounded were left behind. The rest broke though the Axis encirclement and fought their way back to rejoin the British. The hard fight did much to impress the Western Allies that *Charles de Gaulle's* men were worthy battlefield comrades. Symbolizing this change, the Free French movement restyled itself "France Combattante" or "Fighting France."

See also Gazala, Battle of.

BIRKE (SEPTEMBER 3–29, 1944)   "Birch." Wehrmacht code name for the evacuation of German forces from Finland to Norway, conducted amidst great confusion. Finland asked for a ceasefire with the Soviet Union on September 2. Moscow demanded as a precondition of any armistice that the Finnish Army attack retreating Germans, with whom the Finns were then still allied. The Finns were reluctant to attack a withdrawing army that remained extremely dangerous, but needed to appease Moscow and leave the war. Joseph Stalin and the Stavka again insisted that Finland actively expel German troops. The High Command in Helsinki reluctantly positioned troops to carry out this mission, but could not prevent continuing fraternization with the Germans by Finnish combat units. The OKH sent the command "Birke anschlagen," or "cut the birch," on September 3, followed the next day by an even more urgent "birch" order to evacuate most of Finland. A formal armistice was signed by Helsinki and Moscow on September 19, as the Germans pulled out. The only serious military clash between the Germans and Finns occurred on September 29, over control of a bridge across the Olhavan-joki River.

See also NORDLICHT.

BIRKENAU   A German *concentration camp* set up in Poland in 1941. It was used by the *Schutzstaffel (SS)* as a death center for eliminating Soviet officers and commissars, then evolved into a main killing area for the *death camp* centered on *Auschwitz*.

BISCARI MASSACRES (1943)   There were two major incidents in Sicily wherein unarmed Axis troops were slaughtered by U.S. soldiers. The first massacre saw 34 Italian prisoners and two Germans shot near the airfield at Biscari, most by a single sergeant who went on a personal murderous rampage. In the second incident an American captain shot 40 Italian prisoners. Both men later cited General *George Patton*'s preinvasion speech not to show the enemy mercy, thereby invoking a defense of *superior orders*. Patton initially tried to cover up the Biscari massacres, but General *Omar Bradley* refused to hide the atrocities. Both incidents were investigated, but punishment of the murderers was light: the captain was acquitted (he later died in action); the sergeant served one year, then returned to active duty as a private.

See also Malmédy massacre; prisoners of war.

BISMARCK, DKM
See Atlantic, Battle of; battlecruiser; Swordfish.

BISMARCK ARCHIPELAGO   Some 200 small islands and atolls in the South Pacific, off the coast of New Guinea. They were occupied by the Japanese in early 1942. ANZAC and American forces retook some islands in 1943–1944, but bypassed others in the latter *island-hopping* campaigns, most notably *Rabaul*. The reconquest of the *Admiralty Islands* was followed by taking Emirau to the east, completing major actions in the Bismarck Archipelago.

See also Bismarck Sea, Battle of the; New Britain campaign; New Ireland.

BISMARCK SEA, BATTLE OF THE (MARCH 2–4, 1943)   A devastating American air assault on eight Japanese troop transports and eight destroyers. The troop convoy was traversing the Bismarck Sea, the open waters separating New Guinea from the Bismarck Archipelago. The U.S. Navy knew from *ULTRA* intercepts that a convoy left *Rabaul* on February 28, carrying a Japanese Army division to reinforce positions at Lae on New Guinea. The first attack wave of U.S. land-based aircraft hit the convoy at night on March 2. Upon first light the next morning, Australian fighters and U.S. bombers brushed aside Japanese land-based air cover from Lae and New Britain to bomb and strafe the transports with remarkable accuracy, including using a new *skip bombing* technique. Raids were also launched against Japanese air bases to suppress fighter cover. On the night of March 3, PT boats made fast torpedo attacks. The Japanese lost all eight troop transports and four destroyers. Only 3,660 men survived out of more than 6,900 troops in the 51st Division, with hundreds more Japanese sailors lost from 12 sunken ships.

BLACK BOOK   British term for a *Schutzstaffel (SS)* list of nearly 3,000 Britons and European exiles who were to be arrested upon German invasion and occupation of Britain.

BLACK ORCHESTRA
    See Schwarze Kapelle.

BLACKOUT   Eliminating light signatures that might be seen from aircraft at night, and therefore provide guidance to bombers looking for major population centers or other targets. Coastal lights also needed to be blacked out as they provided guidance for enemy submarines. Blackouts became standard procedure for all belligerents, but not before very costly learning took place. For instance, the United States failed to black out east coast cities in the first months of 1942, badly exposing passing tankers and cargo ships to U-boats and easing the latter's navigation problems.

BLACK PIT   "Azores Gap." An area of ocean between Iceland and the Azores uncovered by Western Allied aircraft until late 1943, when pressure on Portugal permitted *VLR (Very Long Range)* aircraft to fly from the Azores. It was referred to as the "Black Pit" by merchants and warships, as well as by U-boat crews, because of the sheer number of ships sunk there from 1939 to 1943.
    See also air gap.

BLACK *REICHSWEHR*
    See Reichswehr.

BLACK SEA OPERATIONS
    See amphibious operations; Kerch-Feodosiia operations; Kriegsmarine; Regia Marina; Sebastopol, siege of; Soviet Navy.

BLACKSHIRTS   "Squadristi." Members of Italy's Fascist Party paramilitary organization, comprising some 300,000 men and boys organized in 177 "legions" in

June 1940. Some formed three Italian *fascist* divisions which fought in Spain during the *Spanish Civil War (1936–1939)* and later in Africa. About 40 blackshirt legions were seeded among regular Italian Army divisions in North Africa from 1940, and on the Eastern Front from 1941 to 1943. Others fought for Benito Mussolini's rump "Salò Republic" from 1943 to 1945. Fascists in other countries also wore monochrome shirts, modeled on the original Italian example: brown shirts were worn by the *Sturmabteilung (SA)* in Germany; blue shirts in Spain and China, and so forth.

See also *Blue Division; march on Rome; Schutzstaffel (SS)*.

BLAMEY, THOMAS (1884–1951) Australian general. A veteran of the Great War, Blamey was brought out of retirement and made commander in chief of ground forces in 1939. In 1940 he commanded the 1st Australian Corps in the Western Desert and the Balkans. He was instrumental in the evacuation of British and Commonwealth forces from *Crete*. He rose to become deputy commander in chief in the Middle East, but returned to Australia along with most "Diggers" following Japan's entry into the war. He was initially named commander of Western Allied ground forces in the *South-West Pacific Area (SWPA)*. After the Buna campaign stalled in New Guinea, General *Douglas MacArthur* assumed personal command of U.S. troops within SWPA. Blamey returned to Australia, although he remained in nominal command in New Guinea. Blamey returned to the field in New Guinea and the Solomons from October 1944 to conduct a bloody set of campaigns against cutoff pockets or garrisons of Japanese. MacArthur sharply criticized these efforts as wasteful and unnecessary. Blamey was also much criticized within Australia. A year before his death he was promoted to Field Marshal, the only Australian to achieve that rank.

BLASKOWITZ, JOHANNES VON (1884–1946) German field marshal. A specialist in armored warfare, he commanded an army in the invasion of Poland in 1939. He served as eastern commander in Poland until May 1940. He protested against atrocities carried out in Poland by the *Schutzstaffel (SS)* and *Gestapo* and was temporarily relieved by an angered Adolf Hitler. In October 1940, Blaskowitz was put in charge of occupation forces in France. From May to September, 1944, he commanded Army Group G in the south of France. In January 1945, he took charge of Army Group H in the Netherlands (or the so-called "Festung Holland"). He surrendered his command to 1st Canadian Army in May. Under indictment for war crimes in 1946, he probably killed himself while awaiting trial. However, there were rumors that he was murdered by SS prisoners.

BLAU (JUNE 28–NOVEMBER 18, 1942) "Blue." Code name for the 1942 German summer offensive in the east. Adolf Hitler wanted BLAU to become a 1942 version of *BARBAROSSA*. Field Marshal *Fedor von Bock* led every available element of a strongly reinforced Army Group South at the start of this swirling, confusing assault. BLAU unfolded in four phases, originally coded by the Wehrmacht as BLAU I, II, III, and IV. BLAU I was subsequently renamed BRAUNSCHWEIG by the

OKH. It corresponded to what Soviet historians call the "Voronezh-Voroshilovgrad defensive operation" (June 28–July 27, 1942), during which Army Group South was opposed by five Soviet armies, comprising Southwestern Front under Marshal *Semyon Timoshenko* and four more armies of Southern Front led by Major General *Rodion Malinovsky*. BLAU I aimed to drive to the Don. The Wehrmacht struck first for Voronezh on the Soviet extreme right flank, reaching that city on the upper Don on July 6. Having flanked the Soviet line, the Germans drive swung south, as Bock carried out a classic series of rolling flank attacks while also bringing pressure to bear toward the middle Don. The result was one of the most terrible Soviet defeats of the entire war, as a yawning hole was ripped open and nearly 400,000 men and over 2,400 tanks were lost. The fact that another *Kessel* was not created by the Panzers was mainly a result of the vast expanse of the battle area, which militated against encirclement. Also, most of the Panzer armies were elsewhere.

BLAU II was planned as a rapid drive over the Donbass to take Rostov. It was later renamed CLAUSEWITZ. The Germans reached Rostov at the mouth of the Don on July 23. Instead of assaulting the heavily defended city they crossed the river to the north, then encircled Rostov from the east. Hitler and the OKH next divided Army Group South into Army Groups A and B. Army Group A was sent into the Caucasus, reaching for the oil fields at Baku, which had drawn Hitler's eye away from Moscow and Leningrad in the first place. Initially called BLAU IV, the OKH retermed the drive *EDELWEISS*. Russian historians call it the "North Caucasus strategic defensive operation" (July 25–December 31, 1942). Meanwhile, BLAU III got underway. Recoded to FISCHREIHER ("Heron") by the OKH, the advance by Army Group B was intended as an auxiliary operation to cover the flank of what Hitler saw as the more critical effort to seize the minerals of the Caucasus. But Army Group B trapped Soviet 62nd Army in the great Don bend in mid-August and crossed the river on August 21. That opened a clear road to the Volga. Russian historians call the Red Army defense against the drive that ensued the "Stalingrad strategic defensive operation" (July 23–November 18, 1942). That was followed by the great Soviet counteroffensive launched on November 19, which smashed several minor Axis armies and trapped and annihilated German 6th Army during the *Battle of Stalingrad*.

During 1942 the Wehrmacht showed that it was still operationally superior to the Red Army. But the series of BLAU operations also demonstrated that German military intelligence was persistently inadequate and that Germany's top political and military leadership was strategically inept. Wehrmacht army groups thus tore through Soviet defenses to reach the Don and the Volga and cut deep into the Caucasus. They encircled and destroyed whole Soviet armies and took vast swaths of territory. The Wehrmacht outran its logistical systems by November, both in the Caucasus and at the Volga, where 6th Army and other forces were badly extended into a deep and vulnerable pocket. The Stavka exploited that vulnerability to smash weaker Axis armies on either side of Stalingrad and entrap 6th Army. The Soviet counteroffensive nearly trapped Army Group Don as well. It was clear by January 1943 that Hitler and the OKH had suffered a strategic defeat and not merely a lost battle or frustrated summer campaign. The Axis order of battle was shy by 50 divisions and irreplaceable stocks of tanks and guns. The Luftwaffe was exposed as an ill-led shell of its former self, with almost no supply capacity and no long-range bombing capability. Gains made in the Caucasus would be surrendered in the spring to pull out of a looming trap. None of the BLAU aims were achieved: Hitler did not have access to Baku's oil or the food stocks of southern Russia, nor could he deny these to the Soviet Union. Worse, the Soviet war economy recovered during 1942 and began outproducing Germany's still underachieving production. And the United States was fully in the war. Hitler turned on his generals: heads rolled on angry orders issued from the Wolfsschanze as Hitler flailed about in face of insurmountable material obstacles. Among the Field Marshals he sacked were *Wilhelm List, Fedor von Bock,* and *Franz Halder.* The OKH fell more firmly under control of the toady tandem of *Alfred Jodl* and *Wilhelm Keitel* and the strategic whims and foolhardy impulses of the Führer.

See also desert campaign (1940–1943).

BLETCHLEY PARK   "Station X." The site of, and usual shorthand reference for, the British Code and Cypher School founded in 1919 and located about 80 miles north of London. During World War II it housed the critical code-breaking operation run by *MI6.* It employed some of the most brilliant British minds of the century—notably Alan Turing, inventor of the first computer—as well as cryptanalysis specialists from Allied countries such as France, Poland, and the United States. The Americans actually took a long time to arrive and longer to be fully integrated: the first U.S. team did not reach Bletchley Park until April 25, 1943. Work at Bletchley Park was compartmentalized by "hut," with groups in different huts listening to various of the hundreds of Luftwaffe, Kriegsmarine, or Wehrmacht codes. Signals were passed to code translators in Hut Three, which accepted its first Americans only in January 1944. There were over 10,000 people working on or otherwise supporting the extraordinarily complex and crucial work done at Bletchley Park by 1945. All their extraordinary work was kept secret for several decades after the war. Outposts of cryptanalysis tied to Bletchley Park were also maintained overseas, such as the "Combined Bureau, Middle East" in Cairo.

See also East African campaign (1940–1941); Enigma machine; Geheimschreiber machine; intelligence; MAGIC; PURPLE; ULTRA.

BLIMPS

See balloons.

BLIND BOMBING   A bombing technique used when ground targets could not be visually confirmed because they were obscured by smoke or clouds. Such targets were *area bombed* by aircraft directed over them by *Gee, Oboe,* or *H2S* navigation aids.

BLITZ   Derived from *Blitzkrieg.* This was common English slang for the German night bombing campaign against London and other British cities lasting from September 1940 until May 1941. It was also used (lower case) as a generic reference to swift-paced, combined arms assaults. The decision to continue bombing British trade and industrial targets followed the failure of the Luftwaffe to win the *Battle of Britain* in 1940. It reflected basic confusion in German strategic thinking: other than the ongoing naval fight on the high seas, Adolf Hitler had no other way to damage the British economy. In addition, he needed a propaganda campaign to counter the effects of RAF Bomber Command's raids on German cities. During the summer and fall of 1940, Hitler hoped that terror bombing might drive Britain from the war. However, the Luftwaffe had nowhere near the capability needed to conduct *strategic bombing* or *morale bombing*, and in any case, the effort was abandoned as limited resources were pulled into new military adventures in the Balkans, the Mediterranean, and finally in the western Soviet Union.

Over the course of the Blitz more than 43,000 Britons lost their lives to bombs and fires. Another 140,000 were hurt. Many houses and factories were destroyed, and Britain was forced to commit a large share of its war effort to homeland air defense. Otherwise, the Blitz did more to steel British resolve than to break it, and hardly slowed aircraft or other key war production. Moreover, the Luftwaffe lost 600 planes it had a much harder time replacing. The German cause would have been far better served had those lost bombers cooperated with the Kriegsmarine to attack vital British convoys, or attacked Soviet strategic targets before the badly smashed VVS recovered during 1942. Fortunately for the British and the Soviet Union, the Luftwaffe high command would not agree to deploy more than a few bombers to attack the convoys. By the time *BARBAROSSA* was launched, over 600 German bombers had been lost over Britain. A second or "mini-Blitz" was conducted by the Luftwaffe from January to May 1944, when its resources were more denuded still. V-1 and V-2 rockets were used instead of bombers from June 17, until their launch sites were overrun by Western Allied ground forces.

See also Baedeker raids; V-weapons program.

BLITZKRIEG "Lightning war." Attack and infiltration tactics developed by the German Army. Some historians have seen it as both an operational and strategic concept, while others have challenged the validity of Blitzkrieg as an explanatory concept of any kind, and even dismissed it as a "myth." The latter is a charge that is sooner or later made against all once-dominant ideas and images by revisionist academics. On the other hand, even Adolf Hitler publicly disavowed Blitzkrieg as a concept. He told a Munich audience in November 1941: "I have never used the word Blitzkrieg, because it is a completely idiotic word." The preferred German term was *Bewegungskrieg*. Yet, enough of the core concept of "Blitzkrieg" remains valid to help elucidate German operations from 1939 to 1941. That is especially so, as Hew Strachan has noted, because astonishingly rapid German victories in Poland, in Scandinavia, and especially over France gave to "Blitzkrieg" an iconic status that was retroactively outfitted as an all-encompassing German military doctrine. It should be noted at the onset that a critical component of the success of

Blitzkrieg was an advance element of political and strategic surprise to lay groundwork for operational surprise by field forces. That was well understood by the war planners of the *OKW*.

Blitzkrieg grew out of new technologies of armored transport; advances in tank speed, design, and firepower; maturation of the tactical bomber; and radio links between ground and air forces. It also spoke to intense need and desire to avoid a descent into trench warfare akin to 1914–1918. Blitzkrieg tactical doctrine drew closely from experience in the closing days of the Great War, where battlefield movement was reestablished by specialized shock troops (German) and concentrated armored formations (Allies). "Lightning" attacks by the Wehrmacht disregarded safety of the flanks of an advance in favor of aggressive tactical breakthroughs and stunningly rapid exploitation. The aim was to "punch a hole" in an enemy's line, then exploit confusion and opportunities in his immediate rear with armor and mechanized infantry. Concentrations of Panzers and Panzergrenadiers would make a lightening breakthrough, closely supported by tactical air power. This was followed by infantry exploitation of any local advantage created, which required exceptional innovation and initiative on the ground by division and corps-level commanders. At its optimum, this tactic might lead to encirclement of enemy armies on either flank of the breakthrough. It is infrequently noted that the role of infantry in Blitzkrieg—especially mechanized or motorized infantry—was just as critical as the part played by armor. In fact, Blitzkrieg demanded fully mechanized forces capable of constant movement in a series of rapid flanking and pincer maneuvers, as well as revolutionary close command and control of ground and air units. Blitzkrieg in this form was inflicted on Poland, Norway, Denmark, the Low Countries, and France in 1939 and 1940. Most spectacularly, it was at the center of *BARBAROSSA* operations in the Soviet Union in 1941.

The best image of Blitzkrieg tactics is of an armored spearhead joined to a stout infantry shaft, capable of piercing the enemy's line rather than assaulting it futilely across a broad front, as had been attempted so often to such little effect during World War I. This new method proved highly effective in *FALL WEISS* in Poland in 1939, and even more so during *FALL GELB* in France in 1940. That was true even though a doctrinally radical and nonconformist French general, *Charles de Gaulle,* found the weakness in Blitzkrieg during the Battle of the Meuse: striking at the junction of armor spearpoint and infantry shaft with a precise armored counterattack. If done properly, such a counterattack could break off the spear tip, leaving it cut off and isolated. Better defenses were developed against armored Blitzkrieg by all major armies by 1943. The new methods involved using armored divisions, artillery, and mines to prepare a defense-in-depth that blunted and absorbed the Panzer thrusts, then counterattacking with an armored and mobile strike force. A hard-learned sense of bitter realism about the goals and nature of Nazi Germany also stiffened anti-German resistance everywhere, as "methodical battle" rather than Blitzkrieg came to dominate fighting. From mid-1943 the Red Army added lessons learned from defending in 1941–1942 to its prewar offensive concept of *deep battle,* then encircled and smashed whole German armies. The

German response was a call for *total war*. As Stalin noted in May 1943, that was a sure signal that the original plan for Blitzkrieg had failed.

See also BAGRATION; *keil und kessel*; *Kesselschlacht*; *kotel*; *Kursk*; *Normandy*; *Pacific War (1941–1945)*; *Sino-Japanese War (1937–1945)*; *Stalingrad*; *Vernichtungskrieg*; *Vistula-Oder operation*.

BLOCKADA

See siege of Leningrad.

BLOCKADE   The Western Allies employed economic and food blockades of the Axis states as a core war policy during World War II. That was partly based on false assumptions of the supposed efficacy of their earlier blockade of Imperial Germany in bringing about capitulation in 1918. The Allied blockade during World War II had multiple aims: to slowly strangle Axis war economies by limiting access to critical raw materials not available in Europe or Japan; to created a "neurosis" of encirclement; to stretch Axis military assets in defense of distant supplies; and to create a real shortage of critical war matériel. The efficacy of the blockade of Germany was greatly reduced from 1939 to 1941 by two things: Germany's conquest and economic exploitation of multiple neighboring states and intimidation of others; and Soviet matériel assistance to Germany under terms of the *Nazi–Soviet Pact (August 23, 1939)*. The Germans counter-blockaded Britain with *unrestricted submarine warfare* during the *Battle of the Atlantic (1939–1945),* but ultimately lost this most crucial campaign of the war in the west. The British were especially careful to ration exports of critical goods to neutrals such as Sweden, to limit potential transshipment to Germany. The Western Allies also used competitive buying from poor countries such as Portugal and Spain to keep stocks of critical supplies of tungsten and wolfram out of German hands. The Germans countered by offering top dollar to the Swedes and others. Following the *DRAGOON* landings in southern France and closing of the Spanish border in August 1944, those supplies stopped. Turkey was also pressured to cease deliveries of chromium to Germany. That also stopped with Western Allied military success in the Mediterranean theater and, to a lesser extent, in the *Italian campaign (1943–1945)*.

The Japanese failed to even consider true economic warfare against the Western powers, either offensive or defensive. That was a remarkable omission considering how access to natural resources of the South Pacific and Southeast Asia was the major war aim pursued by Imperial General Headquarters in 1941. The omission continued throughout the war. For instance, Japan failed to assign IJN submarines to intercept Pacific or Indian Ocean convoys, retaining them instead as fleet auxiliaries for an illusory "decisive battle" to be waged by the main war fleets. Sea blockade was not critical to the ultimate defeat of Germany for reasons described previously. But savaging the Japanese merchant marine by mining Japan's home waters from B-29s, combined with economic blockade via cargo ship and tanker interdiction by submarines and naval and land-based air power, proved a major contribution to the collapse of the Japanese war economy. As one result, in 1945 American bombs often fell on idled Japanese factories whose workers had already run away to the countryside to look for food and that in any case lacked resources to continue production. Blockade thus not only seriously disrupted Japanese production, it reduced the population to near-starvation levels by mid-1945.

See also blockade runners; convoys; Leningrad, siege of; Phoney War; Switzerland; U-boats.

BLOCKADE RUNNING Smuggling is an ancient and honorable profession. Blockade running is smuggling by neutrals or belligerents in time of war. In a truly global war such as World War II, that became a far more deadly game than usual. Sometimes, it was a last resort. For instance, the British used submarines to run critical aircraft fuel into Malta during the siege of that island base because their tanker convoys were savaged by Italian and German air attack. Americans used private ships from the Dutch East Indies to move supplies in to *Corregidor* and fast PT boats to get General *Douglas MacArthur* out. Smuggling operations supported isolated *coast watchers* in the South Pacific. The British also used submarines and small craft to smuggle in spies and commando teams and to supply resistance movements with arms in German-occupied Europe. Résistance leaders were smuggled in to take control of fractious local movements in France and out to brief officials in London. Several Norwegian surface blockade runners made a dangerous passage from Sweden, carrying vital finished war matériel to Great Britain in January 1941. They were bombed, but survived. A second run from Sweden in March 1942, by 10 Norwegian ships with British crews, was a disaster: only two vessels completed the voyage after encountering neutral Swedish and hostile German armed opposition. Later in the war, as Sweden sidled more toward the Western Allies with the obvious approach of German defeat, British *Motor Gun Boats (MGBs)* operated by the *Special Operations Executive (SOE)* made a number of dashes to Sweden and back.

Blockade running was mostly unattractive to neutral shipping once Allied naval supremacy was established. But Axis blockade runners—on and below the water—operated wherever enemy surface navies or land-based aircraft intercepted regular maritime traffic. They concentrated on critical raw materials and other contraband goods. One German blockade runner was caught disguised as a U.S. ship. Japanese–German blockade breaking was facilitated by the Soviet Union until June 1941. The Japanese also ran materials to Germany by surface ship, especially natural rubber but also vegetable oils. The first surface blockade runner left Japan for France on December 28, 1940. It did not arrive in Germany until April 4, 1941. Operation *BARBAROSSA* shut down the trans-Siberian rail route from Manchuria to Germany from the end of June 1941. Seventeen Japanese ships were then sent west, carrying enough natural rubber to serve as a base for the German synthetic rubber program for two years. The Germans asked for even more blockade runners, but only a few Japanese dozen ships were sent out in 1942. Their loses rose steeply during 1943. German goods went back to Japan in surviving ships. This surface trade ceased entirely in January 1944. Yet, the small amounts of rubber, tin, and wolfram sent to Germany before then proved critical to continued war production in 1944. After cancellation of the surface trade, U-boats and converted Italian submarines were used. Obvious limitations of space and improved Western Allied *anti-submarine warfare* capabilities meant that U-boat blockade runners proved decreasingly effective and were frequently sunk. On occasion, U-boats also carried German military officers and Japanese diplomats. One transported *Subhas Chandra Bose* from Germany to the Pacific. In the case of isolated Japanese garrisons in the Pacific, blockade running by submarine was vital to even minimal resupply of starving troops.

BLOCKING DETACHMENTS "zagraditelnyi otriad." Zagradotryady were Red Army troops positioned in the immediate rear of frontline combat troops to block mass desertion and to shoot stragglers, or anyone else who could not explain why he was there and not at the front killing Germans. Sharpshooters and machine gun crews picked off would-be mass deserters, while firing squads dealt with individual stragglers. Discipline was enforced by the harshest means to prevent mass desertion, panic, and surrender that threatened to lead to strategic defeat. The role of Zagradotryady was thus expanded during the great crisis of mass surrenders in the opening months of the German invasion. Too many had surrendered overly easily in 1941; more would do so in the first half of 1942. As historian Evan Mawdsley aptly put it, Soviet soldiers at that time were "demoralized troops in a demoralized society." On September 12, 1941, Joseph Stalin and the Stavka therefore issued a harsh directive establishing "blocking detachments." Their role was only strengthened by his July 28, 1942, *Order #227*.

The men of blocking detachments were drawn directly from Red Army units. They were not *NKVD* troops, but operated under NKVD control and in the shadow of their own potential execution by Red Army officers or by the NKVD. Behind dragooned detachments of Zagradotryady were still harder NKVD troops and firing squads, ready to shoot even senior officers or any Zagradotryady who failed to do their duty as defined by the Stavka and by Stalin. The Stavka issued orders to reduce the number of executions from October 1941, cautioning that officers should instead try to persuade men to stand and fight. Recruitment of *krasnoarmeets* from regular units into blocking detachments was ended one year later. Thereafter, NKVD troops alone filled the enforcement role of Order #227, with their usual utterly ruthless disregard for individual pleadings or special cases. Such extraordinary measures were continued even after the open wound of mass surrenders by Red Army soldiers was stanched. That was because suspicion remained among the NKVD, and in Stalin's mind, that too many Ukrainians, Belorussians, Poles, and Balts were actively hostile to the Soviet system—which many of them were—and hence could not be trusted to fight. Blocking detachments were finally disbanded in October 1944, as final victory came into view.

BLOMBERG, WERNER VON (1878–1946) German field marshal. A veteran of the Great War, Blomberg served on the secret *Reichswehr* General Staff in the 1920s. He was minister of defense, then of war, from 1933 to 1938. He supported the ascent to power of Adolf Hitler, seeing the Nazis as a bulwark against social chaos and as the wrecker of the Weimar Republic, which he and other generals so despised. In turn, Hitler saw Blomberg as a useful link to the old Prussian officer corps. Blomberg applauded destruction of the *Sturmabteilung (SA)*—a potential Nazi Party rival to the Reichswehr—which Hitler gutted during the *Night of the Long Knives* in 1934. Blomberg then led the Wehrmacht in swearing loyalty oaths to Hitler's person. Hitler never trusted Blomberg, but nonetheless elevated him to become first Generalfeldmarschall of the Third Reich. Blomberg was highly nervous about the reaction of the Western Allies to Hitler's remilitarization of the *Rhineland*, and even more about the prospect of war over Czechoslovakia in 1938. His opposition to Hitler's hopes for a more aggressive foreign policy led Hitler to use pornographic blackmail to force Blomberg out. Hitler named himself minister of defense in place of the Field Marshal and took over personal control and direction of the OKW. Blomberg never held another active command. He died in an Allied prison at Nuremberg in March 1946.

BLOOD PURGE
See Blomberg, Werner von; Hitler, Adolf; Nazi Party; Night of the Long Knives; Schutzstaffel (SS); Sturmabteilung (SA); Wehrmacht.

BLÜCHER II (SEPTEMBER 1942)   Wehrmacht code name for the crossing of the Kerch Straits in September 1942.
See EDELWEISS.

BLUE (1942)
See BLAU; EDELWEISS.

BLUE DIVISION   "División Española de Voluntarios (DEV)." A full infantry division sent by General *Francisco Franco* to fight alongside the Wehrmacht on the Eastern Front, ostensibly in belated response to Soviet intervention in the *Spanish Civil War (1936–1939)*. It was not a division of the Spanish Army, though all its officers were regular Army at Franco's insistence. Its enlisted men initially comprised a great majority of Spanish *Falangist* volunteers. The party uniform of these former *blueshirts* lent the division its popular nickname. Not all its members were volunteers, even at the start: Franco forced men into the division that included a number of his most bitter, left-wing opponents. The DEV was organized from June 27, 1941, by Franco's brother-in-law and foreign minister, the committed *fascist* Serrano Suñer. He provided enthusiastic political support while regular officers shaped some 18,000 Falangist volunteers into a reinforced fighting division. Most of the original contingent were radical Falangists, many students from the universities but also men of the middle class and workers. Motivations of those joining the DEV were a mix of fascist enthusiasm, expectation of German victory, and anti-Communist and anti-Soviet feeling dating to the Civil War. While Franco was well pleased to see such committed revolutionaries depart Spain, his other interests were to soften the impact on German relations of Spain's long-postponed entry into the war and repay the blood debt owed to the *Kondor Legion*. DEV participation in fighting on the Eastern Front would mark the height of

Spanish collaboration with the Axis. No other nonbelligerent country raised an entire division for Adolf Hitler.

In Bavaria for basic training by July, the DEV was registered as the 250th Division of the Wehrmacht and reorganized to fit within the German order of battle. It took nearly two months for it to reach the front due to terrible German logistics. Most DEV troops prudently discarded their Spanish blue uniforms once they reached the Eastern Front, switching to German feldgrau. Some still wore blue shirts, however, when the DEV saw first combat on October 7. The 250th fought well but was badly bloodied as part of Army Group North, fighting around Leningrad for the next two years. By the end of 1941 it had suffered 1,400 dead, but also made a strong impression on local German commanders and on Hitler. The Blue Division saw more heavy action in the first months of 1942. It experienced especially heavy fighting over the next winter, when it was finally cracked by a Red Army assault in a bloody fight at Krasny Bor on February 10, 1943. On that single day the DEV lost 2,252 men, including over 1,100 dead. That was one-quarter of all casualties it suffered over two years. Its last seven months on the Eastern Front were more quiet. As casualties rose fewer Falangist volunteers could be found. More conscripts or regular army troops and more enemies of the regime were shipped out instead. During 1943 the Division was wholly reformed with replacements. Spain paid all wages and maintenance costs, but Germany provided weapons and military equipment.

Once Franco finally realized that Germany was going to lose the war, and as he came under increasing pressure from the Western Allies to end collaboration with the Hitler regime, he disbanded and recalled the Blue Division in October 1943. Over two thousand committed Spanish fascists refused to leave. Reinforced with conscripts, they were reorganized as part of German 121st Division under the designation "Spanish Legion" (Legion Españolo de Voluntarios), or "Blue Legion." Even that small force was ordered dissolved by Franco and to return to Spain in March 1944, as Western Allied pressure on Madrid increased and Franco feared invasion and overthrow of his regime. The last surge of ideological enthusiasm among Blue Division veterans came in mid-1944, as 300 crossed into southern France looking to join Wehrmacht units readying to fight the Western Allies. A last few true fanatics were still in the east in 1945: 243 men who had not had enough of war in the fascist cause refused Franco's 1944 order to return to Spain, staying on to form the "Spanish Volunteer Unit." They and other Spaniards recruited separately into the *Waffen-SS* fought in the east until the final *conquest of Germany* in 1945. Almost none saw Spain or family again.

Of more than 45,000 men who served one-year enlistments or longer in the DEV just under 5,000 were killed, 8,700 were wounded, about 400 were captured by the Red Army, and another 8,000 had severe frostbite or other front-related illnesses. A vast praise literature later developed in Spain that portrayed Blue Division men as unusually kind to Russian civilians, absolving them from known German atrocities carried out in the east. The moral difference of the DEV from the behavior of other Wehrmacht units or Waffen-SS men was exaggerated in this nationalist revisionism, but the charge of somewhat greater decency was not wholly baseless. Most Spanish fascists who volunteered for the DEV were anti-Communist ideologues rather than Nazi-style race-haters, and not a few DEV men were unwilling working class conscripts who had no loyalty to the fascist cause whatsoever. Several hundred DEV prisoners were returned to Spain by the Soviet Union in 1954 and 1959.

See also Blue Squadron.

BLUE LEGION   "Legion Españolo de Voluntarios (LEV)."
See Blue Division.

BLUE PLAN
See Force Française de l'Intérieur (FFI).

BLUESHIRTS   *Fascist* street organizations that engaged in political thuggery and even murder of political opponents. In China in the 1930s, Whampoa Military Academy cadets and graduates were organized as leaders of death squads and political intimidation units by the Academy's erstwhile first commandant, *Jiang Jieshi*. He dressed them in blue shirts in admiring emulation of Benito Mussolini's *blackshirts* in Italy. Many blueshirts later served Jiang's regime as secret police. Before, during, and after the *Spanish Civil War (1936–1939)*, Falange Party radicals organized in blueshirt clubs and street gangs across Spain to intimidate political enemies. Some later fought as volunteers in the *Blue Division* on the Eastern Front.

BLUE SQUADRON   "Escuadrilla Azul." Five squadrons of Spanish volunteer fighter pilots, many of them former *blueshirts,* who joined the Luftwaffe on the Eastern Front.

See also Blue Division.

BLUM, LÉON (1872–1950)   French socialist. He came to prominence on the French left during the Dreyfus Affair before World War I. Blum rejected Vladimir Lenin's hard ideological line in 1921, splitting democratic French socialists from far left fanatics who started to call themselves Communists. Blum opposed French occupation of the *Ruhr* in the 1920s. In 1936 he headed a Popular Front government, becoming the first socialist premier of France. He was unable to garner support for strong opposition to Adolf Hitler: the *Spanish Civil War* badly divided French public opinion and made it impossible to form an antifascist front with other democracies. The democratic right in France also failed to understand that the real danger to national liberty was not internal but external: not French socialists but German and Italian fascists and their building armies, made more threatening by fifth columnists and future eager collaborators among domestic fascists. Blum became premier again in 1938, but he still could marshal almost no support for a policy of active resistance to Nazi Germany's growing aggression in Central Europe. Blum condemned the *appeasement* policy of the *Munich Conference*. Despising his socialist politics and his Jewish faith, the extreme right in France instead embraced the defeatist slogan: "Better Hitler than Blum." Following *FALL GELB,* the campaign that led to the defeat and surrender of France, Blum opposed the right-wing turn by Vichy. Tried by Vichy at Riom, he masterfully turned the proceedings into a judgment on the regime. That led to embarrassed cancellation of the trial. Blum was subsequently imprisoned by the Germans at *Dachau* for the duration of the war. Blum briefly headed a caretaker government in 1946.

BM "boevaia mashina" or "combat vehicle." Soviet weapons designation for multiple types of armed vehicles, but excluding tanks.
See also katiusha.

BOCAGE
See Normandy campaign.

BOCK, FEDOR VON (1880–1945) German field marshal. He was highly decorated for bravery during World War I, including with the "Blue Max." Bock commanded Army Group North in Poland in 1939, Army Group B in France in 1940, and Army Group Center during the *BARBAROSSA* invasion of the Soviet Union in 1941. He took the classic route into Russia, trod in both directions by Napoleon's troops in 1812. In just four months Bock's Army Group Center totally destroyed 18 Soviet armies, some in cooperation with *Gerd von Rundstedt's* Army Group South. But Bock was halted short of Moscow by strained logistics, severe weather, and Russian courage. Bock was exhausted, fell ill, and was replaced on December 19 by *Günther von Kluge.* A month later Bock was put in command of Army Group South when its commander, *Walter von Reichenau,* was killed. Bock was forced to defend against two major Soviet offensives in 1942, the second occurring at Kharkov. He counterattacked and inflicted severe casualties on enemy Fronts led by Marshal *Semyon Timoshenko.* During the complex *BLAU* operation Bock deviated from strict orders issued by Adolf Hitler, who blamed him for the delay and failure that followed. Although Bock smashed through Soviet lines on a nearly 300-mile front and raced ahead to the Donets River, Hitler forced him to retire that July. Bock never returned to active command. He was always suspect to Hitler and other top Nazis because of his aristocratic origins and privately held, but intense, anti-Nazi views. His professional ethics and opinions once led him to file a mild protest over mistreatment of civilians in the east. But he never tipped into outright opposition, falling back on an officer's code of political neutrality that the Nazis had long since gutted of principle or moral content. Bock thus declined to cooperate with the German military resistance that organized the *July Plot* in 1944, the only group that might have given his supposed principles iron teeth. Bock was killed when his car was strafed by a British fighter in May 1945.
See also TAIFUN.

BODYGUARD A series of *deception operations* designed to mask the *OVERLORD* invasion of France in mid-1944. BODYGUARD comprised three major operations:

ZEPPELIN, FORTITUDE North, and *FORTITUDE South.* These helped ensure total surprise for Western Allied forces that landed in Normandy on *D-Day (June 6, 1944),* and further delayed German reinforcements for weeks after that as Adolf Hitler remained persuaded the main attack would come at the Pas de Calais.

BOFORS

See anti-aircraft guns; pom-pom.

BOGEY

BOGEY   Or "bogie." Western Allied tag for any unidentified aircraft picked up at a distance on *radar* or by the naked eye. If subsequently identified as an enemy plane the designation swiftly changed to *bandit.*

BOHEMIA-MORAVIA   A protectorate set up by the Nazis during the German occupation of Czechoslovakia from 1939 to 1945. The territories reverted to Czechoslovakia after the war.

BOHR, NIELS (1885–1962)

See nuclear weapons programs.

BOLERO   Code name for the build-up of U.S. forces in Great Britain pending the invasion of France.

BOLIVIA   This isolated South American country declared war on the Axis states in April 1942, under great pressure from the United States. A pro-Nazi military coup briefly threatened to reverse course in 1944, but Axis-leaning members of the junta were quickly purged to placate Washington. Bolivia made no significant military contribution to the Allied war effort.

BOMBARDIER   American term for the bomber crew position the British called "bomb-aimer." The latter did not appear in RAF bombers until 1942, before which bomb aiming was the job of the navigator.

BOMBER COMMAND

See Royal Air Force (RAF). See also airborne; area bombing; Combined Bomber Offensive; Harris, Arthur; morale bombing; Portal, Charles; strategic bombing; thousand plane raids.

BOMBERS   The *Red Army Air Force (VVS)* built four and six-engine experimental bombers in the 1930s. Otherwise, "heavy" bombers on all sides at the start of the war were mostly two-engine models with a relatively small payload, rarely exceeding 5,000 lbs. Two-engine models were reclassified as medium bombers once four-engine "heavies" were developed that had a much larger carrying capacity and range. The Western Allies built 50,000 four-engine heavy bombers by the end of the war. Most bombers were not armored before 1938. U.S. aircraft were built to a standard of protection from .50 caliber ordnance beyond a range of 200 yards from 1941, while canopies were made with bullet-resistant glass. Other armies and navies adopted variations of armor protection, but continued to build all or partly wooden aircraft as well in an effort to maximize speed over defense. Only Japanese Army and Navy bombers remained without armor throughout the war. The Luftwaffe was the first air force to install self-sealing fuel tanks. The VVS and Western Allied air forces followed suit, but the Japanese again lagged in this aircraft technology.

Soviet aircraft production was advanced from the moment the regime emerged from the Russian Civil War (1918–1921). Technical help was provided from 1922 by Germany under terms of the *Treaty of Rapallo (April 16, 1922)*. A modified medium bomber, the TB-1, flew from Moscow to New York in 1929. That demonstrated to the Japanese that they were vulnerable to strategic attack by the VVS, which also built the world's first four-engine bomber in 1930: the ANT-6. The Soviets built a six-engine version, the ANT-16, in 1933. They built a four-engine *float plane* heavy bomber four years later. By 1941, however, the most numerous Soviet bomber was the light SB2. A few larger Il-4s were also available. Both types proved technically inadequate. In any case, thousands were thrown away in poor attack plans over the first months of the German–Soviet war or were destroyed on the ground by the Luftwaffe or overrun on their airfields by the Wehrmacht. Production of all types of VVS bombers was greatly slowed by relocation of major factories from Moscow to the Urals over the winter of 1941–1942. Bomber production recovered and then excelled from the end of 1942. For medium bombers the VVS relied on 6,800 Il-4s, 3,000 American-built Douglas A-20 Arados, and 900 *Lend-Lease* B-25s. VVS planners and Red Army generals wanted bombers mostly for close tactical support. Perfect for this role was the two-seater Il-2 "Shturmovik" attack bomber, of which 36,200 were built. The IL-2 was heavily armored, which served it well in its primary ground attack role. Another 10,600 Petliakov Pe-2 dive bombers were produced. The generic Soviet term for "assault" or "attack" aircraft, "shturmovik," became most closely identified with the Il-2.

"Stuka," the German equivalent to "shturmovik," similarly came to be used almost exclusively in reference to the prewar Ju-87, of which 5,700 were built for the Luftwaffe. The Ju-87 "Stuka" proved vulnerable and inadequate during the *Battle of Britain,* but it found a new role in the east as a *tank-buster*. The Luftwaffe entered the war with two other main bombers, both medium in range and payload: the Dornier Do-17 (1,100 built to 1942) and the Heinkel He-111 (7,300 in service to 1945). Neither proved adequate to the bombing missions ordered by Adolf Hitler over Britain in 1940, nor promised by *Hermann Göring* for the war in the east. The Germans built 14,676 Ju-88-A4 twin-engine aircraft, of which 9,000 were designated bombers while the rest served as transports. Another 1,000 model Ju-88-E-1s were built from 1943, too few to have a real impact on the bombing war. About 2,000 Do-217s were built from 1941, but that model was only a marginal improvement on the Do-17 prewar version. The 1,146 He-177s built from 1942 had a significantly longer range at over 3,000 miles, but they were badly designed had poorly performing engines and many other technical problems. In any case, not enough left the assembly line to fulfill a *strategic bombing* role.

German bomber production declined from mid-1943. It fell sharply in 1944 as fighter production was greatly increased at the expense of new bombers to deal with vast Western Allied air fleets carrying out the *Combined Bomber Offensive* over Germany. Other aircraft production also suffered. For instance, only 900 heavily armored, twin-engine Henschel Hs-129 attack planes were built. The He-178 jet bomber prototype had flown as early as August 1939, but German jet production waited several more years as Luftwaffe designers concentrated on a dive bombing role on the express orders of Hitler. Of the several models of jet bombers designed in Germany, two eventually became operational. Paucity of numbers and major design flaws limited their combat impact. Germany's first operational jet bomber was the twin-engine Arado Ar-234 light bomber and reconnaissance aircraft. It was capable of speeds over 500 mph. It first saw service in 1943, but bombing of its main factory forced dispersal of production and delayed operational status into 1944. Just 210 Ar-234s left underground Luftwaffe factories by the end of the war. Research was begun on a long-range "Amerika bomber" in 1937, but it came to naught. Several prototypes were developed, including a Sänger Amerika Bomber and a Junkers Ju-390. The Sänger project was canceled in 1941. The Ju-390—which evolved from the Ju-290 transport plane—was canceled in 1944 after construction of just two prototypes.

Among other Axis states, Italy's Regia Aeronautica concentrated on torpedo bombers in the prewar period, building 1,330 three-engine wooden Savoia-Marchetti SM-79s to support Benito Mussolini's ambitions to dominate the Mediterranean. Italy built just 600 Fiat BR-20Ms, twin-engine medium bombers that saw action over Britain in 1940 and in North Africa to 1943. Italy built under 700 CRDA (or Cant) Z1007 wooden, three-engined medium bombers. These were used to harass and attack Mediterranean convoys but soon proved highly vulnerable to RAF fighters. The Japanese had a wider range of bombers. English-language terms for these aircraft derived from Western Allied identification codes, in which female names were given to bombers and male names to fighters. The Japanese Army's Mitsubishi "Betty," or Type-1 G4M, was famed for flaming out. It was underarmored, with almost no cockpit protection and mounted highly vulnerable fuel tanks that did not self-seal. Similar problems attended the twin-engine Mitsubishi "Sally" and "Peggy" models, with the latter appearing in small numbers from October 1944. Some thought was given to developing an interoceanic bomber called the "Fugako," but Japan's limited aircraft industry could not spare the needed resources. The Japanese Navy deployed several bombers, including the "Kate" torpedo bomber, "Judy" dive bomber, and "Val" altitude or level bomber.

France and Britain started the war with several single-engine and two-engine bomber types. Heavy losses in France in May–June, 1940, revealed that most of these were inadequate, especially older French models. The British single-engine Fairey "Battle" and twin-engine Bristol "Blenheim" were shot out of the sky in large numbers. "Hamden," "Whitley," and "Wellington" twin-engine bombers fared somewhat better, but were still inadequate to the evolving strategic role envisioned by RAF Bomber Command. These older models were phased out as new four-engine heavy bombers were brought into production. Nearly 4,000 "Sterling IIIs" became operational after February 1941. The first of 6,176 operational "Halifax VIs" rolled off the assembly line the next month, followed by 7,377 "Lancaster Is" from March 1942. In German street slang, these British heavy bombers and their U.S. counterparts lumbering across Germany's skies were called "dicke Autos" ("fat cars"). The British also built 7,781 De Havilland "Mosquitos" from May 1942. These fast, twin-engined light bombers found a special role as *pathfinder* aircraft. They also served as daytime tactical strike bombers. Differently armed, they proved excellent heavy fighters and effective long-range night-fighters. The RAF also developed the "Typhoon" as an effective fighter-bomber after 1941.

The USAAF built 12,731 four-engine heavily armed B-17s starting in 1935. The B-17 "Flying Fortress" had a relatively small bomb load at just 6,000 lbs at shorter ranges, or 4,000 lbs for a run over Germany from bases in Britain. If a B-17 was fitted with special external racks its bomb payload rose significantly. About 7,400 two-engine medium Douglas A-20s were built; in British units, these Lend-Lease aircraft were called "Boston IVs." The single most numerous USAAF bomber was the B-24 "Liberator." Over 18,300 of these four-engine heavies were produced from 1942 to 1945. They were joined by 11,400 four-engine B-25 "Mitchells" starting in February 1942. Over 5,100 B-26 "Marauders" were built and deployed from April 1942. Finally, 3,970 B-29 "Superfortresses" were constructed specifically to reach Japan. Originally conceived as a Japan bomber in 1939 but not built until several years later, they were used only in the Pacific theater of operations. The program was well funded and widely publicized, but also plagued with design and engine problems. B-29s finally rolled off the assembly line in large numbers in late 1944. They mined waters around Japan's home islands and burned out Japanese cities during 1945, culminating in delivery of two atomic bombs in early August. The United States also commissioned two true intercontinental bombers in 1941 for use against Germany should Britain be knocked out of the war: the B-32 "Dominator" and B-36 "Peacemaker." Fewer than 120 B-32s were built owing to the success of the B-29. Only a handful reached the Pacific, to fly a few missions against Japan in mid-1945. The B-36 prototype was not ready until 1946. The USAAF also developed a series of highly effective fighter-bombers, notably the P-47 "Thunderbolt" and the remarkably powerful and long-range P-51 "Mustang." In addition to superlative performance as a fighter in Europe and the Pacific, the P-51 could carry a 2,000 lb bomb and place it precisely on target or use wing-mounted rockets in a tank-busting role. The U.S. Navy deployed a variety of torpedo and dive bombers that improved in capability as the war progressed. They were highly effective in destroying Japanese warships, merchantmen, and tankers.

See also air power; anti-aircraft weapons; anti-submarine warfare; bombs; morale bombing; thousand plane raids.

Suggested Reading: W. Green, *Warplanes of the Second World War*, 4 vols. (1961).

BOMBER STREAM

See area bombing; Kammhuber Line; Ruhr; strategic bombing; thousand plane raids; Wilde Sau.

BOMBES   British copies of the *Enigma machine*.

BOMBING

See air power; anti-aircraft weapons; anti-submarine warfare; area bombing; Berlin bomber offensive; blind bombing; bombers; Britain, Battle of; cab rank system; CLARION; Combined Bomber Offensive; Coventry raid; creep back; Direction-Finding (D/F); Dresden raid; FALL GELB; FALL WEISS; FIDO; flak; Flak Towers; Freya; Fugo; Gee; Guernica; Harris, Arthur; Hiroshima; IFF; Knickebein; leaflet bombing; LeMay, Curtiss; Lichtenstein-Gerät; Light Night Striking Force; LORAN; Lorenz; Luftwaffe; Molotov breadbasket; morale bombing; Nagasaki; Norden bombsight; Oboe; Pathfinders; pattern bombing; Pointblank Directive; Red Army Air Force (VVS); Royal Air Force; Shaker technique; shuttle bombing; skip bombing; strategic bombing; Tedder's carpet; thousand plane raids; Unit-731; United States Army Air Force; window; Würzburg; X-Gerät; Y-Gerät.

BOMBS   The types of bombs used in World War II were many and varied. High explosives were used to shatter buildings or implode field fortifications. Incendiaries were dropped to burn the kindling produced by high explosives. Armor-piercing bombs were used against tanks. The power of comparably sized bombs grew markedly as the war progressed. High explosive filling of a 500 lb bomb might be only 300 lbs in 1939. High explosive charges improved in destructive power as the amount of high explosive filler increased, meaning that smaller bombs in 1945 did more damage than heavier types at the start of the war. Most early-war bombs ranged between 100 and 500 lbs. The RAF went further than any air force in increasing bomb weight, as heavy bombers were developed that increased load capacity. The RAF introduced a 1,000 lb bomb in early 1941 and a 2,000 lb high explosive bomb later that year. In July 1942, the RAF first deployed 4,000 lb bombs called "Cookies." The RAF regularly delivered 8,000 lb bombs after that. It dropped 12,000 lb "factory busters" or "Tallboys" from June 1944. Made by bolting three "Cookies" together, "Tallboys" were used against V-3 bunkers in the Pas de Calais. A few dozen 22,000 lb "Grand Slams" were dropped on Germany by the RAF in March 1945.

Time-delayed explosive bombs were dropped by all belligerents to kill rescue workers and firefighters who moved into bombed areas after an attack. A high percentage of duds among high explosive bombs added to problems on the ground: was an unexploded bomb a dud or time-delayed? Other major bomb types included antipersonnel fragmentation bombs used against infantry and antistructure incendiaries. It took many missions and improved intelligence before the RAF discovered that incendiaries were far more likely to destroy a target than high explosives. Improvements soon followed so that smaller incendiaries did far more damage at the end of the war than large ones when it began. The Luftwaffe also turned to incendiaries as a means of achieving more destruction with its numerically and qualitatively smaller bomber force. The Germans developed innovative incendiaries, including water-resistant metallic magnesium bombs, which burned more slowly than thermite bombs and therefore were more likely to start fires. The British and Japanese stuck mostly to thermite, with the Japanese also developing an early cluster-type incendiary. The USAAF used napalm as the main fuel in its incendiaries It dropped giant fire bombs that spread napalm when they hit German targets, starting in 1943. An admixture of types was most often used when bombing cities: fragmentation to create rubble and incendiaries to burn it. The Western Allies worked out special bombing techniques over time. These included first dropping high explosives to seal off part of an urban area and create kindling, something much harder to do in Germany than in Japan. Follow-on waves of high altitude bombers saturated the target area with incendiaries. This method elevated incendiary attacks to lethal levels that equaled, and in several cases exceeded in destruction and lethality, the atomic attacks of 1945.

The Western Allies were the principal bombing powers and therefore developed many specialty bombs, including colored targeting and smoke bombs. The RAF developed bouncing drums bombs for use against the Ruhr dams, in a marked adaptation of the *skip bombing* method. Special bombs developed to destroy U-boat pens in France and the Low Countries were completely ineffective. The U.S. developed the preset GB-1 (Glider-Bomb) in 1941. It was essentially a wing and tail assembly fitted to a standard 2,000 lb gravity bomb. Because it proved inaccurate it was not used until a raid on Cologne on May 28, 1944, well after the USAAF had abandoned its goal of *precision bombing*. Over 1,000 GB-1s were dropped on Germany. They proved less accurate even than "dumb" gravity bombs, as their fins carried them off course. The GB-4 television-guided model was in service by 1945. The GB-8 was radio-controlled. The USAAF also converted damaged or old B-17s, planes it called "war-weary," into huge glider bombs for use in Europe at stand-off distances. The intent was to preserve crew lives. Stripped-down and stuffed with 10 tons of high explosives, B-17s were flown toward the target by a minimal crew of two. The men bailed out during the approach, after which the B-17 was guided via radio signals from an accompanying manned bomber. These special "APHRODITE" and "CASTOR" missions were flown against V-1 and V-2 launch sites, but without success. The JB-2 ("jet bomb") was an American copy of the V-1 rocket. The USAAF used VB-1 "Azon" ("azimuth only") semiguided vertical bombs against bridges and other precision targets in Burma, the only theater where guided bombs enjoyed any success. The Luftwaffe also experimented with guided bombs, or air-delivered guided torpedoes: it deployed two aircraft-delivered, radio-controlled torpedoes that the Luftwaffe called "glider bombs." The Hs-293A was equipped with a rocket-booster. It and the Fritz-X glider bomb enjoyed some success against enemy warships. The main German missile-glider bomb effort came through the *V-weapons program*.

See also biological warfare; Fugo; Unit 731.

BONHÖFFER, DIETRICH (1906–1945)
See resistance (Germany); Schwartz Kapelle.

BORIS III
See Bulgaria.

BORMANN, MARTIN (1900–1945) *Nazi Party* official. Bormann served in the *Reichswehr* in World War I. He joined a *Freikorps* unit before joining the *Sturmabteilung (SA),* or Nazi "Brownshirts." Thereafter, he rose in the Nazi Party bureaucracy, overseeing its finances and the personal accounts of Adolf Hitler. He always kept close to Hitler, but avoided the public limelight that so many top Nazis could not resist. When *Rudolf Hess* flew to Britain in an abortive effort to negotiate a separate peace, a move Bormann may have encouraged to rid himself of a rival, Bormann moved into a commanding position as successor to Hess at Party headquarters. Bormann gained enormous power by controlling access to Hitler, even by powerful Nazi leaders such as *Heinrich Himmler* and *Hermann Göring.* Concerning Hitler's *"special order"* to the Wehrmacht to live off the land in the Soviet Union while shipping millions of tons of grain back to Germany, Bormann contentedly and characteristically commented on the fate of Soviet civilians: "Many tens of millions will starve." Bormann had nothing to do with military affairs, seeing the war always through a political and personal prism. Nevertheless, in the wake of the *July Plot* (1944), he was named commander of the *Volkssturm* ("People's Army") in September 1944.

Borman's main interest was always to control Hitler's staff and Party bureaucracy, and to stay in the direct shadow of his lord and master. During Hitler's final days in April 1945, Bormann continued byzantine maneuvering for power. He secretly encouraged efforts by Himmler to obtain a separate peace with the Western Allies, which eventually eliminated Himmler as Hitler's successor. When Göring tried the same thing, Bormann persuaded Hitler to have the Luftwaffe chief arrested and argued that he should be executed. It was Bormann who arranged Hitler's bizarre marriage to *Eva Braun* and later oversaw disposal of the twisted couple's bodies after their joint suicide. Bormann ordered bunker survivors to try a mass breakout as Berlin fell to the Soviets. He was tried in absentia by the *Nuremberg Tribunal,* found guilty as a major war criminal, and sentenced to death. The sentence was never carried out because Bormann was never located. A skeleton was unearthed by an excavation crew in Berlin in 1972. It was identified through forensic evidence as Bormann's. DNA testing in 1998 confirmed that the corpse was Bormann's. Circumstances and some eyewitness testimony strongly suggest that he committed suicide with a cyanide capsule once it became clear he could not get out of Berlin. As is common in such cases, for some these facts were not permitted to overcome belief that Bormann had somehow escaped to South America after the war.

BOSE, SUBHAS CHANDRA (1897–1945) Indian nationalist. Bose split with the policy of nonviolence upheld by the *Congress Party* after the Amritsar massacre of unarmed Indian civilians by British and Indian Army troops in 1919. He nevertheless became party president in 1938. He broke with *Mohandas Gandhi* before the war, calling openly for armed insurrection by Indians against British rule. He escaped a British jail in early 1941 and fled in disguise to Afghanistan. From there he traveled to Moscow and thence to Berlin. He was an admirer of European *fascism* in general, and of Adolf Hitler in particular. Bose therefore claimed the title "Netaji" ("Leader") of the Indian Independence League, in emulation of the Italian "Il Duce" and German "Führer." In February 1943, a U-boat carried Bose on a three-month voyage around Africa (the Suez Canal was closed to his host's warships). He proclaimed an end to the Raj in India in October, and declared war on the Western Allies. He traveled to Singapore to attend the only conference held to plan Japan's *Greater East Asia Co-prosperity Sphere*. Bose led the *Indian National Army (INA)* "on to Delhi" during 1944–1945, alongside Japanese forces against British and *Indian Army* troops in Burma. He set up a provisional capital in Rangoon and briefly invaded northeast India in March 1944. The INA surrendered in 1945, but Bose did not. He died in a plane crash on August 18, 1945, while trying to flee into Manchuria, possibly to arrange Soviet sponsorship for his anti-British movement.

See also Andaman and Nicobar Islands.

BOSNIA This Yugoslav province was annexed by the Nazi puppet regime in Croatia following the German invasion in April 1942. It was the scene of vicious guerrilla warfare and multiple ethnic massacres. It was liberated in 1945 by Yugoslav partisans and the Red Army.

See also Tito; Yugoslavia.

BOUGAINVILLE CAMPAIGN (NOVEMBER 1943–AUGUST 1945) This island in the Solomons was occupied by the Japanese in early 1942. The Japanese strongly reinforced Bougainville and several small offshore islands, raising their garrison to 37,000 men. The Western Allied campaign to retake Bougainville was preparatory to a planned assault against the main Japanese base at *Rabaul,* with the immediate object being to secure existing air fields and build more on Bougainville to suppress dangerous Japanese land-based aircraft based at Rabaul. Longer term, the intention was to cut off, isolate, and neutralize the 100,000 man garrison and air fields on Rabaul. New Zealand troops took the adjacent *Treasury Islands* in late October 1943, while U.S. marines conducted a diversion in force on *Choiseul* from October 28 to November 3. The main attack hit Bougainville on November 1, when 14,000 men from U.S. 3rd Marine Division and the U.S. Army's 37th Division landed at Cape Torokina. They faced hand-to-hand fighting along the coast, but came ashore in strength by nightfall. The landings led to a naval night fight at *Empress Augusta Bay* that night, when a Japanese surface attack force was driven off before it could savage the landing zone. A fierce, week-long battle took place for control of Piva Forks from November 19–25. When it ended the Japanese no longer resisted or threatened the landing sites in Empress Augusta Bay. The Japanese tried a second time to intercept Western Allied shipping supporting ground forces on Bougainville, leading to a small naval battle at *Cape St George* off New Ireland on November 25.

U.S. marines and army troopers beat back Japanese 6th Division attacks on a slowly expanding perimeter that was soon reinforced and protected by 50,000 men. Once the Americans advanced four miles from the beachhead Seabees began building two airstrips. The first plane landed on December 19. After that, air supremacy was established and the Japanese retreated into the jungle, many dying there from illness rather than enemy firepower. The last major Japanese assault was made on March 9, 1944, after Lieutenant General Hyakatake Harukichi marched 19,000 exhausted, demoralized, and undersupplied men over rugged mountains to assault a force of 60,000 well-prepared and dug-in enemy troops around Empress Augusta Bay. A bloody four-day fight followed over possession of two key hills, designated #700 and #260 on Western Allied maps, connected by a low "saddle." Heavy artillery was the deciding factor, in support of tanks and well dug-in infantry. Increasingly desperate, often suicidal Japanese probes were made to March 23, until even Hyakatake's men could take no more. When the remnant of the Japanese force withdrew, it left over 5,500 dead behind for just 263 Americans killed. More Japanese died of wounds, disease, and despair in the backward trek. After that disaster the rump of the Japanese garrison was a spent force in terms of future offensive action.

With the Western Allies no longer pressing to clear the island each side settled in for a war of desultory patrols and occasional perimeter skirmishes, while both suffered from debilitating tropical heat and diseases. Neither force had the power or the will to attack and overrun the other. Japanese supply sharply deteriorated as the main fighting in the Pacific moved farther north over the course of 1944, making the last defenders on Bougainville more pathetic than threatening. In December 1944, Australian 2nd Corps took over Bougainville from the Americans. The Australians were given a mission to suppress the last pockets of enemy resistance by General *Thomas Blamey*. The bitter, and some say mostly useless, fighting that resulted lasted into August 1945. It cost 500 Australian dead and another 1,500 wounded. Contemporary Australian opinion, and many later historians, regarded the Australian portion of the Bougainville campaign as wasteful of lives and strategically unnecessary.

See also African Americans; CARTWHEEL.

Suggested Reading: Harry Gailey, *Bougainville, 1943–1945* (1991).

BRADLEY, OMAR (1893–1981) U.S. general. Bradley was an infantry officer by training and inclination, a fact reflected in his affectionate nickname among troops and the news media: the "G.I.'s General." That spoke to his genuine solicitude and expressed concern for minimizing casualties. The image of Bradley as a general who always strove to do the right thing by his men was greatly enhanced by the self-portrait he drew in postwar memoirs and while advising on portrayal of himself and other commanders in the highly influential 1970 feature film "Patton." Subsequent studies by military historians have been less kind to

Bradley, notably over his several command failures and exceptional jealous command attitude during and after the *Ardennes offensive* (1944). Bradley began the war in North Africa in November 1942 as a special advisor sent into the field by General *Dwight Eisenhower* to find out why the U.S. Army did so poorly in its first encounters with the Wehrmacht. He was soon made General *George S. Patton*'s deputy at 2nd Corp. He replaced Patton as 2nd Corp commander in April 1943, and led 2nd Corps through the invasion of Sicily that July (*HUSKY*). He is widely praised by military historians for his excellent performance in North Africa and again in Sicily. Bradley notably refused Patton's order to cover up the *Biscari massacres* of unarmed Axis prisoners on Sicily. That led to the first real break between the two men.

Bradley left Sicily for Britain to prepare to lead 21st Army in the invasion of France. On *D-Day (June 6, 1944),* he was in command of the American assaults on Omaha and Utah beaches. He is also judged to have been a solid commander during the campaign for the Côtentin peninsula in Normandy from June to July, 1944. He was promoted to command U.S. 12th Army Group in the Allied command shuffle that followed the breakout from Normandy. That made him Patton's direct superior, with both generals serving under ground forces commander *Bernard Law Montgomery* until September 1944, and Eisenhower after that. Bradley is usually blamed for excess caution during the fight to seal the *Falaise pocket.* His relations with Montgomery began to go south in August, worsened markedly during the failed Operation *MARKET GARDEN* in September, and collapsed totally into bitter resentment during the Ardennes fight in December 1944. Bradley never forgave Eisenhower for transferring command of U.S. 1st Army to Montgomery during the opening days of the "Battle of the Bulge." Nor did he forgive Monty for helping to recover the situation in the broken Ardennes. Monty's truly unforgivable sin was to publicly claim credit for that feat, and thereby severely embarrass Bradley. During the *conquest of Germany* in 1945 Bradley argued for the main push to head into southern Germany, away from the northern road favored by Montgomery. It is not clear whether his motives were primarily personal or strategic. Bradley led 12th Army Group into the *Ruhr,* thence to the Elbe, where his forces linked with the Red Army at Torgau on April 25. After the war Bradley was promoted to the rank of General of the Army. He oversaw formation of NATO as head of the Joint Chiefs of Staff from 1948 to 1953.

BRANDENBURGERS Special operations units of the Abteilung II department of the *Abwehr*. It was common for these initially small units to secure enemy uniforms to work behind the frontier or lines. Several teams were sent into Poland in advance of the *FALL WEISS* invasion to secure key bridges. Brandenburgers also captured crucial bridges in Denmark on the first day of *WESERÜBUNG*, April 9, 1940. In the opening hours of *FALL GELB* on May 10, Brandenburgers crossed the River Mass in an armored train, leading 9th Panzer Division into the Netherlands. These successes led to expansion to regimental size in October 1940. They also caused the British Army to model its *commando* units on the Brandenburgers. Brandenburgers mainly operated among local ethnic groups on the Eastern Front in 1941, stirring anti-Soviet sentiment as well as conducting sabotage missions in rear areas. During 1942 some saw action against the British in North Africa. During 1943 most were used in dirty, antipartisan fighting or to shepherd non-German POW units into combat. The Brandenburgers numbered close to a full division by 1944 and were used as a rearguard during a chaotic German retreat from the Crimea. Shortage of manpower in the Wehrmacht thereafter wasted their special capabilities by converting Brandenburgers into emergency regular infantry, a shift perhaps also hurried along by professional jealousy. The loss of special status was confirmed when the *Schutzstaffel (SS)* took over the Abwehr following the *July Plot* (1944), after which most Brandenburgers were converted into Panzergrenadiers.

BRATISLAVA–BRNO OPERATION (MARCH–MAY, 1945)

See Czechoslovakia; Red Army; Schörner, Ferdinand.

BRAUCHITSCH, WALTER VON (1881–1948)

German field marshal. He served as an artillery officer in the Reichswehr during World War I. He struck the usual Junker pose as a disdainer of *Nazism,* but in fact supported Adolf Hitler's program of rearmament and militarization of German society in the 1930s. He was commander in chief of the *Heer* (OKH) from 1938 to 1941. That appointment followed the purge that ousted *Werner von Blomberg,* whose opposition to Hitler's aggressive plans Brauchitsch replaced with servile and unquestioning devotion. He oversaw an uninterrupted spate of Wehrmacht victories from 1939 to 1941, in Poland, Denmark, Norway, the Low Countries, and France. For those achievements he was promoted to field marshal. Brauchitsch next carried out Hitler's orders to invade Greece and Yugoslavia in April 1941, and the Soviet Union in June. Brauchitsch was sacked in December, as Army Group Center stalled before Moscow and then was thrown back in the *Moscow offensive operation (December 5, 1941–January 7, 1942).* Hitler assumed personal command of the Heer, while Brauchitsch never again held an active command. His loyalty to Hitler—and disloyalty to military honor—led him to testify against old Wehrmacht comrades implicated in the *July Plot* in 1944. Brauchitsch was charged with *war crimes* by the Allies. He took the stand as a witness at the *Nuremberg Tribunal* and lied to exonerate himself and the Wehrmacht from the horrific crimes of the regime, which he helped plan and carry out. He died before he could be prosecuted.

BRAUN, EVA (1912–1945)

Adolf Hitler's mistress, 1932–1945, and his wife for less than two days before they committed suicide together in a display of vulgar nihilism beneath the ruins of Berlin. She was by all accounts a stupid, vain, and notably uneducated woman. She was not even permitted the role of bauble on the great man's arm: she was never seen with Hitler in public and spent most of her time pining for his rare attentions. Her sister married Hermann Fegelein, an aide to *Heinrich Himmler.* Eva Braun's influence with the dictator was so low she could not even persuade him to spare Fegelein from a firing squad while Berlin burned all around the Führerbunker. She married Hitler below ground on April 29, 1945. A day later, she happily took cyanide while he shot himself.

BRAUN, WERNER VON (1912–1977) German scientist. Braun was fascinated by rocketry from his boyhood. He founded a Society for Space Travel in 1930 and established an experimental rocket base outside Berlin, and he soon was at work for the *Reichswehr*. Once the Nazis came to power, Braun's career became a testament to the cold careerism of many German scientists and the mere technical interests of his rocket scientist soul: he moved to *Peenemünde* in 1936 to direct secret weapons research for Adolf Hitler. He headed the team developing the *V-weapons program,* which built the V-1 and V-2 rockets, as well as Germany's jet fighters. Braun's main frustration before and during the war was that Hitler did not appreciate the potential of the weapons he designed. He was briefly imprisoned on espionage charges in 1944 for refusing to cooperate with an effort by *Heinrich Himmler* to transfer the V-2 project to *Schutzstaffel (SS)* control. He was released on the personal order of Hitler and returned to Peenemünde. Braun was captured along with his research team by the U.S. Army at the end of the war. His service to the Nazis was overlooked in favor of future service to America under the postwar imperatives of the Cold War: he was made a U.S. citizen in 1955 and later headed the U.S. Ballistic Missile Agency. He was singularly responsible for development of America's early intercontinental ballistic missile (ICBM) force and oversaw the launch of the first American satellite, Explorer I, in 1958. Braun headed the Marshall Space Flight Center from 1960 to 1970, guiding the "Mercury," "Gemini," and "Apollo" launch programs. His "Saturn V" rockets carried Apollo astronauts into orbit on their way to the Moon.

BRAUNSCHWEIG (JUNE 1942) "Brunswick." Revised code name for the Wehrmacht summer offensive in the southern Soviet Union during June 1942.
See BLAU.

BRAZIL Under the dictator Getúlio Vargas (1930–1945), Brazil was run as a corporatist state. When war broke out it declared formal neutrality, while continuing to assert neutral rights to trade with states in Europe. In January 1942, Rio de Janeiro broke off diplomatic relations with Berlin following multiple sinkings of Brazilian ships in the Gulf of Mexico. When a single U-boat sank seven more ships off the coast of Brazil, Vargas declared war on Germany on August 22, 1942. He had bent to American and public pressure to declare war, although his personal sympathies leaned toward the *Axis*. Thereafter, Brazil was one terminus of the vital *Takoradi air route* and greatly benefited economically from the war. Unlike most South American countries that declared war on the Axis only to please Washington, Brazil sent troops to fight in Italy in 1944. The last battles fought by the "Brazilian Expeditionary Force," which served under U.S. 5th Army, were over control of the *Argenta Gap* and through the *Adige Line* in April 1945. In the last days of the war the Brazilians took nearly 14,000 German prisoners. The

Brazilian Air Force and Navy made more limited contributions. Varga was ousted in 1945.

BRAZZAVILLE DECLARATION (OCTOBER 27, 1940)   *Charles de Gaulle,* supported by colonial governors and officials from *French Equatorial Africa* and the Congo, announced at this conference that the Vichy regime was illegitimate and did not represent France. The conference then established a Council for Defense of the Empire, which became the kernel of the *Free French* political structure and movement.

BRENNER PASS   A strategic Alpine pass between Austria and Italy. Its access and control was a major objective of both countries during World War I, leading to repeated futile mountain battles at Isonzo which cost hundreds of thousands of lives. Italian concern that Germany would control the pass led to initial opposition to the *Anschluss* of Austria with Germany. Adolf Hitler and Benito Mussolini met in the Brenner Pass on June 2, 1941. U.S. armies in Italy and Austria linked there on May 4, 1945.

   See also Switzerland.

BRERETON, LEWIS (1890–1967)   U.S. general. Commander of USAAF forces destroyed in the Philippines in 1941–1942. He next commanded 9th Air Force in North Africa. Promoted to lead Allied 1st Airborne Army in August 1944, he was in charge of drops at Arnhem and other sites during *MARKET GARDEN* that September. He oversaw the marginally more successful Rhine drop in March 1945.

BRESKENS POCKET

   See Scheldt Estuary campaign.

BRESLAU, SIEGE OF (1945)

   See Germany, conquest of.

BREST-LITOVSK   This Polish city was annexed by the Soviet Union in September 1939, under terms of the *Nazi–Soviet Pact (August 23, 1939).* A ferocious fight broke out over control of the 18th-century citadel during the first hours of *BARBAROSSA* on June 22, 1941. Desperate Soviet defenders held out in the citadel for five days. During the fight, *NKVD* troops slaughtered all their prisoners rather than see them freed by the Germans. Such resistance was only a burr in the rear of the Wehrmacht juggernaut, but it was also a portent of bitter fighting to come. The city was not retaken by the Red Army until July 1944. The NKVD returned to take control of its old jail cells and execution chambers—which the Germans had used extensively in the interim. A handful of survivors from the fight at Brest-Litovsk were found in 1945, having survived four years of gross mistreatment in German POW camps. They were immediately arrested by *SMERSH*. Most were either executed or shipped off to forced labor camps in the *GULAG*, probably to conceal the lack of preparedness caused by Joseph Stalin's blunders four years before.

BREST-LITOVSK, TREATY OF (1918)
 See *BARBAROSSA; Hindenburg, Paul von; Soviet Union; Stalin, Joseph; Ukraine; Versailles, Treaty of (1919).*

BRETTON WOODS CONFERENCE (JULY 1–22, 1944)   A planning meeting for the postwar world held in Bretton Woods, New Hampshire. The purpose of the conference was to establish a cooperative postwar system to monitor exchange rates, maintain liquidity, and prevent balance of payment problems. The aim was to assist postwar reconstruction, ease a transition back to a market economy from wartime command administration, and encourage integration of the major trading economies on liberal principles and away from renewal of the tariff wars of the 1930s. It laid groundwork for creation of the International Bank for Reconstruction and Development and the International Monetary Fund. A proposed International Trade Organization failed to gain approval; it was replaced by the General Agreement on Tariffs and Trade. Bretton Woods arrangements rebuilt the postwar monetary system on dollar convertibility to gold. Because Britain was economically weaker than first thought and the Soviet Union refused to join, the Bretton Woods system evolved from a plan for international management to dependence on primary U.S. management, lasting to 1971.

BRIANSK
 See *BARBAROSSA; TAIFUN.*

BRICKS   British beach organizations that solved many of the early problems encountered in *amphibious operations*. They first proved effective at Salerno on September 9, 1943.
 See *Combined Operations Pilotage Parties.*

BRIGADE   Complement of a brigade varied from army to army, but generally ranged from 1,800 to 3,000 men organized into two or three *battalions*. Independent specialized brigades were often attached to regular *divisions* or *corps* to beef up combat power.
 See also *regiment.*

BRITAIN, BATTLE OF (JULY 10–SEPTEMBER 17, 1940)   This prolonged air battle between the Luftwaffe and Royal Air Force was one key to Adolf Hitler's planned invasion of Britain (*SEELÖWE*) and thus a major turning point in the war. Only if the RAF was eliminated and Luftwaffe air superiority established would the Kriegsmarine dare to escort an invasion force across the Channel with any chance of success against the Royal Navy. After initial skirmishes over the

Channel during July and early August, the battle began officially for the Luftwaffe on *Adlertag* ("Eagle Day"), or August 13, 1940, which commenced the protracted Operation *ADLERANGRIFF* ("Eagle Attack"). Although the fight in the sky was extremely dramatic at the time and in later recollection, at no point was the RAF on the verge of defeat. It lost many aircraft and good men in fighting over the south, but it was able to replace both without drawing down its main reserves by depleting the defense of the north of Britain. The fundamental problem for the Germans was a basic failure to understand that air warfare by its nature was attritional and therefore, that the RAF could not be eliminated in a single "decisive battle." The Luftwaffe was also ill-equipped for the mission, with slow medium bombers with inadequate bomb loads and fighters escorts of still more limited range. That was true even though it had tried to develop a strategic bombing capacity before the war and had a significant lead in long-distance navigation and other blind-bombing aids.

There were several keys to the outcome. The RAF fighter force was larger than the Luftwaffe realized when the fight began, despite heavy losses over France and the Low Countries in May and June. Also, Britain was able to significantly outproduce Germany in fighter aircraft throughout the campaign: Luftwaffe intelligence calculated a fighter replacement rate of 180–300 per month, whereas the RAF actually achieved a rate of nearly 500 per month. The Wehrmacht held back resources from German fighter production, which underachieved its goal by 40 percent in the summer of 1940. The RAF thus readily replaced its aircraft losses where the Luftwaffe did not. Similar erroneous estimates of RAF losses marked incompetent Luftwaffe intelligence reports throughout the battle. Also, the fight took place over Britain. That meant the RAF recovered many downed pilots but the Luftwaffe lost aircraft and crews: nearly 1,400 aircraft all told and many crews killed, taken prisoner, or lost in the Channel. British training schemes were already operating at full tilt, whereas the Luftwaffe's were not. The RAF therefore did not have to draw down main reserves from the center and north of the country without also replacing those more idle squadrons with fresh aircraft and pilots. Fighter Command was further aided by a series of bad decisions born of sheer Nazi arrogance and the erratic decision-making system in Germany. The most fateful of these was Hitler's choice—provoked by rage over two small British raids against Berlin—to switch bomber targeting from RAF airfields to attacks on British cities. That caused many civilian deaths but allowed the RAF to continue to attrit German bombers and fighters alike. The fundamental reason for the German defeat was the fact that the Luftwaffe was asked to improvise a strategic air campaign for which it did not have the right planes or doctrine, against sophisticated British air and ground defenses in preparation over several years. Finally, the Luftwaffe had no precedent, let alone direct experience, in attacking an enemy that waited behind a comprehensive early warning radar system and had an excellent command-and-control radio net with which to direct fighter air defenses.

When Luftwaffe losses became intolerable Hitler called off the air battle and invasion and turned instead to planning *BARBAROSSA*, the great attack on the Soviet Union by which he intended to deny Britain its last available continental ally and bring about its acceptance of terms. Hitler continued to harbor the delusion that Britain might agree to a separate peace, which he wanted for tactical reasons. That and overcommitment of limited Luftwaffe resources in Russia left Britain free to rearm and recover and to serve as a platform for punishing Anglo-American air raids from 1942 to 1945. Winston Churchill aptly said of the British nation: "This was their finest hour." Of the British, Commonwealth, and other airmen who won the battle and helped save civilization from Nazi barbarism, he memorably said: "Never in the field of human conflict was so much owed by so many to so few." Along with the role played by "the few," less well-acknowledged is the anti-invasion role played by the Royal Navy, which was the truly effective deterrent to Hitler. The Royal Navy was far superior to the Kriegsmarine in numbers of destroyers and capital warships. It is difficult to imagine an invasion fleet borne across the Channel—mainly on Rhine barges—surviving against the determined effort by the Royal Navy with which it surely would have met. That case was well-argued in 2006 by historians Brian James, Richard Overy, and Andrew Gordon of the Joint Service Command Staff College.

See also Blitz; Regia Aeronautica.

Suggested Reading: Richard Overy, *The Battle of Britain: Myth and Reality* (2000).

BRITISH ARMY As it had done during the Great War of 1914–1918, the British Army entered a second world war as a small professional force: in 1939 the British Army numbered under 160,000 men. The formation deployed in France from 1939 to 1940 was known as the British Expeditionary Force (BEF). It was organized into two infantry Corps, with plans for rapid expansion as new divisions were raised. As also happened during World War I, the BEF was to be reinforced by Australian, Canadian, and Indian Commonwealth divisions. In prewar planning the French Army initially looked to the British to provide a mobile striking force for counteroffensive operations against a German invasion. But the British were still constituting their first mobile division in 1938 and had only two semimotorized infantry divisions ready for deployment. The French concluded that the initial British contribution in the event of war would be "limited and tardy." They therefore shifted to building their own mobile forces while asking BEF divisions to replace French divisions moving out of static positions to counterattack the Wehrmacht. Only from March 1939, with German occupation of the rump of Czechoslovakia, did the British government decide that a credible deterrent must include a greatly expanded land force as well as the threat of bombing by the RAF and blockade by the Royal Navy. Rapid progress was made in assembling scratch infantry divisions from the *Territorial Army* and from conscripts. The Territorial Army was quickly doubled, and it was announced that Britain would ultimately ready a BEF of 19 divisions. But that prospect was still two years away in mid-1939. British planners told their French counterparts that at the outbreak of war they could provide just two infantry divisions and one mobile division within the first 30 days, to be followed by a fourth division within three months. Territorial divisions would follow up to a year after that.

Led by Field Marshal *John Gort,* the BEF began deployment to France on September 4, 1939. By October 12, Britain sent four regular infantry divisions across the Channel, supported by 12 squadrons of RAF fighters and bombers. The BEF expanded over the winter as poorly trained Territorial Army divisions were hurriedly shipped to France to comprise an all-infantry force of 10 divisions by May 1940. At the time, the BEF was the only major power army whose artillery was fully mechanized. However, the first British armored division did not embark for France until the German attack was already underway. Although British infantry were well-motorized, the BEF thus lacked effective armored mobility despite years of prewar discussion with the French. While all BEF divisions were expected to play a defensive role, they were also asked to move into neutral Belgium as soon as Germany violated that country's borders. From September 1939 to May 1940, during the so-called *Phoney War,* the BEF settled into defensive positions it expected to have to abandon once real fighting began. By May 1940, the British Army had 395,000 men in France. Of these, 150,000 were still largely untrained. All were under overall French command. At the start of *FALL GELB,* the German invasion of France and the Low Countries, the plan to move into Belgium was implemented. But after advancing to the *Dyle Line* at the start of May, the BEF was forced to fall back and then to evacuate from France at *Dunkirk* to avoid being cut off and annihilated. An effort was made to reconstitute a fighting field force south of the German breakthrough line, but in mid-June the French indicated the fight was lost. Gort was replaced by Lieutenant General *Alan Brooke.* A second evacuation of 136,000 British and Canadian troops, as well as 20,000 Poles, was made from Cherbourg.

Desperate need led to a desperate measure in mid-1940: organization of the *Home Guard,* quaintly known as "Dad's Army." It was never a serious force beyond providing an early warning observer corps, although later in the war some Guardists provided needed service as anti-aircraft crews. Such ad hoc measures reflected a deep structural problem in the British Army left unresolved from 1918: it had no single interwar mission that defined doctrine, training, equipment, or weapons programs. Instead, it was charged with homeland defense as well as an imperial garrison and policing role. The Army therefore had to relearn how to fight a large-scale war by fighting and did not really find its feet until mid-1942. For the rest of the war it was afflicted by a different set of organizational problems that attended growing British casualties in a protracted *total war.* The problem surfaced during the *Italian campaign (1943–1945).* Within a few weeks of *D-Day (June 6, 1944),* attrition and exhaustion of British forces and lack of any replacements reached crisis point. The British had little choice but to cannibalize some divisions to keep others going. The first unit to disappear from the Army's order of battle was 59th division. More followed, as the British saw their heaviest fighting of the war in France and the Low Countries in 1944. Still more casualties were taken in northwest Germany in 1945, though fewer than anticipated as the pace of the British advance slowed as many men became understandably combat shy once they realized the end of the war was in sight.

Other Britons continued to bleed in bombers over Germany and on the ground in Italy to the end of April. Still more fought and died in Southeast Asia into

August 1945. The last major controversy of the war came when London decided to release all long service troops, defined as men with three years and four months overseas. That immediately gutted the Southeast Asia command of veteran troops needed to carry out the final clearances of Burma, and units readying for *ZIPPER*, the planned invasion by British 14th Army of Malaya and Singapore. The British Army was spared more hard fighting in Asia by the sudden Japanese surrender on August 15, 1945: large-scale British forces were slated to go ashore on Honshu as part of *DOWNFALL*, but the operation was canceled.

See also airborne; Alexander, Harold; armor; Auchinleck, Claude; Balkan campaign; Brooke, Alan; Burma campaign (1941–1942); Burma campaign (1943–1945); CHARN-WOOD; chemical warfare; Chiefs of Staff; commandos; Crete; desert campaign; desertion; Dodecanese campaign; East African campaign; Germany, conquest of; Gideon Force; GOOD-WOOD; Gurkhas; HUSKY; Indian Army; Irish Free State; Jewish Brigade; Long Range Desert Group; Maginot Line; Malaya; MARKET GARDEN; Montgomery, Bernard Law; Mountbatten, Louis; Normandy campaign; OVERLORD; prisoners of war; Raiding Forces; rations; Singapore; Wavell, Archibald.

Suggested Reading: S. Bidwell and D. Graham, *Firepower: British Army Weapons and Theories of War, 1904–1945* (1982); Raymond Callahan, *Churchill and His Generals* (2007).

BRITISH ARMY AID GROUP (BAAG) An escape organization set up in southern China to aid British and Western Allied escapees and pilots. It continued operations until near the end of the war in Asia.

BRITISH BORNEO A British colony comprising Brunei, Sarawak, and the northern half of Borneo—the southern half was part of the *Dutch East Indies*. The Japanese invaded on December 16, 1941, and quickly overran Brunei and Sarawak. The American *island-hopping strategy* bypassed the garrison, isolating over 30,000 Japanese. A rebellion by local Chinese was crushed by the garrison in late 1943. Native guerilla resistance continued into June 1945, when Australian 9th Division landed. The Australians pushed slowly inland, careful of their own casualties while killing many still resisting Japanese. The last Japanese units did not surrender until October 1945, and only after killing several thousand Western Allied prisoners of war in terrible death marches away from their pending liberation.

BRITISH COMMONWEALTH
See Commonwealth.

BRITISH COMMONWEALTH AIR TRAINING PLAN The *Royal Canadian Air Force (RCAF)* agreed to provide training for 50 RAF pilots per year in April 1939. When war broke out in September, the RCAF agreed to host an empire-wide air crew training program: the "British Empire Air Training Scheme." The scheme was renamed the "British Commonwealth Air Training Plan" in mid-1942. Most of its training bases were located in Canada. Some were in Australia, New Zealand, and South Africa. The air scheme was costly and did not get underway until 1940, training just 1,100 pilots and navigators that year. But by September 1944, the Plan trained 168,000 pilots, navigators, and other specialist crew from Canada (116,417), Australia (23,262), South Africa (16,857), Rhodesia (8,235), and New Zealand (3,891).

BRITISH COMMONWEALTH OCCUPATION FORCE
See Japan.

BRITISH EMPIRE
See Commonwealth; Great Britain.

BRITISH EMPIRE AIR TRAINING SCHEME
See British Commonwealth Air Training Plan.

BRITISH EXPEDITIONARY FORCE (BEF)
See British Army.

BRITISH FREE CORPS   "Britisches Freikorps."
See Waffen-SS.

BRITISH SOMALILAND   This east African colony was overrun by Italian forces in August 1940. Less than a year later, Benito Mussolini and the Italian Empire lost the territory when *Indian Army* troops were landed by the Royal Navy and retook the colony.

BRITISH UNION OF FASCISTS   A British *fascist* movement founded in 1932 by Oswald Mosley. It never became a mass party, peaking at a 1934 membership of about 50,000, then declining as Britons grew more wary of its fascist cousins on the continent and more put off by its rising *anti-Semitism*. Its most famous member was the propagandist *William Joyce,* known as "Lord Haw Haw" for his broadcasts from Berlin during the war. Mosley and other top leaders were arrested in May 1940, as Britain faced possible defeat and invasion. They were released in 1943. Nearly 800 BU members were preventively detained at some point.

BRITISH WEST AFRICA
See Gold Coast; Nigeria; Sierra Leone; West African Military Labor Corps.

BRITISH WEST INDIES   The various British island colonies of the West Indies provided oil, bases, and *anti-submarine warfare* facilities to the British effort from 1939. They contributed to the American naval effort after U.S. bases were established under the *destroyers-for-bases deal* in 1940. The islands also provided some troops. For instance, Bermuda supplied a Volunteer Rifle Corps as part of a larger British regiment, and several islands together provided men for the *Caribbean Regiment*.

BROAD FRONT DEBATE (1944)

See Ardennes offensive; *Bradley, Omar*; *Eisenhower, Dwight*; *MARKET GARDEN*; *Montgomery, Bernard Law*; *Patton, George*.

BROOKE, ALAN (1883–1963)   British field marshal. Chief of the imperial general staff (CIGS). A veteran of the Somme in 1916, Brooke was an artillery specialist by training and experience. During the 1930s he commanded Britain's limited mobile forces, then its anti-aircraft artillery. He led II Corps of the British Expeditionary Force (BEF) in France from September 1939 to June 1940. He took overall command of the BEF upon relieving Field Marshal *John Gort* in mid-June, 1940, during *FALL GELB* but following *Dunkirk*. Brooke convinced Winston Churchill not to try to hold Cherbourg, then oversaw a second but more orderly evacuation of 160,000 BEF and Western Allied troops from the Côtentin peninsula. As commander of the *Home Army* during the summer of 1940, he prepared against a possible German invasion. In December 1941, he found his true role as CIGS, the principal military adviser to the prime minister and war cabinet. Brooke proved an essential brake on Churchill's frequent amateurish military enthusiasms and impulses. He was less successful, and perhaps less right, in opposing the prime minister's political vision for the postwar settlement in Germany. Brooke was highly respected by top British and American leaders for his role on the *Combined Chiefs of Staff*. He protected British interests well and saved several British generals from themselves, especially *Bernard Law Montgomery*, on more than one occasion. The shifting weight of Britain's contribution to the Western Allied war effort denied him the role he coveted as supreme commander for the invasion of France in 1944, but he was partly compensated with promotion to field marshal.

BROOKE-POPHAM, HENRY R. (1878–1953)   British air chief marshal. His primary experience was in imperial administration. Accordingly, he helped set up the *British Commonwealth Air Training Plan* in Canada and other British "white dominions" in 1939–1940. In late 1940, he was made commander in chief of air and ground forces in the Far East, with responsibility for British Borneo, Burma, Hong Kong, Malaya, and Singapore. The post held little real authority, and he did little to prepare for the coming onslaught by the Japanese. He was sacked on December 27, 1941, and forced to retire in May 1942.

BROWNING, FREDERICK (1896–1965)   British general. Browning led British airborne forces in drops in North Africa, Italy, France, and the Netherlands. He was closely involved in planning the airborne missions in *OVERLORD* and *MARKET GARDEN* in 1944. After the disaster in the Netherlands, about whose dangers he had forewarned Field Marshal *Bernard Law Montgomery,* Browning was sent to Southeast Asia to serve as chief of staff to *Louis Mountbatten.*

BROWNSHIRTS
See Freikorps; Night of the Long Knives; Sturmabteilung (SA).

BRÜCKENSCHLAG (1942)
"Bridge-Building." A proposed Wehrmacht offensive in the spring of 1942. It was to be launched against the *Toropets step,* where the Red Army bulged into the German line.

BRÜNING, HEINRICH (1885–1970)
See Germany.

BUCHENWALD
Among the first Nazi *concentration camps,* Buchenwald was located near Weimar. It was a labor and slave camp for men and boys working for the *Schutzstaffel (SS)* and the munitions industry. Although it was not a *death camp* per se, many thousands per month died there over a number of years, most from extreme mistreatment, harsh conditions, and poor food. Some 20,000 emaciated inmates were liberated by the U.S. Army in April 1945, after staging a successful revolt against the camp's dispirited guards.

BUCKET BRIGADE
An ad hoc American coastal *convoy* system set up in April 1942, in response to enormous shipping losses of unescorted *independents.* It encouraged clustering of ships to be escorted by any available armed vessel by day. At night, the group took refuge in a local anchorage, then resumed the journey with new daylight. It was a stopgap measure kept in place until Admiral *Ernest King* and the U.S. Navy accepted the need for a full convoy system and had the escorts to provide one.

BUDAPEST, SIEGE OF (DECEMBER 1944–FEBRUARY 1945)
See Hungary; KONRAD.

BUDAPEST STRATEGIC OPERATION (1944–1945)
See Hungary; KONRAD.

BUDYONNY, SEMYON M. (1883–1973)
Marshal of the Soviet Union. He fought in the Tsarist Army in the Russo–Japanese War (1904–1905) and during World War I. A commander of Red cavalry during the Russian Civil War (1918–1921), Budyonny was an old comrade of Joseph Stalin. He held high military rank throughout the 1930s, yet did not disappear into the *GULAG* or an unmarked grave during the *Yezhovshchina* or other blood purges of the Red Army. He started the *Great Fatherland War* as a member of the Stavka, with a focus on overseeing

fighting by the Southwest *Direction*. Budyonny was in command at Kiev, with *Nikita Khrushchev* as political commissar, when the great encirclement battle for the city began on September 21, 1941. Budyonny quickly proved less than capable as an operational commander, showing no comprehension of new forms of armored and mobile warfare. He was quickly shifted to the Reserve Front. In 1942, he briefly held Direction and Front commands in the Caucasus, again faring poorly before moving back to the cavalry. He never again held a real command.

See also EDELWEISS; TAIFUN.

BUFFALO

See Landing Vehicle Tracked.

BUFFALO

See BÜFFEL.

BÜFFEL (MARCH–APRIL, 1943)   "Buffalo." Code name for the Wehrmacht spring withdrawal from the *Rzhev balcony* west of Moscow. It was proposed by General *Günther von Kluge* on January 26, 1943. It began on March 1 as Adolf Hitler agreed to withdrawal from salients precariously held by Army Group Center. The retreat from Rzhev and Viazma cut 230 miles from the line. As the Germans pulled out they burned everything and forced nearly 200,000 civilians to leave with them. The decision to withdraw was prompted by the defeat and surrender of German 6th Army at *Stalingrad* to the south, and by a lesser but still important defeat in front of Leningrad to the north. As important, attrition of Wehrmacht forces along the entire Eastern Front made it critical to rationalize and shorten defensive lines. After BÜFFEL, Moscow was no longer threatened by the Wehrmacht.

See also Haltebefehl orders.

BUKA   A Japanese naval and air base off New Georgia. It was strafed and bombed intermittently, but not assaulted directly. Its ragged garrison surrendered to the Australians at the end of the war.

See island-hopping.

BUKOVINA   The northern part of this ethnically Ukrainian but historically Rumanian province was annexed by the Soviet Union in June 1940, along with *Bessarabia*. That act of aggression—Bukovina had never been part of the old Tsarist empire—provoked Rumania into the war on the Axis side a year later, even though Italy and Germany had secretly supported the Soviet annexation. Bukovina was recovered by Rumanian troops at the end of July 1941, during the opening offensive of *BARBAROSSA*. There followed progressive *nazification* of Rumanian policy in the province, especially toward Jews and Roma. Bukovina was retaken by the Soviet Union after heavy fighting in late 1944.

BULGANIN, NIKOLAI ALEXANDROVICH (1895–1975)   Onetime mayor of Moscow, he was active in the high *Military Council* during World War II. He became defense minister in 1946. He served as vice-premier after Stalin's death in 1953 and was a figurehead premier of the Soviet Union from 1955 to 1958.

BULGARIA   Boris III (1894–1943) was the last king of Bulgaria (r. 1918–1943). He tried to keep Bulgaria out of the war, but the country was closely linked to Germany by trade and propinquity, and too many of his countrymen nursed strong grievances over lost territory dating to defeat at the side of Germany during World War I. The influential Bulgarian officer corps also wanted to catch a ride on the fast-moving Wehrmacht military train. After the Soviet annexation of *Bessarabia*, the Red Army loomed near Bulgarian borders. Sophia was courted by Germany and the Soviet Union over the winter of 1939–1940. The question was, which alliance should it make? After Adolf Hitler's victory over France and Britain in *FALL GELB* (1940), it seemed prudent to come to terms with such a dominant and aggressive power. King Boris therefore joined the Axis, adhering to the *Tripartite Pact* on March 1, 1941. Thereafter, he permitted German troops to cross Bulgarian territory to invade Greece and agreed to occupy Macedonia. Bulgaria joined the German invasion of Yugoslavia on April 24, 1941, and benefited from the partition of that state. However, Boris stayed out of the German war with the Soviet Union. He was convinced that the Bulgarian Army was not capable of fighting against a modern Great Power. But he allowed Luftwaffe and Kriegsmarine units to operate in the Black Sea from Bulgarian ports. He also declared war on Britain and the United States on December 13, 1941, pushed hard to do so by Hitler. Hoping that Bulgaria would rescind its declaration, the United States did not declare war on Bulgaria until June 5, 1942. Pressure from Hitler and internal support for the Axis meant that Boris could not take advantage of American hopes to separate Bulgaria from Germany.

Domestically, Bulgaria resisted *nazification* despite hosting local fascists who would have been happy to comply with Hitler's vision for Europe. Anti-Semitic laws were passed under German pressure that were modeled on the *Nuremberg Laws*. However, the King refused demands to deport Bulgarian Jews to German *death camps*. Most Bulgarian Jews therefore survived the *Holocaust*. The King's judgment about the Bulgarian Army was borne out, as it had great difficulty dealing even with Greek and Macedonian partisans in its annexed territories. Otherwise, although a full member of the Axis, Bulgaria made a minimal commitment to the war effort. Boris refused to allow any Bulgarian troops to engage the Red Army and repeatedly declined to declare war on the Soviet Union. He had ferocious rows with Hitler over this issue and over his Jewish policy. Some believe that Hitler had Boris poisoned after the King refused concessions in 1943, but conclusive evidence is lacking. A weakened three-man regency governed into 1944, with Prime Minister Bogdan Filov the de facto ruler. As the German–Soviet war turned against Hitler, pro-Soviet partisans of the "Fatherland Front" (Otechestven) began operations in eastern Bulgaria. Western Allied bombing raids increased in intensity from late 1943. The Bulgarians sent out peace feelers to the Western Allies through the Greeks and Yugoslavs, but were rebuffed.

Meanwhile, Moscow threatened war if Bulgaria did not remove all German forces from its soil. The Soviets finally declared war on Bulgaria on September 5, 1944. Three days later Bulgaria was invaded by 3rd Ukrainian Front in a lightning offensive commanded by no less a figure than Marshal *Georgi Zhukov*. Bulgarian border forces were easily brushed aside, offering little real opposition: the Soviets suffered under 1,000 casualties to overrun all Bulgaria. A formal ceasefire was arranged after five days, just two of which that saw real fighting. The pro-Soviet "Fatherland Front" took power in Sophia in a bloodless coup on September 9. Red Army units entered the capital six days later. Bulgaria thereupon renounced the Tripartite Pact and formally switched sides by declaring war on Nazi Germany. Bulgaria signed an armistice with Moscow and the Western Allies on October 28. Soviet 37th Army remained in the country as a guarantee of loyalty, while 340,000 Bulgarian troops participated in Soviet invasions/liberations of Serbia, Hungary, and Austria. The Bulgarian Army suffered over 32,000 dead during those campaigns. The Soviets then oversaw postwar establishment of a Communist state in Bulgaria, starting with Fatherland Front trials and executions of wartime "collaborators" with the Germans. The Communist-run country that emerged was melded into the postwar "Soviet bloc" in eastern and central Europe. The monarchy was formally abolished in 1947.

BULGE, BATTLE OF (1944–1945)
See Ardennes offensive.

BUNA
See New Guinea.

BUND DEUTSCHER MADEL   "League of German Girls."
See Hitlerjungend.

BUREAU CENTRAL DE RENSIGNEMENTS ET D'ACTION (BCRA)   The intelligence service of the *Free French*.

BÜRGERBRÄUKELLER BOMB   An attempt to assassinate Adolf Hitler probably occurred on November 2, 1939, though some doubt remains as to whether the attempt was staged. A bomb placed in the Bürgerbräukeller, or beer cellar, in Munich detonated just after Hitler finished speaking and left the building. It killed seven Nazis. The incident was blamed on a Bavarian carpenter and Communist. Some suspected that the device was planted with Hitler's knowledge, as a prelude to new intimidation and purges of the German civil service. That suspicion was deepened by the fact that the accused was never tried, but was instead kept alive in various KZ (*concentration camps*) until he was murdered in 1945.

BURMA   Britain governed Burma as part of its larger empire in India, but never persuaded the Burmese to accept direct rule from London. From 1931 to 1933, Burmese peasants actively resisted British rule and especially British land policy. In 1937 Burma was administratively separated from India. It was invaded and occupied by the Japanese Army during the *Burma campaign* of 1941–1942. Some Burmese, led by *Aung San,* fought alongside the Japanese early in the war. A collaborationist government led by *Ba Maw* was rewarded with a territorially truncated and politically false "independence" in 1943, and formally declared war on the Western Allies. Heavy fighting accompanied the disastrous Japanese *Imphal offensive* in 1944. Three Japanese armies failed to keep British, Indian, and Chinese troops from advancing northward in 1944–1945. The Western Allies were supported by 13 battalions of Burmese troops drawn exclusively from the Chin, Kachin, and Karen ethnic minorities, serving under British officers with 14th Army. In March 1945, Aung San and the *Burma National Army* switched sides upon seeing that Japan would surely lose the war and realizing that some new deal would have to be made with the victorious British. The last 30,000 men of Japanese 28th Army made a desperate attempt to break out of Burma in July 1945. They sought to reach and cross the Sittang, fighting past the end of the war elsewhere. They failed at terrible cost: only 1,400 weak survivors were taken prisoner out of 30,000 who made the final trek. British losses were under 100 men. The British reoccupied Burma at the end of the war, but the return was tentative. As Burma sank into civil war, London negotiated a reasonably graceful departure. It acceded to formal independence in 1948.

See also Admin Box; Arakan campaign; biological weapons; Burma Road; Burma-Siam railway; Ichi-Gō; Ledo Road; X Force.

BURMA CAMPAIGN (1941–1942)   The Japanese assault on Burma was first assayed on December 14, 1941, along with attacks on *Pearl Harbor, Malaya, Hong Kong,* and the *Philippines.* The main aims of the invasion of Burma were to cut off supplies to the *Guomindang* in southern China, buffer the conquest of Malaya, and threaten and tie down British forces in India. Japanese 15th Army was led by General Shojiro Iida. Opposing the Japanese was a single Indian Army division of 12,000 men and an even less well-trained or properly armed Burmese division of 15,000. A Japanese assault on Indian troops along the Sittang wiped out most defenders by February 23, 1942. The key moment came when a panicked British commander blew a major bridge, thereby stranding most of his Indian troops on the wrong side of the river. General *Archibald Wavell,* commander in chief of the hastily organized *ABDA Command,* ordered Rangoon defended at all cost. The city fell on March 8, with a British motorized column escaping when the Japanese uncharacteristically failed to complete their attack with sufficient speed or aggression. The Britain retreat was protected by fighters of the *American Volunteer Group,* the famed "Flying Tigers."

A British armored brigade arrived in-country, but an Australian division never made it in time. *Guomindang* troops were seconded to the British front from China under their American commander, General *Joseph Stilwell.* Japanese troops overmatched all these forces in morale and training, superior commanders, and especially local air power. Japanese aircraft sowed panic in enemy columns, further eroding morale. The oil fields at Yenangyaung were fired by the retreating British. A sharp battle was fought among the flames at Yenangyaung, in which British and Chinese units finally rescued the broken remnants of the 1st Burma Division. But other Chinese units were beaten by Thai intervention in the west—the Thais would be rewarded with two Burmese provinces. Others were handily defeated by the Japanese near Mandalay. Most Chinese troops thereupon pulled back into Yunnan. Before the first Burma campaign ended the British Army made the longest retreat in British military history: over 900 miles back into India. When ragged British and Commonwealth survivors staggered into Bengal they were short 13,000 dead comrades. Tens of thousands of civilians had also perished along the way. A poorly planned effort by Wavell to retake Akyab in December was beaten back by the Japanese. For the whole campaign, Japanese casualties reached just 2,000 dead.

BURMA CAMPAIGN (1943–1945) The Western Allies wanted to retake Burma for the same reason the Japanese sought to retain control: only through Burma could large-scale military supplies be sent overland to *Jiang Jieshi* in southern China. The Americans were especially interested in opening the *Ledo Road* in northern Burma. They did not achieve that objective until January 1945, by which time president Franklin Roosevelt had given up hope that any significant contribution to the defeat of Japan would be made by the *Guomindang*. The British had never been convinced that FDR's faith in China or Jiang was well placed. They were far more interested in Burma as a buffer for British interests in India and as a route back into old possessions in Southeast Asia and coastal China. They did not like Jiang's rhetorical support for Indian nationalism and had extremely low regard for Guomindang armies. But the British needed Americans elsewhere, and so went along with Washington's call for a push in Burma. This resulted in the second Burma campaign, an effort that Winston Churchill had little interest in unless easy victories could be achieved that promised good press.

In February 1943, *Orde Wingate* led his *Chindit* force into northern Burma. He lost one-third of his men but showed that air resupply might be used to maintain a powerful striking force that could threaten Japanese rear areas. The Japanese reinforced and reorganized during the first half of 1943, as did the British. Behind the lines, special forces in Burma—SOE Force 136 for the British and OSS Detachment 101 for the Americans—benefited from close cooperation with the Kachin and Karen minorities. Both sides were exhausted from the first year of war in Burma and suffered unusually high attrition from the difficult tropical environment. Japan compensated by striking a political blow: Tokyo agreed to sham Burmese independence in August. Meanwhile, the Americans built up an air supply route to China from bases in India and continued extraordinary work on the Ledo Road. But even the Americans realized by the end of 1943 that the main campaign against Japan was taking place in the Central Pacific, where it was proceeding faster than anticipated or planned when the commitment to take the offensive in Burma was first made. In sum, Burma had fallen to secondary importance in a tertiary theater of operations. The campaign continued nevertheless, partly from inertia and partly because the Japanese retained a sizeable army in Burma. By early 1944 the Western Allies had built up sufficient forces under General *William Slim* and were ready to assault the main Japanese force.

The Western Allied thrust had three spear points. The first was led by Slim in Arakan, aiming for Akyab. The second was a combined Chinese, American, and Chindit operation toward Myitkyina on the Irrawaddy (Ayeyarwady) River. The third was an *Indian Army* assault out of bases in Assam. The Chindits fought a 79-day battle at Myitkyina from May 17 to August 3, 1944, before the broken Japanese garrison pulled out. The Chindits were near broken and deeply exhausted by that fight. The Japanese did not intend to defend everywhere in Burma. Instead, with typical offensive spirit, but against all material logic, they launched their own *Imphal offensive* in 1944. It began with a diversionary attack in Arakan in February, meant to draw British troops away from the main area of the offensive. The Japanese called the Arakan portion of their operation "Ha-Gō." The British called the fight the *Battle of the Admin Box*. The Japanese were beaten soundly in the Arakan after making initial gains. Their main Imphal, or "U-Gō," offensive failed even more miserably. The breakdown in Japanese command, supplies, and morale that followed failure of the Imphal offensive permitted the Western Allies to push deep into Burma in early 1945. But first the British had to meet and defeat more Japanese at Meiktila in February–March. British 14th Army then crossed the Irrawaddy in chase of Japanese 15th Army, which was falling back in disarray after the failure at Imphal. Slim threw a strike force around the retreating Japanese through the Myittha Valley, while his armor raced ahead to Meiktila. British tanks smashed the poorly equipped *Indian National Army* and sundry Japanese defenders and took Meiktila on March 3. Seeing that Japanese collapse was imminent, the *Burma National Army* switched sides. A Japanese counterattack briefly threatened Slim's position, but Indian 17th Division held as it was reinforced by air. The Japanese withdrew on March 28, leaving the road open to Mandalay and Rangoon. The last months for the Japanese in Burma were catastrophic: remnants of broken armies, beyond supply or hope, tried to fight their way out but only suffered enormous loss of life. Some units lost 60 to 90 percent of their complement. A ceasefire was signed in Rangoon on August 28. Resistance by some frightened or diehard Japanese continued into October.

See also ZIPPER.

Suggested Reading: Louis Allen, *Burma: The Longest War, 1941–1945* (1984); William Slim, *Defeat Into Victory* (1956); Donovan Webster, *The Burma Road* (2003).

BURMA NATIONAL ARMY (BNA) A pro-Japan Burmese force led by *Aung San,* who held the rank of general in the Japanese Army. A small Japanese-sponsored and supplied force called the "Burma Independence Army" fought alongside the Japanese invaders in 1942, but was militarily ineffective. It was replaced by Aung San's modest force, which fronted as a Burmese "national army" upon Japan's permission to declare formal "independence" in August 1943. Aung San and the

BNA changed sides in March 1945, once it became clear that Japan was losing the war. The BNA then fought against the Japanese in support of British and *Indian Army* forces.

BURMA ROAD   The supply line to China used by the British to support *Jiang Jieshi* from December 1938, during the *Sino-Japanese War (1937–1945)*. Built with conscripted "coolie" labor, it ran for over 350 miles through dense jungle and over high, jagged mountains. Wartime extensions stretched it to over 700 miles. It was closed for several months in 1940 when Winston Churchill was compelled to bow to Japanese pressure following the German victory in *FALL GELB*. It was closed again in 1942, after the Japanese pushed the British out of Burma in the first *Burma campaign (1941–1942)*. That seriously threatened *Guomindang* forces by cutting their main overland supply route: the only one left ran 3,000 miles from Alma Ata through outer Mongolia to Chongqing (Chungking). To compensate, the Western Allies flew military supplies and fuel in unpressurized aircraft "over the Hump," as pilots called the air route over the Himalayas from India to southern China. By 1944, China and the Guomindang ceased to figure prominently in Western Allied plans or expectations for final victory over Japan. When the Burma Road was finally reopened by American *Mars Task Force* and engineers in January 1945, it permitted additional supplies to be delivered to the Guomindang in southern China but did little to affect the final outcome of the war.

See also *Ledo Road*.

BURMA–SIAM RAILWAY   A Japanese military railway built during the war with "coolie" forced labor and by Australian, British, and Dutch *prisoners of war*. It was built between July 1942 and October 1943. It ran for 260 miles, spanning many gorges and rivers, including the Mae Klong ("River Kwai"). Louis Allen, leading historian of the war in Burma, places the total lives lost at over 12,000 prisoners and more than 90,000 forced laborers from all over Japanese-occupied Southeast Asia. Although true totals remain unknowable, it has been calculated that one man died for each 17-foot section of track laid. The main causes of death were brutal mistreatment and execution by Japanese guards, deliberate starvation, and disease. Western Allied air forces bombed the line repeatedly and with success. The railway was abandoned by the Japanese in early 1945, as they fell back under pressure from enemy offensives.

BURP GUN   Any of a variety of submachine pistols. The most famous were the American "Thompson," British "Sten," German MP40, Italian "Beretta," and Soviet PPsH (M1941). Western Allied soldiers named the class of submachine pistols "burp guns" after the short, loud bursts of fire they characteristically produced.

See also *grease gun; machine guns*.

BUSCH, ERNST (1885–1945)   German field marshal. He was a corps commander during the invasion of Poland in 1939. He led 16th Army in the invasion of

France in 1940, and again as part of Army Group North during the *BARBAROSSA* invasion of the Soviet Union in 1941. He was promoted to field marshal in 1943 and took command of Army Group Center, replacing *Günther von Kluge*. During Operation *BAGRATION* in 1944, Busch proved that he was not capable of commanding the main German army group on the Eastern Front. He was sacked by Adolf Hitler in June, although Hitler bore at least as much responsibility for the disaster suffered by the Wehrmacht in Belorussia. In the last desperate weeks of the Third Reich, Busch was restored to command of Wehrmacht forces fighting in northwest Germany. On May 4, 1945, he surrendered all Axis forces there, in Denmark, and in the Netherlands to Field Marshal *Bernard Law Montgomery*.

BUSHIDŌ

See Imperial Japanese Army.

BUSTARD HUNT

See TRAPPENJAGD.

BUTT REPORT

See area bombing.

BUZZ BOMB British slang for the V-1 rocket.
See V-weapons program.

BYRNES, JAMES F. (1879–1972) American statesman. A close friend and confidant of President Franklin Roosevelt, Byrnes left the Supreme Court to direct the Economic Stabilization Office in 1942. In May 1943, he was also appointed to head the War Mobilization Board. That gave him unprecedented power for an appointee. His principal role and contribution was directing the extraordinary war economy of the United States, which he did remarkably well. Byrnes also had enormous influence over planning for postwar reconstruction. He informed newly sworn-in President Harry Truman about the existence and meaning of the *Manhattan Project*. Byrnes served as secretary of state from 1945 to 1947.

C

C-47 DAKOTA Military designation for the originally civilian, twin-engined Douglas DC-3 built in the United States. C-47s were used as troop and cargo transports and for delivering airborne assaults.

CAB RANK SYSTEM A ground control system developed by the Royal Air Force (RAF) in North Africa. It provided two-way communication between air and ground forces, with the latter identifying targets against which they directed tactical air strikes. In the final battles in the west in France and Germany in 1944–1945, RAF Typhoons and USAAF P-47s and P-51s fitted with rockets circled in cab ranks waiting to be called down for surgical tactical strikes against enemy targets identified by friendly ground forces.

CACTUS American code name for the August 7, 1942, marine landings on *Guadalcanal*.

CACTUS AIR FORCE Marine term for the hodgepodge of aircraft defending American ground forces on *Guadalcanal*. It flew out of a captured Japanese air strip that was renamed "Henderson Field."

CAIRO CONFERENCE (DECEMBER 3–6, 1943) "SEXTANT." Franklin Roosevelt and Winston Churchill met for a second time in Cairo on their return from the *Tehran Conference* with Joseph Stalin. They mostly discussed joint command appointments and other matters pertaining to the pending invasion of Europe, then set for May 1944. They were joined by President Inönü of Turkey, whom they failed to persuade to bring 40 Turkish Army divisions into the fight against Germany in the Balkans. The question of who would command *OVERLORD* was settled: General *Dwight Eisenhower* selected as supreme commander and General *Bernard Law Montgomery* as ground forces commander. Eisenhower was replaced in the Mediterranean theater by British General *Henry Wilson*. Operations in the CBI (China, Burma, India) theater were downgraded in favor of using scarce *landing craft* in OVERLORD, and in the follow-up *DRAGOON* landings in southern France.

See also Potsdam Declaration.

CAIRO CONFERENCE (NOVEMBER 22–26, 1943) "SEXTANT." Franklin Roosevelt met Winston Churchill and *Jiang Jieshi* in Cairo from November 22–26, 1943. The president and prime minister were en route to the *Tehran conference,* where they met Joseph Stalin. Discussions at Cairo focused on the war with Japan, including conversations with *Louis Mountbatten* and *Joseph Stilwell*. The three Western Allied leaders issued a joint "Cairo Declaration," which stated four common positions on the postwar settlement in Asia: Japan would lose all territories in the Pacific acquired since 1914, including the old German mandates it held in *League of Nations* trust from 1919; all lands taken from China were to be returned, including Taiwan, Manchuria, and the Pescadores; Japan was to be expelled from any territory it had acquired by force, including Sakhalin Island and the Kurils; Korea was to become independent "in due course." Joint operations were also agreed for Burma in 1944, over strong British reservations.

CAIRO DECLARATION

See Cairo Conference.

CAMOUFLAGE As late as 1939 some inept Red Army senior officers still regarded camouflage as akin to cowardice and at best as a retardant of offensive spirit. Nonetheless, camouflage was adopted by the Red Army and all other armies fighting during World War II. It was used on equipment, vehicles, aircraft, ships, in uniform design, and by individual soldiers. It was mostly accomplished with paints in varying combinations and disruptive displays such as "dazzle" patterns, or with nets used to support natural foliage covering vehicles, machine gun nests, trenches, and even helmets. It was commonplace to wear uniforms and paint vehicles to fit the main color of the natural background. Sand was preferred for desert campaigns, white for the Arctic, and olive drab or brown in forested and temperate areas. Not all camouflage was effective: the first jungle-camouflage, one-piece suits issued to U.S. forces in the Pacific, actually made the wearer easier to see while moving. They were replaced in 1944 by an olive-drab, two-piece jungle uniform.

See also elephants; punji stakes; snipers.

CAMPAIGN

See military strategy; operational art.

CANADA Under Prime Minister Mackenzie King, the Canadian government shared the isolationist outlook of its southern neighbor during the interwar years. The population was even more heavily weighed down by memories of national division and terrible casualties incurred during World War I, in which Canadians fought from 1914 to 1918. Canada remained badly divided politically and culturally between its French minority and English-speaking majority, especially over a potential new war and the return of conscription. Yet, along with other Dominions, it moved away from isolationism from late 1938. Mackenzie King even warned Adolf Hitler on August 25, 1939, that Canada would fight if war broke out with Britain. Hitler was unfazed. He did not comprehend the latent military and economic power even of the United States and therefore, completely underestimated the role that Canada would play in the war against Germany over the next six years.

Canada followed its Imperial lode star and declared war on Germany on September 10, a week after declarations by Britain and other Dominions. That merely decorous delay was a token of symbolic foreign policy independence, dating to the constitutional revisions of the *Statute of Westminster*. But Canada committed to wage war without benefit of conscription for overseas service. Its government at first seemed far less committed to victory than its armed forces, as evidenced in drawn-out negotiations with Commonwealth allies for payment for hosting the *British Commonwealth Air Training Plan*. That reticence did not change until Britain and the Commonwealth stood alone against Nazi Germany in the summer of 1940, following the fall of France in *FALL GELB*. From that point, resolve in Canada firmed, just as it did in Britain. Although conscription remained a bitterly divisive issue throughout the entire war, by 1940 most Canadians understood the grim stakes and committed to the hard slog that eventual victory would require. The same cannot be said of their wartime prime minister, who never seemed to attempt half leadership measures where quarter ones sufficed, especially on the key issue of conscription—although that was a problem on which irresolution was shared by the Cabinet and the country. King was mystically inclined and developed a grossly exaggerated private sense of his importance to the alliance, and as a mediator in Anglo-American relations. A more positive, but also desperate, sign of determination on either side of the Imperial pond was the transfer of Britain's gold reserves and negotiable securities to Canada. These were loaded into a battleship, two cruisers, and three cargo ships and delivered for wartime safe-keeping in Canadian vaults. Britain would have the financial resources to fight on from overseas, even if the home island fell under German jackboots in 1940.

The most immediate impact of the war on Canadian national life was the great stimulus it gave to a still-depressed economy. Long term, the war provided an impetus to economic and defense integration with the United States, away from the old Imperial trading system and defense arrangements. Improved and expanded relations with the other North American democracy were partly codified in the "Hyde Park Declaration" of April 20, 1941. In addition, Canada and the United States established a "Permanent Joint Board on Defense" in 1940. This contrasted with a lingering aloofness and even disdain in London toward a former colony pulling away toward full independence, but still seen largely through imperial lenses. By 1945 Canada's prewar agrarian economy would be supplemented by new industrial production and make a significant contribution to the Allied war effort. Canadian food surpluses were critically important to sustaining Britain's population. Food also made up the lion's share of Canada's *Mutual Aid* program, a miniature version of *Lend-Lease* to the Soviet Union. As a result of expanding economic activity, Canada saw its standard of living rise significantly during the war. On the other hand, Canada was not important enough to Washington to be included in all Western Allied conferences or to be consulted directly on wartime or postwar planning: Washington still tended to see Canada as an appendage of the British Empire and to negotiate most directly with London. However, military cooperation with U.S. forces expanded from 1942, in both the Atlantic and Pacific theaters.

From 1939 to 1945 Canada expanded its total military personnel from under 10,000 to over one million. Its main military contribution came in the *Battle of the Atlantic (1939–1945)*, which saw the *Royal Canadian Navy (RCN)* expand over 50 times its original size—the greatest wartime expansion of any navy in history. Hugely expanded Canadian shipyards turned out large numbers of vital light escort ships such as the *corvette*, when they were most desperately needed in 1940 and 1941. The RCN then filled these little ships with crews, some barely trained in the rush to protect the convoys. There were frictions with the British into 1943 over the inexperience and training of some Canadian crews, but overall the naval contribution—including that of the merchant marine—was disproportionate to Canada's size and military weight. The home front was a different story. Rather than uniting in a common cause and shared sacrifice of a hard war, Canada's 11.5 million people were once again bitterly divided over the issue of overseas conscription. Even after introducing conscription the government shied away from forcing men to serve overseas. Canada therefore fought most of the war with an all-volunteer combat force, which was undermanned and probably took heavier casualties as a result. All Canadian combat troops were still volunteers as late as 1945. That brought the government and military under intense pressure from veterans and families of active duty volunteers. Still, it was only when the problem of replacements reached crisis level in November 1944 that King's government finally agreed to send 16,000 conscripts to fight in Europe.

The war in Europe led the *Canadian Army* and *Royal Canadian Air Force* to make significant contributions to the Allied effort in Italy in 1943, in France and the Low Countries in 1944, and in the Netherlands and the *conquest of Germany* in 1945. Canadian pilots fought in the *Battle of Britain* in 1940 and in North Africa. Bomber crews flew deep over Germany in units attached to RAF Bomber Command and separately in an all-Canadian, RCAF Group. A Canadian division was sacrificed and savaged at *Dieppe* in 1942, a wasteful fight that is still bitterly recalled. Canadians fought more successfully with British 8th Army in the *Italian campaign (1943–1945)*. One of the five beaches on *D-Day (June 6, 1944)* was taken by Canadian troops, who next fought around Caen and to close the *Falaise pocket* during the *Normandy campaign*. By September 1944, Canadian troops were fighting under their own generals: some were excellent, others were very poor. Canadian 1st Army fought on the left wing of the advance through the Netherlands, thence into northern Germany in 1945. It had its hardest fight in taking the *Scheldt estuary campaign* in 1944, and in liberating the Netherlands over the winter of 1944–1945.

Canadians also fought in the Pacific, suffering early defeat alongside British forces in late 1941 and early 1942. Canada reacted even more harshly than did the United States to a perceived threat from Japan to the west coast of North America in December 1941: *Japanese Canadians* were dispossessed and interned, then dispersed across the country. They were discriminated against in law for many years after the war, longer than *Japanese Americans*. The first joint military effort with the United States in the Pacific came during the battle for Attu in the *Aleutian Islands,* where the *Devil's Brigade* first saw action. More battles followed, mainly in Italy, France, the Low Countries, and on the ground and in the skies over Germany. Canadians would have participated in the invasion of Japan, but *DOWNFALL* was canceled after the atomic attacks and Soviet *Manchurian offensive operation* in August 1945. By the end of the war Canada suffered 42,000 dead and 54,500 wounded in battle. That was a terrible cost, but still fewer men than it lost in the Great War.

See also various battles and campaigns, and *air gaps; Air–sea rescue; convoys; Devil's Brigade; merchant marine; prisoners of war; Red Devils; zombies.*

Suggested Reading: Charles P. Stacey, *Six Years of War* (1955).

CANADIAN ARMY In mid-1939 the Canadian Army fielded under 4,300 officers and men. It had fewer than 100 machine guns and just two light tanks. Another 51,000 were in reserve in poorly trained militia units. Two new divisions were quickly raised from volunteers at the start of the war, though there were not as many volunteers as the government hoped. The first enthusiastic—but still raw and poorly equipped—Canadian division embarked for Britain in December 1939. Remarkably, after the defeat of France in June 1940, volunteers and general Canadian commitment to the war increased (outside Québec). The government in Ottawa deeply feared a rerun of the great conscription crisis that tore apart Canadian society during World War I and therefore, did not introduce conscription for overseas service until late 1944. It also preferred to enlist for the RCAF and the RCN rather than the army, expecting to incur fewer casualties at sea and in the air. By 1944, over 530,000 Canadians volunteered for the Army. Some were retained for homeland defense but many saw combat overseas. Canadian forces arriving in the Pacific in late 1941 were unfortunate to reinforce Hong Kong just before that colony surrendered to the Japanese, after heavy fighting in December. Much worse was the disaster for the Canadian Army at *Dieppe* in 1942, the low point of the war for the country. Canadians next saw bloody fighting in central Sicily, and again as a discrete corps in central Italy during the *Italian campaign (1943–1945)*. Fighting in Italy brought heavy casualties but taught hard and necessary lessons that enabled the Army to fight well and hard in France and the Low Countries in 1944, then in the Netherlands and Germany in 1945.

Like other minor Allies—and like American forces in World War I—there was growing domestic political pressure to have Canadian troops fight under their own general officers. That led to formation of Canadian 1st Army, which fought on the left wing of the British advance through the Netherlands and northwest Germany. Unfortunately, while some Canadian officers such as Lieutenant General Guy Simonds were top drawer, the main commander was not: General Henry Crerar proved a failure as a battlefield commander. Field Marshal *Bernard Law Montgomery* held him in especially low regard and might have sacked him but for the political pressure not to embarrass Canada. The reputation of Canadian troops was mixed. The Canadian Army was responsible for taking JUNO beach on *D-Day (June 6, 1944),* from whence its men reached farther inland than any landing force. Canadians fought hard and sometimes without mercy against *Waffen-SS* and other German Panzer and infantry divisions at Caen, and again at the *Falaise pocket* during the *Normandy campaign.* Following the breakout and during the pursuit of the Wehrmacht out of northern France, Canadian 1st Army took Dieppe and Calais before advancing into Belgium. After the failure of *MARKET GARDEN* in September, it was 1st Army that slogged through the *Scheldt Estuary campaign* in November, then slowly liberated the Netherlands from February to April, 1945. As with other western and especially British troops during the last months of the war in Europe, there was a growing reluctance in Canadian ranks to take risks or press attacks hard. Despite his poor reputation with Montgomery, Crerar commanded 13 Allied divisions in northwest Germany comprising Canadian 1st Army, including several divisions of Americans and other non-Canadian troops. Lieutenant General Charles Foulkes, commander of Canadian 2nd Division, accepted surrender of all German forces in the Netherlands in early May 1945.

See also prisoners of war; Red Devils; TRACTABLE; zombies.

CANARIS, WILHELM FRANZ (1887–1945) German admiral. He enlisted in the Imperial Navy in 1905. As a young officer he was aboard DKM Dresden, one of four German cruisers sunk or scuttled during the Battle of the Falklands in 1914. He spent part of the Great War organizing secret naval supplies from South America. His Latin successes drew him into intelligence work, which he pursued after the war. In 1934 he assumed command of the *Abwehr,* or German military intelligence. From the beginning of the Nazi period he rejected Adolf Hitler and most of the core ideas of *Nazism,* although he shared Hitler's anti-Bolshevism. Canaris was aghast at the prospect of war with the Western Allies in 1938. Therefore, he took part in the first of several Abwehr-organized plots to kill Hitler. Canaris is widely remembered for using his position and Abwehr contacts to protect anti-Nazis, especially among the Junker class, and for involvement in plots to assassinate Hitler. There are many myths that go much further, asserting that Canaris supposedly passed intelligence directly to the Allies and warned *Francisco Franco* to keep Spain out of the war. There is little to no evidence to support most of the claims. Less widely remarked is his active participation in odious and even criminal preparations for the invasions of Poland (*FALL WEISS*) in 1939 and the Soviet Union (*BARBAROSSA*) in 1941.

Canaris lost control of the Abwehr when Hitler transferred its powers and assets to *Heinrich Himmler* and the *Sicherheitsdienst (SD)* in early 1944. Canaris does not appear to have been directly involved in the *July Plot* (1944). However, because his loyalty was already suspect among senior Nazis, he was among those arrested following failure of the coup. Confined to a concentration camp, he was not cruelly tortured or hanged in the aftermath as were other suspected conspirators. In part, that was because of Hitler's fear of the propaganda damage that surely would have ensued from any public trial. For the same reason, General *Erwin Rommel* was allowed to commit suicide and given a state funeral. It is also likely that Himmler kept Canaris out of court because the Admiral knew details of the SS leader's sympathy for prior Hitler assassination plots. Canaris remained a prisoner in various camps until April 1945. Toward the end, he may have been seen as an asset in Himmler's extraordinary late-war delusions that he could personally negotiate a separate peace with the Western Allies. As U.S. forces neared *Flossenbürg* concentration camp, Canaris was summarily tried and murdered to prevent his liberation.

Suggested Reading: H. Höhne, *Canaris* (1979).

CANARY ISLANDS

See Franco, Francisco; Kriegsmarine; Spain.

CANNIBALISM

See concentration camps; Imperial Japanese Army; Leningrad, siege of; New Guinea campaign; prisoners of war; Sino-Japanese War (1937–1945).

CANNON

See anti-aircraft guns; armor; fighters.

CANOES   Small electric-motor or paddled canoes were used by *special forces* in the Pacific to insert or extract operatives, clandestinely lay mines close to ships or docks, and other small-scale operations.

CAPE ESPERANCE, BATTLE OF (OCTOBER 11–12, 1942)   A naval fight off *Guadalcanal*. A U.S. Navy task force of cruisers and destroyers intercepted a Japanese fleet that included two seaplane carriers. The Japanese were attempting a typical night shelling of American ground forces on the island, while also bringing in Army reinforcements. The U.S. ships were unable to stop the landings, but broke up the bombardment run. The Japanese lost a heavy cruiser and one destroyer, with another heavy cruiser badly damaged. They sank one American destroyer. Land-based U.S. aircraft spotted the retreating enemy fleet after dawn on the 12th, and bombed and sank two more Japanese destroyers.

CAPE MATAPAN, BATTLE OF (MARCH 28, 1941)   A small but important surface battle between the Royal Navy and the Regia Marina. The British knew from *ULTRA* intercepts where the Italians would be: steaming in three groups, one including the battleship "Vittorio Venito." They intercepted with a strong fleet of cruisers, destroyers, battleships, and the carrier HMS Formidable. In a confused action that lasted into the night, Admiral *Andrew Cunningham* vectored carrier aircraft to torpedo and bomb the "Vittorio Venito" and damage an Italian cruiser. The wounded cruiser fell behind the withdrawing battleship and escorts. When two more cruisers and two destroyers were sent to aid the stricken ship, the British caught the flotilla in the open and sank all three cruisers and both destroyers. The outcome encouraged the Regia Marina to keep its most valuable ships in port.

CAPE ST. GEORGE, BATTLE OF (NOVEMBER 25, 1943)   A small naval battle that resulted from Japanese efforts to attack supply ships supporting American forces early in the *Bougainville campaign*. Five Japanese destroyers engaged five U.S. destroyers off New Ireland. Three Japanese ships were sunk.

CAPITAL   Code name for the Western Allied operation that took Rangoon. It began on November 19, 1944. "Extended Capital" took the fight to Meiktila.
   See Burma campaign (1943–1945).

CARIBBEAN REGIMENT   A *British West Indies* regiment that was formed in 1944 from troops raised from several island colonies. It was deployed to Africa and the ETO, but never entered combat.

CARIBBEAN SEA
   See Atlantic, Battle of; British West Indies; Caribbean Regiment; convoys; destroyers-for-bases deal; U-boats.

CAROLINE ISLANDS   Some 600 small islands and coral atolls forming a large, but widely scattered, archipelago between the Marianas and New Guinea. The Carolines were originally settled by Spain but were sold to Germany in 1899. During World War I they were seized by Japan. In 1921 they became a Japanese mandate territory under the *League of Nations*. The Imperial Japanese Navy maintained a major base on Truk Island, with garrisons on Yap and Ponape. U.S. forces established an air base and anchorage at Ulithi, but otherwise bypassed the Carolines as they *island-hopped* through the Central Pacific. In 1947 the Carolines became part of the Trust Territory of the Pacific Islands, governed under United Nations authority by the United States.

CARPATHIAN BRIGADE
   See Polish Army.

CARPATHO-UKRAINE   An alternate name for Ruthenia, an area ceded by Czechoslovakia to the Soviet Union in 1945.

CARPET BOMBING   American term for the practice of large groups of bombers dropping ordnance in planned destructive patterns along a designated "carpet," or wide dispersal area, rather than aiming for specific targets as in *precision bombing*. The British called such wide patterns "*area bombing*." A special British form of tactical bombing developed by the RAF was known as *Tedder's carpet*.
    See also air power; strategic bombing; thousand bomber raids; total war.

CARRIER PIGEONS   Homing pigeons were used nearly universally in World War II by air forces, armies, and navies, as well as by *resistance* fighters, newsmen, and in *air–sea rescue*. The American, Australian, and Japanese navies all used carrier pigeons for island communication during the Pacific War. Carrier pigeons ranged up to 1,000 miles from their lofts and could fly over terrain no other courier could cross. At short ranges they might fly at 60 mph, carrying coded messages or hand-drawn maps several miles in just minutes. The U.S. Army Signal Corps maintained an extensive Pigeon Service. Its more than 50,000 birds were deployed in Africa, Europe, and Asia. Some paratrooper vests had specially adapted pockets to carry pigeons during combat jumps. The British maintained a feathered air fleet called the "National Pigeon Service." An additional, secret pigeon intelligence wing was known as "Source Columbia." It operated the "Confidential Pigeon Service" behind German lines from 1940. Its most basic method was to drop hundreds of carrier pigeons in parachute cases at night. Each case included a bird, a message tube, ultrafine paper, a special pencil, detailed instructions in several languages, and a copy of a London newspaper to establish authenticity. The Germans set up a counter-pigeon service in March 1944, wherein German birds were dropped across France replete with English cigarettes and a request for return of the names of *Résistance* members. The Résistance council advised those who found German birds to eat them.
    See also falcons; Gibson Girl.

CARRIERS
    See aircraft carriers; Catapult Aircraft Merchant (CAM); escort carriers; float planes; Merchant Aircraft Carrier (MAC).

CARTWHEEL (1943)   Code name for an offensive against the Japanese that originally planned to retake *Rabaul*. It was modified when the Western Allies decided to bypass Rabaul as part of their *island-hopping strategy*. That decision led to continued heavy fighting in the *New Guinea campaign*, fresh island and naval combat in the *New Georgia campaign*, but more limited ambitions for the *New Britain campaign*. These operations ultimately isolated and contained over 100,000 Japanese troops until they surrendered in August 1945. From the Japanese point of view, New Guinea and the Solomons were reduced in strategic importance by September 1943, as the Imperial General Headquarters struggled to conserve limited resources for the main fight to come in the Central Pacific theater.

CAS   Chief of Air Staff (Britain).

CASABLANCA CONFERENCE (JANUARY 14–24, 1943)   "SYMBOL." Franklin Roosevelt and Winston Churchill met in Casablanca from January 14–24, 1943, to discuss and coordinate strategic policy. Joseph Stalin was invited but declined to attend. The main topic was the ongoing *Battle of the Atlantic (1939–1945)*, which received top resource priority thereafter. The key decisions taken were: (1) agreement to demand *unconditional surrender* from all Axis powers; (2) invasion by the Western Allies of Sicily and Italy, to precede invasion of France; (3) issuance of the "Casablanca Directive" ordering a sustained *Combined Bomber Offensive* against Germany, with priority assigned to destruction of U-boat yards and fighter production; and (4) approval of a U.S. Navy proposal to advance toward Japan via the Central Pacific. That signaled the formal adoption of the great *island-hopping strategy*, which greatly shortened the Pacific War. The most important decision concerned the invasion of Sicily. Churchill pressed for it in part with the intention of deflecting the Americans from their determination to open a *second front* in France in 1943, which he feared could not be opened until 1944 without sustaining severe casualties. It was also agreed that the main invasion of Europe must await victory over the U-boat threat in the Atlantic. Obtaining U.S. agreement to the Sicilian invasion, to be followed by an Italian invasion, was the last time the British viewpoint prevailed on a major strategic decision.

   See also Québec Conference (1943); VLR (Very Long Range) aircraft.

CASABLANCA DIRECTIVE
   See Casablanca Conference; Combined Bomber Offensive.

CASH AND CARRY
   See Neutrality Acts; Roosevelt, Franklin Delano (1882–1945).

CASSINO
   See Clark, Mark; Italian campaign; Monte Cassino.

CASUALTIES
   See individual countries, discrete battles and campaigns, and Appendix E.

CATAPULT AIRCRAFT MERCHANT (CAM)   During 1940-1941, the Royal Navy (RN) rushed into service 35 merchants converted to carry catapult-launched fighters in addition to their cargo. This was an interim response to the new *Kondor* long-range reconnaissance threat to convoys. Four CAMs manned by RN crews were known as "Fighter Catapult Ships" and considered military vessels. The rest were crewed by the merchant marine, with RN pilots aboard. Of the 35 converted CAMs, 13 were sunk by U-boats or bombers. Few fighters launched from CAMs scored Kondor kills, but they did chase many away. CAMs were progressively replaced by true *escort carriers* starting in 1942.

See also Merchant Aircraft Carrier (MAC).

CATCHPOLE   Code name for the assault on Eniwetok.
See Marshall Islands.

CAT GEAR
See Foxer.

CATHOLIC CHURCH

See *anti-Semitism; concordats; corporatism; Franco, Francisco; Lateran Treaties; Lend-Lease; Mussolini, Benito; Neutrality Acts; Pétain, Henri Philippe; Pius XI; Pius XII; ratlines; Résistance (French); resistance (German); Saar; Spanish Civil War (1936–1939); Uštaše; Vatican; Waffen-SS.*

CATROUX, GEORGES (1877–1969)   French general. He was governor of French Indochina, where he was unable to forestall Japanese occupation. He was replaced by a Vichy appointee in August 1940. Catroux immediately joined the fledgling *Free French* movement, the only prewar French general to do so (*Charles de Gaulle* was promoted general during *FALL GELB* in 1940). Catroux commanded the Free French campaign that took Syria from Vichy. He was less successful as governor of Algeria, where his fierce reimposition of colonial rule provoked Western Allied criticism and much local resistance.

CAUCASUS

See *BLAU; Eastern Front; EDELWEISS; MOUNTAINS; Red Army; Wehrmacht.*

CAVALLERO, UGO (1880–1943)   Italian field marshal. Chief of the *Comando Supremo* from December 1940 to February 1943. A veteran of World War I, he took over from *Pietro Badoglio* in Italian East Africa in 1937. Cavallero served Benito Mussolini in various administrative jobs until the end of 1940, then emerged as the main military adviser to "Il Duce." He led Italian forces fighting against the Greeks in Albania, where his troops had to be rescued by German intervention. He next oversaw successive defeats and loss of colonial territory to the British in East Africa and North Africa. He again lost face during the *desert campaign (1940–1943)* when the Germans sent the *Afrika Korps* to Tunisia to shore up his failing Italian forces. He was sacked shortly after the defeat at *Second El Alamein* in late 1942. He was briefly arrested by Badoglio after the fall of Mussolini. Cavallero was released by the Germans following Badoglio's flight from Rome, but Cavallero refused to fight for the Germans and was either murdered by them or killed himself on September 13, 1943.

CAVALRY   The Polish Army used cavalry against German infantry in the opening battles of the war in Europe in 1939. Some Polish cavalry units were assaulted by Panzers that overran them or broke into rear assembly areas. Others were smashed bloody by Ju-87 "Stuka" dive bombers. Otherwise, the widespread story that foolhardy Polish cavalry charged German tanks is untrue. Cavalry was used most effectively in the winter conditions and vast expanses of the Eastern Front from 1941 to 1945. Just before the German invasion of June 22, 1941, the Red Army had 13 cavalry divisions. Four were trained for mountain warfare. That large number reflected abiding influence on the Red Army of older commanders from the *Konarmiia* of the Russian Civil War (1918–1921). Each Soviet cavalry division had a paper strength of nearly 10,000 men and 64 light tanks, but more often a cavalry division actually fielded 5,000–6,000 troopers and fewer tanks, along with light horse-artillery and anti-aircraft guns. The paper number was cut to just 3,000 troopers within a few months, as cavalry units were cannibalized or lost in defensive battles. However, in December 1941, *Cossack* cavalry gave the Red Army a mobility denied to frozen German vehicles. Cossacks overran immobilized German guns and outflanked trenches, notably during the *Rzhev-Viazma strategic operation (January 8–April 20, 1942)*. Soviet cavalry was mainly used in a traditional horse soldier role: to exploit initial breakthroughs with deeper mobile penetrations, and to skirmish and harass enemy rear areas. By the end of 1943 the Red Army had 26 cavalry divisions comprising 8 cavalry corps, with most divisions reorganized as reinforced mechanized units. These *KMG*, or "cavalry-mechanized corps," were extensively used in great encirclement offensive operations from 1943 to 1945, notably in Ukraine and Hungary. Soviet *partisans* rode as dragoons deep into Ukraine in 1943 and 1944. The Germans and their lesser Axis partners also used cavalry in the east. The last ever Italian Army cavalry charge was made directly into the guns of a Soviet infantry division in 1942.

Cavalry played a significant role in the war in Asia, providing mobility to an undermotorized Japanese Army and to wholly footborne Chinese forces. The Red Army deployed KMG against the Japanese in the last major action of the war, the *Manchurian offensive operation (August 1945)*. The U.S. Army began the war with 12 million horses and 4 million mules. The 26th Regiment of the Philippine Scouts was the last cavalry unit in the U.S. Army to fight from horseback, facing the Japanese on the Bataan peninsula in early 1942. Smaller mounted units were used in the North African desert and during the *Italian campaign (1943–1945)*, but they were locally improvised for mobility in difficult terrain rather than cavalry units per se. The discrete prewar cavalry command was eliminated in March 1942, as the U.S. Army mechanized nearly all its cavalry units to serve in reconnaissance. Men were retrained in "infiltration" and "fire and maneuver" behind enemy lines, tactics necessary to support a primary recce mission. Mechanized cavalry units were attached to each armored and infantry division, with nondivisional cavalry assigned to Army HQs. Just two cavalry divisions of 13,000 men apiece were maintained as horse soldiers into 1944, at great cost in maintenance of their animals with no combat punch in return. Shipping shortages made it impossible to ship out so many horses—each man needed at least two mounts—and attendant fodder. The 1st Cavalry Division was therefore sent to the Pacific without horses to fight as dismounted light infantry. The all *African American* 2nd Cavalry Division suffered a more ignominious fate, partly because it was a cavalry division and in part due to racial prejudice: it was sent to North Africa in 1944, only to be broken up to provide replacements for theater service units.

CBI Western Allied shorthand for the "China-Burma-India" theater of operations.

CCS
See Combined Chiefs of Staff (Allies).

C-ELEMENT
See Belgian Gate.

CENT FORCE The Gela assault force during the invasion of Sicily.
See HUSKY.

CERBERUS Kriegsmarine code name for the naval operation the British call the "Channel Dash." It was undertaken on the direct order of Adolf Hitler, but over the objection of Admiral *Karl Raeder*. On February 11, 1942, the *battlecruisers* DKM Scharnhorst and DKM Gneisenau, the heavy cruiser DKM Prinz Eugen, and 9 destroyers all slipped out of Brest under cover of night and made for Norway at high speed. A British comedy of errors combined with German skill and a good deal of luck to allow the squadron to escape notice until it was already well underway. The RAF scrambled bombers while the Royal Navy sent various small, fast ships to intercept. The two battlecruisers were damaged by mines, but all German ships eventually reached safety. The "Channel Dash" greatly embarrassed the Royal Navy, while also revealing operational inadequacies in RAF Coastal Command. Yet, it hardly constituted a victory for the Kriegsmarine, even though it was portrayed as such in Germany.
See also JUPITER.

ČETNIKS
See Chetniks; Yugoslavia.

CEYLON Following the Japanese attack on British colonies in Southeast Asia and China, Australian troops were dispatched to garrison Ceylon. The island also hosted a small Royal Navy fleet—Ceylon was an important naval guard of the main routes from Australia to India, thence to the Middle East and East Africa. And it was a major exporter of rubber. A Japanese fleet bombarded Colombo and sank a number of RN warships in nearby waters in April 1942. However, the *Battle of the Coral Sea* ended any IJN aspiration to take Ceylon for use as an Indian Ocean naval and air base. A brief mutiny by pro-Japanese Ceylonese on the Cocos Islands was forcibly suppressed. Several of the mutineers were hanged.

CHAFF
See window.

CHAIN HOME RADAR   A system of early warning, homeland air defense radar stations deployed around the British coast. The key to the success of the system was that Chain Home radars were linked directly to air controllers who could "scramble" fighters to intercept incoming enemy bombers.

CHALLENGER   Code name for a proposed British contingency plan to seize the Spanish enclave of Ceuta on the North African coast, across from Gibraltar. It was never implemented.

CHAMBERLAIN, ARTHUR NEVILLE (1869–1940)   British statesman. As prime minister from 1937 to 1940, Chamberlain took control of British foreign policy. Although inexperienced in diplomacy, he was convinced he could avoid a general war by face-to-face negotiation with the dictators Benito Mussolini and Adolf Hitler. Chamberlain is usually portrayed as the main dupe of the *Munich Conference* (1938), where he agreed to hand the *Sudetenland* to Germany as the price of general peace. He appears to have genuinely believed that Germany had legitimate grievances arising from the *Treaty of Versailles* and that territorial concessions at the expense of the Czechoslovaks might satisfy Hitler. But more profoundly, Chamberlain feared the carnage of another Great Power war in Europe and the damage to the British Empire and civilization that he was certain another war would bring. Back in Britain, he self-consciously echoed the words of Benjamin Disraeli after the Congress of Berlin 50 years earlier. He announced that he, too, had achieved "peace with honor" and "peace for our time." He then advised the British : "Go home and get a nice, quiet sleep."

Chamberlain's animosity for the Soviet Union prevented him from seeing the utility and necessity of an alliance with that state, which was the only other continental power besides France that had the raw military capabilities to possibly deter Germany, and which prior to Munich actively sought a compact with the West. Britain's policy of *appeasement* predated Chamberlain's prime ministership and was an honorable and effective tradition in the diplomacy of the British Empire. But it was so discredited by the events that followed in 1939 that statesmen have ceased to use the term out of fear of damaging association with

Chamberlain and the disastrous outcome of the Munich Conference. Chamberlain himself reluctantly abandoned appeasement of Germany—but not of Italy—in January 1939, even before Hitler occupied the rump of Czechoslovakia in March. He was determined to fight if Britain must, and he belatedly offered security guarantees to Greece, Poland, and Rumania. He also introduced peacetime conscription and accelerated rearmament and preparedness measures. In late March, he issued a British guarantee to Poland. In part that was done to preempt Soviet influence in east and central Europe, but partly, Chamberlain used Poland as a test case: if Hitler stopped, a deal might yet be had; but if he attacked and eliminated Poland, then Nazi Germany was a fundamental threat to all Europe.

With deep aversion for any real fighting, Chamberlain cautiously led Britain into World War II when Germany attacked Poland on September 1, 1939. He appeared weak and indecisive during the period derisively known in the press as the *Phoney War*, but behind the scenes his government was working hard to speed rearmament and expand the BEF in France. Remarkably, into the late spring of 1940, Chamberlain remained convinced that continuing appeasement of Mussolini was necessary and possible and that Italy could be lured out of alliance with Germany. That extraordinary belief was based on continuing overestimation of Italy's real military power and potential—an error shared by others in his government and in the British military—and an utter misreading of Mussolini, who had already turned away from cooperation with London and Paris. Chamberlain's views of Italy were importantly misshaped by singularly inaccurate reporting by Britain's ambassador in Rome, Sir Percy Loraine. They were also distorted by the wishful thought that, because Britain could ill-afford to fight Italy in the Mediterranean while it was dangerously threatened in the North Sea and North Atlantic by Germany and potentially in the Far East by Japan, terms could be had with Rome to keep that theater closed.

On April 4, 1940, Chamberlain said that Herr Hitler had "missed the bus" of opportunity to attack in the west. Five days later the Wehrmacht began *WESERÜBUNG*, a bold operation that conquered Denmark in a day and most of southern Norway inside a month. As fighting continued in northern Norway, a crisis of confidence overtook Chamberlain's government. On May 10, as Hitler unleashed *FALL GELB* (1940) against France and the Low Countries, Chamberlain stepped down and was replaced as prime minister by his longtime nemesis Winston Churchill. Chamberlain died from cancer on November 9, 1940. Whatever his failings of prewar vision and diplomacy, there can be no doubt that his motives were the highest: to preserve a peaceful and great democracy, and empire, from the barbarization and carnage that war with Nazi Germany would surely bring. He was wrong, but so were the times. As Churchill graciously put it in his eulogy in the House: "It fell to Neville Chamberlain in one of the supreme crises of the world to be contradicted by events, to be disappointed in his hopes, and to be deceived and cheated by a wicked man."

Suggested Reading: Robert Caputi, *Neville Chamberlain and Appeasement* (2000); Robert Shay, *British Rearmament in the Thirties* (1977).

CHAMBERLAIN, HOUSTON STEWART (1855–1927) English philosopher whose rambling, racist theories of international affairs were picked up by the Nazis—who needed intellectual cover for their own specious race claims. Chamberlain developed a "Theory of Race," which he claimed explained all major historical developments. It placed Germanic peoples at the apex of all civilization. He had a significant influence on the thinking, such as it was, of Adolf Hitler. Both men also shared a fascination for the composer Richard Wagner (1813–1883), whose daughter Chamberlain married.

CHANG HSÜEH-LIANG Zhang Xueliang, the "Young Marshal."
See Manchuria.

CHANGKUFENG, BATTLE OF (1939)
See Nomonhan.

CHANG TSO-LIN Zhang Zuolin, the "Old Marshal."
See Manchuria.

CHANNEL DASH
See CERBERUS.

CHANNEL ISLANDS These small British islands, which lie closer to France than to England, were occupied by Germany a week after the armistice with France was signed on June 22, 1940. They were the only part of Great Britain to be occupied by the enemy. Adolf Hitler intended to keep the Channel Islands and ordered them fortified from mid-1941. The Germans therefore introduced slavery to the islands in 1942, as the *Todt Organization* imported Soviet *prisoners of war* and Jews to work on the new defenses. Some of the 60,000 islanders who were not evacuated resisted the occupation; about 2,200 were deported to Germany for their troubles, or as hostages. Most collaborated at levels great or small to survive. British commandos conducted several harassment raids against the German garrisons, for which the Islanders suffered the usual retaliations. The Islands were bypassed in *OVERLORD* in 1944. In March 1945, the German garrison conducted a raid into the rear of U.S. forces on the Cherbourg peninsula. The garrison surrendered along with all other German forces in May 1945.
See also Jerry Bag.

CHARLEMAGNE DIVISION
See Waffen-SS.

CHARNWOOD (JULY 7–8, 1944) Code name for a British Canadian operation to take Caen halfway through the *Normandy campaign*. Preceded by a heavy air bombardment that later proved to have been ineffective, CHARNWOOD also saw an infantry and armor advance under a *creeping barrage* by the artillery. Further fire support came from warships off the Normandy coast, which proved highly effective in blunting an advance to reinforce Caen by a freshly arrived Panzer division. The main fighting in Caen was done by a weak *Luftwaffe field division* but also by young and skilled fanatics of 12th *Waffen-SS* (Hitlerjungend) Division. When the operation was halted, Caen was left divided, with German and Western Allied forces in possession of different sections of the badly bombed city.

CHELMNO   The first of the *death camps* in the Nazi *concentration camp* system. Sited outside Lodō, it was designed to kill all Jews residing in western Poland, a territory annexed to Germany in October 1939. It opened in December 1941. Probably 150,000 people were murdered at Chelmno, most by gas.

CHEMICAL WARFARE   The Italians used gas against Abyssinian troops during the *Abyssinian War (1935–1936),* crop dusting a retreating column of 20,000 with blister agents. Lethal chemical and gas weapons were much feared but hardly used during World War II, despite the fact that all major armies carried defensive equipment and were prepared to use gas weapons if the other side used them first. Nonuse was not due to moral restraint on the part of belligerents, but because most tacticians deemed chemical weapons to be militarily ineffective. Massive stockpiles of chemical weapons by the major powers also proved a mutual deterrent to actual use. Still, there were times when use of poison gas was actively contemplated. On June 30, 1940, the War Cabinet in London authorized use of gas against any German beachhead established on the English coast. It did so upon the recommendation of General John Dill and the Imperial General Staff. The Germans anticipated British use of gas and issued gas masks to all troops slated for the invasion, though they neglected to provide masks for tens of thousands of horses that would accompany the troops into battle. They also failed to ever supply gas masks to most of their civilian population. In contrast, the British were so concerned about Axis gas bombs they issued gas masks to all civilians during the *Blitz.* London also increased its own lethal gas stockpiles, mainly of phosgene and mustard gas, by thirty-fold from 1940 to 1941. That meant the British had enough poison gas to supply the USAAF with 10,000 gas bombs, sufficient until American gas production got underway in 1942. Germany also ordered massive production increases as of June 1, 1940: Adolf Hitler hoped to use gas to strike a "death blow" against Britain after conventional bombing failed in 1940. However, the Luftwaffe never overcame problems of poison gas production or delivery-to-target.

The British repeatedly announced that they would massively retaliate with chemical bombs should Germany use them first, including German first use on the Eastern Front. Winston Churchill wrote secretly to Joseph Stalin in 1942, promising that the RAF would use gas against Germany if Hitler used gas against the Soviet Union. He added: "I have been building up an immense stock of gas bombs for discharge from aircraft." The British Army also kept ground force gas weapons and specialists close to *combat zones,* ready for use in the event of German or Japanese first use of battlefield chemical weapons. That led to the tragedy of the *Bari Raid* on December 2, 1943, when British mustard gas was accidentally released by Luftwaffe bombing of cargo ships in the harbor. Over 2,000 were killed, including 1,000 British sailors and troops. The Germans considered using gas against the landings in France in 1944, but decided against it out of fear of massive retaliation. Churchill seriously considered dropping gas on German cities in direct retaliation for *V-1* and *V-2* attacks on London in September 1944. He was stopped from doing so by the *Chiefs of Staff,* who had a veto on use of gas and who understood that RAF gas attacks would provoke Luftwaffe retaliation, with some bombers surely getting through RAF fighters and barrage balloons. American officials also objected, mainly because German retaliation would expose GIs to gas attack. Hitler was also deterred from using gas in 1944, when told that the RAF had a far greater capacity to deliver gas bombs than the badly attrited Luftwaffe.

The U.S. Army prudently kept Chemical Warfare Service (CWS) units in all theaters, to retaliate in the event the enemy chose to use gas weapons, and to defend by providing troops with gas masks and chemical warfare clothing. By 1943 the CWS comprised 70,000 officers and men. U.S. Chemical mortar battalions were armed to fire toxic bombs if needed. Americans called this weapon "casualty agent," while British parlance perhaps more honestly called it "war gas." Actual use of chemical weapons had to be agreed in advance with the British, and never was. Retaliation did not require joint approval, but it never took place either. Instead, American CWS teams fired smoke bombs to screen maneuvering infantry and armor and used their 4.2-inch mortars in high explosive pin-point tactical bombardments that reached out to 5,000 yards. The main role of CWS teams was thus deployment of nonlethal chemical weapons and traditional mortar close-support fire. The units were only "chemical" when they fired smoke bombs or used generators to produce chemical or oil *smokescreens.* The Western Allies jointly developed, but did not manufacture or use, crop killing chemicals that would have destroyed German and Japanese food supplies.

Mutual deterrence also prevented battlefield use in the east, where there were otherwise no moral qualms about the character of fighting and little mercy on either side. The Red Army had a significant gas weapon capability before the war, but chose not to use gas even during the most desperate battles waged on the Eastern Front in 1941–1942. The Wehrmacht had several thousand tons of lethal gas, but no effective battlefield delivery system. The one exception to nonuse came in the Crimea when the Germans piped lethal gas into caves during the *siege of Sebastopol* in 1942, murdering thousands of civilians trapped inside. During the war, German chemists continued to develop ever more lethal types of poison gases, but these were not used either. The other main type of technically chemical weapon was the highly lethal *flamethrower.* All armies used flamethrowers to ferret out enemy strongpoints. However, flamethrowers were seen as an infantry weapon that did not break the chemical weapon taboo. There was also precedent for their use in battle dating to Verdun in 1916.

Japanese chemical warfare research was German in inspiration and origin, including testing on *prisoners of war* and *concentration camp* inmates. By the early 1930s all Japanese Army divisions deployed chemical warfare specialists called "gas personnel." Japan used chemical weapons extensively in China, although this was denied by its military leaders. Lewisite and mustard gas shells were used to bombard Chinese defenders on numerous occasions—the decision was left to local commanders. The main reason for extensive battlefield use of gas weapons on the Asian mainland by the Japanese was that they had no fear of Chinese or Mongolian retaliation in kind. Other lethal weapons actually used by the Japanese Army included toxic "special smokes," prussic acid grenades and bombs, and poison gas issued from "candles" into Chinese strongpoints, pill boxes, and tunnels. However, from 1942 the Japanese feared U.S. chemical retaliation and therefore abjured from use of chemical weapons in the Pacific, even though some island garrisons had chemical capabilities in their arsenal. On rare occasions, Japanese troops in the Pacific used a "chibi-dan" bomb: a glass ball filled with liquid poison that gasified on contact with air. The Western Allies reciprocated nonuse of lethal chemical weapons, even though they had a significant advantage in quantity and delivery systems. The source of restraint was Franklin Roosevelt, who publicly renounced "first use" and personally vetoed proposed use of gas to winnow the Japanese out of caves on *Iwo Jima,* despite the inability of the Japanese Army to massively retaliate on that island or elsewhere. There is evidence that, were the Japanese home islands invaded in 1945–1946, each side was prepared to use chemical weapons in all-out fighting. The Allies would also have used atomic weapons behind the battlefield.

See also Badoglio, Pietro; Italian Air Force; nerve agents; white phosphorus.

CHENNAULT, CLAIRE (1890–1958) American general. Chennault was a retired U.S. pilot and fighter tactician. He served as a colonel in the *Chinese Air Force* and as adviser to *Jiang Jieshi* while the United States was still neutral. He learned much from observing Soviet pilots of the VVS flying for Jiang against the Japanese, thereafter developing disciplined tactics that used team and formation fighting to counter initial Japanese advantages in speedier and more agile aircraft. In 1940 Chennault organized a volunteer pilot scheme that led to creation of the *American Volunteer Group,* or "Flying Tigers." He was recalled to the USAAF and promoted to general in April 1942. He was named commander of the China Air Task Force, later redesignated the 14th Air Force, in July. Based at first in India, the 14th flew supplies "over the *Hump*" to Jiang's forces in Chongqing. From October 1942, Chennault organized efforts to bomb Japan with long-range aircraft based in southern China. The project was not a success, but provoked the Japanese *Ichi-Gō* campaign that was hugely damaging to the *Guomindang* in 1944. Unlike his superior *Joseph Stilwell,* Chennault got along well with Jiang, but the intense personal frictions that dominated the CBI theater led him to resign in July 1945. By that time his air bases had been overrun by the Japanese Army, the USAAF had long since lost faith in the China route for bombing Japan, and B-29s had already ravaged Japan's cities from bases in the Central Pacific.

CHEN YI (1901–1972) Chinese communist general. He was a leading Chinese general during the *Sino-Japanese War (1937–1945)* and in the *Chinese Civil War (1927–1949)*. He was defense minister of the People's Republic from 1958 to 1966. Despite his decades of service, he was stripped of power and publicly humiliated during *Mao Zedong's* "Great Proletarian Cultural Revolution" of the late 1960s.

CHERNIGOV-POLTAVA OPERATION (AUGUST–SEPTEMBER, 1943)
See RUMIANTSEV.

CHERNYAKOVSKY, IVAN D. (1906–1945) Soviet general. Chernyakovsky joined the Red Army in 1924, too late to participate in the Russian Civil War (1918–1921). He studied mechanized warfare during the 1930s. Younger than most Front commanders, Chernyakovsky was only a colonel when the *Great Fatherland War* began in 1941. He rose rapidly as he repeatedly proved his mettle in the field. From a tank division command, he was promoted to lead 18th Tank Corps. He next led 60th Army from mid-1942 to mid-1943. From April 1944, he commanded Western Front—later renamed 3rd Belorussian Front—battling Army Group North. He was severely wounded in fighting over the *Heiligenbeil pocket* near Königsberg on February 18, 1945, and died soon after. He was one of three Front commanders to be killed in the war, along with Generals *Nikolai Vatutin* and *Mikhail Kirponos*. After the war, Insterburg was renamed Cherniakhovsk in his honor.

CHETNIKS Originally, Serbian radical nationalists who fought the Ottomans before 1918. The term *"Četnik"* was revived by General Draza Mihailovic´ (1893–1946) during World War II, for non-Communist Serbs who fought Italians, Germans, and Yugoslav and Albanian Communists. At first, the Chetniks were actively and materially supported by the British. Mihailovic´ was opposed by Moscow, however, which increasingly threw its diplomatic and material support behind an ongoing civil war against the Chetniks conducted by Communist *partisans* led by *Tito*. The Chetniks made local truces with the Italians, which enabled them to solidify a territorial base in western Serbia. Mihailović may have wanted to spare the civilian population from German reprisals—something Tito showed little concern for—and to preserve Chetnik military power for a critical point later in the war. But the British wanted more anti-Axis partisan activity from the Chetniks and finally switched support to Tito and the Communists, largely in response to pressure from Moscow. That hung the Chetniks out on a limb that Tito then happily sawed off. Withdrawal of British support and continuing fighting against Tito's men also pushed the Chetniks further toward accommodation and *collaboration* with the Axis occupation in 1944, a path Tito also actively pursued but for which he paid no price at all. Many thousands of Chetniks were "liquidated" by Tito after the war. Mihailović was captured in 1946, tried for treason, and shot.

CHIANG KAI-SHEK
See Jiang Jieshi.

CHIANG, MADAM (1897–2003)   Née Christian Soong Mei-Ling. American-educated and highly influential wife of *Jiang Jieshi* (Chiang Kai-shek). Her most important role, beyond influencing her husband's policies, was in carrying out pro-*Guomindang* propaganda in the United States.

CHIEFS OF STAFF COMMITTEE (COS)   The interservice committee that directed the British war effort. It sent representatives to work with the American *Joint Chiefs of Staff*, forming the *Combined Chiefs of Staff* at the end of 1941. That joint committee ran the war waged by the Western Allies in Europe and the Pacific.
   See also chemical warfare; Churchill, Winston; CULVERIN; intelligence.

CHINA   In August 1914, the Japanese and British expelled German forces from the Shandong leasehold. As Europe descended into total war, Japan emerged as the main threat to China's unity, security, and independence. Tokyo's ambition to dominate and exploit large parts of China was revealed in the "Twenty-one Demands" it made in 1915, which would have reduced much of China to a Japanese protectorate. The United States moved into the power vacuum left in North Asia by the wartime withdrawal of European assets. Washington's concern was to defend its perceived interest in keeping an "Open Door" of free trade in China, as opposed to a closed Japanese imperial trading system. Washington also sought to uphold an Asian balance of power by supporting China's territorial integrity. However, fractured and warlord-riven China proved to be unsupportable. Internal fragmentation and instability climaxed after 1911, following decades of radical decentralization and militarization of the Chinese countryside, which marked the mass violence of the calamitous "Taiping Rebellion." The process culminated in the 20th-century division of China among competing warlords, accompanied by subjugation of coastal regions to foreign powers. The situation worsened in 1916 with the death of the strongest warlord, the dictator Yuan Shikai. Hundreds of regional warlords clashed, devastating the countryside. Then the "May 4th movement" erupted. That ferociously nationalist and antiforeigner social and political movement began in protest over Allied treatment of China at the Paris Peace Conference in 1919. It left the intellectual classes in ferment and deeply divided over whether or not China should adopt a Marxist path to modernization, but unified in rejection of all foreign influences, concessions, and unequal treaties. Communist and *Guomindang* armed forces worked jointly to defeat the southern warlords. However, in 1927 *Jiang Jieshi* carried out the Shanghai massacres, signaling the start of the protracted *Chinese Civil War (1927–1949)*. The Guomindang did not reestablish central authority over northern China until the defeat of most of the northern warlords in 1928, then turned its resources to crushing surviving Communists, most of whom had taken refuge in isolated "soviets" in the countryside.
   Radical officers in Japan directed increasing economic, diplomatic, and military pressure toward northern China following their takeover of Manchuria in 1931. Even nationalists were dismayed at the decision by the Guomindang, led by Jiang Jieshi, to appease the Japanese to keep his forces free to pursue southern

Communists. After the fifth "bandit suppression campaign" in 1934, Jiang drove *Mao Zedong* and other Communists onto the "Long March" to northwest China, away from their southern mountain base in the Jiangxi Soviet. The Guomindang and Communists nominally put aside differences to fight parallel wars against the Japanese following the extraordinary *Xi'an incident (December 1936),* although open fighting against the Japanese did not begin for another six months. It was instead hotheads in Japan's *Guandong Army* who sought advantage from Chinese internal divisions to attack in the north in 1937. The *Marco Polo Bridge incident* they provoked and exploited began the *Sino-Japanese War (1937–1945).* The swift and brutal Japanese occupation of northern China, and total disregard for the value of Chinese lives, was communicated to the world by indiscriminate bombing of Shanghai. There followed the atrocity of the *Rape of Nanjing.* The conflict raged through 1938 and 1939, with heavy loss of life. With the Japanese ascendant, the war settled into a sustained stalemate that took millions of lives. China's war merged with the still-wider conflict of World War II upon the Japanese attack on Pearl Harbor, Hong Kong, and other Western outposts in Asia. Even before that, informal American military aid was sent to China. This increased from 1942, but was largely wasted by Jiang and the corrupt leadership of the Guomindang. Through deep and open animosity and fighting among various Chinese forces, and an eventual loss of faith in Chinese efforts by Washington, Chinese armies held down a major share of the Japanese Army. Yet, China was unable to liberate itself from Japanese occupation. That feat was accomplished by Westerners in the Pacific and by *strategic bombing* of Japan. But at least Chinese efforts prevented even larger transfers of Japanese troops to distant island garrisons or Japanese-occupied Southeast Asia.

There was extensive *collaboration* along the seaboard of China and by puppet regimes set up in northern and central China. Elsewhere, the Chinese response to Japanese occupation was revulsion and resistance. In occupied areas and under the puppet regimes, many types of "passive resistance" took place, from drivers wrecking Japanese trucks to small gestures of personal and moral defiance. Meanwhile, outside China Jiang Jieshi was treated as one of the *"Big Four,"* consulting at several wartime conferences. This contrasted sharply with his shrinking control of Chinese territory and population, a reality noticed by the British and other Chinese, but which took longer to be recognized in Washington. Upon the defeat of Japan in 1945, the Chinese Civil War flared back into the open, starting with a race to reoccupy Manchuria. The war years had greatly drained Guomindang morale and manpower, while the Communists learned new military skills, which they used to effect against fellow Chinese to 1949. With captured Japanese military equipment and Soviet aid, the Civil War was won by the Communists by January 1949. After Mao Zedong proclaimed establishment of the "People's Republic of China," there followed an orgy of executions of political and class enemies during what is often glibly called the "consolidation phase" of the Chinese or Communist Revolution. That upheaval took another several million Chinese lives, perhaps as many as 10 million. But at long last, China was unified and no longer at war with itself.

See also ABC-1 Plan; American Volunteer Group; biological warfare; chemical weapons; Ianfu; Lend-Lease; Mukden incident; Three Alls; Unit 731; Wang Jingwei; Zhu De.

Suggested Reading: Lloyd Eastman, *The Nationalist Era in China* (1991); Lloyd Eastman, *Seeds of Destruction* (1984); Paul Sih, ed., *Nationalist China During the Sino–Japanese War, 1937–1945* (1977).

CHINA-BURMA-INDIA THEATER (CBI)

See ABDA Command; Admin Box, Battle of; American Volunteer Group; Arakan campaign; Arcadia Conference; Ba Maw; biological weapons; Bose, Subhas Chandra; Burma; Burma campaign (1942); Burma campaign (1943–1945); Burma National Army; Burma Road; Burma–Siam railway; Ceylon; chemical warfare; Chennault, Claire; China; China War; Chindits; Chinese Civil War (1927–1949); Chinese Communist armies; Congress Party; French Indochina; GALAHAD; Guandong Army; Guomindang; Hô Chí Minh; Hong Kong; Ichi-Gō; Imperial Japanese Army; Imphal offensive; India; Indian Army; Indian National Army; Jiang Jieshi; Ledo Road; Malaya; Manchuria; Manchurian offensive operation; Mars Task Force; Mongolia; Nanjing, Rape of; Nomonhan; Singapore; Sino-Japanese War (1937–1945); South East Asia Command; Stilwell, Joseph; Thailand; Unit 731; Viêt Minh; Wingate, Orde; X Force; Zhu De; ZIPPER.

CHINA INCIDENT (1937)

"Shina jihen." Japanese term for what Western historians call the *Marco Polo Bridge incident* (1937). It is sometimes extended to include the entire *Sino-Japanese War (1937–1945).*

CHINA WAR

The term preferred by some Japanese for the war with China that began in 1937, as distinct from the *Pacific War* fought against the Western Allies from December 1941 to August 1945. China officially terms its long war against Japan: "Chinese People's War of Resistance Against Japanese Aggression." In most English-language histories the conflict is recorded as the *Sino-Japanese War (1937–1945).*

CHINDITS

From the Burmese "chinthe" or leogryph, the unit insignia. Officially known as "Long-Range Penetration" groups, and later as "Special Force," Chindit units were organized by British General *Orde Wingate* to fight behind Japanese lines in Burma. They relied on aircraft resupply to achieve mobility and surprise and to survive deep jungle harassment operations. The first Chindit raid was mounted in February 1943. It was a failure that lost over 850 men out of a starting force of 3,000. Many survivors were too sickened to fight again for many months. They had spent weeks marching over 1,000 miles through heavy jungle, had unhealed jungle sores and tropical diseases, and suffered from malnutrition and low morale. Some never recovered. That did not prevent the British government and press from portraying the first Chindit raid as a signal victory. With enthusiastic backing by Winston Churchill, Wingate put together a second Chindit unit—an operation by "Special Force." Plans for a much larger "deep penetration" raid by 20,000 British, Gurkha, and West African troops were subsumed under the larger *GALAHAD* operation commanded by General *Joseph Stilwell*. When Wingate was killed in a plane crash, the resulting operation turned into a disaster in which light infantry Chindits were wrongly used as regulars, poorly supplied, left unrelieved for far too long, and suffered terrible casualties as a result. The major effect of Chindit raids was to encourage the Japanese to undertake a comparably bad plan for a deep jungle operation: the *Imphal offensive* in 1944.

CHINESE AIR FORCE   The Republic of China Air Force (ROCAF) had only 700 obsolete warplanes when China was attacked by Japan at the start of the *Sino-Japanese War (1937–1945)*. Established on paper in 1920 but only taking real form in 1928, the ROCAF was a hodgepodge air force assembled from the private air forces of conquered and coalition warlords, as well as some military aircraft purchased by the *Guomindang* from Britain, France, and the United States. During the mid-1930s the Soviet Union provided fighters and bombers to the Guomindang, as well as pilots to fly them against the Japanese early in the war. Soviet and other foreign trainers taught dog-fighting skills to Chinese pilots, who engaged Japanese Zeros in Russian biplanes and old American P-26 Boeing and Curtiss Hawk fighters. While Soviet pilots impressed many, their aircraft were inferior to more nimble Japanese fighters. The ROCAF was more effective in bombing Japanese shipping on the Yangtze and strafing and bombing Japanese trenches during the siege of Shanghai. As Joseph Stalin looked to secure his Far Eastern frontier through rapprochement with Japan, Soviet air force aid, advisers, and pilots were withdrawn from China in 1940. From 1938 American advisers arrived in China. Most prominent was *Claire Chennault*, who organized the *American Volunteer Group* to fly 100 P-40 fighters out of Burma and southern China starting in September 1941.

CHINESE ARMIES
   See *Chinese Civil War; Chinese Communist armies; Guomindang; Sino-Japanese War (1937–1945)*.

CHINESE CIVIL WAR (1927–1949)   The *Guomindang* turned on its erstwhile ally of convenience, the Chinese Communist Party (CCP), starting with the "Shanghai massacres" of 1927, when CCP cadres were wiped out in a blood purge conducted in the major cities. Survivors fled to the countryside, setting up small "soviets." *Mao Zedong*, an unforgiving romantic and ideologue in his theory and later governance, became one of several leaders of the "Jiangxi Soviet," located in the southern mountains. In 1928 China was mostly reunified under *Jiang Jieshi* with defeat of the last northern warlords by *Guomindang* forces. That allowed Jiang to apply increasing military pressure against the CCP holdouts in a series of so-called "bandit suppression campaigns." These finally forced the Jiangxi Communists onto the deadly "Long March," starting on October 16, 1934. That fighting trek northward by 100,000 cadres and family covered 6,000 bloody miles to Yenan in Shanxi. Mao emerged as the principal Communist leader at the "Zunyi Conference," held during the Long March from January 15–18, 1935. He superceded *Zhou Enlai, Zhu De, Lin Biao*, and others, some of whom had been his Party superiors.

The Long March ordeal—about 90 percent of the original marchers died or deserted along the way—became a central legend of the 1949 Communist Revolution, a heroic myth of the triumph of class-infused will over harsh reality. In fact, Mao became ill and was carried part of the way in a litter borne by peasant porters. There was much real heroism and sacrifice, however, as the Long Marchers were pursued and constantly harried by their Guomindang enemies. Several times they had to break through defensive positions set up to block their path. During the fighting, Zhu De emerged as the most able field commander among the Communists. Jiang pressed the fight from a distance, insisting on eliminating his domestic enemies before engaging against Japanese encroachments into northern China. But at the end of 1936, Jiang was forced by the remarkable *Xi'an incident* to make common cause with the Communists and Manchurians fighting to free their country from Japan. When the Japanese directly invaded northern China in 1937, following the *Marco Polo Bridge incident*, Communists and Guomindang fought against the foreign enemy in parallel campaigns. The fragile truce among the Chinese broke down from early January 1941; when Guomindang troops massacred a Communist column in the "New Fourth Army Incident" (also known as the "Wannan Incident"). The complex episode bitterly divided Chinese. It was followed by cessation of intra-Chinese negotiations and curtailment of supply to the Communists. Longer term, it gave the Communists fresh legitimacy among anti-Japanese nationalists, who tended to blame the Guomindang for the bloodletting. From that point, the Civil War resumed, while the war against Japan split into discrete Communist and Guomindang wars against the Japanese that competed for China's scant military resources.

Fighting in China merged with World War II following Japan's assault on the Western Allies in the Pacific in December 1941. *Lend-Lease* was sent to the Guomindang, a few American bomber bases were set up in southern China, and some Chinese divisions were sent into Burma. Otherwise, the China War and Pacific War were fought as discrete conflicts. The war inside China had two critically important consequences for China's internal divisions and the long-term outcome of the Civil War. First, the Japanese drove the Guomindang far inland from their main coastal bases by mid-1938, to mountainous Chongqing. Then they cut the Guomindang off from foreign resupply by taking Guangzhou and Nanning in the south while forcing Britain to close the *Burma Road*. Air links were established to Jiang by the Western Allies that brought in some supplies, but the *Ledo Road* did not open until late in the war. Outside supplies were supposed to be used to fight the Japanese, but as often as not were diverted into Jiang's anti-Communist efforts or simply stolen or wasted by corrupt generals. In the summer of 1944 the Japanese southern offensive, or *Ichi-Gō*, was launched. It aimed at taking out air bases in Guomindang zones of control. That greatly relieved pressure on the Communists in the north by drawing off Japanese troops while further decimating Jiang's armies.

Thereafter, the Communists were able to move out of enforced isolation deeper into central China and to pick up additional support among the peasantry by instituting ever more radical land reform programs. The CCP and People's Liberation Army increased tenfold in eight years, to over 900,000 troops. Upon the Japanese surrender the United States sent marines to hold Beijing and Tianjin and airlifted

Guomindang troops from southern bases to secure northern cities and to accept the formal Japanese surrender. Meanwhile, Red Army forces already in Manchuria allowed in large numbers of Chinese Communist troops. The Guomindang rushed several divisions to Manchuria as a counter, becoming badly overextended as a result: Manchuria was reoccupied contrary to American advice to consolidate on the other side of the Great Wall. At first, Washington called for a coalition government to be formed with the Communists. On the other side, Joseph Stalin switched from prewar backing of the Guomindang to postwar support for Mao and the Communists, supplying them with massive stocks of captured Japanese war matériel and surplus Soviet weapons. That did not prevent Stalin from also occupying former tsarist territories in Manchuria under cover of expelling the Japanese in August 1945.

All out civil war resumed in China as Jiang moved to reconsolidate the Guomindang military dictatorship and attacked Communist formations in November 1945. But the fight was now engaged on more nearly equal military terms. Jiang grew desperate, while long-exiled landlords moved back to reclaim estates in central and northern China. Guomindang secret police and private warlord armies engaged in massive repression, assassination, murder, and terror among peasants grown used to better behavior by the Communists. That further corroded Jiang's already tarnished legitimacy. In the end, the civil war was as much lost by the Guomindang as won by the Communists. Jiang and other Guomindang were mostly incompetent. They were also massively corrupt, which cost support at home and abroad and brought on a debilitating hyperinflation. Guomindang troops stayed in the cities—much as the Japanese had done—where they were soon besieged. Garrison after garrison in the north was isolated and forced to surrender during 1947–1948. The Civil War then changed character, as confident and well-equipped Communist armies moved to conventional operations against demoralized Guomindang garrisons. In the fall, Lin Biao destroyed an army of 400,000 Guomindang in Manchuria. In another huge battle, Zhu De committed over 600,000 Communist troops to inflict huge damage on the Guomindang. The Civil War climaxed as these battles overlapped in early 1949.

The Huai-Hai campaign (November 1948–January 1949) was the decisive operation during the final phase of the war. In successive engagements the Guomindang lost almost 500,000 troops, while its corporate will and ability to resist was fatally damaged. Underlying the military collapse was a regime crisis brought on by unmitigated corruption of Guomindang government and party officials. Beijing fell to the Communists on January 31, 1949. Communist troops then advanced rapidly from north to south, following the ancient path taken centuries before by the Manchus and other conquerors. Nanjing fell on April 23. On October 1, Mao declared the "People's Republic of China" (PRC). Remaining Guomindang forces retreated to Taiwan, where they established—or as they said, continued—the "Republic of China" (ROC), clinging to a claim to be the legitimate government of all China. Jiang hoped to rearm and return to the mainland, but he only ever received enough American support to survive, never enough to restart the war.

Suggested Reading: Stephen Levine, *Anvil of Victory* (1987); Suzanne Pepper, *Civil War in China* (1978).

CHINESE COMMUNIST ARMIES Chinese Communists fielded a force called "Red Army" until that nomenclature was changed to "Eighth Route Army" during the *Second Sino-Japanese War*. In 1949 the Eighth Route Army and its associates were collectively retermed "People's Liberation Army." During the war of resistance to the Japanese the armed forces of the Chinese Communist Party (CCP) in northern China were designated "18th Group Army" by the *Guomindang,* but were known to the Communists as "Eighth Route Army." The formation comprised three divisions in 1937. A smaller Communist army, "New Fourth Army," was formed to fight along the lower Yangtze in central China in 1938. A handful of Communist guerilla units operated in the south, but for the most part that region was far too hostile and contained too many Guomindang troops, who usually shot Communists on sight or even just suspicion. Also, both "Army" designations are misleading: with rare exceptions, Chinese Communist troops did not organize or fight at divisional or army levels. They scattered into many small units, usually company-size or smaller, to conduct guerilla operations in Japanese rear areas or just to garrison and protect Chinese Communist interests and holdings.

Communist troops who did engage the Japanese specialized in ambushes along roads and in attacking isolated pill boxes and communications along railway lines. After an attack, small units retreated to secure rural base areas that the CCP effectively governed and where large numbers of peasant refugees found sanctuary. CCP troops fought on foot. Some had rudimentary local mobility provided by bicycles or horses. Communist troops had very few trucks and no mechanized weapons. They lived off the land and from captured Japanese supplies. Many "soldiers" served often or even primarily as laborers helping to bring in the harvest or performing military labor. CCP forces expanded greatly after 1938. They drew recruits from among refugees, conscripted peasants, and Guomindang deserters or broken units left behind Japanese lines during the first year of losses in north and central China. Recruits were slowly moved through the militia into regular units. That process was far less shocking and dispiriting to peasants than the Guomindang method of forcible roundups, followed by immediate shipping out of peasant boys under armed guard to some distant, unknown camp. As a result, Communist desertion rates were much lower than those of the Guomindang. By 1945 the CCP had nearly three million men under arms in regular or militia units.

See also Chinese Civil War (1927–1949); Lin Biao; Mao Zedong; Xi'an incident; Zhou Enlai; Zhu De.

CHINESE NATIONALIST ARMIES
See Guomindang.

CHIR LINE An advanced German defensive line behind the confluence of the Don and Chir rivers. Hastily improvised Wehrmacht battle groups, formed mostly from service troops ("alarm units"), struggled to hold the line until December 23,

1942. The Chir position was held initially to support relief operations for German 6th Army at *Stalingrad*, but later it was needed to forestall Soviet encirclement of German armies around Rostov. Each side reinforced the Chir fight with regular units in mid-December so that the line saw heavy and desperate combat. In January 1943, the Red Army massively assaulted and swept over the Chir position, driving the Wehrmacht back to the Donets and thence to the Mius.

CHOIBALSAN, KHORLOGIN (1895–1952)   Marshal of the Mongolian People's Republic. Commander in chief of the Mongolian Army, 1924–1928; prime minister, 1939–1952. He led Mongolian troops alongside the Red Army against the Japanese at *Nomonhan* in 1939 and again in the last two weeks of the war during the *Manchurian offensive operation (August 1945)*. After the war he served as Moscow's puppet, overseeing a client dictatorship on the Soviet far eastern frontier.

CHOISEUL   The Japanese garrisoned this small island in the Solomons with too few men to threaten Western Allied operations, but too many to keep properly supplied once Japan lost most of its merchant marine. On October 28, 1943, 650 U.S. marine parachutists landed in a raid in force intended to divert attention from major landings about to take place on *Bougainville*. The marines harassed the Japanese garrison until they were pulled out on November 3. The New Zealand Air Force bombed and strafed Choiseul intermittently during 1944. The Japanese withdrew a much diminished garrison in mid-1945.

CHOU EN-LAI
   See Zhou Enlai.

CHUE TEH
   See Zhu De.

CHUIKOV, VASILY I. (1900–1982)   Marshal of the Soviet Union. He joined the Red Army at the start of the Russian Civil War (1918–1921), taking command of a regiment at age 20. During the interwar years he served mostly in the Far Eastern Army, including as adviser to *Jiang Jieshi*. He returned to lead occupation troops into Poland in September 1939. He was promoted to command 9th Army during the *Finnish–Soviet War (1939–1940)*. When 9th Army was humiliated by the Finns, Chuikov was among those blamed by Joseph Stalin for initial defeat and losses. Chuikov spent 18 months banished to the Far East as a military adviser in China. In 2007 historian Michael Jones disputed the idea that the China position was a punishment post, but he also neglected to mention Chuikov's earlier role in Poland in his relentlessly admiring and heroic account of Chuikov's leadership at *Stalingrad*. During the summer of 1942 Chuikov headed a reserve force that was then designated 64th Army, one of two Soviet armies soon enmeshed in extraordinarily desperate fighting inside the city on the west bank of the Volga. On September 12 he was given command of decimated 62nd Army, which had retreated inside Stalingrad and was just then reaching crisis. He led that force in increasingly desperate and bloody fighting, until the Stavka launched *URANUS* in relief of the city on November 19. His 62nd Army continued to fight inside Stalingrad, finally helping to crush German 6th Army during Operation RING in January 1943. It was renamed 8th Guards Army in recognition of its vital role as the fractured anvil of Stalingrad, against which other Soviet armies hammered the Germans into submission. Chuĭkov led 8th Guards Army through 1945 in offensive operations that took it through Ukraine from the Black Sea to the Dnieper, then on to Warsaw, and thence all the way to Berlin. He served in the postwar occupation of Germany and rose to the rank of Marshal of the Soviet Union in 1955. Upon his death in 1982 he rejoined veteran dead from 62nd Army in the great burial mound at Stalingrad, in the Mamaev Kurgan.

CHURCHILL, WINSTON SPENCER (1874–1965) British statesman. First lord of the admiralty, 1911–1915, 1939–1940; minister of munitions, 1917; secretary for war, 1918–1921; chancellor of the exchequer 1924–1929; minister of defense and prime minister, 1940–1945, 1951–1955. He was the son of an aristocratic English family descended from the Duke of Marlborough and an American mother. A poor student, he struck out to make his own mark in the world. He attended Sandhurst military academy, rather than Oxford or Cambridge, and took a junior commission in the British Army. He was briefly a war correspondent in Cuba in 1895, but rejoined his regiment in time to see service in India on the Northwest Frontier in 1897. Churchill joined Lord Kitchener's romantic and bloody expedition into the Sudan the next year. He saw his only battlefield action at Omdurman. He resigned from the Army to run for Parliament, but lost. He next went to South Africa as a war correspondent during the Second Boer War, was captured by the Boers, and dramatically escaped. His breathless account of that adventure and heroic newspaper self-portrait did much to make him a national figure. That fitted with a vision he had as a small boy and kept all his life, that he was destined for greatness. Churchill was often personally abrasive, yet he made intensely loyal friends and had many admirers. He was frequently emotional, weepy, and drunk: he suffered from deep depression ("my Black Dog"), which he self-medicated with alcohol, travel, and intense devotion to work, writing, and hobbies such as painting. He was a talented amateur artist and often, but not always, an extraordinary orator. He was a gifted though deeply biased and nationalist amateur historian and a first-rate political opportunist: he switched parties twice to stay near the centers of power. Above all, Churchill was the outstanding statesmen of the 20th century.

Propelled by his feats and reporting to celebrity status, Churchill was elected to Parliament as a Conservative in 1900. In 1904 he crossed the floor to join the Liberals and was rewarded by elevation to undersecretary for the colonies. In 1910 he became home secretary. In 1911 he was named first lord of the admiralty, a post he much coveted and used well to modernize the Royal Navy. He was in that key office at the start of World War I, but was compelled to resign in 1915 over the fiasco and bloody outcome of the invasion of Gallipoli. He had urged that failed assault against the Ottoman Empire as a support for Tsarist Russia and to break the stalemate on the Western Front by a strategic flanking movement. Throughout the interwar years he was closely identified with, and deeply mistrusted because of, the failure at Gallipoli. That remained true although Churchill returned to the War Cabinet in 1917, albeit in a diminished role as minister of munitions. He served as minister for war and air from 1918 to 1921, gaining a personal respect for the role and promise of air power. He returned to his old place in charge of the colonies after that, overseeing the end of the Irish War of Independence and partition of that island in 1922. He managed consolidation of imperial gains in Africa and the Middle East that resulted from the *Treaty of Versailles* with Germany and the Treaty of Sèvres with the Turks. During the Russian Civil War he argued unsuccessfully for massive intervention to strangle the Bolshevik infant in its revolutionary cradle. He lost his seat in the massive defeat of Lloyd George's Liberal government in 1922. Showing his usual political dexterity, Churchill returned to Parliament in 1924 upon crossing the floor to rejoin the Conservatives. He was chancellor of the exchequer from 1924 to 1929, during which term he tried to return Britain to the gold standard. He won the lasting enmity of the working classes for responding harshly to a bitter general strike in 1926. Such failures and policies added apparent weight to arguments made by his many critics—that he was at the same time a reactionary conservative and an incompetent adventurer, not to be trusted with great national responsibility.

Churchill spent most of the 1930s without public office—or as he put it, "in the wilderness." He reached the low point of his career and popularity. Still he voiced deeply unpopular opinions, views that kept him outside the Cabinet and in disfavor within his own party but in which he believed fervently. He was frequently booed and even shouted down when speaking in the House of Commons. Among his most controversial views was adamant refusal to support concessions to India on "home rule," or even to agree to Dominion status for India within the British Commonwealth. That went against the postwar tide of Wilsonianism and shifting fortunes of all empires in face of the new American idea of the "self-determination of nations," as well as the challenge of Bolshevik internationalism. Least popular were Churchill's warnings against taking Adolf Hitler lightly and attendant alarms that Britain must rearm to deter, and if necessary even to fight, a second war with Germany. As early as October 1930, Churchill correctly identified Hitler as planning to wage war to reverse the judgment of Versailles. At that time, most observers of European affairs had not even heard of Herr Hitler, while those who had saw him as merely a minor Bavarian politician with little future and no international importance.

Like Churchill, Hitler also believed himself to be a "man of destiny." But by 1937, it looked like Churchill's sense of personal fate was faulty, while Hitler was vaulting through and reshaping history with every new day. At the very moment that Hitler was telling his generals to prepare for inevitable war, Churchill reached the nadir of his political career. He was mistrusted, isolated, disbelieved, even loathed. He was denounced as a "warmonger" and half-baked adventurer. And that was within his own Conservative Party. More broadly, he was seen as a social reactionary wholly out of touch with the new progressive times and reform demands of an era of economic contraction. He certainly parted from the national mood of the nation on foreign policy and its rising interest in *appeasement* of Hitler. Depressed but undeterred, Churchill called for stepped-up military preparedness for what Prime Minister *Neville Chamberlain* and many others feared would be another general and "Great War." Churchill's insistence that the Western states embrace *collective security* was scorned. From the backbenches, he sounded a lonely clarion call to arms. Booed regularly in the House, he was dismissed as a bitter personal critic of Chamberlain, frustrated at the dismal end of a career that had fallen short of the prime ministership. If not his finest hour, certainly his most prophetic moment came when the nation and most of Europe was loudly cheering the outcome of the surrender of the *Sudetenland* to Hitler at the *Munich Conference*. Churchill publicly called the deal a "total and unmitigated defeat" for Britain and for peace. As German troops and stormtroopers moved into the rump of the Czech lands and then beat the drum for war with Poland during the first half of 1939, Churchill's warnings were revealed to have been prescient and wise. More people in power began to pay attention. But it was too late. World war was coming.

Churchill was recalled to the War Cabinet to take charge of the Royal Navy as First Sea Lord on the first day of the *Battle of the Atlantic,* September 3, 1939. He was elevated to prime minister on the day Hitler attacked France and the Low Countries: May 10, 1940. The shift came because Chamberlain was forced to pay the price for a military fiasco in Norway, which Churchill had also strongly supported. While resolute, in the first hours of battle in the west Churchill was not certain of the outcome of his leadership. He said: "I hope it is not too late. I am very much afraid that it is." In the darkest hour of need and looming defeat, Britain's people turned to Churchill. But it was a closer-run decision than was publicly known at the time or appreciated since: there was bitter division in the Cabinet over whether to fight or negotiate with Hitler after the disaster that befell the British Expeditionary Force (BEF) heading to *Dunkirk* and the surrender of France. Churchill won the argument and moved to form a truly national government to fight a protracted war to final victory, though he did not yet know how that might be achieved. Playing the role of his lifetime as prime minister, Churchill embraced what he had privately always believed was his "destiny" to serve as a great national leader in wartime. In public, however, he more soberly warned: "I have nothing to offer but blood, toil, tears and sweat." His most memorable turn of phrase about the national character of the British applied as well to his own: the country's "finest hour" during the *Battle of Britain* was also surely his. There can be no doubt about the value of Churchill's leadership as Britain stood alone, along with its Commonwealth and Empire, against Hitler's legions in the summer and fall of 1940. Nor is there any just doubt about his great contribution to the survival of civilization itself in keeping alive armed resistance to *Nazism* until the Soviet Union and the United States entered the war to ensure Hitler's defeat and burial of the Nazi idea. The point is not that Churchill or Britain alone won the war. Victory was always beyond British reach in the absence of any major Allies, a strategic fact Churchill knew acutely well. The main point is that Winston Churchill, at the head of building British and Commonwealth forces, did not lose the war. For Britain might well have succumbed to despair in its defeat and strategic solitude of the dark year from mid-1940 to mid-1941.

Instead, during the second half of 1940, the War Cabinet and nation rallied around Churchill's policy of defiance and endurance, of determination that only deepened once the die was truly cast for protracted war with Germany. Resolve only deepened as German bombers hit London and other British cities. The development of RAF Bomber Command as the principal British instrument for striking back at Germany over the next two years owed much to Churchill, a longtime proponent of bombing, who threw his full political weight into the balance. The strategy of attacking the periphery of Hitler's empire with what land and sea forces were available also owed much to Churchill's vision, even as they spoke to basic geopolitical and military realities. Churchill's war leadership was greatly aided by wise council from close advisers that balanced the impulsive, overly sentimental, manipulative, and bullying side of his character. No one better served him by standing up to him than Field Marshal *Alan Brooke,* CIGS. Another key adviser was General *Hastings Ismay.* During *FALL GELB,* or what Churchill called the Battle of France, RAF Fighter Command chief *Hugh Dowding* restrained Churchill from hurling into a lost battle fighter squadrons desperately needed for homeland defense. Churchill might have done just that had any Frenchman accepted his quixotic offer for a full political and military union of France and Britain. Others fought off impulsive decisions by Churchill later in the war. Failure to stop his push for an invasion of Italy following the Sicilian campaign has been seen by many as a major failure of his and British strategic vision, but the more fair judgment is probably that Churchill insisted on continuing the *Italian campaign (1943–1945)* on an over-large scale too long after the success of *OVERLORD* in June 1944.

Churchill wisely cultivated, and most fortunately already enjoyed by 1940, the special favor of the American president, Franklin D. Roosevelt. Their summit meetings even before America entered the fight and their constant correspondence throughout the war were the real axis around which a world war revolved, from Africa and Western Europe to China and the Pacific. Churchill's relationship with FDR well served his most basic strategic goal in 1940–1941: to persuade the United States to enter the war against Germany and *fascism,* to save the British Empire and civilization from the dark night of Nazism and German hegemony over Europe. He threw his support behind a major British bombing campaign and naval blockade, partly as the only means then available to strike at Germany but also to signal to Roosevelt and the American public that Britain was committed to the fight for the duration. Into mid-1941 Churchill had no other real hope of final victory than U.S. belligerence. To that end, he alternately promised Roosevelt that Britain would not quit and darkly hinted that, under anyone but him, it might. If persuasion failed, he planned to entangle the United States in the war and a martial alliance its people still did not want as late as December 6, 1941. His chosen means were close naval cooperation in the Atlantic, effectively ceding American hegemony in the Pacific and encouraging Roosevelt to break down the *Neutrality Acts* and pass *Lend-Lease* legislation and other acts that incrementally edged the United States toward war with the Axis. Well before *Pearl Harbor (December 7, 1941)*, Churchill made great progress on those fronts, but neither he nor Roosevelt could overcome the resistance of the American public to entanglement in another European war. It took the Japanese attack on Hawaii and Hitler's reckless declaration of war against the United States four days later to accomplish that goal. Churchill also coveted a military alliance with the Soviet Union after Hitler launched Operation *BARBAROSSA* in June 1941. The treaty was signed in May 1942. Churchill twice flew to Moscow to meet with Joseph Stalin without Roosevelt present, in August 1942 and October 1944.

Over the five years of his prime ministership, Churchill drew upon deep lessons learned from his time in government during the Great War and at the Admiralty in 1939. He applied these lessons in waging the new war against Germany. Sometimes his insights were correct and led to success, but at other times he pushed wrong ideas with a procrustean insistence and bullying petulance that defied military and strategic circumstances. Among his unshakable views about war were: a real and sound appreciation of the role of civilian command over the largest strategic issues and stakes, but respect for military professionalism in the conduct of operations; skepticism about the role of air power as a war-winning weapon, though perhaps he did not hold this view deeply enough given his commitment to RAF Bomber Command; awareness of the vital importance of keeping open Britain's sea lanes, and of sea power more generally in a truly global conflict; a core belief that Britain needed major allies to win the war, that alone it could do little more than survive and stave off defeat; confidence in the deep resources of the British Empire and Commonwealth, and of the United States; and that the politics of coalition warfare was at least as important as coalition generalship and hence, that political compromise was essential. Churchill was modern enough to appreciate that the role of science in developing new weapons and in actionable intelligence was critically important, but not decisive. While he was keenly interested in weapons research and technical breakthroughs, he did not make the basic error Hitler did by looking to *Wunderwaffen* to correct more fundamental strategic disadvantages. Most of all, Churchill knew already in 1940 that the war Britain must fight would be protracted and attritional and that it could not be won by succumbing to the allure of any single "decisive battle" or decisive campaign, what German theory called *Vernichtungskrieg*. He also understood that the inevitable slaughter of *total war*, an experience burned into the memory of the nation from 1914 to 1918, might be reduced by reliance on firepower over manpower. That is an important reason why he embraced *strategic bombing* and *morale bombing*, though even he came to have doubts that RAF Bomber Command cleaved to the latter policy too long in the face of evidence that it was not working.

An example of several of these principles and lines of thought in real action was Churchill's embrace of Stalin once the Soviet Union was attacked by Hitler. Although Churchill was a life-long anti-Bolshevik, he immediately agreed to send all possible aid to the Soviet Union and even flew there to personally consult (and to console) Stalin. In a realpolitik explanation of breathtaking clarity and simplicity, he remarked on the night of the German attack: "If Hitler were to launch an attack on Hell itself, I would contrive to make at least a favorable reference to the Devil in the House of Commons." His policy of endurance and preparation for protracted war bore fruit when news arrived about the Japanese attack on Pearl Harbor. Even as Britain still suffered terrible defeats of its own in Asia in the days and weeks that followed, Churchill felt great private relief. He understood that with the addition of America's overwhelming military power to the Allied side of the scale, the British Empire would not only survive but would surely defeat Hitler in the end. His role was not so honorable or effective when it came to the loss of *Singapore,* however, where he ordered a futile last stand after having significantly contributed to the catastrophe.

In response to the Pearl Harbor attack, Churchill immediately flew to Washington to consult Roosevelt and to establish joint command structures and agreed strategic aims. Thereafter, he made full use of an exceptionally close relationship with the President to advance Britain's strategic plans and ideas, and sometimes his own that were not endorsed by his military advisers. The latter included a repeat attempt to confirm his long-held conviction that the Mediterranean was the "soft underbelly of Europe," through which a body blow might be struck at Germany. That idea had failed disastrously at Gallipoli in 1915. Churchill's core strategic conception of how to defeat Nazi Germany, which he first articulated in late 1940, was to first weaken Hitler internally with sustained morale bombing, while choking off external links and lopping off minor allies through blockade and limited direct action. While chopping away vulnerable extensions of the Nazi empire and fomenting resistance and uprisings, he looked to some unspecified and distant future when main forces could land on the continent to strike the mortal blow to the head of the beast. Churchill first assayed his renewed peripheral strategic approach in Greece in the *Balkan campaign* in 1940, once again disastrously. Undeterred, he persistently argued for a Mediterranean strategy, persuading Roosevelt to go along with invasions of North Africa in November 1942, and of Sicily and Italy in 1943. Independent British operations were also conducted, against American advice and with mixed results, in the eastern Mediterranean.

Hitler played directly into Churchill's strategy by garrisoning and even reinforcing nonvital promontories of German occupation. As a result, in 1944–1945 large German garrisons would be isolated in Greece, the Balkans, and Scandinavia; more German troops remained tied down in northern Italy after Churchill's indirect strategy successfully knocked Italy out of the war in 1943. However, the peripheral strategy proved harder to implement and costlier than Churchill imagined, not least because the Wehrmacht proved remarkably adept at defense. Churchill's strategic plan also ran into American impatience to land engorged armies in France and strike out for Germany as soon and as directly as possible. In contrast, the British service chiefs envisioned that Germany must be primarily defeated by bombing and subversion before a main force landing took place. All these considerations were in play during the disastrous *Dodecanese campaign* in October 1943, where the prime minister imposed his strategic will against strong military advice. Some 4,800 men, 113 aircraft, and 6 destroyers were lost.

By the end of 1943, Churchill was deeply frustrated by the relative decline of Britain's power among the *Big Three*. He realized that his own influence over Roosevelt and Allied strategy and policy was fading, just as the opportunity to begin shaping the postwar period appeared over the horizon of war. He thought he understood better than did the genial but naïve American president the nature of Stalin's personality, regime, and geopolitical ambitions. Yet, Churchill also indulged a personal view of Stalin that held him to be a reasonable man and leader, and too often absolved the great dictator from blame for Soviet decisions. He tended to attribute Soviet errors to hidden influences with the Soviet state, a view that could not have been more wrong. Churchill's growing differences from Roosevelt also reflected a wider gulf of vision about postwar international affairs, in which Churchill initially was prepared to make territorial and other concessions to the Soviet Union at the expense of minor states, in a manner traditional among Great Powers. Roosevelt wished to defer all such decisions to a postwar conference comparable to the Paris Peace Conference after World War I and was warily suspicious of strategic decisions he thought primarily motivated by postwar British imperial interest.

Churchill shifted his position as the Red Army readied to advanced into Central Europe. He now seemed to argue for peripheral operations in the Balkans and eastern Mediterranean more for postwar political reasons than wartime military reasons, to forestall excessive Soviet influence in those regions that must come with liberation. Roosevelt did not share so dire a view of the likely Soviet shaping of the postwar world in the east and thought that Churchill was trying to delay the invasion of Europe to avoid British casualties. Worse, some advisers to the President argued that Churchill and the British were unreconstructed imperialists who wanted to spend American lives to secure restoration or even expansion of the British Empire. Churchill accomplished what he could against this prejudice during key conferences with Roosevelt at *Cairo* and *Casablanca,* and with Roosevelt and Stalin at *Tehran* and *Yalta*. But already by 1943, Roosevelt was disenchanted with the Prime Minister and disinclined to listen to him as the American contribution to the war effort greatly exceeded that of Britain. Churchill was able to persuade reluctant American leaders to invade Italy after Sicily was cleared of Axis forces, but he promised much that the Italian campaign failed to deliver. That made the Italian campaign the last time Americans deferred to him or the British chiefs on any major strategic decision.

Churchill was therefore unable to delay the invasion of France in 1944, although he tried to do so until just weeks before *D-Day (June 6, 1944)*. He next failed to persuade Roosevelt or General *Dwight Eisenhower* to drive straight for Berlin in 1945, to deny that great political prize to the Soviets and thereby strengthen the negotiating position of the Western Allies in the coming confrontation with Stalin, which he foresaw. Churchill managed to preserve Greece from falling into the Soviet sphere, in part by extraordinary personal intervention in the midst of fighting in Athens.However, he could not prevent communization of Albania and

Yugoslavia, or heavy-handed Soviet treatment of Poland and Rumania. He was less concerned with Soviet influence in the Far East. He instead welcomed Stalin's commitment to join the war against Japan as alleviating Britain's need to transfer large armies to Asia and incur heavy casualties by reinforcing Burma and invading Japan's home islands. Churchill was abruptly dismissed by the electorate at the moment of triumph in 1945, during the Allied summit meeting at *Potsdam*.

Often rash and always mercurial, prone to significant military mistakes from which he had to be rescued by others, Winston Churchill was nevertheless the most essential statesman of the war. Without his long-term vision and uncrushable spirit, Britain might have sought a settlement with Nazi Germany in 1940. It did not, in no small measure because of Churchill's understanding and powers of persuasion about the ultimately unappeasable character of Hitler. Staying in the fight meant the British defended their vital home interests against the Axis while attacking opportunistically at the periphery of Hitler's empire, until they were joined by far more powerful allies who enabled them to switch to permanent offensive operations in pursuit not merely of survival, but of final victory. The British nation was grateful to Churchill for his wartime leadership, and much of the world has been ever after. Yet, Britain was so war-weary by 1945, its people wanted above all to plan for the coming peace. It was thus left to Churchill's successor, *Clement Attlee,* to finish the Potsdam Conference and Britain's war with Japan. Winston Churchill was later honored as the first ever "honorary U.S. citizen."

See also *Atlantic Charter; Bletchley Park; broad front; commandos; Coventry raid; CULVERIN; Declaration on Liberated Europe; Dresden raid; El Alamein; Halifax, Lord; Irish Free State; nanshin; second front; SLEDGEHAMMER; TORCH; unconditional surrender; War Office; Warsaw Rising.*

Suggested Reading: Winston S. Churchill, *The Second World War,* 6 Vols. (1953); Martin Gilbert, *Winston Churchill's War Leadership* (2004); R. Lewin, *Churchill as Warlord* (1972).

CHURCHILL RATION   A mocking Japanese term for food and other valuable supplies captured from retreating British and Commonwealth forces in Malaya and Burma in the first months of 1942.

CIANO, GALEAZZO (1903–1944)   "Count Galeazzo." Son-in-law to Benito Mussolini from 1930; Italian minister of propaganda, 1935; foreign minister, 1936–1943. Ciano was a strong supporter of Mussolini's imperial wars in Africa, even volunteering to fly with the Regia Aeronautica during the brutal aggression by Italy in the *Abyssinian War (1935–1936).* He also supported Mussolini's *Axis alliance* with Germany. He later shifted to an anti-German stance over concern that Adolf Hitler was establishing Germany as the new hegemon of Europe and that Hitler's recklessness would lead Italy into a war with the Western Allies that it could not win. Ciano therefore tried to block Italy's adherence to the *Pact of Steel* in 1939. Instead, he sought to distract Mussolini and counter Hitler by proposing an Italian invasion of Albania. Ciano helped keep Italy neutral over the winter of 1939–1940, but the total German victory in *FALL GELB* proved too tempting to his father-in-law, who hurriedly attacked France so as not to "miss the bus" of conquest. Ciano came to share that view as well, as German hegemony became a fact and Italy looked to share in the kills made by its more powerful partner.

Ciano was at heart a raw opportunist. Once Italy was in the war and the Axis appeared to be winning, he actively endorsed an expansionist policy in Africa, annexation of Albania, and aggression against Greece. All that was planned to take advantage of German victory in the west. His diary, which later became a prime source on Italy's wartime politics and policy, soon recorded disillusionment with Mussolini as Italian arms failed repeatedly first in East and North Africa, then across the Mediterranean. Once bombs began to fall on Italy itself, Ciano's mood grew dark. Mussolini took away the foreign ministry from Ciano in February 1943, appointing him to the harmless post of ambassador to the Vatican. Ciano subsequently repaid the slight by voting with the rest of the Fascist Grand Council to overthrow Mussolini. As things fell apart in Rome in September, Ciano fled into Germany. He was arrested by the *Gestapo* and delivered to Italian fascists. They tried him for treason at Verona. He was convicted and shot on January 11, 1944, upon his father-in-law's nominal approval. Ciano wrote a self-consciously Roman and self-pitying imperial lament in his final diary entry: "Victory finds a hundred fathers, but defeat is an orphan."

See also chemical warfare.

CIGS   Chief of the Imperial General Staff.
See Brooke, Alan.

CINCAF (1)   Commander in Chief, Allied Forces. A Western Allied command.

CINCAF (2)   Commander in Chief, Asiatic Fleet. A U.S. Navy command.

CINCPAC   Commander in Chief, Pacific.
See Nimitz, Chester.

CINCPOA   Commander in Chief, Pacific Ocean Area.
See Nimitz, Chester.

CINCSWPA   Commander in Chief, Southwest Pacific Area.
See MacArthur, Douglas.

CINCUS   U.S. Navy designation for "Commander in Chief, United States." It was used until December 1941, when it was changed to the less-unfortunate sounding *COMINCH*.
See King, Ernest.

CINMED   Commander in Chief, Mediterranean.
See Alexander, Harold; Eisenhower, Dwight.

CIPHER MACHINES

See Bletchley Park; Combined Cypher Machine; Enigma machine; Geheimschreiber machine; JADE; MAGIC; PURPLE; SIGABA; Typex; ULTRA; VENONA.

CIRCUS   Or "flying circus." Royal Air Force term dating to World War I, applied during World War II to combined bomber-fighter sorties across the Channel from March 1942 to mid-1944. These operations were intended to draw Luftwaffe fighters into unequal combat, to attrit enemy air strength, and to draw German fighters away from the Eastern Front as a British contribution to the Soviet war effort.

CITADEL (JULY 1943)

See Kursk; ZITADELLE.

CIVIL AIR PATROL   An all civilian—pilots and planes—coastal patrol and freight service in the United States. It relieved military assets for use overseas. A significant number of CAP pilots were women.

CIVIL DEFENSE   All measures to protect the civilian population in wartime.
See various country entries.

CIVILIANS

See individual country entries, and *see also Air Transport Auxiliary; area bombing; atrocities; bandits; BARBAROSSA; BBC; Berlin bomber offensive; biological warfare; Blitz; Bormann, Martin; BÜFFEL; Burma campaign (1941–1942); chemical warfare; Civil Air Patrol; civil defense; CLARION; collaboration; Combined Bomber Offensive; concentration camps; conscientious objection; Courland pocket; death camps; desertion; Doolittle raid; Dresden raid; Dulag; Dunkirk evacuation; Dunkirk spirit; Eastern Front; Einsatzgruppen; ethnic cleansing; food supply; Geneva Conventions; Germany, conquest of; Gestapo; Goumiers; Graziani, Rodolfo; Guernica; Hague Conventions; Halder, Franz; Harris, Arthur; Heiligenbeil pocket; Hiroshima; Hitler, Adolf; Holocaust; Imperial Japanese Army; Jiang Jieshi; Keitel, Wilhelm; kokubō kokkai; Korück; Kriegsmarine; Leningrad, siege of; Luftwaffe; medals; merchant marine; morale bombing; Morgenthau Plan; Nagasaki; Nanjing, Rape of; NKVD; Nuremberg Tribunal; Okinawa campaign; Ostarbeiter; partisans; Philippines campaign (1944–1945); Pripet Marshes; radio; rape; Rassenkampf; rations; Red Army; Red Cross; resistance; Résistance (France); resistance (Germany); Rikusentai; Saipan; Schörner, Ferdinand; Sino-Japanese War (1937–1945); Slovak Uprising; special orders; Stalingrad; strategic bombing; Tatars; Tosui-ken; total war; Ukraine, First Battle of; Unit 731; unrestricted submarine warfare; Uštaše; war crimes; Warsaw Ghetto; Warsaw Uprising; Wehrmacht.*

CLARION (1945)   Code name for a massive air strike against German communications and transportation networks deemed to be still operating after earlier bombings. It also represented continuing hopes for breakthrough *morale bombing* among the bomber chiefs. CLARION raids were carried out on February 22 and 23, 1945. These were assessed as ineffective in achieving destruction of precision targets or eroding morale, though a few historians demur from the latter judgment.

CLARK, MARK (1896–1984)   American general. A veteran of World War I, Clark was deputy commander under General *Dwight Eisenhower* in North Africa, where he negotiated a truce with Vichy authorities. He was promoted to command U.S. 5th Army during the *Italian campaign (1943–1945)*. He oversaw the landings at Salerno on September 9, 1943. He then led 5th Army in failed, flawed, and brutal efforts to break through a succession of German defensive lines, most notably the *Gustav Line*. Clark attacked frontally into fixed fortifications, behind which Field Marshal *Albert Kesselring's* tough veterans barred the road to Rome. Clark carried out landings at *Anzio* in January 1944, then bogged down inside a small lodgement, which he failed to compel his subordinates to speedily expand before the Germans recovered. He then repeatedly sent another part of his divided force up the slopes of *Monte Casino,* incurring heavy casualties to no gain. Clark's worst failure was personal: he was obsessed with reaching Rome before General *Bernard Law Montgomery* and the British. He developed a venomous loathing for Montgomery far beyond normal or healthy rivalry among allies. His jealousy caused him to disobey direct orders in May 1944, driving directly for Rome instead of completing an encirclement of German 10th Army as he had been instructed to do by Field Marshal *Harold Alexander*. Clark beat the British to Rome, arriving in the city on June 5, 1944. That was one day before all newspaper headlines back home trumped the Roman news with announcement of the *OVERLORD* invasion of France.

Historians have not judged Clark kindly. He is severely criticized for blunt and bloody tactics, little grasp of operational opportunities, ever-rising vanity, damaging Anglophobia, and personal and reputational fixation on the empty symbolic prize of Rome. Most importantly, he is widely criticized for wasting assets and lives while failing to destroy Kesselring's armies when he had the main chance. Many believe General *George S. Patton* would have performed much better, but he was in partial disgrace at the time and not eligible for the Italian command. Clark's failure meant that Western Allied troops had to slog through northern Italy and into the Alps against well-defended German positions, manned by enemy soldiers who should have been in prisoner of war camps instead. Controversy about Clark's actions and reputations continued for decades after the war. He has some defenders, but his critics are more numerous. They render harsh judgment of his command abilities, decisions, and personality, notably when compared to the greater vision and generosity of spirit displayed by Eisenhower.

CLARK FIELD
See Philippines campaign (1941–1942).

CLAUSEWITZ (JULY 1942)   The 1942 summer offensive operation by the Wehrmacht, originally code named *BLAU* II, that advanced through the Donbass region toward Rostov.

CLAY, LUCIUS D. (1898–1978)   Clay was an engineer by training and an administrator, rather than combat soldier, by inclination and talent. His main responsibility was the massive procurement program that underwrote the American war effort and fed *Lend-Lease* aid to Allied states. His most public role came after the war as military governor of the American zone of occupation in Germany from 1945 to 1949.

CLAYTON KNIGHT COMMITTEE   From 1939 to 1942, the RAF and RCAF covertly recruited American pilots though this shadow organization. It was named for the American World War I ace who organized it with Billy Bishop, his Canadian friend and top Allied ace of the Great War. It operated discretely to avoid legal complications that the *Neutrality Acts* posed for any U.S. citizen fighting with a foreign military. Before those U.S. laws were repealed, the Committee recruited over 6,700 American volunteers.
   See also Eagle squadrons.

CLOSE AIR SUPPORT   Tactical bombing and strafing in support of specific and individual enemy battlefield targets in support of one's own ground forces.
   See also interdiction.

COASTAL COMMAND
   See air–sea rescue; Atlantic, Battle of the (1939–1945); Royal Air Force (RAF).

COAST WATCHERS   Western Allied military personnel and civilians who stayed behind on Japanese-occupied islands in the South Pacific to report on enemy air, ship, and troop movements. The Japanese also used coast watchers to observe enemy shipping. Most of the several hundred Allied coast watchers were Australian. Australian naval intelligence had organized a coast watch service after World War I. It built on that foundation from 1941. Some coast watchers were native to the South Pacific islands or colonists there before the war. Others were escaped prisoners or soldiers who evaded capture. Other watchers were organized under the intelligence branch of *South West Pacific Area (SWPA)* command. From mid-1942 coast watchers of several nationalities worked for the *Allied Intelligence Bureau*. They were especially effective in warning of Japanese ship and aircraft movements during the early Solomons campaign, around *Bougainville* and *Guadalcanal*. Some branched into rescuing downed Allied—and even Japanese—air crew. The Japanese rigorously hunted coast watchers and were merciless when they caught them, despite Western Allied attempts to give them military rank and legal protections. Many were killed. The service disbanded in October 1944, as the war moved away to the Central Pacific.

COBRA (JULY 25–AUGUST 13, 1944)   Code name for the American operation to break out of the bocage country during the *Normandy campaign*. After seven weeks of close and heavy fighting along the perimeter of the lodgement in Normandy, on July 25 some 600 fighter-bombers blasted a path for American armor through German artillery positions and strongpoints held by the Panzer-Lehr Division and supporting elite infantry of the 5th Parachute Division. The "Jabos" were followed by 1,800 heavy bombers from U.S. 8th Air Force, unusually attempting to bomb tactically rather than strategically. The heavies devastated defending Germans, but short-bombing killed over 100 Americans and wounded nearly 500. Before noon, U.S. 1st Infantry Division and 2nd Armored advanced, fighting through strong German resistance and large minefields for the rest of the day. Over the next two days the advance picked up speed as the German left flank collapsed and U.S. 4th Armored Division joined the fight. German armored counterattacks were beaten back, with the Americans enjoying air supremacy. By the third day, most German units were fighting to escape rather than hold the line. Panzer Lehr was nearly totally destroyed, along with several other German divisions. On July 30th, British and Canadian assaults in support of the left flank of the COBRA advance further attrited the Germans. Avranches fell to U.S. 8th Corps, and the next day the last major German counterattack was blunted. On August 1, the Western Allied and American command structures in Normandy were altered. Lieutenant General *Courtney Hodges* took over U.S. 1st Army, while General *George S. Patton* took command of a newly activated U.S. 3rd Army, with General *Omar Bradley* rising to command newly designated 12th Army Group. Thus began the "breakout" phase of the Normandy campaign, with Patton sending a corps into Brittany while other large formations raced across Normandy and curled behind broken and retreating divisions of the Wehrmacht and *Waffen-SS*. Adolf Hitler ordered a foolhardy Panzer counterattack that was stopped at Mortain on August 7, with heavy German losses. Fighting in the Mortain Pocket lasted until August 13. After that came the disappointment of failing to close the *Falaise gap* in time to trap all the Germans trying to escape encirclement.

COCKADE   A series of *deception operations* intended to take German pressure off ground forces in Sicily and on the Red Army during 1943, by suggesting impending assaults on the coast of France or the Balkans. It was also hoped to lure Luftwaffe forces into a major air battle that would establish Allied air superiority over Western Europe. COCKADE was implemented by an admixture of double agents, fake wireless traffic, false troop concentrations, and increases in aerial reconnaissance and bombing of decoy areas. Its sub-operations were: STARKEY, a fake Anglo-Canadian amphibious landing at Boulogne, prepared by actual heavy bombing; WADHAM, a dummy American invasion of France at Brest, replete with easily spotted fake landing craft; and TINDALL, a leaked, detailed plan for an Anglo-American invasion of Norway, working on knowledge from *ULTRA* intercepts that Adolf Hitler had exaggerated strategic views about Norway. None of these operations worked, mainly because the OKW correctly did not believe the basic premise that the Western Allies would invade anywhere other than Italy in 1943. However, the *Abwehr* was convinced that the Western Allied order of battle in Britain was far larger than it was: 51 divisions rather than the actual 17 divisions based there. That fact aided successful deception operations concealing *OVERLORD* in 1944.

See also FORTITUDE North.

CODE TALKERS   Navajo Indian teams were recruited by the U.S. Marine Corps to broadcast battlefield intelligence and fire-control information "in the clear" in the Navajo language, in the certain knowledge that Japan did not have experts who understood any Native American language. About 400 Navajo were recruited; 300 saw action in the Pacific War, first on *Guadalcanal* and later on *Iwo Jima*. The U.S. Army used Choctaw signal men during World War I. Despite great field success, during World War II the Army reverted to traditional codes and signals. Only 17 Comanche code talkers were recruited by the Army, of whom 13 saw service in the ETO. The Comanche language had no words for some modern weapons, so imaginative substitutes were invented: bombers were called "pregnant birds" while their bombs were "baby birds." Panzers were called "turtles." Neither Navajo nor Comanche "code talking," which did not actually involve use of codes, was ever penetrated by the enemy.

COLDITZ   A special German *prisoner of war* camp located in Colditz Castle in Saxony. It housed captured officers: Polish, Belgian, French, British and Commonwealth, then American. Its isolated location, high security, and boastful commander all caused it to be used as a warehouse for "escape specialists." Some 20 escape attempts from Colditz succeeded, or about 10 percent of those assayed.

COLLABORATION   Cooperation with the officials of a foreign occupation government. In writing about World War II, the term is almost always used to mean cooperation with one or other members of the *Axis alliance*. Cooperation with an occupier was often viewed at the time as implying economic or political opportunism on the part of collaborators, though it sometimes clearly arose from ideological affinity or antipathy to the Western Allies or Soviet Union. Since the war, historians have portrayed collaboration as far more extensive than most nationalists in once-occupied countries still care to recall. Historians also portray the phenomenon in shades of moral gray, as they have done also with the related concept of *resistance*. At the least, there was both voluntary and involuntary collaboration, as the French social scientist Stanley Hoffmann once put it. The latter was forced on most people by sheer force of circumstance. In eastern Europe, the Balkans, and the Soviet Union, collaboration was often a basic survival technique by ordinary people facing extraordinarily brutal and harsh times and conditions. There was also involuntary cooperation of forced laborers and forced military service offered under threat of starvation or execution. Identified motives for voluntary collaboration ranged from genuine ideological enthusiasm to strictly opportunistic affiliation with the new power, especially in German-occupied

Europe. There was fatalist accommodation to the reality of military occupation by some, notably before the turning of the tide against the Axis in 1942. And there were those who adopted an attitude the French called *attentisme,* or a prudential "wait and see" view about which side would win the war.

Three key factors appear essential in any assessment of collaboration. First, the character of the local Axis administrator was key. The nature of German occupation varied greatly. Traditional military officials might govern relatively benignly in one province of Adolf Hitler's hodgepodge administrative empire, while some Nazi thug governed malignantly in another. In not a few countries, a murderous psychopath like *Reinhard Heydrich* ruled in terror of a type that makes comparison to other parts of German-occupied Europe difficult or impossible. Second, the behavior of local elites mattered greatly. Some national elites in Japanese-occupied Asia initially welcomed, or at least accommodated themselves to, Japanese displacement of older European colonial regimes. That was also true in France and other West European countries occupied by Germany, where some elites used occupation as an opportunity to settled old scores with their domestic enemies on the left. Lastly, the conditions suffered by the mass of a civilian population affected how ideas of resistance or collaboration were received. After liberation, real as well as merely accused collaborators were subjected to rough justice—and often, injustice. Males were most often executed, summarily or after trial. Over 310,000 were formally accused of collaboration in the purges that followed liberation in France, and just over 171,000 actually faced tribunals or Maquis or FFI courts. Of those tried, 40,000 were sent to prison, 50,000 sentenced to "degradation," and 10,500 were condemned and executed. Women accused of "horizontal collaboration" were more usually publicly shamed and punished by mobs, rather than by courts. In France, an old punishment from the Great War, and long before that, was revived: shaving women's heads and social shunning. Sometimes women were also killed, even after such public humiliation.

See also individual countries, and *Aung San; Axis Sally; BARBAROSSA; Bose, Subhas Chandra; Burma National Army; Cossacks; Darlan; fascism; final solution; Greater East Asian Co-Prosperity Sphere; Hiwis; Holocaust; Indian National Army; Joyce, William; Laval, Pierre; Mussolini, Benito; NKVD; Ostarbeiter; Ostlegionen; Osttruppen; partisans; Pétain, Henri; prisoners of war; Quisling, Vidkun; repatriation; Russian Liberation Army (ROA); Sino-Japanese War (1937–1945); Smersh; Sonderkommando; Sudetenland; Tatars; Ukraine; Vlasov, Andrei; Vlasovites; Vichy; Waffen-SS; Wang Jingwei; war crimes trials.*

Suggested Reading: Peter Davies, *Dangerous Liaisons: Collaboration and World War II* (2005).

COLLECTIVE SECURITY A 20th-century theory of international security that aimed at preservation of peace through shared deterrence of aggression. It aimed to achieve that goal by promising to produce an imbalance of power against any would-be aggressor in the form of a grand coalition of all or most other states. Its offer of an advance guarantee to all peaceful states would take the form of overwhelming diplomatic opposition to aggression, followed by the escalating disapproval of economic sanctions and, ultimately, collective use of military force. With these measures certain to be brought to bear against aggressors, the theory held, all would-be aggressors must be deterred from acting. This was the central security doctrine promoted by Woodrow Wilson and embedded in the Covenant of the *League of Nations.* However, the League never met a key precondition of collective security: membership of all Great Powers. It also suffered from a lack of will to enforce sanctions against violators, then was faced with several powerful aggressors all at once: Japan (1931, 1937), Italy (1935, 1940), Germany (1939–1941), and the Soviet Union (1939–1940). The theory was probably fundamentally unsound on political and psychological grounds.

See also Abyssinian War (1935–1936); Churchill, Winston.

COLMAR POCKET A small German pocket in Alsace, west of the Rhine. It held out against the *broad front* advance of the Western Allies in the last quarter of 1944. Bitterenders of German 19th Army in the pocket faced French 1st Army and U.S. 21st Corps at the start of January 1945, part of General *Jacob Devers'* 6th Army Group. The Germans attacked toward Strasbourg from January 7, 1945. Hard fighting to blunt the thrust and compress the pocket lasted until February 9. Paralleling the crushing denouement of the *Ardennes offensive,* the Western Allies took over 18,000 combat casualties in the Colmar pocket while inflicting 35,000 German casualties.

COLOMBIA Like several other Latin American countries, Colombia used U-boat sinkings of some of its ships as an excuse to appease the United States by declaring war on the Axis states in November 1943. It made no military contribution to the Allied war effort.

COLOSSUS I AND II Revolutionary British code-breaking computers.
See Bletchley Park; Enigma machine; Geheimschreiber machine.

COMANDO SUPREMO The usual term of reference for the Italian General Staff. The official title was "Stato Maggiore Generale." The Comando Supremo was led by Marshal *Pietro Badoglio* from its founding by Benito Mussolini in 1925. Badoglio fell from favor in December 1940. He was replaced by Marshal *Ugo Cavallero* from December 1940 to January 1943. Cavallero was followed by Marshal *Vittorio Ambrosio* to the end of the fascist regime. Under Badoglio, the Comando Supremo had little influence over military affairs because Mussolini personally occupied the chairs of the air force and navy and served as war minister as well as prime minister. It was also Il Duce's habit to control all military decisions large and small, and routinely to bypass the Comando Supremo. Cavallero had more administrative influence from 1941, but still not enough to stave off continuing military and imperial catastrophe flowing from earlier commitments in the Mediterranean and on the Eastern Front. After Italy formally switched sides in September 1943, the Comando Supremo had nominal charge of a handful of antifascist divisions fighting alongside the Western Allies into 1945.

COMBAT AIR PATROL (CAP)   A standard operating procedure for all major air forces in which a protective cover of fighters remained airborne above anticipated ground targets, or to protect their home carrier and other high value ships at sea. The Luftwaffe deployed a CAP of nightfighters that circled inside grid boxes waiting to be vectored onto bombers by ground controllers.
  See also cab ranks; Kammhuber Line.

COMBAT CAR   A peculiar U.S. Army category that called light tanks operated by cavalry units "combat cars," solely not to violate a 1920 law that said only the infantry could have tanks.

COMBAT ECHELON   The term used by U.S. forces for the lead element in an advance, moving ahead of the reserves. British and Commonwealth forces called this a "fighting group."

COMBAT FATIGUE
  See battle fatigue.

COMBAT LOADED   Also known as "combat stowed." Loading an amphibious assault vessel in the reverse order in which supplies and equipment would be needed by the assault force so that the most essential items would be unloaded first.

COMBAT WING
  See air division; group (air force).

COMBAT ZONE (CZ)   U.S. forces term for what the British Army called a "forward area," or that part of an active front in direct contact with enemy troops.

COMBINED ARMS ARMY   The basic Soviet fighting formation. Armies were not assigned permanently to *Fronts* or *Directions,* but were shifted by the Stavka to support a specific sector or campaign. Specially equipped and well-proven veteran armies were designated with the honorific "*Guards Army.*"
  See also Shock Army.

COMBINED BOMBER OFFENSIVE (CBO)   When Western Allied leaders met at the *Casablanca Conference (January 14–24, 1943)* the *Combined Chiefs of Staff* agreed that the USAAF and the RAF should coordinate bombing of Germany. The USAAF agreed to bomb by day—the preferred method of those who still believed in *precision bombing*—while RAF Bomber Command conducted *area bombing* by night.

The directive for the CBO combined all threads of thinking about the functions of *strategic bombing*: destruction of enemy transportation and communications nets, retardation of war production, and conscious and deliberate suppression of civilian morale. Within the overall strategic directive given to the Western Allied air forces was a list of "primary objectives." Listed by priority, these were: U-boat pens, the German aircraft industry, transportation and communications targets, synthetic oil facilities, and oil fields. The "Casablanca Directive" gave the CBO more apparent coherence than bombing yet displayed in fact, or was capable of achieving. Tensions persisted between airmen intent on using *morale bombing* as a supposed war-winning weapon and those who saw bombing's major contribution to the war as wrecking critical areas of enemy production and preparing the way for a ground invasion through carefully targeted tactical strikes. *Arthur Harris* of RAF Bomber Command reinterpreted the Directive in ways that allowed him to continue to conduct the morale bombing he preferred. Though not as baldly, USAAF chiefs similarly interpreted the Directive to fit what they were already doing.

Harris launched a series of "air battles" during 1943, which he argued would prove decisive. The first was fought in the smog-filled skies above the Ruhr Valley, starting on March 5. Over the next four months bombers pounded Ruhr cities and industries, taking heavy casualties over the most heavily defended territory in Germany. Nuremberg, Essen, Dortmund, Duisburg, and Düsseldorf were all attacked multiple times. Bochum, Oberhausen, and smaller cities were also hit. Over 1,000 Allied aircraft were lost in the Ruhr campaign. While heavy damage was done and much loss of German life incurred, the Ruhr continued to produce critical resources for the German war economy. Harris ordered bombing of other German cities, including Cologne. A series of four great raids (GOMORRAH) by 3,000 heavy bombers of RAF Bomber Command carried out from July 24 to August 2, 1943, destroyed half of Hamburg. The raids created a firestorm that burned out hundreds of war factories and killed thousands of workers, while "de-housing" many thousands more. That set back German war production in Hamburg, making the argument over targeting doctrine even more complicated.

At the first *Québec Conference (August 17–24, 1943)*, official emphasis on morale bombing was dropped in favor of attacking clearly listed, high-value targets. Among these, the highest priority was given to smashing the Luftwaffe's fighter force and slowing fighter production by bombing aircraft factories. In fact, such priority targeting had been undertaken since May. But in accordance with the Québec directive, U.S. 8th Air Force attempted two precision raids on the critical and heavily defended fighter and ball-bearing works at Schweinfurt, with a companion raid against Regensburg. Carried out on August 17 and October 14, 1943, the Schweinfurt raids were a turning point in the air war. Out of 376 American bombers that made the first raid, 147 never saw their home airfields again. The second raid was even more disastrous: 60 bombers were shot down and 142 badly damaged out of a force of 291. The Americans did not try to hit Schweinfurt again until February 1944. The focus of Bomber Command turned to the *Berlin bomber offensive* through the winter of 1943–1944, while the USAAF reconsidered the wisdom of its entire approach to bombing Germany.

The official 1944 focus on reducing German fighter production and luring existing fighters into battle to be destroyed before the *OVERLORD* campaign was made possible by the advent of long-range American fighters. P-51 Mustangs equipped with drop tanks capable of escorting bombers deep into Germany turned the air war decisively and permanently in favor of the Western Allies. Rising confidence and air dominance led to the "Big Week" operation, a massive six-day bombing campaign (February 20–25, 1944) code named AR-GUMENT. It was carried out by the U.S. 8th, 9th, and 15th Army Air Forces based in Britain and Italy and by RAF Bomber Command. Over 6,150 bombers were involved in a week-long assault on Luftwaffe fighter factories and bases. The Western Allies lost 411 aircraft, including several dozen fighters. It is believed that "Big Week" seriously interrupted fighter manufacture for several months, although production did not begin terminal decline until September. "Big Week" certainly damaged Luftwaffe morale, which was already low from chronic attrition and persistent failure to stop the bombers. This phase of the CBO was crucially important. It severely attrited Luftwaffe pilots and thereby established air supremacy over the landing zones in France in time for the invasion of Normandy in June. The air battle over Germany also eliminated many experienced Luftwaffe pilots. Thereafter, German fighter pilot skills were noticeably lessened and Western Allied kill ratios climbed. With long-range escort fighters available by mid-1944, even Bomber Command began carrying out more daylight precision raids. Fighter attrition continued over Germany during the last months of 1944 and into 1945, when the hugely controversial—though operationally not distinctive—*Dresden raid* was carried out, among other city bombings.

See also anti-aircraft weapons; bombers; creep back; Direction-Finding (D/F); flak; Flak Towers; GEE; Kammhuber Line; Knickebein; LeMay, Curtiss; LORAN; Lorenz; Norden bombsight; Oboe; Pathfinders; pattern bombing; Peenemünde; Ploesti; Ruhr Dams; shuttle bombing; Target Indicators (TIs); window; Würzburg; X-Gerät; Y-Gerät.

Suggested Reading: Tami Biddle, *Rhetoric and Reality in Air Warfare: The Evolution of British and American Ideas about Strategic Bombing, 1914–1945* (2002).

COMBINED CHIEFS OF STAFF (CCS)   The supreme command committee of the Western Allies, comprising a joint board formed by the top service chiefs of the British *Chiefs of Staff* and the American *Joint Chiefs of Staff*. The Combined Chiefs advised Prime Minister Winston Churchill and Presidents Franklin D. Roosevelt and Harry S. Truman on formulation of military *grand strategy* and oversaw implementation of strategic operations. Founded by agreement at the *Arcadia Conference* in December 1941, the CCS met weekly in Washington throughout the war. The British chiefs were represented by a commission ("Joint Staff Mission") that was in constant contact with London. The CCS was supported by a large body of talented and pooled planning staff who coordinated war production overseen by civilian joint boards, filtered critical top secret military intelligence, and advised on priorities for deployment of air, land, and sea forces. The CCS traveled with top civilian leaders to all the major wartime summits.

COMBINED CYPHER MACHINE A shared Western Allied cipher machine in service from 1943. It combined the American *SIGABA* code machine with the British *Typex*. It was used on warships in the Atlantic from November 1943. Older SIGABA and Typex machines were converted so that they could talk to the new Combined Cypher Machine.

COMBINED FORCES Western Allied term for multinational troops under a unified command, that might or might not include *joint forces* but did not normally include *strategic air forces*.

COMBINED OPERATIONS The preferred British and Commonwealth term for *amphibious operations*.

COMBINED OPERATIONS PILOTAGE PARTIES British *amphibious operations* specialists who scouted out landing beaches in advance—often by landing from offshore *submarines* or operating special *midget submarines* of their own. They also sat just off the beaches during landings, directing naval gunfire and seeking to ensure that troops landed in the right sectors. The first Pilotage Parties saw action in the Aegean, then during the *TORCH* landings in North Africa. Teams operating from midget submarines scouted landing sites and assisted major landings at Sicily, Salerno, and in Normandy on *D-Day (June 6, 1944)*. They scouted from boats before British troops crossed the Rhine in March 1945.

COMFORT WOMEN
See Ianfu.

COMINCH U.S. Navy designation for "Commander in Chief, United States Fleet" from December 1941, when it was changed from the unfortunate-sounding "CINCUS."
See Ernest King.

COMINTERN The Third (or Communist) International, 1919–1943. The Comintern was founded by V. I. Lenin and the Bolsheviks as a breakaway movement from the democratic-socialist Second International. That split institutionalized a division extant in socialism since 1903 in Russia, and 1914 more generally. Lenin's group sought immediate revolution and insisted upon a dictatorial party model. His faction thereafter styled itself "Communist." The majority sought basic reform through union action and the ballot box and remained "socialists." The Comintern was feared by Western governments prior to World War II and was a favorite target of Axis propaganda. In reality, it was a not-too-effective front for rather clumsy and heavy-handed prewar policies of the Soviet Union. In China, Comintern agents helped found both the Chinese Communist Party and the *Guomindang* on Leninist lines. The principal and myopic aim of the Comintern was to counter the electoral appeal of social democracy as a rival to Communist parties for working class support. That was most often done at the price of not combating the rising and more urgent threat of militant *fascism*.

The Comintern came to international prominence as a vehicle for Moscow's support of Spanish Republicans during the *Spanish Civil War (1936–1939)*. Joseph Stalin exported terror tactics of the *NKVD* through the Comintern, exterminating foreign Communists and antifascist partisans in Spain. That brutal purge of leftists who refused to adhere to Moscow's party line led to widespread ideological disillusionment. The shift was notably recorded in the war writings of George Orwell, a volunteer in the *International Brigades*. By pursuing aggressive tactics and open subversion of foreign governments, the Comintern misled foreign leaders about the essentially defensive strategic posture of the Soviet Union in the 1930s. It then lost much popular support among ordinary Communists as it followed the tortured maneuvers of Stalin's foreign policy, especially when the Comintern supported Stalin's alliance with Adolf Hitler in the *Nazi–Soviet Pact (August 23, 1939)*. Recently released documents from Soviet archives showed that the Comintern was caught utterly unprepared by the German victory over France in 1940 and was slow to connect with stunned French Communists. It was less slow off the mark in June 1941, instantly reversing its propaganda course upon the German invasion of the Soviet Union. The Comintern was dissolved by vote of its Presidium on May 15, 1943. The news was published a week later in *Pravda*. Dissolution was a placatory gesture to President Franklin Roosevelt. He had expressed concern to Stalin that long-standing hostility might threaten U.S. postwar cooperation with the Soviet Union should the Comintern persist in activities that overexcited anti-Communist public opinion. The decision also reflected Stalin's personal disdain for members of the Comintern, and his pragmatic sense that its work of subversion was best accomplished by more discreet means as long as the Soviet Union needed the support and aid of the Western Allies in the war effort.

COMMANDO ORDER "Kommandobefehl." Issued by Adolf Hitler on October 18, 1942, it directed that all captured British *commandos* were to be summarily executed. Commandos were shot by German troops or by the *Gestapo* on at least two occasions, with the Gestapo victims first undergoing torture. The *Nuremberg Tribunal* held the "commando order" to be illegal and that instances of obedience to it were *war crimes*.

See also prisoners of war.

COMMANDOS Initially called "sea raiders" by the British, these special forces trained to conduct lightning raids against Axis coastal installations—or what Winston Churchill called "butcher and bolt" missions. The British Army and the Royal Marines both developed commando raider units. Raiding was part of Churchill's early strategy to attack the periphery of the Nazi empire while bombing its heartland, preparatory to a main assault at some future opportune moment (that moment came only after the Soviet Union and United States entered the war). The

U.S. Army modeled its six battalions of *Rangers* on British commandos. The Soviet Navy deployed units of amphibious special forces known as *spetsnaz*. The Italians also had naval commandos and strange ideas about using *divers* as underwater infantry. Wehrmacht special forces included the initially elite *Brandenburgers*, but their role shifted to a regular infantry function as German fortunes deteriorated. The Japanese Army generally did not train or field specialty commandos. Instead, it formed ad hoc units. It also experimented with recruitment of violent criminals for special forces, but the idea never amounted to much. The Imperial Japanese Navy fielded *Rikusentai*, or specialist naval marines that had something of a commando ethos and style early in the Pacific War, but who were later used as base defense troops.

See also airborne; Argenta Gap; Channel Islands; Chindits; commando order; Dieppe raid; Elba; Raider Battalions; Raiding Forces; Sacred Band; Skorzeny, Otto; St. Nazaire raid.

COMMAND POST (CP) The position among U.S. forces occupied by an officer in command of a local area of the frontline. The British called this a "Tactical HQ."

COMMAND RESPONSIBILITY The practical obligation of officers for the disposition, discipline, protection, and use of troops and weapons in war. Also, a moral and legal obligation of officers to ensure that troops under their command perform wartime tasks according to humanitarian principles and the laws of war.

See also special orders; superior orders; war crimes trials.

COMMERCE RAIDING

See Atlantic, Battle of; auxiliary cruiser; cruiser warfare; submarines; war crimes; Z-Plan.

COMMISSAR ORDER "Kommisarbefehl." One of the *special orders* given to German officers just prior to the launch of *BARBAROSSA*, issued on June 6, 1941. It required that all political officers—*Commissars* and *politruks*—who were taken prisoner be handed over to *Sonderkommando* units for "special action"—a euphemism for summary execution. Wehrmacht commanders accepted this criminal policy almost without exception or demur. The illegal and barbarous "Kommisarbefehl" was one of the definitive criminal acts of the OKH (German Army High Command), which instigated and circulated the order. The absence of professional or moral objections reflected a wider agreement of the officer corps with a vision of harsh *Vernichtungskrieg* ("war of annihilation") against "Jewish-Bolshevism" purveyed by Adolf Hitler and Nazi ideologues. Among other things, the "Kommisarbefehl" assumed a military victory over the Soviet Union would be achieved so quickly and completely that no advance thought was given to conducting political warfare, to winning "hearts and minds" of conquered non-Russian populations who were intensely hostile to the Soviet system and Communist idea. In short, there was to be no repetition of the political settlement attempted in the east in 1918, no vassal regimes created in conquered non-Russian lands. There was to be only deportation, occupation, slavery, mass death, and criminal brutality, without thought to the long-term moral, political, or military consequences.

See also Küchler, Georg von; prisoners of war.

COMMISSARS   Communist Party officers assigned to Red Army units at the battalion and regimental level or above. Their function was to spy on commanders and monitor morale, report upon flagging officer zeal for official doctrine, and conduct "political education" of troops. Commissars harkened to direct political oversight of the Red Army dating to the Russian Civil War (1918–1921). The office was abolished in the aftermath of a poor military showing during the *Finnish–Soviet War (1939–1940),* but reinstated by the Stavka on July 16, 1941. That was a response to catastrophic collapse of morale and discipline among many shattered Red Army units in the opening weeks of *BARBAROSSA*. Senior commissars were thereafter attached to Fronts as part of *Military Councils*. As in any human activity, but especially true of official "revolutionary" activity, some commissars were helpful to commanders but most were not. All commissars captured by the Germans were murdered in accordance with the criminal "Kommisarbefehl" or "*Commissar order.*" The office of commissar was once again abolished, and the dual command system ended on October 9, 1942, as part of major Red Army reforms. Political work was thereafter carried out at the highest level by senior Party officials on the Military Councils. But those officials were no longer called commissars.

See also politruk.

COMMITTEE TO DEFEND AMERICA BY AIDING THE ALLIES   A pro–*Lend-Lease* and pro-British, but noninterventionist, group founded to oppose isolationist lobbying by the *America First Committee*.

COMMONWEALTH   An association of self-governing territories (Dominions) of the British Empire. In contrast, overseas colonies were still directly governed as imperial territories to the end of World War II. The evolution from Empire to Commonwealth began with passage of the British North America Act (1867). It gained a head of steam during and after World War I, when the "white dominions" found men fighting in far away fields and countries of which they knew little, for imperial causes not understood, or in many cases not deemed worth the blood price that was paid. Disgruntlement across the Empire led to passage of the *Statute of Westminster* and the later "India Acts." The first devolved power from the Privy Council to governments in the various Dominions: Australia, Canada, the Irish Free State, New Zealand, Newfoundland, and South Africa. All but one of those territories supported Britain in declaring war on Germany in September 1939: Ireland remained neutral. India and other directly governed colonies still had no say on issues of imperial war and peace, despite the marginal advances of the various India Acts. The process of decoupling Britain from its expansive overseas empire accelerated after World War

II, greatly expanding the Commonwealth and changing it into a wholly voluntary association of former British colonies and dependencies.

See also British Commonwealth Air Training Scheme; Japan.

COMMUNISM/COMMUNISTS

See Albania; Allied Control Commissions; Anti-Comintern Pact; Blum, Léon; Bulgaria; Bürgerbräukeller bomb; Chen Yi; Chetniks; China; Chinese Civil War (1927–1949); Chinese Communist armies; Comintern; Commissar order; commissars; concentration camps; concordats; Croatia; Czechoslovakia; de Gaulle, Charles; desertion; Eighth Route Army; Estonia; fascism; fifth column; France; Franco, Francisco; Frank, Hans; Freikorps; Germany; Gestapo; Giáp, Nguyên Võ; Golikov, Philipp; Great Fatherland War; Greece; Green Gang; Guomindang; Hiroshima; Hiss, Alger; Hitler, Adolf; Hô Chí Minh; Holocaust; Hoxha, Enver; Hungary; International Brigades; Italian Army; Italy; Jiang Jieshi; Katyn massacre; Kodo-ha; Komsomol; Kulik, Grigory; Lin Biao; Lublin Poles; LUCY; Malaya; Manchuria; MANNA; Manstein, Erich von; Mao Zedong; Marshall, George Catlett; Masaryk, Jan; Morgenthau Plan; Nationalkomitee Freies Deutschland; Nazi Party (NSDAP); Nazi–Soviet Pact (August 23, 1939); Occupation Zones; OSMBON; partisans; Pius XI; Pius XII; Poland; Polish Army; politruk; Pomeranian Wall; prisoners of war; Red Army; Reichstag; resistance; Résistance (French); resistance (German); Rumania; Serbia; Siam; Sino-Japanese War (1937–1945); Slovenia; Soviet Union; Spain; Spanish Civil War (1936–1939); special orders; Stalin, Joseph; Steiner, Felix; Tito; United States; Uštaše; Viêt Minh; volksdeutsch; Warsaw Uprising; Xi'an incident; Yezhovshchina; Yugoslavia; zaibatsu; Zhou Enlai; Zhu De; Zog I.

COMPANY   In most armies a company was a small tactical unit formed from three to five *platoons* of 120–200 men at full paper strength. For example, a U.S. Army infantry company had three rifle platoons and a weapons platoon. A company might comprise armor, cavalry, or infantry, with numbers varying by national army and greatly dependent on time spent in combat and available replacements.

See also battalion.

COMPASS   Code name for the British and Commonwealth operation fought in the Western Desert from late 1940 to early 1941.

See desert campaign (1940–1943).

COMPIÈGNE

See armistices.

COM-Z   Communications Zone. U.S. term for the senior logistical command in charge of supplying field armies. There was significant tension between field commanders and officers in charge of the Com-Z, as there was also between combat troops and rear echelon service troops under control of GHQ Reserve. British and Commonwealth forces used the traditional "lines of communication" as an equivalent term for an American Com-Z.

CONCENTRATION CAMPS "Konzentrationslager (KZ)." Detention centers used to concentrate a civilian population under political or military control existed before the Nazis introduced them to Europe. The Qing Empire used concentration camps to deny political and material support to White Lotus and Taiping rebels in the 19th century by forcibly depopulating territories in which they operated and from where they drew recruits and supplies. Concentration camps were used by the Spanish in Cuba in the 1860s and again in the 1890s. Lord Kitchener coined the term in English, while "concentrating" Boer women and children in camps to break Afrikaner resistance during the Second Boer War, as a result of which Boer civilian death rates from camp diseases were very high. Similar camps were used by other armies fighting guerrillas, including Italians in North Africa from 1922. Barbed wire—a late 19th-century invention of American cattle ranchers—and the guard towers typical of concentration camps became a visual metaphor for all extraordinary horrors and the moral collapse of much of the world in the mid-20th century. Benito Mussolini and the Italian Army used concentration camps in *Tripoli* in 1933 and again during the *Abyssinian War (1935–1936),* in which tens of thousands of Africans died. The Vichy regime set up concentration camps in France to hold 40,000 Jews, of whom about 3,000 died even before the *Milice Française* began deportations to Nazi control. But it was Nazi Germany that gave the term "Konzentrationslager (KZ)" (concentration camp) an indelible and almost ineffable meaning. The *Schutzstaffel (SS)* network of slave labor and then mass extermination camps knows no parallel in history—not even the vast *GULAG* of the *NKVD* had anything like Nazi *death camps.*

The Nazis began planning the concentration camp system before they took power, a fact revealed in "Boxheim papers" uncovered in 1931, two years before Hitler became chancellor of Germany. The immediate purpose of the camps was to isolate political enemies of the regime: opposition Reichstag deputies, mayors, Socialist Party (SPD) and Communist Party (KPD) officials, as well as personal enemies of top Nazis. Political detention camps were set up in March 1933, by the Nazi Ministry of Justice. The first government camp was located at Esterwegen. However, other camps were set up spontaneously by thugs in the *Sturmabteilung (SA),* who began rounding up "enemies of the state" and Nazi Party on their own. These ad hoc SA camps were wild and brutal detention centers, reflecting the brutish nature of their overseers. Most did not last. The official camps built later were instead modeled on the main camp built at *Dachau,* which along with Oranienburg was the only original camp to operate during all 12 years of the "Third Reich." Within 12 months, tens of thousands of Germans were imprisoned at Dachau, Oranienburg, Gross-Rosen, and *Sachsenhausen.* The number of camps and the system's capacity thereafter increased in bursts, corresponding to political purges or new repression of German Jews. Their main purpose was still to warehouse the rising number of victims of a widening and deepening police state, not yet to kill them systematically.

As newly annexed and occupied territories came under Nazi control from 1938, the major camps and proliferating set of satellite camps (Aussenlager) responded to fear among top Nazis about dissent among non-German minorities.

Individuals who expressed personal political or moral disagreement with the regime, or who were just caught grumbling about rationing while riding a Berlin tram or turned in by a jealous or zealous neighbor for listening to the BBC, were usually kept in the vast stone prisons of the *Gestapo*. But even before the war, there were not fewer than 100,000 non-Jewish Germans in any given year in concentration camps such as Dachau, *Flossenbürg, Buchenwald,* and *Bergen-Belsen.* So many women were arrested over time that special women's camps were established at Moringen (1938), Lichtenburg (1938), and finally and most infamously at *Ravensbrück* (1939). These were not yet—or in some cases, ever—death camps. Nonetheless, tens of thousands died in "ordinary" concentration camps from beatings, shootings, or casual extrajudicial murder by guards who knew that no punishment would ever be exacted for brutality against declared enemies of the Hitler regime. There was haphazard and sadistic murder in all camps in Germany right from the start, with more regular murder programs in several. Sadism and murder became more rigorously planned and systematic once the timorous dullard and mystic *Heinrich Himmler* and the savagely cold *Reinhard Heydrich* took over the camp system for the SS. General conditions also worsened from 1939 under pressures of war and, later, looming defeat.

The Nazis used some camps to kill tens of thousands of mentally or physically handicapped in a secret *euthanasia program,* including relatives of serving Wehrmacht and SS men. Next, they began to kill the socially despised and inconvenient, as the system moved toward systematic "extermination" of whole populations. Jews, Roma, and others defined racially as *Untermenschen* were euphemistically ordered "resettled" in the east. New camps were built in occupied-Poland to serve sinister new purposes. Most camps were organized along military lines, and nearly all used prisoners to keep basic order at the barracks level. But there emerged a division and argument within the SS as to the best use of Jewish prisoners, which deepened as the war progressed. Some SS saw the camps as holding pens for huge pools of slaves. They were untroubled by high death rates caused by malignant guards and conditions but looked to rent out prison labor to German industry at varying daily rates, or to use prisoners in SS munitions and other factories. This faction saw the camps as serving the singular profit of the SS and a secondary benefit of war production. The SS therefore set up vast slave camps surrounded by dozens of satellite work camps, whose production of war matériel grew as bombs destroyed Germany's cities and above-ground factories. Camp production was never great or efficient, despite the effort invested in the factories. Some SS slave camps operated right to the end of the war.

In a perverse way, the SS labor camps competed for Jews with another type of camp run by the SS: death camps. The sole raison d'etre of the death camp system was to implement a grand plan for total extermination of targeted populations, above all of Europe's 11 million Jews. The plan was detailed to the whole regime and government apparatus at the *Wannsee conference* in January 1942. Death camps were subsequently built that had the single purpose of killing Jews on an industrial scale. Several smaller populations deemed undesirable by the Nazi hierarchy were also slated for death: Roma, Jehovah's Witnesses, "mental defectives," Communists, and homosexuals. Inmates in these camps wore colored cloth triangles to signify their status: red was worn by "politicals," usually Socialists or Communists; pink denoted homosexuals; violet was for religious dissenters; black adorned the prison costume of "antisocials"; green marked off ordinary criminals; while blue was for stateless persons. Yellow was reserved for Jews, for whom two cloth triangles formed the Star of David on their ragged camp clothes. The death camp system as it ultimately developed was designed and run by the SS under the distant direction of top SS men such as Himmler, Heydrich, and *Adolph Eichmann*. Individual camps came under the immediate supervision of various brutal commandants, who oversaw thousands of savage guards. Some of the men who ran the camps were common criminals, sentenced for life but employed by the SS as guards and administrators. Others were drawn from *Waffen-SS* punishment details, men who wanted to evade combat service or to climb back into favor by doing the dirtiest work of the SS. They were joined by volunteer units of Balts, Ukrainians, and other designated "racial Germans" who shared the Nazis' murderous anti-Semitism. There were also SS women camp guards.

The first of the death camps was *Chelmno*. By mid-1941 there were 10 main camps and 25 smaller ones. During 1942–1943, 10 more main camps were added along with 40 more satellite camps. At its greatest extent, the death camp system totaled 20 main killing and slave labor camps and some 500 satellite work camps. The most infamous and prolific death camp was *Auschwitz,* where 1.5 million human beings were methodically murdered in huge gas chambers (capacity 2,000 each). Remains were picked over by *Sonderkommando* and SS plunderers before incineration in specially designed crematoria, or buried under lime in mass graves formed from anti-tank trenches. The average life expectancy of a prisoner in a slave labor camp was about nine months, though many barely survived three. In a death camp, women with small children and the old were selected for immediate extermination and usually died on the day of their arrival, trekking from the train platform directly to the gas chambers. The young and able bodied who were judged fit to work 18–20 hours every day for the benefit of the SS and private German industry were tattooed with a serial number, overcrowded into rough barracks, and fed at starvation levels. They worked until they died or became so weak that they, too, were herded into a gas chamber, replaced by new arrivals on an endless procession of trains. At larger death camps murder targets were set at 15,000 to 20,000 per day. That figure was actually reached at some camps in 1944, as the Jewish population of Hungary was fed into the mechanized Moloch devised by leading German engineers, scientists, doctors, bureaucrats, and criminals. The death network was so vast and required so many locomotives and rail carriages to feed its insane and utterly evil appetite, the Wehrmacht protested against a drain of resources from the war effort. Calculations as to the final toll of the murdered vary, but reliable and nearly universally accepted estimates are that at least six million Jews were killed during the *Holocaust,* of whom about one million were murdered by the *Einsatzgruppen* and another five million were killed in the camps. Also murdered were several million non-Jews from abused and targeted ethnic or religious minority populations or socially detested groups.

See also Belzec; Birkenau; chemical weapons; Eisenbahntruppen; euthanasia program; Graziani, Rodolfo; Jewish Brigade; Lublin-Majdanek; Mauthausen; nerve agents; Sobibor; Theresienstadt; Tripoli; Uštaše.

Suggested Reading: Raul Hilberg, *The Destruction of the European Jews* (2003); Michael Marrus, *The Holocaust in History* (1987).

CONCENTRATION OF FIRE British term for a concentrated artillery barrage designed to hammer an enemy at a specific point. Its primary purpose was to deny enemy forces access to a targeted area. U.S. artillery called this tactic "interdiction fire."

CONCORDATS Papal treaties agreed with Fascist Italy and Nazi Germany. They were negotiated by Cardinal Pacelli, who became *Pius XII* in 1939. Many top Nazis such as *Martin Bormann* and *Heinrich Himmler* were fanatic opponents of all religion, not just Judaism. Adolf Hitler intended to crush the Christian clergy and churches in Germany after he won the war, but did not move against them before or during it out of concern for the effect on national morale. Yet, the Vatican signed a formal treaty with Hitler and the Nazis. The main motive was to gut social and political Catholicism in Germany of its independence from the papacy—in an older language, to firm papal authority over "Ultramontane" churches outside Italy. This worked in one sense. In Italy and Germany, long-standing Catholic political parties were swept aside without papal objection, and the Vatican regained status as the sole voice of Catholic authority in those countries. In return, the Faithful were assured that it was morally permissible for them to tolerate, and even to serve, reprehensible dictatorships. Another Vatican aim was to retain traditional Church privileges in the face of Nazi paganism. A still deeper fear concerned what the Vatican saw as the far greater moral and political threat of official atheism in the Soviet Union, and the Communist movement generally.

Upon agreement to the 1933 concordat, the Vatican ordered German priests to refrain from all involvement in politics—thereby limiting public moral objection to Nazi policies. For its trouble, the papacy was guaranteed special legal status by the Nazi state, retained Church property, and was allowed to operate parochial schools. By 1937 dissatisfaction with Hitler's violation of some terms of the concordat led to issuance of a papal encyclical. The next year, Pope *Pius XI (1857–1939)* publicly condemned the *Nuremberg laws* and drafted a major statement of papal opinion denouncing *anti-Semitism,* which was then reaching a crescendo within Germany. But Pius XI died in 1939. His successor as Pius XII was Cardinal Pacelli. He declined to publish the pastoral letter or to reconsider his diplomatic work. It is noteworthy that German Protestant churches and ministers also made peace with Nazism. Only a few heroic individuals—representing either side of the Reformation divide—spoke out at great personal risk and cost, notably against the Nazi *euthanasia program.*

See also Lateran Treaties.

CONDOR LEGION
See Kondor Legion.

CONGRESS PARTY   The Indian National Congress Party was dominated by the personality of Mohandas Gandhi—the "Mahatma" ("Great Soul"). Gandhi was a shrewd politician and nationalist leader, but also a fundamentalist social reformer, extreme moral idealist, and Hindu holy man. Most of Gandhi's ideas and accomplishments are unrelated to World War II. His main impact on the war was to continue to seek independence for India without incurring attendant mass violence. That process began in 1920 when he inspired organizational reforms within Congress that made it a true mass party, mainly by persuading its original company of mostly well-educated and higher-caste Hindus to accept membership for low-caste harijan. That shift allowed Congress to appeal to substantial numbers of lower castes and Muslims and to emerge as a genuine national independence party. After failure of negotiations with Britain over proposed "home rule" for India—the Round Table Conferences (1930–1932)—Congress was banned by the British until 1937. London instead experimented with unilateral reforms and contemplated carving India into sectarian electorates. Such policies spurred violent demonstrations across India, a protest fast nearly to-the-death by Gandhi, then an archetypical Gandhian pact with harijan leaders calling for proportional representation.

In 1937 Congress won an impressive, nationwide victory in provincial legislatures set up under the India Act of 1935. But the next year it split between violent radicals led by *Subhas Chandra Bose* and the more traditional and moderate nationalists led by Gandhi. During 1938 Gandhi worked to drive Bose—who embraced violent resistance to the Raj—from the presidency of the Congress Party. When war broke out in 1939, Congress ordered noncooperation with Britain's war effort, and all Party leaders resigned office. Gandhi broke with other Congress leaders who supported armed resistance to a Japanese invasion of India, which he opposed on the basis of strict adherence to nonviolence. He was jailed by the British for most of the war, notably for organizing a new mass movement demanding that Britain "Quit India" (1942–1945). That followed another breakdown in talks with Congress about India's path to postwar independence. Gandhi was basically pro-Western, within a context of profound philosophical pacifism. Forfor the most part, he kept a prudent public silence about the moral consequences of the British waging a war against *fascism* and Nazi Germany. He was released from jail in May 1944. Congress and the Muslim League divided over India's independence, which therefore began tragically with an awful and bloody partition of the subcontinent.

CONINGHAM, ARTHUR (1895–1948)   RAF air marshal. An Australian by birth but raised in New Zealand, Coningham was a veteran of World War I who joined the Royal Flying Corps after being wounded and invalided out of the ANZAC infantry. He commanded a *Group* in Britain from 1939 to 1941, before taking charge of the *Western Desert Air Force*. He played a key role in planning and carrying out air operations at *El Alamein*. During the advance of British 8th Army across North Africa, he pioneered breakthrough ground-to-air targeting cooperation. The Western Allies later used his method as a model of tactical air support. Coningham directed air operations in Sicily and Italy in 1943, then helped plan air operations for the *OVERLORD* campaign in 1944. He was given command of 2nd Tactical Air Force during the 1944–1945 drive into Germany.

CONSCIENTIOUS OBJECTION (TO MILITARY SERVICE)   Ethical objection to participation in war arising from religious or philosophical conviction, deep-seated pacifism, or some other ethical objection to killing. Most democracies permitted individuals who raised such objections sincerely to serve in noncombat roles in the military, such as with a medical unit. Over 100,000 Americans registered as conscientious objectors during World War II. Most served in medical units or with a Civilian Public Service organization. More radical, or principled, depending on one's point of view, objectors refused even nonlethal military duty. They were usually jailed: about 6,000 were imprisoned in the United States. Britain, Canada, and other Western powers recognized conscientious objection and offered more or less the same range of options, from medical service to ordinary jail time. Dictatorships did not respect conscientious objection to military service, or to any kind of compulsory state service. Objectors in the Soviet Union and Nazi Germany were simply executed. So too were some Italians. Guerillas and other insurgents did not generally respect matters of individual conscience and usually treated moral objectors roughly or even lethally.

See also desertion.

CONSCRIPTION

See individual country and armed forces entries. *See also conscientious objection; Guomindang.*

CONSEIL NATIONALE DE LA RÉSISTANCE (CNR)

See de Gaulle, Charles; Force Française de l'Intérieur (FFI); Free French; Moulin, Jean; Résistance.

CONTINUATION WAR (1941–1944)   Finnish term for the war with the Soviet Union lasting from 1941–1944.

See armistices; Finland; Finnish–Soviet War (1939–1940); Mannerheim, Carl Gustaf von (1867–1951).

CONVOY RESCUE SHIPS   Small liners or freighters with enlarged berthing that sailed in rear of a *convoy* to rescue merchant sailors when ships were sunk or damaged and abandoned. They permitted rescue even though the rest of the convoy maintained its speed and zigzag course. Convoy Rescue Ships also freed warship escorts to suppress or hunt attacking U-boats. The British commissioned 30 Convoy Rescue Ships starting in early 1941, of which 6 were eventually sunk.

Together with other escort vessels, they pulled 87 percent of merchant crewmen out of the Atlantic after U-boat sinkings during the height of the *Battle of the Atlantic* in March–April 1943. Convoy Rescue Ships alone saved over 4,000 men over the course of the war.

See also air–sea rescue.

CONVOYS Convoys increased security of vulnerable merchant shipping by lowering the probability that an enemy surface raider or submarine would spot a merchantman: 100 ships sailing separately along a known trade route presented 100 possible instances of an enemy making contact with a target, whereas 100 ships sailing together presented only one opportunity. Despite this statistical fact, psychologically it was hard for seamen and naval leaders struggling through the desperate *Battle of the Atlantic (1939–1945)* to appreciate that, in the vastness of a great ocean, a large convoy is nearly as hard to spot as a single ship. The arguments had been aired before, during World War I. The Royal Navy (RN) had correctly concluded that convoys were the best defense of merchant shipping: of more than 16,500 ships that sailed in convoy in the Great War only 102 were lost to U-boats, a loss rate barely more than 0.6 percent. Nevertheless, Western Allied navies and their political masters went through a second bitter debate about the utility of convoys before World War II. In 1935 the RN decided that convoys might not be needed at the onset of the next war. In March 1938, the Admiralty reluctantly conceded that a partial convoy system might be needed from the outset. Real controversy waxed and waned with rising and falling monthly shipping loss rates during the first two years of war against the U-boats. After the war, the RN's official history balefully concluded that "the comparative neglect of escort vessels in between the wars surely indicates that the lessons of 1914–18 were ignored or misinterpreted." The same argument took place within the U.S. Navy into 1942, despite the benefit of British experience to that point in the war.

The RN initially accepted that convoys were the best defense for slower merchantmen against U-boats. However, insufficient escorts compelled it to convoy only medium speed ships—those capable of sustaining 9–15 knots—through the *Western Approaches*. Faster or slower ships were ordered to steam as "independents." Speed, blackout, and zigzagging were their only defenses against surface raiders or U-boats, the "grey wolves" of the sea. Even that compromise bothered some officers, who resisted all convoying. Their influence cut the top convoy qualifying speed to 13 knots to allow "fast independents" capable of greater speeds to steam alone. Many "slow independents"—ships that could not maintain nine knots—also sailed alone. They made up the majority of U-boat kills. Slow convoys also had a higher loss rate than fast ones, which superficially appeared to confirm the anticonvoy thesis that speed was the best defense. In 1940 more than 660 convoys were sent out, making just less than 18,000 ship voyages. Just 126 ships in convoy were sunk that year. In stark contrast, as many as one in four "slow independents" was sunk while many so-called "fast independents" were also lost. From September 1942 to May 1945, of all ships in convoy, 99.4 percent arrived safely at their destination. Experience over the course of the entire war showed that fast convoys suffered

50 percent fewer losses than slower convoys and that ships in convoys of any speed fared far better than when they steamed as independents.

Neutrals were initially told to steam outside convoys, relying on German respect for neutral flag status. Loss rates for all types of independents, Allied and neutral, soon reached triple that for ships in convoy, so that the experiment with solitary sailing was halted after just a few months. Neutral ships also joined convoys as more were sunk without warning or recourse and Germany expanded its declared *War Zones* on the high seas. Convoys were formed for passage from Britain to and from North America and for voyages to and from Scandinavia. Coastal shipping sailed as independents until the surrender of France in June 1940. That victory greatly increased the threat to coast-hugging ships because it permitted the Kriegsmarine to base U-boats out of French ports, as well as ports in Denmark and the Low Countries. Ships that skirted Scotland and made passage up or down the Channel, and along the south coast of England, were ordered into convoy whenever possible. British coastal convoys included a wide range of local ship types, but especially colliers. Bigger ships from ocean-going convoys heading in or out of port often joined the coastal convoys. A severe lack of small warships meant that many early convoys still sailed unescorted.

All convoys received a letter-code designation. Until the United States entered the war and much of the Atlantic convoy traffic was redirected to American ports, eastbound convoys were designated "HX" from their universal departure point of Halifax, Nova Scotia. Convoys assembled at Bermuda and routed to join the transatlantic conveyor at Halifax were denoted "BFX." Westbound convoys were coded "OB" if leaving Liverpool and "OA" if forming at Southend, until October 1940. A new route for slow convoys was eventually added from Sydney, Nova Scotia. Sydney convoys were designated "SC." Convoys to and from Gibraltar were "OG" and "HG," respectively. Arctic convoys were first tagged as "PQ," but later took the appellation "JW" for outward bound voyages and "RA" on the return leg. Northbound convoys plying coastal waters from the Thames to Scotland were designated "FN," while those heading south were coded "FS." A special oil convoy was established from Curacao to New York, thence to Britain. Convoys totaling more than 350 ships per month also traveled between Freetown and Britain. Transoceanic convoys sailed from New York and other American cities to and from various destinations in Africa and Europe starting in 1942. All late-war convoys were designated by special prefixes that indicated origin and direction. Westbound convoys were tagged "ONS" from March 1943.

Convoys zigzagged according to an agreed speed and course set at a presailing conference of captains and masters. That meant a slower or damaged ship that fell out of order might be able to catch up—albeit, at increased risk—by steaming directly to the next waypoint. Convoys might remain at sea for 10–15 days, depending on average ship speed, wide diversion around known *wolf packs,* and weather. Ships spent another 13–18 days in British ports unloading. Cargo ships made three transatlantic round-trips per calendar year on average. At any given moment, 8–10 convoys might be passing in either direction across the Atlantic, with escort groups coming and going as fuel needs dictated or passover points from the USN or RCN to the RN were reached. The "Western Ocean Meeting Point" (WOMP) off Newfoundland and the "Mid-Ocean Meeting Point" (MOMP) at 35° west of the British Isles were the key rendezvous coordinates for escort groups. At the "East-Ocean Meeting Point" (EOMP) at 18° West, one RN escort group based in Iceland handed over to another from the Western Approaches. In 1941 a new arrangement saw RCN escorts hand over fast convoys to "neutral" USN destroyers at the WOMP. The Americans then escorted British convoys as far as the handoff to RN escorts at a more easterly located MOMP. From the new MOMP, RN escorts could steam all the way to Britain without leaving the convoy to refuel. Troop convoys from North America received the most protection throughout the war.

A bloody U-boat campaign was fought along the U.S. eastern seaboard once the United States was fully in the war. It began on December 8, 1941, when Hitler released the U-boats to attack American shipping even before he formally declared war on the United States. It took many months for a complex, interlocked system of convoys to be formed linking all routes of the North Atlantic. Sydney, Halifax, and Cape Breton Island were replaced as western termini by the vastly larger dock and cargo facilities of New York. Halifax was restored as the termini for slow convoys in March 1943, because even New York's docks were by then hugely congested by the vast stores of war matériel pouring out of American factories. Convoys from South America were linked to the main Atlantic routes via Trinidad and the Panama Canal, thence up the eastern seaboard of North America. Similarly, convoys from the Caribbean formed at Aruba or Port of Spain. Better airborne *Direction-Finding (DF)* equipment, 10-centimetric radar, *Leigh Lights,* shipborne *Huff-Duff,* and other technical advances reinforced the *anti-submarine warfare* capabilities of a growing number of purpose-built escorts and *escort carriers* during the second half of 1942. That permitted Western navies to take the war to the U-boats by forming "Support Groups" of hunter-killer ships and aircraft. These operated outside the convoy escort system, but in fundamental support of it. As the U-boat threat declined with more submarine sinkings, and as Allied shipping capacity increased with production of *Liberty Ships* and other vessels, oceanic convoys increased in size until some exceeded 100–120 ships.

The Soviet Navy formed several desperate evacuation convoys in the eastern Baltic in August 1941. That campaign witnessed the single worst convoy action of the war, in which 60 ships were lost and 12,000 died. Neutral Sweden convoyed in the Baltic against the Soviet Navy later in the war. The main convoy activity in the north saw *Lend-Lease* aid carried in Western Allied ships to Soviet Arctic ports. Convoys left Scotland or Iceland, heading to Russia via the North Sea and Arctic Circle routes, across the Barents Sea between Norway and Russia. Surviving ships pulled in to Murmansk, Archangel, or Molotovsk. The first Arctic convoy set out carrying British weapons to Russia in August 1941, within just two months of the start of *BARBAROSSA*. These convoys were threatened by German surface warships longer than were convoys in the Atlantic, from which the Kriegsmarine withdrew its major surface ships. Arctic convoys ran the risk of interception by powerful warships such as "Tirpitz," "Scharnhorst," "Lützow," "Hipper," and "Admiral Scheer." Arctic convoys were twice suspended as naval demands in other theaters drew escorts away from the passage around northern Norway in 1942, to even more desperate duty around Malta, then to protect the *TORCH* landings in North Africa. A third suspension of Arctic convoys was instituted from March to November 1943, as the U-boat war in the Atlantic crested and Allied navies were stretched to escort ship-bound armies from North Africa to Sicily, thence to Italy.

Northern convoys also faced greater danger from German aircraft over longer stretches of their routes. As soon as feasible they were provided with anti-aircraft escort ships and a few catapult-launched fighters. So important were the early Arctic convoys that some British aircraft were allowed by Moscow to base on Soviet territory. Arctic convoy escorts included surviving ships of several conquered northern nations, including Norway. Some were British warships with exiled Norwegian or other European crews. But most ships—surface escorts and merchantmen—were British. A few Soviet surface escorts joined some convoys. Several Soviet submarines also patrolled in support of British submarines, on the watch as late as 1943 for German surface raiders hiding at anchor in Norwegian waters. Some Soviet Navy submarines traveled across two oceans to get to the Barents Sea from their prewar assignment with the Soviet Pacific Fleet. They traveled down the west coast of North America to cross through the Panama Canal, resupplied at U.S. and British bases along the way, passing through the Panama Canal into the Atlantic and thence to Soviet bases around the Barents Sea.

Loss rates on the treacherous Arctic routes in Europe were higher than any other convoy route, at nearly 8 percent. That aggregate figure for shipping losses meant further loss of many thousands of fighters, tanks, trucks, and huge amounts of raw material produced by the Western Allies and shipped out as Lend-Lease, sunk before it reached Soviet ports. Half a world away, American Lend-Lease convoys traveled up the Pacific coast of the United States before plying the rough and frigid waters of the Bering Sea, en route to Vladivostok. Many convoys made long legs of either northern route shrouded in the 24-hour blackness of northern winter nights. During summer, however, they were illuminated 24 hours per day as they passed over pale seas lit by the midnight sun. Losses on the northern Pacific route were insignificant compared to the high Atlantic, in part because the Imperial Japanese Navy preferred to hoard its highly capable submarines for fleet actions rather than disperse them as commerce raiders. Japan also respected U.S. and other neutral ships heading into Soviet ports before December 1941. Thereafter, the IJN feared the consequence of provoking Moscow by attacking U.S. Lend-Lease convoys, and abjured. That meant a great deal of war matériel was transhipped to Soviet Pacific ports, thence by the Trans-Siberian Railway to the Eastern Front where Russians used it to kill German soldiers. As with Atlantic convoys, as more and better small escorts became available in the Pacific later in the war they reinforced convoy protection. *Escort carriers* proved invaluable in both theaters. Lasting improvement in Allied convoy security arrived in the north once German air power was mostly bled out of Norway by transfers of Luftwaffe squadrons into brutal attritional combat in the Mediterranean and on the Eastern Front.

See also anti-submarine warfare; Armed Merchant Cruiser; ASDIC; balloons; Bucket Brigade; Catapult Aircraft Merchant (CAM); intelligence; radio; Replenishment-at-Sea; troop ships.

Suggested Reading: Arnold Hague, *The Allied Convoy System, 1939–1945* (2000); Bernard Ireland, *Battle of the Atlantic* (2003); Marc Milner, *North Atlantic Run* (1985); B. Schofield, *The Arctic Convoys* (1977).

CORAL SEA, BATTLE OF THE (MAY 3–8, 1942) This carrier battle in the Coral Sea was provoked by a Japanese plan to land an invasion force at Port Morseby on Papua New Guinea, with a smaller force ordered to set up a seaplane base at Tulagi in the southern Solomons and another in the Louisiades Islands ("Operation MO"). The Western Allied fleet was under overall command of Admiral *Chester Nimitz*. It comprised two carrier task forces and a third strike force of Australian and U.S. cruisers. Nimitz knew the Japanese were on their way from key breakthroughs in *ULTRA* naval intelligence, which provided the Americans with an immense—but not decisive—advantage in the engagement. The Japanese commander was Vice Admiral Inoue Shigeyoshi. His two invasion groups started from Truk and Rabaul, rendezvousing with escorts at sea. The escort was composed of a light carrier, four cruisers, and a destroyer, while a separate strike force comprising two fleet carriers, two heavy cruisers, and six destroyers looked to surprise Nimitz and his Task Force commander, Admiral *Frank Fletcher*.

In operations preliminary to the main carrier action, a Japanese troop convoy arrived unopposed at Tulagi on May 3. Its support ships were bombed by U.S. carrier-based aircraft the next day. Fletcher steamed for Port Moresby on May 6, separating his cruiser task force and sending it ahead to catch the other Japanese troop transports, while his carriers looked to engage their counterparts in the Japanese battlefleet. Identification errors and weather played major roles, as Fletcher's planes mistook the convoy escort for the enemy carrier fleet and attacked. The Japanese troopships pulled back out of range to await the outcome of the carrier fight. Meanwhile, Fletcher's planes found the light carrier IJN Shōhō and sank her. Japanese carrier planes were simultaneously making a mistake of their own. They sank two small American escorts but in the process revealed the approximate location of their home carriers. At dawn on May 8 both sides launched all-out strikes, looking to find and sink the other side's fleet carriers. American planes damaged one Japanese carrier but could not find the other. Better trained Japanese pilots flying superior naval aircraft found the U.S. carriers. They sank USS Lexington with bombs and torpedoes and damaged USS Yorktown with bombs, forcing Fletcher to withdraw his reduced fleet under cover of a smoke screen.

Although Coral Sea would eventually be assessed as a strategic draw, American losses were felt to be more grievous at the time. The battle was fought inside six months of the shock of losses at *Pearl Harbor,* and no one yet foresaw the great U.S. victory at *Midway* the following month. Instead, the loss of an invaluable fleet carrier was thought to have tipped the naval balance in Japan's favor, even if an overly timid Japanese commander failed to follow through with planned ground invasions. The U.S. Navy also lost a destroyer and a hugely important fleet oiler at Coral Sea, and suffered heavy damage to a second fleet carrier. The Japanese canceled the Port Moresby amphibious invasion while losing a light carrier, one destroyer, and several small transports. But two fleet carriers were badly damaged, and they lost many carrier planes and irreplaceable pilots. The battle is usually counted as a technical victory for the IJN but also a strategic failure, because it stopped the momentum of the Japanese advance into the South Pacific. Coral Sea also marked the end of U.S. naval decline, if not yet the reassertion of U.S. sea power. It spared northern Australia from attack by Japanese bombers that would have based around Port Moresby. Most importantly, damage to two Japanese fleet carriers subtracted those key assets from the coming battle at Midway in June. Coral Sea was the first naval battle in history in which ships were never in sight of one another, with all damage done by carrier-based aircraft. That was a portent of things to come in the Pacific War, which would see six battles between carrier fleets. The outcome also changed the way carriers fought by revealing to each side that it relied on carriers that were hugely powerful ships, but also highly vulnerable to dive bomber and torpedo plane attack. The Americans, in particular, responded by surrounding carriers with much thicker anti-aircraft screens.

CORFU
See Mussolini, Benito.

CORK PATROLS   Unofficial term for *anti-submarine warfare* sweeps of the Channel prior to the *OVERLORD* landings. They were designed to stop U-boats from penetrating to Normandy by keeping multiple aircraft in the area constantly, each sweeping the surface with search radar to force U-boats to submerge and to find and fix their position. Below the planes were destroyer patrols and six ASW Support Groups. Cork patrols intercepted and sank or damaged 10 U-boats in the first five days of the landings. Not one U-boat got through to attack the invasion convoys.

CORN COBS
See GOOSEBERRY.

CORONET   Code name for the planned Western Allied invasion of Honshu originally scheduled for December 1, 1945.
See DOWNFALL; Potsdam Conference.

***CORPO DI TRUPPE VOLONTARIE* (CTV)**   The Italian corps committed to the *Spanish Civil War (1936–1939)*. It totaled 75,000 men, of whom 49,000 served in Spain at the same time at the peak of its involvement. It fielded 700 aircraft, 2,000 artillery tubes, and many ineffective tankettes. It suffered about 16,000 casualties, including 4,300 fatalities. Its battlefield performance was better than is often reported, but wider lessons of its experience with poor equipment and doctrine were not learned by the Italian Army.

CORPO ITALIANO DI LIBERAZIONE
    See Italian Army.

CORPORATISM   The vague ideology of Italian *fascism* that viewed society as an organic whole with mutually reinforcing, functional parts called "syndicates" or "corporates." These comprised obligatory combines of labor and capital, ostensibly fairly mediated by the state. Corporatism mainly reinforced Benito Mussolini's personal dictatorship and the endemic corruption of his regime. It had roots in Catholic social doctrine and therefore was also experimented with in Portugal under António de Oliveira Salazar and in Spain under *Francisco Franco*.

CORPS   An operational unit controlling two or more divisions, numbering anywhere from 20,000 to 50,000 men at full strength. Actual corps might be overstrength or understrength and have many nondivisional troops attached. The Red Army eliminated the corps level of organization during the first two years of the war due to a shortage of officers caused by massive early casualties. Western Allied corps tended to expand in the last year of the war, while Wehrmacht corps contracted until they hardly counted as division strength. Japanese armies were two-division formations that would have been termed corps in Western Allied parlance.

CORREGIDOR, BATTLE OF (1942)   A fortress island in the mouth of Manila Bay, across from the Bataan peninsula. Corregidor was the locale of fierce fighting in the first five months of 1942. Its shore batteries held off the Japanese Navy while an American and Filipino garrison held out against the Japanese Army for several months. The defense was overseen by Lt. General Jonathan Wainwright, who held out for an additional month after General *Douglas MacArthur* was ordered to leave the Philippines. The Japanese landed on the island on May 5. The garrison—starving and with over 1,000 wounded men huddled in dank tunnels—surrendered the next day. The prisoners suffered terrible abuse while in Japanese hands. Survivors were liberated in March 1945. An emaciated Wainwright stood behind MacArthur during the Japanese surrender ceremony aboard the USS Missouri in Tokyo Bay on September 2, 1945.
    See also Philippines campaign (1941–1942).

CORSICA   This French island was governed by *Vichy* from June 1940, until it was occupied by Italian forces in November 1942. Local *maquis* carried out small attacks against the Italians. The island had no strategic importance to the Western Allies while they were bogged down in Italy during 1943. Upon the Italian surrender to the Allies that September, the Wehrmacht transferred its Sardinian garrison to Corsica as part of Operation ANTON. The Germans arrived before the Allies could get men onto the island, then quickly decided to leave. A *Free French* battalion landed on September 15, in the middle of a hasty German evacuation of only recently disembarked troops. As the Germans pulled out, they were harassed by the French, by the Maquis, and even by some Italian troops who switched sides. However, the Wehrmacht got most of its men off the island by the first week in October. The Western Allies subsequently installed 12th Tactical Air Command on 14 Corsican airfields.

CORVETTES   A series of escort ship types that began with the "Flower" class, which first saw service in July 1940. The top speed of a "Flower" was reduced to just 16 knots by prewar design errors that aimed at enabling it to perform secondary roles in minesweeping and as a fleet tug. Flowers proved nearly unseaworthy in bad North Atlantic weather, and at least one broke in half in a storm. They were usually built in smaller British yards that could just manage their frames, thereby freeing main yards to build bigger warships. Some were built in Canada. Longer, faster, twin-screwed "River" class corvettes were built to make up early deficiencies of the "Flowers." From 1942, "River" ships were reclassified as *frigates*. A third "Castle"-class of corvette was still built for a time in small yards. It was longer than a "Flower"-class ship by 35–50 feet and armed with the latest *anti-submarine warfare* weapons, notably a *Squid* three-barreled mortar. However, frigates proved more capable and stable than any corvette. All corvette construction was therefore halted in 1943 to build more "River"-class frigates.

COSSAC   "Chief of Staff to the Supreme Allied Commander." An Anglo-American joint planning group established in March 1943. It arose from a decision on invasion planning made at the *Casablanca Conference (January 14–24, 1943)*. It preceded establishment of *SHAEF* in February 1944. COSSAC set out preliminary plans for the *OVERLORD* invasion of France and for a supporting series of *deception operations* that came to be collectively called *FORTITUDE*. The COSSAC plan for the main invasion was approved at the *Québec Conference* in August 1943, but substantially modified by General *Bernard Law Montgomery* and others in early 1944.

COSSACK POST   U.S. forces term for a night-time observation post. British troops called this a "listening post," befitting a natural reduction in visual acuity at night.

COSSACKS   Many Cossacks fought against the Germans on the Eastern Front. Their horses could maneuver around frozen German guns and vehicles, as during the *Moscow offensive operation* (December 5, 1941–January 7, 1942). More than 50,000 Cossacks joined an anti-Soviet army set up by the Germans from Soviet prisoners of war and led by ex–Red Army General *Andrei Vlasov*. The Western Allies deported tens of thousands of Cossack survivors to the Soviet Union after the war. Joseph Stalin ordered them all shot.

See also Osttruppen.

COUNTERBATTERY FIRE   When divisional artillery batteries fired against enemy batteries to suppress fire. If additional artillery at corps level was called in, the practice was referred to as "counter-bombardment."

See also radio.

COUNTER-INTELLIGENCE CORPS (CIC)   The U.S. Army counterintelligence organization. It operated wherever the U.S. Army went.

COURLAND   As part of Latvia, Courland was annexed to the Soviet Union in 1940. It was overrun by the Wehrmacht in the opening phase of *BARBAROSSA* in 1941. It was reattached to Soviet-occupied Latvia at the end of the war.

See also Baltic offensive operation (1944); Courland Pocket.

COURLAND POCKET   Under overall command of Marshal *Alexander M. Vasilevsky,* the Red Army's Baltic Front broke through to the Baltic coast on the west side of Riga on July 31, 1944. It had made a bloody and arduous trek to reach the coast, so Vasilevsky paused to regroup and rest the troops. By mid-September he was ready to resume the advance, joined now by the Leningrad Front under Marshal *Leonid A Govorov.* The Soviets struck on September 14, launching the *Baltic offensive operation (September 14–November 24, 1944),* which drove the remnants of Army Group North into a shrinking pocket on the Courland (Kurland) peninsula, a feat achieved only after ferocious infantry and tank battles and heavy Russian losses. Most of the dreaded and despised Army Group North, which tormented Leningrad for 28 months, was shattered. By October, remnants of 33 badly attrited Wehrmacht divisions crowded into a shrinking pocket on Courland. They were led by *Ferdinand Schörner,* who had been forced out of Riga by relentless Red Army pressure. Schörner asked Adolf Hitler for permission to pull out of Courland as well, but was given a *Haltebefehl order.* Worse, he was stripped of several divisions, which Hitler pulled out to reinforce Army Group Center, which was then being driven back across Poland and east-central Germany by massive rolling offensives by the Red Army. Hitler again forbade evacuation of Schörner's 300,000 men in January 1945. Instead, he uselessly renamed Schörner's command "Army Group Kurland."

It became increasingly difficult to feed hordes of German civilian refugees who crowed into the pocket, fleeing ravages of the Red Army in East Prussia. Hitler replaced Schörner with a new commander in January and ordered "Army Group Kurland" to attack out of the pocket. When the assault failed bloodily, Hitler sacked the new commander as well. In the last months of the war, Hitler made wholesale changes in command all around the Wehrmacht, often out of desperate and impulsive rage. As several giant Fronts of the Red Army raced for Berlin from January to April, 1945, Russian and German troops in the Courland Pocket waged an almost separate and terrible war of their own that is often forgotten today. Meanwhile, the *Kriegsmarine* battled ferociously against Soviet submarines and VVS bombers, sacrificing its last surface ships in desperate evacuations of civilians and wounded soldiers from Courland, along with numerous panicked Nazi Party fat cats. The worst maritime disasters in history occurred during these evacuations, each counting lost lives many times greater than the tragedy of the "Titanic." The last Germans in Courland surrendered on May 10, 1945.

COVENANT OF THE LEAGUE OF NATIONS
See League of Nations; Versailles, Treaty of (1919).

COVENTRY RAID (NOVEMBER 14–15, 1940)   Coventry was a small British city in the midlands famed for its medieval cathedral. It was attacked by Luftwaffe bombers using new target finding aids for the first time. *Hermann Göring* was so pleased with the destructive results he spoke afterward of "coventrieren," or dealing out similar treatment to other British cities. In a war that saw far more destructive air raids in a hundred other locales, Coventry stands out in popular memory for two reasons. First, its great cathedral was destroyed by the bombs. Second, a false story circulated after the war that Winston Churchill knew about the raid in advance but refused to vector in fighters to defend the city to protect the more important secret of *ULTRA* intelligence. That tale was proven false by the release of British intelligence documents in 1979. The British knew a major raid was coming but did not know its target, and Churchill certainly did not know that the Coventry sky was where Göring's new *Knickebein* beams intersected.

COVERING FIRE   A basic small-unit, infantry assault tactic. A squad of 12–15 men divided into sections. One scouted, the second advanced, while the third supplied covering fire. In company-sized infantry assaults it was common for tanks to provide close support while infantry protected the tanks from anti-tank guns and enemy infantry. Among Western Allied infantry in the late stages of the war in Europe, this had the deleterious effect of infantry too often waiting for tanks to clear all opposition before advancing. That reduced aggression and slowed the advance.
See also marching fire.

CREEP BACK   Bomb aimers in the main Allied bomber stream over Germany often dropped their loads as soon as they saw marker fires in the bombsight reticule. Follow-on bombers would then drop upon sighting the first fire, which caused the bombing pattern to "creep back" from the target marked by the *Pathfinders*. Compensation for this effect was achieved by having Pathfinders mark beyond the intended target and by using colored flares and other markers or *Target Indicators (TIs)*. But in a very large raid creep back by many bombers in the stream was nearly inevitable. That reduced precision and increased collateral damage and civilian deaths in the suburbs. Alternately, it just cratered the countryside.

CREEPING BARRAGE   When artillery bombarded an enemy position according to a *fire plan*, "walking" the shelling up and over his lines at a measured and predetermined pace. Friendly infantry advanced behind the barrage, hoping to come upon the enemy before he recovered from its stunning effects. The technique was developed during World War I but perfected in World War II.

   See also rolling barrage; standing barrage.

CRERAR, HENRY (1888–1965)   Canadian general. Chief of the General Staff; commander of Canadian 2nd Division in Britain and of 1st Corps in Italy; commander of Canadian 1st Army in Normandy, the Low Countries, and Germany. He was not held in high regard as a field commander by Field Marshal *Bernard Law Montgomery,* but that was not known in Canada during the war.

   See also Canadian Army.

CRETE   This eastern Mediterranean island was captured by German *Fallschirmjäger* in the first ever large-scale paratroop assault in history, Operation MERKUR carried out in May 1941. On the ground there were 35,000 British, New Zealander, and Greek troops. The British forlornly hoped to hold onto Crete as a base for bombing Italy and the crucially important Rumanian oil fields at *Ploesti,* but their forces were in bad shape. Most had been recently driven out of Greece and were demoralized. They also lacked heavy weapons and motor transport. Their commander was a New Zealander, General *Bernard Freyberg.* The RAF had only 24 outmoded fighters on the island, mostly Fulmars and Gladiators. The Luftwaffe brought to the fight over 400 bombers, 180 modern fighters, and 500 transports—mainly older Ju-52s. Fallschirmjäger and their equipment were delivered by parachute and a fleet of 80 gliders. However, German military intelligence failed—as it so often did—to correctly estimate the large size of the garrison on Crete. Fortunately for the Wehrmacht, Freyberg had widely scattered his men and had too little transport to quickly concentrate once the Germans landed. Controversy still attends his decision to disperse. Some historians claim he had access to *ULTRA* intelligence but failed to act on it, but his biographer maintains that he was forbidden to do so to protect the ULTRA secret.

   Germans began falling from the sky on May 20. Although they captured the main airport at Maleme, they suffered staggering losses from ground fire. The British counterattacked the airport but failed to retake it. More German troops and heavy weapons landed once exhausted New Zealanders were pulled off a nearby hill by the local commander. Control of the airfield quickly turned the tide of the entire battle, as it permitted heavy reinforcements and weapons of the German 5th Mountain Division to be flown in to support the light infantry Fallschirmjäger. With Western Allied commanders looking to a German seaborne assault, they failed to concentrate against the growing threat building at Maleme, while suffering greatly from Luftwaffe bombing and strafing. Within five days the Germans were in clear control of the fight. On May 26 Freyberg signaled that the battle was lost and requested a seaborne evacuation. The British retreated to Sphakia on the southwest coast, from whence they were taken off the island. The evacuation was carried out under constant German artillery fire and bombing. The Royal Navy lost 9 warships defending Crete or during the evacuation; 17 more were badly damaged, most by land-based enemy aircraft. Of the ground forces, the British and their allies lost over 1,700 killed or missing, 2,200 wounded, and more than 11,300 prisoners.

About 5,000 British and Commonwealth troops were left ashore at Sphakia once the RN's ship losses became insupportable and the sea evacuation was halted. Most left behind were quickly taken prisoner, but some hid in the mountains. Many joined the local resistance to Axis occupation, fighting Germans and then Italians after Italy jointly occupied Crete until its own surrender to the Western Allies in September 1943. The Wehrmacht did not pull out of Crete until 1944. In the interim, the Western Allies were deprived of use of Crete's air fields to bomb Germany's vital oil supplies at Ploesti. Nor was Crete available as a base from which to support Churchill's strategy of supporting Balkan resistance groups harassing Axis occupation forces, or threaten the strategic southern flank, which was exposed by Germany's invasion of the Soviet Union in June 1941. Adolf Hitler drew very different lessons about the utility of airborne operations than did the British and Americans from MERKUR. He never trusted airborne assault again, while the Western Allies built up a large airborne army and carried out several major drops in Western Europe. Control of the island reverted to Greece after the war.

See also Malta.

CRIMEA The Crimean peninsula saw a great deal of fighting, starting with spectacular success by the Wehrmacht's Army Group South during *BARBAROSSA* (1941). The Red Army fought desperately to hold the Soviet Navy's Black Sea Fleet bases and defend the peninsula during the *Donbass-Rostov defensive operation (September 29–November 16, 1941)*, but its forces were crushed. That led to the *Kerch defensive operation (November 1941)* and an awful, seven-month long *siege of Sebastopol* that only ended on July 4, 1942. Adolf Hitler had plans for colonization of the conquered Crimea by ethnic Germans, and to that end committed large forces to take and to hold it—many critics say too large and for too long. He was concerned in the short-run that the Red Army Air Force (VVS) would use Crimean bases to bomb Germany's oil supplies drawn from *Ploesti*, Rumania. In any case, the Wehrmacht used the conquered Crimea as a major base for forward operations into the Caucasus in 1942.

The Red Army returned to the Crimea in November 1943. The Soviets assaulted under the false impression that Hitler intended to evacuate the peninsula. Instead, Hitler ordered the Taman peninsula on the Crimean side of the Kerch Straits held while the main fight in the east took place at *Kursk,* followed by the *Second Battle of Ukraine*. The Black Sea Fleet failed to prevent a spectacular evacuation of over 250,000 Axis troops of Army Group A across the Kerch Straits during September–October, while losing three new destroyers. North Caucasus Front put 150,000 men into the Crimea by amphibious assault across the Kerch Straits in early November, as the Wehrmacht finally evacuated Taman. This "Independent

Coastal Army" saw heavy fighting around its several beachheads and lost one of them, along with 7,000 casualties. The main Soviet assault on the Crimea awaited a spring offensive from the north, in tandem with a breakout by Coastal Army. Liberation of the peninsula began in April 1944, as the Red Army launched a massive offensive employing 470,000 men against 200,000 poorly supplied German defenders. Soviet successes in Ukraine sealed the top of the peninsula, although the Germans held the Perekop Isthmus for five months in 1944.

Five German and seven Rumanian divisions were trapped in the Crimea, but Stalin and the Stavka refused to permit any major surface ships to operate under fire, recoiling in dismay from the naval losses of October. That excess naval caution lessened the victory that came at Sebastopol in May 1944. A flotilla of small German ships and barges was massively bombed and shelled by air, but about 130,000 German and Rumanian troops of 17th Army escaped to Constanta on the far Rumanian shore. They could have been stopped by the big guns of Soviet destroyers, cruisers, and the Black Sea Fleet's single dreadnought, but none of those ships was allowed to fight. Another 21,000 Axis troops made it out by air. After the liberation of Sevastopol on May 9–10, Axis survivors who missed the sea and air evacuations fled to Kherson. Some 25,000 were trapped on the cliffs and slaughtered or taken prisoner on the 12th. The whole of the Crimea was liberated by May 13. Five days later, Stalin began forced deportations of 200,000 *Tartar* civilians. They were shipped to Siberia in cattle cars under *NKVD* supervision. At least 10,000 died during the voyage, most from typhus. Soviet military losses in liberating the Crimea were about 18,000.

See also amphibious operations; Kerch-Feodosiia operations; Kulik, Grigori; Soviet Navy; Yalta Conference.

CRIMES AGAINST HUMANITY   In a "London Agreement" signed by the major Allies in 1945, several postwar conventions were signed that governed legal trials of captured war criminals. One of the London agreements defined certain acts as "crimes against humanity." The original definition included wartime acts of enslavement, extermination, forcible deportation, and genocide. The first formal charge was made before the *Nuremberg* and *Tokyo Tribunals*. The intention was to elevate respect for ideas of the rule of law and inalienable human rights by focusing attention on heinous acts against whole populations, rather than individuals. In 2001 certain acts of rape were added to the definition, which expanded to include "sexual slavery."

See also crimes against peace; war crimes.

CRIMES AGAINST PEACE   In a "London Agreement" signed by the major Allies in 1945, certain acts were defined as crimes against peace. The definition was vague and remains controversial, but at its core was prohibition of "planning, preparation, initiation or waging a war of aggression." Since aggression remains singularly ill-defined in international law, and because preparations for self-defense or deterrence may be markedly similar to preparations for offense and aggression, some legal thinkers still reject this category of international crimes. Others argue that it became settled law after World War II led to trial precedent, court rulings, convictions, and executions.

See also crimes against humanity; Nuremberg Tribunal; Tokyo Tribunal; war crimes.

CRIPPS, RICHARD STAFFORD (1889–1952) British ambassador to the Soviet Union, 1940–1942; member of the War Cabinet; minister of aircraft production, 1942–1945. A fierce critic of Winston Churchill's war management and tendency to concentrate all important decisions in the prime minister's office, Cripps was a shrewd thinker, a capable diplomat, and a highly valuable manager of war industry.

CROATIA In 1939 Croatian *fascists* led by Ante Pavelic launched a terrorist campaign that aimed at secession and independence from Yugoslavia. In 1941 a puppet regime working for the German occupation accepted divided German and Italian authority over Croatia. The new regime took Croatia into the *Axis alliance* when it signed the *Tripartite Pact* on June 15, 1941. Extremists in the *Ustaše* committed wartime atrocities against Serbs, Jews, Muslims, and Communist *partisans,* murdering perhaps half a million. Croatia was forced back into Yugoslavia upon Germany's defeat in 1945. *Tito* ordered bloody reprisals against tens of thousands of Croatian collaborators.

See also Yugoslavia.

CRUISER A medium tonnage and medium-armored warship, capable of high speeds and independent cruising. In traditional fleet actions, cruisers were used to locate the main capital ships of the enemy fleet. Unlike simple scouts or destroyers, a cruiser was expected to be capable of *cruiser warfare* as well as independent action against significant warships when necessary, to be able to defend against more powerful ships, and to disengage quickly without being crippled and speed away to report. The *Five Power Naval Treaty* (1922) limit of 10,000 tons for cruisers made it impossible during the interwar years to design a properly balanced yet fully legal heavy cruiser, in terms of speed, armor, and armament. The Italian and Japanese Navies simply ignored the limit. Japan then withdrew from the treaty system in 1936. The Germans built a "Hipper class" of 14,000-ton heavy cruisers. The three Western signatories observed the limit, building cruisers up to it but packing them with additional armament. Of course, all limitations were abandoned once the war began. During the war most new heavy cruisers built by the Western Allies sported eight-inch guns, while those newly classed as light cruisers mounted six-inch guns. However, overall tonnage increased dramatically, with some American heavy cruisers reaching close to 20,000 tons and light cruisers topping out at 10,000 tons. Two truly outsized "large cruisers" were built by the United States to compete with so-called *pocket battleships*. The U.S. large cruisers did not see action against those German ships, which were instead dealt with by the Royal Navy. The Kriegsmarine had built pocket battleships before the war to a standard that heavily outgunned all enemy *treaty cruisers*. They were intended to serve as unstoppable commerce raiders, in which role they very much frightened the British until they were knocked out.

See also Armed Merchant Cruiser; auxiliary cruiser; battlecruiser.

CRUISER WARFARE Also known as "commerce raiding." These rules were formally set in the 19th century. They required that a surface raider must give enemy merchantmen fair warning and make provision for the safety of enemy or neutral crew and passengers before sinking a ship. That could mean transporting civilians and crew to a neutral port, but at least providing lifeboats, food, and water. Such rules could not be followed by submarines due to their inherent vulnerability to ramming by any larger surface ship, or to fire from armed merchantmen or escort vessels. Submarines had extremely limited internal space and supplies, which did not permit taking survivors onboard. The resulting tension between law and reality led to enormous friction between the United States and Germany during World War I, culminating in issuance by Woodrow Wilson of the "Lusitania Notes" in 1915. U.S. entry into the war in 1917 was provoked by Imperial Germany's resumption of *unrestricted submarine warfare.* A renewed effort to apply rules of cruiser warfare to submarines was made in the *London Submarine Agreement (1936).*

At the start of World War II, all major navies avowed adherence to the London rules. Adolf Hitler initially ordered his U-boats not to sink passenger liners even if they traveled with convoys. His concern was strictly to avoid incidents that might provoke the United States. Not for a moment was Hitler or the U-boat command of the Kriegsmarine constrained by moral or legal considerations: Hitler's order was rescinded within a month. On September 23, 1939, after just three weeks of war, Germany warned that it would sink any ship that used its radio for any reason once it was located by a U-boat. A week later unrestricted submarine warfare was declared in the North Sea. In mid-October, U-boat captains were told they could sink any ship running blacked out to 20° West. A month later, the last restrictions were lifted on sinking identified passenger liners. That left only the U.S.-declared *War Zone* restricted to U-boats, and even there Germany warned that it would *sink on sight* any ship that zigzagged or ran blacked out. Subsequently, all combatant navies on both sides—without exception—abandoned cruiser rules in the conduct of submarine operations.

Also *see anti-submarine warfare; Armed Merchant Cruiser; Athenia, sinking of; Atlantic, Battle of; auxiliary cruiser; Dönitz, Karl; Laconia Order; merchant marine; neutral rights and duties.*

CRUSADER (NOVEMBER 1941) A British offensive operation assayed in November 1942, during the *desert campaigns (1940–1943).* British 8th Army pressed a real advantage in numbers of tanks against the *Afrika Korps* and Italians, for once taking General *Erwin Rommel* by surprise. But British armored doctrine, officers, and training had not mastered combined-arms operations, and the advantage was wasted in sequential brigade-sized tank assaults that were often unsupported even by infantry. The Germans also made mistakes, such as a wasteful counterattack without proper intelligence or air cover. The British offensive failed, possibly along with the command nerve of General *Alan Cunningham*. The main failure came in the face of heavy casualties inflicted by enemy resistance along the Sidi Rezegh ridge. Hesitation in continuing the advance led to Cunningham's dismissal and replacement by General *Claude Auchinleck,* who resumed the attack on November 26. The New Zealand 2nd Division retook the ridge line in a bloody fight, but was assaulted and thrown off the ridge on December 1 by a German counterattack. That rebuff cut the corridor to the besieged British garrison of *Tobruk.* British and Commonwealth forces suffered nearly 18,000 casualties in CRUSADER while inflicting over 24,000 on the Germans and Italians. Even so, Rommel had again unnerved an offensive by a much larger British 8th Army.

CRYPTANALYSIS The science and study of all methods of code making, *ciphers,* and rendering secret writing and of all procedures used in code breaking and analysis of secret writing.

CULTS OF PERSONALITY

See Emperor cult; fascism; Hitler, Adolf; Mussolini, Benito; Stalin, Joseph.

CULVERIN Code name for an invasion of Sumatra proposed by Winston Churchill in late 1943, and pushed by him in the face of mounting and finally bitter opposition from the *Chiefs of Staff.* Churchill promoted the invasion plan even after the Chiefs pointed out that it would require such massive shipping it could not be mounted before March 1945. It was finally canceled, but not before there were threats of resignations from the COS and the prime minister's relations with his military chiefs reached their nadir.

CUNNINGHAM, ALAN (1887–1983) British general. He commanded in the *East African campaign* against the Italian Army and briefly commanded British 8th Army in the *desert campaign* from August 1941. He fell out with his superiors, especially General *Claude Auchinleck,* and was sacked after a perceived failure in the defeat endured by 8th Army in *CRUSADER.* He never held another field command.

CUNNINGHAM, ANDREW (1883–1963) British admiral. First Sea Lord, 1943–1945; member of the *Chiefs of Staff* and the *Combined Chiefs of Staff.* Cunningham started the war as commander of Royal Navy forces in the Mediterranean. He masterminded the naval air strike against the Italian Army at *Taranto* in November 1940. His most critical job was keeping open the sea lanes to *Malta* and escorting convoys there under heavy air and submarine attack. He lost many ships, notably in the evacuation of ground forces from *Crete,* but won the naval war. Over nearly three years his Mediterranean fleet progressively reduced the Regia Marina, until its major ships ceased to venture from their home ports. In June 1942, Cunningham was sent to Washington to help organize the new Combined Chiefs of Staff committee. He then led all naval forces during the *TORCH* landings in North Africa in November 1942. There followed more amphibious operations in Sicily and at Salerno in 1943. He accepted the surrender of the Regia Marina at Malta in September 1943. He returned to London as First Sea Lord and oversaw the vast *NEPTUNE* naval operations of *OVERLORD* in 1944. He managed the final two years of the *Battle of the Atlantic (1939–1945)* and dispatch of the RN's *Task Force 57* to the Pacific in 1945. He was one of the outstanding naval figures not just of World War II, but in all British naval history. His younger brother was General *Alan Cunningham*.

See also Cape Matapan.

CURTIN, JOHN (1885–1945)   Australian prime minister, 1941–1945.
See Australia.

CURZON LINE   Named for British foreign secretary George Curzon (1859–1925), the Curzon Line was a proposal for settlement of the frontier between Poland and Russia after World War I. It was drawn up by the victorious Allies. It adhered roughly to the principle of self-determination by excluding from Poland certain eastern areas populated mainly by non-Poles. Poland rejected the proposal, keeping and expanding those territories during the *Polish–Soviet War* of 1920. In October 1939, the Curzon Line served as the boundary between western Polish lands annexed by Nazi Germany and eastern Polish territory annexed to the Soviet Union under terms of the *Nazi–Soviet Pact (August 23, 1939)*. In 1945 the Curzon Line marked the new border between postwar Poland and a greatly expanded Soviet Union. It was settled upon by the major Western Allies and Soviet Union over vehement objections of Polish nationalists and the government-in-exile.

See also Tehran Conference.

CYPRUS   During World War II this British colony in the eastern Mediterranean hosted RAF air bases flying convoy protection missions. Later, it served as a base for launching an ill-advised operation against isolated German garrisons in the Aegean Islands. It was bombed only a few times. Greek Cypriots were staunch supporters of the British after the fall of Greece in 1940. By 1945 over 30,000 volunteered to serve with British military forces.

CZECHOSLOVAKIA   Historic Bohemia was joined to Moravia and Slovakia to form the new state of Czechoslovakia in the last days of the Austro-Hungarian Empire in 1918. Led by *Tómaš Masaryk* and *Eduard Beneš* during the 1920s and 1930s, this small democracy joined the *Little Entente* in 1920. In the 1930s it sought security guarantees from the Western Allies as *Nazi Party* agitators and *fifth columnists* stirred secessionist sentiment in the ethnically German border country of the *Sudetenland*. At the *Munich Conference (September 29–30, 1938)*, to which Czech representatives were not invited, the Sudetenland was handed to Adolf Hitler by the leaders of France, Britain, and Italy. *FALL GRÜN* (Case Green) was the German war plan for invasion of Czechoslovakia in 1938, but Hitler was frustrated in his desire to implement it because of the policy of *appeasement* pursued by the Western Allies at Munich. There were some in the Czech government and Army who wanted to depose Beneš and fight in 1938, despite full knowledge of certain defeat. Beneš won out, but the settlement with Germany was fleeting: Hitler quickly moved to occupy the rump of the Czech state that remained when his Panzers rolled into Prague on March 15, 1939. There was no armed resistance of any kind. The Germans seized Czech foreign reserves, the extensive Czech armaments industry, and all weapons and military supplies. Evidence emerged after the war that, had Hitler and Germany won, there were Nazi plans in place to deport most of the non-German population of Bohemia and resettle the region with "German stock."

Czechoslovakia was divided into puppet states of the Nazi empire from 1940 to 1945. President Emil Hácha was the Nazi puppet in Bohemia and Moravia. The occupation was brutal, especially under the "butcher of Prague," *Reinhard Heydrich*. But with the obvious exception of Czech Jews, it was less horrific than the fate suffered by Poles or Ukrainians, as most Czechs actually benefited from economic expansion tied to German war production. During *FALL WEISS (1939),* the Wehrmacht used parts of Slovakia as assembly areas and jump-off points for the invasion of Poland. Participation of some Slovak soldiers in the assault earned that puppet state 300 square miles of Polish territory and de jure recognition from Moscow. Czech resistance to the Nazi occupation was limited, but still 350,000 of its citizens died during the war. With the Beneš government in exile in London, Czech pilots flew for the RAF in the *Battle of Britain* and thereafter. A Czech armored brigade of 5,000 men fought as part of the British Army in France in 1944. Some units of ethnic Ukrainians from eastern Slovakia formed under auspices of the Red Army and fought on the Eastern Front from 1941 to 1945. Larger units of Slovaks and Jews formed the Czechoslovak Independent Brigade, which fought at Kiev in 1943. The Brigade rose to a full corps under Ludvik Svoboda in 1944, once it was reinforced by Slovaks released by Stalin from *NKVD* prisoner of war camps. Other Czechs and Slovaks formed a VVS fighter air division.

Unlike the *London Poles,* the Beneš government was unable to sustain a significant military contribution to the war effort made in the West. Instead, it spent most time and energy planning for postwar recreation of an independent Czechoslovakia. Beneš obtained a meaningless repudiation of Munich from the British government and Free French in late 1942. He agreed to a deeply controversial treaty with the Soviet Union on July 18, 1943. Critics note that although it was basic realpolitik to foresee that a Soviet victory was the essential precondition to restoration of Czechoslovakia after the war, placing so heavy a wager on Joseph Stalin and a paper agreement was more misguided even than the bet Beneš made on the Western powers in 1938. The Beneš government also turned its back on prewar conceptions of Czechoslovak nationalism. It made its own plans to *ethnically cleanse* the Sudetenland of *Volksdeutsche.* That action was in fact carried out in 1945, in spite of clear knowledge of the fact that during the 1938 war scare most Sudeten Germans reported for military duty and were prepared to fight alongside their Czech and Slovak countrymen. Beneš and his advisers also were prepared to cede "Sub-Carpatho Ruthenia" to Stalin, a region they did not want because it contained mainly ethnic Ukrainians.

Meanwhile, the Nazi puppet state in Slovakia sent small ground and air units to fight against the Soviet Union. Formerly a province of the Austro-Hungarian Empire, after World War I Slovakia shared the twists and turns of the history of the Czech state. But during World War II the two provinces were split when a Nazi protectorate was set up in Slovakia under a local priest and *fascist* leader, Josef Tiso (1887–1947). Slovakia adhered to the *Tripartite Pact* and Axis alliance on November 23, 1940. In June 1941, it declared war on the Soviet Union. There followed declarations of war against the Western Allies in tandem with the German declarations of December 11, 1941. The Slovak population did not so readily embrace these pro-German policies. At the end of August 1944, the *Slovak Uprising* broke out. Like the *Warsaw Rising* in Poland, the Slovak rebellion was savagely crushed by the Germans by the end of October: it was as hard for small powers to leave the Axis at the end of the war as it was to resist annexation at its beginning. Slovakia was defended against the assaulting Red Army by German 1st Panzer Army. That was a misnamed force without any tanks which had no chance against the combat power it faced in Soviet 1st and 4th Ukrainian Fronts. Three Soviet armies broke part way into the Carpathians in September–October during what Russian historians call the "East Carpathian operation." After a two-month pause, a complimentary "West Carpathian operation" was launched in January–February, 1945. It was temporarily blocked by a stiffened defense by 600,000 Axis troops led by General *Ferdinand Schörner*. Stalin and the Stavka sacked the original Soviet commander, replacing him with General *Andrei Yeremenko*. He also had trouble with Slovakia's terrain: mountain fighting was new to much of the Red Army, while in Slovakia the Soviets faced German and *Waffen-SS* bitterenders. Yeremenko was reinforced and attacked again from March to May, 1945. His *"Bratislava-Brno operation"* went around the German flanks and up the Danube valley. Bratislava fell on April 4. Brno was taken on the 28th. Tiso was found hiding in a cellar. He was hanged as a traitor in 1947.

Prime Minister Winston Churchill urged the new American President, Harry Truman, to send American forces to take Prague. American 3rd and 7th Armies had advanced through Bavaria against light resistance and reached the border of western Bohemia on April 25, 1945. By Allied agreement, liberation of Prague was left to the Red Army. Citizens of the city had other ideas and rose on May 4, though perhaps more in celebration of expected liberation than in violent determination to liberate themselves. The rising cut off remnants of Army Group Center from escape to the west or back to Germany, so German troops tried to retake Prague. The Red Army arrived five days later, one day after a formal ceasefire and surrender agreement at Reims went into effect across Germany. The Soviets took down the last German resistance after a blistering artillery barrage. There was heavy fighting in other parts of Czechoslovakia by bitterenders in Army Group Center, especially among Waffen-SS units. More famously, there was some fighting with a demoralized division of the *Russian Liberation Army* that lasted until May 11. All that made Czechoslovakia the first territory invaded by German troops and the last from which they were violently expelled.

When the fighting ended, almost 720,000 Germans were marched off to Soviet POW camps. Most remained in harsh captivity for years, working as forced laborers in the Soviet Union. The Red Army put its losses for nine months of the Czech and Slovak campaigns at 140,000 men. When the Soviets withdrew their armed forces from the country, Beneš returned as president of a restored Czechoslovakia. The dawn of liberation did not last long: in 1946 Beneš appointed a Communist prime minister in yet another foolhardy placatory gesture toward Moscow. In February 1948, a Communist coup forced Beneš to resign. Klement Gottwald, a harsh Stalinist, thereafter embedded Czechoslovakia deep inside an emerging postwar "Soviet bloc."

Suggested Reading: Chad Bryant, *Prague in Black: Nazi Rule and Czech Nationalism* (2007); Vojtech Mastney, *The Czechs Under Nazi Rule* (1971).

D

DACHAU   One of the first *concentration camps* set up by the Nazis after they took power, Dachau was located just outside Munich. Its regulations were developed by *Schutzstaffel (SS)* commandant Theodore Eicke. At the end of 1933 the Dachau model was imposed on other SS detention camps and camps set up by the *Sturmabteilung (SA)* and Ministry of Justice. Dachau evolved into the main administrative center for a circle of slave labor camps throughout southern Germany and Austria. Most of the killing was done in the satellite camps. Dachau was not a *death camp* per se, but many died there anyway. At first they were beaten to death or shot. Most later murders were by hanging from a great beam installed specifically for that purpose next to crematoria used to burn remains, which were installed in 1942. Dachau was also used to house prominent political and military prisoners, including Austrian Chancellor *Kurt von Schuschnigg,* French Premier *Léon Blum,* and several out of favor Wehrmacht generals, notably *Franz Halder.* It was the scene of some of the worst medical experimentation of the *Holocaust,* competing with barbarities at Auschwitz in depravity and cruelty. Upon liberation by U.S. forces in 1945, most citizens of Munich claimed they knew nothing about Dachau. General *Dwight Eisenhower* was so angered by that falsehood he ordered local civilians walked through the camp and made them help with disposal of the last corpses so that they could never again disown what had been done within range of the spring breezes that had carried the stench of the dead to their comfortable homes.

See also Malmédy massacre.

DAKAR   In August 1940, British leaders were determined to establish General *Charles de Gaulle* in a major French overseas base. They also wanted to prevent Vichy forces in Senegal from lending aid to German U-boats hunting off the coast of Africa and in the South Atlantic. They therefore sent a joint British and *Free French* expedition to take Dakar by land and sea. De Gaulle was onboard ship along with 7,000 Anglo-French troops. A four-cruiser squadron of the Marine Nationale slipped out of the Mediterranean in September en route to support Vichy ground forces in Gabon and to try to retake French Cameroun. It paused in Dakar. It was met there by the Anglo-French force attempting to take the port. The Vichy squadron fled on September 19, but two ships were forced back into port. The other two were forced to surrender later at Casablanca. The Vichy battleship "Richelieu" and other ships in the harbor at Dakar fired on the British and Free French convoy, severely damaging a cruiser and an old dreadnought. A partial landing was carried out on September 23, but effective resistance from the alerted Dakar garrison caused the main landing to be canceled two days later. The debacle severely damaged de Gaulle's prestige in London. The Dakar failure also caused the British to withhold advance operational information from Free French forces for the remainder of the war, further exacerbating Allied tensions.

DALADIER, ÉDOUARD (1884–1970) French premier 1933, 1934, and 1938–1940. Leader of the Radical Socialist party, he played second fiddle to *Neville Chamberlain's* lead at the *Munich Conference*. He had earlier supported the British policy of *appeasement* of Adolf Hitler, but without the same enthusiasm as his British counterpart as Daladier had fewer delusions about Germany or Italy. Daladier acted with increasing authoritarianism at home after Munich, presenting himself as savior of peace and defender of the Empire, but presaging to some degree Vichy's later turn against foreigners and Jews. Daladier's foreign policies firmed from March 1939, in tandem with Britain's. In late August he declined an Italian invitation to a conference on the building Polish crisis, saying that he would resign before attending a "second Munich." Daladier took over the post of foreign minister from Georges Bonnet 10 days into the war, on September 13, 1939. He refused to consider peace talks unless Hitler first withdrew from all conquests in the east. Daladier resigned as premier in March 1940, citing refusal by his cabinet to support Finland in the *Finnish–Soviet War (1939–1940)*. However, he remained minister of war and foreign minister for much of the catastrophic defeat suffered by France during *FALL GELB*. Along with *Léon Blum* and General *Maurice Gamelin*, Daladier was put on trial at Riom in 1942, as Vichy officials looked to fix blame for France's defeat in the "War of 1939–1940" on its internal enemies. The trial was canceled when Blum's brilliant oratory turned it into a showcase against Vichy's policy of *collaboration*. Daladier was deported to Germany, where he remained a prisoner until 1945. He resumed his political career after the war during the shaky "Fourth Republic." He retired from politics in 1958.

DALMATIAN ISLANDS The *Treaty of Rapallo* (1920) split the Dalmatians between Yugoslavia and Italy. Germany and Italy jointly governed the islands and the Dalmatian coast of occupied Yugoslavia from April 1941. Most Croats left the Italian zone, or "Governatorato di Dalmazia." The Italian occupation ended in September 1943, and German troops garrisoned some islands after swiftly disarming the Italians. British troops occupied Vis, where *Tito* established a partisan headquarters for five months starting in May 1944. British relations with antifascist partisans in the Dalmatian Islands were often fractious and deeply suspicious. The British used Vis as a base to launch amphibious raids against surrounding island and mainland garrisons. The most notable action was a three-day assault on Brac. The German base on Brac was finally overrun in October 1944. An airfield on Vis hosted elements of the *Balkan Air Force* and serviced wounded bombers returning from Germany. Western Allied bombers hit the island of Zara in 1944. It was "ethnically cleansed" of Italians by the Yugoslavs in 1945.

DAM BUSTERS
See Ruhr dams.

D'ANNUNZIO, GABRIELE (1863–1938) Italian nationalist. A 52-year-old poet who urged war against Austria in 1915, he volunteered when war came and was wounded in combat. Fiume had long been coveted by Italian nationalists but was not ceded to Italy as hoped at the Paris Peace Conference, causing the Italian delegation to storm out in April 1919. D'Annunzio led a handful of fanatics in seizure of Fiume. He held the city for a year in spite of opposition by the main Allied powers. Benito Mussolini learned much from D'Annunzio's cult of "action." They also shared utter contempt for democracy.
See also mutilated victory.

DANZIG Polish: Gdańsk. Detached from Germany and declared a demilitarized and "free city" at the Paris Peace Conference in 1919, Danzig was placed under the administration of a *League of Nations* commissioner. Poland took charge of its customs and exports, gaining access to its port facilities through the *Polish Corridor,* which connected Danzig to the rest of Poland. German–Polish relations suffered greatly from this unwieldy arrangement. Danzig was a hated symbol for almost all Germans of the hypocrisy of the Western Allies as encoded in the *Treaty of Versailles* (1919), in the German view a clear violation of the promise of self-determination for nations and peoples. In the 1930s the status of Danzig became an international question pregnant with the possibility of a general European war, as Adolf Hitler instructed local Nazis to agitate for reunion with Germany. Those who feared war would result from the crisis and preferred *appeasement* asked rhetorically: "Who wants to die for Danzig?" In fact, quite a few in the West were prepared to do so: a French poll taken in 1939 found that 76 percent agreed that force should be used to stop Germany from taking the city. Hitler launched *FALL WEISS* against Poland on September 1, 1939, ostensibly to free the persecuted German population of Danzig. In 1945 the city reverted to Poland, which was moved north and west and given a long stretch of formerly German coastline along the Baltic. The

German population was roughly expelled so that the city became ethnically as well as legally Polish.

See also Teschen; Volk; volksdeutsch.

DARLAN, JEAN LOUIS (1881–1942) French admiral. Until the defeat of France in *FALL GELB* in June 1940, Darlan urged Paris and London to take a stronger line against Italian aggression and ambitions in the Mediterranean. He was not listened to, as *Neville Chamberlain* and his own government were bent on *appeasement* of Benito Mussolini to the moment Italy attacked France in June 1940. Darlan ordered the *French Navy* (Marine Nationale) scuttled should the Germans try to seize its ships, but he refused British entreaties to steam for French overseas ports. He was infuriated by the British assault on the French fleet at *Mers El-Kebir*. Darlan headed the Vichy navy and served as defense minister in Marshal *Henri Philippe Pétain's* government. He was also the great man's designated successor. Darlan moved into open, even eager, collaboration with Nazi Germany after he met Adolf Hitler in May 1941. He agreed to the *Paris Protocols* that conceded bases and military rights to Germany in French colonies in Africa and the Middle East. Without reciprocity or prompting, he warned the Kriegsmarine that its U-boats were signaling excessively and thereby giving away their positions. He even promised Berlin to destroy a French aircraft carrier and cruiser marooned in Martinique should the United States try to seize the ships. He was in Algiers visiting his son when Anglo-American forces landed on November 8, 1942, to carry out Operation *TORCH*. Darlan ordered the *Armée d'Afrique* to fire on the Western Allies. Some did, but most French defenders had little stomach for more than brief resistance. Some went over to the invading side within a day. Darlan then negotiated a cease-fire in exchange for recognition of his authority over Algeria as Allied appointee. That infuriated *Charles de Gaulle* but well-suited Franklin Roosevelt, who despised de Gaulle and long had sought another French leader. Darlan continued to enforce Vichy's anti-Semitic laws during his short rule in Algiers. On December 24, 1942, he was assassinated by a befuddled monarchist, an act that greatly relieved the Western Allies of an embarrassing arrangement.

DARWIN
See Australia.

***DAS REICH* DIVISION**
See Schutzstaffel (SS); Waffen-SS.

DAVITS Shipboard cranes employed to lower and raise smaller craft over the side of troop carriers, cargo, or warships.

DAWES PLAN
See Germany.

DAZZLE PATTERNS
    See camouflage.

D-DAY Western Allied term designating any given date for which a planned assault or invasion was set. "D" simply stood for an as yet to be determined "Day." Similarly, "H" stood for the anointed Hour of attack, as in "H-Hour." Days before the attack were referenced as D-1, D-2, and so on. Follow-on operations and target goals were counted as D+1, D+2, and so forth.
    See also J-Jour.

D-DAY (JUNE 6, 1944) The most famous *D-Day* of the war was June 6, 1944, marking the invasion of France and breaking into *Festung Europa* by the Western Allies. The term was permanently attached to that extraordinary day after the Western Allies disembarked five infantry divisions and three British armoured brigades onto five beaches in Normandy: "SWORD," "GOLD," "JUNO," "OMAHA," and "UTAH." The Western Allies landed 156,000 men by the end of the day, a powerful wedge of fighting men along with support personnel and thousands of military vehicles of all types. To move this massive force they assembled an enormous armada of 5,333 ships—ranging from battleships, cruisers, light cruisers, and destroyers, to PT boats, miniature submarines, and many types of specialized landing craft. Escorting and protecting the invasion fleet or bombing shore positions in advance of the landings were 12,837 aircraft ranging from reconnaissance and artillery fire-support scouts to heavy bombers and tactical dive bombers, as well as nearly 4,000 fighters. The Western Allies lost 127 aircraft on D-Day to all causes: accident, technical failure, and enemy action. The air armada included over 1,000 C-47s and nearly 900 gliders to transport 23,000 airborne troopers to the flanks of the invasion beaches during the night of June 5–6. British 6th Airborne Division, the "Red Devils," landed east of the Orne River in advance of three British and Canadian divisions set to land on the left flank on SWORD, GOLD, and JUNO. The U.S. 101st and 82nd Airborne Divisions were dropped on the right flank behind OMAHA and UTAH, but were widely scattered across the Côtentin peninsula from Ste. Maire Eglise to Carentan. Paratroopers and glider troops on the left flank took critical objectives during the night, notably the Orne River bridge brilliantly captured by British 6th Airborne. U.S. airborne troops took some of their objectives on the right flank of the invasion, but were mostly so scattered that their main effect was to sow confusion among the Germans as to what those objectives actually were. The chaos usefully delayed and confused German reinforcements heading to the beaches. Adding to that effect, thousands of "paradummies" equipped with fake machine gun noise and other battle sounds were dropped in areas the Western Allies had no intention of reaching with ground forces on D-Day.

    As the airborne troops reassembled on the ground and concentrated to take critical bridges and crossroads to permit ground forces egress from the coast, or fought sharp but isolated actions against surprised but recovering German troops, the invasion fleet approached. Above the warships, transports, and landing craft many hundreds of barrage balloons were anchored by cable to disrupt low-flying strafing runs by *Luftwaffe* aircraft. Only a handful of squadrons were available to Luftflotte 3 at forward airfields in Normandy, most of which were heavily bombed over the prior weeks and days. Other aircraft and forward air bases, including hurried reinforcements flying to Normandy directly from Germany, were destroyed before dark closed out "the longest day" in the West, as Field Marshal *Erwin Rommel* once called D-Day. Neither the Luftwaffe nor the Kriegsmarine seriously disrupted the invasion, despite fanatical orders to spare no air assets or U-boat crews in the effort to do so. Facing the Western Allies along the shore was a mainly infantry German defense force of just three divisions, including several battalions of demoralized or forcibly conscripted *Osttruppen* who surrendered as soon as feasible. The defense was supported by a paltry 169 aircraft. There were a total of 50 German divisions nearby to reinforce and stiffen resistance. The main question was: could German reinforcements arrive fast enough to block and defeat the invasion before the Western Allies put enough men ashore to hold the beachhead, then expand it into a lodgement to provide operational room to move inland?

Advice from senior officers experienced in amphibious assaults in the Pacific theater of operations, notably Major General Charles Cortlett, had been brushed away in the planning phase by Generals *Dwight Eisenhower, Omar Bradley,* and other overseers of the OVERLORD landings. Contrary to experience that showed the critical role of protracted naval fire, the D-Day bombardment was too short as well as imprecise: the beach assaults thus began with quick naval bombardments that proved mostly ineffective, as huge shells overflew defenses to kill trees and cows well behind the coast. It was not a mistake that would be repeated in later landings in France during *DRAGOON*. But on that terrible day in Normandy, insufficient naval support meant that most German defenses were intact when the infantry climbed out of their landing craft and headed ashore. British and Canadian troops were able to quickly overcome German obstacles and defenses in part through use of the excellent collection of specialized armor and other vehicles known as "Hobart's Funnies." These specialized armored vehicles included "swimming" tanks fitted with rubber floats and canvas screens; "crab" tanks, equipped with thrashers and flails for clearing mines; "bobbin" tanks that rolled out mesh as a temporary road over sand or clay; armored bulldozers; "Crocodile" flame-throwing tanks; "Armored Ramp Carriers" to bridge gullies and ditches; and other specialty tools such as demolition frames or fascine layers. One modified Churchill tank sported a petard spigot mortar that fired a 40 lb bomb for demolishing pillboxes.

Earlier *X craft* advance reconnaissance made of the British and Canadian beaches proved extremely valuable, ensuring that engineers had real success clearing obstacles and mines on D-Day. The Canadians were additionally fortunate that the OKW had just transferred to the Eastern Front a crack German division that had been defending the JUNO position, replacing it with a much weaker division. Canadian 3rd Division moved off JUNO while taking casualties of 340 killed, 574 wounded, and 47 taken prisoner. British 3rd Infantry Division suffered just over

600 casualties on SWORD but also cleared it relatively quickly, to press inland by mid-day. British 50th Infantry Division, 8th Armoured Brigade, Royal Marine Commandos, and elements of 79th Armoured Division together suffered 1,000 casualties on GOLD, but still made it off that beach more or less on schedule. They pushed hard against and past German 716th Infantry Division and elements of the crack 352nd Infantry Division. These casualties make clear that the impression that the other Western Allies somehow had it "easy" on D-Day compared to Americans must be set aside: by nightfall on June 6, British and Canadian casualties reached 4,300. There were also a number of Polish and Free French troops killed, wounded, or missing along the left flank of the invasion.

In the American sector, UTAH was taken relatively quickly by the U.S. 4th Infantry Division, which suffered 197 KIA and 60 missing against a weak and un-inspired defense by reluctant Osttruppen. Part of the reason for the rapid success at UTAH was good luck; to wit, an 1,800-yard navigational error in landing, which positioned 4th Division landing craft and assault waves outside presited ranges of German beach artillery. In addition, key German batteries behind UTAH were put out of action by the 101st Airborne. The worst fight of the day was on OMAHA, where the U.S. 1st Division and a regiment of 29th Infantry Division were mauled: most of the nearly 5,000 American casualties suffered on D-Day came fighting against the first-rate 352nd Wehrmacht division, which Allied intelligence had failed to identify. American troops were also denied critical on-beach assistance from "Hobart's Funnies" because of an earlier, purblind decision by Bradley not to accept the British offer to use them. Just as he had turned aside from other advice gleaned through experience in the PTO, Bradley cavalierly rejected the offer of Hobart tanks. Instead of "Funnies" on OMAHA, 1st Division immediately lost 29 amphibious Shermans, which were deployed too far out in heavy swells and went under with their crews. Only five 1st Division tanks reached the beach, though more arrived later from 29th Division. These few tanks then spun and ground steel treads in fine wet sand that had not been properly assessed in advance, until they were all knocked out by German anti-tank fire from pillboxes and beach guns left undamaged by the short naval bombardment. The infantry on OMAHA was therefore left exposed to pillboxes and other fortified defenses they did not have the weapons to overcome. Bradley's arrogance about how to conduct amphibious operations cost men's lives and nearly led to disaster at the outset of OVERLORD, as observers on either side of the fighting reported back to respective HQs that the OMAHA landing had failed. Lack of beach firepower was made up by several destroyers which disobeyed their orders not to approach too close to the beach for fear of hitting mines. Traveling forward and then in reverse up and down the length of OMAHA, their 5- and 6-inch naval guns blasted pillboxes while providing cover to infantry crawling through several defiles leading out of the dunes.

With five small beachheads established, troops and war matériel poured ashore. Some 23,000 airborne went in ahead of the assault: 15,500 Americans, 7,900 British, and some Canadians and Poles. By the end of D-Day, another 23,000 American troops landed on UTAH, while 34,250 made it onto OMAHA. The British and Canadians put 83,115 troops into France that first day, about

3/4s of them British: 21,400 on JUNO, 24,970 on GOLD, and 28,845 on SWORD. The invaders spent the next several days moving inland from five distinct beachheads, straining the individual perimeters in an effort to link them into a continuous front against rapidly stiffening German resistance. The Germans launched a Panzer thrust to prevent enlargement of the beachhead. It looked to reach the sea and split apart the British and Canadian left flank, a preliminary to rolling up the OMAHA and UTAH line and defeating the invasion in detail. But the Panzers failed in hard fighting against the British and Canadians: Hitler's "Atlantic Wall" was breached, the beaches were linked into a continuous front, and the *Normandy campaign* was underway. It was an astonishing achievement of technical and organizational skill, as well as of mass production, personal and collective heroic effort, and democratic leadership in a world war. Stalin himself said of the D-Day landings: "the history of war has never seen a comparable undertaking."

Western Allied air casualties included not just the 127 aircraft and crews lost on June 6, but 12,000 men and 2,000 planes lost in preparatory bombing operations from April to June. The air battles included wide-ranging bombing in the heavily defended Pas de Calais prior to and after the invasion, conducted as part of a key *deception operation*. There was also heavy bombing of French railheads, Luftwaffe air bases, and other rear area targets to disrupt German movement once the invasion began. The Allies lost 59 large and mid-sized ships on D-Day, along with over 100 more damaged to some degree. Best estimates of ground forces and airborne casualties suggest the British lost 2,700 men killed, wounded, or missing, while the Canadians lost another 946 men. The Americans suffered 6,600 casualties, of whom just over 2,400 were killed; the rest were wounded or missing. A large number of missing men later turned up alive or as German prisoners of war, most notably paratroopers from badly scattered light infantry that went in first and deepest on D-Day. German casualties are not reliably known, but best estimates place them at well over 5,000.

See also DD tanks; Widerstandsnest.

Suggested Reading: John Keegan, *Six Armies in Normandy* (1994); Cornelius Ryan, *The Longest Day: June 6, 1944* (1959).

DD TANKS "Duplex Drive tank." A Western Allied "swimming tank" adaptation in which a tank making an amphibious landing was kept afloat with an inflated and detachable apron. DD tanks were used in the *D-Day (June 6, 1944)* landings in Normandy. They had some success on the Canadian assault beach at JUNO but many floundered and sank at American landing sites on OMAHA.

DEAD ZONES
See partisans.

DEATH CAMPS Major *concentration camps* set up by the *Schutzstaffel (SS)* in pursuit of "final solution" of the latter stages of the *Holocaust.* In "regular" concentration camps many tens of thousands died, but detention rather than direct mass murder was the main function. "Death camps" were specially adapted or purpose-built camps of the *Aktion Reinhard* program, whose main function was "extermination" of entire populations and ethnic groups, principally but not exclusively Jews. They had attendant facilities for disposing of masses of human remains by industrial methods.

See Auschwitz; Belzec; Birkenau; Chelmno; Lublin-Majdanek; Sobibor; Sonderkommando; Theresienstadt; Treblinka; Zyklon-B.

DEATH MARCHES

See Bataan death march; British Borneo; concentration camps; Einsatzgruppen; Hungary; Vistula-Oder operation.

DEATH'S HEAD UNITS

See Totenkopfverbände.

DEBACLE, LE   French term for the defeat of 1940, which led to a great national debate about its causes.

See FALL GELB; France.

DEBRECEN OFFENSIVE OPERATION (OCTOBER 1944)

See Hungary.

DECEPTION OPERATIONS   Deception is as old as war. In World War II it was ubiquitous. It could be as simple as passive deception using natural foliage to *camouflage* machine gun nests or vehicles. Or it might employ sophisticated signals intelligence or double agents to plant false impressions that aimed to deceive an enemy into believing he knew future operational plans, or to mislead him about the size of opposing forces by either exaggeration or underestimation. The British were especially adept at turning enemy agents into double agents, and other imaginative planting of false information. They left dead officers in damaged vehicles, with false battle plans and misleading maps planted on the corpse that concealed sand traps or mine fields. On one occasion that later became famous, they sent a body and fake plans ashore from a submarine off Spain. Breaking light security and erecting false lighting over islands or starting fires in farmer's fields to lead enemy bombers to harmless areas away from high-value targets was commonplace, both in Britain and Germany. Although not subject to enemy air raids, the United States built some aircraft factories underground. These were covered with elaborate canvasses painted to look like a small town if seen from the air, replete with painted roads, canvass tent-houses, but real shrubbery. The Soviet Union also painted public squares to look like buildings, preventing their use as guideposts by Luftwaffe navigators. The Japanese Army used real treetops that were chopped off in some other locale, then transported to airfield construction sites and suspended by wires to conceal runway construction. The British disguised troop and tank movement behind the *El Alamein line* by leaving tents in place, along with canvas replicas of 400 tanks and over 2,000 heavy trucks, dummy supply depots, and even a 20-mile long dummy pipeline.

World War II saw several of the largest and most successful active deception operations in military history, involving large-scale false SIGINT and radio patterns; multiple fake airfields and a few fake ports; and nonexistent armies replete with unit insignia and identifiable signals traffic emanating from mobile radio units with recorded and piped-in truck and tank sounds overheard by enemy microphones. With deception often succeeding only through detail, large-scale operations deemed subject to enemy air reconnaissance added inflatable rubber tanks and trucks, fake submarines, and even a dummy battleship as a deterrent added to a convoy escort or parked off the Suez Canal. Deception operations near the battlefield or prior to launching or defending against a major offensive were often critical to success, helping shape the battlefield and providing surprise or security for ongoing military operations. Camouflage and movement at night were the simplest form of frontline deception, but dummy radio traffic was almost constant. The Wehrmacht started the war with several successful deception operations, but more often by 1945 was the victim of sometimes quite spectacular deceits. Great Britain, the United States, and the Soviet Union all began the war with limited deception plans, concepts, or capabilities. The Red Army learned how to integrate its *maskirovka* operations into successful battle plans that repeatedly fooled Wehrmacht commanders, starting with the *Moscow offensive operation (December 5, 1941–January 7, 1942)*. Red Army maskirovka operations grew increasingly more sophisticated and successful as the war proceeded, as German military intelligence repeatedly failed to pierce the veil that covered Soviet movements, concentrations, and dispositions.

The Western Allies learned to integrate evermore sophisticated deceptions into planning for offensive campaigns. From 1942 they carried out major deception operations in every joint campaign they conducted. For instance, *BARCLAY* and *BODYGUARD* twice deceived Adolf Hitler and the OKW about where landings would occur in 1943 and 1944. The Western powers also ran a highly successful deception operation in Burma in 1944–1945. On the other hand, the series of *COCKADE* deceptions in 1943 all failed. The Western Allies received Soviet cooperation in carrying out successful deceptions of Hitler and the OKW on several occasions in 1944.

For other examples of deception *see Abwehr; BARBAROSSA; biological weapons; Brandenburgers; convoys; COSSAC; Devil's Brigade; El Alamein, Second; FORTITUDE North; FORTITUDE South; FUSAG; KREML; Kursk; intelligence; MI6; MINCEMEAT; Quaker gun; Special Operations Executive; Stalingrad; Targul-Frumos; ULTRA; XX Committee; ZEPPELIN.*

Suggested Reading: Charles Cruickshank, *Deception in World War II* (1979); David Glantz, *Soviet Military Deception in the Second World War* (1989); Michael Handel, ed., *Strategic and Operational Deception in the Second World War* (1987); T Holt, *The Deceivers: Allied Military Deception in the Second World War* (2004); Michael Howard, *British Intelligence in the Second World War, Vol V: Strategic Deception* (1990).

DECLARATION ON LIBERATED EUROPE (1945)   An endorsement of the loose war aims of the *Atlantic Charter* and concomitant promise of free elections to be held in Eastern Europe after World War II, signed by the "*Big Three*" at the *Yalta Conference* in February 1945. Charges were quickly made that the Soviets willfully violated it, starting with their occupation of Rumania in March. On the hard right in the United States, it was even said that Franklin D. Roosevelt and Winston Churchill had "sold out" Eastern Europe to Joseph Stalin. Given physical occupation of that region by the Red Army, it is hard to see what might have been done short of starting another major war that no one wanted and the populations of the West would not have supported, even while Japan remained undefeated in Asia. The Declaration was often cited in later political and diplomatic quarrels and remained highly controversial during the early years of the Cold War.

DECORATIONS
   See medals.

DEEP BATTLE   Like other armies that had experienced the carnage of trench warfare during World War I, in the interwar period the Red Army sought to develop operational doctrine that would permit it to break through static defenses in any future war. It developed a combined-arms offensive operations doctrine that called for deep penetrations into the enemy's flanks and rear areas by mechanized and airborne forces, interrupting resupply and communications and paralyzing any response to encirclement. This idea was closely associated with Marshal *Mikhail Tukhachevsky* and his circle, before he was purged. There is debate among military historians as to whether the idea itself became dormant as a result of the Red Army purges, with some arguing that the core problem caused by the purges was a disjuncture between Soviet doctrine and leadership capabilities. Another problem was that this doctrine assumed it would be the Soviet Union that chose the time and place of war and, therefore, that there would be time to fully mobilize. The events of *BARBAROSSA* left no time to do so in late June 1941, while the enemy seized the strategic and operational initiative. It was thus the Red Army that was surprised and stunned by the heaviness of an opponent's opening blows and deep operational thrusts. However, by 1943 the Red Army was a much different and vastly more capable force: its men and commanders were experienced and more skilled, and better trained and armed. The Red Army therefore implemented a revised version of its prewar doctrine during the second half of the war, several times creating great *kotel* upon encircling whole German armies.
   See also BAGRATION; Blitzkrieg; Germany, conquest of; Historikerstreit; keil und kessel; Kesselschlacht; Lend-Lease; mines.

DEEP OPERATIONS
   See BAGRATION; BARBAROSSA; BLAU; Blitzkrieg; deep battle; Kesselschlacht.

DEFENSIVELY EQUIPPED MERCHANT SHIP (DEMS)   Allied designation for an armed merchantman.

DE GAULLE, CHARLES ANDRÉ (1890–1970)   French general; war theorist; *Free French* leader; statesman and president of the "Fifth Republic" from 1958 to 1969. De Gaulle fought as a junior infantry officer during World War I. He was wounded and captured at Verdun in 1916. He was deeply impressed by the advent of sophisticated mechanized warfare in the last days of the Great War. He developed a theory of armored tactics in the interwar years and generally sought to modernize and professionalize the French Army, but his proposals were mostly ignored by his superiors before 1935. They were studied more closely by German armored theorists and Panzer commanders such as *Heinz Guderian.* De Gaulle's 4th Armored Division was one of the few French units to successfully counterattack exposed Panzer columns during *FALL GELB* in 1940. In the middle of the battle, on June 1, de Gaulle was promoted brigadier general, making him the youngest general in the French Army. Five days later he became undersecretary of state for war in the short-lived government of Prime Minister *Paul Reynaud.* De Gaulle thus served in the last government of the Third Republic, although he would later refuse to recognize that the Third Republic had ended in 1940, to be replaced by Vichy. The promotion and political office came too late, and gave him far too little power, to make reforms necessary to forestall defeat.

Determined to prolong the fight against Germany despite his junior political and military rank, de Gaulle greatly impressed Winston Churchill at their first three personal meetings in June 1940. It greatly helped that he endorsed Churchill's quixotic idea for a constitutional union of Britain and France, and their empires and armed forces, to continue the fight. De Gaulle's temperament and positions suited Churchill's own determination that merely a battle, but not the war, had just been lost in France. Refusing to accept defeat, de Gaulle resigned from the cabinet of Marshal *Philippe Pétain* and left for London: he was flown out by the RAF on June 18. He subsequently broadcast over the BBC a call for patriots to rally to his *Free French* movement. Ten days later, Great Britain recognized him as the true representative of France. Almost no one inside France or across the Empire accepted the grand claim by France's youngest general, whose political legitimacy rested on serving as a junior minister in a defeated government for just 10 days and on Churchill's personal support.

De Gaulle needed troops and at least some French overseas territory to sustain even a faint claim to British recognition and aid. In September 1940, he accompanied a British expedition that failed to capture *Dakar* in Senegal. The disaster of the failed landings at Dakar badly hurt his reputation in London. However, French Cameroon, Chad, and the French Congo quickly rallied to his cause, not least because of astute action by General *Philippe Leclerc,* whose forces invaded and took control of Gabon after four days of fighting in November. The territory of the French Empire in West Africa, along with a single Legion from the *French Foreign Legion,* became the basis of de Gaulle's late 1940 claim to represent France. He proved his mettle when he sent French troops to fight other French troops in the Levant and Syria in June 1942, with assistance from British and Commonwealth troops. He was enraged with the settlement arranged by the Britain with the local Vichy governor, who surrendered authority over the French colonies not to de Gaulle but to London. That nearly led to a formal breach with Churchill's government. A compromise was ultimately reached in which de Gaulle agreed that the Middle Eastern theater of operations was a special case concerning territory of the French Empire, where pressing and wider security interests required the British government to promise postwar independence to Syria and Lebanon. A similar dispute marked the British invasion of Madagascar in May 1942, but was abated in November when London handed the colony to the Free French. At the time, and even in hindsight, this appeared to outsiders as two failing and even moribund empires quarreling over bits of an old corpse.

A prickly and driven person, de Gaulle deeply loved France but disdained many French. He got on reasonably well with Churchill under tough circumstances of a losing war effort from 1940 to 1942, although the British prime minister considered removing recognition from de Gaulle more than once and they had several bitter arguments. Most damaging for de Gaulle were terrible personal relations with Franklin Roosevelt, who froze him out of the North African *TORCH* landings in 1942 while looking for another Frenchman to represent France. Roosevelt, Churchill, and General *Dwight Eisenhower* were even prepared to work with Admiral *Jean Louis Darlan* in preference to de Gaulle, until Darlan was fortuitously assassinated. Roosevelt then tried to elevate General *Henri Giraud* above de Gaulle during the first half of 1943, ordering Eisenhower to ignore the Free French governing committee and instead deal directly with French commanders in the field, including former Vichy generals. At the *Casablanca Conference (January 14–24, 1943)*, de Gaulle fended off intense pressure to accept subordination to Giraud. Churchill was also ready to break with de Gaulle in favor of Giraud as late as May 21, but the proposal to do so was rejected by the War Cabinet. Roosevelt cabled Eisenhower a month later that a formal break was coming. Instead, de Gaulle completely outmaneuvered Giraud and had him removed from office by November. He then roughly patched relations with Churchill, and less well with Roosevelt. The "National Committee of French Liberation (CFLN)" he headed was recognized by Britain as the provisional government of France on August 26. De Gaulle and the CFLN thereafter received enough material support to field eight divisions of merged, Fighting France-Vichy forces.

Why was de Gaulle so difficult? One biographer put it this way: "de Gaulle bit the hand that fed him because it was his only way of showing that France still had teeth." Important in the process was establishing effective political control in Normandy and elsewhere in liberated France in the wake of the Western Allied advance. De Gaulle achieved this by relieving Allied commanders of the burden of imposing a military government, while creating new political facts and legitimacy for themselves, not least by preempting a possible French Communist grab for power. De Gaulle landed in Normandy on June 14, and set up his own headquarters in Bayeux. Paris was retaken on August 25, 1944, by an armored division spearhead of "France Combattante" forces led by Leclerc. De Gaulle paraded under the Arc de Triumph the day after that, subject to German sniper fire. It was a heroic gesture that cemented his image as the embodiment of French resistance and liberation for many French. But it only partially reinforced de Gaulle's claim to political leadership. In fact, most in the *Force Française de l'Intérieur (FFI)* did not accept his assertion of personal authority, least of all the large bloc of Communist fighters and party members. De Gaulle nevertheless established himself as head of a de facto provisional government, was recognized by the Western Allies, and governed France to the end of the war and into 1946. A large and heroic reinterpretation of the "Dark Years" was later assayed by his political supporters, pointing to the fact the General refused to declare the Republic reestablished in Paris in August 1944, on the ground that it never ceased to exist but was embodied overseas in his person and the Free French movement.

Suggested Reading: Charles de Gaulle, *Memoirs*, 3 vols. (1955–1960; 1984); Julian Jackson, *De Gaulle* (2005).

DEGAUSSING Reducing the magnetic signature of individual ships as a defense against magnetic *mines* by passing a current around the hull.

DEGRELLE, LÉON (1906–1994) Belgian fascist. He formed the volunteer "Légion Wallonie" in 1941 to fight alongside the Wehrmacht in the Soviet Union. In 1943 this unit was transferred into the *Waffen-SS*. He escaped to Spain in 1945, where he remained for 40 years.

See also fifth column.

DE GUINGAND, FRANCIS (1900–1979) British general. His war record was closely tied to that of General, later Field Marshal, *Bernard Law Montgomery,* whom de Guingand served as chief of staff with 8th Army during the *desert campaigns (1940–1943).* He stayed with Montgomery through the fighting in Italy, France, and Germany from 1943 to 1945. He enjoyed a high reputation with other general staff officers. He quarreled badly with Montgomery after the war over the facts of certain wartime events.

DEKANOZOV, VLADIMIR (1898–1953) Soviet ambassador in Berlin. A squat Georgian, as a senior member of the *NKVD* Dekanozov earned the title "Hangman of Baku" during the great purges of the late 1930s. He was a leading protégé of *Lavrenti Beria,* and about as vicious: he had a torture and execution chamber built in the Berlin embassy that he used against local Soviet citizens. During receptions and other formal events, Hitler enjoyed humiliating the five-foot Dekanozov by flanking him with the tallest *Schutzstaffel (SS)* guards available. Like his master in Moscow, on the eve of *BARBAROSSA,* Dekanozov clung to the conviction that all warnings about German intentions were part of a British plot to draw the Soviet Union into war. He held onto that view in spite of fervent belief in imminent danger voiced by his intelligence staff and the fact that the German ambassador in Moscow, *Count von der Schulenburg,* personally warned him about the coming invasion two weeks earlier during a private lunch in Moscow.

DEMIANSK OFFENSIVE OPERATION (MARCH 6–APRIL 9, 1942) A failed Red Army offensive conducted by Briansk Front. The conception for the ground campaign was both audacious and ferocious. It aimed at replicating the German encirclements of Red Army troops that marked the five-month battle before Moscow that began in November 1941. General *Nikolai F. Vatutin* enveloped a large German pocket—six divisions and nearly 100,000 troops—centered on the small town of Demiansk, south of the *Toropets bulge*. Joseph Stalin and the Stavka decided to crush it totally. To accomplish this, three brigades of airborne were dropped inside the 35-mile wide pocket while Soviet ski troops infiltrated its perimeter. Their orders were to attack the Demiansk encirclement from inside, while Red Army main forces hammered at the outer German lines. The Ostheer and Luftwaffe determined to fight for the pocket, rather than fight out of it. Luftwaffe transports flew in supplies and Wehrmacht armor and infantry drove a road into the Demiansk Pocket in early March. Over 7,000 Soviet airborne died in the botched operation at Demiansk. Fighting continued in the area until a second, smaller German pocket at Kholm was also relieved on May 1.

DEMIANSK POCKET A German pocket that withstood the Soviet *Demiansk offensive operation* of March–April, 1942. Marshal *Semyon Timoshenko* then failed to reduce it in the late autumn of 1942, which proved the final blow to his reputation with Joseph Stalin. Adolf Hitler agreed to allow the OKH to abandon the exposed Demiansk salient in mid-February 1943, and to pull back to a more defensible line along the Lovat River.

DEMILITARIZATION OF THE RHINELAND
See Rhineland.

DEMOLITION
See engineers.

DEMPSEY, MILES (1896–1969) British general. Well regarded as a battlefield commander, his career followed that of his superior, General and later Field Marshal *Bernard Law Montgomery*. Dempsey succeeded to progressively more important commands in France in 1940, North Africa from 1940 to 1942, Sicily and Italy in 1943, and France and Germany in 1944–1945.

DENAZIFICATION A screening system was set up by the Allies in Germany in 1945 to ensure that senior *Nazi Party, Wehrmacht,* and *Schutzstaffel (SS)* men did not escape trial, should they deserve to be charged with *war crimes* or *crimes against humanity*. It was hoped to also remove tens of thousands of lesser Nazis from public office as a prerequisite to eventually reconstructing Germany along liberal and democratic lines in the Western occupation zones (American, British, French). In the three Western zones there was real controversy by 1946. Instead of removing all former Nazi officials from public positions, they were instead classified into four groups according to Allied perceptions of their degree of commitment to the defunct regime and its murderous ideology. These were: major offender; lesser activist or war criminal; minor offender or simply Nazi Party member, not thought to have committed serious crimes; and innocent. Simply holding Nazi Party membership was not assumed to mean automatic culpability in crimes of the regime or unfitness for postwar office. In other cases, including several members of the *Krupp* family, erstwhile Nazis and close collaborators were given early release because their skills were needed for economic reconstruction or for political reconciliation. That meant all but a few of the greatest offenders, and by no means all of them, got away with terrible crimes.

In the Soviet occupation zone denazification was more brutal, and perhaps arguably more just. The same procedure was carried out as in the Western zones, but from a harder realpolitik view of the rights of the conqueror. That attitude was also present in the three non-Soviet zones among occupation officials in the various military Western governments, and especially the French zone. But it reached levels of unparalleled and arbitrary harshness: Soviet-style denazification included large-scale summary executions and forced deportations by the *NKVD* of Nazi Party members, former SS and Wehrmacht officers, or anyone else deemed a threat to long-term Soviet control of what would in time become East Germany. In addition, the Soviets proceeded to systematically replace Nazis with German Communists, though not yet to replace their own military authority with a German Communist government. And even in the Soviet zone, former Nazis were just too numerous and practically useful to running the area on a daily basis to permit a total purge. Austria was occupied separately from Germany after the war and not officially required to denazify. In Japan, a similar, and similarly short-circuited, postwar process of first purging then dealing with the wartime culpable in American occupation policy became known as the *"reverse course."*

See also Gestapo; Office of Strategic Services; Nuremberg Tribunal; Patton, George; Rabe, John.

DENMARK   In 1939 neutral Denmark agreed to a *nonaggression treaty* with Nazi Germany. That pact did nothing to prevent Adolf Hitler from invading Denmark on April 9, 1940, in Operation *WESERÜBUNG.* The German assault began at first light with *Fallschirmjäger* drops around key bridges. Copenhagen was occupied within a few hours. After offering minimal resistance the Danes agreed to a cease-fire by the end of the day. The occupation was unusually lenient, partly because of the attitude of the local German commander. In addition, in specious Nazi "race" theory, Danes were considered full *"Aryans."* Danes did not establish a *government-in-exile* or present an active initial *resistance* to the occupation. Instead, there was broad *collaboration* with the occupiers, though under subdued protest by many. The Danes upheld a legal fiction until late summer 1943 that they were still neutral rather than occupied. That gave Germany what it wanted: quiet and order in Denmark. It also helped relations with Berlin that the collaborationist government of Eric Scavenius signed the *Anti-Comintern Pact,* while some Danes volunteered to serve in the *Waffen-SS*. On the other hand, and to his lasting credit, King Christian X (1870–1947) defied Nazi orders to round up Danish Jews and refused to collaborate with more brutal aspects of the occupation. Many Danes followed that lead: some heroically and successfully hid the majority of the small Danish Jewish community from the *Gestapo*, then helped many Jews escape to Sweden in October 1943.

A more active resistance movement grew slowly, notably after an "August Uprising" of strikes and other unrest in 1943 unsettled the tacit bargain with Germany, a deal in any case deteriorating from the moment it was struck. The Germans took over local administration on August 19. The small Danish Navy scuttled its ships or steamed them at flank speed for neutral Swedish ports. Most of the merchant marine had already joined the Western Allies in 1940, either out of free choice or more often as a result of chance location overseas at the outbreak of the naval war. Danish ships were already steaming in Allied convoys in the *Battle of the Atlantic (1939–1945)*, and some Danes died at sea in the merchant marine. But only a handful of Danes fought in Western armed forces. Among Denmark's overseas territories, the Faeroe Islands were occupied by Britain in 1940. In 1944 Iceland declared independence from Denmark, under heavy Anglo-American pressure: it was already in use as a naval base. As Allied victory approached, a small popular resistance broke out in Denmark, encouraged and supplied by drops of weapons organized by the British *Special Operations Executive (SOE)*. German occupation forces surrendered on May 4, 1945, except for the garrison on Bornholm. It was heavily bombed by the VVS, after which the Soviet Union occupied Bornholm until April 1946.

DEPORTATION

See individual countries and colonies. *See also Action Françaises; Barbie, Klaus; Belorussian offensive operation; Beria, Lavrenti Pavlovich; Bessarabia; Channel Islands; Commissar order; Cossacks; Crimea; crimes against humanity; denazification; Eichmann, Karl Adolf; ethnic cleansing; FALL WEISS; fifth column; forced labor; Gestapo; GULAG; Himmler, Heinrich; Holocaust; Italian Army; Japanese Canadians; Lebensraum; Madagascar; Night of the Long Knives; NKVD; Oder–Neisse Line; Ostarbeiter; prisoners of war; Red Army; Roma; Schutzstaffel (SS); Stalin, Joseph; Tatars; treason; Ukraine; Volga Germans.*

DEPRESSION

See Great Depression.

DEPTH CHARGES A weapon first used by the Royal Navy in *anti-submarine warfare* during World War I. Depth charges were drums or "ashcans" of 200–300 pounds of high explosive that were initially rolled off racks at the rear of a ship. They were later dispersed by side throwers (Y-guns) that supplemented the centerline racks. The charge was set off by a hydrostatic pistol actuated by water pressure. The pistol could be set to explode the main charge at a series of predetermined depths. Escort ships dropped ashcans in a spread pattern around the last sited location of a U-boat, then along its suspected course. Such attacks were often ineffective before new technologies came on stream that permitted a more certain U-boat location to be determined. Even then, laying down a pattern of depth charges might consume hundreds of ashcans and draw attacking escorts far away from their main responsibilities to the convoy. The central technical problem with depth charging an area where a rapidly submerging and turning U-boat was last seen, or was thought to be lurking, was the slow sink rate of 300 feet in about 30 seconds. In early 1942, U.S. Navy depth charges still used TNT and were only capable of final sink depths of 300 feet, when U-boat technology already permitted deeper escape dives. One advantage was that depth charges were proximity fused rather than contact weapons, which provided additional chance of cumulative damage to U-boat hulls and works. Still, when laid in patterns of 12 or 14 each, an escort would quickly exhaust its supply of a bulky weapon.

The problem was partly solved in 1943 by new designs with faster sink rates. New depth charges such as the British 450 lb Mark VII Heavy and the American Mark XI also replaced TNT with more powerful and compact Torpex explosive. The late-war British Mark X contained one ton of high explosive but did not deliver more effective bang for the pound. Better shaped weapons permitted light and heavy charges to be dropped at the same time, to achieve depth bracketing of a submerged enemy. The core problem remained, however, that the weapon could not be deployed forward of a charging ship. That meant most attacks were delayed as the escort was forced to pass over the dive spot of the U-boat and then drop blind: *ASDIC* (or Sonar) went deaf at around 200 yards range as the pulse and echo merged. Depth charges were thus dropped astern on the last estimated position of a U-boat. Their explosion then masked further ASDIC readings for many minutes. Given the time it took a depth charge to sink to explosive depth, U-boats most often escaped destruction: the average kill ratio achieved by depth charge attack throughout the war was about 6 percent, or 1 in every 16 attacks. The ultimate solution was forward throwing weapons such as the *Hedgehog* and *Squid*. The Royal Air Force modified depth charges for delivery by aircraft even as its researchers worked to develop a better anti-submarine bomb. The technical problem for aircraft was actually to slow the sink rate, because U-boats were usually attacked on the surface when taken by surprise by an aircraft, or just after diving and therefore likely to be a shallow depth. That problem was resolved later in the war by using better bombs and homing *torpedoes*.

See also balloons.

DESERT CAMPAIGNS (1940–1943)   The contest in Tripoli (today, Libya) and Egypt originally was between British and Commonwealth forces on one hand and Italy on the other. The Italians were later supported by the German *Afrika Korps*. It is also worth recalling that through mid-1940 the Italian Army in North Africa was readying to fight France's *Armée d'Afrique,* not the British Army. For the Italians, the object of the desert campaign was prestige and expanded Mediterranean empire in a "parallel war" to German conquests in continental Europe. That goal was reinforced by old hatreds for the Western Allies dating to frustrations with the 1919 territorial settlement, and to naval rivalries in the Mediterranean. The British were partly supplied by the United States with new and better tanks during 1942–1943. The Western Allies also jointly carried out the *TORCH* landings in Algeria and Morocco, which culminated in defeat of all remaining Axis forces in Tunisia by early May 1943. But British and Commonwealth forces were not supported by American troops in the longer desert campaign that ranged from Tripoli to Egypt. In that fight the main strategic asset at stake was the Suez Canal, with Gibraltar and Malta important assets to the British and threats to long-term Italian strategic ambition but of lesser interest to the Germans.

Fighting began with a desultory and ill-prepared Italian advance into Egypt from Tripoli that ended in disaster for Italy. The British struck back in Operation COMPASS starting on December 8, 1940. The British counteroffensive saw a breakthrough assault by the *Western Desert Force* at *Sidi Barrani*, 60 miles inside the Egyptian border. In the first week of January 1941, Major General *Richard O'Connor* sent freshly arrived Australians into their first offensive action in the desert at *Bardia*. More sharp fighting and additional Italian defeats followed at *Tobruk* and *Beda Fomm* in February. O'Connor hoped to press the attack to Benghazi, but was held back by shortages of supplies and men as he reached the end of a stretched logistical tether—pulled even thinner because Britain simultaneously mounted another assault on the Italian empire in East Africa. The Western Desert Force thus halted at El Agheila. It had lost just over 1,700 total casualties while inflicting over 130,000 Italian casualties, killed or wounded or taken prisoner. The cumulative effect of COMPASS was destruction of Italian 10th Army and large stocks of Regio Esercito war matériel. The Western Desert Force also advanced nearly 500 miles, the first of several lateral movements across the top of Africa that would become a singular mark of the desert campaign. At the time, it remained to be learned by both sides that desert advances might be just as quickly turned into comparable or even worse reverses.

The first elements of the small Afrika Korps were deployed in haste to Tripoli in April 1941, as Adolf Hitler rushed to shore up the Regio Esercito in Africa to prevent a collapse of the Italian position in the Mediterranean. Its commander was General *Erwin Rommel*, who immediately went on a surprise offensive that threw back British and Commonwealth forces during April. The British returned to the offensive with *BATTLEAXE* in mid-June. However, that operation failed when Rommel set a tank trap in the *Halfaya Pass* south of Bardia, while sending his own Panzers to maul enemy infantry. The rebuff led Winston Churchill to sack General *Archibald Wavell* as supreme commander in the Mediterranean and replace him with General *Claude Auchinleck*. The British launched a new offensive in November 1941, code named *CRUSADER*. It sent one armored column toward the Sidi Rezegh ridge south of Tobruk while another moved along the coast road. But it was an ill-planned and poorly conducted operation, throwing away a heavy advantage in armor. Rommel's counterattack threw the British back yet again, as General *Alan Cunningham* wavered and was sacked. By early December, British and Commonwealth forces suffered 18,000 casualties, though they had inflicted over 24,000 on the Germans and Italians, who retreated to El Agheila. Despite the numbers, the outcome hardly felt like a British victory.

Despite the main forces of the Wehrmacht bogging down in front of Moscow in November, Hitler sent reinforcements to Rommel, most importantly Luftflotte 2 under Field Marshal *Albert Kesselring*. The intervention made strategic sense, as the rapid collapse of Italy in 1943 would later confirm: Hitler could not allow an Italian collapse in North Africa because a defeat there threatened the whole edifice of the Italian empire erected by Mussolini, and that would in turn permit the Western Allies to threaten Germany's southern strategic flank with air power, commando raids, and aid to insurgent populations. But Rommel exceeded his defensive brief, eventually talking Hitler into going along with a renewed offensive with the an expanded Afrika Korps. Rommel pushed hard for the great prize of Egypt, against original OKW intentions and in the face of logistical realities of extended and vulnerable German and Italian supply lines. Accompanying Rommel's Panzers and Kesselring's aircraft were Hitler's rising hopes to take the Suez Canal and link with the Japanese, whom he encouraged to cross the Indian Ocean and occupy Madagascar. That strategic dream was distant as well as desperate, though not wholly farfetched. However, the opportunity slipped away with crippling losses incurred by the Imperial Japanese Navy in the Pacific at *Coral Sea* and *Midway,* a preemptive British invasion of Madagascar, and reversal of Axis fortunes in the Middle East due to British intervention in Iraq and invasion of Syria. The loss of Italian East Africa to the Axis foreclosed any strategy to conquer the Middle East and thereby isolate the Soviet Union from *Lend-Lease* supplies arriving overland via Iran. Axis losses were only marginally offset by naval successes in the Mediterranean, where the aircraft carrier HMS Ark Royal and a British battleship were sunk by Luftwaffe bombers, while Regia Marina mini-submarines sank two more British battleships at anchor in Alexandria harbor.

By mid-1942 British and Commonwealth ground and air forces were more numerous than the German-Italian opposition, but they still lacked adequate equipment and were poorly led and still badly demoralized. Having reinforced the Afrika Korps, Rommel led it and four Italian divisions in an attack on British 8th Army that began on May 26. The British were positioned along the *Gazala Line*. The ensuing battle lasted until June 17. Each side had advance intelligence about the other gleaned from code-breaking successes, but neither used it well. Axis forces comprised about 90,000 men supported by fewer than 600 tanks. The British and their allies had 100,000 men and almost 1,000 tanks, including some better quality "General Grant" M3s. Rommel struck first at the extreme British left where the Gazala Line was anchored by a Free French brigade that contained Spanish Republicans and Foreign Legion troops, and a Jewish unit, which Adolf Hitler furiously ordered exterminated. Rommel hoped to take Tobruk by an armored swing around the southern end of the Gazala Line, a turning movement that would trap 8th Army and then release the Panzers to race ahead for Egypt. The Free French at *Bir Hakeim* were quickly surrounded, before the attacking Panzers turned for the coast. The French held against follow-on assaults by the elite Italian Ariete armored division, then fought their way out to rejoin the British line. Meanwhile, 8th Army blunted the German attack in the north by May 29 in a series of vicious tank fights. Rommel made a tactical withdrawal to "the Cauldron," located between Tobruk and Bir Hakeim. That move was mistaken by the British commander, Lieutenant General Neil Ritchie, for a full disengagement by the Afrika Korps. Rommel renewed his attack, forcing a general retreat by the British from June 13. Tobruk fell to the Axis on June 21.

The Axis victory at Gazala and the fall of Tobruk had major implications. After those defeats and another rout of 8th Army at *Mersa Matruh* in June, there was a wholesale shakeup in the British desert command. Auchinleck was sacked in his turn, replaced by General *Harold Alexander*. But it took more time for 8th Army to find its true commander. General William Gott was killed in an air accident before he took effective charge of 8th Army. That meant command was shifted in August to General *Bernard Law Montgomery*. Meanwhile, Axis leaders divided over what to do next in the Mediterranean theater. The Italians wanted Operation *HERCULES* to go ahead, their plan for invasion and reduction of Malta. Newly promoted Field Marshal Rommel and his Führer wanted to press the attack into Egypt. Hitler believed that Operations *BLAU* and *EDELWEISS* on the Eastern Front would soon open a route for a northern pincer from the Caucasus to reach into the Middle East. After much discussion, he persuaded Mussolini to abandon the Malta invasion and transfer forces instead to support Rommel, then preparing for another a hard drive to capture Egypt. The British fell back in a fighting retreat in front of the renewed Axis offensive, fighting a successful holding action at the *First Battle of El Alamein* from July 1–3. A stalemate ensued along the frontier as Rommel looked to reinforce and resupply, while 8th Army dug in along a front that ran from the *Qatarra Depression* in the south to the coastal village of El Alamein.

Montgomery used the time to rebuild the material and morale base of 8th Army, waiting for Rommel to attack before he counterpunched along the *El Alamein line*. The first big fight came at *Alam el-Halfa* from August 30 to September 7, 1942. Rommel took Montgomery's proffered bait, sending two Panzer divisions into a flank attack through a dense minefield that the German commander sorely underestimated. The German tanks were savaged by well-positioned British defenders, who poured in concentrated artillery and anti-tank fire. After Alam el-Halfa, Montgomery steadily built his force until he was ready to go over to the permanent offensive in North Africa. The shift to Allied offense began with the critical, set-piece *Second Battle of El Alamein*. That fight broke German and Italian offensive capability in Egypt and Tripoli. It also confirmed Montgomery's restoration of 8th Army morale and demonstrated a major improvement in British air–land coordination and combined arms combat skills. Even as Rommel ordered full retreat westward from El Alamein with what remained of his mobile forces, abandoning the Italian infantry to capture, the Western Allies carried out the TORCH landings in Morocco and Algiers at the other end of North Africa. From that point, Rommel and the Axis armies in North Africa had more powerful armies pressing them from either side of the continent.

See also British Army; Egypt; Italian Army; Leclerc, Philippe; nanshin; Tripoli; Tunisia.

DESERT FOX
See Rommel, Erwin.

DESERTION   *Guomindang* armies in China employed such brutal conscription methods they suffered a death and desertion rate near 45 percent even before conscripts reached frontline units. Desertion was chronic thereafter. The situation was so bad that peasant boys were sometimes brought to the front in lines of 100 or more, tied together with ropes. Communist forces also saw desertions, but on a smaller scale that reflected their much smaller size and the physical remoteness of their bases in northwest China. A unique feature of Chinese desertion was that whole units facing annihilation in battle defected to join Chinese puppet armies, then later switched back to the Guomindang. That was especially the case on the central China front after 1939. This practice was viewed as prudent and not usually punished, although Communist leaders charged and suspected that it reflected continuing reluctance by *Jiang Jieshi* to fight the Japanese and was only a ploy to preserve his formations to later fight them.

Japanese Army recruits also deserted in growing numbers during the last peacetime years of the 1930s, usually to return to starving families in Depression-era Japan. From 1937, Japanese desertion rates were remarkably low relative to other armies: just 1,085 deserted by official count over the first six months of 1944, a time of terrible defeat and worsening conditions for Japanese troops in Southeast Asia and the Pacific, though one of victories in southern China. Japanese desertion rates stayed low in the Pacific until the last days of the war. That resulted partly from inability to escape isolated island duty, but also hostility of the populations of occupied territories such as New Guinea or the Philippines where Japanese deserters were most often killed once they left their bases or strayed from a jungle path. The story was different in China and Manchuria and on the Japanese home islands, where escape and survival was more likely and desertion more common.

Desertion was not common among Western Allied armies in the Pacific, once again because there was often no place to which one might desert. Europe was a much different story. Some 12,000 men deserted the armies of the Western powers in Italy during 1943–1944. Over 21,000 deserters from the U.S. Army were formally convicted and 49 sentenced to death by firing squad. American armies generally tried to give men a chance at redemption, however: the U.S. Army executed only one man for desertion, Private Eddie Slovak on January 31, 1945. That was the first U.S. Army execution since 1864. By the end of the campaign in France it is thought the equivalent of a full infantry division, over 18,000 men, were AWOL from the U.S. Army in that theater alone. There were also tens of thousands of desertions from the British Army during the course of the war, probably 2.5 times as many as from American armies. The higher number reflected the longer duration of the war for most British soldiers: the U.S. Army was only in combat in Africa and Europe from November 1942 until May 1945, with most men not in action before 1944. Higher British desertion rates—the British Army probably saw close to 100,000 deserters in Africa and Europe by 1945—reflected the strain of 6.5 years of war. This showed up in exhaustion, demoralization, and desertion during heavy fighting in France and more desultory action in Germany in 1945. Many men returned to their units after a few days of being classified as *AWL*; others took to the forests as some British troops did during the Great War. The death penalty for desertion or cowardice was abolished in the British Army in 1930. There was some discussion of reviving it after the disaster at *Tobruk,* but this was not done. Some British and American soldiers stayed away from their units but remained in theater for months, living by theft from local civilians or by stealing supplies from Allied depots. Some of these men were ordinary criminals who had been drafted into service but who reverted to character once overseas, where they escaped into the anarchic conditions of logistical abundance that marked Western Allied rear areas. Conversely, at least 7,000 Irishmen deserted their national army to volunteer and serve in British armed forces.

Desertion rates from minor Axis states were high, and grew higher as catastrophic defeat hit the Rumanian, Hungarian, and Italian armies on the Eastern Front. A number of Wehrmacht conscripts who were also committed Communists deserted to Soviet lines just before *BARBAROSSA,* on the night of June 21–22, 1941. Some *Hiwis* took the opportunity of a return to the frontlines to cross back to the Soviet side, an act for which they were seldom rewarded and more often brutally punished by the Red Army. From mid-1943, Wehrmacht desertions across Soviet lines rose dramatically, as despair and too much fighting took a toll on troops tasting defeat more often than victory. Also, German desertions rose as the Red Army sent out instructions against killing prisoners, which had been common practice over the first six months of the German–Soviet war. Adolf Hitler and German officers had tens of thousands of men shot for desertion: at least 15,000 after formal Wehrmacht trials, but uncounted numbers by summary execution. Nevertheless, German desertion rates climbed dramatically in 1945 as men and boys fighting on their home soil saw that the war was lost or tried to sneak home to protect their families. Many were caught out of uniform and shot by fanatic SS or Nazi Party officials; others were shot by roving Wehrmacht firing squads. This type of desertion was common in western Germany from January 1945, more so than in the hard-fought eastern half of the country. In the east deserters ran a gauntlet formed by vengeful *krasnoarmeets,* brutal Nazi bitterenders, and desperate officers who ordered men summarily shot. In many cases, men were shot for desertion after being cutoff from their unit, without ever trying to desert.

In the Red Army, desertion was closely monitored by the *NKVD.* It also numbered among *"extraordinary events,"* which Soviet authorities automatically punished with death. In the first year of the war especially, merciless *blocking detachments* were deployed in the immediate rear of frontline troops. Soldiers most likely to desert in the opening weeks and months of the German invasion were new conscripts from recently annexed—and deeply embittered—Baltic States and Bessarabia. In addition to individual Baltic and Rumanian desertions, some whole Baltic units turned their guns against the Red Army. Men from other Soviet populations likely to desert were Belorussian and Ukrainian peasants who despised the collective farms and remembered the great and artificial famine of the 1930s carried out by Joseph Stalin and the Soviet state. Some also initially thought Germans might be liberators and shared German hatred for "Jewish-Bolshevism." The problem of desertion by western ethnic groups was so severe that on August 12, 1941, soldiers from those regions were barred from serving in reorganized Red Army tank corps. The ban was later lifted as the real impact of Nazi occupation was felt in Ukraine and Belorussia. Senior commanders were given power to summarily execute subordinate officers, and lesser officers were granted authority to shoot their men without trial. Summary executions for those suspected of desertion, which included surrender, was ordered by Joseph Stalin in Order #270 issued on August 16, 1941. On July 28, 1942, Stalin signed an even more draconian *Order #227*, which demanded of all Soviet troops: "Not one step back!" Order #227 designated military or political officers who removed insignia or surrendered as "malicious deserters" and extended severe punishment to the families of all Soviet deserters. In practice, that included families tied by blood relation to unrecovered corpses in areas overrun by the enemy. The stigma and economic punishment that attended the charge of desertion lasted many years, even decades, after the war. Soldiers cut off by German action who strove to return to their unit were sometimes shot for desertion upon achieving that goal. Knowing that, others preferred to remain with partisan units rather than chance a return to the line. Many stayed with their unit as raw winter closed down any real chance of escape and made solitary survival a gamble not worth taking.

Despite brutal countermeasures, Red Army desertion rates climbed into early 1942. Even Stalin recognized that Soviet official terror was ineffective in the face of the natural terror of battle. He approved a switch in emphasis from October 1941, calling for more propaganda and less persecution. Even so, in the battle before Moscow that month, 5,000 Red Army soldiers were arrested for desertion and 12,000 more were arrested for evasion of military service. Death sentences continued to rise until February 1942, when the Eastern Front stabilized. Desertion remained a problem throughout the war, though it abated somewhat during 1942 as German atrocities were uncovered in liberated territory and a desire for revenge overtook fear of battle, or of Stalin, among many Soviet troops. As combat intensified in 1943, Red Army desertion rates climbed once more. Thousands per month crossed to the German lines; others ran into nearby woods; some befuddled peasant boys naively tried to go home. Still others formed armed gangs that operated behind German and Soviet lines. They were led by hard criminals from the *GULAG* who escaped from *penal battalions* and were determined never to obey another order from anyone. Over the course of the war at least 158,000 Red Army soldiers were formally sentenced and executed for desertion, self-mutilation, or "cowardice." No one knows, or at least NKVD files have yet to be released that would confirm, how many tens or hundreds of thousands more were summarily executed or shot down by blocking troops.

See also Burma National Army; Indian National Army; Manteuffel, Hasso von; Polish Army; Ukraine, First Battle of; Waffen-SS.

DESERT RATS Originally and most properly, British 7th Armoured Division commanded by General William Gott. The sobriquet was later applied more generically to all British and Commonwealth forces who fought in the North African *desert campaign,* especially British 8th Army under General *Bernard Montgomery.*

See also *Afrika Korps.*

DESTROYER ESCORTS   Smaller *destroyers* with lighter armor and reduced firepower. They had less powerful and more fuel efficient engines but enhanced speed. Originally termed "fast escort vessels," they were built with lighter armor and armament than older fleet destroyers. Critically, they did not strain their engines or overconsume fuel, as did fleet destroyers when tasked to operate at *convoy* speeds. Many destroyer escorts eschewed torpedoes in favor of more effective *anti-submarine warfare* equipment and weapons, as well as anti-aircraft guns.

See *Atlantic, Battle of; Royal Navy.*

DESTROYERS   Small, fast warships originating in a late 19th-century protective role for battleships and other capital warships against fast-attack torpedo boats. During World War I destroyers gained an additional role in *anti-submarine warfare (ASW).* Despite that experience, in the interwar years most major navies continued to see destroyers as primarily supporting fleet operations. The Royal Navy was especially lax given its Great War experience. It failed to adapt interwar destroyer designs and training to likely future *convoy* escort duties. British destroyers were nevertheless forced into protection of merchant shipping and troop convoys from submarine attack from the first days of the war. Their high-speed engines quickly proved unable to operate well at the much lower speeds of convoys. They also devoured precious fuel at rates that made it necessary to leave convoys unguarded for extended periods while the destroyers refueled. Most older destroyers, or "four-stackers," were refitted for convoy duty by removal of one or more of their funnels to accommodate larger ASW crews and add new weapons, or to decrease topweight. A few destroyers had their boilers reduced to accommodate the men needed to operate ASW weapons. Other adaptations were made to new destroyers to improve ASW capabilities: the superstructure was pared down and some guns removed to make way for racks of depth charges or other ASW or anti-aircraft weapons. Western navies combined destroyers and *destroyer escorts* with *escort carriers* and some larger warships from April 1943, forming hunter-killer groups that found and finished off many U-boats in the second half of the war. The USN had so many destroyers available by mid-1943, it used the old four-stackers to form U-boat screens for escort carriers at the center of each hunter-killer Support Group, rather than as sub-chasers.

See *also* various navies and naval campaigns, and *ASDIC; destroyers-for-bases deal.*

DESTROYERS-FOR-BASES DEAL   In July 1940, Franklin Roosevelt agreed to send 50 World War I–vintage USN destroyers to the Royal Navy for use in *convoy* duty, in exchange for 99-year leases on eight naval bases in the Atlantic and Caribbean: Bermuda, British Guiana, Newfoundland, and five *British West Indies* islands.

Roosevelt also insisted on a guarantee that the transferred ships would be scuttled rather than surrendered to the Kriegsmarine in the event of a British defeat and exit from the war. It was a clever way around restrictions on arms sales imposed by the *Neutrality Acts* and addressed an immediate and desperate British need in the *Battle of the Atlantic (1939–1945)*. Acquisition of naval bases spoke to FDR's career-long naval power theories and interest in a permanent expansion of American sea power, as well as short- and medium-term interest in securing a hemispheric defense perimeter. Winston Churchill initially opposed the swap, but relented for larger reasons of engaging the United States in the war effort. The transferred destroyers were manned by crews from the Royal Navy, Royal Canadian Navy, and Norwegian, Dutch, and other Western Allied navies-in-exile. Once the escort crisis in the Atlantic passed, several were transferred to the Soviet Union. Others were assigned skeleton crews to less important roles, replaced in convoy duty by purpose-built *destroyer escorts*.

DESTROYER-TRANSPORT
See Tokyo Express.

DEUTSCHES JUNGVOLK   "German Young People."
See Hitlerjungend.

DEUTSCHE VOLKSSTURM   "German Peoples' Storm."
See Volkssturm.

DE VALERA, EAMON (1882–1975):
See Ireland.

DEVERS, JACOB (1887–1979)   American general. He was the youngest major general in the U.S. Army. He was in charge of the rapid expansion of the Army's armored divisions from 1941 to 1942. He was elevated to deputy supreme commander in the Mediterranean in 1943. Then he oversaw ground forces planning for the *OVERLORD* campaign. He commanded 6th Army Group from September 15, 1944, to the end of the war. That was a very large Army Group comprising U.S. 7th Army and French 1st Army. Devers led this force in the south of France before turning into southern Germany. He was privately criticized by General *Dwight Eisenhower* for sluggish command during the battle for the *Colmar Pocket* in January–February, 1945.

DEVIL'S BRIGADE   "Die schwarzen Teufel," or the "Black Devils." A nickname coined by German forces in Italy for the 1st Special Service Force (SSF). The brigade was a 1,600-man, joint Canadian American, special forces commando unit that trained in Montana and fought in both the Pacific and European theaters of operations. Canadians formed about one-fourth of the unit. The SSF originally trained to fight in Norway. When that scheduled deployment turned out to be a *deception operation* to cover the *TORCH* landings, the unit was deployed to the *Aleutian Islands* instead. The brigade landed on Kiska in 1942 as part of a larger Can-Am naval operation to drive the Japanese from the Aleutians. It moved to Casablanca in November 1943, and thence to Italy. It scaled high cliffs to successfully assault a section of the *Bernhardt Line* from December 3–6, 1943. It was withdrawn from the Italian mountains in January 1944, then sent into action against *Waffen-SS* along the Mussolini Canal and to defend a hard-pressed section of the *Anzio* perimeter. It was one of the first units to enter Rome on June 4. On August 14, 1944, the brigade landed in southern France as part of Operation *DRAGOON*. After fighting in the Rhineland and along the Franco–Italian border with U.S. 7th Army, it was broken up on December 5, 1944. Its Canadian troops were sprinkled across 1st Canadian Army as replacements. Most of the Americans were reassigned to airborne divisions, but some finally saw late-war action in Norway.

Suggested Reading: Kenneth Joyce, *Snow Plow and the Jupiter Deception* (2006).

D/F

See Direction-Finding (D/F); Huff-Duff.

DIEPPE RAID (AUGUST 19, 1942) The largest *commando* raid of the war, and the most disastrous. The landings were made near the historic coastal city of Dieppe in occupied France. The raid may have been intended as a strategic diversion to relieve pressure on the Red Army. It was justified by those who planned it as a large-scale test of amphibious capabilities and as an offer of bait to draw the Luftwaffe into a major air battle. General *Bernard Law Montgomery* strongly urged that it be canceled, then left to take charge of British 8th Army in Egypt. Admiral *Louis Mountbatten* ordered the raid carried out, acting with unusual personal control and secrecy during planning of such a major operation. Originally scheduled for July 7, the raid was postponed due to bad weather and not undertaken until six weeks later. On August 19, 4,963 men of Canadian 2nd Division, 1,075 British commandos, and 50 U.S. Rangers—all under British command—hit landing sites along 10 miles of French beaches, but without a preliminary air bombardment and after only a light naval bombardment by destroyers from the escort. The assault was caught on the beaches by well-prepared German defenders. Nearly two-thirds of the attackers were slaughtered or captured as they stumbled ashore. Confusion reigned as fresh waves of commandos reinforced beaches where the first wave was pinned down. Tanks floundered in the water or were hung up on the sea wall. A withdrawal was attempted under heavy fire. When the raid was over the Canadians counted 3,367 casualties, the British suffered another 275, while the Germans lost fewer than 600. The Allies also lost one destroyer, 33 landing craft, and over 100 aircraft. The Luftwaffe lost 48 planes.

Much was learned from the Dieppe disaster that would prove useful on *D-Day (June 6, 1944)* and in other seaborne invasions, but those lessons came at high and bitter cost due to command ineptitude. The raiders also suffered the usual misfortunes of war and were met by a sharp response by well-trained defenders. The central operational lesson from the failure was that any landing needed to achieve surprise to be successful: all surprise had been lost at Dieppe, despite which failure of the landing was reinforced by rigid commanders. It was also concluded that landings must be preceded by intense bombing and naval bombardment. Smaller lessons concerned prior close scouting of the gradient and weight-bearing load of the beach, continuing need for close support fire in the initial phase, quick clearance by engineers of beach obstacles and mines, and improved shore-to-ship communications. British and Canadian troops would apply all those lessons with real success on three of the five D-Day beaches. In September 1944, Canadian troops entered and liberated Dieppe. The raid was a key event for Canada: it reinforced a rising national demand that Canadian troops be allowed to fight under their own generals, and a growing sense of nationhood and political distinction from the interests of Great Britain. Decades after the war there was still great bitterness in Canada about the role played by an ambitious but unqualified member of the royal family, Louis Mountbatten.

See also MULBERRY harbors; Pétain, Henri Philippe; prisoners of war.

DIETL, EDUARD (1890–1944)   German general. An ardent *Freikorps* member and early Nazi in the 1920s, Dietl was a divisional commander during the invasion of Poland in 1939. He led his Gerbirgsjäger (mountain troops) to northern Norway in 1940. He failed to take Murmansk in an advance out of Norway in 1941. He spent the remainder of his war in Karelia, celebrated as a Nazi hero but in fact confined to a minor command in a peripheral theater. Dietl was killed in an air accident in June 1944.

DIETRICH, SEPP (1892–1966)   *Schutzstaffel (SS)* general. He fought in World War I and was an early and enthusiastic Nazi. He rose along with the SS, at the head of Adolf Hitler's personal SS bodyguard or *Leibstandarte*. After leading an SS death squad that killed *Sturmabteilung (SA)* men in the *Night of the Long Knives* in 1934, he became a personal favorite of the Führer. Dietrich was brutish in appearance and manner. That only endeared him to his street fighter Führer, a former corporal who despised buttoned-up and aristocratic Prussian officers. Dietrich commanded the Leibstandarte SS division from 1940 to 1942. He ordered his men to commit atrocities against captured Red Army soldiers at the *Second Battle of Kharkov*. He was one of Adolf Hitler's true favorites by 1944, and was promoted to command 1st SS "Leibstandarte Adolf Hitler" Panzer Korps, a large formation far beyond his abilities. He commanded the same outfit, renamed 6th SS Panzer Army, during the *Ardennes offensive,* during which some of his men carried out the *Malmédy massacre.* His unit was transferred to the southern front in March 1945. Instead of fighting to the bitter end as Hitler expected, Dietrich retreated into Austria to surrender to U.S. forces in May. He served less than 10 years for his *war crimes,* plus another 18 months on domestic charges for his part in the 1934 "Blood Purge."

DIGGER   Term of colloquial affection for Australian soldiers, dating to the trenches of World War I.

DILL, JOHN (1881–1944)   A respected commander in World War I, he was in charge of 1st Corps of the British Expeditionary Force (BEF) from September 1939 to April 1940, during the so-called *Phoney War*. In poor health, he was recalled to serve as CIGS just before *FALL GELB* in 1940. He was CIGS from May 1940 to December 1941, when he went to Washington with Winston Churchill in the wake of *Pearl Harbor (December 7, 1941)*. He was promoted to field marshal and remained in Washington as British representative to the *Combined Chiefs of Staff*. The real reason for the promotion was that Churchill had lost confidence in Dill as a military adviser and wished to replace him as CIGS with General *Allan Brooke*. In a remarkable sign of the respect Dill subsequently gained among American leaders, and in tribute to his contribution to the joint war effort, he was buried at Arlington National Cemetery in 1944.

DIME FORCE   The assault force that targeted Scoglitti during the invasion of Sicily by the Western powers.

DIPLOMACY   World War II evolved into a *total war* in which diplomacy was important at the start and at the end, but during which the main course and consequences of the war were driven by larger material causes and the sheer scale of fighting and destruction. The *Axis alliance* hardly had internal diplomacy worth recording. Adolf Hitler treated all minor Axis states, a category that came to include Italy from late 1943, essentially as vassals. In any case, he had no conception of a political exit from the war, even after it was clear Germany was losing it. For that reason he never seriously contemplated Japanese and Italians proposals made in 1943 that he negotiate an armistice with Joseph Stalin to fight the Western Allies alone. On the other hand, the Japanese and Italians were principally interested in opposing the Western powers rather than in Germany's main fight with the Soviet Union. The diplomacy of the *Allies* was far more complex, involving world-spanning empires, numerous American powers, and deep ideological differences from the Soviet Union. Inter-Allied relations also had to deal with extraordinary complexities of coordinating logistics and *grand strategy* in a global war and across ideological lines. The Allies quickly agreed on a core policy of *unconditional surrender* of the Axis states, a position that precluded much discussion about alternate peace terms or conditions and militated against talking separately or directly with the major Axis states.

See also specific states, treaties, conferences, leaders, diplomats, summits, and countries, but see especially *Anschluss; Anti-Comintern Pact; appeasement; Atlantic Charter; Axis alliance; Baldwin, Stanley; Balkan Pact; Casablanca Conference; Chamberlain, Arthur Neville; Churchill, Winston Spencer; collective security; Comintern; concordats; Declaration on Liberated Europe; Dekanozov, Vladimir; Dulles, Allan; Dumbarton Oaks Conference; Enigma machine; FALL GELB; Five Power Naval Treaty; Four Power Treaty;*

grand strategy; Greater East Asia Co-Prosperity Sphere; Harriman, W. Averell; Hendaye protocol; Hitler, Adolf; Hoare-Laval Pact; Hoover-Stimson Doctrine; Hopkins, Harry; Hull, Cordell; Imperial Japanese Army; intelligence; Japanese Peace Treaty; Jiang Jieshi; Konoe Fumimaro; League of Nations; Lend-Lease; Litvinov, Maxim Maximovich; Lytton Commission; MAGIC; Maginot spirit; Montreux Convention; Moscow Conference; Munich Conference; Mussolini, Benito; Nazi–Soviet Pact; Nine Power Treaty; nonbelligerence; Placentia Bay Conference; Potsdam Conference; PURPLE; Québec conferences; Rapallo, Treaties of; Red Cross; Rhineland; Ribbentrop, Joachim; Roosevelt, Franklin; sanctions; San Francisco Conference; Stalin, Joseph; Stimson, Henry; Tehran Conference; Tōgō, Shigenori; Tripartite Pact; VENONA; Wallenberg, Raul; Washington Naval Conference; World Economic Conference; Yalta Conference.

DIRECT FIRE   Aimed artillery fire at specific targets, usually in a close support role during an infantry assault.

See artillery; assault guns; indirect fire; self-propelled guns.

DIRECTION   During 1941–1942, the Red Army used this designation for operational commands of groups of armies, or "Fronts." Each Direction or Front was roughly equivalent to what other major powers called *Army Groups*. Three Directions were established on July 10, 1941, as part of emergency defensive reforms undertaken even as much of the Red Army was collapsing under three simultaneous Wehrmacht advances in *BARBAROSSA*. The Northwestern Direction under Marshal *Kliment Voroshilov* faced German Army Group North. Western Direction defended against Army Group Center all the way to the suburbs of Moscow, first led by Marshal *Semyon Timoshenko* then by General *Georgi Zhukov*. Southwestern Direction was badly led in the fight against Army Group South by Marshal *Semyon Budyonny*, then was handed off to Timoshenko. It was driven beyond Kiev, losing vast numbers of men and tanks in some of the largest encirclements in the history of war. A fourth Direction was set up in the Soviet far east on July 30, 1945, under Marshal *Alexander Vasilevsky* to prosecute the short *Manchurian offensive operation* against the Japanese in August. It was dissolved on December 20, 1945.

DIRECTION-FINDING (D/F)   Locating the source of a radio transmission by triangulating its position from two listening posts or receivers. *Huff-Duff* was the Western term for detection equipment that pinpointed high-frequency transmissions, especially from U-boats. Shipborne Huff-Duff went operational in July 1941. This was a critical advance over older medium-frequency detection equipment, since U-boats communicated with their HQ by high-frequency transmissions. The habit of Admiral *Karl Dönitz* of insisting on regular U-boat tracking reports thereafter enabled Western navies to locate boats by listening from shore stations. Reliable shipborne D/F was introduced in combination with new *radars*. That permitted anti-submarine escorts to establish an initial bearing, then estimate range, enabling them to force a U-boat to dive or allowing them to *depth charge* it. By the fall of 1944 the Western Allies had 20 shore stations tracking U-boat transmissions. Once enemy captains became aware of the vulnerability of their signals, they seldom made any, sharply curtailing intelligence by either side but also dramatically reducing the effectiveness of the U-boats.

DIRLEWANGER BRIGADE

See Slovak Uprising (1944); Waffen-SS; Warsaw Uprising (1944).

DISARMAMENT

See aircraft carriers; Anglo-German Naval Arms Agreement; chemical weapons; Five Power Treaty; Geneva Disarmament Conference; Geneva Protocol; Imperial Japanese Navy; Kriegsmarine; Luftwaffe; nerve weapons; Nine Power Treaty; pocket battleships; Rapallo, Treaty of; Rhineland; treaty cruisers; U-boats; Versailles, Treaty of; Washington Naval Conference.

DISEASE, EFFECTS ON MILITARY OPERATIONS

See various campaigns. *See also* cross-references listed under *medical issues.*

DIVE BOMBERS

See aircraft carriers; bombers.

DIVERS   Most major navies employed divers ("frogmen") in underwater demolition work; to spy on enemy ships and bases; to examine underwater damage on friendly ships; to secretly survey landing beaches, or later as "clearance divers" to detonate or otherwise eliminate underwater obstacles, or to defuse mines; or as guides, suicide or not, for manned torpedoes and *mines.* All divers trained in combat swimming and silent insertion. The Regia Marina had elaborate prewar plans to deploy thousands of frogmen as aquarian infantry, but like most of Benito Mussolini's military dreams, nothing came of that wild idea.

See also Fukuryu; Marshall Islands; radar.

DIVISION   In most armies this was the lowest-level unit to command organic artillery, anti-tank units, and anti-aircraft guns in support of its infantry or armored operations. Western Allied division commanders also could call on corps-level artillery support when needed. Division combat power varied greatly from army to army, as did strength. For instance, U.S. Army infantry divisions started the war at 15,500 men. That was reduced by 8 percent to an official 14,253 in a reform begun in 1943. The actual size and armament of real divisions was different by country and year, as combat eroded strength. Paper strength and actual strength thus varied greatly according to the misfortunes of war. For example, on *D-Day (June 6, 1944),* assaulting American and British divisions were overstrength at 15,000 to 20,000 men each, in the belief initial casualties would be severe. Canadian divisions in Normandy were smaller, however, in part because they were all-volunteer formations, a fact that reduced initial recruitment and then sharply limited replacements. Western Allied airborne divisions at full-strength numbered 8,000 to 10,000 men, but all were elite volunteers. Wehrmacht field divisions waiting ashore on D-Day were generally at a strength of 10,000 men or fewer, including garrison divisions of mixed nationality and limited effectiveness. These included *Osttruppen* conscripts from a dozen conquered nations who fought alongside Russian "volunteers" drawn from prisoner of war camps. Because of a personal reluctance of Adolf Hitler to ever dismantle combat-shattered divisions, the Wehrmacht continually added new units, until it had 313 divisions on paper by 1945. Most were at half-strength or less, mere shadows of the powerful German divisions of 1939–1941. By 1945 it was not uncommon for a Wehrmacht or *Waffen-SS* division with a paper strength of 10,000 to actually field just 1,000–2,000 battle-weary men.

The Japanese army began the war with heavy divisions averaging 22,000 men, each with its own artillery, engineers, tanks, and support troops. The Guomindang began the *Sino-Japanese War (1937–1945)* with 191 divisions of 11,000 men each. Most Chinese divisions were ill-trained and only 80 were decently equipped with basic weapons, while almost none had organic transport, armor, or artillery. The Red Army formed and reformed combat-destroyed (or surrendered) divisions and whole armies several times during the war. By 1945 the Red Army had 550 divisions listed in its paper order of battle, although just like many Wehrmacht formations, some of these units were severely understrength. Even officially, Soviet divisions of 1944–1945 were smaller than those of 1941. The British Army put 50 divisions into service before the end of the war. Most were partly understrength from August 1944, when the British were forced to deactivate some field divisions to provide replacements for others. Canadian divisions were usually understrength due to a failure to introduce overseas conscription. The U.S. Army fielded 92 Army divisions, of which 88 saw some combat. That number does not include Marine divisions, five Army airborne divisions, or nondivisional combat troops equivalent to a further 26 divisions. U.S. formations were maintained full strength throughout the war through an efficient replacement system. They were also far and away the most heavily motorized or mechanized of any in the war. U.S. divisional artillery was especially impressive: nearly 2,200 men per division handled three dozen 105 mm guns and another dozen 150 mm guns, in addition to many more mortars scattered among infantry companies. From 1944 it was common to have an additional artillery battalion attached to almost every U.S. division in a combat zone, with heavy mortar *chemical warfare* battalions attached to some.

See also binary division.

DIVISIONS LÉGÈRES MÉCHANIQUES   Mobile, light armored cavalry divisions of the French Army. They were designed to carry out deep reconnaissance missions, to screen slower moving infantry divisions, and to quickly move into Belgium in support of that country in the event of a German invasion. Two prewar *divisions légères méchaniques* were established, in 1935 and 1937.

DJEBEL Arabic term for hills and mountains in North Africa. They proved hard for the Western Allies to overcome, as German defenders were well positioned above the valley floors and early British and American tactics were unimaginative and ineffective.

DNIEPER, BATTLE OF (AUGUST 13–SEPTEMBER 22, 1943) One of several massive, rolling offensives that together retook western Ukraine from the Germans by April 1944. An initial thrust was launched toward the lower Dnieper on August 13, 1943. This was intended to take advantage of *RUMIANTSEV* and the *Donbass offensive operation* elsewhere on the Eastern Front, while preceding the awkwardly named *Offensive in Right-Bank Ukraine (1944)*. The attack bogged down by the first week of September, stymied in the attempt to fight directly across the Dnieper. The Stavka therefore settled on an alternative stratagem: on September 24–25 a large airborne assault was undertaken in an effort to leap the Dnieper, with major ground forces to follow once a lodgement was established on the far bank. Unfortunately as well as unwisely, a scratch and temporary airborne corps was used: most men involved made their first jump of any kind, not just their first combat jump. They dropped across the river at Kanev in support of a ground assault already underway. The airborne assault was repelled with such heavy losses that Joseph Stalin forbade all future night jumps. Land forces that had crossed three days earlier managed to hold onto a small bridgehead, but came under sustained German counterattack over the next several weeks. The bridgehead was saved by success elsewhere, notably in the *Second Battle of Ukraine (1943–1944)*. That fight drew off German reinforcements and supplies while the Soviets slung to the western bank of the Dnieper. Reinforced over the winter, the position provided a base for more offensive operations in 1944.

DOCTRINE Recommended tactical procedures passed on to new recruits in training and, on a grander scale, operational principles taught to the officer corps and employed by staff officers in planning operations. Not all armies followed or even understood strategic doctrine. Tactical and operational doctrine varied significantly from army to army, largely according to national historical experience. At the level of *operational art*, doctrine reflected guiding principles about how to maneuver and fight large formations. Such principles were, at their best, derived from close study of historical operations as well as intelligent adaptation to new technology and circumstances.

For examples, successful or not, *see Blitzkrieg; deep battle; Gefechtstreifen; schemes of maneuver; Schwerpunkt; Vernichtungskrieg; Vernichtungsschlacht.*

DODECANESE CAMPAIGN (SEPTEMBER 9–NOVEMBER 22, 1943) When Italy surrendered to the Western Allies on September 9, 1943, 7,500 Germans of the "Sturm-Division Rhodos" overwhelmed and disarmed the Italian Dodecanese garrison of 30,000 men. Winston Churchill, fixated as always on military activity in the Mediterranean, ordered in British and Greek commandos with an eye to forcing the Germans from the Dodecanese and from Crete. By mid-October some 4,000 British commandos were spread over eight small islands, though none landed on Rhodes. Elements of the German 22nd Infantry Division from Crete crossed to Kos on October 3 to eliminate the only British airfield in the Dodecanese. They forced the isolated British garrison of under 1,400 men to surrender, took an additional 4,000 Italian prisoners, and summarily executed over 100 Italian officers. Churchill's advisers recommended withdrawal from the Dodecanese, but the Prime Minister pressed ahead with the campaign, essentially reinforcing failure. In his defense, he hoped to provoke Turkey into the war against Germany. He also saw the island campaign as a preliminary to a larger and long-cherished Balkan campaign, a proposal repeatedly rejected by American military and political leaders. The Germans assaulted Leros (Operation LEOPARD) on November 12, overrunning the British garrison of 3,000 men and taking prisoner another 8,500 Italian soldiers and sailors. The campaign was over by November 22. Elements of the British and Greek navies took serious losses, mostly from Luftwaffe bombing but also strikes by new radio-controlled missiles used by the Germans for the first time.

Suggested Reading: Jeffrey Holland, *The Aegean Mission* (1988).

DOGFIGHT Aerial combat between or among opposing fighters; so termed for its twisting, snarling action.

DOGS Dogs were used by every army in World War II, as indeed they have been by nearly every army that has ever gone to war. They served a variety of purposes, some noble and others savage. The most common use was to guard *prisoner of war* camps, *concentration camps,* or key installations. Dogs also served morale purposes as unit mascots. Well-trained dogs could act as couriers and, in exceptional circumstances or terrain, as pack or draft animals. They were used to sniff out booby traps, caches of explosives, or to locate wounded men or civilians buried in rubble. The Red Army trained dogs in packs to search out wounded and drag them to safety on their own, with one or two harnessed to sledges and the rest scouting and pulling wounded men onto a travois-style litter or sledge. Dog teams recovered corpses in the same manner. They could also locate concealed enemy troops or escaped prisoners and were adept at detecting mines. The Soviets also experimented with training dogs to deliver explosives. Literal "dogs of war" were harnessed with mines and deployed against German units in several areas of western Russia during heavy fighting in 1941. Some were trained to crawl under vehicles while wearing bombs that trailed wires back to their master's position, where the wires connected to manual detonators. Other dogs were harnessed with bombs equipped with contact detonators rising above their back or head. In almost all cases these bomb dogs were shot by the Germans before any damage was done, though some accounts credit Soviet dogs with destroying several dozen Panzers. Others blew up Soviet tanks instead, or their handlers. U.S. Army dogs were trained to locate and attack snipers and did so with real success in Italy and France. U.S. Marines used dogs extensively in the Pacific to locate hidden Japanese positions. British dogs were used to detect mines and find wounded in Normandy, the Netherlands, and later in Germany.

DOLLFUSS, ENGLEBERT (1892–1934)   Foreign minister and chancellor of Austria, May 1932–July 1934. Suspicious of both left and right-wing political parties, he tried to govern directly without parliamentary support. He used the Army freely against demonstrators, unions, and workers' groups. This played into the hands of the *Nazis,* whom he fatally underestimated: in 1934 he was killed during a Nazi coup attempt.

See *Anschluss; Schuschnigg, Kurt von.*

DOLSCHTOSS   "stab-in-the-back."

See *Freikorps; Germany; Hitler, Adolf; Nazism; unconditional surrender; Versailles, Treaty of (1919).*

DOMBÅS, BATTLE OF (APRIL 14–19, 1940)   A five-day fight between German *Fallschirmjäger* and elements of the Norwegian Army, south of Trondheim. The Germans were eventually surrounded and pounded with artillery. The survivors surrendered. A number were rescued as Norwegian resistance elsewhere collapsed. Some went on to fight and die at Narvik.

DON (JANUARY–FEBRUARY, 1943)   Code name for the Soviet winter offensive operation that struck out toward Rostov in an effort to cut off the escape route of Field Marshal *Erich von Manstein's* Army Group Don. The attack was badly conducted. Its failure allowed most German units to escape the trap first sprung at *Stalingrad.* The operation is notable for Adolf Hitler's agreement to allow Manstein to withdraw to the Mius River, rather than lose another field army with a *Haltebefehl order.* On the Soviet side it is memorable for dismissal of General *Andrei Yeremenko* and his replacement by General *Rodion Y. Malinovsky,* leading to the retaking of Voroshilovgrad, Rostov, and most of the Donbass coal region.

DONBASS OFFENSIVE OPERATION (AUGUST 13–SEPTEMBER 22, 1943)   One of several rolling Red Army offensives undertaken in the aftermath of the German defeat at *Kursk,* this one against Army Group South. It was planned as a two-part southern flanking maneuver in coordination with a larger offensive along the entire Eastern Front over the summer and fall of 1943. The first part of the Donbass operation was a diversionary attack along the Mius River by Southern Front, designed to tie down Army Group South and prevent transfer of any of its forces to the larger battle at Kursk. That opening operation was marginally effective, leaving a weakened German position in the western Donbass to face the main assault by Southwestern Front under General *Nikolai Vatutin,* supported by Southern Front. Field Marshal *Erich von Manstein* commanded the German defense. He asked for an additional 12 divisions from Adolf Hitler necessary to hold the Donbass, but there were no troops to spare. The Wehrmacht was reeling backward from defeat of Army Group Center at Kursk and unfolding Soviet counteroffensives in Operations *KUTUZOV* and *RUMIANTSEV.* Manstein's 6th Army, reformed after the original was lost at *Stalingrad,* and his 1st Panzer Army were pushed back from the Mius River by the end of August. Southwestern Front then broke through the German lines to take Stalino (Donetsk) on September 8. Lead Soviet elements advanced 190 miles to reach the Dnieper on September 22. The speed of the advance induced a panicked German retreat. Yet, Hitler decided against issuing another *Haltebefehl order.* Instead, he allowed Manstein to pull back to the *WOTAN Line,* a position whose supposed strength existed more in the Führer's mind than on the ground. But by then, there were few strong German positions left along the Eastern Front and a yawning gap between the southern and central sectors of the German line.

DONBASS-ROSTOV DEFENSIVE OPERATION (SEPTEMBER 29–NOVEMBER 16, 1941)   Soviet nomenclature for the southernmost Red Army defense against Army Group South during Operation *BARBAROSSA.* The Germans call their early success in this sector and period of the campaign the "Battle of the Sea of Azov." Generals *Erich von Manstein* and *Ewald von Kleist,* acting under the command of Field Marshal *Gerd von Rundstedt,* trapped two Soviet armies in a pocket at Melitopol' and proceeded to cook them inside the great *Kessel* that formed there. German records assert that 100,000 Red Army soldiers surrendered, and list capture of the usual complement of huge quantities of tanks, guns, and even aircraft. There is no doubt material and troops losses were a major blow to the Red Army, which was already nearly bled to death along the entire Eastern Front. As the last Soviet reserves were drawn into a great fight along the route to Moscow, Soviet forces in the south thinned and finally broke. The German breakthrough came at the end of October, after weeks of heavy fighting along the Perekop Isthmus at the top of the Crimean peninsula. Manstein rushed forces into the Crimea, pressing the last peninsular defenders into the southwest corner of the peninsula while other Soviet troops who landed in relief were instead hemmed inside a coastal pocket during the *Kerch defensive operation.* The fearsome *siege of Sebastopol* began as the Germans invested and mercilessly pounded that fortified naval base. To the north, Kleist sent his Panzers racing ahead to Rostov. The city fell to *Waffen-SS* elements on November 21. However, the aggressive thrust left Kleist's flanks exposed and his troops in Rostov vulnerable in a deep salient. Soviet Southern Front attacked the salient, prompting Rundstedt to ask Adolf Hitler for permission to withdraw to a more defensible line. Hitler refused. When Rundstedt ordered a tactical retreat anyway and the Red Army subsequently liberated Rostov, Rundstedt was relieved by an angry Führer. He was replaced by Field Marshal *Walter von Reichenau.*

DÖNITZ, KARL (1891–1980)   German admiral. Commander of the Kriegsmarine *U-boat* arm from 1935; commander in chief of the Kriegsmarine, 1943–1945. He served in U-boats during World War I. In 1918 his boat was surfaced, and he was captured and imprisoned in Great Britain. After the war, the *Treaty of Versailles*

(1919) forbade Germany from building or operating any U-boats. Dönitz emerged from the Great War as perhaps the world's most accomplished student of submarine warfare. He was the obvious person to head a secret planning group within the Kriegsmarine, which spent the 1920s in U-boat research and planning, using front companies located in Denmark and the Netherlands. Nine training boats were thus already built in secret and serviceable when the *Anglo-German Naval Agreement* lifted the U-boat ban in 1935. Dönitz oversaw construction of an expanded U-boat fleet leading into the war, though he failed to make his view prevail with Adolf Hitler that U-boats would be the main challengers to British sea power in the event of war. Well before the war Dönitz envisioned a navy made up primarily of U-boats, supported by air reconnaissance and naval intelligence. But, until 1943, Hitler remained committed to the ill-timed and even fantastical *Z-Plan*. He was also held back during most of the prewar period by the parity clause of the 1935 agreement, which limited German U-boats to the same tonnage as submarines of the Royal Navy. He therefore opposed plans to build "U-cruisers" or super U-boats, as these took up too much of the permitted tonnage.

From the start of the *Battle of the Atlantic (1939–1945)*, Dönitz was the most important figure in the Kriegsmarine, personally directing all U-boat operations. When the United States fully entered the fight in December 1941, Dönitz promised Hitler "einen kräftigen Paukenschlag" ("a mighty drumroll") of U-boat sinkings off the American coast. His captains did indeed enjoy their second "happy time" of the war, but Dönitz was held back by Hitler's insistence on deploying U-boats to defend iron ore supplies from Sweden that passed through Norwegian waters, while others were diverted into new campaigns in the Mediterranean. Dönitz replaced Admiral *Erich Raeder* as commander in chief of the Kriegsmarine on January 30, 1943, and immediately ordered a halt to construction of capital warships. He transferred all work and combat crews to submarines, thereby finally achieving his dream of a vast submarine fleet of at least 300 U-boats. Organized to fight in *wolf packs* to hunt down and mass attack convoys, it was already too late: Dönitz's U-boats lost the battle that summer. He recalled all boats from the deep Atlantic and ordered them to prowl only in coastal waters.

A fanatic Nazi and fierce anti-Semite, after failure of the *July Plot* Dönitz broke with German military tradition and joined the *Nazi Party* in 1944. He was named Hitler's successor on April 30, 1945, after spending many of the final days with his lord and master deep underground in the Führerbunker in Berlin. Upon Hitler's suicide, Dönitz was briefly the last Führer of the Third Reich. His signature act as leader was to order Operation *REGENBOGEN*. Then he formally surrendered all German armed forces to the Allies. He was retained for two weeks by the Allies to assist with physical surrender of German ground forces, then arrested. He was tried by the *Nuremberg Tribunal* as a major *war criminal*, largely on the insistence of Soviet and British authorities. He was acquitted of crimes against peace and against humanity, but convicted of palling a war of aggression. He was also charged with war crimes for orders to U-boat captains to ignore rules of *cruiser warfare* specified under the *London Submarine Agreement (1936)*, notably explicit instructions not to rescue enemy or neutral crew and passengers from any ships sunk. A specific citation was made of his *Laconia Order* issued in September 1942. It was a cruel war: well before the "Laconia" incident, Dönitz told his captains in December 1939, "Rescue no one and take no one with you. Have no care for the ships' boats." That was long before he lost two sons serving aboard U-boats. He was sentenced to 10 years, the lightest sentence given to any convicted major defendant. Mitigating his punishment was a letter from *Chester Nimitz* admitting that the USN conducted comparable submarine warfare practices against Japan. Released in 1956, Dönitz's clipped German tones became familiar in oral histories and English-language film narratives of the naval war.

See also *ASDIC; Direction-Finding (D/F); Enigma machine; Leigh Light.*

Suggested Reading: Peter Padfield, *Dönitz: The Last Nazi Leader* (1984).

DONOVAN, WILLIAM (1883–1959) "Wild Bill." Chief of the *Office of Strategic Services (OSS)*. In 1940 he was sent to London by President Franklin D. Roosevelt to learn tradecraft from the *Special Operations Executive (SOE)* and other British intelligence branches, preparatory to setting up American counterpart organizations. He then helped found the OSS in mid-1942, and ran it throughout the war.

DOODLEBUG British slang for the V-1 rocket.
See *V-weapons program.*

DOOLITTLE RAID (APRIL 18, 1942) A daring first bombing of Tokyo and other Japanese cities conducted on April 18, 1942, within just a few months of the attack on Pearl Harbor. It was named for its initiator and commander, James Doolittle (1896–1993). Land-based, long-range, heavy B-25 bombers were used rather than naval aircraft. The B-25s were modified and launched from an aircraft carrier, which steamed in secret to reach maximum range from Japan. Doolittle achieved total surprise by flying just above water level until his attack force made landfall, then climbing and separating to acquire targets. Most of the planes dropped small bomb loads that did minor military and economic damage, then flew on to land safely at airfields in Nationalist China. The Japanese scrambled every available ship and plane to find the American carrier, without success. Of the 80 crew involved in the raid, 3 were killed and 8 were captured. The rest survived to eventually return home and rejoin the war. One bomber landed in Soviet territory, where its crew was interned because the Soviet Union was not then at war with Japan. Eight aircrew survived crashes in northern China. They were tried and convicted of "*war crimes*" by ad hoc Japanese military courts; one flyer was executed in violation of his status as a *prisoner of war.* The Japanese Army in China carried out severe reprisals against villages accused of hiding the Doolittle raiders: unknown thousands of Chinese civilians were murdered.

The Doolittle Raid had two purposes: raise home front morale and demonstrate to the Japanese that the United States would not soon or easily quit the war. Too many in Japan's war party had hoped that the shock of the *Pearl Harbor* attack and loss of the Philippines, Guam, and Wake would convince the Americans to make an early peace that left Japan in control of its new Pacific empire. Instead, the Doolittle raid carried to Japan an important and decisive message: the United States would prosecute the war by any and all means available until complete victory was achieved over the Empire of Japan. News of the raid thrilled American troops and civilians while stunning many Japanese civilians and damaging the prestige of the military. The raid also shocked Japan's leaders: *Hideki Tōgō* witnessed it from the air while circling to land on a routine flight. It provoked Admiral *Isoroku Yamamoto* to attack Midway Island in search of a decisive naval battle that instead led to the disaster of the *Battle of Midway* in June. The Japanese had discovered in the starkest manner possible that, despite assurances from their leaders that the home islands were invulnerable to enemy air attack, families, homes, and cities would indeed be bombed by the enemy. For the Doolittle Raid was only the first small taste of blood in the mouth, the initial promise of mass death falling from the sky yet to come in 1944–1945. Before the war was over hundreds of thousands of Japanese on the home islands would die from tens of thousands of tons of high explosives, incendiaries, and then two atomic bombs delivered by American warplanes.

DORA

See V-weapons program.

DORA

An 800 mm German rail gun, the largest and most famous artillery piece of World War II. It was built to smash the *Maginot Line* with seven-ton shells hurled over 23 miles. But "Dora" was not ready in time for *FALL GELB*. Its less well-known companion was called "Schwerer Gustav" ("Heavy Gustav"). It saw much more action than "Dora," notably during the *siege of Sebastopol*. Both giant guns were built by the Krupp works. Because "Schwerer Gustav" and other German siege guns were used in the Crimea, they were unavailable to reduce the defenses of Leningrad in 1942. They were moved north only after the Red Army had already pushed back the Leningrad perimeter. The main problem with these and other giant guns built for the Wehrmacht was lack of mobility. That meant they rarely saw action and probably did not warrant the research, engineering, and transport dedicated to them.

See also V-weapons program.

DOUBLE CROSS SYSTEM

See XX committee.

DOUBLE ENVELOPMENT

A *scheme of maneuver* seeking to surround and entrap whole enemy formations, even those as large as armies or army groups.

See also Blitzkrieg; envelopment; operational art; Schwerpunkt; Vernichtungsschlacht.

DOUBLE-L SWEEP
See mines; minesweepers.

DOUGLAS, WILLIAM SHOLTO (1893–1969) RAF Air Chief Marshal. A Great War fighter ace, Douglas was deputy chief of air staff during the *Battle of Britain* in 1940. He succeeded Air Chief Marshal *Hugh Dowding* as head of Fighter Command in November 1940, and was in charge of fighter defenses during the *Blitz*. He served in the Middle East and eastern Mediterranean from January 1943, then as head of RAF Coastal Command from 1944 to 1945.

DOWDING, HUGH (1882–1970) RAF Air Chief Marshal. Originally trained as an officer of artillery, he took to the air as an austere, even aloof, member of the Royal Flying Corps in World War I. Dowding became head of Fighter Command in 1936. In that role he was principally responsible for the RAF's edge in radar and ground-to-air control during the *Battle of Britain* in 1940. He was responsible for trenchant advice to Neville Chamberlain not to throw away additional fighter squadrons in Norway and to Winston Churchill not to do the same in France once the Battle of France was lost by the end of May 1940. Dowding was nearing retirement age even before the great summer fight with the Luftwaffe, to which he made an invaluable contribution. But he was not without critics, notably those such as *Leigh-Mallory* who championed the "Big Wing" approach to concentrated fighter defense. Dowding was pushed out of Fighter Command on November 24, while the *Blitz* was still underway. He was treated quite shabbily, especially given his enormous service in the RAF's and the British nation's hour of greatest need. In July 1942, he formally retired.

DOWNFALL Code name of the planned invasion of Japan's home islands. It was subdivided into discrete invasions of Kyushu and Honshu. U.S. 6th Army and the Marines would provide 14 combat divisions for landings on Kyushu in OLYMPIC, a huge amphibious operation based in the Philippines and Okinawa. OLYMPIC was to be an all-American show on land, though other Western Allied naval assets would be involved. It was originally scheduled for September 1, 1945, but was rescheduled to November 1. Not all Kyushu would be occupied, just enough of a lodgement to secure air bases for land-based aircraft to support the invasion of Honshu by over 25 combat divisions in an operation code named CORONET. CORONET was set to take place on December 1, 1945. It was rescheduled for March 1, 1946, once logistical problems and resistance on Okinawa forced a reconsideration of plans. The main assault was to be carried out by U.S. 8th and 10th Armies, which were already in the Pacific. U.S. 1st Army was in Germany but was pulled out of fighting on May 1, one week before the German surrender, to ready for embarkation to the Pacific. Some 1.5 million Americans and half a million additional troops from various Western Allied nations were designated for transfer to the Pacific theater. That prospect embittered many who felt they had "done their bit" but were told they could not yet go home. An oversized

British and Commonwealth corps of up to five divisions and a French corps were slated to participate in the CORONET invasion. Allied ground forces were to be supported by massive air and sea assets, including Royal Navy and other Western Allied ships in support of the main force provided by the U.S. Navy.

General *Douglas MacArthur* would have commanded the planned invasions, with Admiral *Richmond K. Turner* designated to take charge of amphibious operations. The Japanese were prepared to defend against DOWNFALL under their *Ketsu-Gō* plan, for which they readied 10,000 aircraft, with 5,000 intended for *kamikaze* pilots. Hundreds of suicide attack boats were also readied, along with *Fukuryu* suicide divers. The main defense would be provided by 10 Japanese Army divisions on Kyushu alone. Two million soldiers altogether garrisoned the home islands, backed by millions of ill-trained and poorly equipped militia of dubious military worth. It was known from intelligence intercepts that the Japanese would fight all out at least against OLYMPIC, but that some top leaders were leaning toward acceptance of some kind of limited surrender. It should be remembered that most military planners preparing the OLYMPIC and CORONET plans were unaware of the existence of the Anglo-American *nuclear weapons program*. They therefore planned the DOWNFALL operation in the full expectation that it would be carried out.

The invasion was canceled when Japan surrendered on August 15, 1945, following stunning atomic attacks on *Hiroshima* on August 6, and *Nagasaki* on August 9, surrounding the Red Army's launch of its *Manchurian offensive operation* on August 8. It is now known that the Joint Chiefs of Staff position shifted away from a June recommendation to President Harry Truman to approve OLYMPIC. Admiral *Ernest King* was joined by Admiral *Chester Nimitz* in early August in opposing the invasion plan: the Navy command wanted to bomb, bombard, and blockade Japan instead. Therefore, it is not certain the operation would have been carried out. But nor is certain it would have been canceled had Japan not surrendered when it did. Finally, it is not clear what the cost in lives would have been if bombing and blockade over many more months were the chosen instrument of coercion of Japan, rather than the sharper end to the war produced by dropping atomic bombs. In any case, as the estimated cost in American lives of carrying out OLYMPIC rose due to the massive Japanese build-up on Kyushu, and in the face of the horrendous battle experience on Okinawa, Truman agreed to drop two atomic bombs on Japan.

See also Sho-Gō.

Suggested Reading: Richard Frank, *Downfall: The End of the Imperial Japanese Empire* (1999).

DP "Displaced Person." Western Allied (and later, United Nations Organization) term for an external refugee, that is, one displaced from his or her home country.

DRAGOON (AUGUST 15, 1944) Code name for the invasion of Mediterranean France by the Western powers. It was code named "ANVIL" during the planning phase. Winston Churchill vehemently opposed the plan to the bitter end, arguing vainly for a continuation of his "flanking strategy" by calling for troops slated for the south of France to instead launch a new offensive in northern Italy. When that was firmly rejected by the Americans, he proposed other schemes for landings in the Aegean, eastern Mediterranean, and, most bizarrely, for a landing in Brittany. Instead, U.S. 7th Army—comprising one American and one French corps—moved from Italy and landed on the southern coast of France on August 15, in the Gulf of Leon east of Marseilles. Little resistance was encountered during the landings. Marseilles and Toulon quickly fell, although the harbors were demolished by retreating Germans. Even so, Marseilles soon proved an essential entry point for supporting logistics. It easily surpassed the Brittany ports and Cherbourg in importance, while partly compensating for Field Marshal *Bernard Law Montgomery*'s failure to clear the Scheldt estuary and open the port of Antwerp until December.

The Italian front was put on hold so that forces in southern France could be expanded until a full French 1st Army and full U.S. 7th Army, together comprising 6th Army Group, were deployed and fighting toward the Rhine. DRAGOON thus enabled the Western Allies to establish a continuous front from the Alps to the Low Countries. Less happily, poorly armed young *Maquis* rose prematurely in the countryside as the Wehrmacht and *Waffen-SS* retreated. Many were slaughtered. Faced with the rapid enemy advance, Adolf Hitler approved withdrawal by Army Group G (1st and 19th Armies) toward new defensive positions along the southern German border. The Germans wrecked the French railway system as they retreated, forcing the Western Allies to rely heavily on motor transport and form several southern variants of the *Red Ball express*. Small German garrisons remained to hold the ports, while other troops were deployed as so-called *Wellenbrecher* to delay the advance. They did not succeed. Instead, they represented more ill-considered wastage of waning Wehrmacht combat strength.

See also Devil's Brigade; Vercors.

Suggested Reading: Alan Wilt, *The French Riviera Campaign of August 1944* (1981).

DRESDEN, BOMBING OF (FEBRUARY 13–15, 1945)   Dresden escaped destruction by the *Combined Bomber Offensive* until a great raid was carried out over three days from February 13–15, 1945. As the last sizeable city in Germany not yet heavily bombed, and as a major rail and road center, Dresden was packed with refugees fleeing the advancing Red Army. Another 25,000 Western Allied prisoners of war were also in or near the city. "Blind illuminator" aircraft marked the target on February 13. Next came Mosquito "visual marker" aircraft, swooping in low to drop thousands of flares and fire-target markers. They were followed by 20 Pathfinder "Lancasters," heavy bombers that dropped high explosive markers from medium altitude. Next to arrive was the main attack bomber stream of 500 "Lancasters." They flew out of a *Mandrel* screen to hit Dresden with a mix of high explosives and incendiaries. The attackers lost just six planes while achieving high accuracy over an exceptionally well-marked target zone. Thousands of small fires quickly merged to form a calamitous firestorm, initially fed by strong natural winds, then creating uncontrolled winds of its own, sucking fuel, broken buildings, and people into the flames. The Germans lighted a decoy fire outside the city, but this was ignored by the Lancasters. The next morning, 311 American B-17s hit the city, while other American bomber streams attacked Magdeburg and Chemnitz. Prague was also bombed, in error. The Americans followed up a day later when planes looking for a secondary target dropped another 400 tons of ordnance on Dresden. The combined effect of the bombing was to create a firestorm in the center of Dresden.

The effectiveness of the follow-on bombing at Dresden was largely determined by the unusual accuracy of the initial target marking and by favorable weather. The proportionate mix of high explosive to incendiaries dropped was not unusual. In fact, fewer incendiaries were used against Dresden than in several other city bombings where firestorms did not result: the usual mix by 1945 of high explosives to incendiaries was 60:40. At Dresden the bombing created a devastating effect that was first seen in Hamburg, but was generally hard to achieve in Germany's largely stone city centers. In other German cities, wide boulevards had retarded creation of firestorms, but these were absent at Dresden. In addition, civil defense measures made things worse: tunnels made to connect cellars in a system of makeshift underground shelters instead funneled the fire into new areas, and onto huddling refugees. The tunnels also channeled large amounts of carbon monoxide into the cellars, poisoning those inside. For decades, there was enormous controversy about casualty figures. Wild claims of 120,000 or more were made at the time by *Josef Göbbels*. These were repeated in the 1960s by the discredited falsifier of records and convicted Holocaust-denier, David Irving. More honest historians have reached a modern consensus of 25,000–35,000 killed at Dresden. Western Allied prisoners in the area, among them the writer Kurt Vonnegut, were forced to clear away charred corpses and rubble.

Controversy also attended responsibility for ordering the raid, with open criticism made shortly afterward in Parliament, from some pulpits, and in the British press. In otherwise comprehensive memoirs, Winston Churchill elided over the bombing of Dresden and appeared to seek to shift blame to others. *Arthur Harris* never repented from the general policy of *area bombing* conducted under his authority by RAF Bomber Command, or the Dresden raid. He also tried to distance himself from criticism by suggesting that higher authorities insisted upon the bombing. There was some effort by the British to later assert that Joseph Stalin specifically requested that Dresden be bombed. That may in fact have occurred: it is certain that Stalin requested specific raids on Berlin and Leipzig, for instance. It has been clearly demonstrated in recent histories that bombing Dresden was part of a more general air campaign to help clear the way for rapid westward advance of the Red Army by creating transportation confusion and otherwise inhibiting Wehrmacht movement in rear areas, including by deliberately sending hundreds of thousands of refugees onto the German road and rail systems. The Dresden raid, above all others, came to symbolize the role that terror bombing played in the strategic air campaign against Germany. It was even upheld by some as a key example supporting a specious moral revisionism that held war crimes by the Western Allies were equivalent to those committed systematically by Germans. In the West, the Dresden raid in particular and the general trend toward *total war* by *strategic bombing* weighed on consciences, including for those who believed bombing to be justified and necessary. Even the British official history ultimately did not disagree that Dresden might be well-described as a "terror bombing."

Judging Dresden by peacetime standards many decades removed from the event is now common. It should also be remembered what was in the minds of planners at the time. The Western Allies were taking their worst casualties of the war in Germany: the U.S. Army alone took 136,480 casualties against the Germans just in December 1944–January 1945, and over 27,000 in the week prior to the raid. And there was real worry at the highest levels that Western armies had lost initiative and that the war would extend into August or later. At least one leading German historian, Goetz Bergander, has argued that the Dresden raid provided a great psychological shock and fear that helped hasten the end of the war. None of that may excuse the methods used by Western Allied air forces in 1945: not seeking to avoid inflicting casualties on civilians but deliberately targeting civilians to wreak havoc among Wehrmacht military transportation and communications systems. Still, contemporary concerns importantly help explain why the policy was adopted. And even Churchill wrote in private shortly after the raid: "The destruction of Dresden remains a serious query against the conduct of Allied bombing."

See also air power; area bombing; morale bombing.

Suggested Reading: Paul Addison and Jeremy Crang, eds., *Firestorm: The Bombing of Dresden* (2006).

DRÔLE DE GUERRE "Mock war." The French equivalent reference to what British and Americans called the *Phoney War*.
See also Sitzkrieg.

DRUMBEAT "PAUKENSCHLAG."
See Atlantic, Battle of the (1939–1945); Dönitz, Karl.

DUCE "Leader"
See Mussolini, Benito. See also fascism; Führer.

DUKW Dual drive heavy amphibian trucks built by General Motors. They were six-wheeled and weighed 2 1/2 tons. The letter designation derived from the model number and was not an acronym per se: D stood for model year, U for amphibian, K for all wheel drive, and W for its dual rear axles. It made for a memorable pun, however, as soldiers watched "ducks" waddle through water. Over 20,000 were built. First used in the *HUSKY* invasion of Sicily, many saw action in Italy, France, and in the Pacific war. Their great advantage was an ability to move directly from offshore supply ships to unload at inland depots, keeping pace as assault troops moved inland from the beaches.

DULAG A German *prisoner of war* transit camp. Western air crew were processed through "Dulag Luft" until they reached a permanent *Stalag* or, if officers, an *Oflag*. Not all prisoners made it to the camps: German civilians sometimes murdered enemy aircrew, accusing them of being "Terrorflieger."

DULLES, ALLEN (1893–1969) A career diplomat from an early age, Dulles served in a minor capacity with the American delegation to the Paris Peace Conference in 1919. He rose to prominence as head of the *Office of Strategic Services* in Berne, the main American intelligence and covert operations agency operating in the European theater during the war. His OSS office ran spies and counterintelligence operations of varying importance. He was also involved in negotiations with the Vatican and concerning the surrender of Axis forces in Italy in 1945. He later helped found, and became first director of, the Central Intelligence Agency. His brother was John Foster Dulles.

DUMBARTON OAKS CONFERENCE (AUGUST–OCTOBER, 1944) A meeting of representatives of the *Big Four* powers held to draft the framework agreement leading to founding of the United Nations Organization. Most major decisions about division of powers, membership and representation, and other guiding principles were taken at Dumbarton Oaks by the Great Powers alone. That left minor adjustments and amendments for the *San Francisco Conference* of 1945, with two key exceptions: the scope of the veto power of Permanent Members of the Security Council and the issue of separate representation for each of the 15 Soviet republics, over which Joseph Stalin threatened to scuttle the entire United Nations. This matter was settled later by a compromise that gave the Soviets three General Assembly seats (Russia, Ukraine, and Belarus). The United States, alone among the Great Powers, pushed to include human rights in the United Nations Charter. It failed at Dumbarton Oaks but succeeded—with considerable small power assistance—in inserting human rights into the United Nations Treaty at San Francisco.

DUNKIRK EVACUATION (MAY 25–JUNE 2, 1940) When Allied defense against the German *FALL GELB* operation broke, London organized Operation DYNAMO: a desperate withdrawal of 340,000 British, Commonwealth, and other Allied (120,000 French and 20,000 Belgian) troops from the beaches and port of Dunkirk. The operation lasted from May 25 to June 2, 1940. Many clamored aboard rescue ships without even basic equipment, while all tanks, trucks, and heavy weapons were abandoned on the beaches. This massive amphibious retreat was made necessary by a German breakthrough that split the British Expeditionary Force (BEF) and some French and Belgian divisions from the rest of the French Army which forced surrender by Belgium on May 28. There was significant misunderstanding and hostility at first between British and French troops in the enclave, as most of the French who were evacuated were not embarked until nearly all British troops had already left. The main reason was that the French High Command refused to accept the need for any evacuations until after the Belgian surrender on May 28, but later used the British evacuation as an excuse for military failure and signature of the armistice on June 22.

The evacuation was accomplished with the aid of hundreds of civilian craft of all types and sizes, the famed "Little Ships" that included personal yachts, London river barges, and fishing vessels. But mainly it was carried out by Royal Navy minesweepers, destroyers, and other warships. A heroic rearguard defense was made by elements of French 1st Army and selected British and Canadian units, while the RAF fended off Luftwaffe attacks on the beaches and ships and the Royal Navy fought off German E-boats. The RAF lost nearly 200 fighters over nine days defending the Dunkirk enclave; the Luftwaffe lost 240 planes attacking it. The Allies also lost 9 large warships ships and 9 destroyers, with 19 more destroyers damaged. Daylight ship runs stopped on June 1. Another 60,000 French troops and elements of the British perimeter force were evacuated under cover of night on June 2.

Escape of over 320,000 enemy soldiers from Dunkirk was made possible by Adolf Hitler's "stop order." For two critical days, May 24–25, he forbade Panzer forces to pursue a retreating and badly demoralized enemy. But it is important to note that the generals of the OKH agreed with Hitler: their attention was drawn south to what they believed would be a large battle in front of Paris. Hitler and the OKH alike wanted to preserve worn and tired Panzer divisions for that fight and to let slower arriving German infantry and the Luftwaffe finish the job along the coast. About 120,000 British troops remained in France after Dunkirk. Smaller evacuations got some men out, but most of the 51st Highland Division was compelled to surrender on June 12. Over 156,000 British, Canadian, and Polish troops were then evacuated from Cherbourg. although 3,000 died when their departing liner was bombed by the Luftwaffe just off the French coast. Behind the German lines, Wehrmacht and *Waffen-SS* carried out several massacres of French civilians—a sign of occupation practices to come. There were also instances along the perimeter of British troops shooting unarmed or individual surrendering Germans. Dunkirk was not the first time that British forces were chased from Europe by the Wehrmacht and forced into desperate evacuation by sea—British failure in northern Norway was contemporaneous. More dark days and forced amphibious departures from Greece and Crete still lay in the future for the British Army and its Commonwealth and minor European allies. And as Churchill told the House of Commons on June 4: "Wars are not won by evacuations."

See also Gort, John.

DUNKIRK SPIRIT A "necessary legend" of class-free, personal and national self-sacrifice by the British born of the *Dunkirk evacuation* in 1940, especially noting the role played by civilian "Little Ships." That was a remarkable psychological achievement in the face of the stark reality of humiliating defeat of the British Expeditionary Force (BEF) in France. Winston Churchill warned those who would turn defeat into a false victory: "wars are not won by evacuations." Still, the "Dunkirk spirit" was crucial in sustaining national morale after France surrendered on June 22, 1940, and as Britain suffered through the *Battle of Britain* and the *Blitz* with little prospect of ultimate victory. It wore thin after that, as the war dragged on and victory seemed a far distant, if not quite impossible, prospect. It was not until the end of 1942 that Churchill could realistically foresee ultimate victory, although most of the hard and bloody slogging done by the British and their allies still remained to be suffered.

DUPPLE

See window.

DUTCH EAST INDIES   This important Dutch colony comprised most of what is today Indonesia. It was defended by the Netherlands East Indies Army, or KNIL ("Koninklijk Nederlands Indisch Leger"), a mixed Dutch and native colonial force of about 40,000 light infantry first established in 1830. The colony's oil resources were a primary target of the Japanese *nanshin* strategy. In August 1940, with the Netherlands under German occupation, the Japanese brought pressure on the Dutch colonial government to make fundamental concessions to the idea of the *Greater East Asian Co-Prosperity Sphere*. Local Dutch authorities were loyal to the government-in-exile in London and refused, knowing that the Japanese were shipping critical East Asian supplies to Nazi Germany via Siberia. Japan's assault on the colony in early 1942 was carried out by General Hitoshi Imamura at the head of 16th Army. The attack was brought forward by a month after offensive operations went so well and so quickly elsewhere the invasion force could be strongly reinforced. The attack began with landings on Borneo on December 15, followed in January by landings on Amboina, Celebes, and Sumatra. The Japanese also landed on Timor in late February. The main fighting centered on a struggle for control of Java, heartland of the archipelagic colony and center of Dutch colonial administration. Loss by the Allies of the naval *Battle of the Java Sea (February 27–28, 1942)* set the stage for a Dutch defeat on land, too. Japanese landings on Java began on March 1. The Dutch surrendered a week later, on March 8. When the brief campaign was over the vital oil fields of the Dutch East Indies were wrecked, but in Japanese hands. The wells were repaired and oil soon poured into Japanese tankers and headed north.

General Hitoshi Imamura at first governed the colony with a light hand, at least by Japanese standards. By 1944 the Japanese recruited 35,000 Javanese into a nominally pro-Japanese militia—PETA, or "Pembela Tanah Air." Another 25,000 "hei-ho," or native auxiliaries, also signed up while Some 50,000 more Javanese enrolled in basic units that were more political in nature than military. As it became clear that the Japanese would lose the Dutch East Indies to the Americans and Australians, with the Dutch in their wake, PETA rose in rebellion against the Japanese in February 1945. The Japanese *merchant marine* was by then mostly on the ocean bottom, and Japan had no way to transport East Indies oil to its home islands; so the Japanese Army blew up the oil fields. Over a confused six months of negotiations mixed with violence and numerous political kidnappings, Japanese occupation forces worked out a modus vivendi with local anti-Dutch nationalists. Achmad Sukarno (1901–1970) declared independence on August 17, 1945, two days after Japan itself surrendered to the Allies. He did so with encouragement from the Japanese. Fighting broke out when Dutch troops and colonial administrators arrived with Western Allied occupation forces, as the Dutch sought to reestablish direct colonial rule. An interim agreement placed the colony in a "special relationship" with the Netherlands, but that agreement quickly broke down and fighting resumed. The postwar Dutch campaign was so brutal and politically untenable the Netherlands government came under strong international pressure and finally agreed to depart the colony by the end of 1949. KNIL was disbanded the next year.

See also Tarakan.

DUTCH NEW GUINEA   Irian Jaya.
See New Guinea campaign (1942–1945).

DUTCH WEST INDIES   Dutch colonies in the Caribbean, but also Dutch Guiana. British and French troops occupied Dutch Guiana in 1940, after the German occupation of the Netherlands. The French component of the garrison was replaced by U.S. troops in 1942.

DYLE LINE   A defensive line in Belgium also called the "KW-Line." It was extended at the last minute into the Netherlands in a failed Allied effort to link with the Dutch Army. The British Expeditionary Force (BEF) and the best and most mobile units of the French Army advanced toward the Dyle Line starting on May 10, 1940, the opening day of the *FALL GELB* invasion of France and the Low Countries. The operational surprise achieved by the Germans in the *Ardennes* made the Dyle Line a trap rather than a defensible position. The BEF, French Army, and most of the Belgian Army all pulled back, with the BEF and some French and Belgians ultimately departing France as well during the *Dunkirk evacuation*.

See also Gamelin, Maurice; Gort, John; Weygand, Maxime.

DYNAMO
See Dunkirk evacuation; FALL GELB; Gort, John.

E

EAGLE DAY "Adlertag"
See Britain, Battle of.

EAGLE SQUADRONS Three squadrons of American fighter pilots recruited into the RAF by the *Clayton Knight committee*. They flew from September 1940 until September 1942, when they were transferred whole into the USAAF.

EAKER, IRA (1896–1987) USAAF general. Eaker headed U.S. 8th Bomber Command in Britain, then all U.S. 8th Air Force from December 1942. He was a powerful proponent of *precision bombing* vs. *area bombing,* insisting that American bombers were so heavily armed they could conduct daylight raids over Germany. During 1943 he was instrumental in effecting the *Combined Bomber Offensive.* At the start of 1944 he replaced Air Marshal *Arthur Tedder* as commander of all Western Allied air forces in the Mediterranean. He remained in that theater until April 1945.

EAST AFRICAN CAMPAIGN (1940–1941) Shortly after Italy declared war on France and Great Britain in June 1940, 25,000 Italian troops moved out of Abyssinia into British Somaliland, while simultaneously occupying several border posts along the border of Sudan. From August 15 the Italians pushed a small British force of 4,000 men, including the Somali Camel Corps, into a considered retreat to Berbera. Benito Mussolini boasted of the conquest and taunted the British over their first lost colony, which he promised and believed would not be the last. Amedeo, Duke of Aosta, was Italian Viceroy and Governor in East Africa. He had available nearly 100,000 Regio Esercito troops in addition to

200,000 unreliable local troops. Many of these men were tied down in garrison duty or fighting rising Abyssinian and some Somali guerilla resistance in Italian rear areas. Still, that was more than six times the initial British total of 42,000 troops, most of whom were African soldiers drawn from Kenya, Tanganyika, and other nearby colonies. This force was eventually reinforced by 4th and 5th Divisions of the *Indian Army*, transported across the Gulf from Aden. South African and *Free French* ground forces also arrived in theater, the latter traveling from French Somaliland. The British were similarly outnumbered in armor and aircraft at first, although the South African Air Force subsequently provided solid air cover and ground support—including with Ju-88 bombers. As the campaign progressed, the RAF in East Africa received more and new models of fighters while the Regia Aeronautica was progressively outclassed and attrited. British control of the Suez Canal and naval dominance of the sea lanes allowed growing ground and armor reinforcement from July to October, 1940. British naval power effectively isolated the Italians, who additionally lacked aggressive commanders and suffered from low morale.

With superior actionable intelligence available because Italian army and air force codes were broken at *Bletchley Park,* the British attacked on November 6, 1940. The Italians quickly pulled back from outposts on the Sudanese border. The British launched their main offensive out of the Anglo-Egyptian Sudan on January 19, 1941. That was three weeks before schedule, an advance of plans made possible because the British learned about the Italian withdrawal from code breakers. They drove into Eritrea and then onto the Abyssinian lowland country. But the Italian garrison in Eritrea was of high quality, which led to several weeks of hard fighting in that colony and then in the Abyssinian highlands. The main battle took place at Keren on March 11, where 13,000 British and Indian troops defeated 23,000 Italians and colonials. Keren was taken on March 27, breaking the back of Italian resistance. Asmara fell to the Indian 5th Division on April 1. Indian Army and Free French troops took Massawa on the coast on April 8.

A second British force of East African, West African, and South African troops attacked into British Somaliland out of Kenya, moving with speed along the coast. The main force was led out of Kenya into Italian Somaliland on January 24 by Lieutenant General *Alan Coningham*. On March 16, APPEARANCE was staged out of Aden. It landed two battalions of Sikhs from the Indian Army, along with a Somali commando unit, on the flanks of Berbera. Caught between two British pincers, the Italians fell back in great disorder, abandoning Mogadishu on February 25 and Berbera on March 16, and thence retreating into Abyssinia. Cunningham's troops pursued, linked with British forces already in Abyssinia, and took Addis Ababa on April 6. From there, they fanned out into the interior, north and south. The Regio Esercito simply collapsed. In part, that was due to thousands of its men falling sick with malaria, for which the Italians lacked medicine: Aosta himself died of malarial fever a few months after the campaign. British and Commonwealth forces advanced over 1,700 miles in just a few weeks. They smashed through Italian defenses and captured most Italian troops in East

Africa at a cost of just 501 Allied dead. Emperor *Haile Selassie* returned to his capital on May 5. He had not seen Addis Ababa since fleeing the country during the *Abyssinian War (1935–1936)*. He was escorted to Abyssinia by *Orde Wingate* at the head of a special forces unit known as *Gideon Force*. The last Italian troops in the country holed up in a mountain fortified zone at Amba Alagi. The British closed on them in two wide columns, accompanied by Abyssinian troops known locally and to the British as the *"Patriots."* A siege of Amba Alagi lasted 25 days before the Italians surrendered on May 16. The last Italian resistance was made by a garrison that held out at Gondar in the northwest for seven months, until November 27, 1941.

The East African campaign was the first real success for the British Army in World War II. It came against a poorly equipped, badly demoralized, and poorly led Italian and colonial army supported by a single German motorized company. Victory in East Africa provided a critical boost to British and Commonwealth morale. Along with victories over Italian armies at *Sidi Barrani* and *Bardia* in North Africa, success in East Africa assured American leaders that Britain was prepared to fight on against the Axis. Most importantly, it secured the Indian Ocean routes to and from India and the Far East, thereby permitting safer transit for Australian troops to Suez, thence to Egypt and into the fight for North Africa. All that enabled President Franklin D. Roosevelt to reclassify the Red Sea as no longer a war zone, despite the continuing presence of Axis submarines. That legalism permitted American merchantmen to ply those waters and the Gulf of Aden. In turn, that released more of the British merchant marine to bring crucial goods across the Atlantic. The victory in East Africa also opened less critical overland and sea routes from South Africa to Egypt.

EAST CARPATHIAN OPERATION (SEPTEMBER–OCTOBER, 1944)
See Czechoslovakia.

EAST CHINA SEA, BATTLE OF (APRIL 1945)
See Okinawa campaign; Yamato, IJN

EASTERN FRONT   German and Western Allied term for the long battle line between Soviet forces and those of Nazi Germany and the minor Axis powers from the opening of *BARBAROSSA* on June 22, 1942, until the formal *unconditional surrender* of Germany on May 8, 1945. Some fighting continued in holdout pockets of resistance in Czechoslovakia and elsewhere in the east for another week after that. At its greatest physical girth in late 1942, the Eastern Front stretched 1,900 miles (2,800 km), from the flat shores of the Barents Sea in the Arctic north, across the vast forests of Belorussia and northwest Russia, down through the steppe lands of Ukraine, to the mountains of the Caucasus in the south. Maximum German penetration was also reached in 1942: at 1,075 miles inside the Soviet frontier. At that extreme, the Eastern Front included rear areas that encompassed over 600,000 square miles, much of it marked by *partisan* activity and mass killings by the Germans. Until the end of the war in 1945, it was not unusual for as many as 10 million soldiers on all sides to be engaged in the east, which saw some of the most sustained savagery in the history of war. From June 1941 to May 1945, at least 50 significant operations or major battles were fought on the Eastern Front, with an unknown number of smaller clashes of arms.

The central frontier between Germany and the Soviet Union lacked sharp natural barriers except for the Vistula and other flatland rivers, along with the roadless, impassible *Pripet Marshes* southwest of Moscow. The northern section of the front was heavily forested until it reached the tundra of the Arctic, where prolonged fighting was conducted under the endless light of "white nights" in high summer and over thick winter ice in the remorseless dark of Arctic winters. At its farthest eastward expanse, the southwestern section of the front brought fighting into the Kerch and Crimean peninsulas and the mountains and valleys of the northern Caucasus. Germans fought in the east as ancient ancestors had: not merely to win or survive, but to exterminate the local inhabitants to clear a way to resettlement of stolen land. This manner of exterminationist warfare had not been seen in Europe since ravages by Mongols, Magyars, or Teutonic Knights. Germans waged that war of extermination on a scale never before imagined: perhaps 40 million people died as a direct result of the German–Soviet war, 31 million of them citizens of the Soviet Union. Merciless fighting was the standard, not the exception, replete with lack of quarter and extermination squads (*Einsatzgruppen*), bitter and killing winters, and mass starvation and malign neglect of civilians. The "Eastern Front" was feared by all troops. It became legendary among Axis soldiers who fought there as a synonym for suffering and death.

See various named battles and operations, and *balcony; Commissar order; Courland Pocket; Demiansk pocket; Haltebefehl orders; Holocaust; horses; NKVD; Order #227; prisoners of war; rasputitsa; Red Army; Rzhev bulge; Schutzstaffel (SS); step; Toropets bulge; Waffen SS; Wehrmacht.*

EASTERN SOLOMONS, BATTLE OF (AUGUST 23–25, 1942)   Japanese historians call this fight the "Battle of the Solomon Sea." It was one of six carrier-to-carrier battles of World War II. It was provoked generally by the contest for control of *Guadalcanal,* but specifically by arrival of a Japanese troop convoy under heavy IJN escort led by Vice Admiral *Chuichi Nagumo.* Both fleets were extremely cautious about exposing their carriers in the wake of damage and losses suffered earlier at *Coral Sea* and *Midway.* The fleets never saw one another, but carrier-based aircraft sank an IJN light carrier and damaged the USS Enterprise, a prewar fleet carrier. The Japanese came off the worst, mainly because of losses of naval aircraft and experienced air crew, which their training system was less able to replace than the USN. The Japanese were also delayed in reinforcing their ground forces on Guadalcanal, and then were compelled to use fast warships rather than slow troopships. That meant the reinforcements landed without most of their heavy weapons, which could not be stored on the decks of warships.

See also Fletcher, Frank.

EAST-OCEAN MEETING POINT (EOMP)
See convoys.

EAST PRUSSIA
See Germany, conquest of; Goldap operation; Heiligenbeil pocket; Insterburg corridor; Insterburg-Königsberg operation; Landwacht; Mlawa-Elbing operation; Nationalkomitee Freies Deutschland (NKFD); Polish Corridor; Samland peninsula; Vistula-Oder operation.

EBAN EMAEL
See FALL GELB.

EBERT, FRIEDRICH (1871–1925) President of the Weimar Republic, 1920–1925.
See Germany.

E-BOAT "Enemy boat." A Western Allied designation for any small Kriegsmarine attack boat, but especially for a class of mid-size, fast attack torpedo boats. The Kriegsmarine called this vessel "S-boot," short for "Schnellboot" or "fast boat." They were larger and more powerful than comparable American PT-boats or British Motor Gun Boats (MGBs). E-boats flocked against Atlantic or Channel convoys in deadly, fast armadas that sometimes were made up of dozens of boats. Close to British home waters they were countered by destroyer escorts and MGBs. Adolf Hitler ordered many more S-boots built from April 1943, after his large surface ships were no longer able to operate outside the Baltic. But there were still too few E-boats, and they were individually too weak to prevent the seaborne invasion of his so-called *Festung Europa*. For several months after the invasion of France flotillas of E-boats made occasional, dashing attacks from bases in the Netherlands against shipping in the Channel.
See also Anzio; Slapton Sands attack.

ECONOMIC WARFARE
See Atlantic, Battle of; autarky; blockade; blockade runners; Combined Bomber Offensive; convoys; food supply; Lend-Lease; sanctions; strategic bombing; total war; unrestricted submarine warfare.

ECUADOR Like most other Latin American states, except Brazil, Ecuador sought to please the United States and obtain a seat at the United Nations postwar table by making a meaningless declaration of war against Japan in February 1945. It made no material contribution to the war effort.

EDELWEISS
See resistance (German).

***EDELWEISS* (JULY–DECEMBER, 1942)** The Wehrmacht summer operation into the North Caucasus in July–December, 1942, formerly code named *BLAU* IV. In Russian histories it is called the "North Caucasus strategic defensive operation" (July 25–December 31, 1942). It was conducted by Army Group A, which was split from the original Army Group South—Army Group B headed to the middle Don, thence to the Volga and Stalingrad, in what was first planned as merely a covering operation for EDELWEISS. As Army Group A advanced under command of Field Marshal *Wilhelm List,* it pulled units and reserves from Army Group B. Opposing the assault were about 820,000 men, after being reinforced, of North Caucasus Front led by Marshal *Semyon Budyonny.* The defenders had available only a few hundred tanks and aircraft because Joseph Stalin expected the main Wehrmacht summer offensive in the north. In addition, fighting along the Volga drew off men and resources intended for the North Caucasus, while the main railways into the Caucasus were cut by German armies farther north. List reached the foot of the Caucasus Mountains by the end of summer. A Panzer column he sent stretching toward the Caspian moved more slowly than Adolf Hitler liked due to heavy Soviet resistance and because List was outrunning his supply lines. List proposed reinforcing the Caspian advance, but Hitler's impatient eye was on the rich oil fields of the southern Caucasus: he sacked List on September 9 and took direct command from afar.

Hitler received spectacular propaganda photos of German troops on the highest peaks of the Caucasus, but his Panzers faced a huge natural barrier in the mountains as well as hard resistance from Trancaucasus Front, the renamed and now reinforced North Caucasus Front. Another four Soviet infantry armies farther south comprised Black Sea Front. A German amphibious thrust, *BLÜCHER II,* brought 11th Army across the Kerch Straits directly into the Caucasus in September, but by early November Army Group A lost all momentum. The German offensive failed even though it faced Red Army units commanded by an inept *NKVD* general, I. I. Maslennikov, through whom *Lavrenti Beria* played at military commander in the south. As the Germans stalled and parked for the winter, Hitler handed off command to General *Ewald von Kleist.* He let Kleist withdraw to defensible positions in December once events around *Stalingrad* turned toward the catastrophic for German 6th Army. Upon the spring thaw of 1943, the overstretched Wehrmacht pulled out of the Caucasus, except for a toehold retained on the Taman peninsula.

See also desert campaign (1940–1943); LACHSFANG; OKH; OKW.

EDEN, ANTHONY (1897–1977) British foreign secretary, 1935–1938 and 1941–1945. Eden made a timely resignation from the cabinet in 1938, just before the *Anschluss* of Austria and Germany. His reason was disagreement with *Neville Chamberlain* on policy toward Italy and over *appeasement* of Nazi Germany. The resignation made his career by establishing his reputation as a tough-minded man of principle, even though Eden had done nothing of particular usefulness when Adolf Hitler earlier remilitarized the *Rhineland* and Italy launched the *Abyssinian*

War. During the war Eden was an important aide to Winston Churchill, with whom he disagreed on several key issues. He attended all the major wartime summits. In 1945 he led Britain's delegation to the *San Francisco Conference.*

EGYPT   A 1936 treaty confined British troops in-country to the Canal Zone and set up a British–Egyptian condominium over the "Anglo-Egyptian Sudan." Egypt thus hosted British military bases during the war. London brought great pressure to bear on King Farouk to conform his government to British security needs, notably breaking with Italy and allowing British forces to base beyond the Canal Zone. On September 17, 1940, troops of the Regio Esercito attacked the British in Egypt, initiating the *desert campaign.* Officially, Egypt remained "nonbelligerent" even as the British used its territory as their main base in North Africa. Public opinion varied, but there was significant pro-Axis sentiment and even cheering as the *Afrika Korps* drove the British out of Tripoli and back to Egypt by the end of 1941. The British effectively engineered another palace coup to ensure a friendly Egypt lay to their strategic rear. There is no doubt that the British would have used force to protect the Suez Canal had a pro-Axis government come to power, as they showed in Iraq and Syria. Many Egyptian army officers were pro-Axis, and some were in secret contact with the Germans, including two later Egyptian presidents, Gamal Abdel Nasser and Anwar Sadat. Pro-Axis sentiment subsided after the Germans were driven from Egypt with the British victory at *Second El Alamein.* Egypt made a formal but meaningless declaration of war against Germany and Japan on February 26, 1945, principally as the price of a seat at the *San Francisco Conference* in April. British forces were again confined to the Canal Zone from 1946. They pulled out of Egypt in 1954, returned as invaders along with the French and Israelis in 1956, then departed for good.

EICHMANN, KARL ADOLF (1906–1962)   *Schutzstaffel (SS)* and *Gestapo* officer. This Austrian door-to-door vacuum cleaner salesman was a lifelong *anti-Semite.* In 1937 he visited Palestine to consult with Arab leaders of like mind, but was expelled as persona non grata by the British. His star rose with that of *Reinhard Heydrich,* though it was always much dimmer and distant. In late 1941 Eichmann was appointed head of the *Reichssicherheitshauptampt (RSHA)* Department IVB4, the so-called "Race and Resettlement Office." That placed him in charge of SS planning for slave labor and extermination camps in the east, though still under supervision by Heydrich. The two men hosted the *Wannsee conference* on January 20, 1942. In that remarkable meeting the SS drew *Nazi Party* officials and all relevant German government agencies into the extermination policy toward Jews and other "undesirables." The meeting thus set in motion construction of the extraordinary *death camp* machinery of the *Holocaust,* later named the *Aktion Reinhardt* program in "honor" of Reinhard Heydrich. As head of the SS Department of Jewish Affairs, Eichmann oversaw mass deportations of Jews from across Eastern Europe to the death camps. He experimented with various killing methods and closely studied the mechanics of killing to improve the murder system at *Auschwitz.* He then replicated the system in other extermination camps. In the last year of the war he headed a special *Einsatzgruppen* charged with deporting 400,000 Jews from Hungary to the camps. In that role, he negotiated blood ransom money in behalf of *Heinrich Himmler* for three trains filled with Jews sent into Switzerland without the knowledge of Adolf Hitler.

Eichmann was captured by U.S. forces in 1945, but he successfully concealed his identity while in detention. Several months later he escaped into hiding. It was later learned that he left Germany for Argentina in 1950: like several other top Nazis, he used a Vatican passport to pass through Western and international checkpoints. Eichmann was tracked down and kidnapped by agents of Israel's Mossad secret service on May 11, 1960. He was smuggled back to Israel on May 20, while drugged and dressed in an El Al airlines flight jacket. His trial was an international spectacular, despite Eichmann's bland and matter-of-fact descriptions of the most sordid acts in history. His defense was that he had only followed *superior orders;* it was rejected by the Israeli court just as it had been for other major war criminals at the *Nuremberg Tribunal*. Eichmann was convicted and hanged in 1962. The social philosopher Hannah Arendt observed the calm and detached Eichmann at his trial and concluded that the most remarkable thing about him and comparable Nazi functionaries was the "banality" of their evil. Israel released Eichmann's personal memoir in 2000 as evidence in a British Holocaust-denial and libel trial. In 2005 Mossad officially acknowledged its role in the Buenos Aires kidnapping.

EICKE, THEODORE (1892–1943)   Commandant of *Dachau* concentration camp, then inspector general of all *Schutzstaffel (SS)* concentration camps. He played a singular role as Adolf Hitler's loyal killer during the *Night of the Long Knives* in June 1934. He was commandant of the *Totenkopfverbände* from 1936. He organized the *Waffen-SS* Totenkopf Division and served with it on the Eastern Front from 1941 to 1943. He was killed when his small aircraft was shot down by the Soviets.

EIGHTH ROUTE ARMY   The name of the Chinese Communist or "Red Army," renamed the People's Liberation Army late in the *Chinese Civil War (1927–1949)*. It was the main Communist force in northern China throughout the *Sino-Japanese War (1937–1945),* when it was nominally under unified command of the *Guomindang* but in fact was tightly controlled by *Mao Zedong* and *Zhu De*. The other major Communist army was designated New Fourth Army, which fought in central China. Together, by 1945 the Communists put 900,000 troops into the field.

EINSATZGRUPPEN   "Action commandos" or "special task forces." The Wehrmacht used this term for antipartisan strike forces, but it is more usually associated in non-German literature with *Schutzstaffel (SS)* death squads. The first SS Einsatzgruppen were formed from Allgemeine-SS and police personnel from the *Sicherheitsdienst (SD)* and *Sicherheitspolizei* ("Sipo"). They later drew in *Waffen-SS* miscreants on punishment detail and non-German volunteers. Each Einsatzgruppe was battalion size, or about 3,000 men. Smaller detachments formed SS Einsatzkommando and Einsatztrupp that branched out during killing operations. Einsatzgruppen followed the wake of advancing Wehrmacht and Waffen-SS into Poland during *FALL WEISS (1939),* rounding up Polish Jews for summary execution by shooting. Mass burials of victims were in standard anti-tank ditches. There were four Einsatzgruppen at the start of the *BARBAROSSA* invasion of the Soviet Union in mid-1941. Like the Wehrmacht, they were ordered in the first instance to summarily execute all commissars and *politruks*. Their core SS character also led to proactive killing of Jews. Jews and Roma were also herded into ghettos where other SS and Nazi Party officials oversaw their mass starvation and death by epidemic diseases of tens of thousands. The four Einsatzgruppen in the field killed probably 500,000 Jews in the western Soviet Union over the second half of 1941. Einsatzgruppen murdered well over 1 million Jews from 1939 to 1942, and perhaps as many as 1.5 million. Most were killed by shootings, some were buried alive, while others were burned alive in locked buildings, or killed inside experimental mobile gas vans or with other improvised methods. We know all this because Einsatzgruppen commanders kept excellent records, filling out and filing in Berlin nearly 200 "Ereignismeldungen" or field reports. Some of these were introduced into evidence at postwar trials.

Einsatzgruppe A struck into Lithuania, Latvia, and Estonia in June 1941, following the tank tracks of Army Group North toward Leningrad. It carried out major massacres in Kovno, Riga, and Vilna. Einsatzgruppe B was based in Warsaw that June. It moved into Belorussia in the wake of Army Group Center, slaughtering its way through Grodno, Minsk, Brest-Litovsk, Slonim, Gomel, Mogilev, and Smolensk. Einsatzgruppe C also started out from Poland, departing Krakow for Ukraine, killing all the way to Kharkov and Rostov after massive Red Army collapses at Uman and Kiev at the hands of the northern detachments of Army Group South. There were large massacres of Jews at Lvov, Tarnopol, Zolochev, Kremenets, Kharkov, Zhitomir, and Kiev. One two-day massacre later became infamous: the killing of 33,771 people, mostly Jews but including some Red Army prisoners, outside Kiev at *Babi Yar*. Einsatzgruppe D followed the other wing of Army Group South into the Donbass and Crimea. It conducted massacres at Nikolayev, Kherson, Simferopol, Sevastopol, Feodosiya, and at dozens of smaller sites. It has long been known that local anti-Semites assisted the Einsatzgruppen in these murders or even carried out spontaneous killings and pogroms as the Red Army withdrew. More recent research, including by the Bundeswehr, confirms beyond doubt that the Wehrmacht also played a key and active role in the killings. It was not merely passive and certainly did not operate in ignorance of events, as was falsely claimed by its surviving generals for decades after the war.

It was partly to relieve SS Einsatzgruppen men of the trauma of having to shoot women and children that SS-Reichsführer *Heinrich Himmler* ordered *Reinhard Heydrich* and other SS planners to come up with other methods of "extermination." Gas vans proved inefficient and wasteful of fuel. SS and German government authorities therefore planned, at the *Wannsee Conference* and elsewhere, and started to build huge *death camps* with permanent gassing and crematoria facilities, located along rail links near large Jewish ghettos. That began the mass extermination stage of the Showa. From 1942 the SS employed poison gas—culminating in *Zyklon-B* pellets—in huge gas chambers at several death camps, disposing of corpses in industrial crematoria. Along with continued mass shootings, the gas chambers permitted killing of up to 20,000 per day at peak performance of the machinery of death at *Auschwitz* alone in mid-1944. *Adolf Eichmann* led a special Einsatzgruppen into Hungary that year to try to murder over 400,000 Hungarian Jews who had finally become available to the SS. Eichmann hoarded transport and men to ship Jews to Auschwitz as the Red Army approached Budapest. When the trains could no longer reach the camp, the Germans took tens of thousands of Jewish prisoners on erratic *death marches* across Hungary. About 200,000 survived, but many thousands did not. Eichmann and other Einsatzgruppe commanders were also involved in Himmler's late-war plots to sell some Jews to the West. About 3,000 escaped death in that manner, shipped by train to Switzerland in the first months of 1945 in exchange for secret payments. The American military tribunal at Nuremberg tried 22 Einsatzgruppen commanders in 1947, of whom 14 were condemned to death; just 4 were hanged in 1951. Eichmann was secretly flown out of Argentina by Israel's Mossad, who found him there and seized him. He was tried, convicted, and hanged in 1962.

See also concentration camps; final solution; Heydrich, Reinhard; Holocaust; partisans; Rassenkampf; Sonderkommando; Wannsee conference.

Suggested Reading: Richard Rhodes, *Masters of Death: The SS-Einsatzgruppen and the Invention of the Holocaust* (2002).

EINSATZKOMMANDO

See Einsatzgruppen.

EINSTEIN, ALBERT (1879–1955) German physicist and peace activist, most famous for the *Theory of Special Relativity* (1905) and *Theory of General Relativity* (1916). He was awarded the Nobel Prize for physics in 1921. A Jew, he was also an enthusiastic Zionist. That enraged *anti-Semites* in Germany, and Einstein lost his university position in the Nazi purge of the Academy, which followed their seizure of power, an anti-intellectual act greeted with enthusiasm by far too many non-Jewish German professors and students, who eagerly filled purged slots. In 1933 Einstein left for America to teach physics at Princeton. That year he coauthored, with Sigmund Freud (1856-1939), the pacifist pamphlet *Warum Kriege?* (Why War?). The Nazis included both men's books—Freud was also a Jew, and an Austrian—in public book burnings. Einstein's impact on world political affairs arose not primarily from his extraordinary scientific achievements or pacifism but from a letter he wrote to President Franklin Roosevelt in 1939 spelling out the theoretical possibility of an atomic bomb. Einstein was made aware of the potential threat by German chemists who feared Germans were ahead of Western scientists in pursuit of atomic fission. Einstein verified their findings and, pragmatically abandoning pacifism for the duration of World War II, informed Roosevelt that Germany was pursuing research that might lead to atomic weapons; he urged that a rival program be started. That encouraged research that ultimately led to the Anglo-American *nuclear weapons program* code named "Manhattan Project," which culminated in atomic attacks on *Hiroshima* and *Nagasaki*.

EIRE

See Irish Free State (Eire).

EISENBAHNTRUPPEN   German special railway troops. They were tasked with the bulk of logistical support for Wehrmacht and *Waffen-SS* forward operations. They maintained and protected trains, stations, and railcars across rear areas of entire fronts. Eisenbahntruppen laid and repaired track, brought supplies to fighting units, and transported friendly wounded and healthy POWs to the rear. During *BARBAROSSA* they hastily reconfigured whole railway networks in German-occupied areas of the western Soviet Union to conform to the different gauge of German railways. They were assisted in this by more technically adept and specialized railwaymen of the Reichsbahn (national railways). Like Wehrmacht troops, many Eisenbahntruppen were complicit in Nazi *war crimes* and *crimes against humanity*. They supervised forced Jewish and Polish labor in building extensions of German railways toward the Soviet border prior to the invasion of the Soviet Union, and they participated in criminal neglect of POWs left to starve or die of exposure in open rail cars. Some, though not all, Eisenbahntruppen also facilitated rail transportation of hundreds of thousands of innocent victims to the *death camps* of the *Holocaust.*

EISENHAMMER (NOVEMBER 1943)   "Iron Hammer." A proposed Luftwaffe deep bombing operation to destroy the power stations of the central Soviet Union. It was never carried out, largely because the Luftwaffe's forward airfields were overrun by the Red Army in January–February 1944.

EISENHOWER, DWIGHT (1890–1969)   "Ike." U.S. general. Supreme commander of Western Allied forces in the Mediterranean, 1942–1943, and all Western Europe (SACEUR), 1944–1945. Eisenhower served as an aide to General *Douglas MacArthur* in the Philippines from 1933 to 1939. MacArthur later referred to Eisenhower as "the best damn clerk I ever had." Eisenhower thought about as highly of MacArthur. But Eisenhower's superb political and administrative abilities were recognized by General *George C. Marshall* at the start of World War II. Marshall immediately brought Eisenhower to Washington as head of the Operations Division of the War Department. "Ike" was subsequently jumped in rank over several hundred more senior officers to become commander in chief of the *ETO*. His first major operation was to lead the *TORCH* landings in North Africa in November 1942, and the campaign into Tunisia that followed. Eisenhower thought that he would be sacked for the initial failure of the U.S. Army against the Germans in Africa. He instead oversaw the *HUSKY* invasion of Sicily in mid-1943, the invasion of mainland Italy, and the initial phase of the *Italian campaign (1943–1945)* that followed. Eisenhower showed rapid growth as a commander and learned much from the fighting in North Africa. But in Sicily and Italy he revealed a harmful tendency to remain much too far from the front-lines, even for a supreme commander. Worse, his command repeatedly demonstrated excess caution and lack of imagination, where the Germans showed tough and innovative adaptability. It became clear in Italy that the Western Allies were going to have a hard slog against the Germans right to the end of the war. Yet, it was also from that point that Eisenhower's excellent personal character allowed him to herd disparate and often vain subordinate commanders of many nationalities, to head them in the direction of ultimate defeat of the enemy. In his dedication to preparation, grasp of crucial military concepts (and military history), understanding of the problems of amphibious and coalition warfare, and keen ability to inspire genuine "teamwork" by talented but egotistical subordinates working under joint operational commands, Eisenhower rose to the greatest challenge ever faced by an American general and succeeded brilliantly in most respects.

Eisenhower's greatest task and achievement came in 1944, with *D-Day (June 6, 1944)*, the *OVERLORD* operation, and the *Normandy campaign*. Eisenhower shone before and during the battle for France, the start of what he later called the "crusade in Europe." He smoothed over command arguments; properly brought the independent-minded and even willful bomber chiefs into line by insisting on direct control of targeting decisions in the pre-invasion period and that they conduct massive preparatory tactical bombing at the expense of *strategic bombing;* made the difficult decision to send in three airborne divisions ahead of the main invasion; and made the call to go on June 6, despite tough weather conditions in the Channel. Notwithstanding personal inexperience, after the breakout from Normandy was achieved and the second battle for France was won, Eisenhower insisted on assuming his first ever combat command. He took over at the very top, as ground forces commander in charge of multiple army groups and several million troops. He did so over the advice and objection of a number of American subordinates and a great many senior British officers. The latter especially did not highly regard his ability as a field commander.

Eisenhower was not a superior or even very good field commander. As a result, in his combined old and new roles he made a number of blunders, notably: approving the narrow and reduced "single thrust" *MARKET GARDEN* offensive to the Rhine through the Netherlands, before assuming a "broad front" approach to the Rhine thereafter; poor disposition prior to the Wehrmacht's *Ardennes offensive,* which his forces were unprepared and slow to meet, before responding well over time; and in some of the final battles that followed during the *conquest of Germany* in 1945. Nonetheless, Eisenhower made an invaluable contribution to the Allied war effort, mainly in his original capacity as manager of the largest and most complex alliance ever assembled. He was well-suited to overall political command, dealing with personal rivalries among prickly generals, most notably, Generals *George Patton* and *Bernard Montgomery,* but also General *Omar Bradley* and others. He was able to sack commanders with appropriate ruthlessness whenever they failed, but more often build up their confidence when they were merely the victims of the inevitable misfortunes of war. Eisenhower dealt exceptionally well with the even more complex political concerns of the U.S. *Joint Chiefs of Staff,* the British *Chiefs of Staff,* and the Western Allied *Combined Chiefs of Staff.* He handled as well as anyone could have such prickly allies as General *Charles de Gaulle,* and his far more powerful but often erratic civilian warlords, Winston Churchill and Franklin Roosevelt. In all that he enjoyed the crucial support of General Marshall.

Eisenhower did less well in his handful of direct dealings with the sinister Joseph Stalin. He even exceeded his authority in personally promising the Soviet dictator that the Western Allies would not drive for Berlin in 1945. On March 28, 1945, in a decision much criticized afterward but largely defensible on military grounds, Eisenhower turned the armies advancing through western Germany southward and away from Berlin. There were good reasons to do so, not least among them the huge price that the Red Army actually paid to take Adolf Hitler's broken capital. Ike chose not to take Berlin against Churchill's strenuous advice, leaving that prize to the Red Army in favor of continuing his broad-front strategy, which aimed at destroying German military forces rather than seizing cities or territory. He subsequently got along very well at a personal level with Marshal *Georgi Zhukov* during the postwar occupation of Germany. In reward for his exceptional service, Eisenhower was promoted to five-star rank as "General of the Army." He was the first commander of NATO, 1950–1952, and was elected twice as Republican president of the United States, 1953–1961.

Suggested Reading: Stephen Ambrose, *Eisenhower,* Vol. I. (1984); Dwight D. Eisenhower, *Crusade in Europe* (1948).

EL ALAMEIN, FIRST BATTLE OF (JULY 1–3, 1942) Following the German and Italian rout of British 8th Army at *Mersa Matruh,* June 26–28, the retreating British finally stopped and dug in along the *El Alamein line.* The *Afrika Korps* and attending Italian divisions that pursued 8th Army were nearly spent. The Germans and Italians were desperately short of men and matériel. Yet, Field Marshal *Erwin Rommel* did what he always did: he attacked. On July 1, Rommel's lead 90th Light Division ran into devastating artillery fire from three concentrated South African brigades. Rommel himself was pinned to the ground that night by enemy shelling. Follow-on attacks the next morning fizzled out, though a British "box" was stormed and 1,200 prisoners taken. Later that day the Panzers were stopped cold by British 1st Armored Division, emplaced on a ridge in a fixed defensive position, supported by small mobile forces to block German movement on the flanks. On the third day Rommel formed an armored fist by combining his last German and Italian tanks into a concentrated mass and unremarkably sent it to directly smash the British line. The attack was quickly defeated when New Zealand mobile columns attacked its southern flank, where the Italian "Ariete" Division was smashed and overrun within an hour. Rommel pulled out his surviving Panzers—just over two dozen—during the night, replacing them in the line with Italian infantry. The Afrika Korps was no longer capable of offensive action. Next, it would be attrited at *Alam el-Halfa,* then smashed in the *Second Battle of El Alamein.* British 8th Army would then pursue the Afrika Korps to its death in Tunisia.

EL ALAMEIN, SECOND BATTLE OF (OCTOBER 23–NOVEMBER 4, 1942) "Operation LIGHTFOOT." Some histories refer to the earlier Battle of *Alam el-Halfa (August 30–September 7, 1942)* as "Second El Alamein." The term is used in this work for the major battle fought from October to November, 1942. British 8th Army retreated from an earlier defeat along the *Gazala line* during the summer of 1942, pursued by the *Afrika Korps* and associated Italian forces led by newly promoted Field Marshal *Erwin Rommel*. The retreat was one of several low points for the British in the *desert campaign*. Another rout was suffered at *Mersa Matruh* from June 26–28, after which 8th Army dug in along the *El Alamein line*. The British fought a holding action there in the first three days of July: the *First Battle of El Alamein*. There followed a series of limited but sharp engagements as the British hammered at Italian divisions in the line throughout July. General *Bernard Law Montgomery* assumed command in August, upon the accidental death of General William Gott. Rommel first faced Montgomery at Alam el-Halfa on August 30. With his encirclement maneuver blunted, Rommel settled in for the *Stellungskrieg* to come. Behind the El Alamein line humbled 8th Army regrouped and rearmed, notably with freshly arrived emergency deliveries of American motor transport, better anti-tank guns, and superior Grant and Sherman tanks. Montgomery oversaw the build-up, refusing to attack Rommel as soon as Winston Churchill wanted. He preferred to first ensure overwhelming superiority—particularly in the air—and thus more certain success. That allowed fresh British and Indian divisions and one veteran Australian division to arrive and take up position in the line. Most importantly, Montgomery unquestionably and significantly raised the morale of British and Commonwealth forces and began the recovery that made British 8th Army one of the great Western Allied armies of the war.

Montgomery had access to *ULTRA* intelligence on Axis strength even as he built up his own. The British also conducted a highly successful *deception operation*, code named BERTRAM, to hide their concentrations. It began with open movement of 10th Corps to one flank, followed by a secret move back over four nights that was covered by use of elaborate dummy facilities: the British left behind 2,400 canvas vehicles, a phantom force linked by elaborate fake HQs and signals traffic. On the eve of battle, Rommel was absent on sick leave. His temporary replacement was General Georg Stumme. Too much has been made of Rommel's absence: far more important was the paucity and imbalance of Axis supplies and their vulnerability to air interdiction along a 1,200-mile-long supply route back to Tunisia. Manpower was another concern. The newly renamed "Panzerarmee Afrika" comprised just 82,000 Germans and 42,000 Italians. Many were sick; others were disheartened. The infantry was put in the frontline behind vast desert minefields containing over 500,000 anti-tank and anti-personnel mines. Some tanks and most of the artillery was kept in immediate support of the infantry for some semblance of defense-in-depth, but the German and Italian mobile and armored divisions were in reserve on either flank. British experience in fighting Germans in two world wars dictated battle doctrine that was slow and methodical, an approach reinforced by Montgomery's personal command style and well-suited to the El Alamein terrain. The main battle thus opened with a massive artillery barrage that began timed to the BBC signal late on October 23, and rained down on the enemy through six hours of night terror. The artillery barrage was reinforced with heavy aerial bombardment by waves of Wellingtons bombing deeper gun positions. The barrage was partly intended to cut a path through the Axis *Minenkästen*. It went unanswered by return fire due to shortages of ammunition on the Axis side and a consequent but controversial decision by Stumme to hold back his artillery from counterbombardment.

As Allied artillery fire moved over intermediate Axis positions, four infantry divisions and then two armored divisions attacked along a concentrated *Schwerpunkt* of just six miles of the Axis line, or *Hauptkampflinie* (HKL). By early morning on the 24th, parts of the northern section of the HKL were overrun by Australian and Scots troops in heavy, bloody, close-in infantry fighting that maximized blunt force and numbers, and sheer guts, over command skill or schemes of maneuver. A counterattack by 15th Panzer Division and the Italian "Littorio" armored division was repulsed with heavy loss of Axis tanks: about 40 percent of the total available. General Stumme was killed by enemy strafing of his scout car. That meant temporary command fell to General Wilhelm von Thoma. In a desperate move to block a British breakthrough along the coast, Rommel—who had hurried back to North Africa—and Thoma ordered 21st Panzer Division holding on the southern flank to race northward. One historian has called this an order for a "Tottenrit" ("death ride"), in a situation the generals already deemed hopeless. The British conducted an operational pause from October 28–29 in the face of an unexpected thickness of the minefields, but more to reorganize for a final breakthrough assault ("Operation SUPERCHARGE"). Most importantly, they did so without stopping heavy bombing and shelling of the now-ragged Axis HKL. The renewed assault was made overnight on November 1, when three armored divisions moved through the blasted German minefields in two massed columns, concealed on either flank by vast *smokescreens*. With the Afrika Korps down to just 30 tanks in the north, Rommel pulled the last armored and mobile divisions up to the coast from the south, including the fine Italian "Ariete" armored division. The "Panzerarmee Afrika," now shorn of most of its tanks and organic transport and under constant lethal harassment by British fighters and bombers, turned to run. As it did so, Adolf Hitler sent a *Haltebefehl order* commanding Rommel to stand and fight where he was. He did, his career as ever foremost in mind even over the welfare of his men. That meant leaving his much reduced and exhausted Panzerarmee in place to be smashed by a British and Commonwealth armored onslaught on November 4. Four days later, Anglo-American forces landed in Morocco and Algeria and began moving toward Tunisia, in Rommel's strategic rear. This time Hitler let Rommel save what he could: he abandoned the Italian infantry and retreated along the coast with all the armor and mechanized forces he had left.

El Alamein was the first major Western victory over the Wehrmacht. The great desert battle was also the greatest solo British and Commonwealth victory over Germans and Italians in World War II. It turned back the Axis threat to Egypt and the Suez Canal; cost Germany invaluable manpower and equipment (200,000 troops and hundreds of tanks and armored vehicles); ended Benito Mussolini's and the Italian military's pretensions to imperial greatness and Mediterranean empire; and opened the path to total clearance of the Axis from North Africa: within months, all Axis forces on the continent would be crushed or captured by a Western Allied vice closing on Tunisia. El Alamein importantly bolstered flagging British morale, elevated Montgomery to premier British field commander, and was the essential prelude to clearance of North Africa and follow-on invasions of Sicily and Italy as the Western Allies knocked the first Axis nation out of the war in September 1943. Winston Churchill famously said of the victory at El Alamein: "This is not the end. It is not even the beginning of the end. But it is, perhaps, the end of the beginning."

Suggested Reading: Robert Citino, *Death of the Wehrmacht* (2007); John Latimer, *Alamein* (2002); J. Strawson, *El Alamein: Desert Victory* (1981).

EL ALAMEIN, THIRD BATTLE OF (OCTOBER 23–NOVEMBER 4, 1942)   An alternate nomenclature in which the fight more usually referred to as *Alam el-Halfa* is designated "Second El Alamein," with the main battle fought in October–November redesignated "Third Battle of El Alamein."

EL ALAMEIN LINE   Located fewer than 100 km west of Alexandria, this British defensive line in western Egypt was anchored by a little rail junction village on the coast called El Alamein. The position was heavy with minefields, stretching from the coast to the *Qattara Depression,* which was impassable by the armor of the *Afrika Korps* and formed the only natural barrier and inland flank in the western desert.

ELBA   This small island in the Mediterranean—host to Napoleon I's first period of exile—was occupied by the Wehrmacht upon Italy's surrender on September 8, 1943. *Free French* commandos assaulted it from Corsica on June 16, 1944. In bloody fighting that saw combined losses of some 1,700 men, the German garrison was overwhelmed and surrendered.

ELECTRONIC WARFARE
    See anti-submarine warfare; artillery; ASDIC; blind bombing; bombs; Combined Bomber Offensive; Direction-Finding (D/F); Enigma machine; Freya; GEE; Gibson Girl; Huff-Duff; IFF; Kammhuber Line; Knickebein; Leigh Light; Lichtenstein-Gerät; LORAN; Lorenz; Magnetic Anomaly Detectors (MAD); Mandrel; Oboe; Pathfinders; Pillenwerfer; radar; RCM; Serrate; Shaker technique; torpedoes; window; Würzburg; X-Gerät; Y-Gerät.

ELEFANT   Also called the "Ferdinand." A large and technically unready anti-tank gun introduced by the Wehrmacht at *Kursk* in mid 1943.
    See anti-tank weapons.

ELEMENT-C
   See Belgian Gate.

ELEPHANTS   In World War II elephants were commonly employed in military labor by both sides in northern India and Burma, as well as French Indochina and other parts of Southeast Asia. They were employed in road, bridge, and air-field construction; in loading and unloading ships; and as pack animals to carry heavy mortars or ammunition over mountains and down jungle trails. The British used elephants extensively during their Burma campaign and were eager to capture them from the Japanese. The Japanese also relied extensively on elephants. As many as 350 were employed to haul supplies during their *Imphal offensive* in early 1944, many painted camouflage green. Several thousand were in use more generally in Japanese rear areas.

ELNIA OPERATION (AUGUST 1941)
   See Yelnia operation.

EMPEROR CULT   A tradition of emperor veneration in Japan was already evolving into an imperial cult of emperor worship before the 1868 Meiji Restoration. This cult drew deeply on *Shinto* and the idea of "yamato damashii" (national, or Japanese, spirit) developed by 19th-century nationalist thinker Shoin Yoshida and his followers. The cult was promoted with state propaganda, censorship, and by repressing Japan's other religious traditions in favor of Shinto. It proclaimed the divine descent of the emperors, reinforcing that notion with rituals that included an annual rice ceremony in which the emperor imbibed the rice spirit ("kami"), taking on its divinity, too. The Emperor cult had a racial aspect: the idea of the Emperor as head of the *shido minzoku* ("leading race") and attendant clamor for "race purity" and "race integrity" in Japan. Such notions were common in many countries during the late 19th and early 20th centuries, but received state endorsement in only a few. These imperial values were inculcated in the education system following the Imperial Rescript on Education issued in 1890, a copy of which was kept in every school.
   See also Hirohito; Imperial Japanese Army.

EMPEROR SYSTEM   The Japanese imperial system, especially from the Meiji Restoration in 1868 to the end of World War II.
   See Emperor cult; Hirohito; Imperial Japanese Army; Imperial Japanese Navy; Japan; kokutai; shido minzoku; Shinto.

EMPRESS AUGUSTA BAY, BATTLE OF (NOVEMBER 2, 1943)   This sea fight took place on November 2, 1943. It evolved out of the U.S. marine landing on *Bougainville* the previous day. USN Task Force 39, comprising four light cruisers and eight destroyers, intercepted four Japanese cruisers and six destroyers. These fast ships of Japan's 8th Fleet were planning a night attack against the beachhead and transports in Torokina Bay. In a confused mêlée fought throughout the night, TF39 sank a Japanese cruiser and destroyer and damaged two more enemy warships. The Japanese commander mistakenly thought he had severely damaged the Americans in turn, and retreated to *Rabaul*. In fact, only one U.S. ship was damaged by a torpedo hit. The battle was a rare night victory for the USN, which for the first time showed a marked improvement in night-fighting skill. It was also the last significant surface fight of the Solomons campaign.

ENABLING LAW (MARCH 23, 1933) "Ermächtigunngsgestz."
See Germany; Hitler, Adolf; Nazi Party; Reichstag.

ENDLÖSUNG "final solution."
See Holocaust.

ENGINEERS Military engineers in all armed forces were primarily engaged in building transport and other facilities to improve movement and combat power of friendly forces, or destroying the same facilities to impede enemy movement. That meant building or repairing roads, railways, bridges, ferries, airfields, ports, and pipelines for water and fuel; or blowing up the same. "Pionier" was the equivalent Wehrmacht term for specialists that Western Allied armies called "combat engineers." Combat engineers by whatever name swarmed over all battlefields of the war, laying or clearing minefields, building or removing beach or anti-tank obstacles, converting villages and towns into strongpoints, or blowing a path through enemy fortifications. All frontline or combat engineers were capable of fighting when necessary, but sought to avoid it in preference for carrying out their assigned mission. Such missions might include: support for amphibious operations such as clearing beach obstacles, wire, minefields, and pillboxes or other strongpoints; laying mines; building HQs, base camps, and depots; and camouflage. Bridge and road building became a key job of combat engineers as mobility was more crucial in World War II than in the more static conditions of World War I. This was especially true for Anglo-American armies for which roads and river crossing had to accommodate numerous heavy vehicles in areas where the retreating enemy's engineers nearly always destroyed both. All major armies and air forces needed advanced airfields built and others repaired, with sturdier runways needed to accommodate heavy bombers. In many parts of Europe, military roads and bridges were wider and better than civilian facilities that existed before an army passed through the area, while pipelines for fuel added unprecedented capacity. The Western Allies also maintained and repaired numerous ports and harbors that German engineers blew apart or blocked as the Wehrmacht withdrew.

By 1945 the U.S. Army Corps of Engineers numbered nearly 690,000 men. It was by far the largest of any engineering corps, but all major armies experienced a comparable expansion of engineer troops in varying degree. German engineers built hundreds of forward airfields prior to *BARBAROSSA* in the spring of 1941, then replaced all Soviet wide gauge track with European narrow gauge railways as the Wehrmacht advanced through the western Soviet Union in the summer and fall. They remained active in both construction and demolition to the end of the war in Europe. Among the Western Allies, engineers were supported by divisions of military laborers. In the Far East, they also employed "coolie" labor from China and India and drawn from local populations. The Japanese and Germans used slaves and forced laborers to carry out backbreaking physical work. The Japanese also ruthlessly forced prisoners of war to work under dreadful conditions, often at the cost of their lives. The Germans employed Soviet prisoners as forced laborers, but did not impose that burden on most Western prisoners. The Soviets used a combination of domestic forced labor and massive voluntary mobilization of Soviet civilians. In Southeast Asia extraordinary military roads, along with bridges, railways and airfields, appeared for the first time in deep jungle, over mountain ranges, and through other previously inaccessible places. Some were built by the Japanese at enormous cost in human lives. Others were laid down by the Western Allies. By the end of the war, for the first time in history there existed logistical support and communications systems that spanned whole regions, continents, and indeed the globe.

See discrete battles, operations, and campaigns. See also African Americans; Aleutian Islands; amphibious operations; Ardeatine Cave massacre; armor; Atlantic Wall; Bailey Bridge; Belgian gate; Blitzkrieg; Burma Road; Burma–Siam railway; concentration camps; D-Day (June 6, 1944); Eban Emael; Enigma machine; flamethrowers; Gothic Line; Hitler Line; Indian Army; Kriegsmarine; Ledo Road; Maginot Line; mines; mouse-holing; nuclear weapons programs; Office of Scientific Research and Development (OSRD); Ostwall; Panzers; Pionier; PLUTO; radar; radio; recoilless guns; rockets; Siegfried Line; signals; Schnorchel; strategic bombing; Todt organization; total war; U-boats; Underwater Demolition Teams (UDT); U.S. Army; V-weapons program; Wannsee conference; Westwall.

ENIGMA MACHINE The main German cipher machine, derived from a Dutch invention that failed in several commercial models in the late 1920s. Various models of increasing complexity were used by the Heer, Luftwaffe, Kriegsmarine, and in diplomatic traffic. It was also used by the Reichsbahn (German railways). The Italian Navy used a derivative machine, the C38M. Polish intelligence partially broke Enigma ciphers in 1932. By 1939 the Poles had a foothold understanding of the original Dutch machine and therefore were able to rig replicas of its German descendants. The French also made headway from 1938. Polish intelligence Enigma replicas, and dearly acquired knowledge of German ciphers, were supplied by trhe Poles to the Western Allies in July 1939. The French and Poles passed additional information to the British in 1940. The British broke the naval code for the Italian C38M in September 1940, a year before that cipher was withdrawn. That greatly aided the Royal Navy in the Mediterranean naval campaign in 1940–1941. Naval Enigma rotors were recovered from a sunken minelayer U-boat off Scotland in February 1940. That told British intelligence that all German ships and U-boats carried them. Thereafter high priority was assigned to capture of U-boats and other enemy craft. German trawlers off Norway proved especially vulnerable: capture of Enigma code books or rotors from two trawlers led to breaking of the Kriegsmarine code. In May 1941, U-110's Enigma machine was captured intact along with all code books. That and such capture or recovery successes were kept at the highest level of secrecy, including by deceit of captured U-boat crews or separate incarceration from other German prisoners.

The British built "bombes"—machines that mimicked and thus helped work out Enigma's rotor sequences. There were never enough bombes to meet the demand of the code breakers at *Bletchley Park,* plus all the armed services and Britain's clamoring allies. If the British had been more willing to provide technical information to the Americans—which they did not for mostly valid security reasons—it is conceivable that many more bombes would have been made much earlier. That was certainly Admiral *Ernest King's* firm view, but in fairness King was not the most cooperative ally either. U.S. intelligence decided to make their own bombes in September 1942, with the first poor quality models available in May 1943. By the end of the year, 75 better quality bombes had been manufactured in the United States, greatly increasing code breaking capacity. It was still an infernal problem to decode: the two inner settings of the German naval cipher were set by officers only every two days, while naval cipher clerks changed the two outer settings every 24 hours. Enigma operators then chose three of the machine's eight rotors, each of which had 26 point positions. All that provided 160 trillion potential combinations. On the receiving end, each U-boat had two nets of six frequencies each ("Diana" and "Hubertus"). And yet, Bletchley Park broke into the cipher.

The Kriegsmarine added a fourth rotor to its ciphers in January 1942, creating a prolonged "information blackout" that reduced enemy ability to detect *wolf packs* and divert convoys around them. The British made it a top priority to capture another machine from a U-boat or weather ship. U-559 was forced to the surface on October 30, 1942, by a sustained depth charge attack by five destroyers and destroyer escorts. Its documents were recovered, but the machine went down with the scuttled submarine. Still, it became clear that German operators were not fully utilizing the fourth rotor. An American ASW Support Group captured U-505 off Cape Verde in June 1944. The haul of Enigma material was enormous. It was also current and forward looking to new naval codes. Deciphering signals was greatly aided by *COLOSSUS I,* the first electronic computer put together by the brilliance of Alan Turing and engineers at Bletchley Park and elsewhere. It made processing and reading German ciphers faster than ever, often close to "real time." *COLOSSUS II* came on line in June 1944. A measure of how Enigma proved vulnerable to stiff-minded German overconfidence is the remarkable fact that the source of most intercepted signals, Admiral *Karl Dönitz,* went to his deathbed in 1980 convinced that no enemy ever read his Enigma ciphers.

See also Geheimschreiber machine; ULTRA.

Suggested Reading: David Khan, *Seizing the Enigma* (1995).

ENIWETOK
See Marshall Islands.

ENORMOUS
See nuclear weapons programs.

ENTRENCHMENTS
See various battles and campaigns, and *foxhole; octopus pot; slit trench.*

ENVELOPMENT A *scheme of maneuver* seeking to flank on both sides and thereby surround and entrap enemy formations facing one's own. A *deep battle* operation might seek a *double envelopment* to trap whole armies or army groups.
See also Blitzkrieg; operational art; Schwerpunkt; Vernichtungsschlacht.

EPSOM (JUNE 26–30, 1944) On D+20 of the *Normandy campaign* General *Bernard Law Montgomery* launched a renewed effort to drive the Germans from Caen. Montgomery was under rising political and military pressure to make gains on the left flank of the lodgement in Normandy, but also feeling the effects of attrition on his infantry divisions and the knowledge that not all British losses could be replaced. British infantry and armor advanced behind a World War I–style *creeping barrage* by the artillery. The attack made good progress over the first three days, then faced savage German counterattacks that impeded further advance. As it was planned, the operation was a failure: Montgomery did not take Caen until July. However, EPSOM had the necessary and beneficial effect of sharply attriting the last available Panzer reserve divisions in Normandy. That helped thin out the German line while preventing reinforcement of the German left flank during a heavy American build-up that preceded the breakout from the Côtentin peninsula.

EREMENKO, ANDREI
See Yeremenko, Andrei I. (1892–1970).

ERITREA
See Abyssinian War (1935–1936); East African campaign (1940–1941).

ERSATZHEER "Replacement Army." The reserve of the *Heer* or German Army, supplementing the *Feldheer* or "Field Army," with the latter comprising the main battle force. In 1941 the Ersatzheer comprised 1.2 million men while the Feldheer was composed of 3.8 million. After the failure of the *July Plot* in 1944, and with Hitler's final turn against the Wehrmacht and the traditional officer corps, command was handed to *Heinrich Himmler,* chief of the *Schutzstaffel (SS).*
See also Volksgrenadier.

ESCALATOR FORCE
See Alamo Force.

ESCORT CARRIERS   Small carriers used on *convoy* duty during World War II as a countermeasure against submarines and long-range reconnaissance aircraft such as the *Kondor* in the Atlantic, a threat that particularly exercised Winston Churchill. From early 1943, hunter-killer *anti-submarine warfare* Support Groups were built around an escort carrier at the center. The Royal Navy initially commissioned 35 *Catapult Aircraft Merchants (CAM)* while it rushed work on small carriers with flight decks and an ability to land aircraft. British escort carriers were mainly equipped with the *Swordfish,* an underestimated aircraft that served on fleet carriers early in the war but really proved its worth as the mainstay of the escort carrier fleet. The first British escort carriers, or CVEs, were based on merchant hulls and were poorly protected. Royal Navy insistence on redesign delayed delivery of the first CVEs until the fall of 1942. These precious ships were almost immediately diverted from the Atlantic to the Mediterranean to cover the *TORCH* landings in Africa in November. They did not arrive back in the Atlantic until April 1943.

The United States built 122 escort carriers during the war, including 50 of the "Casablanca class." They were short-decked and tended to pitch wildly in heavy seas. The British made several internal changes that improved stability but decreased space for aircraft. The USN did not. Most British CVEs carried a complement of 6 "Martlet" fighters (known as F4F "Wildcats" in U.S. service) and 9 TBM "Avenger" torpedo planes for ASW work. The decks of USN escort carriers were modified to carry 9 F4Fs and 12 TBM bombers. Escort carriers supported numerous amphibious operations with air cover over landing sites in the Pacific. They also provided air ferry services of fighters to defend and reinforce various island airstrips. Later in the war escort carriers arrived in such abundance that they joined task forces tied to major fleet actions, including the *Battle of Leyte Gulf.* The Japanese did not deploy their first escort carrier until July 1944. Because of lack of interservice cooperation and the fact that the Japanese navy still sought "decisive battle" with the Americans, the Japanese Army deployed its own escort carriers. They were armed with JAAF fighters and bombers to protect troop convoys.

See also Merchant Aircraft Carrier (MAC); tankers.

ESCORT SHIPS
See Armed Merchant Cruiser (AMC); Atlantic, Battle of; Catapult Aircraft Merchant (CAM); anti-submarine warfare; convoy; corvettes; destroyer escorts; destroyers; escort carriers; frigates; Replenishment-at-Sea; Royal Navy.

ESTONIA   A Russian province from 1721, Estonia was occupied by Imperial Germany during World War I. When German troops withdrew it declared independence. With Russia deep in civil war until 1920, Estonia succeeded in asserting that claim by force of arms. In 1932 it signed a nonaggression pact with Moscow. On

September 29, 1939, Estonia was forced to sign an agreement permitting Red Army bases on its soil. Estonia was compelled to accept the Red Army troops by threats from Joseph Stalin, who acted under the assurance of German acquiescence flowing from terms of a secret protocol to the *Nazi–Soviet Pact (August 23, 1939)* that granted Estonia to the Soviet sphere of influence. In June 1940, the Red Army moved into the rest of Estonia. The troops were accompanied by the *NKVD,* which began an immediate purge and deportation of all identified as anti-Soviet, with ethnic Germans deported to the greater Reich with the assistance of the *Schutzstaffel (SS).* The forward move importantly exposed large numbers of Soviet troops in less well-prepared positions than the ones they departed, a fact that cost the Red Army dearly when Germany launched *BARBAROSSA* on June 22, 1941. Estonia was overrun by the Wehrmacht by July and was soon annexed to Germany as part of the *Reichskommissariat Ostland.*

Many Estonians welcomed the Germans. Some assisted in the Nazi extermination of Estonian Jews, while others later joined the *Waffen-SS.* About 8,000 Estonians were executed by the Germans during three years of occupation, including 7,000 Communists. Estonia was now trapped between two warring totalitarian empires, neither of which planned to permit an independent Estonian state to exist after the war. When the Red Army returned in January 1944, most Estonians did not view the event as an unadulterated liberation. And indeed, Soviet troops rampaged through the country. Once again, the Red Army was accompanied by brutal agents of the NKVD, which was even more violent and repressive after three years of hardening in a total war farther east. The Soviet Union reaffirmed its annexation of Estonia, asserting the 1940 frontiers and shooting or deporting to the *GULAG* all identified by *Smersh* or the NKVD as dissidents or potential leaders. The United States and some other Western powers refused to recognize that annexation as legal, maintaining ritualistic diplomatic relations with an Estonian government-in-exile in Washington throughout the entire Cold War. Most non-Western states simply accepted Estonia as part of the Soviet Union, until it reemerged in 1990 during the first stage of the process of legal extinction of the Soviet Union, which was completed in 1991.

See also Einsatzgruppen; ethnic cleansing.

ETHIOPIA
See Abyssinia.

ETHIOPIAN–ITALIAN WAR
See Abyssinian War (1935–1936).

ETHNIC CLEANSING A term that came into currency concerning the Balkans in the 1990, but a practice centuries old. The forcible deportation and intimidation of civilian populations "pour encourager les autres" was commonplace in World War II. At its most extreme it reached to industrialized genocide of unarmed populations. It began with Nazi deportations from annexed areas of Poland and corresponding importations to Germany of Baltic Germans. These transfers were overseen by *Heinrich Himmler* and the *Schutzstaffel (SS),* while Himmler's import of Germans was happily accommodated by the *NKVD.* The Nazis subsequently moved millions of people out of "Greater Germany" into ghettos in the east, then into *concentration camps* for use as slaves or for extermination. The SS drafted a "General Plan for the East" ("Generalplan Ost") in July 1941, that called for deportation to Asia or other forms of elimination of over 30 million Slavs from areas soon to be conquered in the Soviet Union. Population transfers were to take place over a period of several decades. More immediately, it was anticipated by Adolf Hitler, other top Nazis, and the leadership of the Wehrmacht, that tens of millions of Soviet civilians should perish from starvation as their food supply was expropriated and they were exposed to the elements over the winter of 1941–1942.

As the Wehrmacht withdrew from the western Soviet Union from 1943 to 1944, more millions of Soviets were forced to march west, driven like cattle to deprive the Red Army of recruits and the Soviet economy of laborers. Within the Soviet Union, whole ethnic populations—Volga Germans, Tatars, and others—whose loyalty Joseph Stalin doubted, without cause, were transported deep into Central Asia or to Siberia or even Sakhalin Island. Mass deportations of ethnic Germans ensued across eastern and central Europe after the war. Some 14–16 million ethnic Germans were forced to leave historic homelands they had inhabited for centuries, and about two million died. Poles and others also left their homes in advance of the Red Army as refugees, or were forcibly expelled afterward as Moscow implemented population transfers agreed to earlier by the Western Allies. Others were trapped abroad by shifting war winds, to eventually settle in Britain, France, Canada, and the United States. Jewish survivors from the *concentration camps* found they were not always welcome when they tried to return to their native cities or villages. Many were turned back east by threats and violence; some continued walking until they found sanctuary farther west, or they died along the road. Seven million Japanese were repatriated from Manchuria, northern China, and other erstwhile bits of the Japanese Empire. Hundreds of thousands of *Ianfu* and Korean forced laborers were removed from Japan or Manchuria.

Suggested Reading: Benjamin Lieberman, *Terrible Fate: Ethnic Cleansing in the Making of Modern Europe* (2006).

ETO   European Theater of Operations. Western Allied theater designation for all active operations in the Mediterranean and Western Europe, as distinct from the Pacific Theater of Operations (PTO).

ETOUSA   European Theater of Operations, United States Army. U.S. Army designation for the build-up zones in Great Britain where troops were based prior to the invasions of Africa and Europe.

EUGENICS
See death camps; euthanasia program; Lebensborn; Nazism.

EUPEN AND MALMEDY   A border area between Belgium and Germany, transferred to Belgium under terms of the *Treaty of Versailles* in 1919. It was reclaimed by Germany immediately upon Belgium's surrender in May 1940. The province was returned to Belgium after Germany's defeat in 1945.

EUREKA   A Western Allied radar navigation system linking a ground beacon with an airborne receiver.

EUREKA   Allied code name for the *Tehran Conference (November 28–December 1, 1943)*.

EUROPEAN ADVISORY COMMISSION   A board of *Big Three* representatives established in 1943 to discuss postwar occupation terms.

EUTHANASIA PROGRAM   The Nazis passed a sterilization law in July 1933 that aimed at stopping procreation by "mental and physical defectives" and at long-term "racial" and eugenic manipulation. In August 1939, registration of all "malformed" and mentally deficient children was made compulsory. Shortly thereafter a secret euthanasia program began at six centers guarded by the *Schutzstaffel (SS)*. This "T-4 program," run out of the Tiergarten, began to sterilize and to kill "incurable" asylum inmates and children in small carbon monoxide gas chambers or by lethal injections. This "social hygiene" program included murder of children of *Nazi Party* members, the *Schutzstaffel (SS),* and *Wehrmacht.* Many doctors beyond those in the SS medical service cooperated with the first director, Dr. Leonardo Conti, and his successor, Dr. P. Bouhler. Some did not, but nor did they speak publicly against T-4, which killed over 70,000 by 1941. A whispering knowledge about the killings, and especially rumors that war-wounded were subject to them, broke into the open once a set of fierce sermons denouncing the killings was delivered by Bishop von Galen of Münster. Afraid that religious opinion in Germany would undermine home front support for the war, one on the regime's worst nightmares, Hitler ordered the program ended on August 16, 1941. However, killings continued in the *concentration camps* to the end of the war, possibly including of some badly wounded veterans. Babies with deformities were routinely killed, while crippled or mentally handicapped old people were simply starved to death. A "Doctor's Trial" was held by the American military tribunal at Nuremberg after the war, but beyond a few suicides and judicial hangings of some medical personnel and administrators, most doctors and nurses involved in the T-4 and other death programs were never brought to account, let alone to justice.

EVACUATION HOSPITAL (EVAC)   A U.S. military hospital of 400 to 750 beds, usually attached to a corps or army. Most were located 25–30 miles from the front along good roads or railways. All casualties went through EVACs, which sorted and cleared wounded men to convalescent or surgical hospitals in-theater, or sent them out of the theater of operations by *hospital ship* or aircraft.

EVAKUATSIIA "The evacuation." The extraordinary relocation of about 10 percent of Soviet prewar military factories from the western Soviet Union nearer to the Urals, along with 10 million people, of whom 3 million were moved from Ukraine. The entire operation was carried out in the teeth of the Wehrmacht advance during *BARBAROSSA* over the second half of 1941. Contrary to some later reports, there was no prewar plan to do this: the entire evacuation was improvised. It was not a complete success, as many trains were misdirected. Some factories stayed out of production for many months as power, fuel, and raw materials strained to reach them over an overtaxed railway system. People who moved with the factories initially toiled and lived in dangerously abject conditions, especially during the first winter of the eastern war.

EXODUS "L'Exode." The extraordinary movement of the French civilian population during the German invasion of May–June, 1940. The flow of refugees primarily comprised women and children, as well as the old.

See FALL GELB.

EXPERTEN

See ace.

EXPLOSIVE MOTOR BOATS The major Axis navies all employed fast attack boats that exploded on contact. In Kriegsmarine and Regia Marina types, which had some success against Royal Navy ships, the pilot bailed out before the explosion. The Imperial Japanese Navy had two types. Both were suicide craft.

EXTRAORDINARY EVENTS A *commissar* and *NKVD* euphemism for what officially were viewed as treasonable acts by troops of the Red Army. These acts included desertion, cowardice under fire, self-inflicted wounds, incompetence on the part of commanders, and, most vaguely but importantly, "anti-Soviet agitation." Often, the last offense amounted to no more than standard grumbling and questioning of officers normal in the ranks of any army, in all times and all wars. In the Red Army, ordinary soldiers could also be shot for drunkenness. Alcoholism was probably worse in the Red Army than in any other major force in World War II, though it was widespread in all. On numerous occasions, drunkenness in the Red Army led to consumption of medical alcohol. That contributed to avoidable deaths among untreated wounded, as well as to mass poisonings of whole units from consumption of deadly chemicals.

F

FACT-FINDING MISSIONS
See Japan; League of Nations; Lytton Commission; Manchuria.

FAEROE ISLANDS   This Danish island group was occupied by the British in Operation VALENTINE on April 12, 1940, three days after Germany invaded Denmark. The Faeroes were returned to Denmark after the war, under conditions of limited autonomy.

FALAISE POCKET   The second largest armored battle of the war resulted from Operation *TRACTABLE,* launched by the Canadians and Poles from the north in an effort to link with American forces holding the lower jaw of the "Falaise gap" in the south. The battle was a two-week mêlée in which elements of 10 Panzer divisions faced 10 Western Allied armored divisions and supporting infantry on an 800-square mile battlefield. Falaise demonstrated an evolution in armored warfare over four years of wartime learning. The shift was from explosive, battle-winning tactics of *Blitzkrieg* to a new style in which tanks were used as a blunt instrument of industrialized, mechanized attrition wherein massed armor was met by anti-tank guns and minefields, tank-busting aircraft, and armored counterattacks. General *George Patton* turned U.S. 3rd Army north from Le Mans on August 10, meeting almost no German resistance until forward units reached Argentan two days later. Bradley stopped the advance there, in an overly cautious decision that remains deeply controversial. The Germans beefed up their threatened southern flank against 3rd Army, fighting past Argentan-Falaise to bleed men out of the "Falaise gap" at the neck of the pocket. A Canadian attack from the north on August 14 was broken up by friendly *short bombing,* but was still pressed until the Canadians took

Falaise after two more days of fierce combat. Hitler finally agreed to let the generals try to pull out men and equipment, in part because he was taken by surprise by the *DRAGOON* landings in southern France on August 15. About 200,000 Axis troops were still inside the Falaise pocket: virtually all German combat forces in northern France. Over four nights the Wehrmacht conducted a remarkably skilled withdrawal. Its men remained subject to massive enemy firepower and constant assault on all sides of the perimeter during the day. About 140,000 Germans got out of the pocket by August 18. Some 10,000 were killed in vicious fighting, especially with determined Poles who held the north lip of the bottleneck against desperate German attacks, until the trap was finally closed by U.S. and Polish troops on the 19th. Some 50,000 Germans were captured, along with most equipment and heavy weapons of the German armies in France.

See also Normandy campaign.

FALANGE   The *fascist* political party of Spain founded in 1933 by José Primo de Rivera (1903–1936). It violently opposed the Spanish Republic and threw its support behind *Francisco Franco's* rebellion during the *Spanish Civil War*. In 1937 Franco merged the Falange with the Carlist monarchist faction.

See also Blue Division.

FALCONS   The British maintained a Falcon Control Unit to control their own *carrier pigeons,* and a Falcon Interceptor Unit to kill German and Italian pigeons. Other armies also used falcons to control pigeons.

FALKENHAUSEN, ALEXANDER VON (1878–1966)
See Belgium; Sino-Japanese War (1937–1945).

FALKENHORST, NICHOLAS VON (1885–1968)   German general. He commanded a corps during the invasion of Poland in 1939. He was commander of the invasion of Norway in 1940, from where he attacked Soviet forces in Karelia in June–July, 1941. He failed to take Murmansk or other northern objectives in the Soviet Union, and commanded only in Norway, confined to a peripheral theater where Adolf Hitler was nonetheless heavily overcommitted on land and at sea. He was dismissed in December 1944. He was tried at *Nuremberg* for ordering shootings of British commandos. He was sentenced to death, but the sentence was commuted in 1953.

***FALL GELB* (MAY 10–JUNE 22, 1940)**   "Case Yellow." German code name for the invasion of France and the Low Countries that began on May 10, 1940. At the time, Winston Churchill called the fight in the west the "Battle of France." That term is still used in many English-language histories, but the battle was for more than France. The end of the *Phoney War,* or what the French called the *drôle de guerre,* came into sight when Adolf Hitler dropped *Fallschirmjäger* over Denmark and assaulted Norway by air and sea on April 9, 1940. Thus began invasions of two small, neutral, democratic countries in what the Wehrmacht dubbed Operation *WESERÜBUNG*. Inactive war ended decisively when Hitler unleashed his armed forces against France itself, attacking into the *Ardennes* while also feinting in sufficient force to trap the main Western Allied armies in the Low Countries. As originally conceived, the German plan for a western *Blitzkrieg* would roll over Belgium and the Netherlands in a few days, then swing south into northern France to cut off Britain from the Atlantic ports it traditionally relied upon for military access to the continent. With the French Army held at bay, the Low Countries would provide a grand platform for the Luftwaffe to pound Britain into submission and for U-boats to throttle the island empire, cutting arteries of food and imports moving through the Channel and across the North Atlantic.

The first Wehrmacht proposal to Hitler did not call for a *Vernichtungsschlacht,* a "battle of annihilation" of the French Army. That had been attempted by the old Reichswehr in the summer of 1914. Its failure trapped Germany in the great *Stellungskrieg* ("war of position") its military men feared most: a vast and protracted war of attrition, a *Materialschlacht* ("material battle") that Germany could hardly hope to win against a more powerful and populous combination of industrial economies and nations. The original operations plan for war in the west in 1940 was much more limited, and certainly not a revisiting of the old "Schlieffen Plan." It proposed only to badly hurt the French Army while occupying Flanders and its immediate environs, the low-lying and coastal regions of Belgium, the Netherlands, and northern France. The Wehrmacht did not propose to take Paris or try to crush all French forces in a vast *Kesselschlacht* ("cauldron battle"). Invasion and occupation of Flanders and northern France was intended to permit the Luftwaffe to reach across the Channel and terror bomb the cities of Great Britain. That OKW proposal was fully in tune with Hitler's strategic thinking. He viewed Britain as the main enemy in the west. Force Britain to terms and Germany would win the war, whatever happened to the French Army. But this original FALL GELB plan was subsequently amended upon the intervention of General *Erich von Manstein* and other, more aggressive German generals. Manstein proposed to switch the main armored thrust, and thereby relocate the *Schwerpunkt* of the attack, away from Army Group B in the north to Army Group A in the south. Hitler liked Manstein's basic idea and added real power to it, ordering that the bulk of armor should be repositioned to strike directly into northern France through the Ardennes. That was a huge gamble, but one that took advantage of German operational and command flexibility at army group, army, and even corps and divisional levels that had not yet been lost to Hitler's propensity to centralize all decision making, as it would be later in the war.

The Wehrmacht would achieve near-complete tactical and intelligence surprise by sending its heaviest armored thrust through the Ardennes. That hilly, wooded region had very few and only narrow roads. It was not thought by all Allied military planners to be impenetrable by armored columns, just that armor could not get through in sufficient force in quick enough time to force the Meuse. Some staff officers within the OKW thought the same thing. But more aggressive thinkers had gone around the OKW to identify the Ardennes to Hitler as the vital location of the whole French defense and Allied position. When Hitler agreed with the dissenters, the changes made to the FALL GELB plan delayed the attack while staff officers hurriedly shifted German dispositions away from the northern axis to make the main attack in the south. That movement went undetected by Allied military intelligence. Gone from German planning was a central intention to seize the Atlantic shelf of northwest Europe as a platform for bombing Britain, though that gain would still accrue to a decisive victory. Hitler and the OKW had decided to seek a Vernichtungsschlacht after all, a great battle of annihilation of the French Army and British Expeditionary Force (BEF). The revised plan was extremely high risk and should not have been fatal for the Western powers. But as the first Panzers poked their snouts into the Ardennes woods and began to rumble along forest roads that were sometimes only one-tank wide, the Allies executed a longstanding plan to move their best armored and mobile forces into Belgium and the Netherlands. Instead of waiting passively for the Germans to arrive at the frontiers of France, the High Commands in the West agreed to advance into the Low Countries to defend prepared positions along the *Dyle Line.* As a result, they readied to move their best divisions directly into a German trap.

The French Army was a magnificent and well-equipped force. In London, Washington, and Moscow it was thought that the French had the best Army in Europe, unit-for-unit as well as in armor, guns, and other equipment. OKW planners also had a healthy respect for the French. The Armée de l'Air (French Air Force) was in the midst of a changeover in aircraft and lacked enough modern types, but it was also a formidable force. When the Armée de l'Air was combined with assets of the RAF, on paper the Western Allies were at least a match in the air for the Luftwaffe. Then the drôle de guerre passed from fall into winter into spring. The delay allowed the BEF to grow its divisions in France and to train. But it also left too many French Army divisions hunkered down inside the *Maginot Line,* where their strength and morale was sapped through ennui and lack of continuous training. When the moment came, the Maginot chain of forts would be circumvented by the Panzers and Panzergrenadiers. Excellent fixed guns, presited kill zones, and large garrisons would be made irrelevant to the operational outcome of the battle for France. Moreover, because the French High Command did not expect that a major armored attack could move through the Ardennes with any speed, their weakest infantry divisions were set to guard the hinge of the Maginot Line where it ended at the unfortified western Belgian frontier, gateway to the open plain of northern France. That was precisely where Hitler and the OKW pinpointed the Schwerpunkt of the looming fight: the point to concentrate greatest stress and the heaviest attack with the main mass of Panzer divisions and German mechanized and motorized infantry.

The French decision to leave only weak infantry divisions holding the Meuse at the foot of the Ardennes hills need not have proven fatal to Allied defenses. Even the great surprise of the majority of Panzers emerging from the Ardennes far sooner than expected might have been countered and the high-risk German attack blunted, if only superb French armored and mobile forces had been held in a mobile operational reserve. French and BEF armored forces might have advanced to the Meuse to counter the German thrust earlier than was in fact attempted, had they been positioned to counter move as soon as the Schwerpunkt was identified by enemy concentrations and advances. Instead, most French armor was aligned farther north, precommitted to a rapid advance into Belgium once an invitation from Brussels was issued to cross the frontier and race ahead to the Dyle Line. Parked alongside the French waiting orders to move into Belgium were the armored and other mobile divisions of the BEF. French 7th Army was positioned even farther north, along the neutral Dutch frontier. When the German feint in force into the Low Countries finally came on May 10, it reinforced Allied preconceptions that Belgium would be the battlefield that decided the outcome of the war in the west.

The German attack was originally scheduled by Hitler for November 1939. Bad weather and planning changes forced him to make no fewer than 29 postponements. Tensions spiked in the west on April 9 with the onset of WESERÜBUNG in Denmark and Norway. It began when Fallschirmjäger dropped around key Danish bridges, allowing Panzers to race across Denmark. Copenhagen was secured within hours, and the whole country was attached to Hitler's empire by the end of a single day. More Fallschirmjäger dropped that day over Norway, seizing air fields for follow-up *air landing* troops, while a secret Kriegsmarine expedition landed more invaders directly into Norwegian ports. Some German officers had traveled in advance to Norway dressed as civilians. Special forces and ordinary *Landser* hid in the holds of merchant ships for days, some peacefully at anchor in Norwegian harbors. Others arrived that morning on destroyer-transports. A critical German supply ship steamed to Norway from a Soviet naval base, revealing the depth of Joseph Stalin's extraordinary misreading of Hitler. The German assault on Norway ran into a simultaneous French and British expedition to secure Norway's northern ports, which aimed to cut off Swedish iron ore supplies to German war industry. After a month of confused fighting the Western Allies pulled out of Norway, a strategic loss that secured Germany's northern flank. Bloody floundering around the fjords of Narvik and Trondheim also forced crises of confidence in Paris and London, leading the governments of France and Great Britain to fall just as the Wehrmacht build-up for FALL GELB ended. Two more small democracies had been forced under the Nazi jackboot, yet the surviving democracies of Europe could not resolve the key issue of coordination of their war plans. The Belgians and Dutch each stood by their desperate formal neutrality. The Allied supreme commander, General *Maurice Gamelin,* thus had no choice but to stick with agreed dispositions for moving his forces to the Dyle Line upon the outbreak of active fighting. The BEF and best French armored divisions remained precommitted to rush into the Low Countries only after the shooting started.

Dutch and Belgian faith in a defense of formal neutrality proved utterly false. Fallschirmjäger again fell out of a western sky early on May 10. The paratroops seized airfields around the Hague preparatory to arrival of Ju-52 transports carrying German 22nd Airlanding Division. They did not have an easy time: the Luftwaffe lost nearly 80 percent of its total air transport capacity, fully 213 aircraft. The

Netherlands was not Denmark: the Dutch fought back, and quickly retook the airfields. However, the distraction caused by the airborne operations was great as forward elements of German 18th Army raced into the Zeeland peninsula, ahead of French 7th Army units that finally began to cross the frontier. The Dutch broke dikes and polders and flooded the countryside in the path of the advancing Germans, but that traditional defense did not stop Fallschirmjäger who dropped near key bridges over rivers and canals at the outset of the attack. *Brandenburgers* in armored trains led Panzer and motorized infantry columns over the Dutch–German border. Several German armored trains were destroyed by the Dutch, but one crossed successfully at Gennep to enable German ground forces to link with airborne troops holding key bridges over the Maas and several major canals. Some of the crossings made swiftly by the Germans in 1940 were over the same rivers and canals that Western armies would fail to take or hold four years later during Operation *MARKET GARDEN*.

The Germans were not successful everywhere: some Dutch battalions fought hard, and isolated groups of surrounded Fallschirmjäger paid a high price in lives, wounded, and prisoners taken. But the Maas Line and Peel Line defenses counted on by the Dutch were breached and abandoned on the first day. Within two days the Ijssel Line was penetrated by forward Wehrmacht units. The Dutch retreated toward their inner sanctuary, or "Fortress Holland," activating more water defenses as they pulled out of Brabant. Their line of retreat forced them away from advancing French 7th Army, while German pursuit was swifter than the Dutch High Command anticipated. The main Dutch armies were soon cut off from Allied assistance. German 18th Army blasted across the Netherlands, moving with remarkable speed over difficult terrain crisscrossed with rivers and canals. Roads channeled movement predictably toward defenses famous for centuries for breaking the momentum of attacking armies, but the Germans overcame those obstacles with stunning swiftness. As Dutch defenses broke and resistance crumbled, Berlin struck a critical psychological blow on May 14: ruthless bombardment was ordered against Rotterdam by the Luftwaffe and Wehrmacht artillery ringing the city. Terror had the desired effect: the Dutch government asked for a ceasefire the next day. Longer term, however, outrage over the bombing and shelling of Rotterdam encouraged the British to lift city-bombing restraints on their bomber force. The seeds of the wind sown by the Luftwaffe in the southern Netherlands would one day bring the whirlwind down upon Germany. In the interim, the ground war also went badly for the Allies in Belgium.

Fallschirmjäger paratroopers and glider troops landed across Belgium on May 10, in advance of thrusting ground forces of Army Group B. As word of the drops and landings reached Belgian frontier guards on the western border, they lifted customs crossing bars to allow British and French armor and troops to move to the Dyle Line. Fallschirmjäger quickly captured two bridges across the Albert Canal, breaching a key Belgian defense line well before that was expected. Most shockingly, just 80 German glider-borne combat engineers took the great fortress complex of Eban Emael, thought capable of withstanding the fiercest bombardment and itself inflicting huge punishment on any invader. The engineers landed in gliders on the fortress roof, achieving complete surprise. Then they rappelled down the walls to penetrate the interior by climbing through the fort's gunports. Once inside they blocked air vents and killed or suppressed defenders with fixed charges and flamethrowers, holding on until regular German infantry reached the complex in large numbers and Eban Emael surrendered on the second day. Meanwhile, the few and narrow roads of the Ardennes conduced to mass traffic jams of German armor, which was advancing in three columns. French military intelligence did not yet recognize the emerging threat in the south: resistance was light, immobile, and poorly organized or reinforced. The lead Panzers broke out of the Ardennes on May 13. There followed two days of hard fighting as elements of three full *Panzergruppe* sought to cross the Meuse between Sedan and Dinant, a full week before even the most optimistic staff officers at OKH thought such a crossing was possible. The breakthroughs and tentative lodgements on the west bank, including that of General *Erwin Rommel's* 7th Panzer Division, were not initially understood by Supreme Allied Headquarters or in Paris or London. A growing depth of armored penetration and the real strength of attacking forces in the Ardennes were revealed by stunning reports of German armor in places far forward from where it should have been and in much greater strength. The armored penetration beyond the Meuse now caused panic in western field HQs and capitals.

General *Heinz Guderian* led the main German breakthrough by 19th Panzer Corps near Sedan, where his tanks first touched the east bank of the Meuse at dusk on May 12. The French High Command thought the Germans must stop at the Meuse for a logistical break. Gamelin did not immediately react or show the panic that all Western commanders would display in another few days. He ordered 11 divisions from his reserve to reinforce Sedan, but only scheduled them to arrive over the week of May 14–21. Nor did he yet recall his main mobile forces from the Netherlands or Belgium. Without waiting for heavy infantry to come up to the Meuse to support his crossing, Guderian ordered combat engineers to lay a temporary bridge over the river and crossed with unsupported armor starting on the evening of May 14. French linear defenses on the west bank, in front of Sedan, cracked the next day: Guderian's tanks were through the thin crustal defense by the 16th and sped off onto the northern plain. Seven Panzer divisions from three different armored corps were soon over the Meuse and racing across France to the Atlantic. Some moved so rapidly and far ahead of follow-on leg infantry that OKH twice tried to halt the advance, from fear of overexposing the thinning and extended flanks of the armored thrusts. As Guderian moved, he ignored the vulnerability of his flanks and two halt orders from OKH. He was ordered to conduct only a "reconnaissance in force." Like *George Patton* in western Sicily in 1943, Guderian carried out the order with his entire armored corps. He lied to his superiors and sent them false reports about his main position. He did so in the grand independent tradition of the Prussian and German officer corps, and suffered no consequences. Rommel behaved similarly with his *Ghost Division,* disregarding halt orders to press on to the coast. Both men were later rewarded for their initiative and success.

General *Charles de Gaulle's* 4th Armored Division nearly fulfilled OKH's worst worry when it counterattacked and disrupted Guderian's supply columns on May 17. But the weight of the German armored thrust was already too great to be stopped by such a localized defense. Swift-moving Panzers reached the Somme River on May 19, an area infamous to German and British soldiers alike for horrid positional warfare from 1914 to 1918. Gamelin was sacked that day, replaced by General *Maxime Weygand* who had flown in from a colonial posting in Syria. German boots dipped in the Atlantic on the 20th. The shock of the German main force punching a giant hole through the Schwerpunkt of the Ardennes knocked the defenders off their preset plans. The entire Anglo-French force that entered Belgium was compelled to turn around in place and retreat. That meant combat elements were at the rear of long columns while the slowest transports—food and medical—were now at the head, blocking the path of the combat units. The retreat was chaotic, carried out in the midst of retreating divisions of the Belgian Army. Hundreds of thousands of panicked civilians clogged roads with horse-drawn carts filled with household goods, or pregnant women or aged parents; many died under strafing attacks by Stukas and German fighters. British armor counterattacked on the 21st, toward Arras. Although the assault was quickly blunted, it increased OKH fear that German armored columns were overextended and exposed. In fact, the entire BEF and large supporting French and Belgian units were already cut off from the bulk of the French Army that was trying to reform a defense line to the south, in open country north of Paris.

Luftwaffe aircraft bombed and strafed enemy columns moving slowly along French roads also clogged with refugees: the great *Exodus* ("L'Exode"), mostly of women and children, was underway across northern France. Late on May 24, General *John Gort* gave the definitive order for the BEF to retreat from Arras toward Dunkirk, as Royal Navy evacuation ships assembled at Dover. The decision caused uproar within Allied councils, and a severe breach of trust between British and French military and civilian leaders. In reality, Gort's order was an entirely necessary response to operational defeat in the "Battle of France," not its cause. Nor was it yet thought by all Allied leaders that the fight for France was over, though it was by many. Initially, the evacuation plan was to ship troops to England then back to France via southern ports, in hopes of firming defenses forming north of Paris. The mass retreat toward the port of Dunkirk was the worst defeat suffered by the British Army in two centuries. When Belgium surrendered on May 28, the BEF and many French and Belgian troops were stranded in a coastal enclave, which the Wehrmacht pressed hard at first. German armored and mechanized units initially harried and pursued the retreating Allied armies, but OKH appetites were already eager for more victories. Hitler's gaze was also drawn south, to the looming battle in front of Paris.

Acting on the advice of Field Marshal *Gerd von Rundstedt,* commander of Army Group A, Hitler halted the Panzers from pursuing the BEF across the sodden Flanders plain. Rundstedt prepared instead to pivot all his armored forces for a push to Paris, and beyond. The decision to leave a large enemy enclave to be pounded by the Luftwaffe, sending only German leg infantry to contain and press the perimeter of the pocket, is usually characterized as a key mistake by Hitler that shaped the rest of the war. That is a highly moot judgment. Whether it is true or not, the decision meant that 240,000 men of the BEF and 120,000 French and Belgians were sealifted to Britain over the several days and nights of the *Dunkirk evacuation*. The halt of the Panzers, tough fighting by French and British troops in defense of the Dunkirk perimeter, close RAF fighter cover to keep off the Luftwaffe, and brave men on Royal Navy ships and even some civilian craft made evacuation possible. On the other hand, Allied troops left France without vehicles, guns, tanks, or in many cases personal weapons. Some exhausted men climbed aboard departing vessels without shoes, having swum out to the last ships. Already there had been two British defeats and evacuations, from Norway and from France. Two more would be suffered by the British Army over the next year of war: evacuations from Greece and Crete lay in the future. And as Winston Churchill said at the time: "Wars are not won by evacuations."

The French lost the best part of their mechanized and mobile forces and the northern third of the country. Still, something was salvaged by evacuation from Dunkirk and less well-known, smaller evacuations from other ports. Nor had the Allies even now accepted defeat. Although defeatist counsel was openly expressed in some quarters on both sides of the Channel, the British still had two fresh divisions in France and were planning to bring in more troops through Cherbourg in Normandy. Even as they desperately pulled men out of the water and off the beaches around Dunkirk, the Chiefs of Staff contemplated setting up a "fighting redoubt" on the Côtentin peninsula. As Rundstedt pivoted, the French Army deployed a much reduced and chastened force, but still one comprising 53 divisions, along a northward-facing front from the Meuse to the Somme dubbed the "Weygand Line." The thin French hope was to hold until Dunkirk evacuees were convoyed south, while reinforcements were rushed from overseas, drawing on the manpower and fighting reserves of the British and French empires. After refitting for a week, Rundstedt sent concentrated armored thrusts against the French line on June 5. Army Group A struck farther south four days later. The OKH assaulted the "Weygand Line" with 119 divisions against just 53 defending divisions. And where the Germans had 23 divisions in reserve, the French threw all they had left into the fight—nearly all their infantry formations except those few standing against potential Italian treachery in the deep south or those still defending the Maginot Line against a potential German flank offensive. There was ferocious fighting before the Panzers broke through improvised French defenses everywhere on June 14, thence to roll on to Paris and into the Après Midi. With the earlier loss of French mobile forces in Flanders, there was no way to counterattack or blunt the fast-moving German armored columns once they were through the crustal defense. Armored spearheads broke past demoralized French infantry, curling around Paris and down the interior side of the Maginot Line. On June 10, Benito Mussolini finally showed his Axis colors when he sent the Italian Army to attack along the French alpine frontier. The inept assault was repelled with heavy losses (nearly 5,000 Italian casualties), despite the defenders being overwhelmingly outnumbered. It mattered little: the main battle for France was already lost to the Wehrmacht in the north.

The Luftwaffe lost 1,400 aircraft over the seven-week fight, but it still had strength enough to attack French cities. For the first time in the war, with Allied air forces pushed away from forward air bases along the German frontier, German bombers struck at strategic targets well behind the front line in early June. They bombed Paris for the first time, along with Marseilles and other cities. Like the earlier German bombing of Rotterdam, these attacks were most important for their psychological effect: they persuaded the French not to defend Paris or other cities, but to declare them "open cities" instead. But they also helped persuade the RAF and the British government to reduce operational targeting limits on bombing German cities in the Ruhr. Meanwhile, the French Army and government fell apart. French leaders were asked directly by Churchill if they intended to continue to fight from the overseas empire. Of special interest to the British prime minister was the fate of the major warships of the Marine Nationale: would they evacuate to ports in the French empire beyond German reach, surrender, or be scuttled? Weygand advised that the land battle for France was over, but the naval question hung in the air. General *Alan Brooke* convinced Churchill to pull out the last BEF troops, just as Air Chief Marshal *Hugh Dowding* had persuaded the prime minister not to send any more RAF fighter squadrons to France: they were needed to defend Britain itself against Axis invasion. The evacuation was organized from Cherbourg; it rescued 156,000 British, Canadian, and Polish troops, some of whom had just been landed in France. On June 16, Marshal *Philippe Pétain,* hero of Verdun and savior of France and its Army in 1916, was recalled from his ambassadorship in Madrid to replace *Paul Reynaud* as leader of the French government. Pétain's deep pessimism during the last years of the Great War had long since morphed into outright defeatism. Defeat was in fact confronting France. In the name of saving the Army and ending suffering of the French people, Pétain asked for an *armistice.*

Hitler accepted the French request to prevent last-ditch resistance, departure for overseas bases by the great warships of the Marine Nationale (which he greatly coveted), or long-term resistance by French overseas garrisons. Hitler especially needed to deny French warships to the British, as he was still contemplating a cross-Channel invasion of Britain. He forced the French and Italians to agree to a second armistice, telling Mussolini to accept limited territorial and other gains in exchange for a minimal Italian effort and achievement. The document of formal surrender to Germany was signed at Compiègne on June 22, in the same railway carriage where German representatives signed the Armistice of November 11, 1918. The car had been preserved as part of a monument to France's victory in the Great War, a conflict in which Hitler served for four years as a trench runner and soldier. He attended the signing but said nothing. He sat briefly where Maréchal Ferdinand Foch had sat in 1918, then abruptly left once the document was signed. Hitler made his only visit to Paris the next day, touring the center of the city with his architect, *Albert Speer.* Afterward, Hitler had the Compiègne monument blown apart. The surrender carriage was taken to Berlin as a trophy, but was later destroyed during an Allied air raid. The armistices with Germany and Italy both came into effect on June 24–25.

Total German losses in the seven-week FALL GELB campaign were 50,000 killed and wounded. Over the course of the battle the BEF lost 64,000 military vehicles, 2,500 guns, 931 aircraft, and 67,000 men killed, wounded, or captured.

French losses were 123,000 dead and many more wounded. Over 1.5 million French prisoners would be held hostage in Germany until 1944, and some until the *conquest of Germany* in 1945. The Wehrmacht had demonstrated ascendant mastery in combined-arms operations, which prewar training, doctrine, organization, and weapons of the Western powers could not yet match, and would not match for another two years. The men of the Wehrmacht also showed a higher ideological commitment to the war. Most had been raised to fight by Nazi organizations and propaganda starting in their boyhood. But the Germans had taken an extreme risk and were simply lucky at several key moments in the battle for France and the Low Countries, as some of their generals later confessed in otherwise mendacious postwar interviews or memoirs.

All across Europe and beyond, leaders of countries not yet involved in the war looked to adjust policies to accommodate new geostrategic and economic realities; to wit: the decided military view that Hitler had already won the war with the Western Allies by mid-1940; the dominant opinion among most diplomats that Britain must come to terms with that fact sooner rather than later; and the seemingly obvious geopolitical conclusion that Nazi Germany and its Axis partners would dominate European affairs for the next generation at least. Neutral states in the Balkans and eastern Europe yet to be attacked thus made gestures of obeisance to Berlin. Some also bowed toward Rome, where Mussolini had shown a comparable reckless belligerence to match Hitler's. On the far side of the Greater German Reich, Moscow moved significant ground forces to its western borders in late May 1940. That was preparatory to Stalin forcing Rumania to cede its provinces of *Bessarabia* and *Bukovina,* as well as physical and military occupation of the Baltic States in accordance with the terms of the *Nazi–Soviet Pact* of August 23, 1939. But FALL GELB meant that Stalin had much less time than he had counted on to repair damage done to the Red Army by his bloody purges, especially the climactic *Yezhovshchina.* Removal of the powerful and modern French Army from the order of battle that opposed Hitler, along with Stalin's military and intelligence assistance to Nazi Germany's project of expelling the British Army from the continent, meant that there was no one left to fight in the West when Hitler turned his Panzers and legions eastward in mid-1941, and that no *second front* could be reestablished there until mid-1944. The peoples of the Soviet Union would pay a dreadful price for that colossal miscalculation by the "man of steel" in the Kremlin, starting with Operation *BARBAROSSA.*

Franklin D. Roosevelt had also relied overmuch on the strength of the French Army to stand against Germany, as it had stood so strongly during the Great War. Now the American president had to consider what he must do beyond making speeches about "moral embargoes" and proclaiming that his nation need serve only as the "arsenal of democracy," when nearly all other free and democratic peoples were in the fight and several were already defeated and occupied by the fascist dictators. Czechoslovakia and Poland no longer even appeared on German maps. The once free populations of Denmark, Norway, Luxembourg, Belgium, the Netherlands, and France were under the thumbscrew rule of the *Gestapo* and local fascist collaborators, while Nazi machinery of death was active across Europe: deportations, swelling *concentration camps,* and the murder brigades of the *Einsatzgruppen.* Sweden was neutral, as was Switzerland, leaving only one democracy still opposing Hitler in Europe at the end of June 1940. And Britain was on its knees in mid-1940, effectively defenseless on the ground, already fighting off the first Luftwaffe swarms to cross the Channel and about to undergo sustained Axis bombing of its major cities. Roosevelt knew the British expected to be invaded at any given sunrise. Against the mortal threat of an invasion fleet, Britain's best defense must be to ask for suicidal sacrifice by the young men of the RAF and Royal Navy. The Channel barrier had to be defended at any cost, because if ever the Germans made a successful lodgement on the British coast it would be a short land war before jackboots were heard tramping down the streets of London.

Before another year passed, Greece would be invaded in an unprovoked aggression by Italy, and Yugoslavia would be smashed to bits by armies from several Axis states, jackals all, snapping at each other over the carcass of the rule of law. Where was America? Every free and once free man and woman outside the United States asked that question. There seemed no other hope but American intervention for the British and Commonwealth struggle to restore decency and law in Europe, in alliance with frail fragments of the broken armed forces of erstwhile allies and occupied or extinguished states: a few brigades and squadrons of exiled *Free French,* Poles, Norwegians, Dutch, and other conquered but still defiant peoples. Echoes of consequence of the defeat of France were felt as far away as China and around the Pacific Rim. Japan was nudged significantly closer by FALL GELB to a decision to follow the *nanshin* path, or "southern advance," toward imperial aggrandizement. The newfound weakness of all European imperial powers in Asia after the German victory in Europe left overripe colonial fruit across Southeast Asia hanging before the Japanese. Tokyo's partner in Berlin seemed to be in cahoots with Moscow, while the Red Army had already proven to the Imperial Japanese Army at *Nomonhan* that the *hokushin* path ("northern advance") was too hard. The first step south for Japan was to force major concessions from a powerless Vichy governor of French Indochina, followed by military occupation of that distant colony, which France no longer had the strength to defend. Dominos were falling all across the world by the end of 1940, toppled by the defeat of France.

See also Finnish–Soviet War (1939–1940).

Suggested Reading: Julian Jackson, *The Fall of France* (2003); Ernest May, *Strange Victory* (2000).

FALL GRÜN (1938) "Case GREEN." German code name for an invasion plan for Czechoslovakia. It was not implemented because Great Britain, France, and Italy instead delivered the *Sudetenland* to Adolf Hitler at the *Munich Conference (September 29–30, 1938).* The Wehrmacht ultimately rolled unopposed into Prague in March 1939.

FALL GRÜN (1940) "Case GREEN." Originally, the German code name for a proposed invasion of Switzerland. It was changed to *TANNENBAUM* when the

Wehrmacht selected *FALL GRÜN* instead for a proposed invasion of Ireland, timed to follow conquest of Great Britain in *SEELÖWE*.

FALLSCHIRMJÄGER   "Flying hunter." German paratroopers. They were highly successful as special forces in targeted drops onto bridges and other key points in Denmark and Norway in April 1940, and again in France and the Low Countries that May. But after suffering heavy losses among Fallschirmjäger in the victory on *Crete* in 1941, Adolf Hitler grew wary of future *airborne operations*. Fallschirmjäger divisions were thereafter used mainly as elite light infantry.

See also *Dombås; MARKET GARDEN; Normandy campaign; recoilless guns; Skorzeny, Otto; Student, Kurt; Vercors.*

FALL WEISS (SEPTEMBER 1–OCTOBER 5, 1939)   "Case White." German code name for the invasion of Poland. So eager was Adolf Hitler for a *Vernichtungsschlacht* ("battle of annihilation") against Poland, he ordered the OKW to draw up invasion plans in early April 1939. Before the *Nazi–Soviet Pact* was signed on August 23, 1939, Hitler set the hour for war as dawn on September 1. He then advanced it to 4:30 A.M. on August 26. Italy was informed of the planned invasion through a late-night phone call to *Count Ciano* on August 24, with a follow-up letter sent the next day to Benito Mussolini. Rome was asked to contribute troops under terms of the *Pact of Steel*. Warnings were sent to four *neutral states* not to permit violations of their territory by Britain and France, along with assurances that Germany promised them peace and security. Similar assurances of peaceful intent were made to Paris and London. Hitler even offered a humbug alliance to Britain—against his Italian, Japanese, and Soviet allies—should London allow him a free hand to deal with Poland. Two key events on August 25 caused Hitler to postpone the attack. Shocked and frightened at the prospect of a general war, Mussolini declined to participate in the invasion. The Italian leader's turnabout greatly surprised Hitler. The second surprise came when London and Paris publicly announced formal military alliances with Poland, affirming on the eve of war that the Western Allies would fight. Meanwhile, Poland hastened to complete a mobilization it had begun far too late. The delay was occasioned by a perceived need in tough economic times to keep Polish workers in factories and rural laborers on farms during the harvest season. Warsaw was also late mobilizing because the Allies asked for a delay to avoid "provoking" Germany during a crisis over *Danzig* that they still hoped to solve through diplomacy. Champing at the bit of war, the German Führer paused only for a few days after losing his main ally and confirming the addition of two Great Power enemies to the opposing order of battle. He abruptly reversed course a second time, ordering that the planned invasion take place on the original target date of September 1.

Hitler's last-minute and extreme command confusion meant that a false start was made by an *Abwehr* field unit that crossed the Polish border on its own. It never received the recall order, and so attacked anyway on the 26th. Abwehr men took their designated target inside Polish territory, but quickly pulled out when they learned that the invasion was postponed. Their attack increased Polish–German border tensions and alertness, but their withdrawal meant it did not precipitate war. For that purpose, the Germans had another plan. On the night of August 31, a gross deceit was perpetrated by a *Schutzstaffel (SS)* special operations squad, under orders to provide a legal pretext for declaring war and a story to arouse Germans to a fight many were as yet reluctant to undertake. Eight SS-men were photographed in Polish Army uniforms, secured for the operation by Admiral *Wilhelm Canaris,* head of the Abwehr. They drove up to Gleiwtz radio station on the German side of the border. Their fake attack was to have been dramatized with a radio broadcast in which they pretended that they were enemy soldiers assaulting a border post on German soil. The SS-men botched the job: their broadcast was so weak it was heard by few people, if anyone at all. To complete the ruse they murdered a *concentration camp* inmate brought along for the purpose, leaving his corpse on display for the cameras of the morning newspapers and for newsreels shot by *Josef Göbbels'* Ministry of Propaganda. The cynical SS plan for a fake attack was the inspiration of *Reinhard Heydrich.* The European war he helped begin would make him infamous as the "Butcher of Prague" and overseer of the *Einsatzgruppen,* then as principal architect of the gas chambers, crematoria, and other machinery of the *death camps* where three million Polish Jews would be murdered.

As three Wehrmacht army groups rolled into Poland with the break of dawn on September 1, German propaganda bellowed that Polish forces had attacked the Gleiwtz customs post and radio station. Later that day, Göbbels broadcast to a hushed and attentive nation and continent that the Wehrmacht had, justly and righteously, moved into Poland in hot pursuit of the attackers and in national self-defense against unprovoked aggression. The three Wehrmacht main columns comprised 60 divisions, including six of Panzers and four of motorized infantry. They faced 30 underequipped and still only partially mobilized Polish divisions. The Poles also fielded 11 cavalry brigades, but had just two mechanized brigades equipped with inferior armor. More Polish infantry divisions were being mobilized when the German hammer struck. A number would be rushed to the frontier only in time for green troops, fresh from the factory or harvest and hardly trained, to be slaughtered by fast-moving advance units of Panzers and Panzergrenadiers. The Poles were not just outnumbered and unready. More importantly, their main defense constituted a woefully improper deployment around much too great an outer perimeter, with virtually no effort at defense-in-depth. The Polish Army stretched and strained to defend the entire Polish frontier, which was now threatened from the start on three sides, partly because of the prior destruction of Czechoslovakia in which Poland had foolhardily participated. The Poles also faced a virtually insoluble problem of defending exposed Danzig and the narrow neck of the *Polish corridor.* Polish dispositions were thus dictated by strategic geography and internal political demands that did not match military capabilities or realities. The result was quick defeat and tragedy for the Polish nation.

The Germans struck hard from the first hours, pounding the small Danzig garrison from the sea while sending *Geschwader* of medium bombers and dive bombers deep into enemy territory to terrorize the population as well as cover ground penetrations by three army groups. The two flank attacks aimed to form a concentric thrust to first crack, and then envelop, the main Polish forces along the northern and southern frontiers. Panzers were quickly through the Polish crustal defense in several places. Once in open country, they showed off the new style of highly mobile and mechanized warfare that marked off the Wehrmacht from all other militaries from 1939 to 1941. Army Group South struck northward from German Silesia, through German-occupied Slovakia. Army Group North linked Pomerania and East Prussia by quickly crossing the Polish corridor and isolating Danzig, then drove hard south. The aim of the German operational plan was to pinch off avenues of retreat into central and eastern Poland. A third attack came directly across the Oder–Neisse river line from the west, forming a central drive on Warsaw intended to fix the bulk of the Polish Army so that the pincers might envelop it. The center was identified as the *Schwerpunkt,* around which the outer pincers would enclose several Polish armies in a giant and decisive *Kesselschlacht.* Wider killing was to begin immediately: Hitler spoke to his generals before the campaign began of the model of the Armenian genocide he wished them to follow in Poland.

The Poles were concentrated largely in the west and center, which perfectly exposed their main force to enclosure by the German pincers. The Panzers now rolled at a speed that astonished the military and political worlds, where many clung to memories of trench warfare from 1914 to 1918. That was true even of those who better appreciated the potential of armored thrusts in theory: this was the first real experience of a renewed "German way of war," of a style of *Bewegungskrieg* ("war of movement") that sought first and foremost to keep Germany out of the *Stellungskrieg* ("war of position") by which it lost the last war, while promising quick operational achievement of a *Vernichtungsschlacht* ("battle of annihilation") over the enemy. The first so-called *Blitzkrieg* of World War II was a stunning success. German armies met at the base of the Polish corridor within three days, then drove on Warsaw from September 6–10. The only reverse of the opening phase of the campaign for the Wehrmacht took place at Kutná, where German 8th Army was counterattacked in its flank on September 9 by Poznan Army. That successful Polish assault forced 8th Army to withdraw 10 miles, pulling away from the outer environs of Warsaw. But the Poles were themselves forced to reverse course on the 14th by a penetrating attack into their exposed position by German 10th Army, strongly supported by Stukas and other air assets. The *Kessel* ("cauldron") was thereafter closed tight, and a triumphant Wehrmacht proceeded to cook the bulk of Polish defenders inside it.

The Polish Navy was small, with just 15 small coastal warships. It was easily overwhelmed by the great battleships and cruisers of the Kriegsmarine, whose powerful surface fleet was fully committed to the brief naval fight in the Baltic Sea. German ships then bombarded fortifications along the short Polish coastline around Danzig. Only a handful of Polish warships escaped, to continue fighting from British ports over the remainder of the war. The Polish Air Force was also weak at just 400, mostly obsolete, warplanes. It was outnumbered in modern aircraft by at least 5:1. Some planes were caught by surprise and destroyed on the ground, but most were subsequently destroyed in the air by superior German fighters and Luftwaffe pilots, some with combat experience from Spain. Within days, a few harried Polish Air Force survivors could do little to stop Stukas and German fighters pounding retreating ground columns, or Do-17 and He-111 medium bombers terror bombing Warsaw. The Poles expected help in the form of immediate Allied bombing of targets in Germany, to be followed by a French offensive along the Rhine agreed to start no later than September 15. Commitment to that date for a proposed French Army offensive—two weeks from commencement of any German attack on Poland—had been promised by the French High Command in May. Timing was based on the French Army mobilization schedule. However, there is no evidence that the Western powers ever seriously contemplated an offensive into Germany in 1939, or for that matter at any time during the *Phoney War*. They decided instead that the only thing to do was hunker down, continue their joint build-up and training of men for the long war of attrition they expected to fight against Germany, and wish the Poles "bon chance" in a sure-to-be-lost cause. That was not mere cynicism: it was probably the only prudent strategy the Western powers could follow.

On September 17 the Soviet Union declared that the state of Poland had legally ceased to exist, and sent the Red Army to slash into eastern Poland to reclaim Tsarist provinces lost during the Polish–Soviet War in 1920. In fact, Soviet troops advanced to a secretly prearranged meeting line with the Wehrmacht established under an unpublished codicil to the Nazi–Soviet Pact. The choice of September 17, with the Polish Army already effectively defeated, appears to have been the result of Soviet surprise at the speed of the German advance and attendant slow Red Army mobilization. In addition, Stalin sought to separate politically and in propaganda terms his invasion from Hitler's naked aggression. Moscow's attention was also drawn away from Poland to the Far East in early September, as the Red Army launched an offensive against the Japanese *Guandong Army* at *Nomonhan*. A ceasefire with Japan was formally agreed on September 15. Assaulted on both sides, the Poles fought bravely but hopelessly to defend Warsaw for 10 days after the Soviet intervention. The Wehrmacht pulled back to the partition line agreed with Moscow during the week of September 20-26. The Polish garrison in Warsaw surrendered on September 27. The rest of the Polish Army formally submitted on October 5. The government had by then slipped into Rumania, thence into exile in Paris. It would move to London the next year, as *FALL GELB* brought Blitzkrieg and death to France and the Low Countries. Fresh Nazi–Soviet border adjustments were agreed in the immediate aftermath of the fighting. There followed mass deportations of ethnic Poles and Jews along the new boundaries, accompanied by importation of ethnic Germans (*Volksdeutsche*) from the Baltic states to Poland. In that brutal, forced movement of whole populations there was extensive cooperation between the Nazi *Gestapo* and the Soviet *NKVD*. Berlin and Moscow then formally declared the Polish war over and Poland extinct as a nation-state. They next called upon the Allies to recognize the new order they had jointly made in eastern Europe, to wit: destruction of Poland and the end of independence for the three Baltic States.

Total German losses in the month-long campaign were 8,100 killed and 32,000 wounded or missing. The Red Army lost 2,600 killed, wounded, or missing. The Poles lost 70,000 killed and 130,000 wounded, with 420,000 prisoners taken by the Germans and 240,000 more falling into Soviet captivity. Hundreds of thousands of Poles escaped to fight and kill Germans another day, in North Africa, Sicily, Italy, at *Falaise* in Normandy, and even inside Germany itself. In 1941 many tens of thousands of Polish prisoners still held in Red Army camps would be freed to join all-Polish or Soviet units to kill Germans on the *Eastern Front*. Most were later allowed to leave the Soviet Union to fight instead under command of the British. However, about 20,000 Polish officers captured by the Red Army were instead murdered in early 1940 at three different sites in the Soviet Union, the most famous of which was in *Katyn* forest outside Smolensk. Many thousands of other Polish resisters died in Gestapo torture cells. Even more—six million Poles died before it was all over—were shot by Wehrmacht execution details and Einsatzgruppen murder squads, as the long dark night of Nazi occupation settled over a benighted and immiserated land.

See also *Czechoslovakia; Hungary; Lithuania; unconditional surrender.*

Suggested Reading: Richard Hargreaves, *Blitzkrieg Unleashed* (1988); Robert Kennedy, *The German Campaign in Poland, 1939* (1956); Alexander Rossino, *Hitler Strikes Poland: Blitzkrieg, Ideology, and Atrocity* (2003); S. Zaloga, *The Polish Campaign* (1985).

FAR EAST COMMAND
See *Manchurian offensive operation (August 1945); Stavka.*

FARUK I (1920–1965)
See *Egypt.*

FASCISM   The term derives from the "fasces," a sheaf of rods carried as a symbol of office by Roman consuls, which was adopted as a symbol by the radical, antidemocratic movement that brought Benito Mussolini to power in Italy in 1922. From this exemplar, in common discourse "fascism" is also applied to *Nazism,* which surpassed the Italian variety in radicalism and depravity. It is also used in reference to only very roughly comparable mid-20th-century movements in Croatia, Rumania, Spain, and on a smaller scale across Nazi-occupied Europe. Burma, China, India, and Japan had "fascist" movements and parties as well, in a broad sense. Milder variants spread to Latin America. There were small fascist movements in Great Britain, Ireland, and even a "greyshirt" movement in Iceland. It is almost impossible to pin down the "essence" of fascism. In general, it was a romantic ideology that looked to obliterate traditional arguments of left and right by upholding veneration of a sacralized state or nation, or people, as in the concept of *Volksdeutsche.* In that regard, fascism has been identified by scholars as partly a response to a broad decline in formal religious belief throughout the West and an attempt to substitute for traditional faith a new civic religion;

or perhaps an older one in Italy: the empire as god, an updated spiritual home for modern Man that was pagan and Roman. Its signature form was a single, permanent political party said to embody the national essence. In one sense, it bound the conservative Hegelian idea of the organic state with a radical notion of the state as the instrument of revolutionary change. All that was captured in the Italian image of the "fasces," which bundled the individual rods of the nation to make a powerful, collective whole. Fascists were not interested in God: the divine existed outside the state. Yet, fascism could associate tactically or strategically with traditional religious belief to identify and isolate "the other" in a given national community, those who were said to exist outside a racial or national covenant.

Fascism exhibited a fascination with modern technology, notably aircraft and air power, but also radio, television, and all other means of the mass politics and propaganda that it championed. It evinced a certain paramilitary style in art, cinema, and especially ritual public displays that made use of mock military uniforms, flags, songs, marching, and very real violence. Its adherents utterly rejected the values of the Enlightenment and French Revolution, displacing the ideals of "liberté equalité, fraternité" with submission to strong leaders and racial and national hierarchy, as in the Nazi slogan "Ein Volk, Ein Reich, Ein Führer" ("One People, One State, One Leader"). Fascism emphasized militarism to the point of cult-like worship of warriors and of war, along with extreme chauvinism, racism, and all types of social-Darwinist and other racialist thinking. *Anti-Semitism* was at the core of German fascism, as well as Rumanian, French, and other versions. Although it infected the Italian and British versions as well, it was never as prominent in Italy or Britain or as widely accepted by the general population. Most Italian and German fascists were both extreme nationalists and imperialists who called for return of all territory ever identified with the dominant ethnic group in their states, but also for acquisition of new territories never part of the historic nation-states of Italy or Germany. Japanese fascists joined their European counterparts in celebrating war as an instrument of imperial expansion, and mass violence as a positive social and moral force. All three movements shared deep anti-Communism, with all fascists evincing an acute fear of the Soviet Union as well as loathing for fellow nationals with leftist political views.

Fascism's revolutionary character and intentions ought not to be underestimated. Fascism was not simply "more conservative" conservatism or far-right reaction—an abusive, trite, and ahistorical misuse common in postwar pejorative speech and writing. Rather, it combined many elements of leftist thinking as well in an utter rejection of democratic norms in favor of mass worship of, and personal surrender to, the ethnic or state collective. In theory, fascism vehemently repudiated both capitalism and Marxism, although in practice its incoherent and inconsistent economic doctrines proved more comfortable with the former. In Italy, the populist socialist component of fascism was strong, though largely ignored by Mussolini after 1928. It did not survive in Germany beyond the *Night of the Long Knives* in 1934. All fascists viewed democracy and any search for tolerant social consensus as weak and decadent. Their movement was spawned by the desolation, nihilism, and despair of World War I, which shattered the weak civil consensus within the newest European nation-states, especially in Germany and Italy but all over Europe in some degree. It thus exerted genuine appeal to tens of millions in the 1920s and 1930s.

Fascism was especially attractive to angry and demoralized middle classes but also rural populations. Many drawn to fascism craved dissolution of bitter class conflicts, personal misfortune, and local and national economic woes into fascism's promised "organic community," supposedly based upon an artificially denied natural unity of the nation, redefined ethnically or even racially and upheld against all other groups. That longing to surrender individuality to some putatively higher and collective purpose was made acute by the travails of the *Great Depression*. During that great social and economic upheaval and overturning of personal hopes, fascism presented itself as a distinct alternative to promotion of class conflict by the Communist left, while still offering radical answers to problems that appeared to defy solution by traditional democratic or capitalist means. Others were attracted to fascism's celebration of the irrational; its declaration of the superiority of emotion, intuition, and will over reasonableness and intellect; its shrill insistence on direct action as against reason; or just because they enjoyed antisocial violence and the feeling of false moral freedom that accompanies belonging to a herd. World War II saw the apex and then military and ideological defeat of the major fascist states and fascist movements.

See individual country entries. *See also Abyssinian War; Action Françaises; arditi; Arrow Cross; Aryan; attentisme; autarchy; Axis alliance; blackshirts; Blue Division; blueshirts; Bose, Subhas Chandra; British Union of Fascists; Ciano, Galeazzo; Comintern; concordats; Congress Party; corporatism; Degrelle, Léon; Falange; fifth column; Freikorps; Graziani, Rodolfo; Guandong Army; Herrenvolk; Himmler, Heinrich; Hitler, Adolf; Imperial Japanese Army; International Brigades; Iron Guard; Italian Army; Jiang Jieshi; Joyce, William; Konoe, Fumimaro; Laval, Pierre; League of Nations; Ligurian Army; Mao Zedong; march on Rome; Nagasaki; Nazi Party; Nazism; New Order; nuclear weapons programs; Nuremberg Tribunal; Pius XII; Popular Front; quarantine; Quisling, Vidkun; Roma; Schutzstaffel (SS); Slovak Uprising; social fascism; Spanish Civil War (1936–1939); Speer, Albert; squadristi; Stalin, Joseph; Tripartite Pact; Übermensch; Uštaše; Verona Trials; Vichy; Victor Emmanuel III; Waffen-SS; Wehrmacht; Zouaves.*

Suggested Reading: A. Hamilton, *The Appeal of Fascism* (1971); P. Hayes, *Fascism* (1973); MacGregor Knox, *Common Destiny* (2000); Robert Paxton, *The Anatomy of Fascism* (2004).

FEBRUARY RISING (FEBRUARY 26–29, 1936)
See Imperial Japanese Army; Kodo-ha; Tosei-ha; total war.

FEDERENKO, YAKOV N. (1896–1947) Marshal of Soviet tank troops. He joined the Red Army at the start of the Russian Civil War (1918–1921). In the 1920s he studied artillery. He moved over to mechanized warfare in the 1930s. In late 1942 he was placed in charge of Soviet tank forces and made deputy minister of defense. Although his main job was not at the front, it was critical: to raise, equip, and train Soviet tank armies. He was singularly responsible for training Soviet tank formations in the new art of *deep battle*. He served as a Stavka representative to various Fronts during the *Moscow offensive operation*, at *Stalingrad*, and at *Kursk*.

FELDGENDARMERIE DES HEERS   Ordinary, uniformed Wehrmacht military police.

FELDHEER   "Field Army." The main battle order of the *Heer*, as distinct from its reserve in the *Ersatzheer* or "Replacement Army." The Feldheer numbered 3.8 million men in June 1941.
   See also Wehrmacht.

FELIX   Code name for a proposed German operation to seize Gibraltar. It was never carried out.

FERDINAND
   See anti-tank weapons; Elefant; Kursk.

FERMI, ENRICO (1901–1954)
   See nuclear weapons programs.

FERNNACHTJAGD   The Luftwaffe "Long-range Night Fighter" force. It carried out *intruder raids* over Britain, looking for bombers leaving their home airfields. Opposition from Adolf Hitler and general Luftwaffe inefficiencies prevented the force from fully developing into a major threat.

FESTE PLÄTZE   "fortified places." Strongpoints declared by Adolf Hitler and erected by the Wehrmacht along the broken southern wing of the Eastern Front from March 1944. The first were centered on various western Ukrainian towns. Hitler said of his "feste Plätze" on April 18: "They are to allow themselves to be surrounded, thereby tying down the largest possible number of enemy forces. They are by this means to establish the preconditions for successful counter-operations." The doctrine might have had a slim chance to work if the Wehrmacht any longer had the mobile and armored forces necessary to link the various strongpoints and concentrate for point defense, but it did not. And the territory defended was too large (as well as strategically unimportant). The original line of "feste Plätze" in far western Ukraine was abandoned after hardly any resistance, as the Red Army broke through and raced for the foothills of the Carpathian Mountains in late March. Only the garrison at Ternopol fought hard, until overwhelmed on April 14. Other "feste Plätze" were declared later, notably contributing to disaster during *BAGRATION* in Belorussia in July–August, 1944. Still more were announced along the extended and bitter line of retreat out of the western Soviet Union back into the Balkans, Central Europe, and Germany itself.

FESTUNG EUROPA   "Fortress Europe." Adolf Hitler's favorite term for his supposedly impregnable continental defenses surrounding Western Europe.
   See Atlantic Wall; Rommel, Erwin.

FESTUNG HOLLAND   "Fortress Holland." A typically exaggerated, late-war Wehrmacht designation for Army Group "H" in the Netherlands in 1945. The Dutch also referred to "Fortress Holland" during *FALL GELB* (1940), but they meant interior defenses where they planned to make a hard stand while British and French forces moved in to support them.
   See also Blaskowitz, Johannes von.

FEUERZAUBER (SEPTEMBER 1942)   "Fire Magic." A German operational plan to finally take Leningrad in September 1942. It was not carried out.
   See also NORDLICHT.

FEZZAN CAMPAIGN (1941–1943)   A series of small scale attacks by *Free French* forces in northern Chad. The French struck into the Italian colony of Tripoli. Most raids were led by Lieutenant General *Philippe Leclerc*. The numbers involved were small, at under 4,000 on the French side. The raids turned into a sustained offensive from December 1942 to January 1943, as Leclerc's men took Tripoli then linked with British 8th Army.

FFI
   See Force Française de l'Interieur (FFI).

FIDO   "Fog Investigation and Dispersal Operation." British system for clearing fog from runways. It greatly assisted returning bombers. It comprised parallel pipes that released fuel vapor. Ignition of the vapor cleared the fog. Not all airfields were equipped with FIDO, but those that were handled heavy bomber traffic when fog socked in other aerodromes.

FIELD GUNS   A subclassification of *artillery* referring to guns that moved "in the field" under control of an infantry or armored division.
   See assault guns; heavy artillery; howitzer; mortars; self-propelled guns.

FIELD SECURITY POLICE   The British Army counterintelligence organization. It operated wherever the British Army went.

FIFTH COLUMN   Saboteurs, activists, or agents behind the lines, drawn from sympathizers for a foreign cause among the local population who work to assist entering political or military forces. The term originated during the *Spanish Civil War* when General Queipo de Llano, who was advancing on Madrid with four columns, was asked which would take the city. He replied: "The fifth, which is already there." Fifth columnists for the Nazis included *volksdeutsch* communities in *Danzig* and the *Sudetenland;* minor fascist movements in France; *Léon Degrelle* and his fellow fascists in Belgium; *Vidkun Quisling* and his helpers in Norway; the *Iron Guard* in Rumania; and others. The Soviet Union feared more fifth columnists for Germany than actually existed. Joseph Stalin and the *NKVD* made entire populations pay the price for paranoia by collective punishment and deportation. Offensively, the Soviets were aided by Communists all over German-occupied Europe. The Western Allies were assisted by Communist and non-Communist *resistance* movements operating behind German lines.

See also *Uštaše.*

FIGHTER CATAPULT SHIPS

See *Catapult Aircraft Merchant (CAM).*

FIGHTER COMMAND

See *Blitz; Britain, Battle of; Dowding, Hugh; Royal Air Force (RAF).*

FIGHTERS Attack aircraft came into their own by the last year of World War I, after first appearing in the skies only a few years earlier. During the 1920s into the mid-1930s, design and development proceeded at a more stately pace. But from 1935 there was a revolution in fighter design and engine power that rendered all earlier fighter models obsolete by vastly improving the key features of any successful fighter: speed, maneuverability, reachable ceiling, and rate of climb. Fighter armament and firepower also made major breakthroughs. The single seat, all-metal monoplane was the culmination of all these trends. Air forces that did not catch this design wave—notably the Regia Aeronautica and large components of the VVS—were blasted from the sky in the first hours and days of their respective wars. Others enjoyed an initial advantage only to lose out as enemies brought superior designs into production over the course of a protracted air war. That was the fate of the Japanese army and naval air forces and of the Luftwaffe, despite the latter's aggressive but scattershot experiments with jets and other innovations.

The Luftwaffe's standard early war fighter was the Meschersmitt Me109C (also known as the Bf109C). It had a top speed of 292 mph, a range of 388 miles, and a ceiling of 32,800 feet. The Bf109E had the same ceiling but could fly at 410 mph. Over 33,000 were built. The Bf110C had a maximum speed of 348 mph, a range of 410 miles, and the same ceiling as the early Bf109 models. It mounted five machine guns and two 20 mm cannon. The Bf109G-10 had a lower top speed at just 385 mph, but could reach 39,400 feet. The Bf109k had a top speed of 450 mph and a ceiling of 41,000 feet. The Focke-Wulf Fw190A-3 "Sturmbock" reached a ceiling of 37,500 feet and flew at 395 mph. It was heavily armed, with devastating firepower from two machine guns and four 20 mm cannon. Its appearance stunned the Royal Air Force (RAF), forcing the British to rededicate significant intelligence resources to winnow out other Luftwaffe secret weapons development they might have missed. The limited production Ta152 flew at 472 mph to a range of 1,250 miles and a ceiling of over 48,000 feet. German jet research began before the war. The late-war Me262 jet fighter—it first flew in July 1943, but was deployed only in the spring of 1944—reached 540 mph with a ceiling just under 38,000 feet. As with other Luftwaffe jets such as the jet-glider Me163, the Me262 was produced in too few numbers far too late in the air war to make any difference to the outcome. Fuel shortages and poor late-war pilots were further handicaps.

The opposing l'Armée de l'Air of France flew obsolescent Moraine 445s that were 80 kph slower than German fighters in 1940. Most did not survive long in the air. Others were caught on the ground in the first hours of *FALL GELB* (1940). The RAF also started the war with several older model biplane fighters such as the "Gladiator," but it had two excellent modern monoplanes: the Hawker "Hurricane" and the elliptical-winged "Supermarine Spitfire." Over 14,200 Hurricanes (all versions) were built between 1935 and 1944, of which 2,800 were shipped to the Soviet Union. Nearly 22,400 Spitfires, built in 24 distinct marks came off British assembly lines from 1936 to 1948. The varying marks included a "Seafire II" naval version capable of aircraft carrier operations, and a special high altitude model. Although the Spitfire remained in production all through the war, the RAF introduced a second generation of modern fighters to compete with improved German models such as the Fw190. These second generation British fighters included the Hawker "Typhoon" and "Tempest." Some 3,300 Typhoons entered service from 1941. They had a maximum speed of 412 mph, heavy weapons and armor, and were equipped with bomb racks to deliver up to 2,000 lbs of conventional ordinance or eight 60 lb rockets. Rocket-armed Typhoons specialized in a ground support role of smashing Panzers and were much feared by the Germans. The RAF also developed the "Meteor" twin-engine jet fighter. It was retained exclusively in British skies for late-war homeland defense.

Joseph Stalin had a longstanding personal interest in aviation, which led to large investment of prewar funds in the Red Army Air Force (VVS). Soviet fighters were therefore plentiful at the start of the German–Soviet war in June 1941, but also mostly obsolete. Thousands of "Stalin's Hawks" were easily destroyed on the ground in the first days of *BARBAROSSA,* and thousands more were blown from the sky or abandoned in panicked retreats and routs. Over 22,000 aircraft (all types) were lost to the VVS in the first six months of war. Soviet fighters were especially inadequate in 1941 because a small number of technically outmoded or design-deficient models had been mass produced prewar. Failure also reflected a dearth of aircraft research and design personnel in Soviet industry in the late 1930s, due mainly to the terrible military purges that hit the VVS particularly hard during the *Yezhovshchina*. The most common VVS fighter type was a small monoplane, the Polikarpov I-16 "Rata." Known derisively as "donkeys" among *krasnoarmeets,* nearly 10,000 were built in the second half of the 1930s. The Rata could not climb with, stay with, or outgun a Bf109. Despondent Red Army soldiers watched thousands of I-16s smoke into the forest or steppe, and abandoned others on the ground as useless. The 1939 model I-153 fighter was also a slow biplane, of which nearly 3,500 had entered VVS service by 1941.

A crucial difference between the VVS and the Luftwaffe was that Soviet fighters improved far more during the war than did German planes opposing them. Designers were released from the *GULAG* after June 1941. New designs were swiftly laid down and completion of old ones greatly speeded into production. New models came on stream during 1942, produced in large numbers mainly in factories relocated to the Urals. In marked contrast, the Luftwaffe mostly made incremental improvements to established fighter models. That decision mainly resulted from pressing need caused by remarkable aircraft attrition at the front, and later over Germany. But the Luftwaffe also wasted design talent on far too many experimental types and on premature production of immature jet technology. VVS fighter pilots thus soon appeared over the battlefield in superior aircraft such as the LaGG-3, which had a top speed of 342 mph, a range of 345 miles, and a ceiling of 31,000 feet. The Yak-1 achieved a maximum speed of 360 mph, a range of 434 miles, and a fighting ceiling of 33,000 feet. The Yak-3 reached a 35,000 foot ceiling and could fly at level combat speeds over 400 mph. The Yak-9D, of which over 14,600 were built, had a lower top speed at just 375 mph, but its range of nearly 900 miles allowed VVS fighters to escort late war Soviet medium and heavy strategic bombers. The MiG-3, one in a long line of Soviet fighters named for their top-drawer designers, (Mi)koyan and (G)urevich, attained level combat speeds of 400 mph, had a range of over 600 miles, and reached a ceiling of nearly 40,000 feet. The "Lavotchkin" or La-5 was an outstanding modern fighter with flying ratings of 405 mph, 475 miles, and 31,000 feet. About 9,900 La-5s were built, plus another 5,800 La-7s, a sleek fighter capable of 425 mph and 32,500 feet, but with a limited range under 400 miles.

All English-language names for Japanese fighters derived from Western Allied identification codes, in which male names were given to enemy fighters and female names to Japanese bombers. The Japanese Naval Air Force (JNAF) *Zero,* or Mitsubishi A6M "Reisen" (Zero-Sen), was the best fighter available in the Pacific in 1941. It was lighter, faster, and more maneuverable than American land-based aircraft. It also had a much greater range and more nimble handling than any U.S. carrier-based fighters. That gave the Imperial Japanese Navy a critical advantage in early carrier vs. carrier fights such as *Coral Sea.* The Japanese Army Air Force (JAAF) flew three models of the Nakajima Ki-43 "Hayabusa" ("Falcon"). Designated alternately as "Jim" or "Oscar" by the Western Allies, these land-based JAAF fighters saw most service in China and Southeast Asia, flying cover over ground forces. They faced handfuls of older Soviet and other fighters in China until the arrival of American pilots and modern aircraft of the *American Volunteer Group,* or "Flying Tigers" ("Fei Hu"). Japanese pilots in Hayabusa also faced RAF Spitfire and Hurricanes in Malaya and over Burma. Western pilots were initially shocked at the excellent performance of the Hayabusa, whose characteristics were not known to British or American military intelligence. The JAAF also flew the very fast "Hein," which reached speeds above 400 mph. The "Frank" (Nakajima Ki84-Ia "Hayate"), introduced in 1944, and the excellent "George" (Kawanishi N1K1-J "Shiden"), introduced in 1944–1945, were also well-known to Allied sailors, troops, and flyers. But as improved as those aircraft were, neither model could match Western Allied fighters by that point in the war: the Japanese planes were relatively underarmored and undergunned, and by 1944 were usually flown by inexperienced, young pilots. However, over Japan the Hayate's ceiling of nearly 38,000 feet and rocket weapons did pose a threat even to American B-29 bombers.

The USN F4F Wildcat was overmatched by Zeros in nearly all ways, an often fatal disadvantage not overcome by introduction of new American fighters for the first two years of the Pacific War. But the USN controlled the skies of the Pacific after powerful Pratt & Whitney engines were put into its heavily armored F6F "Hellcats" and F4U "Corsairs." The combination of power, climb rate, ceiling, and arms and armament allowed those aircraft to master the fast but lightly armored Zero and to splash hundreds of slow IJN and Japanese Army bombers. The USAAF also had inadequate and mostly short-range fighters at the start of the war. But by war's end, the USAAF boasted several of the finest and most effective fighters in the world. Many U.S. fighters were shipped to the Soviet Union under *Lend-Lease,* including 4,700 Bell P-39 "Airacobras" personally requested by Stalin. The P47 "Thunderbolt" and P51 "Mustang" dominated the skies of Italy, France, and Germany almost as soon as they were introduced in 1943. The P51 may have been the finest fighter of the war. It was equipped with long-range drop tanks that permitted it to escort strategic bomber formations deep into Germany and to the home islands of Japan. Both the P47 and P51 were also fitted with rockets and used in a *"tank buster"* role. In combination with late-war deterioration in Japanese aviator skills, better trained American pilots with new and better tactics in much improved machines achieved a 10:1 or higher kill ratio in Pacific War dogfights. Tallies were not as high over Germany, but even there kill ratios climbed to high levels as thousands of barely trained Luftwaffe recruits flying outdated aircraft proved easy marks in late-war dogfights. So many were killed that Luftwaffe veterans wistfully referred to the young replacements as "Nachwuchs" ("new growth"). During the final month of the war, missions flown by Luftwaffe pilots against heavily escorted bomber streams were cynically called "Himmelfahrtskommando" ("missions to heaven"). Other U.S. fighters bore feral names such as the P61 "Bearcat," P61B "Black Widow," and the jet-engined P80 "Shooting Star," which never saw combat.

See also aircraft carriers; air power; Catapult Aircraft Merchant (CAM); escort carriers; Kammhuber Line; Raumnachtjadg; Taitari; Wilde Sau; Zahme Sau.

Suggested Reading: W. Green, *Warplanes of the Second World War,* 4 vols. (1961).

FIGHTING GROUP
See combat echelon.

FIJI   This British colony served as a Western Allied base in the South Pacific. In addition, over 10,000 Fijians volunteered to fight. They saw action at *Guadalcanal, Bougainville,* on *New Guinea,* and in several smaller Pacific War battles.

FILLER REPLACEMENTS   Unfortunate U.S. Army term for what British and Commonwealth forces more happily called "first line reinforcements."

FINAL SOLUTION   "Endlösung," or "final solution to the Jewish problem." The main Nazi euphemism for the genocide against the Jews of Europe.

See anti-Semitism; concentration camps; death camps; Einsatzgruppen; Heydrich; Reinhard; Himmler, Heinrich; Hitler, Adolf; Holocaust; Madagascar; Nazism; Nuremberg Laws; Schutzstaffel (SS); Wannsee conference.

FINLAND   In the interwar period Finland maintained an uneasy neutrality. In 1939–1940 it fought the defensive *Finnish–Soviet War (1939–1940).* Its territorial losses as a result of that conflict were an outcome foreordained by the demographic reality that just 4 million Finns faced a population of 171 million in the pre-1941 Soviet Union, and that the Red Army was the largest armed force in the world. Finland did not have German support while fighting the Soviets in 1939. Adolf Hitler began to view Finland differently as he prepared to launch Operation *BARBAROSSA,* starting as early as July 1940. German arms were delivered to the Finns, transit agreements were signed permitting German troops to move across Finnish territory to and from conquered Norway, and full military staff conversations began in December. Moscow did not know the full extent of Finish–German military coordination, but even its fear of Germany's unabated appetite for ever more territory was finally aroused. Hitler's creeping influence in a country that Joseph Stalin viewed as within his sphere of influence, as previously agreed between Moscow and Berlin, raised anger and fear in the Kremlin. The question of which Great Power would exercise ultimate hegemony over Finland thus became a critical diplomatic issue in the year between the fall of France in June 1940 and the Axis invasion of the Soviet Union in June 1941. Finland joined the Axis attack on the Soviet Union after a strictly operational delay of a few days, but Finland was never a full Axis state in spirit or intent. For the Finns, resumption of active hostilities with the Soviet Union was solely an effort to reverse their loss of 1940, a strictly limited war aim reflected in their term for the conflict: "Continuation War."

The Finnish Army of 1941 was greatly expanded from its dispositions of 1939: it fielded 16 excellent divisions equipped with modern German weapons. Wehrmacht land, air, and naval forces took up attack positions in northern Finland in April–June, 1941. Preparatory to BARBAROSSA, four German divisions were allowed into Lapland to open a high Arctic front. On the opening day of the campaign, June 22, the Finnish Navy occupied the Aland Islands without interference by the Soviet Navy. German troops also attacked out of Lapland toward Murmansk and the Kola Peninsula. Finnish troops opened a southern front in Karelia a few days later. Once the Finns reached their old 1939 boundary they stopped, encouraged to do so by heavy pressure from the United States, but not before Great Britain declared war on Finland in solidarity with the Soviet Union. In that desperate hour for London, any enemy of Hitler was Britain's ally, and any ally of Germany was necessarily Britain's enemy. The Finns did not advance farther during the rest of the war. Trying to take Leningrad and Moscow were German, not Finnish, war aims. Even so, the effort to recover lost territory by swimming with the turn of the geopolitical tide in 1941 engaged the Finns in a long war on what became the northernmost section of the *Eastern Front*: fighting against the Red Army lasted from June 1941 to September 1944, with more limited fighting against the Germans after that.

Over the course of the naval war, the Finnish Navy lost one monitor, six mine-sweepers, and 50 merchantmen and coastal patrol ships. Finland lost far more men in land combat, as Hitler's BARBAROSSA operation failed by the end of November 1941. The Red Army counterattacked in the *Moscow offensive operation (December 5, 1941–January 7, 1942)* and the *Rzhev-Viazma strategic operation (January 8–April 20, 1942)*. The Finnish front thereafter stretched from German positions outside Leningrad, across southern Karelia and along the forest zone of the eastern frontier, to a distant fight by mainly German troops in the high Arctic Circle. The Finns again held back from advancing toward Leningrad, but their presence in southern Karelia completed a three-sided German lock on that starving city throughout the 900-day *siege of Leningrad*. The Finns also placed restrictions on permitted Wehrmacht operations in their high Arctic territory, including during Operation *LACHSFANG*. By the end of 1942 the Finns were in the increasingly difficult position of waiting to see which of their vastly more powerful neighbors would win the war along the Eastern Front. They were also influenced by pressure from Washington not to exceed recovery of their national territory, on pain of incurring American displeasure or even a declaration of war to match Britain's.

Germany was clearly losing the war at the start of 1943, a fact brought home to the Finns by German defeats at *El Alamein* and *Stalingrad*. The Finns opened secret talks with Moscow in an effort to withdraw from the war by negotiating a limited frontier settlement. But Moscow and Helsinki could not agree on where to draw the border in Karelia, the mutual casus belli in 1939 and again in 1941. The Red Army went over to the permanent offensive all along the Eastern Front in the late summer of 1943, following another great victory at *Kursk* and follow-on counteroffensives in the north and in Ukraine. Finnish–Soviet talks broke down in February 1944, even as German Army Group North was pushed back from Leningrad to the *Panther Line* section of the *Ostwall*. The Red Army attacked the main Finnish position on the *Mannerheim Line* on June 10, 1944, achieving complete operational surprise. Soviet tanks and mobile infantry broke through the next day. The Finns now discovered how greatly improved in combat performance the Red Army was since the winter of 1939–1940. Soviet forces were far superior in weapons, veteran troops, and proven commanders. General Leonid A. Govorov's Karelian Front took Vyborg within two weeks, a triumph for which he was promoted to "Marshal of the Soviet Union." The Stavka launched the second phase of the "Svir-Petrozavodsk operation," a full-scale invasion of lower Finland, through the southern forests on June 21. At first, Hitler sent German reinforcements to Finland in exchange for agreement that Helsinki would not accept a separate peace with Moscow. But the combat pressure from Karelian Front was relentless, while the Germans were themselves knocked backward 300 miles by the stunning Soviet achievement of

Operation *BAGRATION* in Belorussia. That marked the start of a cascading series of Soviet victories and catastrophic German defeats in the center of the Eastern Front, which left the more northern German and Finnish flank hanging.

Compared to its performance in Finland in 1939–1940, the Red Army's second campaign in Karelia was a superior example of combined arms warfare, or *Blitzkrieg*. Yet, Moscow did not pursue total war against Finland the way it did against all other Axis states. Stalin was prepared to offer terms to the Finns partly in response to intervention by President Franklin D. Roosevelt and the wider issues of alliance politics that might be adversely affected. Nevertheless, events on the ground had a life of their own. Elements of the powerful Karelian Front crossed the Svir River, forcing the Finnish Army back under great pressure. The Soviets took the provincial capital of Petrozavodsk on June 28. Other Red Army Fronts simultaneously attacked in central and northern Finland, at Salla and Petsamo, where they battered German 20th Mountain Army. That isolated 200,000 Axis troops, left guarding a peripheral position by Hitler, while the center and south of the entire Eastern Front were collapsing for want of men. By August 9, the Red Army achieved all goals set by the Stavka for the summer campaign in the north. Events outside Finland also conduced to lessened Soviet operations. German resistance in Estonia and Latvia collapsed during late July, in tandem with a general military crisis for the Germans attendant on the devastation of Army Group Center in BAGRATION. That defeat signaled to Helsinki that it needed to get out of the war before Finland, too, was wholly overrun. Mannerheim was brought back to the presidency on August 4, tasked to negotiate an exit from the war. On August 24 the cabinet agreed to seek a ceasefire and armistice with Moscow. Soviet troops stopped advancing five days later. On September 2 the Finns formally severed alliance ties to Germany. A ceasefire was agreed with the Soviets three days after that. Retreating Germans tried to seize the critical Finnish island of Suursaan (or Hogland) in the Gulf of Finland. The attempt was beaten off by Soviets and Finns fighting in tandem against the Germans for the first time.

Finland signed a formal armistice with Moscow on September 19, 1944. The agreement restored the expanded Soviet border of 1940, confirming that Finland had lost the "Continuation War" as well as the earlier Finnish–Soviet War. Helsinki surrendered rights to a Soviet naval base at Petsamo and to a Red Army and VVS air base outside Helsinki. The key to the armistice was that it required Finland to declare war on Germany and the Finnish Army to actively expel all Wehrmacht and SS troops from the country. But Finnish soldiers proved lax about enforcing that clause against men who were comrades-in-arms just days earlier. Instead, the Finnish Army simply watched German troops flee the country. In some cases, the Finns peacefully escorted rather than harried German troops on their way out during the Wehrmacht's *BIRKE* withdrawal operation (September 3–29, 1944). There was only one serious armed clash during September between Finnish and German troops. More serious clashes between Finns and Germans marked the later *Lapland War*, fought during the winter of 1944–1945 with the last German troops in the high Arctic. Under great Soviet pressure, Finland formally declared war on Germany on March 3, 1945. The last German troops left the high north a month later.

American support for Finland's independence helped prevent its incorporation into the Soviet Union as another lost tsarist province and kept it outside the quickly forming bloc of Soviet client states. In 1947 a formal peace treaty was signed between Finland and those Allied states with which it had been formally at war. Helsinki permanently surrendered its disputed Karelian territory to the Soviet Union. It was thereafter compelled to adopt the Soviet foreign policy line throughout the Cold War, but it was not forced to host Soviet armed forces beyond a single base at Porkkala. That base was later exchanged for a Soviet lease on Hangö, which was in turn given up by Moscow in 1955. Unlike Czechs, Poles, or Rumanians, the Finns did not have to adopt Soviet domestic policies and were never ruled by a puppet Communist Party. Similar Cold War arrangements in which foreign policy obeisance to a Great Power was combined with domestic independence became known internationally as "Finlandization."

See also *Tripartite Pact.*

FINNISH–SOVIET WAR (1939–1940) "Winter War." In November 1939, Joseph Stalin demanded that Finland provide a military base for the Red Army on its territory and cede the portion of Karelia where the border came within 30 miles of Leningrad, as well as the western portion of the Rybachi peninsula. He offered part of eastern Karelia in exchange. He may have been genuinely concerned about a German attack from so close a starting point, as he reportedly said: "We cannot move the city, so we must move the border." However, Stalin's gross overconfidence in the *Nazi–Soviet Pact (August 23, 1939)* concerning changes to other borders, his contemporaneous success in imposing far more draconian settlements on the Baltic States and Rumania, and his deep interest in further cooperation with Adolf Hitler all strongly belie that idea. In either case, Stalin overestimated the capabilities of the Red Army. Finland adamantly refused to cede any part of Karelia or to allow a Soviet base or any Red Army troops on its soil. Talks broke off on November 9.

Taking a leaf from Hitler's book of provocations, a border incident was fabricated by the Soviets on November 26, diplomatic relations with Helsinki were broken, and Finland was attacked on November 30, 1939. The conflict immediately and badly damaged Soviet relations with all the Great Powers of the West: France, Great Britain, the United States, and Germany. Franklin D. Roosevelt was roused to deep personal anger toward Moscow, but his "moral embargos" and angry speeches availed Finland nothing. Western volunteers for Finland sought to replicate the experience of the *International Brigades* of the *Spanish Civil War (1936–1939)*. Their effort was illegal in their home countries, and they never made it across the Atlantic or the Baltic Sea in time to take up arms. Premier *Édouard Daladier* of France was so incensed he resigned over his cabinet's refusal to directly aid the Finns. Britain also showed restraint, worried about taking on another Great Power opponent and already feeling overstretched in its military commitments. Besides, the *Phoney War* was still underway in the west. Nor did Berlin welcome a war on Germany's northern strategic flank. The conflict threatened to interrupt Soviet supplies of raw materials flowing into Germany and possibly to invite Western Allied intervention in Scandinavia that might threaten critical iron ore imports from Sweden. But nor did Hitler aid or arm the Finns against the Soviets. The only foreign assistance to Helsinki came from about 10,000 Swedes who volunteered to fight for Finland and who were able to walk across the border in time to participate in arms. The Swedish government also kept superb armaments flowing into Finland. But Stockholm refused to come directly to its neighbor's aid or formally abandon neutrality. Whatever happened on the Karelian front and in eastern Finland once the fighting began, the Finns were on their own against the largest military in the world.

From the first day of what turned into a bitter winter campaign, the Red Army revealed that real damage had been done by the blood purge of its top officers during the *Yezhovshchina*. Led by Stalin's old cavalry crony from the Russian Civil War (1918–1921), Marshal *Kliment Voroshilov,* Soviet forces displayed a singular lack of tactical imagination in attacking prepared Finnish defenses. They took very heavy casualties as a result. Advancing predictably, with heavily motorized and mechanized columns strung out along the few forest roads that existed in southern Karelia, Soviet troops were harassed, bloodied, and blocked by the Finns. Especially effective were Finnish ski troops. They flitted among the trees, employing hit-and-run tactics and carrying out forest ambushes in a fight-and-maneuver scheme the lumbering Soviet columns proved incapable of matching. Then, in late December, the Finns mounted a large conventional counterattack, scoring multiple stunning victories over now isolated and broken Soviet columns. Entire Red Army divisions were annihilated. Over nearly four months of hard winter fighting the Finns held out unexpectedly well and exacted a heavy price in Soviet lives and war matériel. Then they fell back behind fixed fortifications of the *Mannerheim Line*. Soviet generals attacked that line of bunkers and machine gun nests with brutal, unimaginative frontal infantry and armor assaults. The Finns sat in fixed positions and proceeded to cut down young Russians by tens of thousands. But Stalin had plenty more young men to hurl at Finnish trenches and muzzles.

The Red Army had failed miserably in its advance intelligence and conduct of operations, as well as in its troop morale, equipment, and resupply operations. It had lost 1,500 tanks and 700 combat aircraft in the first four months of fighting. Worse, its divisions, corps, and armies proved less mobile and flexible than Finnish Army divisions. Soviet commanders showed themselves to be tactically rigid, notably when ordering by-the-book infantry attacks into nimbly defended forests and thickly defended fixed fortifications. Soviet tanks and other armored vehicles were utterly inadequate to the winter conditions, and tank and vehicle repair and recovery was woefully inept. Frostbite cases revealed inadequacies in the Red Army medical corps. Desertion rates were high among conscripts, sometimes of whole units. That was true in spite of the remarkably difficult physical conditions, the fact the woods were swarming with angry Finns, and severe punishments meted out to any *krasnoarmeets* caught while trying to get back to their homes. In the end, however, sheer manpower was an overwhelming and decisive advantage: Moscow brought to bear a weight of 1.2 million men and thousands more tanks and combat aircraft. The Soviets also changed theater commanders and adjusted their tactics in January 1940. With weight of men and metal, they broke through the Mannerheim Line on February 11. Its Finnish defenders were exhausted. After months of heavy resistance they now ran low on stamina as well as ammunition. The Finns were thus forced to ask for terms. They signed them on the night of March 12–13, 1940, in Moscow. Sweden brokered the deal.

With victory, Stalin's demands went beyond his 1939 claims for territory in southern Karelia. He also revoked the earlier offer of "compensation" with territory from eastern, Soviet Karelia. Finland instead ceded to the Soviet Union most of the southern Karelian isthmus, which Field Marshal *Carl Gustaf von Mannerheim* had captured in the campaign of 1919–1920 during the Russian Civil War. The ceded land thereafter formed a widened buffer zone covering the northern approach to Leningrad. Helsinki also surrendered land in central Finland, as well as lease rights to a Soviet naval base protecting the Gulf of Finland. The Red Army occupied all surrendered territories, but no more. It even pulled back to the agreed settlement line where it had overrun it during fighting in the north. Estimates of Soviet dead range from 126,000 to 200,000, but are not reliable due to Soviet propaganda interest in concealing the full extent of casualties. Finland's losses were about 30,000 dead and 45,000 wounded. The Finns were also left to care for 400,000 refugees and other civilians displaced by the border adjustments.

The apparent weakness of Soviet arms in the Finnish campaign made an impression on Hitler. It may even have hastened his decision to attack eastward before driving Britain out of the war, by reinforcing his belief that Soviet strength was an illusion and that all he needed to do was "kick in the door" for the Soviet edifice to fall. The outcome also left all Finns unalterably hostile to the Soviet Union and determined on ultimate reversal of the forced territorial settlement. On June 25, 1941, Finland therefore launched what it officially called the "Continuation War." Its small but excellent armies waited just three days to join the Axis attack against the Soviet Union launched by Hitler in Operation *BARBAROSSA*. Thereafter, the Finns fought on the northeastern flank of the *Eastern Front,* supported by the Wehrmacht but not sharing its methods or goals of extinction of the Soviet Union. All the Finns wanted was their national territory back: once they advanced to 1939 frontiers, they stopped.

See also Molotov breadbasket; Molotov cocktail; motti; Soviet Navy; Tripartite Pact.

Suggested Reading: Carl van Dyke, *The Soviet Invasion of Finland* (1997).

FIRE CONTROL CENTER (FCC)
See artillery.

FIRE FOR EFFECT   Artillery term for when a forward observer confirmed that batteries had found the right range and elevation to the target and were instructed to maintain continuous fire at their maximum rate to suppress or destroy the enemy.

FIRE PLAN   Using mapped *indirect fire,* or otherwise "predicted fire," by one or more artillery batteries to blast preselected areas or precise targets, rather than firing for opportunity's sake or employing *direct fire* against moving or line-of-sight targets. Fire plans were used in offensive and defensive operations to suppress or "soften up" the enemy before assaulting him or to disrupt his troops and armor as they formed to attack. The British tried out quick fire plans during the fighting in North Africa that used simplified and standardized methods to support infantry up to the battalion level. These were later expanded to larger formations. Defensive fire plans were also preset, to be called in by radio on an "SOS" basis.

See also creeping barrage; murder; rolling barrage; serenade; standing barrage; stonk; time on target.

FIRESTORM
See area bombing; Combined Bomber Offensive; Dresden raid; strategic bombing.

FISCHREIHER (AUGUST–SEPTEMBER, 1942)
"Heron." Formerly *BLAU III*. The rapid, steppe-crossing Wehrmacht offensive that brought German 6th Army to the outskirts of *Stalingrad*.

FIUME
See Italia irredenta; march on Rome; Mussolini, Benito; mutilated victory.

FIVE POWER NAVAL TREATY (1922)
Negotiated at the *Washington Conference*, it set up a 10-year moratorium on building capital warships and further established a *battleship* and *aircraft carrier* ratio of 5:5:3, corresponding to limits on these classes for the United States, Britain, and Japan; France and Italy were limited to a capital warship ratio of 1.75:1.75. In addition, all battleships were limited to 35,000 tons and 16-inch guns; *cruisers* were limited to 10,000 tons and 8-inch guns. The treaty was hailed by many as a breakthrough for the disarmament promises of the *League of Nations* since it appeared to forestall an Anglo-American naval race, with Britain accepting an end to its old "two-power naval standard" (which it was financially no longer able to maintain in any case). It also promised to avoid a budget-busting Pacific naval arms race among Britain, the United States, and Japan. Finally, it capped the extant naval arms race in the Mediterranean between France and Italy by promising broad strategic equilibrium of their navies. However, its terms permitted Japan to build more capital warships than it could actually construct in the time allotted, a loophole that Tokyo leaped through in its naval construction plans. The Five Power treaty also left outside its regulation entire classes of important auxiliary warships, most notably *destroyers* and *submarines*. Finally, Japan only accepted its lower ratio vis-à-vis the United States and Great Britain in exchange for agreement that certain key territories in the Pacific be excluded from any additional fortification; to wit: for the United States, the Aleutians, Guam, Midway, Pago-Pago, the Philippines, and Wake Island; for Great Britain, Hong Kong and most other imperial colonies and dependencies east of 110 degrees longitude; for Japan, Taiwan, and the Bonins, Kurils, Pescadores, and Ryukyu island chains. British Empire territories near Australasia and the Pacific coast of Canada were excluded from the ban on

fortification, as were the key American and British naval stations on Hawaii and Singapore, respectively. An effort to extend the 5:5:3 ratio to other classes of warship in the Pacific failed at Geneva in 1927. A compromise was reached at the London Naval Disarmament Conference, but it did not survive the crisis-riven mid-to-late 1930s. When the Five Power treaty expired on December 31, 1936, a building naval arms race was already underway among all the major navies.

See also pocket battleship; treaty cruiser.

FLAK High-altitude explosive anti-aircraft shells that produced expanding bursts of metal shrapnel capable of shredding the skins of enemy aircraft. The term was used by most major armies and air forces in Europe. It derived from the German acronym for *anti-aircraft gun,* "*Flieger-Abwehr Kanone,*" but soon achieved near-universal usage among air crew of non-German speaking nations. Allied slang also referred to anti-aircraft fire onomatopoeically as "*ack-ack.*" Among the best Flak guns of the war was the dual-purpose German 88 mm. Late-war models reached nearly 15,000 meters vertical range with a muzzle velocity of 1,000 meters per second while firing 15–20 rounds per minute (rpm). The Luftwaffe also employed 105 mm and 128 mm Flak guns for high altitude targets. At low- and mid-level ranges, Luftwaffe crews fired 20 mm and 37 mm guns to 2,200 vertical meters at up to 1,800 rpm, and 50 mm Flak guns to 9,400 meters at 130 rpm. The maximum vertical range of Soviet 1944 model 85 mm guns was 10,500 meters.

See also Flakhelfer; Flak towers.

FLAKHELFER "Anti-aircraft helpers." Starting in 1943, teenage German boys were enlisted as auxiliaries in service with anti-aircraft crews. They dug trenches and gun pits and, later, manned the guns and gun searchlights. From October 1944, girls and women were also enlisted. By the end of 1944, out of 1.1 million crew used on over 31,000 anti-aircraft guns in Germany, about 45 percent were teens or women.

FLAKSTAND A German anti-aircraft gun position.
See Flak; Flak Towers.

FLAK TOWERS "Flaktürme." Large, hugely strong concrete anti-aircraft towers built by the Luftwaffe in Berlin, Hamburg, and Vienna. They concentrated defensive fire in key regions, successfully discouraging bombers from overflying and bombing them. Flaktürme were used as mass air raid shelters from 1944. As many as 10,000 people crowded into standing-room-only areas, standing for hours in total darkness and with little air as bombs fell all around. Flaktürme were also used as bunkers and shelters during the battle for Berlin in 1945. Much heavy fighting took place around them. They survived postwar attempts at demolition and still stand, mute testimony to total war.

FLAMETHROWERS The Imperial German army introduced the French to flamethrowers at Verdun in 1916. All armies used them after that, with some adapting the original World War I two-man weapon to a single-man device and others enlarging flamethrowers for use by tanks. The Japanese were shocked when they encountered Soviet flame-throwing tanks at *Nomonhan* in 1939. Japanese Army engineers were unable to make a working prototype of a tank flamethrower until 1942, and never deployed this weapon in combat. However, the Japanese did develop a one-man infantry flamethrower. Their main enemies in the Pacific War, the U.S. Army and Marine Corps, used three models of flamethrowers, all with double fuel tanks and a third pressure tank. These weapons weighed 70 lbs loaded, carried four gallons of flammable fuel, but had a firing duration of just 8–10 seconds. They were the preferred method of winnowing Japanese out of bunkers and caves: unlike conventional weapons, flames reached around bends and deep into tunnels. Their bearers had an exceptionally short combat life expectancy, often dying horribly when a sniper round ripped open their fuel tanks. The U.S. M3–4 tank-mounted flamethrower had a range of 60 yards. It was used to burn Japanese infantry out of *octopus pots* and other positions in the open field.

Flamethrowers were used extensively in fighting in Europe as well. Manned portable units and flamethrower tanks were used in the western *desert campaigns (1940–1943)* and in the *Italian campaign (1943–1945)* by all sides. They were used again by all sides to bust bunkers in Normandy and elsewhere in France and the Low Countries in 1944, and during the *conquest of Germany* in 1945. On the Eastern Front the most memorably horrific use of flamethrowers was the protracted *Rattenkrieg*, or "war of the rats," fought to the death in the sewers of *Stalingrad*. But flamethrowers were far more widely used in the east, including routinely against trenches, bunkers, and in cellars in extensive urban fighting in many other cities on that vast front. In 1940 the British Petroleum Warfare Department deployed a different type of flame weapon, a blunt device for use along the English coast against a possible German invasion. Dating to the late 17th century, this "flame fougasse" was more an incendiary bomb or mine than a flamethrower per se. A 40-gallon drum of fuel oil, petrol, and tar was buried like the old black powder fougasse of early modern times, or a modern mine. When triggered, it released a wall of flame. A variant of the fougasse used a mechanical launcher to hurl the fuel drum onto its target, again engulfing it in flame. It was not used because the German invasion was postponed.

See also chemical weapons.

FLASH SPOTTING   Estimating distance to enemy guns by watching the flash from distant muzzles. U.S. forces called this "flash ranging."

FLEET   A large, unified naval command, comprising all ships and shore establishments necessary to its appointed tasks.

FLEET AIR ARM   British and Commonwealth term for naval aviation, used by British writers about the naval air detachments of other navies as well.
See aircraft carriers; bombers; fighters; float planes.

FLEET BOAT   Common term for the most modern U.S. submarines, notably of the "Tambor," "Gato," and later classes. Late-war boats had very long ranges, enabling them to reach Japanese home waters. The Japanese equivalent was the I-Class submarine.

FLEET TRAIN   The logistical support ships and services that sustained Western Allied fleets in the Pacific War, mainly those of the USN but also the Royal Navy's *Task Force 57* from the end of 1944 and elements of the Royal Australian Navy. Improvised in 1942, the Fleet Train was fully organized by the end of 1943. The British developed a smaller version of nearly 100 ships over the course of 1945. That was important to Royal Navy participation in the Pacific War, as there had been concern that the British could not adapt from their Atlantic and Mediterranean practice of using bases to support distant fleets.

FLETCHER, FRANK (1885–1973)   "Black Jack." U.S. admiral. He saw extensive action as a carrier fleet commander during 1942. He was widely blamed for delaying arrival at *Wake Island* until after the Japanese landed there. He then participated in carrier raids on the Marshall and Gilbert islands in February 1942, the first offensive actions by the USN in the Pacific War. He was sharply criticized for several decisions made during the *Battle of the Coral Sea* in May 1942, where his command lost the USS Lexington. His sharpest and most influential critics were official military historians Samuel Eliot Morrison and Richard Bates. Fletcher fared far better at *Midway* the next month even though he lost the USS Yorktown (and with it, all his command diaries and records). The outcome of that battle, his severest critics say, had most to do with U.S. breakthroughs in naval intelligence and varying degrees of good or ill combat fortune that he did not control. At *Guadalcanal,* they add, he precipitously withdrew his carriers, leaving marines on the island and their transports unprotected by naval air cover. A new biography by John Lundstom argues that, to the contrary, Fletcher successfully led a weakened and inferior American force against a highly aggressive and superior Japanese force during these early battles and campaigns. Fletcher saw another sharp carrier action in the *Battle of the Eastern Solomons* before being transferred to the northern Pacific. His final combat posting was as one of the commanders at *Okinawa* in 1945. In the postwar occupation government he was responsible for northern Japan.

FLIEGERDIVISION   A Luftwaffe unit made up of several *Gruppes*. It was roughly equivalent to a *Wing* in the RAF or to a Red Army Air Force *air division*.

FLIEGERKORPS   A large Luftwaffe organizational unit made up of several *Geschwaders* or *Fliegerdivision* and roughly comparable to a Soviet *air army*.

FLINTLOCK (1944)   Code name for the U.S. campaign to take control of key atolls in the *Marshall Islands* in 1944.

FLOAT PLANES Also known as "seaplanes," these were essentially ordinary aircraft adapted to land on water using wing floats. Most navies and coastal defense commands used float planes for reconnaissance, *anti-submarine warfare,* and in *search and rescue.* For instance, Kriegsmarine *auxiliary cruisers* sported the "Arado" float plane to scout out prey and warn against the approach of enemy capital ships. Luftwaffe reconnaissance squadrons used several models of float planes including a Dornier 18 and a Heinkel 115. Minor Axis states also used these craft. The Royal Navy deployed a float model of the Fairey "Swordfish" biplane torpedo bomber. The RN also deployed a wartime-produced "Albacore" and a float version of the "Spitfire." The Japanese had many float plane models, starting with the "Jake" or E13AI "Aichi" with which they began the war. They purpose built nine seaplane carriers to carry or deliver seaplane fighters, in addition to converting multiple other hulls into seaplane carriers. The Japanese employed float planes in coastal defense spotting roles over the home islands and various South Pacific holdings and used them in anti-submarine warfare. The Italian Cant Z506 was pressed into service on both sides of the war in the Mediterranean, first by the Axis then by the Western Allies after the Italian surrender in September 1943.

See also flying boats.

FLOSSENBÜRG German *concentration camp* set up in Bavaria in 1938. It was used as a slave labor camp, but also by the *Gestapo* for incarceration and execution of high profile political and military prisoners, including enemy agents and resistance leaders. Among those murdered there were Admiral *Wilhelm Canaris* and *Dietrich Bonhöffer.* Its inmates were liberated by the U.S. Army on May 4, 1945.

FLYING BOATS All major power coastal defense forces and major navies employed versions of "flying boats" for naval reconnaissance, *anti-submarine warfare,* and in *search and rescue.* These were much larger than *float planes* and were designed to both take off and land on water. The RAF's "Sunderland" was developed prewar for use as a civilian plane in Australia. It was quickly modified to wartime use and saw action from September 1939. Its 1,000-mile range allowed it to play a critical role in the *Battle of the Atlantic (1939–1945).* Eccentric designer Howard Hughes built an eight-engine prototype HK-1 "Hercules" flying boat popularly known as the "Spruce Goose," the largest aircraft every built. It never flew until after the war and then only once, to prove that it could. The Western Allies and Soviet Union relied principally on flying boats known by different names: "Catalina" (UK), "Cansos" (Canada), and "PBY" (USN). This aircraft played a critical role in spotting the Japanese fleet at *Midway* in June 1942, and in anti-submarine warfare more generally. The Soviet Union imported PBYs and manufactured them from American design plans given to the Soviet aircraft industry. The Japanese flew several types of flying boats. They started the Pacific war with the "Mavis" or H8K1/5 reconnaissance plane. They added the faster "Emily" or H8K1/4 in 1943. Luftwaffe versions of flying boats such as the Dornier Do24 were large enough to transport small numbers of troops. The Dornier Do23 was mainly a reconnaissance aircraft. Other types included the Blohm and Voss Bv138 and Bv222 models, with the latter capable of transporting several dozen men and their equipment.

See also IFF.

FLYING FORTRESS   The USAAF B-17 bomber.
See bombers.

FLYING TIGERS
See American Volunteer Group.

FOOD SUPPLY   Access to food was a critical strategic stake in World War II, and hence a geopolitical and military issue as well. The United States produced food in great abundance, as did Canada and Australia. All three countries provided food to Great Britain. After the war they continued to deliver food to civilians in liberated Europe and parts of Asia. The Japanese and German war efforts were in good measure driven by social-Darwinist notions of competitive control of food-producing regions. Japanese expropriations caused massive famine in China, especially. But Japanese suffered, too, as Pacific garrisons were isolated and left to starve and the population of the home islands could not be properly fed after Japan's *merchant marine* was mostly sunk. Germany was able to maintain high levels of food supply to its population until the winter of 1944–1945, basically by stealing food from all over occupied Europe. It did this better in some areas than others: German rule was so harsh and destructive in Belorussia and Ukraine, and the *Ostheer* lived so closely off the land, that those areas shipped back to the Reich only about 1/7th of the food expropriated from France. The Soviet Union lost vast food-producing regions from 1941 to 1943, yet managed to maintain a basic supply that was a fundamental precondition of final victory in the east. It did so by rationing and by literally harnessing women to take the place of draught animals that had been slaughtered for food over the hard winter of 1941–1942, or wantonly slaughtered by the retreating Germans in 1943 and 1944. Women's labor also replaced tractors as tractor factories instead turned out battle tanks.

See *Canada; convoys; Atlantic, Battle of; autarky; BARBAROSSA; Bengal; biological warfare; chemical weapons; ethnic cleansing; geopolitik; Germany; Great Britain; Hitler, Adolf; Japan; kulaks; Lebensraum; Lend-Lease; merchant marine; Mutual Aid; Nazism; Nazi–Soviet Pact; OSMBON; Philippines campaign (1941–1942); prisoners of war; rations; Soviet Union; special orders; U-boats; United States; unrestricted submarine warfare.*

FORCED LABOR
See *Burma–Siam railway; concentration camps; death camps; GULAG; Hiwis; Holocaust; Imperial Japanese Army; Ostarbeiter; Peenemünde; prisoners of war; Schutzstaffel (SS); Todt organization; Vichy; V-weapons program; war crimes; Wehrmacht.*

FORCE FRANÇAISE DE L'INTÉRIEUR (FFI)   The organized, unified command of the underground *Résistance* in France. It was formed on Western Allied insistence and with British and American financial backing in 1944. In support of Operation *OVERLORD* the Western powers passed an "Instruction" to the FFI that laid out objectives for it to accomplish during a three-stage liberation plan: the fight to establish a lodgement on the coast, wherever and whenever that might come; the fight to enlarge the bridgehead and a breakout into the northern French plains; and protracted rear area support for the battle to liberate the remainder of France, perhaps over a six-month period. The invasion phase, or "Tortoise," called for FFI interdiction and disruption of German ability to reinforce coastal defenses. "Green" asked for critical sabotage of the railway and communications networks feeding into Normandy and the Pas de Calais. "Violet" told the FFI to blow apart telegraph and phone systems, while "Blue" signaled French fighters to target electricity generation and distribution. "Yellow" called for Résistance attacks on Wehrmacht HQs. "Red" was the code to attack ammunition dumps, while "Black" sent Résistance fighters to destroy German fuel supplies. The southern Maquis were asked to conduct mobile operations by flying columns, which they were told would be supplied by air drops. Alternately, Maquis were instructed to stand in fortified mountain redoubts in the event the code "Caiman" was received.

Communist networks within the FFI did not like the Instruction. They wanted all-out insurrection behind the lines, as did a number of non-Communist networks. But the color plan was set. On June 5, 1944, the BBC broadcast the color codes and the FFI went to work. Over the following week, nearly 1,000 predetermined acts of railway sabotage were carried out, including derailments, blowing up railway bridges, and destruction of rails and ties. The other color plans were similarly implemented, significantly assisting the invasion forces. Truth be told, however, the FFI did not really control the Résistance fighters. It was therefore unable to prevent the insurrection that most wanted, which broke out in Paris prior to the arrival of friendly armies. The Western Allies arrived in a number of large French cities in the south and along the coast to find Germans gone and the FFI mobilized and in charge. That happened in the Brittany ports, at one time a major target of Allied OVERLORD planners and logisticians. The FFI fought a number of sharp engagements with the Germans that resulted in perhaps 24,000 French casualties between June 6 and the end of August 1944. General *Dwight Eisenhower* was later extremely complimentary in his assessment of the many contributions of the FFI. Some military historians are more skeptical.

See also France; Jedburgh teams; Special Operations Executive (SOE).

FORCE H A Royal Navy battle squadron based at Gibraltar from June 1940 to October 1943. It engaged in operations in the Atlantic, but its primary mission was to contain and combat the Regia Marina after the severe weakening of Western Allied naval forces in the Mediterranean that attended the fall of France. That task was completed by September 1943, when the Italian fleet surrendered at Malta.

FORCE K A Royal Navy battle squadron operating from Malta against the Regia Marina from October to December, 1941. A lesser "Force K" was reformed at Malta in 1943.

FOREIGN LEGION (FRANCE)   Technically, part of the *Armée d'Afrique*. After the defeat of France in June 1940, Vichy authorities repatriated ethnic German and Italian Legionnaires to their national armed forces. But *Free French* officials encouraged Italian and German *prisoners of war* to join those units of the Legion that had crossed over to support *Charles de Gaulle*. At first, most overseas Legionnaires remained loyal to Vichy. The 13th demi-brigade joined the Free French, after by chance finding itself in England upon the surrender of France in June 1940. It became the nucleus of Free French military forces. It supported de Gaulle's claim on continuing French alliance with Great Britain at a critical moment. It also made a fighting contribution to the Allied war effort: the 13th campaigned in Eritrea alongside the British, then largely separately to seize Syria from Vichy control. In the Syrian desert it met and defeated Legion units fighting for Vichy, then welcomed survivors into its ranks. It went on to fight in West Africa, North Africa, and in Normandy.

Suggested Reading: Douglas Porch, *The French Foreign Legion* (1992).

FOREIGN LEGION (SPAIN)
See International Brigades.

FORMATION   "soedinenie." A Red Army subdivision made up of several "units" (chast). Due to inevitable confusion with English-language nomenclature, neither translated term is employed in this work.

FORMATIONS
See discrete entries for unit designations used by various major armies in World War II, such as *Army Group* or *Front, division, corps,* or *regiment* and *brigade.* Refer to entries on major air forces and navies and the subreferences therein for similar specialized air and naval terminology.

FORMOSA
See Taiwan.

FORRESTAL, JAMES (1892–1949)   U.S. undersecretary of the navy, 1940–1944; secretary of the navy, 1944–1947. His main wartime contributions were in streamlining USN procurement, reforming Navy justice, and partially improving conditions for *African Americans* and for women. His main contribution was to oversee development of a superior logistics system. He frequently argued with Admiral *King.* Forrestal landed under fire on *Iwo Jima* in February 1945, where the sights he saw left him permanently shaken. While serving as secretary of defense in the Truman administration, he committed suicide in 1949.

FORTIFICATIONS, FIXED
See Adige Line; Aliakmon Line; Alpenfestung; Atlantic Wall; Belgian Gate; Bernhardt Line; Dyle Line; feste Plätze; Festung Europa; Festung Holland; Five Power Naval Treaty; Gothic Line;

Guam; Gustav Line; Hagen Line; Hindenburg Line (China); Hitler, Adolf; Hitler Line; howitzer; Ijssel Line; Insterburg corridor; Iwo Jima; Jitna Line; Königsberg Line; Maas Line; Maginot Line; Mannerheim Line; Mareth Line; Metaxas Line; Molotov Line; Monte Cassino; Mozhaisk Line; National Redoubts; Norway; Okinawa campaign; Ostwall; Panama Canal; Panther Line; Pomeranian Wall; Quaker gun; Scheldt Estuary campaign; Siegfriedstellung; Stalin Line; Stalluponen Defensive Region; Tarawa; Vercors; Westwall; Widerstandsnest; Winter Line; Wotan Line.

FORTITUDE NORTH   A highly successful Western Allied *deception operation* in 1944. It was carried out with elaborate fake SIGINT, as well as direct access to the perception and thinking of Adolf Hitler and the OKW through double agents run by the *XX Committee.* Its premise was a sham attack on Norway by a fictitious Anglo-American "4th Army" in Scotland, which supposedly comprised 250,000 troops in three Corps, two of them British. The Red Army and Soviet intelligence cooperated by faking offensive operations into Finland and northern Norway. Its effectiveness was checked by *ULTRA* intercepts. Success sprang in part from the *COCKADE* plan, which left the *Abwehr* with a gross misreading of the size of the Western Allied order of battle in Britain from 1943. The deception appears to have helped lock down 12 Wehrmacht divisions in Norway long after the main threat to Germany in the west was firmly established in Normandy. Eight divisions were still in Norway when the war ended.

FORTITUDE SOUTH   A highly successful Western Allied *deception operation* in 1944. It was carried out with elaborate false SIGINT traffic, the aid of double agents, and fake units, camps, weapons, and airfields comprising "1st U.S. Army Group," or *FUSAG,* under General *George S. Patton.* In a two-phase operation, FORTITUDE South persuaded Adolf Hitler and the OKW that the *OVERLORD* landings were merely a feint and that the main landings would occur in late July at the Pas de Calais. This fact was confirmed by ULTRA intercepts. Hitler therefore held back German 15th Army for seven weeks, until July 25. That allowed the Western powers to build out their lodgement in Normandy, and then to break out into northern France. This was the most effective of the three major *BODYGUARD* operations. Success was built in part on an earlier *Abwehr* overestimation of the Western order of battle in Britain, which it assessed as 79 divisions when in fact there were only 52 in May 1944.

FORTRESS EUROPE
See Atlantic Wall; Festung Europa.

FORTRESS HOLLAND
See Festung Holland.

FORWARD AREA
See combat zone.

FORWARD DEFENDED LOCALITIES
See main line of resistance.

FORWARD OBSERVER
See artillery; fire for effect; flash spotting.

FOUGASSE
See flamethrowers.

FOUR FREEDOMS   A vague set of postwar ambitions announced by Franklin D. Roosevelt on January 6, 1941: freedom of speech and of religion, freedom from want (poverty) and from fear (of aggression). These principles set the tone for the *Atlantic Charter* and subsequent declarations of Allied war aims. They also found some resonance in the 1945 Charter of the United Nations.

FOUR POWER DECLARATION (OCTOBER 1943)   A statement of Allied principles and war aims issued at the close of the *Moscow Conference* in October 1943. It reaffirmed basic, but also most vague, Allied war aims: the principles of the *Atlantic Charter* and *United Nations Declaration;* the call for *unconditional surrender* of all Axis states; and foundation of a postwar international security organization. Such a statement was much desired by President Franklin D. Roosevelt, who often valued paper summaries over hard agreements. In particular, Roosevelt was pleased that Joseph Stalin agreed to elevated China to the level of the *"Big Three"* and about Soviet agreement to a postwar security organization.

FOUR POWER TREATY (1922)   Negotiated at the *Washington Naval Conference,* it abrogated the 1902 Anglo-Japanese Alliance. The 1902 treaty aimed at defending Great Britain against Germany's Kaiserliche Marine, but in 1922 its terms could only adversely affect American naval interests in the Pacific and thus might damage Anglo-American relations. Its abrogation was relatively easy, since no one expected Britain to honor alliance terms with Japan in the event of a Japanese–American war. Instead, the United States, Britain, Japan, and France mutually guaranteed the status quo in the Pacific. That promise included China's continuing territorial integrity, independence, and mutual maintenance of the principle of the "Open Door" in regional commercial relations.

FOXER   A British towed pipe-array housed in a semifloating frame. The clanging of its pipes detonated acoustic *mines.* In later *anti-submarine warfare,* Foxer arrays were added to escort ships to confuse Kriegsmarine acoustic *torpedoes.* A major disadvantage was that Foxer interfered with detection of *ASDIC* (sonar) return signals. The RCN called Foxer equipment "CAT gear."

FOXHOLE   American term for a one- or two-man shallow pit dug to provide minimal protection against snipers or shelling.
See also octopus pot; slit trench.

FRANCE The French nation was bled white during World War I in protracted battles along the Western Front. France would have lost the Great War without the aid of its allies, though it was also the principal contributor to the defeat of Imperial Germany. The British Empire brought to the World War I alliance manufactures and dominant sea power, and from 1916 also a mass army. Tsarist Russia provided huge manpower reserves and a second front against Germany until March 1918. The United States supplied war finance, at a price, then fresh reserves of unbloodied and desperately needed troops. France's near defeat at the Marne in the summer of 1914, and horrific loss of manpower over the rest of the war, made the French the most intransigent of all victors except for Italians. At the Paris Peace Conference in 1919, France sought to engage its wartime allies in long-term containment of Germany, but failed: Russia had succumbed to revolution the prior year and was immersed in a terrible civil war; the United States did not ratify the *Treaty of Versailles* and withdrew all its troops from Europe in 1923; the British disdained French security concerns, reengaged imperial rivalries, then withdrew from the Rhineland in 1926.

The Americans and British together wrecked the security bargain struck with their French ally in 1918–1919. That left France alone and unable to enforce the Versailles settlement unilaterally. It could not sustain occupation of the Rhineland after 1926, and ceased trying in 1930. Even counting renewed closeness to Great Britain from the mid-1930s, as Germany directly challenged the Versailles system after Adolf Hitler came to power in 1933, France was bereft of two of its three World War I main allies. It was unable to call upon the huge economic, demographic, and military reserves of America or Russia to deter, let alone to fight, any new military threat from a revanchist Germany. France faced a double military and political crisis in the 1930s. It needed to upgrade and modernize its armed forces, especially its land forces, while contending with a grave fiscal crisis. In addition, it suffered declining manpower as new recruit streams came into line 20 years after the birthrate fell by 50 percent during World War I. The Army delayed conscription of those young men eligible in the call-up years 1932–1935, desperately trying to create a reserve. Under these multiple constraints, France was left alone to face an expanded German population and resurgent military. Bereft of allies with powerful land forces, France's security policy in the early 1930s looked to military self-reliance, principally by building up the *Maginot Line* as a means of saving its manpower in a future war that the French Army intended to fight on the strict defensive. The French hoped to keep Britain engaged on the continent and tried to prop up the *Little Entente* in Eastern Europe. But the minor and mutually hostile states of that alliance were a poor substitute for the vast numbers of the Russian Army. Nor was it until months after the *Munich Conference* that the British finally decided to end *appeasement* of Germany.

For political and diplomatic reasons, the French could not extend the Maginot Line in the north after Belgium annulled a 1920 convention on mutual defense. Nor did Paris decide on building up a powerful mobile force to counterattack a German invasion: after the bloodletting of 1914–1918, the French Army was fundamentally committed to defense over offense. The Army set up a weak alternative of secret but nonbinding military conversations with Britain and Belgium, intended to lead to full cooperation in the event of a German attack. The French deployed several armored divisions, while hoping the British would provide more for a greatly needed Allied mobile force. In the end, the British proved less interested in building up land forces than in expanding the Royal Navy and Royal Air Force (RAF) over the second half of the 1930s. The widespread idea that a "Maginot Spirit" of defeatism infected the French military and nation in the interwar years is wrong. It is true that France adopted a defensive posture in its military planning and that it pursued a diplomatic policy of appeasement of Italy and Germany. But a defensive posture did not mean the French were unwilling to fight, while political appeasement was first and foremost the policy of France's only important ally, Great Britain.

Without the British alongside, the French Army could hardly hope to prevail over the Germans in any future war. Nevertheless, during the second half of the 1930s France doubled, then tripled, its defense spending. It was the French Army that initiated General Staff talks with its British counterpart and proposed fairly aggressive plans for forward combat in the event of war. It was the British Army that failed to develop a sufficiently mobile armored force to make such plans viable, or to put enough men in uniform in time to serve as a possible deterrent to war. Britain's lack of preparedness did not provide any additional incentive to those few senior officers in the Wehrmacht who considered killing Hitler in 1938, out of fear of war with the Western Allies. It is true that there was near panic in governing circles in Paris in mid-September 1938, when London announced before the Munich Conference that it would fight Germany if necessary. That reflected momentary internal divisions and awareness of lack of readiness more than lack of pluck. Paris moved away from appeasement in tandem with London from January, and certainly by March 1939. When Hitler occupied the rump of the Czech state and began to threaten Poland, the Anglo-French front firmed in support of Poland. Premier *Édouard Daladier's* government was badly shaken by announcement of the *Nazi–Soviet Pact* on August 23, 1939, but most French leaders were by then already resigned to war. Paris therefore reaffirmed its old alliance with Warsaw on August 25, reinforcing an announcement by Britain that it agreed to formal alliance with Poland. When the final crisis broke a week later, France chose honor and decency and declared war on Nazi Germany at 5 P.M. on September 3, 1939, six hours after the British declaration.

After Germany and the Soviet Union together dismembered France's only eastern ally, Poland, the Wehrmacht transferred the bulk of its forces west. As the Germans planned more aggressive war, French Army discipline and morale deteriorated badly the next eight months of the *Phoney War,* or "drôle de guerre." Until May 10, 1940, a large part of the French Army sat in clean, well-lighted subterranean bunkers along the Maginot Line. A few divisions guarded the Alpine Frontier against Italy. The best divisions waited for neutral Belgium to give permission to move through that country once it was attacked, to forward positions with the British Expeditionary Force (BEF) and Belgian Army along the *Dyle Line.* A key problem was that prewar planning positioned the French Army to avoid defeat, but not to take assertive action to defeat Germany until both Britain and France were fully mobilized and deployed, which might take two years. Reliance on a static defense along the Maginot Line also limited French preparation for mobile counteroffensive operations. For long-term victory, French planners relied on the Royal Navy to choke Germany's trade and raw material supply, while awaiting the slow build-up of British land forces on the continent prior to launching a joint offensive. However, ongoing and eager economic cooperation of Moscow with Berlin gutted the Allied blockade of much of its effect, while the BEF remained under-armed, undermanned, and poorly trained, even as it built to 10 divisions in France by May 1940.

The first blows in the West came against Denmark and Norway on April 9, 1940. Real war then crossed the French border on May 10. The French Army was strategically surprised, outmaneuvered, and very badly led throughout the campaign that followed. The BEF was not much better off. Still, many French and British soldiers fought with great courage and skill alongside their Belgian allies during *FALL GELB,* the invasion of France and the Low Countries. Yet, Belgium was quickly defeated and sued for terms, and most of the BEF vacated the continent at *Dunkirk,* after which French resistance collapsed when the Germans broke past Paris and into the south. FALL GELB was a stunning military achievement, surprising the Germans at least as much as the Allies. No one expected mighty France to be knocked out of the war so quickly that the French called the conflict "la guerre de 1939–1940," or that most would come to accept that "la Patrie" had lost decisively. Not everyone agreed to submit to cold reality. The political intervention of Marshal *Philippe Pétain,* especially his implied threat to remain in France under German occupation whatever the rest of the government decided, ended cabinet debate over whether to accept the *armistice* or fight on from the overseas Empire. The French Army laid down its arms one day after France was proffered terms by Hitler on June 21. The Army had inflicted 27,000 casualties on the Wehrmacht and several thousand more on the Regio Esercito after Italy attacked in the south on June 10. It suffered over 100,000 dead of its own. That was far fewer than the butcher's bill of 1914–1918, a key fact that provided some relief to the French and gave Pétain and his Vichy government an initial claim on loyalty. That only faded slowly for most French over four years of occupation. The armistice with Germany was signed under humiliating conditions in Hitler's presence on June 22. Two days later, France and Italy also agreed to an armistice. The military defeat that produced the bastard political child called "Vichy" entered French history as the "Debacle," while the period that followed from mid-1940 to mid-1944 is known to the French as the "Dark Years."

Hitler immediately annexed Alsace-Lorraine, from which non-Germans were expelled as refugees into the *zone libre* left under Vichy administration. Motives among early supporters of Vichy, and that meant a resounding majority of the French people until at least 1942, were wide-ranging. Most ordinary folk were simply relieved that the war had ended mercifully quickly. They were intensely grateful to Pétain for sparing the lives of their fathers, husbands, brothers, or sons by not prolonging a lost war. On the political right, feelings ranged from deep antipathy for the Third Republic to open *fascist* sentiment. The new Vichy Army reclaimed a "Dreyfus Affair" heritage when it purged all Jewish officers and NCOs. Within the reduced armed forces, and especially the Marine Nationale, there was contempt and even hatred for the British. That feeling only intensified after the Royal Navy attacked the French fleet at *Mers El-Kebir*. It is noteworthy how many French officers were prepared to fight and kill British and American soldiers in the years that followed the defeat of 1940 but not more recent enemies: the Germans, Italians, and Japanese. In the *Protocols of Paris* signed on May 27, 1941, the Vichy regime thought it stood at the edge of military alliance with Germany. However, all such efforts to collaborate with Germany's *New Order* in Europe were strictly one-sided: Hitler despised the French and had long-term and brutal plans to reduce France to a minor agrarian province servicing the Greater German Reich. He had no intention of partnering with Vichy, in war or peace. Yet, in the vain hope of partnering with Hitler, Vichyites demolished France's democracy; persecuted tens of thousands of fellow countrymen (mainly Jews, Communists, Freemasons, and Socialists); and oversaw deportation of 650,000 French to compulsory labor in Germany and 75,000 French and foreign Jews to the *death camps*.

The Vichy regime was coldly antirepublican and at least partly fascist. Vichy police aided *Gestapo* deportation of French citizens—workers, political prisoners, and *Résistance* fighters—to forced labor camps in Germany. They helped deport 76,000 Jews, including 11,000 children, to Nazi *concentration camps*. Fewer than 3,000 returned to France alive. A leading historian of France, Julian Jackson, reminds readers that "Vichy emerged not only from what divided the French but also what united them: pacifism, fear of population decline, loss of confidence in national identity, anti-Semitism, discontent with existing political institutions, ambivalence about modernity." Pétain's declared reason for heading the armistice government, that it would preserve at least part of France (the "zone libre") from direct occupation, was invalidated when the Germans occupied all of France from November 1942 in response to the *TORCH* landings in Algiers and Morocco. A smaller zone in the south was occupied by the Italians until September 1943. In a letter to Pétain, the Führer proclaimed his decision to obliterate the zone libre as necessary "to arrest the continuation of Anglo-American aggression" against France. Despite the absurd claim that the conqueror of France was now its greatest defender, Pétain meekly protested a "decision incompatible with the armistice agreement." Then he and the rest of the Vichy regime continued baleful *collaboration,* still overestimating the extent to which Hitler and Germany valued any cooperation by France. The truncated, 100,000 man "Armistice Army" did not fire a shot in resistance to the German occupation, though Vichy forces were everywhere in the overseas empire ordered to defend against landings by the Western Allies or their countrymen in "France Combattante," or *Free French* movement. The Pétain and Vichy myth of undertaking a "National Revolution" was exposed as Vichyites collaborated with increasingly harsh German occupation authorities through 1943-1944, until compelled to flee in disgrace to Germany as the Western Allies advanced across France in July-August, 1944.

By the end of 1942, Vichy no longer controlled any French territory: it lost the overseas empire to the Free French and Western Allies, or to Japan, and surrendered the zone libre in southern France to the Germans. It was no longer permitted even the 100,000 man "Armistice Army" of 1940, and lost control of the *French Foreign Legion* and the *Armée d'Afrique*. Some Vichyites went far beyond necessary accommodation to defeat, and the reality of a German-run Europe, to eagerly embrace Hitler's "*New Order*" in its ugliest racial and anti-Semitic meanings. A significant minority of the population embraced fascism, a French version of which had thrived before the war. Other French men and women morally but silently rejected Vichy. A few kept alive or salvaged a measure of national honor by continuing to actively fight inside France in the *Résistance,* or outside it with General *Charles de Gaulle* and Free French forces. But resisters were a tiny and unpopular minority until the end of 1942, after which the occupation grew more harsh as Germans realized they might lose the war. Most French still adopted an attitude of "wait and see" (*attentisme*). The key issue moving a minority away from collaboration and support for Vichy into passive or active resistance was mass conscription of French males—and later, also of women—for forced labor in Germany. The trend was exacerbated by brutally exploitive German economic practices within France, by the sadism and arbitrary rule of the *Gestapo* and *Milice,* and by a growing awareness among occupied and occupiers alike that Germany was going to lose the war. Even so, attentisme governed the attitude of most French until the Western Allies landed on the coast of Normandy on *D-Day (June 6, 1944),* then liberated most of France during the *Normandy campaign* and with Operation *DRAGOON* landings in the south in August 1944.

General *Dwight Eisenhower* and SHAEF were contemplating bypassing Paris as they pursued the broken Wehrmacht out of the country and to the German border. They planned to return to a vacated city, probably in early September. However, the *Force Française de l'Intérieur (FFI)* rose against the German garrison on its own. The insurrection started with a general strike in the capital on August 14, violently supported by Communist networks of the Résistance. The Prefecture of Police was occupied on the 19th, followed by occupations of other key buildings. Elements from the German garrison of about 15,000 men attacked the Prefecture that afternoon, sparking barricades to go up and a full insurrection to play out. It was lead by 35,000 FFI members, both men and women. A truce was agreed on the 20th, but some hotheads in the Résistance refused to accept it and small-scale fighting continued in the streets. Fortunately, General Dietrich von Choltitz, Wehrmacht commandant of the city garrison, refused Hitler's direct orders to destroy Paris. He did so despite a comparable act of barbarism and brute revenge then underway in Warsaw. The insurrection and threat of a Warsaw-like fate forced Eisenhower to turn some divisions toward the great city. He dispatched General Leclerc's French 2nd Armored Division to lead Western Allied armies into Paris. A small reconnaissance unit arrived late on the 24th. The rest of the division pulled into the city on the 25th, and in the afternoon von Choltitz signed an instrument of surrender. French 2nd Armored was promptly lost to the Allied order of battle for many days due to an abundance of wine and joyous liberation. British troops took

Amiens and crossed the Somme on September 1, areas and names etched in bloody memories of failed offensives during the Great War. U.S. 1st Army approached the Meuse and Ardennes, while U.S. 3rd Army took Verdun and closed on Metz. Farther south, U.S. 7th Army and French 1st Army pushed the Germans back to the border. All France was not freed until 1945, and about 1.5 million French prisoners and hostages remained in German labor and prison camps. By the end of 1944, fresh divisions of French soldiers were under arms and fighting the enemy. But for most French, the worst of the war was over by the autumn of 1944.

Liberation of most of France by the Western Allies brought widespread retribution against collaborators. Reconciliation was subsequently achieved by rallying around an exaggerated legend of wartime resistance, a certain collective forgetfulness about the extent of collaboration and of its shades of meaning, and intermittent embrace by many French—though by no means all—of the charismatic leadership of de Gaulle in the postwar era. Above all, many among the French elite were determined to restore to France "la gloire" (glory) and "rayonnement" (radiating influence), and thereby shed the twin humiliations of German occupation and Allied liberation. That impulse contributed much to terrible tragedies and brutal colonial wars in French Indochina to 1954, and again in Algeria until 1962. In 1995 President Jacques Chirac was the first French leader to publicly admit that Vichy deported Jews to concentration camps during the war. Compensation of F500 million ($645 million) was paid by a state commission established in 2000. In 2009 France's highest judicial body, the Council of State, ruled that the deportations were carried out "in an absolute rupture with the values and principles . . . of the dignity of the human person." France's Jewish population had recovered to 500,000 persons by then, making it the largest in Europe.

See also Alsace-Lorraine; armistices; Atlantic Wall; Blum, Leon; concentration camps; Daladier, Édouard; Darlan, Jean Louis; Exodus; French Air Force; French Army; French Cameroun; French Equatorial Africa; French Expeditionary Corps; French Indochina; French Navy; French Somaliland; French West Africa; Gamelin, Maurice; limited liability; Milice; OVERLORD; Resistance; Tirailleurs Senagalese; Todt organization; Weygand, Maxime.

Suggested Reading: Sarah Fishman et al., eds., *France at War* (2000); Julian Jackson, *France: The Dark Years, 1940–1944* (2001); Robert Paxton, *Vichy France* (1972).

FRANCE, BATTLE OF (MAY–JUNE, 1940)

A term applied contemporaneously by Winston Churchill to the main events of the German invasion of France and the Low Countries that began on May 10, 1940, and ended with French representatives signing an armistice in the presence of Adolf Hitler on June 22, 1940.

See FALL GELB.

FRANCE COMBATTANTE

See Free French.

FRANCO, FRANCISCO (1892–1975) "Caudillo." Spanish dictator. He fought in Morocco in 1912, taking command of Spanish forces there in 1920. He was in command during the Rif Rebellion, 1921–1926. He fell out of favor in Madrid during the early years of the Spanish Republic, but was still named chief of staff of the Army in 1935. He was exiled to the Canaries by the leftist Popular Front government. In 1936 he flew from there to Morocco to rally his old units, then landed with those elite troops in Spain. He marched on Alcazar before moving against Madrid to overthrow the Republic. His military actions began the *Spanish Civil War*. Franco was declared head of state by Nationalist forces in October 1936. With significant matériel help from Benito Mussolini and Adolf Hitler, Franco led a right-wing coalition to victory in the civil war by April 1939. His supporters included Carlists, *Falange,* military men, industrialists, as well as the hierarchy and many ordinary members of the Catholic Church.

Franco was as ruthless in peace as he was in war. He consolidated personal dictatorship by executing 30,000 republican prisoners while tamping down Falangist expectations of social revolution of the *fascist* sort. He then kept a wary eye on the rising international catastrophe all around Spain, looking out for danger while straining for imperial opportunity out of the unfolding aggression of the Axis powers. He called this policy "hábil prudencia," or "adroit prudence." It was marked by a pronounced tilt toward the Axis, most notably a marked affinity for Fascist Italy. Franco was governed in his social policy by traditional authoritarian Catholicism, not the more radical ideas of fascist revolution. He borrowed from the Italian fascist movement insofar as he concluded that he needed a unifying national idea and party, but he always kept Falangists at arms length within his government and worked to counter their influence with contrarian appointments. Franco was a traditional nationalist when it came to economics, although he indulged some borrowings from Italian corporatism. He tried to fend off German efforts to buy up key Spanish industries, but basic economic weakness worked against that effort. All threads of his social and economic thinking came together in a state party he established on the Italian model to institutionalize his rebellion and provide a vehicle for a semblance of unity: the FET. He never understood the moral and ideological opposition of the Western powers to the *Axis alliance.* He saw World War II instead in traditional balance of power terms, with the Axis states in a revisionist role. He sought to maneuver within that perception to maximize Spanish gains: he was always a strong imperialist, eager to expand Spain's empire in Africa and jealous of Madrid's claimed sovereign rights and interests. That was the rock upon which potential Spanish belligerence on the Axis side foundered, producing the "felix culpa" of formal Spanish neutrality throughout the war.

As the Wehrmacht prevailed in the *FALL GELB* conquest of France and the Low Countries in May 1940, Franco indicated his willingness to enter the war against the Western Allies. Eager as he was to share spoils of the French and British defeat, he made Spain's offer to Hitler sternly conditional. He demanded significant military aid and rejected Hitler's entreaties for cession of one island and military bases in the Canaries, and cession of other minor Spanish territories in Africa. A precise date was never set for Spain's entry into the war. With France broken and Great Britain seemingly teetering on the edge, Hitler did not see much to be gained for Germany by allowing another hyena to feed off the carcass of his French kill: he was already contending with Mussolini's uninvited entry into the battle for France on June 10, and with Joseph Stalin taking the opportunity to move against Rumania and other eastern states. From then until December 1940, Franco was willing and eager to join the Axis for ideological and opportunistic imperial reasons. But he was much too skillful to make Mussolini's grave error of going to war alongside Hitler without prior assurances of territorial and other gains, or the likelihood that these could be held onto in the long term. Franco therefore kept Spain out of war, while awaiting a more opportune entry point. During 1941 and 1942 he retreated from the prospect of belligerency without finally rejecting it, and allowed fascist volunteers to fight on the Eastern Front against the Soviet Union under auspices of the *Blue Division*. He cooperated with Axis intelligence and sabotage projects, but not to the point of provoking major British or American retaliation against exposed Spanish interests. He was especially sensitive to the possibility that the Western Allies would seize the Canary Islands.

Franco met Hitler only once, at Hendaye on the Spanish border on October 23, 1940. Their meeting became subject to much later mythologizing by Franco's admirers, who claimed he outwitted the Führer and most cleverly kept Spain out of the war. In fact, Franco pledged to enter the war, but once again no specific date was set. Franco bored Hitler to frustration with endless chatter about minor issues, especially about Moroccan history and Spain's rightful claim to that African colony. They discussed plans to jointly seize *Gibraltar* and settled the outline of the *Hendaye protocol* committing Spain to join Germany's war at some future date. Shortly thereafter, Franco told his generals to prepare plans to invade Portugal. Neither war came about, as Spain instead retreated into a claim of unreadiness by December 1940. Franco left the meeting still remarkably naïve about Hitler and the likely future for Spain in a Europe dominated by Nazi Germany. He viewed the "Third Reich" mainly as a source of technical, military, and economic aid for Spain, not as any kind of threat as a dangerous hegemon if left unchallenged by other major powers. He never understood that Hitler and other top Nazis viewed Spain as a neocolonial source of raw materials and cheap labor, not as a strong country they would help lift into conservative modernity as Franco wished. Franco's fellow dictator in Portugal, Antonio de Oliveira Salazar, did not share such naïvete or false optimism about future Iberian life inside a German-occupied Europe. The crest of Spanish collaboration with Nazi Germany was reached over the two years that followed the Hendaye meeting, without Spain ever entering the war but with Franco still looking to do so if he could negotiate the right price. A real shift in Spanish–German relations did not occur until the tide of battle turned against Italy and Germany at *El Alamein* and *Stalingrad*. The *TORCH* landings in North Africa in November 1942 then persuaded Franco and other Spanish leaders to stay out of the war.

From 1943 to 1945, Franco deflected Hitler's repeated request that Spain enter the European war, having decided that would be imprudent as the tide of war turned to favor the Allies. Franco was a canny and wary nationalist, sensitive to any threat to Spain's overseas empire. Yet, he was also a gushing enthusiast for Nazi Germany's revisionist cause for most of the war. His repeated refusal to enter the fight had most to do with Hitler's demands for basing rights in the Atlantic and colonial concessions in Africa. For similar reasons, Franco refused Hitler permission to garrison German troops inside Spain. However, rejection of active belligerence was not the same as true neutrality and certainly did not reflect a late-war tilt of any kind toward the cause of the Western Allies. Spain's revisionist interests and membership of the Soviet Union in the anti-German wartime alliance prohibited an even-handed policy. Instead, Franco allowed Axis agents to use Spain as an intelligence outpost and proffered covert aid and supplies to U-boats and to minor Kriegsmarine supply and sabotage ships into 1944. He also defied Allied demands to stop shipping Spanish wolfram to Germany. Spain benefited greatly from selling that and other rare and critical mineral resources to Hitler's war industries. Madrid also sold wolfram to Allied purchasing agents at extremely high wartime prices. Clearly pro-German, and while hoping for and for far too long also expecting an Axis victory, Franco never got the right offer from Hitler at the right time to trigger Spanish belligerence. Had the German dictator early on offered Franco assistance in taking Gibraltar and agreed to cede to Spain certain Vichy French and British territories in Africa, Franco probably would have brought Spain into the war. And that would have surely meant an early end to his regime.

Suggested Reading: Sheelagh Ellwood, *Franco* (2000); Stanley Payne, *Franco and Hitler* (2008); Paul Preston, *Franco* (1994).

FRANK   Western Allied term for the Nakajima Ki-84-Ia "Hayate" Japanese fighter.
See fighters.

FRANK, HANS (1900–1946)   Nazi governor of Poland, 1939–1944. A member of one of the *Freikorps,* he joined the *Nazi Party* even before it took that name, in time to participate in Adolf Hitler's failed Beer Hall Putsch in 1923. Frank was utterly unmerciful as governor of Poland during the war, enthusiastically exterminating Jews, Roma, Communists, homosexuals, intellectuals, and all other designated victims of Nazi race and political ideology, in an effort to convert the entire Polish nation into slaves. He secretly investigated Hitler's ancestry during the war. After the war, while awaiting trial, he claimed to have discovered that Hitler might be descended from an Austrian Jew. Hitler's most respected biographer, Ian Kershaw, does not give Frank's tale any credence. Frank fled Poland ahead of the Red Army in 1944. He was convicted as a major *war criminal* by the *Nuremberg Tribunal* and hanged in 1946.

FRASER, PETER (1884–1950)
See New Zealand.

FREEDOM   Signals code for Western Allied HQ in Algiers.

FREE FRENCH   "Forces Françaises Libres." French forces that refused to accept the armistice with Germany of June 22, 1940, or took up arms after German occupation of the so-called *zone libre* once governed from Vichy. From August 1940 to June 1944, some French continued the fight from Britain and bases in the overseas French Empire. They were principally led by Brigadier General *Charles de Gaulle*. On June 18, 1940, as the German *FALL GELB* operation ended in disaster for France, the then nearly unknown de Gaulle broadcast from London a rejection of any surrender to Germany. Ten days later Winston Churchill's government recognized de Gaulle as the true representative of France. On August 7 agreement was reached to arm and support "Free French" forces. The first unit was the 13th demi-brigade of the *French Foreign Legion,* which was in England when the armistice was signed. Most of the *Armée d'Afrique* was initially fiercely loyal to Vichy, reflecting the influence within it of colonial elites and a conservative officer class. However, some later joined and served with the Free French. On the other hand, nearly all evacuees from *Dunkirk* chose to ignore de Gaulle and return home, as did luminary French politicians and civilians in London, though some went to the United States instead. It was the foreigners of the Legion and black soldiers and colonial nations of *French Equatorial Africa* who first and most critically rallied to de Gaulle, starting in August 1940. That was a crucial moment, as most of the Empire and nearly all *Troupe Coloniales* and *Tirailleurs Senagalese* remained loyal to Vichy. General *Georges Catroux,* former governor of French Indochina, was the only prominent military man to join de Gaulle in the early days.

Some Tirailleurs joined the Free French in August. That permitted de Gaulle to launch the first of several small but politically significant military campaigns. The failure of the first, the *Dakar* expedition undertaken with the British in September, led London to conclude that the Free French should not be trusted with advance information about military operations. Next came invasion and conquest of Gabon from French Cameroun in November, a try made against British advice. However, French West Africa failed to rally. Operating from desert bases in Chad, the Free French waged an independent and ultimately successful *Fezzan campaign,* attacking into Italian Tripoli from 1941 until early 1943. The Free French also undertook an unopposed occupation of the tiny islands of St. Pierre-et-Miquelon off Newfoundland in December 1941. That action raised the ire of President Franklin D. Roosevelt, who early on took an intense personal dislike to de Gaulle. The *Brazzaville Declaration (October 27, 1940)* initiated a political as well as military Free French movement, but it remained feeble until the end of 1942. Tensions with the British grew as the Free French looked to chop off more French colonies from the body of Vichy, while Churchill wished to avoid colonial distractions from the main fight in the Middle East. Nevertheless, it was agreed to jointly invade Syria in June 1942. That same month a Free French brigade distinguished itself at *Bir Hakeim,* significantly boosting de Gaulle's prestige in London. On July 13, 1942—the same day that Vichy forces surrendered in the Levant—the Free French movement changed its name to "Fighting France" ("La France Combattante"). It did so as "a symbol of resistance to the Axis of all French nationals who do not accept the capitulation and who by all means at their disposal contribute . . . to the liberation of France." The change meant that the British recognized de Gaulle as speaking for all resistance to the Germans, inside France and across the French Empire. After tough three-way negotiations, 6,000 former Vichy troops in the Levant switched over to Fighting France. On September 28, "Fighting France" repudiated the pact signed at the *Munich Conference* in 1938.

Then everything achieved in the Empire appeared threatened—not by the Axis or Vichy, but by the *TORCH* landings in Morocco and Algeria in November 1942. As always following the fiasco at Dakar, the Western Allies did not inform de Gaulle in advance of the operation. The Free French still had only about 50,000 fighting men available. Most were colonial troops or turn-coat Vichyites from a hodge-podge of overseas units, some with men still exhibiting divided loyalties. That hardly comprised a significant military force when the need to garrison the overseas Empire was considered. The *Armée d'Afrique* was larger and more formidable at over 250,000 men and quickly became available to the Western Allies in North Africa. The Free French movement momentarily looked likely to be bypassed in the negotiated ceasefire with the Vichy colonial government in Algiers, as Admiral *Jean Louis Darlan* was recognized as governor of French North Africa instead of de Gaulle. When the difficult Vichyite Darlan was assassinated a few weeks later, the Western Allies elevated as the representative of France a general superior in rank to de Gaulle, who like Darlan was a former Vichy collaborator: *Henri Giraud.* On the other hand, during 1943 Free French contacts with the metropolitan *Résistance* grew, then formal ties were established with organization of the *Force Française de l'Intérieur.* Another critical moment came in 1943 when Roosevelt agreed to arm 11 French divisions, in a promise made to Giraud rather than to de Gaulle. But where de Gaulle proved a first rate politician, Giraud was inept and easily and quickly outfoxed. Giraud was dismissed in November and de Gaulle was back in charge, forcing the Allies to recognize him.

Eight Free French divisions were subsequently formed, following merger with former Vichy troops. They were armed and equipped by the Western Allies. Three were armored divisions driving Sherman tanks and American halftracks. While a *French Expeditionary Corps* fought in Italy in 1943, French 1st Army landed alongside American 7th Army on the south coast of France on August 15, 1944, in Operation *DRAGOON.* A French armored division led by General Leclerc was permitted by General *Dwight Eisenhower* to spearhead the liberation of Paris on August 25, 1944, where the FFI had already risen against the Germans. Reinforced with French troops from Italy, 1st Army fought its way through southern France into Alsace-Lorraine in late 1944. As part of U.S. 6th Army Group under *Jacob Devers,* French 1st Army fought across the Rhine and into southern Germany in 1945. The formation of a postwar government in France was a more muddled affair, as the Free French movement split into the usual fractious components of French political life.

See also French Army; French Indochina; French Navy; Moulin, Jean.

Suggested Reading: M. Thompson, *The French Empire and War, 1940–1945* (1998).

FREE GERMANY COMMITTEE
> *See Nationalkomitee Freies Deutschland (NKFD).*

FREIES DEUTSCHLAND
> *See Nationalkomitee Freies Deutschland (NKFD).*

FREIKORPS "Free Corps." The term originally referred to Prussian volunteers who rose to help expel French garrisons during the chaotic retreat from Moscow by Napoleon in 1812, and again in the great campaign against the French by the Prussian Army during 1813–1814. It was revived by private armies of right-wing militia in Weimar Germany after World War I. General Kurt von Schleicher took the lead organizing Freikorps to fight on Germany's chaotic eastern frontiers following the Versailles settlement, and to suppress potential Socialist and Communist revolution at home. Most Freikorps recruits were drawn from rootless ranks of unemployed and discontented Great War veterans. The Freikorps were thus a specific German example of a more general historical phenomenon: angry men used to combat and the comradery of the barracks, but no longer in military service and posing a real threat of deadly political violence, anarchy, and even social revolution following a bitterly divisive and losing war. Similar men backed Benito Mussolini in Italy in 1922.

Given their status as veterans and the strict 100,000-man limitation on the *Versailles Army,* many Freikorps were secretly paid and supported by the *Reichswehr* High Command. Some were active in defending the eastern border from spillover violence from chaotic wars in Latvia, Lithuania, Poland, Ukraine, and Russia. Others became notorious for domestic street violence and sheer joy of thuggery. The more politically aware attempted several Putsches (coups) against Weimar democracy. They also helped state governments put down attempts at left-wing revolution. The two most important instances were repression of an effort to set up a Communist government in Bavaria in 1919, put down violently by 30,000 Freikorps, and repression of the "Spartacists revolt" in Berlin. The unsavory historical reputation of the Freikorps arises from their frequent participation in street combats in behalf of antidemocratic political parties in the 1920s and 1930s, especially but not exclusively for the *Nazi Party.* After Hitler's seizure of power in 1933, those Freikorps not absorbed into the *Sturmabteilung (SA)* were banned. From 1935 many former Freikorps men were inducted into the expanded *Wehrmacht.* Among the many top Nazis, Waffen-SS, and some Wehrmacht officers who served in a Freikorps unit were *Hans Frank, Rudolf Hess, Wilhelm Keitel, Georg von Küchler, Hasso von Manteuffel, Ferdinand Schörner,* and *Felix Steiner.*
> *See also blackshirts; brownshirts; Stahlhelm.*

> **Suggested Reading:** R. Waites, *Vanguard of Nazism* (1952).

FREMDE HEERE OST (FHO) The German Army intelligence unit that concentrated on assessment of the intentions, capabilities, and plans of the Red Army.
> *See also Abwehr.*

FREMDE HEERE WEST (FHW)   The German Army intelligence unit that concentrated on assessment of the intentions, capabilities, and plans of the Western Allies.

See also Abwehr.

FRENCH AIR FORCE   The "Armée de l'Air" grew out of the great land battles of World War I, where it played a major role in Army reconnaissance and tactical support. It won paper independence from French Army ground force commanders in 1933, but unity of command with the Army was retained in fact. That meant that in any future combat the Armée de l'Air would be assigned a dispersed ground forces support role comparable to the way French armor would be deployed. Political problems retarded French aircraft production, notably a delay in nationalizing the aircraft industry that was not overcome until early 1940. At the start of the war, the Armée de l'Air was organized into day and night fighter, bomber, and reconnaissance "Escadres." An Escadre was formed by two to three "Groupes" of about 30 aircraft each. Smaller tactical units were "Escadrilles," each comprised of three "Patrilles" of three aircraft apiece, with three more held in reserve. The Armée de l'Air had 1,790 first-line aircraft available when France declared war on Germany on September 3, 1939, though not all were combat ready. It hoped to modernize during the *drôle de guerre* by purchasing aircraft from the United States. Meanwhile, no offensive operations were undertaken as the Armée de l'Air instead prepared solely for a ground support role in the coming fight with the Wehrmacht.

By May 1940, the total number of French combat aircraft was 2,200. Of these, fewer than 640 were modern fighters. Worse, the Armée de l'Air lacked coherent tactical doctrine. Although it was expected to serve a ground support role, its assets were not concentrated to that end. Instead, many fighters were deployed too near the front to escape surprise German attacks on May 10, 1940. Others were destroyed when their airfields were overrun as the Wehrmacht advanced faster than any Allied commander thought possible. About 750 French aircraft were destroyed in aerial combat or on the ground during the onslaught of Operation *FALL GELB* during May–June, 1940. More were blown up by their owners after the *armistice* was signed on June 22. In the week before the surrender, some planes were flown to Britain or to French colonies in North Africa. Those that remained in country and were not blown apart by the Germans or by the French at the surrender were operated by the "Armée de l'Air de Vichy." Elements of that renamed air force flew against the Western Allies during the *TORCH* landings in North Africa. Other French pilots continued to fight the Luftwaffe, flying "Spitfires" or "Hurricanes" for the *Royal Air Force (RAF)* in several theaters of operations; a few went to Russia and flew "Migs" and "Yaks" for the VVS as part of the *Normandie-Niemen* squadron. Others served in air units attached to the *Free French,* flying aircraft supplied by the Western Allies.

See also ace; fighters.

FRENCH ARMY   "l'armée de terre Française." The largest conscript force in Europe for most of the 1920s and 1930s: it fielded five million men in 1939, including overseas forces in the *Armée d'Afrique* and *Troupes Coloniales*. That vast assembly comprised 94 frontline or reserve divisions, of which 63 were infantry, seven were motorized infantry, five were cavalry, and three were mechanized. The great and proud victor of 1918, the French Army was far more heavily armed and better equipped at the end of the 1930s, with better tanks and more artillery than the tiny British Expeditionary Force (BEF). The French Army was also superior in most material respects to the smaller German *Heer*, its main rival and enemy. The great deficiencies of the French Army were not numbers or quality of men or weapons, but poor operational doctrine and weak military intelligence. The French failed to penetrate or understand prewar German operational planning. Worst of all, they did not identify or properly defend what the Germans regarded as the *Schwerpunkt* of the coming fight during *FALL GELB:* the weakly defended Ardennes Forrest route to the Meuse. That failure would lead to poor initial disposition of the French Army, then to its being split. In turn, disaster in the north led to surrender by its Belgian ally and expulsion of most of the BEF from France at *Dunkirk,* followed by total collapse of the rest of the French Army when the Wehrmacht punched through a hasty infantry defense line laid out north of Paris.

The French had hoped that the BEF would send a large number of conscript divisions to France to form a 12-division force of Regular and *Territorial Army* troops. But just four BEF divisions were deployed by mid-October 1939. The French Army was nevertheless confident that it could withstand a German assault and that it would not lose the war even without a major British contribution to the defense. British troops would be needed later, for the Allies to go over to the offensive and win the war, but that was not thought likely before 1941. In overestimating the own strength of the French Army, the generals in Paris and at the front were not alone. Winston Churchill, Franklin Roosevelt, and Joseph Stalin all believed that the French Army was at least a match for the Wehrmacht, if not more. No one in the West or in Moscow during the winter of the *Phoney War* in 1939–1940, and only ever a minority of the most senior Wehrmacht officers in the OKW, thought that the French might be defeated quickly by a new style of war that would come to be called *Blitzkrieg*. Those who understood the reality of the Great War rather than its engrained myths knew that the French had done most of the fighting on the Western Front from 1914 to 1918, had supplied more than their share of Allied war matériel, and had taken the greatest relative losses. Therefore, few military professionals underestimated the French Army. Given those facts, it is understandable why many overestimated its 1939 capabilities.

The French distributed their fine Char B and other tanks among the infantry as fire support, where the Wehrmacht concentrated its armor into a steel fist that punched out of the Ardennes to the Atlantic coast. The French were also inadequately supplied with *anti-tank guns,* while the French Air Force—the Armée de l'Air—was as poorly deployed and quickly overwhelmed as French armor. While still fighting the Wehrmacht in the north, the French Army was compelled to defend against the Regio Esercito in the south when the Italians attacked along the Alpine frontier. In the south, unlike along the Meuse, the French battered and bloodied the invaders although massively outnumbered. The *armistice* signed with Germany on June 22, 1940, forced the Vichy government to reduce the armed forces to a 100,000-man "Armistice Army" (Armée de l'Armistice) that had no real fighting capabilities. That figure deliberately echoed the limitation placed on the *Reichswehr* by the *Treaty of Versailles* (1919). Even that truncated force was abolished by the Germans in November 1942, when they occupied all of France in the immediate wake of the *TORCH* landings in North Africa. In 1944 *Free French* forces landed with the Americans in the DRAGOON landings in southern France on August 15, 1944. Some Free French divisions drove hard to Paris from Normandy, thence to the northern Rhine. Others drove from the Mediterranean coast to the southern Rhine, then into Germany in 1945.

See also *French Expeditionary Corps; French Foreign Legion; Force Française de l'Intérieur (FFI); Gamelin, Maurice; Giraud, Henri; Goums; Juin, Alphonse; Koenig, Marie Pierre; Lattre de Tassigny, Jean-Marie de; Leclerc, Philippe; Maginot Line; prisoners of war; Tirailleurs Senegalese; Zouaves.*

FRENCH CAMEROUN   The colonial governor of this West African colony opposed the armistice of June 22, 1940. He was pushed aside by pro-Vichy officials, but they were in turn set aside when *Free French* forces under General *Philippe Leclerc* took control in August 1940.

FRENCH EMPIRE   The various overseas possessions of France reacted differently to the armistice of June 22, 1940.

See individual colonies and territories, and *see also de Gaulle, Charles; Free French; French Foreign Legion; Tirailleurs Senagalese; Vichy.*

FRENCH EQUATORIAL AFRICA   A large, composite French colony in West Africa. It was the first part of the overseas empire to rally to the *Free French*, led by the governor of Chad. That was no coincidence: its territory included former German colonies seized during World War I whose French administrators feared would be reclaimed in the event of a German victory. A greater fear elsewhere in the French Empire was that Britain had designs on French colonies, an idée fixe that induced many to remain loyal to Vichy. On October 12, 1940, advance units of Free French troops from French Cameroun entered Gabon even as a Vichy naval squadron raced to the colony from Dakar and another steamed from Toulon. *Charles de Gaulle,* then in Douala, and the Free French were opposed by the local garrison of *Tirailleurs Senagalese,* while other Tirailleurs fought on the Free French side. The main Free French forces under General *Philippe Leclerc* and General *Marie Pierre Koenig* arrived in early November, unsupported by any British troops. Fighting lasted from November 8–12, but Libreville finally fell. Most captured Vichy troops refused to enlist with the Free French and were kept as prisoners in Brazzaville until 1945.

FRENCH EXPEDITIONARY CORPS   "Corps Expéditionaire Français." Western Allied nomenclature for a hodgepodge of *Free French*, French colonial, former Vichy regular army, and more-or-less mercenary North African troops thrown together to fight in the *Italian campaign* from 1943–1944. The Corps saw heavy fighting in the Liri Valley and ultimately stormed and breached the *Hitler Line*. Their commander was General *Alphonse Juin*. Most of Corp's divisions were transferred to take part in *DRAGOON* landings in southern France that began on August 15, 1944. Thereafter, as part of an expanded French 1st Army, the old Corps fought to the Rhine and into Germany by May 1945.

FRENCH INDOCHINA   This composite French colony, comprising modern Cambodia, Laos, and Vietnam, did not come under *Vichy* control for some months following the French armistice with Germany of June 22, 1940. Meanwhile, Governor and General *Georges Catroux* closed the border with China in a vain effort to forestall Japanese pressure for concessions by ending French resupply of *Jiang Jieshi* and the *Guomindang*. French Indochina was a key launchpad for Japan's *nanshin* strategy, and therefore the gesture proved futile. Upon receiving a Japanese ultimatum in July, Catroux was forced to agree to permit Japanese military bases in the north (Tonkin) at the end of August. His Vichy successor, Vice Admiral Jean Decoux, was not given a chance to complete peaceful negotiations even though he signed a base agreement on September 22 and accepted Japanese troops who crossed the northern border that day. Despite the absence of French resistance, local Japanese commanders conducted an active amphibious assault on Haiphong the next day. They probably sought to create a provocation for war akin to the *Mukden incident* in Manchuria in 1931 and the *Marco Polo Bridge incident* in northern China in 1937. But the French garrison did not oppose the landings. Imperial General Headquarters was greatly displeased with the local Japanese commanders. Some officers were court-martialed, a rare thing in an Army used to disobedience from junior officers and its overseas garrisons. French forces fought against a Thai invasion of Laos and Cambodia in 1941, but the Thais had Japanese support and five Laotian and Cambodian provinces were ceded to Thailand. On July 21, 1941, the French agreed to Japanese occupation of the south (Annam and Cochin China). Japanese troops entered Saigon on July 24. In March 1945, the Japanese ended the long fiction of French authority by dismissing the French colonial government. As the French reoccupied the composite colony later that summer and fall, some Japanese deserters fought against them alongside the *Viêt Minh*. The Laotian and Cambodian provinces seized in 1941 by the Thais were returned to French control after the war.
   See also Hô Chí Minh.

FRENCH MOROCCO
   See Morocco.

FRENCH NATIONAL COMMITTEE
   See Free French.

FRENCH NAVY   "Marine Nationale." Under terms of the *Washington Naval Treaty* of 1922, the Marine Nationale was the world's 4th largest navy in the interwar period. Like other major navies, it expanded significantly over the second half of the 1930s as Washington protocols broke down. In 1939 it had several new and older model battleships, two battlecruisers, numerous heavy and light cruisers, a seaplane carrier, dozens of destroyers and smaller ships, and 80 submarines. The great advantage enjoyed by the Marine Nationale over potential enemies in the Regia Marina and the Kriegsmarine was working with the Royal Navy. French sailors and ships worked closely with the Royal Navy against the Kriegsmarine in the early months of the *Battle of the Atlantic (1939–1945),* although the principal French mission was to contain the Regia Marina in the Mediterranean. Elements of the Marine Nationale engaged the Italian fleet after Italy entered the war on June 10, 1940. Other French ships aided the evacuation from *Dunkirk* then ferried French and British troops to Calais. When France signed an armistice with Germany on June 22, 1940, *François Darlan* refused to order all ships to steam for colonial ports as requested by Winston Churchill. Instead, he gave orders to scuttle the fleet should the Germans attempt to seize it.

All Marine Nationale ships either took refuge in unoccupied French ports or steamed anyway for overseas territories, ignoring Darlan. The aircraft carrier "Béarn" left Halifax with 40 new American fighters on her deck, only to spend the rest of the war at anchor in Martinique. The unfinished battleship "Jean Bart" and the newly commissioned "Richelieu " left France, the former for Casablanca and the latter for *Dakar.* Both battleships later engaged Western invasion fleets attempting to take those colonial ports: the "Richelieu" fired on a British convoy carrying *Charles de Gaulle* and *Free French* and British forces to Dakar; the "Jean Bart" fired on USN ships during the *TORCH* landings in November 1942, but was battered into silence by the battleship USS Massachusetts. Meanwhile, 10 French surface ships and three submarines steamed all out for England, upon learning of the armistice, to serve in the Free French Navy. On July 3, 1940, a Royal Navy flotilla attacked French warships unscuttled and at anchor at *Mers El-Kebir.* Other French ships were seized in British ports, while a smaller fleet based at Oran escaped destruction, as did some French cruisers at Algiers. On July 5 the "Richelieu" was attacked at Dakar. French ships in port at Alexandria agreed to disarm and fighting was avoided.

Mers El-Kebir and other incidents created deep and lasting hostility between the Vichy navy and the Royal Navy. Vichy ships fired on British and Free French landing ships at Dakar in 1940, at Algiers in 1941, and at Madagascar in 1941. They fired on British and American landing craft and escort ships in Algiers in November 1942. When the Wehrmacht occupied the so-called *zone libre* of Vichy following the Allied invasion of North Africa, some German ground units raced to Toulon to seize French ships still in harbor, several of which had returned from Mers el-Kebir. With armed Germans literally on the docks, the fleet at Toulon was scuttled on November 27, 1942. Out of nearly 80 warships in port, only 5 submarines escaped the carnage. The Germans were able to take control of only a few French warships in dock at Tunisia. Several tankers and warships in the Caribbean whose crews mutinied against Vichy, and other warships interned in Alexandria, finally went over to the Allied cause in May 1943.

See also Laconia Order.

FRENCH SOMALILAND   This small colony in the Horn of Africa evidenced divided loyalties over the armistice of June 22, 1940. Its civilian governor turned it into a minor Vichy outpost, but the local commander led most of his men to join the British and *Free French* forces fighting the *East African campaign (1940–1941)*. The Royal Navy blockaded the colony, which lay across the gulf from the major British naval base at Aden. Force of changing strategic circumstance occasioned by defeat of the Axis states in East and North Africa led the colony's elite to switch loyalty from Marshal *Philippe Pétain* and Vichy to General *Charles de Gaulle* and the Free French in December 1942.

FRENCH WEST AFRICA   A large, federated French colony spanning a vast area. It had few yet widely diverse peoples. The most important French West African port was *Dakar* in Senegal. Its white colons and garrison held for Vichy, repelling a British and *Free French* invasion in September 1940. Many *Tirailleurs Senagalese* subsequently fought for the Free French, as the region generally went over to *Charles de Gaulle*. That included Dakar from November 1942 as Vichyite while colonists realized the significance of the *TORCH* landings in North Africa and their own increasing strategic isolation.

FREYA   A Luftwaffe long-range early warning radar system, comprising a network of ground-based stations. It provided the first instance of tracking bombers as they approached Germany, and as such was an integral part of the *Kammhuber Line*.
    See also IFF; Würzburg.

FREYBERG, BERNARD (1889–1963)   Highly decorated, British-born, New Zealand general. He led the New Zealand contingent in the fight on *Crete* in May 1941, in a command performance that became even more controversial among historians than it was among his contemporaries. He did not hold broad Western Allied commands. However, he led the New Zealand Expeditionary Force (later renamed 2nd Division) well in hard fighting in Greece, at *El Alamein*, across North Africa, up the hardscrabble slopes of *Mount Casino*, and through the *Gothic Line* in Italy. He led the New Zealanders again in their assault on the Senio Line in 1945.

FRICK, WILHELM (1997–1946)   Nazi lawyer.
    See Nuremberg Laws.

***FRIDERICUS* (MAY 17–29, 1942)**   Code name for the Wehrmacht offensive launched in May 1942, seeking to trap Soviet forces in the *Barvenkovo salient*, or what Germans called the "Izium pocket."
    See also Kharkov, Second Battle of; KREML.

FRIEDEBURG, HANS VON (1895–1945)   German admiral.
    See U-boats.

FRIENDLY FIRE   Death and wounds from friendly fire is commonplace in combat. Among major World War II incidents, the following are illustrative of the problem. At the start of the *Second Sino-Japanese War* in 1937, Chinese planes attempting to bomb a Japanese fleet at Shanghai instead bombed the city, killing hundreds of civilians. In July 1943, the U.S. Navy shot down 23 USAAF planes ferrying paratroopers from the 82nd Airborne in support of the invasion of Sicily, killing 229 men. During the *Normandy campaign* in 1944, U.S. artillery mistakenly killed 111 American GIs and wounded 500 more. A month later the RAF accidentally killed or wounded several hundred Canadians it was supporting during the battle to close the gap at *Falaise*. Those incidents might be compared to an official French Army study made in 1921, which concluded that French artillery inflicted 75,000 casualties on friendly troops over the course of the Great War.

See also Aleutian Islands.

FRIGATE   A Royal Navy (RN) class of *anti-submarine warfare* escort and hunter. Larger, faster, "River"-class *corvettes* were reclassed as frigates by the RN from 1942. Over 150 were built by 1944. They were smaller than *destroyer escorts* and *destroyers* and did not have the range to serve with a battlefleet. But they were more heavily armed and more stable in open ocean than were "Flower"-class corvettes. Frigates were deployed by seven Allied navies by war's end. The new "Loch"-class, built in modular fashion from 1943, was equipped with the six-barreled or double *Squid* ASW mortar. Three dozen "Bay"-class frigates were modified for service as anti-aircraft gun platforms in 1945. They were intended for use by the Royal Navy in the Pacific War.

FRITSCH, WERNER VON (1880–1939)   German general. As commander in chief of the *OKW*, he opposed and feared the plans of *Adolf Hitler* to make war against the Western Allies, believing that Germany could not win such a war. He was pushed into retirement when Hitler engineered a purge of top Wehrmacht officers in 1938, including accusing Fritsch of concealed homosexuality. Fritsch was acquitted by a Wehrmacht court but forced into retirement as Hitler took charge of the OKW himself. The bloodless coup against the OKW cleared the last real obstacle to Hitler's total control of Germany's grad strategy, such as it was, and its war policy.

FRITZ   Russian slang for a German soldier. The German equivalent for a Soviet soldier was "*Ivan.*" After the great battle in front of Moscow in December 1941, and then at *Stalingrad* over the winter of 1942–1943, Soviet propaganda frequently portrayed "the Fritzes" as frozen and pathetic to undermine the earlier widely held view that they were super soldiers.

FROGMEN

See divers; Fukuryu.

FRONT   The forward positions where armies were in close proximity, as in "frontlines." The continuous zone of combat contact in a given region might be called the "*Eastern Front*" (by far the largest and longest) or "Baltic front" or "Italian front." For soldiers, "front simply meant the area of gravest danger and closest fighting, as in a tightening sensation felt when receiving fresh orders to "return to the front," or a threat of being sent "back to the front" as punishment. Americans tended to use "line" in this sense, as in "the 101st airborne spent ten days in the line."

See also *combat zone; frontovik; Frontsoldaten; main line of resistance (MLR); trench warfare.*

FRONT Red Army nomenclature for what most other armies called an *army group*. A Front was in theory a self-contained and independent fighting group controlling its own armor, infantry, artillery, and air units. However, early attrition and then the sheer scale of fighting and Soviet offensive operations along the Eastern Front meant that, in practice, the Red Army often operated two, three, or even four Fronts under a combined command that aimed at a single operational or strategic goal. The size, combat power, and number of Fronts varied with each period of the German–Soviet war. By 1945 the Red Army fielded 15 Fronts, each on paper hosting from five to nine armies, usually air, tank, and infantry. A Front had a large standard complement of artillery forces and administrative, medical, and other support units. In addition, a Front might have auxiliary combat units below army level, such as an attached cavalry or tank corp, or be temporarily assigned a *Combined Arms Army* for a specific campaign. The largest Fronts fielded two air armies, three tank armies, and four or five infantry armies, with some exceeding 900,000 men in the final battles of the war in the Baltic, Poland, and Germany.

See also *Direction; Vistula-Oder operation.*

FRONTLINE Any contiguous line across which enemy troops faced and fought each other.

See also *combat zone; front; frontovik; Frontsoldaten; main line of resistance (MLR); trench warfare.*

FRONTOVIK A Red Army frontline soldier. "Frontoviki" shared the usual view of rear area troops and officials common to combat troops in all armies that "shirkers," "cowards," and black marketeers made up most of the rear echelon personnel.

FRONTSOLDATEN Frontline German soldiers. The term dated to the trenches of World War I.

FRÜHLINGSERWACHEN (MARCH 6–15, 1945) "Spring Awakening." Code name for the desperate Wehrmacht operation launched south of Budapest just weeks before the total collapse of Germany and the suicide of Adolf Hitler. It was the last German offensive of the war. It was conducted by 6th SS Panzer Army under *Sepp Dietrich,* only recently retired from heavy fighting in the Ardennes, alongside the third incarnation of German 6th Army. Defending was 3rd Ukrainian Front, in a campaign official Russian histories term the "Balaton defensive operation." The Panzers were an impressive force on paper: 10 Panzer divisions, including three *Waffen-SS* Panzer divisions. But they were badly attrited, undermanned, and most of all, they lacked tanks. As in the Ardennes, an additional lack of fuel and air cover and bad weather that turned roads to mud all hampered movement and maneuver. The Germans mounted small diversionary attacks on the far flanks. None of it mattered: the Red Army was then an experienced and overwhelmingly powerful force; it shattered the weak German thrust. It was all over by March 15. The main effects of spending Germany's last reserves on this futile effort was to open the road to a rapid Soviet advance on Vienna and to denude the defenders of Berlin of any hope of relief or reinforcement.

See also Vienna offensive operation.

FUBAR U.S. slang, standing for "F——ed Up Beyond All Recognition." There were multiple colorful variations on this general sense. For instance, JANFU stood for "Joint Army-Navy F——ed Up."

See also SNAFU.

FUCHIDA, MITSUO (1902–1976) Japanese naval aviator and master battle planner of carrier operations. He helped plan the *Pearl Harbor* and *Midway* attacks.

FUCHS, KLAUS (1911–1988)

See nuclear weapons programs.

FUGO Japanese balloon bombs. They were made from heavy bonded Mulberry paper, in many cases by schoolchildren. When inflated they stood nearly 100 feet high. From November 1944 to April 1945, Japan launched more than 9,000 Fugos into the jet stream heading to North America. Most carried incendiaries intended to set fire to the forests of an enemy continent. Several were shot down by the "Tundra Army," or Alaska Territorial Guard. About 1,000 are thought to have landed across the western United States and Canada, including one as far east as Michigan. A few started small fires, a far cry from the vast infernos the Japanese hoped would scorch North America on an unprecedented scale. Fugo attacks did minimal damage. One hit electricity lines in Washington State, causing a power outage that closed the Hanford nuclear reactor for three days and briefly halted its plutonium production. Some personnel and other resources were diverted to deal with the Fugo threat. News of the attacks was heavily censored. One result was that five children and a young woman chaperon were killed when they accidentally set off a downed Fugo in the woods near Bly, Oregon. The Japanese additionally hoped to use Fugo to deliver *biological weapons* to the United States. They halted the operation in April 1945, partly because effective American censorship blocked feedback information on what the first wave or Fugos achieved. B-29s subsequently destroyed the Fugo manufacturing plant. The British also experimented with balloon bombs, hoping to burn down the Black Forest in Germany.

FÜHRER "Leader." The official title adopted by Adolf Hitler when he abolished the office of president upon the death of Field Marshal Paul von Hindenburg in 1934. He then combined the dead president's position with his own as chancellor of the Third Reich. The full, new title was "Führer und Oberster Befehlshaber der Wehrmacht" or "Leader and Supreme Commander of the Armed Forces." "Führer" mimicked "Il Duce," the appellation used by Hitler's fellow dictator, Benito Mussolini. The title fell to Admiral *Karl Dönitz* for a short span after Hitler's death on April 30, 1945. It was cast on the dust heap of history with Dönitz's acceptance of the *unconditional surrender* of the moral and physical rubble to which Germany was reduced by slavish devotion to the cult of the Führer. The *Nazi Party* and *Waffen-SS* added "führer" as a component of various Party and military titles, in accordance with the *Führerprinzip*.

FÜHRERPRINZIP "Leader principle." The idea in *Nazism* that the entire nation was to be organized along military lines and in absolute obedience to the supreme *Führer* and national leader, Adolf Hitler. Lesser "führers" were in charge at all lowers levels. The "leader" was thus conceived not so much as a head of state or government, but as a combination of tribal chieftain, high priest, and warlord. The essence of the principle was an utter contempt for democracy and for individualism. Hitler's rule was supported by five chancelleries that administered his Führer orders, rather than giving any input to policy. The two principal ones were concerned with political and military affairs and were headed by *Martin Bormann* and *Wilhelm Keitel*, respectively. Other ad hoc agencies, commissioners, or inspectors were set up by Hitler to oversee special tasks.

    See also fascism.

FUKURYU "Special Harbor Defense and Underwater Attack Units." Japanese suicide divers. The Imperial Japanese Navy developed a plan for hundreds of divers armed with mines to wait in neat lines underwater at likely landing sites on the home islands. Their duty and discipline was to stay submerged until enemy invasion ships passed overhead, then blow up themselves along with one enemy ship.

FUNKSPEIL "Radio game." *Abwehr* counterintelligence ran several "radio games" against British intelligence after turning several captured British SOE and M16 agents, whom the Germans tortured into cooperation. The most successful Funkspeil operation was run from the Netherlands against the *Special Operations Executive (SOE)*. Like German double agents run by the British *XX Committee*, British agents turned by the Abwehr passed military and political disinformation back to the host agencies. Other radio games were played against the Red Army in the east, including turning some anti-Nazi guerillas of the *Nationalkomitee Freies Deutschland (NKFD)* who were captured along with their transmitters after being air dropped into East Prussia by the Soviets.

FUNNIES

See armor; Bradley, Omar; D-Day (June 6, 1944).

FUSAG "First United States Army Group." The fake U.S. Army formation that lay at the heart of the successful *deception operation* code named *FORTITUDE South,* deployed to conceal real preparations for operation *OVERLORD.* The huge success of this deception arose partly from the fact that General *George S. Patton* was identified by German double agents as the FUSAG commander. Field Marshal *Erwin Rommel* was among the few who were suspicious, noting that Luftwaffe reconnaissance over the FUSAG assembly areas was easy but that dense resistance was encountered over other areas of southern England. The latter turned out to be the true OVERLORD zones, where *sausages* were stuffed with men, guns, tanks, and war matériel for the invasion of Europe.

G

G-1 Administrative and personnel section of a U.S. corps, army, or army group command staff. Within *SHAEF,* G-1 was additionally responsible for issues pertaining to *prisoners of war* and care of inmates liberated from *concentration camps.*

G-2 Intelligence section of a U.S. command staff; alternately, the principal intelligence officer on staff. Within *SHAEF,* G-2 was responsible for general military intelligence analysis, counterintelligence on a theater level, and for coordinating liaison with *resistance* movements behind enemy lines.

G-3 Operations and training section of a U.S. corps, army, or army group command staff. Within *SHAEF,* G-3 was responsible for the full range of grand operations involving multiple army groups and armies from many nations.
   See also Sitrep.

G-4 Supply and maintenance section of a U.S. corps, army, or army group command staff. Within *SHAEF,* G-4 was responsible for the extraordinary job of coordination of *OVERLORD* logistics. After that came the unsolvable problem of maintaining the momentum of the advance after *MARKET GARDEN,* while Antwerp remained closed to the end of November 1944.
   See also Red Ball Express.

G-5 Civil Affairs and Military Government section of a U.S. corps, army, or army group staff. Within *SHAEF,* G-5 was responsible for liaison with many governments-in-exile, most problematically that of *Charles de Gaulle* and the *Free French.*

GABON
See Free French; French Equatorial Africa.

GALAHAD   Western Allied code name for a "deep penetration" *Chindit* and U.S. special forces operation in Burma in late 1943 and early 1944. Its mission was adjusted to support Chinese forces under General *Joseph Stilwell* advancing into northern Burma during March–August 1944. The plan was readjusted on the fly, and fortuitously ran into the ill-conceived Japanese *Imphal offensive*. The operation penetrated to the airfield at *Myitkyina* on May 17, 1944, and took the town on August 3. The Chindits and GALAHAD were both light infantry forces that were handled badly and suffered grievous losses during the second *Burma campaign (1943–1945)*.
See also Merrill's Marauders.

GALLAND, ADOLF (1912–1996)   Luftwaffe ace and head of fighters. Galland emerged as a brilliant fighter ace and tactician during the *Battle of Britain* (1940). A harsh critic of *Hermann Göring*, his combat skill and reputation enabled him to rise to head the Luftwaffe's fighter arm in homeland defense against the *Combined Bomber Offensive*. Despite his record, Galland was sacked in January 1945. He returned to combat as a pilot and head of a Me262 jet squadron. He was shot down and captured 10 days before the war ended. Well-respected by the RAF pilots he fought, he became familiar to millions through postwar interviews on television and in documentary films.

GALLOP (FEBRUARY 1943)   "Skachok." A failed Red Army offensive operation that endeavored to dash ahead to seize several crossings over the Mius River then drive hard for the Sea of Azov, while a second Soviet pincer reached and bounced the Dnieper. The gallop for the Mius was undertaken by "Special Group Popov," a task force comprising several tank corps and mobile infantry divisions. The Dnieper pincer was composed of 1st Guards Army and the armies of 6th Front. All these formations were combat weary and at the end of stretched lines of resupply and communication. There were few reserves because Operation *POLAR STAR* and the *Orel-Briansk offensive operation* were launched around the same time. Worse for the attackers, Soviet intelligence failed to perceive a Wehrmacht build-up of Panzer reserves in the area. GALLOP failed when the Red Army was caught off guard as hidden Panzers unexpectedly counterattacked, beginning the *Third Battle of Kharkov* on February 19. Most of Special Group Popov was encircled and wiped out. Elsewhere, 4th Panzer Army blunted the other Soviet pincer as it stretched for the Dnieper crossings.

GALVANIC (1943)   U.S. Central Pacific operation aimed at taking *Nauru* and *Tarawa*. The assault on the *Gilbert and Ellice Islands* was the first transoceanic amphibious operation conducted by U.S. forces. The operation to take isolated Nauru was cancelled, and the Army's 27th Division was instead sent to assault *Makin Atoll*. After bloody fighting on Betio Island within Tarawa Atoll, U.S. forces captured the Apamama, Makin, Ocean, and Tarawa atolls. The next Pacific stepping stone toward distant Tokyo was the *Marshall Islands*.

GAMELIN, MAURICE (1872–1958) French general. A veteran staff officer from World War I and of colonial fighting in the 1920s, he was rare within the French military in being an open supporter of the Third Republic. As commander in chief of the French Army, he led military modernization efforts in the latter 1930s, stressing armor and combined arms tactics that were resisted by more staid officers. In 1939–1940 he resisted wilder British proposals to intervene in Norway or Greece, properly concentrating instead on frontier defense of France. However, he never resolved the key issue of Belgian military cooperation. He also failed to revise a disposition plan that sent his heavy left flank and mechanized and mobile reserve, along with the British Expeditionary Force (BEF), forward to the *Dyle Line* at the onset of active fighting. That led to catastrophe during *FALL GELB* in May 1940. Gamelin was relieved of command in the midst of the crisis on May 19. During the rest of the war and for many years after it, he received primary blame from historians for losing the Battle of France though poor deployments and muddled command and control. More recently, that judgment has been somewhat modified.

GAMMON BOMB "No. 82 Grenade." A homemade bomb created by a British parachute officer, Lt. Jock Gammon. It was comprised of a 2 lb high explosive charge in an elastic stockinette, set off by gun cotton and an igniter. It fused while airborne by means of a clever weighted tape, and exploded on impact.

GANDHI, MOHANDAS KARAMCHAND (1869–1948)
See Congress Party; India.

GAP
See Air Gap; Atlantic, Battle of; Azores; Black Pit.

GARDEN Code name for the land force component of the Western Allies operation that aimed to seize a series of bridges culminating in crossing the Rhine at Arnhem.
See MARKET GARDEN.

GARDENING RAF code for sea mining operations. They were conducted all through the war. The huge minefields that were laid were an effective means of sinking German cargo ships early in the war and U-boats in the latter years. However, Western Allied ships also occasionally struck "friendly" mines.

GARIBALDI DIVISION
See Italian Army.

GAS WEAPONS
See Abyssinian War (1935–1936); Badoglio, Pietro; Bari Raid; chemical warfare; chemical weapons; Churchill, Winston; Geneva Protocol; Kerch defensive operation; Mussolini, Benito; prisoners of war; Rapallo, Treaty of; Tripoli.

GAU
See Gauleiter.

GAU "Glavnoye Artilleriyskoye Upravlenie" ("Main Artillery Directorate"). The central coordinating body of Red Army artillery and armaments manufacture. It oversaw design, production, and supply of artillery tubes and ammunition as well as small arms and rockets, both ground-based and mounted on aircraft. It was commanded during the war by General N. D. Yakovlev.

GAULEITER "District Leader." A regional chief of the *Nazi Party* who headed an administrative district called a "Gau."
For an example, *see Generalgouvernement.*

GAZALA, BATTLE OF (MAY 26–JUNE 17, 1942)
See desert campaigns (1940–1943); Gazala Line.

GAZALA LINE British desert defense position about 30 miles west of *Tobruk.* It was formed by loosely connected "boxes" of infantry and minefields supported by dispersed armor. After stopping General *Erwin Rommel's* initial assault on Tobruk the British dug in along the Gazala Line in February 1942. The box defense around Gazala was broken by the Germans in May, after which British 8th Army fell back to *Mersa Matruh.*
See also desert campaigns (1940–1943).

GEE First operationally tested in August 1941, this RAF navigation aid was named for the first letter in "grid." It used a "master" ground station and two "slave" stations to send out a web of radio beams over Germany. Bombers received GEE's signal passively, following the grid until they located their target for that night. Only a plane equipped with a GEE receiver could make sense of the radio grid the system produced. The Germans did not discover that the RAF was using GEE until 1942, and did not understand or effectively jam it until early 1943. That was well after the time the RAF originally anticipated GEE should have been found out by the Luftwaffe and rendered useless. With new countermeasures against effective jamming, GEE was used by the RAF and USAAF in combination with other navigation and targeting aids until the end of the war. By then it had a broadcast range of about 450 miles.

GEFECHTSTREIFEN "Combat strips." In German tactical doctrine, local superiority could be achieved even in the face of operational and strategic inferiority by use of narrow strips, or Gefechtstreifen, into which the attack was developed by channeling forces from deeper reserves.

See also *Schwerpunkt*.

GEHEIME FELDPOLIZEI (GFP) "Secret Field Police." Wehrmacht military police, dressed in plain clothes not uniformed like the normal military police. Much GFP policing of Wehrmacht field units was usurped in 1942 by the *Nazi Party* secret police overseen by the *Reichssicherheitshauptampt (RSHA)*. The *Nuremberg Tribunal* determined after the war that the GFP was not a criminal organization.

GEHEIME STAATSPOLIZEI

See *Gestapo*.

GEHEIMSCHREIBER "Secret writing machine." A German cipher machine that turned patterned holes in paper ribbons into transmittable radio pulses, or back into readable messages. Its 10-rotor system made the code-breaking task of British intelligence at *Bletchley Park* extremely difficult. The British did not break the Geheimschreiber until they developed the *COLOSSUS I and II* mechanical computers by mid-1944. When the Western Allies did break the code, they gleaned much information of high value, for the Wehrmacht used Geheimschreiber machines for its top level headquarters' communications.

GENERALGOUVERNEMENT The Nazi administrative state in German-occupied Poland, under the brutal Gauleiter *Hans Frank*. In typically ridiculous Nazi terminology that also garbled the history it purported to reference, it was called the "Gau of the Vandals."

GENERAL OF THE ARMY U.S. five-star general rank. It was restored by Congress as a temporary grade in December 1944. It was made permanent in March 1946. It was awarded to five World War II generals: *Henry "Hap" Arnold, Dwight Eisenhower, Douglas MacArthur,* and *George C. Marshall,* all in December 1944, and to *Omar Bradley* in September 1950.

GENERALPLAN OST

See *ethnic cleansing*.

GENERAL STAFF The General Staff, the brain of Prussian military operations for a century, was banned by the Allies in the *Treaty of Versailles (1919)*. The General

Staff of the Reichswehr therefore operated in secret, honing the exceptional skills of Wehrmacht leadership cadres during the interwar years. In 1938 it was reshaped into the *OKW* by Adolf Hitler. Other armies also had General Staffs, though not always under that name. The chief of the General Staff of the Red Army was *Marshal Georgi Zhukov* from January 1941, although Joseph Stalin named himself supreme commander (*Verkhovnyi*) in July 1941. The U.S. equivalent to the Wehrmacht and Red Army General Staffs was the *Joint Chiefs of Staff (JCS)*. The JCS combined the heads of all major branches of the U.S. military. Similarly, the British relied on a *Chiefs of Staff Committee*. In 1942 the British and Americans combined their chiefs of staff to form the *Combined Chiefs of Staff*. The term "general staff" was also used for lower levels of the U.S. Army, with every corps, army, and army group served by a field general staff of five sections: *G-1* Personnel, *G-2* Intelligence, *G-3* Operations, *G-4* Supply, and *G-5* Civil Affairs and Military government. The *Imperial Japanese Army* and *Imperial Japanese Navy* did not have a joint command, despite nominal unity of a shared Imperial General Headquarters. Ferocious interservice rivalry in Japan precluded all but minimal intelligence and operational cooperation. On planning, war production, and resource allocation—even of oil, steel, and other vital materials—the Japanese Army and Navy essentially ran separate wars. Partly for that reason, it lost them catastrophically.

See also Nuremberg Tribunal; Stavka.

GENEVA CONVENTIONS   A series of agreements setting out the humane and permissible treatment of individuals in wartime, drawing often from the tenets of the just war tradition. The first was drafted in 1864. It principally concerned treatment of wounded soldiers. Other conventions followed in 1906 and 1929, the latter especially regarding *prisoners of war*. Superceding earlier efforts, four summary conventions were drafted in 1949 to take into account developments during World War II. Often referred to as the "Red Cross Conventions," they were mainly a response to extraordinary outrages against prisoners of war and civilians that occurred from 1937 to 1945.

See also mines.

GENEVA DISARMAMENT CONFERENCE (1932–1934)   The *Treaty of Versailles (1919)* and later the *Geneva Protocol (1925)* called for a full disarmament conference, but this was delayed until February 1932. With 59 state delegations attending Geneva, the conference was the largest international gathering to that point in history. It was sponsored by the *League of Nations,* but nonmembers such as the United States and Soviet Union also participated. Conferees agreed to release Germany from unilateral disarmament provisions of Versailles by accepting a principle of staged equality in armaments. But the agreement floundered upon French insistence on a prior general scheme of international security. It was beached for good with the ascent to power of Adolf Hitler on January 30, 1933. He pulled Germany out that October, denouncing Geneva for not giving Germany immediate parity in arms.

GENEVA PROTOCOL (1925) "Protocol for the Prohibition of the Use in War of Asphyxiating, Poisonous or Other Gases, and of Bacteriological Methods of Warfare." A post–World War I effort to establish a legal regime banning gas, chemical, and biological warfare. Its major flaw—beyond overly optimistic faith in the power of declaratory law to restrain aggression in pursuit of national self-interest—was to ban use but not manufacture or storage of these weapons. As a result, massive stockpiles were retained by most major belligerents in World War II, along with a policy of no first-use but massive retaliation if attacked with banned weapons. What in fact limited use in almost every case was mutual deterrence.

GENOCIDE
See Aktion Reinhard; anti-Semitism; Auschwitz; Babi Yar; Belzec; Buchenwald; Chelmno; concentration camps; death camps; Eichmann, Adolf; Eicke, Theodor; Einsatzgruppen; Eisenbahntruppen; ethnic cleansing; Genocide Convention; Gestapo; Göring, Hermann; Heydrich, Reinhard; Himmler, Heinrich; Hitler, Adolf; Holocaust; homosexuals; Iron Guard; Kristallnacht; Lebensraum; Lublin-Majdanek; Nazism; Nuremberg laws; Pius XII; Reichssicherheitshauptampt (RSHA); restitution; righteous Gentiles; Schutzstaffel (SS); Sobibor; Sonderkommando; Sonderweg; Theresienstadt; Totenkopfverbände; Treblinka; Uštaše; Vernichtungskrieg; Wannsee conference; Warsaw Ghetto rising; Zyklon-B.

GENOCIDE CONVENTION Adopted by the General Assembly of the United Nations in 1948, in direct response to revelation of the full horrors of the *Holocaust,* it entered into effect in 1951. The Convention broadly defined acts of genocide to include killing; causing serious mental or physical harm; deprivation of the "conditions of life" sufficient to cause physical destruction of the group; efforts designed to prevent births within the group; and forced transfers of children outside the group. It criminalized acts of genocide by stripping away the traditional defense against extradition of claiming genocidal acts were political, not criminal, in nature. The Convention included provision for holding individuals directly accountable by national courts, without establishing corresponding international enforcement. While it advanced codification of moral norms and standards of state conduct, it had little immediate and no practical impact. However, by the 50th anniversary of the Convention its prohibition against genocide was widely regarded as jus cogens (a peremptory norm) in international law, and new national and international tribunals began to cite its provisions in bringing charges of genocide.
See also crimes against humanity; ethnic cleansing; war crimes.

GENRŌ "Meritorious elders." The elder statesmen of Meiji Japan. As young men they oversaw the historic reforms that followed the Meiji Restoration of 1868. They had constitutional status and significant influence on Japanese policy into the early 1920s, including selection of prime ministers and of cabinets. The "Twenty-One Demands" made on China in 1915 and reckless intervention in Siberia from 1918 to 1922 signaled their loss of guiding control over Japan's foreign policy. In the end, the *Genrō* failed to oversee a transition to stable constitutional government or a moderate foreign policy.

GEOPOLITIK   A variant of Halford Mackinder's (1861–1947) thesis about the "Heartland"—the Eurasian landmass, or "world island," whose control he saw as the key to all successful historical empires. An even more skewered adaptation was devised by Karl Haushofer (1869–1946), playing off work done by Friedrich Ratzel (1844–1904) and other German theorists. Haushofer added crude social-Darwinist notions of race to extant factors of territory and food supply, and elevated the thesis of "geography as destiny" to a quasi-mystical level. Adolf Hitler absorbed these rough notions into his own intellectually crude, and historically errant, idea of *Lebensraum*. Geopolitik ideas thereby inflamed the pathological insistence of Hitler and the *Nazi Party* on economic *autarky,* which translated into German conquest and exploitation of Slav lands east of historical Germany. That nazified geopolitik vision foresaw a postwar world in which the Germanic peoples lived within a "Grossraum" ("great realm" or space), atop a base of reduced and enslaved non-German populations supplying coarse labor services, while raw materials were expropriated from across Eurasia and production organized by a command economy at the center of the German system. Hitler's fanatic belief in this fantastic nonsense of grand imperial conquest and exploitation encouraged him to launch *BARBAROSSA* against the Soviets as the centerpiece of his strategic policy. Thereafter, he used geopolitik justifications to argue for southern military operations to hold oil fields in Rumania, others to penetrate eastward to the oil fields of Azerbaijan, and more to hold the vast food producing regions of Poland, Belarus, and Ukraine. Haushofer collaborated fully with Hitler, but privately balked at attacking the great expanse of the Soviet empire. Haushofer committed suicide in 1946.

GEORGE   Western Allied code name for the Kawanishi N1K1-J "Shiden" Japanese fighter. "George" was also American slang for an automatic pilot, as in "George is flying the plane."
   See fighters.

GERBIRGSJÄGER   German mountain troops.
   See Dietl, Eduard; EDELWEISS; Greece; Norway; Schörner, Ferdinand.

GERMAN–AMERICAN BUND   An ethnic German, pro-Nazi American organization. It disbanded soon after Nazi Germany declared war on the United States on December 11, 1941.

GERMANICS   An *Schutzstaffel (SS)* racial concept championed by *Heinrich Himmler* and other top SS crackpots proposing that certain nations besides Germany hosted the "best Nordic blood." These were: Britain, Denmark, Flemish Belgium,

Iceland, Liechtenstein, Luxembourg, the Netherlands, Norway, Sweden, and Switzerland. The *Waffen-SS* was able to recruit exclusively from the populations of these areas without direct competition from the Wehrmacht, excepting Luxembourg after the duchy was annexed to Germany in 1940. During the war Himmler added the Walloon population of Belgium and Finns to the list of "Germanics." Ultimately, the Waffen-SS employed four times as many "non-Germanics" as "Germanics," but did so mainly in rear areas so that true "Germanics" could serve at the front. As a result, the supposed racial elite of the Waffen-SS died in large numbers.

See also Aryan.

GERMAN RESISTANCE

See resistance (German).

GERMAN–SOVIET WAR (JUNE 22, 1941–MAY 8, 1945)

For causes and effects see the main entries *BARBAROSSA, Germany, Soviet Union,* and related cross-references. On strategy, operations, leaders, battles, and campaigns, see the following entries and internal cross references: For the Germans, *see Germany, conquest of; Heer; Hitler, Adolf; Kriegsmarine; Luftwaffe; OKH; OKW; Waffen-SS;* and *Wehrmacht.* For the Soviets see: *Great Fatherland War; Red Army; Red Army Air Force (VVS); Soviet Navy; Stalin, Joseph; Stavka.* Also see relevant sections of the main entries for the major and minor allies of Germany, and major allies of the Soviet Union. On matters of specialized interest, *see anti-tank weapons; armor; artillery; battle stress; Blitzkrieg; blocking detachments; bombers; cavalry; Commissar order; Eastern Front; Einsatzgruppen; evakuatsiia; extraordinary events; fighters; Haltebefehl; Historikerstreit; horses; krasnoarmeets; Lend-Lease; NKVD; opolchentsy; Order #227; partisans; politruks; Pripet Marshes; prisoners of war; rasputitsa; Rassenkampf; Schutzstaffel (SS); Schwerpunkt; second front; Second Imperial War; Smersh; special orders; Vernichtungskrieg; Yezhovshchina.*

GERMANY There are several versions of a highly deterministic thesis that share a notion of the so-called "Sonderweg," or "special path," which supposedly lead inexorably through modern German history directly to the Nazi Revolution of 1933. One way or another, Sonderweg arguments posit that *Nazism* was the only possible outcome of centuries of preceding German history. In extreme form, the Sonderweg thesis asserts that all prior great events in that history—from the Lutheran Reformation to the long-postponed unification of the nation and state under the domination of Prussia—moved toward the rise to power of Adolf Hitler. All serious historians reject that thesis as reductionist and ahistorical. Events of the Great War and *Great Depression,* among many others, were critical factors in perverting the politics of the *Weimar Republic* and clearing Hitler's path to power. And on innumerable occasions, choices were made by individuals that might well have been made differently and could have greatly affected events in other directions. Only in German military history is there a more-or-less direct line of thought and action that leads from late 19th-century Prussian military thinking—or even from

18th-century, Frederickian operational doctrine—to the characteristic Nazi way of war in World War II. The ideas of *Vernichtungsschlacht* ("battle of annihilation") and *Vernichtungskrieg* ("war of annihilation") gripped the Reichswehr and the General Staff and Prussian officer corps long before Hitler was anything more than an obscure trench runner in a Bavarian regiment, or gave implementation of those doctrines a peculiarly racial, vicious, and exterminationist twist.

Between the world wars Germany was widely loathed in Europe. It was a pariah nation, detested by many because of the calamity of casualties suffered by all participants in the Great War. Rightly or not, Germans were held principally responsible for those losses in the eyes of Allied populations and the governments of rival empires. Loathing was perhaps also a natural psychological detritus of wartime. For millions of Europeans, wartime hate for Germans lingered long after the fighting was done. Many in Germany felt the same toward the victors, with an extra spur of anger and humiliation over defeat and imposition of a peace settlement seen as utterly unfair. Yet, Germany was more feared than loathed. After all, it had won the Great War in 1917 on the Eastern Front. It nearly won in the west in 1914, and less clearly, again in 1918. Widespread fear was also rooted in the reality that Germany was actually in a stronger geostrategic position after World War I than before it. It was surrounded by weak minor states to the east and south and much weakened Great Powers in the west. And all its enemies were more strategically distant from one another than in 1914. The small states of Western Europe—Belgium, the Netherlands, Denmark—feared for national survival should Germany revive. The new states of eastern Europe and the Balkans—Latvia, Estonia, Lithuania, Czechoslovakia, Poland, Yugoslavia—were trapped between fear of German revanchism, suspicion of each other, and fright that Russia was under Bolshevik rule. Russia itself was a wounded empire withdrawn into bitter isolation, turmoil, and mass violence. France was still militarily strong, but not powerful enough to contain Germany alone. The United States and Great Britain withdrew from any continental engagement during the 1920s. Germany's much-discussed postwar territorial and population losses were actually relatively slight, though they were psychologically preeminent and grossly exaggerated in the minds of most Germans. When Hitler came to power in 1933, the German economy was already emerging from depression and was in any case still regionally dominant in Central and Eastern Europe. The Nazis would reap much credit from merely riding the wave of economic recovery that followed.

Internally, matters were not so clear. Friedrich Ebert took charge of the government on November 9, 1918, just in time for the Kaiser to abdicate and for Ebert to agree to the armistice and oversee Germany's surrender in World War I. Ebert was a tough-minded socialist who appreciated the need for law and order. He understood the threat of violence posed by the leftist Spartacist revolt in Berlin and from the most radical of the right-wing *Freikorps*. Over time, he laid the basis in Weimar of what might have evolved into a parliamentary democracy with more good will and better luck. Instead, the experiment with democracy from 1919 to 1933 was handicapped from the start by Weimar's opening association with the armistice and the hated *Treaty of Versailles (1919)*. Postwar leaders could never shake the accusation from the far right that in signing the armistice of November 11, 1918, civilian politicians had lost the war through a "stab-in-the-back" of the *Reichswehr*. That was nonsense: the war was lost in the field when the Allies broke through in the west in September–October, 1918. It was the German High Command who told the Kaiser just that, and asked the civilians in Berlin to make the best peace they could. But the generals never told their soldiers or the public the same truth, about refusals of whole units to any longer obey orders or the fact naval crews mutinied. Instead, the military dictators of Imperial Germany—General *Erich von Ludendorff* and Field Marshal *Paul von Hindenburg*—allowed a "stab-in-the-back" ("Dolschtoss") accusation by the far right to stand against the reputation of Weimar democrats, socialists, and Jews. That helped a scurrilous libel take root in German political discourse, and not just on the far right, that served to absolve military leaders from responsibility for defeat in November 1918. Instead, a fiction became widely accepted that said Weimar's liberal and socialist politicians lost a winnable war by signing the Armistice. To that bald lie was added a more noxious charge: standing behind and manipulating weak leftist politicians were scheming Jews and traitorous Communists. The officer corps and *General Staff*, which had in fact lost the war, was thereby elevated above grubby political quarrels, unbowed and undefeated. Meanwhile, street-level scapegoating was already moving past political blame to racial redefinition and segregation of Jews from "normal" German society.

The Nazis and other antidemocratic rightists made much of the bitter myth of the "stab-in-the-back." They fed off the wounded nationalism and economic despair of millions of former *Landser,* men who had not personally surrendered or tasted final battlefield defeat. Bereaved families of the dead and of severely wounded men were an additional population that remained psychologically open to blaming anyone but the officer corps for their new lives of worry or woe. The German people were not alone in cleaving to that twisted view of the outcome of the Great War. Many veterans and others in Italy—a nation actually on the winning side in 1918—held a comparable notion about Italy's war and harbored ill feelings of having been cheated during the end game of that great conflict by their Allies. That feeling was summed up in Italian political arguments in the phrase "*mutilated victory*." In both countries, leftist politicians, especially the Communists, and Jews were blamed for an unsatisfactory peace. In addition to aiding Hitler's rise to power, this firm popular belief had a crucial impact on his later conduct of military operations. It notably led him to underestimate the military impact of American belligerence. Why? Because he did not attribute the defeat of 1918 to two million doughboys arriving in France just in time to stanch the Reichswehr's spring offensives and to contribute to decisive enemy breakthroughs that summer and fall. That misapprehension of the causes of defeat in World War I significantly influenced Hitler's reckless declaration of war on the United States on December 11, 1941.

Long before that, Weimar authorities were saddled with special blame for Versailles. Instead of appreciating that Germany lost the war for military reasons, Weimar was held responsible for the loss of *Alsace-Lorraine* and the deeply unpopular "war guilt clause" of the Treaty, which was used as a legal basis to compel Germans to pay their former enemies extensive reparations. Forgotten was the fact that Germany extracted punitive reparations from Russia via the Treaty of Brest-Litovsk, imposed on the Bolsheviks in March 1918. That highly punitive settlement revealed how France would have been treated had Germany won the war. Under the Treaty of Versailles, reparations were divided into several categories: cash payments; payments in kind (principally, coal, timber, chemicals and pharmaceuticals); and credits for occupied or lost territories. The issue was greatly complicated at the Paris Peace Conference by British Prime Minister David Lloyd George, who introduced the idea of German compensation for British widows and payment of BEF veteran pensions. He did so because Britain suffered little direct war damage. Reparations to Britain increased London's share of the total bill paid by Germany. But contrary to a famous calculation and claim of the economist John Maynard Keynes, they did not increase the overall German burden. Historians also later demonstrated that French Premier George Clemenceau put forward quite moderate demands on Germany. And despite tough public talk from the "Tiger" of France, during the 1920s the French were open to economic cooperation with Germany in ways that presaged post–World War II founding of the Coal and Steel Pact and eventual formation of the European Community. Finally, Germany was assigned a level of reparations payments that it could indeed afford to meet, since assessments were not based on Allied claims but on realistic calculations of German ability to pay.

In 1922 Germany achieved a rapprochement of the mutually alienated by signing the *Treaty of Rapallo* with Russia. The Reichswehr thereupon initiated secret military cooperation with the Red Army, which it would fight in extraordinary combat 20 years later. At the same time, Germany chose not to pay its reparations bill to the Western Allies, at least not in full. When Berlin defaulted on payment in January 1923, French and Belgian troops occupied the *Ruhr* to extract reparations directly and compel additional cash payments. More international confrontation and deep bitterness followed as Germany experienced hyperinflation. The mark traded at 4:1 to the U.S. dollar in 1914, but it dropped to 160,000:1 in July 1923, and 130,000,000,000:1 (in short, it was worthless) by November. Some research suggests that Weimar politicians deliberately caused the terrible hyperinflation to pay back war reparations in inflated Reichsmarks. In either case, the inflation proved catastrophic. It demoralized the middle classes, deprived and radicalized the working classes, and severely undermined any chance for democracy to bloom in Germany or for Weimar to be accepted by traditional social and military elites. Ebert's hopes and reforms quickly fell victim to the hyperinflation, along with the hopes, savings, and prospects of much of the middle class. The economy was rescued only by the Dawes Plan hosted by the United States, which provided hefty American bridge loans to Germany.

Matters briefly improved in the mid-to-late 1920s. Under Gustav Stresemann, Germany enjoyed economic recovery, the diplomatic success of *Locarno,* new legitimacy with entrance into the *League of Nations,* and better relations with France. But then hope was flattened by the onset of the *Great Depression*. That downturn in trade and massive increase in unemployment hit Germany first and hardest. It did irreparable harm to Weimar's tenuous hold on democracy by aggravating economic despair and putting an end to confidence in the country's institutions and politicians. Because reparations payments were also used by Britain and France to pay war debts owed to the United States, and with President Calvin Coolidge and his successor, Herbert Hoover, refusing to waive Allied war debts, the reparations crisis came to affect the entire international economic system. A complex interplay of Allied war debts, German reparations, and international balance of payments issues dominated German politics and world affairs into the early 1930s. The problem of deepening ill will was compounded by the unemployment and trade effects of the American "Hawley-Smoot Tariff," which further depressed the world economy by throwing up high tariff barriers to trade. The delegates to the Lausanne Conference (1932) recognized hard reality and brought German reparations payments to an effective end. That provided temporary relief but also presaged collapse of the Versailles system, the underpinning of the entire postwar international order. Allied blindness to popular resentment in Germany, along with poor as well as willful German leadership in the early years, had by then cracked the foundation of the Weimar Republic. Street violence now threatened to bring the whole structure down.

The world financial crisis took form in Germany as a sudden rise in unemployment and increase in general hopelessness. The Weimar Republic was perpetually weakened by an inability of any from a multitude of small democratic parties to secure a parliamentary majority. Its institutions faced open and unremitting hostility from virtually all center-right and conservative parties, as well as rising street violence from *Freikorps* and Communist Party thugs. By 1930 there was a sharp increase in the number of political murders and destabilizing street violence that centered on elections. Paramilitary groups supporting various parties clashed bloodily, especially the Nazi *Sturmabteilung (SA)* and the Communist Party's Red Front—organized thugs from the antidemocratic parties, which benefited most from a rising mood of despair in Germany. Weimar was deeply handicapped during its time of crisis by the poor quality of its president: the vain, hostile, monarchist and authoritarian, and increasingly senile Paul von Hindenburg. Its parliamentary leadership was not much better. Heinrich Brüning (1885–1970), leader of the Catholic Party, was chancellor from 1930 to 1932. As the world financial crisis deepened, Brüning's efforts at moderate domestic reform came to naught. Unable to form a majority, he chose to govern by decree in an attempt perhaps best described as an effort to save German liberalism via illiberal means. That meant invoking an emergency provision of the Weimar constitution dismissing the *Reichstag*. Such a departure from parliamentary practice in favor of centralized decision making further weakened Weimar's shaky democratic credentials. It also set a precedent for Hitler's coming rule-by-decree.

The *Nazi Party* and the Communist Party alike increased popular support and representation in the ensuing election. The Nazis had emerged into national prominence when their representation rose from 12 to 109 seats in the 1930 elections to the Reichstag. The Nazis gained 230 seats in 1932, making their party the largest in the country, though leaving it well short of a majority. Meanwhile, Brüning used his expanded powers in a failed effort to ban paramilitary gangs, including the SA and other right-wing Freikorps. But he was unable to forestall collapse of the economy or what little remained of German democracy. He was abruptly forced out by Hindenburg on May 30, 1932, after failing to convince the old man that his hope to restore the Hohenzollern monarchy required skipping over exiled Kaiser Wilhelm II in favor of a younger prince. Arguing over the succession of a disgraced and exiled royal family was no recipe for political success. It instead revealed how out of touch with events Hindenburg already was. Brüning was followed into office by Chancellor Franz von Papen. He proved no more successful. On January 30, 1933, power was finally handed to Herr Hitler by German conservatives led by von Papen. The men who stood aside for the strange Austrian-born radical who had tried to seize power in Bavaria by force wrongly believed that they could manipulate and control "the little corporal." They held Hitler in contempt; but some thought they could use his populist movement to repress socialist yearnings of the working class. Seldom have men been so awfully or consequentially wrong in their tactical judgment. Within six months Hitler destroyed all institutions of Weimar. With the Republic disappeared hope of democracy and the rule of law within Germany, and any chance of peaceful international adjustment of the Versailles treaty system. Within six years Hitler would lead Germany into a world war that killed tens of millions of Germans of all political stripes, gutted its historic cities, left its borders at the mercy of foreign force majeure, put all Germans under occupation by alien armies, and forevermore stained the country's moral escutcheon.

Inside a month of taking power, the Nazis used a minor arson in the Reichstag as an excuse to ban the Communist Party and suspend most civil liberties. On March 23 they passed an extreme Enabling Law ("Ermächtigunngsgestz"), through a stripped-down Reichstag intimidated by the presence of sneering stormtroopers and a political class stunned and reeling from efficient Nazi ruthlessness. The Enabling Law destroyed the Weimar constitution by giving Hitler effective dictatorial powers. On April 1, anti-Jewish regulations were decreed from the top. That started Germany and all Europe down the road to the *Holocaust,* by scapegoating and purging from public office and jobs the 1 percent of Germany's population that was Jewish. It was a popular program with widespread support across class lines, but it was most clearly aimed to appeal to peasants, Christians, and the jealous among the middle class. All other political parties were banned by July, as the Nazi dictatorship and police state was secured. The next year saw the *Night of the Long Knives,* Hitler's blood purge of the SA that bought him peace with the Army and began the rise to preeminence of the even more sinister *Schutzstaffel (SS).*

In August 1934, President Hindenburg died. The title "President of the Republic" was abolished and no successor named. Instead, Hitler was proclaimed *Führer* of the Third Reich, as well as supreme commander of the Wehrmacht. Officers and ordinary soldiers were compelled to take an oath of personal loyalty to Hitler. Some later reported taking mental reservations, but most did not. In January 1935, a plebiscite in the Saar rejoined that territory to Germany. Hitler repudiated all disarmament clauses of the Treaty of Versailles by March, introduced conscription, and announced plans for a peacetime army of one million men. Britain aided

Hitler tear up the disarmament clauses of the Treaty of Versailles by agreeing to the *Anglo-German Naval Agreement* (1935). London signed that understanding without consulting other naval or treaty powers or its major allies. Hitler passed the *Nuremberg Laws* in September, stripping Jews of what few remaining legal protections they still had. The new laws allowed the Nazis to also rob Jews of their property and drive them out of the country. The bent cross of the swastika was made the official national flag. The Nazi revolution was complete.

Hitler benefited greatly from the peaceful return of the *Saar,* and to some extent from Germany's withdrawal from the League of Nations. He was forced to back away from immediate *Anschluss* with Austria due mainly to Italian threats of military intervention. But Italian–German relations grew warmer as Hitler gave diplomatic support to Benito Mussolini during the *Abyssinian War.* In March 1936, the Führer took his riskiest gamble to date by openly renouncing Locarno and remilitarizing the *Rhineland.* Fresh from that unchallenged diplomatic triumph, Hitler hosted the 1936 Olympic Games in Berlin. That November, the *Axis alliance* was proclaimed and the *Anti-Comintern Pact* signed with the Empire of Japan. Hitler and Mussolini separately sent military aid and "volunteers" to aid the military rebellion of *Francisco Franco* against the Spanish Republic that initiated the *Spanish Civil War (1936–1939).* It had been just three years since Hitler's assumption of power, but already Germany was threatening to pass Britain, France, and Italy to become, as it had been from 1871 to 1914, the leading military power in Europe. By 1936 Hitler had discarded, torn up, or ignored every formal diplomatic, economic, or military restriction that the Versailles settlement imposed on Germany.

Leading conservatives and industrialists learned that the Führer controlled them rather than the reverse. The original conceit of some that they could use the Nazis to crush the Communists helped grease Hitler's path to power, though his major business support was actually from owners of small and medium-size companies rather than the largest concerns. The old social and political elites grumbled, and they worried, about the anticapitalist radicalism and rhetoric of the Nazi state, which had its own hot language of concentrated economic and political power and had elevated a new social elite of brutes and thugs to the upper strata of German national life. Some industrialists and most Wehrmacht officers were also genuine admirers of Hitler's vaunted *"New Order,"* and not a few Junkers agreed with his harsh policy toward Jews. That was not just true of Germany: many in Western elite circles disliked Senor Mussolini and Herr Hitler, not least disdaining the personal vulgarity of the dictators. But they also thought that Italian *fascists* and German Nazis were perhaps necessary barriers to the expansion of Communism within Europe. Self-described worldly men in Paris and London fretted about "excesses" in Germany regarding the Jews. Yet, on the whole, even foreign elites were prepared to give Herr Hitler the benefit of whatever small doubt remained.

The depth of interwar German national and revanchist ambitions was so great that it is difficult after the fact to see how it could be satisfied other than by a policy of war. Most disagreements between Hitler and his top military and civilian advisers were about which war to wage, against whom, and when to begin it, not about the core policy of martial aggrandizement. A faction within the leadership of the *Wehrmacht*—the new name given by Hitler to the old Reichswehr—was appalled at the risks of war he took toward the Western Allies. Yet, few objected to his plans for the small states of eastern Europe, and none cared about the fate of Poland. Hitler took a close and direct interest in the armed forces, the one national institution in Germany that could possibly get rid of him by violent action. He named himself minister of war in February 1938. The following month he carried out the long-sought Anschluss with Austria. Shortly thereafter, *fifth-columnists* in the *Sudetenland* were told to agitate for their own Anschluss with the "Third Reich." Germany mobilized for war against Czechoslovakia in April, prompting anti-Hitler plotters inside the Wehrmacht to prepare a coup to remove this reckless man from national leadership. However, they stood down that September when, instead of the European war the General Staff feared and Germany was quite unready to fight, the Western Allies delivered the Sudetenland to Hitler at the *Munich Conference*. The majority of the German officer corps was deeply impressed, even as a few old men at the top who had opposed Hitler and even contemplated a coup were purged. Nazis were jubilant, celebrating the year's multiple triumphs with an obscene premonition of greater horrors yet to come: *Kristallnacht*.

On January 30, 1939, Hitler made a public pronouncement that in any future German war all the Jews of Europe would be exterminated. There could be no denying foreknowledge of his plans after that, though in later years many would deny it nonetheless. In March the Wehrmacht occupied the rump of the Czech lands left after Munich. Hitler openly displayed utter contempt for the Munich agreements and those Western leaders who had robbed him of the war he wanted against the Czechs. Immediately after sending the Wehrmacht to occupy Prague, where the Czechs offered no resistance, Hitler agitated for surrender by Poland of *Memel, Danzig,* and the *Polish corridor*. There was no institution left within Germany or inside the Wehrmacht to stop him from pursuing his course toward war. Germany had no strategic or military planning bodies—before or during the war— comparable to the War Cabinet in Britain, the Joint Chiefs in the United States, or the *GKO* in the Soviet Union. Besides, most of the officer corps and much of the nation shared Hitler's hatred for Poland and were enthusiastic about war, or at least were fearfully silent if they opposed it. Most ordinary Germans were further reassured by Hitler's promise of a short and successful war. Germans were stunned when he announced to them and the world a spectacular diplomatic and strategic volte face in form of the *Nazi–Soviet Pact (August 23, 1939)*. That assured Wehrmacht officers that the assault on Poland, which they launched for Hitler a week later, would not lead to the war with Russia that few of them yet wanted. But the Western Allies had at last read the Nazi scrawl upon the wall. All that year they had stepped up preparations for war and steeled a determination to wage it if they must. The test case was Poland. Should Hitler assault Poland, even Prime Minister *Neville Chamberlain* agreed that action would prove his regime was a threat to all Europe. Britain and France had extended military guarantees to Poland earlier in 1939. They reaffirmed these in late August in a last-minute attempt to avoid war, but it was far too late to try deterrence. On September 1, 1939, Germany invaded

Poland. British and French diplomats delivered ultimata in Berlin that day. These were contemptuously ignored until they expired on September 3, five hours later for the French than for the British. By evening, most of the Great Powers of Europe were once again at war.

In the first two years Hitler's legions overran Poland, Norway, Denmark, Holland, France, Belgium, Greece, and Yugoslavia; chased the British from the continent; and assaulted and conquered one-third of European Russia. Behind the advancing Panzers the Nazis began systematic liquidation of Jews, as well as of Roma, Jehovah's Witnesses, many Communists, "mental defectives," homosexuals, and any others they deemed undesirable. Germany reintroduced slavery to areas that had not seen it for 1,000 years: by 1944, 25 percent of the German economy depended on forced labor, mostly Slavic *Ostarbeiter* but also tens of thousands of Jews reimported to Germany to be worked to death. From Western Europe, too, they came, forced and conscripted laborers by the hundreds of thousands, including French conscripts and over 600,000 Italian prisoners of war from 1943. They were shipped into Germany from Belgium and across the Balkans, from any place SS jackboots stamped and *Gestapo* agents spread terror and instilled compliance. Most were forced to labor in Germany under terrible conditions that cost many thousands of lives. By war's end the slave labor system in Germany would use up and discard millions of human beings from nearly all occupied nations. It was especially severe for any one hailing from Poland, Belorussia, or Ukraine. Even erstwhile allies were not safe: some 200,000 Italians, nearly all former comrades in arms of Wehrmacht soldiers, died in German forced labor camps from September 1943.

With the strategic failure of *BARBAROSSA* in front of Moscow in December 1941, Hitler and his generals already faced the prospect of total defeat in place of the total victory their methods demanded. All their core assumptions of "Vernichtungskrieg"—of a quick "war of annihilation" in the east—were proven false. Germany instead found itself caught in the very type of war its military leaders long feared most: a vast *Stellungskrieg*, a great war of attrition and *Materialschlacht* it could not really hope to win. The German economy was unprepared to sustain such a protracted war, and too small in any case to win production battles against the enormously powerful enemies that Hitler and the Wehrmacht arrayed against Germany. A head start in war production actually turned against the German war economy by 1942, as enemies brought into action newer and better weapons, while the Heer and Luftwaffe retooled for slight modifications of existing designs and systems. Germany faced a power in the east alone that had twice its prewar population, vastly greater reserves of natural resources, and *total war* mobilization capabilities of a comparably savage and brutal terror state. Moreover, the Soviet Union was allied to the British Empire as a direct consequence of German aggression. Upon Hitler's declaration of war on the United States on December 11, 1941—made without a corresponding declaration of war on the Soviet Union by Japan—Germany faced in war the three greatest industrial empires in the world. Its diplomacy and ill-conceived grand strategy gathered around it only distant Japan, militarily weak Italy, and a few yet weaker, reluctant, and increasingly distraught minor European satellite states. Even so, Germany's broad leadership embraced the reality of a total war of attrition and dedicated the country to waging it.

Germany achieved a substantial economic expansion after 1942. That was led by the *Todt organization* and directed by *Albert Speer*. By September 1943, Speer controlled the German war economy, except for the subeconomy of slave laborers and factories owned and run by the SS. Speer's insistence on exemption from military service of millions of skilled workers needed to keep up war production caused great tension with the Wehrmacht over its recruitment needs. As skilled men were pulled into the armed forces, Speer replaced them with women, with forced labor by prisoners of war, and with slaves brought in from the occupied east and from the concentration camps. The *Combined Bomber Offensive* by the Western Allies began to take a heavier toll on German production from mid-1943, especially after the Western Allies agreed to concentrate on high priority targets such as synthetic oil plants and fighter factories. Deployment of long-range fighters, thousands of heavy bombers, and the introduction of improved navigation aids made bombing economic targets much more effective in 1944. That drove German factories to disperse to multiple sites, and many also to go underground. Despite great pressure from bombing, German production of certain key weapons systems such as fighters actually increased in 1944. Germany surpassed Soviet production that year in small arms manufacture and towed artillery, although a critical fuel shortage was increasingly felt on all fronts. The German economy even continued to produce high levels of consumer goods late into the war, primarily because Hitler feared a repeat of the collapse of the home front like that he blamed for defeat in 1918.

Hitler's mistakes were mounting. By the end of 1942 Germans were starting to understand the meaning of war with Great Britain and the United States as they suffered the first Anglo-American *thousand bomber raids*. German and Italian armies were trounced by the British at *Second El Alamein,* and German 6th Army surrendered to the Soviets at *Stalingrad*. Two more German armies were lost in Tunisia to the Western Allies in early May 1943. The Soviets won the greatest single battle of World War II at *Kursk* that July. In September, Italy switched sides, an antifascist Italian government declared war on Germany, and the Wehrmacht had to disarm and replace Italian troops in Italy and across the Balkans. Rome fell to the Western Allies on June 4, 1944. Two days later the Western powers breached Hitler's vaunted *Atlantic Wall* to establish a beachhead in France. Once the *Normandy campaign* was in full swing, Germany was well-advanced toward losing a vast *two-front war,* having repeated Imperial Germany's great strategic error of 1914–1918. Germans were in fact fighting on a third front in the bitter *Italian campaign (1943–1945)* and an effective fourth front in the air above the homeland. Hitler and the Wehrmacht knew the dangers of a two-front war and swore to avoid the strategic trap. Yet, everything they did by way of serial aggression ensured a grand anti-German coalition would come into existence, then close all around them with superiority in every measure of military power.

On August 25, 1944, French troops liberated Paris. The city of light did not burn despite Hitler's order to set it on fire. But Warsaw did, as Hitler and his most fanatic followers indulged old hatreds of Poles in a departing orgy of violence.

By the end of 1944, German armies were retreating across domestic soil for the first time in the war. The Red Army attacked into East Prussia in January 1945. The Western Allies crossed the Rhine in March. By late April, Soviet troops were in Vienna while others fought to the Reich Chancellery in Berlin. American and French armies swept through the Ruhr into Bavaria and thence to Czechoslovakia, while British and Commonwealth forces pushed deep into northwest Germany. Hitler and some other top Nazis killed themselves inside the Führerbunker under the Chancellery on April 30. Others fled incognito, from all across what was left of German-occupied Europe. Most were captured; a few committed suicide while in Allied hands, including *Heinrich Himmler*. Some of the captured were tried later for *war crimes* and *crimes against humanity*. A few escaped into hiding or exile, while still others disappeared, forgotten corpses buried by the ruins and rubble of Berlin. The last fanatic holdouts in the capital were killed or surrendered to the Red Army on May 2. The costly and bloody *conquest of Germany* was nearly over, with only sporadic fighting over the next few days along the Baltic coast and a few other small pockets of bitterender resistance. On May 7 Hitler's surviving admirals and generals formally accepted *unconditional surrender*. The Nazi dream of a "Thousand Year Reich" was over. It had lasted just 12 nightmarish years.

At war's end Germany was eviscerated: large pieces were torn off and distributed to neighboring states. The Anschluss was reversed and Austria reestablished as a separate republic, though under Allied occupation for 10 years. Austria was then neutralized. The Sudetenland was returned to Czechoslovakia, which immediately forcibly deported its *Volksdeutsche* population. East Prussia as historically known disappeared, much of its population expelled and old German cities renamed in Polish or Russian. Silesia mostly disappeared into Poland, its ethnic German population uprooted and roughly expelled, the innocent along with the guilty and with much loss of civilian life. Germany was then ripped down the middle by a four-power occupation that was left unresolved for four decades by the Cold War, which subsequently broke out among the victorious Allies. Hitler's immediate legacy was thus a divided country, split into two hostile states under close foreign domination for the next 44 years. Berlin was also divided in occupation zone by the four occupying powers, France, Great Britain, the United States, and the Soviet Union; then into eastern and western halves by the Cold War from 1948, and physically by the Berlin Wall from 1961 to 1989.

Germany was formally disarmed by the occupying powers in 1945, although there were hoards of weapons all over the country and trouble with a few hundred young *Werwolf guerrillas* for several years. The much bigger quandary was that the victorious Allies quickly fell out over what to do about the "German problem." Two German states thereby emerged out of the postwar occupation, without any formal agreement made to partition Germany. On May 23, 1949, federation of the three western occupation zones formed the Bundesrepublik Deutschland (FRG), or Federal Republic of Germany, or "West Germany." On October 7, 1949, the Soviet occupation zone was reconstituted as the Deutsche Demokratische Republik (DDR), or German Democratic Republic (GDR), or "East Germany." The FRG became independent of Allied controls in 1955, pursued limited rearmament, and was admitted to NATO. The West German military was carefully reconstituted as the Bundeswehr. Meanwhile, in the DDR the Nationale Volksarmee (NVA) was tightly controlled by the Soviets inside the Warsaw Pact. It was dissolved upon German reunification in 1990, with only a minority of its officers and men admitted into the Bundeswehr.

See also July Plot; Kapp Putsch; Minorities Treaties; Morgenthau plan; National Socialism; Nuremberg Rallies; Potsdam conference; resistance (Germany); Yalta conference.

Suggested Reading: Gordon A. Craig, *Germany, 1866–1945* (1978); Richard Evans, *The Coming of the Third Reich* (2004). Hajo Holborn, *Germany and Europe* (1970); Ian Kershaw, *The Nazi Dictatorship* (1985); Dietrich Orlow, *A History of Modern Germany,* 4th ed. (1999).

GERMANY, CONQUEST OF (1945) The Allies pressed on either side of Nazi Germany by January 1945, grimly determined to complete their version of *Vernichtungskrieg* ("war of annihilation"), or *total war,* to drive Germans to accept *unconditional surrender* and evermore foreswear war as an instrument of national policy. A double-invasion of Germany ensued on a scale unimaginable by any party to the war just four or five years before, and certainly not imagined by its instigators now huddled beneath Berlin or dying in vast multitudes along the frontiers of the "Greater German Reich." Out of the east came the Red Army, engorged with desire for blood revenge for tens of millions of Soviet dead, for destroyed cities and burned out fields, for their own lost youth and ineffable suffering. Millions of heavily armed men with red stars on their caps surged into Germany, bluntly forcing a way across the Oder with blood and brute force, crashing tanks and artillery into cities crowded with the terrified refugee flotsam of broken Nazi ambition for empire. Out of the west came the armies of democracy, pouring through the *Westwall* and over the Rhine. Their rage was not as great, but all war is cruel and most wanted to kill as many Germans as it took to end the fight and buy their ticket home. And whatever the quality of mercy on the ground for some poor *Landser* conscript seeking to give himself up, above advancing Western armies roamed enormous fleets of bombers heading out to burn down Germany's cities and terrorize its civilian population. For even the great democracies of the West had descended into ruthlessness that brooked little resistance and abjured almost no method of destruction that promised to shorten the war. The greatest armies known in the history of war had a singular mission and one destination in 1945: to meet in the center of Germany, astride the fetid corpse of the Nazi idea.

The Soviets had to move millions of men and thousands of war machines hundreds of miles across the devastated eastern half of Europe. The Western Allies moved vast forces in huge armadas that steamed over thousands of miles of ocean, thence by ground through heavily populated and river-crossed terrain in France and the Low Countries. German forces defending against these massive assaults had the classic advantage of interior lines of movement and supply. However, they had few supplies left and limited means of moving what little they had. Matériel production in Germany no longer provided tanks, artillery tubes, or aircraft in any number from January 1945. Even small arms and other ammunition stocks were growing scarce. There was almost no fuel and no mobile reserve left at all: the last sizeable Panzer and Panzergrenadier divisions were thrown away by Hitler, the OKH, and OKW in three vain offensives that only accelerated military defeat: the *Ardennes offensive* in Belgium in December 1944, and the *KONRAD* and *FRÜH-LINGSERWACHEN* counteroffensives in Hungary in January and March, 1945. German forces were also gravely reduced in quality of arms and men even from just one year earlier. The Wehrmacht still had many highly skilled and experienced veterans in its ranks, but it increasingly filled out its order of battle with weak *Volksgrenadier* divisions and militarily useless *Volkssturm*. Wehrmacht and *Waffen-SS* divisions were all much reduced by the great attritional battles of 1944. They were filled out in 1945 with too many second- and third-rate German recruits, or with *Hiwis* or scrapings of foreign volunteers. Some divisions comprised pathetic former Soviet prisoners of war, men who fought only for a crust of black bread and to stay alive one more day, coerced soldiers of the Reich with no zeal to fight for cause or country. After the collapse of Hitler's reckless gamble in the Ardennes there was some question about how hard even veterans would fight against Western armies. It would be learned that Germans fought ferociously in the east to the bitter end, from fear of retribution and out of belief in their own anti-Soviet terror propaganda. It also became clear, once the Rhine barrier was overcome, that there was merely sporadic fight left in formations still standing in the west. Even hard "men of will" in volunteer formations of the Waffen-SS would reach the limits of what flesh could do as the greatest industrialized war in history crossed into the country that had set the world aflame five years before.

The East

No one knew how much fight remained in the "fascist beast," as Joseph Stalin called Nazi Germany. In Moscow, as in London and Washington, it was thought the war was nearly over. As early as October 1944, the Stavka planned for a two-stage *deep battle* operation into Germany it predicted would last just 45 days. Stavka planners foresaw a set of cascading operations from the Vistula to the Oder, with more movement through the Baltic States and into East Prussia. Powerful armored spearheads would also plunge into western Poland and Silesia. Reinforced by a second tier advance by additional reserve Fronts, the Soviets would drive to the upper Elbe and thence to Berlin. Although the Nazi beast was severely wounded it was still snarling and dangerous and was now defending its lair. The Stavka plan was nevertheless put into effect as the *Vistula-Oder operation*, originally intended to be the last Red Army campaign in Europe. It opened on January 12, 1945, while the fight in the Ardennes was still underway. The main Soviet assault was undertaken in the north by 1st Belorussian Front under Marshal *Georgi Zhukov*, with 1st Ukrainian Front under Marshal *Ivan S. Konev* moving in tandem farther south. Both Fronts were immense, several times larger than comparable formations in 1941. The speed of the initial advance to the Oder was spectacular, accompanied by attendant collapse of German Army Groups Center and "A." Remnants of Army

Group "A" were hemmed into a series of isolated pockets along the Baltic shore. Parts of Army Group North were crushed and broken off by simultaneous Soviet operations in Pomerania and into East Prussia. But several of the pockets held out, supplied by the *Kriegsmarine*. The German Baltic fleet was very active throughout the last months of the war, bringing out refugees and wounded from the *Courland pocket,* Königsberg, and other enclaves. In a series of bloody fights to crush the larger coastal pockets, 3rd Belorussian Front defeated opposing Wehrmacht forces in detail in eastern Pomerania before driving into western Prussia, then turning back to fight through East Prussia. The *Insterburg-Konigsberg operation* and *Mlawa-Elbing operation* were over by the end of January. The *Heiligenbeil pocket* and hold-out remnants of German divisions on the *Samland peninsula* took longer to reduce. The cost to the Wehrmacht was dozens of divisions and surface warships. The price paid by the attacking Red Army in these operations approached 200,000 lives.

The speed of the main Vistula-Oder operation surprised the Soviets and stunned the Germans, but it also meant that the second part of the Stavka plan had to be shelved. The axis of attack by Marshal *Konstantin Rokossovsky's* 2nd Belorussian Front—fighting on Zhukov's right flank—had swiveled north to cut off East Prussia from Pomerania during operations in January. That movement opened a gap that left Zhukov's advanced positions uncovered on the right. Fortunately, Zhukov faced newly formed "Army Group Vistula," a much weaker force briefly headed by no less a Nazi personage but military incompetent than SS Reichsführer *Heinrich Himmler*. Stavka planners later explained that Phase II was canceled because moving past dangerous German pockets in Poznan, Königsberg, and the old *Polish corridor* posed too great a threat to the exposed flanks of advancing spearheads. There is support for that conclusion in the German SONNENWENDE counteroffensive assayed by "Army Group Vistula" from February 15–18, into the flank of 1st Belorussian Front in Pomerania. SONNENWENDE was tactically insignificant and was beaten off in just a few days, but it probably influenced the Stavka operational decision to now pause along the Oder. Some western historians believe that the plan was simply implemented too soon, possibly to take advantage of the Wehrmacht's failure in the Ardennes or out of fear that the German defeat in Belgium might permit the Western Allies to bounce the Rhine and get to Berlin first.

In either case, bypassing still dangerous German coastal pockets meant that the tips of the Soviet spearheads were weakened by growing need to strip away assault troops to protect the flanks of the advance. The Red Army was also, and for the first time, fighting beyond the reach of reliable intelligence previously supplied to it by anti-German partisans. That failing was not compensated for by parachuting in teams of *Nationalkomitee Freies Deutschland (NKFD)* and German Communist Party guerrillas. The intelligence blackout meant the Stavka did not realize how weak the Wehrmacht order of battle actually was. In addition, the VVS flew from muddy and improvised forward strips, while the Luftwaffe took off on paved airfields in central Germany, reversing the situation of the two air forces in late 1941. Natural obstacles of local terrain and dozens of blown bridges slowed supply to forward Red Army units that had already raced hundreds of miles ahead of schedule in just three weeks. All these factors likely conditioned the pause order sent to

Zhukov by the Stavka. Konev pushed to the Western Neisse farther south and then also stopped. In mid-February the Stavka decided to secure the flanks of its great advance before striking out for Berlin. Zhukov therefore pivoted his left flank due north, taking Stargard on March 4 and attacking into the outskirts of Stettin. By March 21 he secured a section of the Baltic coast east of the Oder. Zhukov's right flank armies, together with Rokossovsky's left flank armies, reached the coast at another point farther east. Trapped in the newly formed pocket these Soviet movements created were broken and ghost divisions of 3rd Panzer Army. Rokossovsky next turned due east and drove hard into the former Polish corridor. Danzig fell on March 30. Thousands of German soldiers and civilians took pathetic refuge from the enemy on two large sand spits off the coast, where they would remain in miserable conditions and under constant harassing fire until the final surrender in May.

Farther south, Konev's left flank had penetrated Upper Silesia in January. Katowice fell on January 28, and most of German 17th Army pulled back. From February 8–24 Konev conducted the "Lower Silesian offensive operation," an action that drove large numbers of ethnic German and other refugees westward. Many completed their journey crowded into the key transportation hub city of Dresden. Tens of thousands died during the *Dresden raid* by RAF Bomber Command carried out on February 13–15, in part to flood the Wehrmacht rear areas with terrified refugees to aid the advance of the Red Army. Some 100,000 civilians remained in Breslau after Hitler declared that city a "Festung" or fortress. They and the city garrison were besieged by the Red Army from February 13 to May 6. While the enemy at the gates pounded the city from without, the population was terrorized from within by a fanatic SS Gauleiter, Karl Hanke. Konev began the "Upper Silesian offensive operation" in mid-March, sending four armies to overwhelm the defenders of the rail town of Oppeln before occupying the rest of that rich province. A key decision was then made by Stalin and the Stavka to deliberately refuse to set a clear demarcation line between the advances of the two major Fronts in northern Germany, while leaving the target of Berlin available to both commanders. That set Konev and Zhukov against each other in a competitive race to be the first into the Nazi capital.

The so-called "Battle of Berlin" was the last major land battle in the European theater during World War II. It was also more of a campaign to occupy central and eastern Germany than a fight over or inside the poorly defended, sprawling, smoldering wreck of the German metropolis. On one side was the assembled might of the Red Army, driving toward ultimate victory against the once-feared but now only hated and despised Wehrmacht. The defenders arrayed around the capital were made up of broken Wehrmacht and Waffen-SS units. Inside the city Hitler and his commanders assembled about 45,000 Wehrmacht and foreign Waffen SS: Baltic, French, Dutch and other fascist volunteers, fanatics, and opportunists of the "New Order" with no place left to run. They were joined in the frontline by raw boys from the city's *Hitlerjungend,* some as young as 12, each armed with a single-shot anti-tank weapon. Another 40,000 *Volkssturm* were herded to the line, mainly old men of the home guard who fought for the Kaiser in the last war, or invalided soldiers dragged back into the new one for Hitler. Nazi Party officials and other fanatics formed roving death squads to round up any suspected deserter. Any man or boy caught in mufti or behind the lines who could not explain his presence was treated without mercy and summarily hanged for treason: Berlin's lampposts were adorned with corpses. The approaching Soviet formations had massive superiority in everything, in most cases by a ratio of 10:1 or greater: more air power, artillery, and armor and better trained and more experienced troops.

As the marshals and generals of the Red Army prepared to encircle Berlin, which they and their men called "berlog" or "beast," the field marshals and generals of the Wehrmacht sank into the worst extremes and criminal excesses of the "catastrophic nationalism" that long engulfed their Führer and themselves. No one in the High Command contradicted Hitler's final rants or sheer military fantasies about phantom relief armies driving on the city, or his promises of war-winning *Wunderwaffen* soon-to-arrive and change the course of the war in Germany's favor. They knew all that to be false, the ravings of a delusional madman who had conquered all of Europe then lost it again inside six years. The men in feldgrau uniforms with red stripes running down their trouser legs instead allowed the protracted and wanton total destruction of Germany, the decimation of its citizens and their own men. Some senior officers ran for cover in the end. Others made vulgar suicide plans; a few carried these out. Most merely waited with fatalistic stoicism for the end of their world and lives, superficially dutiful at their posts but as morally insensible at the end of Hitler's serial wars of genocidal aggression as they were at the start.

The Red Army paid a bloody price for the honor of delivering Hitler's capital to Stalin, who ordered the attack accelerated when he met with his Front commanders on April 3. The reason for the shift in gear was almost certainly the Kremlin master's concern over the rapid progress being made by the Western Allies, as resistance collapsed into small unit action and a few holdout pockets in western Germany. Two huge Fronts launched the final attack on "berlog" on April 16. Konev's 1st Ukrainian Front attacked from the south out of Silesia with over half a million men. Zhukov's massive 1st Belorussian Front struck westward from the Neisse and Oder with over 900,000 men and thousands of tanks and attack aircraft. Rokossovsky's 2nd Belorussian Front at 480,000 men attacked along the Baltic coast starting on April 18. Rokossovsky tore across Brandenburg and smashed right through immobile 3rd Panzerarmee, which was trying to flee west to surrender to the Anglo-Americans but lacked transport even for that. The three Fronts that closed the ring around Berlin brought to the fight over 6,200 tanks, 7,500 combat aircraft, and 41,000 artillery tubes. Together, they comprised 171 divisions and 21 more mobile corps. Attacking on all sides of the city simultaneously, these vast armies overwhelmed and crushed the last defenders in the outer ring around Berlin. Tactics were crude, frontal, and blunt, especially in Zhukov's opening assault on the Seelow Heights. Heavy Soviet casualties resulted as the attack initially failed against a layered and effective German defense. The main force defending the city was fragments of Army Group Center—not the original force that invaded the Soviet Union in 1941, but a renamed hodgepodge of units cobbled together and led in futile resistance by a fanatic Nazi. General *Ferdinand Schörner* was one of Hitler's' vaunted "men of will." He tried to hold the line of the River Neisse, but failed against unstoppable brute force and more skilled Soviet commanders and troops. German 9th Army also fought hard to pull itself westward from the Oder, inflicting heavy casualties on Konev's lead units. The two main Soviet thrusts, by Konev and Zhukov, linked on April 24 just south of Berlin. Soviet troops entered the outer suburbs two days later.

Army Group Vistula totally collapsed overnight on April 28–29, and the fight for Berlin was effectively over. It had been waged and won outside the city. A few more days of fighting remained as hundreds of thousands of *krasnoarmeets* moved through broken urban neighborhoods and the rubble of earlier Allied bombing to blast away the last resistance from a few thousand fanatics. Through it all Hitler brooded in his "leader bunker" beneath the rubble, under the Reich Chancellery. In the end even he stopped ordering mirage armies to counterattack this street or district, or to break out from some Baltic envelopment and fight through to Berlin. He instead ordered total demolition of the city and of Germany, of all its infrastructure and facilities, just as he had ordered Warsaw destroyed in 1944. The German nation, Hitler pronounced without a shred of self-awareness or irony, had proven "unworthy" of his greatness and failed the test of his social-Darwinist view of war and history. At last, a Führer order was countermanded: his court architect and minister for armaments and munitions, *Albert Speer,* finally disobeyed the man he had followed for over a decade into utter moral and physical ruin. Speer secretly called and circulated to stop the wanton destruction of the means of survival for any German who lived past the end of the war. Other top Nazis deserted their Führer in different ways, with several seeking to contact the Western Allies in vain hopes of negotiating a truce. Hitler condemned them all, married his mistress, then killed himself on April 30. That same day Soviet soldiers tore down the Swastika flag from the Reichstag roof and raised their own in its place. Two days later the last resistance inside Berlin ended. The tiny garrison that remained made an offer of surrender. It was accepted, and a formal ceasefire went into effect at 3:00 P.M. Berlin time. The garrison survivors and hundreds of thousands more Germans taken captive outside the city were marched to the east, most into years of captivity and forced labor.

The conquest of eastern Germany and the Battle of Berlin was accompanied by mass rapes and murder of civilians and prisoners by Soviet troops on a scale so vast that there is little doubt it hardened German resistance, and therefore also cost many tens of thousands of krasnoarmeets their lives. Taking Berlin by direct assault to meet Stalin's advanced schedule cost the Soviets 300,000 casualties, including 78,000 dead. Desperate Germans with *Panzerfäuste* or *Panzerschrecke* knocked out over 2,000 Soviet tanks. More than 900 VVS aircraft were also lost, principally to ground fire. Some killed and wounded on the Russian side were soldiers from all-women Red Army regiments. Yet, despite the presence of these female comrades-in-arms among Soviet formations, as the men of the Red Army advanced toward and through Berlin there was mass drunkenness, gang rape, and killing of civilians. More forgivable mass looting was also carried out by Soviet officers, followed by ordinary soldiers who scuttled among the scraps left them as trainloads of loot pulled away to the east. Some historians argue that the biting memory of the vicious behavior of many Red Army soldiers in East Prussia, Berlin, and other German towns and cities was a contributing factor in cementing West German public opinion within NATO after the war. The reverse is certainly true: victory in the Great Fatherland War against Nazi Germany and memory of the terrible crimes of the Wehrmacht and Waffen-SS in the Soviet Union gave the Soviet system a rare legitimacy and genuine popular support it had never previously enjoyed.

The West

In the fall of 1944 the Western Allies were also convinced the war with Germany was effectively over. They were shocked back to reality by attritional battles in the *Huertgen Forest* in November 1944, and the last-gasp *Ardennes offensive* of the Wehrmacht in the west. On December 16, 1944, Hitler threw all remaining strategic reserves into an offensive he called the "Wacht Am Rhein" ("Watch on the Rhine"), including most remaining Panzer and mechanized divisions and over 1,000 carefully hoarded aircraft. His proposed armored thrust to split the enemy armies in the north and take back Antwerp was both fanciful and a dismal failure that spent Wehrmacht reserves to no operational or strategic purpose. That did much to break the will of many German fighting men to continue resistance in the West, after they were pushed back to the start line in Belgium over the course of January 1945. The southern front around Metz was quiet for a time as elements of U.S. 3rd Army were diverted north during the "Battle of the Bulge" in the Ardennes. Still farther south, U.S. 6th Army Group—which incorporated French 1st Army and U.S. 7th Army—cleared the *Colmar pocket* from January 7 to February 9, with hard fighting along the left bank of the Rhine.

Canadian 1st Army was reinforced by three veteran Canadian divisions transferred from Italy to assist the push into northern Germany. The shift was made over strong objections by Churchill, who wanted offensive action on the Italian front but clearly failed to appreciate how truly overstretched and undermanned both British and Canadian formations were in France and the Low Countries. Canadian 1st Army conducted Operation VERITABLE from February 8 to March 3, pushing the Wehrmacht back east of Nijmegen to the lower Rhine. The attack was coordinated with simultaneous advances by other Allied armies forming Field Marshal *Bernard Law Montgomery's* 21st Army Group, itself reinforced by two British divisions from Italy. The main advance to the northern Rhine was code named GRENADE and conducted from February 23 to March 23. The Canadians, strongly supported by British armor, tied down the bulk of German forces in the flooded Roer Valley during VERITABLE. Then they slowly pushed east of Nijmegen to the Lower Rhine to link with U.S. 9th Army. Canadian and British casualties were 15,000 men, but 70,000 Germans were killed, wounded, missing, or taken prisoner. On the British right flank U.S. 12th Army Group under General *Omar Bradley* reached Cologne during Operation LUMBERJACK

(February 21–March 7). GRENADE and LUMBERJACK together brought U.S. 9th Army into contact with Canadian 1st Army on March 3, straddling the west bank of the Rhine near Dusseldorf. The Americans inflicted 16,000 Wehrmacht and Waffen-SS casualties and took 29,000 prisoners at a cost of 7,500 casualties in 9th Army. Hitler's decision to stand fast on the open west bank of the Rhine was proving disastrous: the Wehrmacht would have been better served to cross to the east bank, blow all bridges, and thereby force the Allies into amphibious assaults against strongly defended positions.

By early March, 100,000 Free French, 400,000 British and Canadians, and 1.5 million American troops were poised for the final push into Germany. Starting in February and lasting to March 9, British and Canadian forces fought to secure the Reichswald Forest. They took heavy casualties while fighting to punch through five German defensive lines inside the heavily wooded battlefield. On March 7 forward elements of 9th Armored Division of U.S. 1st Army captured the Ludendorff railway bridge over the Rhine at Remagen. The bridge was badly damaged by Wehrmacht engineers who tried to bring it down. Judged by American engineers as sound enough to take the weight of tanks and trucks, American troops quickly moved across to establish a weak bridgehead on the east bank. Over 8,000 U.S. troops crossed by the end of the first day, somewhat widening the lodgement. They failed to expand or exploit their early advantage before the German defenders threw strong reinforcements against the perimeter. Less usefully, Hitler ordered V-2 rockets fired at the bridge, a useless gesture made with widely inaccurate missiles: no hits were scored. The loss of the railway bridge at Remagen to the Americans enraged Hitler, who sacked Field Marshal *Gerd von Rundstedt* on March 11, replacing him with Field Marshal *Albert Kesselring:* Hitler's favorite "fireman"was called home from Italy to put out the conflagration that threatened to break out on the east bank of the Rhine. Not even the masterful Kesselring could stop five American divisions from crossing the Rhine before the Remagen bridge collapsed on March 17. By then, U.S. engineers spanned the river inside the bridgehead with a pontoon replacement. Barges and boats were also sallying back and forth with men and supplies, protected by total Allied air supremacy.

French 1st Army fought its way to the Rhine in the south, then crossed on March 19. General *George Patton* simultaneously led U.S. 3rd Army to the Moselle (Mosel), then over the river to make a tearing run right across the rear of German Army Group "G." That truncated formation was positioned along the Rhine. It was already hard pressed from the front by U.S. 6th Army when Patton and 3rd Army smashed into its rear echelons to cross the Rhine at Oppenheim on March 22. Patton paused only long enough to symbolically urinate in the river. Germans turned to run in front of these advances by an enemy whose mobility surpassed anything achieved by the Wehrmacht in its Blitzkrieg operations earlier in the war. Retreating German columns were strafed and bombed not by hundreds, but by thousands of Allied aircraft, including fighters, high-altitude bombers, and low-altitude *tank busters*. Far behind the front lines, *thousand bomber raids* incinerated Hamburg, Dresden, and other German cities even as Allied armies pushed into western Germany. With the French and Americans already over the Rhine in three places, Montgomery finally moved 21st Army Group to the river in the north, fully two weeks after the surprise crossing and quick exploitation at Remagen. After exhaustive preparation Montgomery launched a two-division airborne drop over the river (Operation VAR-SITY) on March 23, which incurred heavy casualties. On March 23–24 his British and Canadian ground forces crossed in Operation PLUNDER.

The exploitation phase was conducted by British 2nd Army and U.S. 9th Army, as Montgomery made a wide turn northeast toward the coast of Germany and pressed into Denmark. U.S. 1st and 9th Armies met beyond the still-unconquered *Ruhr,* encircling German forces in the "Ruhr pocket." At that moment Eisenhower gave transferred 9th Army back to Bradley, shifting it from Montgomery's 21st Army Group where it had resided since early in the battle in the Ardennes. Eisenhower told a surprised Montgomery and a greatly distressed Churchill that he did not intend to press an attack to Berlin, but would leave the Nazi capital to conquest by the Red Army. A delighted Bradley turned 9th Army south, away from the short route to Berlin. The entire American advance into Germany now pivoted toward the southeast, leaving British and Canadians to more slowly advance into the Low Countries, Denmark, and northwest Germany. The decision was deeply controversial, at the time and during the early Cold War. However, it reasonably took account of the fact that Berlin lay within the agreed future Soviet zone of occupation. Besides, the armies of the Western Allies were frayed and showing signs of deteriorating morale and decreased combat power. Overwhelming air power and artillery were sustaining the ground advance, whose movement was much slower than the light German resistance alone explained. Why take Berlin then hand it back to Stalin's control? The price in lives paid by the Red Army to take the city the next month must be kept in mind in any consideration of whether Churchill or Eisenhower was right.

Canadian 1st Army marched into northern Holland and Brabant in April, relieving a desperate Dutch population just emerging from its worst winter of the war, the hunger winter of 1944–1945 that followed the great disappointment of the failure of *MARKET GARDEN* in September 1944. The fight to compress German Army Group "B" inside the Ruhr pocket was the largest *Kessel* of the war in the west. When the German command in the Ruhr surrendered on April 18, over 317,000 men were taken prisoner; most had no fight left in them. U.S. 9th Army advanced to the Elbe and into the Harz Mountains, while U.S. 1st and 3rd Armies drove deep into Saxony against minor resistance, briefly reaching beyond the agreed Soviet occupation line. Patton's 3rd Army then turned into western Austria, where it eventually embraced advancing Soviet forces. On April 20, Hitler's last birthday, U.S. 7th Army occupied the spiritual home of Nazism at Nuremberg. Engineers blew up the giant concrete eagles and Swastikas that ordained the football stadium where the *Nuremberg rallies* had been held before the war. U.S. 7th Army turned next toward the frontier with Italy, seeking to prevent any retreat of Wehrmacht holdouts from Italy into southern Germany. Caught in the Alps between two powerful Allied armies, one descending from Germany and the other finally breaking through German defenses in northern Italy, Kesselring's former command in Italy surrendered on May 6. U.S. 5th and 7th Armies met at the *Brenner Pass*. During this southern operation French 1st Army was pushed southeast along the flank of the American turn. The French were permitted to occupy Stuttgart for many months in compensation, which sometimes took a rough form of vengeance against local Germans.

The End

Allied armies from east and west met at Torgau on the Elbe on April 25, just 70 miles from Berlin. The first cautious encounter occurred as reconnaissance units from Soviet 5th Guards Army met American troops waiting for them at the river: the Americans had stopped their advance to prevent possible friendly fire incidents by forward units, errors of identification, or other potentially lethal accidents that might have dire political implications. Hitler now accepted that the end had come to his regime and life. He married *Eva Braun* deep inside the Führerbunker on April 29. The twisted couple committed joint suicide the next day. Formal surrenders of German forces were accepted for northwest Germany at Lüneburg (Montgomery) on May 4, and by Allied commanders in Bavaria on May 6. Formal capitulation of all German armed forces on air, land, and at sea everywhere ("Act of Military Surrender") took place at SHAEF headquarters at Rheims on May 7. The brief ceremony was repeated at Karlshorst late at night on May 8, hosted by the Soviets at Stalin's insistence. Germany's unconditional surrender became effective at 23:01, just 18 minutes after the second ceremony ended.

There was still fighting after the surrender to suppress diehard Waffen-SS units struggling to escape Soviet captivity at Prague. When all the shooting stopped, millions of German soldiers were taken prisoner, most surrendering to the Western Allies. Individual soldiers and small units continued to move westward after the formal surrender on May 8, hoping to escape capture by the Soviets by surrendering instead to one of the Western powers, or just looking to discard their uniform and sneak home. Not all proffers by Germans were accepted. Some were refused by Anglo-American troops or local commanders, who forced German troops—especially Waffen-SS men—back east at gunpoint to surrender instead to the allied soldiers of the gallant Red Army. The ends of all wars are messy affairs, far less clearly demarcated than their formal end date suggests. But the war in Europe was finally over. Nazi Germany and its vaunted Wehrmacht had been totally defeated at sea, in the air, and on the ground. This time, no doubt was allowed to remain about that fact in the minds of Germans: the Allies ensured defeat was driven home by calculated, lasting physical occupation. Besides, all around German survivors was strewn the literal rubble and ruin of Nazi defeat: 520 million cubic yards of it, which took years to clear. Moral disrepair caused by the Nazi experience may yet prove impossible to fix.

See also Goldap operation; Jewish Brigade; Siegfriedstellung; Vienna offensive operation.

Suggested Reading: Antony Beevor, *The Fall of Berlin, 1945* (2002); Jeffrey Clarke and Robert Smith, *Riviera to the Rhine* (1993); V. I. Chuikov, *The End of the Third Reich* (1967); J. Erickson, *The Road to Berlin* (1983); Max Hastings, *Armageddon: The Battle For Germany, 1945* (2004); Charles Macdonald, *The Last Offensive*

(1993); Tony Tissier, *Battle for Berlin, 1945* (1988); Georgi K. Zhukov, *Memoirs of Marshal Zhukov* (1969).

GERMANY FIRST STRATEGY   Even before the outset of war in 1939, the British—like the Soviets and Americans—were threatened in Europe and Asia simultaneously. London saw the more vital threat as emanating from Germany and concentrated its armed forces in Europe even before the outbreak of fighting. The British thus recalled most Royal Navy assets from Asia; shipped Australians, New Zealanders, and Indians to the Middle East in 1940; and only belatedly and weakly reinforced garrisons scattered across Southeast Asia in 1941. Even after Japan attacked and overran British and American territories in Asia, for Britain the propinquity of the Nazi threat meant that it had no other real choice but to seek the defeat of Italy and Germany at the expense of almost all other considerations. Most top American civilian and military leaders agreed with that strategy, though only after intense internal debate and protracted tension between commands in the ETO and PTO throughout the war. The Germany first strategy was opposed by a powerful *Asia first* media and Congressional lobby, which had internal support from Admiral *Ernest King* and General *Douglas MacArthur*. The key decision was made by President Franklin Roosevelt, who concurred with British Prime Minister Winston Churchill that the war had to be conceived and fought as a truly global conflict, with the primary emphasis on winning in the ETO first.

At the end of 1941 Churchill and Roosevelt agreed on an explicit "Germany first" strategy, which promised to concentrate Western Allied power and resources in the ETO even if that incurred real costs and slowed the pace of the Pacific War. That led to tensions between Admiral King, speaking for the U.S. Navy, and the *Combined Chiefs of Staff*, which took a more global view. And it led to sharp interservice and theater rivalries throughout the war. But it was a policy adhered to, reaffirmed, and proven correct by the course of events. The Soviet Union also concentrated its forces prewar against Germany, although it maintained significant armies in the east to fend off a possible attack into Siberia by Japan. That remained true even after the Red Army bloodied the Imperial Japanese Army at *Nomonhan* (1939), and was still the case while facing catastrophic defeat in front of Moscow in October 1941. A month later, however, the Soviets moved some Siberian divisions west, as intelligence confirmed that Japan would take the *nanshin* path south. It might even be said that the Soviet Union pursued a "Germany only" strategy until August 1945, when Moscow finally declared war on Japan.

See also ABC-1 plan; Rainbow plans; Three Demands.

GERM WARFARE
See biological warfare.

GESCHWADER   The largest mobile Luftwaffe unit. It was normally comprised of one-type of aircraft, whether attack planes, medium bombers, or fighters. At the start of the war a Geschwader comprised three or more *Gruppen* totaling 90–100 aircraft. A Geschwader was roughly equivalent to a *Wing* in the Royal Air Force or an *air regiment* in the Red Army Air Force. Later in the war numbers fell sharply.

See also *Jagdgeschwader; Kampfgeschwader; Schlacht.*

GESTAPO "Geheime Staatspolizei." The Nazi secret and political police. The Gestapo is properly infamous for the barbarism and sadism of its members—self-selected and vicious anti-Semites, routine torturers, and frequent murderers. It was founded by *Herman Göring* in Prussia. It was taken over by the *Schutzstaffel (SS)* under *Heinrich Himmler* and expanded into a national secret police force. At first the Gestapo concentrated on rounding up Communists and activist Social Democrats inside Germany, the early political enemies of the *Nazi Party*. Then its agents moved against Jehovah's Witnesses and other pacifists who opposed Adolf Hitler's preparations for war. But always, it persecuted Jews, orchestrating round-ups and assisting with deportations to the *concentration camps*. Ultimately, it participated in mass killing of Roma and Jews: grey Gestapo functionaries knew about and assisted operations of SS *Einsatzgruppen* and the later *death camps*.

From 1938 the Gestapo expanded along with Hitler's swelling empire, moving behind the advancing Wehrmacht into annexed and conquered lands. Everywhere, it brought suspicion and intimidation, torture prisons, and the terror of sudden or capricious arrest. During the war the Gestapo was synonymous with torture and murder of *resistance* fighters or their sympathizers across German-occupied Europe, hunting resisters down with the help of the worst local collaborators or cowed and terrified witnesses. At its apex the Gestapo had 45,000 members. They routinely threatened incarceration in some concentration camp to control prisoners and extract information, or just to obtain sexual or financial favors. Gestapo officers were allowed by law to beat prisoners until they confessed to some crime, as often as not made up to stop the beating. Many thousands were beaten or tortured to death in terrible Gestapo prisons. That included hundreds of Wehrmacht senior officers, especially after the failure of the *July Plot* to kill Hitler in 1944. The Gestapo was identified by the *Nuremberg Tribunal* as one of six Nazi "criminal organizations." That meant membership alone was deemed a criminal act. However, most agents never saw inside a court of justice or paid a price for their wartime crimes. The worst and most infamous, such as *Klaus Barbie,* hid or fled into foreign exile. The majority lived out postwar lives in untroubled comfort, many on West German state pensions.

See also *commando order; kempeitai; skip bombing; Tokkō.*

Suggested Reading: Eric Johnson, *Nazi Terror* (2000).

GHETTOS The Nazis herded Jews into ghettos wherever they went, but especially starting in the large Polish cities that fell under their control in September 1939. That represented a policy of social and physical separation of Jews from the German population, then from areas intended for *Volksdeutsche* resettlement. Death rates from disease and starvation in the ghettos were high.

See also *concentration camps; death camps; Einsatzgruppen; Holocaust; Schutzstaffel (SS), Warsaw Ghetto rising.*

GHOST DIVISION   German 7th Panzer Division in France during *FALL GELB*.
See *Rommel, Erwin.*

GHQ   General Headquarters.

GI   "Government Issue." The term "GI Joe" came to mean an ordinary American soldier, an enlisted man whose worldly possessions—from his underwear and socks to his rifle and tin hat—were all issued to him by the government. It could be used ironically, sentimentally, or disparagingly—and sometimes with all these intonations at once. It was the U.S. Army equivalent of the German term *Landser*. There were many subsidiary usages. For instance, a "GI bride" was any foreign woman who married an American soldier. After the war U.S. veterans became eligible for educational aid under the "GI Bill." Another use derived from a wholly different source: a "GI can" was slang for a German artillery round, a bitter reference to galvanized iron (GI) from which industrial waste containers were made. The term was also used in the U.S. Navy, but in its original sense of a metal waste container. The equivalent naval term to "GI" was "swabbie," while in the USMC "gyrene" was used.

GIÁP, NGUYÊN VÕ (B. 1911)   Vietnamese Communist general. Giáp left Tonkin for China in 1939, where he met Chinese Communist leaders including *Mao Zedong* and *Zhu De*. He also met *Hô Chí Minh* in China. Giáp then returned to French Indochina to organize the military wing of the *Viêt Minh* and to fight the Japanese. After the war he emerged as the principal military leader of the North Vietnamese Communists fighting the French to 1954 and Americans from 1964 to 1973.

GIBRALTAR   "The Rock." A key British naval base located on a small Spanish peninsula guarding entrance to, and egress from, the Mediterranean. It was bombed by French naval aircraft following the British attack on the French fleet at *Mers el-Kebir* in July 1940. It was bombed more regularly by the Regia Aeronautica until 1942. Gibraltar was critical to British defense of Malta and the Suez Canal in Egypt. During the *desert campaign* it was a vital stopping point for military aircraft being ferried to Malta or on to North Africa. It hosted the Royal Navy's *Force H* to 1943, and watched for Italian submarines and German U-boats running the gauntlet of minefields and patrols in the narrow channel between two great seas. It also served as an intelligence outpost for double agents and other secret operations run through Spain. And it was a haven for Western Allied pilots and other escapees allowed by the Spanish to find a way south. General *Francisco Franco* wanted to seize Gibraltar, but insisted the job be done by his own troops. A Wehrmacht study team concluded the Spanish Army was not up to the task, and Hitler insisted on using German troops. The impasse meant that an assault was never made. The Italians and Germans carried out a number of sabotage operations against Gibraltar installations or shipping, but these did not fundamentally threaten the base's functions.

During the *TORCH* landings in Morocco and Algeria in November 1942, Gibraltar was used by General *Dwight Eisenhower* as the forward invasion headquarters. Adolf Hitler long wanted to eliminate the British base on Gibraltar, but he never received the go-ahead from *Francisco Franco* while his own military advisers cautioned that the Spanish Army could not do the job alone. The Spanish and Germans developed discrete contingency plans to take Gibraltar, but none were effected. The British also drew up several contingency plans based on Gibraltar that aimed to counter any German invasion of Spain or an assault on the peninsular fortress. They went by various code names, including BACKBONE, BACKBONE II, BALLAST, BLACKTHORN, *CHALLENGER*, and SAPPHIC. Those plans varied from reinforcing defense of Gibraltar, to seizing Ceuta and other Spanish territory in Africa, to invading Spain itself to establish a beachhead around Gibraltar in the event Madrid declared war or any German troops entered Iberia.

See also ISABELLA.

GIBSON GIRL   An hourglass-shaped portable radio transmitter issued to all RAF air crews by mid-1942. It was copied from a German radio captured earlier in the war, replacing the original RAF reliance on *carrier pigeons*. Used upon ditching an aircraft in open water, the Gibson Girl communicated crash site location to friendly *air–sea rescue* units. With a wire antenna elevated high above a dinghy by balloon or kite, late-war models achieved a range of up to 1,500 miles.

GIDEON FORCE   A British special forces unit of about 1,700 men led by *Orde Wingate* during the *East African campaign (1940–1941)*. It brought Emperor Haile Selassie back to Addis Ababa.

GILBERT AND ELLICE ISLANDS   A group of small British island and atoll colonies in the South Pacific, immediately southeast of the *Marshall Islands*. They were occupied by the invading Japanese in the initial wave of imperial expansion in early 1942, making them the closest Japanese-occupied territory to Hawaii. On December 9, 1941, two days after *Pearl Harbor,* Japanese naval aircraft bombed Banaba, or Ocean Island. Reconnaissance teams were landed on some atolls. Early in 1942 occupation forces arrived to take control of the undefended Gilberts, the group today forming the state of Kiribati. Japanese mistreatment of the native population included forced labor in phosphate mines and other brutalities. New

Zealand *coast watchers* kept an eye on the chain until the Western Allies took most of it back during Operation *GALVANIC*. That involved bloody fights on *Makin* and *Tarawa* in late 1943, supported by long-distance bombers from the Ellice Islands. A small Japanese garrison on distant Banaba was bypassed. It surrendered at the end of the war in 1945. The next jump took the Western Allies into the Marshall Islands.

GIRAUD, HENRI (1879–1949)   French general. He was captured at the Battle of Guise in August 1914, but escaped two months later. He fought again in Morocco against the Rif in the 1920s, then became military governor of Metz. He commanded French 7th Army in the Netherlands early in *FALL GELB* (1940), then headed 7th and 9th Armies in a vain effort to stop the German breakthrough in the Ardennes. A supporter of motorized infantry but unsure about mobile and mechanized tactics, he quarreled with *Charles de Gaulle* about both. Reprising his Great War experience, he was captured along with his headquarters on May 19. He was held as a prisoner near Dresden until he escaped on April 17, 1942, with aid from friendly agents. He met General *Dwight Eisenhower* in Gibraltar on November 7, a day before the *TORCH* landings in Morocco and Algeria. He agreed to take command of French forces in North Africa, but they would not recognize his authority. After *Darlan* was assassinated, however, Giraud took over both civil and military affairs. He immediately alienated Eisenhower by arresting several former Vichyites whose cooperation was needed by the Western Allies. Giraud attended the *Casablanca Conference* (January 14–24, 1943), where Franklin D. Roosevelt and Winston Churchill moved to elevate him over de Gaulle, then backed down to a copresidency of the Free French with de Gaulle. However, de Gaulle easily outmaneuvered the politically clumsy Giraud over the following months. Giraud was placed in active charge of those members of the *Armée d'Afrique* who turned coat from Vichy to join Fighting France. He led them well enough in Tunisia, fighting on the American southern flank. However, his right-wing sympathies and rivalry with de Gaulle led to personal conflict with General *Philippe Leclerc*. Giraud was forced out of political office in November 1943. He led the minor French invasion of Corsica but was forced from military office as well in April 1944, just before the "big show" of *OVERLORD*.

GISELA
   See *ISABELLA*.

GKO   "Gosudarstvennyi Komitet Oborony" ("State Defense Committee"). The "war cabinet" that advised Joseph Stalin on military policy. It was established on June 30, 1941, one week into the German invasion of the Soviet Union, or Operation *BARBAROSSA*. *Lavrenti Beria*, head of the *NKVD*, sat on the GKO alongside other advisers. There was no German equivalent.
   See also General Staff; Stavka.

GLAVNYI UDAR "main effort."
See Schwerpunkt.

GLIDERS
See airborne; Air Commando; airlanding; bombs; ohka; torpedoes.

GMC A six-wheeled-drive, 2 1/2 ton heavy truck used as the mainstay of U.S. military transport.

GNEISENAU Wehrmacht code name for the German defensive line in the Crimea in 1944.

GNEISENAU, *DKM*
See Atlantic, Battle of; battlecruisers.

GÖBBELS, JOSEF (1897–1945) Nazi "minister of enlightenment and propaganda," 1933–1945. He was a member of Adolf Hitler's inner circle from the early 1920s. He earned a doctorate in philosophy at Heidelberg in 1921. He drifted aimlessly until he met Adolf Hitler, his leading light and master for whom he developed a permanent and fatal attraction. Hitler affirmed Göbbels rabid *anti-Semitism* and gave him *Nazi Party* responsibilities, eventually as *Gauleiter* of Berlin. Göbbels was elected to the Reichstag in 1928, but served only on the margins of Hitler's cabinet once the Nazis took power in 1933. Still, he importantly shaped the internal culture of Nazi Germany. On May 10, 1933, he organized mass, public burning of all books despised by the Nazis, notably those by Jewish authors but also any that challenged Nazi militarism or other dogmas. He introduced the "Heil Hitler!" greeting as standard, deepened and cultivated the *Führerprinzip,* and took direct control of production of books, newspapers, museum exhibits, orchestra programs, dance, painting, all public art, film, and *radio.* He earned a street and Nazi Party nickname of "poison dwarf." He was a self-consciously short and gaunt man, physically unimpressive and partly crippled, his gait interrupted by an obvious limp from a club foot. His chickenhawk civilian rhetoric and withered character made him despised by the Wehrmacht officer corps, who saw him as a mere civilian who paraded violent rhetoric while limping about in make-believe military costume of the Nazi Party. Göbbels loathed all officers in return.

During the war Göbbels directed all civilian propaganda. His main technique was the "Big Lie," a tale so monstrous and clearly false as to be rationally unbelievable, which yet came to be believed through its shock content and constant repetition. He pioneered the use of radio and film to reach a mass audience and introduced the first primitive TV system in 1935. Göbbels was a frantic as well as fanatic organizer of the home front, becoming personally identified with a call for ideological *total war* after making an infamous "totalen Krieg" speech in the Berlin Sportpalast on February 18, 1943: "Do you want total war? If necessary, do you want a war more total and radical than anything that we can even yet imagine?" He asked the question 10 times, and 10 times the answer was "Yes!" Total war was a concept that he defined more in terms of determination and radical idealism than material means. He had no military experience and no understanding of the coming destructiveness of Allied air power, or he might not have so unwittingly invoked total war or invited its visitation upon Germany. Despite his gross inadequacies, Göbbels was made "minister for total war" in 1944. That promotion was part of a much wider and deeper *nazification* of the military that followed failure of the *July Plot* to kill Hitler. Göbbels' main contributions to the war effort were all grim. He organized relief convoys to the frontlines, raised the maximum age limit for compulsory labor for older men and women, and shut down all cultural activities in the name of total dedication of remaining resources to the war effort. The day after Hitler's suicide, on May 1, 1945, Göbbels and his equally twisted wife had their six children poisoned by an SS doctor, declaring that they could not contemplate the children living "in a world without Hitler." Göbbels ordered an aide to shoot him and his wife, an act regretted or mourned by no one then or since.

See also BARBAROSSA; Holocaust.

GOERING, HERMANN

See Göring, Hermann.

GOLD   Code name for a set of British assault beaches in Normandy on *D-Day* *(June 6, 1944).*

GOLDAP OPERATION (OCTOBER 16–27, 1944)   Also called "Gumbinnen operation." Little is known or published about this Soviet offensive into central Prussia. It began with an assault by two Guards Armies into the Insterburg corridor on the 16th, supported the next day by two more infantry armies. The assault was ferociously resisted at the Prussian border from behind a well-prepared defensive line that took four days to overwhelm. A second, interior line was even tougher. It took assault by an entire Tank Army to break through, and then not before October 20. Over the next week heavy Panzer reinforcements arrived to block any further advance through the *Stalluponen Defensive Region,* inflicting heavy Soviet casualties in the defense. Historian David Glantz argues that the failure of the operation taught Soviet planners that far more careful preparation would be needed to overrun East Prussia and Germany. The cost of that lesson and failure was some 17,000 casualties. The Goldap offensive also witnessed some of the first Red Army reprisal atrocities carried out on German territory.

GOLD COAST   This small British colony in West Africa (modern Ghana) provided troops for the 81st and 82nd West African Divisions, which saw action in East Africa and Burma. Others served in the *West African Military Labor Corps.* The Gold Coast hosted the key way station in the *Takoradi air route.*

GOLIKOV, PHILIPP I. (1900–1980)   Soviet general. He joined the Red Army in 1918 at the start of the Russian Civil War (1918-1921). In the early 1930s he studied mechanized and tank warfare. A committed Communist, he survived the purges of the late 1930s and rose to command a mechanized corps, then 6th Army. A year before *BARBAROSSA* he was made deputy chief of the General Staff and head of the *GRU*. He was commander of 4th Shock Army from February to April, 1942, then of successive Fronts fighting around Voronezh and Stalingrad during the balance of 1942. From October 1942 to March 1943, he commanded Voronezh Front along the upper Don River. He held mostly political offices in the last years of the war, including organizing repatriation of millions of Soviet *prisoners of war* and other citizens from liberated territories. That was not always done gently: many prisoners were swept into the *GULAG* or simply shot outright as traitors. Golikov was promoted Marshal of the Soviet Union in 1961.

GOLOVANOV, ALEXANDER Y. (1904–1975)   Chief marshal, *Red Army Air Force (VVS)*. He fought against the Japan at *Nomonhan* in 1939 and against the Finns in the *Finnish–Soviet War* (1939–1940). From 1942 to 1944 he was in charge of planning long-range bombing operations, then took command of 18th Army. He planned VVS long-range bombings of Königsberg and Berlin that were carried out in 1945.

GONA, BATTLE OF (1942)
See New Guinea, Dutch.

GOODWOOD (JULY 18–29, 1944)   General *Bernard Law Montgomery* authorized a major assault to overrun the last defenses in and around Caen. His intent was to break through German lines from the Orne bridgehead to meet the Americans who were closing on Falaise. As too often happened during the last year of the war, Montgomery would make a partial operational success appear as a complete failure to his critics and personal enemies by exaggerated promises of much greater success against a floundering enemy. Ferocious German resistance instead met the attack, which cost nearly 5,000 casualties and 500 tanks, or about one-third of all British armor in Normandy. GOODWOOD began with the heaviest air assault against enemy ground forces yet seen, a massive saturation raid by over 1,000 heavy bombers. That was followed by a huge artillery bombardment by concentrated artillery. Neither firestorm knocked out the main German batteries on Bourguebus Ridge, and many German infantry and tank strongpoints were left untouched. British tanks initially advanced steadily despite traffic and command confusion, but so slowly that the Germans recovered from the heavy bombing and shelling and were waiting in fixed anti-tank positions when the tanks arrived. British armor advanced slowly elsewhere, usually in penny packets and in the face of stiffening resistance by Panzers and soldiers of the Waffen-SS. Skilled and experienced German anti-tank gunners ran up terrible totals of knocked-out enemy tanks. The Panzers counterattacked late on the 18th, leading to swirling tank fights over the next two days. GOODWOOD ended as another operational disappointment for the Western powers. It secured the other half of Caen, although it spent British armored combat power to little additional territorial gain and certainly far less than Montgomery promised his superiors. On the other hand, GOODWOOD and similar thrusts toward and around Caen on the left flank of the lodgement in Normandy held the great bulk of Panzer divisions in front of the British and Canadian sectors, leaving thinner crustal defenses for American armies to punch through on the right flank.

GOOSEBERRY   Five artificial breakwaters formed by "corn cobs" (74 sunken blockships) that steamed or were towed into position along the Normandy coast, then sunk off the invasion beaches during the *OVERLORD* operation. GOOSEBER-RIES were used in construction of each of the two *MULBERRY* artificial harbors.

GOOSE-STEP   The high-kicking, formal marching style adopted by the *Nazi Party* and later also the Wehrmacht in Germany. Benito Mussolini was so impressed that he introduced it to all parades in Italy from February 1938. But he renamed it the "passo romano," or "Roman step."

GÖRING, HERMANN (1893–1946)   Nazi air minister, 1933–1945. Göring was a renowned and highly decorated ace in World War I, with 22 confirmed kills as a member and last leader of the famed "Flying Circus" of Baron Manfred von Richthofen. Göring joined the *Nazi Party* in 1922 and helped plan the 1923 Beer Hall Putsch, during which he was wounded. He retired to Italy and Sweden to recover, where he became addicted to morphine and was intermittently confined to sanatoria. He returned to Germany to stand for election to the Reichstag in 1928; he rose to president of the Reichstag in 1932. He was minister president in Prussia from 1933, occupying one of the most powerful positions in the new Germany. Göring founded the *Gestapo* and approved of the new *concentration camp* system. He was for a decade a very large pillar of the regime, second only to Adolf Hitler in power and public prominence. Göring was thoroughly corrupt: he used his offices to accumulate great wealth, including wartime plundering of the art galleries and museums of German-occupied Europe. In 1935 he took charge of the *Luftwaffe,* eventually rising to the unique position of "Reichsmarschall," a rank Hitler created solely to soothe Göring's insatiable vanity. His aircraft first terrorized civilians during the *Spanish Civil War* when he ordered the bombing of *Guernica* in 1937. They did so again in Poland, France, and the Low Countries during the lightning campaigns of *FALL WEISS* in Poland (1939) and *FALL GELB* in France and the Low Countries (1940).

Göring had sent secret peace feelers to the Allies before FALL GELB, mainly because he wanted more time to mobilize Germany's aircraft industry and war economy before war began. But once committed to war he indulged every Nazi instinct he had, including enthusiastic embrace of plans for physical extermination of the Jews of Europe. From the first days of war, Göring's jealous suspicion that the Kriegsmarine wanted to establish a separate air force caused him to block any effort that fit that phantom of his mind. He refused or severely limited Luftwaffe cooperation in the U-boat war against enemy convoys and hunter-killer groups, while simultaneously blocking creation of a German naval air arm or serious coastal command. His position slipped, however, when his boast that the Luftwaffe would handily win the *Battle of Britain* was hollowed out by the fighters of the RAF. He was humiliated by that failure and further reduced in status and prestige when RAF Bomber Command bombed Berlin. He again boasted to his Führer, and once more failed to deliver on the promise, that the Luftwaffe could by itself supply encircled troops at *Stalingrad*. His understrength transport aircraft never came close to supplying the required tonnage. German 6th Army was lost and with it Hitler's favor. More failure followed Stalingrad, so that Hitler lost all confidence in Göring by 1944 and even ordered the Luftwaffe disbanded during one fit of rage. Göring was able to forestall that bizarre decision by appealing to past Nazi loyalties. Even so, Hitler took more operational control of air deployments upon himself.

Göring never recovered his early influence with Hitler. In 1944 and 1945 his humiliation and increasing withdrawal from active control of Luftwaffe management deepened as Germany's cities were successively pounded into rubble by *thousand bomber raids*. Göring had once said, citing a common Jewish name: "If a single bomber reaches the Ruhr, you may call me Meier!" By 1945 Allied bombers had been pounding the Ruhr—and penetrating much deeper into Germany—for five years. As Germans huddled in inadequate bomb shelters, of which Göring and the Luftwaffe had built far too few, or as thousands crammed inside airless *Flak Towers,* many muttered bitterly: "Where is Meier?" Göring concluded earlier than most top Nazis that the war in the east could not be won. Göring was vain and crudely ostentatious, corpulent and cruel, a morphia addict and thief, endlessly ambitious but never hardworking. He surrounded himself with amateur administrators less qualified than himself because he could not stand to be outshone in any room, except one occupied by his Führer. By late 1944 he did not even try to command the Luftwaffe. He showed little interest in operations as he retreated into drugs and other coarse physical indulgences. Göring had an extraordinary personality and keen intelligence that was on full display even during his trial by the *Nuremberg Tribunal,* where it affected some prosecutors and witnesses against him. Göring was convicted as a "major war criminal" and condemned to hang. He cheated justice by drinking a vial of cyanide a few hours before he was due to be executed. In the mid-1990s it was learned that he obtained the poison by charming a foolish and gullible American officer, who smuggled it into his cell.

See also Coventry raid.

Suggested Reading: David Irving, *Göring* (1989).

GORT, JOHN (1886–1946) British field marshal. General Gort was the highly decorated (Victoria Cross) commander of the British Expeditionary Force (BEF) from 1939 to 1940. He was replaced during *FALL GELB*—the battle for France and the Low Countries in May–June, 1940—by Lieutenant General *Alan Brooke,* after Gort revealed an incapacity to handle large formations in the field. His decisions in the last week of May enabled and required that the BEF evacuate from *Dunkirk.* His early warning to the War Cabinet of a potential need to evacuate the BEF caused the Royal Navy to gather evacuation ships at Dover even before the departure order was given. It is hard to see how Gort should be held accountable for the larger disaster suffered by the Allies in FALL GELB, but blamed by many he was. Through 1944 Gort was permitted only minor Army commands: defense of Gibraltar and Malta. Both were primarily Naval operations and obligations. He ended the war in Palestine, which was also a backwater theater.

GORY

See MOUNTAINS.

GOTENKOPF "Goth's Head." Wehrmacht code name for the German defensive line on the Taman peninsula, which the Wehrmacht occupied from 1943 to 1944.

GOTHIC LINE A powerful set of Wehrmacht defensive works in northern Italy, running from Massa on the Ligurian Sea eastward to Pesaro on the Adriatic. Field Marshal *Albert Kesselring* renamed it the "Green Line" in mid-1944. The Western Allies assaulted it on both sides of the Apennines that fall. But given withdrawal of seven American and Free French divisions to take part in the *DRAGOON* landings in southern France on August 15, 1944, they no longer had enough combat punch in Italy to achieve a decisive breakthrough. Fighting continued along the Gothic (or Green) Line into 1945.
See also Italian campaign (1943–1945).

GOTT, WILLIAM (1887–1942) British general.
See desert campaign (1940–1943); Desert Rats; El Alamein, Second Battle of (October 23–November 4, 1942).

GOUMIERS Native North African troops in France's *Armée d'Afrique.* Goumiers initially were irregular Moroccan troops, mainly from the Atlas Mountains, who served with French forces in various colonial campaigns and kept the interiors of French colonies pacified. They were organized as regulars by the Western Allies and *Free French* from November 1942, taking advantage of a specialization in mountain warfare. They first fought in the Allied cause in Tunisia in early 1943, as part of a French composite force put together from units of Free French and of the Armée d'Afrique. They were called "Goums" by Western soldiers who fought alongside them. Over 10,000 were deployed in two "Moroccan Infantry Divisions," which formed part of the *French Expeditionary Corps* in Italy in 1943–1944. Some earned a reputation for rape, thievery, and murder among the Italian population and with other Allied troops. Many fought hard at *Monte Casino*. About 2,000 Goumiers comprised the bulk of the Free French force that assaulted *Elba* in June 1944; others saw action on Corsica. Goumiers participated in the *DRAGOON* landings in southern France in August 1944, thence fighting to the Rhine and into Germany in 1945.

GOUMS
See Goumiers.

GOVERNMENTS-IN-EXILE "Absentee government."
See Agency Africa; Belgian Congo; Belgium; Beneš, Eduard; Czechoslovakia; de Gaulle, Charles; Denmark; Dutch East Indies; Free French; G-5; Greece; Greenland; Jiang Jieshi; Katyn massacre; Lithuania; London Poles; Lublin Poles; Masaryk, Jan; Merchant Aircraft Carrier (MAC); Netherlands; Norway; Pétain, Philippe; Philippines; Poland; Quezon, Manuel; Royal Hellenic Army; Selassie, Haile; SHAEF; Sikorski, Wladislaw.

GOVOROV, LEONID A. (1897–1955) Marshal of the Soviet Union. Like so many Soviet senior offices, he joined the Red Army in time to fight in the Russian Civil War (1918–1921). He studied tank warfare and artillery in the early 1930s and General Staff operations later in the decade. He served as an artillery staff officer with 7th Army during the *Finnish–Soviet War (1939–1940)*. He held varied and rapidly changing command positions during *BARBAROSSA*, including as deputy commander in front of Moscow to October 1941. He was commander of the Leningrad Front from 1942 to 1944, during the desperate siege of that city. In January 1943 his command finally broke the blockade of Leningrad, though the siege and German trenches remained in place for another year. His men overran Karelia in just two weeks in June 1944, and he was promoted to Marshal of the Soviet Union. In late 1944 he was put in charge of defensive operations of two Baltic Fronts in addition to his duties with Leningrad Front. He spent most of the rest of the war, from September 1944 to May 1945, compressing the *Courland Pocket*.

GPF (*GRANDE PUISSANCE FILLOUX*) A 155 mm cannon, backbone of French Army heavy artillery in 1940.

GPU
See NKVD.

GRAND ALLIANCE
See Allies; United Nations.

GRAND MUFTI The spiritual leader of Muslims in Jerusalem. The Grand Mufti who held office during World War II, Amin al-Husseini (d. 1974), secretly conspired with Adolf Hitler in search of military aid for his opposition to Jewish immigration to Palestine. After fleeing Palestine for Iraq in 1938, he fled Iraq for Germany in 1941. Despite a long personal talk with Hitler on November 28, 1941, about the global ambition of the genocide underway against the Jews, al-Husseini clearly did not understand how Nazi occupation must have led to mistreatment of Jerusalem's Arabs after disposing of local Jews.

GRAND SLAM   *See bombs.*

GRAND STRATEGY   The highest level of war-making, above *operational art* and *military strategy*. Grand strategy concerned defining and setting the main political and strategic goals to be achieved, or at least assayed, by endeavors of military art and science.

See ABC-1 Plan; ARCADIA conference; autarky; BARBAROSSA; BLAU; Casablanca Conference; Chiefs of Staff; Churchill, Winston; Combined Chiefs of Staff; geopolitik; Hitler, Adolf; hokushin; Italian campaign (1943–1945); Joint Chiefs of Staff; Lebensraum; Maginot Line; Mussolini, Benito; nanshin; OKH; OKW; Potsdam Conference; Québec Conference (1943); Québec Conference (1944); Roosevelt, Franklin; second front; Stalin, Joseph; Teheran Conference; Tōjō, Hideki; war plans; Yalta Conference; Z-Plan.

GRAPESHOT   Code name for the last Allied offensive of the war in Italy.
See Argenta Gap.

GRAZIANI, RODOLFO (1882–1955)   Italian field marshal and chief of staff, and dedicated *fascist*. A veteran of World War I, Graziani waged a brutal campaign against tribal rebels in Tripoli in the 1930s. He carried out indiscriminate reprisals and introduced civilian *concentration camps* of the type the British had used to defeat the Boers three decades earlier. In 1935 he moved to Italian Somaliland. Along with *Pietro Badoglio*, Graziani invaded Abyssinia in 1935. He was a brutal military governor of occupied-Abyssinia from 1936 to 1938. He was elevated to chief of staff of the Regio Esercito in October 1939. In June 1940, he took personal charge in Tripoli. He attacked the British in Egypt in September, carrying out the orders of Benito Mussolini. He was quickly routed by British and Commonwealth forces at *Sidi Barrani, Bardia, Tobruk,* and *Beda Fomm,* and retired as the *Afrika Korps* came to Mussolini's aid in North Africa. Graziani came out of retirement to serve Mussolini's German puppet regime in northern Italy, the so-called "Salò Republic." After the war he was imprisoned until 1950.

GREASE GUN   American slang for the short-range M3 automatic rifle.
See also burp guns.

GREAT BRITAIN   Successive British governments and prime ministers pursued a policy of *appeasement* of Italy, then of Germany, from the *Hoare-Laval Pact (1935)* during the *Abyssinian War (1935–1936)*, through the *Anglo–German Naval Agreement (June 18, 1935)*. Britain remained neutral toward the *Spanish Civil War (1936–1939)* as Italian, German, and Soviet forces intervened. Appeasement culminated with an extraordinary deal made by Prime Minister *Neville Chamberlain* at the *Munich Conference* in September 1938. Cabinet appeasement of Germany ended even before Adolf Hitler ignored the Munich agreements and occupied the rump of Czechoslovakia in March 1939. No military aid could be offered to the Czechs with Bohemia exposed once the *Sudetenland* was surrendered to Hitler, but the understanding Chamberlain thought he had reached with Hitler at Munich was thereafter a dead letter. London stepped up rearmament and other readiness measures, preparing for likely war with Germany. When Hitler almost immediately made fresh threats to use force against Poland, even public sentiment in favor of appeasement evaporated, replaced by dread but also firming conviction that Hitler must be stopped. The government reacted by extending an offer of firm military alliance to Poland and quickening the pace of military conversations with France.

In January 1939, the Chamberlain government made the decision to fight Germany should the Polish test case make that necessary. That was two months before Hitler occupied the Czech rump lands. What prompted the newfound resolve? Credible though false rumors had reached London that Hitler intended to attack the Netherlands. The Cabinet therefore voted in secret that Britain would come to the military aid of any nation in Europe that henceforth resisted German aggression. Chamberlain and his principal advisers still hoped to strengthen deterrence and avoid war by not repeating what was seen by many as the great British error of 1914: not announcing Great Britain's determination to fight until it was too late to change minds in Berlin or otherwise alter the course of events and mobilization for war. On February 6, 1939, London publicly declared Britain's military commitment to France, thereby strengthening French resolve to also stand and fight if it must. Britain and France belatedly extended formal military guarantees to several eastern European nations, including Poland, while also counseling Warsaw to tread lightly in its own talks with Berlin. Much of the British cabinet's and of Chamberlain's personal faith—too much, as matters turned out—was ensconced in efforts to detach Italy from the *Axis alliance* to completely isolate Germany. Secret talks began with Hitler asking him to reverse the unilateral German occupation of Bohemia and warning him against any attack on Poland. For the first time, negotiations with Herr Hitler were coupled with a public declaration made in late March that Britain and its Empire, along with France and its Empire, would indeed fight Germany should it attack Poland. The next time either diplomacy or deterrence of Hitler failed, it would mean a European war.

There followed introduction in Britain of peacetime conscription, hastened expansion of the British Expeditionary Force (BEF), and intense military and diplomatic talks with France, Belgium, the Imperial Dominions, and other potential allies. Belated approaches were also made to the Soviet Union, a state and regime detested and deeply distrusted by Chamberlain and many others in British ruling circles. Through all these sets of parallel talks, London was determined that

Germany must be opposed in its ambition to overturn the post–World War I balance of power in Europe and the international status quo, of which Britain was a principal architect and supporter. Preferably, stern opposition to German revanchism would come from a powerful alliance pursuing a modified form of *collective security*. But already the government was committed to the stance that Germany would be opposed by the British Empire alone, if necessary. The stunning surprise of announcement of the *Nazi–Soviet Pact (August 23, 1939)* did not shake that British determination. In fact, London correctly saw that Hitler would become even more aggressive now that he was free of short-term fear of a two-front war. The government sent urgent diplomatic dispatches to Berlin and Moscow on August 25, stating that Britain would indeed fight for Poland. That surprised Hitler, who momentarily delayed his attack plan when Italy also surprised him by saying it would stand aside from any Polish war. Could deterrence and diplomatic isolation of Germany work after all? Not as long as Hitler was Führer and supreme military commander of the Wehrmacht. After but a few days delay, on September 1 Hitler unleashed *FALL WEISS,* his long-planned and much longed-for invasion of Poland. Britain waited two days for its ultimatum to expire, while insisting that Germany must immediately remove all troops from Poland. Then Britain declared war. France followed that lead a few hours later, as did the Commonwealth nations within hours, days, or a week. The sole exception among the latter was the *Irish Free State,* which remained neutral.

The first U-boat sinking of the liner *Athenia* took place within hours, signaling that the *Battle of the Atlantic* would be fought in earnest. It engaged the *Royal Navy* against German surface raiders and U-boats to the last day of the war. The land battle was a different story: as Poland was overrun, the French Army refused to advance into combat by the agreed date of September 15. That was the deadline for a western offensive Paris had falsely promised the Poles, but prudently refused to meet that September. The French High Command understood that the Western Allies, especially the British, were wholly unprepared to seek a "decisive battle" with the Wehrmacht. They must instead ready their peoples, economies, and armies for a long war of attrition. Nor was Britain in a position to argue the point: it had only the tiny BEF to offer to aid the French Army in any land offensive. The few divisions of the BEF were hurriedly trained and transported to the continent, to wait alongside French mobile forces for Belgium to be invaded and Brussels to invite the Western powers to move to the *Dyle Line.* Thus followed the so-called *Phoney War,* to May 1940. It was not a phoney war at sea, however, where the Royal Navy hunted down German *auxiliary cruisers* and *U-boats.* Nor was it "phoney" to Luftwaffe pilots and anti-aircraft gunners who shot down Bomber Command air crews conducting futile *leaflet bombing* of the Ruhr. Any delusion that serious bloodletting might yet be avoided ended in the spring of 1940. On April 4 Chamberlain made the forever-after mocked assertion that Hitler had already "missed the bus" in the west. Five days later the Luftwaffe dropped *Fallschirmjäger,* not leaflets, over Denmark and Norway. The paratroopers were quickly followed by full-scale land and seaborne invasions of those small democratic countries, as the Wehrmacht unfolded Operation *WESERÜBUNG.*

Desultory, confused fighting would engage British forces on the periphery of Europe over the next five years. It began with an expedition to Norway that quickly became a debacle as it ran into the simultaneous German invasion. Failure among the fjords led to a crisis of confidence in the government, which forced Chamberlain to resign on May 10. He was replaced by Winston Churchill just as Panzers rolled into France, Belgium, and the Netherlands, and in spite of the fact that Churchill was complicit in the military failure underway in Norway. With Operation *FALL GELB* underway, the Phoney War was truly over and the British nation turned to the man who rang a clarion bell of warning about Hitler and Nazi Germany for the better part of 10 years. Meanwhile, on the ground in Belgium and France matters went from bad to appalling. The long-planned movement of the BEF and French mechanized forces into Belgium was initiated as German troops violated the Belgian frontier and the expected invitation to move arrived from Brussels. Within days the move into Belgium led to catastrophe. The Germans had settled on a different *Schwerpunkt* in the overall Allied position, attacking with the bulk of their armor through the *Ardennes* and thence across the Meuse, and more importantly, doing so far more swiftly than anyone on either side had anticipated. The disaster along the Meuse was only partly salvaged by the bold evacuation of over 300,000 troops from *Dunkirk*. By then the major fight Churchill called the "Battle of France" was already lost, decided well before the French government asked for and signed an *armistice* with Germany and France exited the war on June 22.

What everyone called the *Battle of Britain* began almost immediately as Luftwaffe and *Royal Air Force (RAF)* fighters battled over the Channel through June and July. The fight in the air was elevated to a new level with a massive German attack against southern England's airfields in mid-August. Still expecting invasion any morning, Britain shipped its gold reserves and foreign securities to Canada. That ultimately signaled to the Empire, and to the government of the United States, a drear determination to fight on even if the island of Great Britain fell under the Nazi jackboot. Britain avoided Hitler's planned invasion—Operation *SEELÖWE*—through aerial victory over southern England and the Channel, and even more importantly because of the strength of the Royal Navy and its ability to intercept any invasion fleet. Had the invasion been assayed, it is certain that scenes of spectacular and even suicidal RN defense would have been seen in and over the Channel. Instead, Britain endured the *Blitz,* or bombing of its cities that was conducted by an ill-prepared German air force over the fall and winter of 1940–1941. When aircraft losses became intolerable, Hitler called off the fight and proposed invasion. He turned instead to planning a great attack on the Soviet Union by which he hoped to deny Britain its last possible continental ally and force London's acceptance of German hegemony in Europe. For some time after that Hitler harbored a delusion that Britain might agree to a separate peace. That thought, along with his overcommitment of limited air resources to war in the east, allowed Britain time to rearm and recover. Thereafter, Great Britain served as a thousand-mile long platform for punishing Anglo-American air raids over Germany, and as the main staging ground for multiple breaches and invasions of Hitler's vaunted but vulnerable *Festung Europa.*

In the meantime, more fighting on the periphery ensued as Churchill pursued a policy of seeking to weaken and break off the outer edges of the overextended Nazi empire. London sought to lop off Germany's minor allies and to foment subversion and armed resistance within German-occupied Europe, while RAF Bomber Command hit hard at Germany's industrial heartland. Bombing would bleed and weaken Nazi Germany while Britain accrued fresh allies, not least to swell new land armies that the British did not possess and could not raise. Only at some distant, undetermined date would a main assault be made into Europe and against Germany with ground forces. That was Churchill's grand strategy. However, events on the ground forced London to commit limited resources pell-mell to defend more small countries that became victims of Axis aggression. Several minor states clung to neutrality until the last minute, as Belgium and the Netherlands had done, begging for military aid only after their borders were breached by the Regio Esercito or Wehrmacht. The British were thus drawn into a perhaps morally noble but strategically losing *Balkan campaign (1940–1941)* when Italy invaded Greece. London won a brief political victory when it successfully sponsored an anti-Nazi coup in Belgrade, but small gains made in Greece and the shift in regime in Yugoslavia were reversed by a German-led Axis invasion of both countries. The Yugoslav Army, one million strong, fell apart inside one week. The Greeks fought better, but could not hold despite rushed British reinforcement. Fleeing defeat in the Balkans, defeated British forces and remnants of the Greek Army evacuated by ship. Hitler followed them to *Crete* with a stunning air assault by Fallschirmjäger and glider troops that took the main airport, then drove the British off the island. Another battle lost, another evacuation: this time to Egypt. And as Churchill had already warned after Dunkirk: "wars are not won by evacuations."

Through all these early defeats the British government kept its resolve, though the decision to continue the fight was a more near-run thing than was known at the time outside the War Cabinet itself. The government may not have held as readily or stoutly as it did had the British people known that the German economy was not yet straining at full war capacity, as the British intelligence community wrongly thought it was. In fact, Germany still had considerable economic slack waiting to be actualized in war production. Nor did London appreciate how effectively *Gestapo* and *Schutzstaffel (SS)* tactics imposed Nazi terror across Europe, cowing entire populations into frightful subservience. If those things were known then as fully as they are today, Churchill and others might not have placed as much early stock as they did in the idea that *Special Operations Executive (SOE)* subversion and pinprick *commando* raids might seriously weaken Hitler's empire, even if just around the edges. Naval blockade, the main British strategic weapon over the centuries and in the last war with Germany, was also unlikely to do fatal damage once Germany bestrode all Europe and could rape the resources of the continent, as it quickly proceeded to do. Instead, the Royal Navy was fully engaged in a desperate fight to break a developing U-boat blockade of Great Britain, and in patrolling the Atlantic and Mediterranean sea lanes against two enemy navies. That left *strategic bombing* as the only realistic means of reaching into Germany to do real damage to its national morale, and perhaps thereby to popular and political support for the war. Germans might be bombed into overthrowing the Nazis, vitiating any need for a future seaborne invasion that was in any case beyond Britain's means. That is what strategic planners wrongly thought and even more fervently hoped, as they searched for some means, any means, to strike a blow that would inflict serious wounds on the enemy.

Defending Britain and fighting around the periphery of the Axis meant making hard choices, including destroying the French fleet at *Mers El-Kebir*. Churchill supported *Charles de Gaulle's* efforts to take control of French colonies in Africa. Rebuffed in the first effort to do so at *Dakar*, Britain gained a minor ally in Africa when *Free French* forces seized Gabon from Vichy, striking out from *French Equatorial Africa* actually against British advice. That victory led the Free French into the *Fezzan campaign (1941–1943)*. More success attended Britain's own military efforts against the Italians in the *East African campaign (1940–1941)*. The first *desert campaign* against the Italians also went well, but it stumbled once the *Afrika Korps* arrived in Tunisia to reinforce the Regio Esercito. The desert campaigns of 1940–1941 were important for restoring British military pride and building command and fighting skills. But they were of minor significant compared to two colossal events that were out of London's control but which, in combination, ensured that Britain would not only survive the war but would win it: Operation *BARBAROSSA,* the German invasion of the Soviet Union that commenced on June 22, 1941, and the Japanese attack on *Pearl Harbor* on December 7, 1941. The entry into the German war of the Soviet Union and the United States as Britain's main allies changed everything. Although the British suffered more humiliating short-term defeats at Japanese hands in *Hong Kong, Burma, Singapore,* and *Malaya,* the Axis powers had fatally overreached. The British Empire would surely survive, as Churchill well knew as he flew off to Washington to coordinate military and economic strategy, even though there still lay ahead years of total war and hard, bloody slogs across North Africa, Europe, and Southeast Asia.

With Japan in the war, the British immediately went over to a limited defense of the Imperial position in the Indian Ocean, occupying Madagascar and reinforcing Ceylon. They also opened the *Indian Army* to mass recruitment. The tide was turned also in the Greater Middle East, as Britain went over to the offensive in the Mediterranean with an impressive victory in the desert at *Second El Alamein* (1942). Operating jointly with the Americans, British-led *TORCH* landings were carried out in North Africa in early November 1942. There followed a tough but successful campaign to drive Axis forces into Tunisia and smash them there. That finished the Italian Empire and expelled the Axis from Africa. Invasion of Sicily was next: Operation *HUSKY*. There followed a less important but exclusively British show in the *Dodecanese campaign*. Lasting controversy attends London's insistence on continuing major operations in the Mediterranean. That policy led most to the problem-filled and problematic, and in many respects also poorly conducted, *Italian campaign* from 1943 to 1945. The British pushed hard for the campaign in Italy, with several top American leaders only reluctantly accepting. A Mediterranean strategy fit Churchill's and the Chiefs of Staff view of the southern theater as providing a great drain on German resources until landings could be made in

France. That may well have been true. It is much harder to defend Churchill's interest in continuing extremely hard offensive operations in Italy well after June 1944, including opposition to additional landings in southern France that August and resistance to reinforcing battered and weakened British and Canadian divisions in France with units bogged down in northern Italy. As the campaign in Italy slowed to a bloody crawl, American leaders—most notably, General *George C. Marshall*—refused to ever again defer to London's strategic preferences.

The Western Allies won the Battle of the Atlantic by mid-1943, though it did not end until the last U-boats surrendered in 1945. The victory permitted Britain to serve as a giant air base supporting great air forces that pounded Germany to the end of the war, as well as a huge staging area for assembling great armies that conducted two invasions of France and Europe in 1944: *OVERLORD* and *DRAGOON*. Germany was not toothless yet, however. Britain was therefore subjected to a second Blitz from January to May, 1944. Then it suffered attacks by Hitler's *V-weapons* from June, after the British took two of the five beaches on *D-Day (June 6, 1944)*, and while they were making a major contribution to the *Normandy campaign* and liberation of France. The RAF defended well against the last few Luftwaffe bombers over England, while the bunkers and bases of the vengeance weapons were soon overrun or bombed into silence. There followed the special disaster for the British Army and Field Marshal *Bernard Law Montgomery* of the failure of Operation *MARKET GARDEN*. British troops saw limited combat in the *Ardennes offensive* at the end of 1944, but saw heavier action during the *conquest of Germany* in 1945. Meanwhile, the Royal Navy continued its vital work securing the seal lanes across several oceans, while Bomber Command conducted the last and most devastating raids of the *Combined Bomber Offensive* against Germany.

Most able British men and women were mobilized in some form during the war—in the armed forces or women's auxiliaries, in the *Home Guard,* or in farm and factory work. By war's end Britain suffered nearly 800,000 casualties, including 383,000 killed in military operations and tens of thousands of civilians killed by bombing and other war-related causes. Food was rationed, consumer goods were scarce, and social life was constrained and dreary. The psychological burden of remaining in a state of war lasting 6.5 years was great. It would have been worse had people known that decisions were taken by the War Cabinet to commit large-scale British and Commonwealth forces to the invasion of Japan, with heavy fighting and losses expected into 1946. Fortunately, Britain had earned many foreign friends with its dedicated early war effort and sustained military commitment, especially in the United States and Commonwealth nations. Much needed aid poured in from abroad during the second half of the war: for the first time in several centuries Britain was itself a recipient of wartime aid, not the mainstay in a grand coalition. By early 1945, with casualties mounting in final battles to cross the Rhine and invade northern Germany, Britain was deeply war weary. The British were tired of blackouts, of bombing and rationing. Several decades later, a school of revisionist historians portrayed Britain as deeply divided during the war by class, criminality, and streaks of pacifism. They argued that many Britons were left unaided in misery and material privation by an indifferent government. At most, that is a greatly exaggerated portrait. The best research, which draws upon wartime files of the Home Intelligence and Mass-Observation departments ignored by the revisionists, demonstrates that the British people as a whole strongly supported the war effort and government and preserved solid national morale to the very end. Of course, it was with feelings of succor as well as joy that they celebrated *VE day* on May 8. And it was with a sense of profound relief that Britain received news of the atomic bombings of *Hiroshima* (August 6, 1945) and *Nagasaki* (August 9, 1945), Soviet entry into the Far Eastern war, and the surrender of Japan that followed those events.

See also ABC-1 Plan; ABDA Command; Air Defence of Great Britain (ADGB); Air Transport Auxiliary (ATA); Allied Control Commissions; Allied Forces Headquarters (AFHQ); Allies; Anderson shelters; Anglo–Soviet Treaty; area bombing; Atlantic Charter; Attlee, Clement; Baedeker raids; Baldwin, Stanley; BBC; Big Four; Big Three; Bletchley Park; British Union of Fascists; Brooke, Alan; Channel Islands; Chiefs of Staff Committee; Combined Chiefs of Staff; Commonwealth; Congress Party; convoys; Cripps, Richard Stafford; Eden, Anthony; Egypt; Enigma machine; Five Power Naval Treaty; Halifax, Lord; India; intelligence; Lend-Lease; limited liability; Malta; merchant marine; MI5/MI6; MI9; morale bombing; National Fire Service (NFS); Neutrality Acts; nuclear weapons programs; Palestine; Royal Air Force; shipbuilding; Special Operations Executive (SOE); strategic bombing; Territorial Army; unconditional surrender; War Office; Westminster, Statute of; XX Committee.

Suggested Reading: Raymond Callahan, *Churchill and His Generals* (2007); Martin Gilbert, *Winston Churchill* (1991); Talbot Imlay, *Facing the Second World War* (2003).

GREAT DEPRESSION (1929–1939) The sharp global economic downturn of the 1930s was marked by high unemployment, declining international trade, and a crisis of deflation. It was worsened, though it was not caused, by the stock market crash that began on Wall Street on "Black Tuesday," October 24, 1929. The crash severely aggravated a recession in the United States that began at least two months earlier. Controversy still attends the question of the Depression's deeper causes. Certainly, they included a radical decline in world money supply; rapidly falling levels of consumption of industrial products; prior depression in agricultural markets and the value of farm land; declines in mining, textiles, and other labor-intensive industries; breakdown of faith in the gold standard supporting major currencies; speculative excesses in financial markets; and a failure of U.S. economic leadership in terms of poor tax and trade policy responses during the first years of the downturn. The consensus view of mainstream economic historians sees the Depression as stemming from the core fact that the international financial system erected after World War I was inherently unstable. Failure to restore the gold standard thus led to seriatim major bank failures, which in turn caused a run on smaller banks and to calls on outstanding loans. In turn, that forced margin calls on stock markets, whose crash converted a steep American recession into a protracted depression. The slowdown in the United States greatly exacerbated the ongoing international financial crisis as still more credit dried up with American banks calling in large international loans, including to the Weimar Republic. As still more banks failed, confidence collapsed. World trade contracted under sharply increased protectionist pressure and beggar-thy-neighbor trade policies that ensued from governments of all the major economic powers.

The Depression's severe dampening effects on prices and trade were felt in all economic subfields and countries. But they were felt most quickly and disastrously in Germany, where core unemployment soared and income fears were added to the burden of an economy barely recovered from the hyperinflation of the early 1920s. Across Europe, international arguments about war debts and reparations were aggravated by new economic woes. In Germany and Japan, radicals found new legs as tentative democracies broke under the strain. In the United States alone, unemployment reached 17 million. Global commodity prices severely contracted, small firms collapsed along with some of the great banking houses, farm income plummeted, and world trade fell off sharply. All that was worsened by a round of mutually destructive, often retaliatory, protectionist tariffs, set off by the Smoot-Hawley Tariff passed in the United States on June 17, 1930. While that only marginally worsened things in the United States, it was disastrous for trading nations in Europe. A *World Economic Conference* in 1933 failed to secure any relief. Broken economic hopes soured political relations among trading nations, splitting the industrial democracies and turning attention away from issues of political and military security, including the rising revanchist and aggressive demands of Italy, Germany, and Japan. Simultaneous and mutually debilitating quarrels over reparations and war debts, a general closing of national markets, and then a complete collapse of the international trading economy handcuffed politicians of left and right, leaving ordinary people in despair that any of the traditional governing elites had real solutions. By 1932 the U.S. economy had contracted by nearly 34 percent. Losses were even worse elsewhere, as international trade fell by over 65 percent from 1929 levels. A year later, U.S. unemployment reached 25 percent.

The Depression radicalized politics everywhere to some degree. In developed economies it led to an enormous increase in direct governmental regulation and control of banking, investment, and the economy. It led to unprecedented efforts at import substitution in the poorest economies and radical demands in several major powers to pursue economic systems that sought *autarchy*. In several countries, most notably Germany and Japan, widespread public despair and anger attended failure of the traditional economy. That greatly encouraged and eased the rise to power of *fascist* and militarist regimes. In China the Depression led to several million peasant deaths from starvation as world crop prices plunged and peasants who had invested everything in now worthless cash crops were left with nothing. The poorest became evermore destitute and desperate. Some turned to follow social and political radicals from the cities. Chinese Communist Party cadres fled *Guomindang* violence in the large cities to set up "soviets" deep in the interior or southern countryside. The Depression also wreaked most colonial economies by depressing prices for all primary product exports, whatever those were in a given colony. The losses severely retarded ongoing development efforts. And that helped accelerate the pace of decolonization after World War II by preventing colonies from achieving financial and tax self-sufficiency, while also encouraging war-weary and fiscally bankrupt imperial powers to shed the financial burden of empire. The Depression put a sudden halt to a prolonged export-fed boom that most Latin American countries enjoyed from 1850 to 1930. Exports grew by a factor of 10 over those decades, an extraordinary rate that greatly expanded light manufacturing, early heavy industrialization, and created a railway and steamship transportation revolution in what were originally almost wholly agrarian economies. This great Latin boom lasted only until the Depression collapsed world commodity prices, compressed primary mineral and agricultural export markets, and erected insurmountable barriers to trade.

Germany was the first major industrial country to recover from the employment slump, though it did not recover on its own from the wider Depression. That was beyond the reach of any single country or policy precisely because the downturn was global in cause and scope. The Nazis decreased German unemployment through massive public spending and works programs, many of them also military spending programs such as the construction of the *Autobahns*. Military and other deficit spending pumped liquidity into the economy, to some degree combating the underlying problem of deflation. By 1935 gross national products were growing in most major economies and some jobs returned. However, in 1937 the U.S. economy reentered recession and unemployment began to rise once more, as some of President Franklin D. Roosevelt's tax and social policies actually undermined a still-shaky recovery. The United States and other industrial democracies did not finally recover until they, too, began to spend heavily on military preparedness measures and weaponry during the late 1930s, carrying military spending over on a still more massive scale during the first half of the 1940s. The Depression then exerted a paradoxical effect: it had produced so much slack in the U.S. and other major economies that conversion to war production proved remarkably fast and efficient, as well as quite popular nearly everywhere.

See individual countries, and *see also appeasement; fascism; Mussolini, Benito; Nazi Party; Nazism; shipbuilding.*

GREATER EAST ASIA CO-PROSPERITY SPHERE   "Dai To-a Kyoeiken." A term minted by Matsuoka Yosuke (1880–1946), the Japanese diplomat who led his country's delegation out of the *League of Nations*. It was used to frame a claim to a "natural" and exclusive sphere of influence in Asia that other Great Powers must respect. It was part euphemism, part slogan, and part theory of *autarky* ostensibly modeled on the British Empire. All of that masked a core reality of brutal imperial expansion by force into Manchuria, China, Southeast Asia, and across the Pacific from 1931 to 1942. On the other hand, for some idealistic Japanese it represented a genuine sense of mission in Asia that was harsher in practice, but no more or less cynical or sincere in theory, than comparable justifications for empire such as the French "mission civilisatrice," British notions of the "white man's burden," or American views of "manifest destiny." The policy was confirmed at an Imperial Conference on July 2, 1941. In the Philippines and across much of Southeast Asia there was armed resistance to Japanese occupation policies and economic exploitation. In some countries, such as Burma, segments of the local population allied with the invaders. That reflected a deep and much older hostility to European empire in Asia, as well as more recent effects of the *Great Depression* on colonial economies. With a fresh and rising set of nationalisms across the region stimulated into political activism by the war, hostility to the return of European empires would find full expression after the Japanese were expelled in 1945. A single "Great East Asia Conference" was held in 1943. It was attended by the heads of various puppet states and minor allies, including Manchuria ("Manchukuo"), several client regimes in occupied-China, Burma, the Philippines, and Siam. *Subhas Chandra Bose* represented India. Japan did not invite representatives from occupied French Indochina, preferring to maintain the fiction that it was still controlled by *Vichy*. Of course, the entire conference was a charade.

See also Asia for Asians; Burma National Army; Dutch East Indies; French Indochina; Hirohito; Indian National Army; Kokutai; Pacific War (1941–1945); Philippines; Sino-Japanese War (1937–1945); Tōjō, Hideki; Wang Jingwei; Yamashita, Tomoyuki.

GREATER EAST ASIAN WAR (1941–1945) Japanese nomenclature for what others call the *Pacific War*.

GREAT FATHERLAND WAR (JUNE 22, 1941–MAY 9, 1945) Or "Great Patriotic War" ("Velikaya Otechestvennaya Voina"), June 22, 1941–May 8, 1945. Soviet and Russian term for the German-Soviet war commencing on June 22, 1941, the date of the German invasion. It lasted until May 8, 1945, when Germany unconditionally surrendered to Soviet representatives in front of Western witnesses a day after surrendering to Western representatives before Soviet witnesses. The term was used contemporaneously, starting with the first edition of *Pravda* to appear after the launch of *BARBAROSSA*. It replaced the cynical term "*Second Imperialist War*" used until then about the conflict in Europe. The new nomenclature reflected realization within the Kremlin—and even by the sharp-knived but dull-witted *NKVD*—that old Communist slogans were insufficient to rouse the population to defense of the state and regime. That insight arose from shocked realization that many Soviet citizens—especially in Belorussia, Ukraine, and in Cossack and other "ethnic" lands farther south—were greeting the Germans not as invaders but as liberators. An even more widespread and profoundly nationalist reaction was manifest among ethnic Russians. Once the war reached the borders of Old Russia a fiercely determined response met Joseph Stalin's call to resist the invaders at all costs. That reaction was evident in ferocious and sometimes suicidal resistance by Red Army soldiers and VVS pilots. The ideological shift led to major changes in propaganda, which celebrated old Russian national heros against Teutonic invaders, notably Alexander Nevsky. Churches reopened in response to a strong revival of religious feeling. The Red Army reverted to issuance of distinct officer uniforms, titles and ranks. A series of personal awards was instituted, in addition to collective awards for valor and honorific titles issued to divisions or armies. The changed approach at the top even admitted celebration of Tsarist military heroes: medals were issued in the name of Alexandr Suvorov, hero of Catherine II's wars against the Ottomans, and Mikhail Kutuzov, hero of the Battle of Borodino and bane of Napoleon during the bloody French retreat from Moscow in 1812.

It is important to note that in Soviet and Russian historiography the German–Soviet war is periodized into three prosaically entitled "First," "Second," and "Third" Periods. During the First Period (June 22, 1941–November 18, 1942), Axis forces held the initiative all along the Eastern Front, driving within reach of Leningrad and Moscow in the north and center, past Kiev and into the Crimea and Caucasus in the south. Wehrmacht combat power greatly exceeded that of the Red Army in the First Period, so that Soviet forces were badly shattered and largely remade, rearmed, and retrained as a result of catastrophic losses. Russian historians consider the Second Period (November 19, 1942–December 31, 1943) to be one of transition by the Red Army from strategic defense to strategic offense with major counteroffensives at *Stalingrad* and *Kursk,* among numerous other campaigns. It was during the Second Period that the Red Army surpassed the Wehrmacht in fighting capabilities and achieved full military modernity. It was also at that time that the ultimate outcome of the war and shape of the peace was decided: total Soviet victory and unconditional and utter German defeat. The Third Period (January 1, 1944–May 9, 1945) was marked by near-continuous, rolling Red Army offensives. Corresponding German retreats and major defeats were occasionally interrupted by mostly failed and always merely local Wehrmacht counteroffensives. Fighting did not end until the Wehrmacht ceased to function as a modern military and the Red Army planted its flags atop the rubble of Berlin and half the capitals of Europe.

Campaigns and battles of the "Great Fatherland War" are dealt with elsewhere in this work under discrete headings. Some use accepted Soviet nomenclature, such as *"Moscow offensive operation"* (December 5, 1941–January 7, 1942). Others are listed under more familiar German terminology, such as *BARBAROSSA.* Cross-references exist to main entries in either case.

GREAT MARIANAS TURKEY SHOOT (JUNE 19–20, 1944)
See Philippine Sea, Battle of.

GREECE On October 28, 1940, Greece was invaded by ill-prepared Italian forces moving out of Albania according to hastily made operational plans. Successful resistance against the Italian Army during the *Balkan campaign (1940–1941)* brought German and Bulgarian troops into Greece on April 6, 1941, in Operation MARITA. The Greek Army discovered that the Wehrmacht was a much tougher foe than the Regio Esercito had proven. While the main Greek force succumbed by April 23, some units and the government left Greece with the British to fight on from *Crete.* After that island was taken by a stunning airborne assault by German *Fallschirmjäger,* the Greeks again evacuated alongside the British for Egypt. Twelve Greek warships also made it to safe harbor in Egypt. The military disaster of 1941 was followed by a famine that took over 100,000 Greek lives over the winter of 1941–1942. The Axis states divided Greece into separate occupation zones until September 1943, when the Italian surrender to the Western Allies led the Wehrmacht to move against the Regio Esercito in Greece and elsewhere in the Balkans and northern Italy. The Germans occupied Greece alone for another year, facing both Communist and Nationalist resistance in the mountains as the tide of war turned against Germany more generally.

The arrival of a British Expeditionary Force and the start of the *MANNA* operation in late 1944 aimed in part at blocking a Communist victory in Greece. At the same time, it led to liberation of Athens from the Germans by October 18, as the Wehrmacht pulled out of the entire country. Civil war broke out immediately between Communists and forces loyal to an anti-Communist government-in-exile based in Cairo and backed diplomatically and militarily by the British. Fierce fighting took place in and around Athens during December, threatening the Balkan strategy, which Winston Churchill still favored. Fighting in Greece thus prompted a remarkable decision by Churchill to fly personally to Athens to mediate a truce. A ceasefire was agreed on January 11, 1945. British support for anti-Communists, some of whom collaborated with the Axis occupation, was bitterly resented in Washington as well as by Greek Communists. Admiral *Ernest King* actually transferred U.S. warships under the British flag rather than supply Greeks with ships flying American colors. Greece thereafter simmered with internal hostilities born of defeat as well as ideology and class conflict. London and Washington subsequently supported the monarchists in a renewed civil war that lasted from 1947 to 1949. Greek Communists were backed by the Soviet Union as the country moved out of World War II into the Cold War.

See also Dodecanese campaign; Greek Sacred Regiment; merchant marine; Moscow Conference; Royal Hellenic Army; Sacred Band.

GREEK SACRED REGIMENT
See Raiding Forces; Sacred Band.

GREEN (1938)
See Czechoslovakia; FALL GRÜN (1938).

GREEN (1940)
See FALL GRÜN (1940); Irish Free State; TANNENBAUM; Switzerland.

GREEN GANG "Qingbang." A secret society of criminal businessmen in Shanghai. They had shadowy dealings with Sun Yixian in the early days of the 1911 Chinese Revolution. The Green Gang participated in *Jiang Jieshi's* purge and murder of Chinese Communists, known as the "Shanghai massacre," in 1928. It then became a principal partner of Jiang Jieshi through the 1930s. Loyal only to money, the gangsters established ties with the *Imperial Japanese Army* during the Japanese occupation of the city.

GREEN ISLANDS   A small group located 60 miles east of New Ireland. In early 1944 the Green Islands lay between two strong Japanese positions on Buka and Bougainville. A 300-man New Zealander reconnaissance team surveyed Nissan, the largest island in the group, on the night of January 30–31. A brigade from 3rd New Zealand Division attacked Nissan on February 15, 1944. The defending Japanese garrison was small and in hiding. Initial resistance was light as the Japanese did not contest the landings. A small fight took place on the islet of Sirot, but the main action on Nissan was delayed until February 20th, when strongly reinforced New Zealanders overwhelmed the remaining Japanese. Ragged Japanese survivors were hunted down over the following months. Over 1,000 Green Islanders were evacuated to Guadalcanal as the Western Allies turned the islands into an air and naval base. New Zealand troops held the group until May 30, 1944, when they handed the islands off to the Americans.

GREENLAND   From April 9, 1940, this Danish colony was cut loose of metropolitan control by the German occupation of Denmark. In April 1941, the Danish government-in-exile signed an agreement with the still-neutral United States to permit "joint defense" of Greenland. That meant hosting U.S. air bases and elements of the Coast Guard. Western Allied planes thereafter flew deep ocean *antisubmarine warfare* patrols during the remaining years of the *Battle of the Atlantic*. Greenland was also important in convoy and invasion weather prediction. Unknown to the Western Allies, its vast and empty east coast hosted several Kriegsmarine weather stations used to alert U-boats about impending storms.

GREENLAND GAP
See air gaps.

GREEN LINE
See Gothic Line.

GREEN PLAN
See Force Française de l'Intérieur (FFI).

GRENADE (FEBRUARY 23–MARCH 23, 1945)
See conquest of Germany (1945).

GRENADES   Hand-thrown bombs. Most grenades used in World War II were high explosive fragmentary bombs or incendiaries using white phosphorus. Some produced smoke. They were used to create local smokescreens or to lay down spotter signals for attack aircraft. The British Army and Wehrmacht used the same types of grenades as they had during World War I. British grenades, notably the *Mills bomb,* were heavier and more explosive, and thus deadlier, than the German "potato masher" M24 stick-grenade ("Steilhandgranate"). The Red Army issued two types of stick grenade: the M1914/30 and the RGD 33. Soviet soldiers had two types of antipersonnel or "pineapple" grenades, an ineffective RPG anti-tank stick grenade used early in the war, a Dyakonov rifle grenade, and several types of smoke and heat bombs. U.S. Army GF-2 "pineapple" grenades were similar in appearance and weight to Japanese Army standard models, with the latter somewhat more square in shape. All armies employed rifle grenades, usually by adding adapters such as the American M7 grenade launcher to a standard infantry rifle. The Japanese used a unique, mortar-like weapon to hurl their Type-89 fragmentation and other grenades up to 650 yards.

GROSSDEUTSCHLAND DIVISION
See Manteuffel, Hasso von; Schutzstaffel (SS); Waffen-SS.

GROSSRAUM
See geopolitik.

GROSSTRANSPORTRAUM   The German lorry (truck) fleet, used to supply formations that had outrun the reach of rail transport. During *BARBAROSSA* this occurred at roughly 500 km from jump off points in eastern Poland, Germany, and the Baltic states. The fleet proved woefully inadequate to the logistic task it was assigned, which significantly contributed to the slowing of attack momentum and then the miserable conditions suffered by German troops who had inadequate shelter and little winter clothing over the winter of 1941–1942. By late November 1941, frontline Wehrmacht units were also running short of ammunition of all types despite frantic railway extensions by German pioneers. They also ran low on fuel for surviving Panzers and other AFVs, and of spare parts for machine guns and vehicles and aircraft of all types. The main fleet was supplemented by trucks commandeered from across German-occupied Europe. That only added to difficulties of upkeep and overly complicated repair and spare parts supply for the logistics service itself.

GROUP (AIR FORCE)   A very large Western Allied air formation, in the RAF comprising several *Wings* and all the base, air crew, repair crew, logistics, and support personnel that supported them. In the French *l'Armée de l'Air* a "groupe" resembled a RAF squadron, but included ground personnel. In the USAAF the group was the principal tactical unit for bombers, comprising 3–4 squadrons of 9–10 aircraft each.
See also carrier air group; Gruppe.

GROUP (U.S. ARMY)   Not to be confused with an *Army Group,* this was a far smaller level of command for nondivisional U.S. combat, signals, and support troops. Each group HQ commanded four or five *battalions,* in particular of tanks and tank destroyers not in regular divisions. This level of HQ replaced a system of organic service and special units attached to each corps and army, serving as a tactical HQ for training and combat without incurring a new level of administration in the field.

GRU "Glavnoye Rasvedyvatelnoye Upravlenie," or "Main Intelligence Directorate" of the *General Staff* of the Red Army. Just before the war the GRU was headed by General *Philipp I. Golikov.* It did not fail to detect German preparations for *BARBAROSSA* on June 22, 1941, but it could not convince Joseph Stalin—and most of its officers were afraid to try—that imminent invasion was Adolf Hitler's true intention. Its General Staff operational work must have been considerable, but it still remains mostly secret and unknown. Inference from the success of late-war Soviet operations suggests that the GRU was quite adept in penetrating, understanding, and predicting German moves on many occasions. But inference is not knowledge. It is known that the GRU was active in running networks of agents scouting German and other military information outside the Soviet Union, from Japan and the United States to Great Britain, Germany, and various neutral countries. Subsequently, the most famous was the *LUCY* network in Switzerland.

GRUPPE The basic Luftwaffe administrative and combat unit, comprising about 30 aircraft early in the war but later dropping well below that number due to heavy attrition. Each Gruppe was formed with a single aircraft type—attack aircraft, medium bombers, or fighters. A Gruppe was roughly comparable to a Soviet *air regiment*. A RAF, RCAF, or USAAF *Group* was a much larger formation.

GUADALCANAL, BATTLE OF (NOVEMBER 12–15, 1942) At the peak of fighting during the *Guadalcanal campaign (1942–1943),* the Japanese tried to supplement inadequate *Tokyo Express* runs to Guadalcanal by bringing in the rest of 38th Army Division. Over 7,000 men moved toward Guadalcanal in a heavily escorted convoy of 11 troop ships. U.S. intelligence learned of the convoy and set to intercept it with two heavy cruisers, three light cruisers, and a number of destroyers. This task force met a Japanese surface bombardment group intending to shell Henderson Field, composed of two older battleships, a light cruiser, and supporting destroyers. In a brutal night action at remarkably and unusually close range, but lasting under 30 minutes, nine warships were sunk. Six of the lost ships were American. Among the IJN losses was one of the battleships, which went under a few hours after taking severe damage. Scouts followed by bombers of the *Cactus Air Force* based at Henderson found the troop convoy on November 14. The bombers sank an escorting Japanese heavy cruiser, damaged three more cruisers, and sank 7 of the 11 troop ships. Most men who went into the water were picked up by Japanese destroyers, but the troop convoy was reduced to just four ships. Two USN battleships and four destroyers reached Guadalcanal that same day. In a rare battleship vs. battleship engagement, three U.S. destroyers were sunk and one battleship was badly damaged. In exchange, the Japanese lost a second battleship, which was supported in the fight by a force of heavy cruisers. The four surviving troop ships beached and hurriedly unloaded their men and cargo.

Suggested Reading: Eric Hammel, *Guadalcanal: Decision at Sea* (1988).

GUADALCANAL CAMPAIGN (AUGUST 7, 1942–FEBRUARY 7, 1943) By mid-summer 1942, the USN had turned the tide of the naval war against the IJN at the *Coral Sea* and *Midway*. However, U.S. land forces had yet to recover from blows suffered in the first *Philippines campaign (1941–1942)*. A hastily organized first counter by the Western Allies in the Pacific struck the *Solomon Islands*. A quickly arranged landing was made, code named Operation CACTUS. The initial aim was to block further Japanese expansion rather than initiate a strategic counteroffensive. Landings of over 14,000 men from U.S. 1st Marine Division were carried out on August 7, 1942, with 11,000 deposited at Lunga point on the northeast corner of the large island of Guadalcanal. About 3,000 marines landed across the New Georgia Sound—called "The Slot" later in the battle—on the small island of Tulagi and on six islets of the nearby Florida (Nggela) Islands. There was a sharp two-day fight on Tulagi against elite Japanese defenders, *Rikusentai* (Special Naval Landing Forces), guarding naval facilities and a seaplane base. There was also resistance—nearly to the last man—by Rikusentai on Guvatu and Tananbogo, in fighting lasting until August 9. Japanese near the main landing site on Guadalcanal were taken by surprise, however. Marines quickly overcame the few defenders and seized an airfield still under construction. Soon renamed "Henderson Field," the air strip became the focus of repeated and ferocious Japanese counterattacks over the following months even as it was expanded by USN Seabees.

Imperial General Headquarters in Tokyo decided to fight all-out for Guadalcanal. Emergency naval and ground reinforcements were sent steaming to the Solomons, while land-based bombers from *Rabaul* immediately struck the beachhead: Guadalcanal was a "triphibious" battle on both sides. On August 9, a strong force of seven IJN cruisers intercepted the warship screen protecting landing and supply ships off Guadalcanal. In the Battle of Savo Island the IJN cruisers again demonstrated superior Japanese night-fighting skills by sinking three U.S. cruisers and damaging another, and sinking a Royal Australian Navy cruiser. Without suffering serious damage to themselves, the Japanese littered "Iron Bottom Sound" with the hulks of four Allied cruisers and the bones of 1,270 enemy sailors. Fortunately for marines on the island, the Japanese cruisers did not steam into the landing zone, where they could have ravaged exposed supply ships and troop transports and pounded the men on shore. Out of fear of daylight air attack from Henderson, the Japanese ships instead withdrew before dawn. In a decision for which Admiral *Frank Fletcher* has been much criticized, supporting U.S. carriers also withdrew beyond range of any Japanese land-based bombers. That rendered them unable to provide naval air cover to marines fighting onshore. All the fighting men could rely on was a scratch force of two squadrons of Marine Corps planes and a few U.S. Army fighters flying out of Henderson Field. This "Cactus Air Force" had been delivered to Guadalcanal on August 20 by a fast escort carrier. Along with the fleet carriers, all partially and some fully unloaded supply ships also pulled out. That left the marines critically short of ammunition and food as their fight continued unabated. Only five days of food supply had been landed before Fletcher left. Captured Japanese stocks and rationing stretched that to two weeks.

A pattern of raids and counter raids along the Matanikau River developed early, as marine patrols encountered Japanese defenders probing the marine perimeter on the Lunga peninsula. The first Japanese reinforcements arrived by destroyer: over 900 men of the "Ichiki Detachment" led by Kiyonao Ichiki, the recklessly aggressive officer who started the *Sino-Japanese War* (1937–1945) by unauthorized and extremely aggressive action during the *Marco Polo Bridge incident*. In a blunt and unimaginative assault, Ichiki and 85 percent of his men were killed in a fierce engagement at what was thought to be the Tenaru River. It was not: neither side had good maps, and mistaken positioning was more the rule than the exception in the first weeks of fighting. More Japanese 17th Army reinforcements, led by Lieutenant General Harukichi Hyakatake, arrived from Truk and New Guinea. The new arrivals included 1,400 more Ichiki men, eager for vengeance, along with 500 more Rikusentai. U.S. forces were strengthened by 1,100 men moved from Tulagi. A critical ground reinforcement race was underway: by the end of August the Allies had 25,000 men engaged while the Japanese built up a force of over 10,000. New Zealander and Australian *coast watchers* looked for Japanese troop convoys and bombardment or attack task forces moving through "The Slot," and gave advance warning of incoming air strikes from Rabaul as daily air battles swirled over Henderson field. From August 23–25, supporting navies fought a carrier action in the *Battle of the Eastern Solomons,* after which each damaged fleet withdrew.

On September 12 a three-column Japanese attack on the perimeter around Henderson Field was repulsed with heavy losses, notably in a fight involving one column assaulting U.S. Army Rangers on "Bloody Ridge" (or "Edson's Ridge"). On September 18, Imperial General Headquarters decided to give Guadalcanal highest priority in the South Pacific. Henderson Field was identified as the main target for renewed attacks by Japanese Army reinforcements to be sent in from all over the *Greater East Asian Co-Prosperity Sphere.* The Allies also poured in reinforcements, bringing in a total of 123,000 men by the end of December. The Japanese brought their strength up to 92,000 over the same period. Protecting or attacking transport of arriving troops and supplies led to several naval battles in the waters around Guadalcanal. Each side also sent submarines and bombers to prowl "The Slot." The IJN landed the Sendai Division near the Matanikau in October, while the USN landed the *Americal Division* on Lunga. The IJN carried out dangerous night runs down "The Slot" with cruisers and destroyers. At the end of the run they bombarded Henderson Field and marine trenches with naval guns, but always pulled out before dawn exposed them to retaliatory air attack. Reinforcements arrived via what Japanese called the "Rat Express" (on destroyers) or "Ant Freight" (on motor torpedo boats). The Allied press dubbed the Japanese supply system the "*Tokyo Express*." On October 11–12 elements of the opposing fleets fought the *Battle of Cape Esperance.* On the 14th, two Japanese battleships bombarded Henderson, followed by IJN cruiser attacks on subsequent nights.

On October 23-24 General Hyakatake launched a major ground offensive seeking to overrun Henderson Field. The assault was badly planned and quickly blunted. The naval *Battle of Santa Cruz* was fought from October 26-27, as the supply struggle continued at sea. General *Hideki Tōjō* and the Army Ministry wanted to cut losses on Guadalcanal and pull the survivors out, but the General Staff decided that the island must be held. A titanic tussle ensued over resupply and reinforcement as the Japanese attempted to land the rest of their 38th Division in November, in a last effort to build up Hyakatake's attacking forces so that he could overrun Henderson Field. The effort to move in more Japanese reinforcements led to the three-day naval *Battle of Guadalcanal* from November 12-15. That conflict saw heavy warship losses by both sides but more critical troopship losses by the Japanese. The failure to reinforce doomed Japanese ground forces on Guadalcanal, as the IJN grew more cautious and made fewer runs of the Tokyo Express—despite their success with one run that developed into the *Battle of Tassafaronga* on November 30. Japanese troops began to doubt their naval support, just as U.S. Marines doubted theirs during the first days of the campaign. The American marines were relieved in December by a fresh corps from the U.S. Army. The Japanese were now the ones hemmed inside a contracting defense perimeter that was pounded daily by the enemy. On January 4, 1943, Tokyo ordered evacuation of all remaining forces. Over 13,000 Japanese crept out of *octopus pots* and sniper pits and headed for the embarkation beaches. Starting on January 23, they were taken off the island by convoys of fast destroyers. The operation culminated in a *Dunkirk*-like night evacuation (Operation Ke) that was carried out without much American interference over several days. The last convoy headed north on February 7. The Japanese Army lost over 25,000 men in the campaign on Guadalcanal, about 40 percent to disease rather than in combat. American casualties were under 1,800 killed but over 4,000 wounded in land combat. Many more were killed at sea, and there were many thousands of marines and soldiers sick with tropical diseases. After Guadalcanal, the Japanese never again held the initiative in the Pacific. The campaign was a critical turning point psychologically as well as strategically: the Japanese were never again seen as invincible fighters, though they always remained tough and relentless opponents.

See also blockade running.

Suggested Reading: Richard B. Frank, *Guadalcanal* (1992).

GUAM Part of the *Marianas Islands* group, this isolated island was an "unincorporated territory" of the United States after its acquisition from Spain during the Spanish–American War (1898). It was seized by Japan on December 8, 1941, a few hours after the attack on Pearl Harbor. Japanese occupation was brutal, not just for American prisoners of war—a number of whom were sadistically murdered—but also for the Chamorro population, which was maltreated and regarded with racist contempt by the new occupiers. Guam was scheduled for invasion on June 18, 1944, but the assault was delayed until the USN countered the threat of IJN intervention in the *Battle of the Philippine Sea (June 19–20, 1944)*. The postponement permitted defenders to reinforce dugouts and pillboxes, but also subjected them to prolonged bombing and shelling. The island was assaulted by U.S. forces starting on July 21, with the attackers immediately running into a fortified beach line. Still, an overwhelming force of over 55,000 Americans came ashore after the most intense naval and air bombardment of the Pacific War. They faced 18,000–20,000 tough defenders in the Japanese garrison.

The 3rd Marine Division landed on the north side of the Orote peninsula while 77th Infantry Division landed on the south side, against strong opposition. The Americans advanced in a pincer maneuver toward the main airfield and population centers. Fighting was hard. The Japanese held fixed positions with their usual tenacity, while infiltrating and counterattacking repeatedly at night. A major fixed-position fight occurred at Mount Barrigada from August 2–4. Once the Japanese line was broken, their resistance rapidly collapsed. A more mobile phase began as American armor and Marines pursued retreating Japanese to the northern tip of the island. The last well-organized Japanese defenders were not finally defeated until August 8. U.S. forces suffered about 1,100 casualties retaking the island, which was formally declared secure on August 10. The Japanese lost nearly all their men, many in futile and bloody *banzai charges* over the first week of August. After the main Japanese resistance was broken, Guam served as a forward logistics base for operations in the second *Philippines campaign* (1944–1945). Several thousand Japanese soldiers retreated into the jungle, where they survived and some continued to fight as guerillas until 1945. One man, Sergeant Shoichi Yokoi, did not emerge or surrender until 1972.

GUANDONG ARMY "East of the Barrier." This quasi-independent army spearheaded Japan's imperial thrust on the Asian mainland during the first half of the 20th century. Its name derived from an original garrison position in the "Guandong Leased Area," between northern China at the Great Wall and three northeastern provinces of China, or Manchuria, that were long coveted by Japan. The Guandong Army was in place in Manchuria from 1905. Over time, it became almost independent of civilian authority, and later even of central military control. It exerted disproportionate influence over foreign and military policy, pushing Tokyo away from international trade toward a policy of territorial expansion and economic *autarky*. Its radical and increasingly *fascist* young officer corps plotted and carried numerous assassinations, provocations of the Chinese, and serial aggression. They attempted unsuccessfully to provoke a war with Nationalist China in 1928 by assassinating Zhang Zuolin, the "Old Marshal." Officers of the Guandong Army then staged the *Mukden incident* on September 18, 1931, as a prelude to conquest of Manchuria on the way to fulfillment of Japan's "unavoidable destiny" of mainland empire.

The Guandong Army next seized Rehe province and skirmished with Chinese Nationalist forces south of the Great Wall. An attempt by Guandong leaders to conquer Mongolia by supporting proxy Mongol forces failed in 1936. The Guandong Army was by then expanded to four divisions and 18 air squadrons. Those troops were supposed to protect against the Red Army in Manchuria, but their local leaders continuously pressed for more expansion into northern China. When Tokyo refused permission, they moved anyway. All-out invasion of northern China was assayed in 1937 following production of another false casus belli, this one created by the neighboring North China Garrison Army: the *Marco Polo Bridge Incident*. The Guandong Army again recklessly committed Japan to military action at *Nomonhan* in 1939, this time against the Soviet Union, whose forces badly bloodied the ill-prepared Japanese. The German Army fought extensively in northern and central China during the opening campaigns of the *Sino-Japanese War (1937–1945)*. During the Pacific War it was held in reserve against a possible Soviet strike, which finally came with the *Manchurian offensive operation* in August 1945. Crushed by the Red Army in just two weeks, the Guandong Army collapsed all along the front. Its last campaign saw mass surrenders to Chinese, Mongolian, and Soviet forces.

See also Imperial Japanese Army; Nanjing, Rape of; Tōjō, Hideki; Unit 731.

GUARDS   A unit-wide honorific granted to certain veteran units of the *Red Army*. Their men were mainly ethnic Russians. Most Guards Divisions contained some formerly wounded men returning to action and valued because of their wounds as veteran and courageous soldiers, whether that was true or not.

See also Guards Army; Guards Corps; Guards Division.

GUARDS ARMY   During 1942–1943 the Red Army granted 11 *infantry armies* the collective honorific of "Guards" for performance in combat. All were thereafter designated "Guards Armies." 1st Guards Army was elevated on August 5, 1942. The 11th and last was designated "Guards" in April 1943. Comprised of all-Guards Corps and Guards Divisions, these elite and veteran armies were usually held in the second echelon or the Stavka reserve until a critical moment of assault, reinforcement, or counterattack. There were no "Guards Air Armies," but some air units were designated "Guards Aviation Corp."

GUARDS AVIATION CORP
See Guards Army; Guards Division.

GUARDS CORPS   Forty out of 140 Red Army rifle corps formed during World War II were granted the collective honorific "Guards" for performance in combat. Nine out of 30 mechanized corps were similarly honored, along with 12 out of 31 tank corps and 7 of 17 cavalry corps.

GUARDS DIVISION   The first elevation of a Red Army division to "Guards Division" status was made on September 18, 1941. The honorific signaled outstanding collective conduct in battle and upheld the division as a model of defensive courage and aggressive offensive spirit. Of 430 *rifle divisions* in the Red Army, over the course of the war 117 were designated Guards Divisions. Another 6 artillery divisions were elevated to Guards status, as were 7 mortar divisions, 6 anti-aircraft divisions, and 17 cavalry divisions. To additionally honor units previously elevated to Guards status, some Guards divisions were allowed to use place names of battles in which they performed well. Others were designated "Guards Red Banner Division." Five airborne divisions were honored as Guards (or battle or place name) divisions. *Red Army Air Force (VVS)* divisions were also designated "Guards Divisions," including 18 divisions each of bombers, fighters, and ground-attack aircraft, and one of mixed aircraft.

GUARDS RED BANNER DIVISION
See Guards Division.

GUDERIAN, HEINZ WILHELM (1888–1954)

German tank commander and Wehrmacht chief of staff. He served as an infantry officer in World War I. In the 1930s he studied the ideas on tank combat of *Charles de Gaulle,* B. H. Liddell Hart, and J.F.C. Fuller, adapting them for the Panzers he later commanded. He made a small splash with his own book: *Achtung Panzer!* After the war he greatly inflated his claim to be the father of the Panzer division and German mechanized warfare. It was instead a fierce personal commitment to Adolf Hitler that was the true underpinning of his professional advancement. He hid that loyalty after the war in numerous interviews and in his mendacious memoirs. Guderian's ideas on tanks but also his evident devotion to the Nazi regime brought him to Hitler's attention. Guderian thereafter gained rapid promotion, initially to command of a Panzer division in time to lead his tanks unopposed into Vienna during the *Anschluss* with Austria, and once again into an unresisting *Sudetenland* in 1938. He was rapidly promoted to General der Panzertruppen then to Chef der Schnellen Truppen, putting him in charge of Germany's developing mobile forces. He thus oversaw tank and mechanized infantry development just before the war began.

Guderian commanded 19th Panzerkorps in Operation *FALL WEISS,* the invasion of Poland in 1939. His tanks dashed through the Polish Corridor and East Prussia to form the outer ring enveloping the last hard-pressed Polish army during that campaign. Playing well to publicity-hungry propagandists inside Germany, Guderian embellished his reputation for skillful daring at that time, repeating his claims after the war. He commanded 19th Panzerkorps again during the invasion of France in May–June 1940, Operation *FALL GELB.* This time he better deserved the reputation he gained for daring and aggressive action. His Panzer divisions emerged from the *Ardennes* and broke through thin French defenses at the edge of the *Maginot Line* at Sedan. His pressed ahead with his tanks while follow-on leg infantry crossed the Meuse, all with a harrowingly narrow margin of success. Guderian then raced his Panzers to the Atlantic coast, in spite of two direct orders from General *Günther von Kluge* and the *OKH* to stop. His superiors at OKH feared that Guderian would outrun his supplies and invite an Allied counterattack into the exposed flanks of his armored columns. When neither event materialized, Guderian's gamble paid off. It was also Guderian's tanks that Hitler and Field Marshal *Gerd von Rundstedt* halted, turning them south to face the remnants of the French Army rather than race to cut off the British from escape from destruction at *Dunkirk*.

During *BARBAROSSA*, the invasion of the Soviet Union in mid-1941, Guderian led 2nd Panzerarmee at the cutting edge of the main assault by Army Group Center. Once again he displayed command dexterity, helping encircle whole Soviet armies at Minsk, Smolensk, and Kiev. Those were some of the most massive victories and prisoner hauls in the history of war. But once more he bickered with superiors, especially von Kluge. Guderian took the disagreement directly to Hitler, but failed to win unequivocal support from his Führer. Moved back to the central front from Ukraine, Guderian's final advance toward Moscow stalled, as did the whole German offensive, during the final phase of Operation *TAIFUN* (September–December, 1941). When he retreated tactically to save his Panzer formations from being overrun during the *Moscow offensive operation (December 5, 1941–January 7, 1942),* he was dismissed for disobeying Hitler's direct *Haltebefehl order* to stand fast. Having lost an active command, Guderian was reassigned to oversee the *Ersatzheer* or Army reserve. In February 1943, in the wake of disaster for the Wehrmacht at *Stalingrad,* he was appointed "Generalinspekteur der Panzertruppen." Working closely with *Albert Speer* to up-tempo the German economy, Guderian was responsible for a number of improvements in tank design and for key production decisions as he set about with his usual energy to reform the armored divisions and *Panzergrenadiers* available to Hitler and the Wehrmacht. None of his reforms did more than delay the fact that the Wehrmacht was already fighting desperate and mostly losing battles all along the Eastern Front.

Following the *July Plot* (1944) to kill Hitler, Guderian was appointed Army Chief of Staff. As such, he participated fully and eagerly in the so-called "Honor Court," which purged the Wehrmacht officer corps, sent many officers to their deaths, and thoroughly deepened final *nazification* of the German military. That dishonorable behavior was fully in character: Guderian was intensely personally loyal to Hitler almost to the end and was always ambitiously pro-Nazi. That reality has been obscured because after the war he successfully portrayed himself as apolitical, a true professional who always stood up to the rank amateur Hitler, but never had the power to carry the argument or block the orders of his Führer. Until he resigned in March 1945, it is true that Guderian engaged in tactical and operational arguments with Hitler, as he had always done with all his superiors. He disputed strategy and late-war, nonsensical dispositions, but he never questioned the morality or purpose of the Nazi cause even while serving up to his master the best technical and operational advice at his disposal. At the end of the war Guderian surrendered to American troops. He was held for three years but never tried. Instead, he wrote a highly influential but lying war memoir. He also gave testimony to interrogators and historians that did much to falsely exculpate Germany's professional officers, to instead lay all blame for crimes and military blunders of the regime solely on Hitler. That self-exculpatory memoir, *Panzer Leader,* was published in 1952. A biographer refined the only possible distinction one may make about Guderian to this conclusion: he was a "Hitlerite" rather than a Nazi, a man moved always by careerism and open to large bribes rather than an ideologue. In the end, that proved a distinction without any moral or practical difference.

See also blitzkrieg; Kursk; Smolensk, Battle of; Ukraine, First Battle of; Yelnia operation.

Suggested Reading: K. Macksey, *Guderian* (1992).

GUERNICA (APRIL 26, 1937)   This Basque town northwest of Bilbao was the first city to experience the ferocity of mass aerial attack, in the first use of deliberate bombing of civilians as a terror weapon. On April 26, 1937, a perfectly clear day, Guernica was overflown and bombed by 43 aircraft of the *Kondor Legion*, attacking in support of *Francisco Franco's* military rebellion that started the *Spanish Civil War (1936–1939)*. Guernica fell to Franco's forces two days later. "Who bombed Guernica?" became an intense international controversy. Spanish Republicans blamed Francoists, while the rebels improbably pointed to anarchist arsonists on the Republican side, denying that a single bomb had even fallen. Also blamed were "volunteer" Germans flying for Franco, and VVS Soviet pilots flying for the Republic. The truth finally emerged at the *Nuremberg Tribunal* when *Hermann Göring* admitted that he had ordered the bombing of Guernica as an experiment in how to destroy an urban target from the air. Yet, not even that confession stopped later extreme right-wing revisionists in Spain from denying the raid even happened.

GUERRA PARALLELA   "Parallel war."
    See Balkan campaign; Italy; Mussolini, Benito.

GUERRILLA WARFARE
    See individual occupied country entries. *See also americanistas; Aung San; Balkan campaign; bandits; Chetniks; Chinese Civil War (1927–1949); Chinese Communist armies; concentration camps; Einsatzgruppen; Force Française de l'Intérieur (FFI); Funkspeil; Hô Chí Minh; horses; Hoxha, Enver; Huk; Korück; Lin Biao; Milice Française; Nationalkomitee Freies Deutschland (NKFD); National Redoubts; NKVD; OSMBON; Palestine; partisans; Philippines; Pripet Marshes; Rassenkampf; réfractaires; resistance; Résistance (French); Sino-Japanese War (1937–1945); Smersh; special orders; Tripoli; Ukraine; Ukrainian Insurgent Army (UPA); Voroshilov, Kliment; Wehrmacht; Werwolf guerrillas; Zhu De; Zog I.*

GULAG   "Glavnoe Upravlenie LAGeri," or "Main Administration of Camps." The most infamous subsection of the vast Soviet labor and prison camp system, which also had extensive "colonies" and "labor settlements." At the start of the German-Soviet war in June 1941, GULAG camps confined at least 2.3 million prisoners and forced laborers. By the end of that year alone, another 1.3 million were sent to the camps, with 2 million more following over the course of 1942. The inmates were charged with anything from ordinary criminal activity to military crimes or "labor desertion." Wartime conditions in the camps were even worse than during the deadly 1930s because GULAG inmates ranked at the bottom of food distribution priority. Camp death rates rose dramatically, corresponding to the worst years of the war and German occupation of the principal Soviet food-producing regions. The camp system was maintained throughout the war, but some prisoners moved in the other direction. A number of former Red Army officers sent to the camps during the *Yezhovshchina* purges were restored to old positions because of the great manpower losses and attendant officer shortages of 1941–1942. Many captive Polish Army men and members of other ethnic groups from the Western Soviet Union were released to kill Germans on the Eastern Front, with tens of thousands of Poles released and eventually allowed to leave the Soviet Union to fight under British command. Many ordinary Russians who were released were sent directly to savage and despised convict military units, which had extraordinarily high casualty rates. Perhaps one million in all were released for one or more of these reasons during the war, their places filled and refilled by incoming prisoners.

See also desertion; Golikov, Philipp; NKVD; penal battalions; Soviet Union; Stalin, Joseph.

GUMBINNEN OPERATION (1944)
See Goldap operation.

GUOMINDANG   China's "National People's Party" and its attendant army, often simplified in English to "Nationalists." The Guomindang was a nationalist and anti-Qing (Manchu) party formed in 1891 by Dr. Sun Yixian (Sun Yat-sen). It played a leading role in the Chinese Revolution that overthrew the Qing in 1911. It won a majority of seats in China's first national elections in 1913. But Sun Yixian and the Guomindang could not overcome the warlord General Yuan Shikai, who defeated Guomindang troops later that year and proceeded to establish a personal dictatorship that lasted until his death in 1916. The Guomindang next failed to subdue numerous successor warlords who devastated and divided much of China, either breaking away from the center or seeking to replace Yuan Shikai in control of it. During the 1920s the Guomindang was structurally reorganized by Sun Yixian along Leninist lines, though he abjured Leninist ideology. In short, the Guomindang was remade as a "vanguard party" claiming to embody the whole national ideal in a small clutch of top leaders. But it was not a Marxist party, even though its leaders tactically and temporarily aligned with the smaller Chinese Communist Party (CCP). Guomindang cadres also accepted arms from the Soviet Union and received military training from *Comintern* advisers. After 1925 the Guomindang was led by General *Jiang Jieshi*. He sent his military forces fanning out from Guangzhou (Canton) to suppress the warlords. Those whom he could not defeat militarily at acceptable costs he simply bought out, restoring immediate peace and order without creating a unified or stable central system.

Jiang set up a national government in Nanjing, then turned on the CCP, killing its urban cadres in the "Shanghai massacre" and other attacks and massacres across China in 1927. Survivors scattered to the fringes of the country, especially deep into the southern countryside and mountains. Jiang's ruthless move against the Communists precipitated the protracted armed struggle known as the *Chinese Civil War (1927–1949)*. During a final "Northern Expedition" led personally by Jiang in 1928, Guomindang troops defeated or bribed, intimidated, and assimilated politically the last northern warlords. That superficially unified most of China under his dictatorship. In turn, general internal peace freed Jiang to attack the rural communal strongholds, or "soviets," of various Communist bands. This action against CCP bases was described by Jiang as a sequence of "bandit suppression campaigns." The prolonged and bloody contest with the Communist was interrupted by Japanese aggression into *Manchuria* in 1931, following the provocation of the *Mukden incident*. Jiang continued his campaigns against *Mao Zedong* and other Communists still holed up in the southern "Jiangxi soviet." That forced Mao and the southern Communists onto the "Long March," all the way to isolated Yenan in northwest China, where they reestablished a base and continued their desultory guerilla war. The exceptional *Xi'an incident* of December 1936, which forced Jiang temporarily to cooperate with the Communists and Mongolians, was followed in mid-1937 by outbreak of the *Sino-Japanese War (1937–1945)*. The Japanese assault proved a severe blow to the Guomindang, pushing its forces away from the coastal cities that formed Jiang's main political base, deeper into southern and western China during a series of brutal retreats.

Guomindang armed forces were developed to fight warlord armies and Communists, not to oppose in battle a more modern force such as the *Imperial Japanese Army*. As head of the National Military Council, Jiang was nominally supreme commander of all Guomindang troops. In fact, his armies incorporated semi-independent warlord formations and were often led by former warlord generals of dubious martial quality, and with political and military agendas all their own. By the mid-1930s the elite core of Jiang's Central Army comprised three heavy divisions of "The Generalissimo's Own," just 80,000 troops trained by German instructors and armed with the best German weapons and equipment. They were surrounded by less well-equipped and barely trained Central Army divisions, bringing the total Central Army force to 300,000 men. Many hundreds of thousands more troops of little to no real quality served in garrisons and lesser Guomindang armies all over China. Many were killed in the opening Japanese siege of Shanghai, or in bloody fighting around the Wuhan cities and industrial area over the first 18 months of the war. The Guomindang lost perhaps one million men in the first year of war.

Troop losses were partly made up by recruiting refugees from the coastal cities and from barely disguised warlord armies, but Guomindang recruitment centered on rough conscription of peasants. Such brutal methods were used that conscripts suffered a death or desertion rate of nearly 45 percent before they reached frontline units. Often starving and seriously ill peasants were taken to the front roped together by the hundreds, which was hardly a prescription for later producing motivated fighting men. Therein lay a good part of the explanation for the Guomindang's continual poor showing against the Japanese. Its conscript divisions never equaled the prewar Central Army in skill or training, while equipment and weapons supplies dwindled as the Japanese brought pressure on Britain to close the *Burma Road* and on French Indochina to stop all rail and road supply to southern China. By 1940 the Sino-Japanese War was stalemated. Jiang had more men than weapons and was waging a strictly defensive campaign. The Japanese were more powerful but greatly overextended. The United States authorized *Lend-Lease* to the Guomindang starting in mid-1941, though delivery remained a problem. The Japanese ended all but minimal air resupply "over the *Hump*" by shutting China's border with French Indochina in August, then invading Burma in December. The Sino-Japanese War thus merged with World War II at the end of 1941, as the Japanese attacked British and other Allied positions across Southeast Asia. The Western powers immediately offered a formal alliance to Jiang and the Guomindang. In return, Jiang desperately offered to send 100,000 troops to fight for the British outside China, on the condition that Britain arm and feed them. Ragged Chinese troops entered Burma just in time to participate in the British defeat in early 1942.

President Franklin D. Roosevelt initially had extremely high hopes for a major contribution by the Guomindang to the defeat of Japan. He authorized a "thirty division plan" to train and equip Chinese troops to engage the Japanese Army on the mainland of Asia. U.S. advisors poured into China in 1942, and Jiang's paper divisional strength soon reached impressive numbers: over 300 divisions by 1945. However, most of those divisions were poorly manned, badly trained, and under-equipped despite the American supply effort, largely because the Japanese Army kept overland supply routes closed for most of the war. Worst of all, too many Chinese soldiers were terribly demoralized. Many fought hard against the ruthless Japanese invader, but others were utterly bewildered and had no understanding of the war or their role in it. Peasant "soldiers" were acquired by brutal conscription methods, with hundreds and even thousands marched out of suddenly surrounded and swept villages and even regions. They were tied together with hemp rope to prevent mass desertion. Many died before reaching their first boot camp. Once in Guomindang uniform, or often still just wearing peasant clothes or rags, Chinese troops were usually poorly led and were hardly fed or clothed. Western soldiers meeting Chinese units in Burma later in the war were shocked to observe that few or none of their allies wore shoes. None had sturdy jungle boots, while many were shod in matted straw. Medical treatment was minimal to nonexistent and death from wounds or disease was ubiquitous. Desertion and attendant executions were therefore chronic.

Nevertheless, with savage conscription methods and brutal discipline, Jiang obtained his needed replacements. By 1941 the Guomindang had nearly six million men nominally under arms. Over the course of the war it conscripted over 14 million into its armies. Most huddled in the south in vast garrisons or were deployed along the extended frontier with Japanese occupation forces. Some carried out effective ambushes and large-scale guerilla operations. But the majority were there to absorb with their suffering and their lives whatever blows the overextended Japanese Army could still deliver. Even if most Guomindang divisions were barely competent as fighting formations and their men deserted at the first—and second and third—opportunity, they were useful to Jiang to suppress local warlords and to threaten the Communists. Most importantly, they kept aid coming into China by impressing with sheer numbers a distant American president eager to avoid casualties, and concerned and committed to train and arm Chinese divisions to fight the bulk of the Japanese Army. The British prime minister and Chiefs of Staff were far less impressed with Jiang's formations. Eventually, even Roosevelt grew frustrated by Guomindang corruption and incompetence. In 1944 he looked instead to the harder slog through the Central Pacific as the road to victory over Japan. Fighting continued in China, but it was no longer seen by Japan or the Western Allies as strategically important to the outcome of World War II.

The Chinese Civil War resumed on a greatly enlarged scale from late 1945, with events and battles initially favoring the Guomindang. The United States helped air lift Guomindang troops into northern cities abandoned by the withdrawing Japanese and into Manchuria. The Red Army permitted Chinese Communist troops to enter the same territories. When serious fighting broke out among competing Chinese forces in 1946, Guomindang reverses in the field revealed depths of political and personal corruption and incompetence that rose into the top leadership. That made victory over the Communists evermore problematic. The civil war culminated in a Communist military triumph in early 1949, followed by the Communist Revolution. The Guomindang was not militarily defeated in the field—though it indeed lost massively during the Huai-Hai campaign (November 1948–January 1949). It was more important that it collapsed from within, morally, fiscally, and politically. Remnant divisions fled to Taiwan, where in later years they were given just enough arms and support by Washington to fend off an expected invasion by Communist forces, but never enough to themselves counter-invade China. The Guomindang remained politically dominant on Taiwan until the mid-1990s.

See also Chinese Air Force.

GURKHAS Tough Nepalese warriors associated with British arms since 1815. They played a key role in repression of the "Indian Mutiny" in the 19th century, for which Queen Victoria gave them the honorific "riflemen." That permitted Gurkhas, alone among sepoy regiments of the *Indian Army*, to eat in the same mess halls as white troops and to ride inside trains rather than atop them. Gurkhas fought in most British wars of the 19th and 20th centuries, including World War I and World War II. They were famed and feared for their frightful kukri (or khukuri) curved knives. Some of the 40 Gurkha battalions raised from 1940 served as garrison troops in India. Others fought against Japanese in *Malaya* as well as during the first and second *Burma campaigns*. Still more fought Germans and Italians in the *desert campaigns (1940–1943),* then in the *Italian campaign (1943–1945),* including at *Monte Cassino* in 1944. Some fought with British and Commonwealth forces in the Balkans. By war's end over a quarter million Gurkhas served in arms, including a brigade of Gurkha paratroopers who saw limited action in southeast Asia.

GUSTAV LINE German fortified defensive works northwest of Naples. The Western Allies ran into the hastily constructed but difficult Gustav Line after they broke though the *Bernhardt Line* during the *Italian campaign (1943–1945)*.
See also *Hitler Line; Monte Cassino; Winter Line.*

GYMNAST
See *TORCH.*

GYPSIES
See *Roma.*

H2S Joke code name (H²S is the formula for hydrogen sulfide) for a critically important RAF Bomber Command navigation radar. It was a real technical breakthrough because it could be carried by an aircraft rather than broadcast from a ground station. An adaptation of RAF night-fighter radar, H2S rotated inside a small dome mounted beneath the aircraft. It pointed at the ground to provide a reasonable picture of terrain features on a cathode-ray tube at the navigator's station. First tested in mid-1942, it was used in Pathfinder aircraft from the end of January 1943. One problem was that Luftwaffe *Lichtenstein* night-fighter radar was configured to home on H2S. The USAAF adopted a version of H2S radar under the code H2X.

See also blind bombing.

HABAKKUK A British proposal for huge aircraft carriers to be made from flattened icebergs, reinforced with wood pulp and ice (Pykrete) construction. The structure was to be topped with wooden flight decks and equipped with hollowed-out ice hangers for scouts and fighters. The core idea was rapid construction to help close the mid-Atlantic *air gap*. Winston Churchill was an enthusiast, as he was for many odd adventures and projects. So, too, was *Louis Mountbatten*. Serious engineering studies were made from January 1942, including of steering, engines, insulation, and refrigeration needs. A model prototype was assembled in Western Canada, and design discussion continued into 1943, but the project was never approved. The air gaps were finally closed and U.S. shipbuilding capacity proved exceptional, so that conventional *escort carriers* replaced the untested Habakkuk idea.

HA **BOMB**

See biological warfare; Unit 731.

HAGANAH
See Palestine.

HAGEN LINE   A Wehrmacht defensive position protecting the key railway junction and supply depots at Briansk during the summer of 1943. General *Walter Model* pulled back to hold the Hagen Line during the Red Army's counteroffensive in July–August, Operation *KUTUZOV*, which broke through the German position north of Kursk.

HA-GŌ **(1944)**   Code name for a Japanese diversionary operation in Burma.
See Admin Box, Battle of; Arakan campaign; Imphal operation.

HAGUE CONVENTIONS   Three sets of conventions dealing with the law of war were agreed in 1899, 1907, and 1954. The third set was the least important but incorporated experiences and lessons of World War II. All three Hague Conventions deplored the recurrence of war but recognized that when a clash of arms occurred it was in the interest of civilization to limit the extent and character of permissible violence. They therefore followed three basic principles. First, no claim is exhaustive: the proper limits of war and interests of humanity are said to extend to implied rules not explicit in treaty form. Second, the right of a belligerent state to inflict harm was upheld, but curtailed. Finally, it was forbidden to use arms to cause "unnecessary suffering" to enemy soldiers or to any civilians. Parties to the Hague Conventions were required to make a prior and reasoned declaration of war, or issue an ultimatum with a conditional declaration of war and communicate its terms to all neutral states. Who did and did not have belligerent rights was defined, and *prisoner of war* rights were agreed. Among battlefield acts forbidden by the Hague Conventions were: use of poison gas, killing or wounding enemies who surrendered or tried to surrender, deceptive use of a flag of surrender, refusing quarter, use of an enemy's flag or uniforms in any ruse de guerre, deceptive use of the symbol of the Red Cross (or Red Crescent) to gain a combat advantage, bombarding undefended towns, pillage (looting), punishing civilians in reprisal for enemy military acts, and refusing to care for enemy wounded. The 1954 convention added protection of cultural property from wanton destruction, recalling how the Nazis deliberately wrecked Russian icons and Jewish and other cultural sites, systematically destroyed Warsaw, and proposed to flatten Paris, Leningrad, Moscow, and other cities.
See also Geneva Conventions; war crimes.

HAILE SELASSIE (1892–1975)   "The Lion of Judah." Né Ras Tafari Makonnen. Emperor of Abyssinia, 1930–1974. He was regent for Empress Zauditu from 1916, and was crowned in 1930. As a young ruler he sincerely tried, though largely failed, to modernize Abyssinia. In 1935 he became an international symbol of resistance to aggression when Abyssinia was invaded by Italy. During the *Abyssinian War* he was forced into exile in England from 1936. He stood before the Assembly of the League of Nations in Geneva and—in a harbinger of coming serial wars of aggression in Africa, Asia, and Europe—poignantly warned that every isolated and small state was a possible future Ethiopia. He returned to Ethiopia in 1941 during the *East African campaign (1940–1941)*. He ruled for another 33 years, turning away from a reformist agenda in later life. He was overthrown by a radical military junta in 1974 and brutally murdered while in confinement in 1975.

HAINAN This large Chinese island was occupied by the Japanese in 1939 during the *Sino-Japanese War (1937–1945)*. Tokyo maintained air and naval bases on Hainan to the end of World War II. The garrison surrendered along with other Japanese forces in late 1945.

HALDER, FRANZ (1884–1972) German general. He served as a staff officer during World War I. Moving into a position vacated by a purged anti-Nazi officer in 1938, he was made Chief of the General Staff. He had sympathy for prewar proposals for a military coup to topple Adolf Hitler and the Nazis, but never acted. His reasons were strategic rather than moral: he feared Hitler was leading Germany into a losing war. However, his opinion was turned by Hitler's bloodless successes in Austria and Czechoslovakia. He then served Hitler with enthusiasm in planning the invasions of Poland in 1939 (*FALL WEISS*), Denmark and Norway in 1940 (*WESERÜBUNG*), and France and the Low Countries, also in 1940 (*FALL GELB*). He next planned Operation *SEELÖWE,* the invasion of Great Britain that was never carried out. He became deeply concerned by the long-term strategic implications of Hitler's Operation *BARBAROSSA* plan to invade the Soviet Union. Yet, once again he did nothing except to serve his master's wishes. He was responsible for much of the operational planning that led to success in the field in the western Soviet Union over the summer and fall of 1941. But his arguments with Hitler continued: where Hitler saw successful encirclement of nearly 700,000 Red Army troops at Kiev as "the greatest victory in world history," Halder worried that it was a colossal strategic mistake to have earlier shifted Panzer forces into Ukraine from Army Group Center, instead of continuing the drive toward Moscow.

Halder was singularly responsible for issuance to Wehrmacht commanders of illegal *"special orders"* prior to and during BARBAROSSA. Those orders approved collective reprisals in response to *partisan* activity and authorized deliberate starvation and malign neglect of Soviet civilians in overrun rear areas. In addition to his early planning successes in BARBAROSSA, he was also largely responsible for errors in the invasion plan, notably in the realm of fantastical logistical assumptions that played out adversely from September to December. He then advised Hitler to continue offensive operations in front of Moscow into the first week of December 1941, long after the overstretched Wehrmacht should have halted and gone over to strict defense. Halder was additionally responsible for excessive offensive optimism about the strategic meaning of operational advances and victories in the southern Soviet Union in the summer offensives of 1942. It was these strategic rather than moral disagreements with Hitler that led to Halder's forced retirement on September 24, 1942. He was dismissed from the General Staff by his Führer just as German 6th Army reached the outskirts of *Stalingrad*.

Always ambivalent about the regime rather than opposed to it, even in retirement, Halder was arrested by the *Schutzstaffel (SS)* in the aftermath of the *July Plot* (1944). He was imprisoned at *Flossenbürg* concentration camp and at *Dachau*. Captured by U.S. forces in May 1945, he testified at the *Nuremberg Tribunal*. It was Halder who planted the first seeds of the officer corp's self-exculpatory thesis that it was Hitler who really lost the war by terrible operational decisions, and the supporting thesis that only dedicated Nazis had waged the war dishonorably. Halder successfully hid facts of his own crimes and those of the Wehrmacht for decades after the war, duping official historians with highly influential memoirs and oral testimony that did much to falsely exculpate the professional officers of the Wehrmacht. Instead, he helped lay all blame for crimes of the regime on Hitler's SS henchmen, while attributing military blunders made by senior officers of the General Staff solely to Hitler's amateurish interventions and decrees. Halder was so successful in that campaign of historical deceit that he was given an award by the U.S. Army, which was then looking for lessons on how to fight a potential war against the Red Army. Later research utterly discredited Halder's moral claims and those of other high-rank Wehrmacht officers that they retained "clean hands" and that they were above and apart from the great crimes carried out in the east on Hitler's orders and their own.

See also autarky; Schwartz Kapelle.

HALFAYA PASS   Or "hellfire pass." A narrow pass through a high escarpment on the border of Egypt and Tripoli. It repeatedly changed hands during the *desert campaigns* in 1940–1942.

See also BATTLEAXE.

HALF-TRACK   An armored troop carrier with rear tracks instead of all-wheels. The standard U.S. Army models were the M2 and M3, in several dozen versions. Many were armed with multiple heavy machine guns, but others carried anti-aircraft mounts, 75 mm or 105 mm howitzers, or 4.2-inch mortars. In addition to its crew of 3, an M3 could carry a squad of 10 men. Other armies had comparable vehicles, such as the British M3A1 and the German SdKfz 251.

HALIFAX, EDWARD WOOD (1881–1959)   Viceroy of India, 1926–1931; foreign secretary, 1938–1941; ambassador to Washington, 1941–1946. Although at first fooled by German assurances, and a strong and long supporter of *Neville Chamberlain's* policy of *appeasement*, from September 1938, Lord Halifax encouraged the prime minister to take a tougher line toward Adolf Hitler. Indeed, what backbone there was in British foreign policy between the *Munich Conference* and the outbreak of World War II may be attributed largely to Halifax. He might have become prime minister instead of Winston Churchill in May 1940, but effectively deferred to Churchill during a War Cabinet meeting. For that reason, and for domestic and internal party reasons in a time of deep crisis, Churchill initially kept Halifax on to serve as foreign secretary. After a decent interval, Halifax was dispatched to the critically important post of Ambassador in Washington that December. In a time when good relations with the United States were vital to Britain's survival, Halifax served his country extremely well in Washington throughout the war, during some of the darkest days in British national history.

HALSEY, WILLIAM (1882–1959) American admiral. "Bull" Halsey rose rapidly in rank and responsibility just before the war because he was a rare prewar senior officer who was a qualified pilot and a specialist in naval aviation. The events of *Pearl Harbor* spared his carrier Task Force, which he immediately took on a series of successful raids of forward Japanese positions. There quickly followed great carrier battles at the *Coral Sea* and *Midway*, which further paved the path to top command by revealing that carriers would be the critical capital warship in the Pacific War. Halsey's route was fully cleared by Admiral *Frank Fletcher's* poor and overly cautious performances at Guam, the Coral Sea, and later during the initial landings on *Guadalcanal*. In contrast, Halsey was always aggressive. For that reason he was promoted to command of all carrier forces in the Pacific and chosen to lead the *Doolittle Raid* in April 1942. However, his aggressiveness did not serve him well as commander of 3rd Fleet at *Leyte Gulf* at the outset of the second *Philippines campaign* in 1944. He was careless about confirming various task force locations and, worst of all, took offered bait and began chasing empty-decked Japanese decoy carriers. Those errors left the landing zones badly exposed to a potential Japanese assault task force. Fortunately, others rescued the day from true disaster with great courage and considerable luck, though at great cost in lives lost. Halsey was also criticized for subsequently brazenly steaming into a typhoon, which took out three U.S. destroyers. His command was part of a larger invasion fleet at Okinawa. On September 2, 1945, he hosted General *Douglas MacArthur* and Allied and Japanese delegations during the surrender ceremony aboard the USS Missouri in Tokyo Bay that formally ended the Pacific War.

***HALTEBEFEHL* ORDERS** "stand fast." A series of infamous "no retreat" orders issued to the Wehrmacht at various times by *Adolf Hitler,* with the first and most important issued to stop panic spreading through the Wehrmacht during the *Moscow offensive operation (1941–1942)*. Hitler was not always inflexible. In the immediate aftermath of the loss of 6th Army at *Stalingrad,* he permitted German armies to pull back from the Crimea and from Rostov in Operation *DON* in the south, and from Demiansk in the north during Operation *POLAR STAR (February 1943)*. But late in the war Haltebefehl orders became more and more his preferred tactic.

For comparable "Not one step backwards!" orders issued to the Red Army by Joseph Stalin *see Order #227. See also Argenta Gap; BAGRATION; Courland Pocket; El Alamein, Second Battle of; Guderian, Heinz; Hungary; OKW; RUMIANTSEV.*

HAMBURG RAIDS (JULY 24–AUGUST 2, 1943)
See Combined Bomber Offensive; strategic bombing.

HANOVER (MAY–JUNE, 1942)   Code name for a Wehrmacht offensive to reduce the Soviet pocket at Viazma during May–June, 1942. It was a follow-up to the failed Soviet *Rzhev-Viazma strategic operation* (January 8–April 20, 1942). HANOVER looked to crush cut-off elements of a Soviet cavalry corps, the "Belov Group," along with a hodgepodge of airborne and other trapped forces. A good number of Soviet troopers managed to escape the trap along with a few airborne troops. Thousands more were killed, wounded, or taken prisoner.

HAPPY TIME
See Battle of the Atlantic; convoys; Dönitz, Karl; King, Ernest.

HARDS   Concrete ramps built in ports all over southern England prior to *OVERLORD*. They were used to load combat vehicles aboard assault ships.

HARPE, JOSEF (1887–1968)   German general. He commanded a division in Poland in 1939. He did not fight in France in 1940, but led a Panzer division again in the invasion of the Soviet Union in 1941, fighting around Minsk and Smolensk. During Operation *BLAU* in 1942 he commanded "Panzerkorps Harpe" in fighting at Kalinin. In mid-1943 he took over 9th Army during heavy defensive fighting in the *Pripet Marshes*. In June 1944, he was put in charge of 4th Panzer Army, which was driven by the Soviets back into Poland during Operation *BAGRATION*. As Harpe's commands grew in title they shrank in real size, as the heavy attrition of the Eastern Front wore down Wehrmacht formations to fractions of their paper strength. In command of Army Group A in September 1944, Harpe could not hold against the combined and truly massive Fronts of Marshals *Ivan S. Konev* and *Konstantin Rokossovsky* during the *Vistula-Oder operation* in January 1945, and Hitler sacked him. He returned to command German forces in the Ruhr in March. He and the remnants of 5th Panzer Army surrendered to U.S. forces the next month.

HARRIMAN, W. AVERELL (1891–1986)   U.S. diplomat. He was sent to London in 1940 to oversee the crucial *Lend-Lease* program to Great Britain. He served as U.S. ambassador to the Soviet Union from 1943 to 1946, and to Great Britain in 1946. Those were critical years of Allied cooperation to win the war, as well as planning for the postwar settlement. Harriman was present at the great summits at *Teheran, Yalta,* and *Potsdam,* as well as the *TOLSTOI* summit. During his time in Moscow he grew increasingly suspicious of Joseph Stalin's postwar intentions. He warned Presidents Franklin D. Roosevelt and Harry Truman that the only way to deal with Stalin was from a position of firm resolve, resistance to bullying, and military and diplomatic strength. Harriman was deeply influential in framing many of the key policies of the early Cold War, including containment of the Soviet Union, the European Recovery Program, and NATO.

HARRIS, ARTHUR (1892–1984) "Bomber Harris." British air chief marshal. Rhodesian born Arthur Harris remains the single most persistently controversial of all senior Western Allied military leaders. Harris was the supreme advocate of *area bombing,* the method of *strategic bombing* evolved by the RAF during his tenure as commander in chief of RAF Bomber Command, from February 1942 to the end of the war in Europe in May 1945. Harris was impressed with the effects of German bombing of London and other cities during the *Blitz,* yet he missed a central fact about those raids: area bombing, or *morale bombing,* did not work against the British. Why should it work against the Germans? Nevertheless, he remained absolutely—one can say with fairness, also blindly—committed to bombing German cities over all other targets, even oil refineries, rail yards, or other high priority strategic targets set by the Joint Chiefs of Staff. Harris deflected nearly all efforts by his fellow air men and his superiors to divert bombers to noncity targets, which he contemptuously dismissed as mere "panacea targets." He notably resisted calls to use heavy bombers for tactical preparation in advance of *OVERLORD,* though he lost that argument to General *Dwight Eisenhower.*

Harris' most blameworthy behavior was to make exaggerated claims about bombing to Prime Minister Winston Churchill, combined with rigid refusal to accept growing evidence that neither area nor morale bombing were working. For instance, he told Churchill in mid-1943 that the Ruhr Valley was "largely out" and that he was "certain that Germany must collapse." He continued in this attitude to the end of the war, often ignoring or outright refusing to believe mounting intelligence that said German war production was expanding and dispersing in response to the area bombing campaign and that enemy civilian morale and even support for the Nazi regime was nowhere near breaking into late 1944. Into 1943 Harris built up Bomber Command to levels capable of conducting *thousand bomber raids* and other operations of the *Combined Bomber Offensive* against German cities. He sincerely thought such devastating bombing could by itself provide decisive victory before *D-Day (June 6, 1944).* His greatest operational failure was the *Berlin bomber offensive (1943–1944),* which cost the Western Allies a great many planes and crews. Harris' name became permanently associated with the great raid on *Dresden,* for which some critics later accused him of carrying out war crimes. In postwar interviews and memoirs, Harris never repented the policy of area bombing or any given instance of it; he defiantly defended it instead.

HAUPTKAMPFLINIE "Defensive Battle Line." A Wehrmacht designation for a fixed defensive position, usually shortened to "HKL."

HAUSSER, PAUL (1880–1972) German general. He served as a young officer on the General Staff during World War I. He retired from the *Reichswehr* in 1932. He joined the *Stahlhelm* the next year and the *Sturmabteilung (SA)* in 1934. He joined the *Schutzstaffel (SS)* in November 1934, and oversaw training of the first small military units that later grew into the *Waffen-SS*. He was an SS division commander in France in 1940, and again at the head of the Das Reich division in the invasion of the Soviet Union in 1941. He lost an eye in October 1941, but took over as commander of SS-Panzerkorps in May 1942. His command saw heavy fighting at *Kharkov* in early 1943, and again at *Kursk* that summer. In March 1944, Hausser led an expanded II SS-Panzerkorps in defensive fighting in Galicia. Transferred with his men to the Western Front in June, Hausser and II SS-Panzerkorps fought the British along the Odon River in Normandy, countering Operation *EPSOM*. When Hausser took command of 7th Army following the suicide of General Friedrich Dollmann, it marked the first elevation of an SS man to command of so large a Wehrmacht force. Hausser was wounded again while leading his troops out of the *Falaise pocket*. He replaced *Heinrich Himmler* as commander of Army Group Upper Rhine in late January 1945. A few days later he was given command of Army Group C, the highest command of any SS officer in the war, though by then a German "Army Group" was a shadow of what it once had been. Not even a dedicated SS man like Hausser could survive the twists of rage and vengeance that coursed through Hitler in the final month of the war. He was dismissed in early April 1945. He testified in defense of the SS at the *Nuremberg Tribunal,* without success. He remained active in SS veterans organizations long after the war. His memoir, *Waffen-SS im Einsatz* (1953), was a long apologia arguing that Waffen-SS men were just like any other soldiers in the war. Most were not.

HAW HAW, LORD
See William Joyce.

HEAVY ARTILLERY
A subclassification of artillery referring to the largest guns available to ground forces, usually under the control of an HQ at the corps or army level.
See artillery; field guns.

HEAVY BOMBERS
See anti-aircraft weapons; bombers.

HEDGEHOG
"Anti-Submarine Projector." Developed by the Royal Navy from 1941 and in service from 1943, the Hedgehog forward-firing spigot-mortar solved the problem of loss of U-boat location when deploying stern-only *depth charges*. Its rod or spigot racks held 24 mortar bombs, each triggered by a contact pistol. When fired ahead of the ship on a known U-boat location, they fell in a controlled circle 40 meters in diameter. This was highly effective because the bombs hit the area around a U-boat before it could dive deeply or turn hard. This markedly improved the kill-per-attack ratio of escorts. The recoil of the Hedgehog placed real strain on smaller ships, and it was initially much disliked by ships' captains. Only once its deadly impact on U-boats became known did it rise in popularity. The kill ratio

achieved by Hedgehog after 1943 reached 30 percent, or almost one out of every three attacks.

See also anti-submarine warfare; ASDIC; Mousetrap; Squid.

HEER The German Army. It was divided into the *Feldheer* or "Field Army," comprising the main battle force, and the *Ersatzheer* or "Replacement Army," which formed the reserve.

See also Heeresgruppe; OKH; OKW; Ostheer; Osttruppen; Volksgrenadier; Volkssturm; Wehrmacht.

HEERESGRUPPE A German army group. In peacetime, Heeresgruppen were responsible for training. They formed field headquarters and nuclei of army groups such as "Heeresgruppe Nord" (Army Group North) once mobilized for war. There were 11 Heeresgruppen situated below the command of the *OKW* or *OKH* by the end of 1944.

See also army group; Front.

HEI-HO Native auxiliaries recruited by the Japanese among occupied populations in southeast Asia, notably on Java.

HEILIGENBEIL POCKET A German pocket of some 15 broken divisions of Army Group North, hemmed by 3rd Belorussian Front along the Baltic coast around Heiligenbeil, near Königsberg, in February–March, 1945. The Kriegsmarine was able to evacuate about 100,000 civilians and wounded from the pocket before it was crushed. The Soviet commander, *Ivan D. Chernyakovsky,* was killed by an artillery round on February 18. After nearly three weeks of extremely heavy fighting, the pocket collapsed on March 29. After a massive artillery preparation by heavy siege guns and thousands of field tubes, Königsberg was assaulted and taken on April 6. The city of Immanuel Kant, and of the Teutonic Knights, yielded 90,000 prisoners.

HELGOLAND Alternately, Heligoland. This North Sea island was an important German naval base from 1900. It was demilitarized by the *Treaty of Versailles* but remilitarized by Adolf Hitler in 1936. It was a target of British bombers during the war and was occupied by the Western powers in 1945. It was again demilitarized in 1947. It was returned to the Federal Republic of Germany in 1952.

HELICOPTERS Helicopter technology was in its infancy during the early 1940s but some models nevertheless made it into active service. On April 20, 1942, the helicopter pioneer Igor Sikorsky successfully demonstrated his HNS-1 model (or R-4 Sikorsky). That persuaded the U.S. Army to order several dozen helicopters for medical air-lift and *air–sea rescue* missions. The United States deployed these small medical helicopters to the Burma theater in April 1944. In tropical and mountain conditions the Sikorsky YR-4Bs could carry only one passenger. A handful of rescue operations were carried out by five small helicopters sent to China in 1945; more were made in central Luzon during the second *Philippines campaign* (1944–1945), where at least 70 men were evacuated by medical helicopter. From 1944 helicopters were also used in air–sea rescue operations by the U.S. Coast Guard. The next year, some flew from the decks of deep sea rescue ships in the Pacific. The Germans introduced a Focke-Achgelis or Fa330 helicopter to their U-boats in mid-1943. This compact, wind-powered machine was tethered to the U-boat while lifting an observer to 500 feet. In the event an enemy escort or aircraft appeared, the tether was invariably cut. Germany and Great Britain each might have done more with helicopters, but the Germans started too late while the British lacked spare resources.

HENDAYE PROTOCOL   A secret understanding of effective but informal Spanish–German alliance, including a commitment by Spain to enter the war against the Western Allies at some future unspecified date. It was agreed to following the only meeting between Francisco Franco and Adolf Hitler, at Hendaye on the Spanish border on October 23, 1940. Spain never lived up to its ultimate terms, remaining neutral to the end of the war.

HENDERSON FIELD
See Cactus Air Force; Guadalcanal.

HENLEIN, KONRAD (1898–1945)
See Sudetenland.

HERCULES   Code name for a proposed German invasion and occupation of *Malta*, preparatory to an effort to link General *Erwin Rommel's* invasion of Egypt with German operations in southern Russia and the Caucasus. It was canceled in favor of a concerted drive on Egypt by Rommel.
See also desert campaigns (1940–1943).

HERO CITIES   On May 1, 1945, four Soviet cities were declared "hero cities" for defensive stands made there during awful wartime sieges: Leningrad, Odessa, Sevastopol, and Stalingrad.

HERON
See BLAU; FISCHREIHER.

HERRENVOLK   "Higher people" or "master race." In spurious *Nazi Party* race theory, the *Aryan* people were considered racially and culturally superior to Jews, Slavs, and other so-called *Untermenschen*. "Master race" thinking was common in the early 20th century, partly driven by social-Darwinist influences seeping out from intellectuals and journalists. Inter alia, Japanese and Serb intellectuals and nationalists developed theories of the putative special place in history, if not biology, of their respective peoples. Such theories led to murderous consequences similar in kind, though not in scale, to those attending Nazism.

See also shido minzoku.

HESS, RUDOLF (1894–1987)   Nazi leader. Hess served in the *Reichswehr* with Adolf Hitler during World War I, and joined one of the *Freikorps* after the war. He was *Nazi Party* member #16, and took part in the Beer Hall Putsch and other early events that became lore among Party members, while cementing his relationship to the Nazi Führer. An utter sycophant, he wrote down Hitler's prison dictation of *Mein Kampf*. Always the loyal cur, he remained Hitler's personal secretary, 1925–1932. He signed the *Nuremberg Laws,* and in every other way was a loyal and fanatic Nazi. He was rewarded in 1939 when Hitler named him "deputy Führer" and designated successor. Yet, on May 10, 1941, Hess flew a Me110 fighter to Scotland and parachuted down on a personal "mission of humanity" to King George VI. He wanted to ask the king to fire the "warmonger," Winston Churchill. The king and prime minister alike refused to meet Hess. It is unclear on what authority, if any, Hess offered his British interrogators a German alliance against the Soviet Union, but it seems most likely he was simply deluded. He would spend the rest of his life in a perpetually addled state, in various British prisons then in Spandau Prison in Berlin. Hitler flew into a classic Führer-rage in private, denouncing Hess as insane. The British also concluded that Hess was demented or simple minded. They confined him under psychiatric care, then moved him to the Tower of London, thence to several other prisons. Convicted by the *Nuremberg Tribunal,* where Hess appeared not fully aware of his surroundings or situation, he was condemned for fomenting a war of aggression but acquitted of *crimes against humanity*. The Soviets dissented from the Tribunal decision not to execute him, and Hess spent the rest of his life in Spandau. From 1967 he was the sole remaining prisoner there: all other convicted Nazis had died or were released. The Soviets refused all requests for clemency. Perhaps that was a vindictive stance toward a mad old man, but it was understandable nonetheless given the great suffering of the German-Soviet war. It was announced in 1987 that Hess had hanged himself in his cell at age 91. That news, too, was received into controversy.

HEYDRICH, REINHARD (1904–1942)   A multitalented youth, Heydrich served briefly in the postwar German navy until he was dismissed by an honor court for unspecified "bad behavior" toward a woman. In 1931 he joined the *Nazi Party* and the *Schutzstaffel (SS),* though it is unclear to what degree he shared their ideology or whether he was merely politically opportunistic. In either case, he rose rapidly within the SS under the close patronage of *Heinrich Himmler* and in spite of the fact that Heydrich likely had a significant Jewish ancestry. That fact was known to Himmler and Adolf Hitler by 1935, but concealed with their connivance because they admired his displays of vicious *anti-Semitism* and his extreme merci-lessness. Heydrich became the top policeman in Germany in 1936, taking control of the *Sicherheitsdienst (SD)*. From 1939 he oversaw the SS *Einsatzgruppen,* the death battalions that killed over one million in the wake of the invasions of Poland and the western Soviet Union. Heydrich was made chief of the *Reichssicherheithauptampt (RSHA)* from 1939 until his death in 1942. In that capacity, he was a principal plan-ner of the machinery of the *Holocaust,* the so-called "final solution to the Jewish problem." He chaired the critical *Wannsee conference* where it was communicated to top Party and government officials that the regime had undertaken to "exter-minate" all Jews. Heydrich had been appointed Protector of Bohemia and Moravia in September 1941. On May 27, 1942, he was shot by a Czech *partisan* team para-chuted in to do the job by the British. He took several days to die. London's mo-tives remain unclear, but may have included an intent to spark German reprisals to stir a more active Czech resistance. Or it may be that the British feared Heydrich's talents and rise as a potential successor to Hitler. The SS indeed retaliated: death squads butchered the population of the village of Lidiče on June 10; others killed over 1,000 innocents in Prague.

See also Aktion Reinhard.

H-HOUR   The moment that the first wave in an American amphibious assault was expected to hit the beaches, or a planned ground forces attack was set to be launched. All supporting operations were timed to this critical moment. British and Commonwealth forces called this "Zero-Hour."

HIGGINS BOATS
   See landing craft.

HIMMELBETT   German nickname for what the RAF and USAAF called the *Kammhuber Line.*

HIMMLER, HEINRICH (1900–1945)   Head of the *Schutzstaffel (SS),* 1929–1945; minister of the interior, 1943–1945. A vicious *anti-Semite,* he joined the *Nazi Party* in 1922. That meant he participated the next year in Adolf Hitler's attempted Bavarian coup, the "Beer Hall Putsch." Himmler rose to lead the SS by 1929, when it was merely Hitler's bodyguard unit numbering under 300 men and still ensconced within the larger *Sturmabteilung (SA).* He worked constantly to split the SS from the SA. He also founded the *Sicherheitsdienst (SD)* and took a direct part in the SS and SD fratricidal massacre of SA men during the *Night of the Long Knives* in 1934. He was named to head the Munich police in 1933, and slowly took control of all other German police outside Prussia, where his great rival *Hermann Göring* held sway. Himmler controlled all German police from 1936, subsequently overseeing the *Gestapo* reign of torture and terror not just in Germany but all over German-occupied Europe. He became Hitler's head butcher, taking deep personal interest in SS and SD *Einsatzgruppen* and in operation of the *death camps* of the *Holocaust.*

He was a fanatic race theorist obsessed with "German blood," who applied "race purity" and other nonsensical theories to the organization and recruitment of the SS. He was also an idiot romantic who indulged prewar fantasies of deporting Europe's Jews to Madagascar, and who sent out expeditions to search for the "Holy Grail" and for lost Atlantis. During the war years he laid methodical plans to "exterminate" all "lesser breeds" within reach of his SS empire, culminating in design of the machinery of mass death at the *Wannsee conference (January 20, 1942)*. Yet, he was personally squeamish and once nearly fainted after watching a demonstration killing of 100 Jews at Minsk.

Himmler's power grew enormously with the creation of *Waffen-SS* units and the economic expansion of the SS through its control of slave labor and *concentration camps,* and war production contracts. In the field, the Waffen-SS never truly rivaled the Wehrmacht or established a separate military authority, other than locally and on an expanded scale only at the very end of the war when command of any type meant little beyond the title. Himmler's SS power relative to the military peaked when he oversaw revenge executions of senior Wehrmacht officers for their role in the *July Plot* in 1944, even though in secret he was not unsympathetic to killing Hitler and to making peace with the Western Allies. In charge of the *Ersatzheer* from that time, he backed the failed experiment of raising *Volksgrenadier* divisions. The Waffen-SS experiment had already revealed Himmler's utter inadequacy in military matters. Yet, he was given a major field command in late 1944, at which he failed quickly and miserably and from which he soon shrank. He evidenced no operational skill whatever as a field officer, blundering repeatedly and needlessly losing men and whole units. On January 23, 1945, he was replaced by SS general *Paul Hausser* as commander of Army Group Upper Rhine facing the Americans. Yet, Hitler again turned to his man of "iron will" as material factors overwhelmed the Wehrmacht in the east, elevating Himmler to command of a mostly fictional "Army Group Vistula." During the *conquest of Germany,* Himmler ineptly faced Marshal *Georgi Zhukov*'s massed tank and mechanized armies. His amateur orders led to quickened defeat for the rump of German military forces facing east. As the battle inside Berlin raged, Himmler sent out diplomatic feelers through Sweden's Count *Folke Bernadotte,* seeking negotiations with the Western powers entirely without Hitler's knowledge. When that fact was discovered and communicated to the Führerbunker, Himmler was summarily dismissed. Hitler demanded immediate execution, but Himmler was already out of his Führer's reach. He was later captured by the British while disguised as one of his own lapdog policeman. He committed suicide in British custody on May 23, 1945, well before he could be tried and executed by the International Tribunal at *Nuremberg*.

HINDENBURG LINE (CHINA)   A set of pillboxes and other strongpoints built by the *Guomindang's* Central Army east of Nanjing. It referenced the World War I German lines of the same name because German advisers, weapons, and ideas were all involved in laying out the Chinese defense line. It was abandoned without a fight in late 1937: Japanese amphibious landings were made in the rear of retreating Chinese troops and a panic ensued.

HINDENBURG LINE (GERMANY)
See Siegfriedstellung.

HINDENBURG, PAUL VON (1847–1934) German field marshal. President of the *Weimar Republic*, 1925–1934. He served as a young officer in the Seven Weeks' War (1866), during which he was wounded at Königgrätz. He served again in the Franco–Prussian War (1870–1871). He joined the *General Staff*, serving first under the famed Helmuth von Moltke and then under Alfred von Schlieffen. Hindenburg retired in 1911, but was recalled upon the outbreak of World War I and the unexpected early Russia success in East Prussia. Along with Erich von Ludendorff, he won great victories over Russia at Tannenberg and the Masurian Lakes in 1914. He was made commander in the east on November 1, 1914, and won again at Gorlice-Tarnow in 1915. He became chief of the General Staff in 1916, replacing Erich von Falkenhayn after the Russian "Brusilov offensive." To break the stalemate on the Western Front, he hoped to defeat Great Britain at sea before the United States entered the war in strength. To do so, he approved resumption of the strategy of *unrestricted submarine warfare* in January, 1917.

Upon the collapse of Russian resistance and German victory on the Eastern Front in 1917, Hindenburg and Ludendorff imposed the diktat of the Treaty of Brest-Litovsk on the Bolsheviks in March 1918. They turned to complete the supreme German effort in the west later that spring. When the *Reichswehr* was defeated in the fall of 1918, Hindenburg and Ludendorff advised the civilians in Berlin to ask for terms. Hindenburg retired from the Army in 1919. He stood for election as president of the Weimar Republic in 1925. He served Germany's young and greatly fragile democracy reluctantly, badly, and with deep contempt for its political class and republican values: he remained an unreconstructed monarchist to his last days. He defeated Adolf Hitler in the presidential election of 1932, but agreed to appoint the *Nazi Party* leader chancellor of Germany in January 1933. Hindenburg may have been senile at the end of his life. He certainly underestimated Hitler, whom he infamously and prematurely dismissed as a mere "Bohemian corporal." Hindenburg's remains—and the victory banners captured from Russians during World War I—were interred in a great tomb and war memorial at Tannenberg. His body was hastily removed to Hamburg, and his tomb was blown up by the Wehrmacht, just before the site was overrun by the Red Army in 1945. Hindenburg was reburied at Schloss Hohenzollern, seat of the defunct Prussian and imperial dynasty.

HIROHITO (1901–1989) "Shōwa" or "Enlightened Peace" emperor ("Tenno") of Japan, 1926–1989. "Hirohito" was his personal rather than reign name. It is generally used outside Japan. "Shōwa" is used within Japan, in a traditional demarcation of generational memory and recounting of historical eras. Hirohito sat on the Chrysanthemum Throne for 63 years, longer than anyone in the history of his dynasty. A figure of continuing historical controversy, he had broad powers under the Meiji constitution. Was he a central decision maker or not? He apparently believed strongly that under *Kokutai* he was obligated solely to his imperial ancestors rather than to mere temporal law or modern constitutional government. His exact role in Japan's imperial surge before and during the first years of World War II is not fully known. Many imperial records were destroyed just before the war ended, while others remain closely guarded still by the Imperial Household. At the least, Hirohito chose not to use his position to deflect Japan's militarists from a course of aggression, even if there is also evidence that he thought the path they took unwise and dangerous for Japan. He may have been a more active and willing participant in councils of war and empire than defenders portray. Contemporary rescripts show that he was deeply satisfied with victories and early conquests by the Army and Navy. Later scholarship also strongly suggests that Hirohito was informed of, and participated in, all Japan's major wartime policies and decisions and many minor decisions as well. He is thus probably fairly implicated in planning wars of aggression—including unprovoked attacks on Manchuria and China—as well as cynical alliance with the *Axis* states in Europe, expansion into Southeast Asia, the attack on the United States at *Pearl Harbor* and other Western powers across Southeast Asia, and possibly even endorsement of mistreatment of *prisoners of war*.

Hirohito might well have been charged as a major war criminal and held to account before the *Tokyo Tribunal*. However, American occupation authority concern over permanently alienating Japan overcame demands from most other Allied nations to have the Shōwa Emperor stand trial. Instead, during the postwar occupation Hirohito's reputation was thoroughly sanitized by General *Douglas MacArthur,* with considerable aid and eager cooperation from conservative Japanese opinion makers. That enabled Hirohito and the Japanese people to be depicted—alongside Chinese, Filipinos, and Koreans—as another set of victims of a minority clique of deviant militarists. Hirohito aided this postwar propaganda effort by posing as a simple gardener—he was in fact a lifelong amateur botanist— who had kept aloof from politics and military decision making on the path to war. His best defense is that the militarists in Japan were indeed in control of policy when he was still a weak ruler and young man, easily influenced by strongwilled generals and admirals and without critical power to intervene under the prewar constitutional system. His strongest defenders also allege that, had Hirohito declined the military's overtures to endorse their aggressive policies, he might have been replaced by another prince. Even if that was true, it only elevates Hirohito's prewar and wartime choices to personal expediency, and certainly not to a position of honor or moral integrity.

Upon the urging and critical tactical manipulation of the decision-making process by *Kantaro Suzuki,* Hirohito finally intervened in a divided War Council on August 10, 1945. His recommendation for peace was decisive, helping to prevent suicidal heroics and mass slaughter of civilians, which would have accompanied Allied invasion of the home islands. A recording of his Imperial Rescript was played over the radio to a nation and its armed forces hearing his "divine voice" for the first time, though even that was only possible after suppression of an attempted coup by young officers who tried to stop the broadcast. The Imperial Rescript was key to convincing bitterenders in the military to surrender. Yet, the address was saturated with breathtaking self-absolution and excuses for past aggression by Japan. It never once used the word "surrender." His portrayal of the China War and Pacific War as noble, even selfless, undertakings by the Japanese military and people in behalf of the liberation of other Asian peoples was nothing less than obscene revisionism that echoed the worst propaganda themes of the *Greater East Asian Co-Prosperity Sphere*. The condition of his continuing reign (Kokutai) during the Allied occupation was open renunciation of any status as a divinity and acceptance of a democratic constitution for Japan. He readily accepted those terms, cleaving to the throne in consequence. In 1946 Hirohito wrote a crafty "Monologue," another self-exculpating document in which he and his advisers claimed that he was not only innocent of participation in all aggressive decisions, but that he actually had opposed war with America and Britain. Once a smart military dresser, after 1945 the ever-adaptable Shōwa Emperor wore only civilian clothes.

See also Kodo-ha.

Suggested Reading: Herbert Bix, *Hirohito and the Making of Modern Japan* (2000); Daikichi Irokawa, *The Age of Hirohito* (1995); Peter Wetzler, *Hirohito and War: Imperial Tradition and Military Decision-making in Prewar Japan* (1998).

HIROSHIMA On August 6, 1945, this hitherto undamaged, mid-sized Japanese city experienced the first use of an atomic bomb in wartime. Making use of *air superiority,* a single U.S. B-29 bomber and its fighter escort dropped "Little Boy," as the first uranium bomb was code-named. The device air-burst over the city. Possibly 75,000–80,000 were killed outright, though some estimates put the number at 66,000, while one Japanese study claims the figure was nearly 120,000. Another 50,000–60,000 may have died within 12 months from burns or radiation poisoning. Many thousands died years or decades later from cancers that likely were caused by radiation exposure. Genetic mutations continued for several generations, at the least. In announcing the attack President *Harry Truman* said: "The force from which the sun draws its power has been loosed against those who brought war to the Far East."

The internal debate among top officials in Washington was fierce over whether or not to drop the bomb on a Japanese city, then over which city to target. Some argued that it would be possible to make a "demonstration" instead. Most were determined on bombing for psychological shock effect, just as they were months earlier when discussing what targets in Germany should be hit once atomic bombs became available. The arguments focused on the need to end the war quickly to avoid further casualties, preserve certain geopolitical interests in Asia, the expected degree of Japanese resistance to a seaborne invasion, benefits to the Western Allies of avoiding an invasion of the home islands and house-to-house fighting through Japan's major cities, and the likely casualties the Western powers would incur should the bomb not be dropped. It was established policy between the United States and Great Britain that the atomic bombs must not be used without joint agreement: they were the final product of a collaborative *nuclear weapons program* that also involved acquiring uranium from Canada and the Belgian Congo. This

"Manhattan Project" was the most closely guarded research program of the war and the most expensive in history, although secrecy did not prevent highly successful penetration and espionage by Soviet agents. The spies were principally British and American Communists with ideological loyalty to the Soviet cause. Soviet nuclear espionage was not wholly unknown at the time to the Western Allies. Therefore, in coming to a decision about atomic bombing, the probable effect on the shape of the postwar peace and the behavior of the Soviet Union was also discussed, as well as what effect an expected Soviet attack into Manchuria might have on the likelihood of Tokyo's early surrender. London gave formal assent to use atomics on Japan in early July. A Soviet declaration of war and massive assault on Japanese mainland forces began on August 8, when Moscow launched the *Manchurian offensive operation*. A second atomic bomb was dropped on *Nagasaki* the next day.

Starting in the 1960s, a ferocious criticism of Truman's decision focused on the idea that Japan was ready to surrender in August 1945, that Truman knew this from intelligence intercepts, and that he dropped the bomb primarily to impress the Soviet Union rather than to end the war. The core thesis was that the atomic bombs were the opening shot in the Cold War rather than the last act of World War II. However, new evidence emerged in the 1970s from secret radio intelligence material—*ULTRA* records and *MAGIC* intelligence summaries—that contradicted such "revisionist" claims. This evidence was barred from publication for decades for security reasons. Still the academic argument raged. A full release of a non-redacted version of MAGIC intercepts in 1995 made it clear that just four messages in the summer of 1945 suggested that Tokyo was amenable to settlement, while 13 said the opposite: Japan planned an all-out fight for its home islands. Moreover, what is now known about the decision of the inner cabinet in Tokyo to approach the Soviet Union to mediate an end to the war does not support the view that Japan was on the verge of surrender before the atomic bombings. Instead, the minimal goal of the leaders of the government was not just to retain the *Kokutai* Imperial system, but the whole militarist structure of the regime and society they governed, the same system that caused the tragedy of war in China, the Pacific, and across Southeast Asia. Finally, military intercepts read in Washington that summer vastly outnumbered the 17 key diplomatic intercepts, and indicated beyond doubt that plans were underway by Japanese forces for a bloody and all-out *Ketsu-Gō* defense.

From the middle of July 1945, ULTRA intercepts revealed that the Japanese Army was already conducting a massive build-up on Kyushu that would have posed enormous difficulty for the invasion scheduled under *OLYMPIC*. Instead of an anticipated 3 Japanese divisions on Kyushu to meet 9 U.S. Army divisions, the Japanese actually had 10 full divisions in place. Those facts fed into ongoing debate between the U.S. Army and U.S. Navy about the wisdom of any invasion, as was revealed in Joint Chiefs of Staff papers released more than 50 years later. General *George C. Marshall* and the Army wanted to invade as the shortest path to ending the war. Admiral *Ernest King* and the Navy brass clung to a long-held view that it was best to blockade, bombard, and bomb Japan into submission precisely to avoid heavy U.S. casualties thought likely to undermine the support of Americans for the war. Admiral *Chester Nimitz* withdrew his support for invasion of Kyushu following the experience of terrible fighting and *kamikaze* threat during the invasion of *Okinawa*. Other intelligence intercepts showed a massive Japanese Army build-up on Kyushu to three times the expected number of defending troops planned for in OLYMPIC. In sum, the U.S. Navy feared exactly the scenario that the Japanese Army hoped to achieve. Intelligence summaries reveal that even after the bombing of Hiroshima it was still believed by top U.S. military leaders that the Japanese were not ready to surrender.

Japanese historians have added much to this picture. Rather than asking only for a symbolic retention of Kokutai on August 10 (or, the "prerogatives of His Majesty as a Sovereign Ruler"), Tokyo was still demanding that an Imperial veto must be allowed over occupation policy and all future reforms. That would have meant the old imperial and militarist order in Japan was retained—a system and order that precipitated a great war in Asia that killed from 17–20 million people. Another group of historians, mainly Westerners, has raised the key moral issue of the attendant cost of continuing the war on the population of Japanese-occupied Asia. Robert Newman, for instance, estimated that cost at 250,000 lives per month, and possibly as many as 400,000. Almost all of those dead would have been civilians from nations victimized by Japanese aggression and occupation. Such a calculus surely must be weighed in any balance that also assesses the cost from dropping the atomic bombs in Japanese civilian lives. Richard Frank has put the case for the current state of knowledge succinctly: "The Japanese did not see their situation as catastrophically hopeless. They were not seeking to surrender, but pursuing a negotiated end to the war that preserved the old order in Japan, not just a figurehead emperor." Finally, as a radio intercept summary of Japanese Army communications put it in July 1945, rather than believing that Japan was on the verge of surrender, American leaders understood that "until the Japanese leaders realize that an invasion can not be repelled, there is little likelihood that they will accept any peace terms satisfactory to the Allies."

See also air power; biological warfare; DOWNFALL; Potsdam Conference; Potsdam Declaration; strategic bombing; thousand bomber raids; total war; unconditional surrender.

Suggested Reading: Michael Kort, *The Columbia Guide to Hiroshima and the Bomb* (2007); Robert Maddox, *Weapons for Victory: The Hiroshima Decision* (1995; 2004).

HISS, ALGER (1904–1996) American spy for the Soviet Union. Hiss had a stellar legal career, clerking on the Supreme Court for Justice Oliver Wendell Holmes and later practicing in Boston and New York. He joined the Department of State in 1936 and rose rapidly. During World War II he was a senior foreign policy adviser and attended several key planning conferences. In 1948 he was accused by a former Communist, Whittaker Chambers, of being a spy for the Soviet Union, a charge Hiss always denied. After a spectacularly controversial trial he was convicted of perjury related to the charge, though not of espionage per se. He was imprisoned from 1950 to 1954. He was always defended by Dean Acheson against fierce attacks from the right, almost certainly because Acheson believed Hiss and had a deep sense of personal loyalty. In 1990 Oleg Gordievsky, a high-ranking KGB defector, stated that Hiss had been a "penetration agent" during and after the war. A year before Hiss died, documents released from Soviet archives confirmed that he was a wartime agent who was later secretly decorated by the KGB, successor agency to the *NKVD* and *NKGB*.

Suggested Reading: Alan Weinstein and Alexander Vassiliev, *The Haunted Wood* (1999).

HISTORIKERSTREIT "Historians' controversy." A bitter academic dispute in the 1980s occasioned by the effort of a Soviet emigré historian, Victor Suvorov, supported by extreme revisionists in Germany, to show that Operation *BARBAROSSA* was a justifiable assault by Germany. Suvorov posited, and the German revisionists embraced, the argument that BARBAROSSA was a preemptive strike by Germany made necessary because Joseph Stalin was purportedly planning to attack. Supporting the thesis was weak circumstantial evidence from Red Army war games and planned dispositions, or wrongly inferred from Soviet weapons experiments and fighting doctrine: the idea of *deep battle*. Other historians of the Soviet war demonstrated conclusively the falsity of the German revisionist claim, originally and most baldly expressed in the Nazi declaration of war on June 22, 1941, in subsequent wartime propaganda, and in Hitler's final "Testament" in April 1945. Underlying the most spurious revisionist writing was a truly pernicious argument: that *Nazism* was essentially a defensive ideology and movement, which understandably took power and aggressive action against the enormous threat presented by Bolshevism to all Western Civilization.

HITLER, ADOLF (1889–1945) Dictator of Nazi Germany, 1933–1945. Adolf Hitler was the son of a minor Austrian customs official, Alois Schicklgruber. Maria Schicklgruber gave birth to Alois illegitimately, with the father left unnamed in parish records. It was later charged that Hitler's paternal grandfather was the young Jewish heir of the Frankenberger family of Graz, whose patron supposedly paid child support to Maria for years. The Schicklgruber family name and baptismal records were retroactively changed by Alois to "Hitler" in 1876, perhaps to facilitate his civil service career. Alois Hitler fathered a son and daughter, Alois Jr. and Angela, by his second wife. He married his third wife, Klara Pölzl, in 1885. The couple had six children. Only their fourth child, Adolf, and one sister, Paula, survived childhood illnesses. Adolf Hitler's father died in 1903. His mother, who always doted on her sickly son, died in 1907. The possibility that the Hitler family included a Jewish ancestor was secretly investigated by *Hans Frank* at Hitler's request in 1930. The *Gestapo* also investigated in the 1930s and 1940s, and declared that all such rumors were false. After the war, while awaiting execution for war crimes as governor of German-occupied Poland, Frank laid out the thinly sourced Frankenberger ancestry. Hitler's major biographer, Ian Kershaw, dismisses the rumor as unsubstantiated. Yet, even the possibility that it was true must have aggravated Hitler's anti-Semitic loathing. Given that he believed in a spurious theory of racial purity transmitted through "blood," he would have seen his personal bloodline as "polluted" by any Jewish entry into the family lineage.

As a young man left on his own, Hitler quickly ran out his small inheritance. He lived for years in vagrant obscurity in Vienna, twice failing to gain admission to the Vienna Academy of Fine Arts. He read anti-Semitic pamphlets, garbled nationalist histories, and too much bad philosophy of the social-Darwinian sort then popular in the brauhaus and cafés of Vienna. He thereby accumulated a hodgepodge of quarter-baked ideas in lieu of the formal education he lacked. He kept body and soul together by selling paintings to tourists that he made on the backs of post-cards, drawing advertisements for local companies, and doing assorted small jobs while sleeping in doss-houses and eating in charity breadlines. He nursed many deep grievances, real and imagined, personal, class, racial, and national. In 1913, at age 24, Hitler moved to Munich to immerse himself in a "German city" and to avoid conscription for service in the multinational Austro-Hungarian Army, where he would have to serve with Slavs and Jews. He later wrote: "My inner aversion to the Hapsburg state was increasing daily. . . . This motley of Czechs, Poles, Hungarians, Ruthenians, Serbs and Croats, and always the bacillus which is the solvent of human society, the Jew." In early 1914 he was located by the Austrian police and recalled to face a conscription board or possible extradition and prison. He was found medically unfit for military service on February 5, 1914. When war came to Europe that August, he was already back in Munich. He immediately volunteered for military service and was accepted into 1st Company of the 16th Bavarian Reserve Infantry Regiment. He was not yet a German, but he was a soldier of the *Reichswehr*. His baptism under fire came at First Ypres in October, just after the slaughter of the child soldiers there, or "Kindermord zu Ypren," that shook all Germany.

Hitler served bravely during World War I, notably in highly exposed work as a trench or dispatch runner ("Meldeganger"). He saw heavy action at Ypres, where just 600 men from his regiment of 3,500 survived. He was also promoted to corporal and received his first combat decoration, for rescuing a wounded officer under fire. He despised the "Xmas Truce" of 1914, refusing to fraternize with the British across No-Man's-Land. He fought the French at Neuve Chapelle and the British at Second Ypres in 1915. In 1916 he was present at the great battles along the Somme. He was wounded quite severely in the leg in October 1916. Though he might have stayed convalescing behind the lines, he volunteered to return to the front in February 1917. That attitude toward the war, along with his odd political views and asocial behavior, marked him as different and distant from his trench mates. He saw more heavy action at Arras and Third Ypres. His regiment fought at Chemin des Dames in 1918, during the final German spring offensives of the war in the west. In June, Hitler's unit advanced to the Marne and he thought Germany would soon win the war. On August 4, 1918, he received the Iron Cross, First Class, for taking a number of French prisoners single-handedly. But Allied counteroffensives and the great collapse of the Reichswehr followed over late summer and early fall. On October 14 Hitler was temporarily blinded by British gas. Also unable to walk, he was sent to the rear to recover. He learned of the civil unrest and mutinies of November 9, and of the Armistice of November 11, 1918, while in a military hospital. Hitler ended the war at the rank of corporal, with multiple decorations for wounds and bravery under fire. His wartime experience was formative. He always spoke of World War I as the happiest time of his life and is not known to have once regretted its destruction of lives, property, and decent personal and social relations. Instead, he seems to have found in martial life the comradery (but not friendship, which he shunned) and a sense of personal purpose in a mass cause that eluded him during his impecunious and secretive youth as a failed artist and vagrant in Vienna.

Like so many German veterans, Hitler could not accept that Germany had been defeated. He instead blamed Jews, socialists, and other "traitors" behind the lines for the so-called "Dolschtoss," the November 1918, "stab-in-the-back" of loyal soldiers like himself. He became dedicated to the "big revenge," a sustained effort to reverse the verdict of the Armistice and the Paris Peace Conference on Germany's imperial drive and national ambition. He worked as a minor propagandist for the Reichswehr in Bavaria after the war, but as an embittered nationalist and pathological anti-Semite he was drawn to become *Nazi Party* member #7 in 1919. Hitler quickly made the ragtag party his own. He soon drew special attention for his spellbinding rhetoric, into which he poured hours of study to perfect dramatic gestures and a monstrous gift for oratory. Hitler's first attempt to take power came in Bavaria with the "Beer Hall Putsch" of November 9–10, 1923. Hitler, *Hermann Göring*, and about 600 *Sturmabteilung (SA)* men burst into a beer hall in Munich and seized the Bavarian State Commissioner who was speaking inside. They forced him to declare the overthrow of the Bavarian and national governments, but he renounced that declaration as soon as the Nazis foolhardily let him go. Hitler thought the Reichswehr would support his revolt. But the Army sat aside, despite the fact that one of its old commanders, Field Marshal Erich von Ludendorff, joined the Putsch attempt.

On November 10, Hitler and about 2,000 supporters were joined by Ludendorff in a march on the Town Hall in Munich. Bavarian police met the Putschists with a hail of bullets, killing 16; 3 policemen were also killed in the gunfight. The man beside Hitler was shot, pulling him to the ground and safety in his death spasm. There had been several episodes in the trenches where Hitler narrowly escaped death. Another close call in Munich was for him more confirmation that he was a "man of destiny," a figure ordained to do great things and rewrite the history of Germany and the world. All subsequent escapes from assassination attempts—there were many over the course of his political career—added layers of conviction to his core belief in a personal destiny. Ludendorff was not touched by any police bullets, but was arrested. Hitler was arrested two days later. He was tried for treason and sentenced to five years in prison. He served just nine months. He used the time in prison to dictate his turgid autobiography *Mein Kampf* ("My Struggle") to *Rudolf Hess*. The Putsch and trial were a political boon: they finally brought Hitler and his revanchist message to national prominence. As important, his failure in Munich decided him against openly illegal methods. Henceforth, Hitler took an electoral and constitutional road to power, supplemented by street violence whenever that proved useful.

In *Mein Kampf,* a rambling and intellectually incoherent work, Hitler laid out many deeply irrational personal and political hatreds. But he also explained his plan to seize power in Germany and what must follow. He expressed contempt for all democracy and especially for the "decadent" Western powers. Most importantly, he explained long-term plans for conquering *Lebensraum* in the east. That was the most essential and persistent of his crude ideas. He did not mean by "Lebensraum" reunification or "self-determination" of all *Volksdeutsche* in a single Reich, as many leaders in the West and perhaps even some naïve early Nazis thought. He meant instead conquest of non-German lands and physical expulsion or extermination of their native populations, to clear "living space" for a "racially purified" German empire. His racism was central to his worldview: he planned more than an expanded Germany; he dreamed of total race war on a global scale until the German "*Volk*" achieved world mastery over a "New Order." To that end, war was not merely an essential instrument behind which one might conceal genocide, a function he praised on several occasions. War was also the "highest expression of the life force" by which racial mastery was to be constructed. Hitler's keenest hatred was reserved for Jews, followed by Communists. He conflated both perceived enemies into a crucially important and ubiquitous propaganda and hate-phrase: "Jewish-Bolshevism." Concerning the general effects of propaganda, he wrote: "the great masses of the people … will more easily fall victims to a big lie than to a small one." The real meaning behind his lust for war probably lies in a revealing remark he made in 1939, that the elimination of people "unworthy of life" was only feasible behind the cover of battle and war. This was the essence of his understanding of the idea of *Vernichtungskrieg* ("war of annihilation").

Hitler was propelled to seek national prominence and power by his fanaticism, anti-Communism, spurious race theories and anti-Semitism, crude social-Darwinism, and personal "will to power." He was obsessed with German greatness defined in terms of "racial purity." He believed race was the underpinning of all higher "Kultur," as expressed by nations through military prowess and triumph in arms in the struggle for "survival of the fittest." His knowledge of the world, even of Europe, was so limited and garbled that he frequently indulged fantastical notions about the history and workings of other nations. The key to all his thinking and political doctrine was race. That meant many nations lay outside his core worldview, even outside history as he understood it: an unfolding of racial conflicts in war. For example, Hitler believed that any greatness Spain ever achieved was due to an early infusion of "Visigoth blood," later "diluted," and to the lingering warrior spirit of the old Muslim caliphate in Cordoba. He appears to have known nothing about Imperial Spain's "Golden Age." Comparable confusions about most other peoples and countries abounded in *Mein Kampf* and in his later voluminous "table talk."

Hitler in Power

Hitler's path to power was made easier by a broad national despair which attended the *Great Depression* in Germany, and by general bitterness with the terms of the *Treaty of Versailles*. The real breakout into national politics came during 1929–1932, as the Nazi Party grew and groomed its appeal to various strata of German society in successive elections to the Reichstag. To run for president of the Weimar Republic in 1932, Hitler needed to become a German citizen. That required him to swear an oath of loyalty to the republic he loathed. Always a crass opportunist, he did so, intending to break his word whenever it suited. He would by the end betray all promises he ever made, including to the people of Germany, whom he led into gross physical destruction and collective moral collapse. In the 1932 election for the presidency, Hitler was defeated by his commander from the Great War, Field Marshal *Paul von Hindenburg*. His old general regarded Hitler with utter class, military, social, and political contempt. However, when the Nazi Party emerged from the 1932 national elections as the largest party in the Reichstag, Hindenburg was persuaded to appoint Hitler chancellor. The teetotaling, nonsmoking, vegetarian, former vagrant, and veteran from rural Austria took power in Berlin on January 30, 1933. Hitler's core thuggery and coarse origins were alike well-hidden beneath a top hat and tails as he swore the oath to serve as Chancellor of the Republic. No one among the men who maneuvered him into power, thinking that they could control the little ex-corporal, expected him to keep his word.

Hitler soon used a small fire started in the Reichstag to single out Communists for arrest and persecution, then to pass the Enabling Law ("Ermächtigunngsgestz") on March 23, 1933. That gave him extraordinary executive powers. Over the next six months he abolished all opposition political parties and established unopposed Nazi Party rule, closely attended by erection of his absolute personal dictatorship. When old Field Marshal Hindenburg died on August 2, 1934, Hitler combined the chancellorship and presidency into a new, all-powerful position: *Führer* ("Leader"). To placate the Reichswehr's concern about the swollen brownshirt ranks of the SA, he ordered SS-men to murder his Nazi Party rivals and their followers over a weekend of killing he called the *Night of the Long Knives*. He showed thereby great political flexibility and a fathomless capacity for ruthlessness, qualities Joseph Stalin expressly admired at the time. In return for eliminating any Nazi Party rival to the military, Hitler exacted an oath of loyalty from all officers and men to himself, personally and by name. The renamed Wehrmacht emerged thereafter as the greatest beneficiary of the Nazi revolution. But Hitler was always deeply distrustful and disdainful of an aristocratic officer corps he knew despised him for lowly origins and his many social crudities. After the war turned against Germany in late 1941, he would dismiss, imprison, and even execute some of the Wehrmacht's top commanders. In the meantime, Hitler and the Nazis deepened legal and social persecution of Jews and began the work of dismantling Germany's conservative civil society, in favor of more radical nazification of all aspects of national life.

Secure domestically, Hitler sought to destroy the Versailles settlement and enact the "big revenge" for Germany's defeat and submission in 1918. Yet, he proceeded cautiously at first, moving only when Western Allied guards went down or resistance to his moves seemed unlikely. He began by withdrawing Germany from membership in the League of Nations in 1933. He greatly stepped-up secret rearmament already underway from the 1920s, but he backed away from a failed Nazi coup in Austria in 1934. The *Saar* was returned to Germany in 1935, following a plebiscite in which 90 percent voted in favor of reunion. That made the Saar the only legal acquisition of territory in Hitler's career. The British helped him erode the Versailles system by signing to the *Anglo-German Naval Agreement (June 18, 1935)*. In a démarche that changed everything in 1936, Hitler reoccupied and remilitarized the *Rhineland*. He was emboldened by the enormous popular support this garnered, including from generals who had feared Western Allied intervention. Some senior military men had actively considered a coup, but backed away after Hitler's stunning diplomatic triumph was confirmed. He was encouraged to further bold strokes by the absence of any foreign resolve or opposition to this clear violation of a territorial clause of the Versailles Treaty. Meanwhile, Hitler supported Italian aggression in the *Abyssinian War (1935–1936)*, maneuvering to split Rome from London and Paris and fatally undermine the *Stresa Front*. When the *Spanish Civil War (1936–1939)* broke out and the Western Allies again displayed irresolution, Hitler agreed to Benito Mussolini's proposal that the *fascist* Great Powers send direct aid to General *Francisco Franco* and the Spanish Falangists and military rebels. Germany's contribution was the *Kondor Legion*. Such relatively low-cost cooperation with Italy led to further negotiations on a broad range of issues. A deeply isolated Mussolini pushed harder than Hitler for a permanent German-Italian understanding. This eventually culminated in creation of the loose, original *Axis alliance*.

In November 1937, Hitler told his generals to begin preparations for a general war in Europe that must result from his plan to redraw Germany's borders by force. He assured them that war was not imminent: Great Britain and France had already decided not to fight for Austria or Czechoslovakia. Be ready for 1941 or 1942, he told them. Time and events proved him prescient about the fate of the small democracies of Central Europe. Hitler completed a mostly bloodless *Anschluss* with Austria in early March 1938. Even Italy withdrew security objections to annexation that had led Mussolini to send troops to the *Brenner Pass* in 1934. Absorption of the German-speaking core of the old Habsburg Empire into the "Greater German Reich" marked a key moment in Hitler's psychological evolution: it confirmed a growing inner conviction that he was a "man of destiny," called upon by history to challenge and change the world. He began to move more quickly after the Anschluss. He was confident that he would meet little opposition from the West, but he was also driven by fear of illness and premature death to accelerate his original timetable. He next sought to destroy Czechoslovakia in a quick war. Misreading his real interest, which was violent conquest, the Western Allies and Italy compelled him to accept annexation of the *Sudetenland* at the *Munich Conference* in September 1938. The last serious internal opposition to Hitler's plans for aggressive war was ushered off the stage after the Munich Conference with forced retirements of Generals *Werner von Blomberg, Werner von Fritsch,* and *Ludwig Beck*. That purge of the High Command was attended by Hitler's personal takeover of the OKW. The old hands were sacked or blackmailed into retirement because they feared and opposed his aggressive diplomacy, thinking it likely to provoke a general and protracted war with the Western Allies, a conflict Germany was always unlikely to win.

Frustrated in his true ambition for war over the Sudetenland, but barely pausing, Hitler sent troops unopposed to occupy the rump of Czechoslovakia in March 1939. That marked the end of the West's policy of *appeasement*. Hitler now threw all caution into the breeze, succumbing to a deep megalomania that haunted him for decades, from the time of his Viennese obscurity and in the trenches of the Great War. He was giddy with triumph. But these extraordinary early successes at home and abroad would in time prove fatal: they led Hitler to believe not just in his personal destiny, but also in the great superiority of all his judgments over those of experienced diplomats, generals, and economic planners. Included in his core delusion was belief in the invincible power of his "iron will" to overcome mere material factors and opposition. This psychological condition was deeply pathological. It ultimately induced him into ever greater errors, though only after it drove him to exceptional victories that other men could not imagine were possible. His coarse romanticism, race ideology, and profound ignorance blinded him to hard realities of the *Materialschlacht* he eventually brought down upon Germany by declaring war on the greatest industrial economies in the world: Great Britain, the Soviet Union, and the United States. His answer was always more war, more risk-taking, ever greater gambles with other people's lives, framed in abulic proclamations of certitude, destiny, and will. Yet, at other times Hitler was consumed and even paralyzed by grave doubt. He vacillated over key decisions, procrastinating to the point of intellectual and psychological dysfunction that might last for weeks. Later in the war, some of those standing in his terrible presence would know what needed to be done but be too afraid of his rage and the secret police of his terror state to speak their mind, in a classic example of an ancient axiom: "the nearer to Caesar, the greater the fear." With war and the first defeats in the east, his increasingly unstable combination of hubris and doubt greatly assisted his enemies overwhelm and crush Nazi Germany militarily. Yet, until the great setback for the Wehrmacht in front of Moscow in December 1941, and even for a time after that, Hitler seemed to himself, to most of those around him, and to many admirers abroad, to be almost incapable of losing.

Worse, Hitler loved the clash of arms for its own sake. He was fatally attracted to war's unique aesthetic of destruction. He would ultimately order systematic destruction of Kiev, Moscow, Leningrad, Warsaw, and Paris, and then of all cities and public works inside Germany itself. In his twisted thinking, war was the essential tool of social-Darwinist selection of strong and fit peoples. Hence, it was also nature's tool for the necessary extermination of the weak. Surrounded by rubble and death in Berlin in 1945, he finally listed Germans as unfit and spoke blankly about their passing from history, while praising the great Slavic power that had arisen in the east and proven itself in a great war for survival. As morally, intellectually, and historically flawed as those ideas were, they gave him a powerful and immediate tactical advantage in the diplomatic run-up to war. Hitler understood that nearly everyone in Europe was so appalled at the prospect of another Great War like that of 1914–1918 that he could bluff and bully, playing the game of "brinkmanship" at its highest level. And he saw that he might win where other politicians and nearly all his generals feared to tread or to try: in remilitarizing the Rhineland in 1936, in the Anschluss with Austria and taking control of the Sudetenland in 1938, and in seizing without any resistance the rump Czech lands in 1939. But his judgment and luck finally ran out: his assault on Poland went a country too far. It was the critical error of his life.

Hitler at War

Insofar as Hitler had any *grand strategy* in 1939, it was this: he decided that he would defeat Germany's main enemy, the British Empire, by overstretching it. He did not believe Britain would fight, but Germany would still threaten it with a powerful navy and air force. Meanwhile, newly forged alliances with two old enemies, Italy and Japan, would tie down British forces in the Mediterranean, Indian Ocean, and Far East. With Great Britain overcommitted to extended imperial defense, Europe would open to German domination and the necessary conquest of Lebensraum in the east. Otherwise, Hitler had little strategic understanding of the ongoing contest for control of the Mediterranean among the navies of Britain, France, and Italy. He had no comprehension whatever of the real balance of forces and power in Asia. Hitler constantly dwelled on lessons he believed sprang from the defeat of 1918. That calamity gnawed at him just as it obsessed other Germans, but far more intimately and intently. A central "lesson" was his deep fear that victory in some foreign field might be snatched away by collapse of morale within Germany. For that reason, he cancelled the secret *euthanasia program* in August 1941, once news of it leaked, Bishop Galen of Münster made brave public protests, and public outrage began to rise over the rumor that wounded veterans were being killed. Fear of internal dissent led him to permit high production of consumer goods and order intense domestic propaganda efforts. It was his fear of domestic collapse, not mythic "Götterdämmerung" fatalism gleaned from a taste for German folk tales and the music of Richard Wagner, that underlay Hitler's ferocious insistence on fighting past the point that even he knew victory was no longer possible. As he characteristically put it during the *Stalingrad* campaign: "Germany at that time [1918] laid down its arms at quarter to twelve—in principle, I always stop only at five past twelve." It was a sentiment and boast he oft repeated. It was not one idly made.

It is widely agreed that from 1938 to 1942, Hitler took repeated rash gambles, risking all on bluffs of war, and then on war itself, against odds that his enemies either would not fight or could not win. But he rolled more than one time too many what another German leader, Chancellor Otto von Bismarck, once called the "iron dice of war." Hitler spoke often of carrying out a succession of discrete wars in which he isolated each victim in turn, so that every victory built strength to take on the next and more powerful opponent. That plan looked to begin spectacularly well. On August 23, 1939, he concluded the *Nazi–Soviet Pact* with Stalin. That freed Hitler to start the first of his serial wars, the attack on Poland on September 1st. But his strategic vision, understanding of enemies in the West, and timetable went wrong right from the start. Rather than stand aside as he predicted, Britain and France declared war on Germany two days later. Hitler was flabbergasted. He had not expected that the West would fight for Poland. Still, Hitler's armies overran Poland and then, far more surprisingly, conquered France and the Low Countries and thus gained for him control of continental Europe. Time to correct errors of planning and strategy was bought for Hitler, the OKW, and the German war economy by the brilliant operational successes of *FALL WEISS* (1939) and *FALL GELB* (1940). Hitler and the killers of the SS instead used that time to launch the first death squads eastward: the SS *Einsatzgruppen* commenced "extermination" of the Jews of Europe, and of Roma, Communists, *homosexuals,* or anyone else they deemed socially undesirable.

Yet, Britain still stood unbowed offshore. Along with its Empire, it set out to choke off the German economy via naval blockade and to hammer the German homeland from the air. The British were determined not merely on survival but on final victory, and readied for a protracted war for which Germany was unprepared. Hitler was right to differ from his top military advisers in believing that Britain, not France, was the main enemy in the west. That was why he struck at Denmark, Norway, and the Low Countries as well as France in 1940: to deny Britain access to the Atlantic coastline and prepare air bases from which the Luftwaffe would cross the Channel to destroy the island empire from the air. Stymied by the Channel and by Royal Navy and RAF strength and Kriegsmarine and Luftwaffe weakness, his basic need to force Britain to seek terms caused him to turn his legions eastward: Hitler determined to invade the Soviet Union in good measure to knock out Britain's last potential continental ally, and thereby force London to accept Berlin's domination of the continent. He said as much at the time in his "table talk." He confirmed that was his "grand strategy" in his final "Testament," dictated before he killed himself amidst the ruin of all his strategies and plans. It is key to note that he was enthusiastically supported in the military turn to the east by nearly all his top military advisers. For two years Hitler let his generals lead the Wehrmacht to triumph upon triumph, while he provided general strategic direction and timing. Yet, neither moral nor strategic distance between Hitler and most of his generals should be exaggerated, as most surviving German commanders did after the war in mendacious memoirs and oral histories. In Hitler's grand strategic idea of breaking the Soviet Union to bring Britain to heel, and in operational planning for the invasion of the Russias, Hitler's generals were almost all in enthusiastic accord with their Führer.

Increasing war production and the growing killing power fielded by Great Britain was supported by mid-1941 by thinly veiled American hostility, active USN involvement in the war at sea, and Roosevelt's preparations for a possible anti-German war by the United States. Those facts alone threatened to overturn Hitler's first victories, to frustrate his grand strategic concept and schedule for conquest, to block Germany's economic absorption of conquered territory, and to prohibit further expansion. In invading the Soviet Union, Hitler therefore made an all-or-nothing gamble to force the British to terms. By then, it was not a wholly irrational decision, given the geostrategic situation he had created around Germany. Still opposing Germany in the west, Britain threatened to coalesce a future "grand alliance" against him. What Hitler did not understand was that rising opposition to his ambition and aggression was fundamentally stimulated into existence by his strategic overreach and compounding errors. The British Empire and Commonwealth was arming and training not inconsiderable field armies. The United States was rearming and beginning limited but active participation in the *Battle of the Atlantic (1939–1945)*. Nor was Hitler wrong that Britain's civilian and military leaders clung to the hope that, if they held on long enough, other Great Powers with larger armies would enter the fight.

It is probably true that Hitler and the OKW were also more comfortable planning a land campaign into Russia than a cross-Channel invasion of Britain. The German Führer and his generals shared a view that the Red Army was ineptly led and ill-prepared for defense. That was not entirely inaccurate. But a larger point is that perception of Soviet weakness persuaded Hitler that an eastern campaign conducted by the Heer would be easier than trying an amphibious operation for which the Kriegsmarine was unprepared and unenthusiastic. And there were underlying and long-term ideological and depraved racial motives for an attack in the east. In the short-run, however, Hitler believed that eliminating the Soviet Union was the only way to extricate Germany from the strategic cul-de-sac it had entered in 1939. A bonus of quickly eliminating the Soviet Union from any potential enemy coalition and order of battle was that a second severe blow would be struck against Britain's other great hope for a war-winning alliance: the United States. With the Soviet threat removed, Hitler's reasoning proceeded, Japan would be freed to turn its full military power against the Americans. Hitler admired the Imperial Japanese Navy and coveted its entry into the war. That is why he still believed as late as his invasion of the Soviet Union in mid-1941 that it was far preferable that Japan attack Great Britain and the United States in Southeast Asia, rather than the Soviet Union in Siberia. His misreading of strategic realities and possibilities was reinforced by a belief that the Soviet Union must collapse militarily in short order, once he kicked in Stalin's front door with Operation *BARBAROSSA*. In his final "Testament" dictated in the ruins of Berlin in April 1945, Hitler openly regretted that Japan did not attack into Siberia in 1941. But such regret still lay a world of death and destruction away. Finally, in the calculus of decision to launch BARBAROSSA and in its operational planning, Hitler and the OKW alike cleaved to a faulty operational doctrine of a "war of annihilation" that foresaw the Wehrmacht easily crushing the Soviet colossus in a matter of weeks, or a few months at most.

At first all went spectacularly well in the western Soviet Union, even better than the campaigns in Poland and France. But as logistics and Soviet resistance hardened over the autumn of 1941, the task looked more daunting. As always, Hitler's answer to shortfalls of men and war matériel was more "iron will." He therefore took personal control of operations. It was his decision to shift two Panzerkorps away from Army Group Center barely a month into BARBAROSSA. Now he shifted them back, ordering a recommencement of the central drive on Moscow in Operation *TAIFUN (September 30–December 4, 1941)*. Why did he make the original shift to the south? One of his generals said after the war that Hitler had an intuitive fear of retracing the invasion route taken by Napoleon. Maybe. More reliably, we know that he believed that he alone truly understood grand strategy and geopolitics, and that he saw urgent capture of the food supply and natural resources of Ukraine as superceding any need to defeat the Red Army in the north. He therefore turned the Panzers to the flanks of the invasion, away from the central thrust to which nearly all his generals pleaded he give priority. Many historians consider that decision to be the main operational blunder of the war in the east, and even of the entire war. On the other hand, Hitler was most likely right to issue his *Haltebefehl* ("stand fast") order during the Soviet counteroffensive, or *Moscow offensive operation (December 5, 1941–January 7, 1942)*. That saved the Wehrmacht's Panzers and artillery and held the line, where his Generalfeldmarschälle and generals all wanted to retreat. But Hitler obliterated that temporary operational success by reinforcing grander strategic failure, as was his wont: just a week into the desperate Moscow battle he declared war on the United States.

The planned knockout blow in western Russia had led to a great crisis for the Heer as Army Group Center reeled backwards, fighting manically to avoid total annihilation while stunned by the appearance of entire Fronts the *Abwehr* could not imagine existed. Where was Hitler? Rushing back to Berlin from his eastern field headquarters. He had heard news of the Japanese attack on *Pearl Harbor (December 7, 1941)* and misread it as a great boon to the Axis alliance. Four days later he announced Germany's declaration of war against the United States, proclaiming that America was "guilty of the most severe provocations toward Germany ever since the outbreak of the European war . . . [and] has finally resorted to open military acts of aggression." Strategic errors were piling up, large and fast. First there was the miscalculation that Britain and France would not fight in 1939, then the mistake of thinking the British would quit after the fall of France in 1940. Next came overestimation of the military capacities of the Italians, followed by embroilment in a wasteful southern front in the Balkans and another in North Africa. That added to overextension of the Wehrmacht through occupation of Norway and holding open a high Arctic front in Lapland. And during what proved to be only the opening campaign of a four-year war in the east, he suffered from such delusions of rapid victory he ordered a shift of war production away from the Heer toward the Luftwaffe and Kriegsmarine, pending new plans for strategic bombing and invasion of Britain in 1942. Worse, after the failure to achieve quick victory over the Red Army, Hitler and the OKH decided to continue a war that was now fundamentally attritional. From 1942 to 1945, Nazi Germany's 80 million people fought a losing Materialschlacht against a stronger and larger Soviet economy, backed by 100 million people even after the loss of 80 million in German-occupied parts of the western Soviet Union. Hitler had also arranged for Germans to fight the British Empire, whose war economy was already outproducing Germany's, while Britain and its Commonwealth allies numbered over 70 million souls (not including India). Hitler then added the economy of the United States, far and away the world's most productive, innovative, and largest, and the military capacity of another 145 million people to the Allied order of battle. That was the most reckless, feckless, and disastrous decision of his wartime leadership. Why did he do it?

Hitler underestimated latent U.S. military and economic power and overestimated that of Japan. He had long planned to go to war against the United States but lacked the blue water navy needed to do so. He once considered a U-boat attack on the U.S. Pacific Fleet at anchor at Pearl Harbor, but was told by naval advisers that it could not work. Now Japan had struck a blow he had only dreamed about and brought its world-class navy into the war. He was excited about fighting the Americans. That is why he raced back to Berlin to announce his latest war: it had broken out prematurely to be sure, but that was nothing iron will and race superiority could not overcome. Even before his arrival in the capital Hitler ordered the U-boat fleet to begin sinking American ships as of December 8, along with ships of eight neutral American states. Beyond welcoming the Japanese navy into the war, Hitler actually believed in incorporeal fantasies like "will," "race" and higher German "Kultur." As in so many areas of his befuddled and frequently contradictory thinking, he cleaved to an erroneous view of American military weakness based on racist conceit about the United States as a "mongrel" and "Jew-ridden" society. That blinding prejudice remained dominant even though he wrote in a secret "second book" in 1928 that the ultimate enemy of German global ambition was the United States.

Nor did Hitler appreciate the degree to which mass mobilization of the U.S. economy and manpower underwrote German defeat in 1918. A mere corporal in the Great War, during World War II he retained a trench-level view of the earlier Allied victory. Dismissing all arguments that Imperial Germany lost the contest of material production, or Materialschlacht, Hitler was convinced defeat in 1918 was solely a consequence of the "Dolschtoss," an imaginary "stab-in-the-back" of the Imperial Army by Jews and Socialists on the home front. He also thought at the end of 1941 that Americans could not mobilize for at least a year, so that during 1942 he had time to finish the job of defeating the Soviet Union. To have viewed the United States as a weak military power was understandable in 1939, when the U.S. Army numbered fewer than 200,000 men and the USAAF was but a fledgling force. But it was unforgivably wrong by December 1941, when the United States was already training new armies and approaching war economy levels of production. Within a year, the American economy would easily surpass all Axis war production combined. Worse was Hitler's misunderstanding of extant and latent Soviet military power.

With failure of Operation *BLAU* and its ancillary offensive operations in 1942, Hitler had lost two giant military gambles in the east (BARBAROSSA and BLAU) and a third in North Africa (*El Alamein*). The minor Axis states were shredded of men and resources and of little aid to his failing cause. Their peoples were war weary and deeply frightened, as increasingly were Germans as well. Hitler's efforts at grand strategic thrusts into Ukraine and the Caucasus, and toward Suez, had all failed. The year of "breathing space" he thought he had during 1942, before the United States fully entered the fight, was wasted. American and British troops landed in North Africa in November 1942, jumped to Sicily in mid-1943, thence to southern Italy in September. Vast air armadas now darkened German skies more than the Luftwaffe had ever done or hoped. By the start of 1943, any grand strategy Hitler ever pursued was done. Thereafter, all he could do was hang on to power until it was wrested from his dead hands by the greatest violence, systematic destruction, and horror the world has ever seen. From 1943 to 1945, his leadership style in field operations thus changed significantly. He became extremely cautious about most proposals for offensives, but also ever more inflexible in defense. Over the second half of the war he was intent on holding what he had gained during its first half, although inflexibility about how to accomplish that cost him whole armies and then entire countries, time and again.

The pattern was first made clear in his refusal to withdraw in front of a series of effective Soviet offensives in Ukraine lasting from November 1943 to March 1944. Hitler insisted on trying to hold at all costs the line of the Dnieper bend. Those operations—the *Second Battle of Ukraine,* the *Zhitomir-Berdichev operation,* and the *Proskurov-Cherovitrsy operation*—drove Army Group South entirely out of Ukraine, leaving it shattered and isolated in eastern Rumania. They also cut off German and Rumanian armies on the Taman peninsula in the Crimea. Again revealing his Great War experience of trench warfare, Hitler hated retreat of any kind, even a successful and necessary one. He could not brook abandonment of a declared but largely imaginary line of *"feste Plätze"* in Ukraine. Field Marshals *Erich von Manstein* and *Ewald von Kleist* were therefore summoned to see Hitler in Bavaria on March 30, 1944, to be dismissed. They were neither the first nor the last of the best German field commanders to be forcibly retired by Hitler's need to blame others for cascading military failures. *Georg von Küchler* had been sacked in February, joining a long list of field marshals and generals fired in the fall of 1941 and winter of 1942. Others followed as the Wehrmacht lost more battles and campaigns on several fronts in 1944–1945. The battlefield skills of such professionals could not have prevented most German losses after mid-1943, and probably not even from the end of 1942. But they would have delayed Nazi Germany's final defeat.

From 1943 to 1945, Hitler repeated a pattern of trying to hold territories of limited strategic importance with diminishing military assets: in the Crimea, the Baltic States, Greece and the eastern Mediterranean, then in Sicily, Italy, Hungary, France, Finland, and Norway. That left large pockets of German forces isolated and cutoff in the Crimea and Lower Dnieper bend, before Leningrad, then at Falaise, the Ardennes, in the Rhineland, and in Courland. Hitler might have learned better from a dead Prussian king he claimed to admire. Friedrich II ("der Grosse") once famously warned: "He who defends everything defends nothing." In 1944 Hitler proposed to hold in northern Italy, give ground slowly as he must in the east, but concentrate to defend against the expected infantry of France by the Western powers. He failed spectacularly in France, not least because he was duped by *deception operations* about where the blow would fall on *D-Day (June 6, 1944).* That and other grave operational errors assisted the Wehrmacht lose the *Normandy campaign* in June–August 1944. Even then, Hitler indulged fantasies of snatching ultimate victory from obvious military catastrophe with spectacular operational blows and *Wunderwaffen* ("wonder weapons"), such as *V-weapons* bombardment of London and Antwerp and contemplation of attacking Britain with *gas weapons*.

As Hitler's wars in the eastern, western, and southern theaters were progressively lost from 1943 to 1945, and as he turned against the professional officer corps toward his fanciful inner lights, he displayed a deepening and fatuously "Nietzchean" superstition about the capability of "superior will" and the putative military utility of ideological resolution. It was other men, most notably *Albert Speer*, who finally put Germany's economy on a full war footing, cutting back civilian goods production and emphasizing defensive weapons systems. It was once argued that Hitler only organized the economy to fight serial short wars, but this is no longer the view of most historians. Instead, it is recognized that while the Nazis made a prewar effort to organize Germany's economy for general war, Hitler and other top Nazis maintained a high level of civilian production to damp down potential unrest. Fear of a second "stab-in-the-back" by dissatisfied folks on the home front was also persistent and powerful. It was more important for German unreadiness that Hitler provoked war with France and Britain years before he expected to have to fight a long war, and in ignorance of the superior capacity for economic mobilization of the British and French economies. He was similarly overconfident in the sure success of Vernichtungskrieg against the Soviet Union: barely a month into BARBAROSSA he ordered some war factories to revert to producing civilian goods. Even on a full war-footing, Germany could not hope to win the great Materialschlacht contest against the Soviets and Western Allies. Hitler instead indulged delusions about supposed limits to Allied production. For example, he rejected Luftwaffe estimates of enemy fighter production as ridiculous; they were not. He relied increasingly on assertions that men inspired by his correct racial ideology should overcome all physical obstacles and powerful opponents, performing feats in battle that were impossible for ordinary men.

Top commands were doled out on the basis of loyalty to the regime rather than military competence, so that even *Heinrich Himmler* received a field command. Hitler habitually encouraged and exploited normal rivalries among generals to maintain overall control. He was assisted in that scheme by sycophantic staff officers on the OKW and OKH who took it upon themselves to stroke his delusions and pass off all blame for failure to field commanders. In the last two years of the war Hitler repeatedly issued orders to whole armies to stand fast, resulting in their premature annihilation. In many cases, all military logic argued for tactical withdrawal to preserve men and weapons to fight another day, or defend from better ground selected for terrain advantages instead of symbolism. Nor had Hitler any real or sound appreciation of military logistics. He grossly overstretched Germany's resources by tying down large garrisons in occupied countries such as Norway, Greece, and Yugoslavia, none of which were significant in the military balance or final outcome of the war. The most spectacular example of his logistical ignorance was invasion of the Soviet Union in the face of information from the Wehrmacht logistical service that it could not support a deeper penetration than 500 km.

Among the major military setbacks for German military fortunes that were caused in whole or in part by Hitler's interference in command decisions were: the switch to city bombing during the *Battle of Britain* in 1940; declaration of war against the United States on December 11, 1941; failure to properly support the *Afrika Korps* in North Africa in 1942; ordering a suicidal stand by German 6th Army at Stalingrad; dividing and weakening attacking army groups on the Eastern Front in 1941, 1942, and again in 1943; refusal to release Panzer reserves early enough in the Normandy campaign to repel the Western Allied invasion of France; and repeated refusal to permit retreat by cut-off German armies in the long, forced withdrawal from the Soviet Union in 1944–1945. His last major blunders included committing Germany's slender reserves during the *Ardennes offensive* then defending along the wrong bank of the Rhine: during the final battles inside the western Reich, armies he had early badly positioned along the Rhine crumbled and started to surrender en masse to advancing forces of the Western powers. Hitler compounded the defeat by transferring the bulk of remaining Panzers to a futile counteroffensive against the Red Army in Hungary, when they were most desperately needed to support the main defense underway in East Prussia. After that, he retreated permanently into his "leader bunker" beneath the bombed-out ruins of the Reich Chancellery. There he awaited total defeat at the hands of either the approaching Red Army or Western Allies, each already deep into the German heartland and intent on prosecuting the *conquest of Germany* to an undeniable conclusion.

Throughout the war, but especially from 1942, Hitler turned his rage and hatred on the Jews of Europe. He held Jews responsible for all his misfortunes, although he was their sole father. Hitler's removal or killing of all Jews from Germany and his police state imprisonment of all dissenters and former political opponents in *concentration camps* eased his fears of home front rebellion by removing from German life all potential "traitors." But the hate was deeper than merely instrumental. Throughout remarkable early victories and calamitous later defeats, Hitler and his murderous henchmen pursued a fanatical hatred of Jews and other so-called "*Untermenschen.*" He enthusiastically listened to reports on the progress of the "final solution" carried out by Einsatzgruppen and in the later *death camps* of the *Holocaust*. To the end of killing Jews he dedicated construction, transportation, and manpower resources that were badly needed by the military. He was essentially unopposed in carrying out that genocidal program. It was only when the hinge of war turned and the door to defeat gaped open that some of his erstwhile admirers in the Wehrmacht at last turned on him, along with a handful of men of conscience. Hitler barely survived the *July Plot* to kill him. He savaged the officer corps in response, purging and murdering respected senior commanders with sadistic tortures, then ending their lives with dishonorable executions by hanging with piano wire from meat hooks, an exercise in sadism he later watched on film.

Thereafter, Hitler and the regime relied most heavily on *Martin Bormann* and the organs of the Nazi Party at home. In the field, they increasingly favored the ideologically reliable alternative to the Wehrmacht of the *Waffen-SS* and turned to the more radical solution of a levée en masse in form of the *Volkssturm*. Nothing availed. As defeat loomed on all fronts and the enemy hosts closed on him, Hitler's perverse sense of destruction overwhelmed all else. He ordered several of Europe's great cities leveled by fire and bomb. Warsaw was in fact systematically razed. Paris was wired for destruction but was spared by a disobedient general, who surrendered it to the *Force Française de l'Intérieur (FFI)* and the Western Allies. In the end, Hitler displayed the same moral indifference to Germans that he showed to millions of non-German victims. As early as January 1942, when it looked as though the Wehrmacht might replicate the defeat of the French Army in the snows before Moscow in 1812, he said to his closest confidants: "If the German people were no longer inclined to give itself [*sic*] body and soul to survive . . . then the German people would have nothing to do but disappear." On March 19, 1945, he tried to implement that contempt for failure in the struggle for the "survival of the fittest" peoples: he ordered wholesale desolation of Germany and smashing of all means of survival left to any postwar Germans. At long last he was disobeyed by a handful of members of a political party, government, and national military who had followed him to physical and moral ruination.

Hitler's Long-Term Aims

Did Hitler seek world conquest? The verdict is not entirely clear, but the evidence strongly suggests that he did, at least in some vague and distant sense. Hitler had once envisaged a two-phase strategy. His "Stufenplan" originally aimed at alliance with Britain, or at least to keep Britain neutral while he crushed France and the Soviet Union and created a Nazi superstate in control of Eurasia. That phase was to be completed by 1943–1945. Next, Hitler would implement his *Z-Plan,* framed in January 1939, which detailed a naval shipbuilding program for super battleships, aircraft carriers, and other blue water ships capable of defeating the Royal Navy. A critical point is that on July 11, 1940, he ordered work on a blue water navy theoretically capable of matching the U.S. Navy. At that moment he believed that the European war he started in Poland in 1939 was already won by Germany: he had wiped Poland off the map, then defeated the Western Allies. The fact that Britain would not quit did not affect his judgment: it was on its knees at the time, being pounded by his Luftwaffe. Further evidence of a long-term plan of world dominion was his insistence on acquiring naval bases in Morocco and the Canary Islands from Spain, a request made of Franco in June 1940. Hitler apparently believed that, in alliance with Japan, the Kriegsmarine should be capable of defeating the Royal Navy and carrying the fight to the United States by 1948. His subsequent forays into North Africa and failed cajoling of Spain to provide his navy with Atlantic bases may therefore have aimed at more than just support of his Italian ally, or a temporary tactical advantage against Britain. Hitler may have intended to keep parts of North and West Africa within a German overseas empire as bases from which to invade South America and to support a prospective anti-American alliance with Mexico. Franklin Roosevelt said about as much at the time and may actually have believed and even feared the possibility.

It is hard to know Hitler's real long-term plans, as he indulged innumerable fantasies that had little basis in reality. For instance, he admired the "jihadist" or holy war spirit of Islam, even speculating that had Germans converted to Islam rather than Christianity in the early Middle Ages they would have conquered the world by his time. What is clear is that, had Hitler won the war in Europe, he would have gained control of an industrial and natural resource base sufficient to make possible a defeat even of the United States—with defeat defined as containment of Washington's influence beyond the Americas. Such a vast resource and industrial base would have given Germany and its Axis partners real domination of the world politically and economically. In time, that would have given them ideological and cultural dominance as well. Add to those distant but real possibilities ongoing Nazi research into nuclear weapons, rocket, jet, and missile technologies, and one reaches the full nightmare: a possible new "Dark Age" descending over most of humanity by the harshest military means, a giant stumble backward from civilization into barbarism, savagery, slavery, and genocide of whole peoples and nations. Even if expansion of the Nazi empire must have spawned local rebellions, the prospect of mass reprisal, destruction, and genocide on a scale greater even than that which actually occurred during World War II must be considered. Facing the possibility of that global threat and the end of its historic independence, the British nation—truly living its "finest hour"—refused to bend or barter, a decisive act that ultimately made all Hitler's megalomaniacal dreams moot. For what came next in fact was not Nazi hegemony over an occupied continent and subservience of a cowed Britain. Instead, Germans lost the remarkably heroic Battle of the Atlantic against the Western democracies at sea, huddled under tens of thousands of enemy bombers streaming through their skies, and saw their armies crushed in a colossal ground war on the Eastern Front in pitiless fighting that has no parallel in human history.

Hitler was the great high stakes gambler of the 20th century. In 1941 he had doubled down on earlier tosses of the "iron dice of war." After the invasion of the Soviet Union, the only choices he had left were world domination through spectacular if farfetched military victories, or total annihilation of his regime accompanied by ruthless Allied destruction and occupation of his smashed empire. At no time did he contemplate a compromise peace. His Weltanschauung demanded nothing less than total victory. The choice was total victory in total war or destruction of the German nation ("der Untergang"). His entire approach to war thus contradicted the core insight and advice of another great Prussian whom Hitler purported to understand and admire, the military thinker Karl von Clausewitz. Where Clausewitz famously admonished that war is a continuation of policy by other means, Hitler had no conception that a political solution might exist for his war problem. He thus rejected all entreaties to negotiate with Germany's enemies: from Stalin in July 1941, from Italy and Japan during 1942, and from some of his own generals in 1943.

For two key psychological reasons, Hitler could not accept that the world balance of power was fatally tilted against his quest for Germany hegemony. First, he believed he was a providential figure of great historical destiny, the only man who could lead Germany from its condition as a second tier power to global dominance. He was the man destined to fulfill the great promise of "Weltmacht oder Niedergang!" ("World Power or Demise!"), in which so many Germans firmly believed during both world wars. Second, he was unable to imagine that men of the decayed old world order could change the world in the radical ways they were in fact doing. How could "reactionary" leaders of "decadent" states such as Winston Churchill and Franklin Roosevelt achieve what must be done? No, the future belonged to him and to Germany. That vision of world revolutionary and historical destiny he reserved unto himself and the *New Order* he planned for all the world; though he sometimes reserved a junior role for a man he once admired, Benito Mussolini. Hitler was moved, in sum, by enormous hubris that fed always on a perverted sense of personal destiny and a twisted and racialized view of history. But he also acted from fathomless hate and a profound fascination with destruction. Hitler thus brought Germany to crushing military defeat even as he led it into moral and physical catastrophe. For all that he was but a man, whom too many Germans followed into desolation for reasons of their own.

Hitler met his end in a subterranean bunker in Berlin, the "Führerbunker," with that great city, the German nation, and a whole continent in ruins around him. By then he was an impotent drug addict, much mentally and physically reduced and deeply shocking in appearance to loyalists who knew him in his prime. With the Red Army a mere 100 meters away, its gunfire audible to Nazi diehards and other bitterenders within the Führerbunker, Hitler made his final and most petty decisions. He dictated a self-justifying "Testament" naming his successor and identifying Germans as undeserving of his greatness, then married his simple-minded mistress, *Eva Braun*. Knowing the physical indignities Italian partisans and civilians inflicted on the corpse of Mussolini just two days earlier in Milan, Hitler ordered his body burned to deny it to the approaching Soviets. On April 30, 1945, Eva Braun took poison and Adolf Hitler shot himself through the mouth. Loyal past the end, SS guards poured petrol on the twisted couple and set them alight, adding more flames to the burning city. Hitler's charred corpse was located and secretly disinterred by the Soviets, although that fact was officially denied for decades. Portions of it were spirited all the way to Moscow, into the hands of the waiting master of the Kremlin. The rest of Hitler's remains were buried in an unmarked grave in an unnamed forest.

See also Atlantic Wall; Auschwitz; autarky; Canaris, Wilhelm; chemical warfare; Dachau; Dönitz; Eichmann, Adolf; Festung Europa; Führerprinzip; geopolitik; Germany; Gestapo; Goebbels, Joseph; Heydrich, Reinhard; Historikerstreit; Jodl, Alfred; Keitel, Wilhelm; National Socialism; Nomonhan; Nuremberg Laws; Nuremberg Rallies; Ribbentrop, Joachim "von"; Rommel, Erwin; Soviet Navy; Third Reich; Wolfsschanze.

Suggested Reading: Alan Bullock, *Parallel Lives: Hitler and Stalin* (1991); Michael Burleigh, *The Third Reich* (2000); Ian Kershaw, *Hitler*, 2 vols. (1999; 2000).

HITLERJUNGEND "Hitler Youth." The Nazi youth organization in which membership was effectively compulsory for all German boys ages 10–18. Boys age 10–13 joined the Deutsches Jungvolk ("German Young People"); those 14–18 served in the Hitlerjungend ("Hitler Youth"). Poorly disguised as athletic and sports clubs akin to the quasi-military Boy Scouts organization of the British Empire, these Nazi fronts trained boys and young men in "war sports" or "military athletics"

("Wehrsport"). Key activities were parade drill, map-reading, long-distance hikes, and weapons drill (with bayonet, grenade, and pistol and rifle marksmanship competitions). Boys also practiced taking cover and erecting camouflage, entrenchment, and defense against gas attack, and some learned to fly gliders as preparation for joining the Luftwaffe. All German boys were taught patriotic as well as Nazi Party songs, and closely indoctrinated in the regime's spurious race theories and radical foreign policy revanchism. There was a parallel organization for *"Aryan"* girls that similarly stressed physical fitness and moral and ideological purity. Girls under 14 joined the Jungmadelbund ("League of Young Girls"), thereafter transferring to the Bund Deutscher Madel ("League of German Girls"). Both groups inculcated a state-defined ideal of maidenhood tied to eventual "German motherhood," all aimed at revolutionary nazification of private and family life. The older boys of the Hitlerjungend were ordered into the *Waffen-SS* on June 24, 1943. They formed SS-Panzer Division "Hitlerjungend" from October 22, 1943. Their first combat came on June 7, 1944, during the *Normandy campaign,* around Caen. Ferocious and fanatic fighters, they stymied the British and Canadians for many weeks, while taking severe casualties themselves. The Division was reformed and fought next in the *Ardennes offensive* in Belgium in December 1944. Reformed for a second time, it was transferred to Hungary in February 1945. Its remnant surrendered to the U.S. Army in Austria on May 8, 1945.

See also *homosexuals; Wehrmacht.*

Suggested Reading: G. Rempel, *Hitler's Children* (1989).

HITLER LINE   Wehrmacht defensive positions built behind the *Bernhardt Line* in Italy in 1943. When the Western Allies threatened a breakthrough in January 1944, the name was changed to "Senger Line." But a defensive position by any other name was still breakable. Western armies got through it later that year.

See also *Adige Line; Gustav Line; Winter Line.*

HITLER'S HEADQUARTERS   Beyond the "Führerbunker" located deep beneath the Reich Chancellery in Berlin, Adolf Hitler kept multiple field HQs. He moved among them by armored train or flew to them by escorted aircraft. His main field HQ was the *Wolfsschanze* in East Prussia. He also had a *Werwolf* forward headquarters at Vinnitsa in Ukraine, following the conquest of that Soviet province. He kept two HQs in occupied Poland, only one of which he ever used. He had two in occupied Belorussia that he never used. Inside Germany, Hitler maintained the Berghof in the mountainous south (former Austria), and the Adlerhorst and three more HQs along the western boundaries of Germany, one of which he never used. Farther west, Hitler had more spartan field HQs at Wolfsschlucht I in southern Belgium and Wolfsschlucht II in eastern France.

HITLER YOUTH
See *Hitlerjungend.*

HIWIS "Hilfswillige" (auxiliaries) or "Hilfsfreiwillige" ("volunteer helpers"). Wehrmacht terms for Red Army *prisoners of war* who agreed to serve in "helper" battalions in exchange for getting out of the brutal camps, and so they might obtain a little more food. Most were used as drivers, cooks, and for basic military labor. By 1943 every Wehrmacht division had an official complement of 2,000 Hiwis, which was a way of making up German manpower shortages arising from mass casualties. By the middle of 1945 there were 500,000 Hiwis working alongside the Wehrmacht. They were dreadfully treated by the Germans while in captivity, then again upon liberation by *Smersh* and the *NKVD*.

See also Osttruppen.

HKL

See Hauptkampflinie.

HOARE-LAVAL PACT (1935) An agreement reached by British Foreign Secretary Samuel Hoare (1890–1959) and French Foreign Minister *Pierre Laval*. It proposed to partition Abyssinia as a means of appeasing Benito Mussolini during the early stages of the *Abyssinian War*. Abyssinia was to be reduced to a rump state, "compensated" with a strip of coastal land ceded from British Somaliland. Public outrage forced renunciation of the pact as well as Hoare's resignation. The agreement did severe damage to the idea of *collective security* without mollifying Mussolini. Indeed, it had the reverse effect of helping persuade him, and indirectly also Adolf Hitler, that the Western Allies were indeed decadent and weak as the fascist leaders suspected.

See also appeasement.

HOBART'S FUNNIES

See armor; Bradley, Omar; D-Day (June 6, 1944).

HÔ CHÍ MINH (1890–1969) Né Nguyên Tât Thành. Vietnamese Communist and nationalist leader. His early adoptive name was "Nguyen Ai Quoc," or "Nguyen the Patriot." That was one of more than 50 nom de guerre he took in the course of his life. In 1943 he changed his name to "Hô Chí Minh," which meant "he who brings/seeks enlightenment." An early Tonkinese nationalist, Hô traveled to Europe in 1911 as a ship's cook. He studied and worked in menial jobs in London and Paris. His ideological commitment deepened in Moscow, where exposure to Leninist ideas converted him into a committed revolutionary. Hô tried unsuccessfully to place Indochina on the agenda of the Great Powers at the Paris Peace Conference in 1919. He was present at the postwar founding of the French Communist Party and later joined the *Comintern*. In 1930 he founded a separate Indochinese Communist Party while still living in the Soviet Union. He made frequent trips to China during that time, but none to Vietnam. He was once jailed in Hong Kong by the British. Hô was fortunate to survive Joseph Stalin's purge of the Comintern. He was not permitted to leave the Soviet Union until the official party line on nationalism changed in 1938. He was dispatched to China to assess the Chinese position in the early *Sino-Japanese War (1937–1945).* In 1940 Hô returned to Vietnam, which he had not visited for 30 years. From 1941 he led guerrilla resistance to the Japanese occupation. In that effort he sought and received weapons, training, equipment, and propaganda assistance from the American *Office of Strategic Services.* After the war he was instrumental in establishing a Communist presence in Tonkin, or North Vietnam. He led the *Viêt Minh* in its armed independence struggle against France and a protracted and ultimately successful war against the United States and other Vietnamese that led to Hanoi extending Communist control over all Vietnam in 1975.

Suggested Reading: Dixee Bartholomew-Feis, *The OSS and Ho Chi Minh* (2006).

HODGES, COURTNEY (1887–1966) U.S. general. A highly decorated veteran of World War I, Hodges directed the Infantry School from 1938 to 1942. His first field command was with 10th Corps; his second was U.S. 3rd Army. He was sent to Britain to served under *Omar Bradley* with U.S. 1st Army in March 1944, then became its commander in August. He led 1st Army during fighting in France, the *Huertgen Forest,* and the *Ardennes offensive.*

HOEPNER, ERICH (1886–1944) German general. He was involved in several plots to overthrow Adolf Hitler, starting in 1938. He placed his conscience in abeyance during the early years of Hitler's military victories in the west and the Balkans. A pioneer of *Blitzkrieg* tactics, Hoepner led Panzer forces in the invasions of Poland in 1939 and of France in 1940. He was promoted to command of 4th Panzergruppe during *BARBAROSSA* in 1941. He was among the top generals purged by Hitler that December, as scapegoats for defeat of the Wehrmacht and near catastrophe during the first days of the Red Army's *Moscow offensive operation (December 5, 1941–January 7, 1942).* Hoepner rejoined the circle of anti-Hitler conspirators after his dismissal from command. He was involved in the *July Plot* to kill Hitler in 1944. After failure of that assassination and coup attempt, Hoepner was arrested, tortured, and hanged.
See also TAIFUN.

HOKUSHIN "northern advance." The geostrategic strategy pursued by the *Imperial Japanese Army* until July 1940. It sought to secure *autarky* within a context of Japanese *total war* theory by directly seizing the raw materials of Manchuria and Northern China. It looked also to Siberia, until the *Guandong Army* was bloodied by the Red Army at *Nomonhan (July–August, 1939).* The full slogan was "nanshu hokushin," or "defense in the south, advance in the north." It still took the grand distraction of a general war in Europe, the fall of France in June 1940, and *BARBAROSSA* against the Soviet Union in 1941 to persuade the Army to instead seek autarky through joining the *Imperial Japanese Navy* in a "southern advance," or *nanshin,* with the recognized condition that would mean war with the United States. On June 24, 1941, two days after Nazi Germany attacked the Soviet Union, the two services agreed to postpone any invasion of the Soviet "Maritime Province" bordering Manchuria until a more "favorable" moment. This strategic shift was confirmed by all decision-making bodies at an Imperial Conference in Tokyo on July 2. Still, the Japanese built up over 850,000 men in Manchuria, ready to strike north should the Wehrmacht assault on Moscow—Operation *TAIFUN*—succeed. But the Red Army withdrew only five divisions to reinforce its *Moscow offensive operation* in December. That left too many highly trained and well-armed Soviet troops in the Far East for the Japanese to confidently assault.

HOLLANDIA
See New Guinea campaign (1942–1945).

HOLOCAUST (1933–1945)   In its primary sense the Holocaust was the systematic persecution of the Jews of Europe perpetrated by the *Nazi Party* and its *collaborators* among "ordinary Germans," and by other Christian European peoples, that culminated in the most calculated and methodical genocide in human history. The full horror of the Holocaust is essentially ineffable; its explanation probably lies beyond human understanding. Some reserve the term "Holocaust" exclusively for the virulent hatred and deliberate and systematic plan by which the Nazis hunted down and murdered millions of Jews, although that sense is now more often communicated by the Hebrew term "Shoah." In the wider Holocaust, the same techniques were also used against many non-Jews, and the end result was the same: mass extermination of whole companies of people singled out for death merely on the basis of group membership. Identifiable groups besides Jews which were systematically annihilated, rather than simply individually murdered, by the Nazis included Roma, Communists, *homosexuals,* Jehovah's Witnesses, and the severely mentally and/or physically handicapped. Even so, Jews were always the central focus of the extraordinary hatred that moved many otherwise ordinary people to commit the most heinous acts imaginable, or previously unimaginable. Without reference to latent and historic *anti-Semitism* that rose up in virulently murderous form under the guidance of the Nazis, one cannot begin to comprehend the origins or meaning of the Holocaust.

The timber of European anti-Semitism in general, and German anti-Semitism in particular, was broad and blunt, but was not usually or overtly murderous or historically "eliminationist," as some have suggested. The leading historian of the Holocaust, Raul Hilberg, has detailed how the "final solution" proceeded by stages as Nazi anti-Semitism evolved from definition of "Jewishness" to facilitate social and then physical isolation from the German population, to culminate during the war in physical elimination of Jews. Moreover, the initial definition was framed in religious terms, evolving into "racial" categories over time. In the 1930s it was sharpened to a lethal point within Germany by fanatic social-Darwinism and venomous personal hatred of Jews on the part of *Adolf Hitler, Hermann Göring, Heinrich*

Himmler, and other leading Nazis. General, latent prejudice was concentrated into active hatred, which drew in more Germans as it combined with elite military and professional acceptance of the overall Nazi project for Germany, then being implemented by an expansive and ruthlessly rationalist bureaucracy. German Jews thus faced ever-diminishing choices of desperate flight, personal resistance (which would likely bring immediate death), or clinging to a fading hope of somehow waiting out events and thereby surviving. Street violence against Jews by the *Sturmabteilung (SA), Sicherheitsdienst (SD),* and *Schutzstaffel (SS)* began even before the Nazi Party's full ascent to power.

The radicalism of Nazi anti-Semitism escalated in stages once the Party achieved control of the apparatus of the state. It began ominously with passage of the *Nuremberg laws,* legally separating Jews from other Germans. Persecution deepened and progressed through social and legal ostracism; confiscation of Jewish property; economic boycott; and finally the orchestrated violence of *Kristallnacht.* Jews were initially encouraged to "voluntarily" leave the Reich lands of Germany and Austria, with every coin possible extorted from any who could afford to pay the bribes necessary to flee. After 1936 Britain limited Jewish immigration to Palestine and most other countries shut their doors as well: the *Great Depression* was underway and unemployment everywhere was at shatteringly high levels. Anti-Semitism was at work as well: Jewish refugees were denied entrance to Canada and the United States due to intense anti-Semitism of several top diplomats and immigration officials. Some refugee ships were forced to return to Germany after being turned away from European, Canadian, or American ports. Jewish passengers were seized from these ships by German officials and deported to concentration camps. There followed forcible ghettoization for the whole Jewish population, daily brutality, and more frequent murders. Finally, it was made a capital offense for any Jew to even set foot on German soil, which by then included annexed Austria. With early German military victories from 1939 to 1941, these horrific conditions pursued Jews across occupied Europe, varying in application with the depth of local hatreds and collaboration with Nazi policies of persecution and deportation. Treatment grew ever more harsh, and death squads moved into areas conquered by the Wehrmacht to begin systematic "extermination" of Jews and other populations unwanted in the *New Order* the Nazis were confidently preparing in Europe.

The Nazi plan for Europe's Jews was genocidal even before Red Army resistance blocked the initial "territorial solution" of deporting Germany's and Europe's Jews into conquered lands in western Russia: once there, they were to be worked to death as slaves. As the war began to go badly for Germany from the *Moscow offensive operation (December 5, 1941–January 7, 1942),* Hitler and the SS returned to their earlier emphasis of the war in the east as a *Vernichtungskrieg* ("war of annihilation") against the "greatest servant of Judaism," the Bolshevik-Soviet state. The Wehrmacht was instructed—it obeyed almost without question, and in many cases with real enthusiasm—to segregate and allow immediate killing of identified Jews, along with Communists, among millions of Soviet prisoners of war. Hitler and his closest Nazi co-conspirators also viewed American hostility toward Nazi Germany as part of a plot by "international Jewry." None of that means Hitler's personal intentions were not murderous from the start, for they were. The shift in Germany's fortunes of war against the Allied powers in 1942 added urgency to Hitler's parallel war against the Jews. Starting systematically from 1942, Jews who had been earlier herded into urban ghettos by Nazi overseers and local collaborators were shipped out of the ghettos to *concentration camps,* including new *death camps* then coming on line for the explicit purpose of industrialized mass murder. The full nightmare of the Shoah would soon be reached.

The use of euphemism about the Holocaust persisted to the top of the Nazi hierarchy, from Adolf Hitler through *Reinhard Heydrich, Adolf Eichmann,* and many others directly involved in its most noxious and heinous acts. Even the vulgar Nazi term "extermination" helped portray Jews as vermin, and thus helped to justify mass murder. One top Nazi who was not shy about committing his murderous thoughts to paper or to openly speak of them to Wehrmacht officers or to Party and government officials was *Heinrich Himmler.* But most shied away in public from expressing the full brutality of language required to describe their crimes. They also shrouded their deeds in quasi-legality, bending laws or writing new ones to fit the desired outcomes of deportation and mass murder of Jews. Later Holocaust deniers thus purveyed the canard that no historian has yet produced a written order from Hitler initiating the "final solution." Yet, everyone involved in carrying it out knew that it was their leader's fiercest wish ("es war des Führers Wunsch"), as indeed it was also their own. If they did not know the mechanics and machinery of the murder plan before the *Wannsee Conference (January 20, 1942),* they knew beyond doubt by the time it ended. Hitler also outlined his intentions clearly in 1939 before the invasion of Poland, and again to several hundred top Wehrmacht commanders on March 30, 1941, when he spoke frankly about their moral duty to conduct a "war of annihilation" in the east against all identified as enemies of the Reich.

The killing program accelerated with the German invasion of Poland in 1939 (Operation *FALL WEISS*). Extraordinary and sweeping German victories in Poland and later in the western Soviet Union gave the worst Nazi fanatics control of most Jews in Europe. As the Wehrmacht advanced into new territories, it was closely followed by special SS murder squads operating under the military euphemism *Einsatzgruppen* (Special Action Groups). These ruthless death commandos went on "Jew hunts" in the countryside, ferreting out refugees in the smallest hamlets. In all, the Einsatzgruppen probably killed 1,500,000 Jews. They also routinely murdered Communists and Roma. More Jews were herded into overcrowded ghettos in the cities. The largest was in Warsaw. There, they awaited more systematic killing machinery in the death camps that would be built by the SS from early 1942. A controversy grew within the SS as to whether it was preferable to kill all Jews immediately, or work the able bodied to death in SS-run slave labor camps. In either case, the long-term ambition was to "resettle" (kill) all Jews in Germany and then in German-occupied Europe. The lands thus "cleansed" and "Jew-free" would be resettled with "racially pure" members of the German *Volk*. Those incapable of work—the very old, children, mothers and their infants—were butchered as soon as possible, in mass shootings in the villages or as soon as the "selection" was made as they detrained at some death camp. At first, most executions even in the camps were by firing squad or machine gun, with thousands of bodies bulldozed into mass graves or anti-tank ditches, such as those used at *Babi Yar*. This was "inefficient," however, even when SS killers jocularly competed to see how many Jews they could dispatch with a single bullet. Mobile gas vans were tried next, mainly to speed up and increase the volume of killings, but also to relieve dutiful SS men of the psychological strains that accompanied shooting tens of thousands of women and children. In addition, Himmler once became hysterical and fainted during a mass execution when two Jewish women failed to die quickly or quietly, writhing and moaning on the ground in front of him during their death agony. He ordered that henceforth women and children should be gassed.

As morale fell among some men of the Einsatzgruppen, but while the prospect of victory over the Soviet Union still seemed possible, a proposal was mooted to resettle all Jews in soon-to-be-conquered Asiatic Russia. There, they would be worked to death as slaves, all dead within a generation. But as the chance for military victory in the east slipped away, SS plans turned to a more immediate and "final solution" laid out ultimately in the *Aktion Reinhard* program: outright extermination of all Jews by mass killings carried out in a new system of purpose-built death camps. Ghetto and labor camp Jews were shipped by sealed cattle car to industrialized death camps such as *Auschwitz*. The killing camps were constructed in accordance with decisions taken at Wannsee that January day to "exterminate" all Jews. The Wannsee plan called for full scale extermination camps, with several capable of killing and disposing of as many as 25,000 people each day. Killings began early in 1942, even before the first death camps were finished and in operation by mid-year. Forced deportations to the camps took place from all over occupied Europe, under the cover of "relocation" and "resettlement." The SS planned to kill as many as 11 million Jews, but they were unable to reach that total once Germany began to lose the war and control of occupied eastern territories. That fact enraged Hitler and his henchmen and speeded the rate of killing. As the advance of the Red Army threatened to overrun the main death camps in late 1944 and early 1945, the SS began destroying physical evidence of their crimes, blowing up gas chambers and crematoria and bulldozing barracks. That also meant accelerating the killing to be rid of witnesses.

What happened next had no precedent in history: severing of families and genders; transport to the camps by packed cattle and freight cars; upon arrival, a selection into those who died immediately—mainly the very old, very young, and mothers with small children—and those fit enough for slave labor until they, too, died or were murdered in turn; slow starvation; sadistic medical experimentation; mass hangings and shootings; and the gross obscenity and indignity of gas chambers and crematoria at sites of horror and suffering that remain unparalleled in all human history. At least six million Jews were murdered by the Germans and local and ideological collaborators. That was an unprecedented attempt at industrialized slaughter of a whole people, stateless and bereft of an army to defend them. Several million non-Jews were also systematically murdered, mainly Russians and Poles starved or worked to death, but also homosexuals, Jehovah's

Witnesses, and Roma who were also shot or gassed. In the scale of lives lost, the Holocaust was possibly surpassed by Stalin's war against the kulaks in the early 1930s and by Mao's depredations that cost so many lives of Chinese peasants in the 1950s. But in its ferocity, sadism, hate, and horror, the Nazi genocide of the Jews of Europe has no peer. Subsequent efforts by neo-Nazis and their fellow travelers to deny the historical reality of the Holocaust are utterly spurious. Worse, they are indicative of the mentality that brought it about.

The Western Allies came in for much postwar criticism about their lack of direct effort to stop the Holocaust or directly come to the aid of its victims. Since publication of a seminal study in 1984, Franklin D. Roosevelt has been heavily criticized for not doing more. However, subsequent scholarship was somewhat more favorable to his contemporary explanation, that the central Western Allied effort to win the war against Germany in the shortest possible time was also his core policy toward the Holocaust. The Western Allies considered diverting bombing and other resources to interdiction of death railways and of the death camps, but they ultimately decided that would only slow the war effort. Primary blame for that inaction has shifted in historical literature from Roosevelt to the State Department, specifically to the deeply anti-Semitic Breckinridge Long, the man singularly responsible for U.S. policy on "Jewish affairs" from 1940 to 1945. Long's personal malignancy was compounded by incompetence or moral diffidence on the part of Secretary of State *Cordell Hull* and others. Other men with similar attitudes worked for the prime ministers of Great Britain, Canada, and other Allied countries, while many anti-Semites of a more murderous sort officered the *NKVD* and other key organs of the Soviet state.

See also Belzec; Buchenwald; Chelmno; Dachau; Eisenbahntruppen; Gestapo; Göring, Hermann; Pius XII; restitution; righteous Gentiles; Sonderweg; Warsaw Ghetto rising.

Suggested Reading: Yehuda Bauer, *Rethinking the Holocaust* (2001); Raul Hilberg, *Destruction of the European Jews,* 3 vols. (1985); Aly Götz, "Final Solution" (1999); Michael Marrus, *The Holocaust in History* (1987).

HOLODOMOR: Ukrainian term for the deliberately induced famine in eastern (Soviet) Ukraine from 1932 to 1933, which took at least seven million lives. Bitterness over the famine induced many Ukrainian nationalists to collaborate with the German occupation, even to volunteer for anti-Soviet Ukrainian divisions of the *Waffen-SS.* Others resisted the return of Soviet rule in arms into the early 1950s.

See Red Army; Soviet Union; Stalin, Joseph; Ukraine.

HOME ARMY "Armia Krajowa."
See Polish Army.

HOME GUARD "Dad's Army." The British civil defense force, founded on May 14, 1940. Originally called the "Local Defense Volunteers," it especially utilized men over normal military age, many of them veterans of the Great War. It kept coastal and air watches, looked out for spies, and trained haphazardly with whatever weapons (or dummy rifles) it could scrounge. From February 1941, its structure became more regular and formal as it served to train underage boys before they were formally conscripted. The Home Guard "stood down" in December 1944.

HOME ISLANDS (OF JAPAN)   By convention, Hokkaido (Ezo), Honshu, Kyushu, and Shikoku. The term usually excluded the Kurils and Ryukyus.
   See DOWNFALL; Ketsu-Gō; Sho-Gō.

HOMING WEAPONS
   See bombs; divers; dogs; torpedoes.

HOMMA, MASAHARU (1887–1946)   Japanese general. He received his commission in 1908, then stood out in studies at the advanced Staff College. During World War I he was liaison to the British Army in Flanders. He maintained his British connections with postwar years spent in India and London—where he nearly committed suicide over social shame at the actress career of his first wife, although he was a poet and playwright himself. He saw field duty escorting the British out of the Tianjin concession two years into the *Sino-Japanese War (1937–1945)*. He served with the Taiwan garrison from 1940 to 1941. Homma led 14th Army in the desultory *Philippines campaign* (1941–1942), during which he moved only slowly to follow-up the conquest of Manila by pursuing retreating American and Filipino forces to Bataan. He was forcibly retired in 1943, basically for insufficient aggressiveness in the Philippines. Homma was tried and shot after the war for allowing the *Bataan death march* in 1942, even though he was among the more humane of Japanese generals and the evidence against him was ambiguous. There was also countervailing evidence that he sometimes sought to prevent atrocities by his troops.

HOMOSEXUALS   Persecution of homosexuals varied in Nazi Germany from unofficial toleration to castration, to death. Adolf Hitler on several occasions used charges of homosexuality to bring down his opponents inside the Nazi Party and the Wehrmacht. The Reichstag fire led to increased persecution right from the outset of the regime. A broad and bloody purge accompanied the *Night of the Long Knives* in 1934. In 1936 German male homosexuals were designated "national pests." They were placed under curfew and close police observation. Hitler harshly denounced homosexuality in August 1941, and imposed the death penalty for male homosexual contact or acts by members of the *Hitlerjungend* or *Schutzstaffel (SS)*. By 1944 at least 7,000 men were purged from the Heer and sent to *concentration camps*. Other inmates arrived by train from across German-occupied Europe. It is not known how many were murdered for being homosexual, but perhaps as many as 15,000 died. Lesbians were not seen as a major threat in the same way male homosexuals were. Many were nonetheless sent to *Ravensbrück*.

See also death camps; Fritsch, Werner von; Holocaust; Nazism; Night of the Long Knives; Rassenkampf; Sturmabteilung (SA).

HONG KONG   This British colony in southern China was attacked by the Japanese in coordination with the attacks on the Americans at *Pearl Harbor, Guam,* and *Wake,* and the British in Malaya and Burma. The colony was captured on December 25, 1941, after just two weeks of Japanese assault. Its small garrison of 12,000 British, Canadian, and Indian troops (Rajputs and Punjabis) was supplemented by local police units. These forces defended with varying degrees of skill or weakness, but were soon isolated and overwhelmed. The formal British surrender was made on December 25, 1941. The conquering Japanese then went on an orgy of rape, pillage, and murder to rival the *Rape of Nanjing* in ferocity and cruelty, though not in raw numbers. Hospitals were raided and patients bayoneted or shot in their beds; convents were singled out by rape gangs; random murder was around every street corner. Some 2,700 Japanese were casualties of the fighting, alongside 4,000 Allied troops. Civilian deaths were extensive. Britain reclaimed the colony in 1945.

HOOD, HMS, SINKING OF
See Atlantic, Battle of the (1939–1945).

HOOVER, HERBERT (1874–1964)
See Great Depression; Hoover-Stimson Doctrine (January 7, 1932); war debts.

HOOVER-STIMSON DOCTRINE (JANUARY 7, 1932)   An announcement by President Herbert Hoover and Secretary of State Henry Stimson, in response to the *Mukden incident* and Japan's follow-on invasion of *Manchuria.* It declared that the United States would refuse to recognize any arrangements in China that were contrary to the "Open Door" principle. That was an ineffective compromise between Hoover's caution and Stimson's desire to carry out sanctions, even though the United States did not belong to the *League of Nations.* The proclamation gave radical Japanese nationalists room to widen a breach with Washington without affecting Tokyo's plans for expansion at China's expense.

HOPKINS, HARRY (1890–1946)   U.S. statesman. He was a close friend and adviser of Franklin Roosevelt. He oversaw the *Lend-Lease* program early in the war, pushing hard for inclusion of the Soviet Union. He also served as FDR's personal envoy to Joseph Stalin and Winston Churchill. Hopkins was a top adviser to the president at the *Yalta Conference.* He was opposed to the hard line on postwar issues toward the Soviet Union advised by *W. Averell Harriman* and others. Hopkins was active at the *San Francisco Conference* and attended the *Potsdam Conference* with *Harry Truman.* He became a hated figure to the American far right during the early Cold War, taking much unfair blame for the supposed "sell-out" of Eastern Europe to Stalin at Yalta.

HORNPIPE   The code signal to be sent to *OVERLORD* invasion forces inside their assembly areas across southern England in the event of a 24-hour delay of the invasion of Normandy.

HORROCKS, BRIAN (1895–1985)   British general. His career was closely aligned with that of his superior, Field Marshal *Bernard Law Montgomery*. Horrocks served with Montgomery in Africa, Sicily, France, and most importantly, as commander of 30th Corps during *MARKET GARDEN* in the Netherlands and in the *conquest of Germany*.

HORSES   Animal power was ubiquitous on World War II battlefields and in rear areas, with horses forming the spine of logistics for several armies. Among major combatants, the Wehrmacht was most reliant on horses for its basic transport. Horses pulled ammunition wagons; towed artillery; and hauled kitchens, food wagons, ambulances, and carts filled with German wounded. During *BARBAROSSA*, most invading Axis infantry that advanced behind the Panzers and mechanized Panzergrenadiers did so on foot, with all their supplies and many of their guns hauled by horse. Over 750,000 horses accompanied the invading Axis armies that summer. Millions more were collected from farms across occupied Europe and the western Soviet Union, thereby greatly reducing agricultural productivity. Most accompanied the Germans eastward into shared death from shellfire, bombs, cold, and starvation. The Red Army also used horses in lieu of trucks and halftracks, which it lacked until *Lend-Lease* trucks began to arrive in large numbers in 1943. It deployed 8 corps of cavalry that year, or some 26 (reduced) divisions. Over the course of the war it is thought that more than 15 million horses died on the Eastern Front. Even the U.S. Army began the war with 12 million horses—and another 4 million mules. Yugoslav partisans, Greek partisans, and all other troops fighting in mountainous areas relied on horses as pack animals. But horses were not important just in transportation. As the Wehrmacht was progressively demodernized by attrition of its armored vehicles on the Eastern Front, in the last year of the war it scrambled to maintain a semblance of mobility through increased used of horses by fighting formations. In Asia, the Japanese Army used large herds of horses extensively while fighting in China, as did opposing *Guomindang* and *Chinese Communist armies*. The Japanese even developed snow-suit camouflage for pack and cavalry horses working in winter conditions.

   See also artillery; cavalry; chemical weapons; Cossacks; tachanka.

HORST WESSEL SONG   The official song of the *Sturmabteilung (SA)*, named for a stormtrooper said by the Nazis to have been killed in a street fight with German Communists. Nazis made the song known all over Europe and much of the world.

HORTHY DE NAGYBÁNA, MIKLÓS (1868–1957)   Hungarian admiral, regent, and dictator, 1920–1944. Horthy commanded the Austro-Hungarian Navy during World War I. In 1920 he was appointed regent of newly independent

Hungary. He moved to quickly crush the Hungarian soviet set up by Béla Kun. He subsequently blocked restoration of the Habsburg monarchy. He thereby found himself in the most unusual situation of serving as a regent in a country without a king. Politically, he governed from the hardline nationalist right during the interwar years. He agreed to join Hungary to the *Axis alliance* in 1941, and sent Hungarian troops to invade Yugoslavia and to fight in the Soviet Union. He tried to withdraw from the Russian war and to negotiate a separate peace with Moscow in 1944, as the Wehrmacht began to fall back all along the Eastern Front and the Red Army approached Hungary's frontier. In response, Hitler ordered the kidnapping of Horthy's son and forced him to abdicate as regent. Horthy was imprisoned by the Nazis. He was captured by the Americans in Germany in 1945. He was called as a witness by the *Nuremberg Tribunal* but was not brought up on any charges. He died in exile in Portugal.

HOSPITAL SHIP   An unarmed, clearly marked—usually with the emblem of the *Red Cross*—medical ship used to transport and treat wounded in a distant combat zone. In legal theory, hospital ships or other ships (or planes or ambulances) displaying medical insignia were immune from all attack. In practice, they were often targeted by excited or confused troops, or deliberately. For example, British fighters shot down clearly marked German rescue aircraft looking for downed pilots in the Channel during the *Battle of Britain,* while German gunboats shot up similarly marked British rescue boats. When the Italians tried to smuggle supplies to North Africa on hospital ships in 1942, the British sank them: they knew of the plan from reading deciphered Italian intercepts.

HOSSBACH MEMORANDUM (NOVEMBER 5, 1937)   A memorandum by Adolf Hitler's adjutant, Friedrich Hossbach, recording a detailed Führer briefing of top Wehrmacht generals on November 5, 1937. Hitler told the gathered generals of plans for a sustained campaign of aggressive war. As commander of German 4th Army in East Prussia, Hossbach abandoned fortified positions during the *Mlawa-Elbing operation.* Hitler sacked Hossbach in January 1945. The 1937 memorandum was cited by the *Nuremberg Tribunal* as a basis for charges of conspiracy to commit aggressive war. Hitler repeated its essential arguments to 200 top Wehrmacht commanders on November 23, 1939, adding that Germany must strike before Britain and France built up their armed forces, German relations with Italy or the Soviet Union soured, or the United States moved away from neutrality. Hitler also expounded at length in the Hossbach memorandum on *Lebensraum,* which he said Germany could not postpone acquiring by an aggressive war that stated later than 1943.

HOSTAGES
See bandit; BARBAROSSA; resistance.

HOSTILITIES ONLY (HO)   Royal Navy term for volunteers, recalled naval retirees, reservists, and fresh conscripts trained by the RN in ship defense. Many were assigned to the *merchant marine*. The term distinguished regular or active-duty career naval personal from those classes called up for the war.

HOTH, HERMANN (1885–1971)   German colonel general. He led a motorized corps during the invasion of Poland in 1939, Operation *FALL WEISS,* and "Hoth Panzergruppe" in the invasion of France and the Low Countries in 1940, during Operation *FALL GELB.* For Operation *BARBAROSSA,* the invasion of the Soviet Union launched in June 1941, he was given command of 3rd Panzergruppe. On the eve of the attack Hoth told his men: "The annihilation of those same Jews who support Bolshevism and its organization for murder, the partisans, is a measure of self-preservation." His command saw major action around Viazma before taking over 17th Army in the Donets regions. He fought at *Kharkov* in the spring of 1942. He commanded German 4th Panzer Army during the *Battle of Stalingrad* and again at *Kursk.* Adolf Hitler relieved him during the *Second Battle of Ukraine* in November 1943. Assigned at first to career oblivion in the *Ersatzheer* or "Replacement Army," Hoth was then dismissed outright. He was recalled in the last weeks of the war to a nearly nonexistent command in the Harz Mountains. In 1948 Hoth was convicted of *war crimes* by the *Nuremberg Tribunal* and sentenced to 15 years. He was released from prison in 1954, after only six years served.

   See also Smolensk, Battle of.

HOWITZER   An *artillery* piece that fired a lower velocity shell at a higher arc than normal, to enable fire over high terrain or artificial obstacles or fortification.

   See also Hobart's Funnies; mortar.

HOXHA, ENVER (1908–1985)   Quixotic, Stalinist resistance leader. He led the main Communist resistance to Italy's invasion of Albania that began upon the launch of the *BARBAROSSA* invasion of the Soviet Union. In 1943 Hoxha broke with the misnamed United Front opposing Axis occupation and attacked non-Communist guerrillas and rivals. He was Communist dictator of Albania from 1945 to 1985.

HUERTGEN FOREST, BATTLE OF (SEPTEMBER–DECEMBER, 1944)   "Hürtgenwald." General *Courtney Hodges* led U.S. 1st Army into the Huertgen Forest along the border of Germany in September 1944, in a vain attempt to flank the German line. The penetration was ill-conceived and poorly prepared, partly from belief that the Wehrmacht was already done as a fighting force after its sharp defeat in the battle for France in July and August. Confined spaces, rolling terrain, and the absence of paved roads in the Hürtgenwald made movement difficult, especially of armor. Meanwhile, the dense Huertgen woods were heavily defended by prepared and well-sited fire positions that could not be easily overcome by American air and artillery superiority. Presited mortars and artillery used tree-bursts to devastate GIs with lethal wood and metal shrapnel, as they plodded forward also under sniper and machine gun fire or stumbled into or across mine fields. Hodges reinforced failure, sending units in piecemeal until he had committed two full divisions against two understrength German divisions, with the latter reinforced during the fight. Casualties were extreme by the standard of the Western Front: over 24,000 combat casualties on the American side, plus many more from frostbite and accident. German casualties were about 13,000. Just as the Germans were cleared from the Huertgen the *Ardennes offensive* began in another dense forest.

Suggested Reading: Robert Rush, *Hell in Huertgen Forrest* (2001).

HUFF-DUFF   "High Frequency Direction-Finder (HF/DF)." *Huff-Duff* was the Western Allied term for detection equipment that located high frequency transmissions, especially from U-boats. Huff-Duff long-range listening stations were set up around the Atlantic. The first reliable shipborne sets appeared in July 1941. A British invention, they were much improved and reduced in size by American engineering and then mass produced.

See also Direction-Finding (D/F).

HUK (*HUKBALAHAP*) ARMY   Anti-Japanese communist guerillas whose main strength was on Luzon. They were more focused on internal "class struggle" and more active against Filipino enemies than against the Japanese. From 1946 to 1950, a Huk rebellion took over most of Luzon. After the outbreak of the Korean War, the United States encouraged the Philippine government to move forcefully against the Huks. They were not defeated until 1954.

See also americanistas.

HULL, CORDELL (1871–1955)   U.S. secretary of state, 1933–1944. Taking office during the *Great Depression,* Hull concentrated on international economic relations. He sought to maintain open trade policies to counteract the harmful effects of the Smoot-Hawley Tariff, though without practical effect. He fleshed out the Good Neighbor policy begun by Presidents Warren Harding and Herbert Hoover in the Americas, making it a signature of Franklin D. Roosevelt's policy. Hull encouraged Roosevelt to open diplomatic and economic relations with the Soviet Union—which the United States did not recognize from 1918 to 1934. He continued the *Hoover-Stimson Doctrine* of a policy of moral and rhetorical condemnation of Japanese aggression in Manchuria and China, again to no real effect. His greatest contribution was to begin early planning for a postwar security organization to replace the failed *League of Nations.* From that initiative came much of the structure of the United Nations Organization after the war. Hull reinforced Roosevelt's antipathy for *Charles de Gaulle* and FDR's suspicion of how colonial interests affected wartime British strategy. However, Roosevelt largely froze Hull out of major decisions, instead employing personal envoys and conducting direct correspondence and negotiations with Winston Churchill and Joseph Stalin. Hull was awarded the 1945 Nobel Prize for Peace.

HUMMEL
  See self-propelled guns.

HUMP   Western Allied term for the Himalayas, over which fuel, men, and war supplies were flown from India to support the *Guomindang* in southern China. It was the only military supply route into China after closure of the overland route from French Indochina and enforced closure of the *Burma Road*. By January 1944, 10th Air Force C-46s flew an astonishing 15,000 tons of supplies per month "over the Hump." Much of that total was aviation and other fuel. In the course of operations, some 500 aircraft were lost for minimal military benefit from the Chinese war effort, or a failed USAAF effort at strategic bombing of Japan from bases in southern China.

HUNDRED DAYS   The blitzkrieg campaign by the Japanese across the Pacific and Southeast Asia from December 1941 to April 1942.
  See Japan; nanshin.

HUNDRED REGIMENTS OFFENSIVE (AUGUST 20–DECEMBER 5, 1940)
  See Sino-Japanese War (1937–1945); Three Alls.

HUNGARY   Hungary fought in World War I as part of the Austro-Hungarian Empire, which lost the war and became extinct in late October 1918. In the wake of that defeat, Hungarian Communist leader Béla Kun briefly set up a "soviet" republic in 1919. This was quickly overthrown in favor of an independent kingdom, which served as a front for the personal dictatorship of the Regent *Miklós Horthy* from 1920 to 1944. Hungary was subject to strictures of the Treaty of Trianon imposed on it by the Allied Powers at the Paris Peace Conference in 1919. As in Germany, there was much bitterness over terms, especially territory lost to several surrounding Balkan states. In the 1920s Hungary came under Italian fascist influence, but the lure of old ties to Germany was much stronger. Some Hungarians shared extreme Nazi views about Jews, while a significant percentage of the officer corps was ethnically *volksdeutsch*. Hungary thus drifted into the Nazi orbit, confirming that it wanted a place in Adolf Hitler's *New Order* in Europe but balking at the prospect of war. That hesitation contributed to Hitler's backdown at the *Munich Conference* in September 1938. Budapest also refused to participate in *FALL WEISS* (1939) and allowed many Poles to escape across its territory. However, Hungary collaborated in dismemberment of Czechoslovakia under terms of the *Vienna Awards,* receiving part of southern Slovakia and Ruthenia on November 2, 1939. The second Vienna Award was made on August 30, 1940, when Hitler compelled Rumania to cede northern Transylvania to Hungary. By then Hungary had signed the *Anti-Comintern Pact*. Still, it was the territorial acquisitions that firmly committed Budapest to Berlin, as a final German victory was thereafter the only outcome that would assure that Hungary kept its new territories. Horthy therefore brought nine million Hungarians formally into the *Axis alliance* on November 20, 1940.

German forces took up attack positions in Hungary in April 1941, preparatory to launching *BARBAROSSA*. Before that attack began, Hungary gained the Banat region from the Axis invasion of Yugoslavia. The Hungarians sent only a token force into the Soviet Union in 1941 (the "Mobile Corps" or "Rapid Corps") after declaring war on June 27. At the end of the year, however, the Wehrmacht was in crisis in the snow in front of Moscow. Horthy bent to the behest of a German Führer desperate for more men. The Hungarians had only about 220,000 regular troops and most were poorly equipped and trained. The Army had fewer than 200 wholly outmoded tanks, and the Air Force almost no modern aircraft. Horthy nevertheless agreed to raise and send Hungarian 2nd Army to the Eastern Front. It comprised 250,000 men, partly armed by Germany but lacking organic transport or sufficient modern weapons. It fought mainly in Ukraine during Operation *BLAU* in the summer of 1942. The commitment in the east left Hungary feeling vulnerable to attack by Rumania, an Axis ally but traditional enemy. Hungary therefore created a home guard of over 200,000 men. By May 1943, most of those would be needed in the east as well because the Hungarian Army was destroyed in heavy fighting around *Stalingrad* over the winter of 1942–1943, where the nation lost perhaps 150,000 men. After that catastrophe Budapest kept back its Army as best it could, under German pressure to replace Wehrmacht losses with Hungarian troops. Berlin noticed and began to plan a change of government in Hungary.

Hitler and the OKH were determined to hold Hungary within the Axis. Hitler was personally fixated on the oil fields at Nagykanizsa, and he was in any case committed to a *Haltebefehl* strategy in the east in 1944. Operation MARGARETHE thus brought German forces into Hungary on March 19, while the Red Army was still advancing through Ukraine. The main results of this operation were to bring Hungary's 400,000 Jews within reach of the *Schutzstaffel (SS)* and to ensure that Hungary would become a battleground that fall and over the next winter. *Adolf Eichmann* personally led a new *Einsatzgruppen* that entered the country and began deporting Jews to *Auschwitz*. As the Red Army approached Budapest, Eichmann hoarded transport and men to ship Hungarian Jews to the great death camp in Poland. When that ceased to be possible, he took tens of thousands on death marches into western Hungary. Meanwhile, another Hungarian Army was destroyed during Operation *BAGRATION* in June–August, 1944. As the center of the Eastern Front collapsed and the Red Army moved into Rumania and Bulgaria that summer and fall, Hungary sought unsuccessfully to negotiate a separate peace with Moscow. In the "Debrecen offensive operation," Soviet forces penetrated to the Pustyna plain starting on October 6, 1944. The Red Army penetrated nearly 80 miles in two weeks, against strong opposition. On the 11th a secret ceasefire was agreed. Horthy announced publicly on the 15th that he was seeking a permanent armistice with Moscow. That provoked a coup by the domestic fascist organization *Arrow Cross,* which was supported by German special forces. The internal conflict briefly threatened to split apart the 25-division strong Hungarian Army. One commander went over to the Soviet side, but his officers did not follow. Most Hungarian troops continued to fight alongside the Wehrmacht and *Waffen-SS* against the Red Army. In part, loyalty to the Axis was sustained by the fact that an ancient enemy, the Rumanian Army, had already switched sides and sent troops into Hungary in the company of the Soviets.

A hard and bitter winter of fighting resulted, lasting into late March 1945. The Soviets struck out for Budapest on October 28, 1944, but were blocked. Two more tries in December were also stymied, for Hitler unaccountably strongly reinforced the Hungarian Army and Army Group South with 2nd Panzer Army, and with the third (and weakest) incarnation of German 6th Army. He even ordered a counter-attack in force in January 1945, reinforced with more Panzer divisions moved in from Belgium after his *Ardennes offensive* failed. Joseph Stalin and the Stavka more sensibly regarded Hungary as a theater useful to draw German reserves away from their main line of advance to Berlin. Budapest was encircled by Christmas, but Hitler issued a *Haltebefehl order* that the city must be held. Because the Hungarian capital bestrode the main avenues of advance into Austria and Bohemia, the Red Army could not circumvent it as it had done in other *deep battle* operations around Smolensk, Minsk, Warsaw, and other major cities. An advance bombardment by massed artillery and bombers announced the start of a siege. A dramatic relief effort by 4th Panzer Corps—Operation *KONRAD*—began on January 1, 1945. But KONRAD's 4th Panzer Corps failed to break in, while the garrison failed to break out. Pest fell in the middle of January. Buda was taken on February 13, after seven weeks of siege. Meanwhile, the *Vistula-Oder operation* benefited by the loss of German combat power to the Hungarian theater, as Soviet tank columns hurtled across Poland at astonishing speed. Official Russian histories claim 49,000 enemy dead in the siege of Budapest, and 110,000 prisoners. Hitler then ordered the last Wehrmacht offensive of the war: *FRÜHLINGSERWACHEN* ("Spring Awakening") from March 6–15, 1945. It failed, but raised total Soviet losses in five months of fighting in Hungary to 100,000 dead. Moscow oversaw installation of a coalition provisional government in Budapest that summer. During 1946–1947, coalition partners of the Communist Party were forced out in rigged elections. Hungary was firmly within the "Soviet bloc" by the end of 1948, and underwent a thorough Stalinization.

Suggested Reading: Mario Fenyo, *Hitler, Horthy, and Hungary* (1972).

HUNTER-KILLER GROUPS
See Atlantic, Battle of the (1939–1945); convoys.

HUNTZIGER, CHARLES (1880–1941)

French general. He led French 2nd Army during *FALL GELB*, then headed the military team that signed the *armistice* with Germany on June 22, 1940. Although *Charles de Gaulle* was an admirer before the war, Huntziger refused to join de Gaulle and the *Free French*. Instead, he became Vichy minister for war, presiding over a truncated republic of ever-declining political and moral legitimacy. He was killed in a plane accident in 1941.

HURRICANE FIGHTER

See Britain, Battle of; fighters; Lend-Lease; Royal Air Force (RAF).

HURRICANE TASK FORCE

See Biak island.

HUSKY (JULY 9–AUGUST 17, 1943)   Code name for the invasion of Sicily that began on the night of July 9–10, 1943, and is officially dated as concluding on August 17. The decision to undertake HUSKY badly divided Western Allied war councils. The British wanted to pursue a Mediterranean peripheral strategy as the primary Western Allied contribution in 1943, possibly continuing through 1944. General *George C. Marshall* and other top American military men objected to the whole idea of a Mediterranean strategy. But they finally agreed to the HUSKY invasion at the *Casablanca Conference (January 14–24, 1943)* when it became clear that heavy and protracted fighting in North Africa, which followed the *TORCH* landings of November 1942, and a shortage of landing craft precluded an alternate invasion of France in 1943. The overall commander of Allied 15th Army Group that conducted HUSKY was Field Marshal *Harold Alexander,* who in turn answered to Mediterranean Theater commander General *Dwight Eisenhower.* The initial plan to land two armies at either end of the island and drive for Messina was derailed by objections from General *Bernard Law Montgomery,* whose alternate plan to land all forces in the southeast corner of Sicily and drive due north along the coast was adopted instead. The invaders did not land directly at Messina because African-based fighters could not provide cover that far north and because of the rugged terrain and poor landing sites in the north. The landings in the south were well-covered by fighters. They were also masked by a highly successful *deception operation,* code named *BARCLAY,* which completely fooled Axis leaders into thinking the Western Allies intended to land in the Balkans instead. On the first day, more men were put ashore over a larger landing area than in any other amphibious operation of the war.

General Alfredo Guzzoni's Italian VI Army would offer resistance of varying quality. Fighting much more fiercely were two German divisions under nominal Italian command, but in fact controlled from mainland Italy by Field Marshal *Albert Kesselring*: the 15th Panzergrenadiers and the Hermann Göring Panzer Division, together comprising about 30,000 troops. The main landings were preceded by separate British and American glider and paratrooper assaults. The British got ashore with relative ease, but the American landings were sharply opposed by beach defense Axis troops. The Americans faced a fierce counterattack while getting onto their invasion beaches. In a close-run fight, they repelled the beach defenders using superior naval and aircraft fire support. Rangers, airborne, and regular infantry then had to fight hard to cling to a shallow lodgement against effective German and Italian armored counterattacks. July 11, the second day, saw especially perilous fighting around the U.S. beachhead. General *George Patton* ordered an emergency drop of 2,000 reserve airborne troops around Gela. Nearly 10 percent of those men were lost when nervous anti-aircraft gunners opened fire on transport aircraft carrying them to the island. General *Omar Bradley* proved an excellent corps commander during HUSKY, starting with close organization of the beach defenses that including scratch forces of logistics and support personnel drafted as ersatz riflemen. Bradley would rise to ever greater levels of responsibility in the last years of the war, during which he would not perform as well or as honorably as he did on Sicily. The U.S. 7th Army took 2,300 casualties that day, but it and British 8th Army had made it ashore to stay, establishing two separate but firm lodgements on the southern coast of Sicily.

Montgomery commanded the main assault toward Messina with British 8th Army, a hodgepodge of British units and Commonwealth forces. Montgomery's task was to advance up the eastern coast road into mountainous country, pass by Mount Etna, and take Messina by the southern landward route. As usual, Montgomery did not fight as well in mountains or when improvising an advance as he did in well-planned set-piece affairs. Patton led his greener U.S. 7th Army in a covering operation on the left flank, the first time in the war an entire U.S. army took the field. Montgomery's progress slowed as Axis defense of the coast road thickened. Heavy resistance was aided by difficult terrain and reinforced by arrival from Germany of the elite 1st Parachute Division. Montgomery persuaded Alexander to shift the boundary line of his operation to the west to Highway 124, to broaden the front of his advance. Thus relegated to a secondary mission and without direct road access to Messina, Patton sent a "reconnaissance in force" northwest toward Agrigento, a prelude and pretext to next send a powerful thrust from the Gela base position 100 miles toward Palermo. He did so largely on his own initiative and partly against explicit orders to instead directly support Montgomery and 8th Army. On the other hand, Alexander had left 7th Army's final objectives less than clear, and the Germans and Italians had largely withdrawn from western Sicily to concentrate in front of the British advancing on Messina. Patton took the empty trophy of Palermo along with over 50,000 Italian prisoners, at a cost of fewer than 300 American casualties. On July 23 he was ordered by Alexander to pivot 7th Army along the northern coast road and advance in a pincer move toward Messina, separately from Montgomery and 8th Army. There was no "race to Messina" against the British as is popularly thought and depicted in the film "Patton," except in the Patton's mind. He was furious that most British generals did not yet respect the fighting ability of American troops and had shunted aside 7th Army to a secondary role in Sicily. He was determined to beat Montgomery to Messina.

Meanwhile, Benito Mussolini was toppled from power in Italy. That greatly affected already low Italian morale and disturbed the Axis command structure in Sicily. General Hans Hube took charge of a newly formed German XIV Panzer Corps that operated independently of the disintegrating Italian command. Henceforth, Hube was the main Axis commander in Sicily. He answered only to Kesselring. German resistance and repeated counterattacks on American columns on the narrow north coast road stiffened so that Patton found making progress toward Messina nearly as difficult as Montgomery. There was especially heavy fighting around the key village of Troina. Two short, amphibious hops around German coastal strongpoints proved successful. As two enemy armies advanced on Messina, Hube and Kesselring made the decision to evacuate Sicily, while leaving strong blocking detachments holding back the enemy on the northern and eastern coast roads. The great failure of the campaign in Sicily was allowing the Germans an escape route across the Messina Strait. Hube and Kesselring effectively conducted a German *Dunkirk,* evacuating 50,000 or more men across the Strait while Western Allied navies and air forces did almost nothing to stop them. Allied commanders chose not to land on the far side of the Strait to block egress from the island. Crack and veteran German troops therefore escaped to kill many more enemy during the follow-on *Italian campaign (1943–1945).* Messina was finally taken on August 17. The first units to enter were American, greatly pleasing Patton. However, with the Germans already gone, Messina was not the prize it could have and should have been.

The cost to the Axis of 38 days of hard combat in Sicily was 29,000 killed and wounded and 140,000 prisoners. The latter were mostly Italians but included some Germans. U.S. losses were just under 2,300 killed and just over 6,500 wounded, missing, or captured. British and Commonwealth forces suffered more than 2,700 dead and 13,000 total casualties. HUSKY quickly affected German strategic perceptions, priorities, and operations. Because of HUSKY, Adolf Hitler cancelled *ZITADELLE* only a few days into that offensive on the Eastern Front that led instead to a severe defeat for the Wehrmacht at *Kursk.* Hitler ordered an entire Luftflotte and a Panzerarmee to Italy from the east, which contributed to the success of Red Army counteroffensives in the immediate wake of their victory at Kursk. Invading Sicily also precipitated an Italian crisis that ended in deposing Mussolini, which in turn led to secret negotiations with the Western Allies to take Italy out of the war. The Regia Marina, Regia Aeronautica, and Regio Esercito were all removed from the Axis order of battle by early September, for within weeks of concluding HUSKY the Western powers landed armies in southern Italy. Italian troops surrendered en masse; some even turned to fight the Germans in Italy and in the Balkans. Sicily served for the rest of the war as a giant fixed carrier, used to bomb Axis forces in the Balkans and the cities of southern Germany. An unintended consequence of liberations was that the Mafia made a major comeback as Western troops passed out of Sicily to mainland Italy and thence to France. Organized criminals in Sicily were surprisingly but effectively suppressed by Mussolini before the war. In a chaotic and often criminalized wake of the 1943 conquest, they enjoyed a strong resurgence.

See also desertion; DUKW.

Suggested Reading: Carlo d'Este, *Bitter Victory* (1988); John Eisenhower, *Allies* (1982); C. Molony, *The Mediterranean and Middle East,* Vol. 5 (1973); G. Nicholson, *The Canadians in Italy, 1943–1945* (1967).

HYPERINFLATION
See Chinese Civil War (1927–1949); Germany; war guilt clause.

I

IANFU "comfort women." Starting during the *Sino-Japanese War (1937–1945)* and continuing through World War II, an estimated 200,000 or more women from Japanese-occupied territories were deceitfully lured or forced into *Imperial Japanese Army* brothels ("ianjo") to sexually service Japanese troops. Most "Ianfu," a euphemism for sex slave, came from Korea, with others abused in the Philippines, China, Manchuria, Mongolia, and Indochina. The Ianfu included some captured Dutch, British, and Australian girls and women from the territorial conquests of 1941. Less well-known is the fact that lower-class Japanese girls and women were recruited into the Army's brothels in Mongolia and had been for years before the war. Mistreatment of women by Japanese soldiers and sailors was decades old, dating at least to the export of impoverished, lower-class Japanese girls to China ("karayuki-san") from the 1870s through the 1920s. The sex trades were actually a significant source of criminal foreign exchange for the Japanese Army and Empire. In the 1930s Japanese women were imported to Manchuria to work as prostitutes. Official organization of sex slavery was carried out by the Army in China, as at Hankou in 1938. That was done partly to prevent worse sexual crimes, such as the bestialities and killings that had attended the *Rape of Nanjing* earlier that year. Mostly the Army maintained control of the sex trade to keep its soldiers amused and in barracks instead of prowling streets of occupied cities. Ianfu were sexually enslaved and routinely raped; some committed suicide as the only way to escape abuse. Others were murdered. A "lucky" few were taken by officers as personal "mistresses," to live in marginally better conditions than in the rape camps, but most girls and women were held in barracks behind the front lines in terrible conditions. They suffered brutal mistreatment and sustained physical, emotional, and psychological wounds that lasted the rest of their lives. Formal

Japanese government acknowledgment of the plight of former Ianfu—the "ianfu mondai," or "sex slave problem"—was begrudging to nonexistent for decades after the war. Some compensation was finally paid and informal apologies were made in July 1992, after three ethnic Korean former Ianfu broke silence and filed a lawsuit a year earlier. Insistence on a full and formal apology, and proper restitution, fueled additional lawsuits in a number of countries lasting into the early 21st century.

Suggested Reading: Yoshima Yoshiaki, *Comfort Women: Sexual Slavery in the Japanese Military,* translated by Suzanne O'Brien (2000).

IASSY-KISHINEV OPERATION (1944)

See Rumania.

IBEX

See STEINBOCK.

ICEBERG   Code name for the invasion of Okinawa.

See Okinawa campaign.

ICELAND   With Denmark under Nazi occupation from 1940 to 1944, Iceland hosted British (from May 1940) and American (from July 1941) troops and bases. The first American troops were a marine brigade landed to defend the island and support USN destroyers and other warships escorting Atlantic convoys of all nationalities to Iceland. Naval and air operations from bases in Iceland were critical to Allied victory in the *Battle of the Atlantic (1939–1945),* first in refueling British destroyers and later in hosting long-range aircraft to compress and close the mid-Atlantic *Air Gap.* Iceland severed formal ties with the Danish crown on June 17, 1944, under American pressure but following a local referendum.

ICHI-GŌ OFFENSIVE (APRIL–DECEMBER, 1944)   "No. 1 Offensive." The last major Japanese offensive operation of the *Sino-Japanese War (1937–1945),* undertaken from April to December, 1944. The Japanese Army drove down the central China coast, smashing *Guomindang* forces in their way, then turned inland and head for *Jiang Jieshi's* base and headquarters at Chongqing. The principal Japanese objectives were to cut all supplies to Jiang, push back American bomber bases in southern China out of range of the home islands, and force the Guomindang to end the China War. The Japanese also needed to clear a land route for forces in French Indochina, where their garrison no longer could be supplied by sea due to great losses suffered by the Japanese *merchant marine*. At first the Japanese enjoyed military success not seen in China since 1937–1938. The first battle of the campaign was fought in central Henan province ("Operation Kodo"), where a rapid encirclement of Chinese forces was effected by Japanese armor. In May the Japanese occupied large swaths of south-central China. In June they began a drive toward Indochina in three connected operations (code named Togo-1, Togo-2, and Togo-3).

Japanese success further undermined respect for Jiang and the Guomindang in Washington, finally ending Franklin D. Roosevelt's exaggerated sense of the importance of the China theater in deciding the war against Japan. Roosevelt relieved General *Joseph Stilwell*. The Joint Chiefs thereafter looked to the drive through the central Pacific as the main war-winning path and strategy.

IFF   "Identification Friend or Foe." An electronic device fitted to Western Allied warplanes to identify them to ground radars in 1939-1940. The USN requested IFF technology from the British in October 1940, before the United States entered the war. American military aircraft began installing IFF in *PBYs* in July 1941. RAF Bomber Command fitted all its bombers with IFF, as did the USAAF and the RCAF. A later British modification was called "Shiver." It was developed to confuse German *Freya* radar. Other Allied air forces adopted similar technology. However, interservice rivalry was so pronounced in Japan that Army and Navy aircraft used different IFF sets and therefore could not identify each other without visual confirmation.

IJSSEL LINE   Dutch defense line along the border with Germany. Defended by three battalions of the Dutch Army, it was quickly breached during *FALL GELB* (1940).

ILONA
See ISABELLA.

IMPERIAL JAPANESE ARMY   "Kogun." The Japanese Army that waged World War II emerged in the 1870s and 1880s during the rapid modernizing period of the Meiji Restoration. Into World War II it retained some pre–20th-century ideas and a unique military culture that had roots in *bushidō* and in other samurai and premodern traditions and views of honor and death in combat. However, that idea should not be exaggerated: in most ways, the Japanese Army emulated the most modern armed forces of the Western world. New shotai (rifle troops) and Kiheitai (shock troops) were shaped into a modern army in the 1860s by Yamagata Aritomo and his Choshu clan disciples, later reinforced by men of the Satsuma clan. The leading clans used modern troops to defeat an only partly reformed army of the Tokugawa shoguns. Over time, these two traditionally dominant clans removed the samurai class from its superior position in the officer corps, replacing many non-Satsuma or Choshu clan samurai—men tied to other feudal and local clan loyalty groups—with a new officer class that was drawn most often from the rising middle classes, men tied more closely to emerging national institutions. In 1878 a General Staff was established on the Prussian model. Ten years later the Army shifted from a regimental and garrison system to a more modern divisional system. Lower ranks were conscripted principally from the middle and lower classes. Officers and men were imbued with national ideals, from the *Emperor cult* and state *Shinto* to the racialist idea of *shido minzoku*. French military advisers were important in the early years of change and reform. They were increasingly replaced by German advisers before World War I, a trend that persisted prior to World War II. Despite self-conscious modernism and a new professionalism, the Japanese Army that entered the 20th century still relied on an old idea of "seishin" ("human spirit") as the driving force behind its tactics and doctrine. That was not especially unusual: most modern militaries heading into the wars of the 20th century retained elements of their premodern warrior ethic, spirit, and origin. In the 1930s the fascist states in Europe would revert to comparable emphasis on "will" and martial or racial "spirit" over material factors in war.

The new Army was tested in the first Sino-Japanese War (1895), during which it swept aside less modern Korean forces and Chinese Qing armies that still fielded some units of archers. After sharp battlefield victories in Korea, the Japanese Army demonstrated what became a pattern of harsh occupation that would mark its history for the next half century, though with important exceptions. Another encounter with Chinese troops occurred when Japan agreed to join an international expedition to suppress the Boxer Rebellion in 1900. During that conflict the Japanese Army was actually the only force to abstain from revenge atrocities against the Chinese. The Japanese Army fared less well militarily during the Russo-Japanese War (1904–1905), taking terrible casualties around Mukden in particular. Its structural weaknesses were covered up in propaganda that celebrated the *Imperial Japanese Navy*'s triumphs at Port Arthur and the Tsushima Strait. Marginal Japanese victory over Tsarist Russia in the war as a whole had contradictory psychological effects on the Army. On one hand, Japanese military thinkers exaggerated the victory and thereby overestimated national military prowess. On the other hand, a deep fear of Russia was confirmed that would underlie Japan's diplomatic and military policies through 1945, and even after that.

Another pattern became evident in Japanese military policy upon the outbreak of World War I: Japan's leaders saw war in Europe as presenting opportunities to make gains in Asia at the expense of European colonial empires. Japan quickly entered the war, taking over German possessions in China and the Pacific. In 1914 the Japanese Army was small, but as modern as any other. It struck against the German concession in China, at Qingdao (Tsingtao) in Shandong. It fought well in Shandong, but not well enough to warrant Tokyo making "Twenty-One Demands" in 1915 that would have reduced all China to vassal status. Over the next three years the Army remained relatively small by world standards. It prepared to fight quick and decisive battles, where armies of the Great Powers evolved into mass forces geared to waging attritional warfare. Most importantly, at the Paris Peace Conference, Japan's diplomatic ambition outpaced its military capabilities, leaving its leaders isolated, embittered, and with feelings of having been cheated of the due spoils of victory in war. Again, that reaction was replicated in Europe, where Italians notably evoked angry denunciations after 1919 of the "mutilated victory" that supposedly cheated Italy of its just reward of other peoples' territory.

The 1920s saw growing civilian opposition to bloated military budgets and more lower-class Japanese avoiding conscription. In 1924 the first real cuts were made to the Army since its founding—four full divisions—to pay for modernizations. It is therefore widely thought that after World War I the Japanese Army faced a dilemma: it needed to invest in more modern technology but lacked the financial resources and technical expertise to make the transition. Some historians argue that the Army turned away from technology it could not afford to embrace "spiritual training" and fantastical ideas about the unique and special power of the Japanese national spirit to overcome a European-style (or American-style) *Materialschlacht*. This shift included posting officers to public schools to ensure martial and imperial indoctrination of the young. In that sense, around the new professionals much of the old Meiji value system survived. On the other hand, Leonard Humphreys argues persuasively that during the 1920s the old Meiji system was displaced by a new "imperial army system" in a reform process that raised up new factions not tied to the old Meiji clans. Instead, by the end of the 1920s the most important factions within the Army were organized around shared professional views about how and where to fight future wars. The most important of these factions was the *Issekikai*, whose members came to dominate the *Guandong Army* in Manchuria, and eventually also the General Staff. From 1931 even Issekikai officers split into *Kodo-ha* and *Tosei-ha* factions whose bitter arguments and conflicts roiled the entire Japanese government through the mid-1930s. These officer cliques provided most of the military prime ministers as well as field commanders who led the Army into a long war in China, then a world war that spread Japanese forces across Southeast Asia and the Pacific.

Many things changed after 1926 as the Army reasserted a leading role in Japanese politics and foreign policy. An important factor in driving Army thinking was a perpetual budgetary struggle with its great rival, and even opponent, the Imperial Japanese Navy. The conflict went far beyond interservice rivalries normal in all national militaries. It would ultimately produce extraordinary irrationalities in the Japanese war effort until total military defeat arrived in 1945, as Army–Navy rivalry led to astonishing duplication in war planning and production. Japan's military leaders would mutually hoard oil and other vital raw materials, refuse to coordinate on weapons design, and most disastrously, follow divergent grand strategy and operational planning. A round of bitter infighting was set off when Issekikai radicals in the Guandong Army assassinated Zhang Zuolin, the "Old Marshal" and warlord of the north of China and Manchuria. That was the first of several key steps that drew Japan into protracted war with China. The next was the *Mukden incident* on September 18, 1931, which led to unauthorized conquest of Manchuria by the Guandong Army. That had the unintended consequence of provoking massive anti-Japanese boycotts and riots in China. On January 28, 1932, anti-Japanese rioting in Shanghai was met by ruthless Japanese bombing of part of the city, then by the IJN landing marines (*Rikusentai*). The *Guomindang* fought hard and threatened to overmaster the outnumbered marines. The Army reinforced with 50,000 men, forcing a truce on *Jiang Jieshi* after defeating his forces inside the city. On either side, the "Shanghai incident" forebode a much wider war to come. The Kodo-ha faction reacted by embracing the idea of war with China. Its radical "war now" agenda led to an attempt to seize power in Japan in 1936, in a rebellion known as the "February Rising." Opposition from the Tosei-ha faction, and refusal by most troops to obey the rebel officers, ended the February Rising in great disgrace and led to executions of 19 young plotters. Enemies of the Kodo-ha then purged other mutinous young officers and thereby partially restored Army discipline and unity under a newly centralized command.

Japanese Army officers were not all samurai. The majority of Army officers came from a range of socioeconomic backgrounds. As early as 1907 fewer than 50 percent were samurai in class origin. By 1931 only about 15 percent were samurai by class, while fully one-third came from the lower middle class. Along with the disappearance of samurai domination, the old regional basis of the Meiji army waned as officer cadets were trained from the age of 14 in six military schools set up on the *Reichswehr* model. The best cadets graduated into the central Military Academy at Ichigaya, where they studied for qualifying exams and learned still deeper devotions of the Emperor cult. Specialist training followed at an Infantry School at Chiba. The true elite went on to the Staff College. While regional dominance of senior commands by Choshu officers continued into the 1930s, more important informal associations of officers emerged in which men aligned by training or ideology. The most notable were Issekikai with their Kodo-ha and Tosei-ha factions, but there were other more fanatic groups known as the "Blood Pledge Corps" and "Young Men's Patriotic Storm Troops." Such personal loyalty cliques meant the Army was almost impossible to control, with different disobedient factions assuming a moral right and duty to set national policy through mutiny and by force. There also developed a wide gulf between senior officers of the General Staff and Imperial General Headquarters who thought about a *total war* strategy, and the majority of lesser and more junior officers who cleaved to a highly aggressive 19th-century ethic of decisive battle through "l'offensive à outrance." The gulf was partly bridged by developing mobile strike forces for future fighting in Manchuria and Siberia. Overall, by the early 1930s the officer corps was contentious, faction-ridden, impatient with civilian authority, and ready to make aggressive war. It had a tradition of officers on the scene outside Japan ignoring and even disobeying orders from Imperial General Headquarters. That tendency would repeatedly draw the Army as a whole, and the Japanese state and people, into military commitments that the Army alone should not have made and could not meet. Simultaneously, the Army declined in general professional competence as it expanded from 24 divisions in 1937 to 51 divisions by 1941. That rapid expansion meant many new officers were not as well trained as older ones, a fact that began to show in the field as early as the first year of the *Sino-Japanese War (1937–1945)*.

A strategy of garrisons and reliance on conscripted civilians in uniform to hold new territorial gains made in China strained old Army identities while eroding established offensive doctrine. On the other hand, the Japanese Army in China had to adapt like other armies to new realities of industrial warfare, facts which militated against blunt infantry assaults in favor of speed and mobility. To facilitate this need in any future war with the Soviet Union, which was thought the most likely next conflict, the Army adopted a three regiment structure for its divisions, replacing the old quadrangular structure. Where earlier Army tactics called for a division to attack in two columns of two regiments each, new doctrine emphasized that one regiment should attack frontally, the second must probe the enemy's flank with an eye to envelopment, while the third was held in reserve to exploit any breakthrough or effected encirclement. The main point was to draw the enemy forward toward the attacking main column, then envelop and destroy him in a battle of annihilation. Although first tried in the field in China, the new infantry doctrine maximized what the Japanese saw as their primary skills and advantages—ferocious fighting spirit married to short-range weapons—when confronted with a Western or Soviet enemy capable of bringing vast advantages in matériel to battle. Other close-in fighting skills were to be used in infiltration along the flanks by smaller units, noisy diversionary assaults, and attacking in successive waves that leapfrogged positions to maintain the momentum of attack. These tactics proved most effective in night-fighting, for which the Japanese Army trained hard and was far more effective than any of its enemies. Nevertheless, some historians sharply criticize Japanese Army command and operational skills as blunt, primitive, and inflexible. When one adds a compounding strategic policy that was reckless rather than bold, and that badly overextended Army capabilities, protracted stalemate in China followed by grinding defeat in the Pacific start to look foreordained.

From 1939 the Japanese Army in China suffered from growing lethargy and ill-discipline among fresh conscripts, as well as the usual desuetude of an occupation force stuck in a strategic quagmire. Adding to the burden was a remarkable level of moral and fiscal corruption at an institutional level as the Army sought to develop and exploit territories it occupied. Notably, the Army partially funded operations through a drug empire run out of the occupied territories. It imported heroin from Europe and raw opium from Iran before the war, expanding on ancient drug trades operated from Korea, Taiwan, Manchuria, and southern Chinese ports. A League of Nations report concluded in 1937 that 90 percent of all illegal drugs sold globally originated with the Japanese. As Japan lost access to European and American markets for its export of heroin and morphine, thousands of "opium dens" were set up in China's cities and in Indochina. Japanese soldiers using these drugs were severely punished: the addictive drug trade was for Army profit and to undermine and humiliate the Chinese and other occupied peoples; its temptations were forbidden to Japanese. The Army also ran prostitution rings and other felonious enterprises across Asia, in partnership with local criminal gangs or client regimes. Prostitution on a grand scale was run at an official level for Japanese soldiers as well as for the Army's profit. In addition to outrages inflicted on kidnapped or coerced non-Japanese *Ianfu* in rape camps in China and Korea, tens of thousands of Japanese girls were lured and imported to Manchuria and Inner Mongolia upon signing five-year prostitution contracts with the Army.

In 1936 Army conscription in Japan produced only 170,000 men per annum. From that point forward the rate of conscription was repeatedly increased as the huge manpower drain of war in China was felt. By the end of 1939 nearly half a million Japanese were casualties of the China War, a conflict for which they were relatively well-trained and equipped but badly overstretched. By 1941 the Japanese Army had 2.25 million men in uniform and under arms. Half were in Manchuria or northern China. The other half were scattered in occupation garrisons across Korea and on Taiwan, or held in reserve on Army bases in Japan. Another 4.5 million men were registered in the reserve. Despite those impressive numbers, when the Army agreed to the Navy's *nanshin* ("southern offensive") strategy in July 1940, it was wholly unprepared for the jungle fighting it agreed to undertake in the South Pacific and Southeast Asia. Weapons and doctrine had been developed to fight on the great dry plains of northern China, Manchuria, Mongolia, and Siberia, not the fetid jungles of Burma or the Solomons. An effort was made to correct this equipment deficiency in 1941, during war games and with some training on Hainan Island. But the training was limited and proved inadequate. Japanese soldiers were therefore asked to fight a new war in distant and alien environments for which they had little tropicalized equipment, precious few medical or other field resources, and almost no specialized training or knowledge. They also knew little about the new enemies they faced and fell back on cultural and racial stereotypes to make up the deficit. Fortunately for ordinary Japanese soldiers, their enemies were no better prepared for jungle fighting at the start. Later in the war, each side fought with hard-gained tactical and environmental experience. However, Japanese defenders by then faced severely adverse conditions of a matériel imbalance that had tipped decisively in favor of their enemies.

The Japanese Army had more motorized infantry capabilities than the Guomindang ever had in China. It reinforced mobility in that theater by highly effective use of local railways. It also used large numbers of horses and bicycles, including towing mortars behind tandem bikes. The Japanese evidenced a pronounced reliance on superior artillery and bombers to suppress poorly equipped Chinese troops during fighting in the late 1930s. Their high mobility and firepower strategy worked initially in *blitzkrieg* campaigns in Malaya and Burma as well. However, that advantage faded by the end of 1942, then disappeared as the Japanese dug in for tough defensive battles where mobility was not an issue, while meeting increasingly better-armed American and other Allied troops who were supported by exceptional air, land, and sea-based firepower. Japanese tanks were all light infantry-support types, or just tankettes: what all other armies called "light tanks" the Japanese Army classed as "medium tanks." Its first two armored divisions were not activated until 1942, only to be broken up a year later. Without decent tanks, lacking armored doctrine, and absent real experience in armored warfare beyond a trouncing by the Red Army at *Nomonhan* in the summer of 1939, the Japanese Army made elementary tactical errors. Most of its armored attacks were conducted by too few tanks employed in an infantry support role. It was not until late 1944 that the Japanese Army finally massed its armor for offensive actions in China. The Japanese also failed to develop or produce anti-tank guns adequate to defend against late-war enemy models such as "Shermans" faced in the Pacific and T-34s and "Stalin" tanks met in Manchuria in August 1945. Nor could Japanese field artillery match the heavier guns Americans brought to the Pacific. Improved tubes available late in the war lacked adequate ammunition supply and had to be fired sparingly. Japanese soldiers therefore suffered under enemy naval gunnery, land-based artillery, and bombing they could not counter or match. Finally, Japanese Army all-arms coordination was less effective than that of late-war Western armies, and that reduced too many Japanese attacks to unsupported all-infantry assaults that were brutally smashed with overwhelming defensive firepower, reversing the early Japanese Army experience in China.

Standard Japanese infantry weapons included the "Arisaka" M-38 rifle, which came in a 6.5 mm sniper version. It was an older model and overly heavy. Infantry were also issued the usual assortment of mines, grenades, and small mortars. These weapons were highly valued and emphasized in Japanese close combat doctrine. Emphasis was also placed on fighting with bayonets. This standard Army infantry weapon—a wicked blade nearly 16" long—added weight to an already heavy rifle. But it proved effective during infiltration night attacks, a Japanese Army specialty never matched by Western troops, and was physically and psychologically intimidating by advance reputation. Carbines with folding bayonets were issued late in the war to some Japanese troops. Infantry companies were issued 6.5 mm and 7.7 mm "Nambu" machine guns. Officers also carried swords, which they sometimes used in combat and at other times to behead prisoners. Enemy troops particularly valued Japanese officer swords as war trophies.

Japanese soldiers conscripted from the countryside had a more favorable attitude toward Army life than many urban conscripts—about 80 percent of Japanese Army recruits came from fishing or farming communities. All received basic training that included the usual physical exercise and weapons learning. Physical fitness was given a premium but independent thinking was discouraged, as was normal in basic units in most armies (though not in the Wehrmacht). In addition, Japanese recruits were trained in traditional virtues and skills of the national infantry tradition dating to Meiji times, notably in small group surprise and night infiltration attacks. Japanese rankers were inculcated with a less-refined version of the officer cult of emperor devotion that placed a premium on blind obedience. This devotion was explicitly spelled out in Army field guides, which built on ideological foundations of military life encouraged in the school system and national press. Discipline was harsh. For instance, it was common practice for soldiers to be slapped across the face by officers for the most minor infraction. It was not unknown for Japanese officers to also kick, beat, or whip their men. General *George S. Patton* might have been justly astonished at those facts, had he served in the Pacific. Regular brutality toward their own men by Japanese officers was passed down the line, to become routine ill-treatment of prisoners and civilians by drunken and often riotous troops. Even so, infractions of military law and rank indiscipline within the Japanese Army increased with each successive year of a corrosive war in China, then with more suffering and defeat across the Pacific and in Southeast Asia.

Indiscipline and violence against non-Japanese was almost never punished, a fact that reinforced hard treatment and conduced to repeated atrocity. However, explaining the frequent barbaric behavior of Japanese troops remains most difficult. Abuse of civilians and *prisoners of war* was routine, but at times exploded into murderous frenzies that nearly defy understanding. Atrocities were probably facilitated by a national education and propaganda system that inculcated feelings of racial superiority in the lowliest Japanese. Beastly acts were also almost always carried out while drunk. But rage was not just a problem of rear areas, where poor quality troops roamed without combat discipline. The worst outrages were actually conducted by frontline combat soldiers, most notably those who took *Nanjing, Singapore,* and *Hong Kong,* then rampaged through those cities. Western armies also carried with them rapists and murderers. With isolated exceptions, however, they did not behave with savagery on a grand scale as did so many ordinary Japanese soldiers. Explanation is not made less difficult, but perhaps it becomes more contextual, if one recalls comparable barbarism, rape, and massacre elsewhere. Ordinary Germans in the Wehrmacht committed comparable atrocities throughout the German–Soviet war, as did *krasnoarmeets* of the Red Army seeking revenge on Axis prisoners in 1941 or against civilians in Silesia and Prussia in 1945. Uniquely among a small minority of Japanese, there were instances of documented ritual cannibalism of enemy prisoners. The main cause does not appear to have been hunger, although starvation seems to have led to at least some cannibalism on a few islands. More usually in cannibalism cases, an Aztec-like ritual superstition about eating parts of a defeated enemy to take on his physical and spiritual powers appears predominant. The practice was apparently supported by special desire for revenge against American air crew: killing and ritual eating of Allied flyers occurred on several unconnected Pacific islands. Both sorts of motive were demonstrated in postwar trials of Major General Yosio Tachibana and several of his men who tortured, murdered, and ate prisoners on Chichi Jima.

Not all men fighting for Japan were ethnic Japanese. Manchurian and Mongolian troops supplemented ethnic Japanese occupation forces in those territories, with the best non-Japanese units sent to Japan to receive some advanced training. The most numerous non-Japanese troops in Japan's service constituted Chinese *"Peace Preservation Armies."* These were ethnic Chinese formations from Japanese client states in occupied-China, primarily in the north and along the coast. They were anything but elite or reliable formations and more than once switched sides en masse. However, they filled essential garrison roles that released Japanese combat troops for active fronts in south and west China against the Guomindang or to conduct antiguerrilla sweeps in the north against smaller *Chinese Communist armies.* Also allied with Japan were about 20,000 Indians recruited into *Indian National Army (INA)* units from among the miserable in prisoner of war camps. They were poorly equipped, low in morale, and hardly trusted by the Japanese. In fact, most Japanese openly despised INA troops doubly, once for having surrendered and a second time for turning their coats. Across Southeast Asia, local nationalist forces who initially believed Japanese anticolonial propaganda, and some minority ethnic groups looking for a chance to improve their lot, provided scouts and some troops. Most such formations in occupied territory, such as the *Burma National Army,* spent the war positioning politically for its end. Some turned on the Japanese as they were exiting in 1945, to curry favor with the returning metropolitan power or to seize political and military ground before Allied forces arrived or colonial forces returned.

The Japanese Army was oddly medically backward in many ways. For example, it did not inject against tetanus. Japanese troops had little choice but to turn to folk prescriptions, or they just suffered greatly, especially in the appalling tropical conditions of Burma or the South Pacific. The main native killers of Japanese troops on New Guinea, New Britain, Guadalcanal, and in Burma were jungle sores and tropical diseases, especially beriberi, typhus, and malaria. Conditions worsened as island garrisons were cut off from access to quinine sources for treating malaria and from other medicines and medical supplies. Japanese soldiers and marines incurred a great many fatal as well as debilitating casualties from unfamiliar tropical conditions, in many locales leading to more dead and men put "hors de combat" than from casualties inflicted by enemy action. Army medics lacked proper medicine or medical knowledge about the theater, and suffered from too little transport for wounded or any ability, beyond a few submarines later in the war, to evacuate sick or injured men. As a result, if defeat or retreat was pending, sick and wounded Japanese might be killed in their beds, including in several known cases by their own medical officers. Chinese troops facing the Japanese on the mainland also suffered terrible medical conditions and lack of medicines, likewise aggravated by hunger and brutal treatment and neglect at the hands of their own officers. Western Allied troops suffered similarly to at least the end of 1942, but thereafter were much better off than the Japanese: they had better access to medical evacuations, field surgeries and hospital ships, and preventive and palliative medicines, especially pioneering antibiotics.

To compensate for losing the war of matériel to the Western Allies, the Japanese Army kept its ratio of support troops to combat troops at 1:1. That was a remarkable figure achieved by no other major combatant. On the other hand, it reflected a general lack of supplies and support available to frontline troops. Another manner of compensating was to inculcate frantic display of superior "spiritual values" in losing campaigns conducted from 1943 to 1945, a shift clearly apparent as a declared *Absolute National Defense Sphere* cracked at *Saipan (June 15–July 9, 1944)*. The Army began moving whole divisions out of Manchuria to the Philippines, Taiwan, Okinawa, and back to the home islands, preparing to defend the inner sanctuaries of a broken Pacific empire and strategy. Exhortation and indoctrination produced many examples of remarkable self-sacrifice and heroism in the face of the enemy by Japanese troops fighting past any hope of survival, let alone of victory. Ultimately, the trend to fanatic devotion found expression in such militarily wasteful tactics as futile *banzai charges,* mass suicides (and mass executions) in bunkers and caves, ritual seppuku by officers at all levels, and the extraordinary strategy of the *kamikaze.* Contrary to popular imagery of unquestioning Japanese soldiers, however, the last year of the war also saw rising refusal to obey stupid orders, increased desertion wherever that was physically possible, and even some killing of unpopular or overly brutal officers. In the end, slogans and exhortation failed in the face of overwhelming enemy material superiority and determination to press home total war to Japan itself. The Japanese Army fought with great tenacity on *Okinawa* and had several million men still in uniform in mid-1945. Nearly half were positioned on the home islands awaiting a series of invasions that never came. Instead, Japan succumbed to a weight of woes, fire, and death too great to be borne: strategic bombing that destroyed dozens of cities; strangulation of its war economy by naval blockade;

collapse of all military, then basic economic, logistics through loss of the merchant marine and tanker fleets; threat of starvation that prompted mass migration into the countryside in search of food; and rising despair and anger that deeply frightened the ruling caste, as defeat threatened to turn into revolution. Then came the last, triple shocks of two atomic bombs and the Red Army's *Manchurian offensive operation* in August 1945. The Shōwa Emperor told his people and Army of several million men, at long last, to lay down arms and "endure the unendurable."

By the end of the war the Japanese Army had raised 170 infantry divisions and 4 armored divisions, though many existed only on paper or as woefully underequipped and unready units. Officially, 1,439,101 Japanese soldiers were killed in the war or went missing and were presumed dead. Offering and accepting surrender was not always neat or peaceful: all wars end more messily than formal dates suggest. It took months to receive formal Japanese surrenders in areas the Western Allies or Soviets had yet to reach, and more time to ship home disarmed Japanese troops. The last Japanese Army units in the South Pacific were not disarmed until October 24. Under surrender terms of demilitarization of Japan, by order of the occupation authority headed by General *Douglas MacArthur*, the Imperial Japanese Army was formally dissolved on November 30, 1945.

See also various named battles and campaigns, Japanese-occupied countries and territories, and *anti-tank guns; artillery; Bataan death march; escort carrier; Homma, Masaharu; intelligence; Japanese Army Air Force; kempeitai; Manchuria; Mutaguchi, Renya; octopus pot; rations; Terauchi, Hisaichi; Tōjō, Hideki; Tosui-ken; Yamashita, Tomoyuki; zaibatsu.*

Suggested Reading: Edward Drea, *In the Service of the Emperor* (2003); Meiron and Susan Harries, *Soldiers of the Sun: The Rise and Fall of the Imperial Japanese Army* (1991); Saburu Hayasi, *Kogun: The Japanese Army in the Pacific War* (1959; 2003); Leonard Humphreys, *The Way of the Heavenly Sword: The Japanese Army in the 1920s* (1995); Gordon Rottmann, *The Japanese Army in World War II: Conquest of the Pacific, 1941–1942* (2005).

IMPERIAL JAPANESE NAVY "Kaigun." From the late 19th century to the cusp of World War II, the Imperial Japanese Navy (IJN) cleaved to an idée fixe that the defense of Japan was principally its task, rather than the Army's. For most of the period IJN leaders also clung to the idea that defense was best achieved by a powerful surface fleet centered on *battleships* that was capable of winning a decisive battle against the U.S. Navy (USN) or the Royal Navy (RN), its two great rivals. In 1907 the idea found numerical expression in a planning ratio of 70 percent or more of the battle power of the USN. The IJN was compelled to accept a more limited fleet under restraints imposed at the *Washington Naval Conference* in 1922. The Washington treaty system split IJN planners and doctrine into three competing factions. In assessing relative naval power in the 1930s, some in the IJN clung to an outdated formula that underlay the Washington treaties: counting capital warships of comparable displacement and gunnery power as the measure of fleet power. This ignored critical developments in *aircraft carriers* and general naval air power and in submarines, two ship classes in which the IJN was itself a leading innovator. This faction drove the decision to order two super battleships: the IJN *Yamato,* launched on December 16, 1941, and IJN *Musashi,* commissioned on August 5, 1942. In addition to super battle-worthiness, they and other armor and gun-engorged behemoths were meant to force the U.S. Navy to build matching ships that would be so large they could not pass through the Panama Canal, thereby in some sense dividing the American navy into discrete, and smaller, two-ocean fleets. Other naval officers formed a still more influential antitreaty faction that griped angrily for two decades about the Washington treaty limits, insisting these were on Japan to leave her vulnerable with a weakened naval defense. This group wanted to break the Washington treaty limits not just in secret, as the IJN was already doing by the early 1930s, but to embark on an open naval arms race. The third faction was smaller. It belonged to the *total war* school, which saw a different type of war-fighting capability as partly obviating the need to match battlefleets with the Americans or British.

Interservice rivalry and differing Navy vs. Army views of who Japan's main "hypothetical enemy" really was—the United States or the Soviet Union—meant IJN relations with the *Imperial Japanese Army* were openly hostile from 1936. The competition went far beyond the most severe interservice rivalries over budgets, influence, and prestige that are common to all militaries. It affected strategy, operational planning, weapons design, hoarding of oil and other strategic resources, economic competition, technical research, and virtually every other vital aspect of Japan's ongoing war effort in China and future war in the Pacific. The pull on Japan by the *Guandong Army* into war for Manchuria in 1931, then more war in northern China from 1937, deeply frightened planners in the IJN. Their rather feeble effort to gain countervailing influence in Imperial Conferences was to base a small fleet on the Songhua (Songari) River in northern China. During the opening campaign of the *Sino-Japanese War (1937–1945),* the IJN was assigned to evacuate Japanese nationals from China's coastal cities. It also supported its own *Rikusentai,* or marines, fighting for nine days in the streets of Shanghai, and flew air cover for the Army's 50,000 man relief force. To interdict supplies to *Jiang Jieshi,* who was holed up in the southern interior at Chongqing, the IJN occupied Hainan Island and the Spratly Islands in 1939. That move was followed by an amphibious operation to land an expeditionary force on the south China coast, which moved inland to take Nanning. This coastal support role continued to the end of the war in China.

Doctrine and interservice rivalry aside, the Japanese economy was unable to sustain a capital warship building program that permitted fulfillment of the IJN's vision of a battlefleet sufficient to defeat the Royal Navy in a "decisive battle," let alone the more likely and generally hypothesized enemy, the U.S. Navy. The IJN kept pace with the Western powers in construction of submarines and carriers until just before war began in Europe in 1939. Its RO-class and larger I-class submarines were superior to any boats in the U.S. Navy; the I-class boats could cross the Pacific without refueling, an achievement denied to American submarines until after the war. The IJN looked to fall behind in quantity of warships of all classes as the USN received huge appropriations from Congress in 1940, while the Royal Navy expanded to meet the German threat in the Atlantic. The prospect of looming numerical inferiority in capital warships pushed IJN leaders closer to the idea of preemptive war against the Americans in the Pacific. Yet, even that prospect did not help the Japanese overcome U.S. shipbuilding capacity. From 1941 to 1945 the IJN would add 171 significant surface ships to its order of battle, about one-third the number of major surface ships launched by the USN over the same period. As the fight in the Pacific commenced, the IJN had the world's third largest battlefleet. Its Combined Fleet was the largest plying any single ocean. In December 1941, the IJN had 10 fleet carriers and 2,200 *Japanese Naval Air Force* planes, including over 500 flying boats and sea planes. However, it had only 2,500 Sea Eagles, or elite pilots, to fly them. It believed it had a two-year reserve of oil for its 10 battleships, 18 heavy cruisers, 20 light cruisers, 112 destroyers, 44 modern and 21 older submarines, and 156 smaller surface craft. Wartime consumption at higher than anticipated rates reduced that estimate to a one-year supply. Oil remained a critical problem in shaping IJN operations throughout the Pacific War, with lack of sufficient tankers a severely aggravating factor that ultimately led to a naval fuel crisis that could not be solved. The IJN equivalent to USN *Seabees* was the "Shipping Regiment" ("senpaku kōhei rentai") of naval engineers.

From 1942 the Japanese floated several large new fleet carriers and built the world's largest carrier—the IJN Shinano—utilizing the hull of an unfinished superbattleship. It would be sunk by a USN submarine while still in harbor. Deeper into the war the IJN concentrated on nine seaplane carriers and on converting various tenders and other large hulls to carriers, including three converted passenger liners. It also partially converted two battleships, the IJN Ise and IJN Hyuga. But when the Navy ran out of naval aircraft, these ships were reconverted to fight as battleships. What the IJN badly neglected before the war, and did not produce during the conflict, was sufficient purpose-built escort ships or a sound *convoy* doctrine. It additionally lacked advanced ship and naval aircraft *radars*. The gap was not made up by trying to acquire enemy naval radar technology by such desperate means as diving to British or American wrecks to recover the technology. The IJN also lacked an adequate pilot training system, so that it would be unable to maintain a supply of quality aviators after losing too many frontline pilots in the great carrier clashes of 1942–1943. Whole Japanese Army garrisons were left unsupplied by the Navy, effectively abandoned as the war passed them by. From 1937 IJN officers felt aggrieved that Japan was dragged by the Army into the quagmire of the China War. After 1941, Army officers believed they had been misled by the IJN into agreeing to a ruinous war in the Pacific. Both views were correct.

The 311,000 officers and men of the IJN at the end of 1941 were high quality: nearly 80 percent of crew had enlisted as volunteers. As the IJN embarked upon the Pacific War it was a highly motivated professional service, confident in its ships, aircraft, and excellent *torpedoes*. It was overconfident in its primary doctrine, however. Because IJN planners realized they could not win a long naval war against the USN, they planned for a war in which they brought the main enemy fleet to a "decisive battle" and destroyed it, thereby evening the naval odds. This doctrine relied overmuch on battleships, even after the Royal Navy showed the vulnerability of large capital ships to naval air attack at *Taranto* in November 1940, and the Japanese demonstrated the same thing at *Pearl Harbor (December 7, 1941)* and in sinking HMS Repulse and HMS Prince of Wales. The first chance to test the doctrine in a fleet action came at the *Battle of theCoral Sea (May 3–8, 1942)*, but that encounter was indecisive. Next came the *Battle of Midway (June 4–5, 1942)*, where the IJN suffered a catastrophic loss of fleet carriers and naval air power from which it never fully recovered. The *Guadalcanal campaign* (1942–1943) provided more opportunities for small fleet actions in the battles of *Cape Esperance (October 11–12, 1942);* the *Eastern Solomons (August 23–25, 1942); Santa Cruz (October 26–27, 1942);* and the naval *Battle of Guadalcanal (November 12–15, 1942).* As Samuel Elliot Morrison noted in his monumental history of the naval war, the old tactics of line of battle were rendered obsolete by advances in antiship aircraft, which demanded evasive action and rendered it "impossible to maintain the line under air attack." Yet, the old battleship wing of the IJN still clung to line of battle dogma and the "decisive battle" delusion as late as the great fight at *Leyte Gulf* in 1944.

Just as tellingly, the IJN deployed its submarines not to intercept enemy troop and resupply columns but to attack and reduce the number of the enemy's capital ships in preparation for the always elusive "decisive battle" it sought between surface fleets. Japanese submarines of all types, including midget submarines, were deployed to harry the ships of the U.S. Pacific Fleet rather than to destroy merchantmen and force the USN to redeploy destroyers and shipyard capacity to building escorts. Even this ill-advised submarine strategy had to be abandoned from 1943, as IJN submarines were converted into supply ships for stranded garrisons along the coast of New Guinea and across the South Pacific. That need also affected construction, so that late-war Japanese submarine designs shifted away from lethality to increased cargo capacity. To partly compensate for lost naval combat power, a base for 11 German attack U-boats and a supply boat was established at Penang in mid-1943. More U-boats arrived later, as Indian Ocean hunting was safer and more profitable for U-boats by that point than plying dangerous Atlantic waters. Effective Axis submarine cooperation did not survive past the destruction of the last Kriegsmarine Milchkühe ("Milk Cows") supply boats in Asia in the spring of 1944. The last four German and two converted Italian submarines in Asia were seized by the IJN when Germany surrendered in May 1945. Efforts to persuade Dönitz to send more boats to the Pacific failed, as he instead instituted *REGENBOGEN,* scuttling the U-boat fleet. At its maximum, the IJN deployed a fleet of 200 submarines. Poor doctrine and the shift from an attack to a supply role meant that Japanese submarines sank only 171 enemy ships to the end of the war. A handful were important warships and a few were military auxiliaries, but nowhere near enough warships were sunk or damaged to turn the fortunes of the naval war. The cost to Japan of that effort was to leave hardly dented the enemy merchant marine. The IJN lost 128 lost boats and crews in a submarine effort that barely registered against the enemy order of battle. The United States captured two I-400 "Toku"-class boats a week after the surrender. At 400 feet in length, they were larger than any submarine built before nuclear vessels in the 1960s. When the Soviet Union asked to inspect them, the USN took the boats to sea and sank them.

The IJN commissioned *kamikaze* suicide pilots in 1944. It also prepared lines of *Fukuryu,* or "Special Harbor Defense and Underwater Attack Units," comprising suicide divers armed with mines or torpedoes. They would have greeted any Allied attempt at amphibious landings on the home islands. The IJN deployed suicide motor boats in the Philippines and at Okinawa, but to little effect. By the end of the war the IJN lost 332 out of 451 warships, including submarines, it put to sea. A paltry 37 warships of the once feared IJN remained operating upon the surrender, and most of those were in safe Korean or Chinese ports, hiding from enemy bombers and submarines. What was left of the Imperial Japanese Navy was formally dissolved on November 30, 1945. Japanese warships were hardly seen again in north Asian waters—beyond minimal coastal patrols—until the 1990s. On June 24, 2008, the first IJN warship since World War II docked in a Chinese port, carrying earthquake relief supplies. Its arrival on a mission of peace was regarded as a major breakthrough in Sino-Japanese relations, dating back over 100 years.

See also Aleutian Islands; escort carriers; Fukuryu; intelligence; Java Sea, Battle of; kamikaze; Kondō, Nobutake; Kolombangara, Battle of; Komandorski Islands, Battle of; Kula Gulf, Battle of; Leyte Gulf, Battle of; London Naval Treaty; Military Landing Craft Carrier; Nagumo, Chuichi; Okinawa campaign; Ozawa, Jizaburō; Rikusentai; Seabees; second front; Tanaka Raizō; Taranto; Tassafaronga, Battle of; Tōgō, Heihachiro.

Suggested Reading: Sadao Asdada, *From Mahan to Pearl Harbor: The Imperial Japanese Navy and the United States* (2006); David Evans and Mark Peattie, *Kaigun: Strategy, Tactics, and Technology in the Imperial Japanese Navy, 1887–1941* (1997).

IMPERIAL WAY

See Kodo-ha; Issekikai.

IMPHAL OFFENSIVE (MARCH–APRIL, 1944) "U-Gō." The Japanese badly misread the lessons of the *Chindit* raid of February–March 1943: they concluded that they, too, could mount a jungle operation supported by air power beyond normal lines of communication and supply. Although the Imphal offensive is often portrayed as an effort to invade India, it is unlikely the Japanese considered an invasion. At most, they thought in propaganda terms to raise morale among their troops and troops of the *Indian National Army,* which accompanied Japanese 15th Army on the campaign. The Japanese goal was to cut-off enemy supplies at Imphal and thereby preempt a Burma offensive by 14th Army under General *William Slim.* Preceding the main assault was a diversionary attack at *Arakan,* which led to the fight over the *Admin Box.* The intent of that diversion was to hold down British and Commonwealth forces and preempt reinforcement of Imphal's defenses. General *Renya Mutaguchi* then drove for Imphal. He began a rapid thrust through the jungle starting on March 7, catching Slim's force by surprise and forcing British 17th Division to retreat pell-mell. A second Japanese formation, the so-called "Yamamoto Force," pushed hard for Tamu but was stopped short. Two divisions of enemy reinforcements arrived by air in the main combat zone, freed from the Arakan by a quick victory there. By March 19 they were positioned in the path of Mutaguchi's advance. Nevertheless, on April 12 the Japanese cut the road from Imphal to Kohima, even as they carved their own road through the jungle using coolie slaves and prisoner labor as well as their own troops.

Meanwhile, a division-sized Japanese third thrust was made toward Kohima by General Kotuku Satō. The Japanese pushed aside an Indian airborne brigade and invested Kohima by April 3. Allied air power made the difference, first in airlifting two divisions to block the way from Imphal then in air resupply as newly arrived troops dug in. The Japanese had no tanks and few anti-tank guns. They were surprised that British tanks operated in Burmese terrain. On April 18 a British relief army broke through to the Indian troops defending Kohima. Three days later the Japanese were ordered to assume the defensive. Satō instead tried to retake Kohima, wasting men and resources that were needed at Imphal, where failure to take British supply depots left the attacking Japanese troops in dire condition. Personal and tactical arguments between the Japanese commander on the ground and his superior hundreds of miles away in Burma boiled over on April 29. Satō directly accused Mutaguchi of incompetence and refused to obey his orders to reinforce the assault on Imphal. A hard four months of perimeter fighting followed, during which the Japanese were slowly ground down by heavier enemy weapons and superior logistics. On May 31, Satō pulled out of Kohima against orders. His effort left 6,000 Japanese and 4,000 enemy casualties in its wake. The Western Allies reopened the main supply road on June 22. Even Mutaguchi admitted failure and pulled his starving, malarial, despondent troops back from Imphal on July 18. The Japanese suffered 60,000 total casualties during the campaign, including 50 percent dead, while inflicting 17,000 British and Indian casualties. After Imphal and because of it, the fight for Burma was won by the British.

See also elephants; mules.

Suggested Reading: David Rooney, *Burma Victory: Imphal and Kohima,* new edition (2000).

INCENDIARIES
See bombs; Combined Bomber Offensive; Coventry raid; Dresden raid.

INDEPENDENT BOMBING
See strategic bombing.

INDEPENDENTS Merchantmen sailing outside of any *convoy.* They were classed as "slow" if incapable of sustaining 9 knots and "fast" if they could exceed 13–15 knots. Neutrals initially sailed as independents but later most joined Allied convoys. Loss rates among independents were enormous compared to ships in convoy, especially for slow ships, which fell easy prey to German surface raiders and submarines. Once the error was recognized in the loss statistics all independents were brought into convoy. That left only the occasional straggler sailing alone.

See also Atlantic, Battle of the; mines; troop ships; U-boats.

INDIA *Mohandas Gandhi* took over leadership of the *Congress Party* just as confrontation between Indians and their British overlords rose at the end of World War I. The situation was made irretrievable by the Amritsar massacre (April 13, 1919) of over 1,000 peaceful demonstrators by *Indian Army* troops under British command. That stimulated open and mass demands for independence by galvanizing Indian outrage and shocking British liberal opinion. Gandhi brought the Indian masses into the nationalist movement with a series of brilliant stratagems, such as the salt march and an electoral deal with the harijans. Before that Congress had been an elitist, even effete, party of pamphleteers, lawyers, and property owners. An effort to deflate the conflict took place at the Round Table Conferences in the early 1930s, but British colonial officers remained unconvinced their day in India was done. Following the failure of the Round Table Conferences, the 1935 "India Act" proposed transforming the Raj into a federation. That included representation for Princely States as well as 11 provinces and an electorate divided along sectarian and caste lines. The scheme was not implemented because of the intervention of World War II and due to opposition from independent princes, Gandhi, and Congress. Significant autonomy was granted to India by 1937, with Aden and Burma severed from jurisdiction of the Raj. World War II then delayed progress toward independence, not least because Prime Minister Winston Churchill was a vehement opponent of any concessions to Indian nationalists. Over the course of the war, India's material and human resources and contributions accelerated demands for a permanent political solution, which must mean some form of home rule or independence. A terrible wartime famine in Bengal cost three million lives. Along with Britain's military and financial exhaustion by 1945, that humanitarian and administrative failure made inescapable British withdrawal from India, as well as from other insupportable commitments to overseas empire. Elections for a constituent assembly were held in 1945. India was partitioned, and it and Pakistan achieved independence in 1947.

From 1939 to 1945 India provided resources and troops vital to the British and Commonwealth war effort in the greater Middle East and SE Asia. India was a vital staging ground for both *Burma campaigns*. It hosted RAF and USAAF bases and one terminus of the *Hump* air supply route to the *Guomindang* in southern China. India's elites argued about whether to support the Allied war effort and to what degree. *Subhas Chandra Bose* led a more radical anti-British faction that sided with the Axis. Bose left India to avoid arrest, living in German and then Japanese exile: he was transferred to Japanese-held territory from Berlin by U-boat in 1943. He revived and headed the militarily weak but symbolically highly significant *Indian National Army,* until it was destroyed in Burma. The rest of India provided two million men to fight and garrison the British Empire under colors of the Indian Army. Other Indians were involved in broad "Quit India" movement inspired by the civilian leadership of Congress. Otherwise, most of India's 800,000 villages and 400,000 million people knew little of grand and far away events, wars and rumors of war, or the rise and fall of other peoples' empires. Moreover, during the war years, the cost of India's defense and its wider military contributions was heavily subsidized by Britain, in a major reversal of the historic financial relationship of the Raj to London. That fact, too, conduced to persuading many British after the war to stop opposing independence for India.

INDIAN ARMY The large force of Indian volunteers and British officers with which Great Britain controlled the subcontinent and manned other posts of its vast empire. The key fact about the Indian Army was that for most of its existence it was supported by Indian taxation, not paid for by London. That gave it a certain independence, while making it an invaluable addition to British imperial power. After the Indian Mutiny ("War of Independence") of 1857–1858, the size of the force was reduced and British troops took exclusive control of artillery and engineering, while Sikhs, Gurkhas, and Pathans—all of whom stayed loyal during the rebellion—replaced Bengalis, Marathas, and other suspect ethnic groups among sepoy units. During World War I sepoy regiments fought in the trenches of the Western Front in faraway battles such as Neuve-Chapelle, Loos, and Ypres, for nations and causes of which they knew little. In fact, only the arrival in France and the Mediterranean of this Indian "territorial force" during 1915 enabled Britain to sustain its commitment to its major ally while it trained its own conscript army for deployment to Flanders in 1916. Some Indian regiments suffered over 100 percent casualties in the Imperial cause during the Great War.

At the start of World War II the Indian Army was still a highly traditional colonial force of about 270,000 men, of whom 64,000 were British. It was just beginning to modernize its training, equipment, doctrine, and social organization. "Indianization" was barely underway, in accordance with the 1919 and 1935 India Acts: just 577 Indians held commissions in a force that had 200,000 soldiers. All that changed with the crisis brought on by France's defeat in June 1940. Suddenly, the Indian Army was essential to hold Britain's lifeline through Suez and its position in the greater Middle East. To expand Indian regiments and recruit new ones to effectively take the place of lost French divisions, Indians had to be accepted as officers in ever greater numbers. Moreover, it was necessary to recruit ordinary soldiers from beyond the select and trusted post-mutiny ethnic and religious groups. Now, Sikhs, Rajputs, and other trusted troops were joined in the Indian Army by long excluded Madrassis and other ill-favored ethnic and social classes. Japan's assault on the British Empire in SE Asia and the Indian Ocean at the end of 1941 accelerated the process of Indianization. It caused new splits as some Indian Army prisoners of war were recruited into the anti-British *Indian National Army* and Japan directly challenged the whole idea of European empire in Asia. Over the course of the war the Indian Army modernized rapidly and expanded dramatically, to 2.5 million troops by 1945. Some 16,000 Indians took full commissions in the Indian Army by that year. Although a majority of officers were still British in 1945, some British junior offices served under Indian superiors for the first time.

In 1940 a small number of Indian troops participated in the fight against the Wehrmacht during *FALL GELB* (1940), the fall of France and the Low Countries. They were more successful, and indeed were critical, in British victory over Italy in the *East African campaign*. At the end of 1941 Indian and British units were overrun by the Japanese in *Hong Kong,* and in early 1942 they suffered more terrible defeats and prisoner losses in *Malaya* and at *Singapore*. Indian Army troops accompanied British regulars in the longest retreat in British or Indian military history in Burma in early 1942. Disaster and defeat reflected lack of preparation for modern combat, for which the Indian Army lacked heavy weapons, motorized transport, or proper training, as did regular British Army forces in Asia. The Indian Army regrouped and rearmed. From 1942 to 1943 it was instrumental in holding off the Japanese in Burma and manning garrisons in the Middle East. Its wartime expansion and modernization was paid for by heavy contributions from Indians, but also by direct British funds and American aid. Better trained and equipped Indian Army divisions were key to retaking Burma in 1944–1945. By the end of the war Indian casualties reached 89,000, including 24,000 killed. In 1947 the Indian Army was divided between independent India and Pakistan. Most of its officers and physical assets remained with India.

See also Admin Box; airborne; Allies; COMPASS.

Suggested Reading: Daniel Marston, *Phoenix From the Ashes: The Indian Army in the Burma Campaign* (2003).

INDIAN INDEPENDENCE LEAGUE

See Bose, Subhas Chandra; Indian National Army.

INDIAN LEGION "Legion Freies Indien." The armed wing of the "Indian Independence League," this small military force comprised deserters and *prisoners of war* from the *Indian Army*. About 6,000 recruits were taken from among disgruntled prisoners captured by the Germans in the North African desert campaigns in 1940–1941. Nominally headed by *Subhas Chandra Bose,* this anti-Raj band had all-German officers. Bose and the *Abwehr* had wild thoughts about parachuting the Legion into India to foment rebellion or marching through the Middle East to India, but nothing came of these. When Bose went to Japan by U-boat in 1943, the Abwehr arranged for *blockade runners* to take the Legion to the Far East. One ship got through, but another was lost at sea. The survivors of the Legion were ordered to the Eastern Front; they mutinied instead. After shooting the ringleaders, the Germans disbanded the Legion, formed its men into a Wehrmacht regiment— "Indisches Infanterie Regiment 950"—and sent the unit to perform garrison duty in France. In a sheer propaganda maneuver on August 8, 1944, 2,500 of these men were absorbed into the *Waffen-SS* as the "Indische Freiwilligen Legion," though they retained Heer uniforms. The unit saw no combat in France, retreated into Germany, and surrendered in March 1945. The Regio Esercito also recruited Indians to form the "Battaglione Azad Hindoustan."

See also Indian National Army.

INDIAN NATIONAL ARMY (INA) "Azad Hind Fauj." The armed wing of the "Indian Independence League," this small military force (about 20,000 at maximum strength) comprised deserters and *prisoners of war* from the *Indian Army* captured by the Japanese at Malaya, Singapore, and Hong Kong. It also recruited some ultranationalist volunteers, including a number of women, when it formed in February 1942. It was largely reformed in 1943 by *Subhas Chandra Bose,* who arrived in Singapore by U-boat from Germany. The INA was always tightly controlled by the Japanese military. Its origins in betrayal and desertion caused Japanese to mistrust it and regard its troops as a collection of dishonorable turncoats and traitors. For the same reasons, the British and many Indians despised the INA. However, other Indians genuinely thought it represented an army of liberation, and to them Bose was a hero. Many of its soldiers were racially abused and mistreated by Japanese officers —who also mistreated their own men. The INA was used as cannon fodder to spare Tokyo's own troops in Burma, or as auxiliaries, scouts, and translators. Its men did not fight well or hard. Nor did it receive the arms or other military capabilities needed to invade or capture India from Britain, as Bose vainly hoped. The INA briefly crossed into Bengal on March 21, 1944, but fell short of establishing a political base after failure of the Japanese *Imphal offensive.* The INA was easily driven out of India, mainly by *Indian Army* troops. Whole brigades surrendered whenever possible, which raises questions about men's motives for joining when the other choice was to remain in Japanese prison camps, while also pointing to chronic low INA morale. The last INA remnants surrendered in Rangoon in May 1945. When INA officers were tried in Delhi in 1945 and 1946, they emerged as popular heroes in the new postwar environment and received suspended sentences.

INDIAN NATIONAL CONGRESS
See Bose, Subhas Chandra; Congress Party; Gandhi, Mohandas; India.

INDIAN OCEAN RAID
See Ceylon.

INDIRECT FIRE   Artillery fire at unseen targets, often with *howitzers* or *mortars.* Indirect fire was guided by recce or a forward observer with line of sight to the target (German practice), or fire was called down on grid coordinates by radio or field telephone to the battery (British and American practice).
See also artillery; assault guns; direct fire; self-propelled guns.

INDISCRIMINATE BOMBING
See area bombing; morale bombing; precision bombing; strategic bombing; V-weapons program.

INDOCHINA
See French Indochina.

INDONESIA
See Dutch East Indies.

INFANTRY The core units of all armies in World War II were infantry divisions, from light infantry with specialized training and roles in battle such as mountain troops, to heavy infantry capable of taking on enemy armor with mines, anti-tank guns, and their own armored vehicles. Leg infantry formations suffered the highest rate of casualties in all armies as they sought to assault or hold key terrain in battle or garrison conquered territory.

For national variations on organization and deployment see entries for discrete armies and military units (*squad, platoon, company,* etc). For the role of infantry in combat see various battles, campaigns, and operations. *See also airborne; amphibious warfare; armored infantry; banzai charges; Blitzkrieg; Brandenburgers; cavalry; Chindits; covering fire; creeping barrage; divers; Fallschirmjäger; Goumiers; horses; infantry army; ironing; Jäger; landing craft; Luftwaffe field divisions; marching fire; marines; mechanized; motorized division; motorized rifle division; Panzergrenadier; Panzerjägdgruppe; Panzerzerstörer; penal battalions; Raider Battalions; rifle division; Rikusentai; storm groups; tank panic; trench warfare; Volksgrenadier; Volkssturm.*

INFANTRY ARMY "obshchevoiskovaia." Although more closely translated as "combined arms" army, and in fact comprising armor and artillery as well as infantry divisions, because these Red Army formations had much less armor or mobility than a *tank army,* this term is most often used.

See also Guards Army.

INFANTRY WEAPONS
See individual armies. *See also anti-aircraft artillery; anti-tank weapons; armor; artillery; assault guns; bangalore torpedo; B.A.R.; bazooka; burp guns; field guns; flamethrowers; grease gun; grenades; machine guns; mines; mortar; Panzerfaust; Panzerschreck; PIAT; punji stakes; recoilless guns.*

INFILTRATION Stealthy movement deep into an enemy position, prior to attacking at a vulnerable time or point with the advantage of surprise. Almost every significant military operation in the war began with at least limited attempts at infiltration, certainly of spies, saboteurs, and *special forces.* Sometimes infiltration was made days or weeks in advance of the main operation. A more blunt tactic to prepare for an attack was massive preliminary artillery and air bombardment followed by a direct frontal assault.

INÖNÜ, ISMET (1884–1974)
See Turkey.

INSTERBURG CORRIDOR A fortified line of German defenses in East Prussia.
See Goldap operation; Insterburg-Königsberg operation; Vistula-Oder operation.

INSTERBURG-KÖNIGSBERG OFFENSIVE OPERATION (JANUARY 13–24, 1945) Soviet 3rd Belorussian Front attacked German 3rd Panzer Army in the *Insterburg corridor*. Insterburg itself fell on January 22. Forward elements of the Red Army reached the outskirts of Königsberg five days later.

See also Vistula-Oder operation.

INTELLIGENCE Accurate military and political intelligence is a "force multiplier" that may be worth many divisions and even whole armies and fleets during wartime. That was certainly the case for all the major *Allies* during World War II, whose intelligence successes were a vital ingredient of success against the armed forces of Germany, Italy, and Japan. It remains unknown how far Soviet political intelligence penetrated German communications, but Soviet military intelligence and counterintelligence regularly outwitted the German *Abwehr*. The story of Western Allied intelligence is better known, though still not fully revealed. Western leaders and commanders probably knew more in real time about their enemies' secret plans and intentions, and field and sea dispositions and operations, than any foe in the history of warfare. Britain and the United States made enormous use of superior intelligence to trick, manipulate, and misdirect the Axis powers in Europe and Asia, most notably during the vital *Battle of the Atlantic (1939–1945)*. The Western Allies also conducted extensive *deception operations* that concealed the true landing sites of the *TORCH* assaults in North Africa in 1942, the *HUSKY* invasion of Sicily in 1943, and the *OVERLORD* invasion of France in 1944.

However, things did not always go the way of the Western powers. During the 1930s French intelligence deliberately overestimated the size of the Wehrmacht in reports to the French government, to sustain a public campaign for budget increases for rearmament. But the tactic backfired by helping weaken national confidence and deepen, in certain political quarters, an already baleful mood that is sometimes called the "Maginot Spirit." American intelligence also began badly. In mid-1940 U.S. diplomatic codes were compromised globally by their betrayal to an Italian spy ring by a clerk in the London Embassy. That may have made the codes available to Germans as well. The United States was also heavily penetrated during the war by agents working for the Soviet Union, including after the two countries became allies in December 1942. Soviet penetration of the Manhattan Project, code name for the Allied *nuclear weapons program,* was especially damaging to long-term U.S. interests. Germany's *B-Dienst* organization broke the Western Allied *convoy* escort code, enabling U-boats to vector in on forward waypoints. The Germans may have had other successes, but many captured German intelligence files still remain closed to protect procedures and spycraft, and possibly also reputations. Best known are several German code-breaking failures, including catastrophic failure to detect that their own naval codes were violated. Such mistakes appear to have resulted not simply from technical problems, but from a systematic failure of German intelligence that arose from the essential sycophancy of Nazi political culture, along with a cultural inability of German officers and agents to self-examine and critique their own operations. The problem flowed from the top, as Adolf Hitler was only ever interested in tactical conclusions from his spies, not in strategic assessments that discomfited his assumptions about relative German economic and military strength. As a result, strategic intelligence was not gathered by Germany, and the self-study that might have revealed systemic failures was not undertaken.

Misunderstanding of latent Soviet economic capacity was one of the gravest errors made by German prewar intelligence. The mistake was tied closely to doctrinaire belief by Hitler and among OKW generals in the so-called *Vernichtungskrieg* ("war of annihilation") they felt able to wage in the western Soviet Union. That meant the Abwehr failed to correctly assess the Red Army order of battle, underestimating the size of the enemy's forces by over 81 divisions, 13,000 tanks, and 10,000 aircraft. From the end of 1942 the Abwehr and its successor, the *Sicherheitsdienst (SD),* suffered an even greater failure to evaluate or appreciate Soviet industrial and manpower capacity to replace the catastrophic losses of 1941–1942. Throughout the war the Wehrmacht assigned a paucity of resources to intelligence gathering and analysis beyond direct operational intelligence. For instance, the Luftwaffe flew very few deep reconnaissance missions into Soviet rear areas. Nor did the Germans ever crack signals codes used by their enemy's field armies. The Wehrmacht was therefore repeatedly caught left-footed by Red Army *maskirovka* operations on the Eastern Front. One of the worst examples came with the Soviet offensive into Belorussia in 1944. Operation *BAGRATION (June 22–August 19, 1944)* found Army Group Center totally unprepared for its timing, strength, dispositions, and operational speed and depth. German military intelligence also miserably failed to understand the location or timing of the invasion of Africa by the Western Allies in 1942, or the invasions of Sicily and Italy in 1943 and the climactic invasions of France in 1944. OKW and Hitler repeatedly fell for major deception operations that included creation of ghost army groups, and persistent overestimation of the order of battle and number of divisions available in Great Britain. The Germans believed much false information supplied by multiple double agents and never realized how deeply their own codes and procedures were penetrated.

Early in the war, German B-Dienst intercepted and decoded much British naval traffic directing convoys. As a result, Admiral Karl Dönitz was able to vector U-boats and then whole wolf packs into the path of Atlantic convoys. On the other hand, Dönitz was greatly overconfident of German radio security and therefore was as badly duped at sea by the Western Allies as were Hitler and the OKW generals concerning land operations. Dönitz's "naval *Enigma*" messages to and from U-boats were sent in short bursts, which he believed could not be intercepted. In fact, British radio intercept stations collected Dönitz's transmissions, which were then deciphered by the great minds gathered at *Bletchley Park*. It still took until August 1941 for the men in the isolated huts at Bletchley Park to report that they could read Dönitz's transmissions, but then they did so nearly on demand. Their work was greatly assisted on several occasions by Royal Navy divers recovering crucial machines from U-boats sunk in shallow waters, or code books from surfaced U-boats boarded at gunpoint. All such successes were closely guarded secrets, such that captured U-boat crews were confined separately from other German *prisoners of war*. Such successes at sea and others in the field in German-occupied Europe kept decoders at Bletchley Park supplied with intermittent changes in German techniques, rotor settings, and codes. For instance, British intelligence is known to have broken simpler German police codes by July 1941. That meant the highest levels of the British government knew something about the heinous actions of the *Einsatzgruppen*. Later, the same sources informed the Western Allies about internal German reports on mass killings in the *death camps*. British military intelligence often reported directly to Prime Minister Winston Churchill, as well as to the *Chiefs of Staff Committee*. The reports were coordinated by *Stewart Menzies*. The main British intelligence agencies were *MI5/MI6* and the *Naval Intelligence Bureau*.

Little is yet known about active Soviet military intelligence, but it may be inferred from the success of many late-war maskirovka operations that it was often of high quality. It is not thought that the Soviets penetrated Enigma, though Soviet intelligence did have access to some captured code books and a key agent, John Cairncross, in place inside Bletchley Park and MI6. Cairncross fed Moscow ULTRA intercept intelligence that contributed directly to the Red Army's success at *Kursk*. More is known about the successes of Soviet political intelligence. That side of the Soviet intelligence game benefited greatly from high-level penetrations of German command and diplomatic circles by ideological sympathizers with the Soviet system, by German and other committed Communists or other anti-Nazis. However, sound military and political intelligence about the timing or Germany's plan to launch Operation *BARBAROSSA* on June 22, 1941, was totally ignored by Joseph Stalin. His singular distrust of all prewar Soviet foreign and internal intelligence ("razvedka") led to spectacular strategic blindness, lasting until just hours before the German invasion of the Soviet Union. Soviet intelligence had provided Stalin with reliable information on the scale of the Axis build-up along the Soviet frontier in April and May. Prime Minister Winston Churchill and President Franklin Roosevelt both warned Stalin directly about Hitler's intentions, and in detail about forward positioning of Panzerkorps. The Western Allies gleaned that information from *ULTRA* intercepts, but could not reveal that fact to Stalin. Even had they done so, there is little to nothing in the record to say that he would have believed them. Alarming build-up reports from the distrusted West were confirmed by *Comintern* agents in Germany. The latter provided even more accurate details about plans for the invasion than did ULTRA readings.

What Stalin and other Soviet leaders failed to appreciate was what the timing of the build-up implied for a pending assault, and just how good German troops would prove to be in action. They also misread how poorly Red Army frontline units would perform, not least because many were still forming from recently arrived conscript, who had less than two months training before the Axis attack began. Evan Mawdsley argues that fact meant "Stalin and the Soviet High Command believed they were dealing with Hitler from a position of strength, not from one of weakness." If true, then Stalin's nearly fatal error was to completely misread Hitler's intention to attack, as well as the deterrent and defense capabilities of the Red Army. Stalin alone may be properly blamed for those errors, as he overcentralized Soviet intelligence operations and denied full information about German dispositions to the professional military men of the *Stavka*. And just like Hitler, he overly trusted his own judgment of foreign leaders whom he had never met, and about countries he had never visited and knew little beyond caricature formulae of Marxist dogma. Soviet master spy Richard Sorge in Tokyo had access to highly reliable intelligence about German plans directly from a foolish German ambassador. Yet, his warnings about BARBAROSSA were also ignored. A few months later, his communiques about Japan's intention to attack southward, including against the United States, were accepted in Moscow but not passed on to Western leaders. Instead, the information enabled Stalin to shift five Siberian reserve divisions to the Eastern Front to help carry out the *Moscow offensive operation (December 5, 1941–January 7, 1942)*.

The "Second Bureau" of the General Staff was responsible for all Imperial Japanese Army intelligence. Its focus prior to 1941 was nearly exclusively on the Soviet threat to Japanese holdings and interests in Manchuria and on possibilities for further Japanese aggression in China. The Japanese view of Soviet military capabilities was quite correct for much of the war. That wartime success came in large part out of the shock of defeat, after the Japanese Army encountered stunning Red Army strength and armored warfare doctrine at *Nomonhan* in 1939. However, Japanese insights about Soviet capabilities were not shared with intelligence officers of the Abwehr or with the Wehrmacht. That was another example of the minimal practical utility or intercourse of the *Axis alliance*. As one result, German leaders cleaved to radically erroneous views of Red Army capability and to grossly faulty assessments of Moscow's deep military and economic reserves. It must be added that the Western Allies at that time did not share with the Soviets information gleaned from Luftwaffe intercepts about Heer formations and deployments: Luftwaffe radio operators were consistently more careless than their Heer counterparts.

Western intelligence about Japan's political intentions was fair through 1941, but knowledge of Japanese military capabilities and audacious initial plans for imperial expansion was very poor. For instance, although the JAAF flew the superb Zero fighter in China in 1940, British intelligence was unaware of its existence. By contrast, Japanese military intelligence about the military assets deployed by the Western Allies in Asia was quite good in 1941. Intelligence therefore played an expected force multiplier role for relatively weak Japanese offensive forces during the "Hundred Days" of initial conquest and expansion in Southeast Asia and the Pacific. Japan's military intelligence officers also enjoyed successes later in the war, although their counterintelligence was spectacularly bad. Urgent needs for information in field operations dictated a focus on recruiting agents among native elites in occupied territories from 1942, to encourage *collaboration* by native militia as well as to preempt any local or nationalist *resistance*. Japanese Army intelligence officers also taught weapons and sabotage skills to collaborationist Asian militias.

Japanese military intelligence fell prey to several Western Allied deception operations during the Pacific War, and made many other major mistakes of assessment and evaluation. One egregious error was to grossly overestimate British forces stationed in India and the number of American divisions actually in Australia in 1942. Another was failure to appreciate a marked improvement in the morale and fighting abilities of British and *Indian Army* divisions in Burma in 1944. Things only got worse for the Japanese Army after February 1944, when enemy troops on New Guinea dug up a hastily buried trunk filled with Japanese Army codes. Capture of the main Japanese Army code, along with cryptographic equipment, was put to immediate battlefield use, as it provided JAAF air raid schedules and troop numbers for Japanese garrisons on the *Admiralty Islands*. Also read were masses of captured military documents and uncensored diaries of dead Japanese soldiers or *Rikusentai* on dozens more Pacific islands. Japanese Army counterintelligence was generally bad, with codes repeatedly broken and read by the enemy without the knowledge of Japanese intelligence officers or commanders.

The *Imperial Japanese Navy (IJN)* was unaware that U.S. naval intelligence had compromised some Japanese naval codes. That work was done by Op 20-G in Washington and by "Station Hypo" working in the Pacific. Both units achieved limited reading of JN-25, the main enemy naval code, before *Pearl Harbor (December 7, 1941*, although that success did not tip them off to the impending attack. American intelligence officers better understood Japanese radio call signs and locale identifiers that preceded or followed coded transmissions. That information was put to spectacular good effect in laying a trap for the IJN at *Midway* in June 1942. Japanese political intelligence against the United States was even less reliable. It relied principally on Spanish journalists recruited to report via Madrid. Much of the information gathered by these distant agents was of poor quality, and some of their reports were made up out of whole cloth to please Japanese paymasters. Tokyo's once intimate and solid understanding of Soviet intentions and military capabilities failed during the last year of the war. Japanese intelligence officers and diplomats badly misread the chances for Soviet mediation of a settlement with Washington. They were, therefore, caught by complete surprise by Moscow's renunciation of neutrality in the Far East conflict, the diplomatic precursor to a massive Red Army attack on Japanese forces during the *Manchurian offensive operation* that began on August 8, 1945.

A fundamental problem with Japanese intelligence was that bitter interservice rivalry meant the IJN maintained a separate General Staff and ran a discrete intelligence operation from that run by the Japanese Army. The IJN concentrated solely on American and British naval capabilities while Army intelligence focused on enemy land forces. That bifurcation did not represent a rational division of labor or allocation of scarce human and technical resources, only professional rivalry. Both operations were characterized by gross technical inadequacies and redundancies relative to enemy capabilities. The Japanese also evinced an arrogant disregard for intelligence as a force multiplier to partially make up for Japan's clear and gross failure in the material contest with its enemies, the *Materialschlacht* that did much to decide the outcome of the war. Japanese code breaking was singularly unimpressive as a result, at least outside China where the Japanese did mange to break weak *Guomindang* codes. Code breaking was also hindered by a relative lack of advanced mathematics in Japanese universities and by failure to develop mechanical computers and other advanced *cipher machines* during the war. Political intelligence was similarly woeful and infected by cultural prejudices. Most Japanese officers knew very little about their Western enemies. That problem was compounded at the highest level by the fact that Japanese generals and admirals hardly ever talked or listened to Japanese diplomats. Too often, they relied on almost childlike cultural and racial caricatures of Westerners, a fact evidenced in multiple internal action reports and intelligence summaries captured after the war.

See also Agency Africa; Canaris, Wilhelm; code talkers; Combined Cypher Machine; Enigma machine; Geheimschreiber machine; GRU; Interallié; JADE; Kriegsorganisationen; MAGIC; nerve agents; nuclear weapons programs; PURPLE; radar; radio; Rote Kapelle; Secret Intelligence Service; SIGABA; Typex; ULTRA; Venlo incident; VENONA; XX Committee; Y service.

Suggested Reading: F. H. Hinsley, ed., *British Intelligence in the Second World War* (1979); David Khan, *Hitler's Spies: German Military Intelligence in World War II* (1978); R. Lewin, *Ultra Goes to War* (1978); R. Lewin, *The American Magic* (1982); R. A. Ratcliff, *Delusions of Intelligence* (2006).

INTERALLIÉ A Franco-Polish intelligence network active in France in 1940, when it was badly disrupted by the Germans. Thereafter, it was run on a smaller scale by the British.

INTERDICTION Using air power to interrupt enemy supplies moving toward the battlefield or, in a strategic sense, into the enemy economy.
See also close air support; strategic bombing.

INTERNATIONAL, THIRD
See Comintern.

INTERNATIONAL BRIGADES (1936–1938) About 42,000 foreign volunteers fought for the Republican cause in the *Spanish Civil War* from 1936 to 1938. Some were liberals or democratic socialists, many were Communists. A considerable percentage were Jews. Over time, Communists brought the International Brigades under control by harsh discipline and superior organization, a parallel to their determined penetration and ultimate control of the government of Republic. Communist tactics and purges alienated and disillusioned many non-Communist volunteers, including George Orwell. All were jeered as Communist dupes upon their return home, and not a few were arrested. For many volunteers, their politics and lost cause were both vindicated by the character of the general war that followed defeat in Spain: a world war against *fascism*. However, that was mostly retroactive reasoning, as the Spanish war actually had little impact on World War II, and *Francisco Franco* abandoned his flirtation with fascists in his government by 1945. It is less well known and hardly celebrated that a significant number of international volunteers fought for Franco and the rebels against the Republic, including thousands of Portuguese who formed two "banderas" of the Foreign Legion of the Nationalist Army.

INTERNATIONAL COMMITTEE OF THE RED CROSS (ICRC)
See Red Cross.

INTERNATIONAL WAR CRIMES TRIBUNALS
See Nuremberg Tribunal; Tokyo Tribunal; war crimes.

INTERNMENT   All belligerents maintained internment camps where they detained enemy aliens, suspected nationals, or whole persecuted or suspect ethnic groups. Conditions varied widely and wildly, from mild in the internment camps of ethnic Japanese in Canada and the United States, to murderous in camps across SE Asia and in China run by the Japanese. Neutral powers interned individuals from belligerent states, though there was often conniving in "escapes" that greatly favored one side over the other. For example, the Irish Free State let Western Allied fliers go free near the border with Ulster, while detaining Germans. Spain generally allowed personnel from both sides to escape: Allied air men and POWs into Portugal, German submariners into German-occupied France. The Swiss and Swedes were also even-handed, until it became obvious that the Allies would win the war and Nazi Germany lost its power to retaliate against a new policy that tilted toward Hitler's enemies.

See also Channel Islands; concentration camps; GULAG; Japanese Americans; Japanese Canadians; NKVD.

INTRUDER RAIDS   British term for Luftwaffe night raiders, including bombers and long-range fighters of the Luftwaffe's *"Fernnachtjagd."*

IONIAN ISLANDS   Italian troops garrisoned these offshore Greek islands from May 1940, until Italy's surrender to the Western Allies on September 9, 1943. In the ensuing Wehrmacht disarmament of Italian forces there was hard fighting and many executions of erstwhile Italian allies by the Germans.

IRAN   Following the Bolshevik Revolution in Russia (1917), the British made a definitive move in the old "Great Game" by moving into all Persia. From bases in northern Persia, the British even intervened in the Russian Civil War (1918–1921). In 1925 Britain assisted Reza Pahlavi make himself Shah of Iran. He began to secularize and modernize the country, formally changing its name from Persia to Iran in 1935. During World War II the new Shah initially backed the *Axis alliance,* thinking that Germany would win the war. When Adolf Hitler launched Operation *BARBAROSSA* into the Soviet Union in June 1941, the British and Soviets set aside their old differences in the Greater Middle East to jointly depose Reza Pahlavi that August and replace him with his young son, Muhammad Reza Pahlavi. The Soviets and British also decided to occupy Iran until the war was over, to preempt a possible pro-Axis coup such as occurred in Iraq. Iran thereafter became an overland and air conduit for up to one-fourth of *Lend-Lease* aid shipped to the Soviet Union.

On September 9, 1942, Iran made a nominal declaration of war against Germany. After the war the Soviet Union applied pressure on northern Iran, but Britain and the United States propped up the young Shah and resisted Russian encroachment. British and Soviet troops alike withdrew in 1946. Iran inherited much modern infrastructure that was left behind by American and British wartime construction of docks, airfields, and roads to service Lend-Lease shipments.

IRAQ In September 1939, a pro-British government in Baghdad was prevented from declaring war on Germany by Arab nationalists. A tug-of-war within the government ensued between pro-British and pro-Axis factions. In April 1941, a coup brought the pro-Axis elements of the Iraqi Army to power, led by Rashid Ali al-Gaylani. Momentarily, it looked as though the British would be expelled with help from Germany. There was fighting around British bases in May. The British landed *Indian Army* troops at Basra to hold the line, then brought in nearly 6,000 more British and Arab Legion troops by truck from Palestine to crush the rebellion. The Germans were refused permission by Turkey to transit troops, but flew in troops and supplies from Italian bases on Rhodes and trucked in more from Vichy-administered Syria. After more fighting, a pro-British regime was restored in Baghdad. Iraq nominally entered the war against the Axis in 1943, but it contributed little. Elements of the British Army stayed in Iraq until 1947.

See also Persia and Iraq Force (PAIForce); Polish Army.

IRELAND

See Irish Free State.

IRGUN

See Palestine.

IRISH FREE STATE (EIRE) In 1937 a new constitution was prepared for the Irish Free State by President Eamon de Valera, former Irish Republican Army (IRA) chieftain and mortal opponent of Michael Collins and the majority IRA faction during the Irish Civil War. The new basic law unilaterally proclaimed sovereignty over the whole of Ireland, including the British province of Ulster, and gave the country its Gaelic name of "Eire." The British did not recognize the expanded claim. Ireland remained neutral when war broke out with Germany in September 1939, and throughout World War II. It was the only part of the British Empire not to declare war on Germany or to be pulled in by the British declaration. De Valera fended off insistent British proposals, which were closely followed by threats, for Irish entry into the war or at least for Royal Navy access to Ireland's "treaty ports." These had been reserved for use of the Royal Navy in the Anglo-Irish Treaty of December 6, 1921, which established the Free State, but which de Valera's faction of the IRA had always rejected. The ports were handed over to full Irish control only in 1938. De Valera's then government denied Britain or its allies use of the ports during the *Battle of the Atlantic (1939–1945)*.

De Valera's anti-British stance was supported by Irish emigré opinion, which hampered the policy freedom of President Franklin Roosevelt. The president argued with Prime Minister Winston Churchill—a signatory of the 1921 treaty—against a contemplated British invasion to secure access to the Irish ports, warning of the adverse effect that would have on *Lend-Lease* legislation in Congress. Adolf Hitler also considered invading Ireland, the historic and strategic backdoor to England. But Hitler lacked the means to invade as long as Britain stood as Ireland's geographical buffer and natural protector. De Valera announced publicly that Ireland would fight whichever army crossed its borders first, whether it wore Feldgrau or khaki. In practice, however, Ireland made prudent provisional defense arrangements only with Britain. It also expanded its armed forces from under 8,000 men in 1939 to over 250,000 at their peak. The new Irish divisions were essentially militia, without modern equipment. That was denied to Ireland by the Western Allies because of the de Valera government's neutral stance. The Irish troops could not have withstood a determined thrust by either side in the war. Had the de facto shield of Great Britain fallen, they could never have stopped German occupation and recolonization of Ireland under a brutal Nazi regime. By not joining the *United Nations alliance* even after the threat of Luftwaffe bombing of Irish cities passed, the Irish government forfeited much good will and economic aid during the war and afterward. It also lost the chance to unify the whole island under one government: London made that remarkable offer in the dark hours of 1940, in exchange for an Irish declaration of war on Germany.

Whether de Valera wanted to permit violations of Irish neutrality or not, he had no means to prevent German U-boats or Royal Navy hunter groups from plying Irish waters, nor any means to shoot down aircraft that violated Irish air space. On the other hand, Allied pilots who bailed out over Ireland were handed across the Ulster border, a violation of neutrality that Germany could not prevent. The Irish Free state also prudently agreed to a contingency "W-Plan" to permit British troops to enter from Ulster in the event of a Wehrmacht amphibious operation occurred in the south. Ireland's gentle tilt toward the Allies became more acute after the United States based troops in Ulster. Over 120,000 Irish left to find work in that province or in England, and nearly 40,000 volunteered for the British Army. Still, de Valera's deep personal animosity to all things British did not abate. He protested Anglo-American use of northern Irish shipyards and of Ulster as a base of air and other military operations against Germany, although he was careful to maintain close ties to the Irish diaspora in the United States. He also maintained diplomatic relations with the Axis states despite strenuous U.S. protests and British sanctions applied in 1943 under the guise of "wartime shortages." So distrusted was the Irish government and elements of the population that in preparation for *OVERLORD* the Western Allies sealed egress from the island in March 1944, to prevent invasion information reaching Germany. Upon Hitler's death on April 30, 1945, de Valera personally delivered a message of condolence to the Nazi ambassador in Dublin. He had not made a comparable gesture on April 12, when Franklin Roosevelt died. His government allowed the German legation to fly the Swastika flag all through the war while denying comparable flag rights to the British, whose ships and airmen thanklessly protected Ireland from Hitler's long-term plans to colonize it in anything but the interest of the Irish people.

See also Abwehr; desertion; FALL GRÜN.

Suggested Reading: Robert Fisk, *In Time of War* (1983).

IRISH REPUBLICAN ARMY
See Irish Free State; MI5/MI6; Mountbatten, Louis.

IRON BOTTOM SOUND
See Guadalcanal campaign.

IRON GUARD   "Garda de Fier." A Rumanian *fascist*, peasant, and nationalist organization founded in 1927 and led by Zelea Codreanu until his assassination in 1938. Its green-shirted members were viciously *anti-Semitic* and participated in murderous blood rituals and slaughtering of Jews. They had secret, prewar ties to the *Schutzstaffel (SS)*. The Iron Guard rose against the government in Bucharest in 1941. Much to its surprise, the insurrection was crushed with the aid of German troops acting to support an allied government: Adolf Hitler wanted stability in Rumania as he prepared to invade the Soviet Union, not local fascists in charge in Bucharest. German support for repression of the Iron Guard was provided despite earlier Guardist massacres of thousands of Rumanian Jews, carried out for hate's sake but also in the expectation of ingratiation with the Nazis.

IRONING   An anti-infantry, close fighting tank tactic in which armor reversed direction back and forth over a foxhole or trench, crushing or burying alive the men inside.

IRONSIDE, EDMUND (1880–1959)   British field marshal. Chief of the Imperial General Staff (CIGS) from September 1939 to May 1940. Already near retirement in 1939, he became CIGS when General *John Gort* headed to France at the head of the British Expeditionary Force (BEF). Ironside presided over the *Phoney War* that followed that first winter of the war, but he was not responsible for it. His error was to overcommit scarce resources to the government's cherished peripheral operation in Norway. When the main German assault arrived in France and the Low Countries, Ironside proved incapable of handling his duties and was relieved by Prime Minister Winston Churchill. He was promoted to field marshal as a face-saving measure.

IRREDENTISM
See Italia irredenta.

ISABELLA   Code name for a Wehrmacht contingency plan to invade Spain and Portugal in the event the British moved into the Iberian peninsula. First framed in

May 1941, it envisioned seven German divisions driving out the British, followed by occupation of most Iberian coastal cities and a likely assault against Gibraltar. With the *BARBAROSSA* commitment to the Eastern Front, ISABELLA was scaled down to a plan to hold the line of the Pyrenees with a much smaller force. It was recoded in July 1942 as "ILONA," which proposed moving into Spain to hold a line from Santander to Zaragoza. The plan was revised again following the *TORCH* landings in North Africa in November 1942, and renamed "GISELA." Once again the Wehrmacht proposed to hold at the Pyrenees, while seizing a few smaller ports in northern Spain. Field Marshal *Gerd von Rundstedt* was charged with overseeing the plan. Then Adolf Hitler changed his mind yet again, ordering Rundstedt to prepare a more aggressive version of GISELA to include a two-corps strong invasion of Spain as far south as Galicia at the end of one thrust, and Valladolid and Madrid by the other. As the Tunisian campaign was lost, Hitler canceled GISELA and reverted to planning a simple fortified line along the Pyrenees, which he coded "NÜRNBERG."

ISHII DETACHMENT
See Unit 731.

ISKRA
See SPARK.

ISLAND-HOPPING STRATEGY Sometimes called "leapfrogging," this was a brilliant strategy of bypassing some Japanese garrisons to attack others far beyond them, thereby moving closer to the penultimate goal of touching Japan with a *strategic bombing* offensive. Garrisons bypassed by this method might be completely cut off on a small South or Central Pacific island or atoll, or left as isolated enclaves along the coast of a large island such as New Guinea.
See also Macarthur, Douglas; Nimitz, Chester; Rainbow Plans.

ISMAY, HASTINGS (1887–1965) British general. Ismay was a close adviser of Prime Minister Winston Churchill, liaising with the *Chiefs of Staff* as deputy secretary to the War Cabinet. He never held a combat command, but was very useful to the Chiefs and prime minister and extremely influential on all war policy made behind the scenes.

ISOLATIONISM
See America First Committee; Canada; Japan; Kellogg-Briand Pact; Neutrality Acts; Roosevelt, Franklin; Soviet Union; Stalin, Joseph; United States.

ISSEKIKAI An association of several dozen field-grade *Imperial Japanese Army* officers formed in May 1929. It included most of the men who became top commanders during the *Sino-Japanese War (1937–1945)* and World War II, including key military thinkers behind the notion of *total war,* commanders of the *Guandong Army,* the architects of the *Mukden incident,* and supporters of other assassinations and military provocations. It split in 1931 into the *Kodo-ha* and *Tosei-ha* factions, each with a following among junior officers as well. Among its most prominent members were *Hideki Tōjō* and *Tomoyuki Yamashita.* Its parallel in the Imperial Japanese Navy was the "fleet faction," which opposed any naval construction restrictions or arms control treaties.

ITAGAKI SEISHIRO (1885–1948)   Japanese general. He was one of the *Guandong Army* plotters who provoked the *Mukden incident (September 18, 1931).* He rose to become minister of war in 1937 and was intimately involved in taking Japan into the *Sino-Japanese War (1937–1945).* He was a proponent of joining the *Axis alliance* but reacted harshly to a perceived German betrayal of Japan in the *Nazi–Soviet Pact (August 23, 1939).* He served as a staff officer in China to 1941, then moved to Korea. In 1945 he took over in Malaya just in time to surrender. He was convicted by the *Tokyo Tribunal* and hanged.

ITALIA IRREDENTA   "Unredeemed Italy." Ethnically Italian areas located mainly in Austria and Yugoslavia that post–World War I nationalists wished to join to Italy after they were frustrated in that ambition at the Paris Peace Conference in 1919: Fiume, Gradisca, Gorizia, Istria, South Tyrol, Trentino, and Trieste.

ITALIAN AIR FORCE   "Regia Aeronautica." The military boastfulness of Benito Mussolini rested to a high degree on the prewar reputation of the Italian Air Force. Italian pioneering aviation in the first decade of flight lingered in international memory, as did for a narrower audience the 1920s theoretical work of Giulio Douhet on principles of *strategic bombing.* The Italian Air Force was original in another way in the 1930s: crop-dusting Abyssinian columns with poison gas during the *Abyssinian War (1935–1936).* The Regia Aeronautica had almost as many aircraft as Great Britain or France in 1940 when it entered the war, but most Italian models were woefully inadequate. Of its several thousand planes, half were biplane trainers and most of the rest were older model biplane bombers and fighters. In 1940 the Regia Aeronautica had only two fighter groups equipped with modern monoplane fighters. In all, it had just 129 frontline fighters and 454 medium bombers, dive bombers, and torpedo bombers. Over the next three years of war the structurally weak, and always resource- and finance-starved, aircraft industry produced only 7,183 new military aircraft, the equivalent of a single month of British production in 1943. The Italians also suffered from too few trained pilots and inadequate repair facilities. Nor did the Regia Aeronautica have effective fighting doctrine or reserves.

Despite these inadequacies, Mussolini insisted on sending several squadrons of obsolete biplane fighters to fly alongside the Luftwaffe during the *Battle of Britain* in 1940. Nearly 20 percent of the planes were lost to accidents en route. Many of the rest were easily shot down by "Spitfires" and "Hurricanes." Italian air attacks were conducted against the Suez Canal and targets in North Africa, to no effect whatever. The Italian Air Force then sent several squadrons to fly on the Eastern Front from 1941 to 1943. Its main wartime achievements came in the Mediterranean, especially against British convoys making the run from Gibraltar to Malta. But even there, undersized bombs and primitive tactics led to minimal success against merchantmen. Almost nothing was achieved against enemy warships before new models of aircraft and bombs were introduced in 1942. Similarly, Italian Air Force ground support capabilities were limited in campaigns in East and North Africa. By mid-1943 the Regia Aeronautica had suffered such losses that it ceased to be a combat factor in any theater, including defending its home skies. Upon the surrender of Italy in September 1943, the Regia Aeronautica had only 447 planes still operating, while its total losses were nearly 5,300 aircraft.

See also ace; airborne; air power; bombers; fighters.

ITALIAN ARMY "Regio Esercito." The Italian Army made a supreme effort in the Great War from 1915 to 1918 during 11 battles along the Isonzo River. It broke at Caporetto in 1917, but recovered with help from the Allies at Vittorio Veneto in 1918. Then it became essentially an imperial-colonial force in the 1920s and 1930s, fighting native armies with harshly brutal methods in Tripoli and elsewhere. The Army again showed a brutal character in the *Abyssinian War (1935–1936),* during which it carried out numerous atrocities. Although the Italian Army was reasonably large at 1.6 million men, it was wholly unready as war in Europe approached in the late 1930s. Most Italian divisions were underequipped as well as poorly equipped. Moreover, the third regiment of each infantry division was actually a "legion" of barely functional fascisti militia. In 1939 Mussolini boasted that he had available 12 million soldiers in over 150 divisions. In fact, he had 160,000 in just 10 divisions. Moreover, the Regio Esercito was the only army to experiment with *binary divisions:* smaller divisions with just two battalions each. Italian motorized or "self-transportable" divisions still did not have sufficient organic motor transport for their regiments in 1940; all other infantry divisions hardly had modern motor transport for their supplies, let alone the men. Many rifles dated to the late 19th century, and other weapons were comparably inadequate. These fundamental weaknesses were first exposed by the sharp repulse handed 30 binary divisions of the Regio Esercito by just four modern French Army divisions defending southern France when Italy attacked on June 10, 1940.

The *East African campaign (1940–1941)* by Italian and colonial troops against British Army, *Indian Army,* and East and South African colonial troops only piled on more military humiliation. So, too, did a losing *desert campaign* in North Africa against British and Commonwealth forces in 1941–1942, where Italian 5th Army was shattered and dissolved and 10th Army was destroyed. Italian tankettes proved wholly inadequate when facing British armored divisions. The elite "Ariete" armored division was high quality, but even it was repulsed by a heroic *Free French* infantry stand at *Bir Hakeim* in May 1942. The "Folgore" airborne division was also a crack Italian unit, but its skills were most often wasted as it was used in battle as a regular infantry division. In July 1941, Italy sent three divisions as an "expeditionary force" to fight in the east against the Red Army during Operation *BARBAROSSA*. Seven more divisions followed in 1942, as Adolf Hitler called upon Italy and the minor Axis powers to replace dead and wounded men of the decimated Wehrmacht. During near simultaneous fights at *El Alamein* and *Stalingrad,* the Regio Esercito had two more divisions fighting Hitler's war in Russia than it did fighting Mussolini's war in Egypt. Moreover, all Italian divisions on the Eastern Front were up to paper strength and far better equipped than those struggling in North Africa. Italians in Tunisia in 1943 did much better than their predecessors in Egypt and Tripoli. Several Italian divisions also fought hard in defense of Sicily. All Italian divisions and supporting units fighting in Russia did so in the southern theater.

A badly botched armistice and handover to the Western Allies placed Italian Army troops in grave danger in September 1943. The Germans began immediate round-ups and disarmament, followed by rough deportations of over 600,000 Regio Esercito soldiers as prisoners to the Reich to work as forced laborers; many never returned. Hitler issued a standing order that Italian officers captured while resisting or aiding the Western Allies must be shot. Hundreds were, along with thousands of Italian soldiers who resisted. In Yugoslavia, Albania, and Greece some 27 Italian divisions were trapped between the Wehrmacht and hostile partisans. Most surrendered meekly to the Germans, but the "Taurinense" and "Venezia" divisions went over almost whole to the partisan and Allied side, then turned to fight the Wehrmacht. Other Italian divisions simply broke apart, with some troops surrendering to the Germans but others—very often comprising large numbers of Italian Communists—heading for the hills to fight as guerillas. These fighters were later formed into the "Garibaldi" division. They fought in Yugoslavia until repatriated to Italy in 1945, by which time Garibaldi suffered 15,000 casualties. Back in Italy, fascist divisions formed around the puppet "Salò Republic" in the north while the Western Allies armed the "Corpo Italiano di Liberazione" in the south. This "Italian Liberation Corps" was six divisions strong, of which four saw some heavy fighting from the fall of 1944, and contributed to the defeat of fascism and expulsion of the Nazis from Italy.

The fighting ability of the Regio Esercito is often written about in derisive terms, especially when compared to the Wehrmacht. That derision was also felt by most German officers and *Landser* at the time. Leaving aside how Italians might have fought better in a cause they believed in, under better political leadership and with first-rate arms, there was a critical difference from the Wehrmacht that some historians have argued constitutes the Italian Army's finest hour: many ordinary soldiers and officers not only refused to kill Jews at German behest, they protected Jews from Wehrmacht or *Waffen-SS* officers intent on *Rassenkampf* and other genocidal fascists such as the Croatian *Uštaše*. The Italian Army possibly saved 800,000 French and Balkan Jews from the *death camps,* at least for a time. That went some way to recovering military honor lost in savage acts of racist violence in Abyssinia starting in 1935. That said, Italian Army did not actively seek to help the Jews under German or Uštaše control. Italian commanders also turned away as many or more Jews than were saved by becoming refugees in Italian occupation zones.

Other commanders did not attack Jewish communities in the Balkans as a tactical matter because they did not want to provoke passive populations to armed revolt. From 1942, Italian knowledge of the Holocaust in the east caused some commanders to worry about issues of prestige if they cooperated with Nazi racial killing. Relative Italian benevolence toward Jews thus has been explained by other historians as primarily a policy of upholding Italian authority against German encroachment, not as motivated by feelings of empathy, sympathy, or humanitarianism. Moreover, Italian occupation policy in the Balkans should not be mistaken for altruism, even if it was less harsh than German occupation. Policies of "Italianization" were carried out by the Regio Esercito amidst mutual incomprehension of local populations, by largely illiterate Italian soldiery. Much brutality resulted, including harsh antipartisan tactics imported from experiences in Africa. The Army also made possible sustained economic exploitation and political repression of occupied peoples.

See also Albania; Ambrosio, Vittorio; Badoglio, Pietro; blackshirts; Cavallero, Ugo; Corpo di Truppe Volontarie (CTV); Dodecanese campaign; Graziani, Rodolfo; Ionian Islands.

ITALIAN CAMPAIGN (1943–1945)   After serious tension and argument over Allied grand strategy at the *Casablanca Conference (January 14–24, 1943),* the Western Allies agreed to invade Sicily from North Africa. Operation HUSKY followed in July 1943. The question of invading mainland Italy arose again, with Winston Churchill and the British Chiefs of Staff pushing hard for what they believed would be a major drain on the Wehrmacht and support to the Red Army, by drawing off divisions from the Eastern Front. As the Allies readied to invade, Adolf Hitler moved significant forces into Italy to reinforce Army Group "C." British 8th Army under General *Bernard Law Montgomery* landed on the toe of the Italian boot across the Strait of Messina on September 3, 1943. Montgomery immediately paused to build up supplies and forces. It was Montgomery at his worst, many have since argued. It certainly cost him support and credit among some American military leaders at the time. Yet, the Americans had little better to offer: Lieutenant General *Mark Clark* also got off to a bad start in Italy, and his performance was arguably a good deal worse for the Allied cause than was Montgomery's in the long run. Clark was in charge of U.S. 5th Army landings near Naples at Salerno (Operation AVALANCHE), carried out on September 9, a day after General *Dwight Eisenhower* announced the Italian surrender. He was inexperienced at that level of command and would ultimately prove to be dangerously vainglorious and careless of soldiers lives. In combination, the Western Allies thus failed to link the two beachheads or to connect promptly or properly with the government of Marshal *Pietro Badoglio,* which had agreed to coordinate an armistice and a quick and bloodless surrender. Instead, the handoff was badly botched by Italians and Western Allies alike, while the Germans moved faster than either to occupy the country.

Heavy naval gunfire helped the Western Allies get onshore and pushed the Germans back from the landing zone perimeters. But Wehrmacht and *Waffen-SS* troops quickly contained and isolated the widely separate beachheads. Just as rapidly, they disarmed the Italian Army across Italy and the Balkans. In several locales,

Germans butchered their erstwhile allies by the hundreds, and even thousands. On the island of Cephalonia, for instance, nearly 5,000 Italian officers and men were executed after offering resistance to the Germans. Within a short time, 650,000 Italian prisoners were entrained for the Reich to work in forced labor camps; some 200,000 died there. Meanwhile, German units moved south to defend a series of fortified lines thrown across the paths that must be taken by the enemy armies as they moved north. The lodgement at Salerno came under brisk attack from German 10th Army as Field Marshal *Albert Kesselring* reinforced and attacked much faster than the deleterious Clark. A major effort to crush the lodgement was made by the Germans on September 12. The situation was recovered for the defenders only by a desperate drop of two battalions of U.S. 82nd Airborne, in combination with concentrated naval and air bombardments. German 10th Army began a phased pullback on September 16, enabling the Americans at Salerno to finally link with British 8th Army.

Hitler had been skeptical about defending south-central Italy. Now he reversed course and told Kesselring to hold south of Rome at all costs, along a hastily constructed set of defensive works dubbed the *Bernhardt Line*. Kesselring bloodied the Allies, then fell back to a stronger position at the *Gustav Line*. This strategy took full advantage of the fact that Italy was crossed by rivers on either side of the Apennines. The river positions were well-defended by the Germans and had to be crossed under fire by Allied troops in terrible and costly small boat assaults. The Italian campaign thus played out as a series of brutal, unimaginative frontal assaults on a series of Wehrmacht fortified lines and river positions. As soon as German defenses looked ready to crack, but just before they did, Kesselring pulled back to a fresh set of lines already prepared to his rear. That essential pattern marked the fighting until the end of the war, which did not come in Italy until just a few days before fighting ended in Germany. Four major and bloody battles were thus fought from January 1944, before the Germans were finally driven from their position atop and around *Monte Casino* on May 18. Each was more like a World War I trench fight than the swift armored advances both sides had seen in the *desert campaign* or later in France and Germany.

The main exception to the pattern of bloody frontal attrition in Italy was the daring but poorly planned and executed landing at *Anzio* on January 22, 1944. That amphibious operation was carried out in an attempt to use superior sea power to outflank Kesselring and cut off and kill his armies in a north Italian *Kessel*. However, the assault troops took too long to expand the Anzio beachhead. They thereby tossed away the advantage of operational surprise, a fact that nearly allowed Kesselring to crush the landing zone and throw them back into the sea. Only superior air power and precise intelligence, gathered through air recce and *ULTRA* intercepts, enabled the Anzio defenders to blunt a major German counteroffensive from February 16–20. Hard fighting continued along a slowly expanding perimeter until late May, when 6th Corps at Anzio finally linked with 2nd Corps of 5th Army and a broad American advance began. Clark's 5th Army was part of Allied 15th Army Group led by Field Marshal *Harold Alexander*. But Clark never really accepted the fact that he was Alexander's subordinate. Over the course of the campaign Clark lied and disobeyed orders while alternately carping that Montgomery was secretly conspiring to beat him to Rome, or alternately, that Montgomery was not moving fast enough. Clark's insubordination and frequent command recklessness broke all bounds once he smelled a Roman triumph for himself following the breakout from Anzio. His disobedience culminated in the liberation of Rome on June 4, 1944, but only because he ignored Alexander's order to cut off and destroy retreating German 10th Army. Instead, Clark took a different road than ordered. That permitted 10th Army to escape north while he personally drove into Rome in the role of conqueror-liberator. History does not record that achievement as decisive. Most historians have judged Clark ever more harshly as time passed, and the cost of his vanity in lives and wasted strategic opportunity became more clear. Clark's own comment on June 6, 1944, that the D-Day landings would steal his headlines from Rome, speaks volumes on its own.

Some Western commanders were exposed in Italy as incompetent, others as vainglorious. A few were both. However, everyone was impressed by the combat power and fighting quality shown by the Wehrmacht in defense, and by the high level of command skill displayed by Kesselring. The Germans had to fight at a growing material disadvantage, but did so with tenacity. Smaller armies, such as the *Canadian Army, Free French,* and *Polish Army,* found lasting moral significance and great pride in blood sacrifices made on the slopes of Cassino and elsewhere in Italy. Some British and French soldiers and many of their officers reacted differently, recalling with bitterness experiences along the Somme and at Ypres during the last war. Most lamented the low command imagination of Clark, the slowness of Montgomery, and lack of closer oversight of subordinates by Alexander. Meanwhile, relations between the British and American armies and among some top officers deteriorated in tandem with a growing gulf between London and Washington over the strategic morass that Italy had become. Arguments that began south of Rome among participants continued for decades after the war among historians. Some viewed the entire campaign as another "Churchillian mistake." Nigel Hamilton even argued that it approximated a replay of Churchill's disastrous Dardanelles campaign during the Great War, with Anzio playing the role of Gallipoli. However, Douglas Porch has argued that the North African, Sicilian, and Italian campaigns sponsored by Churchill and the British High Command were all essential preludes to the decisive *Normandy campaign* in France in 1944.

While U.S. 5th Army was driving to break out of the Anzio perimeter, British 8th Army—with units of Free French, Canadians, Poles, New Zealanders, and others included—drove up the Adriatic coast of Italy, making comparably slow progress against the *Hitler Line*. There followed two failed American assaults on Monte Cassino. Fresh New Zealand and Polish attacks were complicated rather than helped by preliminary heavy bombing that destroyed the monastery and gave more effective cover to the defending Germans. The Poles finally took the heights, at great cost in casualties. The Germans, too, were nearly broken by the defense of Cassino. The *French Expeditionary Corps* stormed and broke the Hitler Line simultaneously with the Anzio breakout, but Clark's fixation on Montgomery and Rome robbed the Western powers of the chance to wipe out German 10th Army and race to the Alps. Instead, a hard slog north resumed after Kesselring fell back to an alpine defense line. Western resources were drawn away to Normandy for the *OVERLORD* invasion in June, then to southern France in August for Operation *DRAGOON*. As a result of the failure to properly pursue a defeated enemy after the fall of Rome, northern Italy would not be liberated until the end of the war in Europe. By then, Italy had become witness to a civil war among fascisti of the Salò Republic and pro-Allied partisans, replete with massacres and reprisals, mass deportation of Italian Jews and former soldiers, and all the other horrors of Nazi occupation and civil war. From February 1945, Alexander was not even under orders to liberate more Italian territory. His instructions were instead to hold as many German troops as he could in Italy while the *conquest of Germany* was underway.

The Mediterranean strategy of 1942-1943 and the invasion of Italy that crowned it incurred great costs, but also brought some strategic benefits: it compelled Hitler to cancel *ZITADELLE* and to transfer elite ground and air forces from the Eastern Front. It knocked Italy and its armed forces out of the war. It provided air bases from which to open a new front in the *Combined Bomber Offensive* and, notably, for successful attacks on the Rumanian oil fields and refineries at *Ploesti*. In addition, it gave Western ground forces combat experience they lacked and needed before the main invasion and fight in France. But while the Italian campaign ground down the Wehrmacht, it also wore out Allied divisions. By May 1944, there were only 27 German divisions fighting in Italy. At that time, there were 156 Axis divisions on the Eastern Front. Stalin had made it clear before the start of the Italian campaign that he did not approve of an invasion that was never part of the grand strategy agreed by all the Allies. But he tempered that view by November 1943, acknowledging that the war in Italy made a real contribution to the larger war against Germany. He said: "The present action of the Allied armies in the south of Europe do not count as a second front. But they are something like a second front."

Even if the Mediterranean path might be justified strategically up to mid-1944, most historians believe it was a misguided and wasteful campaign after the OVERLORD and DRAGOON landings established a true and continuous second front in France. Although the Western Allies reduced their effort in Italy once they got ashore in France, they still incurred many casualties over the final 11 months of the war. It took a bloody campaign to batter and break through the *Gothic Line,* then to fight into well-defended northern valleys and take the many cities of northern Italy. The last Allied offensive broke through at the *Argenta Gap* from April 9-19, 1945. Once Western armies also broke the *Adige Line,* they took just over a week to encircle most remaining German units. Bologna, Ferrara, Genoa, Milan, and Venice were liberated in rapid succession. On April 29, 1945, all German forces in Italy surrendered effective at 1200 hours on May 2. In all, Allied casualties in Italy numbered 312,000. The Germans lost 435,000 men over the course of the Italian campaign, excluding large prisoner totals from the final surrenders.

Suggested Reading: D. Graham and S. Bidwell, *Tug of War: The Battle for Italy, 1943–1945* (1986); Richard Lamb, *The War in Italy, 1943–1945* (1993).

ITALIAN EAST AFRICA   A short-lived union of Italy's east African posses-sions: Eritrea, Italian Somaliland, and the newly but only briefly conquered Abys-sinia, from 1936 to 1942.

See East African campaign.

ITALIAN NAVY   "Regia Marina." The Italian Navy was the great rival of the French Navy in the Mediterranean, and a lesser rival of the Royal Navy. It was consid-ered one of the world's top five navies in the interwar period and was therefore sub-ject to restrictions of the *Washington Naval Treaty* of 1922. As naval arms control broke down from 1935, the Italian Navy struggled to keep pace with shipbuilding programs of its rivals. Work on aircraft carriers was set aside because Benito Mussolini believed that land-based bombers would suffice. At the start of the war the Regia Marina had no aircraft carriers and poor to no radar, but it did have 2 modern battleships and 4 rebuilt dreadnoughts; 19 cruisers (including 7 *treaty cruisers*); 3 *auxiliary cruisers;* 113 submarines; and about 100 destroyers, motor torpedo boats, and small coastal craft. However, its tactics and doctrine were outmoded and extremely cautious. Over objections of the Kriegsmarine, and in particular Admiral *Karl Dönitz,* Benito Mus-solini insisted on sending a significant number of Italian submarines into the *Battle of the Atlantic (1939–1945).* The Regio Marina also maintained a "Red Sea Flotilla" of destroyers, submarines, and motor torpedo boats at Massawa and Assab in Eritrea, to protect that colony and its conquest of Abyssinia. These bases and most of the Flotilla were isolated and wiped out during the *East African campaign (1940–1941).* In 1941 an Italian small craft flotilla was shipped overland to operate in the Black Sea under Kriegsmarine command. From 1940 to 1943 about 30 Italian submarines op-erated out of a base at Bordeaux shared with Dönitz's U-boats. Dönitz thought they hampered rather than helped Atlantic operations. At the end of 1941 he confined the Italian boats to a marginal southern zone and no longer even tried to include them in Kriegsmarine hunts. They still sank 350,000 tons of shipping.

The Italian Navy had some success in its more familiar Mediterranean waters, especially in the use of small attack boats and manned torpedoes. Its "10th Light Flotilla" made surprise attacks on British warships at anchor in Alexandria, Malta, and other Mediterranean ports. However, the Italians suffered a catastrophic defeat at *Taranto* in November 1940, which exposed a critical lack of aircraft carriers and naval air defenses. Its merchant marine and transports were savaged repeatedly in convoy duty to North Africa, and its warships were under constant air threat when seeking to intercept British convoys to Malta. About half the prewar tonnage of the Italian Navy was lost by mid-1943, though most of its capital warships were preserved by the expedient of keeping them in harbor most of the time—a pattern of nonuse reminiscent of the Imperial German Navy's behavior before and after Jut-land in 1916, but also dictated in the Italian case by a severe lack of fuel oil. Under the final armistice agreement, all Italian ships steamed all-out to surrender to the Allies at Malta. One battleship was sunk by the Germans en route. Joseph Stalin was subse-quently denied any Soviet claim to a share of the Italian fleet. He was given a number of older Western Allied vessels and captured German ships in compensation.

See also airborne; BARCLAY; explosive motor boats; Schnorkel.

ITALIAN SOMALILAND   An Italian protectorate since the late 19th century, it was used as a jump-off base for the invasion of Abyssinia in 1935. It was invaded and occupied by British and Commonwealth forces in February 1941.
   See Abyssinian War (1935–1936); East African campaign (1940–1941).

ITALO-ETHIOPIAN WAR
   See Abyssinian War (1935–1936).

ITALY   Italy was bitterly disappointed by its territorial gains from the Paris Peace Conference in 1919, though its war record did not warrant more than it received and its demands flew in the face of Allied pledges to apply Woodrow Wilson's "Fourteen Points" on issues of territorial settlement. Many Italians nevertheless nursed a deep grudge about their so-called *"mutilated victory."* Matters were not helped by the "biennio rossa" ("two red years") of 1918–1920, which were marked by violent agrarian unrest and postwar urban unemployment. The *march on Rome* brought *Benito Mussolini* to power as prime minister, under the constitutional monarch *Victor Emmanuel III*. It took four more years for Mussolini to institute a *fascist* dictatorship and consolidate personal power. It is important to note that while he freely used murder and violent street tactics to do so, his rise to power was entirely constitutional, as would be his dismissal in 1943. That did not mean Mussolini was not a true revolutionary, for he was.
   In 1929 Italy signed the *Lateran Treaties,* regularizing its relations with the Vatican. Outside the peninsula, Mussolini engaged in an aggressive diplomacy in the disastrous tradition of some earlier Italian leaders. He lost to Greece under great international pressure during the "Corfu incident." He consolidated colonial holdings with a savage war in Tripoli, then expanded them in the *Abyssinian War (1935–1936).* That was a critical turning point that shifted Italy out of the *Stresa Front* into alliance with, and dependence on, Nazi Germany. From 1935 Mussolini was a fundamental revisionist and aggressive imperialist in foreign policy, although he never gave the Italian military the proper tools to implement his overly grandiose visions of empire, and the Italian economy could never have sustained his ambitions in any case. For Mussolini envisaged a new Italian Empire with an inner sphere from the Dalmatian coast to Nice and Savoy reserved for "racial" Italians, and an outer sphere of colonial conquests in the Balkans, North Africa, East Africa, and the Middle East (Egypt, Iraq, and Palestine). Unlike the Nazis, Italian authorities did not foresee genocide as an essential part of their plans for empire. They did, however, plan "population transfers" and to export racist policies to African conquests and colonies designated for white settlement. Still, the Italian vision was fairly traditional: an empire of protectorates and colonies closer to that of the extant British and French empires than to the radical and genocidal plans for *Lebensraum* of Nazi Germany. Mussolini thought he could acquire that empire in a series of wars fought parallel to the German wars in Europe ("guerra parallela"). In the end, however, Italians fought not as equals to the Germans but

as their despised subordinates, and then on both sides as an occupied people and nation.

Mussolini was afraid of the war that began in September 1939, and was restrained from joining it by knowledge that the Italian military was unready. Utterly unprovoked, however, Italy invaded Albania on April 7, 1939. Even against that militarily weak opponent, the Regio Esercito (Royal Army) had trouble that should have warned against further martial adventures. Nor did Italy's only true conquest in Europe prove much of an economic gain for the empire: Albania was an overall drain on Italy's limited economic resources. Italy received only two days advance warning of Adolf Hitler's intention to launch *FALL WEISS* against Poland. Angered and fearful of facing the Western Allies alone while Germany concentrated on reducing Poland, Rome tipped off London and Paris. Most critically, Rome declined to fight alongside Nazi Germany under terms of the *Pact of Steel* it had earlier signed, a decision for "nonbelligerence" that surprised Hitler and caused him to delay the invasion of Poland to September 1. Italy later warned the *neutral states* of Belgium and the Netherlands that a German attack would come sometime in the spring of 1940. The truly essential and irrevocable decision that tied Mussolini to Hitler, and Italy to Nazi Germany, came when Italy declared war on Great Britain and France on June 10, 1940. Giving up neutrality to enter a general European and even world war, Mussolini ordered the Italian Army to attack the French along the Alpine frontier, to take advantage of the fact that the German *FALL GELB* operation had already ensured victory over the Western Allies. The march from a rhetorical *Axis alliance* with Berlin to active belligerence was slow and unsteady, reflecting fits and starts of Mussolini's increasingly erratic personal diplomacy after 1938, as well as his impulsive and foolhardy military aggressions in the Balkans as he sought a "parallel war" to Hitler's. Mussolini led Italy into war in mid-1940, but not into the war he expected. He thought the war in Europe was already effectively over when he joined it, to share in the spoils. It was, in fact, just beginning.

From 1935 to 1940 the British, and to a lesser extent the French, had consistently overestimated Italian military power. As a result, instead of facing Mussolini down, the Western Allies sought to appease him. That posture continued even after the *Munich Conference,* where Mussolini pirouetted in his diplomacy and fear of German power and aided the betrayal of Czechoslovakia to Hitler. When war broke out over Poland in 1939, Mussolini wisely remained neutral. But as Hitler rolled up victories and brought mighty France to its knees in May 1940, Mussolini threw away all caution. Thereafter, he would pin his fate and Italy's to the success of Hitler's "*New Order*" and to the martial fortunes of the Third Reich. Mussolini thus gave into the temptation of apparently easy conquest and declared war on France and Britain. He did so because he reasonably viewed France as defeated and no longer a threat to Italy, but under the false assumption that Britain was a spent power that could no longer stand against Italian grand designs for a new empire in the Mediterranean. That decision was critical, for it converted British war aims from strict defense of the homeland and status quo ante bellum into an imperial war with worldwide implications for transfers of territory and the global balance of power.

Despite Mussolini's rhetorical and diplomatic swagger, the Italian military was always woefully underequipped for the modern war in which it in fact was now engaged. Italy faced a core strategic problem that Mussolini never admitted or overcame: it was not militarily equal to Britain or France, the powers which stood in the way of any imperial plan for domination of the Mediterranean and expanded Italian empire in Africa. That says nothing about the Soviet Union and United States, whose armies Italy would later face as a result of the extraordinary miscalculation and uncontrolled bravado of the Italian "Duce" (Leader). The Regio Esercito was barely a modern force and had mostly outdated equipment. For example, the standard rifle first saw active service at Adowa in 1898. The Regia Marina (Royal Navy) was superficially impressive. In fact, it was grossly out-gunned by the combined Mediterranean fleets of Britain and France. Until the defeat of France in 1940 removed the French navy from the Allied order of battle, Italy's naval enemies could expect to bring major reserve flotillas into any Mediterranean conflict. Finally, the Regia Aeronautica (Royal Air Force) was wholly outclassed by every other major air force in Europe, in quantity and quality of aircraft, productive capacity, and pilot training schemes.

The hoped-for spoils that Mussolini sought were not easily secured. The French badly bloodied Italian troops on the alpine front where the Italian Army managed to advance just two miles and capture only one significant town, yet paid dearly in blood even for that. France agreed to an armistice with Italy on June 24. Hitler was annoyed by Italian intervention and rewarded Mussolini with only a small section of alpine southern France. Henceforth, the only Italian territorial gains would be the least economically desirable bits of German conquests that Hitler saw fit to toss to Mussolini. Meanwhile, Italy's war with Britain continued in the Mediterranean and East Africa. The Royal Navy savaged the Italian Mediterranean Fleet from the start. The first blows to Mussolini's imperial ambition were felt during the *East African campaign* in 1940–1941, at the end of which Italy lost all its old colonies in East Africa along with its most recent conquest in Abyssinia. Next came the early desert campaign, during which the Italians were repeatedly defeated by British forces, and even the weak Free French made real gains at Italian expense. Hitler would eventually be obliged to send the *Afrika Korps* to Tunisia to support his flailing ally. Despite those martial failures—but also because of them—Mussolini greatly desired to attack Greece and Yugoslavia. Italy's feelers to Berlin about starting a fresh Balkan war met with a stern German veto and Hitler's insistence that the Balkans must remain quiet. Hitler did not tell Mussolini that he was already planning to use the northern Balkans as a launch pad for the southern wing of his *BARBAROSSA* offensive into the western Soviet Union. The Italians were stunned and infuriated when they learned that German troops were moving into jump-off positions in Rumania, Bulgaria, and Hungary. Mussolini decided to pay back his Axis partner in similar coin by launching an Italian-only "parallel war" in the Balkans: he gave Hitler no advance warning when he sent Italian forces to attack Greece on October 28, 1940.

Italian armies were again humiliated. They were not just beaten back by the Greek Army, but were left in dire need of rescue and reinforcement by German troops during the *Balkan campaign (1940–1941).* The Regia Marina was savaged by the British at *Taranto (November 11–12, 1940),* and thereafter in a protracted naval war for control of the Mediterranean. Inside two years the Regio Esercito was defeated in East Africa and North Africa. Mussolini's humiliation was deep, but worse was to come. Italy sent a sizeable "Expeditionary Force" to support Hitler's invasion of the Soviet Union in 1941. The 60,000 man "Corpo di Spedizione Italiano (CSIR)" fought on the southwest flank of the invasion. Italy's commitment grew significantly during 1942 as a second great offensive failed to knock the Soviets out of the war. The German dictator pressured his Italian counterpart to send more reinforcements. Mussolini raised the Italian contribution to a full, but badly underequipped, army during 1942. By the end of May 1943, Italian 8th Army was utterly destroyed in heavy fighting that followed the Soviet breakthrough and encirclement of German 6th Army at *Stalingrad.* By the middle of the year Italian armed forces overall had demonstrated little but martial incompetence, despite solid performance and the often heroic character exhibited by select units. The inescapable conclusion of most Italians was that Mussolini had dragged them into a protracted war with the Western powers and Soviet Union solely to support German ambitions in the east, in which they had no interest. The combination of military failure and political contempt that resulted proved fatal to the fascist regime. Moreover, Mussolini had recklessly accepted Japan's invitation to declare war on the United States in the wake of *Pearl Harbor (December 7, 1941).* To many Italians with an auntie in Boston or a brother in San Francisco, the United States was the last country considered an enemy nation. Bombing of Rome and other Italian cities later blunted the edge of benevolent views of the Western Allies. Still, when American and British invaders arrived in Italy in September 1943, most Italians greeted them as liberators.

On July 10, 1943, Anglo-American armies landed in Sicily (Operation *HUSKY*). Allied armies arrived in southern Italy in separate British (September 3) and American (September 9) landings. Mussolini had already been legally and constitutionally dismissed in a palace coup on July 24–25, a move instigated by a 19:8 vote of the Fascist Grand Council. The votes against him included that of his son-in-law, *Count Ciano.* Marshal *Pietro Badoglio* promised Hitler that Italy would stay in the war. In secret, Badoglio prearranged an armistice and surrender to the Western Allies. Unfortunately, the handover was botched by both sides. Badoglio, the King, and government fled Rome as German forces moved quickly to free Mussolini and disarm Italian armed forces in Italy, southern France, and across the Balkans. Hundreds of thousands of former comrades in arms were corralled for deportation as forced laborers in the Reich, revealing what most Germans really thought of most Italians. About 200,000 died in slavery to the Germans. Meanwhile, the Regia Marina steamed to Malta, subject to heavy German bombing that sank several ships, including one battleship. Most of the fleet managed to surrender to the Western Allies. About 400 planes of the Regia Aeronautica flew to Western bases or were already in the south of Italy when the Allies landed. In parts of Italy and the Balkans there was armed resistance by Italian soldiers to the German takeover and attempt to disarm them, notably in the Ionian islands, Greece, and Yugoslavia. Thousands of Italian soldiers were murdered by the Germans in reprisal.

The bitter, always dogged *Italian campaign* was fought up the length of Italy by Western Allied armies and the Wehrmacht, intensely to June 1944 then on a reduced scale to the end of April 1945. Rival Italian regimes appeared on either side of the fighting lines, one backed by the Western Allies in the south and nominally led initially by Badoglio. The other was based at Salò in the north, backed by the Germans with a powerless and broken Mussolini as its ostensible head. Neither regime was fully trusted by its supporting alliance nor in control of much Italian territory—in the case of the Salò Republic, none at all. Both "governments" sought to purchase legitimacy with their respective partners by paying the blood tax, through raising small armies (under close supervision) and joining the fight. Italians thus found themselves on both sides of the lines over the last 18 months of the war. Badoglio's government formally declared war on Germany on October 13, 1944. After Badoglio was removed from power, the antifascist government made a rising military contribution to slowly driving the Germans out of Italy. The northern third of the country was riven by civil war to the end, cursed by German occupation, and saw protracted fighting between slowly moving Allied armies and the fading Wehrmacht. The last Allied offensive in Italy was fought over the *Argenta Gap* starting on April 9, 1945. All German and other Axis forces surrendered on April 29, effective at 1200 hours on May 2. In the immediate postwar period the Fascist party was banned, the monarchy was abolished by referendum, and the Communist Party emerged as Italy's largest.

See also nonbelligerence.

Suggested Reading: David Ellwood, *Italy, 1943–1945* (1985); MacGregor Knox, *Common Destiny: Dictatorship, Foreign Policy and War in Fascist Italy and Nazi Germany* (2000); Davide Rodogno, *Fascism's European Empire: Italian Occupation During the Second World War* (2006); Reynolds Salerno, *Vital Crossroads: Mediterranean Origins of the Second World War* (2002).

IVAN German slang for a Red Army soldier. It was directly comparable to German use of "Tommy" for a British soldier and "Amis" for Americans. Russians called German soldiers "Fritzes."

See Red Army.

IWO JIMA (FEBRUARY 19–MARCH 24, 1945) "Sulfur Island" was the Japanese name for this tiny island of surreal ash and slag in the Volcano Island group, 660 miles from Tokyo. Iwo Jima was strategically important because it lay on the air route from Saipan to Tokyo. Japanese fighters based on Iwo could intercept U.S. bombers on the way to *strategic bombing* raids of the Japanese home islands. It was part of Japan's "inner ring" of defenses, remarkably well fortified with steel and concrete bunkers connected to natural caves and crannies chock full of concealed and protected snipers, and machine guns nests of defenders manning presited gun pits. A desperate fight thus ensued when U.S. marines landed. Iwo Jima was defended ferociously—most often, to the death—by highly motivated and even suicidal Japanese troops. Over 72 days a powerful flotilla pounded Iwo Jima with big naval guns and navy bomber and strafing missions. The defenders rode it out, deep inside 5,000 pillboxes or natural caves that had been enlarged and connected with 11 miles of tunnels. On February 19, 1945, two divisions of U.S. marines, with a third division in reserve, hit the ash beaches of Iwo Jima. As the marines crossed over the first 300 yards the Japanese held fire. Japanese tactics were different on Iwo Jima: Lieutenant General Kuribayashi Tadamichi decided against active defense on the beaches. Instead, landing sites were presited for murderous barrages once the enemy landed. Mt. Suribachi was riddled with connected tunnels, strongpoints, and defended caves, as were other parts of the island. Unlike at *Tarawa* or *Peleliu* or on *Saipan,* at Iwo the Japanese defense was purely static: they did not mount assaults or night attacks, but waited in ambush and in their caves for the Americans to winnow or blast them out, or popped out of concealed *octopus pots* to blow up a passing "Sherman" or shoot marines in the back. The first of three air strips fell on D+1 and a second was overrun on D+4. The main fight then shifted to two heavily fortified lines and the hard climb up the slopes of Mt. Suribachi.

It took 36 days to secure the island, three weeks longer than anticipated. Over 6,000 marines were killed and another 17,400 wounded. Only 216 Japanese surrendered or were taken prisoner from a garrison of over 21,000. Overall casualties measured per square yard rank Iwo Jima among the most bloody battlefields of the war. Subsequent efforts to justify the losses suffered by the marines assert that thousands of B-29 crew were later saved by opening Iwo Jima's airfields. Those claims are undermined by research that shows most B-29 landings were not emergency landings. On the other hand, any such calculus of whether or not the islands should have been bypassed or assaulted must bear in mind that planners had in mind that Iwo would play a key role in invasions of the Japanese home islands. That it did not reflected subsequent changes in the course of the war neither side knew at the time. Iwo Jima was returned to Japan in 1968. The first memorial visit by a Japanese prime minister was made in 2005.

See also chemical weapons.

IZIUM-BARVENKOVO OPERATION (1943) A small Red Army offensive in mid-1943 by Southwestern Front. It was designed to tie down Army Group South forces and prevent their transfer to the larger battle at *Kursk.* It was marginally effective.

IZIUM POCKET
See Barvenkovo salient; FRIDERICUS; Kharkov, Battle of.

J

JABO
See Jagdbomber.

JABO-REI   Luftwaffe night fighters with extended range.

JACOB'S LADDER   A wire or rope ladder with wooden rungs. Slung over the side of the hull, it was used to board a warship or to disembark assault troops into *landing craft*.

JADE   U.S. code name for an Imperial Japanese Navy cipher machine in use from 1942 to 1944. JADE was also briefly the code name given to Soviet ciphers, later recoded as *VENONA*.

JAGDBOMBER   German term for a fighter-bomber. Such attack aircraft were commonly referred to as "Jabo," whether they belonged to the Luftwaffe or to some Allied air force.

JAGDFLIEGER   German fighter pilot.

JAGDFLUGZEUG   German fighter aircraft.

JAGDGESCHWADER   A German fighter group, or *Geschwader*. Equivalent to a *Wing* in the RAF. Other fighter units of varying size were similarly designated by adding "Jagd" ("hunt") before the normal nomenclature.

JAGDPANTHER
See anti-tank guns.

JAGDPANZER   A German armored vehicle of a type Americans called "tank destroyers." There were various types, but their common and essential feature was mounting of a turretless anti-tank gun on a tank chassis. This made Jagdpanzer cheaper and faster to build, demanding less skilled labor and steel from a German economy hard-pressed to supply either.
See also anti-tank weapons; self-propelled guns.

JAGDSTAFFEL   A Luftwaffe fighter unit originally comprised of three *Schwarm* (12 fighters). As the Luftwaffe built up fighter defenses in lieu of bombers, in 1943 every Jagdstaffel was expanded to four Schwarm (16 fighters).

JAGDVERBAND (JV 44)   An all-jet fighter *Gruppe* led by *Adolf Galland* over Germany in 1945. It was the only Luftwaffe unit so designated.

JAGDVERBÄNDE   *Waffen-SS* special forces units. Most concentrated on anti-partisan warfare. Others carried out spectacular special missions, notably those commanded by *Otto Skorzeny*.

JÄGER   German light infantry. Often employed in reconnaissance, they were notable for sniping skills. The term "Jäger" was widely employed by other specialized German units, including "Gerbirgsjäger" light mountain troops and *Fallschirmjäger* airborne infantry. It was even used by some poor quality *Luftwaffe field divisions*. From 1942, newly raised Wehrmacht light infantry divisions were designated "Jäger" divisions.
See also Panzerjägdgruppe; Panzerjäger.

JAPAN   The Meiji Emperor died in 1912, after a long and remarkable reign that saw transformational reform in many areas, but also much official repression and a huge gulf left between the governing elite and middle and lower social orders. The succession led to a period of relative liberalism ("Taishō democracy") from 1912 to 1922, including the epochal premiership of Hara Takashi. However, constitutional order and effective party government never really stabilized. Instead, Japan cycled through multiple cabinets and prime ministers: from 1885 to 1945 there were 43 cabinets and 30 prime ministers in Tokyo, several of whom were assassinated. Foreign policy remained crucially concerned with the collapse of China, and how Japan's interests there affected relations with other Great Powers. Japan had entered World War I after invoking its 1902 alliance with Great Britain, seizing the opportunity to attack and occupy German interests in the Shandong concession. In 1915, with Europe utterly absorbed with the Great War, Japan tried to force "Twenty-one Demands" on China that would have reduced its giant neighbor to the status of a bloated vassal state. The United States intervened to compel Tokyo to back down. That crisis raised American ire and opposition to Japanese encroachment in China, along with Japanese antipathy to American usurpation of what the Japanese saw as their natural sphere of influence on the Asian mainland. Another blow to American–Japanese relations came when Tokyo dispatched 75,000 troops to Siberia in 1918. It did not pull out until 1922, long after all other powers withdrew and only after the end of the Russian Civil War (1918–1921).

Japan pursued three goals at the Paris Peace Conference in 1919, two of territory and one of prestige: gain legal title to former German islands in the Pacific, win recognition of wartime gains in Shandong, and secure acceptance of an international principle of racial equality. Japan was partially successful on the first two items, but was rebuffed on the third. That proved an unnecessary blow to Japanese prestige by Woodrow Wilson and other Western diplomats. Japanese umbrage deepened in 1924 when the U.S. Congress passed "oriental exclusion" laws and severely restricted all immigration from Asia. Japan's wars with China and Russia, and then World War I, had provided real economic stimulus. The boom ended in a severe postwar depression made worse by the Tokyo earthquake of 1923. Animosity toward the United States grew even as Japan's export trade slackened. Nevertheless, Japan was a key participant in the *Washington Naval Conference* (1922). The several treaties agreed there required Japan to retrench its naval build-up but not to surrender its underlying ambition to achieve economic hegemony over the adjacent Asian mainland. The treaties benefited Japan, especially in its weakened economic condition. However, many naval officers and other Japanese saw the Washington treaty system more as a major humiliation than a reasoned compromise. Relations with Great Britain also deteriorated in the angry wake of British hostility to the "Twenty-One Demands," Japan's refusal to provide troops to the fight on the western front, and especially Japanese sympathy for decolonization by European empires in India and elsewhere in Asia. More diplomatic distance was added with lapse of the 1902 Anglo–Japanese alliance. That was a legality necessary to clear the way for the more general agreements of the Washington conference, but it was also a shift reflecting Japanese perceptions about a rising relative threat from the United States. Civilian ascendancy in domestic Japanese politics during most of the 1920s then led to military budget cuts that partly concealed this growing animosity.

Much changed from 1927, starting with a national bank crisis. A "Resources Bureau" was founded to ensure total mobilization for *total war*. This included industrial, labor, and manpower mobilization plans. However, the *zaibatsu* were not tamed but remained free to pursue economic goals outside the planning system. Worse, the onset of the Great Depression in 1929 ended the international consensus on an open world trading order that was the main support of civilian ascendancy within Japan. Trade shrank, overseas markets were closed, and unemployment rose. By the early 1930s civilian ideas were discredited by economic failure and threatened by a series of political assassinations carried out by junior military officers, sometimes with behind-the-scenes support from superiors, but at other times acting on their own initiative. As militarism revived, a form of local *fascism* found a home among young officers of the *Imperial Japanese Army* and *Imperial Japanese Navy,* and among some elite civilians. Some Japanese civilian leaders were genuine internationalists, but their position was gutted by economic downturn and the closing of foreign markets after 1929. Other liberals and moderates differed from the militarists not in their final goals, but in a preference for diplomacy over direct military action to achieve them. As long as international cooperation worked to advance regional hegemony the sword could remain sheathed. But there was little disagreement about the desirability of hegemony as a first order principle. Japan sought rapprochement with the Soviet Union while its civilians were still in charge, starting with recognition of the Bolshevik government in 1925. At a deeper level, however, that was just a tactical diplomatic move that disguised an elite consensus that war with the Soviet Union was almost inevitable. The main differences within governing circles persisted mainly over whether that war should be feared or embraced. Rising Chinese nationalism in the wake of the "May Fourth Movement" and attendant anti-Japanese sentiment among Chinese, along with revival of Soviet military power in the late 1920s, increased a rising sense of urgent insecurity among informed Japanese.

In 1927–1929 Japanese troops occupied Jinan (Tsinan), leading to skirmishes with Chinese forces. Under the growing influence of aggressive young officers in the *Issekikai,* the military acquired a growing share of the budget and more directly influenced foreign policy. In 1931 all restraint was abandoned by the Army, at home and abroad. A series of assassinations, attempted assassinations, and would-be coups d'etat struck down several prime ministers in the early 1930s, starting with Osachi Hamaguchi. Plotting within the *Guandong Army,* for what Japanese would later call the "China War," began when the most radical faction among Issekikai officers, young turks of the *Kodo-ha,* staged the *Mukden incident.* Anti-Japanese sentiment in China in the wake of the invasion of Manchuria led to boycotts and riots. In turn, these caused the Japanese to terror bomb Shanghai on January 28, 1932, then follow-up with an intervention by marines (*Rikusentai*) and then 50,000 Japanese Army troops. Heavy fighting with *Guomindang* forces around Shanghai led to diplomatic ruination of the coup de main in Manchuria: Japanese aggression and brutality in Shanghai permanently shifted world opinion against Tokyo's war to expand into the Asian mainland. Undeterred, Kodo-ha officers in the Guandong Army and government set up a puppet state of "Manchukuo." Their policy of forcible imperial expansion enjoyed wide popular support. Mutinous young officers killed another prime minister, Inukai Tsuyoshi, in 1932. That effectively replaced the civilian party system, though not yet the constitution, with de facto military rule. Objecting to mild criticism of its Manchurian policy by the *Lytton Commission,* Japan gave notice of withdrawal from the *League of Nations* on March 27, 1933. Where once Japan proudly served as a prestigious and permanent member of the Council, it was henceforth an international pariah and rogue state. The Army consolidated gains in Manchuria from 1932 to 1937. Possession of that province gave the Army a decided advantage over the Navy in Imperial Conferences and strategic planning.

Finance Minister Takahashi Korekiyo (1854–1936) dramatically reflated the economy to increase employment, in an effort to also steer Japan toward becoming a command economy, one geared for eventual total war. In fact, the zaibatsu still conducted themselves as almost sovereign entities, refusing to bend to a total war concept of the state: economic unity and rational planning remained mostly illusory. A "February Rising" in 1936—essentially a coup attempt by the Kodo-ha clique—was put down with *Hirohito's* (the Shōwa Emperor) decisive, even angry assistance. However, mutiny by junior officers fatally weakened civilian authority, giving license to imperial ambitions of other military and ultranationalist elites, especially as represented in the so-called *Tosei-ha* faction. Even after Kodo-ha radicals were executed or banished, Japan had a fundamental problem of disobedience within its officer corps and overall military rejection of civilian authority. After the February Rising, Japan was a military dictatorship in all but name, without real restraint exercised by civilians or the Chrysanthemum Throne. Policy increasingly reflected the military's belief in *Tosui-ken,* or complete strategic independence. Japan hence launched a propaganda policy of *"Asia for Asians"* and a newly territorial definition of the old economic dream of *autarky* under proposals for a *Greater East Asia Co-Prosperity Sphere.* More controversially, Japan also adhered to the *Anti-Comintern Pact.* Not wanting to be left out of the new militarism, the Navy insisted on abrogation of the Washington Treaty system as of January 1, 1937, so that it was no longer bound by warship building limitations.

Under Prime Minister *Fumimaro Konoe,* Japan next stepped into the "China quagmire," at one and the same time willingly and unintentionally: it embarked on the *Sino-Japanese War (1937–1945).* Starting with the *Marco Polo Bridge incident,* arrogant officers in the Guandong Army drew Japan into war deeper in China. They did so despite a consensus among their superiors that the ultimate enemy was the Soviet Union, and the fact that the IJN was mostly uninterested in Manchuria or northern China. The Japanese took heavy casualties from the start and lost enormous international prestige when news broke of the *Rape of Nanjing.* The die was cast: Japan was pulled ever deeper into China in a war it could not win but also could not leave, which soured its relations with the Western powers and opened new vulnerabilities along the Manchurian–Mongolian–Soviet border. The Guandong Army was then humbled by the Red Army in a bloody, undeclared border war along the Amur River in 1938 and at *Nomonhan* in July–August 1939. Even as that fight was underway, the shock of the *Nazi–Soviet Pact*—announced one day after a ceasefire was agreed at Nomonhan—left Japanese leaders feeling betrayed by their principal ally, strategically confused and even frightened, and extremely cautious about any new war with the Soviet Union. Fearing that Adolf Hitler had left Joseph Stalin free to attack Japan in the east, and hamstrung by crop and economic failures from Taiwan and Korea to Manchukuo, even core Army militarists became less provocative.

When war broke out in Europe a week later, Japan was gravely damaged economically. Overnight, it was mostly cut off from traditional continental markets and found itself more dependent than before on the United States. This shift occurred even as the administration of Franklin D. Roosevelt moved toward a view of Japan that drew fewer distinctions between aggressive decision makers in Tokyo and the fascist warmongers in Berlin and Rome. That marked a critical turn in American–Japanese relations that did not bode well for peace in Asia. Meanwhile, production irrationalities abounded in Japan's war economy. Navy and Army planners rarely consulted, except when grand strategy coincided. In weapons design, economic planning, and raw materials allocation, the two services operated more like rival empires. Research data was not shared, while human and material resources were hoarded from the rival service. That was especially true of oil, with neither armed service knowing the other's true reserve stocks or willing to share supplies. Competition led to multiple research and production redundancies, weapons design blunders, and failure to develop advanced new war-fighting technologies to keep pace with other major military powers after 1938. This bizarre state of affairs was also characteristic of powerful economic barons in the perverse Nazi managerial system in Germany. It continued in Japan to the end of the war, even after a central Ministry of Munitions was established in 1943.

The United States began to selectively but progressively embargo exports of war matériel to Japan, starting with aircraft in 1938. The next year, Roosevelt abrogated a commercial treaty dating to 1911. The main tension was still over Tokyo's ongoing aggression against China, but disputes also arose from American suspicions of larger and longer Japanese ambitions to close the "Open Door" in Asia through such initiatives as the Greater East Asian Co-Prosperity Sphere. By late-1939 Japan was already turning the focus of its aggressive urge southward, away from Siberia toward more lightly defended and newly vulnerable colonies of the European enemies of its ally in Berlin. European weakness in Asia presented Tokyo's restless warlords with a grand strategic opportunity, and a dilemma. By 1940 the Army was bogged down in the "China quagmire" and already looking for a way out by negotiation, since final victory seemed impossible. The Army had always seen the future of Japan's martial empire in a strike against the Soviets in Siberia. The Navy was instead drawn southward, toward action against its main European maritime rivals and away from a land war with the Soviets. By early 1940 the Asian outposts of the British, Dutch, and French Empires were only lightly defended; by June two of those mother countries were under Nazi occupation. Which direction should Japan strike? Deeper into China or south, over the water? The Army remained unconvinced by the Navy's arguments until Germany's *FALL GELB* operation overran France and the Low Countries, expelled the British Army from Europe, and forced Britain to husband its naval and air resources for defense against a possible German invasion.

With a further drawing back of British forces from Burma, Hong Kong, and Singapore to shore up homeland defense after the defeat of France, potential colonial pickings in the south reached full ripeness. By occupying French Indochina and attacking into Malaya and Burma, Japan could also cut the main overland supply routes to *Jiang Jieshi* and Guomindang armies in southern China. Fumi-maro Konoe returned to the prime minister's office on July 14, determined on a dramatic shift in Japanese policy at home and abroad. The key decision came on July 27, 1940. Konoe obtained formal agreement by the Army for a strategy that abjured the *hokushin* ("northern advance") in favor of accepting a version of the Navy's old proposals for a *nanshin* ("southern advance"). In return, the Navy dropped opposition to joining the *Axis alliance.* Japan signed the *Tripartite Pact* on September 27. Like Mussolini in Italy, Japan's leaders concluded that Hitler had already succeeded in establishing a "*New Order*" in the world and, therefore, that it was time to strike against the decadent, declining democratic empires of the pre-war, ancien regime. Japan turned away from the fearful prospect of fighting a terrible land war against the Soviets. As late as October 1941, as Moscow desperately sought to fend off a ferocious Nazi onslaught during Operation *BARBAROSSA,* it kept a superb and tested army group in Siberia. The Japanese Army had by then agreed to support an oceanic war against Great Britain and the United States. The former was already staggering in Asia and showed signs of strategic intimidation and inability to defend its distant interests. Perhaps, like Vichy France, London would not defend the outer empire at all? The United States was the only potential enemy with sufficient naval resources, but perhaps not the will, to stand against a determined thrust of the blade into Southeast Asia. In other words, the Army and Navy agreed on an astonishing new strategy wherein fresh wars against Great Britain and the United States were seen as the solution to stalemate in China, while also satisfying Japan's dire need to acquire resources from somewhere in Asia that would be sufficient to eventually fight and defeat the Soviet Union.

During the second half of 1940 Japan became more aggressive in Southeast Asia. Tokyo forced Vichy authorities in Saigon to allow Japanese troops into northern Indochina. Japan also put great pressure on Britain, counting on the fact that overstretched British naval assets would not allow London to resist pressure in Asia. Tokyo was right: Winston Churchill agreed to close the *Burma Road.* Such easy conquest as represented by the occupation of northern Indochina confirmed the Army's acceptance of the Navy view within the war party in Japan. But this pressure on the beleaguered British changed important minds and firmed opposition in Washington. Western Allied volunteers arrived to support the Guomindang, later becoming official in status and support. Meanwhile, the anti-Japanese compromise enforced in northern China by the *Xi'an incident* in 1936 more-or-less held until January 1941. Tokyo also felt increasing pressure from a massive U.S. Navy warship construction program approved by Congress in July 1940. U.S. naval expansion promised to turn the Imperial Japanese Navy into a second-rank force within two years, and thereby close out Japan's opportunity to expand at the expense of the beleaguered European empires in Southeast Asia. By mid-year, the IJN High Command concluded that the optimum time for war was the end of 1941. The Army came to the same conclusion by November, when it was made clear from ongoing diplomatic negotiations that the United States would not accept a settlement in Asia that left the Japanese in control of northern China, a holding that was the sine qua non of Japanese ambitions to autarky and empire.

Washington offered a diplomatic and strategic accommodation to Japan throughout 1940, but on terms that ultimately insisted on Japanese withdrawal from China. That was deemed unacceptable by aggressive imperialists in the

Japanese Army, even as they sank ever deeper into the China quagmire. The government of Abe Noboyuki held to a strict neutrality toward the war in Europe. Although Noboyuki fell from office in January 1940, his government's formal affirmation of a desire for a nonaggression pact with Moscow survived as a guide to policy. On April 13, 1941, Japan signed a five-year neutrality pact with Moscow that set the stage for the turn southward, where only the United States barred Japan's path to fresh conquests. The great lure was possible economic autarky, and maybe escape from the trap of the China War and the constant threat of war with the powerful and feared Soviet Union. That last ambition was to be achieved by partitioning China with the Soviets: the northern provinces already occupied by Chinese Communist forces would be given to Moscow, while Japan took what it wanted among the rest. Japanese troops from northern Indochina marched south and occupied Saigon in July 1941, over strenuous objections from Washington. Japan then threatened action against the Dutch East Indies. An Indochinese move was seen as a necessary preliminary to the larger military offensive to come: air bases in southern Indochina would extend the strategic reach of Japanese bombers over territories targeted for later conquest. The Roosevelt administration responded with an ever-tighter embargo on Japan's purchase of war matériel. Roosevelt embargoed copper, iron ore, nickel, oil drilling equipment, and uranium and increased informal military aid to Jiang Jieshi and the Guomindang from December 1940. His hope was to tie down one million Japanese troops in China by propping up the Guomindang. A freeze on Japanese assets in the United States was imposed on July 26, 1941. The most critical embargo, on exports of oil, was announced six days later and formally enacted on September 5.

The Japanese were stunned. Few in the leadership expected so severe a reaction to occupation of southern Indochina. An Imperial Conference convened on September 6 to consider the American demands: total withdrawal from Indochina and China and an end to the idea of a closed Japanese sphere in Asia. Tokyo saw the conditions, especially the oil embargo, as unfairly constricting its ambitions and economic needs and as threatening its war effort in China and plans for further expansion. The Imperial Conference concluded that war with the United States was inevitable, though the chance of final victory remained uncertain. Military preparations began that looked to open hostilities in October, though the Navy warned it could not be ready until November. General *Hideki Tōjō* replaced Konoe as prime minister on October 17. The "peace party" insisted that a final overture be made to Washington. The terms Tokyo offered were little changed, however. They amounted to a demand that the United States accept Japanese hegemony throughout Asia. Roosevelt rejected the Japanese offer, partly from fear that any such deal would free Japan to attack the Soviet Union, a development that would threaten far greater American interest in the ultimate defeat of Nazi Germany in Europe. A key psychological and strategic linkage of two otherwise largely unconnected theaters of war—dating back to Japan's accession to the Axis alliance—had taken firm hold on both sides of the Pacific. Given the enormous attention to last-minute negotiations that has been paid by historians, it is important to recognize that the impasse reached between Tokyo and Washington was strategic and not merely perceptual: the interests and values at stake were incompatible, and each side determined that they warranted defense by force if necessary.

An IJN carrier task force secretly left the Kuriles on November 26, 1941, headed toward Hawaii. Strangely believing that Japan was the provoked and aggrieved party, on December 1 another Imperial Conference affirmed the decision to attack. Six days later carrier-based planes struck the U.S. Pacific Fleet at anchor at *Pearl Harbor*. Apologists for the Japanese decision argue that Tokyo had no other way out of its strategic cul de sac than to take the nanshin road. They point to Roosevelt's creeping embargos, the growing strength of the USN, and stalemate in China as the main inducements. However, the documentary evidence clearly shows there was real eagerness for war in high councils of the Navy, Army, and civilian elite in Japan. The Shōwa Emperor had doubts, as did Admiral *Isoroku Yamamoto* and some others within the top military and civilian leadership. Otherwise, a real consensus existed on war to secure an expanded empire of expropriation in the Pacific and Southeast Asia. The temptation created by German victories in Europe lured Japan into a wider war that both seemed to afford a unique opportunity to seize a huge Asian empire and a path out of the quagmire in China. Japan's launch of the Pacific War directly linked hitherto disjointed wars in Europe and China and completed conversion of all ongoing conflicts into the true world war begun by Germany when it embarked on a new kind of war, a *Vernichtungskrieg* ("war of annihilation") in 1939.

Japan at first enjoyed victory after victory in a seaborne storm: it took *Guam, Wake,* and the *Philippines* from the United States; *Hong Kong, Burma, Malaya,* and *Singapore* from the British; and the *Dutch East Indies* from the Netherlands, as well as assorted minor islands and territories. In most of the early military campaigns, conquest of territory was accompanied by ferocious atrocities against non-Japanese civilians and soldiers, notably at Hong Kong and Singapore and in the Philippines during the *Bataan death march* and after. In later years, the Japanese military added to that shameful list *biological warfare* and use of lethal *chemical weapons* against the Chinese and some South Asian populations, and heinous medical experimentation at *Unit 731*. The Japanese were stunned by the *Doolittle Raid (April 18, 1942)*. The next month, an ambition to carry the war into the Indian Ocean was set back by the naval battle in the *Coral Sea (May 7–8, 1942)*, where U.S. carrier air power prevented Yamamoto from luring his enemy into a close-range fight where battleships could destroy the American fleet. In a grievous overreaction to the Doolittle Raid, Yamamoto argued for a strike into the Central Pacific. That led the carrier fleet into a trap at *Midway (June 4–5, 1942)*. Four fleet carriers were lost, a catastrophe from which the IJN never recovered. The Japanese also became bogged down in a protracted and useless campaign in the western *Aleutians*.

The IJN outperformed the USN in a number of smaller actions, especially night fights, through the end of 1942 and into 1943. But after Midway, it increasingly succumbed to the allure of the search for a "decisive battle" against the USN that it never achieved. The Army also suffered from starvation and loss of supply when the Allies adopted Admiral *Chester Nimitz*'s "island-hopping" strategy. Entire garrisons were bypassed as enemy forces leapfrogged up the coast of large islands like New Guinea, or bypassed the Japanese on isolated islands and atolls to move to more distant islands, finally reaching those from which *strategic bombers* could pound the Japanese homeland. Meanwhile, the United States outbuilt Japan in every important category of war production, often by hundreds of percent or even hundreds of times. The Americans thereby achieved a staggering advantage in war matériel, to go along with their greater numbers of conscripted and volunteer manpower. For instance, in 1943 Japan built just 122 warships to America's 2,654 of all types; by 1944 Japan had built 4 new aircraft carriers, to 90 commissioned by the United States. The United States also conducted *unrestricted submarine warfare* to devastating effect against Japan's tanker fleet and *merchant marine,* strangling overseas island garrisons of supplies and the military and home islands of essential fuel and food. Overall, the United States defeated Japan while expending just 15 percent of its total war effort in the Pacific theater of operations.

The Japanese Army was met by ANZAC and U.S. forces in hard fighting at Buna and Gona in the *New Guinea campaign* and in the Solomons in the *Guadalcanal campaign.* On March 15, 1943, Imperial General Headquarters announced a new defensive strategy wherein it would hold central New Guinea and the rest of the Solomons to make the enemy pay for every inch of sand and ash or jungle they took while moving across the South Pacific. In awful jungle fighting from 1943 to 1944, British and *Indian Army* troops threw Japanese 15th Army back from Bengal and India's northeastern frontier and began to drive it from Burma as well. Some Indians, in the *Indian National Army,* fought alongside Japan against the British, but more fought against them. Garrison after garrison fought and died on Pacific islands and atolls like *Peleliu* and *Tarawa,* not in hope of victory but merely to delay the enemy advance toward the *Absolute National Defense Sphere.* Some in the Army protested this wasteful strategy, preferring to fall back to big islands such as the Philippines or Taiwan, to meet the Allies in more regular combat. But the Navy lacked transport to supply even small isolated garrisons, let alone to pull them out or supply a major stand on the Philippines or Taiwan. A turning point came with the fall of *Saipan* in July 1944: the inner defense perimeter was breached and round-trip bombing of Japan from the Marianas became possible, a fact that toppled Hideki Tōjō's government on July 18. The Philippines was subsequently invaded by U.S. forces led by General *Douglas MacArthur,* provoking the spectacular naval battle of *Leyte Gulf* in October 1944. Land fighting in the Philippines archipelago lasted deep into 1945. Combat included house-to-house engagements that destroyed most of Manila, where Japanese troops also ran amok and carried out a fresh wave of atrocities, as other troops did across the Pacific. Fighting continued in the mountains and on a number of Philippine islands until Japan's final surrender.

The threat of pending invasion and demodernization through attrition of its armed forces—as happened on *Iwo Jima*—pushed Japan's military to truly desperate measures. These included the futile effort to lure the U.S. Navy into a "decisive battle," which led only to more attrition of the IJN at Leyte Gulf. *Area bombing* of Japan's cities started in earnest on March 9, 1945, with a low-level incendiary attack by B-29s on Tokyo that destroyed one-quarter of the city's buildings. A mass flight from the cities began: ultimately, over 10 million fled into a forlorn countryside denuded of young men and already straining to feed the population of the home islands. Within six months, one quarter of a million Japanese were dead from bombing; another 300,000 were wounded and millions were homeless. War production went into steep decline as factories were burned out and raw materials were blocked from reaching the home islands by sea. Japan responded with air and naval *kamikaze* attacks against the invasion fleet, most powerfully at *Okinawa* in mid-1945. Imperial General Headquarters feared that Okinawa would be used by the Allies as a base to bomb Japan and to threaten the Empire in northern China and Manchuria. That revealed a basic unreality about the progress and looming end of the war that defied rational assessment of what Japan might expect from any future peace.

The military instead prepared for a final, cataclysmic bloodbath to greet any invasion of the home islands, to salvage national "honor"—which was no longer possible after the manner in which Japan had fought the war—and perhaps to influence surrender negotiations. "People's Volunteer Combat Corps" ("Kokomin giyō Sentōtai") were established in June, many armed solely with bamboo sticks. They were told that the Japanese must prepare for "the glorious death of one hundred million" to stop the enemy on the shores of the home islands. American planners set November 1 as the date for invasion of Kyushu. Meanwhile, bombing continued until every major Japanese city and significant town was smoldering, millions were without shelter, the economy effectively shut down, and nearly every thought was about fire, starvation, and death. The bombing torment of Japan might have begun much earlier than it did: the Soviet Union refused permission to the United States to fly bombers to Manchuria or Japan from bases in Siberia. The benefit on the other side of the ledger was that Japan did not interfere with deliveries of *Lend-Lease* to Vladivostok, destined for transshipment to help kill Germans on the Eastern Front. But by May 1945, the German war was over and the full fury of all the Allies, including the Soviet Union, was set to burn out and crush the last resistance by Japan.

On August 5, 1945, Moscow told Tokyo that it would not renew the joint neutrality pact signed in 1941. Some Japanese leaders were already considering capitulation when the United States dropped atomic bombs on *Hiroshima* and *Nagasaki,* on August 6 and 9, 1945, respectively, and promised to bring down upon Japan a further "rain of death never equaled in history" if Tokyo did not surrender. In the interim, the Red Army struck at Japanese forces in Manchuria on August 8, easily overwhelming them in two weeks of fighting during the *Manchurian offensive operation* of August 1945. The Soviet assault was on a massive scale, smashing outmoded Japanese armies in Manchuria and northern China. The atomic bombs and the Soviet attack together persuaded Japan's political leaders to surrender. Because the enemy possessed such awesome weapons, the Western powers would not need to invade the home islands; and there was no withstanding the power of the reformed Red Army. The great enemy Japan long feared at last joined the war in Asia. The Soviet offensive into Manchuria provided additional psychological shock, piled atop the atomic bombings, and broke the back of the Japanese on the mainland during just two weeks of fighting. Any final defense of the home islands from invasion, a bloodbath the militarists hoped to use to extract concessions from the Allied powers, was no longer a viable option. Yet, the War Cabinet remained evenly divided over surrender, at three-to-three. The decision was made only following personal intervention by the Shōwa Emperor. The first peace feelers were sent out on August 10. Japan agreed to terms five days later.

Japan had endured months of fire-bombing and destruction of 60 cities, and instant incineration of two more. It now faced a whole new front and a determined and vastly more powerful Soviet enemy on the mainland. Yet, even then there was last-ditch resistance to surrender by thousands of fanatic officers. Some junior officers in Tokyo attempted a coup to prevent broadcast of Hirohito's call for Japanese to "endure the unendurable." Their effort was foiled, and the Japanese people heard their god-emperor's voice for the first time in their lives. Japan accepted to lay down arms on August 15, 1945 (August 20th in Korea). The United States and the other major Allies at the end conceded continued reign of the Shōwa Emperor and the nominal survival of the imperial system (*Kokutai*). On September 2, 1945, representatives of Imperial Japan signed the instrument of surrender to the Allied powers in Tokyo Bay aboard the battleship USS Missouri, in the presence of representatives from many nations. Over the following months formal surrenders were accepted in the field across the South Pacific, Southeast Asia, China, and Manchuria. They netted some 5.4 million Japanese Army prisoners of war and 1.8 million more from the Japanese Navy. By the end of the war over 1.14 million Japanese soldiers died, with another one-quarter million missing. More died in service with the Navy, and still more civilians under Allied bombs, conventional and atomic, and from great hunger.

American troops began landing in Japan and disarming the Japanese Army in the home islands starting on August 21. By October the entire country was under occupation, and fundamental reforms were initiated. From September 1945 to April 28, 1952, most of Japan was occupied by American troops. The British Commonwealth Occupation Force was limited to Shikoku and western Honshu. The occupation was technically conducted in consultation with an Allied Council for Japan, comprising Britain, China, France, and the Soviet Union. It was nearly exclusively an American effort run by the *Supreme Command, Allied Power (SCAP)*, headed by General *Douglas MacArthur*. During November 1945, when Operation *OLYMPIC* would have been bloodily underway on Kyushu had Japan not surrendered, the Japanese Army and Navy were formally dissolved. Japan lost significant territory by virtue of decisions taken at the earlier *Casablanca, Yalta* and *Potsdam* conferences, which shank Japan to its mid-19th-century borders. An initial effort was made to break up the zaibatsu, but in 1947 a "reverse course" decision was made in Washington whereby emphasis shifted from postwar reform and rehabilitation of Japanese society to Cold War rapid economic recovery, to remake Japan into a North Asian bulwark against the Soviet Union. By then much of Asia that had been touched by Japanese armies was again ablaze in war: civil war was underway in China and Manchuria; anticolonial wars were being waged with bitter cruelty on both sides in Malaya, French Indochina, and the Dutch East Indies; India was torn asunder by sectarian massacres and war with the new state of Pakistan. All that was, in real measure, the still-burning legacy of the meteor that was the impact of the Japanese Empire violently impacting European colonies and deeper Asian nationalisms in the 1930s and early 1940s.

Japan would gain much of lasting value from the occupation: internal stability, prosperity, rehabilitation, security, democracy, and a sure path back to regional acceptance and international respect. Japan was demilitarized and a democratic "peace constitution" passed that made Hirohito a figurehead monarch. Article Nine limited the military to a strictly self-defense role. That was interpreted until 1992 as blocking deployment of any troops overseas, even in a peacekeeping role. Among major achievements of the occupation were democratization, but also land reform and enfranchisement of women. In 1951 the *Japanese Peace Treaty* was signed. On the same day, a security treaty with the United States affirmed siting of U.S. military bases and a formal alliance that required limited rearmament by Japan. Japan had allied with Great Britain 50 years before and progressed haltingly toward democracy. After World War II, Japan absorbed additional liberalizing influences under an umbrella of military security provided by the United States, and completed the journey.

See also DOWNFALL; Emperor cult; Genrō; Ianfu; intelligence; kokubō kokkai; Nanjing, Rape of; Sho-Gō; Tanaka Memorial; Tokkō; Tokyo Tribunal; unconditional surrender; war crimes trials; Yamashita, Tomoyuki.

Suggested Reading: Haruko Cook and Theodore Cook, *Japan at War: An Oral History* (1992); John Dower, *Japan in War and Peace* (1995); Richard Frank, *Downfall: The End of the Imperial Japanese Empire* (1999); T. R. Havens, *Valley of Darkness: The Japanese People and World War II* (1978); Daikichi Irokawa, *The Age of Hirohito* (1995); Louise Young, *Japan's Total Empire* (1998).

JAPANESE AIR FORCES
See Japanese Army Air Force; Japanese Naval Air Force.

JAPANESE AMERICANS
Unlike Americans of German or Italian descent who were vetted for loyalty as individuals, Japanese Americans were interned as a group for a time during the war by order of President Franklin Roosevelt, starting on February 19, 1942. Many Japanese Americans volunteered for military service, and by 1944 the camps were closed.
See also Argenta Gap (1945); Japanese Canadians; Merrill's Marauders; Saipan.

JAPANESE ARMY
See Imperial Japanese Army.

JAPANESE ARMY AIR FORCE (JAAF)
The *Imperial Japanese Army* first began training pilots in France and Germany in 1909. Before World War I it experimented with several types of dirigibles. It acquired its first fixed-wing aircraft from France. In 1913 Japan had just five military aircraft. The JAAF grew rapidly

under the impetus of participation in the Great War, as did all other major power air forces. In 1915 the Army Flying Corps was founded. It reached a size of two battalions by 1918. The Army founded a formal and permanent air bureau in 1919, which then developed into the postwar JAAF. The JAAF saw more combat flying in Siberia from 1920 to 1922 than it had during World War I. Imperial General Headquarters looked to air power as an equalizer against larger armies, and as a critical means of maintaining lines of supply and affording close support to Army ground forces. Japan produced its first military aircraft in 1916. It expanded overall aircraft production greatly over the next five years as several *zaibatsu* entered the industry. The JAAF itself expanded with renewed funding in the late 1920s and 1930s, reaching 54 squadrons by 1937.

The JAAF was given equal status within the Imperial General Headquarters with other Army branches. Engaged in deep rivalry with its IJN air counterpart, far beyond anything normal in other armed forces, much technical work was duplicated within Japan's limited aircraft industry and scientific community. Because the JAAF was controlled by ground force commanders it concentrated in the prewar period on acquisition of a force of medium bombers, dive bombers, and attack fighters, but eschewed strategic bombers. JAAF maintenance, repair, resupply of parts, and overall support was inadequate even to the war in China from 1937. Its support systems were wholly unsuited to the air war fought in the Pacific from 1941. In addition, once Japan's mostly imitative aircraft industry was cut off from the main technical innovations of western powers, it proved incapable of keeping pace with rapid technological change. The early lead the Japanese enjoyed in aircraft design was therefore lost. This problem was compounded by wartime shortages in matériel caused by enemy blockade, a backward or at least undeveloped industrial sector, shortages of skilled labor, and extraordinary interservice rivalry with the IJN naval air arm. There was also a shortage of trained pilots: the JAAF began the Pacific War with just 3,500 pilots, although these were better trained than those of any other major power except Germany. But it refused to relieve combat crew, keeping them at the front until they were killed or wounded. The JAAF compounded progressive loss of crew skill by failing to adequately expand its training program. New pilots were entering combat with as few as 60 hours experience by 1944. In the final year of the war they did not have even those many hours in a cockpit, while even rookie pilots opposing them averaged 250 hours flying time.

Most squadrons of the JAAF were deployed in Manchuria and northern China from 1937, both for combat operations and in readiness against possible war with the Soviet Union. The Japanese–Soviet nonaggression pact of April 13, 1941, freed about 700 planes for redeployment to Southeast Asia. Most JAAF squadrons remained in China and Manchuria nonetheless. The fundamental problem for the Japanese was that their aircraft industry could not compete with that of the United States, even though Americans devoted just 15 percent of their resources to prosecuting the Pacific War. Only 40,000 aircraft were built in Japan for the Army and Navy combined by the end of the war, and most of those were light "Zero" fighters built after mid-1942. Such planes proved inadequate for homeland defense against American high-altitude bombers and vastly improved long-range fighters. The problem was made worse by a failure to build enough air engines to supply new air frames, while also providing replacements in the field for damaged or worn-out aircraft. As a result, even new warplanes became unserviceable very quickly. Finally, the Japanese Army and Navy could not cooperate on aircraft design, resource allocation, or economies of scale and shared production. The result was a colossal muddle in which some level of production was initiated on 90 different aircraft types in 164 variations.

By November 1941, the JAAF had 151 squadrons. Most comprised fighters, notably of the famed "Zero" model. Others were squadrons of inadequate medium bombers, such as the highly vulnerable "Betty." A sizeable force of short-range JAAF aircraft was based at Rabaul from late 1941. More squadrons fought in New Guinea from 1942. As the Pacific War approached the home islands, new squadrons had to be retained in Japan for home air defense. The largest formation in the JAAF was the "kōkōgun" or Air Army, of which six were formed by 1944. Next came the "hikōshidan" or Air Division, composed of two or three "hikōdan" or Air Brigades. A hikōdan comprised three "sentai" or Groups, which was the main JAAF tactical unit of medium bombers, attack bombers, or fighters. Every sentai comprised three chōtai or squadrons of 9–12 fighters or bombers each. By the end of the war the JAAF raised 13 hikōshidan. But by 1944 most of its light fighters were badly overmatched by superior enemy aircraft, and offered only minimal resistance to strategic bombing of Japan's cities in 1945. For instance, the JAAF could put only two groups of night-fighters into the air over the home islands, and even these had very poor radars. The JAAF followed the IJN's desperate lead and also founded a suicide or *kamikaze* division in October 1944. The JAAF unit was known as the "Banda Special Attack Corps," or "Ten Thousand Pilots," who sought to crash into enemy ships. It also employed *Taitari*, pilots who sought to intercept and ram B-29s with their own aircraft. None of these last-stand tactics availed to stop the invasion of *Okinawa*, firebombing of nearly all of Japan's cities, or atomic incineration of *Hiroshima* and *Nagasaki*.

Suggested Reading: Richard Overy, *The Air War* (1980).

JAPANESE CANADIANS Japanese Canadians were removed from the west coast to east of the Rocky Mountains, or interned or internally exiled in small groups starting on January 14, 1942, all by order of Parliament. That was unlike any treatment of Canadians of German or Italian descent, who were vetted for loyalty to Canada on an individual basis. Internal deportations at first drew in only young Japanese men. They were expanded to include all ethnic Japanese of any age or gender from late February 1942. In 1944 the Canadian Parliament decided to deport after the war all ethnic Japanese deemed "disloyal to Canada," including many people born in Canada who had never seen Japan. Such treatment was harsher than that meted out to *Japanese Americans*.

JAPANESE NAVAL AIR FORCE (JNAF) The Naval Air Service was founded in 1912. During the 1914 Japanese attack on the German concession at Qingdao

(Tsingtao) in Shandong, the *Imperial Japanese Navy (IJN)* flew light bombers off a converted merchantman. The IJN established a permanent air bureau in 1916. Its early experiment in carrier flying expanded during the 1920s and 1930s into a major commitment. In 1936 the IJN settled on massed carrier task forces as its principal strike force and as the main instrument of defense of the outer perimeter of the new empire that was to be established in the South Pacific and Southeast Asia. By November 1941, the JNAF had ready about 1,750 frontline fighters, torpedo planes, and navy dive bombers, as well as over 500 flying boats or sea planes. These were deployable to forward sea bases and on six fleet carriers and four larger fleet carriers. The JNAF organized its planes into *kokutai* or air corps, usually of all one-type, either of fighters or bombers. In 1941 all JNAF pilots were highly trained—at a minimum of 800 hours flying time—and some JNAF planes were superior to anything the U.S. Navy could then put into the air. That gave the JNAF an initial skills and numerical advantage in the Pacific War. However, Japanese reserves were insufficient to sustain a long war with the U.S. Navy: the entire aircraft industry produced under 1,500 military planes in 1937, which had to be divided with the Japanese Army. Production rose to 4,768 aircraft by 1940, again divided between the JAAF and JNAF. Just 5,088 military aircraft left the assembly lines in 1941. Japan also uniquely failed to expand its pilot training schools. It began the Pacific War with just 2,500 Navy pilots—the Sea Eagles—to fly its aircraft, and throughout the war suffered from a shortage of pilot training plans or facilities.

The use of IJN carriers to create local air superiority during the "Hundred Days" campaign at the start of the Pacific War was brilliantly executed. However, losses of aircraft and pilots then and later at *Coral Sea* and *Midway* was critical, given the low level of reserves. Even worse was the decision by Admiral *Isoroku Yamamoto* to order fleet planes to operate from land bases in support of the Japanese Army and *Rikusentai* during the *Guadalcanal campaign (1942–1943)*. That left the fleet dangerously low on air cover and vulnerable to air attack. That wrongheaded policy was also pursued by his successor, Admiral Mineichi Koga, who lost two-thirds of all fleet aircraft in air battles in defense of *Rabaul*. By January 1943, American aircraft in the Pacific theater of operations exceeded those available to Japan in all East Asia. A year later the U.S. Army and U.S. Navy together fielded 11,442 planes against Japan, while the JAAF and JNAF had only 4,050 increasingly outclassed aircraft flown by pilots with progressively diminishing skills. JNAF "Special Attack Corps" of *kamikaze* or suicide pilots was formed in 1944 and first deployed in defense of the Philippines. While partly successful and very much feared by the U.S. Navy, kamikaze for the most part accelerated Japanese naval aircraft losses beyond hope of redemption or recovery. Japan's defense strategy was reduced to desperate attacks by poorly trained pilots flying outclassed bombers and fighters in the *Battle of the Philippine Sea* and again at *Leyte Gulf* in 1944. There, the last of the IJN's fleet carriers were lost: the central IJN strike force in 1941, the carriers were reduced to mere unprotected bait for American naval air power to sink at Leyte. By the end of 1944, all 15 post-1941 Japanese carriers were sunk or otherwise knocked out of action, along with the whole prewar carrier fleet. In exchange, the Japanese had by that point sunk only 1 of 27 newly floated U.S. fleet carriers.

Suggested Reading: Richard Overy, *The Air War, 1939–1945* (1980); Mark Peattie, *Sunburst: The Rise of Japanese Naval Air Power, 1909–1941* (2007).

JAPANESE NAVY

See Imperial Japanese Navy.

JAPANESE PEACE TREATY (SEPTEMBER 8, 1951)

The treaty ending World War II for Japan and most of the states with which it was at war, though not with China or the Soviet Union. It was signed at San Francisco by Japan and 49 belligerent states on September 8, 1951. The Soviet Union and several of its client states in Eastern Europe attended the negotiations but refused to sign the final draft. Neither Chinese government—in Beijing or Taipei—was included in the ceremony. Its terms included a promise by Japan to uphold human rights at home and abroad. Japan renounced territorial claims beyond its home islands and minor attachments, as decided by the Allies at the *Cairo Conference* and confirmed at the *Potsdam Conference*. That is, it surrendered all Antarctic claims; all claims to mainland China, Taiwan, and Korea; all former Pacific mandates from the *League of Nations;* and the Paracels, Pescadores, Spratly Islands, and south Sakhalin. It retained "residual sovereignty" over the Bonins and Ryukyus. The issue of the Kurils stayed moot. Tokyo and Moscow disputed possession of the southernmost islands of that chain into the 21st century. Japan retained a right of self-defense of its home islands, but was required to renounce the use of force in foreign policy. That promise was already contained in Article Nine of its postwar "Peace Constitution." Occupation armies agreed to withdraw, although the United States quickly leased a base on Okinawa. Japan pledged to join the postwar bloc of free trade nations. Reparations were prescribed, but payment was indefinitely postponed. The Treaty came into force on April 28, 1952, upon receiving all necessary ratifications. Countries not signing but which later negotiated ad hoc settlements or joint declarations with Japan included: India (1952), Burma (1954), the Philippines (1956), the Soviet Union (1956), and Indonesia (1958). The Guomindang government on Taiwan signed the Treaty of Taipei with Japan on April 18, 1952. That agreement was not binding on the Communist government in Beijing.

JAPANESE–SOVIET MILITARY CLASHES (JULY–AUGUST, 1939)

See Imperial Japanese Army; Nomonhan.

JAVA

See Dutch East Indies.

JAVA SEA, BATTLE OF (FEBRUARY 27–28, 1942)

The first major naval fight after *Pearl Harbor (December 7, 1941),* with Western Allied naval forces of the *ABDA Command* facing a battlefleet of the Imperial Japanese Navy. The battle was an all-round catastrophe for the Allies. In an all-night action in which the IJN excelled, an ABDA flotilla of five Australian, Britain, Dutch, and U.S. cruisers and nine destroyers under Dutch command engaged the escort force of one of two large troop convoys heading to invade Java in the *Dutch East Indies*. The Japanese escort comprised four cruisers and 14 destroyers. The Western flotilla had no air cover and was disadvantaged by relatively shorter-range guns and ineffective torpedoes. Two Dutch cruisers and three destroyers were sunk and a British cruiser severely damaged. The Japanese suffered damage to a single destroyer. The surviving Australian and American cruisers located the second convoy the next day and sank or damaged five ships at anchor, before they were intercepted by the Japanese escort and sunk themselves. The wounded British cruiser and two more destroyers were sunk by Japanese aircraft on March 1.

JCS
See Joint Chiefs of Staff.

JEDBURGH TEAMS "Jeds." Western Allied *special forces* operations that inserted three-man teams behind enemy lines in advance of major ground operations such as *OVERLORD* and *MARKET GARDEN*, as well as in advance of smaller operations. They were operated and manned jointly by the British *Special Operations Executive (SOE)* and the American *Office of Strategic Services (OSS)*, but always contained at least one French member. Each "Jed" comprised a *resistance* liaison officer, a communications specialist, and a team leader. Their main task was to coordinate sabotage and other resistance. In all, 93 Jedburgh teams were dropped into German-occupied territory in July–August, 1944. They suffered high casualties. One "Jed," William Colby, subsequently became head of the Central Intelligence Agency.

Suggested Reading: Will Irwin, *The Jedburghs* (2005).

JEEP U.S. Army scout and staff car. It was capable of towing small artillery or anti-aircraft guns and often mounted a .50 caliber anti-aircraft machine gun. Over 630,000 were built during the war. A good number were supplied to British and Commonwealth forces and some to the Red Army via *Lend-Lease*.

JERRY British slang for a German soldier; comparable to "Tommy" or "Ivan."

JERRY BAG A British woman from the *Channel Islands* accused of "horizontal collaboration" with members of the German garrison, whether she "collaborated" in fact or just in nasty rumors.

JERRY CAN British slang for the much admired standard petrol can issued by the Wehrmacht.

JESCHONNEK, HANS (1899–1943)
See Luftwaffe.

JETS

See Air Transport Auxiliary; bombers; fighters; Jagdverband (JV 44); Luftwaffe; V-weapons program.

JEWISH BRIGADE   An all-Jewish unit of the British Army formed in Palestine and Egypt. It served in North Africa and Italy. Prime Minister Winston Churchill was a strong proponent who simply overrode prejudiced objections to Jewish soldiers within the War Office. After the war, members of the Brigade aided still-illegal immigration of Jewish refugees to the British mandate territory in Palestine. They also formed groups to hunt down escaped Nazis, later calling themselves "Nokmim" ("Avengers"). Initially Nokmim units tracked, captured, and turned over to the various major Allies ex-*Schutzstaffel (SS)* men, focusing on those known to have run *Einsatzgruppen* or worked in the *concentration camps* and *death camps*. When some of these men were released by Allied authorities instead of being charged with war crimes, Nokmim units decided to hunt down and kill SS murderers summarily. As many as 1,000 of the worst SS met justice at Nokmim hands.

JEWS

See individual countries, and *anti-Semitism; Axis alliance; concentration camps; death camps; Eichmann, Adolf; Einsatzgruppen; Eisenbahntruppen; ethnic cleansing; fascism; Gestapo; ghettos; Grand Mufti; Heydrich, Reinhard; Himmler, Heinrich; Hitler, Adolph; Holocaust; International Brigades; Italian Army; Iron Guard; Jewish Brigade; Judenräte; Korück; Madagascar; Manstein, Erich von; Mussolini, Benito; National Socialism; Nazi Party; New Order; Palestine; Patton, George; Polish Army; Pripet Marshes; Reichenau, Walter von; Reichssicherheitshauptampt (RSHA); Schutzstaffel (SS); Sicherheitsdienst (SD); Stalin, Joseph; Vichy; volksdeutsch; Waffen-SS; Wannsee Conference; Wehrmacht.*

JIANG JIESHI (1887–1975)   Known outside China during the war as "Chiang Kai-shek," Jiang Jieshi was a Chinese warlord and dictator. As a youth he studied in Chinese and Japanese military academies and alongside the *Imperial Japanese Army*. In 1905 he joined the Revolutionary Alliance, an anti-Manchu coalition organized among Chinese students studying in Japan. He deserted in 1911 to return to China, then deep in the throes of Sun Jixian's nationalist revolution. In 1913 Jiang took part in a failed revolt, after which he fled back to Japan. He returned to China in 1915 to join the "Third Revolution," which preserved the Chinese Republic from an imperial restoration under the warlord Yuan Shikai. Jiang's corruption showed early: he was involved with the infamous "Green Gang" underworld in Shanghai and involved in manipulating China's currency markets. From 1918 to 1923 he rose through the ranks of the *Guomindang* and consolidated his power in southern China. Sun Yixian sent him to Russia for several months in 1923 to study Leninism in practice and for military training, after which Jiang returned to become the first head of the Whampoa Military Academy. From that influential position, where he also received considerable military aid from the Soviet Union, Jiang built up a base of personally loyal supporters in the new officer corps.

After Sun Yixian died in 1925, the politically cunning and nimble Jiang showed that he learned much from Bolshevism as he set out to unify China. His principal means were military, but he also emulated V. I. Lenin's tight, dictatorial control of the governing Guomindang. Unlike Lenin, who delegated military matters to Leon Trotsky and others, Jiang was a competent field general. He personally led the "Northern Expedition," which ended resistance by several dozen warlords by 1928 and unified most of China under a Guomindang dictatorship. Jiang bloodily purged the Guomindang and China's cities of members of the Chinese Communist Party (CCP), starting with the "Shanghai massacre." He expelled Soviet advisors from his army and marched against surviving Communist strongholds organized in "soviets" in the countryside (revolutionary communes governed by Party committees and cadres). In 1927, he married a Wellesley College graduate. "Madam Chiang" (Jiang) was a well-spoken Chinese Christian, with the latter fact helping enormously with an American public that still saw China largely through the eyes of missionaries. She helped secure U.S. diplomatic and military support for her husband from the late 1930s onward. From 1930 to 1934 Jiang conducted five "bandit suppression campaigns" against the Communists, driving *Mao Zedong* and *Zhu De* and their followers onto the "Long March." Jiang led the Guomindang throughout the long *Chinese Civil War (1927–1949)*. During the 1930s he introduced faintly *fascist* overtones to Guomindang propaganda and ideology, but mostly he was a militarist in the broad tradition of Chinese warlordism.

In 1931, a more immediate threat appeared. Following the *Mukden incident,* Japan's *Guandong Army* invaded Manchuria. Fighting later broke out at Shanghai, where Jiang's forces fought hard but were defeated. Thereafter, a tense compromise was reached, but a Japanese military threat was constantly and directly posed to northern China. Jiang hoped that the Soviet Union would fight and contain Japan, as Japanese troops intermittently pressed against China's border and threatened to plunge deep into the country. Nationalist and Manchurian troops were unhappy that Jiang insisted on pursuing a more vigorous war against the Communists in the south instead of concentrating on expelling the foreign enemy looming over northern China. A Manchurian unit detained Jiang in December 1936 and held him for nearly two weeks during the remarkable *Xi'an incident*. During his detention he met *Zhou Enlai* and the local Manchurian commander, the "Young Marshal" Zhang Zuolin. They tried to persuade him to sign an agreement on a common anti-Japanese front. He finally verbally agreed to join with the Communists in fighting the Japanese, but would not sign anything to that effect. Jiang understood that China was not a military match for Japan. Still, within six months he thought he saw an opportunity to unify northern warlords, make fresh gains against the hated Communists, and curry international favor and military aid. He thus decided, after all, to make a military stand against the Japanese. His chance came with the *Marco Polo Bridge incident* that initiated the *Sino-Japanese War (1937–1945)*. As with Joseph Stalin's stand against Adolf Hitler, Jiang turned early catastrophic defeats into a long-term victory over Japan by refusing to quit or negotiate, no matter how many millions of Chinese died or how many cities and provinces were lost. From the first day of the war he determined to fight with as much ruthlessness as the Japanese displayed. That included a decision to break the dikes holding back the Yellow River to block a Japanese advance, an act that killed as many as one million Chinese civilians. Jiang still was forced to move his capital deep into the mountains at Chongqing.

Pragmatic and crafty, Jiang walked a tightrope for eight years between domestic and foreign enemies, and between domestic and foreign allies, from local warlords to Franklin D. Roosevelt. He was always most interested in pressing the internal war against Chinese Communists, often at the expense of not defending ordinary Chinese against depredations of the Japanese. He had little interest in the wider world war, despite attending several Allied summits and being portrayed in American propaganda as one of the "Big Four." With the main Chinese armies forced to retreat into the southern mountains, Jiang lost access to China's coastal cities and fertile plains. Even so, the tenuous and coerced Xi'an contract was only loosely adhered to by Jiang during the first years of the Sino-Japanese War. It collapsed in January 1941, when Jiang ordered an ambush of Communist troops: 3,000 were killed in an attack known as the "New Fourth Army Incident." The Sino-Japanese War merged with the larger course of World War II once Japan attacked the British and Americans in the Pacific in December 1941. Jiang thereafter received American aid to supplement British supplies and Western volunteers. The new aid arrived via aircraft flown over "The Hump" of the Himalayas, until the Americans completed the *Ledo Road* in 1944. In the meantime, Jiang was elevated by Roosevelt into a major Allied leader, and attended the *Cairo Conference*. Winston Churchill was far less impressed with Jiang than was Roosevelt. Also, Jiang quarreled badly with the American theater commander, "Vinegar" *Joseph Stilwell,* who did not regard the Chinese leader highly. From 1944, even FDR lost interest in the Guomindang war effort.

Jiang's postwar regime received strong initial support from President Harry Truman, as civil war with the Communists was renewed and intensified from 1946. By then, Jiang's regime was so evidently corrupt and brutal as it moved back into formerly Japanese-occupied territory that its renewed effort against the Communists was militarily weak, politically ineffectual, and socially unpopular with most Chinese peasants. American support waned as Jiang proved incapable of working for national reconciliation, or of managing the economy or conducting successful military operations against the Communists. Jiang's forces were defeated by the end of 1948. He led two million Guomindang into armed exile on Taiwan, where he headed a government-in-exile that asserted it was the sole legitimate government of all China. He vainly sought to continue the fight to "recover" the mainland from Mao. However, after 1950 that posture was mostly rhetorical: the Guomindang turned strictly toward defense of Taiwan, while the United States and Chinese Communists committed against each other militarily in Korea and, later, in Indochina. Jiang and his wife remained favorites of hardline anti-Communists in the United States, and elsewhere in the West, throughout the

Cold War. Jiang was president of the Republic of China (Taiwan) from 1950 until his death in 1975.

See also *Green Gang; Three Demands.*

JINRAI "thunder."
See *ohka.*

JITNA LINE A fortified British defensive line in northern Malaya. It failed to stop or even much slow the Japanese, who punched through it in under 72 hours.

J-JOUR The French term for *D-Day (June 6, 1944).*

JODL, ALFRED (1890–1946) German general. Chief of staff of Wehrmacht operations, 1939-1945. As a young officer Jodl was wounded in the leg during World War I. The rest of his career was spent in staff duties. As an antidemocratic nationalist and racist, though not originally a full-fledged Nazi, Jodl was deeply attracted to Adolf Hitler. He became morally and intellectually mesmerized by the Führer and stayed totally loyal to the Nazi vision to the last hours of the regime. Jodl was the top operations planner and key military adviser to Hitler, and thus shares major responsibility for strategic and operational blunders made by Hitler, the *OKW,* and *OKH.* Jodl was intimately implicated in most of the major crimes and atrocities of the regime, not just by his knowledge of them and passivity toward them, but often by active engagement. He personally recommended terror bombing of British and other European cities, signed orders for illegal executions of *prisoners of war,* and sent atrocity orders out over his name and with full OKW authority. He requested a field command after falling out with Hitler in 1942 over dismissal of Field Marshals *Franz Halder* and *Wilhelm List,* but was refused. Jodl was standing beside Hitler when the bunker bomb planted during the *July Plot* exploded, but was not seriously injured. He then served on the "Honor Court" that purged the Wehrmacht officer corps and deepened its nazification. At the end of the war Jodl signed the instrument of *unconditional surrender* in behalf of the German government and military at Rheims. At the *Nuremberg Tribunal* he was charged with war crimes and with planning and carrying out an aggressive war. His plea that he had merely followed *superior orders* was rejected and denounced by the Tribunal. Jodl was convicted and hanged. In 1953 a Munich court posthumously declared that he was not, after all, a "major offender" as the Nuremberg Tribunal found. That reversal remains moot—certainly morally, if not also legally.

JOINT CHIEFS OF STAFF (JCS) The *General Staff* of the U.S. armed forces, comprising the top service chiefs plus General *George C. Marshall* and, later, Admiral *William Leahy.* Together with the British *Chiefs of Staff,* the JCS formed the *Combined Chiefs of Staff* that ran the war for the Western Allies in consultation with top civilian leaders. Throughout the war the JCS consistently affirmed that the only path to final victory was land invasion of the German and Japanese homelands. The JCS did not regard *strategic bombing* as a war-winning strategy, no matter what individual air chiefs said.

JOINT FORCES   Western Allied term for multiservice (air, land, sea) forces under a unified command. These did not include *strategic air forces* but might include *combined forces*.

JOSS   Western Allied code name for the Licata assault carried out during the invasion of Sicily.

JOYCE, WILLIAM (1906–1946)   "Lord Haw Haw." British propagandist for Nazi Germany. A vicious anti-Semite, he was an early admirer of Benito Mussolini and the Italian *fascist* movement. He started his political career on the hard right as deputy to Oswald Mosley in the *British Union of Fascists*. American-born, he grew up mostly in Ireland. He left Britain for Germany in late August 1939. He acquired German nationality the next year. Joyce made hundreds of radio broadcasts ("Germany Calling") from Berlin to Britain. He also broadcast to approaching Western forces as they liberated Western Europe. His last broadcast went out just days before the war ended. It repeated all his themes: Germany had never sought war, which was the creation of Jews; the real enemy of the West was Bolshevik Russia; the Western powers would pay the postwar price of not joining Nazi Germany to oppose the Soviet Union; and so forth. Joyce was captured by a British unit at the end of May 1945, while trying to escape by hiding among crowds of refugees. He was returned to Britain to be tried. Convicted of treason, Joyce was executed on January 3, 1946.
See also Axis Sally; Tokyo Rose.

JU-87   "Stuka." Junkers-87 German dive bomber.
See bombers.

JU-88   Junkers-88 German medium bomber. Twin-engined, it also served in a fighter role.
See bombers.

JUDENRÄTE   Jewish Councils set up across German-occupied Europe to administer Jews herded into ghettos and camps.

JUDY   Western Allied code name for the Yokosuka D4Y3 "Suisei," a Japanese dive-bomber.
See bombers.

JUIN, ALPHONSE (1888–1967)   French general. During *FALL GELB,* the invasion of France in 1940, he led the defense of the perimeter around *Dunkirk* to permit more evacuations. He was taken prisoner by the Germans. After the *armistice* of June 22, 1940, Juin stayed loyal to Vichy in North Africa, into whose hands he was released. In November 1941, he took command of ground forces of the *Armée d'Afrique.* Upon the *TORCH* landings in Morocco and Algeria in November 1942, Juin turned coat and commanded French forces fighting in Tunisia alongside the Western Allies. He commanded the *Corps Expéditionaire Français* in the *Italian campaign* in 1943. He was promoted Maréchal de France in 1952.

JULY PLOT (JULY 20, 1944)   The main assassination and coup attempt by the "Resistance Circle" of mostly retired, but also some active, German officers, on July 20, 1944. The "July Plot" was the most significant and most nearly successful effort by German officers to kill Adolf Hitler and push the Nazis from power. The aim of the key plotters, comprising anti-Nazi resisters inside the Wehrmacht as well as a number of more opportunistic officers, was to kill Hitler, seize power from the *Nazi Party* in a military coup, and negotiate an end to the war with the Western Allies before Germany suffered catastrophic defeat. It was not the first attempt by the *German resistance* to kill Hitler. There were several other attempts assayed by political opponents in the 1920s, even before he came to power. There was contemplation of a coup by senior Wehrmacht officers in 1938, including discussion of assassination of Hitler. That scheme was prompted by Hitler's highly aggressive stance toward the Western Allies leading into the *Munich Conference* that September. Fear of war against the Western democracies brought the first plotters together. But Hitler moved more quickly, purging and taking personal control of the *OKW.* Another possible close call occurred on November 2, 1939, when the *Bürgerbräukeller bomb* went off in Munich. In March 1943, a bomb placed on Hitler's plane by a small conspiracy of anti-Nazi officers failed to detonate. It had to be physically retrieved for the plotters to remain undetected. Starting in April 1943, the *Gestapo* and *Sicherheitsdienst (SD)* penetrated the German resistance, made multiple arrests of religiously motivated and other anti-Nazi Germans, and scattered and frightened many more resisters into silence and submission. Early in 1944 resisters with the *Abwehr* were hamstrung by the dismissal of Admiral *Wilhelm Canaris* and absorption of the Abwehr into the SD.

But a new group of plotters grew up around the forceful personality and moral drive of Count and Colonel Claus von Stauffenberg, a Württemberger and General Staff officer who had been severely wounded in North Africa in April 1943. Stauffenberg convalesced on the roll of the *Ersatzheer,* during which time he came to the decision that Hitler must be deposed. Making contact with other officers he knew belonged to the German resistance, Stauffenberg organized an assassination and coup attempt code named "Operation Valkyrie." On July 20, he personally placed a briefcase bomb beneath a heavy wooden conference table inside the *Wolfsschanze* headquarters, next to where Hitler was then standing. Stauffenberg was missing an eye, one arm, and two fingers on his remaining hand. But he pressed down a specially made chemical trigger, then left the room. A powerful explosion followed that killed several Wehrmacht officers and aides who remained inside. But due to a sequence of chance small events the blast only slightly wounded and shook Hitler but did not kill him. Had the bomb done its job and killed the German Führer, its detonation was to have been followed by simultaneous seizure of power in Berlin, proclamation of a military government, and an immediate offer to Western Allied governments to negotiate an end to the war. Stauffenberg believed that Hitler was dead and showed great energy and drive racing to Berlin to organize the coup. But some of the other plotters failed to move quickly, while others hedged their bets while waiting for different men to move events. Loyal Nazis in Berlin, not least a most unlikely man of action, *Josef Göbbels,* took advantage of the hours-long delay to organize SS units and the commander of the Berlin garrison, and acted against the plotters. Hitler's supporters moved with ruthless and effective force once telephone calls were received from Hitler at the Wolfsschanze and a radio broadcast made it clear to everyone that he was still alive.

The events of July 20 may have helped mislead leaders of the Polish *Home Army* that the end was near for the German war effort, and encouraged them to mistime the *Warsaw Uprising.* Its most important outcome was that, after July 1944, there was no hope that the German officer corps would act to remove Hitler and his Nazi regime. Instead, in an apt phrase by historian Michael Geyer, only those generals who believed in the "catastrophic nationalism" of the Nazi elite henceforth were permitted near the German Führer or to hold active command. Such men helped Hitler exact a terrible vengeance on survivors, trying hundreds of officers and other suspects in front of Nazi "people's courts," then butchering many with cruel tortures and without the usual military dignities: executions were by firing squad in a few cases, but by axe or slow strangulation by piano wire while hanging from meat hooks in others. The scenes of slow murder were later watched on film by Hitler. *Heinz Guderian, Alfred Jodl,* and *Wilhelm Keitel* served on the "Honor Court" that purged the Wehrmacht officer corps and thereby deepened its nazification during the last year of the war. Murder and vulgar nihilism in all the German armed forces thus reached a crescendo, as the Wehrmacht paid with the flesh of its officers and men the blood debt it owed Hitler and the Nazis from the Faustian bargain its leaders had struck in 1934.

See also Abwehr; Beck, Ludwig; Brandenburgers; Himmler, Heinrich; Paulus, Friedrich von; Rommel, Erwin; Volksgrenadier; Witzleben, Erwin von.

JUNGMADELBUND   "League of Young Girls."
See Hitlerjungend.

JUNKERS   The east-Prussian landed aristocracy, many descended from the medieval Teutonic Knights. They were closely bound to service to the Prussian monarchy from the 16th century, in exchange for autocratic rights over peasants on their large estates. As the main defenders of agrarian interests, they were increasingly at odds with the 19th-century German state as it industrialized. Junkers officers were also uneasy with the rough social upstarts who populated the top of the *Nazi Party,* but accommodated quickly once Adolf Hitler brought the *Wehrmacht* fiscal and social ascendancy in the 1930s, and then diplomatic and military victories. Junker influence was already largely broken by the Nazis before it ended with Allied occupation of Germany after 1945. In some areas it disappeared with annexation of parts of old East Prussia into Lithuania, Poland, and the Soviet Union, territorial adjustments attended by expulsion of ethnic Germans from those regions.

JUNKERS AIRCRAFT
See bombers; fighters.

JUNO   Code name of the Normandy beach attacked by Canadian 3rd Division on *D-Day (June 6, 1944)*.

JUPITER (1942)   Code name for a proposed British landing in northern Norway. It was a favorite project of Winston Churchill, but was never carried out in face of equally strenuous opposition from the *Chiefs of Staff*. Instead, a cross-Channel project few wanted led to disaster at *Dieppe*. Fear of just such an operation in Norway led to *CERBERUS,* intended to shift powerful German naval assets to the north.

JUPITER (1943)   "Iupiter." It is speculated by some historians that the Red Army considered a major operation to follow Operation *MARS.* That Red Army counteroffensive began on November 25, 1942, but ran out of steam by mid-December. David Glantz has suggested that the Stavka canceled the larger operation JUPITER after MARS failed west of Moscow. It is thought the main objective of JUPITER would have been to envelop and destroy Army Group Center around Viazma. The evidence cited by proponents of this view is mainly circumstantial but not unpersuasive. The Stavka concentrated vastly greater forces around the *Rzhev balcony* than were then available for the counteroffensive that began at *Stalingrad* on November 19, and was generally committed to offensive operations in that sector. Also, there were operational similarities to the double-encirclement of large German forces that the Red Army successfully conducted at Stalingrad and Rostov in the linked operations *URANUS* and *SATURN.* If the parallel to SATURN is correct, then JUPITER should have sought to encircle and smash the outer formations of Army Group Center once MARS smashed innermost forces in the Rzhev salient. When MARS failed to make sufficient headway, the Stavka is said to have canceled JUPITER.

KACHIN RANGERS   Kachin tribesmen working as scouts and auxiliaries for the Western Allies in Burma.

KAITEN
   See torpedoes.

KALININ, MIKHAIL IVANOVICH (1875–1946)   Soviet statesman. Nominal head of state, 1922–1946. A long-time member of the Politburo, Kalinin survived the great purges and terror under Joseph Stalin in the 1930s, mainly through sheer toadyism. He slavishly supported Stalin at every presented opportunity, and on occasion invented some of his own. Emulating the behavior of Foreign Minister *Vyacheslav Molotov*, Kalinin also failed to object when his wife was arrested and sent to the *GULAG* in 1938.

KALKIN GOL, BATTLE OF (1939)   The preferred Russian terminology for what Japanese refer to as *Nomonhan*.

KALTENBRUNNER, ERNST (1903–1946)   *Schutzstaffel (SS)* leader and secret policeman; head of the *Gestapo, Sicherheitsdienst (SD)*, and *Reichssicherheithauptampt (RSHA)*, 1942–1945. An Austrian by birth, Kaltenbrunner joined the *Nazi Party* and SS in 1932. He was involved in the attempted Nazi Putsch in Austria in 1934 that led to the murder of Chancellor *Englebert Dollfuss.* Following the 1938 *Anschluss,* he headed the SS inside the former Austrian territories. He succeeded to the post of chief murderer for the Nazi state upon the assassination of *Reinhard*

Heydrich in 1942, continuing oversight of the *death camps* and other SS *concentration camp* enterprises. His SD absorbed the *Abwehr* once Adolf Hitler turned against that Wehrmacht military intelligence arm and abolished it in early 1944. He was the leading SS figure to be convicted as a "major war criminal" by the *Nuremberg Tribunal*. He was hanged in October 1946.

See also *Kugelerlass*.

KAMIKAZE "Divine wind." The original kamikaze was a typhoon that destroyed a Mongol invasion fleet in 1281. The term was revived in reference to Japanese suicide pilots who crashed planes loaded with ordnance into enemy warships starting in 1944 in the skies around the Philippines. A strictly military reason for deploying kamikaze was that the tactic could make use of trainer aircraft and outmoded "Zeros," "Kates," and "Vals." That spoke to the overall inefficiency of the Japanese aircraft industry and its dramatic decay and decline in warplane production during 1944. While militarily ineffective, kamikaze addressed Japanese national morale, which was badly in decline by late 1944 but rallied to some degree around the sacrifice and symbolism of the young kamikaze. On the other hand, it is important to note that not all kamikaze were volunteers: attack squadrons were escorted by fighters ready to shoot down those who faltered, while any pilot who returned to base was imprisoned. Even among those who were volunteers, social shame and peer pressure on young men heavily conditioned their choice. Moreover, many officers in the Army and Navy air forces regarded the exercise as morally vulgar and militarily wasteful. The Navy founded its suicide wing, the "Special Attack Corps," in 1944. The Army followed suit, founding its "Banda unit"—or the "Ten Thousand Pilots"—in October 1944. Kamikaze and Banda tactics formed part of a larger pathology of death that saturated Japan in the closing months of the war, conducing to many other types of suicide attacks, slaughtering of *prisoners of war,* and a pervasive fatalism and resignation about looming individual death and national defeat, all mixed with rising popular dissatisfaction with Japan's war leaders and growing elite unease over possible rebellion.

The first kamikaze attack may have been made on October 21, 1944, against an Australian cruiser. Attacks against U.S. warships four days later during the fight at *Leyte Gulf* were certainly official kamikaze, and scored the first ship kill: a U.S. escort carrier. By the end of the war, 1,388 Japanese Army pilots died in suicide attacks. Thousands more naval aviators died, 4,000 or more. Few kamikaze pilots were military professionals. Most of the original group of 1,000 "tokkotai" ("special attackers") were college students in their early 20s, drawn directly from officer candidate programs of Japan's elite universities. Later groups were mostly lower-class boys, often as young as 16 or 17 years old, enlisted directly out of high school air cadet programs. Tactics were simple: a high, unrecoverably steep dive that targeted the enemy amidships; or a low-level, water-skimming approach that came in beneath defending anti-aircraft guns, then popped up at the last second to ram the ship while carrying a 500 lb bomb. Kamikaze attacks were often part of larger air assaults that included conventional bombing runs by pilots and air crew who fully expected, or hoped, to return to base.

The greatest kamikaze effort was made against the invasion fleet off *Okinawa* from April to June, 1945. Kamikaze attacks sank 38 warships, though none larger than a destroyer; they damaged nearly 200 more, while killing 4,907 U.S. sailors. The Japanese plan was to allow an initial landing, then isolate and destroy it by driving away the supporting fleet. A naval task force centered on the giant battleship *IJN Yamato* sailed south with only enough fuel to reach and attack the invasion fleet. Some dispute that its mission may be fairly characterized as a suicide run as the apparent intention was to beach "Yamato" and fight it out with its massive deck guns. Before that could happen the task force was met by several hundred U.S. naval aircraft and the "Yamato" and its escorts were sunk with great loss of life. About 25 percent of all enemy ships struck by kamikaze were sunk. Kamikaze hit 402 enemy warships in all, putting 375 out of action for some period of time, including 12 carriers of various type. That still left thousands of enemy warships and transports hovering around Japan's home islands, readying to support invasion. After the surrender, Allied inspectors found over 5,000 aircraft ready for kamikaze service.

Allied countermeasures against kamikaze were highly effective. They included deploying decoy ships to steer inexperienced pilots away from major capital warships, increased anti-aircraft guns on all ships, and provision of an especially heavy Combat Air Patrol (CAP) by dozens of carriers. The CAP was maintained over the fleet at Okinawa to shoot down suicide attacks at safe distances. It also should be remembered that the vast majority of unskilled kamikaze pilots who tried to hit enemy ships instead missed and splashed, or were shot down during the attempt. The danger from kamikaze at Okinawa diverted a number of B-29 raids intended to pound Japan's cities to instead bomb kamikaze and Banda airfields, although given the enemy's overwhelming superiority in the air that temporary shift of the strategic bomber force hardly mattered to the outcome. Some 10,000 obsolete old trainers, along with a few new aircraft, were held in reserve for use as kamikazes pending invasions of the home islands that never took place. They were captured and destroyed after the occupation of Japan.

See also DOWNFALL; ohka.

Suggested Reading: Rikihei Nakajima, et al., *The Divine Wind: Japan's Kamikaze Force in World War II* (1958; 2003); M. Sheftall, *Blossoms in the Wind* (2005).

KAMINSKI BRIGADE
See Warsaw Uprising (1944).

KAMMHUBER LINE German air defense system for night fighter interception of RAF Bomber Command flights over the Low Countries into northern Germany. It was basically in place by the middle of 1941, and complete and growing in sophistication by September 1942. It was named for Luftwaffe General Josef Kammhuber, General of Fighters in the Luftwaffe and the man in charge of Germany's homeland defense. Night fighters circled inside grid pattern boxes (Räume) until vectored onto approaching bombers by ground control intercept (GCI) radars, with ground units also illuminating the target plane with radar-guided searchlights. Once in range, the night fighter's own *Lichtenstein-Gerät* air radar located the target. The Kammhuber Line also had an integrated ground defense system of *Flak* guns, searchlights, and search radars. It was highly successful until Bomber Command adopted the bomber stream as a countermeasure. This risked more mid-air collisions, but it effectively punched through thin Kammhuber crustal defenses and provided bombers relative safety in numbers, much like the protection provided by a school of fish. As long as individual bombers did not stray from the stream, the Räume-based single-fighter system was swamped. The Kammhuber Line was made obsolete by later mass raids that fed into all-out *area bombing* from early 1943. However, its technology formed the basis for more sophisticated *Raumnachtjadg* tactics employed against the RAF and USAAF to the end of the war.

See also *Freya; Himmelbett; Wilde Sau; Würzburg; Zahme Sau.*

KAMPFGESCHWADER (KG)   Any normal Luftwaffe bomber wing, with one exception. Kampfgeschwader 200 was a unique, top secret group formed in February 1944. It was essentially a Luftwaffe special forces *Geschwader*. In coordination with the *Sicherheitsdienst (SD)*, it flew special deep reconnaissance and agent insertion missions, long-range delivery of strategic supplies to and from the Japanese, and one failed long-range bombing mission in late 1944 against power stations deep in Soviet rear areas. It sometimes flew captured or repaired Western and Soviet aircraft. It had a small component of volunteer suicide pilots, who seem to have spent more time contemplating bizarre ideas such as crashing into the Kremlin to kill Joseph Stalin than conducting viable military missions. A suicide ramming mission was flown on April 7, 1945, that knocked out several heavy bombers, but it had no real impact on the air war.

KAMPFGRUPPE (KG)   A Wehrmacht combined arms battle group. Alternately, any ad hoc and mixed German battle formation, including Luftwaffe or Kriegsmarine units. The term was also used by the *Nationalkomitee Freies Deutschland* for small units infiltrated or parachuted into Wehrmacht rear areas with the intention of establishing contact with partisans, carrying out guerrilla attacks, and conducting forward reconnaissance for the advancing Red Army.

KANNALFRONT   German term for the Atlantic frontier of the Nazi empire formed by the English Channel.

KAPP PUTSCH (MARCH 1922)   A failed coup attempt against the Weimar Republic by the *Freikorps*. Supporters included Field Marshal *Erich von Ludendorff*. The main leader was the journalist Wolfgang Kapp (1868–1922). The rebels briefly held Berlin but fled when popular support failed to develop. Though it failed, the Putsch revealed how thin public support was for Weimar. Adolf Hitler drew dark lessons from the Putsch attempt, which he emulated with his "Beer Hall Putsch" in Munich in 1923.

KARELIA   The heavily forested Finnish peninsula and isthmus that abutted Leningrad before 1940. Joseph Stalin forced cession of the lower portion of Karelia at the conclusion of the *Finnish–Soviet War (1939–1940)*. Karelia was retaken by the Finns during the "Continuation War" from June 1941, until September 1944. Permanent territorial transfer to the Soviet Union was confirmed in 1944.

KASSERINE PASS, BATTLE OF (FEBRUARY 19–22, 1943)   A German counteroffensive against the inexperienced, poorly led, and still largely unbloodied U.S. 2nd Corps in Tunisia led to this sharp American defeat. Elements of German 4th Panzer Army led by General *Hans-Jürgen von Arnim* joined with elements of Field Marshal *Erwin Rommel's* German-Italian 1st Panzer Army in an effort to split the Western Allies by driving through the Americans via the Kasserine Pass. Rommel broke through the pass, severely mauling a hodgepodge of American defending units. But hurried reinforcements, air power, the approach in Rommel's rear of British 8th Army, and miscommunication among German and Italian commanders meant the breakthrough was not properly exploited. Rommel pulled back on February 22. The Americans reoccupied the pass two days later.

The defeat was a psychological shock to top U.S. Army commanders in the theater, to the War Department in Washington, and to the general public in the United States. It led to important long-term changes in command personnel: General Lloyd Fredendall of 2nd Corps was sacked and replaced by General *George S. Patton,* while General *Omar Bradley* was given an active command. Kasserine also led to a more realistic American understanding of German combat skills and the likely length and costs of the pending European campaign. Finally, the defeat conduced to important technical changes and improvements in future production of American armor: the M3 "Lee" and M3 "Stuart" tanks that fought at Kasserine were found wanting in several respects, and were shortly thereafter replaced. On the other side of the ledger, British General *Bernard Law Montgomery* and Field Marshal *Harold Alexander* formed a lasting impression of poor training and combat quality of American troops. That perception would distort and complicate Allied war councils during operations in Sicily and Italy, and even as late as the *Normandy campaign.*

KATYN MASSACRE   On April 13, 1943, Germany announced that it had uncovered a mass grave of 4,000 Polish officers said to have been murdered by the Soviets in the Katyn Forrest, west of Smolensk. Moscow denied the charge. It accused Germany of the killings instead, issuing the cynical statement: "The hand of the Gestapo can easily be traced in this hideous frame-up." The Polish government-in-exile in London was suspicious, as the Soviet Union never made an accounting of more than 20,000 Polish officers seized during its invasion of eastern Poland in September 1939. In fact, all those men had been murdered by the Soviets, either in the Katyn Forest or outside Kharkov or Tver in April 1940: Stalin decided to close prisoner of war camps after the Nazi–Soviet invasion of Poland and to simply murder the prisoners, potential leaders of a future Polish resistance movement. On April 26, 1943, Stalin used a Polish request for a Red Cross investigation into the Katyn mass grave as a pretext to break relations with the *London Poles*. In their place, he recognized in-house Communist Poles, whom he later hoisted as puppets in the medieval city of Lublin.

The move to empower the *Lublin Poles,* rather than the massacre per se, caused the first real rift between the Western Allies and the Soviet Union. At the *Nuremberg Tribunal* the Soviets cynically included Katyn as a count in the indictment of German defendants charged with war crimes. With Soviet domination of Poland a fait accompli after the war, the Katyn massacre became a focal point of Cold War politics and of historical controversy. For more than 40 years Moscow denied culpability. In 1989 the first non-Communist government of postwar Poland released previously suppressed evidence that identified the Soviet Union as perpetrator of the forest killings. In April 1990, the Soviet government, staggering toward extinction, finally admitted full guilt for the massacre. The confession was provoked by Russian Federation President Boris Yeltsin, who released top secret documents confirming *NKVD* culpability for massacres of Polish officers at Katyn, Kharkov, and Tver. Yeltsin did so not out of dedication to historical truth or any moral regret but to discredit his political rival, Mikhail Gorbachev, the last Soviet leader. The documents conclusively proved that the decision for mass murder was rubber-stamped by the Politburo on March 5, 1940, at Stalin's personal direction.

See also Sikorski.

KATYUSHA "katiusha." The nickname "little Kate" was given by soldiers of the Red Army to the top secret BM-13, a truck-mounted multiple rocket launcher, and later, to all larger cousins of the BM-13. The name recalled the high whining sound the rockets made in flight, as well as more sentimental memories. Germans called the katyusha "Stalin organ" ("Stalinorgel"), for the organ-like appearance of its multitubed launcher. A katyusha was inaccurate as a single weapon. Katyusha launchers instead fired all rockets within seconds of each other. This battery-fire technique laid down a saturation barrage in a tight pattern. Even if a target was missed, the effect was psychologically intimidating to Germans while greatly encouraging to Soviet troops. Katyusha barrages could destroy virtually anything in the target area. Some launchers were mounted on tractors and the sides of tanks, but most were truck-mounted, including on *Lend-Lease* vehicles. Katyusha artillery batteries first saw action during the *Battle of Smolensk* in July 1941. They went into mass production that August. The BM-13 model mounted 32 tubes, each firing a small rocket with a 4 lb warhead. Early, smaller versions had a limited range of just 5 km. By 1945 much larger versions mounted 16 tubes that fired solid-fuel rockets capable of propelling a 40 lb warhead to 9,000 meters. Some 10,000 katyusha of all sorts—mainly BM-13 and BM-8 models—were produced by 1945. They fitted out more than 500 rocket artillery batteries.

See also Nebelwerfer.

KEIL UND KESSEL "wedge and cauldron." A Wehrmacht battle doctrine wherein a mechanized Panzer wedge punched through an enemy line, with follow-on motorized infantry support on the expanding flanks and rear supplied by Panzergrenadiers. The armored wedge itself was called the "Panzerkeil."

See also Kesselschlacht; kotel.

KEITEL, WILHELM (1882–1946) German field marshal; chief of staff of the *OKW,* 1938–1945. Keitel served with an artillery unit in World War I. He joined the *Freikorps* after the war and thereafter served in the *Reichswehr* and Wehrmacht, rising to a top General Staff posting in 1938 after Adolf Hitler purged the most senior officers who were resisting his aggressive foreign policy. Keitel played an important role in operations planning for the invasions of Poland, Denmark, Norway, France, and the Low Countries. He was promoted to Field Marshal upon arranging the surrender of France in June 1940. He was involved in all major operations planning for the duration of the war. He was therefore knowledgeable about and wholly complicit in the worst crimes and atrocities of the regime. Specifically, he signed several illegal orders leading to mass murder, including executions of prisoners of war and mass death by execution or malign neglect of civilians on the Eastern Front. He also signed the infamous "Nacht und Nebel" ("Night and Fog") order by which any opponents of the Hitler regime could be seized and executed in secret, without trial or evidence beyond mere denunciation. Totally loyal to the regime, he served on the "Honor Court" that purged the top ranks of the Wehrmacht officer corps and deepened nazification of the military after the *July Plot* was foiled in 1944. While serving on that "court," he voted to execute numerous fellow officers. That deepened the contempt in which he was already held by most other German officers, who viewed him as Hitler's talentless lackey , even though most of them also lacked courage to oppose the most reckless or criminal decisions of their Führer. After Hitler's death, Keitel coordinated the formal military surrender of Germany. He was tried by the *Nuremberg Tribunal,* convicted as a "major war criminal," and hanged in 1946.

See also Jodl, Alfred.

KELLOGG-BRIAND PACT (1928) "General Treaty for the Renunciation of War" or "Pact of Paris." In March 1927, French Foreign Minister Aristide Briand floated the idea of a defense pact with the United States that called for joint renunciation of war as an instrument of policy. Secretary of State Frank Kellogg objected to Briand appealing over his head directly to American public opinion, and thought the proposal represented an "entangling alliance." Senator William Borah, a powerful isolationist, suggested deflecting the idea into a multilateral declaration outlawing war. The French were greatly displeased. However, as holder of the 1926 Nobel Prize for Peace, Briand could hardly spurn a formal renunciation of war—no matter how little he actually believed in it. France agreed to a multilateral pact, though with reservations, which suggested that it reserved a right to use force for "legitimate self-defense." Kellogg had by then naïvely come to believe that the Pact would be a benediction for humanity. It was duly agreed by 65 states, including such later aggressors as Italy, Japan, and Germany. It had no provision for enforcement. It was touted by liberal-internationalists in the interwar period as an advance for moral consciousness among states, while criticized by believers in realpolitik as a prime example of legalistic and moralistic folly in statecraft. Neither view seems entirely merited. The Pact was actually a low-cost, even clever, security gambit by Briand. It failed because he did not foresee that isolationists in the United States would deflect it into an innocuous public relations exercise—that Kellogg would gut it by making it general instead of bilateral. Despite this checkered history and its utter inconsequence in real-world affairs, the Pact achieved public acclaim. It was cited by the *Nuremberg Tribunal* and *Tokyo Tribunal* to support post facto charges of *crimes against peace* against Axis defendants. Its wording was later added to Article 9 of the post–World War II Japanese "Peace Constitution."

KEMPEITAI Or "kempei-tai." The military police of the Imperial Japanese Army. They enforced rough discipline on soldiers in the field and investigated and arrested rebellious officers. Their most important role during the war was to investigate and repress dissent of all kinds. They were much feared by soldiers and civilians alike, and bore close comparison in their methods and reputation to the *Gestapo* in Europe or the *NKVD* in the Soviet Union. In Manchuria and Inner Mongolia they ran independent opium and heroin networks that paralleled the larger drug trade by which the Japanese Army financed its mainland operations. Kempeitai were brutal torturers of enemy *prisoners of war*, specializing in water and electric tortures. They were formally demobilized on October 30, 1945.

See also Tokkō.

KERCH DEFENSIVE OPERATION (NOVEMBER 1941)
One of Joseph Stalin's favorites, Marshal *Grigory I. Kulik* represented the Stavka in operations in the Crimean and Kerch peninsulas in November 1941. Kerch was a 60-mile long eastward abutment of the larger Crimean peninsula. Initial fighting at Kerch was part of the much wider *Donbass-Rostov defensive operation (September 29–November 16, 1941)*. The town of Kerch fell to the Germans on November 15. Three thousand soldiers and civilian refugees who remained alive were then trapped in a nearby quarry at Adzhimuskai, or in labyrinthine tunnels in hills around the city. They survived for three months by eating horse flesh, until most were killed by ferocious *NKVD* guards who would not permit the weakened survivors to surrender. The miserable few who lived though massacre by their own side were subsequently killed by poison gas piped into the caverns by the Germans.

See also Crimea; Kerch-Feodosiia operations; Sebastopol, siege of.

KERCH-FEODOSIIA OPERATIONS (DECEMBER 1941–MAY, 1942)
Soviet amphibious and supporting airborne operations took the Germans by surprise at Kerch and Feodosiia, located on the Kerch peninsula, in the last week of December 1941 and first two days of January 1942. Larger landings were planned

but were canceled when the weather and military situation at Feodosiia worsened. However, more troops were sent in via an ice road over the Kerch Straits until more than 250,000 men, or 21 divisions organized in three armies, were crowded into the bridgehead by May. In February, Stalin sent Lazar Mekhlis to Kerch as the new Stavka representative, replacing the disgraced and demoted former Marshal, *Grigory I. Kulik*. Among Russian historians, Mekhlis receives much of the blame for the disaster that followed, possibly in part because he was Jewish and a fierce Communist. Western military historians are more balanced, usually assigning responsibility for the failure to a badly divided command. Even so, it was blunt incompetence on the part of Mekhlis to deny permission to entrench across the 10-mile wide isthmus at the western end of the Kerch peninsula. Instead, he and other Soviet commanders clung to the offensive spirit of prewar Red Army doctrine and ordered repeated frontal infantry assaults into the teeth of the attacking Germans, starting on February 27. More bloody assaults on German positions were launched in March and April, with both sides heavily reinforcing with tanks and aircraft. General *Erich von Manstein* launched Operation TRAPPENJAGD ("Bustard Hunt") on May 8. That drove the Soviets reeling backward, and in short order forced a sea evacuation across the Kerch Straits. Those left behind were crushed or surrendered to Manstein. At least 162,000 Red Army soldiers were lost in the fighting on the Kerch peninsula in less than two weeks in May 1942. About 240,000 became casualties over the course of the campaign. Also lost were more than 1,200 guns and hundreds of tanks. The defeat was catastrophic and allowed Manstein to renew the *siege of Sebastopol*. The city fell on July 4.

KEREN, BATTLE OF (MARCH 11, 1941)

See East African campaign (1940–1941).

KESSEL "Cauldron." Wehrmacht term for a battle of encirclement.
See keil und kessel; Kesselschlacht.

KESSELRING, ALBERT (1885–1960)

German field marshal. Originally trained in the *Heer*, he transferred to the *Luftwaffe* upon its formation in 1935. He served with the Luftwaffe during *FALL WEISS*, the invasion of Poland in 1939, and again in *FALL GELB*, the invasion of France in 1940. After the French campaign he was promoted to Field Marshal. He saw more active duty during the *Battle of Britain* that summer. He commanded large Luftwaffe assets in *BARBAROSSA*, the invasion of the Soviet Union in 1941. He is best known to Westerners as overall commander of German forces, air and ground, during the fight for Sicily (*HUSKY*) and the *Italian campaign (1943–1945)* that followed. Salvaging what he could on Sicily, he carried out a German *Dunkirk* by evacuating across the Strait of Messina in the face of far superior enemy air and naval forces. His alacrity in disarming the Italian Army in September 1943, after the surrender of Italy by Marshal *Pietro Badoglio*, foiled Allied plans for quick conquest and set the stage for two years of hard fighting.

Hitler ordered Kesselring to hold the *Bernhardt Line* north of Naples in October 1943. He subsequently fell back to the *Gustav Line*. During hard fighting at *Anzio* and *Monte Cassino,* Kesselring made his reputation as a tough and resourceful defender. After Rome fell on June 4, 1944, he withdrew to alpine defenses from which his forces continued to resist to the end of April 1945. In the interim, he was injured in an accident in October 1944, and did not return to active duty until March 1945, when he took over as commander in chief of all German forces and Hitler's last best hope in northwest Europe. In 1947 a British military court convicted Kesselring of ordering shootings of 335 Italian hostages, Jews, and prisoners at the *Ardeatine Cave massacre* outside Rome in 1944. He was sentenced to death, but Winston Churchill and others intervened to save the so-called "good German" of the Wehrmacht, and the court's judgment was commuted to life imprisonment. Kesselring was released from prison in 1952. He published mendacious memoirs—as did most surviving German generals—and served as the head of the German veterans' organization until his death. In 1997 clear proof was produced undoubtedly linking Kesselring to an order for summary execution of 15 OSS agents captured in U.S. uniform behind German lines in Italy. For that and other war crimes, he received minimal or no punishment.

KESSELSCHLACHT   "Cauldron fighting." Wehrmacht term for a battle of envelopment or encirclement.

See BARBAROSSA; *Donbass-Rostov operation; Germany, conquest of; keil und kessel; kotel; Ruhr; Sumi-Kharkov operation; TAIFUN; Ukraine, First Battle of.*

KETSU-GŌ (1945)   "Decisive Operation." The Japanese Army plan for defense of the *home islands*. It was scheduled to be implemented should the first phases of the planned *Sho-Gō* defense (1944–1945) of the Philippines, Taiwan, and the Ryukyus fail to deter the Allies from invasion or induce them to negotiate a compromise settlement. In addition to bringing several divisions of the Japanese Army back to the home islands from China, Korea, and Manchuria, the plan proposed sending millions of ordinary Japanese in barely armed "People's Volunteer Combat Corps" (Kokomin giyō Sentōtai) to meet any invaders on the beaches. The plan's key assumption was that American morale and willingness to fight was brittle and would shatter if it met such stiff and bloody resistance. Ketsu-Gō was upstaged by Anglo-American atomic bombs dropped on *Hiroshima* and *Nagasaki,* and by the Soviet *Manchurian offensive operation*.

See also DOWNFALL.

KETTE   A standard Luftwaffe flying formation of three fighters.

See also Rotte; Schwarm.

KHALKIN-GOL, BATTLE OF (1939)

See Nomonhan.

KHARKOV   This Ukrainian industrial city changed hands four times over the course of the German–Soviet war, three times in 1943 alone.

See, for operational details, the entries and references under the various Battles of Kharkov, and *see BARBAROSSA; KREML; Kursk; Orel-Briansk offensive; RUMIANTSEV; Sumi-Kharkov defensive operation.*

KHARKOV, FIRST BATTLE OF (OCTOBER 1941)

See BARBAROSSA; Stavka; Sumi-Kharkov defensive operation.

KHARKOV, SECOND BATTLE OF (MAY 12–29, 1942)   Second Kharkov

remains one of the most controversial battles of the war in Soviet and Russian historiography. Blame for another catastrophic defeat of the Red Army was laid on Joseph Stalin by *Nikita Khrushchev* in 1956, after the great dictator's death. Marshals *Boris M. Shaposhnikov* and *Semyon Timoshenko* and their immediate subordinates have been blamed by others, with Stalin in a supporting role. The origins of the controversy lie in the fact that, despite massive losses suffered in 1941 and again over the first four months of 1942, Stalin and some members of the Stavka insisted on fresh spring offensives all along the Eastern Front. Among these operations, the most important turned into the disastrous Second Battle of Kharkov. Timoshenko pushed especially hard for this fight. General *Georgi Zhukov* and some other Stavka members seem to have opposed an unwise dispersal of sparse forces among too many, and also overly ambitious, operations. A compromise was reached by limiting the operation in eastern Ukraine to a push to retake Kharkov, which was held by German 6th Army under General *Friedrich von Paulus.* It was simultaneously proposed to straighten the line and protect the *Barvenkovo salient* southeast of Kharkov. Meanwhile, the Germans were planning their own Operation *FRIDERICUS,* a limited offensive intended to trap Soviet forces in the "Izium pocket," or "Barvenkovo salient." Neither side knew the others' plans. Soviet military intelligence failed to detect the German offensive intention to cut off the Barvenkovo salient and additionally fell victim to a German deception campaign that effectively concealed the Barvenkovo build-up.

Each side was about equal in numbers of men and guns involved as the battle was engaged. The Soviets moved first, though not well or fast. Many of the more than 1,100 Soviet tanks at Kharkov were in newly organized and still experimental formations. Formed into two armored pincers, they reached deep into the German defenses. The first pincer was a strong formation of three armies from Southwestern Front that attacked on either side of Kharkov on May 12. Soviet 6th Army formed a smaller pincer that struck farther south, directly out of the Barvenkovo salient. Within five days, Soviet 6th Army ran into the planned FRIDERICUS attack, which was strongly supported by Panzers and by the Luftwaffe. The Germans achieved complete surprise, as General *Ewald von Kleist* sliced into the thinned southern flank and rear of the still-advancing Soviet 6th Army. The left pincer of the Soviet Kharkov operation was thus forced to reverse, fighting desperately to return to its jump-off positions in the Barvenkovo salient in an effort to prevent being totally cut off. The fighting retreat by Soviet 6th Army was delayed by lack of timely orders from the Stavka or from Timoshenko. Some 20 divisions and thousands of guns and tanks were thus encircled by the Germans on May 23, as Kleist closed the trap around a Soviet force that had advanced directly into it. Very heavy fighting followed in another great *Kessel,* which cooked to death all Soviet 6th Army. Loss of the southern Soviet pincer eviscerated the effect of any advance farther north, around the city. Worse, vast losses of men and matériel opened a wide gap in the Soviet line. Through that gap, von Paulus and German 6th Army pushed their advantage later that summer, along what turned out to be a deadly, one-way road to *Stalingrad.*

Much of the controversy about the Soviet failure at Second Kharkov attends the delay in ordering a pullback by Soviet 6th Army. More attention might be usefully paid to the lack of Red Army mobility even with a large tank force at hand, and to the readiness with which large numbers of Red Army conscripts still surrendered, as they had done during 1941. The Red Army lost at Kharkov not merely because of intelligence and command failures, but more fundamentally because it was still bleeding men and machines that operated with overly blunt tactics, and because it had yet to recover fighting morale: as many as 214,000 *krasnoarmeets* gave up the fight at Kharkov. As for the Wehrmacht, while its military intelligence showed its usual inability to penetrate Soviet planning, its field commanders again displayed superior operational command and control and its field units performed with remarkable mobility and better basic fighting skill than their opponents. That disparity in battle performance would remain into late 1942, and even to mid-1943.

See also KREML; Sepp Dietrich.

KHARKOV, THIRD BATTLE OF (FEBRUARY–MARCH, 1943) A major Soviet intelligence failure led to the conclusion that the Wehrmacht lacked reserves and was withdrawing behind the Dnieper River. In fact, three elite *Waffen-SS* Panzer divisions had been brought east from France. Field Marshal *Erich von Manstein* unexpectedly counterattacked toward Kharkov on February 19. Well-supported by the Luftwaffe, he drove elements of two Panzerarmee, the 1st and 4th, into the flanks of advancing Soviet spearheads. "Special Group Popov" was quickly surrounded and wiped out while another pincer was blunted before it could reach the Dnieper. SS 2nd Panzer Corps retook Kharkov on March 14; the city had fallen to the Red Army on February 16. Voronezh Front was propelled backwards to Belgorod, then held. Manstein's mobile successes were later much admired, not least by himself, and upheld as models of skilled operational art. His maneuvers certainly interrupted and contributed to the failure of two Soviet offensive operations, one in the high north and the other reaching for the Dnieper: *STAR* and *GALLOP.* Manstein also bled four more Soviet armies, while his counteroffensive straitened part of the German line and recovered a previously broken southern position. However, the main factor in the Soviet defeat was that Stalin and the Stavka simultaneously conducted too many large operations too far forward of bases just established during the *Stalingrad* campaign. In short, the Soviets overreached in early 1943 following their victory at Stalingrad, as they had also done in January 1942, upon winning in front of Moscow. By rushing forward more reserves to stop Manstein's counteroffensive, a large bulge was created in the line around the junction town of Kursk. That fact invited the Wehrmacht to attack later in the year, in the overly ambitious Operation *ZITADELLE*. The Third Battle of Kharkov thus set the stage for the greater *Battle of Kursk* in midsummer, which was followed by the even more decisive Soviet counteroffensives *KUTUZOV* and *RUMIANTSEV*.

KHOLM POCKET

See Demiansk offensive operation.

KHRUSHCHEV, NIKITA SERGEYEVICH (1894–1971)

During the first part of the war, this future leader of the Soviet Union served as a commissar under Marshal *Semyon Timoshenko*. Khrushchev was present during the great disasters for the Red Army in the south at Uman and Kiev in 1941, and again at the *Second Battle of Kharkov* in 1942. He was also present at *Stalingrad* and during the reconquest of Ukraine. His wartime service as commissar helped him rise to the pinnacle of power after Joseph Stalin died.

See also NKVD.

KIEV ENCIRCLEMENT

See *Ukraine, First Battle of.*

KING, ERNEST (1878–1956)

U.S. admiral. King was appointed USN Commander in Chief (COMINCH or later just CINC) on December 30, 1941. That gave him strategic direction of naval wars in the Atlantic and Pacific as well as command of the Coast Guard. Three months later he replaced Admiral Rainsford Stark as Chief of Naval Operations (CNO), the first time those two posts were combined under one man. King distrusted Royal Navy arguments about evasive *convoy* routing and so initially insisted upon a policy of running convoys at high speed along the U.S. eastern seaboard without employing evasive techniques. That policy, and the large number of *independents* forced to sail outside convoy protection, allowed enemy U-boats their second "happy time" of the *Battle of the Atlantic (1939–1945)*. Although King agreed with the *Germany first strategy*, great tension with the British arose over his constant push for more resources to be sent to the Pacific. Specifically, he never forgave refusal of his May 18, 1942, request for one of three Royal Navy aircraft carriers stationed off Africa—the British were deeply concerned at the time about a Japanese foray into the Indian Ocean. King was personally abrasive and intolerant. Nonetheless, he worked closely with General *George C. Marshall*, the *Joint Chiefs of Staff*, and the *Combined Chiefs of Staff*. He was always a powerful voice for the interests of the U.S. Navy in the Pacific War, sometimes to a fault. He retired in December 1945.

See also Bucket Brigade; Hiroshima; Québec Conference (1944).

KING, MACKENZIE (1874–1950)   Canadian wartime prime minister.
See Canada.

KIRIBATI   A British protectorate from 1892, forming part of the *Gilbert and Ellice Islands,* it was made an outright British colony in 1916. It was occupied by Japan early in World War II. It was liberated by U.S. forces in 1943.

KIRPONOS, MIKHAIL (1892–1941)   Soviet general. He fought for the Reds in the Russian Civil War (1918-1921). Surviving the *Yezhovshchina,* he saw action in the *Finnish–Soviet War (1939–1940).* He was commander of Southwestern Front at the start of *BARBAROSSA* in June 1941. He was in command during the disastrous encirclement at Kiev and to nearly the end of the *First Battle of Ukraine (June–September, 1941),* in which he was killed.

KISKA
See Aleutian Islands.

KLEINKAMPFVERBÄNDE   Kriegsmarine *special forces.* Mainly *divers,* they operated manned torpedoes, explosive motor boats, and midget U-boats in a variety of demolition and scouting roles. Although they were notably active against shipping during the long siege of the perimeter at *Anzio* and again in the English Channel after the *D-Day (June 6, 1944)* landings, they did little damage. Their Royal Navy counterparts were far more successful, as were their erstwhile partners in the Regia Marina.

KLEIST, EWALD VON (1881–1954)   German field marshal. Raised in a traditional *Junkers* and monarchist family, Kleist served with a cavalry unit then with the artillery during World War I. He rose quickly with the expansion of the Reichswehr into the Wehrmacht in the 1930s, but was forced to retire in 1938 by Adolf Hitler, who distrusted all aristocratic officers on principle and detested Kleist personally. He was recalled to a corps command for the invasion of Poland the next year. During the invasion of France he headed Panzer Group Kleist, which he led across the Meuse at Sedan in a daring operation critical to German success. He argued throughout the campaign against the more reckless tactics of his unrestrained subordinate *Heinz Guderian.* But together, they touched the coast of France before any other German force. Kleist commanded 1st Panzer Group in the Balkans in operations that began in April 1941, and again during the opening phase of *BARBAROSSA* in June. In August his Panzer Group was part of the vast encirclement of four Soviet armies at Kiev, to that point the greatest mass surrender in military history. Kleist took Rostov in October by crossing behind the Soviet lines. He then lost the city to a counterattack during the winter. At the head of a renamed 1st Panzer Army he led the spearhead of Operation *BLAU,* driving into the Caucasus in Operation *EDELWEISS.* He spent the rest of 1942, all of 1943, and the spring of 1944 as commander of a constantly attrited and isolated Army Group A. The command was mostly defensive, fighting off heavy Soviet counteroffensives in the Caucasus and Crimea. Hitler promoted Kleist to the rank of field marshal on February 1, 1943, for his excellent defensive campaign and withdrawal of two armies from the Crimea. However, Hitler later blamed him for the pending loss of the Crimean peninsula in early 1944. At the end of March, Kleist was summoned to see Hitler in Bavaria and dismissed. He was assigned to the *Leader Reserve* and never again held an active command. In 1946 Kleist was convicted of *war crimes* by the Yugoslavs, then convicted a second time by the Soviets. He died in a Soviet prison in 1954.

See also *Donbass-Rostov operation; Kharkov, Second Battle; Ukraine, First Battle of.*

K-LINE

See *Königsberg Line.*

KLUGE, GÜNTHER VON (1882–1944)   German field marshal. He served with an artillery unit in World War I, then stayed in the *Reichswehr* after the war. He was dismissed by order of Adolf Hitler in 1938 for insufficient enthusiasm for the regime's aggressive plans for war. He was recalled to command 4th Army for the invasion of Poland in 1939. He still held that command during the invasion of France in May–June 1940. During Operation *BARBAROSSA* in 1941, he led 4th Army within Army Group Center, until given that higher command in December. He quarreled all the way to Moscow with General *Heinz Guderian,* as did most officers who ever suffered Guderian as their subordinate. An outstanding field commander, Kluge remained with Army Group Center for the next 18 months, through the *Demiansk offensive operation,* the *First Rzhev-Sychevka offensive operation,* Operation *ZITADELLE* and the attendant great fight at *Kursk* in mid-1943, and the long German fighting retreat from Kursk. He was badly hurt in a car accident in October 1943. He was transferred to the west after the *July Plot* in 1944, near the end of the *Normandy campaign.* He replaced *Erwin Rommel,* whom Adolf Hitler compelled to commit suicide for his role in the attempted July coup. Kluge took command of a rapidly declining force that had been engaged in weeks of desperate fighting and was on its last combat legs. Still only partially recovered from his accident, he despaired of containing the Western Allies in Normandy. He was sacked by Hitler on suspicion of seeking a local truce, although there is no evidence that he did so. Kluge wrote a long apologia for his actions to Hitler, then poisoned himself.

See also *BÜFFEL.*

KMG   "Konno-Mekhanizirovannaya Gruppa" ("Cavalry-Mechanized Group"). Red Army designation for mid-to-late war mobile groups of joint cavalry, motorized, and mechanized forces. They were an adaptation of the prewar strength of Soviet cavalry forces, reinforced with more tanks and additional artillery. They were used extensively in fighting against the Wehrmacht and other Axis armies in Ukraine and Hungary, and in the *Manchurian offensive operation* against the Japanese in August 1945.

KNICKEBEIN A Luftwaffe electronic navigation aid for night bombers in which two directional radio beams were broadcast to intersect over a target in Britain. The bombers followed one beam—guided by Morse dots and dashes—until it met the second, then released their bomb load. It was an advance in both range and accuracy on the prewar *Lorenz* blind-landing system used by civil aviation. By July 1940, the RAF developed a counter, code-named "Aspirin," which imposed a British beam atop the German beam in a process called "bending the beam," although the German beam was never actually "bent." The Luftwaffe next moved to the *X-Gerät* system, as the "battle of the beams" continued.

KNIL "Koninklijk Nederlands Indisch Leger," or Netherlands East Indies Army. *See Dutch East Indies.*

KODO-HA "Imperial Way." An ultranationalist clique within the Imperial Japanese Army formed when the *Issekikai* association split. Kodo-ha officers backed General (later, Prime Minister) Sadao Araki. He was slightly more moderate than most Kodo in the 1930s, but strongly favored immediate action against Japanese Communists over the long-term and patient preparation of the nation for *total war,* probably against the Soviet Union. The Kodo-ha promoted aggressive expansion on the Asian mainland even as they anticipated and sought a decisive war with the Soviet Union as the main enemy of Japan. Young turks of the Kodo-ha were thus highly active in violent intervention in Japanese politics, in provoking war with Manchuria in the *Mukden incident,* and in fighting with Chinese troops at Shanghai. Such aggression reflected the core beliefs of its members, including *Tomoyuki Yamashita.* Araki recognized the Kodo coup de main in creating "Manchukuo." He then extended Japanese aggression into northern China by invading Jehol (Chengde) province and forcing the Chinese to accept a demilitarized zone in part of Hopei province. Even that was not enough for Kodo fanatics, who broke with Araki in 1934.

On February 26, 1936, Kodo-ha officers launched the largest insurrection in Japan since the failed Satsuma rebellion following the Meiji Restoration. Squads of Kodo-ha assassins killed several top military and civilian leaders, including two former prime ministers. They just missed killing a man who would later become prime minister and preside over Japan's surrender in 1945: *Kantaro Suzuki.* Kodo-ha assassins at the head of commandeered infantry, most of whom did not understand or share Kodo-ha beliefs, quickly secured control of key buildings in central Tokyo. They hoped to present a fait accompli to the military and thereby gain wider support for the goal of open military government and more speedy imperial aggression. But they failed to convince the Army High Command or the Shōwa Emperor, *Hirohito,* who uncharacteristically intervened against them. Loyal troops were called into Tokyo to repress the uprising on February 29. Most of the faction's junior leaders—none ranked higher than captain—were arrested within two days. They were tried, and 19 Kodo-ha were executed. A purge of the Army followed that destroyed the Kodo-ha so decisively that some conspiratorially minded believe the coup attempt was allowed to set the stage for restoring Army discipline. In any event, the imperial cause within the Army passed over to the slightly less extreme *Tosei-ha* or "Control Faction" of the Issekikai. In the end, the shift proved a distinction without much of a difference. The "February Rising" had done permanent damage by physically eliminating several key proponents of constitutionalism, exposing a fragile illusion of civilian control in Japan itself, and accelerating militarization of Japanese society and foreign policy.

KOENIG, MARIE PIERRE (1898–1970) *Free French* general. He led *Foreign Legion* forces to Norway and in France in 1940. Upon the armistice, he was one of the few officers to follow the call for continuing resistance made by *Charles de Gaulle*. Koenig fought in Syria in 1941, then led a Free French brigade in a fierce fight at *Bir Hakeim* in 1942 that won much for the Free French fighting reputation, and hence for de Gaulle. Koenig served as the "Fighting France" ("France Combattante") representative to *SHAEF* in 1944, and as nominal commander of the *Force Française de l'Intérieur (FFI)*. After the war he served as military governor in French-occupied Germany.

KOGUN

See Imperial Japanese Army.

KO-GŌ

See Ichi-Gō offensive (1944).

KOHIMA

See Burma campaign (1943–1945); Imphal offensive (1944).

KOISO KUNIAKI (1880–1950) Japanese general. Prime minister, July 1944–April 1945. Koiso Kuniaki was chief of staff of the *Guandong Army* from 1932 to 1934, during the *Mukden incident*. He never showed real military talent: his main expertise was in colonial government. After replacing *Hideki Tōjō* as prime minister in mid-1944, Koiso Kuniaki presided over the illusory victory of the *Ichi-Gō offensive* and a more strategically important trail of defeats in the Pacific along with heavy US bombing. His main policy was to try to split the *Guomindang* in China from the Western Allies. When that failed, he resigned. He was convicted by the *Tokyo Tribunal* and sentenced to life in prison.

KOKODA TRAIL

See New Guinea campaign (1942–1945).

KOKUBŌ KOKKAI "national defense state." The imperial idea, cleaved to most strongly in the Imperial Japanese Army but widely believed by civilians as well, that Japan needed to seize and hold by force sufficient territories to maintain a powerful martial state and autarchic economy.

KOKUTAI "National Essence." The term had multiple meanings in Japanese: linguistic, cultural, and uniquely political. It underlay the Meiji imperial system after 1868, serving as a unifying national ideology that responded to the Western challenge in a spiritual–political manner that celebrated the immutable native virtue of the Japanese, centered on the unbroken succession of emperors descended from the Sun Goddess. Kokutai as an underpinning of the imperial system was revived by prewar militarists to inform a broad "return to Japan" movement in politics and culture. It had irrational components derived from its religious (or metaphysical) origins, myths taught by the government and military as the factual history of Japan as confirmed by a special committee of scholars in 1937. That permitted a view of the Meiji constitution as less than fundamental law while upholding sovereignty as enshrined in the imperial family as the central condition of the "national essence." During World War II the term usually referred to the imperial Japanese principle, or ideology, of a "family state," which had the emperor at its summit as both a "divine" and human father figure to the nation. Its retention in 1945 was the single condition asked for by the Japanese in surrender talks: how could Japan surrender if its "national essence," as housed in the imperial system, was not guaranteed? After the war, "Kokutai" was redefined in a more modern and democratic form that helped secure legitimacy for those Japanese cooperating with occupation authorities, although its meaning was undercut for purists by the Shōwa Emperor, *Hirohito*, being forced to renounce any claim to divinity.

See also Hiroshima; Japan; Nagasaki; unconditional surrender.

KOKUTAI "Air corps." The principal organizational unit of the *Japanese Army Air Force,* usually formed from one aircraft type and attached to a specific fleet or tactical land-based command.

KOLOMBANGARA, BATTLE OF (JULY 13, 1943) A small action between a U.S. Navy task force composed of light cruisers and a destroyer squadron and Japanese escorts of a *Tokyo Express* "destroyer transport" convoy speeding reinforcements to New Georgia. The IJN again demonstrated its superiority in night actions, exchanging one light cruiser for an enemy destroyer and severe damage to three USN cruisers. The troop reinforcements got through.

KOMANDORSKI ISLANDS, BATTLE OF (MARCH 26, 1943) A rare North Pacific naval battle in which a U.S. Navy task force of two cruisers and four destroyers sought to block Japanese reinforcement of garrisons in the *Aleutian Islands*. A larger and more powerful IJN task force escorting two fast transports chased the Americans away and badly damaged a heavy cruiser. Before retiring, the American ships did enough damage to the Japanese escorts that the IJN task force turned back.

KOMMANDATURA
See Allied Control Commissions.

KOMMANDOBEFEHL
See commando order.

KOMMISARBEFEHL
See Commissar order.

KOMOROWSKI, TADEUSZ (1895–1966)   "General Bor."
See Warsaw Uprising.

KOMSOMOL   A division of the Communist Party of the Soviet Union that recruited youth, or "Young Communists." The recruits were used for many public functions during the war, and often became ardent *krasnoarmeets* in the Red Army.

KONARMIĬA   The Red Army cavalry arm, dating to the original Bolshevik force during the Russian Civil War (1918–1921). Its veteran officers exerted disproportionate influence over Joseph Stalin and Red Army policy in the 1930s. Some of those who survived the *Yezhovshchina* had influence beyond their talents—usually based on personal ties to Stalin—all through World War II.
See Budyonny, Semyon; Kulik, Grigory; Meretskov, Kiril; Timoshenko, Semyon; Voroshilov, Kliment; Yeremenko, Andrei.

KONDŌ, NOBUTAKE (1886–1953)   Japanese admiral. He led Imperial Japanese Navy task forces in multiple actions from 1941 to 1945, mainly in a support role to some larger command. His most notable and numerous command actions occurred during the *Guadalcanal campaign* (1942–1943).

KONDOR   This Fw-200 four-engined bomber greatly extended German reconnaissance for *U-boats* far out over the Atlantic. However, jealousy on the part of *Hermann Göring* and lack of interservice cooperation between the Luftwaffe and Kriegsmarine limited its numbers and effectiveness. The appearances of "Kondors" at first greatly alarmed Winston Churchill and the Royal Navy, which was inexcusably ill-prepared for its predictable arrival over the convoy routes. By the end of 1941 the threat was contained, mainly by better naval air defenses and direct support to convoy air defense by RAF Coastal Command.
See also Catapult Aircraft Merchant (CAM); escort carrier.

KONDOR LEGION   "Condor Legion." Wehrmacht "volunteers" fighting for General *Francisco Franco* in the *Spanish Civil War* from November 1936 to May 1938.

The Kondor Legion numbered about 6,500 men operating several squadrons of bombers and fighters, as well as two tank brigades. In all, 16,500 served of whom about 300 were killed. The Kondor Legion brought combined arms skills to Spain, as well as terror bombing, but little that it learned was considered of relevance to the German wars that followed from 1939. The Kondor Legion always fought in Spain under exclusive German command.

See also Blue Division; Guernica; Sperrle, Hugo.

KONEV, IVAN S. (1897–1973)   Marshal of the Soviet Union. He was drafted into the Tsarist army too late to fight in World War I. He fought for the "Reds" during the Russian Civil War (1918–1921), seeing action mainly in Siberia. Like so many World War II Soviet commanders, he studied tank and mechanized warfare during the 1920s and 1930s. He also served in the Soviet far east and the Caucasus. He was one of the younger officers who benefited from the *Yezhovshchina* and other purges of the Red Army. During *BARBAROSSA* he was appointed to command Western Front in the desperate fighting retreat before Moscow. He was replaced by General *Grigori Zhukov* in October. He was reappointed to command of Western Front from August 1942 to February 1943, when he was sacked for failure during the *MARS* operation. He returned to a command in the Caucasus from March to June, 1943, before taking over Steppe Front for the great fight at *Kursk*. He was in command of 2nd Ukrainian Front from October 1943 to May 1944, during a series of rolling offensives that pushed the Wehrmacht back hundreds of miles. During the *Zhitomir-Berdichev operation* he worked well with General *Nikolai Vatutin* to trap German 8th Army in a *kotel* just west of the Dnieper. Konev was unfairly given all credit for the victory by Joseph Stalin, and promoted to Marshal of the Soviet Union. He also took over 1st Ukrainian Front from Vatutin, combining command with his 2nd Ukrainian Front for the invasion of Poland in 1944. During the *conquest of Germany* in 1945, he was ordered by Stalin and the Stavka to pivot north, putting him in a race for Berlin with Zhukov. Konev was finally redirected south of the city, which fell to Zhukov. After the war Konev served in the Soviet occupation zone in Austria, then as the top officer in the Red Army from 1946 to 1955. He was commander in chief of Warsaw Pact ground forces from 1956 to 1960.

See also Rzhev-Sychevka offensive operation, First; TAIFUN.

KÖNIGSBERG

See East Prussia; Germany, conquest of; Heiligenbeil pocket; Vistula-Oder operation; Samland peninsula.

KÖNIGSBERG LINE   "K-Line." A hastily and ill-prepared defensive line established by the Wehrmacht during the great fight in front of Moscow in December 1941. It ran from Rzhev to Iukhnov, west of the city. During the Red Army's *Moscow offensive operation (December 5, 1941–January 7, 1942)*, there was argument between Hitler and some of his generals over withdrawal to the K-Line. Hitler refused permission at first. He relented in mid-January 1942, during the *Rzhev-Viazma strategic operation (January 8–April 20, 1942).*

KONOE, FUMIMARO (1891–1945) A Kantian philosopher by training and prince of the Imperial family, Konoe served as Japan's prime minister during the early stages of the *Sino-Japanese War (1937–1945).* He was popular within the Imperial Japanese Army because he headed a "New Order" movement—the Imperial Rule Assistance Association—which mimicked *fascist* party organizations in Italy and Nazi Germany. Imperial General Headquarters saw Konoe's movement as facilitating mobilization of the Japanese for *total war.* Within a month of taking office in June 1937, the *Marco Polo Bridge incident* was provoked by the *Guandong Army.* Konoe thereafter led Japan into war with China, a quagmire from which Tokyo did not come unstuck until the defeat of 1945. It was not the last time Konoe allowed the Army to set policy by acting unilaterally in the field. His direct responsibility for the disaster of the Sino–Japanese War dates to January 16, 1938, when he issued an infamous "we will not meet" decree refusing to negotiate a settlement with Chinese authorities. His subsequent political efforts focused on breaking China apart by working with hand-picked collaborators, notably *Wang Jingwei.* Such men commanded no loyalty in China and could never make a real peace with Japan. Konoe resigned as premier in January 1939. He returned to the premiership at a critical moment on July 22, 1940, just as the Army and Navy agreed to pursue new aggressions into Southeast Asia: the *nanshin* road. Konoe thereafter presided over sharp deterioration in Japan's relations with the United States. He was replaced as premier by General *Hideki Tōjō* in October 1941, just weeks before the attack on *Pearl Harbor* in the first week of December. In July 1945, Konoe was appointed to lead a mission to Moscow to seek Soviet mediation of Japan's surrender to the Western Allies, but Joseph Stalin refused to receive him. Konoe committed suicide in prison in mid-December 1945, while waiting to be brought before the bar of justice at the *Tokyo Tribunal.*

KONRAD (JANUARY 1945) "Conrad." Code name for the German counter-offensive in Hungary mounted on January 1, 1945, by 4th Panzer Corps. It goal was to relieve a siege of four German and two Hungarian divisions fighting desperately in surrounded Budapest. The transfer of an entire Panzer corps to Hungary from Army Group Center seriously weakened Wehrmacht and *Waffen-SS* forces defending against the Soviet *Vistula-Oder operation* launched 11 days later. KONRAD failed, as did a belated breakout attempt by the garrison. The last resistance in Buda ended on February 13.

KONZENTRATIONSLAGER (KZ)
See concentration camps; death camps; Holocaust.

KOREA Having cleared the way diplomatically with agreements with Russia, Britain, and the United States, in 1910 Tokyo ended the legal fiction of

Korean independence that persisted from its initial occupation in 1895 and formally annexed the "Hermit Kingdom." Korea remained under harsh Japanese occupation—and was brutally and ruthless exploited economically and for forced labor—until 1945. Korea was partly developed and modernized in some respects, but always to the advantage of Japanese overlords rather than that of its native population. Japanese language was compulsory in all government and education. Agricultural production increased, but was skimmed off to feed Japan—leaving Koreans near starvation levels as Japan's own food production declined in the last years of the war. At the *Cairo Conference* (1943) it was decided that Korea would become independent "in due course." At *Potsdam* (1945) it was determined to share the surrender of Japanese forces in Korea: the United States would take control south of the 38th parallel while the Soviet Union accepted all Japanese surrenders in the north. The Soviets and Americans duly occupied the Korean peninsula after the war. The promised unified independence then fell victim to the burgeoning Cold War in Asia. On August 15, 1948, the Republic of Korea (South Korea) was proclaimed under American auspices. On September 9, 1948, the Democratic People's Republic (North Korea) was established in the Soviet occupation zone. Those states fought the Korean War from 1950 to 1953 and remained hostile into the 21st century.

KORÜCK "Kommandant des rückwärtigen Armeegebiets." Wehrmacht term for the command of the rear area of a field army, with responsibility for guarding transport and supply lines. Other responsibilities included gathering intelligence and provision of medical and other necessary services. Where a Korück overlapped a German civilian administrative area, as in the case of the *Reichskommissariat Ostland,* the Wehrmacht retained control of all civilians. Early in the German-Soviet war, the Wehrmacht criminally allowed millions of *prisoners of war* to die of malign neglect within its vast Korück, and allowed or participated in murder of *partisans* and Jews by *Einsatzgruppen.*
See also military district; Wehrkreis.

KOSCIUSZKO DIVISION
See Polish Army.

KOTEL Red Army term for a battle of encirclement. It was the Soviet equivalent to *keil und kessel* and *Kesselschlacht* ("cauldron fighting"). The greatest was the double encirclement of German 6th Army and supporting Axis forces at *Stalingrad.* The next attempt to form a kotel failed, however: *POLAR STAR.* Obstruction of the German *ZITADELLE* offensive led to creation of another great kotel after *Kursk,* flowing from Operations *KUTUZOV* and *RUMIANTSEV.* Subsequently, the Red Army carried out repeated, even rolling, kotel operations to the end of the war.
See also deep battle.

KRASNOARMEETS "Red Army man." The official Soviet term for an ordinary soldier, the equivalent of German *Landser* or "GI" in the U.S. Army. The Germans called krasnoarmeets "Ivans."

See Red Army.

KREISAU CIRCLE

See resistance (German).

***KREML* (MAY 1942)** "Kremlin." Code name of a Wehrmacht *deception operation* carried out against the Red Army in May 1942. Its purpose was to persuade Soviet military intelligence that the main Wehrmacht offensive of 1942 aimed at Moscow, when in fact it was directed by Adolf Hitler to drive on the Caucasus. KREML may have deflected Soviet forces away from a German attack launched in June, when Operation *FRIDERICUS* surprised and cut off Soviet 6th Army in the *Barvenkovo salient* and opened the road east to Stalingrad on the Volga.

See also Kharkov, Second Battle of; Rzhev-Sychevka offensive operation, First.

KRIEGSMARINE The German Navy. From 1872 to 1918 the Imperial German Navy was known as the Kaiserliche Marine; from 1919 to 1921 as the Vorlaeufige Reichsmarine; from 1921 to 1933 as the Reichsmarine. In the Nazi period, from 1933 to 1945, it was called Kriegsmarine. During World War I the Kaiserliche Marine put to sea a "High Seas Fleet" of powerful capital and other surface warships. It was not the equal of Britain's "Grand Fleet," but effectively forced the Royal Navy to concentrate its great battlefleet in home waters from 1914 to 1918. Germany also commissioned 419 *U-boats* during the Great War, of which 186 were lost to enemy action by aircraft and escorts, or to other submarines. The *Treaty of Versailles* (1919) forced the surrender or internment of 74 named German surface ships and over 200 U-boats. Naval aviation was forbidden under terms of the Treaty, but the ban was later circumvented through efforts of a private company, the Luftdienst, which supplied aircraft to the Reichsmarine. Admiral *Erich Raeder* was Fleet Commander in Chief of the Kriegsmarine during the interwar years and deep into the naval war. The submarine arm was commanded by Admiral *Karl Dönitz* from its creation.

Shipbuilding was severely limited by Versailles to surface warships no larger than 10,000 tons and no U-boats at all. To counter these limits, the Kriegsmarine secretly preserved ship design expertise by establishing a front company and naval design bureau in the Netherlands that took commissions for foreign navies. Special machine tools and other U-boat components were stored in secret by another company in Denmark. Work on new submarines for Finland and Spain thus simultaneously advanced eventual German designs. Serious secret planning for resumption of naval construction began in 1927, including plans for an initial force of 16 U-boats. Some were built in secret before the diplomatic coup for Germany of the *Anglo-German Naval Agreement* in July 1935. Within two months of that breakthrough, Germany openly declared that it possessed a fleet of 9 U-boats and announced a construction program for two "Scharnhorst"-class capital ships and another 28 U-boats. At the start of World War II German naval air power was limited to 15 squadrons of reconnaissance and anti-submarine aircraft. Nine training U-boats were already serviceable when the Anglo-German Naval Agreement allowed Germany to build in the open. Construction continued on the "Scharnhorsts" and other major surface ships. German naval aviation was always sharply limited by *Hermann Göring's* jealous suspicion that the Kriegsmarine wanted to operate a separate air force. That interservice and personal rivalry was more limiting than production or design problems.

A critical moment came in May 1938, when Raeder was told by Hitler to prepare for war. He was ordered to speed completion of two "Bismarck"-class battleships and build U-boats to parity with the Royal Navy. The quasi-debate between Hitler and Raeder that ensued led the former to adoption of the latter's 10-year capital shipbuilding program, or *Z-Plan*. Hitler told Raeder that war with Britain was a distant prospect and approved this plan for a battlefleet of aircraft carriers, battleships, battlecruisers, and heavy cruisers. But he also decreed that yards should speed completion of several pocket battleships and of more U-boats, to be employed alike as commerce raiders. Dönitz oversaw expansion of the U-boat fleet, always protesting the waste of resources spent on surface ships. Still, by September 1939, he had 57 operational boats plus two large experimental Type-Is. Although Hitler's confidence in the Z-Plan slipped and it was later modified, until 1943 he remained committed to its vague strategic vision and allowed some costly work on capital ships to continue. In addition, work began in mid-1940 transforming the Norwegian port of Trondheim into a German city and major Kriegsmarine base, continuing until March 1943. That was only the first of several major bases planned for construction around the world. They were all proposed by the Kriegsmarine to sustain a world-class blue water navy that would eventually be able to challenge and defeat the Royal Navy and U.S. Navy. Other bases were planned for Morocco and the Canary Islands. The idea of bases from which to launch the final naval war against the United States was so important to Raeder and Hitler that the latter forewent facilitating Spanish entry into the war in mid-1940 when Madrid refused to permit a Kriegsmarine base in the Canaries. In the interim, most wartime experience and energy centered on the *Battle of the Atlantic (1939–1945)*. That saw progressive diminution and withdrawal of Germany's surface fleet from 1939 to 1942, alongside all-out *unrestricted submarine warfare* against *convoys*.

At the start of the German–Soviet war in June 1941, the Kriegsmarine had 404,000 personnel, many still deployed in the surface navy on ships concealed from the British in Norwegian fjords or operating from safe Baltic bases. The main shift in Kriegsmarine personnel and strategy occurred on January 30, 1943, when Raeder was wildly berated by Hitler and resigned. Dönitz replaced Raeder as supreme commander. He immediately halted all construction on capital warships, including the vain but by then 95 percent completed aircraft carrier DKM Graf Zeppelin. Crews were reassigned to U-boats and all yards turned to building a warfleet of over 400, mostly Type IX, U-boats by the end of 1943. Work continued on new long-range and other experimental designs, but not all were successful. Hitler approved a new base plan in April that refused materials or labor for any surface craft other than E-boats, destroyers, and minesweepers. All other effort went into floating Type IX U-boats, ordered built at a rate of 30 per month into 1944, when the advanced Type XXI "Elektroboote" was expected to be ready for mass production. *Albert Speer* subsequently authorized increased production to 40 U-boats per month. That strained labor and material resources without addressing the worsening issue of training sufficient U-boat captains and crews. Nor did the proposed fleet and kill rate come close to matching enemy replacement cargo and escort construction. German yards did not begin a shift to modular construction techniques until April 1943, when the change was driven by a need to disperse production to escape mounting bombing. None of the reforms made any difference: the U-boat arm failed to interfere with, let alone stop, the *OVERLORD* invasion and remained mostly confined to base or coastal waters. Despite new boats and technologies it was savaged even in the Channel when the invasion came. Still, U-boats made a major contribution to the overall German war effort by slowing supplies of war matériel to Britain and Russia from 1939 to 1943 and thus delaying the Anglo-American build-up needed to launch a *second front*. The Kriegsmarine thereby greatly prolonged the war and the agony of all participants.

German naval cooperation with the Italians and Japanese was minimal throughout the war, even concerning joint amphibious, convoy, and extraction operations with the Italians in the Adriatic and Mediterranean. Italian submarines operating in the Atlantic were ignored by Dönitz and then relegated to marginal areas. Italian and Rumanian coastal patrols and submarines came under Kriegsmarine command in the Black Sea. The Kriegsmarine could never persuade Hitler that the Mediterranean was a theater where the Royal Navy could be seriously threatened: he saw it as an Italian problem. U-boats were sent into the Mediterranean in larger numbers from 1942—as were large Luftwaffe formations—only after the Italian position in North Africa had already crumbled. After the start of BARBAROSSA, several hundred small German patrol craft were transported overland and deployed in the Black Sea, along with six U-boats and an entire Italian light flotilla. From September to December 1943, the German boats were used to ferry 250,000 Axis troops and their equipment across the Kerch Straits—a true German *Dunkirk* that exceeded the evacuation from Sicily. After that, the boats ran supplies into ground forces cut off in the Crimean peninsula, operating from Odessa to Sebastopol. When Hitler finally permitted the evacuation of Sebastopol on May 6, 1944, the order came too late for many: a flotilla of small ships and barges was massively bombed as it loaded desperate men. About 130,000 German and Rumanians got out, but at least 8,000 drowned or were killed by bombs and 80,000 were left behind. Few efforts were made to link with the IJN beyond token long-range U-boat cruises in Southeast Asia and some late-war technological exchanges. That was true despite Hitler's initial exuberance about Japanese naval power adding weight to the Axis order of battle.

The Kriegsmarine made its last major surface effort in the Baltic during the last months of the war. Dönitz concentrated all remaining surface ships along the southern Baltic coast, covering retreat and evacuation of cut off garrisons and civilian refugees. Evacuations totaling 1 million troops and 1.5 million civilians were carried out under intense Soviet bombing and submarine attacks, altogether forming the single largest maritime evacuation in history. Soviet submarines caused three of the greatest maritime disasters in history when they sank three German liners packed with troops and refugees. Each sinking cost several times the peacetime casualties lost on the far more famous civilian ships "Titanic" and "Lusitania": over 9,000 died in the frigid Baltic when the "Wilhelm Gustloff" was sunk by three torpedoes. There were only 900 survivors. The Kriegsmarine continued to run the gauntlet to Courland until the end of the war, supplying the shrinking pocket and removing wounded and refugees. By the end of the Baltic campaign the Germans had lost 1 old battleship, 7 U-boats, 12 destroyers, and nearly 200 smaller warships (minelayers, minesweepers, and various landing craft).

When the end came, Dönitz ordered the U-boat fleet scuttled in Operation *REGENBOGEN*. Some captains disobeyed or never got the signal. They surrendered their boats in Western Allied or neutral ports. Surviving U-boats were divided among the major Allied navies, including the Soviet Navy, but most were simply taken to sea and destroyed by January 1946. The few remaining German surface ships all went to the Soviet Navy, except for minesweepers, which were taken by the Royal Navy. Using German naval munitions, British engineers blew up all Kriegsmarine docks, pens, yards, barracks, and even several military hospitals in a demolition and disarmament program that lasted into mid-1946.

See also ace; aircraft carriers; air–sea rescue; amphibious operations; ASDIC; Athenia; auxiliary cruisers; BdU; Britain, Battle of; Channel Dash; cruiser warfare; E-boat; Enigma machine; explosive motor boats; Kleinkampfverbände; Laconia Order; London Submarine Agreement; mines; minesweepers; neutral rights and duties; Pillenwerfer; radar; radio; Replenishment-at-Sea; Schnorchel; Seekriegsleitung; shipyards; torpedoes; treaty cruisers; WESERÜBUNG.

Suggested Reading: Howard Grier, *Hitler, Dönitz, and the Baltic Sea* (2007); J. P. Malcolm Showell, *The German Navy in World War II* (1979).

KRIEGSORGANISATIONEN (KO)   "War organizations." A set of German intelligence units established in 10 major neutral states. The most important was in Spain, where a staff of 220 ran up to 2,000 agents and oversaw dozens of transmission and observation stations. That made "Kriegsorganisationen-Spanien" the single largest German state organization outside Nazi-occupied Europe.

KRIMINALPOLIZEI   "Kripo" or criminal police. The ordinary, local German police. It was subsumed into the *Sicherheitspolizei* under the *Schutzstaffel (SS)*.

KRIPO
See Kriminalpolizei; Sicherheitspolizei.

***KRISTALLNACHT* (NOVEMBER 9–10, 1938)**   "Night of broken glass." Leaders of the *Nazi Party* arranged this vulgar orgy of pillage of Jewish shops and property and rape and murder of some Jews. The terror of that night was named for the broken windows from some 7,500 Jewish shops, which left shards of glass littering the streets of German and Austrian towns. Nearly 200 synagogues were desecrated and burned and nearly 100 Jews murdered. Some 20,000 more were arrested and confined in *concentration camps*. The rest were collectively fined a billion marks to pay to repair the damage, which allowed many more Jewish businesses and homes to be confiscated by the Nazis. Kristallnacht marked a new phase in Germany's descent into barbarism. The pogrom was a signal, if one was still needed, that the position of Jews within the "Third Reich" was set to deteriorate dramatically. Thereafter, Jews could not make a living or feel even minimally secure on the streets, or in their persons or homes. Those who could do so sold whatever they were permitted to, at larcenously low prices, to pay huge bribes to Nazi officials who otherwise blocked them from leaving the country. With characteristic cynicism, the Nazis encouraged the refugee outflow through a "Ministry for Jewish Emigration" that extorted the last pfennig from those departing. Franklin Roosevelt recalled the U.S. ambassador to Germany in protest and publicly condemned the pogrom, but no outside help arrived as the long Nazi night fell over the Jews of Germany, presaging the darkness that was coming over all of Europe.

KRN   "Polish National Council of the Homeland."
   See London Poles; Lublin Poles; Poland.

KRONSTADT NAVAL BASE
   See Soviet Navy.

KRUPP FAMILY   Alfred Krupp (1812–1887) was a principal steel maker and arms manufacturer. He developed the vast Krupp steel and armaments works, which fed the German war machine during its rapid expansion under Chancellor Otto von Bismarck in the late 19th century and during both world wars. His descendants made the firm the largest armaments conglomerate in the world. Gustav Krupp (1870–1950) initially opposed the Nazis as vulgar, but as head of the Association of German Industrialists, he embraced Adolf Hitler in 1933. He was essential to smoothing the great dictator's relations with other major capitalists. His son, Alfred Krupp (1907–1967), was Hitler's minister for war economy, 1943–1945. He was convicted of war crimes by the *Nuremberg Tribunal,* including the use of *slave labor* from *concentration camps* in munitions factories and mines. He was sentenced to 12 years and had his property confiscated. He served four years, was pardoned and released in 1951, and most of his property was restored to him. He played a leading role in West Germany's postwar industrial revival. The Krupp firm became a public corporation in the 1960s.
   See also denazification; Speer, Alfred.

KÜCHLER, GEORG VON (1881–1968)   German field marshal. He saw heavy fighting on the Western Front during World War I before becoming a staff officer. After the war he joined a *Freikorps* and fought briefly in Poland. He participated in the occupation of Memel in March 1939, and commanded 3rd Army in the invasion of Poland in September. He led 18th Army in the invasion of Belgium in 1940, advancing to the Scheldt and taking Antwerp before turning south into France. His troops were among those halted outside *Dunkirk*. After the Anglo-French evacuation, 18th Army moved south to Paris and beyond. Küchler again led 18th Army, through the Baltic states and into the Soviet Union, during Operation *BARBAROSSA* in 1941. His command formed the northernmost flank of Army Group North. It was during this campaign that Küchler approved various *war crimes,* including use of Soviet prisoners to walk across minefields to clear them for his tanks, and enforcement of the *Commissar order*. He was promoted to command Army Group North in December 1941. For the next two years he fought a mostly static battle centered on the long *siege of Leningrad*. He was abruptly sacked and briefly "retired" in January 1944, on the order of Adolf Hitler. His offense was to approve a wholly essential tactical withdrawal by 18th Army as the Red Army broke out of the Leningrad enclave. He did so over enraged objections and a direct "stand fast" order by his Führer. Captured by U.S. forces at the end of the war, Küchler was convicted of war crimes in 1948. Sentenced to 20 years, he was released in 1955.

KUGELERLASS   "bullet order." A *Schutzstaffel (SS)* decree issued by *Ernst Kaltenbrunner* on March 4, 1944, commanding that escaped prisoners of war were to be taken to Mauthausen concentration camp and shot. Most escapees from the armed forces of the Western Allies were exempted, but not all. The order was routinely enforced against Red Army men.

KULA GULF, BATTLE OF   A minor night action in the Solomons provoked by a small U.S. Navy task force seeking to intercept a destroyer transport run by the *Tokyo Express* on the night of July 6, 1943. The Japanese displayed still clearly superior night-fighting skills, exchanging one destroyer lost for an American cruiser sunk.

KULAKS   "Tight-fisted ones." A Bolshevik pejorative for "rich" peasants: those with property beyond subsistence or who employed other peasants as farm laborers. They had benefited most from agrarian reforms in 1906 and again after 1917. They bitterly resisted collectivization of Soviet agriculture ordered by Joseph Stalin from 1931 to 1933. Stalin retaliated by ordering kulaks "liquidated as a class" and "dekulakization" of all agriculture. The term "kulak" was never precisely defined, which suited Stalin's simultaneous campaign against Ukrainian nationalism and his paranoid delusion that failure to meet unrealistic requisition quotas was due to kulak "sabotage" and "counterrevolution." As a result, middle peasants were also swept into the net and destroyed. By 1933 the scale of peasant resistance and state repression approached that of civil war, but it was a war that the kulaks could not win. Kulaks were banned from the Red Army until desperate need opened recruitment and they were conscripted from April 1942. Many served with sullen resentment. Others deserted. Some switched sides and fought alongside the Germans.

KULIK, GRIGORY I.   Marshal of the Soviet Union, deputy commissar for defense. An old comrade of Joseph Stalin from the days of the *Konarmiia,* Kulik was one of four prewar Red Army marshals. He served on the Stavka at the start of the German-Soviet war, but was demoted and expelled from the Central Committee of the Communist Party after his disastrous leadership led to the loss of the Crimean peninsula. He was especially inept during the *Kerch Defensive operation* in November 1941.

See also *Yezhovshchina.*

KUOMINTANG

See *Guomindang.*

KURIL ISLANDS   A chain of 30 small islands north of the Japanese home islands, disputed by Japan and Russia from the late 18th century. The Soviets seized the islands as part of their *Manchurian offensive operation* (August 1945). They were then ceded to Moscow in accordance with decisions taken by the Allies at the *Cairo Conference* and *Yalta Conference.* Four more southern islands—Etorufo, Habomai, Kunashiri, and Shikotan—were claimed by Moscow to be part of the Kuril chain and also occupied, with the Japanese population forcibly ejected. But those islands were deemed its "Northern Territories" by Japan and not part of the Kurils. They were not, therefore, included in the territorial terms of the *Japanese Peace Treaty.* The Soviets pledged to return Habomai and Shikotan once a separate treaty could be negotiated, which was partially achieved in 1956. In 1960 Moscow added a precondition of abrogation of the 1951 Japan-U.S. security treaty, though that proviso was quietly abandoned in 1973. But in either case, Moscow was adamant that return of Etorufo and Kunashiri was permanently out of the question. Even after the breakup of the Soviet Union these disputed islands remained a source of angry contention between Russia and Japan.

KURLAND POCKET

See *Courland Pocket.*

KURSK, BATTLE OF (JULY 5–23, 1943)   The greatest armored battle in history and one of the largest battles ever fought. The limited success of the Soviet *Orel-Briansk offensive operation* under General *Konstantin Rokossovsky* in February and March, along with Field Marshal *Erich von Manstein's* successful southern operations (*DON* and the *Third Battle of Kharkov*), set the lines of the Kursk bulge, a Soviet salient that projected 100 miles deep into German lines. The Wehrmacht built up unprecedented forces around Kursk from March to June. The great mass of German armor was ordered to the area, to ready to slice off the salient. Meanwhile, the Red Army also built up huge forces inside the bulge as well as along its wider flanks. The Soviets knew of the German plans and intended to meet them with even larger, well-hidden tank and air formations under Marshal *Georgi Zhukov*. These were deployed in a deep defensive field designed to absorb and bog down the German assault in its earliest stages. After strategically overreaching and failing in December 1941–February 1942, and again in January–March 1943, Joseph Stalin and the Stavka had at last recognized a deep truth about the war: it was fundamentally an exercise in sustained attrition necessary to wear down the Wehrmacht before any decisive thrust could be made into the vitals of Nazi Germany. Soviet forces therefore deployed in an extraordinarily deep set of seven defensive belts designed to absorb, bog down, and kill German armored thrusts at price of massive but accepted Soviet casualties and loss of equipment. The armor, artillery, infantry, and air combat that ensued combined to form the largest battle ever fought. Some 3.5 million troops in total fought at Kursk, nearly half the 8.5 million positioned that summer along a 1,500-mile long Eastern Front.

The German offensive plan, *ZITADELLE,* was delayed several times from April to July, partly for technical reasons and to refit on the German side but also because of the spring *rasputitsa*. During the postponements German and Soviet casualties dropped significantly. But there was also a building sense of violent tension as each side waited for the summer explosion into combat. Where Adolf Hitler grew evermore cautious and dubious about ZITADELLE as time passed, the Stavka had to restrain Stalin's urge to attack prematurely. Zhukov's plan was to draw the German armor into the Soviet defensive belts, in some places 175 miles deep. Only then would he spring a great trap around the Panzer columns with simultaneous counteroffensives on either side of the salient. For that, he held back huge Fronts whose presence was hidden from *B-dienst* and the *Abwehr* by some of the most elaborate and successful *maskirovka* operations of the war. In the south, the counteroffensive was given the additional task of retaking Kharkov and Belgorod, which had been lost to Field Marshal *Erich von Manstein* and the SS 2nd Panzer Corps in March. Soviet intelligence was unusually good at Kursk, although it mistook the *Schwerpunkt* as the north side of the salient whereas the Germans believed it was in the south and concentrated their effort there. Information came from multiple sources that allowed the VVS to catch the Luftwaffe on the ground, attacking forward airfields in a set of preemptive strikes carried out from May 6–8. And it then gave the Stavka three days advance notice of the precise hour of the German assault. That enabled Soviet artillery to hammer the armor spearheads at their jump-off points before dawn on July 5. Shelling massed Wehrmacht and *Waffen-SS* formations just 10 minutes before they were set to attack the first defense belt according to the usual, precise German instructions staggered the attacking troops, upset timetables, and shook the confidence of Hitler and the OKH. The armor and artillery battles that followed, as Panzer columns cut into the salient and through the first defensive belts, were bloody and destructive. The climax came in an armor battle at Prokhorovka, still the single greatest armored battle in history. From that point, Kursk became a vast and chaotic *Kesselschlacht* —or rather, a great *kotel*—that engaged over 5,000 tanks and lesser armored vehicles, thousands of guns, several thousand combat aircraft, and several million troops. The air battle was also huge.

The Red Army suffered about 70,000 casualties of all types in the fighting at Kursk, excluding the wider Soviet counteroffensives on either side of the salient, which cost another 100,000 men. The Soviets lost nearly 500 aircraft and more than half the armor force they deployed, or over 1,600 tanks. In the main battle the Germans lost 57,000 men and considerably fewer tanks and planes, about 300 and 200, respectively. However, they lost so many tanks and planes in the related Soviet counteroffensives that followed Kursk—Operations *KUTUZOV* and *RUMIANTSEV*—that the Wehrmacht never again launched a strategic offensive operation on the Eastern Front. Instead, it surrendered the initiative and was confined to local counterattacks. Germany was already being outproduced in major weapons systems. Despite temporarily regaining a technical advantage with its Panthers and Tigers, it was outproduced in armor in such quantities by the Soviet Union and Western Allies that it never recovered its relative position from the loss of combat power in men and war machines suffered in the summer of 1943. For that reason, Kursk is often identified as the major turning point along the Eastern Front, more so even than Stalingrad. The Red Army for the first time at Kursk succeeded in physically blunting a major German offensive, rather than just defending desperately against it until the Wehrmacht ran out of momentum, as happened before at Moscow in December 1941, and at Stalingrad in November 1942. Then the Stavka launched a set of massive counteroffensives, which completely fooled the Germans in their direction, intentions, and timing. Kursk was, in *Heinz Guderian's* expert estimation, the decisive defeat for Germany to that point in the war. After Kursk, the Soviets took the strategic offensive, starting a long and bloody drive that ended only with Hitler's death in the "Führerbunker" beneath the ruins of Berlin in May 1945.

And yet, arms and aircraft production for both armed forces increased to the end of 1943 and again in 1944, while enlistments swelled new divisions, armies, and army groups. Most casualties suffered along the Eastern Front in World War II still lay in the future. Kursk no doubt massively accelerated the pace of destruction of German military power. But it cannot be argued that, had the Soviets lost at Kursk, the final outcome of the war would have been placed in grave doubt. Not even the greatest battle ever fought was sufficient to decide the larger armed struggle between mighty industrial empires. To decide the war in the east it would take a series of additional battles—a full campaign—fought hard to the end of 1943, then more savage campaigns along several axes of Soviet advance and German counterattack in 1944, and yet more thrusts and fighting and destruction over the first four months of 1945. Meanwhile, the air war continued over Germany and heavy fighting took place in Italy, while the Western powers did not invade France until mid-1944, after which there remained 11 months of fighting in the west. While it cannot really be said, therefore, that Kursk was "the" decisive victory or defeat of World War II, it certainly numbered among its greatest battles and did much to confirm and accelerate the trajectory of attrition that led to ultimate Soviet victory and German defeat.

See also Donbass offensive operation; HUSKY; intelligence; Izium-Barvenkovo operation; Ostwall; Schwerpunkt; ULTRA.

Suggested Reading: Walter S. Dunn, *Kursk: Hitler's Gamble, 1943* (1997); David M. Glantz and Harold S. Orenstein, eds., *The Battle for Kursk, 1943* (1999).

KURSK SALIENT   A great Red Army bulge into German lines formed during fighting along the Eastern Front in the first half of 1943. It centered on the important junction town of Kursk. It was the locale of the great *Battle of Kursk* in July 1943, and focal point of two related and even more important Red Army counteroffensives that followed: *KUTUZOV* and *RUMIANTSEV*.

KUTNÁ, BATTLE OF (SEPTEMBER 1939)
See FALL WEISS.

KUTUZOV (JULY 12–AUGUST 18, 1943)   Soviet code name for the Red Army counteroffensive launched to reduce the "Orel balcony"—a German salient around Orel—simultaneously with the *Battle of Kursk*. It was fully planned before Kursk by a Stavka determined to first hold the Germans up, attrit them badly, then counterattack in massive force along multiple fronts. It was executed by the Western, Central, and Briansk Fronts against German forces in the Orel balcony. Western Front's 11th Guards Army broke through the weakly defended German line north of the Kursk salient. The breakthrough was quickly exploited by three *tank armies* and additional mobile corps, which pushed aside 5th Panzer Division and advanced on Orel. Having smashed though the German lines, the Guards captured Orel on August 5. But the operation failed in a much greater objective: to encircle all German forces. That was because Adolf Hitler had earlier ordered the exposed defenders withdrawn from a potential *kotel,* and because he needed to reinforce elsewhere along the Eastern Front and in Sicily, where the Western Allies were engaged in Operation *HUSKY* landings. When the Soviets arrived the Germans had already pulled back from Orel to the *Hagen Line*. More rolling Red Army attacks were made farther north, which drew in more German reserves and additional Soviet tank and infantry corps. KUTUZOV was more important in persuading Hitler—whose attention was strangely drawn away to the landings in Sicily—to cancel *ZITADELLE* and seek to disengage his Panzers from Kursk. It also prepared the way for liberation of Smolensk in September. Reflecting the fact that the Red Army was on the offensive north of the Kursk bulge, it lost nearly twice as many men and tanks in KUTUZOV than it did at Kursk: 113,000 compared to 70,000 men, and 2,600 tanks lost compared to 1,600. The complementary operation on the southern flank of the Kursk salient was *RUMIANTSEV*.

KWAJALEIN ATOLL
See Marshal Islands.

KWANTUNG ARMY
See Guandong Army.

KW-LINE   A Belgian anti-tank barrier constructed in 1939–1940, better known to English-language readers as the *Dyle Line*.
See also FALL GELB.

L'ARMÉE DE TERRE FRANÇAISE
  See French Army.

LACHSFANG (1942) "SALMON CATCH." German code name for a proposed corps-level operation to destroy the Soviet railway to Murmansk by advancing through northern Finland. It was intended to completely cut the supply line of *Lend-Lease* aid to Russia, which was already being interdicted by Luftwaffe patrols and U-boats. Similarly, Adolf Hitler hoped that *EDELWEISS* would cut southern supply lines in the Caucasus, even as it brought him closer to the oil fields at Baku. LACHSFANG was reliant on the prior success of a planned *NORDLICHT* offensive to take Leningrad in September. The Finns refused to participate in LACHSFANG if Leningrad was not taken first, an objective they doubted the Wehrmacht could achieve. When NORDLICHT was preempted by the Soviet *Siniavino offensive operation,* so too was LACHSFANG stymied and canceled.

LACONIA ORDER (SEPTEMBER 1942) On September 12, 1942, U-156 sank the Cunard liner "Laconia" northeast of Ascension Island off the West African coast. The liner was blacked-out and zigzagging and hence a legitimate target under the rules of *cruiser warfare.* Among its more than 2,500 passengers were 1,800 Italian prisoners of war, 160 Polish troops, and about 350 British soldiers and their families. Once U-156 Captain Werner Hartenstein realized the dire situation of over 2,000 survivors in the water, he decided to stay on site and rescue as many as he could. He radioed to *BdU* for help. Admiral *Karl Dönitz* vectored in three more U-boats. An Italian submarine also arrived on scene. However, Dönitz ordered his U-boats to cut tow lines set up for "Laconia" lifeboats full of Poles or British subjects: U-boat crews were told to use "Laconia" ship's boats to save Italian prisoners first. Dönitz radioed that Vichy warships would be sent from Dakar to rescue any remaining Italians or non-Axis personnel still alive: because Vichy was technically neutral, its warships would face lessened hazard from Allied attacks than Dönitz's U-boats. But Hartenstein would not simply abandon the rest of the passengers in the water. He made a desperate SOS broadcast in the clear and in English, calling vessels of all nations to assist under a flag of truce that he promised to respect: "If any ship will assist the ship-wrecked 'Laconia' crew, I will not attack providing I am not attacked by ship or air forces. German submarine."

U-boats on the scene displayed the Red Cross emblem as they worked on the surface among the human flotsam of "Laconia." Hundreds stood on the decks of the four submarines; others clung to hulls or bobbed along in crowded lifeboats. A series of grave and tragic misunderstandings ensued over the next several days to spoil the rescue. On September 15, and again two days later, American B-24s from Ascension Island bombed and strafed the surfaced U-boats. As the submarines dived hundreds fell from their sinking decks into the sea. Dönitz reacted by ordering a halt to all rescue efforts, for "Laconia" survivors and for the rest of the war. He cabled his captains: "Rescue remains contrary to the primary demands of warfare for the destruction of enemy ships and their crews." He also ordered provision of lifeboats with food and water to halt: the practice depleted his U-boats' supplies. The captains cut cables, left the survivors to drift, and departed the area. Vichy warships arrived on the 19th and rescued 1,100 souls. The rest perished. The "Laconia order" was raised in evidence against Dönitz during his *war crimes trial* by the *Nuremberg Tribunal* in 1945. He was censured for issuing illegal orders, a reduced penalty because Admiral *Chester Nimitz* and other Western Allied naval leaders testified that it was also policy of Western navies not to attempt rescue of passengers or crew from enemy ships sunk by their submarines. U-156 was depth-charged in the Caribbean on March 8, 1943, while on her fifth war patrol. It sank with Captain Hartenstein and all hands.

LAGG
  See fighters.

LAKE KASAN, BATTLE OF (1939)   Also called "Changkufeng."
  See Nomonhan.

LAMP   Soviet code name for a major partisan operation carried out in November 1942.

LANDING CRAFT   Any flat-bottomed small craft or larger ship used to bring troops, vehicles, and equipment onshore in an amphibious assault, from where they sought to drive inland to press home an attack. The Japanese pioneered large landing craft with the *Military Landing Craft Carrier*. It was first used at Shanghai in 1937. Japan also built the first bow-ramp landing craft. The Western Allies developed several classes of landing craft, from large ships to small beachable types, in several cases copying the Japanese bow ramp innovation into their designs. Landing Craft Control (LCC) carried special forces (usually, Rangers) and small radar. Their essential job was to find paths through obstacles and minefields for other landing craft to follow. Landing Craft Navigation (LCN) were British boats that performed the same mission. Landing Craft Assault (LCA) ran small numbers of infantry directly onto the beach, with each carrying about 35 troops. Landing Craft Infantry (LCI) carried as many as 200 infantry or 75 tons of cargo, unloaded by two gangways off the sides. They were used to ferry wounded back to Britain during the *D-Day (June 6, 1944)* landings and throughout the *Normandy campaign*. Ambulances could drive across a beach right up to the extended ramp of an LCI, transferring wounded men directly to a ship capable of taking them all the way back to the United Kingdom. Still larger versions were capable of long-distance ocean ferrying, including carrying troops directly to North Africa from the United States and Great Britain. Landing Craft Personnel, Large (LCPL) was the U.S. version of the British LCA. Landing Craft Mechanized (LCM) carried one tank or about 100 infantry. Each Landing Craft Tank (LCT) could carry four Shermans or other medium tanks. Late-war mark LCTs carried up to six tanks. Landing Craft Vehicle Personnel (LCVP) were multipurpose assault ships capable of carrying three dozen men, along with four tons of supplies or a jeep or 3/4-ton truck. Later versions delivered men and cargo directly onto beaches via a wide front ramp. LCVPs were popularly known as "Higgins' boats," a term that also covered all-metal adaptations of the original wooden craft. Armed variations of some British landing craft mounted spigot mortars, anti-aircraft guns, and even four- or five-inch naval guns for close beach support. Others were fitted out as rocket bombardment ships. Landing Craft Flak (LCF) and Landing Craft Gun (LCG) were small, close fire-support ships.

See also amphibious operations; DUKW; landing ships; Landing Vehicle Tracked (LVT).

LANDING SHIPS   Numerous specialized amphibious warfare ships were developed during the war, especially by the Western Allies. Among the most important types was the Landing Ship Tank (LST), an ocean-capable ship that carried up to 20 medium tanks. It delivered its cargo via a remarkable two-piece bow that swung open. Smaller ships included the Landing Ship Medium (LSM) and Landing Ship Infantry (LSI). The first British LSI were converted cargo ships and ferries. The Western Allies later purpose-built hundreds of LSI. The Landing Ship Dock (LSD) was capable of partial rear flooding to deliver smaller *landing craft* into the water at some distance from the beach. The United States purpose-built several additional landing ships, including the Auxiliary Personnel Attack Ship (APA), essentially an assault troop carrier, and the Attack Cargo Ship (AKA), which carried landing craft and priority cargo needed at the outset of a beach assault.

See also Military Landing Craft Carrier.

LANDING VEHICLE TRACKED (LVT) The British called this amphibious assault vehicle the "Buffalo." It was primarily a cargo carrier capable of driving supplies out of the water directly onto the beach, or beyond if a breakout had been made. A later version added a ramp for easier unloading. The LVT (A) mounted a cannon, making it something of an amphibious tank.

LAND MINES
See mines.

LANDSER Affectionate nickname for an ordinary German soldier. The American equivalent was "Yank." The British parallel was "Tommy," the French term was "poilu." Germans called Russian soldiers "Ivans" and Americans "Amis." Russians called Germans "Fritzes."

LANDWACHT Traditional Prussian country militia. They were mobilized to hunt down *Nationalkomitee Freies Deutschland (NKFD)* guerillas in East Prussia in the summer of 1944. They were absorbed into the *Volkssturm* from September 25, 1944.

LAPLAND WAR (1944–1945) A series of armed clashes between Finnish troops and erstwhile allies in the Wehrmacht. It began with the prolonged German withdrawal from Finland from September 3–29, 1944, in Operations *BIRKE* and *NORDLICHT*. The Germans speeded the evacuation following a ceasefire between the Finnish army and Red Army on September 5, 1944. A formal armistice followed two weeks later. The Finns were mostly content to let the Germans leave, although some fighting broke out in the Gulf of Bothnia at the end of September. *Waffen-SS* troops remained in parts of northern Finland until evacuated to Norway in November 1944. As they pulled out, they scorched the land of their erstwhile ally. The last few Wehrmacht soldiers left the far north in April 1945. Long before then, whole Soviet armies were transferred away from the quiet Finnish theater to fight in Hungary. One was sent to Manchuria to prepare for war against Japan.

LARGE CRUISERS
See cruisers.

LATERAN TREATIES (FEBRUARY 11, 1929) Agreements between the Italian state and the "Holy See" signed on February 11, 1929. They resolved a conflict that had dragged on since the unification of Italy in the time of Pius IX. The treaties established the Vatican as an independent city-state within the city of Rome and granted generous financial compensation to the popes for the lost territories of the old Papal States. In return, the Vatican recognized the Italian state, and the Catholic Church was formally established in Italy. In 1984 a revision to the treaty was agreed that nullified the article establishing Catholicism.
See also concordat; Mussolini, Benito; Pius XI.

LATTRE DE TASSIGNY, JEAN-MARIE DE (1889–1952)   French general. He led a division against the Germans during *FALL GELB* in 1940. He served in the Vichy "Armistice Army," then in the *Armée d'Afrique* in Tunisia. He was arrested for resisting German occupation of the *zone libre* of France in November 1942. Tried and sentenced by a Vichy court, he escaped to Britain to join the *Free French*. He fought with the *French Expeditionary Corps* in the *Italian campaign* in 1943–1944, then led Fighting France ("France Combattante") forces in *DRAGOON*, the Franco-American landing in the south of France on August 15, 1944. At the head of French 1st Army, he fought into Germany in 1945. He was promoted Maréchal de France after his death.

LATVIA   This small Baltic state was a battleground for Russian and German armies during World War I. After fending off the Red Army and lingering German forces in 1918–1919, it was independent from 1921 to 1939. In 1934 its fledgling democracy ended, and Latvia saw institution of an authoritarian regime. It was secretly assigned to the Soviet sphere of influence by the *Nazi–Soviet Pact (August 23, 1939)*. On October 5 Latvia was forced to sign an agreement permitting Red Army bases on its soil. In June 1940, the Red Army moved into the rest of Latvia. It was formally annexed in August, whereupon the worst excesses of the *NKVD* were imposed on the country. The Germans occupied Latvia from 1941 to 1944, as part of the *Reichskommissariat Ostland*. There was extensive *collaboration* by some Latvians not just with the occupation but with the worst crimes of the Nazi regime. Latvians also volunteered for two Baltic divisions within the *Waffen-SS*. Soviet control was reestablished in 1944–1945. The United States and some other Western countries never accepted the legality of the postwar Soviet annexation because it was based on the Nazi–Soviet Pact and 1940 border claimed by Moscow.

   Suggested Reading: Valdis Lumans, *Latvia in World War II* (2006).

LAVAL, PIERRE (1883–1945)   French politician. Prime minister of Vichy, 1942–1944. Originally a socialist, Laval drifted toward the far right in the 1920s, then raced there in the 1930s. He thought he saw the handwriting of German victory on the walls of Europe, but believed that he could keep France secure. He was prime minister of the "Third Republic," 1931–1932, and 1935–1936, and foreign minister, 1934–1936. He negotiated the *Stresa Front* and *Hoare-Laval Pact*. He joined Marshal *Philippe Pétain's* government in 1940, but was indifferent to Pétain's ideal of "National Revolution." Laval was arrested under suspicion of plotting a putsch and dismissed from the government on December 13, 1940. He was reinstalled as prime minister from 1942 to 1944. He concentrated power and ministerial portfolios in his own hands and instituted and administered an aggressively authoritarian regime. He enthusiastically collaborated with the Nazis. He tried to obtain concessions from the Germans for each collaborationist step he undertook, but nearly always failed: he never won more than the most minor concessions from Hitler, who had no interest in seeing

France restored to anything like its prewar status within his planned *New Order* in Europe. Nevertheless, Laval approved shipping foreign Jews and then French Jews to the *death camps,* and accepted deportations of other French nationals to work as forced laborers in Germany. Not even that saved him from the ire of the most extreme French collaborationists, for whom he did not move far or fast enough toward accommodation of Germany and of domestic *fascism.* Always the schemer, Laval adopted a more neutral stance after *D-Day (June 6, 1944).* For that he was briefly arrested by the Germans. He fled to Spain upon the breakout of Western Allied armies in Normandy in mid-1944. *Francisco Franco* refused to provide sanctuary, so that Laval was forced to return to France via Austria. He was arrested, tried for treason, and executed on October 15, 1945.

LAWS OF WAR

See Geneva Conventions; Hague Conventions; Laconia Order; Nuremberg Tribunal; Tokyo Tribunal; unrestricted submarine warfare; war crimes; war crimes trials.

LCA

See landing craft.

LCC

See landing craft.

LCF

See landing craft.

LCG

See landing craft.

LCI

See landing craft.

LCM

See landing craft.

LCN

See landing craft.

LCPL

See landing craft.

LCT

See landing craft.

LCVP
See landing craft.

LEADER RESERVE   A pool of senior Wehrmacht commanders dismissed from active combat or staff positions. This was a different status than convalescent leave or full retirement. At various points in the war any number of field marshals were placed in the Leader Reserve because they had displeased or disobeyed Adolf Hitler, among them: *Heinz Guderian, Ewald von Kleist, Georg von Küchler, Wilhelm von Leeb,* and *Erich von Manstein.*
See also Ersatzheer.

LEAFLET BOMBING   Operation "NICKEL." During the *Phoney War* (1939–1940), the Ruhr was heavily leafleted by RAF Bomber Command. The policy derived partly from French fear of provoking total war before the Western Allies were ready and from *Neville Chamberlain's* continuing reluctance to see real hostilities commence. Millions of leaflets were dropped explaining the peaceful intentions of the Western Allies and calling for Germans to rise up and overthrow Adolf Hitler and the Nazis. The leaflet campaign was carried out at real cost in RAF aircraft and lost crews to no political or military gain at all, beyond perhaps some operational experience for surviving crews. The assumption behind leafleting was that no civilized population that had experienced World War I could possibly support another war. That assumption was wrong. Yet, it was not wholly abandoned until much later in the war, after Germans showed every sign of supporting the Nazi regime. Early bewilderment in Britain thus turned into hatred and desire for revenge against Germans, in tandem with newly indiscriminate *area bombing* and *morale bombing* doctrine, determination, and RAF capabilities.

LEAGUE OF NATIONS   Intended to be history's first permanent conference, or international security organization, the League was the great innovation in the conduct of world affairs that Woodrow Wilson most wanted from the Paris Peace Conference. Its "Covenant"—the term arose from Wilson's insistent Presbyterianism—was made an integral part of the text of the *Treaty of Versailles* with Germany and other treaties with lesser defeated Central Powers. That was a tactical mistake of the first order, as was revealed when the United States failed to ratify the Versailles treaty, and thus never joined the League. The original 42 member states met in Geneva in 1920. At no time were all Great Powers members: the United States never overcame its isolationism and stayed outside the League throughout its entire existence. Germany was admitted in 1925 and given a permanent seat on the Council, but Adolf Hitler withdrew Germany from membership in 1933. Japan pulled out in 1933 to protest the League's mild condemnation of Tokyo's aggressive mischief in Manchuria. The Soviet Union joined in 1934 but was expelled in 1940, for its unprovoked attack on Finland. Italy withdrew in 1937 over sanctions introduced in response to its invasion of

Abyssinia. The League therefore never met even the preliminary conditions of *"collective security,"* its proclaimed and cardinal doctrine.

Many measures the League took in the interwar years were designed to prevent the last war, not the one that was looming. Sending fact-finding missions and offering diplomatic "good offices" were measures supposed to lead to "cooling-off" periods in a crisis, presuming that states would then see reason and submit disputes to arbitration. That practice reflected a widespread belief that World War I had resulted from international "tensions" and even hot-tempered accident, not any deliberate plan of aggression by any major power. The League achieved minor successes in the Balkans and Latin America with such measures, but made little headway on matters deemed of vital national interest by any Great Power. It was helpless when several of the major powers began to plan deliberate war in the 1930s. Similarly, League disarmament resolutions and conferences aimed to end arms races, which many thought led directly into World War I. One result of preoccupation with arms control was that public opinion in the Western democracies was unprepared to face the great crisis of the 1930s. In that decade, several aggressive Great Powers rearmed for planned wars of aggression. That meant rearmament for deterrence—not disarmament and *appeasement*—was the security policy called for by the facts, which hardly needed finding out after 1935. Instead, the League was not used by the Western powers in any significant way to affect the outcomes of the Japanese conquest of Manchuria, the Italian conquest of Abyssinia, or multiple interventions in the *Spanish Civil War*. Finally, the League never enjoyed the confidence of *fascist* leaders in Rome and Berlin, who openly despised it. It lost whatever confidence it ever enjoyed in Moscow when Joseph Stalin early on recognized its vacuity. In any case, Stalin only relied on Soviet military strength and bilateral diplomacy, not international cooperation. As for the West, failure of the League became a self-fulfilling prophesy resulting from failure to employ it effectively.

During World War II the League convalesced as a shadow of its former self, concentrating on operating its "functional agencies" in an utterly dysfunctional era. After the war it was discarded by the Great Powers. The Soviet Union would not consent to rejoining an association that had shamed it with expulsion; the United States did not wish to revisit its failed ratification debate of 1919; and "world public opinion" was in any event utterly uninspired by the League's record in the 1930s. The League of Nations was therefore formally dissolved in 1946. For all that failure, the League of Nations was a real advance for the idea of permanent international conferencing and negotiations, and long-term peaceful resolution of interstate disputes through multilateral diplomacy. Many of its organs dealing with labor regulation, health, social, economic, and other international regulatory issues were of immediate and lasting benefit to humanity. The United Nations Organization therefore carried forward many basic League structures and ideas, as well as its most successfully agencies.

See also Danzig.

Suggested Reading: F. P. Walters, *History of the League of Nations,* 2 vols. (1952); Inis Claude, *Swords Into Ploughshares* (1974).

LEAHY, WILLIAM (1875–1959)   U.S. admiral. A close friend of President Franklin D. Roosevelt, Leahy held top naval commands until FDR sent him to Vichy as ambassador. In 1942 he was appointed chairman of the *Joint Chiefs of Staff*. He was highly influential in that position as well as privately with the president, attending all major military and diplomatic conferences during the war.

LEAPFROGGING
   See island-hopping; passage of lines.

LEBANON   Lebanon became a League of Nations mandate territory following World War I, governed by France. In 1926 it became a republic while remaining a French mandate. After the fall of France to the Wehrmacht in June 1940, Lebanon was briefly governed by Vichy. In July 1941, *Free French* forces took control of Lebanon with British support, as part of the larger *Syrian campaign*. In 1946 Western troops withdrew and Lebanon became independent.

LEBENSBORN   "Spring of life" or "Source of Life." The *Schutzstaffel (SS)* eugenics program that sought to produce "racially sound" German babies, mainly by selective breeding with SS-men based on quack race theories but also by kidnapping "German-looking" children from occupied countries and even the *concentration camps*. As many as 300,000 children may have been abducted. About 12,000 Lebensborn children are believed to have been sired by SS fathers, then "baptized" into *Nazism* in an SS ceremony. After the war, many Lebensborn children were disowned, shunned, or even institutionalized in psychiatric facilities. Some later sued their Nazi adoptive parents.
   See also Aryan.

LEBENSRAUM   "Living space." The euphemism used by Adolf Hitler for land to be taken by force from the Slavic and other peoples (Jews, Roma) of central Europe and the Soviet Union. For Hitler and his military advisers the immediate purpose of acquiring Lebensraum was to gain access to the food and mineral resources of a continental empire sufficient to permit a future war with the United States. Hitler's vision of Lebensraum was therefore closely related to his strategy of achieving *autarky* for the German economy and *Volk*, and was the most persistent and essential idea in his crude ideology. Among the *Nazi Party* elite the idea of Lebensraum had a more romantic meaning. It captured a dream of *Aryan* soldier-farmers expanding a racial and agrarian empire eastward, as ethnic Germans resettled conquered lands whose native populations had been expelled or killed. Hitler laid out plans for war and radical expansion of the Greater Reich's "Lebensraum" in the "*Hossbach memorandum*," a two-hour rant delivered to an audience of unprotesting generals in November 1937. First the Czech lands and Austria would be absorbed, he said. Non-German populations would be deported or used as forced labor, their agricultural and manpower bounty added to the power of the "Third Reich." Early in the war, the *Schutzstaffel (SS)* began to settle Germans on expropriated lands to the east. It even received initial cooperation from the *NKVD* during 1939–1940: in accordance with the terms of the *Nazi–Soviet Pact*, the NKVD was also busy deporting anti-Soviet Balts and Poles from newly annexed territory, and facilitated SS population transfers in those and related areas.

It is crucial to understand that Hitler saw Great Britain and France, not the Soviet Union, as standing in the way of Germany's imperial expansion. That remained true into the late 1930s, even as he came to despise the Western Allies as unlikely to ever oppose him with force. He intended to destroy the minor enemies of Czechoslovakia and Poland, a timetable he accelerated from 1938 after being frustrated in his hope for war by the settlement arranged at the *Munich Conference*. He wanted Germany fully rearmed by 1943, at which point he foresaw war in the west to complete his dream of a new *Mitteleuropa*. That would be followed by an all-out assault on the Soviet Union, but in a secondary war that he regarded as less immediate, important, or potentially difficult than the critical fight against the French and, especially, the British. That vision was shared by most of his advisers and Feldmarschälle following his 1938 purge of top Wehrmacht leaders who opposed plans for war with the West, a move that led to Hitler's personal takeover of the OKW. Moreover, Hitler repeatedly rejected Japanese proposals for a joint war against the Soviet Union because he feared that a premature attack would force Moscow into the arms of the Western Allies. Instead, to the great consternation of Tokyo, Hitler agreed to the Nazi–Soviet Pact on August 23, 1939.

See also autarky; Einsatzgruppen; geopolitik; Nazism; Rassenkampf; volksdeutsch.

LECLERC, PHILIPPE (1902–1947) Né Philippe Hauteclocque. French general. As a junior officer, Leclerc joined General *Charles de Gaulle* in Britain immediately upon the fall of France in June 1940. He was sent to French Equatorial Africa and quickly showed political and military acumen by securing a West African base for the *Free French* movement. He led Free French forces in the *Fezzan campaign* in 1941–1943, then held a subordinate command in Tunisia. He next led French 2nd Armored Division in France from the end of July 1944, taking the honor of liberating Paris on August 25. His division fought as part of U.S. 3rd Army into southern Germany in 1945. Leclerc was sent to French Indochina after the war, where he was less than solicitous of local Viet or Cambodian rights and freedoms than he had been those of Frenchmen. He was posthumously elevated to the rank of "Maréchal de France."

LEDO ROAD A high mountain road, and parallel pipeline, built by the Americans through northern Burma in 1943–1945, to bring supplies to *Jiang Jieshi* and the *Guomindang* in southern China. It was planned to replace a cut-off section of the *Burma Road*, which fell under Japanese control in 1942. It was a hugely expensive engineering effort that led to little or no strategic gain, as the fulcrum of the war against Japan moved to the Central Pacific.

See also Burma campaign (1943–1945); Hump; Stilwell, Joseph.

LEEB, WILHELM VON (1876–1956) German field marshal. He served with the Imperial German expedition in China, 1901–1902, then as a staff officer during World War I. A Bavarian by birth, in 1922 he helped put down Adolf Hitler's *Beer Hall Putsch*. He was one of several top commanders sacked in 1938 for opposing Hitler's aggressive plans for war. Recalled in 1939, he opposed the invasion of Poland. But he saluted his superiors and his Führer and agreed to command Army Group "C" in *FALL GELB* in 1940. During *BARBAROSSA*, the mid-1941 invasion of the Soviet Union, Leeb set aside all strategic objections and any lingering moral qualms to command Army Group North in the drive through the Baltic states, then on to Leningrad. Despairing of victory in the snows of Russia during the *Moscow offensive operation*, Leeb requested retirement in January 1942. Hitler eagerly granted the request. After the war Leeb was convicted by the *Nuremberg Tribunal* for acceding to illegal orders from Hitler and the OKW. He was sentenced to time served and released in 1948.

LEESE, OLIVER (1894–1978) British general. His career closely followed that of General *Bernard Law Montgomery*, who was an early admirer when Leese was one of his corps commanders in Africa, Sicily, and Italy. Leese was a competent and tough general officer who succeeded Montgomery as commander of British 8th Army in December 1943. During the *Italian campaign*, Leese and 8th Army finally broke though the *Gustav Line*. In November 1944, he was promoted to command 11th Army Group in Burma. But after he criticized *Louis Mountbatten*, he was relieved in July 1945.

LEGION OF ST. GEORGE "St. Georgs-Legion."
   See Waffen-SS.

LEIBSTANDARTE-SS "Adolf Hitler Division." One of the elite Panzer divisions of the *Waffen-SS*. Originally, it was a small personal *Schutzstaffel (SS)* bodyguard to Adolf Hitler led by *Otto Skorzeny*. It supplied the murderers who gained Hitler's favor by killing former comrades in the *Sturmabteilung (SA)* during the *Night of the Long Knives* in June 1934. The unit was rewarded with expansion to battalion size, then with the right to form a full-scale, armed SS-division. In 1943 a "Leibstandarte Adolf Hitler" 1st SS Panzer Korps was formed. Undersized and therefore overnamed, it fought in Ukraine in 1943, in Normandy in mid-1944, and along the Rhine in late-1944. Rested and refitted, it was one of the crack units (though always much smaller than a full corps) that launched the *Ardennes offensive* in December 1944. Badly attrited in that fight with the Americans, it was pulled out of Belgium in January 1945. Its last battles were in Hungary and Austria. Its remnants surrendered near Vienna in May 1945.

LEIGH LIGHT A powerful searchlight fitted to the wings of British bombers to illuminate surfaced U-boats that had been first fixed by ASV (Airborne Surface

Vessel) *radar*. The Leigh Light was attached to the standard gun mount. Hence, the beam was adjustable by the flight crew. The first generation needed a large aircraft to house its generator. It was simple and effective but late to be deployed: the first working sets were mounted only in June 1942. Leigh Lights thereafter caught stunned U-boats and crews in bright beams as bombs or *depth charges* were dropped. That development led Admiral *Karl Dönitz* to order all U-boats to remain submerged at night, using daylight to surface and recharge batteries while anxious scouts scanned the sky for aircraft. But daylight surface running had other dangers, and put a severe limitation on U-boat operations even as it exposed many U-boats to being caught and destroyed on the surface by warships.

LEIGH-MALLORY, TRAFFORD (1892–1944)   RAF air marshal. He commanded No. 12 Fighter Group during the *Battle of Britain* in 1940, during which he argued persistently with Air Marshal *Hugh Dowding* over "Big Wing" vs. squadron fighter tactics. Leigh-Mallory won the political argument and rose to head Fighter Command in November 1942. Neither RAF Bomber Command nor the USAAF would agree to hand authority over their bomber forces to a man whose sole experience was with fighters, so the command of tactical bombing leading into the invasion of Europe went to *Arthur Tedder* instead. Leigh-Mallory's most important contribution came during the *OVERLORD* landings and campaign, when he commanded all tactical air forces in the northwest theater. He was killed in an air crash in November 1944, while on his way to take up a new command in Southeast Asia.

LEMAY, CURTIS (1906–1990)   USAAF general. LeMay led the early American bombing effort from England in 1942, evolving his views about *area bombing* vs. *precision bombing* along with the capacity and experience of the USAAF. His most important role came in Asia from August 1944, first in China then over Japan. LeMay took command of U.S. 20th Air Force bombing operations and shifted the whole style of B-29 bombing of Japan from high altitude to low-level. Yet, he was not the revolutionary he is often said to have been: he did not change bombing tactics for two months, and not before he was threatened with being sacked by his dissatisfied superiors. In response to pressure to perform as well as to monsoon conditions that lowered the bombing ceiling, LeMay stripped B-29s of much of their armament and brought them down into fighter and anti-aircraft range. That displeased crews but enabled them to devastate Tokyo and over 60 other Japanese cities with massive incendiary raids that created terrible firestorms. Although he was not original in developing the theory or operations of low-level firestorm bombing—the USAAF was aware for many years of the potential to burn Japanese cities—he oversaw implementation of the policy on a massive scale.

See also pattern bombing.

LEND-LEASE   President Franklin Roosevelt was desperate to extend aid to Britain for its war effort against Germany, but he faced enormous opposition within

Congress. In a close vote in March 1941, he obtained authority to extend food and matériel assistance to all countries he deemed "vital to the defense" of the United States. This "Lend-Lease" aid was also supposed to help bring about "the end of compromise with tyranny," which made the policy an act of effective intervention while the United States was still formally neutral. The political and psychological effect in Tokyo was to advance a sense of encirclement by hostile powers and persuade the Japanese Army that the Japanese Navy's belief in inevitable war with the United States was correct. In stark contrast, already deep into preparations for invasion of the Soviet Union, Adolf Hitler reinforced a standing policy of avoiding provocation of the United States in the Atlantic. He even ordered additional restraints on the attack authority given to U-boat captains. Other military effects of Lend-Lease took longer to manifest. Significant aid was sent to Britain immediately, growing to huge amounts over the course of the war. Some aid was also quickly sent to China, but delivery by air over the *Hump* to southern China was much more difficult than delivery to Britain. Aid to the *Guomindang* was curtailed in 1944 as FDR realized his military hopes for a major Chinese contribution to the defeat of Japan were largely illusory. Lend-Lease was also given in small amounts to many minor states, including Abyssinia, several Latin American belligerents, Allied provisional governments, Allied governments-in-exile, and even discrete colonies of occupied European powers. Countries occupied by the Allies, such as Iran and Iraq, also received some aid. Important shipments of Lend-Lease went to the Soviet Union in a flow that expanded from a trickle in 1941–1942 under the first two of four "protocols," to a river of aid from 1943 under the third and fourth protocols.

Where the British moved immediately to supply Moscow with what aid they could, and fought through heavy German opposition to desperate Arctic *convoys* to deliver it, Roosevelt was compelled to engage in deep and creative deceit to undercut isolationist and Catholic opposition to aiding Stalin fight Hitler. Lend-Lease was thus extended to the Soviet Union only on November 7, 1941, several months after it was invaded by Germany and other Axis states. Lend-Lease provided to the Soviet war effort included: 25 percent of all food supplies available in the Soviet Union from 1942 to 1945; 2.6 million tons of oil; 12,200 armored vehicles, including "Valentine," "Matilda," and "Churchill" British tanks, and "Lee," "Stuart," and "Sherman" American tanks; 132,000 machine guns; more than 18,000 combat aircraft and nearly 15,000 aircraft engines; 1,860 train locomotives—the Soviet Union produced only 32 locomotives domestically during the war—and almost 12,000 boxcars; 410,000 heavy trucks and jeeps; 420,000 field telephone sets; bolts of cloth sufficient for millions of uniforms; 15 million pairs of military boots; millions of tons of rails, steel, explosives, metals, and minerals; and one million miles of telephone cable and 35,000 radio stations essential to command and control of the expanding Red Army. Of this war matériel, the locomotives and trucks had the most direct impact on Soviet fighting power by greatly improving battlefield and rear area logistics.

Aid moved to Soviet frontiers via three main routes: Arctic convoys (about 25 percent), overland through Iran (another 25 percent), and across the Pacific to Vladivostok, thence via the Siberian railway to the Eastern Front in Europe (half of all shipments). The Siberian route remained open despite Japan's membership in the *Tripartite Pact* and *Axis alliance*: the Imperial Japanese Navy did not interfere with American Lend-Lease supplies shipped into Vladivostok. Tokyo feared Soviet bombing of the Japanese home islands if it did try to stop the aid, or an attack into Manchuria or northern China, or Moscow's agreement to allow American bomber bases in Siberia. In exchange, the Soviet Union remained officially neutral in the Pacific War and refused to allow American aircraft to bomb Japan from bases located on Soviet territory. No Soviet second front was opened in the Pacific until August 9, 1945. The fact that the Pacific route stayed open to the end of the German–Soviet war, helping Russians killed very large numbers of Germans, was a source of much argument and friction between Tokyo and Berlin. It also typified the failure of the Axis powers to coordinate military strategy or view or run their separate wars in Asia and Europe as a connected, world conflict. The Western Allies did not make that mistake.

One sign of prominence of certain types of Lend-Lease was the American words that entered Russian daily speech during the war, including "Studabaker" for heavy truck, as well as "Spam." Driving those trucks and fighting and dying inside uniforms made of American cloth or while wearing U.S. combat boots were millions of ordinary Soviet soldiers. For that reason, Soviet official accounts of the war downplayed the contribution of Lend-Lease to final victory. Academic controversy in the West also waxed and waned over the importance of Lend-Lease. The most recent Russian official history broke with old denials of the significance of Lend-Lease to note that 70 percent of the Red Army's transport was composed of Western-made vehicles. Studebaker and GM heavy trucks were especially important in the spectacular Red Army *deep battle* operations of 1944, and may have been critical. A leading historian of the Soviet war effort, David Glantz, summarized the contribution this way: "Without Lend-Lease trucks, rail engines, and railroad cars, every Soviet offensive would have stalled at an earlier stage . . . forcing the Soviet Army to prepare and conduct many more deliberate penetration attacks to advance the same distance." A balanced view should recognize that Lend-Lease aid did not arrive in enough quantity or in time to stem the initial heavy onslaught of the Wehrmacht in the east. Only an ocean of Soviet blood and raw courage did that during the 18 dark months that followed the Axis invasion. However, given the enormous economic damage and dislocation of the Soviet economy suffered into 1942, the importance of Lend-Lease as a bridge to recovery in the second half of the war, then continuing supply of vital raw materials in support of Soviet war production, should not be doubted. Lend-Lease was not critical to the survival and recovery of the Soviet Union in the darkest days of 1941–1942, but it certainly speeded Soviet victory in the second half of the war.

Overall, Lend-Lease provided Britain, the Commonwealth Dominions, and other smaller Allies with badly needed supplies far beyond British or others' ability to finance or produce. As importantly, it placed the U.S. economy on a near-war footing heading into the second half of 1941, and thus quickened vital conversion of factories to full war production many months before the United States entered the war. It provided real, though not decisive, assistance to the Soviet Union, helping it recover military production from the desperate days of shortage in 1941–1942. It matched thereby Soviet manpower with American industrial power in a mutually reinforcing combination that proved lethal to German ambitions. By the end of the war the United States provided sufficient war matériel of all kinds to its many allies for them to raise and equip 2,000 division equivalents. That was the single most decisive economic fact determining the final outcome of the war. The aid supplied was most important in sustaining British and Commonwealth forces. Great Britain received 43 percent of Lend-Lease supplies. By comparison, the Soviet Union received 29 percent of all Lend-Lease aid.

President Harry Truman announced on August 1, 1945, that Lend-Lease would end within the month. It had cost the United States $48.5 billion. The program formally ended on August 21, reputedly causing deep rancor in Moscow for which some have sharply criticized Truman. Unpersuasively, some academics even pointed to the decision as a supposed cause, or at least trigger, of the Cold War. That conclusion ignores the fact that Lend-Lease was always intended to be a strictly wartime program and that it was cut off to Britain and 36 other nations at the same time. More fundamentally, the argument trivializes Stalin's postwar intentions and ambitions by attributing his actions almost to pique over American policy. Great Britain repaid in full and retired its last Lend-Lease war debts to the United States on December 31, 2006. A smaller, Canadian aid program that paralleled Lend-Lease was known as *Mutual Aid*.

See also Air Transport Auxiliary; Air Transport Command; Alaska; America First Committee; amphibious operations; ARCADIA conference; Atlantic Ferry Organization; BAGRATION; Churchill, Winston; Free French; Guomindang; Leningrad, siege of; Polish Army; radio; Roosevelt, Franklin D.; sub-chasers; War Zones.

Suggested Reading: Alan Dobson, *U.S. Wartime Aid to Britain, 1940–1946* (1986); George Herring, *Aid to Russia* (1973); Roger Muntin, *Feeding the Bear* (1989).

LENINGRAD, SIEGE OF (SEPTEMBER 8, 1941–JANUARY 27, 1944)   The great siege of Leningrad is known in Russia as the "blockada." Army Group North approached Leningrad in mid-August 1941. It was urged forward by a fascination the city exerted for Adolf Hitler as a long-despised source of Slavic influence over Europe, as well as Leningrad's strategic importance as a major Baltic port and center of Soviet war manufacture, especially of heavy KV-1 tanks. It was surrounded by Army Group North on three sides by September 1941. Leon Gure argues that Leningrad should have fallen to the Wehrmacht that autumn. It did not because defenses firmed as the front contracted and because Hitler transferred key Panzer and mobile forces south to reinforce the renewed Army Group Center attack on Moscow (Operation *TAIFUN*). Half a million people fled or were evacuated from the city before it was cut off, including many children whose parents remained to work in the city's factories. Except for barge traffic across Lake Ladoga, remaining civilians could not get out once the Germans and Finns closed on three sides of the city, and precious little food, fuel, or ammunition arrived. German artillery kept up a near-constant bombardment until they were pushed back to extreme range by local Soviet counterattacks. Another limiting factor on the artillery threat was a lack of heavy siege guns in the batteries of Army Group North: most of the Wehrmacht's siege train was far to the south, hard-pounding *Sebastopol*.

Inside the besieged northern city conditions grew progressively worse at the approach of the first winter of the German–Soviet war. Heavy ammunition and food trucks ran in endless columns, unloading vital cargo onto lake barges until Lake Ladoga grew treacherous with ice. Barge traffic was limited by a lack of harbors and lake craft, which Soviet authorities now scrambled to build. During that dread first autumn and again in the spring, before Ladoga fully froze and just after it began to melt, the only way to bring in supplies to Leningrad was by air, but by then the VVS had been ravaged in fighting all along the Eastern Front. When deep winter set in during December, long columns of trucks navigated a treacherous and constantly shifting ice trail, the "Road of Life" ("doroga zhisni"), across Lake Ladoga, for that was the only way into the city after the Germans occupied the last land bridge, the Shlisselburg corridor. Fortunately, the Luftwaffe was far less effective in bombing the city, barges, or truck convoys than *Hermann Göring* promised his Führer: the Germans had too few planes in the north and the wrong types for effective city bombing. More docks and barges were added, protected by anti-aircraft guns. Over time, lighter Soviet trucks would be replaced on the ice road by heavier American 3-ton and 5-ton models, shipped to the Soviet Union under the *Lend-Lease* program. But during the first winter of the siege there was not enough transport and far too few goods arriving, especially food and fuel, to both sustain Leningrad's swollen civilian population and supply its defenders with the means to hold out.

Even as much larger battles before Moscow and at Viazma-Rzhev were underway, Joseph Stalin and the Stavka ordered an attack to relieve Leningrad: the result was the failed and costly *Liuban offensive operation (January 7–April 30, 1942)*. While it was in progress the population of the old imperial capital suffered the worst winter of starvation and death of its nearly 900-day siege. Food and fuel were quickly exhausted by a city population bloated with refugees. Trucks traveling the "Road of Life" that winter carried mostly ammunition. The trickle of food that arrived was given, out of military necessity, mainly to soldiers manning trenches and batteries along the perimeter defense or struggling through forest and bog in weak, premature offensive operations. More than a million civilians starved or froze to death during that first dread winter of the siege. Two million more emerged in the spring as mere skeletons, having eaten rats, polish, boiled leather soup, tree bark, anything. Some had consumed human flesh. Order was kept by the *NKVD*, which did not let up arrests or executions even as those dead from more natural causes piled all around the city's prisons and in its parks and streets. Yet, Leningrad and its defenders held out until spring reopened the Lake to barge traffic. Then barges took out 500,000 civilians over the first half of 1942, reducing the population from a presiege level of well over three million (mainly women engaged in war work, and their dependents) to just under 800,000 in July, then to a sustainable 600,000 by the end of the year. Leningrad stayed under siege, but it became a symbol of Soviet resolution and much more, of an extraordinary capacity of ordinary people to endure calamitous evil and suffering, and to survive.

For 28 months Leningrad was besieged. Repeated efforts to break through the German encirclement failed. Its defense turned into a World War I–style fight of trenches, mortars, shelling, and frozen mud. The defenders in Leningrad Front would lose 317,000 men, while Volkhov Front lost just under 300,000 before the siege was lifted. The Red Army's *Siniavino offensive operation (August 19–October 20, 1942)* to break the German hold on the Shlisselburg corridor failed dismally, but had the merit of interrupting a German offensive to envelop Leningrad slated for September: *NORDLICHT*. In January 1943, the Red Army began a third counteroffensive to relieve Leningrad: *SPARK* was a concerted drive to restore a land link to the city. Guided by freshly promoted Marshal *Georgi Zhukov*, the attack began on January 12, 1943. Six days later Shlisselburg fell. The siege was not over, but a critical land bridge varying from five to seven miles wide was opened, curving around the south shore of Lake Ladoga. Engineers speedily laid a new rail line through the corridor. During the *Battle of Kursk* and follow-on operations *KUTUZOV* and *RUMIANTSEV* in July–August, 1943, a small offensive was also assayed to widen the land corridor of Lake Ladoga and to prevent Army Group North from reinforcing German positions farther south. It was minimally effective, but cost over 21,000 Soviet casualties. More relief came as a result of Operation *SUVOROV (August 7–October 2, 1943)*: two tank armies attacked the hinge of the two Wehrmacht army groups, Center and North, and pushed the Germans from Nevel.

On January 4, 1944, the Red Army began its "Leningrad-Novgorod offensive operation." It was conducted by three Fronts comprising 1.25 million men and 1,600 tanks and self-propelled guns, spread across a frontage of 300 miles. The VVS flew nearly 1,400 aircraft over the operation, a figure the Luftwaffe could no longer match. Army Group North had 740,000 men but few tanks, guns, or aircraft. Among its units were less reliable or competent *Luftwaffe field divisions* and inexperienced Nordic troops of the *Waffen-SS*. The offensive unfolded as three loosely coordinated operations by the separate attacking Fronts. Instead of starting from the Shlisselburg corridor—the jump-off position of three earlier and failed Soviet offensives in the Leningrad region—the attack came from the southwest: 44,000 troops struck out from the Oranienbaum (Lomonosov) pocket. A second thrust started in the outer suburbs of Leningrad. Together, these two attacks overran the German siege guns that had plagued the citizens of Leningrad for two years. Army Group North hastily evacuated its last toehold in the Shlisselburg corridor and was harried back to the Neva and Luga Rivers. Novgorod was liberated on January 20. A week later the blockade of Leningrad was finally broken when the Moscow railway was reopened. The Soviet breakthrough and pursuit of German 18th Army was not a complete victory, however: the Germans were not encircled or smashed, but instead slipped away in a fairly orderly withdrawal. Many lived to fight and kill Russians on some future bloody day.

During the first two weeks of February German 18th Army fell back another 100 miles to the old border with Estonia, for a total retreat distance of 150 miles in some places. Hitler still would not grant the urgent request by Army Group North commander, Field Marshal *Georg von Küchler,* to be allowed to withdraw to the more defensible position of the *Panther Line.* Instead, Hitler sacked Küchler and replaced him with Field Marshal *Walter Model.* The new commander was able to halt the Soviet offensive in front of Narva and Pskov during the first week of March. Model was greatly aided by an early onset of the northern *rasputitsa,* well-prepared field positions, and the heavily wooded and swampy terrain that impeded Red Army tank movement. By April, with Model called south to put out another of the fires then breaking out along the Eastern Front, most of German 18th Army had escaped the planned Soviet trap and fallen back to the Panther Line. Hitler demanded that new position be held, issuing another *Haltebefehl order.* The line was held, until July 1944. The Red Army was thus stopped shy of its short-term goal of reentering Estonia. After 28 months of siege—nearly 900 days—Leningrad surged back to life, 150 miles behind the frontline and safe from German guns and bombs.

Suggested Reading: Leon Goure, *The Siege of Leningrad* (1962); Bruce Lincoln, *Sunlight at Midnight* (2002).

LENINGRAD-NOVGOROD OFFENSIVE OPERATION (JANUARY–FEBRUARY, 1944)
See Leningrad, siege of.

LÉOPOLD III (1901–1983)
See Belgium.

LEYTE GULF, BATTLE OF (OCTOBER 23–26, 1944)
The largest of all naval battles in history, and among the most confusing to follow and difficult to report. Like many naval battles, Leyte was decided as much by sheer luck, mistaken identity, and miscommunication as it was by the fear, courage, and skill that were also evident in abundance on both sides. Before it was over, Leyte Gulf—or "Second Battle of the Philippine Sea"—saw major engagements in the Sibuyan Sea, the Surigao Strait, and off Samar Island, as three Japanese task forces were sent to intercept a large U.S. invasion force converging on Leyte. The Imperial Japanese Navy devised a complex battle plan that called for decoy action to lure away the powerful American carrier forces. U.S. 3rd Fleet was commanded by Admiral *William Halsey,* whom the Japanese knew to be recklessly aggressive. Their decoy maneuver was to be followed by closely coordinated pincer attacks against the landing force and its U.S. 7th Fleet escort. The strike on the landing force was to be made by two different surface groups of the IJN Combined Fleet, under overall command of Admiral Soemu Toyoda.

The action began with Japanese deployment of an immensely powerful flotilla of five battleships, including the two largest in history, the sister ships "Yamato" and "Musashi," and 16 heavy cruisers. This was Admiral *Jizaburō Ozawa's* 1st Mobile Force, sent to pound the landing zones and supporting ships of U.S. 7th Fleet.

Ozawa split his complement into two strike forces. Meanwhile, a four-carrier decoy force—there were no longer enough Japanese pilots or planes to operate the ships as carriers—and escorts set out to lure U.S. 3rd Fleet's massive and powerful carrier forces north. Halsey bit hard on the bait of another prospective carrier vs. carrier victory for the U.S. Navy. The critical result was to draw the main strength of the American fleet away from the landing sites. That was a tactical error of the first order, from which Halsey's reputation never recovered. It very nearly led to a major Japanese naval victory while exposing the landing forces to a potentially terrible and bloody naval bombardment. Halsey compounded his error by not ensuring that a designated task force, TF-34, was actually where he thought it was and told his superiors it was: readying to defend the landing zones and ships against the Japanese "Center Force" of battleships and cruisers led by Vice Admiral Takeo Kurita, then headed straight for the invasion area. In fact, Halsey's excessive aggression and reporting errors about TF-34 meant the path to the invasion beaches was wide open to Kurita's ships.

The first naval action took place in the Palawan Passage on October 23, when U.S. submarines on picket patrol spotted "Center Force" steaming at high speed and sank Kurita's heavy cruiser from under him. Kurita was rescued, transferred his flag to a destroyer, and remained in command. But he was shaken and now more full of doubt and caution than before the submarine attack, a factor that played a vital role in the outcome of the larger fight. American naval air superiority and a new capability in night fighting on the surface ensured that Kurita would not succeed. USN pilots caught Kurita's strike force steaming at high speed across the Sibuyan Sea. They sank the "Musashi," scored hits on the "Yamato," and damaged several cruisers. These severe losses caused Kurita to turn back. The second Japanese strike force was then caught in the Surigao Strait and utterly savaged by PT-boats and a wave of USN destroyers that made high-speed torpedo runs, followed up by pounding from U.S. battleships and cruisers. It was the last time battleships engaged battleships in naval history. Only a single Japanese destroyer survived the terrific onslaught. In the meantime, Kurita turned around and again raced through the San Bernardino Strait, heading for the landing zones that were still exposed by Halsey's error.

A small task force of U.S. escort carriers was caught by surprise by the appearance of "Center Force" close to the Leyte landing sites. Kurita chased the slow carrier group down and hit it hard off Samar Island, sinking two escort carriers, two destroyers, and a destroyer escort. One of the small carriers was sunk with aid of a new force that first appeared earlier in the battle: land-based *kamikaze*. However, a combination of bravery, skill, and luck allowed aircraft from the escort carriers to sink two of Kurita's cruisers, while a U.S. destroyer attacked, damaged, and slowed a third. The little carriers and their escorts had defended themselves so well Kurita thought the naval forces between him and the landing zones were more powerful than they actually were. He believed the slow escort group was actually the U.S. fast carrier force, TF-58, which was in fact far to the north chasing the Japanese decoy carriers. The landing sites, troop transports, and supply ships were utterly exposed, had Kurita chosen to assault them. Instead, his losses persuaded Kurita to turn around for the second time and seek safety for his surviving ships by retraversing the San Bernardino Strait.

While those desperate actions were underway around the landing zones, Halsey caught and sank the four Japanese decoy carriers. The IJN thus lost two of its last surviving fleet carriers, including the "Zuikaku," which had launched strikes at *Pearl Harbor*. In addition to these vital carriers, Japan lost 3 battleships, 6 heavy cruisers, 3 light cruisers, and 10 destroyers. Yet, an even greater defeat could have been inflicted on the Japanese had Halsey not steamed so far north that Kurita was able to escape with a flotilla of important surface ships intact. Also escaping was part of Ozawa's northern group. American forces were hard hit in return for their victory, which was a much closer-run affair than the final tally of lost lives and 300,000 lost Japanese tons to 38,000 American tons of warships suggests. Even so, the victory for the U.S. Navy and accompanying Australian and other Allied warships at Leyte effectively ended Japan's naval air presence in the Pacific. It thereby opened up an unimpeded invasion of the Philippines and cleared a path for later invasions of *Okinawa* and the Japanese home islands.

Suggested Reading: Thomas Cutler, *Battle of Leyte Gulf, 23–26 October, 1944* (1994); H. P. Willmott, *The Battle of Leyte Gulf: The Last Fleet Action* (2005).

LIBERTY SHIPS Technically, the EC2 cargo ship built by the U.S. Maritime Commission. The term was also popularly used for all prefabricated, modular cargo ships turned out by U.S. *shipyards* during the war. Rather than building more slowly from frames, as was common in Britain and Canada, U.S. companies mass produced the EC2 in assembly-line fashion by welding together 250-ton modules brought to the yards by train. Initially built to fill orders placed by Britain, the first EC2 was launched in September 1941. Another 2,750 followed, each completed in 70–90 days, at up to three ships per day at peak production. Each Liberty Ship could carry 9,000 tons of cargo, or nearly 3,000 crated jeeps or 450 Sherman tanks or gross equivalent, while making 12 knots fully loaded. They were armed for antisubmarine and anti-aircraft defense, which meant that in addition to a *merchant marine* crew of 52, they carried a naval party of 29 men. They served in all naval theaters of operations.

See also troop ships.

LIBYA
See Tripoli.

LICHTENSTEIN-GERÄT German night-fighter air-to-air *radar*. It was very short-range, at about two miles. It was countered by the RAF *Serrate* receiver.

LIDICE MASSACRE
See Heydrich, Reinhard.

LIECHTENSTEIN
See neutral states.

LIGHT NIGHT STRIKING FORCE (LNSF)   An RAF light bomber force founded in 1943. It employed "Mosquito" bombers to conduct "spoof raids" as diversions from the main bomber attacks. Initially attacking with just two or three aircraft, LNSF raids utilized one or more of 11 squadrons of "Mosquitos" available by late 1944.

LIGURIAN ARMY   The last organized Axis force left in Italy at the end of the war. It was comprised of one Wehrmacht corps and the *fascist* Italian "Lombardia Corps." It surrendered along with other Axis remnants in Italy effective May 2, 1945.

LIMITED LIABILITY   The prewar defense policy of Great Britain, under which no formal alliance was agreed with France and all joint military arrangements were considered contingent, not binding.

LIMPET MINE
See mines.

LIN BIAO (1907–1971)   Also known as Lin Piao. Communist marshal. Born into a working-class family, Lin Biao graduated from a leading *Guomindang* military academy in 1926. As a young officer he fought in the Northern Expedition, 1926–1927, before leading his regiment out of the Guomindang to join the armed forces of the Communist Party. He supported *Mao Zedong* in the Jiangxi Soviet, in 1927–1934, and fought against *Jiang Jieshi* in the "bandit suppression" campaign of 1934. He commanded a corps during the "Long March" and held combat commissions again during the *Sino-Japanese War*. He scored a notable victory against the invading Japanese in 1937 but fared less well in the 1940 campaign. He spent much of the remainder of the war organizing Communist guerrillas behind Japanese lines.

LINDEMAN, FREDERICK (1886–1957)   "Professor Lindeman." The head of a team of eight academic statisticians who advised Winston Churchill on any technical or scientific matter he cared to ask them to assess, from domestic material and food consumption rates, to bombing accuracy, to the German *V-weapons program* and Western Allied secret weapons research. His team's baleful but highly influential report on *precision bombing* reinforced the Butt Report and persuaded Churchill and RAF Bomber Command to switch to a clear policy of *area bombing*.

LINE   The most dangerous area of the front when strategic maneuver was replaced by static defense, and friendly units were in direct proximity to enemy troops.
See combat zone; front; frontline.

LION Signals code for British 21st Army Group.

LIST, WILHELM (1880–1971) German field marshal. He led an army in the invasion of Poland (*FALL WEISS*) in 1939, and in the invasion of France in 1940 (*FALL GELB*). He achieved real prominence with his swift assault on Yugoslavia and Greece in April 1941. He returned to France in early 1942. His first command on the Eastern Front was to lead Army Group "A" in the *EDELWEISS* offensive into the North Caucasus in July 1942. He was dismissed by Adolf Hitler on September 9, along with *Franz Halder*. Both firings were made over vehement objection by *Alfred Jodl*. List never again was given an active command. He was captured by the Western Allies in 1945. After the war he was convicted of war crimes committed in the Balkans. He was sentenced to life but was released on grounds of ill health in 1952.

LISTENING POST
See cossack post.

LITHUANIA Lithuania was assigned to Germany under the original terms of the *Nazi–Soviet Pact (August 23, 1939)*. It was then traded in future consideration to Moscow in an addendum agreed at the end of September, in exchange for the central section of Soviet-occupied eastern Poland. The swap may have been intended by Adolf Hitler as punishment for Lithuania refusing to participate in his invasion of Poland, or as a ruse because he fully intended to retake the territory at some future date. In June 1940, the Red Army moved into Lithuania and the *NKVD* began a purge and deportation of all Lithuanians identified as anti-Soviet. Lithuania was annexed by the Soviet Union in August 1940. Moscow offered to buy that piece of Lithuania promised to Germany, which its troops had also occupied in August. Berlin accepted in principle, but stalled in practice while it prepared to retake all Lithuania once it attacked the Soviet Union in *BARBAROSSA* in June 1941.

The Soviet move into Lithuania exposed large numbers of Red Army troops in less well-prepared positions than the ones they departed, a fact that cost the Soviets dearly when Army Group North attacked. Lithuania was quickly overrun by the Germans, a fact greeted by many of its citizens as constituting a liberation. Instead, Lithuania was soon thereafter annexed to Germany as part of the *Reichskommissariat Ostland*. It was occupied by Germany from 1941 to 1944. Collaboration with Nazi authorities was extensive: some Lithuanians joined the *Waffen-SS;* others assisted in extermination of Lithuanian Jews. The Red Army returned in January 1944, again accompanied by the NKVD. The second Soviet occupation was more brutal in its repression, after three years of hardening of Soviet attitudes in a total war with Germany. The Soviet Union proclaimed that its annexation of Lithuania stood, asserting the 1940 frontiers. The United States and some other Western states refused to recognize any of the Baltic annexations as legal and maintained relations with a Lithuanian government-in-exile throughout the Cold War. Most non-Western states accepted Lithuania as part of the Soviet Union until that empire became extinct in 1991.

LITTLE ENTENTE (1920–1939)   A system of interwar alliances among several small, post–World War I states lying between Germany and the Soviet Union. Czechoslovakia and Yugoslavia signed the first treaty in 1920. Both powers allied with Rumania in 1921. Separate agreements were incorporated into a single treaty system in 1929. The main purpose of the Little Entente was to prevent Austria or Hungary from reclaiming Habsburg lands lost in the Treaties of St. Germain and Trianon in 1919, at the end of the Great War. With the rise to power of Adolf Hitler in Germany, efforts were made to negotiate a defense pact with France. A right-wing shift in Yugoslavia after the assassination of Alexander I, marked by a new willingness to collaborate with aggrandizement by Germany, shook the Little Entente. The alliance did not survive the far more stunning Great Power outcome of the *Munich Conference* (1938), which shattered Czechoslovakia. Germany cunningly compounded that result by inviting other Little Entente powers to share in the Czech spoils. The alliance was formally dissolved in February 1939.

LITTLE SATURN (DECEMBER 1942)   Soviet code name for the offensive operation launched in December 1942, leading to an outer encirclement of German 6th Army and other Axis forces at *Stalingrad*.

LITVINOV, MAXIM MAXIMOVICH (1876–1951)   Soviet diplomat. Deputy foreign commissar, 1921–1930, 1939–1946; foreign commissar, 1930–1939; ambassador to the United States, 1941–1943. He consistently argued for closer Soviet ties to the Western powers. He got on superficially well with President Franklin D. Roosevelt while serving as the first Soviet ambassador in Washington. Litvinov argued for Moscow to support *collective security* measures under the auspices of the *League of Nations,* until the Soviet Union was expelled by the League for its aggression against Finland during the *Finnish–Soviet War (1939–1940)*. Following the *Munich Conference* in September 1938, Litvinov was replaced as foreign minister by *Vyacheslav Molotov*. The change appears to have been made in good measure to signal to Berlin that Joseph Stalin had real interest in a spheres of influence arrangement with Germany. Molotov negotiated the deal a few months later in the *Nazi–Soviet Pact*. Litvinov's survival of the purges of the 1930s, given his known Western proclivities and personal heritage as a Jew, was itself a singular political accomplishment. He was replaced as ambassador to United States on August 22, 1943, by Andrei Gromyko.

LIUBAN OFFENSIVE OPERATION (JANUARY 7–APRIL 30, 1942)   A failed Red Army operation on the northern flank of the *Moscow offensive operation (December 5, 1941–January 7, 1942)*. It was launched upon the demand of

Joseph Stalin that the Red Army stop defending and instead attack. It was conducted by a newly formed and understrength Volkhov Front under Marshal *Kiril A. Meretskov*, who was released from torture sessions in an *NKVD* prison to take command. Meretskov's weak attack was feebly supported by Leningrad Front under General M. S. Khozin. The initial aim of the offensive was to push the Germans back from the main Leningrad–Moscow railway, which they had cut, and thereby relieve the *siege of Leningrad*. Its larger aim was a premature insistence by Stalin that Army Group North must be enveloped and wiped out. The offensive failed in both ambitions, even though the Red Army enjoyed superior numbers in tanks and other ground forces. A lack of reliable air cover was part of the problem, as was timing. Meretskov was ordered to attack too soon, and therefore could put just two infantry armies into the opening assault. The real cause of failure, however, was excess strategic ambition by Stalin and some on the Stavka that led to dilution of Soviet forces across too many counterattacks at once along too many hundreds of miles of the Eastern Front. This problem was compounded by a still incoherent command structure, which overtaxed the Stavka with too many simultaneous operations, sapped initiative from on-scene commanders, and permitted the Germans to concentrate inferior forces to repeatedly achieve local superiority of numbers and combat power. The defeat for the Red Army that ensued at Liuban was hard and bitter. It was also essentially predicted by General *Georgi Zhukov*, who was still angry decades later about Stalin's wastage of lives and military effort.

Meretskov made little headway in the dense forests and sparsely populated bog land around Leningrad, as fighting degenerated into endless small-unit actions that were bloody and exhausting in their cumulative effect. During the campaign nearly 100,000 Red Army casualties were added to a list already comprising millions of names from the defeats of 1941. Meretskov was reinforced by an elite force, 2nd Shock Army, which broke through the German line. Command and control of the advance was shoddy, however, as two flanking armies failed to support this breakthrough, thereby dangerously exposing 2nd Shock Army's flanks. Nor did the lead units properly exploit their new position. After some confused movement, the campaign centered on a fight for control of the critical rail junction at Liuban. A counterattack by elements of Army Group North, code named RAUBTIER or "Predator," began in March. It cut off 2nd Shock Army along the Volkhov River, preempting the possibility that the Germans might themselves be trapped. The ground attack was strongly supported by the Luftwaffe, which outclassed and outperformed the VVS throughout the Liuban operation. The spring *rasputitsa* began early and soon stopped movement by either side. Soldiers resorted to huddling in trenches, while the population of Leningrad suffered its worst months of the siege and war. Not even Stalin's emissary, General *Andrei A. Vlasov*, who was flown in to assist defense of the contracting pocket, could save 2nd Shock Army from being pounded into submission from April through June. The loss of 2nd Shock Army ended and then gutted the Soviet offensive. The result was a loss of another 55,000 officers and men, including Vlasov. Failure at Liuban was matched on the far southern flank of Army Group Center by defeat of yet another understrength and overly ambitious thrust made on Stalin's order: the *Orel-Bolkov offensive operation*.

LOCARNO, TREATIES OF (1925)   Belgium, France, and Germany agreed on the permanence of their mutual frontiers and on demilitarization of the *Rhineland*. The treaties were guaranteed by Britain and Italy. Germany also signed treaties of arbitration with Czechoslovakia and Poland. Those states were in turn assured by French treaties of guarantee. Germany was admitted to the *League of Nations* on the basis of the "Locarno Pact." There was much talk of a new "spirit of Locarno" in Europe, but it did not last. Adolf Hitler hated rapprochement with the Western powers and explicitly renounced Locarno. In 1936 he sent a small number of troops into the Rhineland, and no one in London or Paris tried to enforce treaties once hailed as a major breakthrough for lasting European peace and security.

LOGISTICS   Famously referred to in Roman times as the "sinews of war," no military action can take place without logistical support. In World War II that meant production, provision, and movement of all supplies necessary to establish and maintain armies, navies, and air forces in the field, at all levels from tactical, to operational, to strategic. Items produced or moved included everything imaginable, from mail and medicine to vehicles, fuel, food, shoes, pack and feed animals, ammunition, and men. Logistics in World War II was necessarily concerned with long-term management of ships, roads, bridges, railways, aircraft, air fields, and all other requirements of transportation necessary to the basic task of moving men, equipment, and supplies into battle. Unintentionally genuflecting before the fact that the gods of logistics dominate all warfare, the U.S. Army referred to its towing vehicles as "prime movers."

For details *see* entries on individual armies and navies and discrete battles, operations, and campaigns. *See also airborne; Air Transport Auxiliary; Air Transport Command; amphibious operations; animals; area bombing; blockade; blockade runners; Burma Road; Burma–Siam railway; Com-Z; convoys; elephants; engineers; Fleet Train; food supply; Grosstransportraum; helicopters; horses; Hump; interdiction; landing craft; landing ships; Ledo Road; Lend-Lease; merchant marine; MULBERRY; mules; panje; PLUTO; Quartermaster Corps; railways; Red Ball Express; Replenishment-at-Sea; Sino-Japanese War (1937–1945); strategic bombing; submarines; Tokyo Express; U-boats; ULTRA.*

Suggested Reading: Roland Ruppenthal, *Logistical Support of the Armies,* 2 vols. (1985).

LÖHR, ALEXANDER (1885-1947)   German general. An Austrian air force officer before the *Anschluss,* Löhr held important commands in the Luftwaffe during *FALL WEISS* (1939), *FALL GELB* (1940), and *BARBAROSSA* (1941). He assumed ground forces command in Greece during the *Dodecanese campaign* in 1943, and in Yugoslavia in 1944. He was tried by a Yugoslav court after the war on charges of ordering atrocities. He was hanged in 1947.

LONDON CONFERENCE (1941) An early meeting of Soviet, British, and Commonwealth representatives, along with governments-in-exile, to discuss mutual interests in the war with Germany. It was occasioned by the Soviet Union's entry into the war.

LONDON CONFERENCE (1945) An immediate postwar conference of the major Allies convened to discuss occupation issues and future peace treaties with the defeated Axis states. Held from September 11 to October 2, 1945, it broke up in serious disagreement. Most notably, the erstwhile Allies could not agree over seating Chinese or French representatives, while the Western powers protested exclusionary Soviet occupation policy already emerging in parts of eastern Europe, notably in Rumania and Poland.

LONDON NAVAL DISARMAMENT CONFERENCE (1930)
See London Naval Treaty.

LONDON NAVAL TREATY (1930) The London Disarmament Conference convened in 1930 as a follow-up to the successful *Washington Conference* of 1922 and a later failed Geneva disarmament conference. A naval treaty was agreed by Britain, Japan, and the United States that extended variations of the 1922 *Five Power Naval Treaty* ratio for battleships (5:5:3 in ships) to heavy cruisers (18:15:12 in ships), light cruisers (1:1.5:0.75 in tonnage), destroyers (1:1:0.66 in tonnage), and full parity in submarines. It also committed naval powers to abstain from *unrestricted submarine warfare* and instead abide by traditional rules of *cruiser warfare*. This apparent victory for arms control and international moderation was short-lived in Tokyo. Senior naval officers split between "fleet" and "treaty" factions, with the latter sharply and even violently opposed to treaty limitations. A number of key political assassinations followed signature of the London Treaty on April 22, 1930. It was formally abrogated by Japan in 1936.
See also London Submarine Agreement; Mukden incident; Yamamoto, Isoroku.

LONDON POLES Unofficial term for the Polish government-in-exile in Paris, then in London, from 1939 to 1945. The "London Poles" were officially recognized by the Western Allies. They broke relations with the Soviet Union over revelation and investigation of the *Katyn massacre* and, later, over Soviet policies toward Poland in 1944–1945.
See also Lublin Poles; Poland; Polish Army; Yalta Conference.

LONDON SUBMARINE AGREEMENT (1936) A procés-verbal whereby submarine nations, by then including Germany, recommitted to rules of the *London Naval Treaty* governing the conduct of submarine warfare. The essential terms applied modified rules of *cruiser warfare,* or prize rules, to all submarines operating in wartime. The agreement had little bearing on the actual conduct of submarine captains during World War II, when navies of all signing and combatant nations essentially ignored it. However, it was cited in the *war crimes trial* of Admiral *Karl Dönitz* after the war.

See also unrestricted submarine warfare.

LONG MARCH

See Chinese Civil War (1927–1949); Chinese Communist armies; Jiang Jieshi; Mao Zedong; Zhu De.

LONG RANGE DESERT GROUP (LRDG)

A British Army special forces unit set up in mid-1940 to operate in the western desert against the Italian Army. It contained a high proportion of New Zealand troops to start, then more British and other Commonwealth forces. Its principal function was long-range espionage, but sabotage missions were also carried out using vehicles adapted for the desert. The LRDG supported British 8th Army from its advance westward following *Second El Alamein* to the *Mareth Line* campaign. It shipped out in 1943 to fight in the *Dodecanese campaign* and the *Italian campaign (1943–1945)*. Elements of the former desert force also fought in Greece and Yugoslavia.

See also Special Air Service.

LONG-RANGE PENETRATION GROUP (LRPG)

See Chindits.

LONG TOM

Nickname of the powerful, long-range U.S. Army 155 mm heavy artillery tube.

LORAN

"LOng-Range Aid to Navigation." A U.S. navigational aid that calculated radio signals from three known points, out to a maximum detectible range of up to 1,500 miles. That permitted long-range aircraft navigators to establish their plane's location to a margin of error of just a few miles. The system was especially useful for guiding bombers onto distant targets or locations of a recent submarine sighting. It was used by all Western Allied navies.

LORD HAW HAW

See Joyce, William.

LORENZ

A prewar, civilian radio beam navigation system adapted as a bomber aid by both the RAF and Luftwaffe. It comprised a radio signal broadcast by the airfield and received passively by approaching aircraft. It had a limited range of about 20 miles. Its main importance was to aid wartime development of the *Knickebein* and *X-Gerät* beam systems.

LOS NEGROS ISLAND
See Admiralty Islands.

LOWER SILESIAN OFFENSIVE OPERATION (FEBRUARY 8–24, 1945)
See Germany, conquest of.

LSD
See landing ships.

LSM
See landing ships.

LST
See landing ships.

LUBLIN-BREST OFFENSIVE OPERATION (1944)
See Poland.

LUBLIN-MAJDANEK   German *concentration camp* set up in Poland in 1942 as an extermination camp. It is believed that 200,000 died there, mostly Polish Jews.
See also Zyklon-B.

LUBLIN POLES   A committee of Polish Communists formed in Moscow on January 1, 1944, as an alternate government-in-exile to the official Polish government-in-exile formed by the *London Poles*. The official reference for "Lublin Poles" was "Polish National Council of the Homeland (KRN)." The KRN moved to Chelm in Red Army–liberated eastern Poland on July 22, 1944. On December 31, 1944, the KRN was formally established in Lublin and unilaterally recognized as the Provisional Government of Poland by the Soviet Union. It was not recognized by the Western Allies. At the end of the war a compromise was arranged, over vehement objections from the London Poles, that admitted a power-sharing or joint government dominated by the Lublin committee but including some members of the original, non-Communist government-in-exile. That agreement was subsequently abrogated as the Communists took full control of Poland with definitive military, political, and diplomatic backing from Moscow.
See also Katyn massacre; Poland; Polish Army; Yalta Conference.

LUCKY   Radio signal code for U.S. 3rd Army.

LUCY   Code name for the main source of the "Rote Drei," a German Communist spy ring run by the Soviet *GRU* out of Switzerland. It penetrated the *Abwehr* at some level, although tales that Admiral *Wilhelm Canaris* used LUCY to actively assist the Soviet war effort appear fanciful. Whatever the actual origins of its inside information, the LUCY source and Rote Drei spy ring provided much invaluable intelligence. Some of it Joseph Stalin actually listened to and acted upon, but only later in the war.

LUDENDORFF, ERICH VON (1865–1937) German field marshal and, with *Paul von Hindenburg*, virtual military dictator of Imperial Germany in the last two years of World War I. He was influential in giving early national prominence and political legitimacy to Adolf Hitler, notably by participating in the failed Nazi "Beer Hall Putsch" in Bavaria.
See also Germany; Materialschlacht; Nazi Party; total war.

LUFTFLOTTE "Air fleet." The largest operational formation of aircraft in the Luftwaffe. Each was supposed to be the rough equivalent of a battle group or army and was in theory assigned to support an army group. Luftflotten varied greatly in size and types of aircraft over the course of the war, as German capabilities were attrited and fighter production was emphasized from 1944 over bombers. From 1943 Luftflotten were spread far more thinly as numbers of operational aircraft declined. Each remained on paper the organizational equivalent to a USAAF formation like 8th or 15th Air Force, but in fact came nowhere close to equivalent combat power or number of planes. Late in the war, downsized Luftflotten were designated "Luftflottenkommando."

LUFTGAU A Luftwaffe regional command or air administrative district comprising several *Fliegerkorps*. During the war the Luftwaffe operated 24 Luftgau, 14 numbered with another 10 named for their region of operational and administrative responsibility. Luftwaffe ground forces were organized into "Feld Luftgau (FLGK)."
See also Luftgaukommandos.

LUFTGAUKOMMANDOS Luftwaffe air administrative commands in forward areas. Their main job was supply and maintenance of the *Luftgau* to which they were assigned. Until mid-1943 they were generally understaffed, poorly run, and their critical maintenance functions woefully underappreciated by either higher Luftwaffe authorities or the OKH.

LUFTSCHUTZ German air defense.
See anti-aircraft guns; fighters; Flak; Flakhelfer; Flak towers; Freya; Kammhuber Line; Lichtenstein-Gerät; Nachtjagd; Ploesti; radar; radio; Raumnachtjadg; Reichsluftschutzbund; Reichsverteidigung; Ruhr; strategic bombing; Wilde Sau; Würzburg; Zahme Sau.

LUFTWAFFE "Air weapon." The air force of Nazi Germany, founded officially in 1935. The old German air force was abolished under terms of the *Treaty of Versailles* in 1919, with additional limits placed on the German civilian aircraft industry. The civilian limits were lifted by the 1926 Paris Air Agreement, the same year that several small airlines were consolidated into a national carrier: Lufthansa. By 1931 the German military operated four secret fighter squadrons and eight light-reconnaissance squadrons. From 1933 to 1935 pilots were trained in "sports clubs" and "glider clubs" run by the Nazi Party Air Corps (NSFK), the German counterpart of the *Osoaviakhim* in the Soviet Union. Nearly 20,000 boys and men were already trained by the time the existence of the Luftwaffe was officially announced by Adolf Hitler in 1935, with World War I fighter ace *Hermann Göring* at its head.

The Luftwaffe never planned or developed a *strategic bombing* capability after its only strategic bombing advocate, and first chief of staff, died in 1935. Air doctrine was heavily influenced by the fact that the first air staff were recruited directly out of the *Heer*. That gave the Luftwaffe a lasting bias toward a ground force support and tactical role. As a result, in the five years before the war the Luftwaffe built up a complement of medium bombers, dive bombers, and heavy attack fighters, but eschewed design or production of strategic bombers. Even so, its prewar research was impressive. By 1939 the Germans were well ahead of their great rivals—the *Royal Air Force (RAF), French Air Force* or Armée de l'Air, and *Red Army Air Force (VVS)*—in navigation and target-finding aids, as well as ground-to-air controls and tactical integration with ground forces. However, technical leads were thrown away over time by incoherent weapons development procedures and political interference that led to faulty strategic decisions. As a result, Germany and its allies soon fell behind the RAF, USAAF, and VVS in air technology and production. Even in the case of jets, the one advanced area where the Germans kept pace with or bettered the RAF into 1945, development was handicapped by insistence by Adolf Hitler that all jets must be built with a bombing capability. A general trend toward comparative technological backwardness was reinforced by the fact that the Luftwaffe was a fully independent air force: it was not tied to the Heer or Kriegsmarine, although it retained a ground support bias all through the war. Also, it was the Nazi arm par excellence: it was led by Nazi-true believers, and its institutional ethos reflected the Nazi cult of heroic battle, rather than understanding that air superiority could be achieved and maintained only over time.

Poor intelligence led the Luftwaffe to believe that the British aircraft industry was incapable of producing more than 3,000 aircraft in 1939–1940, when in fact the British permanently surpassed German aircraft production in late 1939. This false view of enemy capabilities caused the Luftwaffe to overestimate its own strength and to delay mass production of bombers and fighters until it was too late to make a strategic difference to the outcome of the war. At the start of *FALL WEISS,* the invasion of Poland in September 1939, the Luftwaffe had 4,036 operational frontline aircraft, of which 1,800 were medium or dive bombers. The Western Allies had 4,100 frontline planes. Luftwaffe command planned ahead based on an assumption that war would not break out in the West until 1942. That left it at 1936 levels of production when war actually came in September 1939, whereas Britain was ramping up to full wartime production. The initial advantage enjoyed by the Luftwaffe was, therefore, not as great as is often stated. It did lead, however, in making the changeover to more modern aircraft types. That gave German pilots an initial advantage in combat from 1939 to 1940, but one squandered during the first two years of the air war as German aircraft production sputtered along at barely more than peacetime levels. This went unnoticed by Hitler until 1941, when he finally intervened in aircraft production. But that was too late to eliminate growing shortfalls in aircraft in the Mediterranean and on the Eastern Front. Luftwaffe servicing and repair was also mismanaged and inadequate.

The first significant military operations by the Luftwaffe came during the *Spanish Civil War (1936–1939)*, as the mainstay of the *Kondor Legion*. Luftwaffe pilots engaged elements of the VVS in Spain and became infamous for the first terror bombing of civilians at *Guernica*. Next came an airlift of 2,000 troops into Austria during the *Anschluss* in 1938. A shock was felt by the Germans in Poland during *FALL WEISS* (1939), even though the Polish Air Force was wholly destroyed, much of it caught by surprise on the ground. Against a Polish defense mounted by 333 mostly obsolete planes, the Germans lost 285 aircraft destroyed and another 279 damaged. That should have served warning about the appalling attrition rates to come against major air forces, yet German production remained relatively low. During the *Phoney War* in the West over the winter of 1939–1940, Hitler directed the Luftwaffe to confine attacks to coastal shipping and interdiction of the RAF *leaflet bombing* campaign in the Ruhr. Just 258 aircraft were devoted to maritime patrol and interdiction duties at the start of the critical *Battle of the Atlantic (1939–1945)*. Yet, Göring vehemently opposed development of any naval aviation, fearing that senior Kriegsmarine commanders would pursued creation of a rival air force. This obstruction badly damaged German antishipping efforts at a time when RAF *convoy* defenses were still primitive. During *FALL GELB* (1940), it was principally the Heer that brought about German success. The Luftwaffe played an important supporting role, however, taking advantage of French dispersal and British reluctance to commit their full fighter force to the battle on the continent. As of May 10, 1940, the Luftwaffe thus enjoyed a local numerical advantage of 2,750 aircraft to 1,200 French aircraft and just 416 RAF planes. That enabled it to achieve air supremacy over active sectors, and to strafe and harass enemy columns and armor. In contrast, having squandered the winter with a leafleting campaign, the RAF dispersed its battle effort by bombing oil and rail targets in the Ruhr, attacks that contributed nothing to forestalling swift defeat on the ground in France.

The Luftwaffe did not fare as well later that summer: having failed to develop a theory or capability for strategic bombing, the Luftwaffe was unprepared for the campaign asked of it during the *Battle of Britain* and the *Blitz*. The attrition rates suffered over *Dunkirk* and then again over Britain in the summer and early fall of 1940 were compounded by dispersal of squadrons to the Middle East and across the Balkans in 1941. All that meant that the Luftwaffe was smaller at the outset of *BARBAROSSA* in June 1941, than when it began FALL GELB in May 1940, despite fielding 1.7 million personnel. With total operational and tactical surprise achieved in the opening battles in the east, the Luftwaffe destroyed over 2,000 VVS planes in the first three days. After two weeks it had destroyed nearly 4,000 VVS planes. However, the Germans lost 550 aircraft in the same period. During 1942 the Soviet aircraft industry produced 25,000 aircraft, solely for use against the Germans. The VVS also took significant deliveries of Western fighters starting late in the year. Total Allied production that year was over 71,000 aircraft. By comparison, the Germans produced just 15,000 aircraft of all types, and spread them over three active fronts: North Africa and the Mediterranean, the German homeland, and the Eastern Front. The Luftwaffe upheld a wholly tactical support role in the east, while scrambling to develop or replace an air transport capacity it sorely lacked. Its loss rate was so high that it never fully replaced its losses. The Germans thus lost air superiority around Leningrad and Briansk over the course of 1942. At *Kursk,* 400 German aircraft faced over 2,000 VVS planes. By mid-1943 Soviet aircraft and pilots had closed the early technical and training gaps with their German counterparts. Luftwaffe crew skills deteriorated further as Göring and Hitler insisted on replacing combat losses by throwing trainer aircraft and instructors into active service.

From mid-1943 many Luftwaffe fighter *Geschwader* were drawn away from the east, to be instead attrited by Western air forces in the Mediterranean, over France, and above Germany. The process began well before the *Normandy campaign,* as the Western Allies made engagement of Luftwaffe fighters and destruction of Germany's fighter production a top priority of their *Combined Bomber Offensive.* The bulk of German fighters and anti-aircraft artillery, which consumed vast quantities of ammunition, were defending the Reich by September 1943. Hence, despite ramping up production to 25,000 aircraft in 1943, hardly any increase was experienced on the Eastern Front. German fighter losses in France and over Germany were so great that by mid-1944, despite greatly expanded production in the most efficient year of the war for the German aircraft industry, the Luftwaffe was no longer a major combat factor on the Eastern Front. Similarly, by mid-1944 half of all artillery tubes were located in the homeland, in use as anti-aircraft guns against Western Allied bomber streams. The Luftwaffe was on the defensive everywhere; airfields and factories were pounded by enemy air forces that seemed to have more and better planes every month. As pilot and crew casualties mounted, the Luftwaffe faced better and more experienced enemy pilots in the east as well as in the west. None of that prevented intense personal conflict within its top ranks, or with other armed services of the Wehrmacht. An extreme example was the suicide by Göring's chief of staff in 1943, on grounds that he could no longer work with the erratic Reichsmarschall. Göring was indeed impossible to work with, a fact that severely retarded new aircraft designs and impeded production of older ones throughout the war.

Hitler's personal interventions and odd theories—for instance, in favor of jet bombers—further aggravated severe irrationalities in aircraft design and production schedules. This problem was eased somewhat from 1943 by the succession of Erhard Milch to the position of chief of staff. Milch was a technically competent man who greatly increased fighter production into 1944, when *Albert Speer* took over the aircraft industry and stretched production to even greater levels. Improved production was achieved by cutting back on bombers and transports, in favor of ramping up output of earlier model fighters that were already outclassed by new planes in all major enemy air forces. Without a strategic bomber force the Luftwaffe had been unable to punish Britain sufficiently to drive that country from the war in 1940. Germans now paid the price in blood and destroyed cities from 1943 to 1945, as the RAF and USAAF flew from Great Britain, and later also from Italy, to destroy dozens of German cities. Nor could the Germans knock out Soviet factories relocated far behind the combat lines, not even at the deepest extent of Wehrmacht penetration on the Eastern Front in 1942. Germany had devoted too much of its limited material and intellectual resources and war production to the Luftwaffe, without developing a decisive air weapon or a sufficient defense to successfully fend off superior and far more numerous enemy aircraft. A fundamental structural flaw was Luftwaffe political isolation within the Wehrmacht and the Nazi political system. The latter was a byproduct of Göring's chronic scheming, which was outmatched by Nazi rivals as his performance and that of the Luftwaffe declined in tandem. That left the Luftwaffe without a clientele base in the war economy or political support when Hitler turned against it, scapegoating the air force for Germany's overall strategic failure.

Unknown to the general German population, Luftwaffe thinking about civil defense dating to 1934 assumed that enemy bombers would always get through. With their usual ruthlessness, prewar Nazi and German state planners set out secret lists of cities to receive funds for priority defense and building of bomb shelters, based on their importance to the future war economy rather than exposure of citizens. They also prepared lists of German towns deemed "expendable." When the bombers came, wave upon wave or in long streams, even in the priority cities there were never enough bomb shelters. The Party stepped in to build some shelters to fill the gap, but as sirens wailed terrified civilians were crammed into the few public shelters that existed. Those who could ran inside the huge and nearly invulnerable, but stifling, *Flak towers* (Flaktürme) in the few key cities that had them. Most just huddled in some nearby basement that was no protection against high explosive bombs. Worse, these basements were connected by tunnels so that people might run from cellar to cellar in front of the bombs, and poisonous carbon monoxide was channeled into cellars to silently kill those inside. Slave laborers, who comprised most foreigners in Germany by 1944, were provided no shelter whatever. They remained in the street when the bombs fell, and suffered commensurately enormous casualties. Most harmful to civilians was that civil air defense ("Zivlier Luftschutz") was left to the Luftwaffe to organize as a military matter. The air force was too decentralized, grossly inefficient, and politically weakened late in the war to obtain or manage the men or material resources needed for the job. Instead, the Luftwaffe turned to women and the *Hitlerjungend* to crew its forests of anti-aircraft guns. These were concentrated in the Ruhr Valley and other industrial areas, then later around Berlin and other repeated urban targets of Allied air raids.

By 1943 the Luftwaffe included hundreds of thousands of ground personnel engaged in air defense of the Reich, as Germany faced *thousand bomber raids* and round-the-clock bombing. Those facts were pointed to by Winston Churchill in 1943 when protesting directly to Stalin that the air campaign constituted an effective "*second front,*" well before the landings in Normandy. As German infantry losses mounted, pressure was brought to bear to surrender some of the Luftwaffe's many nonflying personnel for the frontlines. Some 200,000 were transferred to the Heer in 1943. Göring's waning political influence was still strong enough in 1944 to ensure that additional infantry units were formed as *Luftwaffe field divisions* that remained under his control. Most were armed into 1943 with captured Czech, French, or Soviet guns, along with various German PAK anti-aircraft guns and horse-towed anti-tank guns. They were not consistently organized until 1944, and were never effective or highly ranked in the Heer's order of battle. In addition to erosion of Luftwaffe manpower on the ground, bomber pilots were transferred to fighter units without real success, and suffered high casualties. The effects of poor planning were felt across the board from the second half of 1944, as fighter production peaked, but there were not enough trained pilots to man new squadrons, while fuel and other supplies reached critically low levels by the autumn. Morale and performance thereafter plummeted in inverse relation to rising battle losses.

The Luftwaffe was progressively overmatched on all fronts from 1943: in Africa and Italy, over the Balkans, in the skies of France and Germany, and all along the Eastern Front. Each of the three main enemy air industries—the RAF, USAAF, and VVS—on its own outproduced Germany's aircraft industry. The Luftwaffe continued to produce many older types of outmoded fighters such as the Ju-88 and Me-109. Failure to stop enemy bombers meant that many of these planes were destroyed on the ground or in factories, so that the fighter loss rate reached an astonishing 73 percent of monthly strength throughout 1944, the peak months of fighter production. The Luftwaffe was the first air force to deploy operational jets, but it produced these in paltry numbers and far too late in the war to have any effect on its outcome. Senior Luftwaffe and political leadership also delayed development of jets by arguing over whether they should be used primarily as bombers or fighters, with Hitler insisting on the former. That meant that those aircraft actually produced had serious design flaws. In any case, there was hardly fuel for aircraft of any kind by early 1945, as the skies over Germany grew dark with enemy heavy bomber fleets and "Jabos" hunted ground forces and Panzers at will.

Toward the end, Hitler took more personal charge of the air war, as he did all aspects of the German war effort. His limited knowledge and bias toward steering resources to the Heer, matched with absolute personal conviction about his own military insights—though these seldom rose above the level of vulgar misunderstanding—exacerbated extant problems in the organization of the Luftwaffe. For instance, he insisted that anti-aircraft guns would suffice to defend cities from bombers and never sanctioned a system of air defense-in-depth. He also utterly failed to appreciate that the air war could be won only by constant and routine daily operations. Instead, he resented what he saw as "hoarding" of reserves, then flung these away in grand but futile spectaculars such as the *Ardennes offensive*. He also wasted precious resources on supposed *Wunderwaffen*. Hitler's growing disgust with Luftwaffe failures led to an order in 1944 to disband the air force and replace it with a huge anti-aircraft army to defend Germany. Only Göring's residual call on past Nazi Party and personal glories in the first years of the war prevented this bizarre Führer order from being carried out.

The defeat of the Luftwaffe was total at all levels, in tandem with the final and utter military rout of Nazi Germany. Its failure was exacerbated by Göring's and Hitler's personal idiosyncrasies and interference, but it had much deeper structural causes. The German air force failed to develop a strong bomber arm, leading to a fundamental imbalance that was never corrected; it fell behind in the "battle of the beams" and *radar* war; it worked on too many and too radical new designs even as it delayed full war production until it was too late to correct for the growing Allied lead; it lost control of training even as it received more fighters, with the end result that pilot wastage rose dramatically in 1944.

See specific battles, and *see also ace; airborne; Baedeker raids; bandit; blitz; Blitzkrieg; bombers; Coventry raid; Crete; Fernnachtjagd; fighters; Flak; Fliegerdivision; Fliegerkorps; float planes; Galland, Adolf; Gruppe; intruder raids; Jaeger; Jagdbomber; Jagdflieger; Jagdgeschwader; Jagdstaffel; Jagdverband; Kampfgeschwader; Kette; Knickebein; Kursk; Lorenz; Luftflotten; Luftgau; Luftgaukommandos; Malta; Nachtjagd; Pulk; Reichsverteidigung; Rotte; Schlacht; Schwarm; shuttle bombing; Sperrle, Hugo; squadron; strategic bombing; Student, Kurt; Stuka; Valhalla; Wilde Sau; X-Gerät; Y-Gerät; Zahme Sau; Zerstörergruppen.*

Suggested Reading: M. Cooper, *The German Air Force: Anatomy of Failure* (1981); John Killen, *The Luftwaffe: A History* (1967; 2003); Williamson Murray, *Luftwaffe* (1985); Richard Overy, *Göring: The Iron Man* (1984).

LUFTWAFFE FIELD DIVISIONS   Units of infantry formed from Luftwaffe ground personnel, of whom there were many due to the Luftwaffe's independent control of air base defenses, anti-aircraft artillery, and prisoner of war camps. The main reason for the odd choice to create Luftflotte infantry divisions was that Reichsmarschall *Hermann Göring* did not wish to surrender any authority over his men, despite the extraordinary need of the Wehrmacht for reinforcements and the poor performance of the Luftwaffe in homeland defense. The new units were unusually poorly trained and ill-equipped, and proved not very battleworthy. Casualties taken by "field divisions" were heavy, and the units often broke while in action.

LUMBERJACK (FEBRUARY 21–MARCH 7, 1945)
See Germany, conquest of.

LUXEMBOURG   This small *neutral state* of fewer than 300,000 people was marched through by German troops on May 10, 1940, as it had been also in 1914. It was annexed to Nazi Germany from 1942 to 1945. That made its citizens legally Germans, and its young males eligible for conscription by the Wehrmacht. As a result, over 10,000 Luxembourgers were conscripted and nearly 3,000 were killed while wearing Feldgrau, either in combat or shot for desertion. Almost all its nearly 4,000 Jews were murdered by the Nazis. Many Luxembourgers supported the anti-Nazi cause. Some were active in local resistance; others served as volunteers in various Western Allied military units. Luxembourg was occupied by American troops on September 10, 1944, as the Wehrmacht retreated without offering much resistance. However, the country was briefly lost to the Germans during the *Ardennes offensive*. It was liberated a second time during February–March 1945, this time after some heavy fighting and destruction of lives and property.

See also Germanics.

LVOV-SANDOMIERZ OFFENSIVE OPERATION (1944)
See Poland.

LVT
See Landing Vehicle Tracked.

LYTTON COMMISSION (1932–1933) A *League of Nations* commission of investigation established in 1932. It was sent to China, Japan, and Manchuria following the *Mukden incident*. It issued a report that mildly criticized Japan. The report was actually intended to appease Tokyo by asserting that Japan indeed had an expectation of "special rights" in Manchuria. But the report did not go so far as to recommend international recognition of the puppet regime set up by the *Guandong Army* in the new colony called "Manchukuo." Knowing the contents of the Lytton Commission report in advance, Japan sent forces deeper into northern China. The League vote was unanimous to accept the final report: only Thailand abstained. Yet, even that mild rebuke was seized upon by hotheads among the militarists in Japan, notably in the "fleet" faction in the Navy and *Issekikai* in the Army, as an excuse to force the Japanese government to withdraw from membership in the League and thereafter to pursue unfettered aggression.